lonely planet

South India & Kerala

THIS EDITION WRITTEN AND RESEARCHED BY

Sarina Singh,

Lindsay Brown, Paul Harding, Trent Holden, Amy Karafin, Kate Morgan, John Noble

PLAN YOUR TRIP

ON THE ROAD

PHOTOSINDIA.COM / GETTY IMAGES ©
AJANTA P100

KEREN SU / GETTY IMAGES ©
DAULATABAD P96

RICHARD I'ANSON / GETTY IMAGES ©

Contents

RICHARD I'ANSON / GETTY IMAGES ©

KERALA P267

MITCHELL KANASHKEVICH / GETTY IMAGES ©

MEENAKSHI AMMAN TEMPLE P384

KATHAKALI PERFORMER P264

ON THE ROAD

DREAMPICTURES / GETTY IMAGES ©

MUMBAI P44

ANDERS BLOMQVIST / GETTY IMAGES ©

PAPANASHAM BEACH, VARKALA P280

Contents

VEGETARIAN THALI P468

ANJUNA P146

GREG ELMS / GETTY IMAGES ©

UNDERSTAND

SURVIVAL GUIDE

SPECIAL FEATURES

Welcome to South India & Kerala

Like a giant wedge plunging into the Indian Ocean, peninsular South India is the subcontinent's steamy heartland, and a lush contrast to the snow-capped peaks and sun-crisped plains of the North.

Expect the Unexpected

India loves to toss up the unexpected. This can be challenging, particularly for the first-time visitor: the poverty is confronting, Indian bureaucracy can be exasperating and the crush of humanity may turn the simplest task into a frazzling epic. Even veteran travellers find their nerves frayed at some point, yet this is all part of the India experience. With an ability to inspire, frustrate, thrill and confound all at once, adopting a 'go with the flow' attitude is wise if you wish to retain your sanity. Love it or loathe it – and most travellers see-saw between the two – to embrace the unpredictability is to embrace India's soul.

Soul Stirring

Spirituality is the common thread that weaves its way through the vast and complex tapestry that is contemporary India. The multitude of sacred sites and time-honoured rituals are testament to a long, colourful, and sometimes tumultuous, religious history. And then there are the festivals! South India hosts some of the nation's most spectacular devotional events – from formidable city parades celebrating auspicious dates on the religious calendar, to simple harvest fairs that pay homage to a locally worshipped deity.

Luscious Landscapes

South India comprises thousands of kilometres of coastline that frame fertile plains and curvaceous hills, all kept glisteningly green by the double-barrelled monsoon. The region's tropical splendour is one of its greatest tourist drawcards with thick coconut groves, luminescent rice paddies, fragrant spice gardens and picturesque tea plantations proffering plenty of green respite. And then there are the waterways. Azure seas gently lap crescents of sun-warmed sand and boats cruise along the slender rivers and glassy lagoons of Kerala's famed backwaters.

Deliciously Festive

With its glorious culinary variety and melange of dining-out options, South India is deliciously rewarding. From traditional southern favourites such as *idlis* (fermented rice cakes) and large papery dosas (savoury crepes) to a mix of inventive fusion creations, there's certainly no dearth of choice for the hungry traveller. Food has also long played a prominent role in many of the region's festivals, with temptingly colourful *mithai* (sweets) more often than not taking centre stage.

Why I Love South India

By Sarina Singh, Author

The moment I start to think I'm right on the precipice of unravelling one of its deep mysteries, India has an uncanny way of reminding me that it would take more than just a few lifetimes to do so. Indeed, demystifying India is a perpetual work in progress. And that is precisely what makes the country so deeply addictive for me. The constant exploration. The playful unpredictability. And knowing that, just when it's least expected, you can find yourself up close and personal with moments that have the power to alter the way you view the world and your place in it.

For more about our authors, see page 560

Above: Kovalam (p276), Kerala

South India & Kerala

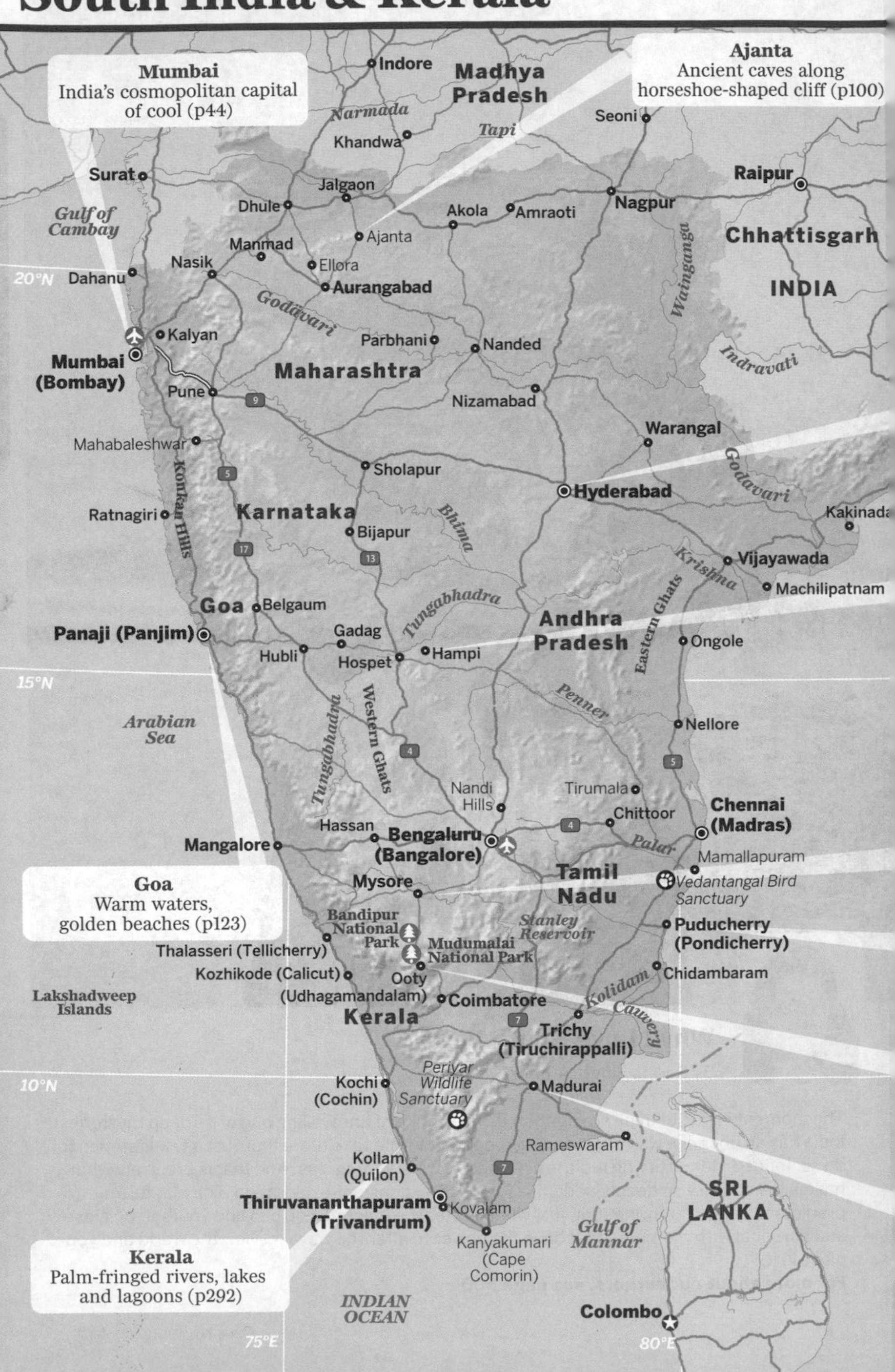

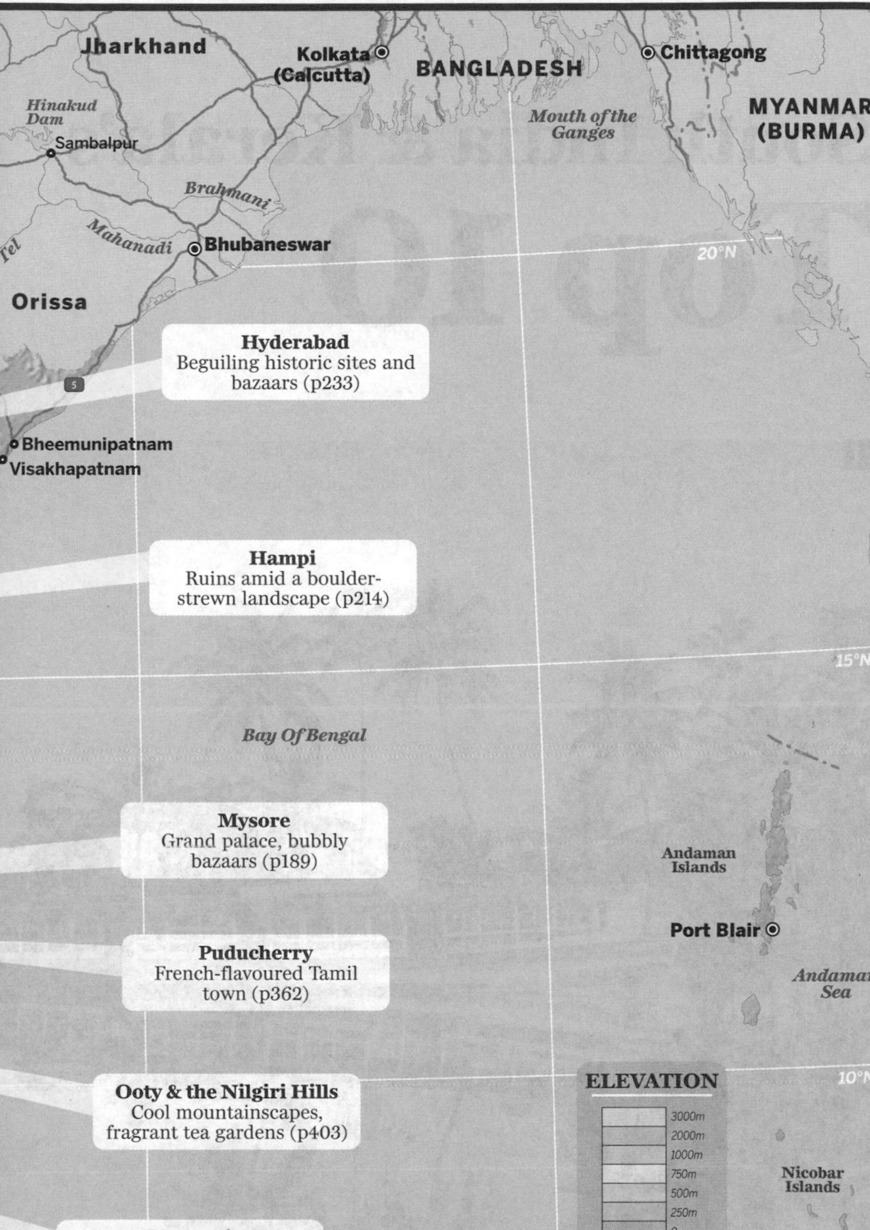

0 400km
0 200miles
Jharkhand
Kolkata (Calcutta)
BANGLADESH
Chittagong
MYANMAR (BURMA)
Hinakud Dam
Sambalpur
Mouth of the Ganges
Brahmani
Mahanadi
Tel
Bhubaneswar
20°N
Orissa
Hyderabad
Beguiling historic sites and bazaars (p233)
Bheemunipatnam
Visakhapatnam
Hampi
Ruins amid a boulder-strewn landscape (p214)
15°N
Bay Of Bengal
Mysore
Grand palace, bubbly bazaars (p189)
Andaman Islands
Port Blair
Puducherry
French-flavoured Tamil town (p362)
Andaman Sea
ELEVATION
3000m
2000m
1000m
750m
500m
250m
0
10°N
Ooty & the Nilgiri Hills
Cool mountainscapes, fragrant tea gardens (p403)
Nicobar Islands
Madurai
Site of stunning Meenakshi Amman Temple (p384)
85°E
90°E

South India & Kerala's Top 10

Kerala's Beautiful Backwaters

1 It's not every day you come across a place as sublime as Kerala's backwaters (p267): 900km of interconnected rivers, lakes and glassy lagoons lined with lush tropical flora. And if you do, there likely won't be a way to experience it that's quite as serene and intimate as a few days on a teak-and-palm-thatch houseboat. Float along the water – as the sun sinks behind whispering palms, while nibbling on seafood so fresh it's still almost wriggling – and forget about life on land for awhile.

Go Goa

2 Silken sand, gently crashing waves, thick coconut groves, hot pink sunsets...yes, if there's one place that effortlessly fulfils every glossy tourist brochure cliché, it's Goa (p123). Apart from a few exceptions Goa's beaches are a riot of activity, with a constant cavalcade of roaming sarong vendors, stacks of ramshackle beachside eateries and countless oiled bodies slowly baking on row after row of sun lounges. Goa is also known for its inland spice plantations and lovely heritage buildings, most notably the handsome cathedrals built during Portuguese reign.
Below: Agonda beach, Goa

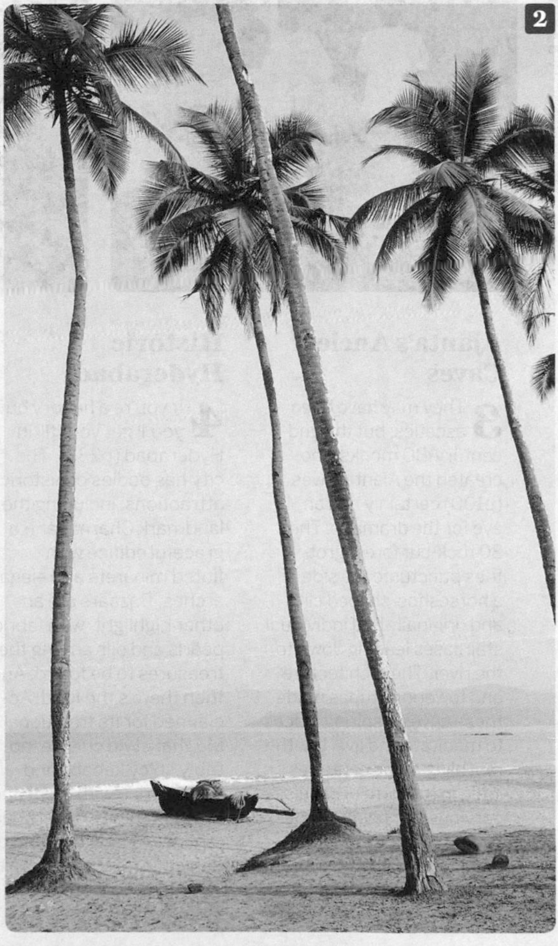

2

3

MARC SHANDRO / GETTY IMAGES ©

4

Ajanta's Ancient Caves

3 They may have been ascetics, but the 2nd-century-BC monks who created the Ajanta caves (p100) certainly had an eye for the dramatic. The 30 rock-cut forest grottoes punctuate the side of a horseshoe-shaped cliff and originally had individual staircases leading down to the river. The architecture and towering stupas made these caves inspiring places to meditate and live, but the real bling came centuries later, in the form of exquisite carvings and paintings depicting the Buddha's former lives. Makes living in a cave look pretty darn good.

Historic Hyderabad

4 If you're a history buff, you'll get your fill in Hyderabad (p233). The city has oodles of historic attractions, including the landmark Charminar – a graceful edifice with fluted minarets and elegant arches. Bazaars are another highlight, with fabrics, pearls and oils among the treasures to be found. And then there's the food. Acclaimed for its traditional Mughal-style cuisine, notably spicy kebabs and biryani (rice with meat and/or vegetables), Hyderabadi fare gets a hearty round of applause for its deliciously inventive preparations. Charminar, Hyderabad

Mumbai's Architectural Gems

5 Mumbai (Bombay; p44) has always had a knack of weaving disparate strands together to make a unique cultural tapestry. The architectural result is a diverse mix of buildings: the art deco and modern towers are flash, but it's the Victorian-era structures that have made Mumbai such a flamboyant beauty. All those slender spires, curvaceous arches and puffy onion domes make for a riveting amble through the city's former incarnations. Taj Mahal Palace Hotel, Mumbai

Puducherry Savoir Faire

6 A little pocket of France in Tamil Nadu? *Pourquoi pas?* In this former French colony, mustard-coloured houses line cobblestone rues, austere cathedrals are adorned with architectural frou-frou, and the croissants are the real deal. But Puducherry (Pondicherry; p362) is also a classic Tamil town – with all the history and hubbub that go along with that – and a classic retreat town, too, with the Sri Aurobindo Ashram at its heart. Turns out that yoga, *pain au chocolat*, Hindu deities and colonial-era architecture make for a *très* atmospheric mix.

CLAUDE RENAULT / GETTY IMAGES ©

Enigmatic Hampi

7 Today's surreal boulderscape of Hampi (p214) was once the glorious Vijayanagar, capital of a powerful Hindu empire. Still glorious in ruins, its temples and royal structures combine with the terrain in mystical ways: giant rocks balance on skinny pedestals near an ancient elephant garage, temples tuck into crevices between boulders, and round coracle boats float by rice paddies and bathing buffaloes near a gargantuan bathtub for a queen. Watching the sunset cast a rosy glow over the extraordinary landscape, you might just forget what planet you're on. Lotus Mahal, Hampi

Madurai's Meenakshi Amman Temple

8 Built in the 17th century, Madurai's brilliant Meenakshi Amman Temple (p384) is dedicated to Sundareswarer (a form of Shiva) and his consort, Meenakshi (an incarnation of the goddess Parvati). 'Meenakshi' means 'fish-eyed', which, in classic Tamil literature, is a reference to perfect eyes. The complex is a feast of deftly crafted pillars, friezes and figurines, which are flanked by ornate *gopurams* (pyramidal gateway towers). A star attraction is the 1000-Pillared Hall, its columns artfully embellished with delicately sculptured celestial beings.

9

10

Ooty & the Nilgiri Hills

9 The plunging valleys, pancake-flat plains and palm-ringed beaches are all well and good, but it can get mighty hot down there! India's princes and British colonials used the country's mountain towns, such as Ooty (Udhagamandalam; p403), as cool refuges from the relentless summer heat, and today the hill stations still have plenty of forests, crisp mountain air and sprawling tea plantations. Curl up under a blanket with a steaming cup of local tea, peer over the misty hills at the mountain birds swooping by and experience India's chilled-out side.

Majestic Mysore

10 Welcome to Mysore (p189), a city whose etymology is linked to the spot where a brave goddess conquered a ferocious demon. Apart from its formidable history, this is the place to take a leisurely wander through frenetic old bazaars filled with the intoxicating aroma of sandalwood, fresh flowers and incense. Mysore is also known for its convivial festivals. Dussehra – which celebrates the triumph of good over evil – is one of the most spectacular occasions, with merry street parades and the dazzling illumination of the city's enormous palace. Mysore Palace

Need to Know

For more information, see Survival Guide (p495)

Currency

Indian Rupees (₹)

Languages

Hindi, English and regional dialects

Visas

Most people travel using a six-month tourist visa, which is valid from the date of issue, not the date you arrive in India.

Money

ATMs in most large towns; carry cash or travellers cheques as back-up. MasterCard and Visa are the most widely accepted credit cards.

Mobile Phones

Roaming connections are usually excellent in urban areas, poor in the countryside. Local prepaid SIMs are widely available but security checks can be complex and time-consuming.

Time

Indian Standard Time (GMT/UTC plus 5½ hours)

When to Go

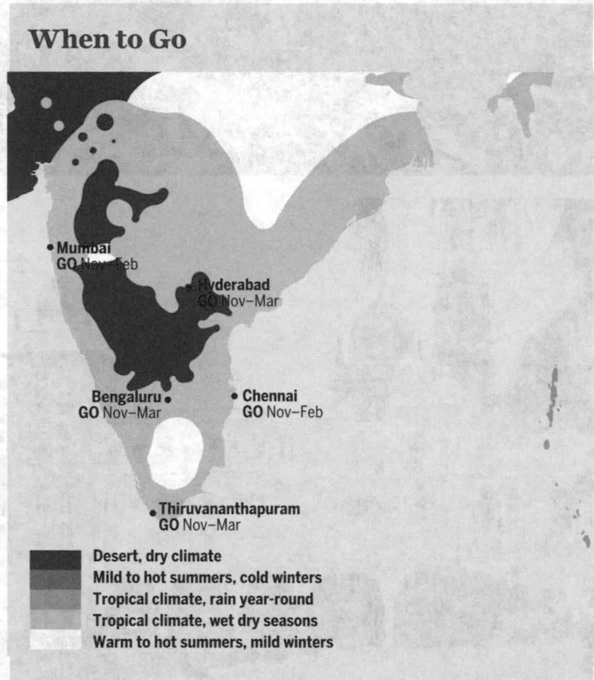

Low Season

(Apr–Jun)

➡ April is hot; May and June are scorching. Competitive hotel prices.

➡ From June, the monsoon sweeps from south to north, bringing draining humidity.

➡ Beat the heat (but not the crowds) in the cool hills.

Shoulder

(Jul–Nov)

➡ Monsoon rain-showers persist through to September.

➡ The southeast coast and southern Kerala see heavy rain from October to early December.

High Season

(Dec–Mar)

➡ Pleasant weather – warm days, reasonably cool nights. Peak tourists. Peak prices.

➡ December and January bring chilly nights further north.

➡ Temperatures climb steadily from February.

Useful Websites

Lonely Planet (www.lonelyplanet.com/india) Destination information, the Thorn Tree Travel Forum and more.

Incredible India (www.incredibleindia.org) Official India tourism site.

Templenet (www.templenet.com) Temple talk.

Rediff News (www.rediff.com/news) Portal for India-wide news.

World Newspapers (www.world-newspapers.com/india.html) Links to India's English-language publications.

Important Numbers

From outside India, dial your international access code, India's country code then the number (minus '0', only used when dialling domestically).

Country code	☎91
International access code	☎00
Ambulance	☎102
Fire	☎101
Police	☎100

Exchange Rates

Australia	A$1	₹54
Canada	C$1	₹54
Euro zone	€1	₹72
Japan	¥100	₹55
New Zealand	NZ$1	₹45
UK	UK£1	₹84
US	US$1	₹56

For current exchange rates see www.xe.com

Daily Costs

Budget: Less than ₹2000

➡ Double room in a budget hotel: ₹300–700

➡ All-you-can-eat thalis (plate meals): ₹120–300

➡ Local transport: ₹250–500

Midrange: ₹2000–7000

➡ Double hotel room: ₹800–4000

➡ Meals in midrange restaurants: ₹400–1500

➡ Admission to historic sights and museums: ₹100–1000

Top End: More than ₹7000

➡ Deluxe hotel room: ₹4000–20,000

➡ Meals at superior restaurants: ₹1000–4000

➡ First-class train travel: ₹800–8000

➡ Renting a car and driver: ₹1000 upwards per day

Opening Hours

Business hours are year-round for banks, offices and restaurants; many sights keep summer and winter opening hours.

Banks 10am to 2pm or 4pm Monday to Friday, to noon or 1pm Saturday

Restaurants noon to 10pm or 11pm (more expensive restaurants may shut 3pm to 7pm)

Bars & Clubs noon to 1am or later

Shops 10am to 7pm or 8pm (some shops close Sundays)

Markets 10am to 7pm in major cities, usually with one closed day; rural markets may be once weekly, from early morning to lunchtime

Arriving in South India

Chhatrapati Shivaji International Airport (Mumbai; p81) Prepaid taxis to Colaba, Fort and Marine Dr cost ₹650/750 (non-AC/AC). Expect to pay ₹395 to ₹495 to southern neighbourhoods.

Chennai International Airport (Chennai; p346) Suburban trains to central Chennai run several times hourly from 4am to midnight from Tirusulam station at the airport. Prepaid taxis cost ₹380 to ₹515.

Getting Around

Transport in South India is frequent and inexpensive, although not always fast. Consider domestic flights or sleeper trains as an alternative to long uncomfortable bus rides.

Air Flights to most major centres and state capitals; cheap flights with budget airlines.

Train Frequent services to most destinations; inexpensive tickets available even on sleeper trains.

Bus Buses go everywhere; some destinations are served 24 hours but longer routes may have just one or two buses a day (typically early morning or afternoon/evening).

For much more on **getting around**, see p514

If You Like...

Forts & Palaces

Historically South India has a uniquely colourful tapestry of wrangling dynasties, interwoven with the influx of seafaring traders and conquerors. Today some of their legacies can be seen in the region's remarkable collection of palaces and forts.

Mysore The Maharaja's Palace is one of India's largest and most spectacular royal buildings. Within the walls of this grand Indo-Saracenic complex are rare artworks, stained glass, mosaic floors and beautifully carved wooden fittings. (p189)

Maharashtra The land of Shivaji is almost as much of a fort junkie as Rajasthan (which has a particularly prolific royal heritage) with defensive masterpieces like Daulatabad (p96), camouflaged on a hilltop, and Janjira, an island fortress.

Hyderabad The rugged Golconda Fort, whose gem vault once stored the Hope and Koh-i-Noor diamonds, complements the ethereal palaces of the City of Pearls. (p235)

Bidar Fort So weathered and peaceful you'll just have to trust that it was once the seat of a powerful sultanate. (p228)

IF YOU LIKE... DIVING

The Andaman Islands have some world-class diving opportunities, with coral gardens and marine life. (p421)

Beaches

South India has the country's most breathtaking stretches of coastline, with standout beaches found in Goa and Kerala. Seaside resort towns usually spring to life around sunset, when locals take leisurely strolls and enjoy beachside snacks sold by roving vendors.

Kerala Kovalam and Varkala, with their gorgeous crescent-shape sugar-white beaches, rustling palm trees, lighthouse (Kovalam; p276) and dramatic cliffs (Varkala; p280), are an absolute vision.

Goa Everything they say about the beaches is true – even when overrun with tourists, they're still somehow lovely. Vagator (p149) and Palolem (p161) are among the prettiest, as is Gokarna, just nearby in Karnataka.

Mumbai Hit Chowpatty beach, as the afternoon melts into dusk, to snack on unusual and creative local delicacies, people-watch, and see just how hot-pink the sunset can get. (p52)

Bazaars

Megamalls may be popping up like monsoon frogs in South India's larger cities, but the traditional outdoor bazaars – with their tangle of lanes lined with shops selling everything from freshly ground spices and floral garlands to kitchen utensils and colourful saris – can't be beat.

Goa Tourist-oriented flea markets have become huge attractions at several spots on the north coast, while the local bazaars of Panjim and, especially, Margao make for atmospheric wandering. (p149)

Mumbai Among modern malls, this megalopolis has wonderful old markets conveniently dedicated to themes: Mangaldas (fabric), Zaveri (jewellery), Crawford (meat and produce) and Chor (random antique pieces). (p79)

Mysore Iconic Devaraja Market is about 125 years old and filled with about 125 million flowers, fruits and vegetables. (p190)

Grand Temples & Ancient Ruins

No one does grand temples (or little temples, for that matter) like the subcontinent. From the psychedelic

(Top) Beach at Vagator (p149), Goa

(Bottom) Pongal festival (p370), Tamil Nadu

Technicolor Hindu towers of Tamil Nadu to the faded splendour of Ajanta and Ellora's Buddhist cave temples, the range is as vast as it is sublime.

Tamil Nadu Tamil Nadu is prime temple territory, with towering, fantastical structures – such as the striking Meenakshi Amman Temple of Madurai – that soar skyward in rainbows of masterfully sculpted deities. (p384)

Ajanta & Ellora These magnificent old rock-cut cave temples, clinging to a horseshoe-shaped gorge, are revered not only for their spiritual significance but also for their architectural prowess. (p100)

Hampi The rosy-hued temples and crumbling palaces of what was once the mighty capital of Vijayanagar are strewn among otherworldly-looking boulders and hills. (p214)

Local Festivals

Apart from embracing a range of countrywide festivals, South India has its own vibrant collection of locally celebrated events. These range from sacred temple processions to flamboyant beachside affairs.

Kerala Keralan festivals are nothing short of fabulous, especially when it comes to elephant processions and boat races. The Nehru Trophy Snake Boat Race sees elegant 125ft-long canoes in a lively rowing showdown. (p289)

Chennai Festival of Music & Dance For six weeks the city fills up on Carnatic (and some non-Carnatic) music, dance and drama. (p340)

Tamil Nadu Pongal, in mid-January, celebrates the close of the harvest season. Pots of *pongal* (a mixture of rice, sugar, dhal and milk) are prepared and fed to decorated cows. (p370)

Goa The four-day Carnival in Goa kicks off Lent with colourful parades, concerts and plenty of merrymaking. (p132)

Mumbai Mumbai (Bombay) hosts interesting art performances and exhibitions during its two-week Kala Ghoda Festival. (p45)

City Sophistication

Most Indians do live in villages, but city people here had attained high planes of sophistication when classiness was just a glimmer in the West's eye. India's cities have riveting arts scenes, terrific multicuisine restaurants and oodles of style.

Mumbai Mumbai has it all – fashion, film, art, dining and a buzzing nightlife scene – on an elaborate stage of fanciful architecture and scenic water views. (p44)

Hyderabad The ancient architecture of several extraordinarily wealthy dynasties sits just across town from a refined restaurant, nightlife and arts scene. (p233)

Bengaluru This cosmopolitan metropolis is the hub of India's IT industry. The city's lungs are its leafy gardens which are sandwiched between knots of high-rise office blocks and peeling apartments. (p176)

Puducherry A pleasant coastal town known for its faded French flavour, Puducherry (Pondicherry) is India at its eclectic best. The French Quarter has charming alleys and mustard-coloured villas. (p362)

IF YOU LIKE... LUXURY TRAIN TRIPS

The 'Deccan Odyssey' is seven nights of the best of Maharashtra and Goa. (p29)

Hill Stations

South India is blessed with sunshine and hills to escape from it when summer rolls in. The foundation for today's hill-station resort culture is largely thanks to locals – especially royalty and colonials – who traditionally fled to escape the heat of the plains.

Tamil Nadu The Tamil hill stations of the Western Ghats are full of thick pine forests, tiny tea houses, sprawling cardamom plantations and architectural Raj-era flourishes. (p393)

Matheran A popular weekend retreat for Mumbaikars, Matheran is not only delightfully scenic and easygoing (largely thanks to its ban on cars) but also has a quaint narrow-gauge toy train plying the 21km to the main road. (p108)

Ooty & the Nilgiri Hills The most renowned hill station of the Nilgiri Hills, Ooty is a lofty, pine-clad retreat popular with honeymooners, families and nature lovers. (p403)

Meditation & Yoga

The art of wellbeing has long been ardently pursued in the South. Today there is a variety of treatments on offer that strive to heal mind, body and spirit, with meditation and yoga courses especially abundant.

Maharasthra The Vipassana International Academy (p92), in Igatpuri, has intensive meditation courses in the Theravada Buddhist tradition. Meanwhile, the famous Osho International Meditation Resort (p114) runs on the teachings of its charismatic founder, the late Bhagwan Shree Rajneesh.

Tamil Nadu Puducherry's Sri Aurobindo Ashram was founded by the renowned Sri Aurobindo. Its courses seek to synthesise yoga and modern science. (p363)

Coimbatore The Isha Yoga Center has a variety of residential courses and retreats. (p400)

Puttaparthi Prasanthi Nilayam is the ashram of the controversial but very popular guru Sri Sathya Sai Baba. (p30)

Traveller Enclaves

Sometimes you don't want to race around in a bid to absorb as much as you can before your trip ends. Sometimes you want to chill with fellow backpackers: swap travel tales, read, take afternoon naps, play cards, drink beer...

Hampi The stunning beauty of Hampi's landscape and architecture makes everyone want to stay for a while, which has led to a well-developed traveller community. (p214)

Arambol Goa is one big traveller enclave, but Arambol may be its epicentre. Lots of shops and services combine with a splendid beach and cheap sleeps; no wonder we all end up there sooner or later. (p153)

Month by Month

TOP EVENTS

Carnival, January or February

Pongal, January

Ganesh Chaturthi, August or September

Navratri and **Dussehra**, September or October

Diwali, October or November

January

Post-monsoon cool lingers throughout the country, although it never gets truly cool in the most southerly states. Pleasant weather and several festivals make it a popular time to travel (book ahead!).

Free India

Republic Day commemorates the founding of the Republic of India on 26 January 1950.

Kite Festival

Sankranti, the Hindu festival marking the sun's passage into Capricorn, is celebrated in many ways across India – from banana-giving to dips in the Ganges. But it's the mass kite-flying in Maharashtra (among other states) that steals the show.

Southern Harvest

The Tamil festival of Pongal (p370), equivalent to Sankranti, marks the end of the harvest season. Families prepare pots of *pongal* (mixture of rice, sugar, dhal and milk), symbolic of prosperity and abundance, then feed them to decorated cows.

Celebrating Saraswati

On Vasant Panchami, Hindus dress in yellow and place books, musical instruments and other educational objects in front of idols of Saraswati, the goddess of learning, to receive her blessing. The holiday may fall in February.

The Prophet Mohammed's Birthday

The Islamic festival of Eid-Milad-un-Nabi celebrates the birth of the Prophet Mohammed with prayers and processions. It falls around 13 January 2014, 3 January 2015 and 26 December 2016.

February

The weather is comfortable in most nonmountainous areas, with summer heat starting to percolate in the south. It's still peak travel season.

Tibetan New Year

Losar is celebrated by Tantric Buddhists all over India for 15 days. Losar is usually in February or March, though dates can vary between regions.

Shivaratri

This day of Hindu fasting recalls the *tandava* (cosmic victory dance) of Lord Shiva. Temple processions are followed by the chanting of mantras and anointing of *linga* (phallic images of Shiva). Shivaratri can also fall in March.

LUNAR CALENDAR

Many festivals follow the Indian lunar calendar (a complex system based on astrology) or the Islamic calendar (which falls about 11 days earlier each year), and therefore change annually relative to the Gregorian calendar. Contact local tourist offices for exact festival dates.

Carnival in Goa

The four-day party kicking off Lent is particularly big in Goa. Sabado Gordo, Fat Saturday, starts it off with elaborate parades, and the revelry continues with street parties, concerts and general merrymaking.

March

The last month of the travel season, March is full-on hot in most of the country. Wildlife is easier to spot as animals come out to find water.

Holi

More widely celebrated in the North but still embraced by many southerners, Holi is an ecstatic festival; Hindus celebrate the beginning of spring according to the lunar calendar, in February or March, by throwing coloured water and *gulal* (powder) at anyone within range. Bonfires the night before symbolise the demise of demoness Holika.

Rama's Birthday

During Ramanavami, which lasts anywhere from one to nine days, Hindus celebrate Rama's birth with processions, music, fasting and feasting, enactments of scenes from the Ramayana and, at some temples, ceremonial weddings of Rama and Sita idols.

April

The hot has well and truly arrived in South India, and with the rise in temperature also comes a rise in competitive travel deals and a drop in tourist traffic.

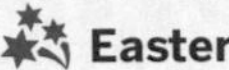

Easter

The Christian holiday marking the Crucifixion and Resurrection of Jesus Christ is celebrated simply in Christian communities with prayer and good food. Easter may also be in March.

Mahavir's Birthday

In April or March, Mahavir Jayanti commemorates the birth of Jainism's 24th and most important *tirthankar* (teacher and enlightened being). Temples are decorated and visited, Mahavir statues are given ritual baths, processions are held and offerings are given to the poor.

May

In most of the country it's hot. Really hot. Festivals slow down as humidity builds up in anticipation of the rain. Hill stations are hopping, though.

Buddha's Birthday

Commemorating the Buddha's birth, nirvana (enlightenment) and *parinirvana* (total liberation from the cycle of existence, or passing away), Buddha Jayanti is quiet but moving: devotees dress simply, eat vegetarian food, listen to dharma talks and visit monasteries or temples.

Ramadan (Ramazan)

Thirty days of dawn-to-dusk fasting mark the ninth month of the Islamic calendar. Muslims traditionally turn their attention to God, with a focus on prayer and purification. Ramadan begins around 28 June 2014, 18 June 2015 and 6 June 2016.

June

June's not a popular travel month in India, unless you're trekking up north. The rainy season, or premonsoon extreme heat, has started just about everywhere else.

July

It's really raining almost everywhere, with many remote roads being washed out. Consider doing a rainy-season meditation retreat, an ancient Indian tradition.

Brothers & Sisters

On Raksha Bandhan (Narial Purnima), girls fix amulets known as *rakhis* to the wrists of brothers and close male friends to protect them in the coming year. Brothers reciprocate with gifts and promises to take care of their sisters.

August

It's still high monsoon season: wet wet wet. Some folks swear by visiting tropical areas, like Kerala or Goa, at this time of year: the jungles are lush, bright green and glistening in the rain.

(Top) Diwali – the 'Festival of Lights'

(Bottom) Celebrating with *gulal* during the Holi festival

Independence Day

This public holiday on 15 August marks the anniversary of India's independence from Britain in 1947. Celebrations include flag-hoisting ceremonies, parades and patriotic cultural programs.

Celebrating the Buddha's Teaching

Drupka Teshi commemorates Siddhartha Gautama's first teaching, in which he explained the Four Noble Truths to disciples in Sarnath. The festival may also fall in July.

Snake Festival

The Hindu festival Naag Panchami is dedicated to Ananta, the serpent upon whose coils Vishnu rested between universes. Women return to their family homes and fast, while serpents are venerated as totems against flooding and other evils. Falls in July or August.

Krishna's Birthday

Janmastami celebrations can last a week in Krishna's birthplace, Mathura; elsewhere the festivities range from fasting to *puja* (prayers) and offering sweets, to drawing elaborate *rangoli* (rice-paste designs) outside the home. Held around 17 August 2014, 5 September 2015 and 25 August 2016.

Parsi New Year

Parsis celebrate Pateti, the Zoroastrian new year, especially in Mumbai (Bombay). Houses are cleaned and decorated with flowers and *rangoli*, the family dresses up and eats special fish dishes and sweets, and offerings are made at the Fire Temple.

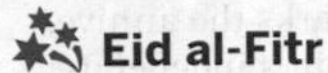

Eid al-Fitr

Muslims celebrate the end of Ramadan with three days of festivities. Prayers, shopping and gift-giving may all be part of the celebrations.

September

The rain begins to somewhat ease up, but with temperatures still relatively high throughout southern India the moisture-filled air can create a fatiguing steam-bath-like environment.

Ganesh's Birthday

In August or September Hindus celebrate Ganesh Chaturthi, the birth of the elephant-headed god, with verve, particularly in Mumbai. Clay idols of Ganesh are paraded through the streets before being ceremonially immersed in rivers, tanks (reservoirs) or the sea.

October

Although the southeast coast (and southern Kerala) can still be rainy, this is when India starts to get its travel mojo on. October (shoulder season) brings festivals, reasonably comfy temperatures, and post-rain lushness.

Gandhi's Birthday

The national holiday of Gandhi Jayanti is a solemn celebration of Mohandas Gandhi's birth, on 2 October, with prayer meetings at his cremation site in Delhi, Raj Ghat.

Navratri

The Hindu 'Festival of Nine Nights' leading up to Dussehra celebrates the goddess Durga in all her incarnations. Festivities, in September or October, are particularly vibrant in Maharashtra.

Dussehra

Colourful Dussehra celebrates the victory of the Hindu god Rama over the demon-king Ravana and the triumph of good over evil. Dussehra is big in Mysore (p195), which hosts one of India's grandest parades. Falls around 4 October 2014, 22 October 2015 and 11 October 2016.

Festival of Lights

In the lunar month of Kartika, Hindus celebrate Diwali (Deepavali) for five days, giving gifts, lighting fireworks, and burning butter and oil lamps (or hanging lanterns) to lead Lord Rama home from exile. One of India's prettiest festivals. Begins around 23 October 2014, 11 November 2015 and 30 October 2016.

Eid al-Adha

Muslims commemorate Ibrahim's readiness to sacrifice his son to God by slaughtering a goat or sheep and sharing it with family, the community and the poor. It will be held around 4 October 2014, 3 September 2015 and 11 September 2016.

November

The southern monsoon is sweeping Tamil Nadu and Kerala, but it's a good time to be anywhere low altitude, as the temperatures are generally pleasant.

Guru Nanak's Birthday

Nanak Jayanti, birthday of Guru Nanak, founder of Sikhism, is celebrated with prayer, *kirtan* (devotional singing) and processions for three days, especially in Punjab and Haryana. The festival may also be held on 14 April, possibly Nanak's actual 1469 birth date.

Muharram

During this month of grieving and remembrance, Shiite Muslims commemorate the martyrdom of the Prophet Mohammed's grandson Imam, an event known as Ashura, with beautiful processions. It begins around 25 October 2014, 13 October 2015 and 2 October 2016.

December

December is peak tourist season for a reason: the weather's glorious (except for the chilly mountains), the humidity is lower than usual, the mood is festive and the beaches are sublime.

Christmas Day

Christians celebrate the birth of Jesus Christ on 25 December. The festivities are especially big in Goa and Kerala, with musical events, elaborate decorations and special Masses, while Mumbai's Catholic neighbourhoods become festivals of lights.

Itineraries

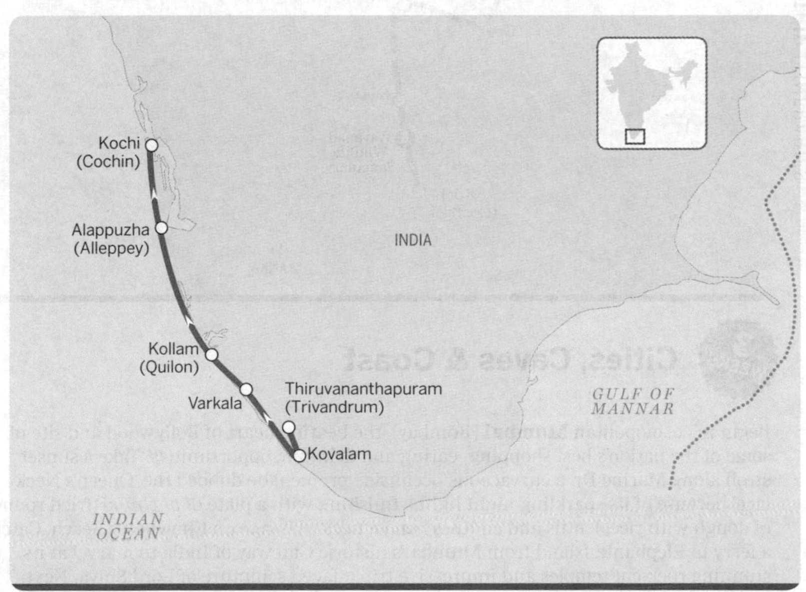

2 WEEKS Classic Kerala

Start your Keralan adventure in the capital, **Thiruvananthapuram** (Trivandrum). Spend a day visiting the zoological gardens and the nearby museums before making the half-hour hop to the beach at the well-developed resort of **Kovalam**. Backpackers might prefer to head further north to **Varkala**, a holy town thanks to its Janardhana Temple and alluring for its dizzying clifftop guesthouse and restaurant enclave. Chill out here with some yoga or surfing for a few days before continuing north to **Kollam** (Quilon), where you can take a canoe tour through the canals and backwaters around Munroe Island. Ditch the bus or train and take the full-day tourist cruise through the canals to Alappuzha (Alleppey) with an overnight stop at the **Matha Amrithanandamayi Mission** (p287), the pink ashram of 'The Hugging Mother'. Moving on to **Alleppey**, you're in houseboat central. Scout out for a houseboat or canoe operator and discover what the sublime backwaters are all about. Continuing north on the rail line to **Kochi** (Cochin), take the short ferry ride to Fort Cochin, Kerala's former colonial outpost. Aromatic seafood barbecues, wonderfully warm homestays, colonial-era mansions, Kathakali shows and the intriguing Jewish quarter at Mattancherry make this a fascinating place to while away a few days.

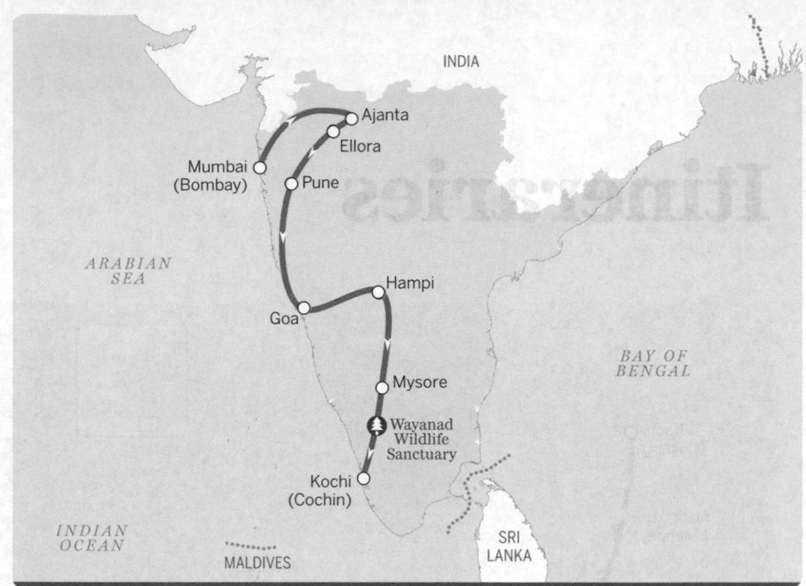

Cities, Caves & Coast

Begin in cosmopolitan **Mumbai** (Bombay), the beating heart of Bollywood and site of some of the nation's best shopping, eating and drinking opportunities. Take a sunset stroll along Marine Dr, a curvaceous oceanside promenade dubbed the 'Queen's Necklace' because of its sparkling night lights, finishing with a plate of *bhelpuri* (fried rounds of dough with rice, lentils and chutney) and a neck massage on Chowpatty Beach. Catch a ferry to Elephanta Island from Mumbai's historic Gateway of India to marvel at its stunning rock-cut temples and impressive triple-faced sculpture of Lord Shiva. Next, head northeast to explore the ancient cave art at **Ajanta** and **Ellora**. Located within 100km of each other, the incredible frescoed Buddhist caves of Ajanta are clustered along a horseshoe-shaped gorge, while the rock-cut caves of Ellora – which contain a mix of Hindu, Jain and Buddhist shrines – are situated on a 2km-long escarpment near Aurangabad. After soaking up cave culture, journey southwest to **Pune**, Maharashtra's IT hub, and its excellent museums, bars and the infamous Osho International Meditation Resort. Next stop is the tropical beach haven of **Goa** for some soul-reviving sandcastle therapy. Wander through a lush spice plantation, visit Portuguese-era cathedrals at Old Goa, shop at Anjuna's colourful flea market and take your pick from dozens of fabulous beach resorts before travelling east to the traveller hotspot of **Hampi** in neighbouring Karnataka. Ramble around Hampi's enigmatic boulder-strewn landscape and imagine what life here was like when it was a centre of the mighty Vijayanagar empire. Make the long trip down to **Mysore** to explore the Maharaja's Palace, one of India's grandest royal buildings, and shop for silk and sandalwood in its colourful markets. From Mysore it's an exciting bus ride into the Western Ghats and across the Keralan border to **Wayanad Wildlife Sanctuary,** a pristine forest and jungle reserve and one of the best places in the south to spot wild elephants. Finally, take the hair-raising road down to the coast and make your way to **Kochi**, Kerala's intriguing colonial city where a blend of Portuguese, Dutch and English history combines with wonderful homestays and a buzzing traveller scene.

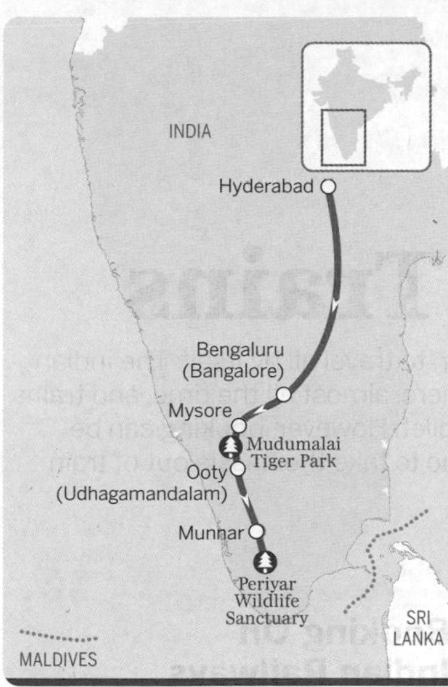

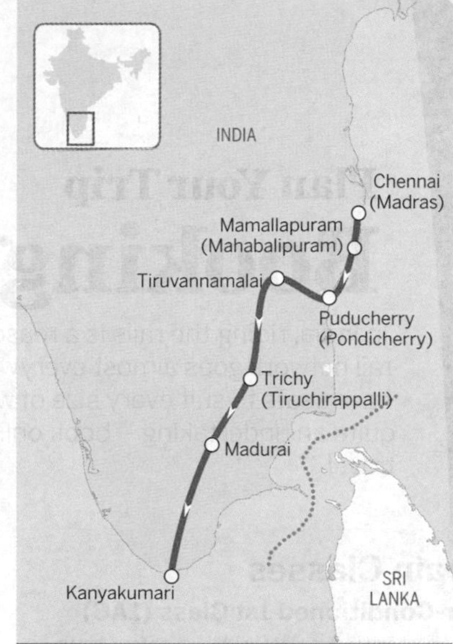

Cities & Sanctuaries

Start in **Hyderabad**, capital of Andhra Pradesh and a wealth of centuries-old Islamic monuments. Don't miss the impressive 16th-century Golconda Fort, then make the long trip south to **Bengaluru** (Bangalore), where you can spend a few days indulging in culinary and shopping delights. For a taste of the city's royal past visit the 18th-century Tipu Sultan's Palace and whimsical Bengaluru Palace. Next stop is the royal city of **Mysore**. Gawp at the Maharaja's Palace, an uber-grand complex topped with rhubarb-red and chalky-white domes. Put on your hiking boots now and head for the hills, south to Tamil Nadu's wonderful **Mudumalai Tiger Park**, where you can spot wild elephants on jeep safaris or trek through pristine jungle. Next stop is the cool hill town of **Ooty** (Udhagamandalam), one of South India's most-loved summer holiday retreats. Take the toy train down to Coimbatore, then cross the border into Kerala and the emerald-green tea-covered hills of **Munnar**, with some fine hiking and secluded accommodation in the surrounding forests. Finish with some optimistic tiger spotting and jungle trekking at pretty **Periyar Wildlife Sanctuary.**

Tamil Nadu's Temples

If temples are your thing, Tamil Nadu is the place to be. Delve into the rich history of **Chennai** (Madras) with a wander around the Government Museum before visiting the ancient Shiva Kapaleeshwarar Temple, San Thome Cathedral, and the military memorabilia at Fort St George museum. Travel south to beachside **Mamallapuram** (Mahabalipuram) to explore the superb rock-cut shrines that hark back to the Pallava dynasty. Time to move on to **Tiruvannamalai** to see the Arunachaleshwar Temple, one of the country's largest sacred complexes. Take a break from Hindu temples at **Puducherry** (Pondicherry) to feast your eyes on the faded buildings of the French Quarter and the 18th-century Church of Our Lady of the Immaculate Conception. For more spiritual sustenance head to **Trichy** (Tiruchirappalli), site of the memorable hilltop Rock Fort Temple and a gaggle of important Hindu shrines. Head south to **Madurai** to savour the incredible Meenakshi Amman Temple, considered by many to be the pinnacle of South Indian temple architecture. Finally, head to the southern tip of India at **Kanyakumari**, home to the Kumari Amman temple.

Plan Your Trip

Booking Trains

In India, riding the rails is a reason to travel all by itself. The Indian rail network goes almost everywhere, almost all the time, and trains have seats to suit every size of wallet. However, booking can be quite an undertaking – book online to take the hassle out of train travel.

Train Classes

Air-Conditioned 1st Class (1AC)

The most expensive class, with two- or four-berth compartments with locking doors and meals included.

Air-Conditioned 2-Tier (2AC)

Two-tier berths arranged in groups of four and two in an open-plan carriage. Bunks convert to seats by day and there are curtains, offering some privacy.

Air-Conditioned 3-Tier (3AC)

Three-tier berths arranged in groups of six in an open-plan carriage with no curtains; popular with Indian families.

AC Executive Chair

Comfortable, reclining chairs and plenty of space; usually on Shatabdi express trains.

AC Chair

Similar to the Executive Chair carriage but with less-fancy seating.

Sleeper Class

Open-plan carriages with three-tier bunks and no AC; the open windows afford great views.

Unreserved 2nd Class

Wooden or plastic seats and a *lot* of people – but cheap!

Booking On Indian Railways

Bookings open 90 days before departure and seats fill up quickly – reserve at least a week ahead where possible. Trains and seats come in a variety of classes, from the crush of unreserved class to the air-conditioned luxury of 1st class. Sleeper trains offer the chance to travel huge distances for not much more than the price of a midrange hotel room.

Express and mail trains form the mainstay of Indian rail travel. Not all classes are available on every train, but most long-distance services have general (2nd class) compartments with unreserved seating and more-comfortable reserved compartments, usually with the option of sleeper berths for overnight journeys.

Shatabdi express trains are same-day services with seating only; Rajdhani express trains are long-distance overnight services between Delhi and state capitals with a choice of 1AC, 2AC, 3AC and 2nd class. More-expensive sleeper categories provide bedding. In all classes, a padlock and a length of chain are useful for securing your luggage to baggage racks.

Booking Online

Booking in-country is a notoriously convoluted process, but you can avoid the hassle

RAILWAY RAZZLE DAZZLE

South India offers an enticing choice of tailored train journeys for tourists seeking to ride the rails with flair. Fares usually include on-board accommodation, tours, admission fees and all or most meals, and there are normally child concessions: enquire when booking.

➡ **Deccan Odyssey** (www.deccan-odyssey-india.com) Seven nights covering the main tourist spots of Maharashtra and Goa. From October to March, fares per person per night start at US$650/500/425 for single/double/triple occupancy (US$500/390/315 in September and April).

➡ **Golden Chariot** (www.thegoldenchariot.co.in) Tours the South in style from October to March, starting Bengaluru (Bangalore); eight-day/seven-night trips visiting Karnataka and Goa, or Tamil Nadu and Kerala. Rates per person per night start at US$754/545/440 for single/double/triple occupancy.

by booking online. Here's the low-down on how to do it.

When booking online, it pays to know the details of your journey – particularly station names, train numbers, days of operation and available classes. Start by visiting http://erail.in – the search engine will bring up a list of all trains running between your chosen destinations, along with information on classes and fares.

Step two is to register for an account with IRCTC (www.irctc.co.in), the government-run ticket booking service. This is required even if you plan to use a private ticket agency. Registration is a complex process, involving passwords, emails, scans of your passport and texts to your mobile phone. The ever-helpful Man in Seat 61 (www.seat61.com/India.htm) has a detailed guide to all the steps.

Once registered, you can use a credit card to book travel on specific trains, either directly with IRCTC or with private agencies. You'll be issued with an e-ticket, which you must print out to present alongside your passport and booking reference once you board the train. Note that the railway reservation system is open from 1.30am to 11.30pm (IST) every day.

Reputable booking agencies include the following:

IRCTC (www.irctc.co.in) Government site offering bookings for regular trains and luxury tourist trains; only American Express cards for international ticketing.

Cleartrip (www.cleartrip.com) Reliable private agency; accepts international credit cards.

Make My Trip (www.makemytrip.com) Reputable private agency; accepts international cards.

Yatra (www.yatra.com) Books flights and trains; accepts international cards.

Reservations

You must make a reservation for all chair-car, sleeper, 1AC, 2AC and 3AC carriages. No reservations are required for general (2nd class) compartments. Book well ahead for overnight journeys or travel during holidays and festivals. Waiting until the day of travel to book is not recommended.

Train Passes

IndRail passes permit unlimited rail travel for a fixed period, ranging from one day to 90 days, but these offer limited savings and you must still make reservations. Prices start at US$19/43/95 (sleeper/2AC and 3AC and chair car/1AC) for 24 hours. The easiest way to book these is through the IndRail pass agency in your home country – click on the Passenger Info/Tourist Information link on www.indianrailways.gov.in/railwayboard for further details.

Plan Your Trip

Yoga, Spas & Spiritual Pursuits

Birthplace of at least three of the world's great religions, India offers a profound spiritual journey for those so inclined. Even sceptical travellers can enjoy the benefits of trips to spas and yoga centres.

What to Choose

Ashrams

South India has plenty of ashrams – places of communal living established around the philosophies of a guru (a spiritual guide or teacher).

Ayurveda

Ayurveda is the ancient science of Indian herbal medicine and holistic healing, based on natural plant extracts, massage and therapies to treat body and mind.

Yoga

Yoga's roots lie firmly in India and you'll find hundreds of schools to suit all levels.

Buddhist Meditation

Various centres in Buddhist areas offer training in *vipassana* (mindfulness meditation) and Buddhist philosophy; many require a vow of silence and abstinence from tobacco, alcohol and sex.

Spa Treatments

South India's spas offer an enticing mix of international therapies and local techniques based on ancient ayurvedic traditions.

Ashrams

Many ashrams (literally 'places of striving') have made a name for themselves – both within India and abroad – thanks to their charismatic gurus, and some tread a fine line between spiritual community and personality cult. Many gurus have amassed vast fortunes collected from devotees, and others have been accused of sexually exploiting their followers. Always check the reputation of any ashram before enrolling in a program.

Most ashrams offer courses of study, typically with elements of philosophy and yoga or meditation, and visitors are usually required to adhere to strict rules, which may include a dress code, a daily regimen of yoga or meditation, and charitable work at social projects run by the ashram. Make sure you're willing to abide by the rules before committing

A donation is appropriate to cover the expenses of your food, accommodation and the running costs of the ashram. The following are some of India's most famous ashrams.

Andhra Pradesh

➡ **Prasanthi Nilayam** (www.srisathyasai.org.in; Puttaparthi) Ashram of the controversial late guru Sri Sathya Sai Baba, revered by six million enthusiastic devotees.

Kerala

➡ **Matha Amrithanandamayi Mission** (p287; Amrithapuri) Famed for its female guru Amma, 'The Hugging Mother'.

Maharashtra

➡ **Brahmavidya Mandir Ashram** (p105; Sevagram) Established by Gandhi's disciple Vinoba Bhave.

➡ **Sevagram Ashram** (p105; Sevagram) The famous ashram founded by Gandhi.

➡ **Osho International Meditation Resort** (p114; Pune) Follows the sometimes controversial teachings of Osho.

Tamil Nadu

➡ **Sri Aurobindo Ashram** (p363; Puducherry) Founded by the famous Sri Aurobindo.

➡ **Isha Yoga Center** (p400; Coimbatore) Offers residential courses and retreats.

➡ **Sri Ramana Ashram** (p361; Tiruvannamalai) Long-established ashram of Sri Ramana Maharsh.

Ayurveda

Ayurveda – Indian herbal medicine – aims to restore balance in the body through two main techniques: *panchakarma* (internal purification) and herbal massage. Centres all over India offer ayurvedic treatments, from *abhyangam* (whole body massage with herbal oils) to *shirodhara* (where warm oil is dribbled onto the forehead from a hanging bowl); the use of enemas is likely to appeal to serious converts only. Here are some recommended centres.

Goa

➡ **Ayurvedic Natural Health Centre** (p142; Saligao) A reputable school with professional courses and treatments.

Karnataka

➡ **Ayurvedagram** (p181; Bengaluru) Varied treatments in a garden setting.

➡ **Soukya** (p181; Bengaluru) Excellent programs in ayurvedic therapy and yoga.

➡ **Indus Valley Ayurvedic Centre** (p194; Mysore) Therapies from ancient scriptures.

➡ **Swaasthya Ayurvedic Centre** (p194; Mysore) Traditional therapies and residential retreats.

➡ **SwaSwara** (p213; Gokarna) Resort combining therapies and artistic pursuits.

Kerala

➡ **Eden Garden** (p280; Varkala) Offers single treatments and packages.

➡ **Santhigiri Ayurveda Centre** (p285; Kollam) Seven- to 21-day packages and day treatments.

➡ **Ayur Dara** (p307; Kochi) One- to three-week treatments on Vypeen Island.

Tamil Nadu

➡ **Ayurveda Holistic Healing Centre** (p365; Puducherry) Treatments and courses in yoga, ayurveda and varma.

Yoga

You can practise yoga almost everywhere in India, from Goan beach resorts to mountain retreats in the Himalaya. Note that some centres are only open to experienced practitioners – seek recommendations from other travellers, and visit several to find one that suits your needs and ability.

Some recommended centres are listed below.

Andaman Islands

➡ **People Tree** (p423; Havelock Island) Offers yoga and meditation retreats in tropical surroundings

Goa

➡ **Himalaya Yoga Valley** (p152; Mandrem) A popular training school with an international focus.

Karnataka

Mysore was the birthplace of *ashtanga* yoga, popularised by K Pattabhi Jois in the 1940s, and the city has numerous centres offering courses.

Above: Take a yoga class in India, the birthplace of yoga
Left: Nilaya Hermitage (p144), Goa

Kerala

Thiruvananthapuram (Trivandrum), Varkala and Kochi (Cochin) are popular places for yoga.

➡ **Sivananda Yoga Vedanta Dhanwantari Ashram** (p276; Trivandrum) Renowned for two-week (and longer) hatha yoga courses.

Maharashtra

➡ **Kaivalyadhama Yoga Hospital** (p110; Lonavla) Offers yogic healing – a combination of yoga and naturopathic therapies.

➡ **Ramamani Iyengar Memorial Yoga Institute** (p114; Pune) Advanced Iyengar yoga courses (for experienced practitioners only).

Mumbai

➡ **Yoga Institute** (p61) Has daily classes as well as longer-term residential programs.

Tamil Nadu

➡ **International Centre for Yoga Education & Research** (p365; Puducherry) Offers three-week introductory courses and advanced training.

Buddhist Meditation

Whether you want an introduction to Buddhism or are seeking something more profound, there are courses and retreats on offer in Buddhist regions across India. We recommend the following centres in South India.

Andhra Pradesh

Numerous centres in AP offer courses in the Burmese-style *vipassana* tradition, including in Hyderabad (p239), Vijayawada (p256) and Nagarjuna Sagar (p250).

Maharashtra

➡ **Vipassana International Academy** (p92; Igatpuri) Offers 10-day courses in the Burmese tradition of *vipassana* meditation free of charge.

Mumbai

➡ **Global Pagoda** (p56; Gorai Island) Has one- to 10-day *vipassana* courses.

Spa Treatments

There are spas all over South India, from accessible spas in big-city shopping centres to indulgence in opulent five-star hotels. Be cautious of dodgy one-on-one massages by private (often unqualified) operators, particularly in tourist towns – seek recommendations from fellow travellers and trust your instincts.

Goa

➡ **Nilaya Hermitage** (p144; Arpora) Enjoy maximum indulgence at this famous celebrity-hangout.

Karnataka

➡ **Emerge Spa** (p194; near Mysore) Offers pampering treatments based on ayurveda and other Asian traditions.

Plan Your Trip
Volunteering

For all India's beauty, rich culture and history, its poverty and hardship are unavoidable facts of life. Many travellers feel motivated to help, and charities and aid organisations across the country welcome committed volunteers. Here's a guide to help you start making a difference.

How to Volunteer

Choosing an Organisation

Consider how your skills will benefit the people you are trying to help, and choose an organisation that can specifically benefit from your abilities.

Time Required

Think realistically about how much time you can devote to a project. You're more likely to be of help if you commit for at least a month, ideally more.

Money

Giving your time for free is only part of the story; most organisations expect volunteers to cover their accommodation, food and transport.

Working 9 to 5

Make sure you understand what you are signing up for; many organisations expect volunteers to work full time, five days a week.

Transparency

Ensure that the organisation you choose is reputable and transparent about how they spend their money. Where possible, get feedback from former volunteers.

Aid Programs in South India

India faces considerable challenges and there are numerous opportunities for volunteers. It may be possible to find a placement after you arrive, but charities and nongovernment organisations (NGOs) generally prefer volunteers who have applied in advance and been approved for the kind of work involved.

As well as international organisations, local charities and NGOs often have opportunities, though it can be harder to assess the work that these organisations are doing. For listings of local agencies, check www.indianngos.com or contact the Delhi-based **Concern India Foundation** (☎26210998; www.concernindiafoundation.org; A-52 Amar Colony, Lajpat Nagar IV). The Delhi magazine *First City* (www.firstcitydelhi.com) also has listings.

The following programs are just some of many that may have opportunities for volunteers; contact them in advance to arrange a placement.

Caregiving

If you have medical experience, there are numerous opportunities to provide health care and support for the most vulnerable in Indian society.

Maharashtra

➡ **Sadhana Village** (☎020-25380792; www.sadhana-village.org; 1 Lokmanya Colony, Priyankit, Pune) A residence for disabled adults; has a minimum commitment of two months for volunteers.

Community

Many community volunteer projects work to provide health care and education to villages.

Karnataka

➡ **Kishkinda Trust** (☎08533-267777; www.thekishkindatrust.org; Royal St, Anegundi; Hampi) Volunteers needed to assist with sustainable community development.

➡ **Equations** (☎080-25457607; www.equitabletourism.org; 415, 2nd C Cross, 4th Main Rd, OMBR Layout, Banaswadi Post; Bengaluru) Volunteers assist with sustainable tourism initiatives.

Working with Children

The following charities provide support for disadvantaged children.

Goa

➡ **Mango Tree Goa** (p139; Mapusa) Opportunities for volunteer nurses and teaching assistants to help impoverished children.

➡ **El Shaddai** (p139; Assagao) Placements helping impoverished and homeless children; one-month minimum commitment.

Mumbai

➡ **Child Rights & You** (p61) Volunteers can assist with campaigns to raise funds for projects around India; six-week minimum commitment.

➡ **Vatsalya Foundation** (p61) Long- and short-term opportunities teaching and running sports activities for street children.

Tamil Nadu

➡ **Rural Institute for Development Education** (RIDE; ☎044-27268223; www.rideindia.org; Kanchipuram) Volunteer teachers and support staff help rural communities and children rescued from forced labour.

Working with Women

Several charities work to empower and educate women.

Mumbai

➡ **Apne Aap Women Worldwide** (www.apneaap.org) Provides education and livelihood training for trafficked women.

Environment & Conservation

The following charities focus on environmental education and sustainable development:

Andaman Islands

➡ **ANET** (p419; North Wandoor) Volunteers assist with environmental activities from field projects to general maintenance.

Maharashtra

➡ **Nimbkar Agricultural Research Institute** (☎02166-222396; www.nariphaltan.org; Phaltan-Lonand Rd, Tambmal, Phaltan) Offers internships in sustainable agriculture lasting two to six months for agriculture, engineering and science graduates.

Tamil Nadu

➡ **Keystone Foundation** (p401; Kotagiri) Has occasional opportunities to help improve

HANDY WEBSITES

➡ **Ethical Volunteering** (www.ethicalvolunteering.org) Useful guidelines for choosing an ethical sending agency.

➡ **World Volunteer Web** (www.worldvolunteerweb.org) Information and resources for volunteering around the globe.

➡ **Working Abroad** (www.workingabroad.com) Volunteer and professional work opportunities in over 150 countries.

➡ **Worldwide Volunteering** (www.wwv.org.uk) Database of worldwide volunteering opportunities.

AGENCIES OVERSEAS

There are so many international volunteering agencies, it can be bewildering trying to assess which ones are reputable. Agencies offering the chance to do whatever you want, wherever you want are almost always tailoring projects to the volunteer rather than finding the right volunteer for the work that needs to be done. Look for projects that will derive real benefits from your skills. To find sending agencies in your area, read Lonely Planet's *Volunteer: a Traveller's Guide*, the *Big Trip* and the *Career Break Book*, or try one of the following.

➡ **Voluntary Service Overseas** (VSO; www.vso.org.uk) British organisation offering long-term professional placements in India and worldwide.

➡ **Indicorps** (www.indicorps.org) Matches volunteers to projects across India, particularly in social development.

environmental conditions, working with indigenous communities.

Working with Animals

From stray dogs to rescued reptiles, opportunities for animal lovers are plentiful.

Andhra Pradesh

➡ **Blue Cross of Hyderabad** (p239; Hyderabad) A shelter with over 1000 animals; volunteers help care for shelter animals or work in the office.

Goa

➡ **International Animal Rescue** (p159; Assagao) Volunteers needed to assist vets and tend to sick strays.

➡ **Animal Rescue Centre** (p159; Chapolim) Animal welfare group that also has volunteer opportunities.

Mumbai

➡ **Welfare of Stray Dogs** (p61; Mumbai) Volunteers can work with the animals, manage stores or educate kids in school programs.

Tamil Nadu

➡ **Madras Crocodile Bank** (p350; Vadanemmeli) A reptile conservation centre with openings for volunteers (minimum two weeks).

Heritage & Restoration

Those with architecture and building skills should look at the following.

Tamil Nadu

➡ **ArcHeS** (p384; Karaikkudi) Aims to preserve the architectural and cultural heritage of Chettinadu; openings for historians, geographers and architects.

Plan Your Trip

Travel With Children

Fascinating and thrilling, South India can be every bit as exciting for children as it is for their wide-eyed parents. The scents, sights and sounds of this part of the country will inspire and challenge young enquiring minds, and with careful preparation and vigilance, a lifetime of vivid memories can be sown.

India for Kids

In many respects, travel with children in South India can be a real joy, and warm welcomes are frequent. Lots of locals will delight at taking a photograph or two beside your bouncing baby. But while all this is fabulous for outgoing children it may prove tiring, or even disconcerting, for younger kids and those with more retiring dispositions.

The key as a parent on the road in India is to stay alert to your children's needs and to remain firm in fulfilling them. Remember, though, that the attention your children will inevitably receive is almost always good-natured; kids are the centre of life in many Indian households, and your own will be treated just the same. Hotels will almost always come up with an extra bed or two, and restaurants with a familiar meal.

Children's Highlights

Best Natural Encounters

➡ **Elephant Encounters** It's possible to see elephants at a variety of southern sanctuaries, including the Nilgiri Biosphere Reserve, which spans Tamil Nadu, Karnataka and Kerala.

Best Regions for Kids

Goa

Palm-fringed, white-sand beaches and inexpensive food make Goa an ideal choice for family holidays. If you're looking to stay for awhile, there's a good selection of apartments and homey guesthouses on offer to suit all budgets.

Kerala

Houseboat adventures, surf beaches, Arabian sea sunsets, snake boat races, ayurvedic massage and elephant festivals. From the Ghats down to the coast, Kerala offers action and relaxation in equal doses.

Maharashtra

Maharashtra has some fabulous options for kids. The mysterious Ajanta and Ellora Caves have plenty of appeal, promising to stir young and old imaginations alike. Meanwhile, a short boat ride to Elephanta Island, just off Mumbai – to see its wonderful rock-cut temples – makes for a relaxing half-day expedition.

➡ **Goa's Dolphins** Splash out on a dolphin-spotting boat trip from almost any Goan beach to see them cavorting among the waves.

➡ **Hill Station Monkeys** Most hill stations proffer the opportunity for close encounters with cheeky monkeys. Be cautious though – these feisty simians can be aggressive and are known to grab food from your hands and even bite unsuspecting visitors.

➡ **Hampi** Make like the Flintstones on the boulder-strewn shores of the Tungabhadra River, crossable by coracle; explore magical ancient ruins.

Fun Forms of Transport

➡ **Hand-pulled Rickshaw, Matheran** A narrow-gauge diesel toy train takes visitors most of the way up to this cute, monkey-infested hill station, after which your children can choose to continue to the village on horseback or in a hand-pulled rickshaw. (p108)

➡ **Backwater Boat, Alappuzha (Alleppey)** Hop on a houseboat to luxuriously cruise Kerala's beautiful backwaters. If you happen to hit town on the second Saturday in August, take the kids along to see the spectacular Nehru Trophy Snake Boat Race. (p292)

➡ **Autorickshaw** Hurtle along city back alleys to create a scene worthy of Indiana Jones.

Best Beaches

➡ **Palolem, Goa** Hole up in a beachfront palm-thatched hut and watch your kids cavort at pretty Palolem beach, featuring the shallowest, safest waters in Goa. (p161)

➡ **Patnem, Goa** Just up the leafy lane from Palolem, quieter Patnem draws scores of long-stayers with children to its nice sand beach and cool, calm, child-friendly beach restaurants. (p161)

➡ **Havelock Island** Splash about in the shallows at languid Havelock Island, part of the Andaman Island chain, where, for older children, there's spectacular diving on offer. (p419)

Planning

Before You Go

➡ Look at climate charts and choose your dates to avoid the extremes of temperature that may put younger children at risk.

➡ Remember to visit your doctor to discuss vaccinations, health advisories and other health-related issues involving your children well in advance of travel.

➡ For more tips on travel in India, and first-hand accounts of travels in the country, pick up Lonely Planet's *Travel with Children* or visit the Thorn Tree Forum at lonelyplanet.com.

What to Pack

➡ If you're travelling with a baby or toddler, there are several items worth packing in quantity: disposable or washable nappies, nappy rash cream (Calendula cream works well against heat rash too), extra bottles, wet wipes, infant formula and canned, bottled or rehydratable food. You can get all these items in many parts of South India too, but often prices are at a premium and brands may not be those you recognise.

➡ Another good idea is a fold-up baby bed or the lightest possible travel cot you can find (companies such as KidCo make excellent pop-up tent-style beds), since hotel cots may prove precarious. A stroller, though, is optional, as there are few places with pavements even enough to use one successfully.

➡ For older children, make sure you bring good sturdy footwear, a hat or two, a few less-precious toys (that won't be mourned if lost or damaged) and a swimming jacket, life jacket or water wings for the sea or pool.

➡ Child-friendly insect repellent, wide-brimmed hats and sun lotion are a must.

Eating

➡ You may have to work hard to find something to satisfy sensitive childhood palates, but if you're travelling in the more family-friendly regions of South India, such as Goa, Kerala or the big cities, feeding your brood is easier. Here you will find familiar Western dishes in abundance.

➡ While on the road, easy portable snacks such as bananas, samosas, *puri* (puffy dough pockets) and packaged biscuits (Parle G brand are a perennial hit) will keep diminutive hunger pangs at bay.

➡ Adventurous eaters and vegetarian children, meanwhile, will delight in experimenting with the vast range of tastes and textures available at the Indian table: *paneer* (unfermented cheese) dishes, simple dhals (mild lentil curries), creamy kormas, buttered naans (tandoori breads), pilaus (rice dishes) and Tibetan *momos* (steamed or fried dumplings) are all firm favourites.

➡ Few children, no matter how culinarily unadventurous, can resist the finger food fun of a vast South Indian dosa (paper-thin lentil-flour pancake) served up for breakfast.

Accommodation

➡ South India offers such an array of accommodation options – from beach huts to heritage boutiques to five-star fantasies – that you're bound to find something that will appeal to the whole family.

➡ The swish upmarket hotels are almost always child-friendly, but so are many upper midrange hotels, whose staff will usually rustle up an extra mattress or two; some places won't mind cramming several children into a regular-sized double room along with their parents.

➡ If your budget stretches to it, a good way to maintain familial energy levels is to mix in a few top-end stays throughout your travels. The very best five-stars come equipped with children's pools, games rooms and even children's clubs, while an occasional night with a warm bubble bath, room service, macaroni cheese and the Disney channel will revive even the most disgruntled young traveller's spirits.

On the Road

➡ Travel in India, be it by taxi, bus, train or air, can be arduous for the whole family. Concepts such as clean public toilets, changing rooms and safe playgrounds are rare in much of the country. Public transport is often extremely overcrowded so plan fun, easy days to follow longer bus or train rides.

➡ Pack plenty of diversions (tablets or laptops with a stock of downloaded movies make invaluable travel companions, as do the good old-fashioned story books, cheap toys and games widely available across India), but most of all don't be put off: it might take you a while to get there (and there are few words more daunting than 'delay' to already frazzled parents), but chances are it will be well worth it when you do.

➡ If you are hiring a car and driver – a sensible and flexible option – and you require safety capsules, child restraints or booster seats, you will need to make this absolutely clear to the hiring company as early as possible. Don't expect to find these items readily available. And don't be afraid to tell your driver to slow down and drive responsibly.

Health

➡ The availability of a decent standard of health care varies widely in South India. Talk to your doctor at home about where you will be travelling to get advice on vaccinations and what to include in your first-aid kit.

➡ Access to health care is certainly better in traveller-frequented parts of the country where it's almost always easy to track down a doctor at short notice (most hotels will be able to recommend a reliable one).

➡ Prescriptions are quickly and cheaply filled over the counter at numerous pharmacies, often congregating near hospitals.

➡ Diarrhoea can be very serious in young children. Seek medical help if it is persistent or accompanied by fever. Rehydration is essential.

➡ Heat rash, skin complaints such as impetigo, insect bites or stings can be treated with the help of a well-equipped first-aid kit.

Regions at a Glance

South India is made up of a wonderfully diverse patchwork of states. The vernaculars are varied, the customs are distinctive, there's a variety of culinary choices and the topography is spectacularly manifold. A mind-shaking mix of state-of-the-art and timeless tradition, no matter where you choose to travel you'll be rewarded with an invigorating assault on all the senses.

For travellers, South India's remarkable diversity is most often apparent in its extraordinary wealth of architecture, wildlife, landscapes, festivals, handicrafts, cuisine and performing arts. And then there's spirituality – the beating heart, indeed, of the entire nation – which faithfully pulsates all the way from the jagged peaks of the snowy Himalayas to the lush, steamy jungles of southern plains.

Mumbai (Bombay)

Architecture
Cuisine
Nightlife

Angels in the Architecture

Thank the British – and Indian stonemasons – for Mumbai's colonial-era architecture, including the Chhatrapati Shivaji Terminus, High Court and University of Mumbai.

Divine Dinners

Flavours from all over India mingle in Mumbai – sample hot and sour *dhansak* (curried lentil stew) in Parsi canteens, *bhelpuri* (fried rounds of dough with rice) on Chowpatty Beach or globe-trotting feasts in a five-star hotel eatery.

Bollywood Beats

Sharing their city with the world's most prolific film industry, Mumbaikars are party people. Keep an eye out for Bollywood stars as you dance till dawn in bars and nightclubs crammed with beautiful people.

p44

Maharashtra

Caves
Beaches
Wine

Caves as Galleries

The World Heritage-listed caves at Ajanta and Ellora hide exquisite cave paintings and rock sculptures dating back to India's golden age.

Secret Sands

Strung out along Maharashtra's Konkan Coast are some of the most secluded beaches in India, custom-made for romantics and adventurers.

Tasty Tipples

Nasik, the *grand cru* of India's up-and-coming wine industry, boasts vineyards that blend California-style new-world attitude with Indian atmosphere.

p85

Goa

Beaches
Cuisine
Architecture

Super Sands

So beautiful they're almost a cliché, Goa's beaches have undeniably been discovered, but with the surf breaking over your toes and palm fronds swaying overhead, it doesn't seem to matter.

Colonial Cookpot

Goa has fresh-off-the-boat seafood and cooks who blend cooking tricks and ingredients from India and Portugal to create a fabulous interplay of flavours.

A Catholic Legacy

When the Portuguese decamped from Goa in 1961, they left behind a grand colonial legacy: mansions in Quepem and Chandor, shop-houses in Panaji (Panjim), stately basilicas in Old Goa and villas scattered along the coastline.

p123

Karnataka & Bengaluru

Temples
Parks
Cuisine

Temple Extravagance

From the Hoysala beauties at Belur, Halebid and Somnathpur to the Virupaksha Temple in Hampi and shrines in Gokarna and Udupi, the temples of Karnataka overflow with carved embellishments.

Pristine Reserves

Draped in tropical vines, the Nilgiri Biosphere Reserve boasts some of the most pristine forests in India; seek abundant wildlife in national parks such as Bandipur and Nagarhole.

Creative Cuisine

Start off with a delectable Udupi vegetarian thali, then move on to some fiery Mangalorean seafood, washing it all down with fresh draught Kingfisher in beer-town Bengaluru (Bangalore).

p173

Andhra Pradesh

Religion
Cuisine
Beaches

Soulful Sites

Hindu pilgrims flock to the Sri Venkateshwara Temple at Tirumala, Buddhists contemplate amid the ruins of monastic centres, and Muslims recall the heyday of Islamic India in monument-crammed Hyderabad.

Brilliant Biryanis

Synonymous with Hyderabad, biryani is a local obsession. The similarly famous Hyderabadi *haleem* (mutton stew) has been patented so that it can't be served unless it meets local quality standards.

Coastal Exuberance

Beach tourism here is geared towards the domestic market, lending a unique and festive atmosphere to the seaside resorts; Visakhapatnam has the most gorgeous coastline.

p230

Kerala

Backwaters
Cuisine
Wildlife

Serene Waterways

Behind the beaches, the inlets and lakes of Kerala's backwaters spread far inland; exploring this waterlogged world by houseboat or canoe is one of India's most relaxing pleasures.

Fire & Spice

Delicious, delicate dishes flavoured with coconut, chilli and myriad spices – the Keralan kitchen is a melting pot of international cultural influences and local ingredients.

Wild Beasts

Kerala has been dealt a fine hand of wildlife-filled national parks, where, amid lush mountain landscapes, you can spot wild elephants, tigers, leopards and other native Indian species.

p267

Tamil Nadu & Chennai

Temples
Hill Stations
Hotels

Towering Temples

The amazing architecture, daily rituals and colourful festivals of Tamil Nadu's Hindu temples draw pilgrims from around India. Major temples are topped by *gopurams* (gateway towers) and carved *mandapas* (pavilions).

Cool Escapes

The hill stations of the Westerns Ghats offer wonderfully cool weather, animated festivals, cosy colonial-era guesthouses with open fires, and the chance to hike to gorgeous viewpoints looking out over the plains.

Heritage Hotels

Elegant spots to lay your head include the picturesque townhouses of Puducherry's French Quarter, grand old palace hotels in the hills, and the Chettiar mansions of the south.

p329

Andaman Islands

Diving
Beaches
Tribes

Undersea Adventures

Explore underwater jungles of coral teeming with tropical fish in jewel-bright colours – India's prime diving spot has easy dips for first-timers and challenging drift dives for veterans.

Superior Sands

If you're searching for that picture-postcard beach, or kilometres of deserted coastline, the Andamans boast some of the most unspoiled beaches in India.

Island Culture

An anthropologist's dream, the Andamans are home to dozens of fascinating tribal groups; most reside on outlying islands, which tourists are prohibited from visiting, but even the major islands offer a beguiling blend of South Asian and Southeast Asian culture.

p410

On the Road

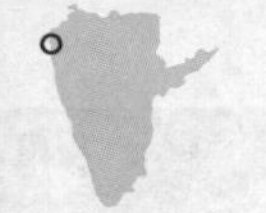

Mumbai (Bombay)

Includes ➡

Best Places to Eat

➡ Koh (p71)

➡ Hotel Ram Ashraya (p72)

➡ Revival (p71)

➡ Pradeep Gomantak Bhojanalaya (p70)

➡ Culture Curry (p73)

Best Places to Stay

➡ Taj Mahal Palace, Mumbai (p64)

➡ Iskcon (p66)

➡ YWCA (p64)

➡ Anand Hotel (p66)

➡ ITC Maratha (p68)

Why Go?

Mumbai is big. It's full of dreamers and hard-labourers, starlets and gangsters, stray dogs and exotic birds, artists and servants and fisherfolk and *crorepatis* (millionaires) and lots and lots of other people. It has the most prolific film industry, some of Asia's biggest slums (and the world's most expensive home) and the largest tropical forest in an urban zone. It's India's financial powerhouse, fashion epicentre and a pulse point of religious tension. It's evolved its own language, Bambaiyya Hindi, which is a mix of…everything.

But Mumbai does not have to be overwhelming: it just has its own rhythm, which takes a little while to hear. Just give yourself some time to appreciate the city's lilting cadences, its harmonies of excess and restraint, and before you know it, Mumbai might just decide to take you in like you're one of her own.

When to Go

Mumbai (Bombay)

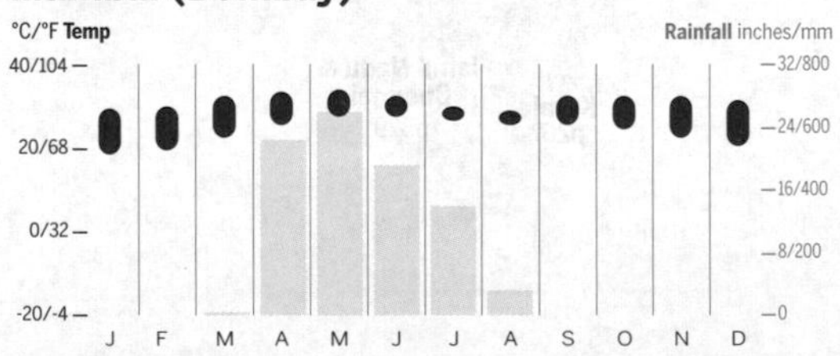

Dec–Jan The very best, least sticky weather.

Aug–Sep Mumbai goes Ganesh-crazy during its most exciting festival, Ganesh Chaturthi.

Oct–Apr Post-monsoon, best for festivals, and bird-watching in Sanjay Gandhi National Park.

Food

Mumbai is a city shaped by flavours from all over India and the world. Go on a cultural history tour by sampling Parsi *dhansak* (meat with curried lentils and rice), Gujarati or Keralan thalis ('all-you-can-eat' meals), Mughlai kebabs, Goan vindaloo and Mangalorean seafood. And don't forget, if you see Bombay duck on a menu, it's actually *bombil* fish dried in the sun and deep-fried. Streetwise, don't miss Mumbai's famous *bhelpuri* (puffed rice tossed with fried rounds of dough, lentils, onions, herbs and chutneys). Stalls offering *bhelpuri*, as well as samosas, *pav bhaji* (spiced vegetables and bread), *vada pav* (deep-fried spiced lentil-ball sandwich), bhurji pav (scrambled eggs and bread) and *dabeli* (a mixture of potatoes, spices, peanuts and pomegranate, also on bread), do a brisk trade around the city.

DON'T MISS

For many, a visit to cosmopolitan Mumbai is all about dining, nightlife and shopping, but the city offers far more than nocturnal amusement and retail therapy. Nowhere is that more evident than in the spectacular maze of Gothic, Victorian, Indo-Saracenic and art deco architecture, remnants of the British colonial era and countless years of European influence. **Chhatrapati Shivaji Terminus**, **High Court**, **University of Mumbai**, **Taj Mahal Palace** hotel and the **Gateway of India** are just the most prominent: the city is laced with architectural jewels, and stumbling upon them is one of Mumbai's great joys.

Top Festivals

- **Mumbai Sanskruti** (Jan; Fort) This free, two-day celebration of Hindustani classical music is held on the steps of the gorgeous Asiatic Society Library.
- **Kala Ghoda Festival** (Feb; citywide, p53) Getting bigger and more sophisticated each year, the two-week-long art fest sees tons of performances and exhibitions.
- **Elephanta Festival** (Mar; Gateway of India, p48) Formerly on Elephanta Island, this classical music and dance festival now accommodates more people on waterfront Apollo Bunder.
- **Nariyal Poornima** (Aug; Colaba) This Koli celebration marks the start of the fishing season and the retreat of monsoon winds.
- **Ganesh Chaturthi** (Aug/Sep; citywide) Mumbai gets totally swept up by this 10- to 12-day celebration of the elephant-headed Hindu god Ganesh. On the festival's first, third, fifth, seventh and 11th days, families and communities take their Ganesh statues to the seashore and auspiciously submerge them.
- **Mumbai Film Festival** (Oct; citywide) New films from the subcontinent and beyond are screened at the weeklong MFF.

MAIN POINTS OF ENTRY

Most arrive at Mumbai's Chhatrapati Shivaji International Airport, Mumbai Central train station (BCT) or Chhatrapati Shivaji Terminus (CST; Victoria Terminus).

Fast Facts

- **Population:** 18.4 million
- **Area:** 444 sq km
- **Area code:** 022
- **Languages:** Marathi, Hindi, Gujarati, English
- **Sleeping prices: $** below ₹1500, **$$** ₹1500 to ₹5000, **$$$** above ₹5000

Top Tips

Many international flights arrive after midnight. Beat the daytime traffic by heading straight to your hotel, and carry detailed landmark directions for your hotel: many airport taxi drivers don't speak English and may not use official street names.

Resources

- **Mumbai Magic** (www.mumbai-magic.blogspot.com) Excellent blog on the city's hidden corners.
- **Mumbai Boss** (www.mumbaiboss.com) The boss of what's on in Mumbai.
- **Maharashtra Tourism Development Corporation** (www.maharashtratourism.gov.in) Official tourism site.
- **Lonely Planet** (www.lonelyplanet.com/india/mumbai) Recommendations, planning advice, reviews, insider tips.

Mumbai Highlights

❶ Marvel at the magnificence of Mumbai's colonial-era architecture: **Chhatrapati Shivaji Terminus** (p49), **University of Mumbai** (p49) and **High Court** (p50)

❷ Get lost amid the millions of things for sale in Mumbai's ancient **bazaars** (p79)

❸ Dine like a maharaja at one of India's best **restaurants** (p68)

❹ Feel the city's sea breeze amongst playing kids, big balloons and a hot-pink sunset at **Girgaum Chowpatty** (p52)

❺ Ogle the Renaissance-revival interiors of the **Dr Bhau Daji Lad Mumbai City Museum** (p53)

❻ Learn to meditate at the awe-inspiring **Global Pagoda** (p56), then see how it was originally done at the **Kanheri Caves** (p61)

❼ Behold the commanding triple-headed Shiva at **Elephanta Island** (p57)

❽ Sleep in one of the world's iconic hotels, the **Taj Mahal Palace, Mumbai** (p64) or have a drink at its **bar** (p74), Mumbai's first

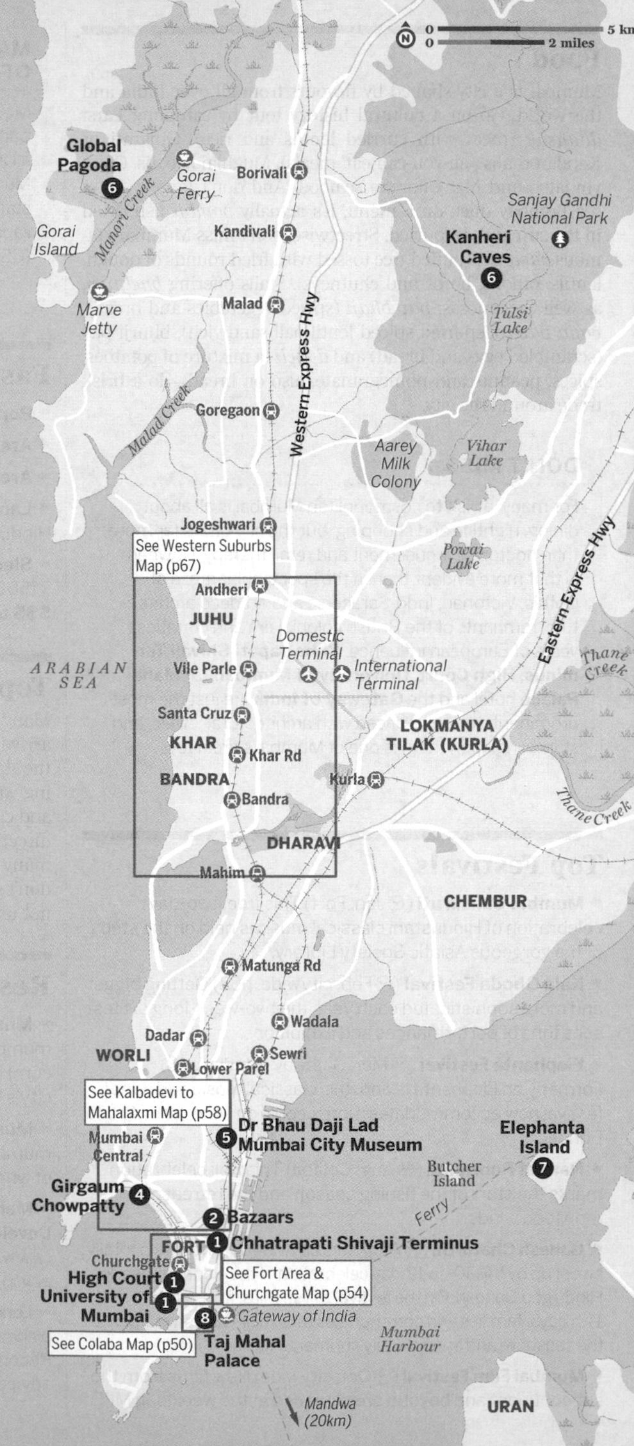

History

Koli fisherfolk have inhabited the seven islands that form Mumbai as far back as the 2nd century BC. Amazingly, remnants of this culture remain huddled along the city shoreline today. A succession of Hindu dynasties held sway over the islands from the 6th century AD until the Muslim Sultans of Gujarat annexed the area in the 14th century, eventually ceding it to Portugal in 1534. The only memorable contribution the Portuguese made to the area was christening it Bom Bahai, before throwing the islands in with the dowry of Catherine of Braganza when she married England's Charles II in 1661. The British government took possession of the islands in 1665 but leased them three years later to the East India Company.

Bombay flourished as a trading port, and within 20 years the East India Company presidency was transferred here. The city's fort was completed in the 1720s, and a century later ambitious land reclamation projects joined the islands into today's single landmass. The city continued to grow, and in the 19th century the fort walls were dismantled and massive building works transformed the city in grand colonial style. When Bombay became the principal supplier of cotton to Britain during the American Civil War, the population soared and trade boomed as money flooded into the city.

Bombay was a major player in the Independence movement, and the Quit India campaign was launched here in 1942 by frequent visitor Mahatma Gandhi. The city became capital of the Bombay presidency after Independence, but in 1960 Maharashtra and Gujarat were divided along linguistic lines – and Bombay became the capital of Maharashtra.

The rise of the pro-Marathi, pro-Hindu regionalist movement, spearheaded by the Shiv Sena (literally 'Shivaji's Army'), shattered the city's multicultural mould by actively discriminating against Muslims and non-Maharashtrians. Following Shiv Sena's rise to power in the city's municipal elections in 1985, communalist tensions increased, and the city's cosmopolitan self-image took a battering when 900 people, mostly Muslims, died in riots following the destruction of Ayodhya's Babri Masjid in December 1992 and January 1993. The riots were followed by a dozen retaliatory bombings in March 1993, which killed hundreds of people and damaged the Bombay Stock Exchange and Air India Building.

Shiv Sena's influence saw the names of many streets and public buildings – as well as the city itself – changed from their colonial names. In 1996 the city's name was officially changed to Mumbai, the Marathi name derived from the Hindu goddess Mumba, who was worshipped by the early Koli residents. The airport, Victoria Terminus and Prince of Wales Museum were all renamed after Chhatrapati Shivaji, the great Maratha leader.

Religious tensions continued to deepen and became intertwined with and supplanted by India's larger national religious tension and its struggles with Pakistan. Bombings in 2006 and 2011, and the 2008 attacks across the city, which lasted three days and killed 173 people, shifted the discussion to terrorism with origins outside Mumbai.

But in late 2012, when the Sena's charismatic founder Bal Thackeray died, the entire city shut down – due as much to fear of riots as to grief – and an estimated 500,000 people attended his funeral. Many predict the decline of the Shiv Sena mission – and a brighter future for harmony among Mumbaikars.

Sights

Mumbai, the capital of Maharashtra, is an island connected by bridges to the mainland. The city's commercial and cultural centre is at the southern, claw-shaped end of the island known as South Mumbai. The southernmost peninsula is Colaba, traditionally the travellers' nerve centre, with many of the major attractions, and directly north of Colaba is the busy commercial area known as Fort, where the British fort once stood. It's bordered on the west by a series of interconnected, fenced grassy areas known as maidans (pronounced may-*dahns*).

Though just as essential a part of the city as South Mumbai, the area north of here is collectively known as 'the suburbs'. The airport and many of Mumbai's best restaurants, shopping and nightspots are here, particularly in the upmarket suburbs of Bandra, Juhu and increasingly, Lower Parel.

Colaba

Along the city's southernmost peninsula, Colaba is a bustling district packed with street stalls, markets, bars and budget-to-midrange lodgings. Colaba Causeway (Shahid Bhagat Singh Marg) dissects the promontory and Colaba's jumble of side streets and gently crumbling mansions.

If you're here in August, look out for the Koli festival, Nariyal Poornima, which is big in Colaba.

★Taj Mahal Palace, Mumbai LANDMARK

(Map p50) This stunning hotel is a fairy-tale blend of Islamic and Renaissance styles jostling for prime position among Mumbai's famous landmarks. Facing the harbour, it was built in 1903 by the Parsi industrialist JN Tata, supposedly after he was refused entry to one of the European hotels on account of being 'a native'. The image of smoke rising from the hotel became an iconic image of the 2008 terrorist attacks, when dozens were killed and much of the hotel was damaged. The hotel partly reopened less than a month later, dedicating the hotel to the victims; the fully restored hotel reopened on Independence Day 2010.

Gateway of India MONUMENT

(Map p50) This bold basalt arch of colonial triumph faces out to Mumbai Harbour from the tip of Apollo Bunder. Incorporating Islamic styles of 16th-century Gujarat, it was built to commemorate the 1911 royal visit of King George V, but not completed until 1924. Ironically, the British builders of the gateway used it just 24 years later to parade the last British regiment as India marched towards Independence.

These days, the gateway is a favourite gathering spot for locals and a top spot for people-watching. Giant-balloon sellers, photographers, vendors making *bhelpuri* and touts rub shoulders with locals and tourists, creating all the hubbub of a bazaar. In March, they're joined by classical dancers and musicians who perform during the **Elephanta Festival** (www.maharashtratourism.gov.in).

Boats depart from the gateway's wharfs for Elephanta Island.

MUMBAI IN...

Two Days

Start at the grandaddy of Mumbai's colonial-era giants, the old Victoria Terminus, Chhatrapati Shivaji Terminus (CST; p49) and stroll up to Crawford Market (p79) and the maze of bazaars here. Lunch at Revival (p71), with a juice shake from Badshah Snacks & Drinks (p70).

Spend the afternoon admiring Mumbai's marvellous architecture at the High Court (p50) and the University of Mumbai (p49). Walk down to the Gateway of India (p48) and Taj Mahal Palace, Mumbai (p48). After sunset, eat streetside at Bademiya (p69). Swap tall tales with fellow travellers at Leopold's Café (p74).

The next day, visit the ornate Dr Bhau Daji Lad Mumbai City Museum (p53), then head to Kemp's Corner for lunch at Café Moshe (p70) and some shopping. Make your way down to Mani Bhavan (p55), the museum dedicated to Gandhi, and finish the day wandering the tiny lanes of **Khotachiwadi** followed by a beach sunset and a plate of *bhelpuri* at Girgaum Chowpatty (p52). A blow-out dinner at Khyber (p71) won't let you forget Mumbai soon.

Four Days

Head out to the Global Pagoda (p56) and learn to meditate, then return in the afternoon to visit the museums and galleries of **Kala Ghoda**. In the evening, head to Bandra for a candle-lit dinner at Caravan Serai, followed by some seriously hip bar action with a view at Aer (p75) in Worli.

Another day could be spent visiting the Dhobi Ghat (p55) and the nearby Mahalaxmi Temple (p55) and Haji Ali's Mosque (p53). Lunch at Olive Bar & Kitchen (p75) at Mahalaxmi Racecourse and then rest up for a night of avant-garde clubbing at Bluefrog (p76) in Worli.

Sassoon Dock WATERFRONT

Sassoon Dock is a scene of intense and pungent activity at dawn (around 5am) when colourfully clad Koli fisher-folk sort the catch unloaded from fishing boats at the quay. The fish drying in the sun are *bombil*, the fish used in the dish Bombay duck. Photography at the dock is forbidden.

Fort Area & Churchgate

Lined up in a row and vying for your attention with aristocratic pomp, many of Mumbai's majestic Victorian buildings pose on the edge of **Oval Maidan**. This land, and the **Cross** and **Azad Maidans** immediately to the north, was on the oceanfront in those days, and this series of grandiose structures faced west directly out to the Arabian Sea.

Kala Ghoda, or 'Black Horse', is a subneighbourhood of Fort just north of Colaba and contains many of Mumbai's museums and galleries alongside a wealth of colonial-era buildings (best seen on a walking tour, p62).

★Chhatrapati Shivaji Terminus (Victoria Terminus) HISTORIC BUILDING

(Map p54) Imposing, exuberant and overflowing with people, this is the city's most extravagant Gothic building, the beating heart of its railway network, and an aphorism for colonial India. As historian Christopher London put it, 'the Victoria Terminus is to the British Raj what the Taj Mahal is to the Mughal empire'. It's a meringue of Victorian, Hindu and Islamic styles whipped into an imposing Daliesque structure of buttresses, domes, turrets, spires and stained-glass windows.

Designed by Frederick Stevens, it was completed in 1887, 34 years after the first train in India left this site. Today it's Asia's busiest train station. Officially renamed Chhatrapati Shivaji Terminus (CST) in 1998, it's still better known locally as VT. It was added to the Unesco World Heritage list in 2004.

★Chhatrapati Shivaji Maharaj Vastu Sangrahalaya (Prince of Wales Museum) MUSEUM

(Map p54; www.themuseummumbai.com; K Dubash Marg; Indian/foreigner ₹50/300, camera/video ₹200/1000; ⏲10.15am-6pm Tue Sun) Mumbai's biggest and best museum displays a mix of exhibits from all over India. The domed behemoth, an intriguing hodgepodge of Islamic, Hindu and British architecture, was opened in 1923 to commemorate King George V's first visit to India (back in 1905, while he was still Prince of Wales). Its flamboyant Indo-Saracenic style was designed by George Wittet, who also designed the Gateway of India.

A recent renovation introduced a fascinating new miniature-painting gallery and a new gallery of contemporary art. Elsewhere, the vast collection includes impressive Hindu and Buddhist sculpture, terracotta figurines from the Indus Valley, porcelain and some particularly vicious-looking weaponry.

There's an outdoor cafeteria here, and the museum shop is excellent.

University of Mumbai (Bombay University) HISTORIC BUILDING

(Map p54) Looking like a 15th-century French-Gothic masterpiece plopped incongruously amongst Mumbai's palm trees, this university on Bhaurao Patil Marg was designed by Gilbert Scott of London's St Pancras Station fame. There is an exquisite **University Library** and **Convocation Hall**, as well as the

MUMBAI FOR CHILDREN

Little tykes with energy to burn will love the Gorai Island amusement parks, **Esselworld** (www.esselworld.in; adult/child ₹690/490; ⏲11am-7pm, from 10am weekends) and **Water Kingdom** (www.waterkingdom.in; adult/child ₹690/490; ⏲11am-7pm, from 10am weekends). Both have lots of rides, slides and shade. Combined tickets are ₹890/690 (adult/child). It's a ₹35 ferry ride from Borivali jetty.

The free **Hanging Gardens**, in Malabar Hill, have animal topiaries, swings in the shade and coconut-wallahs. **Kamala Nehru Park**, across the street, has a two-storey 'boot house'.

BNHS (p60) and Yuhina Eco-Media (p60) often conduct nature trips for kids, while **Yoga Kids by Shraddha** (Map p58; ☎9820349688; shraddha@yogakidsworld.com; Chinoy Mansion, Warden Rd, Cumballa Hill; drop-in classes ₹500, Yoga Kids kits ₹2000; ⏲under 6yrs/over 6yrs 9.45am/10.30am Sat) has kids' yoga classes, taught in English.

Time Out Mumbai (₹50) often lists fun things to do with kids.

Colaba

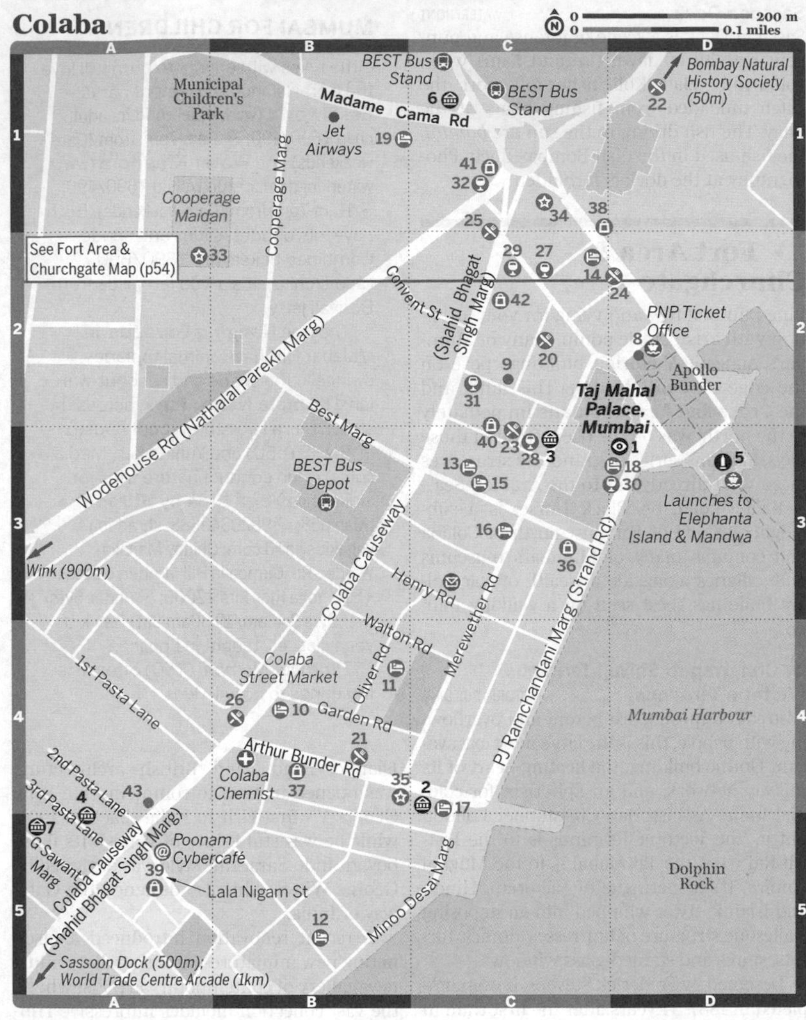

80m-high **Rajabai Clock Tower** (Map p54), decorated with detailed carvings, however, since the 2008 terror attacks, the public is not allowed inside the grounds. Admire the architecture on a stroll along Bhaurao Patil Marg (trees obscure much of the splendour when viewed from the Oval Maidan).

High Court HISTORIC BUILDING

(Map p54; Eldon Rd) A hive of daily activity, packed with judges, barristers and other cogs in the Indian justice system, the High Court is an elegant 1848 neo-Gothic building. The design was inspired by a German castle and was obviously intended to dispel any doubts about the authority of the justice dispensed inside, though local stone carvers presumably saw things differently: they carved a one-eyed monkey fiddling with the scales of justice on one pillar. You are permitted (and it is highly recommended) to walk around inside the building and check out the pandemonium and pageantry of public cases that are in progress – just walk right in! You'll have to surrender your camera to the guards, then make your way through the mazelike building to the original building's courtyard opposite Court 6.

Colaba

Top Sights
1 Taj Mahal Palace, Mumbai D3

Sights
2 Chatterjee & Lal C4
3 Galerie Mirchandani + Steinruecke C3
4 Gallery Maskara A5
5 Gateway of India D3
Guild .... (see 2)
6 National Gallery of Modern Art C1
7 Project 88 .... A5
Volte .... (see 2)

Activities, Courses & Tours
8 Maharashtra Tourism Development Corporation Booth D2
9 Reality Tours & Travel C2

Sleeping
10 Ascot Hotel B4
11 Bentley's Hotel B4
Carlton Hotel .... (see 3)
12 Fariyas Hotel B5
13 Hotel Moti C3
14 Hotel Suba Palace C2
India Guest House .... (see 17)
15 Regent Hotel C3
16 Salvation Army Red Shield Guest House C3
17 Sea Shore Hotel C4
18 Taj Mahal Palace, Mumbai D3
19 YWCA B1

Eating
20 Bademiya C2
21 Basilico B4
Café Moshe .... (see 24)
22 Hotel OCH D1
23 Indigo C3
24 Indigo Delicatessen D2
Koyla .... (see 2)
25 Saharkari Bhandar Supermarket C2
26 Theobroma B4

Drinking & Nightlife
27 5 All Day C2
28 Busaba C3
29 Cafe Mondegar C2
30 Harbour Bar D3
31 Leopold's Café C2
32 Woodside Inn C1

Entertainment
33 Cooperage Football Ground A2
34 Regal Cinema C1
35 Voodoo Pub B4

Shopping
36 Bombay Electric C3
37 Bungalow 8 .... B4
Central Cottage Industries Emporium .... (see 2)
38 Central Cottage Industries Emporium C1
39 Colaba Market A5
40 Cottonworld Corp C2
41 Phillips C1
42 Search Word C2

Information
43 Akbar Travels A1
Thomas Cook .... (see 26)

Transport
IndiGo .... (see 23)
Maldar Catamarans Ticket Office .... (see 8)

Mumba Devi Temple HINDU TEMPLE
(Map p58; Bhuleshwar) Pay a visit to the city's patron goddess at this 18th-century temple, about 1km north of CST. Among the deities in residence is Bahuchar Maa, goddess of the transgender *hijras*. Puja (prayer) is held several times a day.

Keneseth Eliyahoo Synagogue SYNAGOGUE
(Map p54; www.jacobsassoon.org; Dr VB Gandhi Marg; admission free, camera/video ₹100/500; 11am-6pm Mon-Sat, 1pm–6pm Sun) Built in 1884, this impossibly sky-blue synagogue still functions and is tenderly maintained by the city's dwindling Jewish community (and protected to Baghdad Green Zone levels by Mumbai's finest).

National Gallery of Modern Art MUSEUM
(NGMA; Map p50; www.ngmaindia.gov.in; MG Rd; Indian/foreigner ₹10/150; 11am-6pm Tue-Sun) Increasingly well-curated shows of Indian and international artists in a bright and spacious exhibition space.

St Thomas' Cathedral CHURCH
(Map p54; Veer Nariman Rd; 7am-6pm) This charming cathedral, begun in 1672 and finished in 1718, is the oldest English building standing in Mumbai: it was once the eastern gateway of the East India Company's fort (the 'Churchgate'). The cathedral is a marriage of Byzantine and colonial-era architecture, and its airy interior is full of exhibitionist colonial memorials.

DHARAVI SLUM

Mumbaikars were ambivalent about the stereotypes in 2008's *Slumdog Millionaire*, but slums are very much a part of – some would say the foundation of – Mumbai city life. An astonishing 60% of Mumbai's population lives in slums, and one of the city's largest slums is Dharavi. Originally inhabited by fisher-folk when the area was still creeks, swamps and islands, it became attractive to migrant workers from South Mumbai and beyond when the swamp began to fill in due to natural and artificial causes. It now incorporates 1.75 sq km of land sandwiched between Mumbai's two major railway lines, and is home to more than one million people.

While it may look a bit shambolic from the outside, the maze of dusty alleys and sewer-lined streets of this city-within-a-city are actually a collection of abutting settlements. Some parts of Dharavi have mixed populations, but in other parts inhabitants from different parts of India, and with different trades, have set up homes and tiny factories. Potters from Saurashtra live in one area, Muslim tanners in another; embroidery workers from Uttar Pradesh work alongside metalsmiths; while other workers recycle plastics as women dry pappadams in the searing sun. Some of these thriving industries, around 10,000 in all, export their wares, and the annual turnover of business from Dharavi is thought to exceed US$650 million.

Up close, life in the slums is strikingly normal. Residents pay rent, most houses have kitchens and electricity, and building materials range from flimsy corrugated-iron shacks to permanent multistorey concrete structures. Many families have been here for many generations, and some of the younger Dharavi residents may work in white-collar jobs. They often choose to stay, though, in the neighbourhood they grew up in.

Slum tourism is a polarising subject, so you'll have to decide your feelings for yourself. If you opt to visit, Reality Tours & Travel (p63) does a fascinating tour, and puts a percentage of profits back into Dharavi. Some tourists opt to visit on their own, which is OK as well – just don't take photos. Take the train from Churchgate station to Mahim (₹6), exit on the west side and cross the bridge into Dharavi.

To learn more about Mumbai's slums, check out Katherine Boo's 2012 book *Behind the Beautiful Forevers*, about life in Annawadi, a slum near the airport, and *Rediscovering Dharavi*, Kalpana Sharma's sensitive and engrossing history of Dharavi's people, culture and industry.

Jehangir Art Gallery ART GALLERY
(Map p54; 161B MG Rd; ⏲11am-7pm) FREE Hosts shows by local artists and students, and the occasional big name. Rows of artists display their work on the pavement outside.

Kalbadevi to Mahalaxmi

★Marine Drive & Girgaum Chowpatty BEACH
(Map p54; Netaji Subhashchandra Bose Rd) Built on land reclaimed from Back Bay in 1920, Marine Drive arcs along the shore of the Arabian Sea from Nariman Point past Girgaum Chowpatty (where it's known as Chowpatty Seaface) and continues to the foot of Malabar Hill. Lined with flaking art deco apartments, it's one of Mumbai's most popular promenades and sunset-watching spots. Its twinkling night-time lights earned it the nickname 'the Queen's Necklace'.

Girgaum Chowpatty (often referred to as just 'Chowpatty') remains a favourite evening spot for courting couples, families, political rallies and anyone out to enjoy what passes for fresh air. Evening *bhelpuri* at the throng of stalls at the beach's southern end is an essential part of the Mumbai experience. Forget about taking a dip: the water's toxic.

Chowpatty's also the place to be on the 10th day of the Ganesh Chaturthi festival (in August or September), when millions come to the shore to submerge the largest Ganesh statues: it's joyful mayhem.

Dr Bhau Daji Lad Mumbai City Museum MUSEUM
(Map p58; www.bdlmuseum.org; Dr Babasaheb Ambedkar Rd; Indian/foreigner ₹10/100; ⏲10am-5.30pm Thu-Tue) Jijamata Udyan – formerly named Victoria Gardens – is a lush and sprawling mid-19th-century garden and zoo. It's home to this gorgeous museum, built in Renaissance revival style in 1872 as the Victoria & Albert Museum. It reopened in 2007 after an impressive and sensitive four-year renovation. In addition to extensive structural work, the building's Minton tile floors, gilt ceiling mouldings, and ornate columns, chandeliers and staircases were restored to their former historically-accurate glory. Even the sweet mint-green paint choice was based on historical research. Also restored were the museum's 3500-plus objects centering on Mumbai's history – clay models of village life, photography and maps, textiles, books and manuscripts, Bidriware, laquerware, weaponry and exquisite pottery, all set against the museum's very distracting stunning decor. The museum has also begun hosting exhibitions of contemporary art and other special shows. Skip the zoo.

Haji Ali Dargah MOSQUE
(Map p58) Floating like a sacred mirage off the coast, this exquisite Indo-Islamic shrine is one of Mumbai's most striking symbols. Built in the 19th century on the site of a 15th-century structure, it contains the tomb of the Muslim saint Pir Haji Ali Shah Bukhari. Legend has it that Haji Ali died while on a pilgrimage to Mecca and his casket miraculously floated back to this spot. A long causeway reaches into the Arabian Sea,

THE ART DISTRICT

India's contemporary art scene has exploded in recent years, and Mumbai, along with Delhi, is the centre of the action. A slew of galleries, mostly in Colaba, are showing incredible work in some gorgeous spaces. Kala Ghoda, meanwhile, Mumbai's traditional art district, has a namesake two-week **festival** (www.kalaghodaassociation.com) each February, with some great exhibitions.

Year-round, the second Thursday of each month is 'Art Night Thursday', when galleries stay open late and the vibe is social. Gallery crawls are sometimes organised; check **Mumbai Boss** (www.mumbaiboss.com) for the latest. *Time Out Mumbai* is another good gallery-hopping guide, as is the latest addition to the family, the free fold-up *Mumbai Art Map*, available at galleries, bookstores and other art-friendly spots around town. To go more in depth, check out the magazine *Art India*, available at most English-language bookshops, which has news, background and criticism on work from across the country.

Or, just read nothing and go see pretty things on your own: most of the following galleries are within walking distance of one another and make for a lovely afternoon art walk.

Chatterjee & Lal (Map p50; www.chatterjeeandlal.com; 1st fl, Kamal Mansion, Arthur Bunder Rd, Colaba; ⏲11am-7pm Tue-Sat)

Chemould Prescott Road (Map p54; www.gallerychemould.com; 3rd fl, Queens Mansion, G Talwatkar Marg, Fort; ⏲11am-7pm Mon-Sat)

Galerie Mirchandani + Steinruecke (Map p50; www.galeriems.com; 1st fl, Sunny House, 16/18 Mereweather Rd, Colaba; ⏲11am-7pm Tue-Sat)

Gallery Maskara (Map p50; www.gallerymaskara.com; 6/7 3rd Pasta Lane, Colaba; ⏲11am-7pm Tue-Sat)

Guild (Map p50; www.guildindia.com; 2nd fl, Kamal Mansion, Arthur Bunder Rd ; ⏲10am-6.30pm Mon-Sat)

Jhaveri Contemporary (www.jhavericontemporary.com; Krishna Niwas, 58A Walkeshwar Rd, Walkeshwar, Malabar Hill ; ⏲11am-6pm Tue-Sat)

Project 88 (Map p50; www.project88.in; BMP Building, NA Sawant Marg, Colaba; ⏲11am-7pm Tue-Sat)

Volte (Map p50; www.volte.in; 1st fl, Kamal Mansion, Arthur Bunder Rd, Colaba; ⏲11am-7pm Mon-Sat)

Fort Area & Churchgate

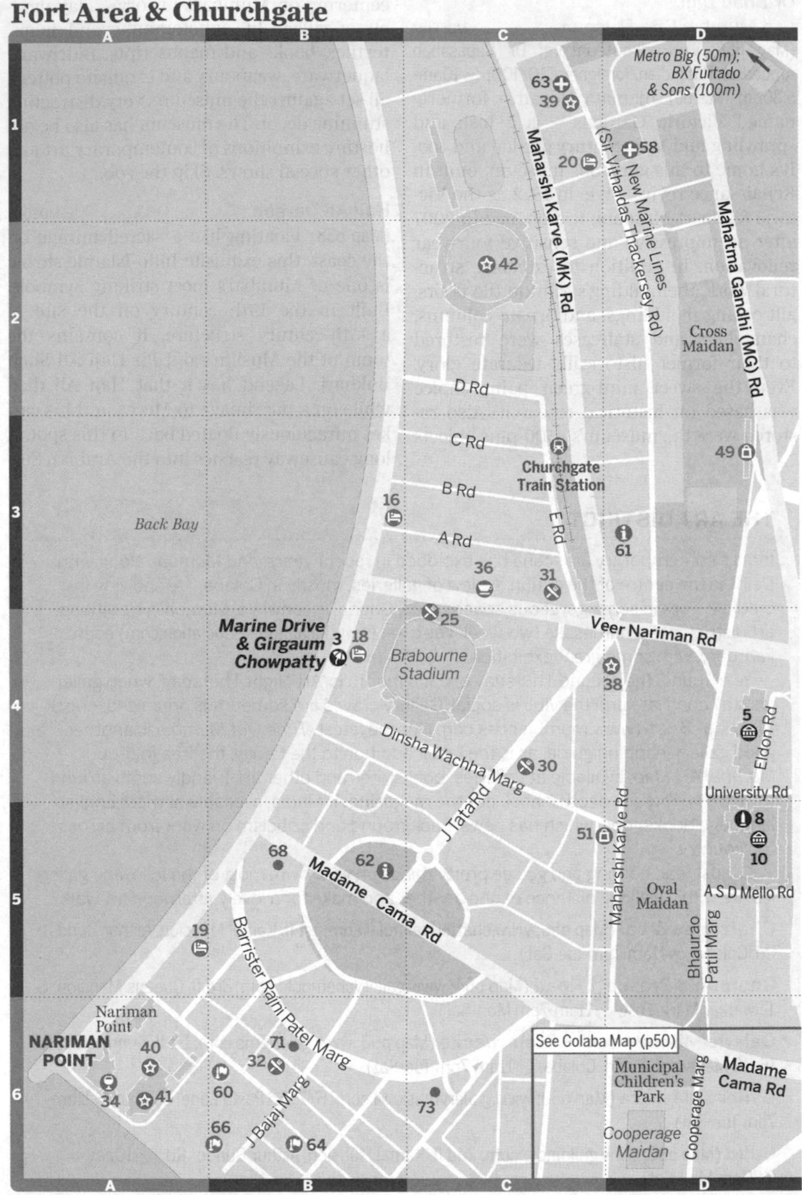

providing access to the dargah and mosque, but at high tide, water covers the causeway and the mosque becomes an island. Thousands of pilgrims, especially on Thursdays and Fridays (when there may also be *qawwali*, devotional singing), cross it to make their visit, many donating to beggars who line the way. Once inside, pilgrims fervently kiss the dressings of the tomb – or at least some do. In 2012, the dargah controversially adjusted its layout to bar women from entering the inner tomb. Discussions are ongoing.

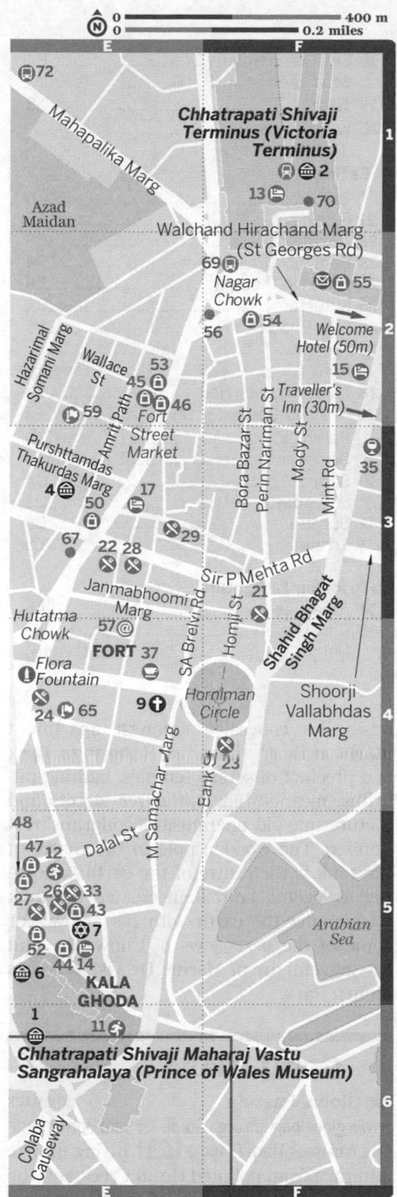

Mahalaxmi Dhobi Ghat GHAT
(Map p58) If you've had washing done in Mumbai, chances are your clothes have already visited this 140-year-old *dhobi ghat* (place where clothes are washed). The whole hamlet is Mumbai's oldest and biggest human-powered washing machine: every day hundreds of people beat the dirt out of thousands of kilograms of soiled Mumbai clothes and linen in 1026 open-air troughs. The best view, and photo opportunity, is from the bridge across the railway tracks near Mahalaxmi train station.

Mani Bhavan MUSEUM
(Map p58; ☎23805864; www.gandhi-manibhavan.org; 19 Laburnum Rd, Gamdevi; donation appreciated; ⊙9.30am-6pm) FREE As poignant as it is tiny, this museum is in the building where Mahatma Gandhi stayed during visits to Bombay from 1917 to 1934. The museum showcases the room where the leader formulated his philosophy of satyagraha (nonviolent protest) and launched the 1932 Civil Disobedience campaign that led to the end of British rule. Exhibitions include a photographic record of his life, along with dioramas and original documents, such as letters he wrote to Adolf Hitler and Franklin D Roosevelt. Nearby, August Kranti Maidan is where the campaign to persuade the British to 'Quit India' was launched in 1942.

Bombay Panjrapole ANIMAL SHELTER
(Map p58; www.bombaypanjrapole.org.in; Panjrapole Marg, Bhuleshwar, near Madhav Baug Post Office; ⊙11am-6pm) In the middle of bustling Bhuleshwar market is, of all things, this shelter for 300 homeless cows. It was founded in the 18th century in response to the British approach to controlling the city's many stray dogs and pigs, which was, according to the Panjrapole, to shoot them. Cows were brought in to provide milk and eventually outnumbered the strays. Today, 1500 cows are cared for in seven centres across Gujarat and Maharashtra. You can wander around and pet the cows and calves and, for a small donation, feed them fresh greens.

Mahalaxmi Temple HINDU TEMPLE
(Map p58) It's only fitting that in money-mad Mumbai one of the busiest and most colourful temples is dedicated to Mahalaxmi, the goddess of wealth. Perched on a headland, it is the focus for Mumbai's Navratri (Festival of Nine Nights) celebrations in September/October.

Babu Amichand Panalal Adishwarji Jain Temple JAIN TEMPLE
(Walkeshwar, Malabar Hill; ⊙5am-9pm) This temple is renowned among Jains for its beauty;

Fort Area & Churchgate

Top Sights
1 Chhatrapati Shivaji Maharaj Vastu Sangrahalaya (Prince of Wales Museum) E6
2 Chhatrapati Shivaji Terminus (Victoria Terminus) F1
3 Marine Drive & Girgaum Chowpatty B4

Sights
4 Chemould Prescott Road E3
5 High Court D4
6 Jehangir Art Gallery E5
7 Keneseth Eliyahoo Synagogue E5
8 Rajabai Clock Tower D5
9 St Thomas' Cathedral E4
10 University of Mumbai (Bombay University) D5

Activities, Courses & Tours
11 Bombay Natural History Society E6
12 Welfare of Stray Dogs E5

Sleeping
13 CST Retiring Rooms F1
14 Hotel Lawrence E5
15 Hotel Oasis F2
16 InterContinental B3
17 Residency Hotel E3
18 Sea Green Hotel B4
Sea Green South Hotel ..... (see 18)
19 Trident A5
20 West End Hotel C1

Eating
210°C ..... (see 30)
21 5 Spice F3
22 A Taste of Kerala E3
23 Bademiya Restaurant F4
24 Food for Thought E4
25 K Rustom C4
26 Kala Ghoda Café E5
27 Khyber E5
Koh ..... (see 16)
28 Mahesh Lunch Home E3
29 Pradeep Gomantak Bhojanalaya E3
Relish ..... (see 30)
Samovar Café ..... (see 6)
30 Samrat C4
31 Suryodaya C3
32 Suzette B6
33 Trishna E5

Drinking & Nightlife
34 Amadeus A6
35 Café Universal F3
Dome ..... (see 16)

given how beautiful Jain temples are, that's saying a lot. Check out the paintings and especially the ecstatically colourful zodiac dome ceiling – you've never seen anything like it. As this is a small temple, with usually a lot of prayer going on, tread lightly; you may wish to refer to the helpful 'Dear Tourist' sign at the entrance for guidelines (which include modest dress).

Nehru Centre CULTURAL COMPLEX

(☎24964676-80; www.nehru-centre.org; Dr Annie Besant Rd, Worli; Discovery of India admission free, planetarium adult/child ₹50/25; ⏰Tue-Sun, Discovery of India 11am-5pm, planetarium English show 3pm) This cultural complex includes a planetarium, theatre, gallery and an interesting history exhibition **Discovery of India**. The architecture is striking: the tower looks like a giant cylindrical pineapple, the planetarium a UFO.

Malabar Hill AREA

(around BG Kher Marg) Mumbai's most exclusive neighbourhood of sky-scratchers and private palaces, Malabar Hill is at the northern promontory of Back Bay. Surprisingly, one of Mumbai's most sacred and tranquil oases lies concealed amongst apartment blocks at its southern tip: **Banganga Tank** is a precinct of serene temples, bathing pilgrims, meandering, traffic-free streets and picturesque old dharamsalas (pilgrims' rest houses). The wooden pole in the centre of the tank is the centre of the earth: according to legend, Lord Ram created the tank by piercing the earth with his arrow. For some of the best views of Chowpatty and the graceful arc of Marine Dr, visit **Kamala Nehru Park**.

Gorai Island

★**Global Pagoda** LANDMARK

(www.globalpagoda.org; Gorai; ⏰9am-7pm, meditation classes 11am & 4pm) FREE Rising up like a mirage from polluted Gorai Creek and the lush but noisy grounds of the Esselworld and Water Kingdom amusement parks, is this breathtaking, golden 96m-high stupa modelled after Burma's Shwedagon Pagoda. The dome, which houses relics of Buddha, was built entirely without supports using an ancient technique of interlocking stones (it just snatched the record away from Bijapur's

36 Mocha Bar C3
37 Starbucks E4

Entertainment

38 Eros D4
39 Liberty Cinema C1
40 National Centre for the Performing Arts A6
41 NCPA Box Office A6
42 Wankhede Stadium C2

Shopping

43 Artisans' Centre for Art, Craft & Design E5
44 Chetana Book Centre E5
45 Chimanlals E2
46 Contemporary Arts & Crafts E2
47 Cotton Cottage E5
48 Fabindia E5
49 Fashion Street Market D3
50 Khadi & Village Industries Emporium E3
Kitab Khana .... (see 24)
51 Oxford Bookstore C5
52 Rhythm House E5
53 Royal Music Collection E2
54 Standard Supply Co F2
55 Tribes India F2

Information

56 Akbar Travels F2
57 Anita CyberCafé E4
58 Bombay Hospital D1
59 Dutch Consulate E2
60 German Consulate B6
61 Indiatourism D3
Israeli Consulate .... (see 66)
62 Maharashtra Tourism Development Corporation B5
63 New Royal Chemists C1
Portasia .... (see 53)
64 Singaporean Consulate B6
65 Sri Lankan Consulate E4
66 Thai Consulate B6
67 Thomas Cook E3

Transport

68 Air India B5
69 BEST Bus Stand F2
70 Central Railways Reservation Centre F1
71 Emirates Airlines B6
72 Chandni Travels E1
73 Thai Airways C6
Western Railways Reservation Centre .... (see 61)

Golgumbaz for being the world's largest unsupported dome), and the meditation hall beneath it seats 8000. A museum dedicated to the life of the Buddha and his teaching is also on site. The pagoda is affiliated with teacher SN Goenka, and two free 20-minute meditation classes are offered daily; an on-site meditation centre also offers 10-day meditation courses.

To get here, take a train from Churchgate to Borivali (exit the station the 'West' side), then an autorickshaw (₹40) to the ferry landing, where Esselworld ferries (return ₹35) come and go every 30 minutes. The last ferry to the Pagoda is 5.25pm.

Elephanta Island

Nine kilometres northeast of the Gateway of India in Mumbai Harbour, the rock-cut temples on Gharapuri, better known as **Elephanta Island** (http://asi.nic.in/; Indian/foreigner ₹10/250; caves 9am-5pm Tue-Sun), are a Unesco World Heritage Site and worth crossing the waters for. The labyrinth of cave-temples, carved into the island's basalt rock, contain some of India's most impressive temple carving. The main Shiva-dedicated temple is an intriguing latticework of courtyards, halls, pillars and shrines; its magnum opus is a 6m-tall statue of Sadhashiva, depicting a three-faced Shiva as the destroyer, creator and preserver of the universe, his eyes closed in eternal contemplation.

The temples are thought to have been created between AD 450 and 750, when the island was known as Gharapuri (Place of Caves). The Portuguese called it Elephanta because of a large stone elephant near the shore, which collapsed in 1814 and was moved by the British to Mumbai's Jijamata Udyan. There's a small **museum** on-site, with informative pictorial panels on the origin of the caves.

Aggressive, expensive guides will meet you at the jetty and try to convince you to employ their services; you don't really need one. Opt instead for Pramod Chandra's *A Guide to the Elephanta Caves*, for sale at the stalls lining the stairway.

Launches (Map p50; economy/deluxe ₹120/150) head to Gharapuri from the Gateway of India every half-hour from 9am to 3.30pm.

Kalbadevi to Mahalaxmi

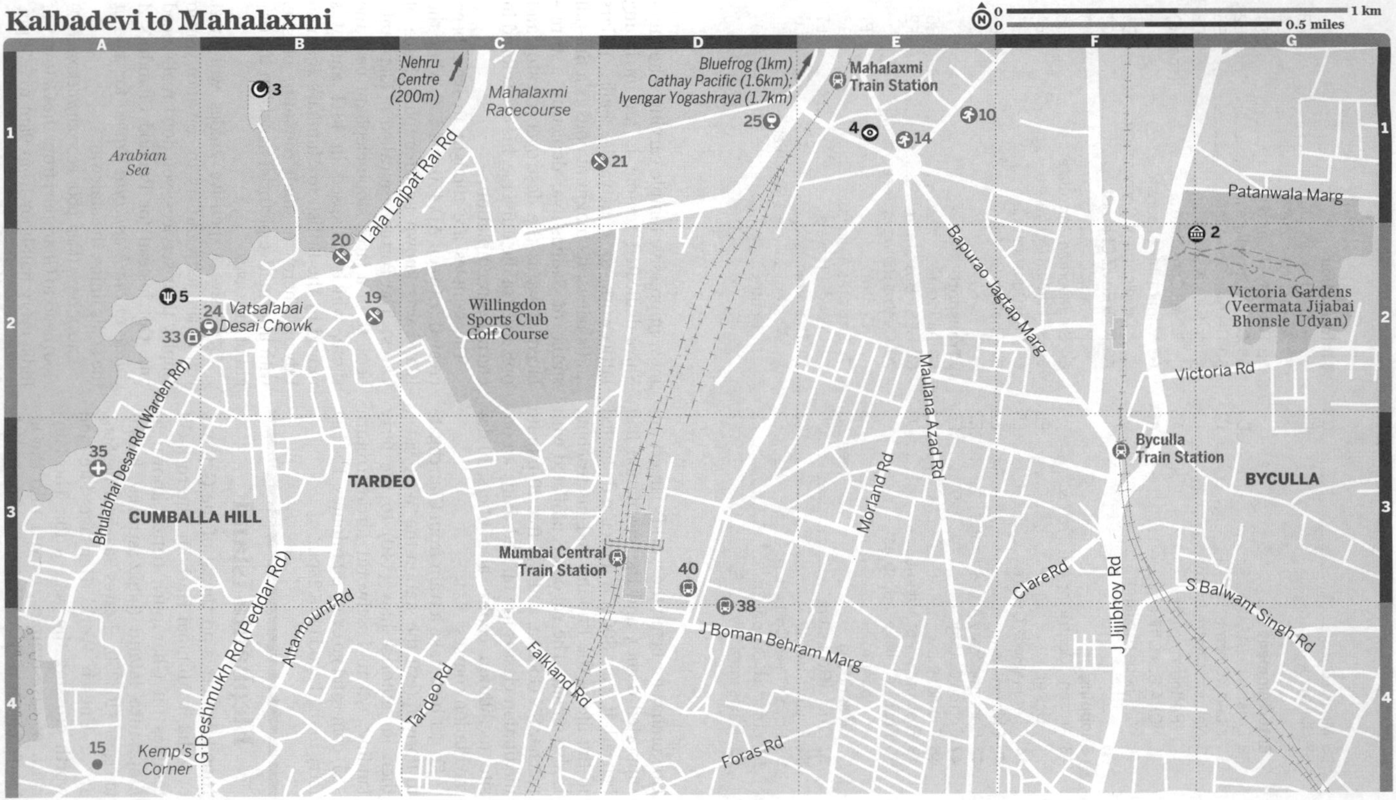

0 1 km
0 0.5 miles

A B C D E F G
1 2 3 4

Nehru Centre (200m)
Bluefrog (1km)
Cathay Pacific (1.6km);
Iyengar Yogashraya (1.7km)
Mahalaxmi Train Station
3
Arabian Sea
Mahalaxmi Racecourse
25
4
14
10
21
Lala Lajpat Rai Rd
Patanwala Marg
2
20
Bapurao Jagtap Marg
Victoria Gardens (Veermata Jijabai Bhonsle Udyan)
5
19
24 Vatsalabai Desai Chowk
33
Willingdon Sports Club Golf Course
Maulana Azad Rd
Victoria Rd
Bhulabhai Desai Rd (Warden Rd)
35
TARDEO
Morland Rd
Byculla Train Station
BYCULLA
CUMBALLA HILL
Mumbai Central Train Station
40
38
Clare Rd
J Jijibhoy Rd
S Balwant Singh Rd
G Deshmukh Rd (Peddar Rd)
Altamount Rd
J Boman Behram Marg
Falkland Rd
Tardeo Rd
15
Kemp's Corner
Foras Rd

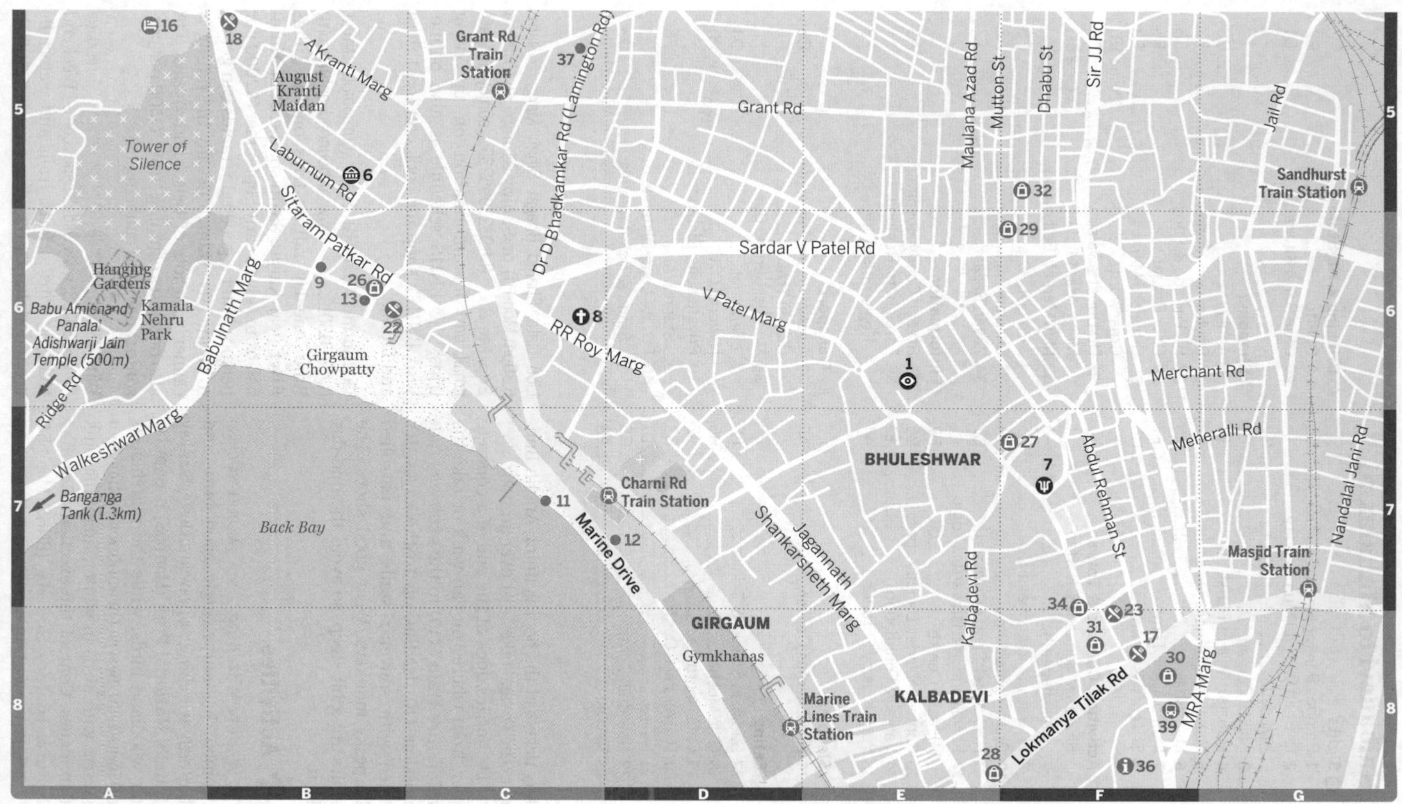
Grant Rd Train Station
A Kranti Marg
August Kranti Maidan
Tower of Silence
Laburnum Rd
Sitaram Patkar Rd
Dr D Bhadkamkar Rd (Lamington Rd)
Grant Rd
Maulana Azad Rd
Mutton St
Dhabu St
Sir JJ Rd
Jail Rd
Sandhurst Train Station
Sardar V Patel Rd
Hanging Gardens
Babu Amichand Panalal Adishwarji Jain Temple (500m)
Kamala Nehru Park
Babulnath Marg
V Patel Marg
RR Roy Marg
Girgaum Chowpatty
Merchant Rd
Ridge Rd
Walkeshwar Marg
Meheralli Rd
BHULESHWAR
Abdul Rehman St
Nandalal Jani Rd
Charni Rd Train Station
Banganga Tank (1.3km)
Back Bay
Marine Drive
Jagannath Shankarsheth Marg
Kalbadevi Rd
Masjid Train Station
GIRGAUM
Gymkhanas
MRA Marg
Lokmanya Tilak Rd
Marine Lines Train Station
KALBADEVI

Kalbadevi to Mahalaxmi

Sights
1 Bombay Panjrapole....E6
2 Dr Bhau Daji Lad Mumbai City Museum....G2
3 Haji Ali Dargah....B1
4 Mahalaxmi Dhobi Ghat....E1
5 Mahalaxmi Temple....A2
6 Mani Bhavan....B5
7 Mumba Devi Temple....F7
8 St Teresa's Church....C6

Activities, Courses & Tours
Bharatiya Sangeet & Nartan Shikshapeeth....(see 9)
9 Bharatiya Vidya Bhavan....B6
10 Child Rights & You....E1
11 H2O Water Sports Complex....C7
12 Kaivalyadhama Ishwardas Yogic Health Centre....D7
13 Sumeet Nagdev Dance Arts....B6
14 Vatsalya Foundation....E1
15 Yoga Kids by Shraddha....A4

Sleeping
16 Hotel Kemps Corner....A5

Eating
17 Badshah Snacks & Drinks....F8
18 Café Moshe....B5
19 Cafe Noorani....B2
20 Haji Ali Juice Centre....B2
21 Neel....D1
22 New Kulfi Centre....B6
23 Revival....F8

Drinking & Nightlife
24 Ghetto....B2
25 Olive Bar & Kitchen....D1

Shopping
26 Anokhi....B6
27 Bhuleshwar Market....F7
28 BX Furtado & Sons....E8
29 Chor Bazaar....F6
30 Crawford Market....F8
Crossword....(see 18)
31 DD Dupattawala....F8
Mangaldas Market....(see 31)
32 Mini Market/Bollywood Bazaar....F5
33 Shrujan....A2
34 Zaveri Bazaar....F7

Information
35 Breach Candy Hospital....A3
36 Foreigners' Regional Registration Office....F8

Transport
37 Allibhai Premji Tyrewalla....C5
Citizen Travels....(see 39)
38 Mumbai Central Bus Terminal....D4
National CTC....(see 38)
39 Private Long-Distance Bus Stand & Agents....F8
40 Private Long-Distance Bus Stand & Ticket Agents....D3

Buy tickets at the booths lining Apollo Bunder. The voyage takes just over an hour.

The ferries dock at the end of a concrete pier, from where you can walk or take the **miniature train** (₹10) to the **stairway** (admission ₹10) leading up to the caves. It's lined with souvenir stalls and patrolled by pesky monkeys. Wear good shoes. The stairs are a bit steep, so avoid the mid-day heat.

Activities

★Wildlife-Watching WILDLIFE-WATCHING

Mumbai has surprisingly good bird- and butterfly-watching opportunities. **Sanjay Gandhi National Park** (Map p58) is popular for woodland birds, while the marshlands of industrial Sewri (pronounced shev-ree) swarm with birds in winter, including pink flamingoes. Contact the excellent **Bombay Natural History Society** (BNHS; Map p54; ☎22821811; www.bnhs.org; Hornbill House, opp Lion Gate, Shahid Bhagat Singh Marg; ⏰9am-5.30pm Mon-Fri) or Sunjoy Monga at **Yuhina Eco-Media** (☎9323995955; sunjoymonga@gmail.com) for information on upcoming trips; the BNHS schedule is also online. Visit BNHS's shop for books on local flora and fauna.

Outbound Adventure OUTDOOR ADVENTURE

(☎26315019; www.outboundadventure.com) Runs one-day rafting trips on the Ulhas River near Karjat, 88km southeast of Mumbai, from July to early September (₹2000 per person). After a good rain, rapids can get up to Grade III+, though usually the rafting is calmer with lots of twists and zigzags. OA also organises camping (from ₹1500 per person per day) and canoeing trips.

Wild Escapes TREKKING

(☎66635228; www.wild-escapes.com) Weekend trekking trips to forts, trails and waterfalls around Maharashtra, from around ₹1500.

OFF THE BEATEN TRACK

SANJAY GANDHI NATIONAL PARK

It's hard to believe that within 90 minutes of the teeming metropolis you can be surrounded by this 104-sq-km **protected tropical forest** (☎28866449; Borivali; adult/child ₹30/15, vehicle ₹100, safari admission ₹50; ⏲7.30am-6pm Tue-Sun, last entry 4pm). Here, bright flora, birds, butterflies and elusive wild leopards replace pollution and crowds, all surrounded by forested hills on the city's northern edge. Urban development tries to muscle in on the fringes of this wild region, but its national park status has allowed it to stay green and calm.

At research time, a trekking ban had been introduced to protect wildlife, but you can get inside the woods if you go with BNHS (p60). On your own, you can take the shuttle to the Shilonda waterfall, Vihar and Tulsi lakes (where there's boating), the zoolike lion and tiger safari and – the most intriguing option – the **Kanheri Caves** (admission/round-trip shuttle ₹5/30), a set of 109 dwellings and monastic structures for Buddhist monks 6km inside the park. The caves, not all of which are accessible, were developed over 1000 years, beginning in the 1st century BC, as part of a sprawling monastic university complex. They're no Ajanta, but worth a visit.

Inside the park's main northern entrance is an information centre with a small exhibition on the park's wildlife. The best time to see birds is October to April and butterflies August to November.

Volunteering

Child Rights & You VOLUNTEERING
(CRY; Map p58; ☎23096845; www.cry.org; 189A Anand Estate, Sane Guruji Marg, Mahalaxmi) Child Rights & You works to raise funds for hundreds of projects India-wide that help marginalised children. Volunteers can assist with campaigns (online and on the ground), research, surveys and media, as well as occasional fieldwork. Note, a six-week commitment is required.

Vatsalya Foundation VOLUNTEERING
(Map p58; ☎24962115; www.thevatsalyafoundation.org; Anand Niketan, King George V Memorial, Dr E Moses Rd, Mahalaxmi) The Vatsalya Foundation works with Mumbai's street children, focusing on rehabilitation into mainstream society. There are long- and short-term opportunities in teaching and sports activities.

Welfare of Stray Dogs VOLUNTEERING
(Map p54; ☎64222838; www.wsdindia.org; Yeshwant Chambers, B Bharucha Rd, Kala Ghoda) This organisation works to help street dogs by eradicating diseases such as rabies, sterilising the animals, educating the public about strays and finding adoptive homes. Volunteers can walk dogs, mind kennels, treat street dogs, manage stores, educate kids in school programs or fundraise.

Courses

★**Yoga Institute** YOGA
(Map p67; ☎26122185; www.theyogainstitute.org; Shri Yogendra Marg, Prabhat Colony, Santa Cruz East; per 1st/2nd month ₹570/400) At its peaceful leafy campus near Santa Cruz, the almost-100-year-old Yoga Institute has daily classes as well as weekend and weeklong programs, and longer residential courses, including teacher training (with seven-day-course prerequisite).

★**Bharatiya Vidya Bhavan** LANGUAGE, MUSIC
(Map p58; ☎23871860; 2nd fl, cnr KM Munshi Marg & Ramabai Rd, Girgaum; per hr ₹500; ⏲4-8pm) Contact the Professor Shukla, a warm and worldly octogenarian, to arrange private Hindi, Marathi, Gujarati and Sanskrit classes here; prices for long-term study are negotiable. Also at the Bhavan is the **Bharatiya Sangeet & Nartan Shikshapeeth** (Indian Music & Dance Institute; Map p58; bhavansangeet@gmail.com; twice-weekly lessons per month ₹1000-5000; ⏲4-8pm). Connect with the friendly Professor Ghosh – a Grammy-winning composer and musician, and the principal – to join an ongoing group class or arrange private lessons in tabla, vocals (from classical Hindustani to playback), sitar, *sarangi* or Kathak or Orissi classical dance.

Yoga House YOGA
(Map p67; ☎65545001; www.yogahouse.in; 53 Chimbai Rd, Bandra; classes ₹600; ⏲8am-10pm) A

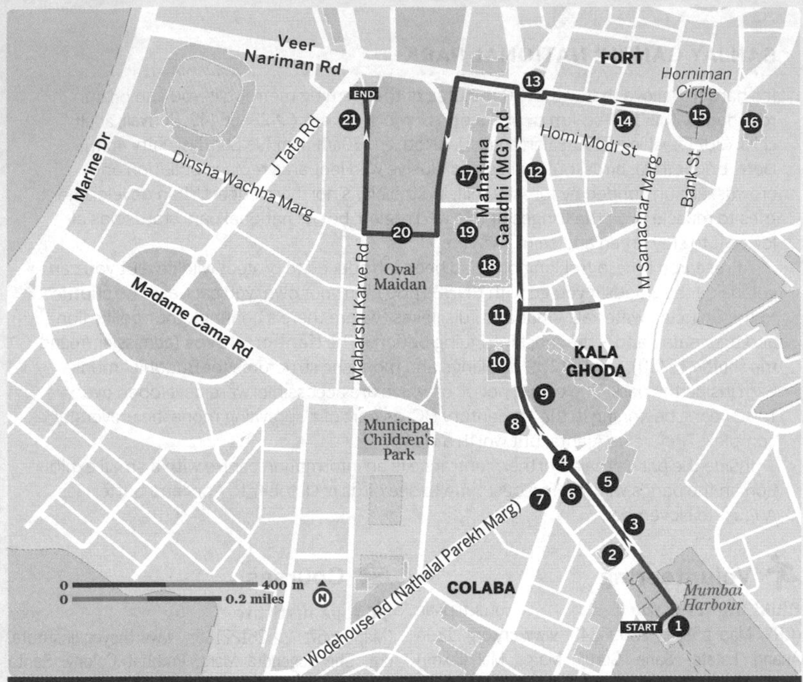

City Walk Architectural Mumbai

START GATEWAY OF INDIA
END EROS CINEMA
DISTANCE 2.5KM
DURATION 1½ HOURS

Mumbai's defining feature is Its distinctive mix of colonial-era and art deco architecture .

Starting from the 1 **Gateway of India** (p48), walk up Chhatrapati Shivaji Marg past the members-only colonial relic 2 **Royal Bombay Yacht Club** and the art deco residential-commercial complex 3 **Dhunraj Mahal**, towards 4 **Regal Circle**. Walk the circle for views of the surrounding buildings – including the old 5 **Sailors Home**, which dates from 1876 and is now the Maharashtra Police Headquarters, the art deco 6 **Regal** (p77) cinema and the 7 **Majestic Hotel**, now the Sahakari Bhandar cooperative store. Continue up MG Rd, past the beautifully restored facade of the 8 **National Gallery of Modern Art** (p51). Opposite is the 9 **Chhatrapati Shivaji Maharaj Vastu Sangrahalaya** (p49). Back across the road is the 'Romanesque Transitional' 10 **Elphinstone College** and the 11 **David Sassoon Library & Reading Room**, where members escape the afternoon heat lazing on planters' chairs on the upper balcony. Continue north to admire the vertical art deco stylings of the 12 **New India Assurance Company Building**. On an island ahead lies 13 **Flora Fountain**, depicting the Roman goddess of flowers. Turn east down Veer Nariman Rd, walking towards 14 **St Thomas' Cathedral** (p51). Ahead lies the stately 15 **Horniman Circle**, an arcaded ring of buildings laid out in the 1860s around a beautifully kept botanical garden. It's overlooked from the east by the neoclassical 16 **Town Hall**, home to the Asiatic Society library. Backtrack to Flora Fountain, continuing west and turning south onto Bhaurao Patil Marg to see the august 17 **High Court** (p50) and the ornate 18 **University of Mumbai** (p49). The university's 80m-high 19 **Rajabai Clock Tower** is best observed from within the 20 **Oval Maidan**. Turn around to compare the colonial edifices with the row of art deco beauties lining Maharshi Karve (MK) Rd, culminating in the wedding cake tower of 21 **Eros Cinema** (p77).

variety of yoga traditions are taught at this homey, Western-style yoga centre, housed in a Portuguese bungalow by the sea. Also has a charming cafe.

Kaivalyadhama Ishwardas Yogic Health Centre YOGA
(Map p58; ☎22818417; www.kdhammumbai.org; 43 Marine Dr; ⏲6am-7pm Mon-Sat) Several daily yoga classes, as well as workshops and special programs, are held here. Fees include a ₹600 monthly membership fee and a ₹500 admission fee. A medical consultation at the on-site health centre, as well as modest dress, are required.

Iyengar Yogashraya YOGA
(☎24948416; www.bksiyengar.com; Elmac House, 126 Senapati Bapat Marg, Lower Parel; 1½hr classes ₹150) The Mumbai centre for the BKS Iyengar tradition of yoga has walk-in classes.

Sumeet Nagdev Dance Arts DANCE
(☎24366777; www.sumeetnagdevdancearts.in; Silver Cascade Building, SB Marg, Dadar West; 1hr classes ₹400) SNDA offers tons of dance classes, from contemporary and ballet to Kalaripayattu (a Keralan martial art) and Bollywood. You can drop in on a class if it's early on in the session (or if you're a quick study); call to inquire. Classes are also held at a **Chowpatty location** (Map p58; Studio Balance, Krishna Kunj, 29/30 KM Munshi Marg).

Tours

Fiona Fernandez's *Ten Heritage Walks of Mumbai* (₹395) contains walking tours in the city, with fascinating historical background. Jumping on a double-decker is an inexpensive and surprisingly good way to see South Mumbai.

The Government of India tourist office (p80) can provide a list of approved multilingual guides; most charge ₹750/950 per half-/full day.

Reality Tours & Travel SLUM TOUR
(Map p50; ☎9820822253; www.realitytoursandtravel.com; 1st fl, Akbar House, Nawroji F Rd, Colaba; short/long Dharavi tours ₹650/1200) Photography is strictly forbidden on Reality's socially responsible tours of Dharavi, and 80% of post-tax profits go to the agency's own NGO, **Reality Gives** (www.realitygives.org), which runs a kindergarten and community centre in Dharavi. Reality also conducts village and Mumbai-by-bicycle tours. Enter the office through SSS Corner store.

Bombay Heritage Walks WALKING
(☎23690992, 9821887321; www.bombayheritagewalks.com) Run by two enthusiastic architects, BHW has the best city tours in heritage neighbourhoods. Two-hour guided tours are ₹2000 for up to four people; longer tours are ₹3000 for three people; both include a 'handy keepsake'.

Mumbai Magic Tours CITY TOUR
(☎9867707414; www.mumbaimagic.com; 2hr tours from ₹1500 per person) City tours, designed by the authors of the fabulous Mumbai Magic blog (www.mumbai-magic.blogspot.com), focus on food markets, traditional dance and music, and Jewish heritage, amongst others, and cover many places you would never find on your own.

Nilambari Bus Tours BUS TOUR
(MTDC; 1hr tours ₹150; ⏲7pm & 8.15pm Sat & Sun) Maharashtra Tourism runs open-deck bus tours of illuminated heritage buildings on weekends. They depart from and can be booked at both the MTDC booth (p80) and the MTDC office (p80).

Cruises CRUISE
(☎22026364; ⏲8am-8pm) A cruise on Mumbai Harbour is a good way to escape the city and see the Gateway of India as it was intended. Half-hour ferry rides (₹70) depart from the Gateway of India; tickets are sold on-site.

H2O Water Sports Complex CRUISE
(Map p58; ☎23677584; www.drishtiadventures.com; Marine Dr, Mafatlal Beach; cruises per person day/night ₹400/500; ⏲10am-10pm Sep-May) Arranges 45-minute day and night cruises (four-person minimum, so you may have to wait for them to fill), plus kayaking and parasailing.

Sleeping

You'll need to recalibrate your budget here: Mumbai has the most expensive accommodation in India, and you'll never quite feel like you're getting your money's worth. Welcome to Mumbai real estate!

Colaba is compact, has the liveliest tourist scene and many budget and midrange options. Fort is more spread out and convenient for the main train stations (CST and Churchgate). Most of the top-end places are dotted along Marine Drive and around the suburbs; Juhu and Bandra are good for nightlife, Juhu Beach and shopping. No matter where you stay, always book ahead.

Rates listed for five-star hotels are rack, but they go down, sometimes by 50%, depending on occupancy.

To stay with a local family, contact **India-tourism** (www.incredibleindia.com) for a list of homes across the city participating in Mumbai's **paying-guest and B&B program** (s/d from ₹400/800).

Colaba

Carlton Hotel HOTEL $
(Map p50; ☎22020642; 1st fl, Florence House, Mereweather Rd; s/d/tr/q without bathroom from ₹900/1400/2150/2850, s/d with AC ₹2750/2950) Rooms here are quirky and tired, with about 100 different bathroom scenarios (most rooms have common showers, though they were recently renovated). But the hotel also has old tile floors, wood-beam ceilings and wooden railings, a balcony with plants and colonial-era Colaba views, and glittery old pictures of gods about – so it goes both ways.

Salvation Army Red Shield Guest House GUESTHOUSE $
(Map p50; ☎22841824; red_shield@vsnl.net; 30 Mereweather Rd; dm incl breakfast ₹250, d/tr/q incl breakfast & lunch ₹850/1150/1600; ❄@) 'Salvies' is a Mumbai institution popular with rupee-pinching travellers. The large, ascetic dorms here are clean but cannot be reserved in advance: come just after the 9am kickout to ensure a spot. Curfew is midnight.

Sea Shore Hotel GUESTHOUSE $
(Map p50; ☎22874237; 4th fl, Kamal Mansion, Arthur Bunder Rd; s/d without bathroom from ₹624/988) The Sea Shore's shoebox-size rooms are simple but nearly hotel-quality, with incongruously high-design communal bathrooms. Interior rooms have no window, but front-facing rooms have (through dingy, tiny screens) million-dollar views of Mumbai Harbour. The same owners run **India Guest House** (Map p50; ☎22833769; s/d without bathroom ₹416/520) downstairs, with similar bathrooms but not-as-nice rooms.

★**YWCA** GUESTHOUSE $$
(Map p50; ☎22025053; www.ywcaic.info; 18 Madame Cama Rd, Colaba; s/d/tr/q with AC incl breakfast & dinner ₹2126/3150/4462/6301; ❄@📶) The YWCA is immaculate – your room is scrubbed down every single day – and ridiculously good-value: rates, which are a good ₹1000 cheaper than most in its class, include breakfast, dinner, early-morning tea, free wi-fi...*and a newspaper*. But there's a trade-off here with the long list of borderline-monastic rules, which some find off-putting.

Bentley's Hotel HOTEL $$
(Map p50; ☎22841474; www.bentleyshotel.com; 17 Oliver Rd; r incl breakfast ₹1675-2295, with AC ₹1990-2610; ❄) People either love Bentley's or hate it, depending on which of the five buildings they end up in. Avoid Henry Rd and JA Allana Marg. The three buildings on Oliver Rd are good, but your first choice is the main building, where big rooms have old-school floor tiles, wooden furniture and colonial-era charm aplenty.

Regent Hotel HOTEL $$
(Map p50; ☎22021518; www.regenthotelcolaba.com; 8 Best Marg; r with AC incl breakfast ₹4579-5284; ❄@📶) The friendly, Arabian-flavoured Regent has marble surfaces and soft beiges aplenty. More-expensive upper floors have tree views. The retro-chic breakfast area fills the 1st floor hallway, so avoid rooms 101–110 if you plan to sleep in.

Hotel Moti GUESTHOUSE $$
(Map p50; ☎22025714; hotelmotiinternational@yahoo.co.in; 10 Best Marg; s/d/tr with AC ₹3000/3200/4500; ❄@) Rooms here, in a gracefully crumbling, colonial-era building in prime Colaba, are simple and slightly overpriced. But all have fridges and some are huge and/or have whispers of charm, like ornate stucco ceilings. It's a family-run place, but the service gets complaints.

★**Taj Mahal Palace, Mumbai** HERITAGE HOTEL $$$
(Map p50; ☎66653366; www.tajhotels.com; Apollo Bunder; s/d tower from ₹27,887/29,649, palace from ₹38,162/39,923; ❄@📶🏊) With its sweeping arches, staircases and domes, the Taj really does feel like a palace. Following the 2008 terrorist attacks here, some 285 rooms were lavishly restored in fuchsia, saffron and willow-green colour schemes (and security is Fort Knox–level). Rooms in the tower wing lack the period details of the palace wing, but some have spectacular, full-on views of the Gateway. The hotel's Harbour Bar (p74), Mumbai's first licensed bar, is legendary.

Hotel Suba Palace HOTEL **$$$**
(Map p50; ☎22020636–9; www.hotelsubapalace.com; Battery St; s/d with AC incl breakfast ₹5519/6341; ❄📶) Teetering precariously on the edge of boutique hotel, the Suba Palace oozes soothing neutral tones, from the tiny taupe shower tiles in the contemporary bathrooms to the creamy crown moulding and beige zebra-print quilted headboards in the tasteful rooms. Plus, wi-fi's free. Comfy, quiet and central.

Fariyas Hotel HOTEL **$$$**
(Map p50; ☎61416141; www.fariyas.com; 25 D Vyas Marg; r with AC incl wi-fi from ₹11,742; @📶🏊) This smart, friendly place has tasteful, traditional-style rooms (prices go up a couple notches for a harbour view) and a small pool, which nonguests can use (₹780 per day). With its peaceful spot on a residential street near the water, it's also a comfortable distance from the fray.

Ascot Hotel HOTEL **$$$**
(Map p50; ☎66385566; www.ascothotel.com; 38 Garden Rd; r with AC incl breakfast from ₹7045; ❄@📶) Marble-meets-modern at this well-designed hotel. Airy rooms have big headboards, bathtubs, desks and lots of natural light and, in front-facing rooms, tree views. Wi-fi's ₹300 per day.

Fort Area & Churchgate

Hotel Lawrence GUESTHOUSE **$**
(Map p54; ☎22843618; 3rd fl, ITTS House, 33 Sai Baba Marg; s/d/tr without bathroom incl breakfast ₹700/850/1050) Tucked away in a little side lane, Lawrence has clean crashpads that are popular with shoestring meditators – and a management that tends to enforce moral judgements on guests.

Traveller's Inn HOTEL **$**
(☎22644685; 26 Adi Marzban Path; dm/d ₹628/1579, d with AC incl breakfast ₹2260; ❄@📶) On a quiet, tree-lined street, the tall and narrow Traveller's Inn has tiny rooms and rain-shower heads in even tinier bathrooms. But everything's squeaky clean, and the location's excellent. Free wi-fi in the lobby.

Hotel Oasis HOTEL **$$**
(Map p54; ☎30227886–9; www.hoteloasisindia.in; 276 Shahid Bhagat Singh Rd; r from ₹1620; ❄) Rooms at this friendly place are incredibly small and need some paint, and some of the standard rooms are low on natural light. But they're spick and span and a stone's throw from CST. Plus, the kooky pastel design scheme makes you feel like you're inside an ice-cream cone. In a good way.

Sea Green Hotel HOTEL **$$**
(Map p54; ☎66336525; www.seagreenhotel.com; 145 Marine Dr; s/d from ₹3974/5063) This excellent art deco hotel, and its twin, **Sea Green South** (Map p54; ☎22821613; www.seagreensouth.com; 145A Marine Dr; s/d from ₹3974/5063), have spacious but spartan air-conditioned rooms, originally built in the 1940s to house British soldiers. Ask for one of the sea-view rooms: they're the same price.

CST Retiring Rooms RAILWAY RETIRING ROOM **$$**
(Map p54; dm/d with AC ₹540/1600) Ticket-holders should try to snag one of VT's quaint and oddly quiet retiring rooms for a night; check in at the enquiry counter/station manager office.

Residency Hotel HOTEL **$$**
(Map p54; ☎22625525; www.residencyhotel.com; 26 Rustom Sidhwa Marg; s/d with AC incl breakfast from ₹3640/3875; ❄@📶) Recent renovations have transformed the friendly Residency into a contemporary design-style hotel, with mood lighting, rain showers and leather-walled elevators. Rooms also have fridges, flatscreens, slippers and wi-fi (free in the pricier rooms). But there are odd oversights (why only a single towel in double rooms?) that shouldn't happen in this price range.

Welcome Hotel HOTEL **$$**
(☎6631488; welcomehotel@gmail.com; 257 Shahid Bhagat Singh Rd; s/d incl breakfast from ₹3082/3611, without bathroom from ₹1644/1820; ❄📶) Though the service needs some work, rooms here are simple and fresh, and shared bathrooms are nicer than most attached baths elsewhere. Top-floor executive rooms are more boutique than midrange, more LA than Bombay. Free wi-fi.

Trident HOTEL **$$$**
(Oberoi Hotel; Map p54; ☎66324343; www.tridenthotels.com; Marine Dr; s/d from ₹22,016/23,480; ❄@📶🏊) The Trident is, along with the Oberoi, part of the Oberoi Hotel complex. But the Trident wins out both on price and on the spiffy, streamlined design of its restaurants, bars and pool area. The rooms, too, are as cool as the Oberoi's, but with earthy elements (and smaller bathrooms).

West End Hotel HOTEL $$$

(Map p54; ☎40839100; www.westendhotelmumbai.com; 45 New Marine Lines; s/d with AC from ₹5871/7045;) The West End's spacious art-deco rooms have modish beds, balconies, and moments of mid-century modern and Hollywood regency. Bless their hearts, the look is totally accidental. The rest of the place is old-fashioned, down to the friendly service and the hotel's taglines: 'Honest Prices' and 'Good VFM' – Value For Money. If the rates were a wee bit lower, that would be TT – totally true.

InterContinental HOTEL $$$

(Map p54; ☎39879999; www.intercontinental.com; 135 Marine Dr; r incl breakfast from ₹22,897;) Very sleek for an InterContinental. All earth tones and East Asian chic, deluxe sea-front rooms are sizeable, with a massive picture window, while half-moon corner suites mirror the curve of Marine Drive. Lower-category rooms have poor views. Its lobby-level Koh (p71) turns Thai food on its head, while stunning Dome (p75) lounge stylishly graces the rooftop.

Western Suburbs

★**Anand Hotel** HOTEL $$

(Map p67; ☎26203372; anandhote@yahoo.co.in; Gandhigram Rd, Juhu; s/d with AC from ₹2348/3875;) The rooms here are so clean, homey and old-fashioned – think embroidered artwork in the rooms, steel clothes-drying rods on the balconies and images of Ganesh everywhere – that they feel like they're in someone's Bombay apartment. It's around the corner from the ISKCON temple and upstairs from the excellent Dakshinayan restaurant, so the location couldn't be any better either.

★**Iskcon** GUESTHOUSE $$

(Map p67; ☎26206860; guesthouse.mumbai@pamho.net; Hare Krishna Land, Juhu; s/d ₹3095/3495, with AC ₹3395/3995;) This efficiently managed guesthouse is part of Juhu's lively ISKCON complex. The lobby overlooks the temple, while rooms have Gujarati *sankheda* (lacquered country wood) furniture; some have balconies with pretty arches. Krishna's birthday (Janmastami; August) and the car festival (Rath Yatra; celebrated in January) are big here; the thrice-daily *aarti* (candle-lighting ritual) is also special.

Western Suburbs

Activities, Courses & Tours

1 Yoga House ... A5
2 Yoga Institute ... C3

Sleeping

3 Anand Hotel ... B1
4 Hotel Columbus ... C2
5 Hotel Neelkanth ... B4
6 Hotel Regal Enclave ... B4
7 Hotel Suba Galaxy ... C1
8 Hotel Suba International ... D2
9 Iskcon ... B1
10 Juhu Residency ... B2
11 Sun-n-Sand ... A1

Eating

12 Adar Udipi Refreshment ... C2
13 Basilico ... B5
Bora Bora ... (see 15)
14 Candies ... B5
15 Caravan Serai ... B5
Dakshinayan ... (see 3)
16 Eat Around the Corner ... B5
17 Mahesh Lunch Home ... B2
Prithvi Cafe ... (see 25)
18 Salt Water Café ... B6
Suzette ... (see 13)
19 Theobroma ... B5
Yoga House ... (see 1)

Drinking & Nightlife

20 Big Nasty ... A4
Elbo Room ... (see 19)
21 Hungry Birds ... B4
22 Mocha Mojo ... B5
23 Olive Bar & Kitchen ... B4
24 Toto's Garage ... B5

Entertainment

25 Prithvi Theatre ... B2
26 Trilogy ... B3

Shopping

27 Indian Hippy ... A4
28 Play Clan ... B5
29 Shrujan ... B1

Information

30 Australian Consulate ... D5
31 French Consulate ... D5
32 Humsafar Trust ... C3
33 Malaysian Consulate ... B5
34 New Zealand Consulate ... C5
35 UK Consulate ... D5
36 US Consulate ... D5

Hotel Kemps Corner HOTEL **$$**
(Map p58; ☎23634646; www.hotelkempscorner.com; 131 August Kranti Marg; s/d with AC incl breakfast from ₹2818/4697; ❄@📶) You can tell this place is a family business from the TLC given to rooms (spick-and-span bathrooms, new TVs) and guests (free breakfast and wi-fi, smiley service). The hotel is also in a shady spot in the Kemp's Corner fashion bonanza, which is much less frenzied than Colaba or Fort, and just 2km to Haji Ali Dargah and Chowpatty.

Western Suburbs

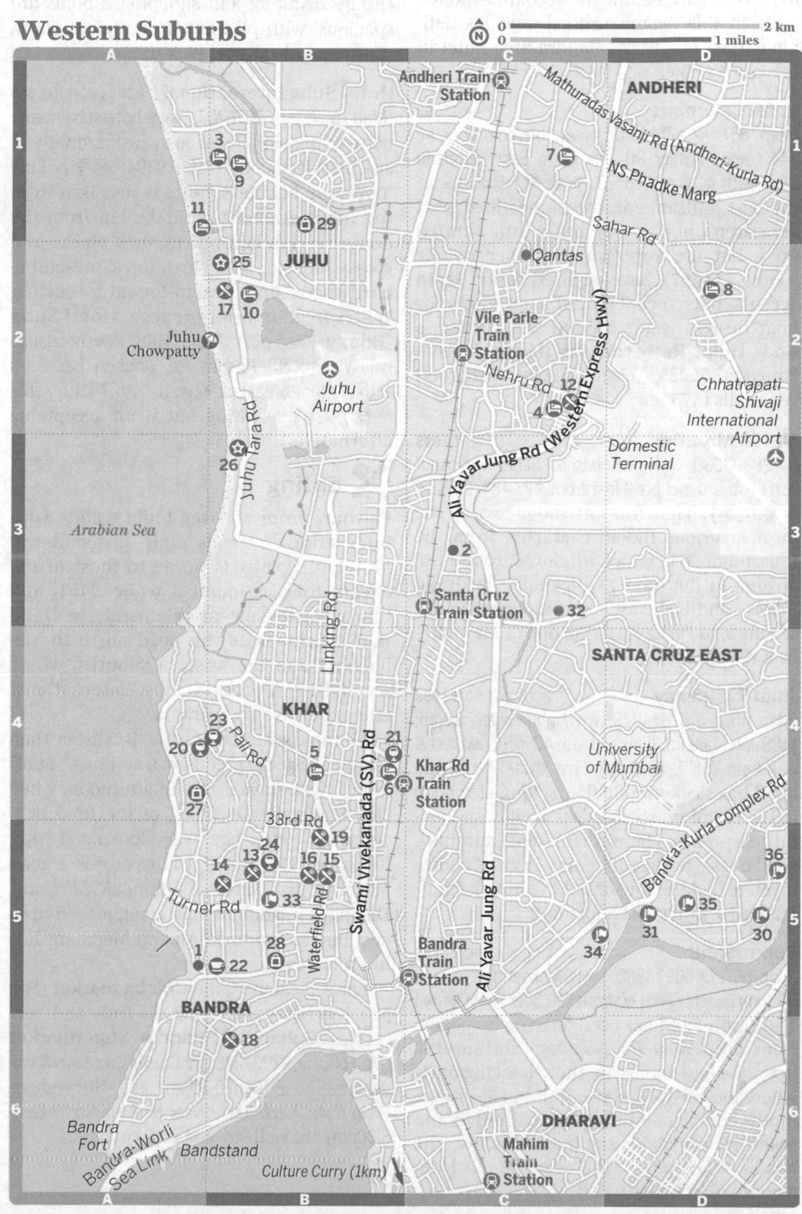

Hotel Neelkanth HOTEL $$
(Map p67; ☎26495566-9; 354 Linking Rd, Khar West; s/d from ₹2231/2935; ❄) Rooms at the friendly Neelkanth are inadvertently retro, with lots of marble, chrome-trimmed wooden furniture and old-school plaid wool blankets. (Check out the sublimely mod logo too.) It might be the most old-fashioned place in this neighbourhood, and it's definitely the only decent Bandra-area hotel in this price range.

Hotel Columbus HOTEL $$
(Map p67; ☎42144343; www.hotelcolumbus.in; 344 Nanda Patkar Rd, Vile Parle East, opposite BP; r with AC from ₹3523; ❄@📶) Rooms at the best midrange in the domestic airport area aren't new – they are a little scuffed up – but are very homey. Super deluxe rooms (₹4697) have stylised wood-grain accents, flatscreen TVs and aspirations for high design. Right around the corner is **Adar Udipi Refreshment** (Map p67; Nehru Rd; mains ₹55-135; ⏰7am-10.30pm), with good veg thalis (₹75).

★**ITC Maratha** HOTEL $$$
(☎28303030; www.itchotels.in; Sahar Rd, Andheri East; s/d incl breakfast from ₹23,484/25,832; ❄@📶🏊) The five-star hotel with the most luxurious Indian character, from the Rajasthani-style lattice windows around the atrium, to the rooms with their silk throw pillows and lush raspberry and grey colour schemes, to Peshawri (p73), one of Mumbai's best restaurants.

Juhu Residency BOUTIQUE HOTEL $$$
(Map p67; ☎67834949; www.juhuresidency.com; 148B Juhu Tara Rd, Juhu; s/d with AC incl breakfast & wi-fi from ₹5871; ❄@📶) This quasi-boutique hotel has sleek marble floors, king-size beds in the premium rooms, dark woods and artful bedspreads. There are three restaurants – good ones – for just 18 rooms. A great choice if you're looking for something hip and intimate that won't cost a fortune.

Sun-n-Sand HOTEL $$$
(Map p67; ☎66938888; www.sunnsandhotel.com; 39 Juhu Beach; r with AC from ₹10,568; ❄@📶🏊) The Sun-n-Sand has been offering up beachfront hospitality for decades. Not surprisingly, the best rooms are the sea-facing ones, where lots of silk and pleasant burnt-orange motifs complement the pool, palm-tree and ocean views outside the huge window. The hotel's off Juhu Tara Rd, near the old Holiday Inn. Rates vary wildly.

Hotel Regal Enclave HOTEL $$$
(Map p67; ☎67261111; www.regalenclave.com; 4th Rd, Khar West, near Khar market; r with AC incl breakfast from ₹6000) Regal Enclave has a stellar location: in an exceedingly leafy part of Khar, right near the station (some rooms have train views) and all of Bandra's best eating, drinking and shopping. Rooms are spacious, with pleasant if unoriginal decor. Rates include airport pick-up.

Hotel Suba International BOUTIQUE HOTEL $$$
(Map p67; ☎67076707; www.hotelsubainternational.com; Sahar Rd, Andheri East; s/d with AC incl breakfast from ₹8102/9394; ❄📶) This 'boutique business' hotel is just 1km from the international terminal, 3km from the domestic. It's laid out in slick blacks and glossy marble, with clean lines, masculine hardwoods and design-forward touches. Wi-fi's free. Its sister property, **Hotel Suba Galaxy** (Map p67; ☎26821188; www.hotelsubagalaxy.com; NS Phadke Rd, Andheri East; s/d with AC incl breakfast & wi-fi from ₹4110/7985; ❄📶), isn't as shiny but is an acceptable alternative.

Eating

Flavours from all over India collide with international trends and tastebuds in Mumbai. Colaba is home to most of the cheap tourist haunts, while Fort and Churchgate skew more upscale, a trend that continues as you head north to Mahalaxmi and the western suburbs, where you'll find Mumbai's most international and expensive restaurants.

Mumbai's street cuisine is vaster than many Western culinary traditions. Stalls tend to get started in late afternoon, when chai complements much of the fried deliciousness (*vada pav*, we're looking at you); items are ₹10 to ₹25. Chowpatty is a good place to try Mumbai's famous *bhelpuri*. During Ramadan, fantastic night food-markets line Mohammed Ali and Merchant Rds in Kalbadevi.

For self-caterers, the **Colaba market** (Map p50; Lala Nigam St) has fresh fruit and vegetables. **Saharkari Bhandar Supermarket** (Map p50; ☎22022248; cnr Colaba Causeway & Wodehouse Rd; ⏰10am-8.30pm) and **Suryodaya** (Map p54; ☎22040979; Veer Nariman Rd; ⏰8am-8.30pm) are well-stocked supermarkets.

Colaba

Hotel OCH INDIAN $

(Map p50; Shahid Bhagat Singh Rd; mains ₹65-110, thalis ₹65-105; ⊙7am-10.30pm) The best of the Colaba cheapies, with decent lunch thalis and evening *pav bhaji* in a cafeteria-like setting. Popular with families and cops working next door.

Bademiya MUGHLAI, FAST FOOD $$

(Map p50; Tulloch Rd; light meals ₹60-150; ⊙8pm-1.30am) Formerly a tiny, outrageously popular late-night street stall, Bademiya recently added a dingy seating area across the street, a tiny eatery around the corner and a restaurant in Fort, which some say have been its downfall. It's true that prices have gone up while portions have shrunk, but the spicy, fresh-grilled kebabs and tikka rolls still hit the spot on a late night.

Theobroma CAFE $$

(Map p50; Colaba Causeway; confections ₹40-95, light meals ₹180-200; ⊙7am-midnight) Perfectly executed cakes, tarts and brownies, as well as sandwiches and breads, go well with the coffee here. The pastries change regularly; if you're lucky, you'll find the Portuguese vanilla cinnamon custard tart (₹70). For brunch, have the *akoori* – Parsi-style scrambled eggs – with green mango. The **Bandra branch** (Map p67; 33rd Rd, near Linking Rd; ⊙8am-11.30pm) is big and airy, with the same menu.

Indigo FUSION $$$

(Map p50; ☎66368980; www.foodindigo.com; 4 Mandlik Marg; mains ₹750-1100; ⊙12-3pm & 6.30pm-midnight) Colaba's finest eating option is a gourmet haven serving inventive European cuisine, a long wine list, sleek ambience and a gorgeous roof deck lit with fairy lights. Favourites include the kiwi margaritas (₹465), Cochin oysters (₹765) and zucchini-wrapped prawns with polenta and saffron butter (₹1100). Reserve on weekends.

Koyla NORTH INDIAN $$$

(Map p50; www.koylaethniccuisine.com; 4th fl, Kamal Mansion, Arthur Bunder Rd; mains ₹280-550; ⊙7.30pm-1am Tue-Sun) This massive rooftop space has fairy lights, plants and sandy paths winding around the tented tables, while Mumbai Harbour and the Taj Palace twinkle in the distance. The menu is strong on tikkas and kebabs.

Basilico MEDITERRANEAN $$$

(Map p50; ☎66345670; www.cafebasilico.com; Sentinel House, Arthur Bunder Rd; mains ₹360-690; ⊙9am-1am) Euro-style Basilico does creative steaks and fresh pastas, but the real draw is for vegies: exquisite salads (from ₹250) like grilled artichoke, Lebanese fattoush or the specials, which might include a spicy brown rice, baked tofu, and green salad in lemon-chilli-ginger dressing. The **Bandra branch** (Map p67; St John Rd, Pali Naka) has outdoor seating.

Indigo Delicatessen CAFE $$$

(Map p50; Pheroze Bldg, Chhatrapati Shivaji Marg; mains ₹425-645; ⊙8.30am-midnight) Indigo's deli and bakery has cool tunes, warm decor and massive wooden tables. It has breakfast all day (₹155 to ₹385), inventive sandwiches and other casual meals, French-press coffee – including some from Andhra Pradesh's Araku region – and tons of teas, wine (₹350 to ₹790 per glass) and, alas, poor service.

DABBA-WALLAHS

A small miracle of logistics, Mumbai's 5000 *dabba-wallahs* (literally 'food container person'; also called tiffin-wallahs) work tirelessly to deliver hot lunches to office workers throughout the city.

Lunch boxes are picked up each day from restaurants and homes and carried on heads, bicycles and trains to a centralised sorting station. A sophisticated system of numbers and colours (many wallahs don't read) identifies the destination of each lunch. More than 200,000 meals are delivered – always on time, come (monsoon) rain or (searing) shine.

This system has been used for over a century and there's only about one mistake per six million deliveries. (In a 2002 analysis, *Forbes Magazine* found that the *dabba-wallahs* had a six-sigma, or 99.99966%, reliability rating.)

Look for these master messengers mid-morning at Churchgate and CST stations.

Fort Area & Churchgate

★ Pradeep Gomantak Bhojanalaya MAHARASHTRIAN $
(Map p54; Sheri House, Rustom Sidhwa Marg; mains ₹60-130; 11am-4pm Mon-Sat) The *surmai* (seer) rice plate here looks plain – a fried piece of fish, some dhal, rice and chutneys on a stainless steel plate – but the meal will transport you. The food is homestyle Malvani cuisine, from coastal Maharashtra, and so fresh you can taste the individual flavours dancing with one another. Savour the sublime, pink *sol kadhi*, a soothing, spicy drink of coconut milk and kokum.

A Taste of Kerala KERALAN $
(Map p54; Prospect Chambers Annex, Pitha St, Fort; mains ₹50-140, thalis ₹80-120; 6am-midnight) This humble little hotel is one of several little Keralan eateries on an alley in Fort and does a fine fish curry rice (if you can handle the bones) and lunch thali, served on a banana leaf. Lots of coconut and southern goodness.

Badshah Snacks & Drinks INDIAN $
(Map p58; snacks & drinks ₹35-120; 7am-12.30am) Opposite Crawford market, Badshah's been serving snacks, fruit juices and its famous *falooda* (rose-flavoured drink made with milk, cream, nuts and vermicelli) to hungry bargain-hunters for more than 100 years. Try the mango *falooda*.

K Rustom SWEETS $
(Map p54; Stadium House, Veer Nariman Rd; desserts ₹25-70; 9.30am-11pm Mon-Sat, 3-11pm Sun) Nothing but a few metal freezers, but the ice-cream sandwich (₹50) has been pleasing Mumbaikar palettes since 1953.

★ Suzette FRENCH $$
(Map p54; www.suzette.in; Atlanta Bldg, Vinayak K Shah Marg, Nariman Point; light meals ₹200-330; 9am-11pm Mon-Sat;) You'll feel like a cool Parisian when you eat here: there are newspapers, really good crepes, croques and coffee, water served in glass bottles, and loungy music that sways from old-timey French to Afropop. Also, a jaggery-and-butter crepe is a really good idea. Just one concern: it has no bathroom. The Bandra **Suzette** (Map p67; St John's St, Pali Naka) has outdoor seating and is open daily.

★ Samrat GUJARATI $$
(Map p54; 42135401; www.prashantcaterers.com; Prem Ct, J Tata Rd; thalis lunch/dinner & Sundays ₹265/330, mains ₹170-250; noon-11pm) If this is your first thali, strap yourself in: the cavalcade of taste and texture (and sweetness – this is Gujarati food) will leave you wondering what just happened. Come hungry. Samrat is also the king of a pure-veg empire that includes **210°C** (Map p54), an outdoor cafe and bakery, and **Relish** (Map p54), with Asian-Mexican-Lebanese fusion, at the same location.

Kala Ghoda Café CAFE $$
(Map p54; www.kgcafe.in; 10 Ropewalk Lane, Kala Ghoda; light meals ₹100-275, dinners ₹375-525; 8.30am-11.45pm;) An artsy, modern and miniscule cafe that's a favourite among journalists and other creative types, who come for the organic coffee sourced from sustainable plantations, organic teas, excellent sandwiches and salads, and charming breakfasts – after fighting for one of the few tables.

Café Moshe CAFE $$
(Map p50; www.moshes.in; Chhatrapati Shivaji Marg; light meals ₹175-375; 9am-midnight) Teeny tiny Moshe's does excellent baked goods, coffees, smoothies, salads, fondue and sandwiches (the whole-wheat bagel sandwich with broccoli tapenade, rocket, basil, feta and mozzarella is to die for). The other outlets – the flagship **restaurant** (7 Minoo Manor, Cuffe Parade; 9am-midnight), in a heritage building, and the bookstore **cafe** (Map p58; Crossword, NS Patkar Marg) at Kemp's Corner – all serve the same great food.

Bademiya Restaurant MUGHLAI $$
(Map p54; 22655657; Botawala Bldg, Horniman Circle; mains ₹110-180; 11am-1am) The grown-up, sit-down version of Bademiya's legendary Colaba streetside stand has the classic rolls and rotis, plus biryanis, tikka masalas and dhals. Delivers.

Brittania PARSI $$
(Wakefield House, Ballard Estate; mains ₹100-350; 12-4pm Mon-Sat) This Mumbai icon and its endearing owner have been going since 1923. The signature dishes are the *dhansak* and the berry *pulao* (from ₹250) – spiced and boneless mutton or chicken, or veg or egg, buried in basmati rice and tart barberries that are imported from Iran – in a shady spot in pretty Ballard Estate.

Samovar Café CAFE $$

(Map p54; Jehangir Art Gallery, MG Rd, Kala Ghoda; mains ₹90-160; ⏱11am-7pm Mon-Sat) This intimate place inside the art gallery, perfect for a snack and a tea, overlooks the gardens of the Prince of Wales Museum.

★ **Koh** THAI $$$

(Map p54; ☎39879999; InterContinental, Marine Dr; mains ₹495-1395; ⏱12.30-3pm & 7.30-midnight) India's first signature Thai restaurant is Mumbai's hottest and most beautifully designed dining destination. Celebrity chef Ian Kittichai works his native cuisine into an international frenzy of flavour with revelatory dishes like wok-tossed black-pepper tenderloin, and oven-roasted aubergine sprinkled with nori (paired with hot-stone garlic rice), throwing preconceived notions about Thai food to the curb.

★ **Revival** INDIAN $$$

(Map p58; 361 Sheikh Memon St, Kalbadevi, opp Mangaldas market; thalis ₹300; ⏱12-4pm & 7.30-10.30pm, lunch only Sun) It turns out that Tamil, Punjabi and Rajasthani food can work together in a jumbo thali if you know what you're doing – and Revival knows what it's doing. Servers in silken dhoti come one after another to fill your golden plates with dozens of dishes, sides and chutneys in a luscious onslaught. The thali changes daily and it's bigger on Sundays.

Khyber NORTH INDIAN $$$

(Map p54; ☎40396666; 145 MG Rd; mains ₹375-725; ⏱12.30-4pm & 7.30-11.30pm) The Afghan-inspired cave-like interior here sets off mouth-watering kebabs, biryanis and curries. Highlights of the meat-centric menu include the *reshmi kebab masala*, a transcendent dish of cream and yoghurt-marinated chicken drowning in the restaurant's intricate red masala; and its pièce de résistance, *raan* (a whole leg of slow-cooked lamb). Veggies, look elsewhere.

Trishna SEAFOOD $$$

(Map p54; ☎22703213/4; Ropewalk Lane, Kala Ghoda; mains ₹260-750; ⏱noon-3.30pm & 6.30pm-midnight) An outstanding and intimate seafood restaurant focused on Mangalorean preparations. The crab with butter, black pepper and garlic, and Hyderabadi fish tikka are house specialities that warrant the hype, while service is underbearing, friendly and helpful. One of the best seafood places in town. Reservations unnecessary before 8pm.

Mahesh Lunch Home SEAFOOD $$$

(Map p54; ☎22023965; www.maheshlunchhome.com; Cowasji Patel St; mains ₹150-475; ⏱11.30am-4pm & 7pm-midnight) A great place to try Mangalorean seafood in Mumbai. It's renowned for its ladyfish, pomfret, lobster and crabs; the *rawas tikka* (marinated white salmon) and tandoori pomfret are outstanding. There's also a **Juhu branch** (Map p67; Juhu Tara Rd; mains ₹200-600; ⏱12-3.30pm & 7pm-12.30am).

5 Spice CHINESE $$$

(Map p54; 296A Perin Nariman St, Sangli Bank Bldg; mains ₹240-635; ⏱noon-3pm & 7pm-midnight) A 30-minute wait is common at this Indo-Chinese godsend whose menu is packed with so many tantalising chicken, lamb, prawn/fish and veg dishes that choosing is an issue. In the end, the chicken in burnt-chilli sauce (₹290) works on a bed of burnt chilli-rice (₹265). Veggies should stick to the **veg branch** (Shalimar Bldg, G Rd) in Churchgate.

Kalbadevi to Mahalaxmi

★ **New Kulfi Centre** SWEETS $

(Map p58; cnr Chowpatty Seaface & Sardar V Patel Rd; kulfi per 100gm ₹35-50; ⏱10am-1am) Serves the best *kulfi* (firm-textured ice cream) you'll have anywhere, which means it's pretty much the best thing in the world. Killer flavours include pistachio, *malai* (cream) and saffron.

Dakshinayan SOUTH INDIAN $

(183 Teen Batti, Walkeshwar Rd, Malabar Hill; light meals ₹75-110; ⏱11am-3pm & 6-11pm, from 8am Sun) This smaller, slightly faded Dakshinayan has the same excellent food as the Juhu branch (p72).

Haji Ali Juice Centre JUICE BAR $

(Map p58; Lala Lajpatrai Rd, Haji Ali Circle; juices & snacks ₹30-180; ⏱5am-1.30am) The Haji Ali Juice folks know all sweet, tasty things: fresh juices, milkshakes, *falooda*, and – don't miss this – fruit with fresh cream (the custard apple is so good you'll die). Strategically placed at the entrance to Haji Ali Mosque, it's a great place to cool off after the pilgrimage.

Cafe Noorani NORTH INDIAN $$
(Map p58; Tardeo Rd, Haji Ali Circle; mains ₹75-275; ⏲8am-11.30pm) This almost-retro diner is a requisite stop before or after visiting Haji Ali Mosque. On the menu is the gamut of Mughlai and Punjabi staples, all done well and cheap. The chicken tikka biryani (₹190) is so good, you'll forgive a bite or two of gristle.

Neel NORTH INDIAN $$$
(Map p58; ☎61577777; Gate No 5 & 6, Mahalaxmi Racecourse; mains ₹445-685; ⏲noon-3pm & 7pm-midnight) Funky, all-white tree-branch interiors and ridiculously beautiful crowds aside, this hip restaurant and lounge dishes out mostly Awadhi/Northwest Frontier cuisine with creative adjustments. The outdoor seating is canopied by grand old trees. Reserve on weekends.

Western Suburbs

North Mumbai is home to the city's trendiest dining, centered on Bandra West and Juhu. Look out for the Juhu branch of Mahesh Lunch Home (p71), and the Bandra outposts of Suzette (p70), Basilico (p69) and Theobroma (p69).

★ **Hotel Ram Ashraya** SOUTH INDIAN $
(Bhandarkar Rd, King's Circle, Matunga East; light meals ₹30-50; ⏲5am-9.30pm) Tucked away in the Tamil enclave of King's Circle, 80-year-old Ram Ashraya is beloved by southern families for its spectacular dosas, *idli* (round steamed rice cakes), *upma* (semolina cooked with onions, spices and coconut) and filter coffee. The menu, written on a chalkboard, changes daily. To get here, take the Central Line from CST; it's just outside the Matunga station's east exit.

★ **Dakshinayan** SOUTH INDIAN $
(Map p67; Hotel Anand, Gandhigram Rd, Juhu; light meals ₹75-110; ⏲11am-3pm & 6-11pm, from 8am Sun) With *rangoli* on the walls, servers in lungis and groups of women in saris lunching (*chappals* off under the table), Dakshinayan channels Tamil Nadu. The delicately textured dosas, *idli* and *uttapam*, fresh coconut chutney, sambar, tomato and onion chutneys all taste homemade. Finish them off with a South Indian filter coffee – served in a stainless-steel set, so you can pour it back and forth to cool just like your grandma in Madras used to do.

Candies CAFE $$
(Map p67; Mac Ronells, St Andrews Rd, Pali Hill, Bandra West; meals ₹70-170; ⏲8.30am-11pm Tue-Sun) Reminiscent of an Escher etching, with outdoor patios, balconies, and interior spaces stacked on top of one another and connected by staircases, Candies is quirky. Each eating area has plants and trees, lanterns and fairy lights, mosaic artwork, and gorgeous students wearing fedoras. The food is self-service, cheap and fine-enough, with sandwiches, rolls, salads and curries well represented. Weekends are crowded.

Yoga House CAFE $$
(Map p67; www.yogahouse.in; 53 Chimbai Rd, Bandra West; light meals ₹140-250; ⏲8am-10pm) On the balcony of Yoga House's bungalow by the sea is a little cafe with tasty and creative veg fare – much of it vegan, much of it raw and all of it wholesome. Designed to complement the yoga on offer, it's possibly the healthiest food in Mumbai.

Prithvi Cafe CAFE $$
(Map p67; Juhu Church Rd; light meals ₹70-165; ⏲9am-11pm) This bohemian cafe attached to the Prithvi Theatre is a cultural hub of

OFF THE BEATEN TRACK

KHOTACHIWADI

This storied *wadi* (hamlet) is a bastion clinging onto Mumbai life as it was before high-rises. A Christian enclave of elegant two-storey wooden mansions, it's 500m northeast of Girgaum Chowpatty, lying amid Mumbai's predominantly Hindu and Muslim neighbourhoods. These winding lanes allow a wonderful glimpse into a quiet life free of rickshaws and taxis. It's not large, but you can spend a little while wandering the alleyways and admiring the old homes and, around Christmas, their decorations.

To find Khotachiwadi, aim for **St Teresa's Church** (Map p58) on the corner of Jagannath Shankar Sheth Marg (JSS Marg) and Rajarammohan Roy Marg (RR Rd/Charni Rd), then head directly opposite the church on JSS Marg and duck down the second and third lanes on your left.

intellectuals, artists and theatre types who tuck themselves away in the lush, bamboo-heavy spot for coffee, sandwiches, *chaat* and Punjabi standards. The food is OK, but the setting is fantastic.

★Culture Curry SOUTH INDIAN **$$$**
(Kataria Rd, Matunga West; mains ₹319-499; ⏲12-3.45pm & 7pm-12.30am) There's a lot more to southern food than *idli* and dosas. Exquisite dishes from all over the south, ranging from Andhra and Coorg to Kerala, are the specialty here. Veggies are particularly well served: the *rajma* curry (kidney and green beans in coconut gravy; ₹259) is extraordinary. The same owners run **Goa Portuguesa**, specialising in fiery Goan dishes, and the Maharashtrian **Diva Maharashtracha**, on the same block. From Matunga station, they're about 750m west along Kataria Rd.

Peshawri NORTH INDIAN **$$$**
(☎28303030; ITC Maratha, Sahar Rd, Andheri East; mains ₹1500-2850; ⏲12.45-2.45pm & 7-11.45pm) Make this Northwest Frontier restaurant, outside the international airport, your first or last stop in Mumbai. It's pricy, but you won't regret forking out the ₹2850 (feeds two) for the exquisite Sikandari *raan* (leg of spring lamb braised in malt vinegar, cinnamon and black cumin). The buttery dhal Bukhara (a thick black dhal cooked for a day; ₹700) is renowned.

Salt Water Café FUSION **$$$**
(Map p67; 87 Chapel Rd, Bandra West; mains ₹320-690; ⏲9am-1am) This foodie find made a name for itself for marrying dramatically opposing flavours (green peppercorn chicken with grape jus, cardamom and carrot mash), but most of the menu is just mouth-watering global fusion. The cool, minimalist design is as nice a change as the recipes – a lovely spot to twist up your tastebuds.

Caravan Serai NORTHWEST FRONTIER **$$$**
(Map p67; ☎42631000; 1st fl, 155 Waterfield Rd, Bandra West; mains ₹225-375; ⏲noon-4pm & 7pm-1am) With white, cave-like walls, gentle lighting and glass beads, Caravan Serai feels like a glamorous desert yurt. The mostly northern cuisine is accessorised with southern dishes and exciting creations like 'tandoori salad'. Also a great place for a drink. Reserve on weekends. Downstairs, **Bora Bora** (Map p67; mains ₹225-375; ⏲noon-1am) is super popular for all-evening-long drinks and starters.

Eat Around the Corner CAFE **$$$**
(Map p67; cnr 24th & 30th Rd; light meals ₹150-200, mains ₹250-600; ⏲7am-1am) The cool decor, cosy outdoor seating, modelesque clientele and novel salad and sandwich options make for a fun lunch, even if the food doesn't quite reach its potential.

Drinking & Nightlife

Mumbai has loads of places to drink – from hole-in-the-wall beer bars and chichi lounges to brash, multilevel superclubs – but the 25% liquor tax can bring bill shock. You're also technically supposed to have a licence to drink in Maharashtra; you won't have any problem without one, but some bars require you to buy a temporary one, for a nominal fee.

Wednesday and Thursday are big nights at some clubs, as well as the traditional Friday and Saturday; there's usually a cover charge. Dress codes apply, so don't rock up in shorts and sandals. The trend in Mumbai is towards resto-lounges as opposed to full-on nightclubs.

If it's the caffeine buzz you're after, Barista and Café Coffee Day cafes are ubiquitous in Mumbai.

Colaba

Cafe Mondegar BAR
(Map p50; ☎22020591; Metro House, 5A Shahid Bhagat Singh Rd, Colaba; ⏲7am-12.30am) 'Mondys' draws a healthy foreign crowd, but with a mix of locals, who all cosy up together in the small space, bonding over the excellent jukebox, one of Mumbai's few. Good music, good people.

5 All Day LOUNGE
(Map p50; www.5allday.in; Lansdowne Rd; ⏲noon-12.30am; 📶) The bartender here takes his work *really* seriously, and it works: the drinks, including several of his own invention, are fabulous, like the whisky crusta (whisky, fresh tomato, mint leaves and sour mix). The food (mains ₹295 to ₹555) is also great, all in a sleek, contemporary, all-white space lit with candles.

Woodside Inn BAR
(Map p50; Wodehouse Rd, Regal Circle; ⏲10am-1am) It's not a sleek lounge filled with Bollywood stars. It's just a cosy, friendly place with a traditional European look, not-too-loud classic rock (think Nirvana, Dire Straits), good wine and drinks (some served

in jars), and excellent food (mains ₹295 to ₹425).

Harbour Bar BAR

(Map p50; Taj Mahal Palace, Mumbai, Apollo Bunder; ⏰11am-11.45pm) The views here – of the Gateway of India and boats in the harbour – are spectacular, and the drinks are reasonably priced (for Mumbai; from ₹350/750 for a beer/wine). Snuggle up in a booth beside one of the big picture windows as the day's winding down on Apollo Bunder.

Busaba BAR

(Map p50; ☎22043779; 4 Mandlik Marg; ⏰6.30pm-1am) Sunken couches and contemporary Buddha art give this restaurant-bar a loungey vibe. Cocktails are pricey but potent (₹425 to ₹550), and a DJ plays house on weekends. The upstairs restaurant serves pan-Asian (mains ₹425 to ₹575); its back room feels like a posh treehouse. Reserve ahead for dinner.

Leopold's Café BAR

(Map p50; cnr Colaba Causeway & Nawroji F Rd, Colaba; ⏰7.30am-12.30am) Love it or hate it, most tourists end up at this Mumbai travellers' institution at one time or another. Around since 1871, Leopold's has wobbly ceiling fans, crap service and a rambunctious atmosphere conducive to swapping tales with strangers. There's food, but the lazy evening beers, especially the 3L yards, are the real draw.

Wink NIGHTCLUB

(Vivanta by Taj - President, 90 Cuffe Pde; ⏰6pm-1am) Weekends, including Sunday, are thumping here, but it's a classy place even then, with its sophisticated decor (low beige sofas, intricately carved screens), long whiskey list and famous Winktinis. A DJ spins nightly, though, to a slightly more grown-up crowd, some of whom are guests at the hotel.

Fort Area & Churchgate

Mocha Bar CAFE

(Map p54; 82 Veer Nariman Rd, Churchgate; coffees ₹60-150; ⏰10am-1.30am; 📶) This atmospheric Arabian-styled cafe is often filled to the brim with students deep in esoteric conversation or gossip. Cosy, low-cushioned seating (including some old cinema seats), exotic coffees, shakes and teas, and global comfort cuisine promote an intellectually chillaxed vibe. Sometimes the wi-fi works.

QUEER MUMBAI

Mumbai's LGBTQ scene is still not as big as you might expect, especially for women, but it's gaining momentum. Start with visiting **Gay Bombay** (www.gaybombay.org) and **Queer Azaadi Mumbai** (www.queerazaadi.wordpress.com) for listings of events and other queer-community info. Queer Azaadi organises Mumbai's **Pride Parade**, usually held in February.

Though published erratically, the pioneering magazine **Bombay Dost** (www.bombaydost.co.in) is a great resource on happenings around town. *Bombay Dost* also founded the **Humsafar Trust** (Map p67; ☎26673800; www.humsafar.org; Old BMC Bldg, 1st fl, Nehru Rd, Vakola, Santa Cruz East), with tons of programs and workshops; one of its support groups organises the monthly gathering 'Sunday High'.

The excellent **Kashish Mumbai International Queer Film Festival** (www.mumbaiqueerfest.com), with a mix of Indian and foreign films, made its debut in 2010 and is held each May.

No dedicated LGBTQ bars/clubs have yet opened, but gay-friendly 'safe house' venues often host private gay parties (announced on Gay Bombay). The only regular club is **Voodoo Pub** (Map p50; ☎22841959; Kamal Mansion, Arthur Bunder Rd; cover ₹300), a dark and sweaty bar that has hosted Mumbai's only regular gay night on Saturdays since 1994. There's a DJ every night (usually free entry) and staff are screened for open-mindedness, so it's gay-friendly all week long too. The sign outside says 'Slip Disc Restaurant Bar & Permit Room'.

One of the best places to hook into the scene (and also buy stuff) is D'Kloset. Most of the merch is for men, but it also has films and books, including the story collection *Out!*, published by **Queer Ink** (www.queer-ink.com).

Starbucks CAFE
(Map p54; www.starbucks.in; Veer Nariman Rd; coffees ₹95-180; ⏲8am-10pm) We were sceptical too, but when this first Starbucks cafe opened in 2012, Mumbai's young, fun and beautiful were so, so happy that it's worth a visit just to see their joy. The coffee is all fair-trade and sourced from India.

Amadeus LOUNGE
(Map p54; NCPA, Nariman Point; ⏲7.30pm-1.30am Fri-Sun) The NCPA's elegant Spanish restaurant opens its lounge, with great DJs, on weekends for the SoBo crowd.

Café Universal BAR
(Map p54; 299 Shahid Bhagat Singh Rd, Fort; ⏲9am-11pm Mon-Sat, 4-11pm Sun) A little bit of France near CST. The Universal has an art nouveau look to it, with butterscotch-colour walls, a wood-beam ceiling and marble chandeliers, and is a cosy place for happy hour and Kingfisher draughts (₹160).

Dome LOUNGE
(Map p54; Hotel InterContinental, 135 Marine Dr, Churchgate; ⏲5.30pm-1.30am) This white-on-white rooftop lounge has awesome views of Mumbai's curving seafront while cocktails beckon the hip young things of Mumbai nightly.

Western Suburbs

★Aer LOUNGE
(Four Seasons Hotel, 34th fl, 114 Dr E Moses Rd, Worli; cover ₹2000-2500 Wed-Sat after 8pm; ⏲5.30pm-1.30pm) With astounding city views on one side and equally impressive sea and sunset views on the other, rooftop Aer is India's tallest and most stunning lounge. You'll need to remortgage your home for a cocktail (₹850), but the ₹350 Kingfishers are a steal at these views. A DJ spins low-key house and techno nightly from 9pm, but Aer is more about the eye candy, both near and far.

Mocha Mojo CAFE
(Map p67; Hill Rd, Bandra West, near Holy Family Hospital; ⏲10am-12.30am; 📶) It's a little rundown, but the Mocha's Bandra branch is still good for coffee, all-day breakfasts or a beer in a funky, futuristic space.

Big Nasty BAR
(Map p67; 1st fl, 12 Union Park, Khar West, above Shatranj Napoli; ⏲7pm-12.30am) The decor may be industrial, but the Nasty is fun and unpretentious. It's best known for its cheap drinks – beers (including, mysteriously, Miller High Life) from ₹160, glasses of wine from ₹350 – and its 'all-American classic beef burger' (₹240).

Trilogy NIGHTCLUB
(Map p67; Hotel Sea Princess, Juhu Tara Rd, Juhu; cover per couple after 11pm ₹2000; ⏲closed Tue) Trilogy was closed at research time for 'renovations' (actually bureaucratic permit snafus), but Mumbaikars expect it to return to its throne as nightclub queen of Mumbai as soon as it's back. The trilevel space, like the clientele, is gorgeous, with a black granite dance floor lit up by LED cube lights that go off like an epileptic Lite-Brite. The imported sound system favours house and hip-hop.

Shiro LOUNGE
(☎66511201; www.shiro.co.in; Bombay Dyeing Mills Compound, Worli; ⏲7.30pm-1.30am) At Shiro, water pours from the hands of towering Japanese faux-stone goddesses into lotus ponds, which reflect shimmering light on the walls. It's totally over the top, but the drinks (as well as the Asian-fusion dishes) are excellent and the DJs spin some mean house (Saturdays) and retro (Fridays).

Ghetto BAR
(Map p58; ☎23538418; 30 Bhulabhai Desai Marg, opposite Tirupathi Apts; ⏲7pm-1am) Just a grungy, graffiti-covered hang-out blaring rock nightly to a dedicated set of regulars.

Olive Bar & Kitchen BAR
(Map p67; ☎26058228; www.olivebarandkitchen.com; 14 Union Park, Khar West; ⏲7.30pm-1am daily, plus noon-3.30pm Sat & Sun) Hip, snooty and favoured by film stars, this gorgeous Mediterranean-style restaurant and bar has light and delicious food (mains ₹595 to ₹1095), soothing DJ sounds and pure Ibiza-meets-Mykonos decor. Thursday and weekends are packed. There's a second **branch** (Map p58; ☎40859595; Gate No 8, Mahalaxmi Racecourse; ⏲noon-3.30pm & 7.30pm-1.30am) in Mahalaxmi.

Toto's Garage BAR
(Map p67; ☎26005494; 30th Rd, Bandra West; ⏲6pm-1am) Forget the beautiful people. Toto's is a down-to-earth local dive done up in a mechanic's theme where you can go in your dirty clothes, drink pitchers of beer and listen to AC/DC. Get there early or you won't get a seat.

Elbo Room PUB
(Map p67; St Theresa Rd, Khar West, off 33rd Rd; ⌚11am-1am) This reminiscent-of-home pub is a good bet for wines by the glass (₹350 to ₹500). The Italian-Indian menu is best enjoyed on the plant-filled terrace, where a screen is often set up for English Premier League and Bundesliga football matches.

Hungry Birds BAR
(Map p67; 3rd Khar Rd, Khar West; ⌚7pm-1am) Conveniently around the corner from the train station in leafy Khar, the Hungry Birds has lots of bright colours, cheap drinks and chicken popcorn.

☆ Entertainment

The *Mumbai Mirror*, an insert of the *Times of India*, lists major events and other Mumbai happenings, as do **Time Out Mumbai** (www.timeoutmumbai.net; ₹50), **www.nh7.in** (live-music listings) and **Mumbai Boss** (www.mumbaiboss.com).

It would be a crime not to see a movie in India's film capital. Unfortunately, Hindi films aren't shown with English subtitles. The cinemas we've listed all show English-language movies, along with some Bollywood numbers.

Mumbai has some great arts festivals: the **Mumbai Film Festival** (www.mumbaifilmfest.org; ⌚Oct) in October is excellent, as is May's Kashish-Mumbai International Queer Film Festival (p74). Prithvi Theatre's November festival (p77) has a packed program of excellent drama, and **Mumbai Sanskruti** (⌚Jan) sees two days of Hindustani classical music.

★Bluefrog LIVE MUSIC
(☎61586158; www.bluefrog.co.in; D/2 Mathuradas Mills Compound, Senapati Bapat Marg, Lower Parel; admission after 9pm Sun & Tue-Thu ₹350, Fri & Sat

BOLLYWOOD DREAMS

Mumbai is the glittering epicentre of India's gargantuan Hindi-language film industry. From silent beginnings with a cast of all-male actors (some in drag) in the 1913 epic *Raja Harishchandra* and the first talkie, *Lama Ara* (1931), it now churns out more than 1000 films a year – more than Hollywood. Not surprising considering it has a captive audience of one-sixth of the world's population, as well as a sizable Non-Resident Indian (NRI) following.

Every part of India has its regional film industry, but Bollywood continues to entrance the nation with its escapist formula in which all-singing, all-dancing lovers fight and conquer the forces keeping them apart. These days, Hollywood-inspired thrillers and action extravaganzas vie for moviegoers' attention alongside the more family-oriented saccharine formulas.

Bollywood stars can attain near godlike status in India and star-spotting is a favourite pastime in Mumbai's posher establishments. You can also see the stars' homes, as well as a film/TV studio with **Bollywood Tours** (www.bollywoodtours.in; 8hr tours per person ₹6000), but you're not guaranteed to see a dance number and you may spend much of it in traffic.

Extra, Extra!

Studios sometimes want Westerners as extras to add a whiff of international flair (or provocative dress, which locals often won't wear) to a film. It's become so common, in fact, that 100,000 junior actors nearly went on strike in 2008 to protest, among other things, losing jobs to foreigners, who work for less money and worse working conditions.

If you're still game, just hang around Colaba (especially the Salvation Army hostel) where studio scouts, recruiting for the following day's shooting, will find you. A day's work, which can be up to 16 hours, pays ₹500. You'll get lunch and snacks but usually no transport. The day can be long and hot with loads of standing around the set; not everyone has a positive experience. Complaints range from lack of food and water to dangerous situations and intimidation when extras don't comply with the director's orders. Others describe the behind-the-scenes peek as a fascinating experience. Before agreeing to anything, always ask for the scout's identification and go with your gut.

₹600; 6.30pm-1.30am Tue-Sat, from 11.30am Sun) Bluefrog is a concert space, production studio, restaurant and one of Mumbai's most happening spaces. It hosts exceptional local and international acts, and has space-age booth seating in the intimate main room. Happy hour – also known as 'one on the Frog' – is buy one, get one free 6.30pm to 9pm.

National Centre for the Performing Arts THEATRE, LIVE MUSIC
(NCPA; Map p54; 66223737, box office 22824567; www.ncpamumbai.com; Marine Dr & Sri V Saha Rd, Nariman Point; tickets ₹200-800; box office 9am-7pm) Spanning 800 sq metres, this cultural centre is the hub of Mumbai's music, theatre and dance scene. In any given week, it might host experimental plays, poetry readings, art exhibitions, Bihari dance troupes, ensembles from Europe or Indian classical music, as well as the occasional dance workshop open to the public. Many performances are free. The **box office** (Map p54) is at the end of NCPA Marg.

Prithvi Theatre THEATRE
(Map p67; 26149546; www.prithvitheatre.org; Juhu Church Rd, Juhu; tickets ₹80-300) A great place to see both Hindi and English-language theatre. Its excellent international theatre festival in November showcases what's going on in contemporary Indian theatre and includes performances by international troupes and artists. The theatre also has film screenings and a charming cafe.

Liberty Cinema CINEMA, LIVE MUSIC
(Map p54; 9820027841; 41/42 New Marine Lines, near Bombay Hospital) The stunning art-deco Liberty was once the queen of Hindi film – think red-carpet openings with Dev Anand – while Bombay's other cinemas were focused on Hollywood. It fell on hard times but has been making a valiant effort to be awesome again and now occasionally hosts film festivals and live music in terribly atmospheric surrounds.

Wankhede Stadium SPORTS
(Mumbai Cricket Association; Map p54; 22795500; www.mumbaicricket.com; D Rd, Churchgate; ticket office 11.30am-7pm Mon-Sat) Test matches and One Day Internationals are played a few times a year in season (October to April). Contact the Cricket Association for ticket information; for a test match you'll probably have to pay for the full five days.

Cooperage Football Ground SPORTS
(Map p50; 22024020; www.wifa.in; MK Rd, Colaba; tickets ₹50-250) The recently renovated Cooperage, home to FC Air India, Mumbai FC and ONGC FC, hosts national-league and local football (soccer) matches between September and April, as well as the Rose Cup in July/August. Tickets are available at the gate, though many local matches are free.

Regal Cinema CINEMA
(Map p50; 22021017; Shahid Bhagat Singh Rd, Regal Circle, Colaba) Check out the art deco architecture.

Eros CINEMA
(Map p54; 22822335; MK Rd, Churchgate; tickets ₹100-150) When in Mumbai it's hard to ignore the fact that you're at the epicentre of the world's biggest film industry. To experience Bollywood blockbusters in situ, the Eros is the place.

Metro Big CINEMA
(39894040; MG Rd, New Marine Lines, Fort; tickets ₹120-600) This grand dame of Bombay talkies was just renovated into a multiplex.

Shopping

Mumbai is India's great marketplace, with some of the best shopping in the country – in its stores, ancient bazaars and on sidewalks.

Be sure to spend a day at the markets around CST for the classic Mumbai shopping experience. In Fort, booksellers, with surprisingly good wares (not all pirated), set up shop daily on the sidewalks around Flora Fountain. Snap up a bargain backpacking wardrobe at **Fashion Street** (Map p54; MG Rd), the strip of stalls lining MG Rd between Cross and Azad Maidans, or on Bandra's Linking Rd, near Waterfield Rd. Hone your bargaining skills. Kemp's Corner has many good shops for designer threads.

Colaba

Bungalow 8 CLOTHING, ACCESSORIES
(Map p50; www.bungaloweight.com; 1st, 2nd & 3rd fls, Grants Bldg, Arthur Bunder Rd, Colaba; 10.30am-7.30pm) Bungalow 8 is so cool, you'll want to be it. Original, high-end, artisanal clothing, jewellery, home decor and

other objects of beauty, spread across three loftlike floors.

Phillips ANTIQUES
(Map p50; www.phillipsantiques.com; Wodehouse Rd, Colaba; ⏱10am-7pm Mon-Sat) The 150-year-old Phillips has nizam-era royal silver, wooden ceremonial masks, Victorian glass and various other gorgeous things that you never knew you wanted. It also has high-quality reproductions of old photos, maps and paintings, and a warehouse shop of big antiques.

Search Word BOOKS
(Map p50; ☎22852521; Metro House, Colaba Causeway, Colaba; ⏱11.30am-9pm) Small and tidy, with a choice selection of books and magazines.

Cottonworld Corp CLOTHING
(Map p50; ☎22850060; Mandlik Marg; ⏱10.30am-8pm Mon-Sat, noon-8pm Sun) Small chain selling stylish Indian-Western-hybrid goods. Entrance is behind State Bank of India.

Bombay Electric CLOTHING
(Map p50; www.bombayelectric.in; 1 Reay House, Best Marg, Colaba; ⏱11am-9pm) High fashion is the calling at this trendy, slightly overhyped unisex boutique, which it sells at top rupee alongside artisanal accessories and a handful of fashionable antiques.

Central Cottage Industries Emporium HANDICRAFTS, SOUVENIRS
(Map p50; ☎22027537; www.cottageemporium.in; Chhatrapati Shivaji Marg; ⏱10am-6pm) Fair-trade souvenirs. Now has a second **Colaba branch** (Map p50; Kamal Mansion, Arthur Bunder Rd; ⏱11am-7pm Mon-Sat).

Fort Area & Churchgate

★Kitab Khana BOOKS
(Map p54; www.kitabkhana.in; Somaiya Bhavan, 45/47 MG Rd, Fort; ⏱10.30am-7.30pm) This new bookstore has a brilliantly curated selection of books, all of which are 20% off all the time. **Food for Thought** (Map p54; www.cafefoodforthought.com; light meals ₹120-180), the little cafe in back, does a mean *sabudana khichdi* (sago fried with spices).

★Contemporary Arts & Crafts HANDICRAFTS
(Map p54; www.cac.co.in; 210 DN Rd; ⏱10.30am-7.30pm) The CAC stocks contemporary, inventive takes on traditional crafts: these are not your usual handmade souvenirs. Home goods fill much of the store, but plenty of pieces will fit in a suitcase.

Artisans' Centre for Art, Craft & Design CLOTHING, ACCESSORIES
(Map p54; ☎22673040; artisanscentre@gmail.com; 1st fl, 52-56 Dr VB Gandhi Marg, Kala Ghoda; ⏱11am-7pm) This heritage space hosts exhibitions of high-end handmade goods – from couture and jewellery to handicrafts and luxury *khadi* (homespun cloth) – by artisans from around the country.

Khadi & Village Industries Emporium CLOTHING
(Map p54; Khadi Bhavan; 286 Dr Dadabhai Naoroji Rd, Fort; ⏱10.30am-6.30pm Mon-Sat) Khadi Bhavan is dusty, 1940s timewarp that's so old it's new again. Ready-made traditional Indian clothing, silk and *khadi*, shoes (including great handmade leather *chappals* for ladies and gents) and handicrafts are sublimely old-school.

Tribes India HANDICRAFTS
(Map p54; Gate No 3, GPO; ⏱10.30am-6pm Mon-Sat) 🍃 Right in the post office, this stall sells handmade goods from tribal communities across India.

Chimanlals HANDICRAFTS
(Map p54; www.chimanlals.com; Wallace Rd, Fort; ⏱9.30am-6pm Mon-Fri, to 5pm Sat) The beautiful traditional printed papers here will make you start writing letters.

Royal Music Collection MUSIC
(Map p54; 192 Kitab Mahal, Dr DN Rd, Fort; ⏱11am-9pm Mon-Sat) Brilliant street stall selling vintage records (from ₹250).

Fabindia CLOTHING
(Map p54; www.fabindia.com; Jeroo Bldg, 137 MG Rd, Kala Ghoda; ⏱10am-8pm) Founded as a means to get traditional fabric artisans' wares to market, Fabindia has cotton and silk fashions and homewares in a modern-meets-traditional Indian shop.

Chetana Book Centre BOOKS
(Map p54; www.chetana.com; K Dubash Marg, Kala Ghoda; ⏱10.30am-7.30pm Mon-Sat) This great spirituality bookstore has lots of books on Hinduism and a whole section on 'Afterlife/Death/Psychic'.

Cotton Cottage CLOTHING
(Map p54; Agra Bldg, 121 MG Rd, Kala Ghoda; ⏱10am-9pm) Stock up on simple cotton kur-

tas and various pants – *salwars, churidars, patiala* – for the road.

Rhythm House MUSIC STORE
(Map p54; ☎22842835; 40 K Dubash Marg, Fort; ⏰10am-8.30pm Mon-Sat, 11am-8.30pm Sun) Nonpirated CDs, plus tickets to concerts, plays and festivals.

Standard Supply Co PHOTOGRAPHY
(Map p54; ☎22612468; Walchand Hirachand Marg, Fort; ⏰10.30am-7pm Mon-Sat) Everything you could possibly need for digital and film photography.

Oxford Bookstore BOOKS
(Map p54; www.oxfordbookstore.com; Apeejay House, 3 Dinsha Wachha Marg, Churchgate; ⏰8am-10pm) Spacious, with a good selection of travel books and a tea bar.

Kalbadevi to Mahalaxmi

Markets MARKET
You can buy just about anything in the dense bazaars north of CST, which tumble one into the next in a mass of people and stuff. **Crawford Market** (Mahatma Phule Market; Map p58; cnr DN & Lokmanya Tilak Rds), with fruit and vegetables, is the last outpost of British Bombay before the tumult of the central bazaars begins. Bas-reliefs by Rudyard Kipling's father, Lockwood Kipling, adorn the Norman Gothic exterior.

Mangaldas Market (Map p58), traditionally home to traders from Gujarat, is a mini-town, complete with lanes, of fabrics. Even if you're not the type to have your clothes tailored, drop by **DD Dupattawala** (Map p58; Shop No 217, 4th Lane, Mangaldas Market) for pretty scarves and dupattas at fixed prices. **Zaveri Bazaar** (Map p58) for jewellery and **Bhuleshwar Market** (Map p58; cnr Sheikh Menon St & M Devi Marg) for fruit and veg are just north of here.

Chor Bazaar (Map p58) is known for its antiques, though nowadays much of it is reproductions; the main area of activity is Mutton St, where shops specialise in 'antiques' and miscellaneous junk. Dhabu St, to the east, is lined with fine leather goods.

Mini Market/ Bollywood Bazaar ANTIQUES, SOUVENIRS
(Map p58; ☎23472427; 33/31 Mutton St; ⏰11am-8pm Sat-Thu) Sells vintage Bollywood posters and other movie ephemera as well as old little trinkets. Call if you get lost.

Anokhi CLOTHING
(Map p58; www.anokhi.com; Dr AR Ragnekar Marg; ⏰10.30am-8pm Mon-Sat) Gets the East–West balance just right, with men's and women's clothes and bedding in block-printed silk and cotton.

Shrujan HANDICRAFTS
(Map p58; www.shrujan.org; Sagar Villa, Bhulabhai Desai Marg, Breach Candy, opp Navroze Apts; ⏰10am-7.30pm Mon-Sat) Selling the intricate embroidery work of 3500 women in 114 villages in Kutch, Gujarat, the nonprofit Shrujan helps women earn a livelihood while preserving the spectacular embroidery traditions of the area. The sophisticated clothing, wall hangings and purses make great gifts. There's also a (hard-to-find) **Juhu branch** (Map p67; Hatkesh Society, 6th North South Rd, JVPD Scheme; ⏰10am-7.30pm Mon-Sat).

Crossword BOOKS
(Map p58; Mohammedbhai Mansion, NS Patkar Marg, Kemp's Corner; ⏰11am-8.30pm) Enormous, with a Café Moshe (p70) inside.

BX Furtado & Sons MUSIC STORE
(Map p58; www.furtadosonline.com; Jer Mahal, Dhobi Talao; ⏰10.30am-7.30pm Mon-Sat) The best place in Mumbai for musical instruments – sitars, tablas, accordions and local and imported guitars. The branch around the corner on Kalbadevi Rd is pianos and sheet music only.

Western Suburbs

Indian Hippy ART
(Map p67; ☎8080822022; www.hippy.in; 17/C Sherly Rajan Rd, off Carter Rd, Bandra West; portraits from ₹10,000; ⏰by appt) Because you need to have your portrait hand-painted in the style of a vintage Bollywood poster. Bring (or email) a photo. Also sells vintage LPs and film posters.

Play Clan SOUVENIRS, CLOTHING
(Map p67; www.theplayclan.com; Libra Towers, Hill Rd, Bandra West; ⏰11am-8.30pm) Mumbai has a slew of stores selling fun, kitschy, design-y goods. Play Clan is the priciest, but also has the best stuff, like tote bags printed with futurist portraits of Vivekananda and pillows embroidered with sequined autorickshaws.

Kishore Silk House CLOTHING, HANDICRAFTS (Bhandarkar Rd, Matunga East; 10am-8.30pm Tue-Sun) Handwoven saris and dhotis from Tamil Nadu and Kerala in all the best old-fashioned styles. But the real star here are the finely woven, surprisingly super-absorbant cotton towels – perfect for travelling.

Information

EMERGENCY

Call the police (100) for emergencies.

INTERNET ACCESS

Anita CyberCafé (Map p54; Cowasji Patel Rd, Fort; per hr ₹30; 9.30am-10pm Mon-Sat, from 2pm Sun) Opposite one of Mumbai's best chai stalls (open evenings).

Poonam Cybercafé (Map p50; Lala Nigam St, Colaba Market; per hr ₹20; 10am-10pm Mon-Sat, 8.30am-2pm Sun)

Portasia (Map p54; Kitab Mahal, Dr Dadabhai Naoroji Rd, Fort; per hr ₹30; 9am-9pm Mon-Sat) Entrance is down a little alley; look for the sign hanging from the covered archway.

MEDIA

To find out what's going on in Mumbai, check out *Time Out Mumbai* and **Mumbai Boss** (www.mumbaiboss.com). The *Hindustan Times* is the best paper; its *Café* insert, as well as the *Mumbai Mirror* insert of the *Times of India*, are good what's-on guides.

Look for the free folding neighbourhood maps by **Locus City Cards** in high-end hotels and restaurants.

MEDICAL SERVICES

Bombay Hospital (Map p54; 22067676, ambulance 22067309; www.bombayhospital.com; 12 New Marine Lines)

Breach Candy Hospital (Map p58; 23672888, emergency 23667809; www.breachcandyhospital.org; 60 Bhulabhai Desai Marg, Breach Candy) Best in Mumbai, if not India.

Colaba Chemist (Map p50; 22832848; 27A Arthur Bunder Rd; 8.30am-11pm) Delivers.

New Royal Chemists (Map p54; 22004051; 41/42 New Marine Lines; 24hr) Free delivery 7am to 11pm.

MONEY

ATMs are everywhere, and foreign-exchange offices changing cash and travellers cheques – including Akbar Travels (p80) and Thomas Cook's Fort (p80) and **Colaba** (Map p50; 66092608; Colaba Causeway; 9.30am-6pm) branches – are also plentiful.

POST

The **main post office** (Map p54; behind Chhatrapati Shivaji Terminus; 10am-6pm) is an imposing building beside CST. **Poste restante** (10am-3pm Mon-Sat) is at the 'Delivery Department'. Letters should be addressed c/o Poste Restante, Mumbai GPO, Mumbai 400 001. Bring your passport to collect mail. Opposite the post office, under the tree, are parcel-wallahs who will stitch up your parcel for ₹40.

Colaba Post Office (Map p50; Henry Rd) Convenient branch.

TELEPHONE

Call 197 for directory assistance.

TOURIST INFORMATION

Indiatourism (Government of India Tourist Office; Map p54; 22074333; www.incredibleindia.com; Western Railways Reservation Complex, 123 Maharshi Karve Rd; 8.30am-6pm Mon-Fri, to 2pm Sat) Provides information for the entire country, as well as contacts for Mumbai guides and homestays.

Maharashtra Tourism Development Corporation Booth (MTDC; Map p50; 22841877; Apollo Bunder; 8.30am-4pm Tue-Sun, 8.30am-9pm weekends) For city bus tours.

Maharashtra Tourism Development Corporation (MTDC; Map p54; 22044040; www.maharashtratourism.gov.in; Madame Cama Rd, opposite LIC Bldg, Nariman Point; 10am-5pm Mon-Sat, closed 2nd & 4th Sat) Maharashtra Tourism Development Corporation has its head office in Mumbai. Most major towns throughout the state have offices, too, but they're generally only useful for booking MTDC accommodation and tours. Sunday is not a business day, and many government offices also remain closed on alternate Saturdays.

TRAVEL AGENCIES

Akbar Travels (www.akbartravelsonline.com; 10am-7pm Mon-Fri, to 6pm Sat) Colaba (Map p50; 22823434; 30 Alipur Trust Bldg, Shahid Bhagat Singh Rd); Fort (Map p54; 22633434; 167/169 Dr Dadabhai Naoroji Rd) Extremely helpful, with good exchange rates.

Thomas Cook (Map p54; 61603333; 324 Dr Dadabhai Naoroji Rd, Fort; 9.30am-6pm Mon-Sat)

VISA EXTENSIONS

Foreigners' Regional Registration Office (FRRO; Map p58; 22620446; www.immigrationindia.nic.in; Annexe Bldg No 2, CID, Badaruddin Tyabji Marg, near Special Branch; 9.30am-1pm Mon-Fri) Technically, the FRRO can issue extensions on tourist visas with 'reasonable grounds of delay' for US$70, but applications are reviewed on a case-by-case basis; don't count on it.

Getting There & Away

AIR

Airports

Mumbai is the main international gateway to South India and has the busiest network of domestic flights. **Chhatrapati Shivaji International Airport** (Map p67; BOM; ☎66851010; www.csia.in), about 30km from the city centre, has been undergoing a $2 billion modernisation since its privatisation in 2006. At press time, the shiny new terminal T2, serving both domestic and international flights, was expected to open in 2014 and the existing domestic terminals converted to cargo.

At time of writing, the airport comprises three domestic (1A, 1B and 1C; Map p58) and two international terminals (2B and 2C; Map p58). The domestic side is accessed via Vile Parle and is known locally as Santa Cruz airport, while the international, with its entrance 5km away in Andheri, goes locally by Sahar. Both terminals have ATMs, foreign-exchange counters and tourist-information booths. A free shuttle bus runs between the two every 30 minutes for ticket-holders.

Airlines

Travel agencies and websites are best for booking flights; airline offices are increasingly directing customers to their call centres. The following domestic and international airlines maintain offices in town and/or at the airport:

Major nonstop domestic flights from Mumbai include the following:

DESTINATION	SAMPLE LOWEST ONE-WAY FARE (₹)	DURATION (HR)
Bengaluru	5500	1½
Chennai	7200	2
Delhi	7600	2
Goa	4000	1
Hyderabad	4000	1½
Jaipur	5500	1¾
Kochi	7200	2
Kolkata	8200	2¾

Air India (Map p54; ☎27580777, airport 28318666; www.airindia.com; Air India Bldg, cnr Marine Dr & Madame Cama Rd, Nariman Point; ⊙9.15am-6.30pm Mon-Fri, to 5.15pm Sat & Sun)

Cathay Pacific (☎66572222, airport 66859002/3; www.cathaypacific.com; 2 Brady Gladys Plaza, Senapati Bapat Marg, Lower Parel; ⊙9.30am-5.30pm Mon-Sat)

Emirates Airlines (Map p54; ☎33773377, airport 26829917; www.emirates.com; 3 Mittal Chambers, 228 Nariman Point; ⊙9am-5.30pm Mon-Sat)

GoAir (☎airport 26264789; www.goair.in)

IndiGo (Map p50; ☎call centre 1800 1803838; www.goindigo.in)

Jet Airways (Map p50; ☎call centre 39893333; www.jetairways.com; Amarchand Mansion, Madame Cama Rd, Colaba; ⊙9.30am-6pm Mon-Fri, to 4pm Sat) Also handles JetLite bookings.

Qantas (Map p67; ☎61111818, airport 66859110; www.qantas.com.au; 4th fl, Sunteck Centre, 37-40 Subhash Rd, Vile Parle; ⊙9am-1.15pm & 2.30-5.30pm Mon-Fri)

SpiceJet (☎airport 9920172863; www.spicejet.com)

Swiss (☎67137200; www.swiss.com; 10th fl, Urmi Estate, Ganpatrao Kadam Marg, Lower Parel ; ⊙9am-5.30pm Mon-Sat)

Thai Airways (Map p54; ☎1800 1021225, airport 26828950; www.thaiairways.com; 2A Mittal Towers A Wing, Nariman Point; ⊙9.30am-5.30pm Mon-Fri, to 4pm Sat)

BUS

Numerous private operators and state governments run long-distance buses to and from Mumbai.

Long-distance government-run buses depart from the well-organised **Mumbai Central bus terminal** (Map p58; ☎inquiry 23024075) right by Mumbai Central train station. They're cheaper and more frequent than private services, but the quality and crowd levels vary; **MSRTC** (Maharashtra State Road Transport Corporation; ☎1800 221250; www.msrtc.gov.in) is not as well developed as some of its counterparts in other states.

Private buses are usually more comfortable and simpler to book but can cost significantly more than government buses. Most depart from Dr Anadrao Nair Rd near Mumbai Central train station, but many buses to southern destinations depart from Paltan Rd, near Crawford Market. To check on departure times and current prices, visit **Citizen Travels** (Map p58; ☎23459695; D Block, Sitaram Bldg, Paltan Rd) or **National CTC** (Map p58; ☎23015652; Dr Anadrao Nair Rd), though most private-bus operators are similar in price and quality. Fares to popular destinations (like Goa) are up to 75% higher during holiday periods.

More convenient for Goa and southern destinations are the private buses run by **Chandni Travels** (Map p54; ☎22713901, 22676840), which depart six times a day from in front of Azad Maidan.

POPULAR LONG-DISTANCE BUS ROUTES:

DESTINATION	PRIVATE NON-AC/AC SLEEPER (₹)	GOVERNMENT NON-AC (₹)	DURATION (HR)
Ahmedabad	500/800	N/A	13
Aurangabad	500/800	461 (four daily)	10
Hyderabad	800/1100	N/A	16
Mahabaleshwar	450/600	302 (three daily)	7
Panaji (Panjim)	600/900	N/A	15
Pune	300 (AC seater)	202 (half-hourly)	4
Udaipur	800/1400	508 (one daily)	16

TRAIN

Three train systems operate out of Mumbai, but the most important services for travellers are Central Railways and Western Railways. Tickets for either system can be bought from any station in South Mumbai or the suburbs that has computerised ticketing.

Central Railways (☎139), handling services to the east, south, plus a few trains to the north, operates from CST. The **reservation centre** (Map p54; ⏲8am-8pm Mon-Sat, to 2pm Sun) is on the southern side of CST. Foreign tourist–quota tickets and Indrail passes can be bought at Counter 52. You can buy nonquota tickets with a credit card (₹90 fee) at counters 10 and 11.

Some Central Railways trains depart from Dadar (D), a few stations north of CST, or Lokmanya Tilak (LTT), 16km north of CST.

Western Railways (☎139) has services to the north from Mumbai Central train station, usually called Bombay Central (BCT). The **reservation centre** (Map p54; ⏲8am-8pm Mon-Sat, to 2pm Sun), opposite Churchgate station, has foreign tourist–quota tickets at counter 14.

MAJOR TRAINS FROM MUMBAI

DESTINATION	TRAIN NO & NAME	SAMPLE FARE (₹)	DURATION (HR)	DEPARTURE
Agra	12137 Punjab Mail	410/1139/1770/3050 (A)	22	7.40pm CST
Ahmedabad	12901 Gujarat Mail	232/616/910/1560 (A)	9	10pm BCT
	12009 Shatabdi Exp	721/1535	7	6.25am BCT
Aurangabad	11401 Nandigram Exp	176/480/715 (B)	7	4.35pm CST
	17617 Tapovan Exp	102/376 (C)	7	6.10am CST
Bengaluru	16529 Udyan Exp	363/1028/1600/2750 (A)	25	8.05am CST
Bhopal	12534 Pushpak Exp	325/889/1345/2295 (A)	13	8.20am CST
Chennai	12163 Chennai Exp	403/1116/1730/2980 (A)	23½	8.30pm CST
Delhi	12951 Rajdhani Exp	1550/2270/3870 (D)	16	4.40pm BCT
	12137 Punjab Mail	442/1231/1925/3330 (A)	25½	7.40pm CST
Hyderabad	12701 Hussainsagar Exp	312/854/1285/2195 (A)	14½	9.50pm CST
Indore	12961 Avantika Exp	320/878/1325/2265 (A)	14	7.05pm BCT
Jaipur	12955 Jaipur Exp	383/1059/1630/2805 (A)	18	6.50pm BCT
Kochi	16345 Netravati Exp	430/1222/1935 (B)	26½	11.40am LTT
Margao	10103 Mandovi Exp	288/811/1235/2105 (A)	12	6.55am CST
	12133 Mangalore Exp	308/842/1265 (B)	9	11.05pm CST
Pune	12127 Intercity Exp	76/277 (C)	3	6.45am CST

Station abbreviations: CST (Chhatrapati Shivaji Terminus); BCT (Mumbai Central); LTT (Lokmanya Tilak); D (Dadar) Fares: (A) sleeper/3AC/2AC/1AC, (B) sleeper/3AC/2AC, (C) sleeper/CC, (D) 3AC/2AC/1AC

Getting Around

TO/FROM THE AIRPORTS

International

The international airport has a **prepaid-taxi booth**, with set fares for every neighbourhood, outside arrivals. Taxis are ₹650/750 (non-AC/AC) to Colaba, Fort and Marine Dr, and ₹380/450 to Bandra, plus a ₹10 service charge and ₹10 per bag. The journey to Colaba takes about 45 minutes at night and 1½ to two hours during the day. Tips are not required.

Meru Cabs (☎44224422; www.merucabs.com) has a counter in arrivals. The air-conditioned metered taxis charge ₹27 for the first kilometre and ₹20 per kilometre thereafter (25% more at night). Routes are tracked by GPS, so no rip-offs!

Autorickshaws queue up at a little distance from arrivals, but they only go as far south as Bandra. They also charge 25% more midnight to 5am, plus ₹3 per large bag.

If you arrive during the day (but not during 'rush hour' – 6am to 11am) and are not weighed down with luggage, consider the **train**: take an autorickshaw (around ₹55) to Andheri train station and then the Churchgate or CST train (₹8, 45 minutes). You can also take bus 308 to Andheri station, or 321 to Vile Parle station; the bus stand is a short walk from the arrivals area.

A taxi from South Mumbai to the international airport should be around ₹500; negotiate a fare beforehand. Add ₹10 per bag and 25% to the meter charge at night, and add an hour onto the journey time between 4pm and 8pm.

Domestic

There's a **prepaid taxi counter** in the arrivals hall. A non-AC/AC taxi costs ₹380/465 to Colaba or Fort and ₹220/265 to Bandra, plus ₹10/15 service charge, ₹10 per bag and 25% extra at night.

Alternatively, catch an autorickshaw (around ₹35) or bus 312 from the airport to Vile Parle station, where you can get a train to Churchgate (₹7, 45 minutes). Don't attempt this during rush hour (6am to 11am).

BOAT

Both **PNP** (Map p50; ☎22885220) and **Maldar Catamarans** (☎22829695) run regular ferries to Mandwa (oneway ₹110 to ₹135), useful for access to Murud-Janjira and other parts of the Konkan Coast, avoiding the long bus trip out of Mumbai. Buy tickets near the Gateway of India.

BUS

Mumbai's great and cheap local buses are run by **BEST** (www.bestundertaking.com), whose website has a useful search facility for city routes. Fares start at ₹5 (day passes are ₹40), which you pay on-board. It's handy to learn Devanagiri numerals so you can read the bus numbers on the front. Beware of 'LTD' buses, which make limited stops.

The following useful buses all stop along Colaba Causeway and outside the museum.

DESTINATION	BUS NO
Breach Candy	132, 133
Churchgate	70, 106, 123, 132
CST & Crawford Market	1, 3, 21, 103, 124
Girgaum Chowpatty	103, 106, 107, 123
Haji Ali	83, 124, 132, 133
Hanging Gardens	103, 106, 108
Mani Bhavan	123
Mohammed Ali Rd	1, 3, 21
Mumbai Central train station	70, 124, 125

CAR

Cars with driver are generally hired for an eight-hour day and an 80km maximum, with additional charges if you go over. For a nonair-conditioned car, the going rate is about ₹1200.

METRO

Construction of a new elevated **metro** (www.mumbaimetroone.com) is under way. Phase One, which links Versova (northwest of Andheri) to Ghatkopar, passing near the airports en route, should be completed in late 2013. The underground Colaba–Bandra–Airport line is several years away.

MOTORCYCLE

Allibhai Premji Tyrewalla (Map p58; ☎23099313/9417; www.premjis.com; 205 Dr D Bhadkamkar (Lamington) Rd; ⏲10am-7pm Mon-Sat), around since 1922, sells new and used motorcycles with a guaranteed buy-back option. For two- to three-week 'rental' periods you'll still have to pay the full cost of the bike upfront. The company prefers to deal with longer-term schemes (two months or more), which work out cheaper anyway. A used 150cc or 225cc Bajaj or Honda costs around ₹50,000, with a buy-back price of around 60% after three months. Smaller bikes (100cc to 180cc) start at ₹25,000. The company can also arrange shipment of bikes overseas (around ₹30,000 to the UK).

TAXI & AUTORICKSHAW

Mumbai's black-and-yellow taxis are the most convenient way to get around southern Mumbai, and drivers *almost* always use the meter without prompting. The minimum fare is ₹19; after the first 1.6km, it's ₹12 per additional kilometre.

Autorickshaws are the name of the game from Bandra going north. The minimum fare is ₹15, up to 1.6km, and ₹10 per additional kilometre.

Taxis and autorickshaws have a combination of mechanical and electronic meters, which are not calibrated to display current fares. Drivers by law should keep the most current conversion chart in their vehicle; don't hesitate to ask to see it, or print out copies from the **Mumbai Traffic Police** (www.trafficpolicemumbai.org/Tariff-card_Auto_taxi_form.htm).

Both taxis and autorickshaws tack 25% onto the fare from midnight to 5am.

Tip: Mumbaikars tend to navigate by landmarks, not street names (especially new names), so have some details before heading out.

TRAIN

Mumbai's suburban train network runs from 4am till 1am and has three main lines. The most useful is the **Western Line**, operating out of Churchgate north to Charni Rd (for Girgaum Chowpatty), Mumbai Central, Mahalaxmi (for the Dhobi Ghat), Vile Parle (for the domestic airport), Andheri (for the international airport) and Borivali (for Sanjay Gandhi National Park), among others.

The **Central Line** runs from CST to Byculla (for Veermata Jijabai Bhonsle Udyan, formerly Victoria Gardens), Dadar and as far as Neral (for Matheran).

From Churchgate, 2nd-/1st-class fares are ₹4/45 to Mumbai Central, ₹7/80 to Vile Parle, and ₹9/110 to Borivali.

To avoid the queues, buy a **coupon book** (₹50), good for use on either train line, then 'validate' the coupons at the machines before boarding.

'Tourist tickets' permit unlimited travel in 2nd/1st class for one (₹50/170), three (₹90/330) or five (₹105/390) days.

Avoid rush hours when trains are jam-packed; watch your valuables, and gals, stick to the ladies-only carriages except late at night, when it's more important to avoid empty cars.

Maharashtra

Includes ➡

Best Places to Eat

- Malaka Spice (p116)
- New Sea Rock Restaurant (p107)
- Khyber (p90)
- Grapevine (p119)
- Dario's (p116)

Best Places to Stay

- Verandah in the Forest (p109)
- Hotel Sunderban (p115)
- Lemon Tree (p95)
- Beyond (p91)
- Hotel Plaza (p103)

Why Go?

India's third-largest and second-most populous state, Maharashtra is an expansive canvas showcasing many of India's iconic attractions. There are lazy, palm-fringed beaches; lofty, cool-green mountains; World Heritage historical sights; and bustling cosmopolitan cities.

A short excursion north of Mumbai brings you to Nasik, a curious blend of spirituality, meditation and India's premier wine region. Further inland are the extraordinary cave temples of Ellora and Ajanta, carved from 'living rock' that celebrate the rich cultural heritage of empires past. If you are looking for a cool change, head to Matheron, Maharashtra's only hill station, where a toy train chugs through verdant forests. Pilgrims and inquisitive souls should head south to cosmopolitan Pune, a city famous for its 'sex guru' and alternative spiritualism. Steer westward and you will be rewarded with a string of golden sands and crumbling forts along the romantic Konkan Coast of the Arabian Sea.

When to Go

Nasik

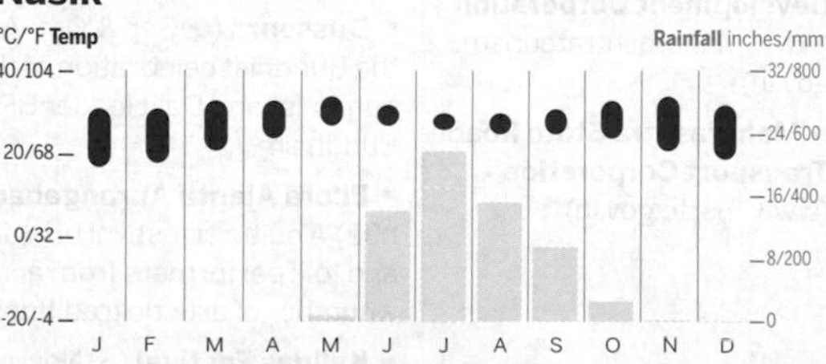

Jan It's party time in Nasik's wineries, marked by grape harvesting and crushing galas.

Sep The frenzied and energetic Ganesh Chaturthi celebrations reach fever pitch.

Dec Winter's a lovely time for the secluded beaches of Murud, Ganpatipule and Tarkarli.

MAIN POINTS OF ENTRY

Mumbai has an international and a domestic airport. Other domestic airports include Aurangabad, Pune and Nagpur. Jalgaon is an important rail hub between Delhi and Mumbai and is convenient to Ajanta and Ellora.

Fast Facts

- **Population:** 112.4 million
- **Area:** 307,690 sq km
- **Capital:** Mumbai
- **Main languages:** Marathi, Hindi, English
- **Sleeping prices: $** below ₹1000, **$$** ₹1000 to ₹4000, **$$$** above ₹4000

Money Matters

Maharashtra is among the most economically well-off states in India. Its per-capita income is 60% higher than the national average.

Resources

- **Maharashtra Tourism Development Corporation** (www.maharashtratourism.gov.in)
- **Maharashtra State Road Transport Corporation** (www.msrtc.gov.in)

Top Yoga & Meditation Centres

The Vipassana International Academy (p92) in Igatpuri has long been a destination for those wishing to put mind over matter through an austere form of Buddhist meditation. The boundaries of yoga, on the other hand, are constantly pushed at the Ramamani Iyengar Memorial Yoga Institute (p114) in Pune and the Kaivalyadhama Yoga Hospital (p110) in Lonavla. For a more lavish and indulgent form of spiritual engagement, there's the superluxurious Osho International Meditation Resort (p114) in Pune, where one can meditate in style, while flexing a few muscles in the unique game of 'zennis' (Zen tennis).

DON'T MISS

The ancient stone temples of **Ellora** and **Ajanta** are among India's top architectural and artistic wonders. Rock carving, sculpture and painting reach sublime levels of beauty and perfection at these World Heritage Sites.

In terms of medieval forts and citadels, Maharashtra comes second perhaps only to Rajasthan. The best of the lot is **Daulatabad**, a bastion that once played a cameo as India's capital. Equally intriguing is **Janjira**, a 12th-century island fortress that was once an outpost for the seafaring African traders. Others include the many forts associated with Chhatrapati Shivaji, including the **Raigad**, and **Shivneri**, where the Maratha leader was born.

Top State Festivals

- **Naag Panchami** (Jul/Aug, Pune, p111; Kolhapur, p120) A traditional snake-worshipping festival.
- **Ganesh Chaturthi** (Sep, Pune, p111) Celebrated with fervour all across Maharashtra; Pune goes particularly hysteric in honour of the elephant-headed deity.
- **Dussehra** (Sep & Oct) A Hindu festival, but it also marks the Buddhist celebration of the anniversary of the famous humanist and Dalit leader BR Ambedkar's conversion to Buddhism.
- **Ellora Ajanta Aurangabad Festival** (Nov, Aurangabad, p92) A cultural festival bringing together the best classical and folk performers from across the region, while promoting a number of artistic traditions and handicrafts on the side.
- **Kalidas Festival** (Nov, Nagpur, p104) Commemorates the literary genius of legendary poet Kalidas through spirited music, dance and theatre.
- **Sawai Gandharva Sangeet Mahotsav** (Dec, Pune, p111) An extravaganza where you can see unforgettable performances by some of the heftiest names in Indian classical music.

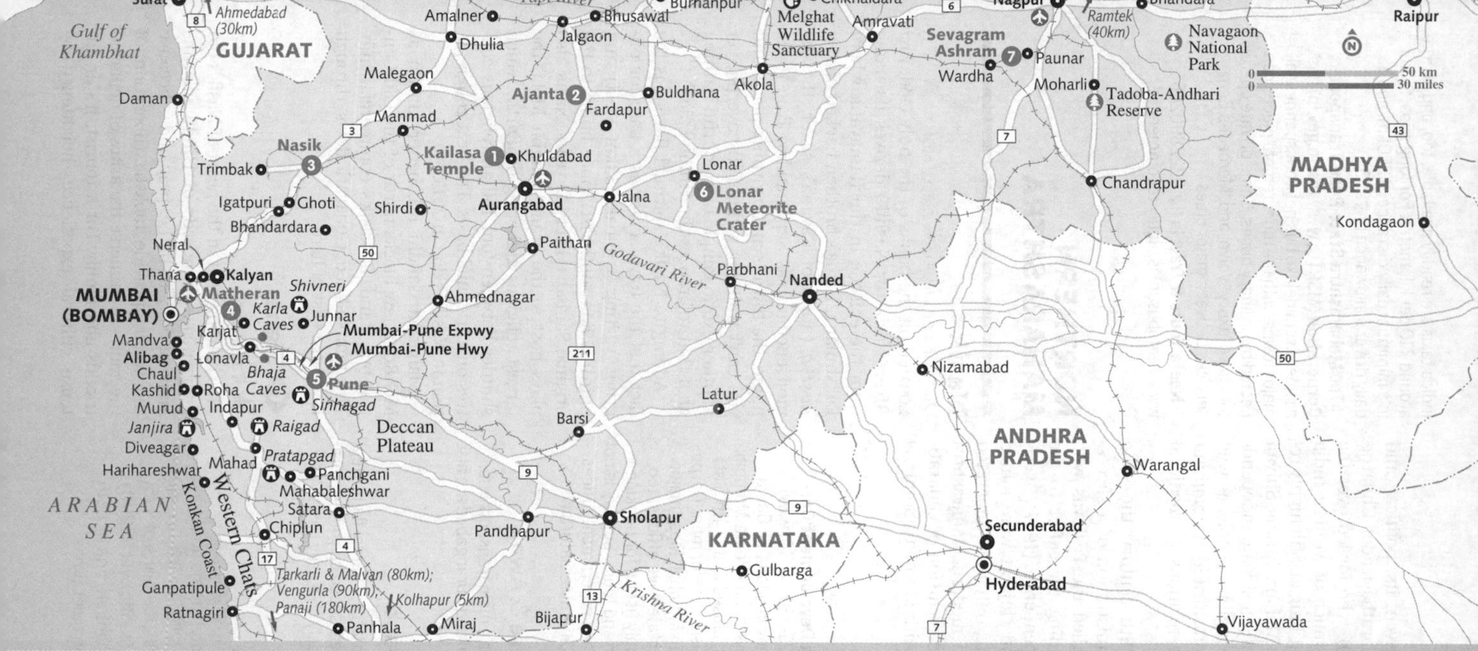

Maharashtra Highlights

1 Be amazed by the intricate beauty of the **Kailasa Temple** (p98), the pièce de résistance in the monumental Ellora temple complex

2 Wander through the ancient cave galleries of **Ajanta** (p100) to admire sublime ancient Buddhist art

3 Sip on a glass of zinfanel, or lose yourself in a holy confluence of faith and ritual in **Nasik** (p88)

4 Take a horse to spectacular viewpoints and breathe in the pollution-free air at the hill station of **Matheran** (p108)

5 Delve into new-age spiritualism and modern Indian cuisine in diverse and bustling **Pune** (p111)

6 Contemplate the power of nature while ambling around the primordial **Lonar Meteorite Crater** (p103)

7 Rediscover the Gandhian way of life at the **Sevagram Ashram** (p105)

History

Maharashtra was given its political and ethnic identity by Maratha leader Chhatrapati Shivaji (1627–80), who lorded over the Deccan plateau and much of western India from his stronghold at Raigad. Still highly respected today among Maharashtrans, Shivaji is credited for instilling a strong, independent spirit among the region's people, as well as establishing Maharashtra as a dominant player in the power relations of medieval India.

From the early 18th century, the state was under the administration of a succession of ministers called the Peshwas who ruled until 1819, ceding thereafter to the British. After Independence (1947), western Maharashtra and Gujarat were joined to form Bombay state, only to be separated again in 1960, when modern Maharashtra was formed with the exclusion of Gujarati-speaking areas and with Mumbai (Bombay) as its capital.

Information

Maharashtra Tourism Development Corporation (MTDC; ☎022-22044040; www.maharashtratourism.gov.in; Madame Cama Rd, opposite LIC Bldg, Nariman Point, Mumbai; ⏲10am-5pm Mon-Sat, closed 2nd & 4th S at) The Maharashtra Tourism Development Corporation's head office is in Mumbai. Most major towns throughout the state have offices, too, but they're generally only useful for booking MTDC accommodation and tours. Sunday is not a business day, and many government offices also remain closed on alternate Saturdays.

Getting There & Away

Mumbai is Maharashtra's main transport hub, although Pune, Jalgaon and Aurangabad are also major players.

Getting Around

Because the state is so large, internal flights (eg Pune to Nagpur) can help speed up your explorations. Airfares vary widely on a daily basis. AC Indica taxis are readily available, too, and charge around ₹10 per kilometre. For long trips, factor in a minimum daily distance of 250km, and a daily driver's allowance of ₹250.

The **Maharashtra State Road Transport Corporation** (MSRTC; www.msrtc.gov.in) has a superb semideluxe bus network spanning all major towns, with the more remote places connected by ordinary buses. Some private operators have luxury 'Volvo' and 'Mercedes Benz' services between major cities.

Neeta Tours & Travels (☎02228902666; www.neetabus.in) is highly recommended.

HOTEL TAXES

In Maharashtra, hotel rooms above ₹1000 attract a 7.42% Service Tax, plus a 'Luxury Tax' of 4% (for tariffs of ₹750 to ₹1200) or 10% (tariffs over ₹1200). Many hotels will negotiate one or both of the taxes away in quiet times.

NORTHERN MAHARASHTRA

Nasik

☎0253 / POP 1.5 MILLION / ELEV 565M

Located on the banks of the holy Godavari River, Nasik (or Nashik) derives its name from the episode in the Ramayana where Lakshmana, Rama's brother, hacked off the *nasika* (nose) of Ravana's sister, the demon enchantress Surpanakha. True to its name, the town is an absorbing place, and you can't walk far without discovering yet another exotic temple or colourful bathing ghat that references the Hindu epic.

Adding to Nasik's spiritual flavour is the fact that the town serves as a base for pilgrims visiting Trimbak (33km west) and Shirdi (79km southeast), once home to the original Sai Baba. Every 12 years, Nasik also plays host to the grand Kumbh Mela, the largest religious gathering on Earth, which shuttles between four Indian religious centres on a triennial basis. The next congregation in Nasik is due in 2015.

Mahatma Gandhi Rd, better known as MG Rd, a few blocks north of the Old Central bus stand, is Nasik's commercial hub. The temple-lined Godavari flows through town just east of here.

Sights

★Ramkund GHAT

This bathing ghat in the heart of Nasik's old quarter sees hundreds of Hindu pilgrims arriving daily to bathe, pray and – because the waters provide moksha (liberation of the soul)– to immerse the ashes of departed friends and family. For a tourist, it's an intense cultural experience, heightened by

Nasik

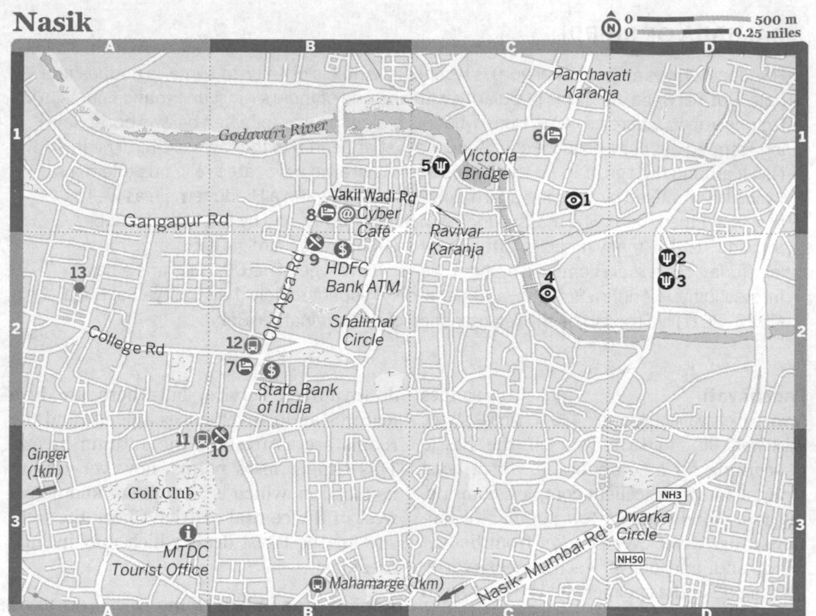

the presence of a colourful **market** downstream. It's OK to take photographs, but try not to be intrusive.

Temples HINDU TEMPLES

(⊙6am-9pm) A short walk uphill east of Ramkund is the **Kala Rama Temple**, the city's holiest shrine. Dating to 1794 and containing unusual black-stone representations of Rama, Sita and Lakshmana, the temple stands on the site where Lakshmana sliced off Surpanakha's nose. Nearby is the **Gumpha Panchavati**, where Sita supposedly hid while being assailed by the evil Ravana.

The ramshackle **Sundar Narayan Temple**, at the western end of Victoria Bridge, contains three black Vishnu deities. The modern **Muktidham Temple**, about 7km southeast of the city near the train station, has 18 muralled chapters of the Bhagavad Gita lining its interior walls.

Sleeping & Eating

Hotel Abhishek HOTEL $

(☎2514201; www.hotelabhishek.com; Panchavati Karanja; s/d ₹335/455, with AC ₹728/775; ❄) Found just off the Panchavati Karanja roundabout, this pleasant budget option packs hot showers, TV and appetising vegetarian food into its spotless, value-for-money rooms. A few minutes' walk uphill from the Godavari River, it sits amid all the spiritual comings and goings, and is therefore a vantage point for familiarising oneself with the colour and ritual of sacred India.

Nasik

Top Sights
1 Ramkund C1

Sights
2 Gumpha Panchavati D2
3 Kala Rama Temple D2
4 Market C2
5 Sundar Narayan Temple C1

Sleeping
6 Hotel Abhishek C1
7 Hotel Samrat B2
8 Panchavati B1

Eating
9 Annapoorna Lunch Home B2
Khyber .... (see 8)
10 Talk of the Town B3

Transport
11 New Central Bus Stand A3
12 Old Central Bus Stand B2
13 Railway Reservation Office A2

SAI BABA OF SHIRDI

His iconic status as a national guru is legendary. And his divinity, to some, is unquestionable. But Sai Baba, for all his popularity, remains one of India's most enigmatic figures. No one knows where he came from, what his real name was, or when he was born. Having stepped out of an obscure childhood, he first appeared in the town of Shirdi near Nasik around the age of 16 (in the mid-1800s). There, he advocated religious tolerance, which he practised by sleeping alternately in a mosque and a Hindu temple as well as praying in them both. The masses took to him right away, and by the time Sai Baba died in 1918, the many miracles attributed to him had seen him gather a large following. Today, his temple complex in Shirdi draws an average of 40,000 pilgrims a day. Interestingly, in Andhra Pradesh, another widely respected holy man Sathya Sai Baba (1926–2011) claimed to be the reincarnation of the original Sai Baba.

Panchavati HOTEL **$$**
(www.panchavatihotels.com; 430 Chandak Wadi, Vakil Wadi Rd) To save yourself the hassle of scouting for a comfy bed in town, head straight for this excellent complex, comprising four hotels (and a few popular restaurants) that cover every pocket from budget to top-end, and deliver each rupee's worth. Kicking off at the cheaper end is **Panchavati Guest House** (☎2578771; s/d from ₹550/650), which has slightly cramped rooms and prompt service. A more inviting option is **Panchavati Yatri** (☎2578782; s/d from ₹1530/1760; ❄), featuring top-notch rooms with hot showers, spot-on service, and an in-house health club. **Hotel Panchavati** (☎2575771; s/d from ₹2000/2410; ❄), fronting the complex, is pricier with classy rooms; it caters largely to business travellers. Last of all is the **Panchavati Millionaire** (☎2312318; s/d ₹2350/2950; ❄), a sumptuous affair where lavish rooms are complemented by cosy breakfast nooks that are perfect for a steaming morning cuppa.

Hotel Samrat HOTEL **$$**
(☎2577211; www.hotelsamratnasik.com; Old Agra Rd; s/d ₹950/1290, with AC ₹1560/1775; ❄) You'll find little to complain about at the Samrat. Inviting rooms have large windows, are decorated in brown and beige, with pine furniture thrown in for good measure. Located right next to the bus stand, its spick-and-span vegetarian restaurant is open 24 hours, making it popular as a refuelling stop.

Ginger HOTEL **$$**
(☎1860 2663333, 6616333; www.gingerhotels.com; Trimbak Rd, Plot P20, Satpur MIDC; s/d ₹2935/3520; ❄📶) Ginger hotels are formulaic, predictable and very, very comfortable. Primarily a business hotel, it features do-it-yourself service, but there are luxe features and conveniences aplenty, and the rooms are as fresh as the autumn breeze. This Ginger loses points, however, due to its location, which is a couple of kilometres west of the central district. Check the website for the latest deals which may include breakfast.

Annapoorna Lunch Home FAST FOOD **$**
(MG Rd; mains ₹50-100) This joint has all the usual quick eats rolling endlessly off its culinary assembly line. No surprises on offer, but it would be hard to find fault with the pan-fresh food that's cheaper than peanuts. We recommend the dosas, but be warned, you might have trouble finding a seat at lunchtime.

★Khyber MULTICUISINE **$$**
(Panchavati Hotel Complex; mains ₹180-300) Taste one succulent morsel of any of Khyber's signature Afghani dishes and you might start wondering if you are actually in Kandahar. The Khyber is one of Nasik's top-notch fine-dining establishments, with a great ambience (soft lighting, sparkling glassware, teak furniture) to go with its wide range of delectable offerings. The *murgh shaan-e-khyber*, juicy pieces of chicken marinated with herbs and cooked in a creamy gravy, is not to be missed.

Talk of the Town MULTICUISINE **$$**
(Old Agra Rd; mains ₹150-280) Next to the New Central bus stand, this multilevel dining experience attracts more tipplers than eaters, although that's no indication of the quality of its food. On offer is a good selection of coastal, North Indian and Chinese dishes, best washed down with a refreshing pint of lager.

Information

Cyber Café (Vakil Wadi Rd; per hr ₹20; ⏲10am-10pm) Near Panchavati Hotel Complex.

HDFC Bank ATM (MG Rd) Twenty-four-hour ATM.

MTDC Tourist Office (☎2570059; T/I, Golf Club, Old Agra Rd; ⏲10.30am-5.30pm Mon-Sat) About 1km south of the Old Central bus stand, behind the golf course.

State Bank of India (Old Agra Rd; ⏲11am-5pm Mon-Fri, 11am-1pm Sat) Opposite the Old Central bus stand. Changes cash and travellers cheques and has an ATM.

Getting There & Around

BUS

Nasik's **Old Central bus stand** (CBS; ☎02532309310) is useful for those going to Trimbak (₹30, 45 minutes). A block south, the **New Central bus stand** has services to Aurangabad (semideluxe ₹216, 4½ hours) and Pune (semideluxe/deluxe ₹230/389, 4½ hours). South of town, the **Mahamarg bus stand** has services to Mumbai (semideluxe ₹220, four hours) and Shirdi (₹90, 2½ hours).

Private bus agents based near the CBS run buses to Pune, Mumbai, Aurangabad and Ahmedabad. Fares are marginally lower than those charged on state buses. Note that buses depart from Old Agra Rd, and that most Mumbai-bound buses terminate at Dadar in Mumbai.

TRAIN

The Nasik Rd train station is 8km southeast of the town centre, but a useful **railway reservation office** (1st fl, Commissioner's Office, Canada Corner; ⏲8am-8pm Mon-Sat) is 500m west of the Old Central bus stand. The Panchavati Express is the fastest train to Mumbai (2nd class/chair ₹85/351, 3½ hours, 7.10am). Tapovan Express departs Mumbai CST at 6.10am, arrives at Nasik Rd at 9.45am, and is a convenient train to Aurangabad (2nd class/chair ₹76/319, 3½ hours, 9.50am). An autorickshaw to the station should cost about ₹80.

Around Nasik

Bhandardara

The picturesque village of Bhandardara is nestled deep in the folds of the Sahyadris, about 70km from Nasik. A little-visited place surrounded by craggy mountains, it is one of Maharashtra's best escapes from the bustle of urban India.

Most of Bhandardara's habitation is thrown around **Arthur Lake**, a horseshoe-shaped reservoir fed by the waters of the Pravara River. The lake is barraged on one side by the imposing **Wilson Dam**, a colonial-era structure dating back to 1910. If you like walking, consider a hike to the

GRAPES OF NASIK

From wimpy raisins to full-bodied wines, the grapes of Nasik have come a long way. The surrounding region had been producing table grapes since time immemorial. However, it was only in the early 1990s that a couple of entrepreneurs realised that Nasik, with its fertile soils and cool climate, boasted conditions similar to Bordeaux. In 1997 industry pioneer **Sula Vineyards** (☎09970090010; www.sulawines.com; Gangapur–Savargaon Rd, Govardhan; ⏲11am-10pm) fearlessly invested in a crop of sauvignon blanc and chenin blanc, and the first batch of domestic wines hit the shelves in 2000. It hasn't looked back.

These days, the wine list in most of Nasik's wineries stretch to include zinfandel, shiraz, merlot and cabernet as well as a few reserves and sparkling wines, and most of these drops can be sampled first-hand by visiting one of the estates. **York Winery** (☎02532230700; www.yorkwinery.com; Gangapur–Savargaon Rd, Gangavarhe; ⏲3-10pm) offers wine-tasting sessions (₹100) in a top-floor room that has scenic views of the lake and surrounding hills. Sula Vineyards, located 15km west of Nasik, rounds off a vineyard tour with a wine-tasting session (₹150) that features four of its best drops. It's also possible to stay among the vines. For an extremely indulging experience, head 3km inland to **Beyond** (☎09970090010; www.sulawines.com; d incl taxes & breakfast from ₹6100; ❄📶), Sula Vineyards' luxury resort set by a lake bordered by rolling hills, where you can roam the landscape on bicycles, go kayaking on the still waters or laze the hours away at the spa.

During harvest season (January to March), some wineries also organise grape-crushing festivals, marked by unbridled revelry. Events are usually advertised on the wineries' websites.

summit of **Mt Kalsubai**, which at 1646m was once used as an observation point by the Marathas. Alternately, you could hike to the ruins of the **Ratangad Fort**, another of Shivaji's erstwhile strongholds, which has wonderful views of the surrounding ranges.

The charming **Anandvan Resort** (9920311221; www.anandvanresorts.com; d from ₹7050; ❄), an ecoresort with a choice of comfy cottages and villas overlooking Arthur Lake, allows you to sleep in style. While the **MTDC Holiday Resort** (02424257032; d from ₹900; ❄), located further down the hill, is a reasonable budget option.

To get to Bhandardara, take a local bus from Nasik's Mahamarg bus stand to Ghoti (₹35, one hour), from where an autorickshaw ride costs ₹70. A taxi from Nasik can also drop you at your resort for about ₹1500.

Igatpuri

Heard of *vipassana,* haven't you? Well head to Igatpuri to see where (and how) it all happens. Located about 44km south of Nasik, this village is home to the headquarters of the world's largest *vipassana* meditation institution, the **Vipassana International Academy** (02553244076; www.dhamma.org), which institutionalises this strict form of meditation first taught by Gautama Buddha in the 6th century BC and reintroduced to India by teacher SN Goenka in the 1960s. Ten-day residential courses (advance bookings compulsory) are held throughout the year, though authorities warn that it requires rigorous discipline. Basic accommodation, food and meditation instruction are provided free of charge, but donations upon completion are accepted.

Trimbak

The moody **Trimbakeshwar Temple** stands in the centre of Trimbak, 33km west of Nasik. It's one of India's most sacred temples, containing a *jyoti linga,* one of the 12 most important shrines to Shiva. Only Hindus are allowed in, but non-Hindus can peek into the courtyard. Nearby, the waters of the Godavari River flow into the **Gangadwar bathing tank**, where all are welcome to wash away their sins. You also have the option of a four-hour return hike up the **Brahmagiri Hill**, where you can see the Godavari dribble forth from a spring.

Regular buses run from the CBS in Nasik to Trimbak (₹30, 45 minutes).

Aurangabad

0240 / POP 1,171,330 / ELEV 515M

Aurangabad lay low through most of the tumultuous history of medieval India and only hit the spotlight when the last Mughal emperor, Aurangzeb, made the city his capital from 1653 to 1707. With the emperor's death came the city's rapid decline, but the brief period of glory saw the building of some fascinating monuments, including a Taj Mahal replica (Bibi-qa-Maqbara), that continue to draw a steady trickle of visitors. These monuments, alongside other historic relics, such as a group of ancient Buddhist caves, make Aurangabad a good choice for a fairly decent weekend excursion. But the real reason for traipsing all the way here is because the town is an excellent base for exploring the World Heritage Sites of Ellora and Ajanta.

Silk fabrics were once Aurangabad's chief revenue generator, and the town is still known across the world for its hand-woven Himroo and Paithani saris.

The train station, cheap hotels and restaurants are clumped together in the south of the town along Station Rd East and Station Rd West. The MSRTC bus stand is 1.5km to the north of the train station. Northeast of the bus stand is the buzzing old town with its narrow streets and Muslim quarters. Interestingly, Aurangabad also has a sizeable Buddhist community who follow in the footsteps of eminent humanist and social leader BR Ambedkar, and celebrate his conversion to Buddhism during Dussehra.

Sights

★**Bibi-qa-Maqbara** MONUMENT

(Indian/foreigner ₹5/100; dawn-10pm) Built by Aurangzeb's son Azam Khan in 1679 as a mausoleum for his mother Rabia-ud-Daurani, Bibi-qa-Maqbara is widely known as the 'poor man's Taj'. With its four minarets flanking a central onion-domed mausoleum, the white structure bears a striking resemblance to Agra's Taj Mahal. It is much less grand, however, and apart from having a few marble adornments, namely the plinth and dome, much of the structure is finished in lime mortar. Apparently the prince conceived the entire mausoleum in white marble, but was thwarted by his frugal father who opposed his extravagant idea of draining state coffers for the purpose. However, despite the use of cheaper material and the obvious weathering, it's a sight far more impressive than the average gravestone.

Aurangabad Caves CAVES

(Indian/foreigner ₹5/100; ⏲dawn-dusk) Architecturally speaking, the Aurangabad Caves aren't a patch on Ellora or Ajanta, but they do throw some light on early Buddhist architecture and, above all, make for a quiet and peaceful outing. Carved out of the hillside in the 6th or 7th century AD, the 10 caves, comprising two groups 1km apart (retain your ticket for entry into both sets), are all Buddhist. Cave 7, with its sculptures of scantily clad lovers in suggestive positions, is a perennial favourite. The caves are about 2km north of Bibi-qa-Maqbara. A return autorickshaw from the mausoleum shouldn't cost more than ₹180.

Panchakki GARDEN

(Indian/foreigner ₹5/20; ⏲6.15am-9.15pm) The garden complex of Panchakki, literally meaning 'water wheel', takes its name from the hydro-mill which, in its day, was considered a marvel of engineering. Driven by water carried through earthen pipes from a reservoir 6km away, it was once used to grind grain for pilgrims. You can still see the humble machine at work today.

Baba Shah Muzaffar, a Sufi saint and spiritual guide to Aurangzeb, is buried here. His memorial garden, flanked by a series of fish-filled tanks, is near a massive banyan tree on the southern side of the main cistern.

Shivaji Museum MUSEUM

(Dr Ambedkar Rd; admission ₹5; ⏲10.30am-6pm Fri-Wed) This simple museum is dedicated to the life of the Maratha hero, Shivaji. Its collection includes a 500-year-old chain-mail suit and a copy of the Quran handwritten by Aurangzeb.

Tours

Classic Tours (p96) and the **Indian Tourism Development Corporation** (ITDC; ☎2331143) both run daily bus tours to the Ajanta and Ellora Caves. The trip to Ajanta Caves costs ₹450 and the tour to Ellora Caves, ₹300; prices include a guide but don't cover admission fees. The Ellora tour also includes all the other major Aurangabad sites along with Daulatabad Fort and Aurangzeb's tomb in Khuldabad, which is a lot to swallow in a day. All tours start and end at the MTDC Holiday Resort. During quiet periods, these operators pool resources and pack their clients into a single bus.

For private tours, try Ashoka Tours & Travels (p96), which owns a decent fleet of taxis and can personalise your trip around Aurangabad and to Ajanta (₹1600 for up to four people) and Ellora (₹1100 for up to four people).

Sleeping

Hotel Panchavati HOTEL $

(☎2328755; www.hotelpanchavati.com; Station Rd West; s/d ₹525/625, with AC ₹775/900; ❄) Panchavati is popular with budget travellers, and for good reason. On offer are a range of compact, colour-themed and thoughtfully appointed rooms, with comfortable beds and balconies. Choose between front-facing, park-view rooms, or the much quieter, tree-view rooms at the rear. There are two restaurants and a bar. The managers are efficient and friendly and the hotel sits easily at the top of the value-for-money class.

Hotel Oberoi HOTEL $

(☎2323841; www.hoteloberoi.in; Osmanpura Circle, Station Rd East; s/d ₹855/969, with AC ₹1082/1197; ❄) Cheekily named, and nothing to do with the five-star chain, this recently renovated hotel is nevertheless a good budget option in a convenient location. Rooms are noticeably modern with flat-screen TVs and comfy beds, and the bathrooms are gleaming, with no loose plumbing! Also on offer is complimentary pick-up from rail or bus stations.

Hotel Nandanvan HOTEL $

(☎2338916; Station Rd East; s/d ₹450/550, with AC ₹650/750; ❄) Unusually large and clean rooms and bathrooms are on offer at this well-run hotel, set in a prime location close to Kailash Restaurant. The noise coming off the main road might get to you at times, though.

Tourist's Home HOTEL $

(☎2337212; Station Rd West; dm ₹375, d ₹500, with AC ₹1000; ❄) This one's as basic as it gets. Most rooms here are simply bare bones, but well-ventilated and clean. There are quite a few rules and regulations to be adhered to, going by the noticeboard at the entrance, but it's close to the train station.

Aurangabad

Hotel Amarpreet HOTEL $$
(☎6621133; www.amarpreethotel.com; Jalna Rd; s/d from ₹3875/5166; ❄@📶) Old-fashioned though spacious rooms might trigger the occasional hunch that you'd have got more bang for your buck elsewhere, but the all-smiles management makes up for it with polite service, excellent housekeeping and a great selection of food and booze. Ask for a room in the western wing, with superb views of Bibi-qa-Maqbara. And look out for the new wing that will double the hotel's size and add a pool, gym and spa. It was all under construction when we visited.

MTDC Holiday Resort HOTEL $$
(☎2331513; Station Rd East; d from ₹1260, with AC from ₹1560; ❄) Set around a verdant lawn and shaded by robust canopies, this curiously disorganised hotel is one of the better state-owned operations in Maharashtra. The rooms, though lacking in character, are spacious and tidy. Couples and solo travellers will be housed in the noisy rooms facing Station Rd; families get the quieter block. There's also a well-stocked bar, a decent restaurant and a couple of travel agencies (for Ellora and Ajanta tours) on-site. Come between March and July and you will pay 20% less.

Aurangabad

Top Sights

Sights

Sleeping

Eating

Information

Transport

★ Lemon Tree HOTEL $$$
(☎6603030; www.lemontreehotels.com; Airport Rd, R7/2 Chikalthana; s/d incl breakfast from ₹7345/8815;) Fresh as lemonade, this swish hotel encircles what we thought was the best swimming pool in the Deccan. The standard rooms, although not large, are brightened by vivid tropical tones offset against snow-white walls. Adding a dash of class is the prim Citrus Café, and the Slounge bar, where you can down a drink while hustling a fellow traveller in a game of pool. It's one place you're sure to have a nice stay.

VITS HOTEL $$$
(☎2350701; www.vitshotelaurangabad.com; Station Rd East; d incl breakfast ₹7632;) Handy to the train station, snazzy-lobbied VITS goes by the motto 'Guest. Rest. Best'. What that basically means is you have a delightfully luxurious room to flop about in, packed with all the usual luxe features you'd find in top-end hotels. Staff are eager to put you up, so it's worth asking for a discount here.

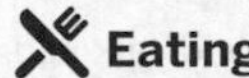

Eating

Hotel Panchavati MULTICUISINE $
(Station Rd West; mains ₹60-280) The 'family' restaurant at this budget hotel has a Chinese and Korean menu in addition to an extensive Indian menu. We can highly recommended its Korean food and tandoori chicken, as well as the cold beer. Ambience isn't a selling point here, but you can watch the soccer on the TV.

Swad Veg Restaurant INDIAN $
(Station Rd East, Kanchan Chamber; mains ₹70-80) Swad offers a great range of Indian snacks and staples, such as dosas, plus a few pizzas, ice creams and shakes, in its clean basement premises. Try the Gujarati thali, an endless train of dishes that diners gobble up under the benevolent gaze of patron saint swami Yogiraj Hanstirth, whose portrait illuminates a far wall of the restaurant.

Kailash INDIAN $
(Station Rd East; mains ₹85-110) Adjacent to Hotel Nandanvan, this busy pure-veg restaurant is a smart glass-and-chrome place where you can sit back after a long day out and wolf down a variety of local delicacies brought to your table by smartly dressed waiters.

China Town CHINESE $$
(Hotel Amarpreet, Jalna Rd; mains ₹180-200) This is one of the two in-house restaurants that sit side by side in Hotel Amarpreet. The other one has the usual Indian and continental dishes, while China Town dishes up surprisingly fine quality Chinese food. A good range of noodles is on offer, which goes extremely well with the numerous chicken and lamb preparations all presented appetisingly in the restaurant's well-dressed interiors.

Tandoor NORTH INDIAN $$
(Shyam Chambers, Station Rd East, ; mains ₹160-290) Offering fine tandoori dishes and flavoursome North Indian veg and non-veg options in a weirdly Pharaonic atmosphere, Tandoor is one of Aurangabad's top standalone restaurants. A few Chinese dishes are also on offer, but patrons clearly prefer the dishes coming out of, well, the tandoor.

Shopping

Hand-woven Himroo material is a traditional Aurangabad speciality. Made from cotton, silk and silver threads, it was developed as a cheaper alternative to Kam

Khab, the more ornate brocade of silk and gold thread woven for royalty in the 14th century. Most of today's Himroo shawls and saris are mass produced using power looms, but some showrooms in the city still run traditional workshops, thus preserving this dying art.

Himroo saris start at ₹1000 (cotton and silk blend). Paithani saris, which are of a superior quality, range from ₹5000 to ₹300,000 – before you baulk at the price, bear in mind that some of them take more than a year to make. If you're buying, ensure you're spending your money on authentic Himroo, and not 'Aurangabad silk'.

One of the best places to come and watch weavers at work is the **Paithani Weaving Centre** (Jalna Rd; ⌚11.30am-8pm), about 6km east of Kranti Chowk (behind the Indian Airlines office), so take a taxi.

ℹ Information

Bank of Baroda, ICICI, State Bank of India (SBI), State Bank of Hyderabad (SBH) and HDFC Bank have several ATMs along Station Rd East, Court Rd, Nirala Bazaar and Jalna Rd.

Ashoka Tours & Travels (☎2359102, 9890340816; atkadam88@gmail.com; Hotel Panchavati, Station Rd West) Personalised city and regional tours, car hire and hotel pick-ups. Run by former *Lonely Planet*–recommended autorickshaw driver Ashok T Kadam.

Classic Tours (☎2337788; www.classictours.info; MTDC Holiday Resort, Station Rd East) Books transport and tours, particularly to Ellora and Ajanta.

Cyber-dhaba (Station Rd West; per hr Rs20; ⌚8am-11pm) Also changes money.

MTDC Office (☎2331513; MTDC Holiday Resort, Station Rd East; ⌚10am-5.30pm Mon-Sat)

Post Office (Juna Bazaar; ⌚10am-6pm Mon-Sat)

Sai Internet Café (Station Rd East; per hr ₹15; ⌚8am-10pm)

State Bank of India (Kranti Chowk; ⌚11am-5pm Mon-Fri, 11am-1pm Sat) Handles foreign exchange.

ℹ Getting There & Away

AIR

The airport is 10km east of town. En route are the offices of **Indian Airlines** (☎2485241; Jalna Rd) and **Jet Airways** (☎2441392; www.jetairways.com; Jalna Rd). There are direct daily flights to Delhi (around ₹7000) and Mumbai (around ₹4000).

BUS

Buses leave roughly hourly from the **MSRTC bus stand** (Station Rd West) to Pune (semideluxe/deluxe/Volvo ₹250/270/530, five hours) and Nasik (semideluxe/deluxe ₹225/250, five hours). **Private bus agents** are located around the corner where Dr Rajendra Prasad Marg becomes Court Rd; a few sit closer to the bus stand. Deluxe overnight bus destinations include Mumbai (with/without AC ₹550/400, sleeper ₹750, eight hours), Ahmedabad (seat/sleeper ₹550/820, 15 hours) and Nagpur (₹450, 12 hours).

Ordinary buses head to Ellora from the MSRTC bus stand every half-hour (₹25, 45 minutes) and hourly to Jalgaon (₹140, four hours) via Fardapur (₹95, two hours). The T-junction near Fardapur is the drop-off point for Ajanta.

TRAIN

Aurangabad's **train station** (Station Rd East) is not on a main line, but two heavily booked trains run direct to/from Mumbai. The Tapovan Express (2nd class/chair ₹112/476, 7½ hours) departs Aurangabad at 2.35pm, and departs Mumbai at 6.10am. The Janshatabdi Express (2nd class/chair ₹142/555, 6½ hours) departs Aurangabad at 6am and Mumbai at 1.50pm. For Hyderabad (Secunderabad), take the Devagiri Express (sleeper/2AC ₹299/1180, 10 hours, 4.10am). To reach northern or eastern India, take a bus to Jalgaon (p103) and board a train there.

ℹ Getting Around

Autorickshaws are as common here as mosquitoes in a summer swamp. The **taxi stand** is next to the MSRTC bus stand; share jeeps also depart from here for destinations around Aurangabad, including Ellora and Daulatabad. Expect to pay ₹600 for a full-day tour in a rickshaw, or ₹1100 in a taxi.

Around Aurangabad

Daulatabad

This one's straight out of a Tolkien fantasy. A most beguiling structure, the 12th-century hilltop fortress of Daulatabad is located about 15km from Aurangabad, en route to Ellora. Now in ruins, the citadel was originally conceived as an impregnable fort by the Yadava kings. Its most infamous highpoint came in 1328, when it was named Daulatabad (City of Fortune) by eccentric Delhi sultan Mohammed Tughlaq and made the capital – he even marched the entire population of Delhi 1100km south to populate it.

Ironically, Daulatabad – despite being better positioned strategically than Delhi – soon proved untenable as a capital due to an acute water crisis, and Tughlaq forced the weary inhabitants all the way back to Delhi, which had by then been reduced to a ghost town.

Daulatabad's central bastion sits atop a 200m-high craggy outcrop known as Devagiri (Hill of the Gods), surrounded by a 5km **fort** (Indian/foreigner ₹5/100; ⏲6am-6pm). The climb to the summit takes about an hour, and leads past an ingenious series of defences, including multiple doorways designed with odd angles and spike-studded doors to prevent elephant charges. A tower of victory, known as the Chand Minar (Tower of the Moon), built in 1435, soars 60m above the ground to the right – it's closed to visitors. Higher up, you can walk into the Chini Mahal, where Abul Hasan Tana Shah, king of Golconda, was held captive for 12 years before his death in 1699. Nearby, there's a 6m cannon, cast from five different metals and engraved with Aurangzeb's name.

Part of the ascent goes through a pitch-black, bat-infested, water-seeping, spiralling tunnel. Guides (₹450) are available near the ticket counter to show you around, and their torch-bearing assistants will lead you through the dark passageway for a small tip. But on the way down you'll be left to your own devices, so carry a torch. The crumbling staircases and sheer drops can make things difficult for the elderly, children and those suffering from vertigo or claustrophobia.

Khuldabad

Time permitting, take a pit stop in the scruffy-walled settlement of Khuldabad (Heavenly Abode), a quaint and cheerful little Muslim pilgrimage village just 3km from Ellora. Buried deep in the pages of history, Khuldabad is where a number of historic figures lie interred, including emperor Aurangzeb, the last of the Mughal greats. Despite matching the legendary King Solomon in terms of state riches, Aurangzeb was an ascetic in his personal life, and insisted that he be buried in a simple tomb constructed only with the money he had made from sewing Muslim skullcaps. An unfussy affair of modest marble in a courtyard of the **Alamgir Dargah** (⏲7am-8pm) is exactly what he got.

Generally a calm place, Khuldabad is swamped with pilgrims every April when a robe said to have been worn by the Prophet Mohammed, and kept within the dargah (shrine), is shown to the public. Across the road from the Alamgir Dargah, another shrine contains strands of the Prophet's beard and lumps of silver from a tree of solid silver, which is said to have miraculously grown at this site after a saint's death.

Ellora

☎02437

Give a man a hammer and chisel, and he'll create art for posterity. Come to the World Heritage Site **Ellora cave temples** (Indian/foreigner ₹10/250; ⏲dawn-dusk Wed-Mon), located 30km from Aurangabad, and you'll know exactly what we mean. The epitome of ancient Indian rock-cut architecture, these caves were chipped out laboriously over five centuries by generations of Buddhist, Hindu and Jain monks. Monasteries, chapels, temples – the caves served every purpose, and they were stylishly embellished with a profusion of remarkably detailed sculptures. Unlike the caves at Ajanta, which are carved into a sheer rock face, the Ellora caves line a 2km-long escarpment, the gentle slope of which allowed architects to build elaborate courtyards in front of the shrines, and render them with sculptures of a surreal quality.

Ellora has 34 caves in all: 12 Buddhist (AD 600–800), 17 Hindu (AD 600–900) and five Jain (AD 800–1000). The grandest, however, is the awesome Kailasa Temple (Cave 16), the world's largest monolithic sculpture, hewn top to bottom against a rocky slope by 7000 labourers over a 150-year period. Dedicated to Lord Shiva, it is clearly among the best that ancient Indian architecture has to offer.

Historically, the site represents the renaissance of Hinduism under the Chalukya and Rashtrakuta dynasties, the subsequent decline of Indian Buddhism and a brief resurgence of Jainism under official patronage. The increasing influence of Tantric elements in India's three great religions can also be seen in the way the sculptures are executed, and their coexistence at one site indicates a lengthy period of religious tolerance.

Official guides can be hired at the ticket office in front of the Kailasa Temple for ₹750. Most guides have an extensive knowledge of cave architecture, so try not to skimp. If your tight itinerary forces you to choose between Ellora or Ajanta, Ellora wins hands down.

Sights

★Kailasa Temple HINDU TEMPLE

This rock-cut temple, built by King Krishna I of the Rashtrakuta dynasty in AD 760, was built to represent Mt Kailasa (Kailash), Shiva's Himalayan abode. To say that the assignment was daring would be an understatement. Three huge trenches were bored into the sheer cliff face with hammers and chisels, following which the shape was 'released', a process that entailed removing 200,000 tonnes of rock, while taking care to leave behind those sections that would later be used for sculpting. Covering twice the area of the Parthenon in Athens and being half as high again, Kailasa is an engineering marvel that was executed straight from the head with zero margin for error. Modern draughtsmen might have a lesson or two to learn here.

Size aside, the temple is remarkable for its prodigious sculptural decoration. The temple houses several intricately carved panels, depicting scenes from the Ramayana, the Mahabharata and the adventures of Krishna. Also worth admiring are the immense monolithic pillars that stand in the courtyard, flanking the entrance on both sides, and the southeastern gallery that has 10 giant and fabulous panels depicting the different avatars of Lord Vishnu. Kailasa is a temple, still very much in use; you'll have to remove your shoes to enter the main shrine.

After you're done with the main enclosure, bypass the hordes of snack-munching day trippers to explore the temple's many dank, bat urine–soaked corners with their numerous forgotten carvings. Afterwards, hike up a foot trail to the south of the complex that takes you to the top perimeter of the 'cave', from where you can get a bird's-eye view of the entire temple complex.

Buddhist Caves CAVE

The southernmost 12 caves are Buddhist *viharas* (monasteries), except Cave 10, which is a *chaitya* (assembly hall). While the earliest caves are simple, Caves 11 and 12 are more ambitious, and on par with the more impressive Hindu temples.

Cave 1, the simplest *vihara,* may have been a granary. **Cave 2** is notable for its ornate pillars and the imposing seated Buddha, which faces the setting sun. **Cave 3** and **Cave 4** are unfinished and not well preserved.

Cave 5 is the largest *vihara* in this group, at 18m wide and 36m long; the rows of stone benches hint that it may once have been an assembly hall.

Cave 6 is an ornate *vihara* with wonderful images of Tara, consort of the Bodhisattva Avalokitesvara, and of the Buddhist goddess of learning, Mahamayuri, looking remarkably similar to Saraswati, her Hindu equivalent. **Cave 7** is an unadorned hall, but from here you can pass through a doorway to **Cave 8**, the first cave in which the sanctum is detached from the rear wall. **Cave 9** is notable for its wonderfully carved fascia.

Cave 10 is the only *chaitya* in the Buddhist group and one of the finest in India. Its ceiling features ribs carved into the stonework; the grooves were once fitted with wooden panels. The balcony and upper gallery offer a closer view of the ceiling and a frieze depicting amorous couples. A decorative window gently illuminates an enormous figure of the teaching Buddha.

Cave 11, the Do Thal (Two Storey) Cave, is entered through its third basement level, not discovered until 1876. Like Cave 12, it possibly owes its size to competition with Hindu caves of the same period.

Cave 12, the huge Tin Thal (Three Storey) Cave, is entered through a courtyard. The locked shrine on the top floor contains a large Buddha figure flanked by his seven previous incarnations. The walls are carved with relief pictures.

Hindu Caves CAVE

Where calm and contemplation infuse the Buddhist caves, drama and excitement characterise the Hindu group (Caves 13 to 29). In terms of scale, creative vision and skill of execution, these caves are in a league of their own.

All these temples were cut from the top down, so it was never necessary to use scaffolding – the builders began with the roof and moved down to the floor.

Cave 13 is a simple cave, most likely a granary. **Cave 14**, the Ravana-ki-Khai, is a Buddhist *vihara* converted to a temple dedicated to Shiva sometime in the 7th century.

Cave 15, the Das Avatara (Ten Incarnations of Vishnu) Cave, is one of the finest at Ellora. The two-storey temple contains a mesmerising Shiva Nataraja, and Shiva emerging from a lingam (phallic image) while Vishnu and Brahma pay homage.

Caves 17 to 20 and **caves 22 to 28** are simple monasteries.

Cave 21, known as the Ramesvara Cave, features interesting interpretations of familiar Shaivite scenes depicted in the earlier temples. The figure of the goddess Ganga, standing on her Makara (mythical sea creature), is particularly notable.

The large **Cave 29**, the Dumar Lena, is thought to be a transitional model between the simpler hollowed-out caves and the fully developed temples exemplified by the Kailasa. It has views over a nearby waterfall. When we visited the footpath to Cave 29 and the Jain temples was closed requiring a short rickshaw ride (₹100).

Jain Caves CAVES

The five Jain caves may lack the artistic vigour and ambitious size of the best Hindu temples, but they are exceptionally detailed. The caves are 1km north of the last Hindu temple (Cave 29) at the end of the bitumen road.

Cave 30, the Chhota Kailasa (Little Kailasa), is a poor imitation of the great Kailasa Temple and stands by itself some distance from the other Jain temples.

In contrast, **Cave 32**, the Indra Sabha (Assembly Hall of Indra), is the finest of the Jain temples. Its ground-floor plan is similar to that of the Kailasa, but the upstairs area is as ornate and richly decorated as the downstairs is plain. There are images of the Jain *tirthankars* (great teachers) Parasnath and Gomateshvara, the latter surrounded by wildlife. Inside the shrine is a seated figure of Mahavira, the last *tirthankar* and founder of the Jain religion.

Cave 31 is really an extension of Cave 32. **Cave 33**, the Jagannath Sabha, is similar in plan to Cave 32 and has some well-preserved sculptures. The final temple, the small **Cave 34**, also has interesting sculptures. On the hilltop over the Jain temples, a 5m-high image of Parasnath looks down on Ellora.

Sleeping & Eating

Hotel Kailas HOTEL $$

(☎244446; www.hotelkailas.com; d ₹1761, with AC ₹2435, cottages from ₹2935; ❄) The sole decent hotel near the site, this place should be considered only if you can't have enough of Ellora in a single day. The comfy cottages here come with hot showers; those with cave views are pricier. There's a good restaurant (mains ₹100 to ₹250) and a lush lawn tailor-made for an evening drink.

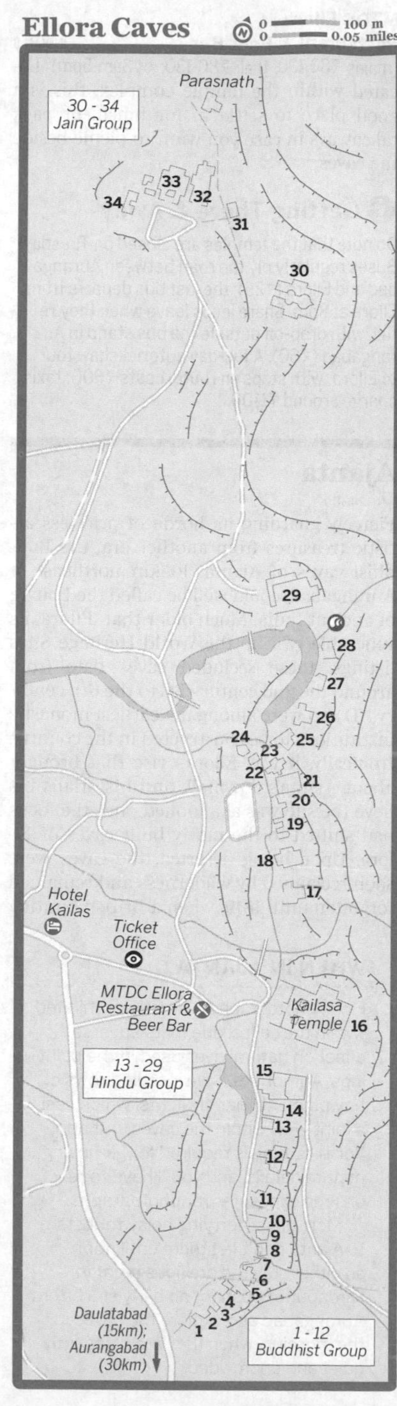

MTDC Ellora Restaurant & Beer Bar INDIAN $
(mains ₹80-130, thali ₹80-130; ⏲8am-5pm) Located within the temple complex, this is a good place to settle in for lunch, or pack takeaways in case you want to picnic beside the caves.

ℹ Getting There & Away

Do note that the temples are closed on Tuesday! Buses regularly ply the road between Aurangabad and Ellora (₹25); the last bus departs from Ellora at 8pm. Share jeeps leave when they're full, with drop-off outside the bus stand in Aurangabad (₹60). A full-day autorickshaw tour to Ellora, with stops en route, costs ₹600; taxis charge around ₹1100.

Ajanta

☎ 02438

Fiercely guarding its horde of priceless artistic treasures from another era, the Buddhist caves of Ajanta, 105km northeast of Aurangabad, could well be called the Louvre of ancient India. Much older than Ellora, its venerable twin in the World Heritage Sites listings, these secluded caves date from around the 2nd century BC to the 6th century AD and were among the earliest monastic institutions to be constructed in the country. Ironically, it was Ellora's rise that brought about Ajanta's downfall, and historians believe the site was abandoned once the focus had shifted to the newly built caves of Ellora. Upon being deserted, the caves were soon reclaimed by wilderness and remained forgotten until 1819, when a British hunting party led by officer John Smith stumbled upon them purely by chance.

The primary reason to visit Ajanta is to admire its renowned 'frescoes', actually temperas, which adorn many of the caves' interiors. With few other examples from ancient times matching their artistic excellence and fine execution, these paintings are of unfathomable heritage value. It's believed that the natural pigments for these paintings were mixed with animal glue and vegetable gum to bind them to the dry surface. Many caves have small, crater-like holes in their floors, which acted as palettes during paint jobs.

Despite their age, the paintings in most caves remain finely preserved today, and many attribute it to their relative isolation from humanity for centuries. However, it would be a tad optimistic to say that decay hasn't set in.

Authorised guides are available to show you around for ₹600.

WHEN IN AJANTA...

Flash photography is strictly prohibited within the caves, due to its adverse effect on natural dyes used in the paintings. Authorities have installed rows of tiny pigment-friendly lights, which cast a faint glow within the caves, but additional lighting is required for glimpsing minute details, and you'll have to rely on long exposures for photographs.

Most buses ferrying noisy tourists to Ajanta don't get there until noon, so either stay the previous night in Fardapur or push for an early start from Aurangabad and explore the caves in the morning, when they are pleasantly quiet and uncrowded.

Sights & Activities

★The Caves CAVE
(Indian/foreigner ₹10/250, video ₹25; ⏲9am-5.30pm Tue-Sun) The 30 caves of Ajanta line the steep face of a horseshoe-shaped gorge bordering the Waghore River. They are sequentially numbered from one end to the other, barring Caves 29 and 30. The numbering has nothing to do with their chronological order; the oldest caves are actually in the middle.

Caves 3, 5, 8, 22 and 28 to 30 remain either closed or inaccessible. Other caves might be closed from time to time due to restoration work. During rush periods, viewers are allotted 15 minutes within the caves, many of which have to be entered barefoot (socks/shoecovers allowed).

Five of the caves are *chaityas* while the other 25 are *viharas*. Caves 8, 9, 10, 12, 13 and part of 15 are early Buddhist caves, while the others date from around the 5th century AD (Mahayana period). In the simpler, more austere early Buddhist school, the Buddha was never represented directly – his presence was always alluded to by a symbol such as the footprint or wheel of law.

Cave 1, a Mahayana *vihara,* was one of the last to be excavated and is the most beautifully decorated. This is where you'll find a rendition of the Bodhisattva Padmapani, the most famous and iconic of the Ajanta artworks. A verandah in front leads to a large congregation hall, housing sculptures and

Ajanta Caves

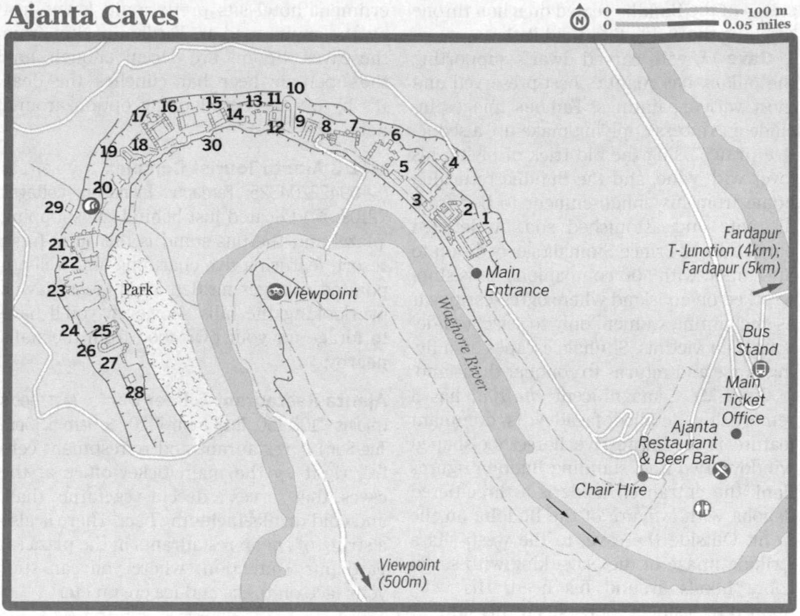

narrative murals known for their splendid perspective and elaborate detailing of dress, daily life and facial expressions. The colours in the paintings were created from local minerals, with the exception of the vibrant blue made from Central Asian lapis lazuli. Look up to the ceiling to see the carving of four deer sharing a common head.

Cave 2 is also a late Mahayana *vihara* with deliriously ornamented columns and capitals, and some fine paintings. The ceiling is decorated with geometric and floral patterns. The murals depict scenes from the Jataka tales, including Buddha's mother's dream of a six-tusked elephant, which heralded his conception.

Cave 4 is the largest *vihara* at Ajanta and is supported by 28 pillars. Although never completed, the cave has some impressive sculptures, including scenes of people fleeing from the 'eight great dangers' to the protection of Avalokitesvara.

Cave 6 is the only two-storey *vihara* at Ajanta, but parts of the lower storey have collapsed. Inside is a seated Buddha figure and an intricately carved door to the shrine. Upstairs the hall is surrounded by cells with fine paintings on the doorways.

Cave 7 has an atypical design, with porches before the verandah leading directly to the four cells and the elaborately sculptured shrine.

Cave 9 is one of the earliest *chaityas* at Ajanta. Although it dates from the early Buddhist period, the two figures flanking the entrance door were probably later Mahayana additions. Columns run down both sides of the cave and around the 3m-high dagoba at the far end.

Cave 10 is thought to be the oldest cave (200 BC) and was the first one to be spotted by the British hunting party. Similar in design to Cave 9, it is the largest *chaitya*. The facade has collapsed and the paintings inside have been damaged, in some cases by graffiti dating from soon after their rediscovery. One of the pillars to the right bears the engraved name of Smith, who left his mark here for posterity.

Cave 16, a *vihara,* contains some of Ajanta's finest paintings and is thought to have been the original entrance to the entire complex. The best known of these paintings is the 'dying princess' – Sundari, wife of the Buddha's half-brother Nanda, who is said to have fainted at the news that her husband was renouncing the material life (and her) in order to become a monk. Carved figures appear to support the ceiling, and there's a statue of the Buddha seated on a lion throne teaching the Noble Eightfold Path.

Cave 17, with carved dwarfs supporting the pillars, has Ajanta's best-preserved and most varied paintings. Famous images include a princess applying make-up, a seductive prince using the old trick of plying his lover with wine, and the Buddha returning home from his enlightenment to beg from his wife and astonished son. A detailed panel tells of Prince Simhala's expedition to Sri Lanka: with 500 companions he is shipwrecked on an island where ogresses appear as enchanting women, only to seize and devour their victims. Simhala escapes on a flying horse and returns to conquer the island.

Cave 19, a magnificent *chaitya*, has a remarkably detailed facade; its dominant feature is an impressive horseshoe-shaped window. Two fine, standing Buddha figures flank the entrance. Inside is a three-tiered dagoba with a figure of the Buddha on the front. Outside the cave, to the west, sits a striking image of the Naga king with seven cobra hoods around his head. His wife, hooded by a single cobra, sits by his side.

Cave 24, had it been finished, would have been the largest *vihara* at Ajanta. You can see how the caves were constructed – long galleries were cut into the rock and then the rock between them was broken through.

Cave 26, a largely ruined *chaitya*, is now dramatically lit, and contains some fine sculptures that shouldn't be missed. On the left wall is a huge figure of the 'reclining Buddha', lying back in preparation for nirvana. Other scenes include a lengthy depiction of the Buddha's temptation by Maya.

Cave 27 is virtually a *vihara* connected to the Cave 26 *chaitya*.

Viewpoints VIEWPOINT

Two lookouts offer picture-perfect views of the whole horseshoe-shaped gorge. The first is a short walk beyond the river, crossed via a bridge below Cave 8. A further 40-minute uphill walk (not to be attempted during the monsoons) leads to the lookout from where the British party first spotted the caves.

Sleeping & Eating

Accommodation options close to the caves are limited and you're better off using Aurangabad or Jalgaon as a base.

MTDC Holiday Resort HOTEL **$$**

(☎244230; Aurangabad–Jalgaon Rd, Fardapur; d with/without AC ₹1262/1577; ❄) This government hotel sits pretty amid lawns just by the main road in Fardapur, 5km from the caves. Rooms are decent enough, and the open-air beer bar clinches the deal. It's by far the best lodging option around here.

MTDC Ajanta Tourist Complex HOTEL **$$**

(☎09422204325; Fardapur T-junction; cottages ₹2103; ❄) Located just behind the shopping 'plaza' and the bus stand is this mint-fresh resort, featuring five charming and well-appointed cottages nestled amid grassy lawns overlooking the hills. However, you'll have to forage for your own food from the stalls nearby.

Ajanta Restaurant & Beer Bar FAST FOOD **$**

(mains ₹100-150, thali from ₹120; ⏲9am-5.30pm Tue-Sun) A restaurant and refreshment centre, right by the main ticket office at the caves, that serves a decent vegetarian thali, and cold drinks including beer. There is also a string of cheap restaurants in the plaza (at Fardapur T-junction) where you can stuff your face on thalis and ice cream etc.

Information

A cloakroom is available at Fardapur T-junction (but not at the caves), where you can leave gear (₹10 per item for four hours), in case you are visiting Ajanta en route from Aurangabad to Jalgaon or vice versa. The caves are a short, steep climb from the ticket office; the elderly can opt for a chair carried by four sweaty bearers (₹600).

On a rather perplexing note, a new tourist complex near the T-junction is under construction, where they reportedly intended to replicate the major caves alongside restaurants and shops!

Getting There & Away

Note that the caves are closed on Monday. Buses from Aurangabad or Jalgaon will drop you off at the T-junction (where the highway meets the road to the caves), 4km from the site. From here, after paying an 'amenities' fee (₹10), walk to the departure point for the green-coloured buses (with/without AC ₹20/10), which zoom up to the caves. Buses return on a regular basis (half-hourly, last bus at 5pm) to the T-junction.

All MSRTC buses passing through Fardapur stop at the T-junction. After the caves close you can board buses to either Aurangabad or Jalgaon outside the MTDC Holiday Resort in Fardapur, 1km down the main road towards Jalgaon. Taxis are available in Fardapur; ₹1200 should get you to Jalgaon.

Jalgaon

☎0257 / POP 460,468 / ELEV 208M

Apart from being a handy base for exploring Ajanta 60km away, Jalgaon is really nothing more than a convenient transit town. It sits on the main line leading northeast from Mumbai, and has rail connections to all major cities across India.

Sleeping

★**Hotel Plaza** HOTEL $

(☎9370027354, 2227354; hotelplaza_jal@yahoo.com; Station Rd; dm ₹200, s/d ₹500/700, r with AC from ₹1000; ❄@) Spending a night here is reason enough to halt in Jalgaon. Stepping into this serene hotel with its clean lines and white interior is just the tonic after a long rail journey. And it is only a short walk from the station. The rooms vary in size and layout but all are kept squeaky clean and fresh. The effusive owner is a mine of useful information and can assist with train reservations and taxi hire.

Hotel Royal Palace HOTEL $$

(☎2233555; www.hotelroyalpalace.in; Mahabal Rd, Jai Nagar; s/d incl breakfast from ₹2320/2436; ❄📶) Luxuriant by Jalgaon's standards, the Royal Palace has bland business-hotel rooms that are adequately comfortable, but don't quite reach the heights promised by the glitzy lobby. There's also a decent pure-veg, multicuisine restaurant serving north Indian, coastal, Chinese and Continental fare.

Eating & Drinking

Hotel Arya INDIAN $

(Navi Peth; mains ₹55-95; ⏲8.30am-10.50pm) Vegetarian-only grub on offer but it's delicious; try one of the lip-smacking Punjabi delights. There's also Chinese and South Indian dishes. It's a short walk south along Station Rd, left at MG Rd, and left at the clock tower. You may have to queue for a table.

Silver Palace BAR

(Station Rd; mains ₹60-190) This restaurant bar's claims of luxury may be stretching things too far. But the beer is cold, and females won't feel like they are trespassing on male-only territory. It is next door to Hotel Plaza.

Information

You can find a couple of banks, ATMs and internet cafes on Nehru Rd, which runs along the top of Station Rd.

Getting There & Away

Several express trains connecting Mumbai (sleeper/2AC ₹286/1035, eight hours), Delhi (sleeper/2AC ₹470/1900, 18 hours), Ahmedabad (sleeper/2AC ₹326/1260, 14 hours) and Varanasi (sleeper/2AC ₹450/1870, 21 hours) stop at Jalgaon train station. The Sewagram Express goes to Nagpur (sleeper/2AC ₹282/1015, eight hours, 10pm), while the Nizamuddin Vasco-da-Gama Express goes to Goa (sleeper/2AC ₹465/1880, 23 hours, 7.55am).

Buses to Fardapur (₹45, 1½ hours) depart half-hourly from the bus stand starting at 6am, continuing to Aurangabad (₹160, four hours).

WORTH A TRIP

LONAR METEORITE CRATER

If you like off-beat adventures, travel to Lonar to explore a prehistoric natural wonder. About 50,000 years ago, a meteorite slammed into the earth here, leaving behind a massive crater, 2km across and 170m deep. In scientific jargon, it's the only hyper-velocity natural-impact crater in basaltic rock in the world. In lay terms, it's as tranquil and relaxing a spot as you could hope to find, with a shallow green lake at its base and wilderness all around. The lake water is supposedly alkaline and excellent for the skin. Scientists think that the meteorite is still embedded about 600m below the southeastern rim of the crater.

The crater's edge is home to several Hindu temples as well as wildlife, including langurs, peacocks, deer and numerous birds.

MTDC Tourist Complex (☎07260221602; d with/without AC ₹1300/1060; ❄) has a prime location just across the road from the crater, and offers eight rooms of relatively good value, considering the location. There are a couple of buses a day between Lonar and Aurangabad (₹150, 3½ hours). It's also possible to visit Lonar on a day trip from Aurangabad or Jalgaon if you hire a car and driver, and don't mind dishing out about ₹2400.

Jalgaon's train station and bus stand are about 2km apart (₹20 by autorickshaw). Private bus companies on Station Rd offer services to Aurangabad (₹140, 3½ hours), Mumbai (₹350, nine hours) and Pune (₹350, with AC ₹550, nine hours).

Nagpur

0712 / POP 2.4 MILLION / ELEV 305M

In the heart of India's orange country, Nagpur is located way off the main tourist routes. Apart from being at its festive best during Dussehra, the city – as such – is hopelessly devoid of sites. Nonetheless, it makes a good base for venturing out to the far eastern corner of Maharashtra. First up, it's close to the temples of Ramtek and the ashrams of Sevagram. Besides, Nagpur is also a convenient stop for those looking for tigers in the isolated **Tadoba-Andhari Tiger Reserve**, 150km south of Nagpur, as well as Pench National Park, just across the border in Madyha Pradesh.

If you have some time to kill in the evening, take a stroll in the city's Civil Lines area, dotted with majestic buildings and mansions dating back to the Raj, now used as government offices. Summer is the best time to sample the famed oranges.

Sleeping & Eating

Nagpur's overpriced hotels cater primarily to business travellers, not tourists. Stay in the Central Ave area if you're on a budget, or have a train to catch in the wee hours. It's a 15-minute walk east of the train station. Otherwise, consider moving to Ramdaspeth, closer to the city centre.

Hotel Blue Diamond HOTEL $

(2727461; www.hotelbluediamondnagpur.com; 113 Central Ave; s/d ₹500/700, with AC ₹1350/1500;) The mirrored ceiling in reception is straight out of a 1970s nightclub, and the rooms are pretty much the type you'd expect above a 1970s nightclub. There's a dungeon-like bar on the mezzanine floor. AC rooms have LCD TVs and crumpled linoleum flooring.

Hotel Centre Point HOTEL $$

(2420910; www.centrepointgroup.org; 24 Central Bazar Rd, Ramdaspeth; s/d incl breakfast from ₹4345/4932;) A trusted address that's been setting the standards of luxury in Nagpur for some time now. Rooms are plush, with fluffy beds and high-speed internet access, and there's a coffee shop and restaurant. It's located in the heart of the business and entertainment district, and airport transfers are complimentary.

Pride Hotel HOTEL $$$

(2291102; www.pridehotel.com; Wardha Rd, opposite airport; s/d from ₹5262/5430;) Located close to the airport and away from the din of the city, this sleek business hotel is a good stopover option for touch-and-go travellers. Royal Lancers, its lobby bar, and Puran Da Dhaba, a dolled-up version of a traditional Punjabi eatery, are good places to settle in for the evening.

Krishnum SOUTH INDIAN $

(Central Ave; mains ₹50-80) This popular place dishes out South Indian snacks and generous thalis, as well as freshly squeezed fruit juices. There are branches found in other parts of town.

Picadilly Checkers FAST FOOD $

(VCA Complex, Civil Lines; mains ₹60-80) A favourite eating joint for Nagpur's college brigade. A good range of all-vegetarian quick bites are on offer.

Information

Numerous ATMs line Central Ave.

Computrek (18 Central Ave; per hr ₹20; 10am-10pm) Internet access on the main drag.

MTDC (2533325; near MLA Hostel, Civil Lines; 10am-5.45pm Mon-Sat)

State Bank of India (Kingsway; 11am-2pm Mon-Fri) A two-minute walk west of the train station. Deals in foreign exchange.

Getting There & Away

AIR

Domestic airlines, including **Indian Airlines** (2533962) and **Jet Airways** (5617888), fly daily to Delhi (from ₹6000, 1½ hours), Mumbai (from ₹5000, 1½ hours) and Kolkata (from ₹8000, 1½ hours), as well as linking Hyderabad, Ahmedabad, Bengaluru, Chennai and Pune. Taxis/autorickshaws from the airport to the city centre cost ₹400/200.

BUS

The main MSRTC bus stand is 2km south of the train station. Ordinary buses head for Wardha (₹65, three hours) and Ramtek (₹40, 1½ hours). There are two buses to Jalgaon (₹370, 10 hours), and three to Hyderabad (₹358, 12 hours).

TRAIN

From Mumbai's Chhatrapati Shivaji Terminus (CST), the Duronto Express runs daily to Nagpur (sleeper/2AC ₹470/1825, 10 hours, 9:15pm). From Nagpur, it departs at 8.50pm and arrives at 7.50am the following morning. Heading north to Kolkata is the Gitanjali Express (sleeper/2AC ₹475/1920, 17½ hours, 7.05pm). Several expresses bound for Delhi and Mumbai stop at Jalgaon (for Ajanta caves; sleeper/2AC ₹282/1015, eight hours).

Around Nagpur

Ramtek

About 40km northeast of Nagpur, Ramtek is believed to be the place where Lord Rama, of the epic Ramayana, spent some time during his exile with his wife Sita and brother Lakshmana. The place is marked by a cluster of **temples** (⏲6am-9pm) about 600 years old, which sit atop the Hill of Rama and have their own population of resident monkeys. Autorickshaws will cart you the 5km from the bus stand to the temple complex for ₹80. You can return to town via the 700 steps at the back of the complex. On the road to the temples you'll pass the delightful **Ambala Tank**, lined with small shrines. Boat rides around the lake are available.

Not far from the main temple cluster, **Rajkamal Resort** (☎07114202761; d without/with AC ₹1050/1410; ❄) has large, featureless rooms with TVs, and a basic restaurant-bar.

Buses run half-hourly between Ramtek and the MSRTC bus stand in Nagpur (₹41, 1½ hours). The last bus to Nagpur is at 7pm.

Sevagram

☎07152

About 85km from Nagpur, Sevagram (Village of Service) was chosen by Mahatma Gandhi as his base during the Indian Independence Movement. Throughout the freedom struggle, the village played host to several nationalist leaders, who would regularly come to visit the Mahatma at his **Sevagram Ashram** (☎284753; ⏲6am-5.30pm). The overseers of this peaceful ashram, built on 40 hectares of farmland, have carefully restored the original huts where Gandhi lived and worked, and which now house some of his personal effects.

Very basic lodging is available in the **Yatri Nivas** (☎284753; d ₹100), across the road from the entry gate (booking recommended), and simple vegetarian meals can be served in the ashram's dining hall with prior notice.

Just 3km from Sevagram, Paunar village is home to the **Brahmavidya Mandir Ashram** (☎288388; Paunar; ⏲4am-noon & 2-8pm). Founded by Vinoba Bhave, a nationalist and disciple of Gandhi, the ashram is run almost entirely by women. Modelled on *swaraj* (self-sufficiency), it's operated on a social system of consensus, with no central management.

Sevagram can be reached by taking a Wardha-bound bus from Nagpur (₹55, three hours).

OFF THE BEATEN TRACK

TADOBA-ANDHARI TIGER RESERVE

Under India's Project Tiger directorate, this little-explored national park – with a healthy population of Bengal tigers – lies 150km south of Nagpur. Less visited than most other forests in India, this is a place where you can get up close with wildlife (which also includes gaurs, chitals, nilgais and sloth bears) without having to jostle past truckloads of shutter-happy tourists. The trade-off is that you'll have to make do with basic amenities and low comfort levels. The park remains open through most of the year.

The **MTDC Resort** (☎9822713201; d without/with AC ₹1645/1996; ❄) in nearby Moharli has decent rooms and dining facilities, though bring your own mosquito net. The resort can arrange jungle safaris in jeeps and minibuses. Bookings can be made at the MTDC's Nagpur office. If you're travelling in groups of six or more, MTDC can arrange an all-inclusive overnight package out of Nagpur, which takes care of logistical hassles.

Several state buses ply the road between Nagpur and Chandrapur through the day (₹124, 3½ hours).

SOUTHERN MAHARASHTRA

Konkan Coast

Despite being flanked on both ends by two of India's top urban centres, it's laudable how the Konkan Coast manages to latch on to its virginal bounties. A little-developed shoreline running southward from Mumbai all the way to Goa, it is a picturesque strip of land peppered with postcard beaches, vivid green paddy fields, rolling hills and decaying forts. Travelling through this tropical backwater can be sheer bliss. However, remember that accommodation is scant, the cuisine unsophisticated though tasty, and the locals unaccustomed to tour groups, especially foreigners. Since transport is both limited and unreliable, a good option is to rent a taxi in Mumbai and drift slowly down the coast to Goa. What you'll get in return is an experience that money can't buy.

Murud

☎02144 / POP 12,700

Even if you don't plan on exploring the whole coast, the sleepy fishing hamlet of Murud – 165km from Mumbai – should be on your itinerary. Once you step on to its lazy beaches and feel the warm surf rush past your feet, you'll be happy you came.

Sight-wise, Murud is home to the magnificent island fortress of **Janjira** (admission free; ⏲7am-5.30pm), standing about 500m offshore. The citadel was built in 1140 by the Siddis, descendants of sailor-traders from the Horn of Africa, who settled here and allegedly made their living through piracy. No outsider ever made it past the fort's 12m-high walls which, when seen during high tide, seem to rise straight from the sea. Unconquered through history, the fort finally fell to the spoils of nature. Today, its ramparts are slowly turning to rubble as wilderness reclaims its innards.

The only way to reach Janjira is by boat (₹20 return, 15 minutes) from Rajpuri Port. Boats depart from 7am to 5.30pm daily, but require a minimum of 20 passengers. You can also have a boat to yourself (₹600), and most oarsmen will double as guides for a negotiable fee (around ₹350). To get to Rajpuri from Murud, take an autorickshaw (₹70) or hire a bicycle from the Golden Swan Beach Resort.

Back in Murud you can waste away the days on the beach, joining in with karate practice or playing cricket with locals. Alternately, you could peer through the gates of the off-limits Ahmedganj Palace, estate of the Siddi Nawab of Murud, or scramble around the decaying mosque and tombs on the south side of town.

Sleeping & Eating

Golden Swan Beach Resort HOTEL $$
(☎274078; www.goldenswan.com; Darbar Rd; d incl full board from ₹4700; ❄) With only waving palms separating it from the beach, this upscale hotel offers accommodation in cosy rooms and cottages looking out to the sea, with views of the Ahmedganj Palace and Kasa Fort. There are also rooms in a charming old bungalow located five minutes away from the main property. Rates increase by 25% on weekends.

THE LEGEND OF 'BABA' AMTE

The legend of Murlidhar Devidas 'Baba' Amte (1914–2008) is oft-repeated in humanitarian circles around the world. Hailing from an upper-class Brahmin family in Wardha, Amte was snugly ensconced in material riches and on his way to becoming a successful lawyer, when he witnessed a leper die unattended in the streets one night. It was an incident that changed him forever.

Soon after, Amte renounced worldly comforts, embracing an austere life through which he actively worked for the benefit of leprosy patients and those belonging to marginalised communities. In the primitive forested backyards of eastern Maharashtra, he set up his ashram called **Anandwan** (Forest of Joy; anandwan@gmail.com). A true Gandhian, Amte believed in self-sufficiency, and his lifelong efforts saw several awards being conferred upon him, including the Ramon Magsaysay Award in 1985.

Amte's work has been continued by his sons Vikas and Prakash and their wives – the latter couple also won the Magsaysay Award in 2008. The family now runs three ashrams in these remote parts to care for the needy, both humans and animals. Volunteering opportunities are available.

WORTH A TRIP

BOUNDLESS BEACHES

Apart from its main sands, the Konkan Coast boasts a string of less-explored but heavenly beaches that host weekend-away-type resorts for stressed-out Mumbai-ites. About 17km north of Murud, well connected by share autorickshaws (₹100), lies **Kashid,** a fantastic beach where you can cosy up with your favourite paperback while sipping on tender coconuts.

South of Murud is **Diveagar**, swarming with colonies of sand bubbler crabs, scenic **Harihareshwar**, famous for its seaside temple, and serene **Vengurla**, 10km from Tarkarli (p108), a place you probably wouldn't mind being shipwrecked. Most of these places are connected by back roads where public transport is scant, so they are best visited in a hired cab.

Sea Shell Resort HOTEL $$
(☎274306; www.seashellmurud.com; Darbar Rd; d without/with AC ₹2280/2500; ❄ 🏊) A cheery place with breezy sea-facing rooms and a multicuisine restaurant, this understated hotel scores quite well with Mumbai's weekend travellers. The swimming pool at the entrance is a welcome addition, and dolphin safaris can be arranged.

★**New Sea Rock Restaurant** INDIAN $
(Rajpuri; mains ₹50-160; ⏱7am-8pm) Perched on a cliff overlooking the beach at Rajpuri, this joint has an awesome view of Janjira. A perfect place to steal a million-dollar sunset for the price of a chai (₹10), though you will probably be tempted to try the Indian or Chinese mains. The proprietors also arrange kayak rides and other water sports during the high season.

Hotel Vinayak INDIAN $
(Darbar Rd; mains ₹70-190; ⏱8am-10pm) A decent place overlooking the beach to tuck into a delicious and fiery Malvani thali, served with pink kokam syrup to smother the spices. Veg and nonveg dishes available.

Getting There & Away

AC catamarans (₹120, two hours) from the Gateway of India in Mumbai cruise to Mandva pier between 6am and 7pm. The ticket includes a free shuttle bus to Alibag (30 minutes), otherwise an autorickshaw will be about ₹200. Rickety local buses from Alibag head down the coast to Murud (₹41, two hours). Alternatively, buses from Mumbai Central bus stand take almost six hours to Murud (ordinary/semideluxe ₹133/180).

Avoid the train. The nearest railhead is at Roha, two hours away and poorly connected.

Ganpatipule

☎02357

Primarily a temple town, Ganpatipule has been luring a steady stream of sea-lovers over the years with its warm waters and lonely stretches of sand. Located about 375km from Mumbai, it's a village that snoozes through much of the year, except during holidays such as Diwali or Ganesh Chaturthi. These are times when hordes of boisterous 'tourists' turn up to visit the seaside **Ganesha Temple** (⏱6am-9pm) housing a monolithic Ganesha (painted a bright orange), supposedly discovered 1600 years ago.

Activities on and off the beach at Ganpatipule include camel (₹50) and boat (₹100) rides. Neither of which are recommended over a long walk on the sand away from the crowd.

About 40km south, **Ratnagiri** is the largest town on the southern Maharashtra coast and the main train station for Ganpatipule (it's on the Konkan Railway). You'll also find several ATMs strung along Ratnagiri's main street. But once you've refilled your wallet and gone shopping for conveniences, the only sight worth checking out – apart from a dirty beach – are the remnants of the **Thibaw Palace** (Thibaw Palace Rd; admission free; ⏱10am-5.30pm Tue-Sun), where the last Burmese king, Thibaw, was interned under the British from 1886 until his death in 1916.

Sleeping & Eating

MTDC Resort HOTEL $$
(☎235248; d without/with AC from ₹1938/2280; ❄) Spread over prime beachfront, this is the best place to stay. It's well kept with a small army of gardeners, and offers an assortment of rooms and cottages. It also packs in a decent restaurant with cold beer. The Konkani

huts, themed on traditional Malvani villages, is an offshoot located well away from the main resort, which offers its own restaurant with beachside dining and a bit more seclusion. The huts themselves are basic concrete blocks, but OK.

Hotel Vihar Deluxe HOTEL **$$**
(☎02352222944; Main Rd, Ratnagiri; d without/with AC ₹1285/1754; ❄) This gigantic operation is one of a few functional hotels that line the main strip in Ratnagiri. It was undergoing extensive renovations when we visited. Rooms reflect the business traveller mindset and are far from luxurious, while the food – especially the seafood – is commendable. A South Indian breakfast is complimentary.

Tarang Restaurant INDIAN **$**
(MTDC Resort; mains ₹80-190) This is just one of several similar places where you can grab a decent, inexpensive meal, such as a thali or Chinese noodles in Ganpatipule.

Getting There & Around

Ordinary buses shuttle between Ganpatipule and Ratnagiri (₹49, 1½ hours). An autorickshaw will cost ₹400. An autorickshaw ride from the MSRTC bus stand to the MTDC Resort will cost ₹25.

One MSRTC bus heads out at 8.45am to Mumbai (₹428, 10 hours), and departs from Mumbai at 8pm. There are three daily buses each to Pune (₹330) and Kohalpur (₹135).

Ratnagiri's train station is 6km out of town on the road to/from Kohalpur. From Ratnagiri, the Mandovi Express goes to Mumbai (2nd class/1st class ₹123/1365, 6½ hours, 2.25pm). The return train heading for Goa (2nd class/1st class ₹105/1125, 3½ hours) is at 1.15pm. From Ratnagiri's old bus stand, semideluxe buses leave for Goa (₹255, seven hours) and Kolhapur (₹150, four hours).

Information

There is a Bank of Maharashtra ATM at the entrance of the Ganesha Temple, and a much more reliable Bank of India ATM in town, about 400m from the MTDC Resort. For internet (₹100 per hour), look for Tapaswi Sandanand Niwas who works in the Spanco office beside the Bank of Maharashtra (not the aforementioned ATM).

Tarkarli & Malvan

☎02365

A government tourism promo parades this place as comparable to Tahiti, which may be a bit ambitious! Within striking distance of Goa, about 200km from Ratnagiri, pristine Tarkarli boasts near-white sands and sparkling waters, but what's lacking is tourist infrastructure and resort-style comforts, but do you care?

The monstrous **Sindhudurg Fort**, built by Shivaji and dating from 1664, lies on an offshore island and can be reached by frequent ferries (₹30) from Malvan. MTDC can arrange snorkelling trips to the clear waters around the fortress.

Of the few hotels and resorts available, the good old **MTDC Holiday Resort** (☎252390; d from ₹2280; ❄) is still your most economical bet. Enquire at the resort about backwater tours on its fabulous **houseboats** (☎8805389003; standard/luxury incl full board ₹7410/9690).

The closest train station is Kudal, 38km away. Frequent buses (₹28, one hour) cover the route from Malvan bus stand. An autorickshaw from Kudal to Malvan or Tarkarli is about ₹500. Malvan has buses daily to Panaji (₹79, three hours) and a couple of services to Ratnagiri (₹147, five hours).

Matheran

☎02148 / POP 5287 / ELEV 803M

Literally 'Jungle Above', Matheran is a tiny patch of peace and quiet capping a craggy Sahyadri summit within spitting distance of Mumbai's heat and grime. Endowed with shady forests criss-crossed with foot trails and breathtaking lookouts, it is easily the most elegant of Maharashtra's hill stations.

The credit for discovering this little gem goes to Hugh Malet, erstwhile collector of Thane district, who chanced upon it during one of his excursions in 1850. Soon it became a hill station patronised by the British and populated by Parsi families.

Getting to Matheran is really half the fun. While speedier options are available by road, nothing beats arriving in town on the narrow-gauge toy train that chugs laboriously along a 21km scenic route to the heart of the settlement. Motor vehicles are banned within Matheran, making it an ideal place to give your ears and lungs a rest and your feet some exercise.

Sights & Activities

You can walk along shady forest paths to most of Matheran's viewpoints in a matter of hours, and it's a place well suited to stress-free ambling. To catch the sunrise, head to **Panorama Point**, while **Porcupine Point** (also known as Sunset Point) is the most popular (read: packed) as the sun drops. **Louisa Point** and **Little Chouk Point** also have stunning views of the Sahyadris, and if you're visiting **Echo Point**, give it a yell. Stop at **Charlotte Lake** on the way back from Echo Point, but don't go for a swim – this is the town's main water supply and stepping in is prohibited. You can reach the valley below One Tree Hill down the path known as **Shivaji's Ladder**, supposedly trod upon by the Maratha leader himself.

A couple of **ropeways** (₹250) have sprung up for those that find the peaceful setting, well, too peaceful. The best of these takes you out between Honeymoon Point and Louisa Point. There's a shorter one at Myra Point that seems to be anchored by a rather wimpy looking tree.

Horses can be hired along MG Rd for rides to the lookout points; they cost about ₹300 per hour (negotiable).

Sleeping & Eating

Apart from a few exceptions, hotels in Matheran are generally overpriced for what's on offer. Many places have a minimum two-night stay, which makes sense, as there's no point in rushing a trip to a place geared for relaxation. Check-out times vary wildly (as early as 7am), as do high- and low-season rates. Matheran shuts shop during the monsoons.

Hope Hall Hotel HOTEL $

(☎230253; MG Rd; d from ₹1000) 'Since 1875', says a plaque at the entrance, and frankly, the age shows! However, going by the 'thank you' notes left by guests, it must be a cheerful place to stay. Be prepared for mosquitoes (and their multilegged friends and enemies), bucket hot water and the lack of an inhouse restaurant.

Lord's Central Hotel HERITAGE HOTEL $$

(☎230228; www.matheranhotels.com; MG Rd; d incl full board from ₹4600; ❄@≋) Owned by a gracious Parsi family for over six generations, this charming colonial-style affair is one of Matheran's most reputed establishments, and guarantees a pleasant stay within its old-world portals. The rooms are comfy, the swimming-pool deck offers fabulous views of the valley and distant peaks, and a jumbo chess board out on the lawns is a nice place to down a beer.

Hotel Woodlands HOTEL $$

(☎230271; www.woodlandsmatheran.com; Chinoy Rd; d 1/2-nights ₹3765/5035) Woodlands is a venerable old homestead with historic charm and enough modern comforts thrown in to keep the most fussy guest satisfied. The forested setting is very relaxing and the playground should keep the kids occupied. But it's the verandah that steals the show; a great place to kick back and dine.

★ **Verandah In The Forest** HERITAGE HOTEL $$$

(☎230296; www.neemranahotels.com; Barr House; d incl breakfast from ₹5883) This deliciously preserved 19th-century bungalow thrives on undiluted nostalgia. Step past the threshold of one of its quaintly luxurious rooms or suites and find yourself reminiscing about bygone times in the company of ornate candelabras, antique teak furniture, Victorian canvases, grandfather clocks and a rush of other memorabilia. The eponymous verandah is probably the most beautiful location from where to admire Matheran's woods, and there's a good selection of food and beverages to keep you company.

Shabbir Bhai INDIAN $

(Merry Rd; mains ₹70-100; ⏰10am-10pm) Known locally as the 'Byrianiwala', this funky joint has a full North Indian menu, but here it's all about the spicy biryanis: chicken, mutton and veg. To find it, take the footpath uphill beside the Jama Masjid on MG Rd and follow your nose.

Rasna INDIAN $

(MG Rd; mains ₹100-150; ⏰9am-11pm) This simple and cheerful restaurant opposite Naoroji Lord Garden serves tasty vegetarian food. Try the popular Punjabi (North Indian) thali.

Information

Entry to Matheran costs ₹40 (₹20 for children), which you pay on arrival at the train station or the Dasturi car park.

You can buy an entertaining, if not entirely accurate, guidebook and map (₹15) at many of the shops along MG Rd. The **Union Bank of India** (MG Rd; ⏰10am-2pm Mon-Fri, to noon Sat) has an ATM.

Getting There & Away

TAXI

Buses (₹25) and share taxis (₹70) run from Neral to Matheran's Dasturi car park (30 minutes). You could take the taxi without sharing for ₹350. Horses (₹300) and hand-pulled rickshaws

(₹400) wait here to whisk you (relatively speaking) to Matheran's main bazaar. You can also walk this stretch in a little under an hour and your luggage can be hauled for you for ₹200.

TRAIN

The toy train (2nd class/1st class ₹35/225) chugs between Matheran and Neral Junction five times daily. The service is suspended during monsoons. From Mumbai, Mumbai Suburban Rail (Central), on the Mumbai CST–Khopoli line, departs Mumbai CST at 12.19pm to arrive at Neral Junction (2nd class/1st class ₹19/155) at 2.03pm.

Express trains from Mumbai CST include the 7.10am Deccan Express and the 8.40am Koyna Express (2nd class/chair ₹56/249, 1½ hours), which stop at Neral junction. Other expresses from Mumbai stop at Karjat, down the line from Neral, from where you can backtrack on a local train or catch a bus to Matheran (₹30). From Pune, you can reach Karjat by the Sinhagad Express (2nd class/chair ₹57/249, two hours, 6.05am). Note: trains from Pune don't stop at Neral Junction.

Getting Around

Apart from hand-pulled rickshaws and horses, walking is the only other transport option in Matheran.

Lonavla

☎02114 / ELEV 625M

Lonavla is an overdeveloped (and overpriced) mercantile town about 106km southeast of Mumbai. It's far from attractive, with its main drag consisting almost exclusively of garishly lit shops flogging *chikki*, the rock-hard, brittle sweet made in the area.

The only reason you'd want to come here is to visit the nearby Karla and Bhaja Caves which, after those at Ellora and Ajanta, are the best in Maharashtra.

Hotels, restaurants and the main road to the caves lie north of the train station (exit from platform 1). Most of the Lonavla township and its markets are located south of the station.

Activities

Founded in 1924, the **Kaivalyadhama Yoga Hospital** (☎273039; www.kdham.com; s/d per week incl full board from ₹4700/8000), set about 2km from Lonavla en route to the Karla and Bhaja Caves, combines yoga courses with naturopathic therapies. Room rates cover accommodation, yoga sessions, programs and lectures over seven days. Two-, three- and four-week packages are also offered.

Mumbai-based **Nirvana Adventures** (☎022-26053724; www.flynirvana.com) offers various paragliding courses (including full board from ₹8000) or 10-minute tandem flights (₹2500) at Kamshet, 25km from Lonavla.

Sleeping & Eating

Lonavla's hotels suffer from inflated prices and low standards. All hotels listed here have a 10am checkout.

Hotel Adarsh HOTEL $$
(☎272353; near bus stand; d from ₹3248; ❄ 🏊) This is clearly the best-value place in town. Centrally located, it has smart rooms and good service, and the terrace pool gives you another good reason to stay.

Hotel Lonavla HOTEL $$
(☎272914; Mumbai–Pune Rd; d from ₹1495, with AC ₹2495) Relatively cheap by Lonavla's standards. Bulk bookings can often leave you without a room, so enquire in advance. They insist that you clear your bills every third day (who stays that long anyway?).

Biso ITALIAN $$
(Citrus Hotel, DT Shahani Rd; mains ₹220-300) This could be a delightfully redeeming feature of your Lonavla trip. A top-class alfresco restaurant thrown around the lawns of a sleek business hotel about 15 minutes east of the bus stand, Biso serves an excellent selection of pastas, wood-fired pizzas and desserts.

Information

The petrol pump opposite Hotel Rama Krishna now has three ATMs dispensing cash. Internet access is available at **Balaji Cyber Café** (1st fl, Khandelwal Bldg, New Bazaar; per hr ₹15; ⌚12.30-10.30pm), immediately south of the train station.

Getting There & Away

Lonavla is serviced by MSRTC buses departing from the bus stand to Dadar in Mumbai (ordinary/semideluxe ₹74/107, two hours) and Pune (ordinary/semideluxe ₹62/91, two hours). Luxury AC buses (₹200) also travel to both cities.

All express trains from Mumbai to Pune stop at Lonavla (2nd class/chair ₹65/273, 2½ hours). From Pune, you can also reach Lonavla by taking an hourly shuttle train (₹15, two hours).

Karla & Bhaja Caves

While they pale in comparison to Ajanta or Ellora, these rock-cut caves (dating from around the 2nd century BC) are among the better examples of Buddhist cave architecture in India. They are also low on commercial tourism, which make them ideal places for a quiet excursion. Karla has the most impressive single cave, but Bhaja is a quieter site to explore.

Sights

Karla Cave CAVE

(Indian/foreigner ₹5/100; 9am-5pm) Karla Cave, the largest early Buddhist *chaitya* in India, is reached by a 20-minute climb from a mini-bazaar at the base of a hill. Completed in 80 BC, the *chaitya* is around 40m long and 15m high, and sports similar architectural motifs as *chaityas* in Ajanta and Ellora. Excluding Ellora's Kailasa Temple, this is probably the most impressive cave temple in the state.

A semicircular 'sun window' filters light in towards a dagoba or stupa (the cave's representation of the Buddha), protected by a carved wooden umbrella, the only remaining example of its kind. The cave's roof also retains ancient teak buttresses. The 37 pillars forming the aisles are topped by kneeling elephants. The carved elephant heads on the sides of the vestibule once had ivory tusks.

There's a **Hindu temple** in front of the cave, thronged by pilgrims whose presence adds colour to the scene.

Bhaja Caves CAVE

(Indian/foreigner ₹5/100; 8am-6pm) Across the expressway, it's a 3km jaunt from the main road to the Bhaja Caves, where the setting is lusher, greener and quieter than at Karla Cave. Thought to date from around 200 BC, 10 of the 18 caves here are *viharas,* while Cave 12 is an open *chaitya,* earlier than that at Karla, containing a simple dagoba. Beyond this is a strange huddle of 14 stupas, five inside and nine outside a smaller cave.

Sleeping & Eating

MTDC Karla Resort HOTEL $$

(02114-282230; d without/with AC from ₹1740/2090;) Set off the highway, close to the Karla–Bhaja access point, this place is much more peaceful than Lonavla. Rooms and cottages are well kept, and there's a good restaurant.

Getting There & Away

Karla and Bhaja can be visited on a local bus (₹15, 30 minutes) to the access point, from where it's about a 6km return walk on each side to the two sites. But that would be exhausting and hot. An autorickshaw should charge about ₹500 from Lonavla for the tour, including waiting time.

Pune

020 / POP 3.1 MILLION / ELEV 535M

Once little more than an army outpost, Pune (also pronounced 'Poona') is a city that epitomises 'New India', with its baffling mix of capitalism, spiritualism, ancient and modern. Today, it is a thriving centre of academia and business. Pune is also famous, or notorious, globally for its number-one export: the late guru Bhagwan Shree Rajneesh and his ashram, the Osho International Meditation Resort.

Pune was initially given pride of place by Shivaji and the ruling Peshwas, who made it their capital. The British took the city in 1817 and, thanks to its cool and dry climate, soon made it the Bombay Presidency's monsoon capital. Globalisation knocked on Pune's doors in the 1990s, following which it went in for an image overhaul. However, some colonial-era charm was retained in a few of its old buildings and residential areas, bringing about a pleasant coexistence of the old and new, which (despite the pollution and hectic traffic) makes Pune a worthwhile place to explore. In September Ganesh Chaturthi brings on a tide of festivities across the city, and provides a fantastic window for exploring the city's cultural side. On a more sombre note, the fatal 2010 terrorist attack on the German Bakery, a once favourite haunt for travellers and ashramites alike, remains a painful memory in this peace-loving city.

The city sits at the confluence of the Mutha and Mula rivers. Mahatma Gandhi (MG) Rd, about 1km south of Pune train station, is the main commercial street. Koregaon Park, northeast of the train station, is the destination for backpackers and pilgrims. Here you'll find numerous hotels, restaurants, coffee shops and of course, the Osho Ashram.

Pune

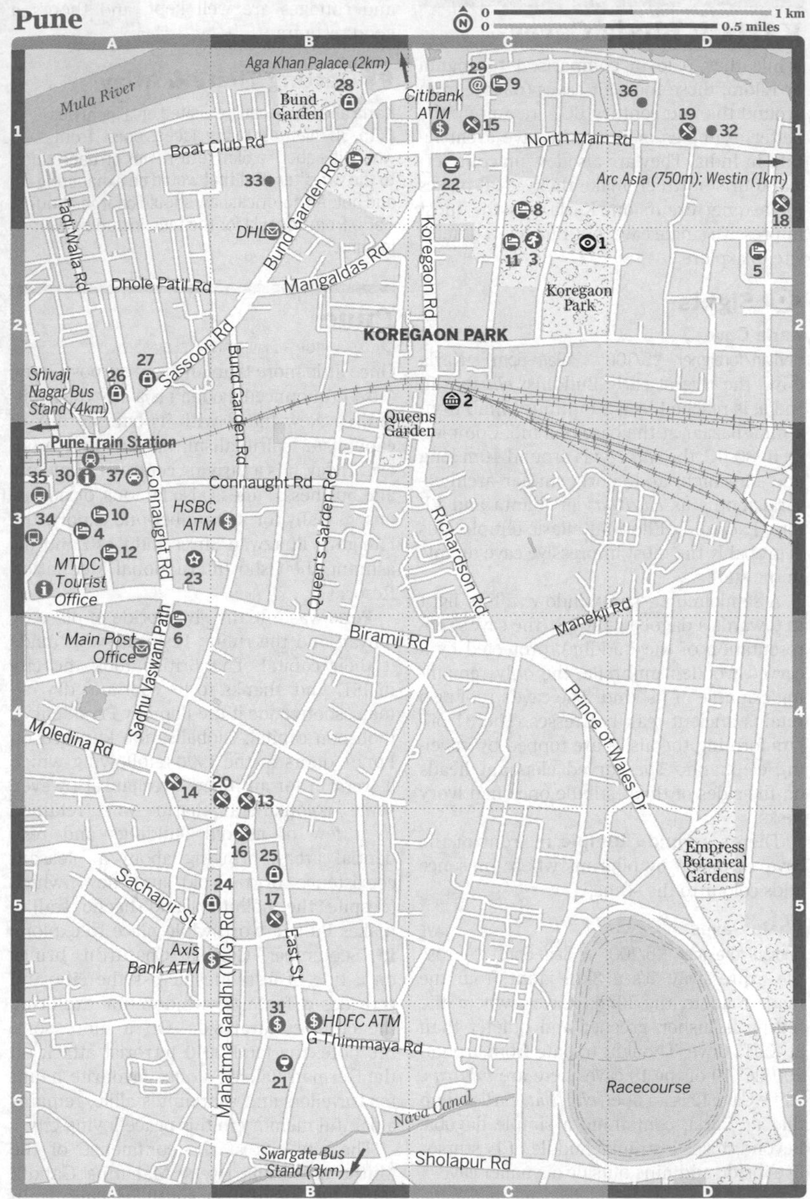

Sights & Activities

Raja Dinkar Kelkar Museum MUSEUM

(www.rajakelkarmuseum.com; Bajirao Rd, 1377-1378 Natu Baug; Indian/foreigner ₹20/200; 9.30am-5.30pm) This peculiar museum is one of Pune's true delights, housing only a fraction of the 20,000-odd objects of Indian daily life painstakingly collected by Dinkar Kelkar (who died in 1990). The quirky pan-Indian collection includes hundreds of hookah pipes, writing instruments, lamps, textiles, toys, entire doors and windows, kitchen

Pune

Sights

1 Osho Teerth Gardens ... C2
2 Tribal Cultural Museum ... C2

Activities, Courses & Tours

3 Osho International Meditation Resort ... C2

Sleeping

4 Hotel Homeland ... A3
5 Hotel Lotus ... D2
6 Hotel Ritz ... A4
7 Hotel Srimaan ... B1
8 Hotel Sunderban ... C1
9 Hotel Surya Villa ... C1
10 National Hotel ... A3
11 Osho Meditation Resort Guesthouse ... C2
12 Samrat Hotel ... A3

Eating

13 Café Barista ... B4
14 Coffee House ... A4
Dario's ... (see 8)
15 German Bakery ... C1
16 Juice World ... B5
17 Kayani Bakery ... B5
18 Malaka Spice ... D1
19 Prem's ... D1
20 The Place: Touche the Sizzler ... B4

Drinking & Nightlife

21 1000 Oaks ... B6
22 Mocha ... C1

Entertainment

23 Inox ... A3

Shopping

24 Bombay Store ... B5
25 Crossword ... B5
26 Crossword ... A2
Either Or ... (see 26)
27 Fabindia ... A2
28 Pune Central ... B1

Information

29 Internet Cafe ... C1
30 MTDC Desk ... A3
31 Thomas Cook ... B6
32 Yatra.com ... D1

Transport

33 Jet Airways ... B1
34 PMT Depot ... A3
35 Pune Train Station Stand ... A3
36 Simran Travels ... D1
37 Taxi Stand ... A3

utensils, furniture, puppets, jewellery, betel-nut cutters and an amazing gallery of musical instruments.

Tribal Cultural Museum MUSEUM
(28 Queen's Garden; admission ₹10; ⏰10.30am-5.30pm Mon-Sat) About 1.5km east of the train station, near the army cantonment, this small museum showcases artefacts (jewellery, utensils, musical instruments, even black-magic accessories) from remote tribal belts. Don't forget to check out the section featuring ornate papier-mâché festival masks, to the rear of the building.

Aga Khan Palace PALACE
(Ahmednagar Rd; Indian/foreigner ₹5/100; ⏰9am-5.45pm) Set amid a wooded 6.5-hectare plot across the Mula River in Yerwada, the grand Aga Khan Palace (housing the **Gandhi National Memorial**) is easily Pune's biggest crowd-puller. Built in 1892 by Sultan Aga Khan III, this lofty building was where the Mahatma and other prominent nationalist leaders were interned by the British for about two years following Gandhi's Quit India resolution in 1942. Both Kasturba Gandhi, the Mahatma's wife, and Mahadeobhai Desai, his secretary for 35 years, died here in confinement. You'll find their shrines (containing their ashes) in a quiet garden to the rear.

Within the main palace, you can peek into the room where Gandhi used to stay. Photos and paintings exhibit moments in his extraordinary career.

Shaniwar Wada FORT
(Shivaji Rd; Indian/foreigner ₹5/100; ⏰8am-6pm) The remains of this fortressed palace of the Peshwa rulers are located in the old part of the city. Built in 1732, Shaniwar Wada was destroyed in a fire in 1828, but the massive walls and plinths remain, as do the sturdy palace doors with their daunting spikes. In the evenings, there is an hour-long **sound-and-light show** (admission ₹25; ⏰8.15pm Thu-Tue).

Pataleshvara Cave Temple TEMPLE
(Jangali Maharaj Rd; ⏰6am-9.30pm) Set across the river is the curious rock-cut Pataleshvara Cave Temple, a small and unfinished (though living) 8th-century temple, similar in style to the grander caves at Elephanta Island. Adjacent is the **Jangali Maharaj**

Temple (⏲6am-9.30pm), dedicated to a Hindu ascetic who died here in 1818.

★Osho International Meditation Resort MEDITATION
(☎66019999; www.osho.com; 17 Koregaon Park) You'll either like it or hate it. A splurge of an institution, this ashram, located in a leafy, upscale northern suburb, has been drawing thousands of *sanyasins* (seekers), many of them Westerners, ever since the death of Osho in 1990. With its placid swimming pool, sauna, 'zennis' and basketball courts, massage and beauty parlour, bookshop and a luxury boutique guesthouse, it is, to some, the ultimate place to indulge in stress-busting meditation. Alternately, there are detractors who point fingers at the ashram's blatant commercialisation and accuse it of marketing a warped version of the mystic East to gullible Westerners.

The main centre for meditation and the nightly white-robed spiritual dance is the Osho Auditorium (no coughing or sneezing, please). The Osho Samadhi, where the guru's ashes are kept, is also open for meditation. The commune's 'Multiversity' runs a plethora of courses in meditation and other esoteric techniques. If you wish to take part, or even just meditate, you'll have to pay ₹1150/1550 (Indian/foreigner), which covers registration, a mandatory on-the-spot HIV test (sterile needles used), introductory sessions and your first day's meditation pass. You'll also need two robes (one maroon and one white, from ₹200 per robe). For subsequent days, a daily meditation pass costs ₹300/700 (Indian/foreigner), and you can come and go as you please. If you want further involvement, you can also sign up for a 'work as meditation' program.

The curious can watch a video presentation at the visitor centre and take a 10-minute silent tour of the facilities (₹10; adults only, cameras and phones prohibited) at 9.15am and 2pm daily. Tickets have to be booked at least a day in advance (9.30am to 1pm and 2pm to 4pm). It's also worth checking out the 5-hectare garden, **Osho Teerth** (admission free; ⏲6-9am & 3-6pm), behind the commune, and accessible all day for those with a meditation pass.

Ramamani Iyengar Memorial Yoga Institute YOGA
(☎25656134; www.bksiyengar.com; Model Colony, 1107 B/1 Hare Krishna Mandir Rd) To attend classes at this famous institute, 7km northwest of the train station, you need to have been practising yoga for at least eight years.

Sleeping

Pune's accommodation hubs are around the train station and Koregaon Park. Most midrange hotels have checkout at noon, and accept credit cards. Many families in

OSHO: GURU OF SEX

Ever tried mixing spirituality with primal instincts, and garnishing with oodles of expensive trinkets? Well, Bhagwan Shree Rajneesh (1931–90) certainly did. Osho, as he preferred to be called, was one of India's most flamboyant 'export gurus' to market the mystic East to the world, and undoubtedly the most controversial. Initially based in Pune, he followed no particular religion or philosophy, and outraged many across the world with his advocacy of sex as a path to enlightenment. A darling of the international media, he quickly earned himself the epithet 'sex guru'. In 1981, Rajneesh took his curious blend of Californian pop psychology and Indian mysticism to the USA, where he set up an agricultural commune in Oregon. There, his ashram's notoriety, as well as its fleet of (material and thus valueless!) Rolls Royces grew, until raging local paranoia about its activities moved the authorities to charge Osho with immigration fraud. He was fined US$400,000 and deported. An epic journey then began, during which Osho and his followers, in their search for a new base, were either deported from or denied entry into 21 countries. By 1987, he was back at his Pune ashram, where thousands of foreigners soon flocked for his nightly discourses and meditation sessions.

They still come from across the globe. Such is the demand for the resort's facilities that prices are continually on the rise, with luxury being redefined every day. Interestingly, despite Osho's comments on how nobody should be poor, no money generated by the resort goes into helping the disadvantaged. That, resort authorities maintain, is up to someone else.

Koregaon Park rent out rooms starting at about ₹500. Rickshaw drivers will know where to find homestays.

National Hotel HOTEL $

(☎26125054; 14 Sassoon Rd; s/d/q ₹750/850, cottages s/d ₹550/650) What the National can't provide in terms of comfort, it compensates for with antique charm. Housed in a crumbling colonial-era mansion opposite the train station, the spacious, low-end rooms in this hotel may not match your idea of 'clean'. The cottages across the garden are more cramped, but come with tiled sit-outs.

★Hotel Surya Villa HOTEL $$

(☎26124501; www.hotelsuryavilla.com; 294/2 Koregaon Park; s/d from ₹1490/1761, with AC ₹1761/2348; ❄) A bright and cheerful place with spotless and spacious rooms, this is one of the best of Pune's midrange options. It stands just off the Koregaon Park backpacker hub, so you're always clued in to the coolest developments in town. Decent breakfasts and other meals are available next door at the associated Yogi Tree Cafe.

★Hotel Sunderban HOTEL $$

(☎26124949; www.tghotels.com; 19 Koregaon Park; s/d incl breakfast from ₹2936/3523; ❄📶) Set around a manicured lawn right next to the Osho Resort, this renovated art-deco bungalow effortlessly combines classy antiquity with boutique appeal. The huge non-AC rooms in the main building sport a variety of dated furniture, and have a generally quaint air. The pricier rooms are across the lawns, in a sleek, glass-fronted building. An additional draw is the in-house fine-dining restaurant, Dario's (p116).

Hotel Lotus HOTEL $$

(☎26139701; www.hotelsuryavilla.com; Lane 5, Koregaon Park; s/d ₹1644/2231, with AC ₹2231/2818; ❄) Hotel Lotus is a sibling to Hotel Surya Villa, and really you are paying a bit extra for the quiet Koregaon Park location, as the rooms are not as spacious here. There's also no attached restaurant, although there are plenty of eating options close by.

Hotel Ritz HOTEL $$

(☎26122995; fax 26136644; 6 Sadhu Vaswani Path; s/d incl breakfast from ₹2348/2936; ❄) Plush, friendly, atmospheric: three words that best describe the Ritz, a Raj-era building that holds its own in town. There are just three Royal deluxe rooms in the main building, while the cheaper ones are located in an annexe next to the garden restaurant, which serves good Gujarati and Maharashtrian food. There's also safe parking and a helpful travel desk.

Hotel Homeland HOTEL $$

(☎26123203; www.hotelhomeland.net; 18 Wilson Garden; s/d ₹1050/1292, with AC from ₹1521/1755; ❄) A surprisingly restful place, Homeland is very convenient to the train station, yet tucked away from the associated din. The labyrinthine corridors lead to rooms with freshly painted walls and clean sheets, and the restaurant downstairs shows movies in the evenings.

Samrat Hotel HOTEL $$

(☎26137964; thesamrathotel@vsnl.net; 17 Wilson Garden; s/d incl breakfast from ₹2114/2583; ❄📶) A slick business-traveller hotel with excellent rooms opening around a central, top-lit foyer, this place sure knows how to make you feel special. The staff is courteous and eager to please, and the well-appointed rooms meet every expectation you could have from hotels in this price bracket. Complimentary airport pick-up.

Hotel Srimaan HOTEL $$

(☎26136565; srimaan@vsnl.com; 361/5 Bund Garden Rd; s/d ₹2936/3405; ❄@📶) A central location, free wi-fi, and a very good Italian restaurant, Little Italy La Pizzeria, earn this place plenty of points before you even step into the compact but luxurious rooms. The pricier rooms have lovely windows with soothing green views outside.

Osho Meditation Resort Guesthouse GUESTHOUSE $$$

(☎66019900; www.osho.com; Koregaon Park; s/d ₹7397/7985; ❄) This uberchic place will only allow you in if you come to meditate at the Osho International Meditation Resort. The rooms and common spaces are an elegant exercise in modern minimalist aesthetics with several ultra-luxe features, such as purified fresh-air supplied in all rooms! Be sure to book well in advance.

Westin HOTEL $$$

(☎67210000; www.starwoodhotels.com; 36/3B Koregaon Park Annexe; d incl breakfast from ₹8983; ❄📶🏊) Sprawled out like a giant luxury yacht on Koregaon Park's eastern fringes is this plush international-standard hotel, combining the best of luxury and leisure with impeccable service. The rooms offer lovely views of the river and city.

Eating

★Kayani Bakery BAKERY $

(6 East St; cakes & biscuits from per kg ₹200; ⏲7.30am-1pm & 3.30-8pm) A Raj-era institution that seems to be stuck in a time warp, where those in the know queue (in the loose sense of the word) for Shrewsbury biscuits (₹240 per kg), bread and Madeira cake.

Juice World CAFE $

(2436/B East St; snacks ₹60-70; ⏲11am-11.30pm) As well as producing delicious fresh fruit juices and shakes, this casual cafe with outdoor seating serves inexpensive but wholesome snacks such as pizza and *pav bhaji* (spiced vegetables and bread).

Coffee House CAFE $

(Moledina Rd; mains ₹60-130; ⏲8am-11.30pm) A calm and clean, coffee-coloured, almost art-deco retreat with booth seating, a huge inexpensive menu and satisfying filter coffee. Dishes include dosas and other excellent South Indian creations, plus North Indian curries and Chinese.

German Bakery BAKERY $

(North Main Rd; dishes ₹80-150, cakes ₹30-70; ⏲6.30am-11.30pm) Pune's melting pot and once compulsory halt on the Koregaon Park backpacker trail, this long-running cafe has reopened after the fatal terrorist attack in 2010. It is known for its light, healthy snacks and a good range of cakes and puddings.

★Malaka Spice ASIAN FUSION $$

(North Main Rd, Lane 5, Koregaon Park; mains ₹275-650; ⏲11.30am-11.30pm) This upscale alfresco restaurant serves mouth-watering Southeast Asian fare that is given a creative tweak or two by its star chefs. There are plenty of seafood dishes, such as the grilled kingfish in banana leaves, or the burnt garlic and shrimp rice, plus vegetarian, chicken, duck and mutton offerings. The air-con section doubles as an art gallery, while outdoor diners are kept cool with an occasional spurt from the mist machine.

Prem's MULTICUISINE $$

(North Main Rd, Koregaon Park; mains ₹140-340; ⏲8am-11.30pm) In a quiet, tree-canopied courtyard tucked away behind a commercial block, Prem's is perfect for a lazy, beer-aided lunch session. Its relaxed ambience attracts droves of loyalists throughout the day, who slouch around the tables and put away countless pints of draught and imported beers before wolfing down their 'usual' orders. The noisy sizzlers are a hit with everyone, so don't leave without trying one.

The Place: Touche the Sizzler MULTICUISINE $$

(7 Moledina Rd; mains ₹310-440; ⏲11.30am-3.30pm, 7-10.45pm) The perfect old-school eating option. A variety of smoking sizzlers (veg, seafood, beef, chicken), and other assorted Indian fare, is on offer at this Parsi-owned, family-style eatery. The ambience is 'quaint mess hall', but the overall experience more than makes up for it.

★Dario's ITALIAN $$$

(www.darios.in; Hotel Sunderban, 19 Koregaon Park, mains ₹310-380; ⏲11.30am-3pm & 7-11pm) This bistro serves only the best of Italian cuisine, made from a selection of local organic produce and hand-picked rations flown straight in from Italy. There's a yummy selection of homemade penne, gnocchi and spaghetti on offer, while dishes such as the *torta di funghi* (mushroom tart with pan-fried mushrooms, garlic, onion and chilli) serenade your palate with delicious flavours. Leave room for the tempting desserts.

Drinking & Entertainment

Pune puts a great deal of effort into its nocturnal activities, yet some pubs tend to shut up shop as quickly as they open, so ask around for the latest hot spots. Most are open from 7pm to around 1.30am.

Café Barista CAFE $

(Sterling Centre, 12 MG Rd; ⏲8am-9pm) A branch of the popular coffee chain that dishes up decent espresso coffee.

1000 Oaks NIGHTCLUB

(2417 East St; ⏲7pm-late) This one is an old favourite among Pune's tipplers, featuring a cosy pub-style bar, a compact dance floor and a charming, foliaged and moodily lit sit-out area for those who prefer it quieter. There's live music on Sundays, to go with your favourite poison.

Mocha CAFE

(North Main Rd, Koregaon Park; ⏲8am-8pm) This popular cafe was undergoing renovations at the time of research, but we expect the friendly staff and brilliant selection of coffees from around the world, from the famed Jamaican Blue Mountain to Indian Peaberry to return. There are flavoured hookahs on offer, too.

Arc Asia BAR
(ABC Farms; ⏲7.30pm-late) A classy affair, in the ABC Farms compound east of Koregaon Park. A great stock of malts, scotches and beers, with grooves on the PA.

Inox CINEMA
(Bund Garden Rd) A multiplex where you can take in the latest blockbuster from Hollywood or Mumbai.

Shopping

Bombay Store SOUVENIRS
(322 MG Rd; ⏲10.30am-8.30pm Mon-Sat) The best spot for quality souvenirs and contemporary furnishings.

Pune Central CLOTHING
(Bund Garden Rd, Koregaon Park) This glass-fronted mall is full of global labels and premium Indian tags.

Crossword BOOKS
(Sohrab Hall, RBM Rd, 1st fll; ⏲10.30am-9pm) An excellent collection of fiction, nonfiction and magazines. There's a smaller **branch** on East St.

Either Or CLOTHING
(24/25 Sohrab Hall, 21 Sassoon Rd; ⏲10.30am-8pm Fri-Wed) Modern designer Indian garments and accessories are available at this popular boutique.

Fabindia CLOTHING
(Sassoon Rd, Sakar 10; ⏲10am-8pm) For Indian saris, silks and cottons, as well as diverse accessories and handmade products.

Information

You'll find several internet cafes along Pune's main thoroughfares.

Destination Finder (₹65) provides a great map of the city, along with some key travel information.

There's a Citibank ATM on North Main Rd. HSBC dispenses cash at its main branch on Bund Garden Rd. You'll find ICICI Bank and State Bank of India ATMs at the railway station, an Axis Bank ATM on MG Rd and an HDFC Bank ATM on East St.

DHL (Bund Garden Rd; ⏲10am-8pm Mon-Sat)

Internet Cafe (Koregaon Park; per hr ₹20) A short stroll from Hotel Surya Villa.

Main Post Office (Sadhu Vaswani Path; ⏲10am-6pm Mon-Sat)

MTDC Tourist Office (☎26126867; I Block, Central Bldg, Dr Annie Besant Rd; ⏲10am-5.30pm Mon-Sat, closed 2nd and 4th Sat) Buried in a government complex south of the train station. There's also an **MTDC desk** (⏲10am-5.30pm Mon-Sat) at the train station.

Thomas Cook (☎66007903; 2418 G Thimmaya Rd; ⏲9.30am-6pm Mon-Sat) Cashes travellers cheques and exchanges foreign currency.

Yatra.com (☎65006748; www.yatra.com; North Main Rd; ⏲10am-7pm Mon-Sat) The city office of the reputed internet ticketing site of the same name.

Getting There & Away

AIR

Airlines listed below fly daily from Pune to Mumbai (from ₹5700, 45 minutes), Delhi (₹6300, two hours), Bengaluru (₹3400, 1½ hours), Nagpur (₹5600, 1½ hours), Goa (₹7500, 1½ hours), Chennai (₹6000, 1½ hours) and hopping flights to Kolkata (₹9000, four hours).

GoAir (☎9223222111; www.goair.in)

Indian Airlines (☎26052147; www.indianairlines.nic.in; 39 Dr B Ambedkar Rd)

IndiGo (☎9910383838; www.goindigo.in)

Jet Airways (☎02239893333; www.jetairways.com; 243 Century Arcade, Narangi Baug Rd)

SpiceJet (☎1800 1803333; www.spicejet.com)

MAJOR TRAINS FROM PUNE

Express fares are sleeper/2AC; Deccan Queen fares are 2nd class/chair.

DESTINATION	TRAIN NO & NAME	FARE (₹)	DURATION (HR)	DEPARTURE
Bengaluru	16529 Udyan Express	414/1735	21	11.45am
Chennai	12163 Chennai Express	465/1880	19½	12.10am
Delhi	11077 Jhelum Express	547/2295	27	5.20pm
Hyderabad	17031 Hyderabad Express	321/1320	13½	4.35pm
Mumbai CST	12124 Deccan Queen	86/355	3½	7.15am

BUS

Several private buses head to Panaji (Panjim) in Goa (ordinary/air-con sleeper ₹650/850, 12 hours), Nasik (semideluxe/deluxe ₹290/500, five hours) and Aurangabad (₹200, six hours). Pune has three bus stands:

➡ **Pune train station stand** (☎ 02026126218) For Mumbai, Goa, Belgaum, Kolhapur, Mahabaleshwar and Lonavla. Deluxe buses shuttle from here to Dadar (Mumbai) every hour (₹296, four hours).

➡ **Shivaji Nagar bus stand** (☎ 02025536970) For Aurangabad, Ahmedabad and Nasik.

➡ **Swargate bus stand** (☎ 02024441591) For Sinhagad, Bengaluru and Mangalore.

TAXI

Share taxis (up to four passengers) link Pune with Mumbai airport around the clock. They leave from the **taxi stand** (☎ 02026121090) in front of Pune train station (per seat ₹750, 2½ hours). Several tour operators hire out long-distance taxis over days or even weeks for intrastate travelling. Try **Simran Travels** (☎ 26153222; North Main Rd, Koregaon Park).

Getting Around

The airport is 8km northeast of the city, and boasts a swanky new building. An autorickshaw there costs about ₹120; a taxi is ₹300.

Autorickshaws can be found everywhere.

A ride from the train station to Koregaon Park costs about ₹40 (₹80 at night).

Turtle-paced city buses leave the **PMT depot** (opposite Pune train station) for Swargate (bus 4) and Shivaji Nagar (bus 5) and Koregaon Park (bus 159).

Around Pune

Sinhagad

The ruined **Sinhagad** (Lion Fort; admission free; ⏰ dawn-dusk), about 24km southwest of Pune, was wrested by Maratha leader Shivaji from the Bijapur kings in 1670. In the epic battle (where he lost his son Sambhaji), Shivaji is said to have used monitor lizards yoked with ropes to scale the fort's craggy walls. Today, it's a sad picture of its past, but worth visiting for the sweeping views and opportunity to hike in the hills.

From Sinhagad village, share jeeps (₹50) can cart you 10km to the base of the summit. Bus 50 runs frequently to Sinhagad village from Swargate (₹25, 45 minutes).

Shivneri

Situated 90km northwest of Pune above the village of Junnar, **Shivneri Fort** (admission free; ⏰ dawn-dusk) holds the distinction of being the birthplace of Shivaji. Within the ramparts of this ruined fort are the old royal stables, a mosque dating back to the Mughal era and several rock-cut reservoirs. The most important structure is Shivkunj, the pavilion in which Shivaji was born.

About 4km from Shivneri, on the other side of Junnar, is an interesting group of Hinayana Buddhist caves called **Lenyadri** (Indian/foreigner ₹5/100; ⏰ dawn-dusk). Of the 30-odd caves, Cave 7 is the most impressive, and interestingly houses an image of the Hindu lord Ganesh.

A bus (₹80, two hours, 7.15am) goes to Junnar from Pune's Shivaji Nagar terminus. A return bus leaves Junnar at 11.30am. A day cab from Pune will cost at least ₹2500.

Mahabaleshwar

☎ 02168 / POP 12,750 / ELEV 1372M

Up in the Western Ghats, Mahabaleshwar – founded in 1828 by British governor Sir John 'Boy' Malcolm – was, at one time, the summer capital of the Bombay presidency. However, what was once a pretty hill station oozing old-world charm is today a jungle of mindless urban construction. Swarms of raucous holiday-makers who throw the place into a complete tizzy only make things worse. Mahabaleshwar's only face-saver is the delightful views it offers, but they're not half as good in practice, given that you'll have to combat the riotous tourists while appreciating them.

The hill station virtually shuts down during the monsoons (June to September), when an unbelievable 6m of rain falls.

The action can be found in the main bazaar (Main Rd, also called Dr Sabane Rd) – a 200m strip of holiday tack. The bus stand is at the western end. You have to cough up a ₹20 'tourist tax' on arrival.

Sights & Activities

Viewpoints VIEWPOINT

The hills are alive with music, though it's usually blasted out of car stereos as people race to tick off all the viewpoints. To beat them, start very early in the morning, and you can savour fine views from **Wilson's**

Point (Sunrise Point), within easy walking distance of town, as well as **Elphinstone**, **Babington**, **Kate's** and **Lodwick Points**.

The sunset views at **Bombay Point** are stunning; but you won't be the only one thinking so! Much quieter, thanks to being 9km from town, is **Arthur's Seat**, on the edge of a 600m cliff. Attractive waterfalls around Mahabaleshwar include **Chinaman's**, **Dhobi's** and **Lingmala Falls**. A nice walk out of town is the two-hour stroll to Bombay Point, and then following **Tiger Trail** back in. Maps (₹20 to ₹65) of varying accuracy are available from several shops within the bazaar.

Tours

Leaving the bus stand thrice from 2.15pm, the MSRTC conducts a Mahabaleshwar sightseeing round (₹80, 4½ hours) taking in nine viewpoints plus Old Mahabaleshwar. Alternatively, taxi drivers will give a 15-point, 2½-hour tour for ₹450. Tours are also available to Panchgani (₹500, 2½ hours) and Pratapgad Fort (₹750, three hours).

Sleeping

Hotel prices soar during weekends and peak holidays (November to June). At other times you might get hefty discounts. Most hotels are around the main bazaar, while dozens of resort-style lodges are scattered around the village. Check out is usually at 8am or 9am. If you're a lone male Indian traveller, be aware that most hotels will be reluctant to rent you a room.

MTDC Resort HOTEL $
(☎260318; Bombay Point Rd; d from ₹1645) This large-scale operation is situated about 2km southwest from town, and comes with quieter and greener surroundings. Rooms come in various grades but all smack of government aesthetics and suffer from the incredibly damp environment. Taxis can drop you here from the city centre for about ₹50.

Hotel Panorama HOTEL $$
(☎260404; www.panoramaresorts.net; 28 MG Rd; d without/with AC from ₹4150/4750; ❄ ≋) Business meets leisure at Mahabaleshwar's most reputed midtown address. Professionally managed, it boasts clean, comfy and tastefully appointed rooms, and there's some great vegetarian food at the restaurant. There's a good-sized pool, and a water channel where you might want to ride a paddle boat.

Hotel Vyankatesh HOTEL $$
(☎260575; hotelvkt@yahoo.com; MG Rd; d from ₹2000) A typically overpriced hotel cashing in on Mahabaleshwar's never-ending tourism boom. Located behind a textile store, this place has slightly dreary, boxy rooms, but so have lots of hotels around town.

BERRY FRESH

Fruity Mahabaleshwar is India's berry-growing hub, producing some of the country's finest strawberries, raspberries and gooseberries. Harvested from November to June, the best crops come around February and can be bought fresh at Mahabaleshwar's bazaar. You can also pick up fruit drinks, sweets, squashes, fudges or jams from reputed farms such as **Mapro Gardens** (☎02168240112; ⏰10am-1pm & 2-6.30pm), halfway between Mahabaleshwar and Panchgani.

Eating & Drinking

Elsie's Dairy & Bakery BAKERY $
(MG Rd; ⏰7.30am-1pm) Since 1849 says the sign. Great for fresh cakes, biscuits, bread and nostalgia.

Aman Restaurant INDIAN $
(MG Rd; mains ₹80-150) Little more than a roadside stall, Aman can pull out some amazing kebabs and other meaty bites.

★**Grapevine** MULTICUISINE $$
(Masjid Rd; mains ₹130-350; ⏰9.30am-3pm & 5-10pm) Skip this place, and you've missed half the fun in town. Tucked away behind the main drag, this tiny restaurant serves a delectable range of Indian, Continental and Thai dishes using organic vegetables and (safe) seafood. Do try the excellent Parsi fare, including the signature *dhansak*, or the cinnamon grilled chicken sticks with harissa. A wrought-iron table set-up at the entrance tastefully lends a Mediterranean air. And the bar boasts cold beer and a smart wine list (which you can purchase by the glass or bottle).

Cafe Coffee Day CAFE
(Masjid Rd; ⌚9am-6pm) Here at Cafe Coffee Day, you may have to tell the staff to turn on the generator first, but a decent espresso is your reward for patience.

Information

Joshi's Newspaper Agency (Main Rd; per hr ₹50; ⌚9am-9pm) Slow internet access if working at all.

MTDC Tourist Office (☎260318; Bombay Point Rd) At the MTDC Resort south of town.

RB Travels (☎260251; Main Rd) Local tours, ticketing, taxi hire and bus services.

State Bank of India (Main Rd; ⌚11am-5pm Mon-Fri, 11am-1pm Sat) Handles foreign currency. ATM on Masjid Rd.

Getting There & Away

From the bus stand, state buses leave regularly for Pune (semideluxe ₹150, 3½ hours) via Panchgani (₹25, 30 minutes). There's one ordinary bus to Goa (₹370, eight hours, 8.30am) via Kolhapur (₹150, five hours), while seven buses ramble off to Mumbai Central Station (ordinary/semideluxe ₹210/275, seven hours).

Private agents in the bazaar book luxury Mercedes and Volvo buses to destinations within Maharashtra, and Goa (seat/sleeper ₹1000/1300, 12 hours, with a changeover at Surur). Remember to ask where they intend to drop you. Buses to Mumbai (₹550, 6½ hours) generally don't go beyond Borivali, while those bound for Pune (₹350) will bid you adieu at Swargate.

Getting Around

Taxis and Maruti vans near the bus stand will take you to the main viewpoints or to Panchgani.

Cycling is also an option, but be careful of speeding traffic, especially on the outskirts. Bikes can be hired from **Vasant Cycle Mart** (Main Rd; per day ₹50; ⌚8am-8pm).

Around Mahabaleshwar

Pratapgad Fort

The windy **Pratapgad Fort** (admission free; ⌚7am-7pm), built by Shivaji in 1656 (and still owned by his descendents), straddles a high mountain ridge 24km northwest of Mahabaleshwar. In 1659, Shivaji agreed to meet Bijapuri General Afzal Khan here, in an attempt to end a stalemate. Despite a no-arms agreement, Shivaji, upon greeting Khan, disembowelled his enemy with a set of iron *baghnakh* (tiger's claws). Khan's tomb (out of bounds) marks the site of this painful encounter at the base of the fort.

Pratapgad is reached by a 500-step climb that affords brilliant views. Guides are available for ₹200 who will take you to 20 points of interest taking nearly two hours. The state bus (₹90 return, one hour, 9.30am) does a daily shuttle from Mahabaleshwar, with a waiting time of around one hour. A return taxi ride (2½ hours' waiting time) is about ₹750.

Raigad Fort

Some 80km from Mahabaleshwar, all alone on a high and remote hilltop, stands the enthralling **Raigad Fort** (Indian/foreigner ₹5/100; ⌚8am-5.30pm). Having served as Shivaji's capital from 1648 until his death in 1680, the fort was later sacked by the British, and some colonial structures added. But monuments such as the royal court, plinths of royal chambers, the main marketplace and Shivaji's tomb still remain, and it's worth a day's excursion.

You can hike a crazy 1475 steps to the top. But for a more 'levitating' experience, take the vertigo-inducing **ropeway** (return ₹175; ⌚8.30am-5.30pm), which zooms up the cliff and offers an eagle-eye view of the deep gorges below. Guides (₹200) are available within the fort complex. **Sarja Restaurant** (snacks ₹30-100), adjoining the ropeway's base terminal, is a good place for lunch or snacks.

Public transport to Raigad is infrequent and the road from Mahabaleshwar is in a terrible state. A return taxi from Mahabaleshwar will cost at least ₹2500.

Kolhapur

☎0231 / POP 549,283 / ELEV 550M

A little-visited town, Kolhapur is the perfect place to get intimate with the flamboyant side of India. Only a few hours from Goa, this historic town boasts an intensely fascinating temple complex. In August, Kolhapur is at its vibrant best, when **Naag Panchami** (⌚Jul/Aug), a snake-worshipping festival, is held in tandem with one at Pune. Gastronomes take note: the town is also the birthplace of the famed, spicy Kolhapuri cuisine, especially chicken and mutton dishes.

The old town around the Mahalaxmi Temple is 3km southwest of the bus and train stations, while the 'new' palace is a similar distance to the north. Rankala Lake, a popular spot for evening strolls, is 5km southwest of the stations.

Sights

★ Shree Chhatrapati Shahu Museum MUSEUM
(Indian/foreigner ₹18/30; ⏲9.30am-5.30pm) 'Bizarre' takes on a whole new meaning at this 'new' palace, an Indo-Saracenic behemoth designed by British architect 'Mad' Charles Mant for the Kolhapur kings in 1884. The ground floor houses a madcap museum, featuring countless trophies from the eponymous king's trigger-happy jungle safaris, which were put to some ingenious uses, including walking sticks made from leopard vertebrae, and ashtrays fashioned out of tiger skulls and rhino feet. Then, there's an armoury, which houses enough weapons to stage a mini coup. The horror-house effect is brought full circle by the taxidermy section. However, don't forget to visit the ornate durbar hall, where the erstwhile rulers held court sessions. Photography inside is strictly prohibited. A rickshaw from the train station will cost ₹30.

Old Town AREA
Kolhapur's atmospheric old town is built around the lively and colourful **Mahalaxmi Temple** (⏲5am-10.30pm) dedicated to Amba Bai, or the Mother Goddess. The temple's origins date back to AD 10, and it's one of the most important Amba Bai temples in India. Non-Hindus are welcome. Nearby, past a foyer in the Old Palace, is **Bhavani Mandap** (⏲6am-8pm), dedicated to the goddess Bhavani.

Kolhapur is famed for the calibre of its wrestlers, and at the **Motibag Thalim**, a courtyard reached through a low doorway and passage beside the entrance to Bhavani Mandap (ask for directions), young athletes train in a muddy pit. You are free to walk in and watch, as long as you don't mind the sight of sweaty, semi-naked men and the stench of urine emanating from the loos. Professional matches are held between June and December in the **Kasbagh Maidan**, a red-earth arena a short walk south of Motibag Thalim.

Shopaholics, meanwhile, can browse for the renowned Kolhapuri leather sandals, prized for their intricate needlework. Most designs are priced from ₹300 to ₹500. The break-in blisters on your feet come free of charge.

Sleeping & Eating

Hotel Tourist HOTEL $
(☎2650421; www.hoteltourist.co.in; Station Rd; s/d incl breakfast from ₹888/1099, with AC ₹1480/1714; ❄) This is one of the better places on the main street, offering cosy though minimalist rooms. There's an acclaimed restaurant serving great veg food, and welcoming staff.

Hotel Panchshil $$
(☎2537517; www.hotelpanchshilkolhapur.com; 517 A2 Shivaji Park; s/d incl breakfast ₹1937/2348, with AC ₹2583/3053; ❄📶) This professionally run business hotel, with a helpful front desk, has an underwhelming plain brown decor. Nevertheless, the spacious, clean rooms with TV and internet are comfortable, there's also a complimentary business centre, and best of all, there's a branch of **Little Italy** (Shivaji Park; mains ₹250-450), the Italian restaurant chain, downstairs.

Hotel Pavillion HOTEL $$
(☎2652751; www.hotelpavillion.co.in; 392 Assembly Rd; s/d incl breakfast ₹1350/1585, with AC from ₹1761/1996; ❄@) Located at the far end of a leafy park-cum-office area, this Mediterranean-style hotel guarantees a peaceful stay in large, clean rooms with windows that open out to delightful views of seasonal blossoms. It's very close to the MTDC office.

Hotel Pearl HOTEL $$
(☎6684451; reservation@hotelpearl.biz; New Shahupuri; s/d incl breakfast ₹2583/2936, with AC from ₹3170/3757; ❄@) Modelled on big-city business hotels, this place has good rooms, a spa, a travel desk and a decent, pure veg, multi-cuisine restaurant.

Surabhi INDIAN $
(Hotel Sahyadri Bldg; mains ₹70-100) Close to the bustling bus stand, Surabhi is a great place to savour Kolhapur's legendary snacks such as the spicy *misal* (puffed rice tossed with fried rounds of dough, lentils, onions, herbs and chutneys), thalis and lassi. Saawan Dining Hall, located alongside, serves nonveg food.

Information

Axis Bank ATM Twenty-four-hour ATM near Mahalaxmi Temple.

Internet Zone (Station Rd, Kedar Complex; per hr ₹20; ⌚8am-11pm) Internet access.

MTDC Tourist Office (☎2652935; Assembly Rd; ⌚10am-5.30pm Mon-Sat) Opposite the Collector's Office.

State Bank of India (Udyamnagar; ⌚10am-2pm Mon-Sat) A short autorickshaw ride southwest of the train station near Hutatma Park. Handles foreign exchange. There's also a 24-hour **ATM** (Indumati Rd), parallel to Station Rd.

Getting There & Around

Autorickshaws are abundant in Kolhapur and many drivers carry conversion charts to calculate fares from the outdated meters.

From the bus stand, services head regularly to Pune (semideluxe/deluxe ₹262/449, five hours) and Ratnagiri (ordinary/semideluxe ₹115/154, four hours). Most private bus agents are on the western side of the square at Mahalaxmi Chambers, across from the bus stand. Overnight services with AC head to Mumbai (seat/sleeper ₹450/750, nine hours) and non-AC overnighters go to Panaji (₹245, 5½ hours).

The train station, which is known as Chattrapati Shahu Maharaj Terminus, is 10 minutes' walk west of the bus stand. Three daily expresses, including the 10.50pm Sahyadri Express, zoom to Mumbai (sleeper/2AC ₹302/1195, 13 hours) via Pune (sleeper/2AC ₹236/855, eight hours). The Rani Chennama Express makes the long voyage to Bengaluru (sleeper/2AC ₹371/1575, 17½ hours, 2.20pm).

Kolhapur airport was not operational at the time of research.

Goa

Includes ➡

Best Places to Eat

- Upper House (p133)
- Fiesta (p145)
- La Plage (p152)
- Plantain Leaf (p145)
- Seafood at seasonal beach shacks (all over)

Best Beaches

- Palolem (p161)
- Mandrem (p152)
- Cola Beach (p160)
- Anjuna (p146)
- Arambol (p153)

Why Go?

Goa is like no other state in India. It may be the Portuguese colonial influence, the endless beaches, the glorious whitewashed churches or the relaxed culture of *susegad* – a uniquely Goan term that translates loosely to 'laid-backness' and is evident in all aspects of daily life and the Goan people themselves.

But Goa is far more than its old-school reputation as a hippie haven or its relatively new status as a package-holiday beach getaway. Goa is as beautiful and culturally rich as it is tiny and hassle-free, so you can go birdwatching in a butterfly-filled forest, marvel at centuries-old cathedrals, venture out to white-water waterfalls or meander the capital's charming alleyways. Add a dash of Portuguese-influenced food and architecture, infuse with a colourful blend of religious traditions, pepper with parties, and you've got a heady mix that makes Goa easy to enjoy and extremely hard to leave.

When to Go

Goa (Panaji)

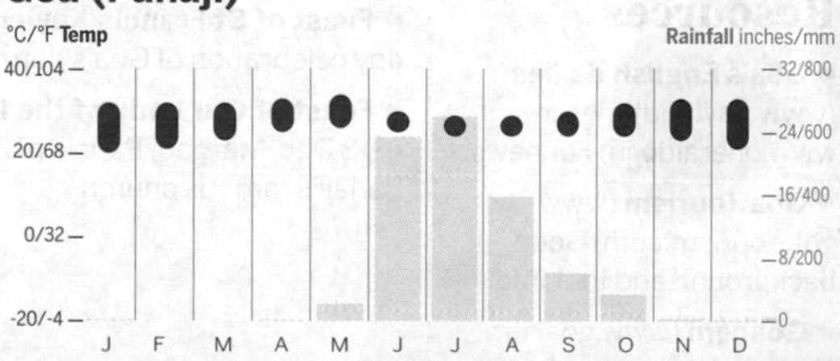

Early Nov Post-monsoon, the shacks and beach huts are up but the crowds are still down.

Early Dec Festivals, Christmas spirit and great weather, before the peak prices and crowds.

Mar Carnival and Easter celebrations as the season winds down.

MAIN POINTS OF ENTRY

Dabolim Airport handles all flights, Margao (Madgaon) Railway Station is the state's largest and best connected; Mapusa, Panaji and Margao bus terminals for long-distance rides.

Fast Facts

➡ **Population:** 1.46 million

➡ **Area:** 3702 sq km

➡ **Capital:** Panaji (Panjim)

➡ **Telephone code:** ☎ 0832

➡ **Main languages:** Konkani, Marathi, English and Hindi

➡ **Sleeping prices: $** below ₹1200, **$$** ₹1200 to ₹4000, **$$$** above ₹4000

Top Tips

➡ Don't swim wasted!

➡ If you can handle the Christmas and New Year crowds, this is a fun time but book well ahead and expect to pay for the privilege.

Resources

➡ **Goa's English dailies** (www.navhindtimes.in, www.oheraldo.in) For news.

➡ **Goa Tourism** (www.goa-tourism.com) Good background and tour info.

➡ **Goacom** (www.goacom.com) Goa's news and views.

➡ **Lonely Planet** (www.lonelyplanet.com/india/goa) For planning advice, author recommendations, traveller reviews and insider tips.

Food & Drink

Goan cuisine is a tantalising fusion of Portuguese and South Indian flavours. Goans tend to be hearty meat and fish eaters, and fresh seafood is a staple, as is the quintessential Goan lunch 'fish-curry-rice': fried mackerel steeped in coconut, tamarind and chilli sauce. Traditional dishes include vindaloo (fiery dish in a marinade of vinegar and garlic) or *xacuti* (a spicy chicken or meat dish cooked in red coconut sauce). For dessert try the layered bebinca.

The traditional Goan drink is *feni*, a double-distilled fiery liqour made from the cashew fruit or palm toddy.

DON'T MISS

There's little chance of missing the **beach** – much of Goa's 100km of Arabian Sea coastline has some spectacular stretches. Dining on **fresh seafood** at one of the many beach shacks up and down the coast is a must. Goa has a fascinating colonial **history** that also shouldn't be missed: set aside some time to explore evocative Panaji (Panjim), Old Goa, Quepem and Chandor.

Top State Festivals

➡ **Feast of the Three Kings** (⏲ 6 Jan, Chandor, p157, & Reis Magos) Boys re-enact the story of the three kings bearing gifts for Christ.

➡ **Shigmotsav (Shigmo) of Holi** (⏲ Feb/Mar, statewide) Goa's version of the Hindu festival Holi sees coloured powders thrown about and parades in most towns.

➡ **Sabado Gordo** (⏲ Feb/Mar, Panaji, p132) A procession of floats and street parties on the Saturday before Lent.

➡ **Carnival** (⏲ Mar, statewide) A four-day festival kicking off Lent; the party's particularly jubilant in Panaji (p132).

➡ **Fama de Menino Jesus** (⏲ 2nd Mon in Oct, Colva, p158) Colva's Menino Jesus statue is paraded about town.

➡ **Feast of St Francis Xavier** (⏲ 3 Dec, Old Goa, p135) A 10-day celebration of Goa's patron saint.

➡ **Feast of Our Lady of the Immaculate Conception** (⏲ 8 Dec, Margao, Panaji, p129) Fairs and concerts around Panaji's famous church.

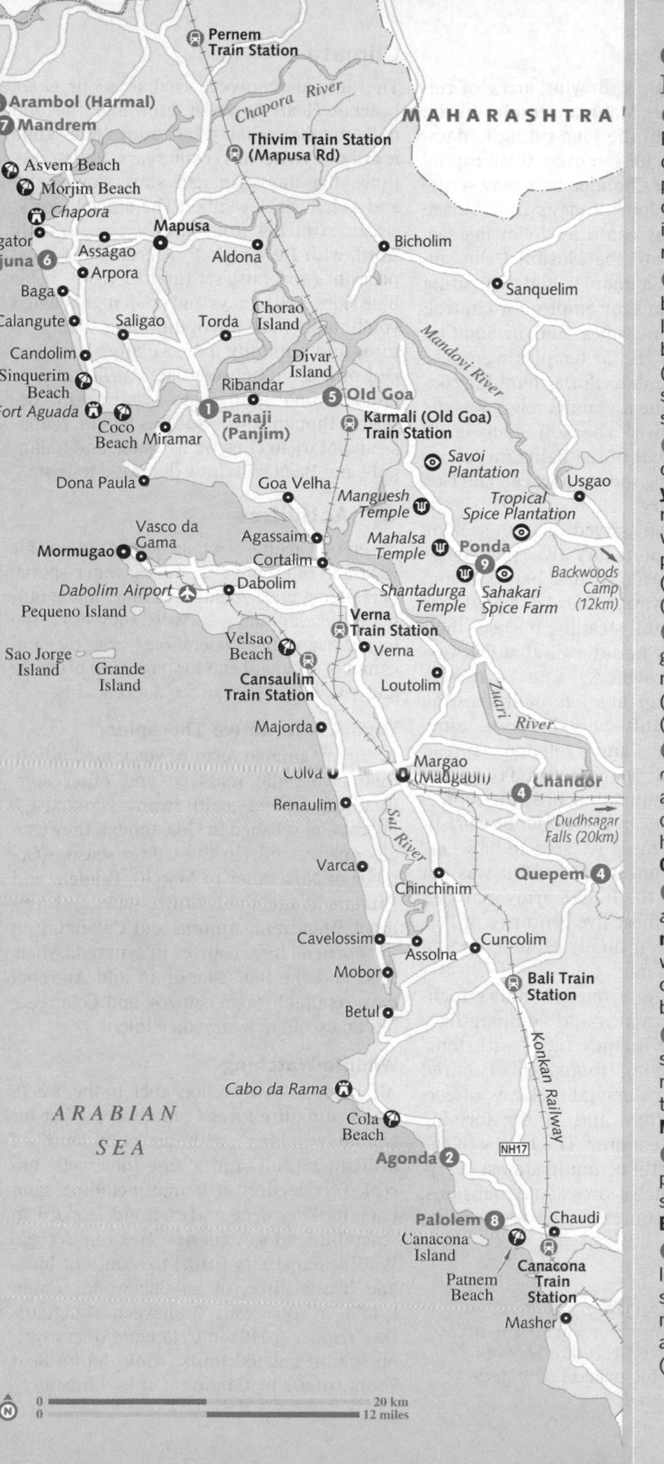

Goa Highlights

1. Wander the Portuguese quarters of **Panaji** (Panjim; p129) and linger over lunch at one of its traditional Goan restaurants
2. Indulge in barefoot luxury on long white-sand beaches, like **Agonda** (p160), in the state's sleepy southern stretches
3. Open up your chakras while doing **yoga** (p126) to the rhythm of ocean waves and swaying palms at Mandrem (p152) and Arambol (p153)
4. Dream of times gone by in the mansions of **Quepem** (p154) and **Chandor** (p157)
5. Bask in the glory of grand cathedrals and observe the countryside from a hilltop chapel in **Old Goa** (p135)
6. Bargain hard at **Anjuna's flea market** (p149) then watch the sunset over a Kingfisher at a beachside bar
7. Worship the sun away from the northern crowds on the beautiful beach at **Mandrem** (p152)
8. Kayak out to see playful dolphins at sunset at **Palolem Beach** (p161)
9. Spend a day learning about the spices that first made Goa famous at a **spice plantation** (p138) near Ponda

History

Goa went through a dizzying array of rulers from Ashoka's Mauryan empire in the 3rd century BC to the long-ruling Kadambas, who in AD 1054 moved their capital from present-day Chandor to a new settlement called Govepuri, today's little village of Goa Velha. The centuries following saw much conflict, with the Muslim Delhi sultanate and then Bahmani sultanate fighting the Hindu Vijayanagar empire for control; these were violent times, and in addition to many deaths, Hindu temples were also razed. (Tiny Tambdi Surla temple, constructed during the Kadamba reign, was the only one to survive.) The Adil Shahs of Bijapur, formerly part of the Bahmani sultanate, created the capital we now call Old Goa in the 15th century.

The Portuguese arrived in 1510, seeking control of the region's lucrative spice routes by way of Goa's wide natural harbours and plentiful waterways. They defeated the Bijapur kings and steadily pushed their power from their grand capital at Old Goa out into the provinces. (The Goa State Museum in Panaji has lots of interesting artefacts from this period.) Soon after, Portuguese rule and religion spread throughout the state – sometimes by force – and the Goan Inquisition brought repression and brutality in the name of Christianity. The Portuguese resisted India's 1947 Independence from Britain and it was not until 1961, when the Indian army marched into Goa, that almost five centuries of Portuguese occupation finally came to an end on the subcontinent.

Today Goa enjoys one of India's highest per-capita incomes and comparatively high health and literacy rates, with tourism, iron-ore mining (though this is mired in political controversy and claims of corruption), agriculture and fishing forming the basis of its economy. The legacy of the Portuguese can still be found almost everywhere, in the state's scores of old mansions, its cuisine, its churches and even in its language.

> **EMERGENCIES**
>
> Dial ☎108 in an emergency. This will connect you to the police, fire brigade or medical services.

Climate

The annual monsoon used to scour Goa's beaches clean between June and the end of September reliably, but things have gone a little haywire in recent years, and sometimes the monsoon can start slowly and end as late as November. The official tourist season stretches from mid-October to early April, with December to February the most pleasant (and busiest) time to visit – clear blue skies, warm days and crisp nights when you'll rarely need airconditioning. Temperatures and humidity increase after February. Out of season, between late April and September, you'll find most coastal resorts deserted, though towns such as Panaji, Mapusa and Margao chug on as usual, and Calangute and Baga still draw domestic tourists.

 Activities

In season Goa has a whole host of options for yoga and alternative therapies, water sports, paragliding and wildlife-watching. Many outfits change annually, so we've only listed the longer-established operations; for the full gamut of options, head to your beach of choice and ask around or scan the noticeboards.

Yoga & Alternative Therapies

Every imaginable form of yoga, meditation, reiki, ayurvedic massage and other spiritually orientated health regime is practised, taught and relished in Goa, though they usually operate only in the winter season (October or November to March). Palolem and Patnem, in the south of the state, and Arambol, Mandrem, Anjuna and Calangute in the north all have courses in ayurveda, yoga, reiki and the like. Mandrem and Arambol have reputable yoga centres, and Calangute has an excellent ayurveda clinic.

Wildlife-Watching

Although many travellers stick to the beach, Goa is a nature lover's paradise, perfect for wildlife-watching, with an abundance of brilliant birdlife and a fine (but well concealed) collection of fauna, including sambars, barking deer and the odd leopard in several inland sanctuaries. Head to Cotigao Wildlife Sanctuary (p161) to scout out birds and beasts alike, or to Backwoods Camp (p137) in Bhagwan Mahaveer Sanctuary. Day Tripper (p142) in Calangute offers various nature-related tours, while John's Boat Tours (p140) in Candolim runs birdwatch-

THINK LIKE THE LOCALS...

Venture beyond the tourist areas and you're sure to find locals who will sadly shake their heads and say that Goa has changed for the worse. The spread of serious drug use amongst locals, overdevelopment and environmental damage, and Goa's growing reputation within India as a place for bad behaviour are the dark underbelly to its tropical paradise. You can help repair Goa's image by following a few simple steps:

➡ Away from the beaches, adopt the same, more modest dress that you would in other parts of the country. This generally means shoulders and knees covered, and keeping your shirt on. Nude or topless sunbathing is illegal in Goa and can result in fines.

➡ Keep your naughtiest behaviour confined to appropriate venues. Partying into the night with illegal substances at a family guesthouse might disturb the owners, not to mention attracting the authorities.

➡ Women should be cautious when partying; rape, sadly, has been an issue in Goa, and though we don't believe (as many do) that bikinis are to blame, it makes sense to be in control of your surroundings.

ing boat trips, along with crocodile- and dolphin-spotting rides.

Water Sports

Based in Baga, Barracuda Diving (p142), offers scuba diving courses and trips. Parasailing and jet-skiing are readily available on the beaches at Baga, Benaulim and Colva, and you can try paragliding at Anjuna and Arambol. Palolem, with its relatively calm waters, is the best place for kayaking.

Dangers & Annoyances

One of the most deceptive dangers in Goa is to be found right in front of your beautiful bit of beach: the Arabian Sea, with its strong currents and dangerous undertows, claims dozens of lives each year, many of them foreigners who knew how to swim. All of Goa's popular beaches are now overseen by lifeguards during daylight hours with patrolled swimming areas marked by flags, but it's extremely important to heed local warnings, and don't venture into the water after drinking or taking drugs, especially at night.

Other dangers and annoyances are of the rather more universal kind. Keep your valuables under lock and key, especially if you're renting an easy-to-penetrate cocohut, and don't walk along empty stretches of beach alone at night.

One of the pleasures of Goa is being able to get around on a cheaply hired scooter or motorbike, but lots of tourists come unstuck on the road. Traffic can be heavy and unpredictable in tourist areas and around towns: ride with care, don't ride intoxicated and wear a helmet (compulsory in Goa since 2012). Also be sure to carry your licence and the bike's registration papers to avoid unwanted police attention.

DRUGS

Acid, ecstasy, cocaine, charas (hashish), marijuana and all other forms of recreational drugs are illegal in India (though still very much available in Goa), and purchasing or carrying drugs is fraught with danger. Goa's Fort Aguada jail is filled with prisoners, including some foreigners, serving lengthy sentences for drug offences, and being caught in possession of even a small quantity of illegal substances can mean a 10-year stretch in a cockroach-infested cell.

Information

The **Goa Tourism Development Corporation** (GTDC; www.goa-tourism.com), also known as Goa Tourism, provides maps and information, operates average hotels throughout the state and runs a host of one-day and multiday tours. Its main office is in Panaji, but you can book tours and get a simple map of Goa at any of its hotel branches. Panaji's Indiatourism (p135) office also has information on Goa.

ACCOMMODATION

Accommodation prices in Goa are generally higher than in most other states of India and vary wildly depending on the season. High-season prices, often more than twice the mid-season rates, run from early December to early February, while prices climb higher to a peak rate during the crowded Christmas and New Year period (around 22 December to 3 January). Mid-season runs from the mid-October through November (when most beach shacks are just being built) and from February to April, and low season runs through the rainy season (April to October). All accommodation rates listed are for the high season – *not* the peak Christmas period, when you'll almost certainly have to book ahead anyway. Prices can still fluctuate from year to year, and some hotels may bump up their high-season tariffs more than others depending on demand. Always call ahead for rates. Most accommodation options have a standard noon checkout, except in Panaji, where many hotels cruelly demand you depart at 9am or earlier.

Getting There & Away

AIR

Goa's sole and diminutive airport, Dabolim, is 29km south of Panaji, 30km north of Margao and an easy taxi ride from any of the state's beaches. Few international flights go here directly; those that do are package-holiday charters, mostly from Russia, Europe and Britain. Independent travellers from the UK could check **Thomson** (www.thomsonfly.com), and from Germany, **Condor** (www.condor.com); both offer direct flight-only fares. Generally, the quickest way to reach Goa from anywhere else overseas is to take a flight into Mumbai (Bombay) or Chennai (Madras), and then a one-hour hop by domestic airline to Goa. There are plenty of domestic flights daily through Jet Airways, SpiceJet, Air India and several other budget airlines to most major capitals.

Dabolim Airport has a money-exchange office, a GTDC counter, charter-airline offices, an ATM and two prepaid taxi booths.

BUS

Plenty of long-distance interstate buses – both 'government' and 'private' – operate to and from Panaji, Margao, Mapusa and Chaudi, near Palolem. Fares for private operators are only slightly higher than for Kadamba government buses, and they fluctuate throughout the year. Long-distance buses can be standard, air-conditioned (AC), Volvo (the most comfortable seater buses) and sleeper. Sleeper buses have improved over the years to include sidebars or even fully-reclining seats, but this is not like travelling on a train – be prepared to be thrown out of your bed while hurtling round a corner at 3am! Most interstate buses depart between 6pm and 10pm.

TRAIN

The **Konkan Railway** (www.konkanrailway.com), the main train line running through Goa, runs between Mumbai and Mangalore. The biggest station in Goa is Margao's Madgaon station, from which there are several useful daily services to Mumbai. Other smaller useful stations on the line include Pernem for Arambol, Thivim for Mapusa and the northern beaches, Karmali (Old Goa) for Panaji, and Canacona for Palolem.

Book tickets online; at Madgaon station; at the train reservation office at Panaji's Kadamba bus stand; or at any travel agent vending train tickets (though you'll pay a small commission). Only the stations at Margao and Vasco da Gama (near Dabolim Airport) have foreign-tourist-quota booking counters. Book as far in advance as possible for sleepers, since they fill up very quickly.

Getting Around

TO/FROM THE AIRPORT

Dabolim's two prepaid taxi counters – one in the arrivals hall and the other just outside – make arriving easy; buy your ticket here and you'll be ushered to a cab. Real budgeteers without much luggage can try walking out to the main road and waving down one of the frequent buses heading east from Vasco da Gama to Margao and catch onward transport from there.

BUS

Goa has an extensive network of buses, shuttling to and from almost every town and village. They run frequently and have no numbers, and fares rarely exceed ₹30. Buses are in fairly good condition and tend to be pretty efficient.

CAR & MOTORCYCLE

It's easy in Goa to organise a private car with a driver for long-distance day trips. Prices vary, but you should bank on paying from ₹1000 (if you're lucky) to ₹1500 for a full day out on the road (usually defined as eight hours and 80km). It's also possible, if you have the nerves and the need to feel independent, to procure a self-drive car. A small Maruti will cost from ₹700 to ₹1000 per day and a jeep around ₹1200 to ₹1400, excluding petrol and usually with a kilometre limit. Your best bet for rental is online at sites like www.mygoatour.com or www.goa2u.com. Note the slightly mystifying signposts posted on Goa's major National Highway 17 (NH17), which advise of different speed limits (on the largely single-carriageway road) for different types of vehicles.

You'll rarely go far on a Goan road without seeing a tourist whizzing by on a scooter or motorbike, and renting (if not riding) one is a breeze. You'll likely pay from ₹200 to ₹300 per day for a scooter, ₹400 for a smaller Yamaha motorbike, and ₹500 for a Royal Enfield Bullet. These prices can drop considerably if you're renting for more than a few days or if it's an off-peak period – it's all supply and demand, so bargain if there are lots of machines around. You'll find them hanging around the taxi/bus stand at any beach resort or near the post office in Panaji.

Bear in mind that Goan roads – while better than many Indian roads – can be treacherous, filled with human, bovine, canine, feline, mechanical and avian obstacles, as well as a good sprinkling of potholes and hairpin bends. Take it slowly, try not to drive at night (when black cows can prove dangerous), don't attempt a north–south day trip on a 50CC scooter, and ask for a helmet – a law which has routinely been ignored by Goans and tourists alike over the years but is now compulsory.

TAXI & AUTORICKSHAW

Taxis are widely available for town-hopping, and, as with a chauffeured car, a full day's sightseeing, depending on the distance, will be around ₹1500. Unlike elsewhere in India, autorickshaws are not much cheaper than taxis and are not as common, but they're still good for short trips. Motorcycles, known as 'pilots', are also a licensed form of taxi in Goa. They're cheap, easy to find and can be identified by a yellow front mudguard – and even the heftiest of backpacks seems to be no obstacle.

CENTRAL GOA

Panaji (Panjim)

POP 115,000

One of India's most relaxed state capitals, Panaji (more commonly known as Panjim) sits at the mouth of the broad Mandovi River, where paddle-wheel boats and floating casinos ply the waters and giant neon advertising signs cast reflections in the night. A glorious whitewashed church lords over the city centre and grand colonial buildings rub shoulders with arty boutiques, old-school bookshops and backstreet bars.

But it's the tangle of narrow streets in the old quarter that really steal the show. Nowhere is the Portuguese influence felt more strongly than here, where the late afternoon sun lights up yellow houses with purple doors, and around each corner you'll find crumbling ochre-coloured mansions with wrought-iron balconies and cats lying in front of bicycles parked beneath oyster-shell windows. Panjim is a place for walking, enjoying the peace of the afternoon siesta, eating well and meeting real Goans. It's not to be missed.

Sights & Activities

One of the pleasures of Panaji is long, leisurely strolls through the sleepy Portuguese-era Sao Tomé, Fontainhas and Altinho districts.

★Church of Our Lady of the Immaculate Conception CHURCH
(cnr Emilio Gracia & Jose Falcao Rds; ⏲10am-12.30pm & 3-5.30pm Mon-Sat, 11am-12.30pm & 3.30-5pm Sun) Panaji's spiritual and geographical centre is its gleamingly white and oh-so-photogenic main church, consecrated in 1541. When Panaji was little more than a sleepy fishing village this place was the first port of call for sailors from Lisbon, who would clamber up here to thank their lucky stars for a safe crossing before continuing to Old Goa, the state's capital until the 19th century, further east up the river. It's usually closed in the evening, but the exterior is wonderfully illuminated at night. Mass in English is held at 8am weekdays and 8.15am Sunday.

Goa State Museum MUSEUM
(☎2438006; www.goamuseum.gov.in; EDC Complex, Patto; ⏲9am-5.30pm Mon-Sat) FREE This spacious museum, in the developing Patto area near the bus stand, has a sleepy feel and an intriguing hodgepodge of exhibits. In addition to Hindu and Jain sculptures and bronzes, the museum has a good collection of wooden Christian sculptures, a room devoted to the history of print in Goa (replete with hulking old-school presses), an exhibition on Goa's freedom fighters, and nice examples of Portuguese-era furniture, including an elaborately carved table used during the notoriously brutal Portuguese Inquisition in Goa.

Secretariat Building HISTORIC BUILDING
(Avenida Dom Joao Castro) This colonial-era building is on the site of Bijapur Sultan Yusef Adil Shah's summer palace. The current structure dates from the 16th century and became the Portuguese viceroy's official residence in 1759. Nowadays it houses less exciting government offices, but as the oldest colonial buildings in town it's worth a gaze. Immediately to the west, the compelling **statue** of a man bearing down upon a supine female form depicts Abbé Faria, a Goan priest, 'father of hypnotism' and friend of Napoleon, in melodramatic throes.

Menezes Braganza Institute HISTORIC BUILDING
(Malaca Rd) This beautiful early 20th-century affair is worth dropping into to see the pretty blue-and-white *azulejos* (glazed ceramic-tile compositions) in the entrance hall.

Campal NEIGHBOURHOOD
The Campal neighbourhood, to the west of Panaji, is home to some green spaces that are perfect for whiling away an afternoon. Goa's premier cultural centre, Kala Academy (p134) has a lovely campus, with an art gallery, a lighthouse, pier and benches along

Panaji (Panjim)

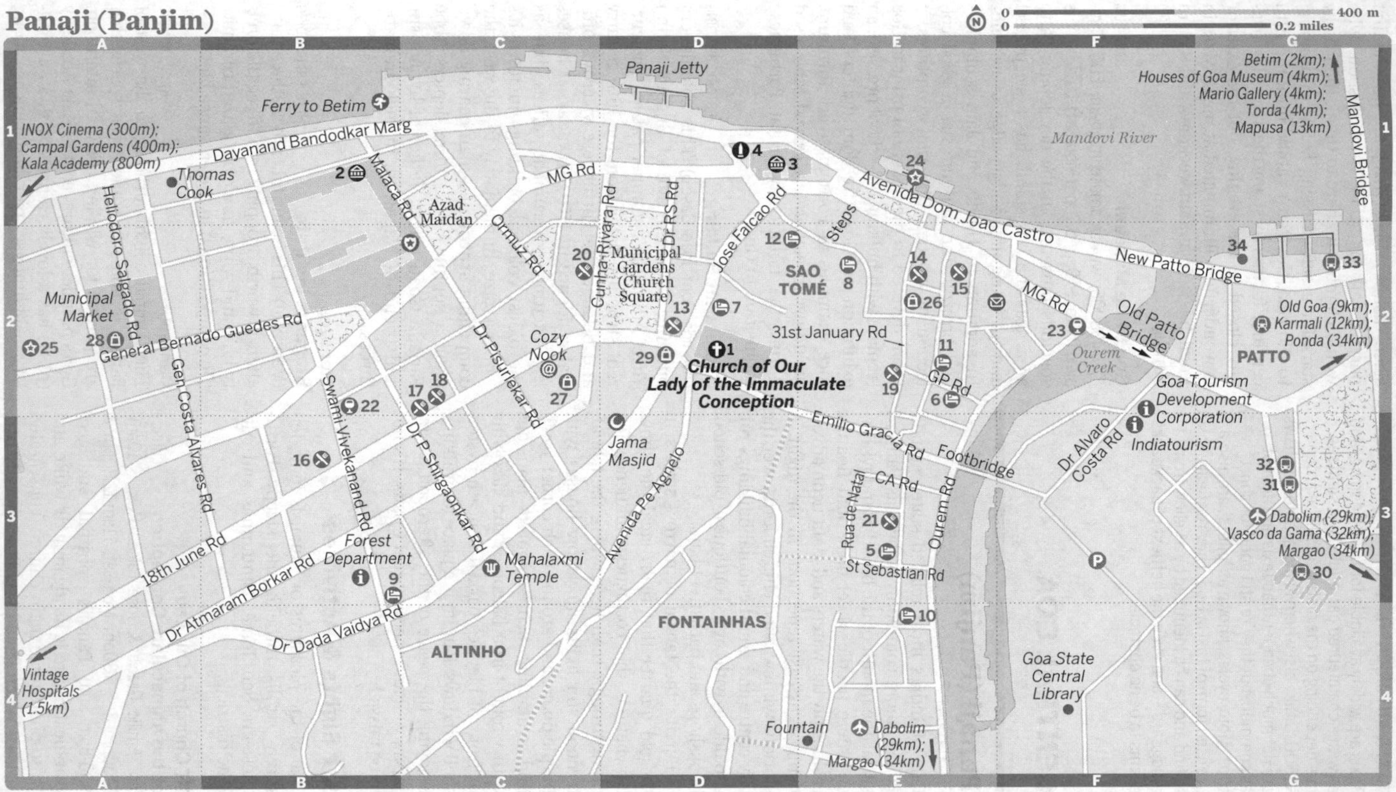

0 400 m
0 0.2 miles

A B C D E F G
1 2 3 4

Panaji Jetty
Ferry to Betim
Mandovi River
Mandovi Bridge
Betim (2km); Houses of Goa Museum (4km); Mario Gallery (4km); Torda (4km); Mapusa (13km)
INOX Cinema (300m); Campal Gardens (400m); Kala Academy (800m)
Dayanand Bandodkar Marg
Thomas Cook
2
Malaca Rd
Azad Maidan
MG Rd
Ormuz Rd
4
3
24
Avenida Dom Joao Castro
New Patto Bridge
34
33
Cunha-Rivara Rd
Dr RS Rd
Jose Falcao Rd
20
Municipal Gardens (Church Square)
12
Steps
SAO TOMÉ
8
14
15
26
MG Rd
Municipal Market
Heliodoro Salgado Rd
28
25
General Bernado Guedes Rd
13
7
31st January Rd
Old Patto Bridge
23
Ourem Creek
Old Goa (9km); Karmali (12km); Ponda (34km)
PATTO
Cozy Nook
Dr Pisurlekar Rd
29
1
Church of Our Lady of the Immaculate Conception
11
19
GP Rd
6
Goa Tourism Development Corporation
Indiatourism
27
17
18
22
Swami Vivekanand Rd
Dr P Shirgaonkar Rd
Gen Costa Alvares Rd
16
Jama Masjid
Emilio Gracia Rd
Footbridge
Dr Alvaro Costa Rd
32
31
CA Rd
Rua de Natal
21
5
Ourem Rd
St Sebastian Rd
Dabolim (29km); Vasco da Gama (32km); Margao (34km)
30
Avenida Pe Agnelo
18th June Rd
Forest Department
9
Mahalaxmi Temple
Dr Atmaram Borkar Rd
Dr Dada Vaidya Rd
10
FONTAINHAS
ALTINHO
Goa State Central Library
Vintage Hospitals (1.5km)
Fountain
Dabolim (29km); Margao (34km)

Panaji (Panjim)

Top Sights
1 Church of Our Lady of the Immaculate Conception....D2

Sights
2 Menezes Braganza Institute....B1
3 Secretariat Building....D1
4 Statue of Abbé Faria....D1

Activities, Courses & Tours
River Cruises....(see 34)

Sleeping
5 Afonso Guest House....E3
Casa Morada....(see 6)
6 Casa Nova....E2
7 Casa Paradiso....D2
8 Crown Hotel....E2
9 Mayfair Hotel....B3
10 Panjim Inn....E4
11 Pousada Guest House....E2
12 Republica Hotel....D2

Eating
13 George Bar & Restaurant....D2
14 Hotel Venite....E2
15 Hotel Vihar....E2
16 Legacy of Bombay....B3
17 Satkar Vegetarian Restaurant....C2
18 Sher-E-Punjab....C2
19 Tea Cafe Goa....E2
20 Upper House....C2
Verandah....(see 10)
21 Viva Panjim....E3

Drinking & Nightlife
22 Cafe Mojo....B2
23 Riverfront & Down the Road....F2

Entertainment
24 Casino Royale....E1
25 INOX Cinema....A2

Shopping
26 Barefoot Handicrafts....E2
27 Khadi Gramodyog Bhavan....C2
28 Municipal Market....A2
29 Singbal's Book House....D2

Transport
30 Kadamba Bus Stand....G3
Konkan Railway Reservation Office....(see 30)
31 Paulo Travels....G3
32 Private Bus Agents....G3
33 Private Bus Stand....G2
34 Santa Monica Jetty....G2

the water, and a library with great books on Indian arts. East of this is **Campal Gardens** (Bhagwan Mahaveer Bal Vihar), a peaceful, expansive park with playgrounds and river views.

Houses of Goa Museum MUSEUM
(☎2410711; www.archgoa.org; Torda; adult/child ₹100/25; ⏲10am-7.30pm Tue-Sun) This little museum, about 8km north of Panaji, was created by a well-known local architect, Gerard da Cunha, to illuminate the history of Goan architecture. Interesting displays on building practices and European and local design will change the way you see those old Goan homes. Next door is the **Mario Gallery** (☎2410711; admission free; ⏲10am-5.30pm Mon-Fri, to 1pm Sat), with works by one of India's favourite cartoonists, the late Mario Miranda (1926–2011). To get here, take a Mapusa-bound bus and get off at Okukora Circle, also known as Kokeru; an autorickshaw from here and back, including waiting time, costs ₹150. From Panaji, a taxi or autorickshaw will cost you about ₹350 one-way.

Courses

On the Menu COOKING
(www.holidayonthemenu.com; courses from US$149) This London-based outfit offers a variety of Goan-cooking holidays (at a price), ranging from a Saturday 'Curry Morning' to a one-week program (US$1599) that includes trips to a spice plantation and a local market.

Tours

The Goa Tourism Development Corporation (GTDC; Goa Tourism) operates a range of popular boat trips along the Mandovi River, including hour-long sunset and evening **cruises** (₹150; ⏲6pm & 7.15pm) and two-hour **dinner cruises** (₹500; ⏲8.45pm Wed & Sat) aboard the *Santa Monica*. All include a live band and dancers – sometimes lively, sometimes lacklustre – performing Goan folk songs and dances. Cruises depart from the Santa Monica jetty beside the New Patto Bridge, where the **GTDC boat counter** (☎2438754; Santa Monica jetty) also sells tickets.

Three private companies offer similar one-hour **night cruises** (adult/child ₹150/free; 6.15pm, 7.30pm & 8.45pm) also departing from Santa Monica jetty. With bars and DJs playing loud music, these tend to be a lot livelier than the GTDC cruises but can get rowdy with groups of local male tourists – avoid on weekends.

GTDC also runs a full-day **backwater cruise** (₹750; 9.30am-4pm) to Old Goa, then a bus to a spice farm where lunch is included.

You can take your own free tour aboard the local ferries that depart frequently (whenever full) at the dock next to Quarterdeck; locals have reported seeing dolphins on evening rides. Avoid rush hour, when the boats are crammed.

Heritage walking tours (9823025748; ajit_sukhija@yahoo.com; per person ₹500, per person ₹250 for five or more), covering the old Portuguese quarter from Tobacco Sq, through Sao Tomé, Fountainhas and the Hindu Mala district, are conducted by experienced local guides on demand.

Festivals & Events

Sabado Gordo STREET FESTIVAL
(Panaji; Feb/Mar) 'Fat Saturday' is a procession of floats and street parties on the Saturday before Lent.

Carnival FESTIVAL
(statewide; Mar) This four-day festival kicks off Lent and is particularly jubilant in Panaji where elaborate floats take to the streets.

International Film Festival of India FILM FESTIVAL
(www.iffi.nic.in; Panaji; Nov) International film screenings and Bollywood glitterati everywhere.

Feast of Our Lady of the Immaculate Conception RELIGIOUS FESTIVAL
(Margao, Panaji; 8 Dec) Fairs and concerts are held, as is a beautiful church service at Panaji's Church of Our Lady of the Immaculate Conception.

Sleeping

As in the rest of Goa, prices vary wildly in Panaji depending on supply and demand. Lots of rock-bottom options pepper 31st January Rd, but most consist of a cell-like room, with a 9am or earlier checkout, for ₹500 or less. Inspect a few before you decide.

Pousada Guest House GUESTHOUSE $
(2422618; sabrinateles@yahoo.com; Luis de Menezes Rd; s/d ₹525/630, d with AC ₹750;) The four rooms in this bright-yellow place in the old quarter are simple but clean and come with comfy spring-mattress beds and TV. Owner Sabrina is friendly and no-nonsense, and at this price it's one of the better budget deals.

Republica Hotel HOTEL $
(2224630; Jose Falcao Rd; s/d from ₹400/800, d with AC ₹1000;) The Republica is a story of unexplored potential, an architectural beauty that's been left to fall apart – but still it was booked out when we visited! Ramshackle it may be, but the location is good and the price acceptable for this part of town.

Afonso Guest House GUESTHOUSE $$
(2222359, 9764300165; www.afonsoguesthouse.com; St Sebastian Rd; r ₹1500-2000;) Run by the friendly Jeanette, this place in a pretty Portuguese-era townhouse offers spacious, well-kept rooms with timber ceilings. The little rooftop terrace makes for sunny breakfasting. It's a simple, serene stay in the heart of the most atmospheric part of town; checkout is 9am and bookings are accepted online but not by phone.

Casa Paradiso HOTEL $$
(3290180; www.casaparadisogoa.com; Jose Falcao Rd; r with AC ₹1575-2100;) The location alone makes this place worth a look. It's a little cramped but just steps away from the Church of Our Lady of the Immaculate Conception, with bright, air-con rooms, cable TV and friendly staff.

Mayfair Hotel HOTEL $$
(2223317; manishafernz@yahoo.com; Dr Dada Vaidya Rd; s/d from ₹980/1180, d with AC ₹1500;) The oystershell windows and mosaic murals in the lobby at this corner hotel are promising but the rooms are not quite as bright – ask to see a few as there's old and new wings with rooms of varying quality. Friendly family owners, a potentially nice back garden and noon checkout.

★**Panjim Inn** HERITAGE HOTEL $$
(2226523, 9823025748; www.panjiminn.com; 31st January Rd; s/d incl breakfast from ₹2900/3450, ste ₹5950;) A long-standing Panaji favourite for its heritage character, this beautiful 19th century hotel has a variety of charismatic original rooms,

along with some newer rooms with more modern touches, but all with four-poster beds, colonial furniture and local artworks. Across the road and run by the same family is the **Panjim Peoples**, with four enormous rooms upstairs and the Gitanjali Gallery downstairs, also across the road is the tranquil nine-room **Panjim Pousada**, in an old Hindu home.

Crown Hotel HOTEL $$$
(☎2400000; www.thecrowngoa.com; off Jose Falcao Rd; d incl breakfast ₹6600-10,450, ste from ₹13,750; ❄@📶🏊) Perched on a hill above the Sao Tomé district, with fine views out over the Mandovi, this spa-hotel-casino is a great option for a little bit of luxury in the heart of the city. Refurbished rooms are airy and tastefully done in mustards and whites (some with balconies) and the pool-bar area is incredibly enticing (nonguests ₹250). There's also a day spa and gym.

Casa Nova GUESTHOUSE $$$
(☎9423889181, 7709886212; www.goaholidayaccommodation.com; Gomez Pereira Rd; ₹4300; ❄) In a gorgeous old Portuguese-style home (c 1831), Casa Nova consists of just one stylish, exceptionally comfy apartment, accessed via a little alley and complete with arched windows, wood-beam ceilings and mod cons like a kitchenette. Sister property **Casa Morada** (☎9822196007, 9881966789; agomes@tbi.in; Gomes Pereira Rd; s/d incl breakfast ₹5000/10,000) is as fancy as Nova is modern. Its two bedrooms and sitting room are full of antique furniture and objets d'art.

Eating

You'll never go hungry in Panaji, where food is enjoyed fully and frequently. A stroll down 18th June or 31st January Rds will turn up a number of great, cheap canteen-style options, as will a quick circuit of the Municipal Gardens.

★**Viva Panjim** GOAN $
(31st January Rd; mains ₹90-120; ⏲11.30am-3.30pm & 7-11pm Mon-Sat, 7-11pm Sun) Though well-known to tourists, this little side-street eatery, in an old Portuguese house, still delivers tasty Goan classics at reasonable prices – there's a whole page of the menu devoted to pork dishes, as well as tasty *xacuti* and *cafreal*-style dishes and desserts like bebinca and *serra durra*. Fair drink prices too.

Satkar Vegetarian Restaurant INDIAN $
(18th June Rd; thalis ₹70-90, mains ₹50-100; ⏲7am-10.30pm) Casual, cheap, pretty good pure-veg and tasty thalis.

Legacy of Bombay INDIAN $
(Hotel Fidalgo, 18th June Rd; mains ₹40-150; ⏲7am-11.15pm) One of several restaurants in Hotel Fidalgo, this street level place serves excellent pure-veg food, including veg versions of pizza and burgers.

Hotel Vihar VEGAN $
(MG Rd; mains ₹40-100; ⏲7.30am-10pm) A vast menu of 'pure veg' food, great big thalis and a plethora of fresh juices make this clean, simple canteen a popular place for locals and visitors alike.

Tea Cafe Goa CAFE $$
(5/218 31st January Rd; cakes from ₹80, meals ₹150-250; ⏲10.30am-6.30pm) This cute modern cafe contrasts with some of the older places, serving excellent sandwiches, quiches, cupcakes and other sweet treats in a charmingly restful air-conditioned interior.

★**Upper House** GOAN $$
(☎2426475; www.theupperhousegoa.com; Cunha Rivara Rd; mains ₹125-385; ⏲11am-10pm) Climbing the stairs to the Upper House is like stepping into a cool European restaurant, with a modern but elegant dining space overlooking the Municipal Gardens at the front, a chic neon-lit cocktail bar next door and more formal restaurant space at the back. But the food is very much Goan – a high standard of regional specialities such as crab *xec xec* (crab cooked in a roasted-coconut gravy), pork vindaloo, and fish-curry-rice done the old-fashioned way. Even the veg adaptations (eg mixed veg and mushroom *xacuti*) are show-stoppers.

Hotel Venite GOAN $$
(31st January Rd; mains ₹210-280; ⏲9am-10.30pm) Atmospheric Venite is a long-time tourist favourite: its tiny, rickety balcony tables make the perfect lunchtime spot. Success may have gone to Venite's head – the Goan food is OK but the prices are exorbitant. We still love the place though – call in for a cold beer or snack and chill out on the balcony before deciding.

Sher-E-Punjab NORTH INDIAN $$
(18th June Rd; mains ₹80-200; ⏲10.30am-11.30pm) Sher-E-Punjab is widely regarded as one of the best North Indian places in

town, catering to well-dressed locals with its generous, carefully spiced Punjabi dishes. There's a pleasant garden terrace out back. The food at the fancier branch of **Sher-E-Punjab** (Hotel Aroma, Cunha-Rivara Rd; mains ₹120-270; ⏲11am-3pm & 7-10.30pm) is equally tasty.

George Bar & Restaurant GOAN $$
(Church Sq; mains ₹90-170; ⏲9.30am-10.30pm) Slightly cramped wooden tables and a healthy mix of drunks and families make for a down-to-earth local vibe, and there's an air-con section upstairs. Seafood and Goan classics are the speciality.

Verandah GOAN $$
(☎2226523; 31st January Rd; ₹150-280; ⏲11am-11pm) The breezy first-floor restaurant at Panjim Inn is indeed on a balcony with Fountainhas street views. Excellent Goan cuisine is the speciality, but there's also a range of Indian and Continental dishes, and local wines.

Drinking & Nightlife

Panaji has pick-me-up pit stops aplenty, especially in the Sao Tomé and Fontainhas areas. Mostly simple little bars with a few plastic tables and chairs, they're a great way to get chatting with locals over a glass of feni.

Cafe Mojo BAR
(www.cafemojo.in; Menenzes Braganza Rd; ⏲10am-4am Mon-Thu, to 6am Fri-Sun) Cafe Mojo is cool. The decor is cosy English pub, the clientele young and up for a party, and the hook is the e-beer system. Each table has its own beer tap and LCD screen: you buy a card (₹1000), swipe it at your table and start pouring – it automatically deducts what you drink (you can also use the card for spirits, cocktails or food). Wednesday night is ladies' night and the weekends go till late.

Riverfront & Down the Road BAR
(cnr MG and Ourem Rd; ⏲11am-3am) The balcony of this bar-restaurant overlooking the creek and Old Patto Bridge makes for a great sundowner spot; the ground-floor bar has occasional live music.

Entertainment

Several casino boats sit moored on the Mandovi, offering a surprisingly entertaining night out.

Casino Royale CASINO
(☎6519471; www.casinoroyalegoa.com; entry Mon-Thu ₹3000, Fri-Sun ₹3500; ⏲24hr) The biggest and best of Panaji's three floating casinos, this upscale floating shrine to all things speculative is as much entertainment as gaming. Admission includes unlimited buffet dinner, free drinks, live music and ₹2000 worth of chips. Various age and dress restrictions apply.

Kala Academy CULTURAL PROGRAMS
(☎2420452; Dayanand Bandodkar Marg) On the west side of the city at Campal is Goa's premier cultural centre, featuring an excellent program of dance, theatre, music and art exhibitions throughout the year. Many plays are in Konkani, but there are occasional English-language productions; call to find out what's on.

INOX Cinema CINEMA
(☎2420900; www.inoxmovies.com; Old GMC Heritage Precinct; tickets ₹160-200; ⏲10.30am-11.30pm) This modern multiplex cinema shows Hollywood and Bollywood blockbusters alike.

Shopping

Panaji's covered **municipal market** (⏲from 7.30am) is a great place for people-watching and buying necessities, while the new **Caculo Mall** (www.caculomall.in; St Inez) is Goa's biggest shopping mall, with designer brands, food courts and gaming arcades.

Singbal's Book House BOOKS
(Church Sq; ⏲9.30am-1pm & 3.30-7.30pm Mon-Sat) Lots of books and newspapers and heaps of character at this slightly grumpy establishment that, incidentally, had a cameo role in the *Bourne Supremacy*.

Barefoot Handicrafts HANDICRAFTS
(31st January Rd; ⏲10am-8pm Mon-Sat) Barefoot is part of Panaji's new wave of very high end shops specialising in design of one kind or another. Barefoot, though pricey, has some nice gifts, ranging from traditional Christian paintings on wood to jewellery and beaded coasters.

Khadi Gramodyog Bhavan HANDICRAFTS
(Dr Atmaram Borkar Rd; ⏲9am-noon & 3-7pm Mon-Sat) Goa's only outpost of the government's Khadi & Village Industries Commission has an excellent range of hand-woven cottons, along with oils, soaps, spices and other handmade products that come straight from and directly benefit – regional villages.

Information

A new tourism complex has been established at Patto on the east side of the Ourem Creek, housing the GTDC (Goa Tourism), Indiatourism and various travel agents. ATMs are plentiful, especially on 18th June Rd and around the Thomas Cook office.

Cozy Nook (18th June Rd; per hr ₹45; ⊙9am-8.30pm) Welcoming internet joint and travel agent.

Goa State Central Library (Sanskruti Bhavan, Patto; ⊙9am-7.30pm Mon-Fri, 9.30am-5.45pm Sat & Sun) Panaji's ultra-modern new state library has six floors of reading material, a bookshop and gallery. Internet access is technically for academic research only.

Goa Tourism Development Corporation (GTDC; ☎2424001; www.goa-tourism.com; Dr Alvaro Costa Rd, Paryatan Bhavan; ⊙9.30am-5.45pm Mon-Sat) Pick up maps of Goa and Panaji here and book one of GTDC's host of tours.

Indiatourism (Government of India tourist office; ☎2223412; www.incredibleindia.org; Dr Alvaro Costa Rd, Paryatan Bhavan; ⊙9.30am-6pm Mon-Fri, to 2pm Sat) Helpful staff can provide a list of qualified guides for tours and trips in Goa. A half-/full-day tour for up to five people costs ₹700/875.

Main Post Office (MG Rd; ⊙9.30am-5.30pm Mon-Sat)

Thomas Cook (☎2221312; Dayanand Bandodkar Marg, 8 Alcon Chambers; ⊙9.30am-6pm Mon-Sat) Changes travellers cheques commission-free and handles currency exchange, wire transfers, cash advances on credit cards, and air bookings.

Vintage Hospitals (☎6644401, ambulance 9764442220; www.vintagehospitals.com; Caculo Enclave, St Inez; ⊙24hr) A couple of kilometres southwest of Panaji, Vintage is a reputable hospital with all the fixings.

Getting There & Away

A taxi from Panaji to Dabolim Airport takes about an hour, and costs ₹600.

BUS

All government buses depart from the huge and busy **Kadamba bus stand** (☎interstate enquiries 2438035, local enquiries 2438034; www.goakadamba.com; ⊙reservations 8am-8pm), with local services heading out every few minutes. To get to south Goan beaches, take an express bus to Margao and change there; Ponda buses also stop at Old Goa. Kadamba station has an ATM, an Internet cafe – and a Ganesh temple.

Calangute (₹15, 45 minutes)

Candolim (₹13, 30 minutes)

Mapusa (₹11, 20 minutes)

Margao (express shuttle; ₹30, 35 minutes)

Old Goa (₹9, 15 minutes)

State-run long-distance services also depart from the Kadamba bus stand. Private operators have booths outside Kadamba, but the buses depart from the interstate bus stand next to New Patto Bridge. One reliable company is **Paulo Travels** (☎2438531; www.paulotravels.com; Kardozo Bldg). Some high-season government and private long-distance fares include the following:

Bengaluru (₹650, 15 hours, five daily)

Bengaluru (private; ₹550 to ₹1000, 14 to 15 hours)

Hampi (private sleeper; ₹700 to ₹800, 10 to 11 hours)

Mumbai (₹650, 12 to 14 hours)

Pune (₹550 to ₹650, 11 hours)

Pune (private; ₹550 to ₹800, 10 to 11 hours)

TRAIN

Panaji's closest train station is Karmali (Old Goa), 12km to the east, where many long-distance services stop (check timetables). A taxi there costs ₹300. Panaji's **Konkan Railway reservation office** (☎2712940; www.konkanrailway.com; ⊙8am-8pm Mon-Sat) is on the 1st floor of the Kadamba bus stand.

Getting Around

Panaji is generally a pleasure to explore on foot, and it's unlikely you'll even need a pilot or autorickshaw, which is good because they charge a lot for short distances: an autorickshaw from Kadamba to the city centre will cost ₹60. Frequent buses run between Kadamba and the municipal market (₹5).

To Old Goa, a taxi or autorickshaw costs around ₹300. Lots of taxis hang around the Municipal Gardens, while you'll find autorickshaws and pilots in front of the post office, on 18th June Rd, and just south of the church.

Scooters and motorbikes can easily be hired from around the post office from around ₹200/300 per day.

Old Goa

From the 16th to the 18th centuries, when Old Goa's population exceeded that of Lisbon or London, this former capital of Goa was considered the 'Rome of the East'. You can still sense that grandeur as you wander the grounds, with its towering churches and cathedral and majestic convents. Its rise under the Portuguese, from 1510, was meteoric, but cholera and malaria

Old Goa

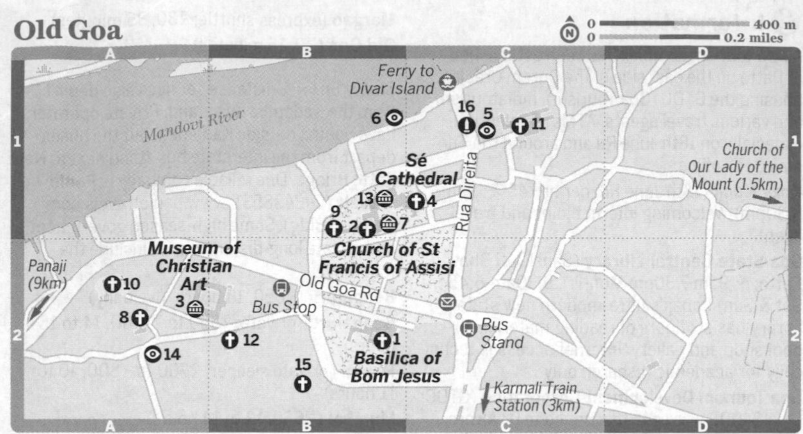

Old Goa

Top Sights

1 Basilica of Bom Jesus B2
2 Church of St Francis of Assisi B1
3 Museum of Christian Art A2
4 Sé Cathedral C1

Sights

5 Adil Shah Palace Gateway C1
6 Albuquerque's Steps B1
7 Archaeological Museum B1
8 Chapel of St Anthony A2
9 Chapel of St Catherine B1
10 Church of Our Lady of the Rosary A2
11 Church of St Cajetan C1
12 Convent & Church of St John B2
13 Kristu Kala Mandir Art Gallery B1
14 Monastery of St Augustine A2
15 Sisters' Convent B2
16 Viceroy's Arch C1

outbreaks forced the abandonment of the city in the 1600s. In 1843 the capital was officially shifted to Panaji.

Some of the most imposing churches, the cathedral and a convent or two are still in use and are remarkably well-preserved, while other historical buildings have become museums or ruined sites. It's a fascinating day trip, but it can get crowded: consider visiting on a weekday morning, when you can take in Mass (in Konkani) at Sé Cathedral or the Basilica of Bom Jesus (remember to cover your shoulders and legs in the churches and cathedral), and definitely stop by if you're around in the 10 days leading up to the **Feast of St Francis Xavier** on 3 December. Once every decade (the next one is 2014), the saint's body is carried through Old Goa's streets.

Sights

★Basilica of Bom Jesus CHURCH

(⏲7.30am-6.30pm; English-language mass 10.15am Sun) Famous throughout the Roman Catholic world for its rather grizzled and grizzly long-term resident, the basilica's vast, gilded interior forms the last resting place of Goa's patron saint, St Francis Xavier (except for his diamond-encrusted fingernail, which sits in Chandor). In 1541, the saint embarked on a mission to put right the sinful, heady lifestyles of Goa's Portuguese colonials. Construction of the imposing red-stone basilica was completed in 1605; St Francis himself is housed in a **mausoleum** to the right, in a glass-sided coffin amid a shower of gilt stars.

Sé Cathedral CHURCH

(⏲7.30am-6.30pm) The largest church in Old Goa, the Sé de Santa Catarina, is also the largest in Asia, at over 76m long and 55m wide. Construction began in 1562, under orders from Portugal's King Dom Sebastião, and the finishing touches were made 90 years later. Fairly plain all-round, the cathedral has three especially notable features: the first, up in the belfry, is the **Golden Bell**, the largest bell in Asia; the second is in the screened chapel inside to the right, known as the **Chapel of the Cross of Miracles**, wherein sits a cross said to have miraculously, and vastly, expanded in size after its creation by local shepherds in 1619. The third is the massive gilded reredos (ornamental screen behind the altar), which depicts the life of St Catherine, to whom the cathedral is dedicated and who came to a sticky end in Alexandria, Egypt, where she was beheaded.

Next to the cathedral, in the old archbishop's house, **Kristu Kala Mandir Art Gallery** (admission ₹10; ⏲9.30am-5.30pm Tue-Sun) has contemporary Christian art and religious objects, including old church confessionals and altar pieces. The decorative wall frescoes may be the gallery's prettiest holdings.

Church of St Francis of Assisi CHURCH
(⏲8.30am-5.30pm) The gorgeous interior of this 1661 church, built over a 16th-century chapel, is filled with gilded and carved woodwork, murals depicting the life of St Francis, frescoes of decorative flowers and various angels, 16th-century Portuguese tombstones and another stunning reredos.

Just behind the church, the former convent houses the **Archaeological Museum** (admission ₹10; ⏲9am-5pm), whose small but worthwhile collection includes a portrait gallery of Portuguese viceroys, a couple of bronze statues, fragments of Hindu temple sculpture and some interesting 'hero stones', carved to commemorate Hindu warriors who perished in combat.

★Museum of Christian Art MUSEUM
(http://christianartmuseum.goa-india.org; adult/child ₹30/free; ⏲9.30am-5pm) This excellent museum, in a stunning space in the restored 1627 **Convent of St Monica**, has a fine collection of 16th- and 17th-century Christian art from Old Goa and around the state. There are some exquisite pieces here – wooden sculptures glittering with gilt and polychrome, processional lamps, tabernacle doors, polychrome paintings and other religious objects from Old Goa's prime – that are almost, but not quite, outdone by the atmospheric interior. The four-storey-high ceilings, exposed wood-beams and terracotta-work, and all-around beauty of the place are worth a visit in their own right.

Church of St Cajetan CHURCH
(⏲9am-5.30pm) Modelled on the original design of St Peter's in Rome, the beautiful Church of St Cajetan (1655) was built by Italian friars of the Order of Theatines, who were sent by Pope Urban III to preach Christianity in the kingdom of Golconda (near Hyderabad). The friars were not permitted to work in Golconda, so settled at Old Goa in 1640.

Church of Our Lady of the Mount CHURCH
For a wonderful view of the city, hike up to this hilltop church, also known as **Capela de Monte**, 2km east of Sé Cathedral; it's especially worth the trip for a spectacular sunset. (Locals will warn you not to go solo; the site is a bit remote.) The church is rarely open but was recently restored and, with its exceptional acoustics, now hosts concerts during the Feast of St Francis Xavier in December, the Monte Music Festival in February, and at other times during the year.

Monastery of St Augustine HISTORIC SITE
The melancholy, evocative ruins of this once vast and impressive Augustinian monastery are all that remain of a huge structure founded in 1572 and abandoned in 1835. The building's facade came tumbling down in 1942; all that remains, amid piles of rubble, is the towering skeletal belfry, though the bell itself was rescued and now hangs in Panaji's Church of Our Lady of the Immaculate Conception.

WORTH A TRIP

BACKWOODS CAMP

In a forest in the Bhagwan Mahaveer Sanctuary full of butterflies and birds, **Backwoods Camp** (☎9822139859; www.backwoodsgoa.com; 2-day ₹6000-7000, 3-day ₹8500-10,000) could hardly be in a more magical, serene spot. The resort is about 1km from Tambdi Surla temple in the state's far east, and for birdwatching enthusiasts it offers one of Goa's richest sources of feathered friends, with everything from Ceylon frogmouths and Asian fairy bluebirds to puff-throated babblers and Indian pittas putting in a regular appearance. Accommodation is in comfortable tents on raised platforms, bungalows and farmhouse rooms (all with attached bathroom), and the camp makes valiant attempts to protect this fragile bit of the Goan ecosystem through measures including waste recycling, replanting indigenous tree species and employing local villagers.

Other Sights

There are plenty of other monuments in Old Goa to explore, including the **Viceroy's Arch**, **Adil Shah Palace Gateway**, **Chapel of St Anthony**, **Chapel of St Catherine**, **Albuquerque's Steps**, the **Convent & Church of St John**, **Sisters' Convent** and the **Church of Our Lady of the Rosary**.

Getting There & Away

Frequent buses from Old Goa head to Panaji's Kadamba bus stand (₹10, 25 minutes) from Old Goa Rd, just beside the Tourist Inn and at the main roundabout to the east.

Ponda & Around

The workaday inland town of Ponda, 29km southeast of Panaji, has two big drawcards in the vicinity – Hindu temples and spice plantations – and is well worth a day away from the beach. Temple aficionados, however, might be a little disappointed; most were built or rebuilt after the originals were destroyed by the Portuguese, so they're not as ancient as those elsewhere in India.

The 18th-century hilltop **Mangueshi Temple** at Priol, 5km northwest of Ponda, is dedicated to Manguesh, a god known only in Goa, while 1km away at Mardol is the **Mahalsa Temple**, also dedicated to a specifically Goan deity. The 1738 **Shantadurga Temple**, meanwhile, just west of Ponda, is dedicated to Shantadurga, the goddess of peace, and is one of the most famous shrines in Goa.

There are regular buses to Ponda from Panaji (₹20, 45 minutes) and Margao, after which you'll need to arrange a taxi to visit the temples or spice farms. Taxis from Panaji charge ₹1200 for a day trip to the area (up to eight hours and 80km).

NORTH GOA

Mapusa

POP 40,100

The pleasantly bustling market town of Mapusa (pronounced 'Mapsa') is the largest town in northern Goa and a transport hub for local and interstate buses. The main reason to visit is for its busy **Friday market** (⏲8am-6.30pm), which attracts scores of buyers and sellers from neighbouring towns and villages, and a healthy intake of tourists from the northern beaches. It's a good place to pick up the usual embroidered bedsheets and the like at prices lower than in the beach resorts.

Mapusa is also home to the exceptionally awesome **Other India Bookstore** (☎2263306; www.otherindiabookstore.com; Mapusa Clinic Rd; ⏲9am-5pm Mon-Fri, to 1pm Sat), specialising in 'dissenting wisdom' and alternative press – a small but spectacular selection of books on nature, farming, politics, education and natural health. To find it, go up the steps next to the old Mapusa Clinic, and follow the signs.

WORTH A TRIP

SPICE OF LIFE

There are several spice farms in the Ponda area that make an excellent day trip. **Tropical Spice Plantation** (☎2340329; www.tropicalspiceplantation.com; admission incl lunch ₹400; ⏲9am-4pm), 5km northeast of Ponda, is one of the most popular with an entertaining 45-minute tour of the 120-acre plantation's 'demo garden' followed by a banana-leaf buffet lunch. Elephant rides (₹600 for 10 minutes) and bathings (₹600) can be fun. **Sahakari Spice Farm** (☎2312394; www.sahakarifarms.com; admission incl lunch ₹400; ⏲9am-4pm), 2km from Ponda, offers a similar experience but with a more traditional hut-style restaurant and the added attraction of folk dances and tree-swinging to collect betel nuts.

The 200-year-old family **Savoi Plantation** (☎2340272, 9822133309; www.savoiplantation.com; ⏲9am-4.30pm), whose motto is 'Organic Since Origin', is much mellower, less touristed and elephant-free. You'll find a warm welcome from knowledgeable guides keen to walk you through the 100-acre plantation at your own pace. Local crafts are for sale, and you're welcomed with fresh kokum juice, cardamom bananas and other organic treats.

Volunteering

If you're interesting in working with disadvantaged children while staying in Goa, there are a couple of well-established options.

El Shaddai VOLUNTEERING
(☎6513286, 6513287; www.childrescue.net; El Shaddai House, Socol Vaddo, Assagao) Runs day-care, night shelters and homes for street children and orphans. Volunteers are required to give a minimum commitment of four weeks, pay a £500 volunteer donation (includes meals and accommodations), and supply background checks. Apply early. You can also sponsor a child via the website

Mango Tree Goa VOLUNTEERING
(☎9881 261886; www.mangotreegoa.org; 'The Mango House', near Vrundavan Hospital, Karaswada, Mapusa) Based at the Mango House near Mapusa, this is another UK-based charity that seeks to help disadvantaged children with shelter, healthcare and education. Visitors are welcome by prior arrangement. Volunteers with teaching and nursing backgrounds are sometimes required.

Sleeping & Eating

There's little reason to stay the night in Mapusa when the beaches of the north coast are all so close and most long-distance transport departs at night. If you do, **Hotel Vilena** (☎2263115; Feira Baixa Rd; d/tr ₹600/750, with AC ₹840; ❄) is central and Mapusa's best budget bolt-hole. There are plenty of decent local cafes within the market area. The thalis are excellent at busy **Ashok Snacks & Beverages** (thalis & mains ₹40-70; ⏰6am-10.30pm Mon-Sat, to 4pm Sun), overlooking the market. **Hotel Vrundavan** (thalis ₹50-75; ⏰7am-10pm Wed-Mon), an all-veg place bordering the municipal gardens, is another great joint with good chai and snacks, while the **Pub** (near the market; ⏰9am-10.30pm) is the best spot for a drink and prime people-watching on market day.

Information

There are plenty of ATMs and a few internet places scattered about the town centre and market area.

Mapusa Clinic (☎2263343; ⏰consultations 10.30am-1.30pm Mon-Sat, 3.30-7pm Mon, Wed & Fri) A well-run medical clinic, with 24-hour emergency services. Be sure to go to the 'new' Mapusa Clinic, behind the 'old' one.

Getting There & Away

If you're coming to Goa by bus from Mumbai, Mapusa's **Kadamba bus stand** (☎2232161) is the jumping-off point for the northern beaches. Local services run every few minutes; just look for the correct destination on the sign in the bus windscreen and try to get an express. For buses to the southern beaches, take a bus to Panaji, then Margao, and change there.

Local services include the following:

Anjuna (₹15, 20 minutes)
Arambol (₹27, 1½ hours)
Calangute/Candolim (₹10/12, 20/35 minutes)
Panjim (₹15, 20 minutes)
Thivim (₹15, 20 minutes)

Interstate services run out of the same lot, but private operators have their offices next to the bus stand. There's generally little difference in price between private services and the Kadamba buses, but shop around as there are various standards of bus.

Long-distance services include the following:

Bengaluru (private; AC or sleeper ₹1400, 13-14hr)
Mumbai (private; non-AC ₹700, AC ₹1200, 12-15hr)
Pune (private; non-AC from ₹650, AC ₹1200, sleeper ₹1000, 11-13hr)

There's a prepaid taxi stand outside the bus terminal with a list of prices. Cabs to Anjuna or Calangute cost ₹300, Arambol ₹500 and Panaji ₹500; autorickshaws typically charge ₹50 less than taxis.

Thivim, about 12km northeast of town, is the nearest train station on the Konkan Railway. Local buses meet trains; an autorickshaw into Mapusa from Thivim costs around ₹200.

Candolim, Sinquerim & Fort Aguada

POP 8600

Candolim's vast beach, which curves round as far as smaller Sinquerim beach in the south, is largely the preserve of older, slow-roasting package tourists from the UK, Russia and Scandinavia, and is fringed with seasonal beach shacks, all offering sun beds and shade in exchange for your custom.

Candolim's beach is pleasant, the town is mellow, there are some very good hotels hidden among the palms behind the beach and the main drag has a good array of restaurants, but it's somewhat fading and lacks the personality of many other beach towns. The post office, supermarkets, travel agents, internet cafes, pharmacies and plenty of banks with ATMs are all on the main Fort Aguada Rd, which runs parallel to the beach.

Sights & Activities

Fort Aguada FORT, AREA

(8.30am-5.30pm) Guarding the mouth of the Mandovi River and hugely popular with Indian tour groups, Fort Aguada was constructed by the Portuguese in 1612 and is the most impressive of Goa's remaining forts. It's worth braving the crowds and hawkers at the moated ruins on the hilltop for the views; unfortunately, there was no entry at research time to the fort's four-storey **Portuguese lighthouse**, built in 1894 and the oldest of its type in Asia. But just down the road is the peninsula's active **lighthouse** (Indian/foreigner ₹10/50, camera ₹25; 3-5.30pm), which you can climb for extraordinary views. It's a pleasant 2km ride along a hilly, sealed road to the fort, or you can walk via a steep, uphill path past Marbella Guest House. Beneath the fort is the **Fort Aguada Jail**, whose cells were originally fort storehouses, and **Johnny's Mansion**, owned by a famously wealthy Goan and often used as a set for Indian films. Neither is open to the public.

Boat Cruises BOATING

Some of the most popular boat trips around town are run by **John's Boat Tours** (9822182814, 6520190; www.johnboattrips.com), including dolphin-watching cruises (₹1000), boat trips to Anjuna Market (₹800), a Grand Island snorkelling excursion (₹1400), and even overnight houseboat cruises (₹5500 per person, full board). For something more low-key (read: cheaper), head to the **excursion boat jetty** along the Nerul River where you can haggle with independent local boats to Anjuna (₹400) and dolphin cruises (₹300) that pass by Coco Beach, Fort Aguada Jail, the fort, and 'Johnny's Millionaire House'.

Sleeping

Candolim has a good range of accommodation, including some of North Goa's top hotels – the southern end is dominated by the Taj hotels. Most of the best-value budget choices are in the lush area in northern Candolim between the road and the beach; wander through the tiny trails off laneways and you're sure to find something.

Beach Nest GUESTHOUSE $

(2489866, 9822381853; Monteiro's Rd, Escrivai Vaddo; d ₹900-1200) There are no sea views here but this is a spotless and friendly little place that's just a quick jungle-footpath walk to the beach. The more expensive upstairs rooms have balcony, kitchenettes and fridges, the owners are helpful, and the atmosphere is serene and homey.

Villa Ludovici Tourist Home GUESTHOUSE $

(2479684; Fort Aguada Rd; d incl breakfast ₹900) The five well-worn, creaky rooms in this grand old Portuguese-style villa have been sheltering budget travellers for years. Back from the beach but a warm place to stay.

★ **Bougainvillea Guest House** GUESTHOUSE $$

(2479842, 9822151969; www.bougainvilleagoa.com; off Fort Aguada Rd, Sinquerim; r ₹2500, penthouse ₹4500;) A lush, plant-filled garden leads the way to this gorgeous family-run guesthouse down a quiet lane off the southern end of Fort Aguada Rd. The eight light-filled suite rooms are spacious and spotless, with fridge, flat-screen TV and either balcony or private sit-out – the top floor penthouse has its own rooftop terrace. This is the kind of place guests come back to year after year. Book ahead.

D'Mello's Sea View Home HOTEL $$

(2489650; www.dmellos.com; Monteiro's Rd, Escrivao Vaddo; d ₹1200-1700; @) The name says it all – rooms in the sea-facing building at family-run D'Mello's are divine, with only three walls: the fourth is your balcony, with ocean views. Even the back rooms are stylish, with perky colours and chic cotton bedspreads. All rooms are fastidiously clean and have mosquito nets but tiny bathrooms. It's a short clamber to the beach and if this place is full, there's a bunch of others nearby.

Candolim Villa Horizon View HOTEL $$

(2489105; www.candolimvilla.com; d with AC ₹2200-2750; @) Simple air-con rooms are set around a small swimming pool at this friendly, professional midranger.

★ **Marbella Guest House** HOTEL $$$

(2479551, 9822100811; www.marbellagoa.com; off Fort Aguada Rd, Sinquerim; r ₹3200-6100;) This stunning Portuguese-era villa, filled with antiques and backed by a lush, peaceful courtyard garden, is a romantic and sophisticated old-world remnant. Rooms are

GREEN GOA?

Goa's environment has suffered from an onslaught of tourism over the last 40 years, but also from the effects of logging, mining and local customs (rare turtle eggs have traditionally been considered a dining delicacy). Construction proceeds regardless of what the local infrastructure or ecosystem can sustain, while plastic bottles pile up in vast mountains. There are, however, a few easy ways to minimise your impact on Goa's environment:

➡ Take your own bag when shopping and refill water bottles with filtered water wherever possible. The 5L Bisleri water bottles come with a deposit and are returnable to be reused. Better yet, bring a water filter with you.

➡ Rent a bicycle instead of a scooter, for short trips at least, and ask around if you don't find any: bicycle rentals are declining as a result of our scooter infatuation and the bikes are poor quality, but they'll bounce back if the demand is there.

➡ Dispose of cigarette butts, which are nonbiodegradeable, and any plastic litter in bins; birds and sealife may mistake them for food and choke.

Turtles are currently protected by the **Forest Department** (www.goaforest.com), which operates huts on beaches, such as Agonda and Morjim, where turtles arrive to lay eggs. Drop into these or check out the website to find out more about the department's work. Also doing good work is the **Goa Foundation** (☎2256479, 2263305; www.goafoundation.org; St Britto's Apts, G-8 Feira Alta, Mapusa), the state's main environmental pressure group based in Mapusa. It has spearheaded a number of conservation projects since its inauguration in 1986, and its website is a great place to learn more about Goan environmental issues. The group's excellent *Fish Curry & Rice* (₹400), a sourcebook on Goa's environment and lifestyle, is sold at Mapusa's Other India Bookstore (p138). The Foundation occasionally runs volunteer projects; call or swing by for details.

individually themed, including the Moghul, Rajasthani and Bouganvillea. Its kitchen serves up some imaginative dishes, and its penthouse suite is a dream of polished tiles and four-posters. No kids under 12.

Eating & Drinking

Candolim's plentiful beach shacks are popular places to eat or relax with a beer.

★Café Chocolatti CAFE, BAKERY **$$**
(409A Fort Aguada Rd; baked goods ₹45-100, mains ₹120-220; ⏲9am-7pm Mon-Sat) Treat yourself at this lovely tearoom, set in a green garden on the main road but light years from the bustle of traffic or the beach. The cafe serves great coffee, sandwiches and salads, but the chocolate cake and waffles are the stars.

Stone House STEAKHOUSE, BAR **$$**
(Fort Aguada Rd; mains ₹150-500; ⏲11am-3pm & 7pm-midnight) Surf 'n' turf's the thing at this venerable old Candolim venue, inhabiting a stone house and a leafy front courtyard. 'Swedish Lobster' cooked in beer tops the list, followed by other beefy plates, seafood and Goan dishes. It's run by the affable Chris and there's quality live music most nights of the week in season.

Bob's Inn MULTICUISINE, BAR **$$**
(Fort Aguada Rd; mains ₹80-300; ⏲10.30am-4pm & 6.30pm-midnight) Great fish dishes, relaxed ambience and old dudes – foreigners and locals alike – chillaxing at the communal table. The African wall hangings, thatch everywhere, and terracotta sculptures are a nice backdrop to the *rava* (semolina wheat) fried mussels or 'drunken prawns'.

Chili Hip THAI **$$**
(☎6650281; www.chilihipgoa.com; Accron Place, Fort Aguada Rd; mains ₹200-380; ⏲noon-3pm & 6.30-10.30pm) Savour authentic, spicy Thai dishes prepared by a Bangkok chef in this stylish new restaurant attached to the Centara day spa. Upstairs, Vibes is a chic cocktail bar.

Republic of Noodles ASIAN FUSION **$$$**
(mains ₹375-450; ⏲11.30am-3pm & 7-11pm) For a sophisticated dining experience, this award-winning pan-Asian place delivers with its dark bamboo interior, Buddha heads and floating candles. Delicious, huge noodle plates, wok stir-fries and clay-pot dishes are the order of the day – consider the coconut and turmeric curry of red snapper – and there are some exciting dishes for the veggies.

Getting There & Away

Buses run frequently to Panaji (₹12, 30 minutes) and Mapusa (₹12, 35 minutes) and stop at the turn-off near John's Boat Tours. Calangute buses (₹5, 15 minutes) start at the Fort Aguada bus stop and can be flagged down on Fort Aguada Rd.

Calangute & Baga

POP 15,800

For better or worse, Calangute and Baga are Goa's most popular beaches – a least with the cashed-up domestic tour crowd and European package tourists. Once a refuge of wealthy Goans, and later a 1960s hot spot for naked, revelling hippies, Calangute has adapted its scant charms to extended Indian families, groups of Indian bachelors and partying foreigners. If you want to experience authentic Indian (or Russian) tourism full-on, come to Calangute. The northern beach area can get crowded – including the water, which fills up with people, boats and jet skis – but the southern beach is more relaxed. Baga, to the north, meanwhile, is the place for drinking and dancing, and Northern Baga, across the Baga River, is surprisingly tranquil, with budget accommodation bargains clinging to the coast.

Activities

Water Sports

You'll find numerous jet-ski and parasailing operators on Calangute and Baga beaches. Parasailing costs around ₹650 per ride, jet-skiing costs ₹1000 per 15 minutes.

Barracuda Diving DIVING
(Map p144; 2279409, mobile 9822182402; www.barracudadiving.com; Sun Village Resort, Baga; courses from ₹4500) This long-standing diving school offers a range of dives and courses, from two-day Discover Scuba (₹4500) to four-day PADI open water (₹20,000). It's also exceptional for its 'Project A.W.A.R.E', which undertakes marine-conservation initiatives and annual underwater and beach clean-ups.

Yoga & Ayurveda

Ayurvedic Natural Health Centre AYURVEDA, YOGA
(08322409275; www.healthandayurveda.com; Chogm Rd, Saligao; 7.30am-7.30pm) This highly respected centre, 5km inland at Saligao, offers a range of massages and other ayurvedic treatments lasting from one hour to three weeks. Herbal medicines and consultations with an ayurvedic doctor are also available. Professional courses are given here in ayurveda, yoga and other regimes; enquire well in advance. For the more spontaneous, drop-in yoga classes (₹300) are held daily.

Boat Trips

Local fishers congregate around northern Baga beach, offering dolphin-spotting trips (₹500 per person), visits to Anjuna Market (₹300 per person) and whole-day excursions to Arambol and Mandrem (₹1100 per person).

Tours

Day Tripper (Map p143; 2276726; www.daytrippergoa.com; Gaura Vaddo, Calangute; 9am-5.30pm Mon-Sat Nov-Apr) runs a variety of trips around Goa, including two weekly to Dudhsagar Falls (₹1330), overnight houseboat trips (₹5300 per person) aboard a Keralan-style rice barge, and a sailing trip through the mangroves of the Cumbarjua River (₹1650).

GTDC tours can be booked online (www.goa-tourism.com) or at **Calangute Residency** (Map p143; 2276024; 24hr), by the main entrance to the beach.

Sleeping

Calangute and Baga's sleeping options are plentiful, lining the main roads and laneways down to the beach for several kilometres. Generally, the quietest hotels lie in south Calangute, and across the bridge north of Baga.

Calangute

★ **Johnny's Hotel** HOTEL $
(Map p143; 2277458; Calangute; d ₹700-900, with AC ₹1100-1300 ;) The 15 simple rooms in this backpacker-popular place make for a sociable stay, with a downstairs restaurant-bar and regular classes available in yoga and reiki. A range of apartments and houses are available for longer-stayers.

Ospy's Shelter GUESTHOUSE $
(Map p143; 2279505; oscar_fernandes@sify.com; d ₹700-800) Tucked away in a quiet, lush little area full of palms and sandy paths between the beach and St Anthony's Chapel, are a bunch of family-run guesthouses. Ospy's, just a two-minute walk to the beach, is a good bet. Spotless upstairs rooms have fridges and balconies, and the whole place has a cosy family feel. Check out the

Calangute

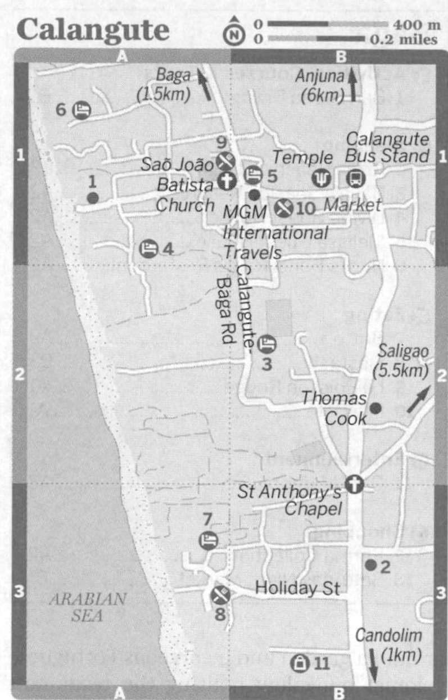

Calangute

Activities, Courses & Tours
1 Calangute Residency A1
2 Day Tripper B3

Sleeping
3 Casa de Goa B2
4 Coco Banana A1
5 Garden Court Resort B1
6 Johnny's Hotel A1
7 Ospy's Shelter A3

Eating
8 A Reverie A3
9 Infantaria A1
10 Plantain Leaf B1

Shopping
11 Literati Bookshop & Cafe B3

gorgeous old floor tiles on the ground floor. Take the road directly west of the chapel but it's tough to find, so call ahead.

Garden Court Resort GUESTHOUSE $
(Map p143; ☎2276054; luarba@dataone.in; r ₹600-1000, with AC ₹700-1200;) Despite being on the busy market road, the rooms here, fronted by a Portuguese-style family home and set amongst pretty gardens, are remarkably quiet. They're not flashy but are reasonable value and come with balconies.

Coco Banana GUESTHOUSE $
(Map p143; ☎2279068; www.cocobananagoa.com; d ₹750-950, with AC ₹1200) Among the palms south of the main entrance to Calangute beach, this tranquil place is run by a friendly Swiss-Goan family who keep the spacious rooms spotless and the vibe mellow. For families or groups it also has an apartment at nearby Casa Leyla, with separate sitting room and kitchen area.

★ **Casa de Goa** HOTEL $$$
(Map p143; ☎6717777; www.casadegoa.com; Tivai Vaddo; r/ste/villa ₹11,500/14,000/15,400; @) The beautiful Casa de Goa is popular with Indian families and books up months in advance for weekends and high season – but at these prices it's really only a bargain from April to October when rates are less than half. Portuguese-style yellow-ochre buildings orbit a pretty pool courtyard, decor is bright and fresh, and the big, clean rooms have safes, flat-screen TVs and other high-end and thoughtful touches.

Baga

Indian Kitchen GUESTHOUSE $
(☎2277555; www.indian-kitchen-goa.com; s/d/chalet ₹770/990/1200; @) If a colourful stay is what you're after, look no further than this family-run guesthouse, which offers basic rooms with much attempt at individual charm, set around a sparkly central courtyard. There's even a small swimming pool out the back, a small gym and a sauna.

Melissa Guest House GUESTHOUSE $
(Map p144; ☎2279583; d ₹600) Small, neat rooms, all with attached bathrooms and hot-water showers, comprise this quiet, excellent-value little place, pleasantly located in a plant-filled garden near the Baga River with views across to the beach.

Divine Guest House GUESTHOUSE $
(Map p144; ☎2279546, 9370273464; www.indivinehome.com; d from ₹800, with AC ₹1200; @) The Divine welcomes you with a 'Praise the Lord' gatepost and keeps perky reminders throughout the place, so only stay here if you don't mind cheerful proselytising. Rooms are sweet and homey, with bright colours, lots of kitsch and the odd individual touch, all at a quiet riverside location. Two-night minimum.

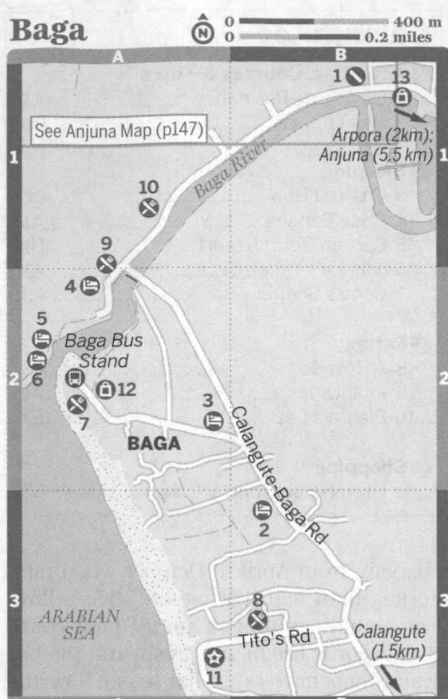

Baga

Activities, Courses & Tours

1 Barracuda Diving B1

Sleeping

2 Alidia Beach Cottages B3
3 Cavala Seaside Resort A2
4 Divine Guest House A2
5 Melissa Guest House A2
6 Nani's Bar & Rani's Restaurant A2

Eating

7 Britto's A2
8 Fiesta B3
9 Le Poisson Rouge A1
10 Lila Café A1

Entertainment

11 Café Mambo A3

Shopping

12 Karma Collection A2
13 Saturday Night Market B1

Alidia Beach Cottages GUESTHOUSE **$$**
(Map p144; ☎2279014; www.alidiabeachcottages.com; Calangute-Baga Rd, Saunta Waddo; d ₹1500, with AC ₹2500-2800, ste ₹3500; ❄📶🏊) Set back behind a whitewashed church, this convivial place has beautifully kept Mediterranean-style rooms orbiting a gorgeous pool. Cheaper rooms are at the back but all are in good conditon, the staff are keen to please and there's a path directly to the beach.

Cavala Seaside Resort HOTEL **$$**
(Map p144; ☎2276090; www.cavala.com; Calangute-Baga Rd; s/d incl breakfast from ₹1050/2100, d with AC ₹3250-5400, ste ₹3900-4750; ❄📶🏊) With its laterite-brick, ivy-clad exterior, Cavala has been charming Baga-bound travellers for more than 30 years, and continues to deliver clean, simple, nicely furnished rooms. The bar-restaurant cooks up a storm, with live music most nights in season. There's a second **pool** (nonguests ₹200) across the road at Cavala's Banana Republic bar.

Nani's Bar & Rani's Restaurant GUESTHOUSE **$$**
(Map p144; ☎2276313; www.naniranigoa.com; r without/with AC ₹1400/1600; ❄@) Nani's is as charming as it is well situated, with nine clean, simply furnished rooms (getting a thorough renovation when we visited), set around a garden and a gorgeous Portuguese colonial bungalow housing the restaurant Balcao, specialising in Goan food. Pricey compared with its neighbours but still a good bet.

★**Nilaya Hermitage** HOTEL **$$$**
(☎2269793, 2269794; www.nilaya.com; Arpora; d incl breakfast, dinner & spa €350; ❄@📶🏊) Ultimate Goan luxury, set 5km inland from Baga beach at Arpora, a stay at this hilltop hideaway will see you signing the guestbook with the likes of Giorgio Armani, Sean Connery and Kate Moss. Ten beautiful redstone rooms undulate around a swimming pool, alongside four luxury tents. The food is as dreamy as the surroundings, and the ayurvedic spa (all inclusive) will spoil you rotten.

Eating

Calangute and Baga have everything from fresh fish cooked up on a beach barbecue to the finest Italian proscuitto in homemade pasta. The main beach strip is thick with vendors selling grilled corn, *pav bhaji* (spiced vegetables and bread) and luminescent candyfloss, as well as the usual beach-shack fare. Dining gets more sophisticated to the north and south – some of Baga's best restaurants are along the road north of the Baga River. Calangute's busy market area, meanwhile, is filled with chai-and-thali joints.

Calangute

★Plantain Leaf INDIAN $

(Map p143; thali ₹100-125, mains ₹80-200; ⊙11am-10pm) On the 1st floor, at a slight remove from the chaos of the market intersection below, is the pure-veg Plantain Leaf. The many Indian families that fill the booths here know a good thing when they see it: cosy, busy and bright, and the veg thali might be the best you'll get in Goa.

Infantaria BAKERY, ITALIAN $$

(Map p143; Calangute-Baga Rd; pastries ₹80-150, mains ₹180-300; ⊙7.30am-midnight) What started out as Calangute's best little bakery has matured and morphed into a fabulous little two-level Italian restaurant. It's still a great place for breakfast, loaded with homemade croissants, flaky pastries and real coffee, but it's also a fine lunch or dinner spot with Goan and Italian specialities, wine and thoughtful cocktails.

A Reverie INTERNATIONAL $$$

(Map p143; ☎9823505550; Holiday St; mains ₹340-600; ⊙7pm-late) A gorgeous lounge-bar, all armchairs, cool jazz and sparkling crystals, this is the place to spoil yourself with the likes of Serrano ham, grilled asparagus, French wines and Italian cheeses. Start with tapas plates and move on to a world menu featuring European, Asian and India flavours.

Baga

Lila Café CAFE $$

(Map p144; mains ₹40-280; ⊙8.30am-6pm) This German-run garden restaurant on the Baga River is a favourite for breakfast with home-baked breads, croissants, perfect, frothy cappuccinos and powerhouse mains like goulash with spaetzle.

Britto's MULTICUISINE, BAR $$

(Map p144; mains ₹100-380; ⊙8.30am-midnight) Britto's is an arena-sized Baga institution at the north end of the beachfront. It's good for breakfast but gets very busy for lunch and dinner. The drinks list is longer than the food menu and there's live music on most nights in season.

★Fiesta CONTINENTAL $$$

(Map p144; www.fiestagoa.in; Tito's Rd; ₹250-600; ⊙7pm till late) Tucked away off noisy Tito's Lane, there's something magical about stepping into Fiesta's candlelit split-level tropical garden. Soft music and exotic furnishings add to an upmarket Mediterranean-style dining experience that starts with homemade pizza and pasta (herb ricotta ravioli or penne with gorgonzola) and extends to French-influenced seafood dishes and some of the finest desserts around. Worth a splurge.

Le Poisson Rouge FRENCH $$$

(Map p144; mains ₹390-480; ⊙7pm-midnight) This Indo-French garden restaurant just across the river is one of Baga's best fine-dining affairs. Simple local ingredients are combined into winning dishes such as beetroot carpaccio, burgundy chicken stew and calamari and prawn risotto, all served up beneath the stars.

Drinking & Nightlife

Baga's club scene bubbles on long after the parties further north have been locked down. If you're up for a night of decadent drinking or dancing on the tables, you're in the right place. Although Tito's Lane in Baga is the hotspot, there are lots of little bars scattered around, many offering live music on weekends.

Café Mambo NIGHTCLUB

(Map p144; ☎9822765002; www.titos.in; couple ₹500; ⊙10.30pm-3am) Mambo's is a slightly sophisticated (relative to Baga) late-night club, with DJs pumping out mostly commercial house and hip hop, and the occasional (Western) retro night. It's strictly 'couples-only', though single women should have no trouble getting in (free); single men can forget it. **Tito's**, just next door, used to be Baga's 'it' club, and is still worth a visit, especially for Bollywood nights. Cover, rules and hours are the same as Mambo's.

Shopping

Both **Mackie's Saturday Nite Bazaar** (www.mackiesnitebazaar.com; ⊙from 6pm Sat Nov-Apr), in Baga, and the larger **Saturday Night Market** (Map p144; www.snmgoa.com; ⊙from 6pm Sat Nov-Apr), in Arpora, about 2km northeast of Baga, set up in season and are fun alternatives to Anjuna's Wednesday market, with food stalls, entertainment and the usual souvenir stalls. They have been cancelled from time to time in recent years for reasons unclear. Ask around to see if they're on.

Karma Collection SOUVENIRS
(Map p144; www.karmacollectiongoa.com; ⏲9.30am-10.30pm) This fixed-price shop near the end of the road to Baga Beach has the usual patchwork wall hangings, but also antiques from across South Asia.

Literati Bookshop & Cafe BOOKS
(Map p143; ☎2277740; www.literati-goa.com; ⏲10am-6.30pm Mon-Sat) A refreshingly different bookstore, this place is in the owners' Calangute home. Ask about readings and other events.

Information

Currency exchange offices, ATMs, pharmacies and internet cafes cluster around Calangute's main market and bus stand area, with several more (of everything) along the Baga and Candolim roads.

MGM International Travels (☎2276037; www.mgmtravels.com; Umta Vaddo, Calangute; ⏲9.30am-6.30pm Mon-Sat) A long-established and trusted travel agency with competitive prices on domestic and international air tickets.

Thomas Cook (☎2282455; Calangute-Anjuna Rd, Calangute; ⏲9am-6pm Mon-Sat) Currency exchange.

Getting There & Around

Frequent buses to Panaji (₹15, 45 minutes) and Mapusa (₹10) depart from the Baga and Calangute bus stands, and a local bus (₹5) runs between the Baga and Calangute stands every few minutes; catch it anywhere along the way. Taxis charge a silly ₹100 between Calangute and Baga. A prepaid taxi from Dabolim Airport to Calangute costs ₹750.

Anjuna

Dear old Anjuna. The stalwart of India's hippy scene still drags out the sarongs and sandalwood each Wednesday for its famous – and once infamous – flea market, and still has that floating in-between-town feel that we love. With its long beach, rice paddies and cheap guesthouses huddled in relatively peaceful pockets, it continues to pull in droves of backpackers and long-term hippies, while midrange tourists are also increasingly making their way here. The village itself might be a bit ragged around the edges, but that's all part of its haphazard charm, and Anjuna remains a favourite of long-stayers and first-timers alike.

Anjuna

Activities, Courses & Tours
1 Oceanic Yoga ... B1

Sleeping
2 Banyan Soul ... C3
3 Casa Anjuna ... A1
4 Elephant Art Cafe ... B3
5 Florinda's ... B3
6 Palacete Rodrigues ... D1
7 Paradise ... B1
8 Peace Land ... B1
9 Vilanova ... C1

Eating
10 Café Diogo ... C3
11 German Bakery ... C3
12 Martha's Breakfast Home ... C2
13 Shore Bar ... B3
14 Whole Bean Tofu ... C3

Drinking & Nightlife
15 Curlie's ... B4

Shopping
16 Anjuna Flea Market ... B4
17 Oxford Arcade ... B1

Sights & Activities

Anjuna's charismatic **beach** runs for almost 2km from the northern village area to the flea market. The northern end is mostly cliffs lined with cheap cafes and basic guesthouses, but the beach proper (starting just south of San Francisco Restaurant) is a lovely stretch of sand with a bunch of beach bars at the southern end. For more action, **paragliding** (tandem rides ₹1800) sometimes takes place on market days off the headland at the southern end of the beach.

Yoga

There's lots of yoga, reiki and ayurvedic massage offered around Anjuna; look for notices at Café Diogo and the German Bakery. Drop-in classes are organised by **Brahmani Yoga** (☎9370568639; www.brahmaniyoga.com), next to Hotel Bougainvillea, and **Oceanic Yoga** (☎9545112278; www.oceanicyoga.com; Anjuna; ⏲1½ hr classes ₹400), which also offers intensive courses and teacher training.

Sleeping

Most accommodation and other useful services are sprinkled along the beach cliffs, on the Anjuna–Mapusa Rd leading to the bus stand or down shady inland lanes. Dozens of rooms of the largely concrete cell

Anjuna

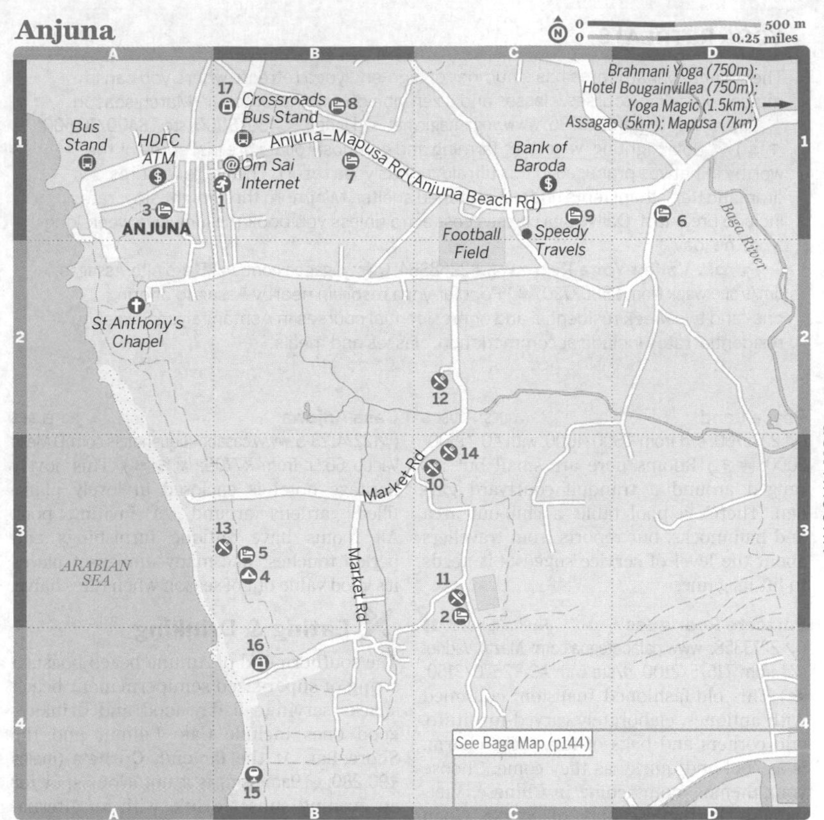

variety run along Anjuna's northern clifftop stretch; most come in at ₹500 to ₹700 per night (more during peak season). There are also plenty of small, family-run guesthouses tucked back from the main beach strip, offering nicer double rooms for a similar price; take your pick from the dozens of 'Rooms to Let' signs.

Elephant Art Cafe TENTED CAMP $
(☎9970668845; elephantartcafe@gmail.com; tents ₹800-1000) The spacious tents here are lined with embroidered fabric, have tile floors and attached bathrooms, and are set in pretty grounds – like a little tent village – with winding, lamp-lit paths. The location, behind the beach shack of the same name, isn't bad either.

Vilanova GUESTHOUSE $
(☎6450389, 9225904244; mendonca90@rediffmail.com; d without/with AC ₹800/1100; ❄) Big, clean rooms have fridge, TV, 24-hour hot water and window screens and are set in three Portuguese-style bungalows in a cute little compound. There are good vibes and a comfortable family atmosphere, with friendly staff and a good-value restaurant.

Florinda's GUESTHOUSE $
(☎9890216520; r ₹400-700, with AC ₹1200; ❄) One of the better cheapies near the beach, Florinda's has a mixed bag of clean rooms, with 24-hour hot water and window screens, set around a flower-filled garden.

Paradise GUESTHOUSE $
(☎9922541714; janet_965@hotmail.com; Anjuna-Mapusa Rd; d ₹1000, with AC ₹2000; ❄@📶) The friendly Paradise is fronted by an old Portuguese house, and its clean rooms are set in rustic grounds full of crowing roosters and sleeping cats. Proprietor Janet and her enterprising family also run a general store, restaurant, internet cafe and more.

YOGA RETREATS

The Anjuna/Vagator area has a number of high-end yoga retreats where you can immerse yourself in courses, classes and a zen vibe during the October–March season.

Yoga Magic (6523796; www.yogamagic.net; s/d lodge ₹6400/8000, ste ₹8400/10,500;) Solar lighting, vegetable farming and compost toilets are just some of the worthy initiatives practised in this ultraluxurious yoga resort. The lodge features dramatic Rajasthani tents under a thatched shelter. Minimum three-night stay; rates include breakfast. Daily yoga classes cost extra unless you book the inclusive week-long 'yoga holiday'.

Purple Valley Yoga Retreat (2268364; www.yogagoa.com; 142 Bairo Alto, Assagao; dm/s one week from £580/720;) Popular yoga resort in nearby Assagao offering one- and two-week residential and nonresidential courses in Ashtanga yoga; weekly residential rates include accommodation, classes and meals.

Peace Land GUESTHOUSE **$**
(2273700; s/d from ₹600/1000, with AC ₹1500-2000;) Rooms here are small but arranged around a tranquil courtyard garden. There's a pool table, a chill-out area and hammocks, but reports from travellers about the level of service suggests it needs to lift its game.

Palacete Rodrigues HERITAGE HOTEL **$$**
(2273358; www.palacetegoa.com; Mazal Vaddo; s/d from ₹1575/2100, d/ste with AC ₹2620/3150;) This old-fashioned mansion, crammed with antiques, elaborately carved furniture, odd corners and bags of fun, tacky charm, is as cool and quirky as they come. Choose your theme: rooms come in Chinese, Vietnamese, Portuguese and, of course, Goan flavours.

Banyan Soul BOUTIQUE HOTEL **$$**
(9820707283; www.thebanyansoul.com; d ₹2200;) A slinky 12-room option, tucked just behind Anjuna's German Bakery, lovingly conceived and run by a young escapee of the Mumbai technology rat race. Rooms are chic and well equipped with cable TV and air-con. It's certainly among the better midrange choices in town.

Hotel Bougainvillea HERITAGE HOTEL **$$$**
(Granpa's Inn; 2273270, 2273271; www.granpasinn.com; Anjuna Beach Rd; d/ste incl breakfast from ₹3950/4450;) This old-fashioned hotel in a 200-year-old yellow mansion is ridiculously pretty. Elegant rooms have that rare combination of charm and luxury, and the pool area is gorgeous. The grounds are so lush and shady that it seems a good few degrees cooler than the rest of Anjuna. The downside is that it's a long way back from the beach.

Casa Anjuna HOTEL **$$$**
(2274123-5; www.casaboutiquehotels.com; D'Mello Vaddo 66; r from ₹7700;) This lovely heritage hotel is enclosed in lovely plant-filled gardens around an inviting pool. All rooms have antique furnishings and period touches; like many upmarket places it's good value out of season when rates halve.

Eating & Drinking

The southern end of Anjuna beach boasts a string of super-sized semipermanent beach shacks serving all day food and drinks – good ones include Cafe Lilliput and the Shore Bar. At the far end, **Curlie's** (mains ₹90-280; 9am-3am) is a notorious spot for an evening sunset drink, with an alternative crowd and the odd impromptu party. While there are plenty of restaurants near the bus stand and along the cliff, Anjuna's best are squirrelled away on the road to the flea market. **Oxford Arcade** (2273436; 8.30am-8pm Mon-Sat), near the Starco Crossroads, is an excellent supermarket where you can stock up on imported goods and cheap alcohol.

Café Diogo CAFE **$**
(Market Rd; snacks ₹60-140; 8.30am-7pm) Probably the best fruit salads in Goa are sliced and diced at Café Diogo, a small locally run cafe on the way to the market. Also worth a munch are the generous toasted avocado, cheese and mushroom sandwiches.

Whole Bean Tofu CAFE **$**
(Market Rd; mains ₹60-150; 8am-5pm) One of the few places in Goa where vegans can eat well, this tofu-filled health-food cafe focuses on all things created from the versatile soya bean.

Martha's Breakfast Home CAFE $$
(meals ₹80-300; ⏲7am-2pm) Martha's specialises in all-day breakfasts, served up in a quiet garden on the way down to the flea-market site. The porridge and juice may be mighty tasty, but the star of the breakfast parade is undoubtedly the piping-hot plates of pancakes and waffles, just crying out to be smothered in real maple syrup. There are a few tidy rooms (₹1000) at the side.

German Bakery MULTICUISINE $$
(www.german-bakery.in; bread & pastries ₹40-80, mains ₹80-270; ⏲8am-11pm; 📶) Leafy and filled with prayer flags, jolly lights and atmospheric curtained nooks, this is a local favourite for breakfast, crepes or a relaxed vegetarian lunch or dinner. Innovative tofu dishes are a speciality.

Shore Bar MULTICUISINE $$
(mains ₹120-400) The Shore Bar has been crowded out by the beachfront competition over the years but it's still an Anjuna institution and with the addition of a soundproof upstairs lounge-bar-nightclub, it's back in the good books. The food here is excellent but pricey, and it's always a cool spot for a sunset drink on market day.

Information

Anjuna has three ATMs, clustered together on the main road to the beach.

Speedy Travels (☎2273266; ⏲9am-6.30pm Mon-Sat, 10am-1pm Sun) Reliable agency for air and train ticket booking, a range of tours, and credit-card advances or currency exchange.

Getting There & Away

Buses to Mapusa (₹15) depart every half-hour or so from the main **bus stand** near the beach; some from Mapusa continue on to Vagator and Chapora. Two daily buses to Calangute depart from the main **crossroads**. Taxis and pilots gather at both stops, and you can hire scooters and motorcycles easily from the crossroads.

Vagator & Chapora

Vagator's twin beaches are small by Goan standards but the dramatic red-stone cliffs, rolling green hills, patches of forest and a crumbling 17th-century Portuguese fort provide Vagator and its diminutive neighbour Chapora with one of the prettiest settings on the north Goan coast. Once known for their wild trance parties and heady, hippy lifestyles, things have slowed down considerably these days. Vagator is still the place of choice for many backpackers and party-goers, and Chapora – reminiscent of *Star Wars'* Mos Eisley Cantina – remains a fave for smokers, with the scent of charas hanging heavy in the air. Vagator has the bulk of eating and sleeping choices, along with what's left of the party scene.

Hang around long enough in Vagator and you'll likely be handed a flyer for a party (many with international DJs), which can range from divine to dire.

Sleeping

Vagator

You'll see lots of signs for 'Rooms to Let' in private homes and guesthouses along Ozran Beach Rd and on side roads too. Most charge around ₹600 per double.

Asterix HOSTEL $
(☎9766267606; www.asterixhostel.com; dm/d incl breakfast ₹500/1300, dm with AC ₹600; ❄@📶) True backpacker hostels are rare in Goa, but Asterix brings the dorm experience and an international vibe to Vagator. Run by a

GOA'S FLEA MARKET EXPERIENCE

Wednesday's weekly **flea market** (⏲8am-late Wed, usually late Oct-late Mar) at Anjuna is as much part of the Goan experience as a day on the beach. More than three decades ago it was the sole preserve of hippies smoking jumbo joints and convening to compare experiences on the heady Indian circuit. Nowadays, things are far more mainstream – the stalls carry crafts from Kashmir and Karnataka and Tibetan trinkets – and package tourists seem to beat out independent travellers in both numbers and purchasing power. A couple of hours here and you'll never want to see a mirrored bedspread, brass figurine or floaty Indian cotton dress again in your life. But it's still a good time, a place to meet and mingle, and you can find some interesting one-off souvenirs and clothing in among the tourist tat. Remember to bargain hard and take along equal quantities of patience and stamina, applicable to dealing with local and expat vendors alike.

Vagator & Chapora

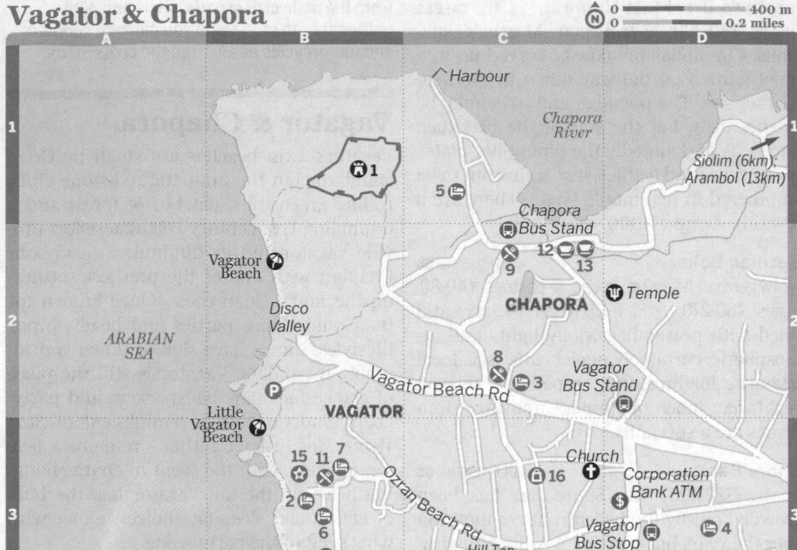

Vagator & Chapora

Sights

1 Chapora Fort B1

Sleeping

2 Alcove Resort B3
3 Asterix C2
4 Bean Me Up D3
5 Casa de Olga C1
6 Paradise on the Earth B3
7 Shalom B3

Eating

Bean Me Up Soya Station .... (see 4)
8 Mango Tree C2
9 Sunrise Restaurant C2
10 Thalassa B3
11 Yangkhor Moonlight B3

Drinking & Nightlife

12 Jai Ganesh Fruit Juice Centre C2
13 Scarlet Cold Drinks C2

Entertainment

14 Hilltop C3
15 Nine Bar B3

Shopping

16 Rainbow Bookshop C3

couple of well-travelled Goans, the six-bed dorms are clean and bright, and things like lockers, wi-fi, communal kitchen and travel advice are free. It's behind the small chapel next to Mango Tree. Bookings via the website only.

Bean Me Up GUESTHOUSE $
(Enterprise Guest House; ☎2273479; www.beanmeup.in; 1639/2 Deulvaddo; d without/with bathrooms ₹475/680; wi-fi) Each of the rooms around the leafy, parachute-silk covered courtyard are simple but themed with their own exotic decor, mosquito nets and common verandas. The mellow, yoga-friendly vibe matches the clientele of the popular vegan restaurant here. Excellent value.

Paradise on the Earth BEACH HUT $
(☎2273591; www.moondance.co.nr; huts without bathroom ₹600-700) Simple bamboo cocohuts (not too common in these parts) clinging to the cliff above Little Vagator Beach are great value for the beachside location, though the name might be a little overkill.

Shalom GUESTHOUSE $$
(☎2273166; jul_and@hotmail.com; d ₹800-1200, with AC ₹1500; AC wi-fi) Arranged around a

placid garden not far from the path down to Little Vagator Beach, this friendly family-run guesthouse has a variety of extremely well-kept rooms, including one with air-con, and a two-bedroom apartment for long-stayers.

Alcove Resort HOTEL $$$
(2274491; www.alcovegoa.com; Little Vagator Beach; d without/with AC from ₹3300/3850, cottages ₹4400/4950;) The location overlooking Little Vagator Beach and a few steps from the popular Nine Bar is hard to beat. Attractively furnished rooms, slightly larger cottages and four suites surrounding a decent pool, bar and restaurant make this a good place for those who want a touch of luxury at reasonable prices.

Chapora

Head down the road to the harbour and you'll find lots of rooms – and whole homes – for rent; check out a few before you commit.

Casa de Olga GUESTHOUSE $
(2274355, 9822157145; eadsouza@yahoo.co.in; r ₹1200, without bathroom ₹600) This welcoming family place has rooms arranged around a pretty garden in a quiet location on the way to Chapora harbour. The cheaper ones are basic (but comfy and clean), while the pricier ones have hot showers, kitchenette with fridge, and balcony.

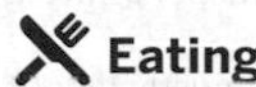

Eating

Vagator

A few eating options cluster around the entrance to Little Vagator Beach, along with the usual slew of much-of-a-muchness beach shacks down on the sands.

★ **Thalassa** GREEK $$
(9850033537; mains ₹180-400; 4pm-midnight) Thalassa has built a solid reputation for authentic and very good Greek food served on a breezy terrace overlooking Little Vagator Beach. Fresh ingredients, expert preparation and imaginative dishes. Reservations essential.

Yangkhor Moonlight TIBETAN, MULTICUISINE $$
(mains ₹70-200) Superfresh food is glorified in the Tibetan and even the Italian dishes here. The veg *momo* (Tibetan dumpling) soup is outstanding. The chairs and tablecloths are plastic and the walls are lime green, but the food and atmosphere are good.

Mango Tree BAR, CAFE $$
(mains ₹50-170; 9am-4am) With loud reggae, crappy service, dark-wood furniture and mango-coloured walls, a sometimes rambunctious bar scene, draught beer, terracotta lanterns and generally a good vibe, Mango Tree is an ever-popular meeting place for all that and its really good food. Films or sports are screened most nights.

Bean Me Up Soya Station VEGAN $$
(1639/2 Deulvaddo; mains ₹120-250; 8am-11pm) Oh, veggies and vegans, you've had a hard time in Goa. In a mellow garden setting, Bean Me Up specialises in vegan and raw foods, including homemade tofu and tempeh, vegan hot dogs and pizza and an internationally-inspired range of meals. There's also health juices, a bar, and an on-site shop selling tofunaise and soysage.

Chapora

Tiny Chapora's eating scene is not as evolved as Vagator's. Little restaurants pepper the main street, but they're reliable only for caloric intake. **Sunrise Restaurant** (mains ₹70-180; 8.30am-10.30pm) is reliable enough, especially for breakfast, while **Scarlet Cold Drinks** (juices & snacks ₹30-50; 8.30am-midnight) and **Jai Ganesh Fruit Juice Centre** (juices ₹25-60; 8.30am-midnight) are both popular meeting places side by side in close proximity to the thickest gusts of charas smoke. Scarlet has an exceptionally good noticeboard, while Jai Ganesh has cold coffee and avocado lassis.

Drinking & Entertainment

Aside from secretive parties, there's not as much going on in Vagator and Chapora these days; gone are the all-nighters and the beach trance is now turned off promptly at 10pm. Still, Vagator's party scene is hanging on, mainly at **Nine Bar** (6pm-4am), a late-night semi-open air bar overlooking the beach, and **Hilltop** (2273025, 2273665; sunset-late), where trance parties are still organised, especially over the peak Christmas/New Year period – the Sunday session is legendary. The Russians, having taken the party crown away from the Israelis, seem to create nightlife in various spots around town.

WHERE'S THE PARTY?

Though Goa was long legendary among Western visitors for its all-night, open-air Goan trance parties, a central government 'noise pollution' ban on loud music in open spaces between 10pm and 6am has largely curbed its often notorious, drug-laden party scene: Goa simply does not party the way it used to. With a tourist industry to nurture, however, authorities tend to turn a blind eye to parties during the peak Christmas–New Year period. Late nights are also allowed in interior spaces, which is why clubs carry on without problems. If you're looking for the remainder of the real party scene, though, you'll need to cross your fingers, keep your ear close to the ground, and wait out for word in Vagator or Anjuna.

Shopping

Rainbow Bookshop BOOKS
(10am-2pm & 3-7pm) In Vagator, near Primrose Cafe, this lovely little shop stocks a good range of secondhand and new books.

Information

Vagator's closest ATM is the HDFC at the petrol station on the back road to Anjuna and Mapusa. Plenty of internet places are scattered around town and lots of accommodation places offer wi-fi.

Getting There & Away

Frequent buses run from Chapora, through Vagator, to Mapusa (₹10) throughout the day, many via Anjuna. The buses start in Chapora village, but there are a couple of other stops in Chapora and Vagator. Scooters/motorbikes can easily be hired for around ₹200/300 per day in high season.

Morjim & Asvem

Morjim and Asvem, a pretty strip of mostly empty sand, are two North Goan beaches where sunbathing doesn't attract hordes of hawkers, dogs and onlookers. The water, though, does suffer from a bit of river run-off pollution and cannot ever be described as crystal clear. Nonetheless, rare olive ridley turtles nest at the beach's southern end from September to February, so this is a protected area, which, in theory at least, means no development and no rubbish. Morjim and Asvem have a handful of low-key beach shacks and several places to stay and eat, including the excellent beachfront **Goan Café & Resort** (2244394; www.goancafe.com; apt & cottage from ₹1050, with AC ₹1250, treehouse without/with bathroom from ₹800/1150;), whose friendly three brother-owners have built a fine array of treehouse huts as well as year-round apartments; **Meems' Beach Resort** (3290703; www.meemsbeachresort.com; huts ₹1500-2500, r ₹2000, with AC ₹3000;), which has a range of huts and rooms also right on the beach, along with free wi-fi and an atmospheric restaurant; and **La Plage** (mains ₹210-320), perhaps the fanciest beach shack in Goa, renowned for its high-calibre French food.

Mandrem

Peaceful, hidden Mandrem has become a refuge for those seeking a break from the traveller scenes of Arambol and Anjuna – and those who avoided the scene to begin with. The beach is beautiful, and there's little to do but laze on it with a good book. Coco-huts can be had from ₹600 to ₹1000. It's not easy to get here by public transport; hire a scooter or cab in Arambol.

There's lots of yoga around, mostly taught by foreigners each season. **Himalaya Yoga Valley** (9922719982; www.yogagoaindia.com) specialises in hatha and ashtanga teacher-training courses, but also has drop-in classes (₹300) twice daily.

Sleeping & Eating

★ **Dunes Holiday Village** BEACH HUTS $
(2247219; www.dunesgoa.com; huts ₹900-1100; @) The pretty huts here are peppered around a palm-forest allée leading to the beach, and at night, globe lamps light up the place like a palm-tree dreamland. Dunes also has friendly, helpful staff, and a good restaurant on the beach.

Cuba Retreat HOTEL $$
(2645775; www.cubagoa.com; d without/with AC ₹1650/2200;) One of a number of fine Cuba properties around Goa, this one really scores for its retro white-and-green exterior, clean

rooms with spring mattresses, kind staff and good bar-restaurant in the courtyard.

Villa River Cat GUESTHOUSE **$$$**
(☎2247928; www.villarivercat.com; 438/1 Junasawaddo; d ₹3015, with bathroom ₹3770-4800; ❄) Styling itself as a retreat for artists, writers and other bohemian types, this unusual circular Portuguese guesthouse is filled with art, antiques and a lot of pets. The riverside location (close to the beach) is lovely but might not justify this price.

Arambol (Harmal)

Beautiful Arambol, with its craggy cliffs and sweeping beach, first emerged in the 1960s as a mellow paradise for long-haired long-stayers, and ever since, travellers attracted to the hippy atmosphere have been drifting up to this blissed-out corner of Goa. As a result, in the high season the beach and the road leading down to it (known as Glastonbury St) can get pretty crowded – with huts, people and nonstop stalls selling the usual tourist stuff. If you're looking for a committed traveller vibe, this is the place to come; if you're seeking laid-back languidness, you might be better off heading down the coast to Mandrem or Morjim.

Activities

The cliffs north of Arambol beach are a popular spot for **paragliding**. **Arambol Paragliding School** (☎9822867570) and **Arambol Hammocks** (☎9822389005, www.arambol.com; per 20min ₹1800; ⏲9am-6pm) both offer tandem flights in season from around ₹1800. Several places also offer **yoga** classes and courses.

Follow the cliff path north of Arambol Beach to pretty **Kalacha Beach**, which meets the small 'sweetwater' lake, a great spot for swimming.

Himalayan Iyengar Yoga Centre YOGA
(www.hiyogacentre.com; Madhlo Vaddo; five-day yoga course ₹3000; ⏲Nov-Mar) This is the winter retreat for the popular Dharamsala-based Iyengar yoga centre. Five-day courses (beginning on Fridays, orientation every Tuesday), intensive workshops, children's classes, and teacher training are all available. The centre is a five-minute walk from the beach, off the main road; look for the big banner. HI also has **huts** (s/d without bathroom ₹250/300) for students.

Sleeping

Arambol is well known for its sea-facing, cliff-hugging budget huts – trawl the cliff-side to the north of Arambol's main beach stretch for the best hut options. It's almost impossible to book in advance: simply turn up early in the day to check who's checking out. The area around the Narayan temple (take a left turn off the main road as you enter town), also has several guesthouses of similar quality.

Chilli's HOTEL **$**
(☎9921882424; d ₹300-450, with AC ₹600; ⏲year-round) The bright yellow house on the main road to the beach, run by the helpful Derick Fernandes, is one of Arambol's best noncliff bargains. Chilli's offers 10 bright, no-frills rooms, all with attached bathroom, fan and hot-water shower, some with fridge and balcony.

Shree Sai Cottages BEACH HUTS **$**
(☎9420767358, 3262823; shreesai_cottages@yahoo.com; huts without bathroom ₹500-600) The last set of huts on the cliffs before Kalacha (Sweet Water) Beach, Shree Sai has a calm, easygoing vibe and basic but cute hut-cottages with little balconies and lovely views out over the water.

Om Ganesh BEACH HUTS **$**
(☎9404436447; r & huts ₹400-800) Popular huts and some more solid rooms on the cliffs overlooking the water, managed by the friendly Sudir. The seaside Om Ganesh Restaurant is also a great place for lunch or dinner. Note that almost everyone in the area will tell you that their place is Om Ganesh.

Famafa Beach Resort HOTEL **$$**
(☎2242516; www.famafaarambolgoa.com; Glastonbury St; r from ₹1200; ❄@) For a little bit of comfort (including some air-con rooms) close to the beach, Famafa is a staid but clean and reliable midranger.

Eating & Drinking

Beach shacks with chairs and tables on the sand and parachute-silk canopies line the beach at Arambol. Many change annually, but **21 Coconuts** (for seafood) and **Relax Inn** (for Italian) are mainstays. There are more restaurants and cafes lining the main road from the village to the beach. For simpler fare, head up to Arambol village, by the bus stop, where small local joints will whip you up a thali and a chai for less than ₹50.

Shimon MIDDLE EASTERN $

(meals ₹70-140; ⏲9am-11pm) Just back from the beach and understandably popular with Israeli backpackers, Shimon is the place to fill up on an exceptional falafel (₹110) or other specialities like *sabikh*, aubergine slices stuffed into pita bread with boiled egg, potato, salad and spicy relishes in pita. Follow either up with Turkish coffee or a fruit shake.

German Bakery BAKERY $

(Welcome Inn; pastries ₹20-70) This rather dim and dingy corner cafe is surprisingly popular, with decent pastries (eg lemon cheese pie, ₹60) and espresso coffee.

Fellini ITALIAN $$

(mains ₹140-300; ⏲11am-11pm) Pizza is the big deal here – the menu has more than 40 different kinds – and they are good. The pastas, calzones and paninis, especially with seafood, are also tasty. The tiramisu will keep you up at night, thinking back on it fondly.

Loeki Café MULTICUISINE $$

(Glastonbury St; mains ₹50-200; ⏲8.30am-late) As much a chill-out and live music joint as a place to eat, Loeki is a very relaxed place with cushions on the floor, regular live music and jam sessions on Thursday and Saturday. Typically extenisve world menu, including Goan dishes.

Double Dutch MULTICUISINE $$

(mains ₹100-290) Longtime popular place for steaks, salads, Thai and Indonesian dishes, and famous for its apple pies, all in a pretty garden setting.

Information

Internet outfits, travel agents and money changers are as common as monsoon frogs on the road leading down to Arambol's beach. The nearest ATM is in Arambol village near the bus stop.

Getting There & Around

Buses to Mapusa (₹27, 1½ hours) depart from Arambol village every half-hour. It's only about 1.5km from the main beach area, but you're lucky if you get a cab, or even an autorickshaw, for ₹60. A prepaid taxi to Arambol from Dabolim Airport costs ₹1000; from Mapusa it's ₹400.

Lots of places in Arambol rent scooters/motorbikes, for ₹200/300, respectively, per day.

SOUTH GOA

Margao (Madgaon)

POP 94,400

Margao (also known by its train station name of Madgaon) is the main population centre of south Goa and for travellers is chiefly a transport hub, with the state's major train and bus stations. Although lacking much of Panaji's charm, it's a bustling market town of a manageable size for getting things done, or for simply enjoying the busy energy of urban India without big-city hassles.

Sights

It's worth a walk around the lovely, small **Largo de Igreja** district, home to lots of atmospherically crumbling and gorgeously restored old Portuguese homes, and the quaint and richly decorated 17th-century **Church of the Holy Spirit**, particularly

THE FOUNDING FATHER OF QUEPEM

When Father José Paulo de Almeida looked out his oyster-shell doors and windows, he saw the Church of the Holy Cross beyond the palm trees out front, the river that functioned as his road into and out of the forest out back, and below, lush gardens elaborately designed with cruciform patterns. The Portuguese priest and nobleman arrived in Goa in 1779 and set up the town of Quepem not long after. Today the **Palácio do Deão** (☎2664029, 9823175639; www.palaciododeao.com; ⏲10am-5pm Sat-Thu) may look a lot like it did when he lived there, with original woodwork, furniture, religious effects and even the garden design all lovingly restored in the past few years by Goan couple Ruben and Celia Vasco da Gama. The Vasco da Gamas also host lunches and teatime on the back verandah; call for reservations and prices. All donations to the Palácio are used to continue restoration work and eventually create a cultural centre here.

A taxi from Margao, 14km away, will cost ₹600 round trip, including waiting time, but the bus (₹10, every few minutes) stops just a few minutes' walk down the road.

impressive when a Sunday morning service is taking place. The church also hosts services at 4pm on weekdays but is open erratically at other times.

The city's business district orbits the rectangular **Municipal Gardens**, a mini-oasis. At the southern end the Municipal Building is home to the dusty and awesome **Municipal Library** (⏲8am-8pm Mon-Fri, 9am-noon & 4-7pm Sat & Sun), which has some great books on Goa and a retro reading room where you can read the paper along with lots of gents in button-downs.

Sleeping

Hotel Tanish HOTEL $
(☎2735656; hoteltanishgoa@gmail.com; Reliance Trade Centre, Valaulikar Rd; s/d ₹650/900, s/d/ste with AC ₹800/1100/1800; ❄) The best budget place to stay in town – incongruously located on the top floor of a mall – has kind staff and tidy, well-equipped rooms with great views of the surrounding countryside. Suites come with a bathtub, big TV and views all the way to Colva. Just make sure to ask for an outside-facing room; some overlook the mall interior.

Om Shiv Hotel HOTEL $$
(☎2710294; www.omshivhotel.com; Cine Lata Rd; d with AC ₹2700-3800, ste ₹4850; ❄) In a bright-yellow building tucked away behind the Bank of India, Om Shiv does a fine line in 'executive' rooms, which all have air-con, balcony and an ordered air. The suites have exceptional views, and it's home to Margao's 'only night hotspot', the Rockon Pub.

Eating

Swad INDIAN $
(New Market; ₹25-110; ⏲7.30am-8pm) Many regard this family-friendly favourite as having Margao's best pure veg food. The North Indian thalis are reliably good, as are the snacks, South Indian tiffins and dosas.

Café Tato INDIAN $
(Valaulikar Rd; thalis ₹60, mains ₹30-70; ⏲7am-10pm Mon-Sat) A favourite local lunch spot: tasty vegetarian fare and thalis in a bustling backstreet canteen.

★**Longhuino's** GOAN, MULTICUISINE $$
(Luis Miranda Rd; mains ₹80-160; ⏲8.30am-11pm) Since 1950, quaint old Longhuino's bar and restaurant, with its old wooden chairs, whirring fans and slow service, has been serving up tasty Goan, Indian and Chinese dishes

Margao (Madgaon)

Sleeping
1 Hotel Tanish B4
2 Om Shiv Hotel B4

Eating
3 Café Tato B4
4 Longhuino's A4
5 Swad B4

Shopping
6 Golden Heart Emporium A3
7 MMC New Market B4

Information
8 Goa Tourism Desk A4
Grace Cybercafe .... (see 1)
9 Municipal Library A4

Transport
10 Paulo Travel Masters A4

popular with locals and tourists alike. It also does a decent job of desserts like bebinca and tiramasu. Great place to watch the world go by.

Shopping

MMC New Market MARKET
(⌚8.30am-9pm Mon-Sat) Margao's bustling covered MMC New Market is one of the most colourful in Goa.

Golden Heart Emporium BOOKS
(Confidant House, Abade Faria Rd; ⌚10am-1.30pm & 4-7pm Mon-Sat) One of Goa's best bookstores, crammed with fiction, nonfiction and illustrated books on the state's food, architecture and history.

ℹ Information

Banks offering currency exchange and 24-hour ATMs are all around town, especially near the municipal gardens and along Luis Miranda Rd. There's a handy HDFC ATM in the Caro Centre near Longuinhos.

Apollo Victor (☎2728888; Station Rd, Malbhat) Reliable medical services.

Cyberlink (Caro Centre; Abade Faria Rd; per hr ₹20; ⌚8.30am-7.30pm Mon-Sat)

Main Post Office (⌚9am-1.30pm & 2.30-5pm Mon-Sat) North of the Municipal Gardens.

Goa Tourism Desk (Margao Residency; ☎2715096; www.goa-tourism.com; Luis Miranda Rd) Book GTDC trips here.

Grace Cybercafe (Valaulikar Rd, 1st fl, Reliance Trade Centre; per hr ₹30; ⌚9.30am-6.30pm) Fastest and friendliest.

ℹ Getting There & Around

BUS

Government and private long-distance buses both depart from Kadamba bus stand, about 2km north of the Municipal Gardens. Shuttle buses (₹30, 35 minutes) run to Panaji every few minutes. For North Goa destinations it's best to head to Panaji and change there. Local buses

MAJOR TRAINS FROM MARGAO (MADGAON)

DESTINATION	TRAIN	FARE (₹)	DURATION (HR)	DEPARTURES
Bangalore	02779 Vasco da Gama-SBC Link	278/779 (D)	15	3.30pm
Chennai (Madras; via Yesvantpur)	17312 Vasco-da-Gama-Chennai Express	343/971/1500 (C)	21	3.20pm Thu
Delhi	12431 Rajdhani Express	2110/3050 (A)	27	10.20am Tue, Thu & Fri
Ernakulum	12618 Lakshadweep Express	325/889/1345 (C)	14½	7.25pm
	16345 Netravati Express	305/858/1315 (C)	15	11.10pm
Hubli	02779 Vasco-da-Gama-SBC Link	144/359 (D)	6½	3.50pm
Mangalore	12133 Mangalore Express	214/564/830 (C)	5½	7.10am
Mumbai (Bombay)	10112 Konkan Kanya Express	288/811/1235 (C)	12	6pm
	10104 Mandovi Express	288/811/1235 (C)	12	9.30am
Mumbai (Dadar)	12052 Jan Shatabdi Express	197/700 (B)	8½	2.30pm
Pune	12779 Goa Express	264/714/1060 (C)	12	3.30pm
Thiruvananthapuram	12432 Rajdhani Express	1405/2005 (A)	19	2.45pm Mon, Wed & Thu
	16345 Netravati Express	347/982/1520 (C)	19½	11.10pm

Fares: (A) 3AC/2AC, (B) 2S/CC, (C) sleeper/3AC/2AC, (D) sleeper/3AC

to Benaulim (₹10, 20 minutes), Colva (₹10, 20 minutes) and Palolem (₹30, one hour) stop at the bus stop on the east side of the Municipal Gardens every 15 minutes or so.

Private buses ply interstate routes several times daily, most departing between 5.30pm and 7.30pm, and can be booked at offices around town; try **Paulo Travel Masters.** (☎2702922; Luis Miranda Rd, 1st fl, Bella Vista Apt; ⏲8am-7pm) The following are sample long-distance high-season fares:

Bengaluru (private; without/with AC ₹600/850, 13 hours)
Hampi (sleeper; ₹750, nine hours)
Mumbai (private; without/with AC ₹700/1000, 14 hours)
Pune (without/with AC ₹500/850, 12 hours)

TAXI

Taxis are plentiful around the Municipal Gardens, train station and Kadamba bus stand, and they'll go anywhere in Goa, including Palolem (₹800), Panaji (₹800), Dabolim airport (₹600), Calangute (₹1100), Anjuna (₹1200) and Arambol (₹1700). Except for the train station, where there's a prepaid booth, you'll have to negotiate the fare with the driver.

TRAIN

Margao's well-organised train station, about 2km south of town, serves the Konkan Railway and other routes. Its **reservation hall** (☎PNR enquiry 2700730, information 2712790,; ⏲8am-2pm & 2.15-8pm Mon-Sat, 8am-2pm Sun) is on the 1st floor. Services to Mumbai, Mangalore, Ernakulum and Thiruvananthapuram are the most frequent. A taxi or autorickshaw to or from the town centre should cost around ₹100.

Chandor

The lush village of Chandor, 15km east of Margao, makes a perfect day away from the beaches, and it's here more than anywhere else in the state that the once opulent lifestyles of Goa's former landowners, who found favour with the Portuguese aristocracy, are still visible in its quietly decaying colonial-era mansions. Chandor hosts the colourful **Feast of the Three Kings** on the 6 January, during which local boys re-enact the arrival of the three kings from the Christmas story.

Braganza House, built in the 17th century, is possibly the best example of what Goa's scores of once grand and glorious mansions have today become. Built on land granted by the King of Portugal, the house was divided from the outset into two wings, to house two

OFF THE BEATEN TRACK

DUDHSAGAR FALLS

On the eastern border with Karnataka, Dudhsagar Falls (603m) are Goa's most impressive waterfalls, and the second highest in India, best seen as soon as possible after the rains. To get here, take the 8.13am train to Colem from Margao (there are only three trains daily in each direction), and from there, catch a jeep for the bumpy 40-minute trip to the falls (₹4000 for the six-passenger jeep). It's then a short but rocky clamber to the edge of the falls themselves. A much easier option is to take a full-day GTDC tour from Panaji, Mapusa or Calangute (₹750, Wednesday and Sunday), or arrange an excursion with travel agencies at any of the beach resorts.

sides of the same family. The **West Wing** (☎2784201; admission ₹150; ⏲9am-5pm, last admission 4pm) belongs to one set of the family's descendants, the Menezes-Bragança, and is filled with gorgeous chandeliers, Italian marble floors, rosewood furniture, and antique treasures from Macau, Portugal, China and Europe. Despite the passing of the elderly Mrs Aida Menezes-Bragança in 2012, the grand old home, which requires considerable upkeep, remains open to the public. Next door, the **East Wing** (☎2857630; admission ₹100; ⏲9am-5.30pm) is owned by the Braganza-Pereiras, descendants of the other half of the family. It's nowhere near as grand, but it's beautiful in its own lived-in way, and has a small but striking family chapel that contains a carefully hidden fingernail of St Francis Xavier – a relic that's understandably a source of great pride. Both homes are open daily, and there's almost always someone around to let you in.

About 1km east of Chandor's church, the original building of the **Fernandes House** (☎2784245; admission ₹200; ⏲9am-6pm), also known as Casa Grande, dates back more than 500 years, while the Portuguese section was tacked on by the Fernandes family in 1821. The secret basement hideaway, full of gun holes and with an escape tunnel to the river, was used by the family to flee attackers.

The best way to get here is by taxi from Margao (₹350 round trip, including waiting time).

Colva & Benaulim

POP 12,000

Colva and Benaulim boast broad, open beaches, but are no longer the first place backpackers head in south Goa – most tourists here are of the domestic or ageing European varieties. There's no party scene as in north Goa and they lack the beauty and traveller vibe of Palolem. Still, these are the closest beaches to the major transport hubs of Margao and Dabolim airport. Of the two, Benaulim has the greater charm, with only a small strip of shops and a village vibe, though out of high season it sometimes has the sad feel of a deserted seaside town. From here you can explore this part of the southern coast (the beach stretches unbroken as far as Velsao in the north and the mouth of the Sal River at Mobor in the south), which in many parts is empty and gorgeous. The inland road that runs this length is perfect for gentle cycling and scootering, with lots of picturesque Portuguese-era mansions and whitewashed churches along the way.

Sights & Activities

The beach entrances at Colva, and to a lesser extent Benaulim, throng with operators keen to sell you **parasailing** (per ride ₹700), **jet-skiing** (per 15 minutes ₹800), and one-hour **dolphin-watching trips** (per person from ₹400).

★**Goa Chitra** MUSEUM
(☎6570877; www.goachitra.com; St John the Baptist Rd, Mondo Vaddo, Benaulim; admission ₹200; ⏲9am-6pm Tue-Sun) Artist and restorer Victor Hugo Gomes first noticed the slow extinction of traditional objects He created this ethnographic museum from the more than 4000 cast-off objects that he collected from across the state over 20 years. Admission to the museum is via a one-hour guided tour (held on the hour). In addition to the organic traditional farm out back, you'll see tons of tools and household objects, Christian artefacts and some fascinating farming implements. Goa Chitra is 3km east of Maria Hall.

Sleeping

Colva

Colva still has quite a few basic budget guesthouses among the palm groves back from the beach; ask around locally.

Sam's Guesthouse HOTEL $
(☎2788753; r ₹500) Up away from the fray, about 1km north of Colva's main drag, Sam's is a cheerful place with good value rooms arranged around a garden. It's a short hop across the road to the beach.

La Ben HOTEL $
(☎2788040; www.laben.net; Colva Beach Rd; r without/with AC ₹860/1300; ❄📶) Neat, clean and not entirely devoid of atmosphere, La Ben is top value for this central Colva location. The rooftop restaurant is a bonus. Wi-fi is ₹40 per hour.

Skylark Resort HOTEL $$
(☎2788052; www.skylarkresortgoa.com; 4th Ward; r without/with AC from ₹2380/2970; ❄🏊) Easily the pick of Colva's hotels for value, Skylark has colourful, immaculate rooms – the more expensive ones face the large pool. Locally-made teak furniture, block-print bedspreads and giant shower heads add to the charm, and Colva's best bar is next door.

Benaulim

There are lots of homes around town advertising simple rooms to let. This, combined with a couple of decent budget options,

> **COLVA'S MENINO JESUS**
>
> Colva's 18th-century **Our Lady of Mercy Church** has been host to several miracles, it's said. Inside, closely guarded under lock and key, lives a little statue known as the 'Menino' (Baby) Jesus, which is thought to miraculously heal the sick. It only sees the light of day during the **Fama de Menino Jesus festival**, on the second Monday in October, when the little image is paraded about town, dipped in the river, and installed in the church's high altar for pilgrims to pray to. At other times of year you can still visit the church in the early evening, and if you have any afflictions, you might choose to stop on your way in to buy a plastic ex-voto shaped like the body part in question or offering to the Baby Jesus.

PUPPY LOVE

International Animal Rescue (IAR; ☎2268328; www.internationalanimalrescue.org; Animal Tracks, Madungo Vaddo, Assagao) runs the Animal Tracks rescue facility is Assagao, North Goa. At Colva's **Goa Animal Welfare Trust Shop** (⏲9.30am-1pm & 4-7pm Mon-Sat), next to Skylark Resort, you can pick up some gifts, donate clothes and other stuff you don't want, and borrow books from the lending library. You can also learn more about the work of **GAWT** (☎2653677; www.gawt.org; Old Police Station, Curchorem; ⏲9am-5.30pm Mon-Sat, 10am-1pm Sun), which operates a shelter in Curchorem (near Margao). At Chapolim, a few kilometres northeast of Palolem, the **Animal Rescue Centre** (☎2644171; arcingoa@gmail.com; Chapolim; ⏲10am-1pm & 2.30-5pm Mon-Sat) also takes in sick, injured or stray animals. Volunteers are welcome at the shelters, even for a few hours, to walk or play with the dogs.

make Benaulim a better bet for backpackers than Colva.

Rosario's Inn GUESTHOUSE $
(☎2770636; r without/with AC ₹400/700; ❄) Across a football field flitting with young players and dragonflies, Rosario's is a big family-run place that's been around for a while and is still a steal at this price.

D'Souza Guest House GUESTHOUSE $
(☎2770583; d ₹700) If you value a homey atmosphere more than proximity to the beach, this traditional blue house is run by a friendly local Goan family but there's just three spacious, clean rooms – book ahead.

Palm Grove Cottages HOTEL $$
(☎2770059, 2771170; www.palmgrovegoa.com; d ₹1450, with AC ₹1730-3100; ❄) Ensconsed in the leafiest garden you'll find, Palm Grove Cottages is close to the Benaulim shops but feels a world away. Guest rooms are atmospheric (some have balconies), and the ever-popular Palm Garden Restaurant graces the garden. The deluxe rooms in the new Portuguese-style building are top notch.

Anthy's Guesthouse GUESTHOUSE $$
(☎0832 2771680; anthysguesthouse@rediffmail.com; Sernabatim Beach; r ₹1400-1950) One of just a handful of places actually on the beach, Anthy's is a firm favourite with travellers (book ahead). Well-kept chalet-style rooms, which stretch back from the beach, are surrounded by a pretty garden and restaurant.

Eating & Drinking

Colva

Colva's beach has a string of shacks offering the standard fare and fresh seafood. At the roundabout near the church, you'll find chai shops and thali places, fruit, vegetable and fish stalls, and, at night, *bhelpuri* vendors. For the less traditional there's even a branch of Subway and Cafe Coffee Day.

Sagar Kinara INDIAN $
(Colva Beach Rd; mains ₹40-160; ⏲7am-10.30pm) A pure-veg restaurant with tastes to please even committed carnivores, this top-floor place is super-efficient and serves up cheap and delicious North and South Indian cuisine.

Leda Lounge & Restaurant CONTINENTAL, BAR
(mains ₹200-600; ⏲7.30am-midnight) The food at stylish Leda – everything from seafood, steaks and Indian standards to pasta – is pricey but the attraction here is the comfy, cosmopolitan bar with live music most nights.

Benaulim

Malibu Restaurant INDIAN, ITALIAN $$
(mains ₹100-180; ⏲8.30am-11pm) With a secluded garden setting full of flowers, cool breezes and butterflies, Malibu is off the beach but still one of Benaulim's tastier and more sophisticated dining experiences, with great renditions of Italian favourites. In season the same owners operate the Malibu beach shack.

Pedro's Bar & Restaurant GOAN, MULTICUISINE $$
(Vasvaddo Beach Rd; mains ₹110-300; ⏲7am-midnight) In a large, shady garden just back from the beachfront and popular with local and international tourists alike, Pedro's offers standard Indian, Chinese and Italian dishes, as well as a good line in Goan choices and some super 'sizzlers'.

Johncy Restaurant GOAN, MULTICUISINE $$
(Vasvaddo Beach Rd; mains ₹110-195; ⏰7am-midnight) At the main entrance to the beach, Johncy has been around forever, dispensing standard beach-shack favourites from its semipermanent location just off the sands.

Information

Colva has plenty of banks and ATM machines strung along the east–west Colva Beach Rd, and a post office on the lane that runs past the eastern end of the church. Benaulim has a '24-hour' Bank of Baroda ATM at Maria Hall and (if that's locked) a HDFC ATM on the back road to Colva. Most useful services (pharmacies, supermarkets, internet, travel agents) are clustered around Benaulim village, which runs along the east–west Vasvaddo Beach Rd.

Getting There & Around

As with other beaches, scooters can be rented at Colva and Benaulim for around ₹200.

COLVA

Buses run from Colva to Margao every few minutes (₹10, 20 minutes) until around 7pm. An autorickshaw/taxi to Margao costs ₹200/250.

BENAULIM

Buses from Benaulim to Margao are also frequent (₹10, 20 minutes); they stop at the Maria Hall crossroads, 1.2km east of the beach. Some from Margao continue south to Varca and Cavelossim. Autorickshaws and pilots charge around ₹200 for Margao, and ₹60 for the five-minute ride to the beach.

Benaulim to Agonda

Immediately south of Benaulim are the beach resorts of **Varca** and **Cavelossim**, with wide, pristine sands and a line of flashy five-star hotels set amid landscaped private grounds fronting the beach. About 3km south of Cavelossim, at the end of the peninsula, **Mobor** and its beach is one of the prettiest spots along this stretch of coast, with simple beach shacks serving good food.

If you're here with your own transport, you can cross the Sal River from Cavelossim to Assolna on the rusting tin-tub **ferry**, which will run until the nearby bridge (you can't miss it) is completed in late 2014. Ferries run approximately every 30 minutes between 6.15am and 8.30pm (free for pedestrians and motorbikes). Continuing south, after about 7km you'll pass the charming fishing village of **Betul**.

From Betul heading south to Agonda, the road winds over gorgeous, undulating hills thick with palm groves. It's worth stopping off at the bleak old Portuguese fort of **Cabo da Rama** (look for the green, red and white signposts leading the way), which has a small church within the fort walls, stupendous views and several old buildings rapidly becoming one with the trees.

Back on the main road to Agonda, look out for the turn-off to the right (west) to **Cola Beach**, one of south Goa's most gorgeous hidden beach gems complete with emerald-green lagoon. It's reached via a rough 2km dirt road from the highway, but it's not totally deserted – a couple of beach shacks and a tent resort set up in season. Agonda is only about 2.5km south of the Cola Beach turnoff.

Agonda

Peaceful Agonda is a small village with a wide, relatively empty stretch of white-sand beach on which rare olive ridley turtles sometimes lay their eggs. Although there's a string of beach huts and restaurants here in season, Agonda is low-key compared with Palolem – strong currents make the water here unsafe for swimming at times, which has kept Agonda from getting too popular.

There's lots of yoga and ayurveda in Agonda – look out for notices – and a community feel among the shops and cafes in the street running parallel to the beach. There's a HDFC ATM near the church crossroads.

Sleeping & Eating

Cocohuts and shack restaurants set up along the beach from November to May, and there are a few more permanent places on the side road running parallel to the beach.

Agonda White Sand BEACH HUTS $$
(☎9823548277; www.agondawhitesand.com; Agonda Beach; huts ₹2800-3500; 📶) Beautifully designed and constructed cottages with open-air bathrooms and spring mattresses surround a central bar and restaurant at this stylish beachfront place. Less than 100m away the same owners have a pair of amazing five-star sea-facing **villas** (₹8500) with enormous beds and cavernous bathrooms large enough to contain a garden and fish pond!

Fatima Restaurant GOAN $
(thalis ₹65-75; ⏲12.30-8pm) Tiny Fatima, with just four tables, is an Agonda institution for its cheap and tasty veg and fish thalis.

Palolem & Around

Palolem has long been 'discovered' but it's still the tropical star of Goa's beaches – a stunning crescent of sand, calm waters and leaning coconut palms lend it a castaway vibe, but it does get crowded in season! It's a backpacker and family-friendly, laid-back sort of place with lots of bamboo-hut budget accommodation along the sands, good places to eat, safe swimming and kayaking in calm seas, and all the yoga, massage and alternative therapies you could wish for. Nightlife is still sleepy here – just beach bars and a couple of 'silent discos'. Many travellers end up staying in Palolem longer than they expected.

If even Palolem's version of action is too much for you, head south, along the small rocky cove named **Colomb Bay**, which hosts several basic places to stay, to **Patnem Beach**, where a fine selection of beach huts, and a less pretty – but infinitely quieter – stretch of sand awaits.

Note that Palolem, even more so than other beach towns, operates seasonally; many places aren't up and running until November.

Activities

Yoga

Palolem and Patnem are the places to be if you're keen to yoga, belly dance, reiki, t'ai chi or tarot the days away. There are courses and classes on offer all over town, with locations and teachers changing seasonally. Bhakti Kutir offers daily drop-in yoga classes, as well as longer residential courses, but it's just a single yogic drop in the area's ever-changing alternative-therapy ocean. You'll find info on daily yoga classes (₹200) and cooking classes (₹1000) at Butterfly Book Shop (p164).

Beach Activities

Kayaks are available for rent on both Patnem and Palolem beaches; an hour's paddling will cost ₹100 to ₹150, including life jacket. Fishermen and other boat operators hanging around the beach offer dolphin-spotting trips or rides to beautiful **Butterfly Beach**, north of Palolem, for ₹1000 for two people, including one hour's waiting time. There are so many outrigger boats around that you should be able to bargain them down.

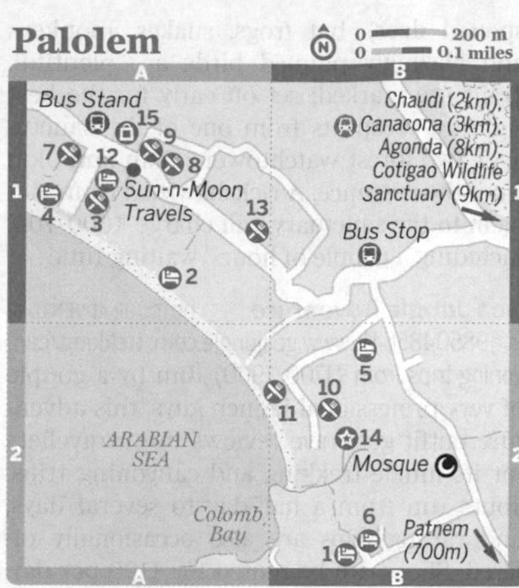

Palolem

Activities, Courses & Tours
Bhakti Kutir (see 1)

Sleeping
1 Bhakti Kutir B2
2 Ciaran's A1
3 My Soulmate A1
4 Palolem Beach Resort A1
5 Palolem Guest House B2
6 Sevas B2

Eating
7 Café Inn A1
8 Casa Fiesta A1
9 Cheeky Chapati A1
10 Fern's By Kate's B2
11 German Bakery B2
12 Magic Italy A1
13 Shiv Sai A1

Entertainment
14 Silent Disco @ Alpha Bar B2

Shopping
15 Butterfly Book Shop A1

Trekking

Cotigao Wildlife Sanctuary NATURE RESERVE
(☎2965601; admission/camera ₹5/25; ⏲7am-5.30pm) About 9km south of Palolem is this beautiful, remote-feeling sanctuary. Don't expect to bump into its more exotic residents (including gaurs, sambars, leopards and

spotted deer), but frogs, snakes, monkeys and blazingly plumed birds are plentiful. Trails are marked; set off early for the best sighting prospects from one of the sanctuary's two forest watchtowers, 6km and 9km from the entrance. A rickshaw/taxi from Palolem to the sanctuary will charge ₹600/700, including a couple of hours' waiting time.

Goa Jungle Adventure OUTDOOR ADVENTURE
(☎9850485641; www.goajungle.com; trekking/canyoning trips from ₹1700/1900) Run by a couple of very professional French guys, this adventure outfit gets rave reviews from travellers for its jungle trekking and canyoning trips. Tours run from a half-day to several days, and rafting trips are also occasionally offered. Shoes can be rented for ₹190 per day. Book or enquire at Casa Fiesta restaurant.

Sleeping

Palolem

Most of Palolem's accommodation is of the simple seasonal beach-hut variety, though there are plenty of old-fashioned guesthouses or family homes to be found back from the beach with decent rooms from ₹500. It's still possible to find a basic palm-thatch hut without bathroom somewhere near the beach for ₹500, but many of the huts these days are made of plywood or timber and come with attached bathrooms and multiple levels. For a quality sea-facing hut in season you can pay more that ₹5000! Since the huts are dismantled and rebuilt each year, standards and ownership can vary – for this reason the places listed here are either permanent guesthouses or well-established hut operations. Popular set-ups include Cozy Nook, Dreamcatcher and Bridge N Tunnel.

My Soulmate GUESTHOUSE $
(☎9823785250; mysolmte@gmail.com; off Palolem Beach Rd; d ₹800, with AC ₹1200-2000; ❄📶) This friendly two-storey guesthouse is down a lane (roughly behind Magic Italy) with easy access to the beach. Clean rooms come with TV and hot water and the newest ones have sexy circular beds!

Sevas HUT $
(☎2639194; www.sevaspalolemgoa.com; huts ₹500-1500; @) Hidden in the jungle on the Colomb Bay side of Palolem, Sevas comprises a village of well-built and maintained huts and cabanas ranging from basic to stylish. Most have attached bathroom, some are built on stilts. Yoga classes, ayurvedic massage and a restaurant are on offer.

Bhakti Kutir COTTAGE $
(☎2643472; www.bhaktikutir.com; Colomb Bay; cottages ₹1000-1600; @) Ensconced in a thick wooded grove between Palolem and Patnem, Bhakti's rustic cottages are looking a little worn, and you might find yourself sharing with the local wildlife, but they still make for a unique jungle ecoretreat. There are daily drop-in yoga classes and ayurvedic treatments, a relaxing vibe, and the outdoor restaurant serves up imaginative, healthful food.

Palolem Beach Resort RESORT $$
(☎2645775, 9764442778; www.cubagoa.com/palolem; r without/with AC ₹1750/2500, cottages ₹2000; ❄📶) You can't beat the location, right at the main beach entrance, and although not flash, Palolem Beach Resort's seasonal cottages are clean and comfortable, and the staff efficient and friendly. It also has some of the only beachfront air-con rooms (which are open year-round). The plywood nonair-com rooms at the back are disappointing for the price.

Palolem Guest House HOTEL $$
(☎2644879; www.palolemguesthouse.com; d ₹1200-1800, with AC ₹1750-2800; ❄) If you can't face another hut or the crazy beach scene, this is a good choice a five-minute walk back from the southern end of Palolem Beach. The variety of rooms are simple but clean and comfortable, some with balconies, and the leafy garden restaurant is a good place to hang out.

★**Ciaran's** BEACH HUT $$$
(☎2643477; www.ciarans.com; huts incl breakfast ₹3500-4000, r with AC ₹3500; ❄📶) Ciaran's has some of the sturdiest and best-designed huts on the beach, with real windows, stone floors, full-length mirrors, wood detailing and nicer bathrooms than you'll find in most hotels, all arranged around peaceful palm-filled gardens and a genuine lawn. It's the perfect balance of rustic and sophisticated. There's also a free library, free breakfast and afternoon tea and two quality restaurants, one of which is Palolem's only tapas bar.

Patnem

Long-stayers will love Patnem's choice of village homes and apartments available for rent. A very basic house can cost ₹10,000 per month, while a fully equipped apartment can run up to ₹40,000.

Micky Huts & Rooms BEACH HUT $
(☎9850484884; www.mickyhuts.com; Patnem Beach; huts ₹300, r & huts with bathroom ₹1500-3000) If you don't mind huts so basic they don't even have electricity, you can sleep cheap here. Fear not: there are also better (pricier) huts with attached bathroom and power, along with the cruisy bar and restaurant, all set in a thick bamboo and coconut grove at the northern end of Patnem Beach.

Papaya's COTTAGE $$
(☎9923079447; www.papayasgoa.com; huts ₹2500-3500;) Lovely huts head back into the palm grove from Papaya's popular restaurant. Each is lovingly built, with lots of wood, four-poster beds and floating muslin, as well as a porch, and the staff are incredibly keen to please.

Sea View Resort HOTEL $$
(☎2643110; www.seaviewpatnem.com; cottage ₹500, d ₹1000-2000, with AC ₹3000;) For year-round accommodation about 100m back from the beach, Sea View is a decent choice with basic cottages, clean rooms – many with balconies, some with kitchens – and a garden setting.

Eating

With limited beach space, restaurant shacks are mercifully banned from the sand at Palolem and Patnem, but there are plenty of beach-facing restaurants on the periphery, all offering all-day dining and fresh seafood. Palolem also has some interesting dining choices back along the main road to the beach.

Shiv Sai INDIAN $
(thalis ₹50-60, mains ₹40-100; 9am-11pm) A local lunch joint knocking out cheap and tasty thalis, including Goan fish and veggie versions.

★**Café Inn** CAFE $$
(www.cafeinn.in; meals ₹110-330; 10am-11pm;) This fun semi-outdoor place has loud music, servers in saris and a cool cafe vibe. The Italian coffee, snacks, shakes, burgers and salads are great, but it's the evening barbecue that stands out: pick your base, toppings, sauces and bread to create a grilled mix-and-match masterpiece.

German Bakery BAKERY, MULTICUISINE $$
(pastries ₹25-80, mains ₹115-180; 8am-10pm) It's worth the trek back from the beach for tasty baked treats, excellent coffee and yak-cheese croissants at the cosy German Bakery. Set breakfasts are good and there's a full menu of Italian, Indian, Chinese and Israeli dishes for dinner.

Fern's By Kate's GOAN $$
(☎9822165261; ₹120-350; 8.30am-10.30pm;) Back from the beach, this solid timber place with a vague nautical feel serves up excellent authentic Goan food such as local sausages and shark *amok-tik*. Upstairs are two beautifully-finished air-con rooms (₹4000) with large bathrooms, four-poster beds and sea views.

Magic Italy ITALIAN $$
(mains ₹230-380; 3pm-midnight) On the main beach road, Magic Italy has been around for a while but the quality of its pizza and pasta is getting ever better, with imported Italian ingredients like ham, salami and olive oil, imaginative wood-fired pizzas and homemade pasta. The atmosphere is busy but chilled.

Casa Fiesta MEXICAN $$
(mains ₹90-280; 8.30am-midnight) Fiesta serves up a bit of a 'world menu' but its

SILENT PARTIES

Neatly sidestepping the statewide ban on loud music after 10pm, Palolem is home to two hugely popular silent rave parties where guests don a pair of headphones and dance the night away in outward quiet. You usually get the choice of two or three channels featuring inhouse Goan and international DJs playing hip hop, house, electro and funk. The parties generally don't fire up till after midnight. Admission includes headphones. **Silent Noise** (www.silentnoise.in; Neptune's Point, Colomb Bay; admission ₹500; 9am-4am Sat Nov-Apr) is the original Saturday night headphone party, in an awesome location at Neptune Point looking back towards Palolem Beach. On Thursday, **Silent Disco @ Alpha Bar** (admission ₹500; 9pm-4am Thur Nov-Apr) kicks off back among the palms at the southern end of Palolem Beach.

speciality (or point of difference) is Mexican, and it makes a pretty good fist of fajitas, burritos and tacos with most dishes under ₹200. The mellow hut ambience is also working, as are margaritas.

Cheeky Chapati MULTICUISINE $$
(mains ₹110-270; ⏲7am-11pm) Expat-run Cheeky Chapati is a rustic, welcoming sort of place offering a full range of Continental and Indian dishes, kebabs and burgers. Sunday is roast night.

★**Home** CONTINENTAL $$
(☎2643916; www.homeispatnem.com; Patnem Beach; mains ₹160-260; ⏲8.30am-9.30pm) A hip, relaxed veg restaurant serving up pasta, salads, Mediterranean-style goodies and desserts, this is a Patnem favourite. Home also rents out nicely decorated, bright rooms (singles/doubles ₹1000/3000); call to book or ask at the restaurant.

Shopping

Butterfly Book Shop BOOKS
(☎9341738801; www.yogavillapalolem.com; ⏲9am-10.30pm) A great bookshop with some neat gifts and a range of books on yoga, meditation and spirituality. You can also arrange yoga and cooking classes here.

Information

Palolem's main road is lined with travel agencies, internet places and money changers. The nearest ATM is about 1.5km away, where the main highway meets Palolem Beach Rd, or head to nearby Chaudi.

Sun-n-Moon Travels (Palolem Beach Rd; per hr ₹40; ⏲9am-10.30pm; 📶) One of several travel agencies with fast internet. Also sells SIM cards and mobile phone top-ups.

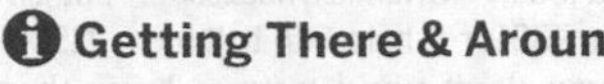

Getting There & Around

Scooters and motorbikes can easily be hired along the main road leading to the beach from ₹200. Bicycles (₹100 per day) can be hired from the shop next to Palolem Dental Clinic.

BUS

Services to Margao (₹30, one hour, every 30 minutes) and Chaudi (₹5, every 15 minutes), the nearest town, depart from the bus stand down by the beach and stop at the Patnem turn-off. Chaudi has good bus connections, but for Panaji and north Goa, it's much better to go to Margao and catch an express from there.

Buses from Chaudi include the following services:

Agonda (₹8, half-hourly)
Cabo da Rama (₹20, 9am; return buses depart Cabo da Rama at 3pm)
Gokarna (₹70, 2pm)
Karwar (₹35, half-hourly)
Margao (₹30, every 10 minutes)
Panaji (₹55, three daily)

TAXI & AUTORICKSHAW

An autorickshaw from Palolem to Patnem costs ₹60, as does a rick from Palolem to Chaudi. To Agonda it's ₹200. A prepaid taxi from Dabolim Airport to Palolem costs ₹1100.

TRAIN

Many trains that run north or south out of Margao stop at the **Canacona Train Station** (☎2643644, 2712790).

ALAN LAGADU / GETTY IMAGES ©

Ancient & Historic Sites

India has a remarkable and extraordinary assortment of historic monuments and ancient ruins that pay testament to this part of the world's prolific architectural and spiritual diversity. Ranging from serene places of worship to remnants of former grandiose empires, there are plenty of opportunities to get lost in time.

Contents

Above Mountain-top temple, near Hampi (p214)

1

2

RELIGIOUS IMAGES/UIG / GETTY IMAGES ©

Hindu Sacred Sites

Hinduism is one of the world's oldest extant religions, and Hindu-majority India is blessed with a suitably impressive mix of sacred sites that showcase the best of devotional architecture: soaring *gopurams* (gateway towers), exquisite *mandapas* (pavilions) and some of the most intricately chiselled sculptures of gods and goddesses you'll ever see.

Madurai

In Madurai, one of India's oldest cities, you'll find the Meenakshi Amman Temple, abode of the triple-breasted goddess Meenakshi. This 6-hectare complex is rated by many as the epitome of classic South Indian temple architecture. The main structure predominantly dates to the 17th century, but the temple's origins are believed to go back around 2000 years when Madurai was the capital of an ancient kingdom.

1. Meenakshi Amman Temple (p384), Madurai **2.** Temple in Hampi (p214) **3.** Shore Temple (p351), Mamallapuram

Hampi

This area's historic World Heritage–listed ruins are strewn amid boulders of all shapes and sizes – the result of hundreds of thousands (if not millions) of years of volcanic activity and erosion. Although now a rather sleepy hamlet, from 1336 to 1565 this region was a thriving centre of the powerful Vijayanagar empire. Some fine examples of Vijayanagan temple art can be seen at the 15th-century Virupaksha Temple and the 16th-century Vittala Temple.

3

Mamallapuram

Today the ruins of Mamallapuram may be a faded reminder of their heyday during the Pallava Dynasty – which flourished in this region from the 7th to the 9th centuries – but they're still mind-stirring. Standouts include the rock-face known as Arjuna's Penance; the Five Rathas, dexterously carved from single slabs of rock; and the Shore Temple, which captures Pallava-era architecture at its zenith. There's also a giant boulder precariously balanced on a stony rise.

1

2

PHOTOSINDIA.COM / GETTY IMAGES ©

1. Buddha statues adorn a cave entrance, Ajanta (p100)
2. Cave mural, Ajanta **3.** Caves at Ellora (p97)

Buddhist, Hindu & Jain Caves

The World Heritage–listed caves of Ajanta and Ellora are a stunning gallery of ancient cave art replete with historic sculptures, columns and natural-dye paintings. Situated within 100km of each other, the caves at Ajanta date back to the 2nd century while those of Ellora trace their origin to the 5th.

Ajanta

The 30 Buddhist caves of Ajanta are clustered along a horseshoe-shaped gorge that overlooks the Waghore River. One of the most renowned features of Ajanta is the natural-dye temperas (similar to frescoes) that decorate many of the caves' interiors. These murals revolve around Buddhist themes and some are even coloured with crushed semiprecious stones such as lapis lazuli. Numbered from one to 30, not all of Ajanta's caves are accessible to the public because of safety, preservation or restoration reasons, although it's possible to visit what is believed to be the oldest cave here, Cave 10. One of the most recent to be excavated is Cave 1, which has some particularly elaborate artwork including a wonderful rendition of Buddhism's Bodhisattva Padmapani.

Ellora

The Ellora caves – a collection of Hindu, Jain and Buddhist shrines constructed over five centuries – are situated on a 2km-long escarpment. There are a total of 34 caves: 17 Hindu, 12 Buddhist and five Jain. Of these, the most famed is the Kailasa Temple (Cave 16), built in honour of the Hindu god Shiva. It is the biggest monolithic sculpture in the world and was skillfully carved into the cliff face by thousands of labourers over a period of 150 years. Ellora's other prominent caves include the Indra Sabha (Cave 32), which is the most ornate of the group's Jain temples, and the Vishvakarma Temple (Cave 10), the only Buddhist shrine in the Ellora group to contain a *chaitya* (assembly hall).

VISAGE / GETTY IMAGES ©

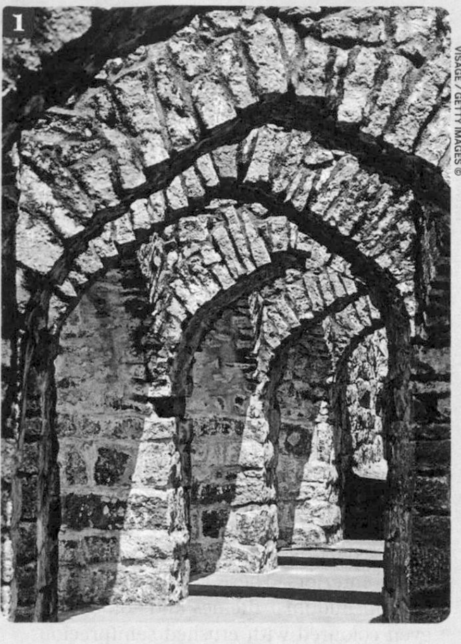

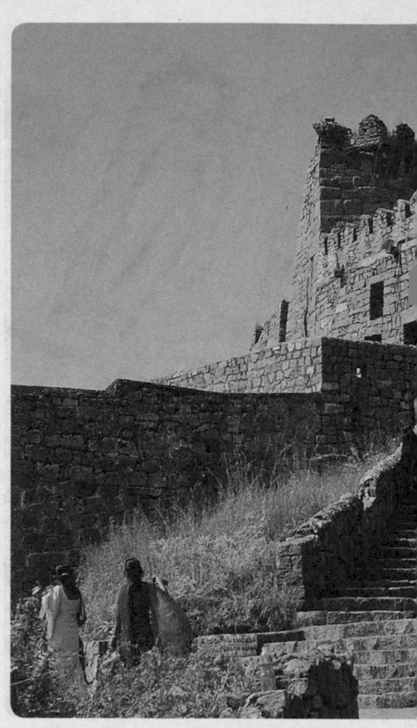

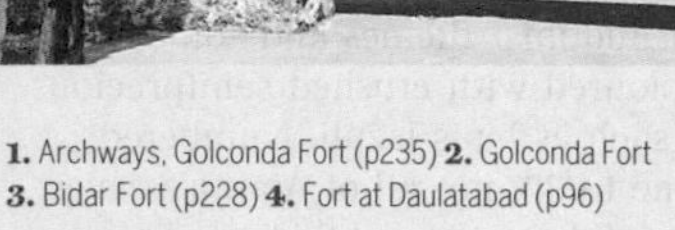

1. Archways, Golconda Fort (p235) **2.** Golconda Fort
3. Bidar Fort (p228) **4.** Fort at Daulatabad (p96)

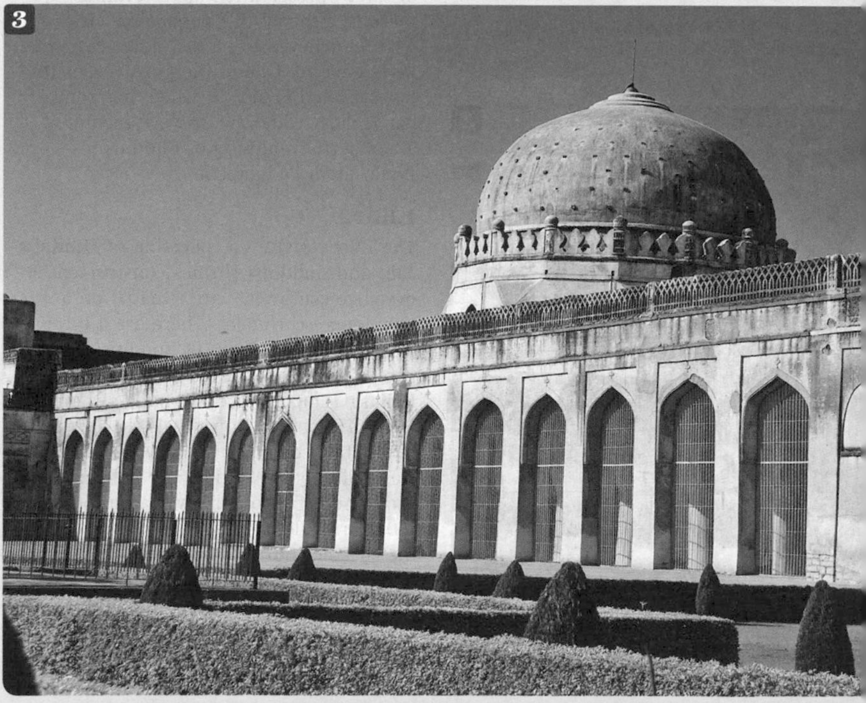

KAY MAERITZ / GETTY IMAGES ©

Forts

Although not as prolific as up north, South India still has its fair share of fantastical forts that have survived the vagaries of time. The vast majority of these are found sprawled across geographically strategic hilltops, wrapped within sturdy walls that protect a treasure trove of buildings and monuments.

Golconda Fort

Hyderabad's majestic 16th-century Golconda Fort was strategically built on a granite hill. Its designers created a clever acoustics system – for that time – which enabled guards to monitor movements from key entry points. Golconda is a fortified feast of crenellated ramparts, cannon-mounted bastions, creaky drawbridges, and imposing gates studded with ominous iron spikes specially designed to thwart raiding war elephants.

Daulatabad

The crumbling 12th-century hilltop fortress of Daulatabad is one of Maharasthra's most historically and architecturally significant sites. Daulatabad's central bastion crowns a 200m-high outcrop, known as Devagiri (Hill of the Gods) and is flanked by a sprawling fort complex. A former ruler – the Delhi sultan, Mohammed Tughlaq – once even had grand plans to transform it into a thriving capital, thanks to its strategic geographical position. However, his dream was swiftly cut short due to a dire water shortage in the area.

Bidar Fort

Bidar is home to the biggest fort in South India. This now forlorn site was once the bustling administrative capital of much of southern India. Although largely in a state of deteriorating disrepair, there are still some noteworthy remnants of its glory days that include Rangin Mahal – with some particularly notable tile designs, woodwork and inlaid panels – and a 16-pillar mosque, with ancient inscriptions.

Above
Buddhist cave, Ellora (p97)

Karnataka & Bengaluru

Includes ➡

Best Places to Eat

- Karavalli (p183)
- Koshy's Bar & Restaurant (p183)
- Sapphire (p197)
- Lalith Bar & Restaurant (p209)

Best Places to Stay

- Casa Piccola Cottage (p182)
- Green Hotel (p195)
- Vivanta (p204)
- Dhole's Den (p201)

Why Go?

Blessed with a diverse geography that takes the highlights from its encompassing states and mixes it in with its own charms, Karnataka is an intoxicating cocktail that is quintessential India. It's a winning blend of palaces, beaches, banana groves, tiger reserves, ancient ruins and legendary hangouts.

At its nerve centre is the silicon-capital Bengaluru (Bangalore), overfed with the good life. Scattered around the epicurean city are rolling hills rife with spice and coffee plantations, the regal splendour of Mysore and jungles teeming with monkeys, tigers and Asia's biggest population of elephants.

If that all sounds too mainstream, head to the countercultural enclave of tranquil Hampi with hammocks, psychedelic sunsets and boulder-strewn ruins. Or the blissful beaches of Gokarna, a beach haven minus the doof doof. Or better yet, leave the tourists behind entirely and take a journey to stunning Islamic ruins of northern Karnataka.

When to Go

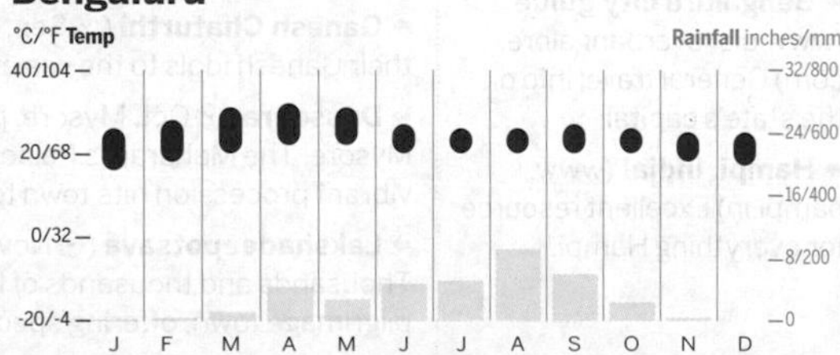

Jan The best season to watch tigers and elephants in Karnataka's pristine national parks.

Oct Mysore's Dasara (Dussehra) carnival brings night-long celebrations and a jumbo parade.

Dec The coolest time to explore the northern districts' forts, palaces, caves and temples.

MAIN POINTS OF ENTRY

Many visitors arrive at Bengaluru's shiny modern airport, 40km north of the city. Mangalore on the western coast serves as a transit point for those going north to Goa, or south to Kerala. Hubli in central Karnataka is also a railway hub that links Hampi with Goa and Mumbai.

Fast Facts

- **Population:** 61.1 million
- **Area:** 191,791 sq km
- **Capital:** Bengaluru (Bangalore)
- **Main languages:** Kannada, Hindi, English
- **Sleeping prices:** **$** below ₹1000, **$$** ₹1000 to ₹4000, **$$$** above ₹4000

Resources

- **Karnataka Tourism** (KSTDC; www.karnatakatourism.org) Sleek government site showcasing state highlights.
- **Bengaluru city guide** (www.discoverbangalore.com) General travel info on the state's capital.
- **Hampi. India!** (www.hampi.in) Excellent resource for everything Hampi.

Food

The diverse and delectable cuisine of Karnataka is perhaps reason enough for you to visit this state. The highest-flying of all local delicacies is the spicy *pandhi* (pork) masala, a flavourful Kodava signature dish. Mangalore, out on the coast, tosses up a train of fiery dishes – mostly seafood. The crunchy prawn *rawa* (semolina) fry and the sinful chicken ghee roast are two of Mangalore's many dishes to have gathered a pan-Indian following. Vegetarians, meanwhile, can head to Udupi to sample its legendary veg thalis. Oh, and did we mention the classic steak-and-beer joints of Bengaluru?

DON'T MISS

The **temples** of Hampi, Pattadakal, Belur and Halebid, and Somnathpur are some of India's best archaeological sites, embellished with sculptures of stellar quality.

Top State Festivals

- **Udupi Paryaya** (Jan, Udupi, p210) Held in even-numbered years, with a procession and ritual marking the handover of swamis at the town's Krishna Temple.
- **Classical Dance Festival** (Jan/Feb, Pattadakal, p225) Some of India's best classical dance performances.
- **Vijaya Utsav** (Hampi Festival; Jan, Hampi,, p214) A three-day extravaganza of culture, heritage and the arts at the foot of Hampi's Matanga Hill.
- **Tibetan New Year** (Feb, Bylakuppe, p206) Lamas in Tibetan refugee settlements take shifts leading nonstop prayers that span the weeklong celebrations.
- **Vairamudi Festival** (Mar/Apr, Melkote, p200) Lord Vishnu is adorned with jewels at Cheluvanarayana Temple, including a diamond-studded crown belonging to Mysore's former maharajas.
- **Ganesh Chaturthi** (Sep, Gokarna, p212) Families march their Ganesh idols to the sea at sunset.
- **Dussehra** (Oct, Mysore, p195) Also spelt 'Dasara' in Mysore. The Maharaja's Palace is lit up in the evenings and a vibrant procession hits town to the delight of thousands.
- **Lakshadeepotsava** (Nov, Dharmasthala, p210) Thousands and thousands of lamps light up this Jain pilgrimage town, offering spectacular photo ops.
- **Huthri** (Nov/Dec, Madikeri, p202) The Kodava community celebrates the start of the harvesting season with ceremony, music, traditional dances and much feasting for a week.

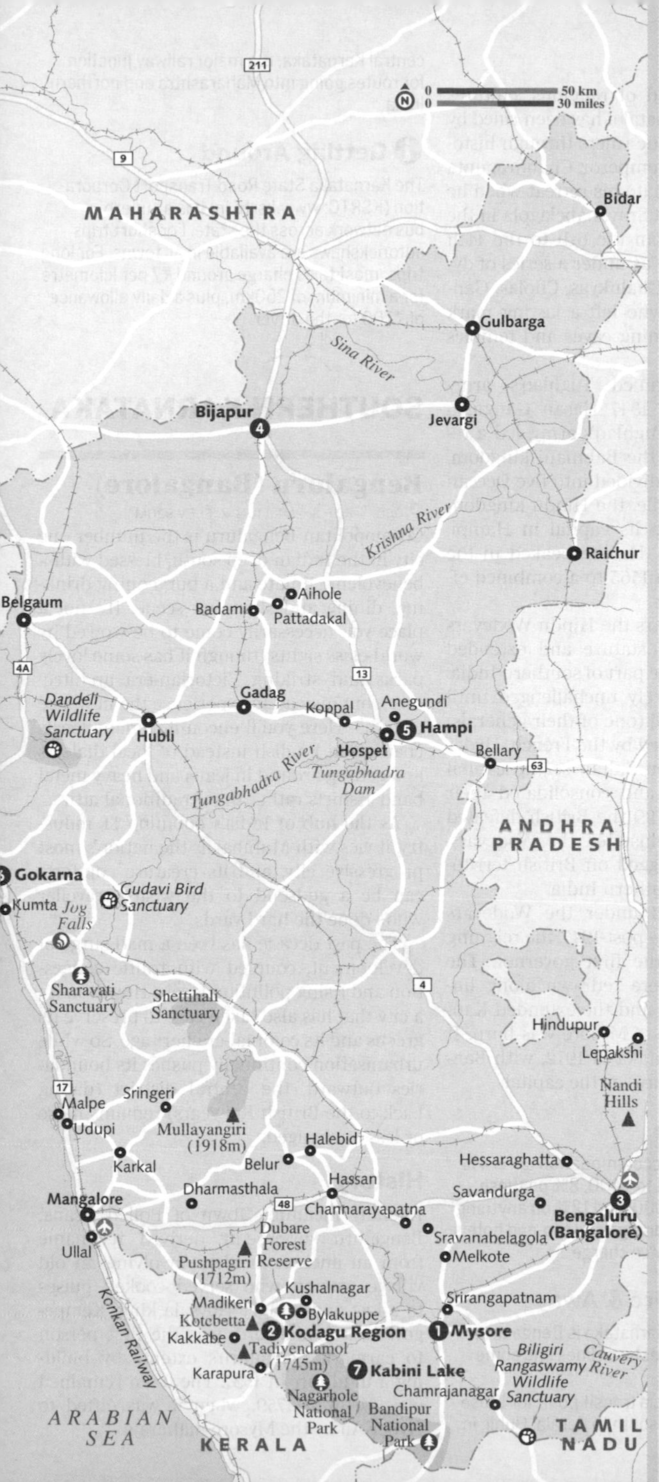

Karnataka & Bengaluru Highlights

1. Be bowled over by the grandiose **royal palace** (p189) in Mysore
2. Savour aromatic coffee while recharging your soul in the cool highlands of the **Kodagu Region** (p202)
3. Drink yourself under the table, or stab into top-notch global cuisine in **Bengaluru** (p183)
4. Stroll peaceful manicured grounds of exquisite 16th-century Islamic architecture in **Bijapur** (p225)
5. Marvel at the gravity-defying boulders, and wander among the melancholic ruins of **Hampi** (p214)
6. Chill the hell out on Om beach in **Gokarna** (p212)
7. Spy on lazy tuskers and listen to exotic birds in the forests bordering the serene **Kabini Lake** (p201)

History

A rambling playfield of religions, cultures and kingdoms, Karnataka has been ruled by a string of charismatic rulers through history. India's first great emperor, Chandragupta Maurya, made the state his retreat when he embraced Jainism at Sravanabelagola in the 3rd century BC. From the 6th to the 14th centuries, the land was under a series of dynasties such as the Chalukyas, Cholas, Gangas and Hoysalas, who left a lasting mark in the form of stunning caves and temples across the state.

In 1327 Mohammed Tughlaq's army sacked Halebid. In 1347 Hasan Gangu, a Persian general in Tughlaq's army, led a rebellion to establish the Bahmani kingdom, which was later subdivided into five Deccan sultanates. Meanwhile, the Hindu kingdom of Vijayanagar, with its capital in Hampi, rose to prominence. Having peaked in the early 1550s, it fell in 1565 to a combined effort of the sultanates.

In subsequent years the Hindu Wodeyars of Mysore grew in stature and extended their rule over a large part of southern India. They remained largely unchallenged until 1761, when Hyder Ali (one of their generals) deposed them. Backed by the French, Hyder Ali and his son Tipu Sultan set up capital in Srirangapatnam and consolidated their rule. However, in 1799 the British defeated Tipu Sultan and reinstated the Wodeyars. Historically, this flagged off British territorial expansion in southern India.

Mysore remained under the Wodeyars until Independence – post-1947, the reigning maharaja became the first governor. The state boundaries were redrawn along linguistic lines in 1956 and the extended Kannada-speaking state of Mysore was born. It was renamed Karnataka in 1972, with Bangalore (now Bengaluru) as the capital.

ℹ Information

In Karnataka, luxury accommodation tax is 4% on rooms costing ₹151 to ₹400, 8% on those between ₹401 and ₹1000, and 12% on anything over ₹1000. Some midrange and top-end hotels may add a further service charge.

ℹ Getting There & Away

The main gateway to Karnataka is Bengaluru, serviced by most domestic airlines and some international carriers.

Coastal Mangalore is a transit point for those going north to Goa, or south to Kerala. Hubli, in central Karnataka, is a major railway junction for routes going into Maharashtra and northern India.

ℹ Getting Around

The Karnataka State Road Transport Corporation (KSRTC; www.ksrtc.in) has a superb bus network across the state. For short trips autorickshaws are available in all towns. For long trips, most taxis charge around ₹7 per kilometre for a minimum of 250km, plus a daily allowance of ₹200 for the driver.

SOUTHERN KARNATAKA

Bengaluru (Bangalore)

080 / POP 8.5 MILLION / ELEV 920M

Cosmopolitan Bengaluru is the number one city in the Indian deep south, blessed with a benevolent climate and a burgeoning drinking, dining and shopping scene. It's not a place you necessarily come to be wowed by world-class sights (though it has some lovely parks and striking Victorian-era architecture), but instead to experience the new face of India. Here you'll encounter many locals chatting in English instead of local dialects and getting around in jeans and heavy metal band T-shirts rather than traditional attire.

As the hub of India's booming IT industry, it vies with Mumbai as the nation's most progressive city, and its creature comforts can be a godsend to the weary traveller who's done the hard yards.

The past decade has seen a mad surge of development, coupled with traffic congestion and rising pollution levels. However, it's a city that has also taken care to preserve its greens and its colonial-era heritage. So while urbanisation continually pushes its boundaries outward, the central district (dating back to the British Raj years) remains more or less unchanged.

History

Literally meaning 'Town of Boiled Beans', Bengaluru supposedly derived its name from an ancient incident involving an old village woman who served cooked pulses to a lost and hungry Hoysala king. Kempegowda, a feudal lord, was the first person to earmark Bengaluru's extents by building a mud fort in 1537. The town remained obscure until 1759, when it was gifted to Hyder Ali by the Mysore maharaja.

The British arrived in 1809 and made it their regional administrative base in 1831, renaming it Bangalore. During the Raj era the city played host to many a British officer, including Winston Churchill, who enjoyed life here during his greener years and famously left a debt (still on the books) of ₹13 at the Bangalore Club.

Now home to countless software, electronics and business-outsourcing firms, Bengaluru's knack for technology developed early. In 1905 it was the first Indian city to have electric street lighting. Since the 1940s it has been home to Hindustan Aeronautics Ltd (HAL), India's largest aerospace company. And if you can't do without email, you owe it all to a Bangalorean – Sabeer Bhatia, the inventor of Hotmail, grew up here.

The city's name was changed back to Bengaluru in November 2006, though few care to use it in practice.

Orientation

Finding your way around Bengaluru can be difficult at times. In certain areas, roads are named after their widths (eg 80ft Rd). The city also follows a system of mains and crosses: 3rd cross, 5th main, Residency Rd, for example, refers to the third lane on the fifth street branching off Residency Rd.

Sights

Lalbagh Botanical Gardens GARDEN
(www.lalbaghgardens.com; admission ₹10; 5.30am-7.30pm) Spread over 240 acres of landscaped terrain, the expansive Lalbagh gardens were laid out in 1760 by the famous Mysore ruler, Hyder Ali. As well as amazing centuries-old trees it claims to have the world's most diverse species of plants. You can take a guided tour with Bangalore Walks (p181), in a ecofriendly buggy (per head ₹100), or otherwise just stroll around at your own pace. On weekends you'll see health-conscious locals jogging and playing badminton all over the park.

National Gallery of Modern Art ART GALLERY
(NGMA; 22342338; www.ngmaindia.gov.in/ngma_bangaluru.asp; 49 Palace Rd; admission ₹150; 10am-5pm Tue-Sun) Housed in a 200 year-old mansion – the former vacation home of the Raja of Mysore – this museum showcases an impressive permanent collection as well as changing exhibitions. The Old Wing exhibits works from pre-Independence, including paintings by Raja Ravi Varma and Abanindranath Tagore (nephew of Rabindranath Tagore, and the avant-garde Bengal School art ment), while the New Wing focuses on po Independence with works by MF Hussain and FN Souza.

Cubbon Park GARDEN
In the heart of Bengaluru's business district is Cubbon Park, a sprawling 120-hectare garden named after former British commissioner Sir Mark Cubbon. Under its leafy boughs, groups of Bengaluru's residents converge to steal a moment from the rat race that rages outside. On the fringes of Cubbon Park are the red-painted Gothic-style **State Central Library**, while at the northwestern end of the park are the colossal neo-Dravidian-style **Vidhana Soudha**, built in 1954, and the neoclassical **Attara Kacheri**, that houses the High Court. Both of the latter are closed to the public.

Government Museum MUSEUM
(Kasturba Rd; admission ₹4; 10am-5pm Tue-Sun, closed every 2nd Sat) In a beautiful red colonial-era building dating from 1877, you'll find a dusty collection of 12th-century stone carvings and artefacts excavated from Halebid, Hampi and Attriampakham. Your ticket also gets you into the **Venkatappa Art Gallery** (admission free; 10am-5pm Tue-Sun) FREE next door, where you can see works and personal memorabilia of K Venkatappa (1887–1962), court painter to the Wodeyars.

Visvesvaraya Industrial and Technical Museum MUSEUM
(Kasturba Rd; adult/child ₹20/free; 10am-6pm) This hands-on science museum makes you feel a bit like you're on a school excursion, but there are some cool electrical and engineering displays, plus kitschy fun-house mirrors and a walk-on piano. There's also a replica of the Wright brothers' 1903 flyer.

Bengaluru Palace PALACE
(Palace Rd; Indian/foreigner ₹210/400, camera/video ₹600/1250; 10am-5.30pm) The private residence of the Wodeyars, erstwhile maharajas of the state, Bengaluru Palace preserves a slice of bygone royal splendour. Still the residence of the 20th maharaja, an audioguide provides a detailed explanation of the building, designed to resemble Windsor Castle, and you can marvel at the lavish interiors and galleries featuring hunting trophies (along with grisly photos of expeditions), family photos and a collection of nude portraits.

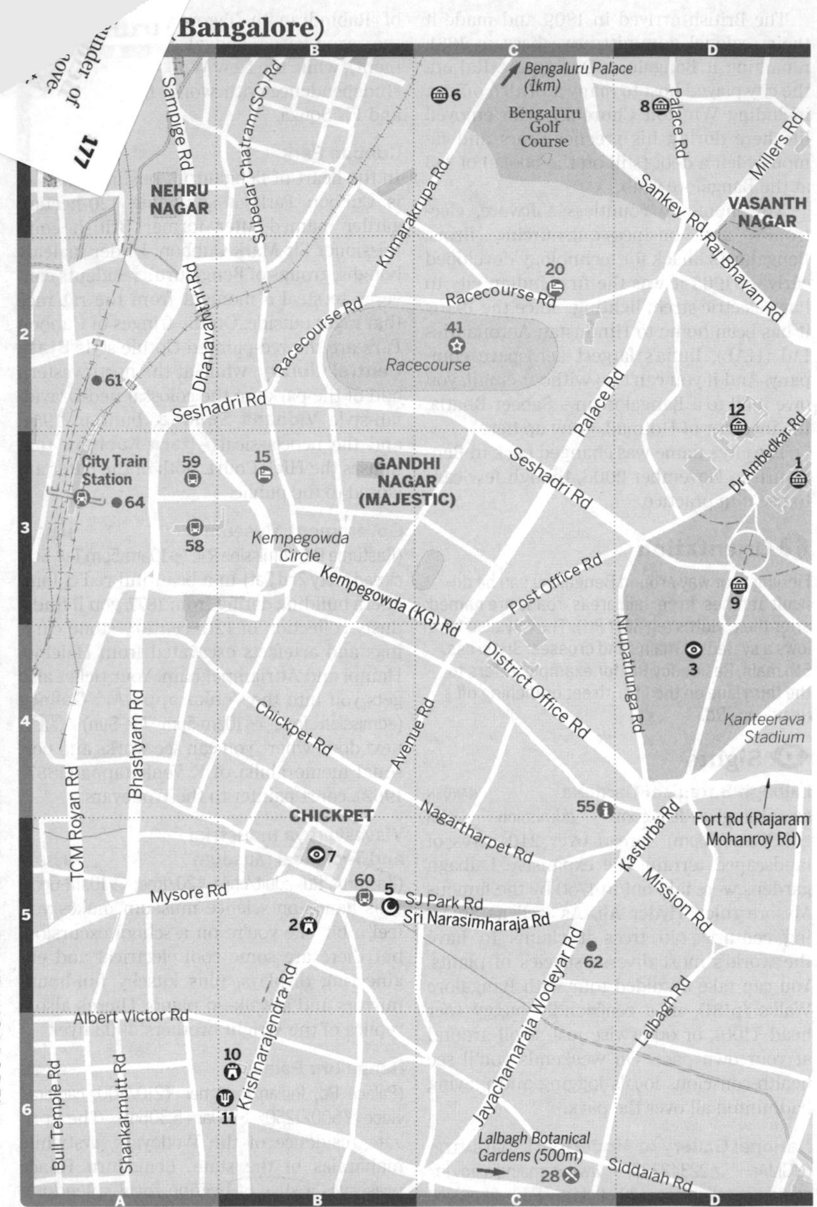

Karnataka Chitrakala Parishath ART GALLERY (www.karnatakachitrakalaparishath.com; Kumarakrupa Rd; admission ₹50; ⏲10am-5.30pm Mon-Sat) One of Bengaluru's premier art institutions, with a wide range of Indian and international contemporary art on show in its galleries, and permanent displays of Mysore-style paintings and folk and tribal art from across Asia. A section is devoted to the works of Russian master Nicholas Roerich, known for his vivid paintings of the Himalayas.

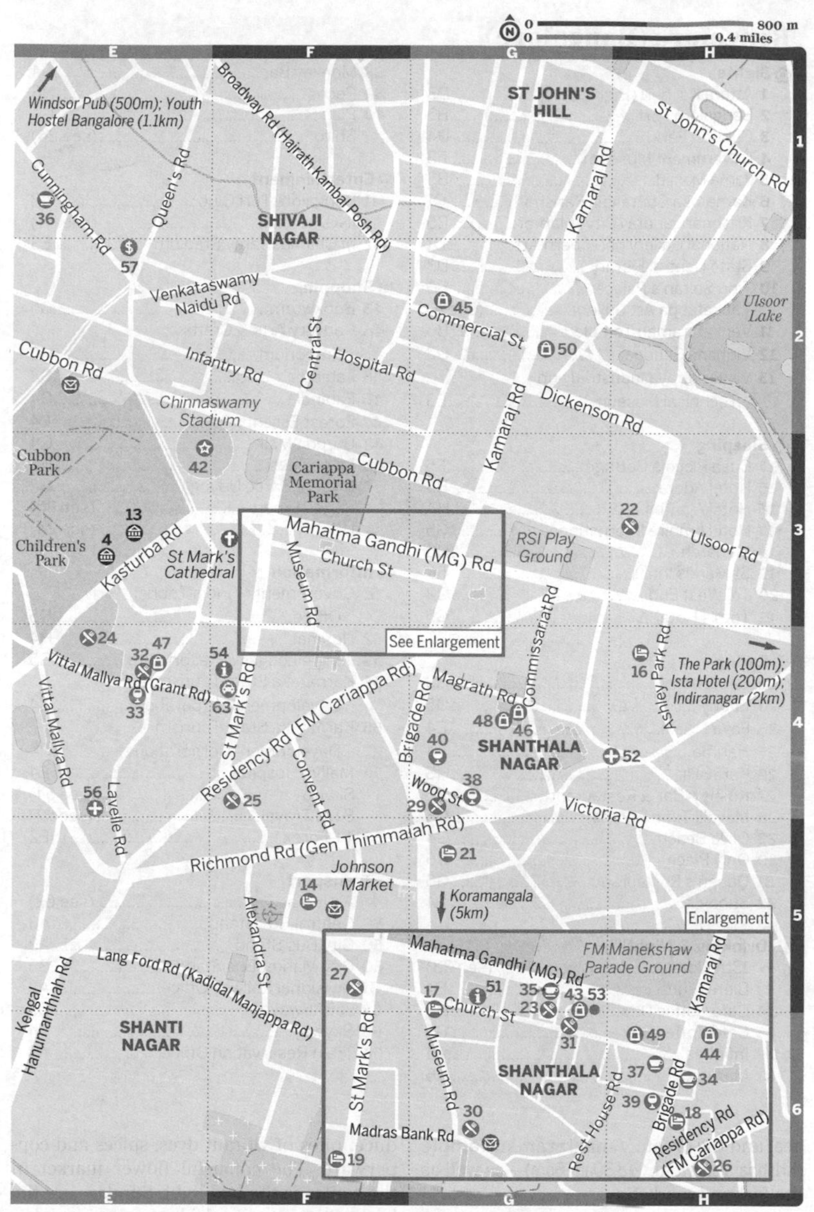

Tipu Sultan's Palace PALACE
(Albert Victor Rd; Indian/foreigner ₹5/100, video ₹25; ⊙8.30am-5.30pm) Close to the vibrant Krishnarajendra (City) Market stands the elegant palace of Tipu Sultan, notable for its teak pillars and ornamental frescoes. Though not as beautiful (or well maintained) as Tipu's summer palace in Srirangapatnam, it's an interesting monument, and worth an outing when combined with other nearby sights such as the massive **Jama Masjid** (Silver Jubilee (SJ) Park Rd; ⊙admission

Bengaluru (Bangalore)

Sights
1 Attara Kacheri (High Court) D3
2 Bangalore Fort B5
3 Cubbon Park D4
4 Government Museum E3
5 Jama Masjid B5
6 Karnataka Chitrakala Parishath C1
7 Krishnarajendra (City) Market B5
8 National Gallery of Modern Art D1
9 State Central Library D3
10 Tipu Sultan's Palace B6
Venkatappa Art Gallery (see 4)
11 Venkataraman Temple B6
12 Vidhana Soudha D2
13 Visvesvaraya Industrial and Technical Museum E3

Sleeping
14 Casa Piccola Cottage F5
15 Hotel Adora B3
16 Hotel Ajantha H4
17 Hotel Empire International G5
18 Monarch H6
19 St Mark's Inn F6
20 Taj West End C2
21 Tom's Hotel G5

Eating
22 Caperberry H3
23 Ebony G5
24 Fava E4
25 Harima F4
26 Karavalli H6
27 Koshy's Bar & Restaurant F5
28 Mavalli Tiffin Rooms C6
29 Olive Beach G4
30 Only Place G6
31 Queen's Restaurant G6
32 Sunny's E4

Drinking & Nightlife
13th Floor (see 23)
33 Biere Club E4
34 Café Coffee Day H6
35 Café Coffee Day G5
36 Infinitea E1
37 Matteo H6
38 Monkey Bar G4
39 Pecos H6
40 Plan B G4
Shiro (see 24)

Entertainment
41 Bangalore Turf Club C2
INOX (see 48)
42 M Chinnaswamy Stadium E3

Shopping
43 Bookworm G5
44 Cauvery Arts & Crafts Emporium H6
45 Fabindia G2
46 Fabindia G4
47 Forest Essentials E4
48 Garuda Mall G4
49 Magazines H6
50 Mysore Saree Udyog G2
Page Turners (see 35)
UB City (see 24)

Information
51 Government of India Tourist Office G5
52 Hosmat H4
53 Jungle Lodges & Resorts Ltd G5
54 Karnataka State Tourism Development Corporation F4
55 Karnataka State Tourism Development Corporation C4
56 Mallya Hospital E4
Skyway (see 54)
STIC Travels (see 57)
57 TT Forex E2

Transport
Air India (see 62)
58 Central Bus Stand A3
59 City Bus Stand A3
60 City Market Bus Stand B5
61 Divisional Railway Office A2
62 Jet Airways C5
63 Skyway F4
64 Train Reservation Office A3

free) and the ornate **Venkataraman Temple** (Krishnarajendra Rd; 8.30am-6pm) – as well as the fort and market.

Krishnarajendra (City) Market MARKET
(Silver Jubilee Park Rd; 6am-10pm) For a pungent taste of traditional urban India, dive into the bustling Krishnarajendra Market and the dense grid of commercial streets that surround it. Weave your way around this lively colourful market past fresh produce, piles of vibrant dyes, spices and copperware. The colourful flower market in the centre is the highlight. Sundays are the best with more roadside vendors opening up.

Bangalore Fort FORT
FREE The last remnants of this 1761 fort is a peaceful escape from the chaotic surrounds, with its manicured lawn and stone pink walls. There's a small dungeon here, and

Ganesh temple with its Mooshak (ratlike creature) statue.

Bull Temple & Dodda Ganesha Temple HINDU TEMPLE
(Bull Temple Rd, Basavangudi; ⏲7am-8.30pm) Built by Kempegowda in the 16th-century Dravidian style, the Bull Temple contains a huge granite monolith of Nandi and is one of Bengaluru's most atmospheric temples. Nearby is the **Swee Dodda Ganapathi Temple**, (Bull Temple Rd, Basavangudi; ⏲7am-8.30pm) with an equally enormous Ganesh idol. The temples are about a kilometre south of Tipu Sultan's Palace, down Krishnarajendra Rd.

Iskcon Temple HINDU TEMPLE
(www.iskconbangalore.org; Chord Rd, Hare Krishna Hill; ⏲7am-1pm & 4-8.30pm) Built by the International Society of Krishna Consciousness (Iskcon), also referred to as the Hare Krishnas, this shiny temple, inaugurated in 1997, is lavishly decorated in a mix of ultra-contemporary and traditional styles.

Activities

Ayurvedagram YOGA
(☎65651090; www.ayurvedagram.com; Hemmandanhalli, Whitefield) Set over 15 acres of tranquil gardens with heritage homes transplanted from Kerala, this centre specialises in specifically tailored Ayurvedic treatments and rejuvenation programs.

Soukya YOGA
(☎28017000; www.soukya.com; Soukya Rd, Samethanahalli, Whitefield; ⏲6am-8.30pm) Soukya offers some fantastic long-term programs in ayurvedic therapy and yoga (seven days from ₹6600) as well as medical and therapeutic skin treatments (₹2750 per hour) at its internationally renowned place set on a picture-perfect 30-acre organic farm.

Tours

In a city lacking in blockbuster sights, the following companies offer fantastic grassroots tours to get under Bengaluru's skin.

Bangalore Walks WALKING
(☎9845523660; www.bangalorewalks.com) Choose between a traditional culture walk, the medieval Old City history walk, garden walk through Lalbagh Gardens or the 19th-century Victorian walk. Held on Saturdays and Sundays (7am to 10am), the walks (adult/child ₹500/300) are all about knowing and loving Bengaluru in a way that many locals have forgotten. There's a delicious breakfast en route. Book in advance.

Art of Bicycle CYCLING
(☎9538973506, 8105289167; www.artofbicycletrips.com; from ₹950 per person) Recommended cycling tours with handcrafted itineraries that explore the city, state and beyond, including Victoria-era tours, challenging routes up to Nandi Hills or 10-day journeys to Gokarna. All equipment is provided, including 21-speed mountain bikes and support vans.

Getoff ur Ass ADVENTURE TOUR
(☎26722750; www.getoffurass.com; 858 1D Main Rd, Giri Nagar 2nd Phase) Getoff ur Ass has perfect recipes for outward-bound adventures, including off-beat cultural trips, rafting and trekking in Karnataka and elsewhere. Also sells and rents outdoor gear.

Bus Tours SIGHTSEEING
The **government tourism department** (☎43344334; www.karnatakaholidays.net) runs city bus tours, all of which begin at Badami House. The basic half-day city tour runs twice daily at 7.30am and 2pm (non AC/AC ₹230/255), while the full-day tour departs at 7.15am (non AC/AC ₹385/485) Wednesday to Sunday.

The day trips are worth considering, particularly the daily departure to the hard-to-get-to Belur, Halebid and Shravanabelagola (non AC/AC ₹910/970). It can also arrange the luxurious **Golden Chariot** (☎11-42866600; www.thegoldenchariot.co.in) rail journeys that head across Karnataka.

Sleeping

Decent budget rooms are in short supply but a stack of dive lodges line Subedar Chatram (SC) Rd, east of the bus stands and around the train station; convenient if you're in transit.

MG Road Area

Hotel Ajantha HOTEL $
(☎25584321; www.hotelajantha.in; 22A MG Rd; s/d incl breakfast from ₹988/1541, d incl breakfast with AC from ₹1899; ❄📶) Stacks of potted foliage welcome you into this oldie located on Ashley Park Rd, with a range of par-for-the-course rooms in a semiquiet compound. Unfortunately they've doubled the prices, so is no longer the steal it once was, but still the best budget option in the Mahatma Gandhi (MG) Rd area.

★Casa Piccola Cottage HERITAGE HOTEL $$
(22270754; www.casapiccola.com; 2 Clapham Rd; r incl breakfast from ₹4300;) Located on a quiet back lane, this beautifully renovated heritage building turned into cute cottages is a tranquil sanctuary from the city madness. Its personalised brand of hospitality has garnered it a solid reputation and rooms come with tiled floors, spotless bathrooms and colourful bedspreads. Deluxe rooms offer the best value with their own verandah sitting area with cane furniture in garden surrounds of papaya and avocado trees. Go for Room 1 with its loft-style bedroom and spacious living and kitchen area. The garden gazebo dining room is the perfect place to tuck into breakfast.

St Mark's Inn HOTEL $$
(41122783; www.stmarkshotels.com; St Marks Rd; r incl breakfast ₹2500;) There are only six smart rooms on offer at this fresh new boutique hotel, so get in fast. Immaculate rooms are decked out with modern decor, big comfy beds, in-room safe and sparkling stainless-steel bathroom fittings, free wi-fi and double-glazed windows.

Hotel Empire International HOTEL $$
(42678888; www.hotelempire.in; 36 Church St; s/d incl breakfast from ₹1789/2135;) Right in the heart of the action and nightlife, Hotel Empire is a sure deal. Rooms vary in size and decency so ask to check a few out before committing. Spacious upstairs rooms are clean, bright and airy, and have good access to wi-fi. The front desk staff are professional and courteous, and there's a busy social restaurant downstairs.

Monarch HOTEL $$
(42507000; www.monarchhotels.in; 54 Brigade Rd; s/d incl breakfast from ₹3060/4285;) The well-located and good-valued Monarch is a top midrange choice with super-comfy rooms that make the most of their innumerable facilities (free wi-fi, 24-hour currency exchange counter, courier service and a dozen others).

Tom's Hotel HOTEL $$
(25575875; 1/5 Hosur Rd; s/d incl breakfast from ₹1632/1924;) Long favoured for its low tariffs, bright and cheerful Tom's allows you to stay in the heart of town in spacious clean rooms with friendly staff. Traffic noise is the only fault here so ask for a room away from the main road.

The Park HOTEL $$$
(25594666; 14/7 MG Rd; s/d incl breakfast from ₹15,000/16,000) A swanky designer hotel with oodles of glitz and glam. Home to the reputed Italian restaurant, i-t.ALIA.

Ista Hotel HOTEL $$$
(25558888; www.istahotels.com; 1/1 Swami Vivekananda Rd, Ulsoor; s/d from ₹8000/8500;) With its name meaning 'sacred space', Ista delivers accommodation happiness in a cool, business-boutique, minimalist style. The smallish but elegant rooms come with king-sized windows and some offer sweeping vistas across Ulsoor lake. The bar and restaurant open on to the infinity pool, and the spa will pamper you with diverse treatments kicking off at around ₹1200.

Other Areas

Hotel Adora HOTEL $
(22200024; 47 SC Rd; s/d ₹546/780, with AC ₹936/1444;) A largish and popular budget option near the station, with unfussy rooms with clean sheets. Downstairs is a good veg restaurant, Indraprastha.

Youth Hostel Bangalore HOSTEL $
(25924040; www.youthhostelbangalore.com; 65/2 Millers Rd; dm/d ₹150/650, d with AC ₹850) One for those watching their pennies, with the very basics on offer, but you can opt in for extras like bucket hot water (₹15), wi-fi (per hour ₹20) and downstairs security lockers (per day ₹15). It's popular with Indian students and discounts are available for YHA members.

★Villa Pottipati HERITAGE HOTEL $$
(23360777; www.neemranahotels.com; 142 8th Cross, 4th Main, Malleswaram; s/d incl breakfast from ₹3000/4000;) Located a little off-centre, this heritage building was once the garden home of the wealthy expat Andhra family. Needless to say, it's flooded with memories in the form of numerous artefacts scattered within its rooms. Dollops of quaintness are added by features such as antique four-poster beds and arched doorways, while the overall ambience gains from a garden full of ageless trees, seasonal blossoms and a dunk-sized pool.

Taj West End HERITAGE HOTEL $$$
(66605660; www.tajhotels.com; Racecourse Rd; s/d incl breakfast from ₹14,000/15,000;) The West End saga flashbacks to 1887, when

it was incepted by a British family as a 10-room hostel for passing army officers. Since then, nostalgia has been a permanent resident at this lovely property which – spread over 20 acres of tropical gardens – has evolved as a definitive icon of Indian luxury hospitality.

Eating

Bengaluru's adventurous dining scene keeps pace with the whims and rising standards of its hungry, moneyed locals and IT expats. You'll find high-end dining, gastro pubs and cheap local favourites.

MG Road Area

Queen's Restaurant INDIAN $

(Church St; mains ₹100-220; 12.30-3.30pm & 7-10.30pm, closed Mon) This reputed joint serves some quick and tasty Indian morsels such as a range of vegetable and dhal preparations, to go with fluffy and hot chapati. The interiors are rustic village-style, with painted motifs adorning earthy walls.

Koshy's Bar & Restaurant MULTICUISINE $$

(39 St Mark's Rd; mains ₹127-380; 9am-11pm) They say half of Bengaluru's court cases are argued around Koshy's tables, and many hard-hitting newspaper articles written over its steaming coffees. Serving the city's intelligentsia for decades, this buzzy and joyful resto-pub is where you can put away tasty North Indian dishes or the popular fish and chips in between fervent discussions and mugs of beer. The decor is old school with creaky ceiling fans and dusty wooden shuttered windows.

Only Place STEAKHOUSE $$

(13 Museum Rd; mains ₹260-540; noon-3pm & 7-11pm) Juicy sirloin steaks, brawny burgers and the classic shepherd's pie – no one serves them better than this time-tested restaurant which has many an expat loyalist in town.

Sunny's ITALIAN $$

(41329366; 34 Vittal Mallya Rd; mains ₹300-700; noon-11pm;) A well-established fixture in Bengaluru's restaurant scene, Sunny's is all about authentic charcoal thin-crust pizzas, homemade pastas, imported cheese and some of the best desserts in the city – go the blueberry crème brûlée. There's atmospheric lounge seating upstairs, downstairs modern dining or often buzzing outdoor tables. There's another branch in Indiranagar.

Ebony MULTICUISINE $$

(41783344; 84 MG Rd, 13th fl, Barton Centre; mains ₹200-450) Despite it's salivating-inducing menu of delectable Indian, Thai and French dishes, here it's all about the luxurious views from its heavenly rooftop location. There's a good alcohol selection too, but skip the syrupy cocktails.

★Karavalli SEAFOOD $$$

(66604545; 66 Residency Rd, Gateway Hotel; mains ₹325-1200; 12.30-3pm & 7-11.30pm) The Arabian Sea may be 500km away, but you'll have to come only as far as this superb spot to savour South India's finest coastal cuisines. The decor is a stylish mash of thatched roofs and vintage woodwork, and does superb fiery Mangalorean fish dishes and the signature Lobster Balchao (₹1200).

Fava MEDITERRANEAN $$$

(UB City; mains ₹350-850; noon-11pm) Sail away to the Med at Bangalore's stylish newcomer. It may be set in a mall but it serves up a classy atmosphere, whether indoors or al fresco on its canopy-covered decking. Feast on large plates of mezze, hummus and pita, fish kebabs, Greek-style moussaka, zatar sausages or something healthier from the organic menu. End the night with a strong Turkish coffee and blueberry panna cotta. If you're up for it, there's two hours of all-you-can-drink alcohol for ₹1200.

Olive Beach MEDITERRANEAN $$$

(41128400; 16 Wood St, Ashoknagar; mains ₹350-400; noon-11.30pm) Lodged in upscale Ashoknagar is this white-washed villa straight from the coast of Santorini, with food that evokes wistful memories of sunny Mediterranean getaways. Try the almond-encrusted kingfish or spinach and goat's cheese pizza and request the indulgent chocolate mousse cocktail for dessert. The fairly lit pebbled al fresco area is ridiculously atmospheric while loved-up couples get romantic in the dimly lit dining room among candles and flowers.

Other Areas

★Mavalli Tiffin Rooms SOUTH INDIAN $

(MTR; Lalbagh Rd; mains ₹40-60; 6.30-11am, 12.30-2.45pm, 3.30-7.30pm & 8-9.30pm) A legendary name in South Indian comfort food, this super-popular eatery has had Bengaluru eating out of its hands since 1924. Head to the dining room upstairs, queue

FOOD STREET

For a real local eating experience, head to Harrar St, aka **Food Street**, where a short strip is home to several hole-in-the-wall eateries serving up classic street-food dishes. Things kick off around 5pm when the stalls fire up and people stand around watching rotis being handmade and spun in the air or bhaji dunked into hot oil before being dished up on paper plates to enjoy standing in the street. It's an all-vegetarian affair with a range of dosas, curries, roti and deep-fried goodies. The street packs out on weekends around 9pm.

for a table, and then admire the dated images of southern beauties etched on smoky glass as waiters bring you savoury local fare, capped by frothing filter coffee served in silverware. It's a definitive Bengaluru experience.

Gramin INDIAN **$$**
(☎41104104; 20, 7th Block Raheja Arcade, Koramangala; mains ₹70-150; ⊙12.30-3.30pm & 7-11pm) Translating to 'from the village', Gramin offers a wide choice of flavourful rural North Indian fare at this cosy, eclectic all-veg place popular with locals. Try the excellent range of lentils and curries best had with oven-fresh rotis and sweet rose-flavoured lassi served in a copper vessel.

Harima JAPANESE **$$**
(☎41325757; Residency Rd, 4th fl, Devatha Plaza; mains ₹250-280; ⊙noon-3pm & 6-11pm) Authentic Japanese staples cooked up by the Osakan owner/chef, including flavourful yakitori, tempura, sushi and sashimi. Wash it down with a few cold Asahis before finishing off with green tea ice cream. The decor here is traditional and atmospheric.

Windsor Pub MULTICUISINE **$$**
(1st Main Vasanthnagar, 7 Kodava Samaja Bldg; mains ₹230-300; ⊙11.30am-3pm & 6-11pm) It's dark pub interior may not inspire, but it has a fantastic menu of regional favourites such as flavoursome Mangalorean fish, or the tangy *pandhi* (pork) masala from Kodagu's hills. Otherwise go the awesome fillet steak, accompanied by a draft beer and a soundtrack of blues, jazz and '70s rock.

Caperberry CONTINENTAL **$$$**
(☎25594567; 121 Dickenson Rd; tapas ₹275-625, mains ₹425-950; ⊙12.30-3.30pm & 7-11.30pm) A smart blend of mod Euro decor and glittering South Indian goldwork create a sophisticated ambience at this fancy restaurant specialising mostly in Spanish food. Pick from grilled lamb chops with garlic and rosemary or squid rings with aioli, accompanied with jugs of sangria. There's also tasting menus from ₹1950. It's tucked away at the back of the block.

Drinking & Nightlife

Bars & Lounges

Despite Bengaluru's rock-steady reputation, local laws require pubs and discos to shut shop at 11.30pm (opening time is usually 7pm). However, given the wide choice of chic watering holes around, you can indulge in a spirited session of pub-hopping in this original beer town of India. The trendiest nightclubs will typically charge you a cover of around ₹1000 per couple, but it's often redeemable against drinks or food.

Monkey Bar PUB
(www.mobar.in; 14/1 Wood St; ⊙noon-11pm) From the owners of Olive Beach comes this chic industrial gastro pub with a stylish vintage feel. Affordable cocktails and good pub classics draws a mixed, jovial crowd to knock back drinks around the bar or at wooden booth seating. Ottherwise head down to the basement to join the 'party' crew shooting pool, playing foosball and rocking out to bangin' tunes.

Shiro BAR
(UB City; ⊙12.30-11pm) A sophisticated lounge to get sloshed in style, Shiro has elegant interiors complemented by the monumental Buddha busts and Apsara figurines. Its commendable selection of cocktails and drinks draws rave reviews from patrons, who often fight off their Saturday night hangovers by converging again for Sunday brunch sessions (₹2200 all you can eat and drink).

Biere Club PUB
(20/2 Vittal Mallya Rd; ⊙11am-11pm) Beer lovers rejoice as South India's first microbrewery serves up handcrafted beers on tap, six of which are brewed onsite. Brewing equipment and large copper boilers sit behind the bar, and renowned DJs and Bollywood stars

are occasional guests. The music pumps in the spacious upstairs room and good pub grub and beer snacks are on the menu. It attracts a good crowd of students, professionals, tourists and IT expats.

Plan B PUB
(20 Castle St, Ashoknagar; ⏲12pm-11pm) Finish your beer. 'There are sober kids in India', says a poster adorning this hip pub's industrial interiors. And to aid you in this eminently enjoyable task, ₹1000 will get you a 3.5L beer tower. There's a whole line of awesome bites from 14 kinds of burgers to porky platters, with rock and metal tunes on rotation.

Pecos BAR
(Rest House Rd; ⏲10.30am-11pm) Hendrix, The Grateful Dead and Frank Zappa posters adorn the walls of this charmingly shabby, narrow tri-level bar. It's a throwback to simpler times where cassettes line the shelves behind the bar, sports are on the TV and the only thing to quench your thirst is one choice of cheap beer on tap. No wonder it's an all-time favourite with students.

13th Floor BAR
(84 MG Rd, 13th fl, Barton Centre; ⏲5-11pm) Come early to grab a spot on the rooftop terrace, with all of Bengaluru glittering at your feet. It attracts a refined, yet lively crowd, sipping on martinis. Happy hour is 5pm to 7pm, with 30% off drinks.

Cafes & Teahouses

Bengaluru is liberally sprinkled with good chain cafes. Café Coffee Day has several outlets across town, including one on **Brigade Rd** (Brigade Rd; ⏲8am-11.30pm) and another on **MG Rd** (MG Rd; ⏲8am-11.30pm).

★**Matteo** CAFE
(Church St; ⏲9am-11pm; 📶) The coolest rendezvous in the city centre where local hipsters lounge on retro couches sipping first-rate brews while chatting, plugged into free wi-fi, or browsing a great selection of newspapers and mags. Also does comfort food such as toasties.

Infinitea CAFE
(Cunningham Rd, 2 Shah Sultan Complex; pot of tea from ₹100; ⏲11am-11pm; 📶) This smart yet homely cafe has an impressive menu of steaming cuppas, including orthodox teas from the best estates, and a few fancy selections such as chocolate-ginger rooibos and blooming flower teas like the peony rosette. Order your pot and team it with a delectable sweet or light lunch.

☆ Entertainment

Cinema

INOX CINEMA
(☎41128888; www.inoxmovies.com; Magrath Rd, 4th fl, Garuda Mall) Screens new releases from Bollywood and the West.

Sport

For a taste of India's sporting passion up close, attend one of the regular cricket matches at **M Chinnaswamy Stadium** (ksca.co.in; MG Rd); check its website for upcoming matches.

Horse racing is also big, and can make for a fun day out. Bengaluru's horse-racing seasons are from November to February and May to July. Contact the **Bangalore Turf Club** (www.bangaloreraces.com; Racecourse Rd) for details.

Theatre

Ranga Shankara THEATRE
(☎26592777; www.rangashankara.org; 36/2 8th Cross, JP Nagar) All kinds of interesting theatre (in a variety of languages and spanning various genres) and dance are held at this cultural centre.

Shopping

Bengaluru's shopping options are abundant, ranging from teeming bazaars to glitzy malls. Some good shopping areas include Commercial St, Vittal Mallya Rd and the MG Rd area. Commercial St is best for clothing and gets packed on weekends.

Some good malls in town include **Garuda Mall** (McGrath Rd), **Forum** (Hosur Rd, Koramangala) and **Leela Galleria** (23 Airport Rd, Kodihalli).

Mysore Saree Udyog CLOTHING
(www.mysoresareeudyog.com; 316 Kamaraj Rd, 1st fl; ⏲10.30am-11pm) A great choice for top-quality silk blouses and men's shirts, scarves and saris, this busy store has been in business for over 70 years and has something to suit all budgets. Ninety-nine percent of the garments here are made with Mysore silk, and the store also stocks 100% pashmina shawls. All fixed prices.

Cauvery Arts & Crafts Emporium SOUVENIRS
(49 MG Rd; ⌚10am-8pm) Showcases a great collection of sandalwood and rosewood products as well as textiles.

Forest Essentials COSMETICS
(www.forestessentialsindia.com; 4/1 Lavelle Junction Bldg, Vittal Mallya Rd; ⌚11am-8.30pm) Smell the lemongrass as you browse the shelves at this tranquil store selling all-organic beauty products.

Fabindia CLOTHING
(www.fabindia.com; 54 17th Main, Koramangala; ⌚10am-8pm) Commercial St (152 Commercial St; ⌚10am-8.30pm) Garuda mall (McGrath Rd, Garuda mall) These branches contain Fabindia's full range of stylish clothes and homewares in traditional cotton prints and silks.

UB City CLOTHING
(Vittal Mallya Rd; ⌚11am-9pm) Global haute couture (Louis Vuitton, Jimmy Choo, Burberry) and Indian high fashion come to roost at this towering mall in the central district.

Magazines BOOKS
(55 Church St; ⌚10am-10pm) An astounding collection of international magazines. Up to 70% discount on back issues.

Bombay Store SOUVENIRS
(100Ft Rd; ⌚10.30am-8.30pm) For gifts ranging from ecobeauty products to linens.

Bookworm BOOKS
(Shrungar Shopping Complex, MG Rd; ⌚10am-9pm) Great secondhand bookstore filled with contemporary and classic literature as well as travel guidebooks.

Page Turners BOOKS
(☎25595111; www.pageturners.in; 89 Kannan Bldg, MG Rd; ⌚10am-8.30pm Mon-Sat, 11am-8pm Sun) Stocks an excellent range of Penguin books from Indian and international writers, set over three floors.

ℹ Information

INTERNET ACCESS
Being an IT city, internet cafes are plentiful in Bengaluru, as is wi-fi access in hotels.

LEFT LUGGAGE
The City train station and Central bus stand have 24-hour cloakrooms (per day ₹10).

MAPS
The tourist offices give out decent city maps and you can find excellent maps at most major bookstores.

MEDIA
Time Out Bengaluru (₹50) is an excellent magazine which covers all the latest events, nightlife, dining and shopping in the city. *080* and *What's Up Bangalore* are great monthly magazines covering the latest in Bengaluru's social life. *Kingfisher Explocity Nights* (₹200) gives the low-down on the best night spots. All titles are available in major bookstores.

MEDICAL SERVICES
Hosmat (☎25593796; www.hosmatnet.com) For critical injuries and other general illnesses.

Mallya Hospital (☎22277979; www.mallyahospital.net; 2 Vittal Mallya Rd) Emergency services and 24-hour pharmacy.

MONEY
ATMs are everywhere, as are moneychangers, including **TT Forex** (☎22254337; 33/1 Cunningham Rd; ⌚9.30am-6.30pm Mon-Fri, 9.30am-1.30pm Sat).

POST
Main Post Office (Cubbon Rd; ⌚10am-7pm Mon-Sat, 10am-1pm Sun)

TOURIST INFORMATION
Government of India Tourist Office (☎25585417; 48 Church St, 2nd level; ⌚9.30am-6pm Mon-Fri, 9am-1pm Sat) Very helpful for Bengaluru and beyond.

Karnataka State Tourism Development Corporation (KSTDC) Badami House; ☎43344334; Badami House, Kasturba Rd; ⌚10am-7pm Mon-Sat) Karnataka Tourism House (☎41329211; 8 Papanna Lane, St Mark's Rd, Karnataka Tourism House; ⌚10am-7pm Mon-Sat) Mainly about booking tours and accommodation, but has a city map and useful website and can provide a general overview of things to do.

TRAVEL AGENCIES
Jungle Lodges & Resorts Ltd (☎25597944; www.junglelodges.com; MG Rd, Shrungar Shopping Complex, Bengaluru; ⌚10am-5.30pm Mon-Sat) Books government-run lodges across the state, including wildlife parks and reserves; however inflated rates for foreigners means they're not cheap.

Skyway (☎22111401; www.skywaytour.com; St Mark's Rd, 8 Papanna Lane; ⌚9am-6pm Mon-Sat) A thoroughly professional and reliable outfit for booking long-distance taxis and air tickets.

STIC Travels (☎911244595300; www.stictravel.com; 33/1 Cunningham Rd, G5 Imperial

Ct; ⌚9.30am-6pm Mon-Sat) For ticketing, vehicles, hotels and holiday packages.

ℹ Getting There & Away

AIR

International flights arrive to Bengaluru's airport in Hebbal, and there are direct daily flights to major cities all across India, including Chennai (₹2500, two hours), Mumbai (₹3000, two hours), Hyderabad (₹2500, one hour), Delhi (₹4500, 2½ hours) and Goa (₹2500, one hour).

Air India (☎22277747; www.airindia.com; JC Rd, Unity Bldg)

GoAir (☎47406091; www.goair.in; Bengaluru airport)

IndiGo (☎9910383838; www.goindigo.in)

Jet Airways (☎39893333; www.jetairways.com; JC Rd, Unity Bldg)

SpiceJet (☎18001803333; www.spicejet.com)

BUS

Bengaluru's huge, well-organised **Central bus stand** (Gubbi Thotadappa Rd), also known as Majestic, is directly in front of the City train station. **Karnataka State Road Transport Corporation** (KSRTC; ☎44554422; www.ksrtc.in) buses run throughout Karnataka and to neighbouring states. Other interstate bus operators:

Andhra Pradesh State Road Transport (APSRTC; www.apsrtc.gov.in)

Kadamba Transport Corporation (☎22351958, 22352922) Services for Goa.

Maharashtra State Road Transport Corporation (MSRTC; www.msrtc.gov.in)

Tamil Nadu State Transport Corporation (SETC; www.tnstc.in)

Computerised advance booking is available for most buses at the station. KSRTC also has convenient booking counters around town. It's wise to book long-distance journeys in advance.

Numerous private bus companies offer comfier and only slightly more expensive services. Private bus operators line the street facing the Central bus stand, or you can book through a travel agency.

TRAIN

Bengaluru's **City train station** (Gubbi Thotadappa Rd) is the main train hub and the place to make reservations. **Cantonment train station** (Station Rd) is a sensible spot to disembark if you're arriving and headed for the MG Rd area, while **Yeshvantpur train station** (Rahman Khan Rd), 8km northwest of downtown, is the starting point for Goa trains.

If a train is booked out, foreign travellers can use the foreign-tourist quota. Buy a wait-listed ticket, then fill out a form at the **Divisional Railway Office** (Gubbi Thotadappa Rd) building immediately north of the City train station. You'll know about 10 hours before departure whether you've got a seat (a good chance); if not, the ticket is refunded. The computerised **train reservation office** (☎139; ⌚8am-8pm Mon-Sat, 8am-2pm Sun), on the left facing the station, has separate counters for credit-card purchase, women and foreigners. Luggage can be left at the 24-hour cloakroom on Platform 1 at the City train station (₹10 per bag per day).

ℹ Getting Around

TO/FROM THE AIRPORT

The swish city **airport** (☎66782251; www.bengaluruairport.com) is in Hebbal, about 40km north from the MG Rd area. Prepaid taxis can take you from the airport to the city centre

MAJOR BUS SERVICES FROM BENGALURU

DESTINATION	FARE (₹)	DURATION (HR)	FREQUENCY
Chennai	363 (R)/650 (V)	7-8	6.35am-11.55pm, every hour
Ernakulam	532 (R)/902 (V)	10-12	7 daily, 4am-9.45pm
Gorkana	517 (R)/650 (V)	12	3 daily
Hampi	444 (R)	8½	1 daily, 11pm
Hospet	411 (R)/381 (V)	8	2pm-11pm, every hour
Hyderabad	640 (R)/904 (V)	11	16 buses daily, from 7.30am-10.30pm
Jog Falls	500 (R)	9	1 daily, 9.50pm
Mangalore	451 (R)/650 (V)	9	every 30min 6.30am-2pm & 7-11.30pm
Mumbai	1200 (V)	19	5 daily, from 3pm
Mysore	180 (R)/290 (V)	3	Every 10min, 24hr
Ooty	360 (R)/600 (V)	8	8 daily, 6.30am-11.15pm
Panaji	602 (R)/847 (V)	15	3 daily, from 5am

R – Rajahamsa Semideluxe, V – Airavath AC Volvo

(₹750). You can also take the hourly shuttle Vayu Vajra AC bus service to Majestic or MG Rd (₹170).

AUTORICKSHAW

The city's autorickshaw drivers are legally required to use their meters; few comply in reality. After 10pm, 50% is added onto the metered rate. Flag fall is ₹20 for the first 2km and then ₹11 for each extra kilometre.

BUS

Bengaluru has a thorough local bus network, operated by the **Bangalore Metropolitan Transport Corporation** (BMTC; www.bmtcinfo.com). Red AC Vajra buses criss-cross the city, while green Big10 deluxe buses connect the suburbs. Ordinary buses run from the **City bus stand**, next to Majestic; a few operate from the **City Market bus stand** further south.

To get from the City train station to the MG Rd area, catch any bus from Platform 17 or 18 at the City bus stand. For the City Market, take bus 31, 31E, 35 or 49 from Platform 8.

METRO

Bengaluru's shiny new AC metro service, known as Namma Metro finally had some lines up and running at the time of research (running from Baiyappanahalli to MG Road) while others are still in development. With trains plying every fifteen minutes and tickets costing marginally more than intra-city buses, upon completion the service will come as a welcome alternative to the city's congested public transport system. For the latest updates on the service, log on to www.bmrc.co.in.

TAXI

Several places around Bengaluru offer taxi rental with driver. Standard rates for a long-haul Tata Indica cab are ₹7 per kilometre for a minimum of 250km, plus a daily allowance of ₹200 for the driver. For an eight-hour day rental, you're looking at around ₹2000. Try **Skyway** (☎22111401) or **Meru Cabs** (☎44224422).

Around Bengaluru

Hessaraghatta

Located 30km northwest of Bengaluru, Hessaraghatta is home to **Nrityagram** (☎080-28466313; www.nrityagram.org; ⏰10am-2pm Tue-Sun), a leading dance academy established in 1990 to revive and popularise Indian classical dance.

The brainchild and living legacy of celebrated dancer Protima Gauri Bedi (1948–98), the complex was designed like a village by Goa-based architect Gerard da Cunha. Long-term courses in classical dance are offered to deserving students here, while local children are taught for free on Sundays. Self-guided tours cost ₹50 or you can book a tour, lecture and demonstration and vegetarian meal (₹1500 to ₹2000, minimum 10 people).

Opposite the dance village, **Taj Kuteeram** (☎080-28466326; www.tajhotels.com; d ₹4000; ❄@) is a hotel that combines comfort with rustic charm. It also offers ayurveda and yoga sessions.

MAJOR TRAINS FROM BENGALURU

DESTINATION	TRAIN NO & NAME	FARE (₹)	DURATION (HR)	DEPARTURES
Chennai	12658 Chennai Mail	193/735	6½	10.45pm
	12028 Shatabdi	529/1155	5	6am Wed-Mon
Delhi	12627 Karnataka Express	546/2485	39	7.20pm
	12649 Sampark Kranti Express	536/2425	35	10.10pm Mon, Wed, Fri, Sat & Sun
Hospet	16592 Hampi Express	191/785	9½	10pm
Hubli	16589 Rani Chennamma Express	203/840	8	9.15pm
Kolkata	12864 YPR Howrah Express	508/2625	35	7.35pm
Mumbai	16530 Udyan Express	363/1600	24	8.10pm
Mysore	12007 Shatabdi	316/665	2	11am Thu-Tue
	12614 Tippu Express	66/233	2½	3pm
Trivandrum	16526 Kanyakumari Express	307/1320	22	9.40pm

Shatabdi fares are AC chair/AC executive; Express (Exp/Mail) fares are 2nd-class/AC chair for day trains and sleeper/2AC for night trains.

OFF THE BEATEN TRACK

LEPAKSHI

While actually located in Andrha Pradesh, Lepakshi is most easily accessible from Bengaluru, and is the site of the **Veerbhadra Temple** (admission free). The town gets its name from the Ramayana: when demon Ravana kidnapped Rama's wife, Sita, the bird Jatayu fought him and fell, injured, at the temple site. Rama then called him to get up; 'Lepakshi' derives from the Sanskrit for 'Get up, bird'.

Look for the 9m-long monolithic **Nandi** – India's largest – at the town's entrance. From here, you can see the temple's **Naga-lingam** (a phallic representation of Shiva) crowned with a seven-headed cobra. The temple is known for its unfinished **Kalyana Mandapam** (Marriage Hall), depicting the wedding of Parvati and Shiva, and its **Natyamandapa** (Dance Hall), with carvings of dancing gods. The temple's most stunning features, though, are the Natyamandapa's ceiling **frescoes**.

To get here from Bengaluru, take a Hindupur-bound bus (₹70, 1½ hours) or train, from where it's a further 11km to the temple. A private car from Puttaparthi is ₹1000.

Our Native Village (9591700577, 080-41140909; www.ournativevillage.com; s/d incl full board & activities ₹5100/7500;), an eco-health retreat situated in the vicinity, is a great place to unwind in style while engaging in yoga, meditation and sound therapies as well as fun activities such as flying kites or riding bullock carts.

From Bengaluru's City Market, buses 266, 253, 253D and 253E run to Hessaraghatta (₹25, one hour), with bus 266 continuing on to Nrityagram. From Hessaraghatta an autorickshaw will cost ₹70.

Nandi Hills

Rising to 1455m, the **Nandi Hills** (www.nandihills.co.in; admission ₹5; 6am-6pm), 60km north of Bengaluru, were once the summer retreat of Tipu Sultan (his palace is still here). Today, it's the Bengaluru techie's favourite weekend getaway, and is predictably congested on Saturdays and Sundays. Nonetheless, it's a good place for hiking, with good views and two notable **Chola temples**. Buses head to Nandi Hills (₹50, two hours) from Bengaluru's Central bus stand.

Janapada Loka Folk Arts Museum

Situated 53km south of Bengaluru, this **museum** (adult/child ₹10/5; 9am-5.30pm) dedicated to the preservation of rural cultures has a wonderful collection of folk-art objects, including 500-year-old shadow puppets, festival costumes and musical instruments. Departing from Bengaluru, Mysore-bound buses (one hour) can drop you here; get off 3km after Ramnagar.

Mysore

0821 / POP 887,500 / ELEV 707M

If you haven't been to Mysore, you just haven't seen South India. Conceited though it may sound, this is not an overstatement. An ancient city with more than 600 glorious years of legacy, Mysore is one of the most flamboyant places in India. Known for its glittering royal heritage, bustling markets, magnificent monuments, cosmopolitan culture and a friendly populace, it is also a thriving centre for the production of premium silk, sandalwood and incense. It also flaunts considerable expertise in yoga and ayurveda, two trades it markets worldwide.

History

Mysore owes its name to the mythical Mahisuru, a place where the demon Mahisasura was slain by the goddess Chamundi. Its regal history began in 1399, when the Wodeyar dynasty of Mysore was founded, though they remained in service of the Vijayanagar empire until the mid-16th century. With the fall of Vijayanagar in 1565, the Wodeyars declared their sovereignty, which – save a brief period of Hyder Ali and Tipu Sultan's supremacy in the late 18th century – remained unscathed until 1947.

Sights

★**Mysore Palace** PALACE

(Maharaja's Palace; www.mysorepalace.tv; Indian/foreigner ₹40/200, children under 10 free, Sound & Light show adult/child ₹40/25; 10am-5.30pm) Among the grandest of India's royal buildings, this fantastic palace was the former seat of the Wodeyar maharajas. The old

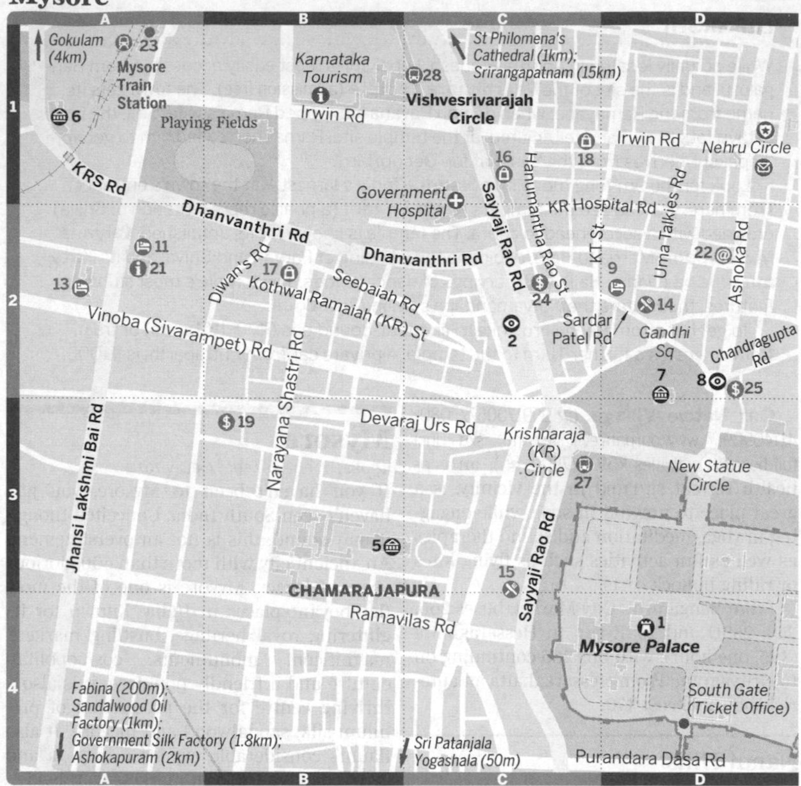

palace was gutted by fire in 1897; the one you see now was completed in 1912 by English architect Henry Irwin at a cost of Rs4.5 million. (See also the illustration, p192.)

The interior of this Indo-Saracenic marvel – a kaleidoscope of stained glass, mirrors and gaudy colours – is undoubtedly over the top. The decor is further embellished by carved wooden doors, mosaic floors and a series of paintings depicting life in Mysore during the Edwardian Raj. The way into the palace takes you past a fine collection of sculptures and artefacts. Don't forget to check out the armoury, with an intriguing collection of 700-plus weapons.

Every weekend, on national holidays, and through the Dasara (Duesshera) celebrations, the palace is illuminated by nearly 100,000 light bulbs that accent its majestic profile against the night.

Entrance to the palace grounds is at the South Gate on Purandara Dasa Rd. While you are allowed to snap the palace's exterior, photography within is strictly prohibited. Cameras must be deposited in lockers at the palace entrance.

Also available within the compound is a multilingual guided audiotour of the palace, the price of which is included in the foreigners' ticket.

A Sound & Light show is held most evenings at 7pm, which narrates the palace's history with effects of illumination; English-language shows were being launched at time of research.

Devaraja Market MARKET

(Sayyaji Rao Rd; ⏲6am-8.30pm) Dating from Tipu Sultan's reign, this lively bazaar has local traders selling traditional items such as flower garlands, spices and conical piles of *kumkum* (coloured powder used for bindi dots), all of which makes for some great photo-ops. Refresh your bargaining skills before shopping.

Mysore

Top Sights
1 Mysore Palace D4

Sights
2 Devaraja Market C2
3 Government House F1
4 Indira Gandhi Rashtriya Manav Sangrahalaya E1
Jaganmohan Palace .... (see 5)
5 Jayachamarajendra Art Gallery B3
6 Rail Museum A1
7 Rangacharlu Memorial Hall D2
8 Silver Jubilee Clock Tower D2

Activities, Courses & Tours
Shruthi Musical Works .... (see 18)

Sleeping
9 Hotel Dasaprakash D2
10 Hotel Maurya Residency E3
11 Hotel Mayura Hoysala A2
12 Parklane Hotel E3
13 Royal Orchid Metropole A2

Eating
14 Hotel RRR D2
15 Hotel Sree Annapoorna C3
Parklane Hotel .... (see 12)
Tiger Trail .... (see 13)

Shopping
16 Cauvery Arts & Crafts Emporium C1
17 Sapna Book House B2
18 Shruthi Musical Works C1

Information
HDFC ATM .... (see 19)
19 HDFC Bank B3
20 ICICI Bank E2
ICICI Bank ATM .... (see 20)
21 KSTDC Transport Office A2
22 Pal Net D2
23 Railway Booking Office A1
24 State Bank of Mysore C2
25 Thomas Cook D2

Transport
26 Central Bus Stand E2
27 City Bus Stand C3
28 Private Bus Stand C1

Chamundi Hill VIEWPOINT
At a height of 1062m, on the summit of Chamundi Hill, stands the **Sri Chamundeswari Temple** (7am-2pm, 3.30-6pm & 7.30-9pm), dominated by a towering 40m-high *gopuram* (entrance gateway). It's a fine half-day excursion, offering spectacular views of the city below. Queues are long at weekends, so visit during the week. You can take bus 201 (₹23, 30 minutes) that rumbles up the narrow road to the summit. A return autorickshaw trip will cost about ₹400.

Alternatively, you can take the foot trail comprising 1000-plus steps that Hindu pilgrims use to visit the temple. One-third of the way down is a 5m-high statue of **Nandi** (Shiva's bull) that was carved out of solid rock in 1659.

Jayachamarajendra Art Gallery ART GALLERY
(Jaganmohan Palace Rd; adult/child ₹100/50; 8.30am-5pm) Built in 1861 as the royal auditorium, the **Jaganmohan Palace**, just west of the Mysore Palace, houses the Jayachamarajendra Art Gallery. Set over three floors it has a collection of kitsch objects and regal memorabilia of the Mysore royal family including rare musical instruments, Japanese art, and paintings by the noted artist Raja Ravi Varma.

Mysore Palace

The interior of Mysore Palace houses opulent halls, royal paintings, intricate decorative details, as well as sculptures and ceremonial objects. There is a lot of hidden detail and much to take in, so be sure to allow yourself at least a few hours for the experience. A guide can also be invaluable.

After entering the palace the first exhibit is the **Doll's Pavilion** 1, which showcases the maharaja's fine collection of traditional dolls and sculptures acquired from around the world. Opposite the **Elephant Gate** 2 you'll see the seven cannons that were used for special occasions, such as the birthdays of the maharajas. Today the cannons are still fired as part of Dasara festivities.

At the end of the Doll's Pavilion you'll find the **Golden Howdah** 3. Note the fly whisks on either side; the bristles are made from fine ivory.

Make sure you check out the paintings depicting the Dasara procession in the halls on your way to the **Marriage Pavilion** 4 and look into the courtyard to see what was once the wrestling arena. It's now used during Dasara only. In the Marriage Pavilion, take a few minutes to scan the entire space. You can see the influence of three religions in the design of the hall: the glass ceiling represents Christianity, stone carvings along the hallway ceilings are Hindu design and the top-floor balcony roof (the traditional ladies' gallery) has Islamic-style arches.

When you move through to the **Private Durbar Hall** 5, take note of the intricate ivory inlay motifs depicting Krishna in the rosewood doors. The **Public Durbar Hall** 6 is usually the last stop where you can admire the panoramic views of the gardens through the Islamic arches.

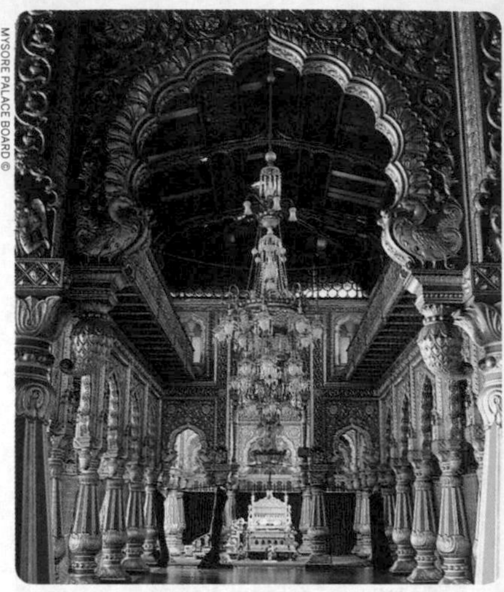

Private Durbar Hall
Rosewood doors lead into this hall, which is richly decorated with stained-glass ceilings, steel grill work and chandeliers. It houses the Golden Throne, only on display to the public during Dasara.

Doll's Pavilion
The first exhibit, the Doll's Pavilion, displays the gift collection of 19th- and early-20th-century dolls, statues and Hindu idols that were given to the maharaja by dignitaries from around the world.

Public Durbar Hall
The open-air hall contains a priceless collection of paintings by Raja Ravi Varma and opens into an expansive balcony supported by massive pillars with an ornate painted ceiling of 10 incarnations of Vishnu.

Marriage Pavilion
This lavish hall used for royal weddings features themes of Christianity, Hindu and Islam in its design. The highlight is the octagonal painted glass ceiling featuring peacock motifs, the bronze chandelier and the colonnaded turquoise pillars.

Elephant Gate
Next to the Doll's Pavilion, this brass gate has four bronze elephants inlaid at the bottom, an intricate double-headed eagle up the top and a hybrid lion-elephant creature (the state emblem of Karnataka) in the centre.

Golden Howdah
At the far end of the Doll's Pavilion, a wooden elephant howdah decorated with 80kg of gold was used to carry the maharaja in the Dasara festival. It now carries the idol of goddess Chamundeswari.

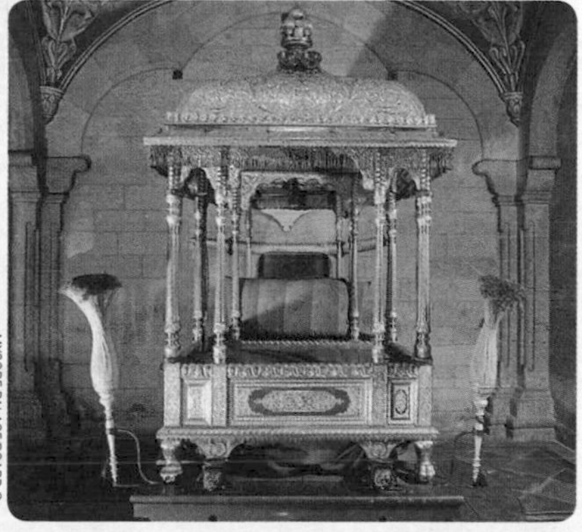

Indira Gandhi Rashtriya Manav Sangrahalaya MUSEUM
(National Museum of Mankind; ☎2448231; www.igrms.com; Irwin Rd, Wellington Lodge; 2-week workshops ₹50; ⏰10am-5.30pm Tue-Sun) As well as excellent rotating exhibitions showcasing arts from rural India, this arts-cultural centre also organises two-week workshops in traditional, folk and tribal art forms, which are open to the public. It could be painting, embroidery, woodwork or paper mâché maskmaking conducted by specialist instructors. You need to book well in advance and commit to full-day workshops over two weeks.

Jayalakshmi Vilas Mansion Museum Complex MUSEUM
(Mysore University Campus; ⏰10.15am-5pm Mon-Sat) FREE Housed in a grand mansion, this museum specialises in folklore with artefacts, stone tablets and sculptures, including a wooden puppet of the 10-headed demon Ravana, and rural costumes.

Rail Museum MUSEUM
(KRS Rd; adult/child ₹5/2, camera/video ₹10/25; ⏰9.30am-6.30pm Tue-Sun) Located behind the train station, this open-air museum's main exhibit is the Mysore maharani's saloon, a wood-panelled beauty dating from 1899 that provides an insight in to the stylish way in which the royals once rode the railways. There are also six steam engines, each with its own story (told effectively through cutesy captions) and memorabilia from the Indian Railways' chequered past. A toy train rides the track around the museum (adult/child ₹5/2).

Mysore Zoo ZOO
(Indiranagar; adult/child ₹40/20, camera ₹20; ⏰8.30am-6.30pm Wed-Mon) Unlike many other pitifiul zoos in India, Mysore zoo conforms to much higher standards, set in pretty gardens that date from 1892. Highlights include white tigers, lowland gorillas and rhinos.

Colonial Architecture ARCHITECTURE
For architecture buffs, Mysore has quite a handful of charming buildings. Dating from 1805, **Government House** (Irwin Rd), formerly the British Residency, is a Tuscan Doric building set in 20 hectares of gardens. Facing the north gate of the Maharaja's Palace is the 1927 **Silver Jubilee Clock Tower** (Ashoka Rd); nearby stands the imposing **Rangacharlu Memorial Hall**, built in 1884. The beauty of towering **St Philomena's Cathedral** (St Philomena St; ⏰8am-5pm), built between 1933 and 1941 in neo-Gothic style, is emphasised by beautiful stained-glass windows.

Activities

Royal Mysore Walks WALKING
(☎9632044188; www.royalmysorewalks.com; 2hr walks from ₹600) A walking tour is an excellent way to familiarise yourself with Mysore's epic history and heritage. Techie-turned-historian Vinay and his team organise weekend walks with a specific focus on either the city's royal history, its markets, its old quarters or its handicrafts. Offbeat walks, such as a yoga and spirituality tour or Mysore silk tour, can also be arranged at extra cost. They also conduct cycling and jeep tours.

Emerge Spa AYURVEDA
(☎2522500; www.thewindflower.com; Maharanapratap Rd, Windflower Spa & Resort, Nazarbad; ⏰7am-9pm) Slick, out-of-town resort offering pampering ayurvedic sessions (try the one-hour Abhayanga massage for ₹1800 which involves two therapists) followed by the steam chamber or a range of Balinese massage, hydrotherapy and beauty treatments. Rates include pick-up and drop off.

Indus Valley Ayurvedic Centre AYURVEDA
(☎2473263; www.ayurindus.com; Lalithadripura) Set on 25 acres of gardens, this classy centre derives its therapies from ancient scriptures and prescriptions. The overnight package (single/double including full board ₹9500/16,900) includes one session each of ayurveda, yoga and beauty therapy.

Swaasthya Ayurveda Centre AYURVEDA
(☎6557557; www.swaasthya.com; No 726/B, 6th Cross, opp Yoganarsimhaswamy Temple; treatments from ₹250) Professional Ayurveda therapists providing traditional treatments and all-inclusive packages that include accommodation and food. Also has a retreat in Coorg.

Karanji Lake Nature Park NATURE PARK, BIRDWATCHING
(Indiranagar; admission ₹20, camera ₹20; ⏰8.30am-5.30pm) Next to the zoo, this nature park is the place to spy on various bird species, including cormorants, herons, rose-ringed parakeets, painted storks and many butterflies.

Courses

Jayashankar, the music teacher at **Shruthi Musical Works** (9845249518; Irwin Rd, 1189 3rd Cross; 10.30am-9pm Mon-Sat, 10.30am-2pm Sun), gets good reviews for his tabla instructions (₹300 per hour).

Tours

KSTDC runs a daily Mysore city tour (from ₹725), taking in the entire city, Chamundi Hill, Srirangapatnam and Brindavan Gardens. It starts daily at 6.30am, ends at 11.30pm and is likely to leave you breathless!

Other KSTDC tours include one to Belur, Halebid and Sravanabelagola (₹450) on Tuesday, Wednesday, Friday and Saturday from 7.30am to 9pm. It requires a minimum of 10 people, so call in advance.

All tours leave from the tours office at Hotel Mayura Hoysala (p195). Bookings can be made at the KSTDC Transport Office (located at the hotel) or at travel agencies around town.

Sleeping

Mysore attracts tourists through the year and can fill up very quickly during Dussehra. Booking early is recommended.

Mysore Youth Hostel HOSTEL $
(2544704; www.yhmysore.com; Gangothri Layout; dm/students from ₹100/75) Set against a patch of green lawns 3km west of town, this hostel has clean, well-maintained male and female dorms. OK, there's a 10.30pm curfew, no alcohol allowed, bucket hot water and no towels, but you can't go past these prices. Take a city bus to Maruthi Temple, from where it's a short walk; an autorickshaw costs ₹60.

Hotel Dasaprakash HOTEL $
(2442444; www.mysoredasaprakashgroup.com; Gandhi Sq; s/d from ₹400/702, d with AC ₹1732;) Popular with local tourists and pilgrim groups, rooms here are a bit rundown, but the building has character and makes for a decent budget option. It has an inexpensive veg restaurant with good dosas.

Hotel Mayura Hoysala HOTEL $
(2426160; 2 Jhansi Lakshmi Bai Rd; s/d incl breakfast from ₹953/1050;) This government-owned hotel continues to offer its blend of mothballed heritage (lace-lined curtains, heavy wooden doors, assorted cane furniture and old photographs lining its corridors) at affordable prices. The bar here is popular with Mysore's tipplers.

★ **Green Hotel** HERITAGE HOTEL $$
(4255000; www.greenhotelindia.com; 2270 Vinoba Rd, Jayalakshmipuram; s/d incl breakfast from ₹3550/4050;) Undergoing several fascinating reincarnations over the years, the character-filled Green Hotel was originally built as the Chittaranjan Palace in the 1920s by the maharajah for his three daughters, before becoming a major film studio from the 1950s to 1987. Today its 31-rooms, set among charming gardens, are all run on solar power and those in the Palace building include themes such as a Writers room or kitschy

JAMBOREE

Mysore is at its carnivalesque best during the 10-day **Dussehra** (Mysore; Oct) (locally spelt 'Dasara') festival in October. During this time the Maharaja's Palace is dramatically lit up every evening, while the town is transformed into a gigantic fairground, with concerts, dance performances, sporting demonstrations and cultural events running to packed houses. On the last day the celebrations are capped off in grand style. A dazzling procession of richly costumed elephants, garlanded idols, liveried retainers and cavalry kicks off around 1pm, marching through the streets to the rhythms of clanging brass bands, all the way from the palace to the Bannimantap parade ground. A torchlight parade at Bannimantap and a spectacular session of fireworks then closes the festival for the year.

Mysore is choc-a-bloc with tourists during the festival, especially on the final day. To bypass suffocating crowds, consider buying a Dasara VIP Gold Card (₹7500 for two). Though expensive, it assures you good seats at the final day gala and helps you beat the entry queues at other events and performances, while providing discounts on accommodation, dining and shopping. It's also possible to buy tickets (₹250 to ₹1000) just for entering the palace and Bannimantap for the final day's parades. Contact the the **Dasara Information Centre** (2418888; www.mysoredasara.gov.in) for more details.

MYSORE ASHTANGA YOGA

It's not just the palace that attracts visitors to Mysore; this city is also famous for yoga, attracting thousands of international students each year to learn, practice or become certified in teaching Ashtanga.

Unlike at casual centres, here students are required to be austerely committed to the art, and will need at least a month's commitment. You'll also need to register far in advance, as courses are often booked out. Call or email the centres for details.

Most yoga institutes, as well as local laws, insist that all visitors arriving in Mysore to train in yoga must do so on a student visa, not a casual tourist visa. You are also required to register yourself at the local police station within 14 days of your arrival.

Yoga Centres

Ashtanga Yoga Research (AYRI; ☎9880185500; www.kpjayi.org; 235 8th Cross, 3rd Stage, Gokulam; 1 month ₹28,600) Founded by the renowned Ashtanga teacher K Pattabhi Jois, who taught Madonna her yoga moves. He has since passed away and the reigns have been handed over to his son, who is proving very popular. A tourist visa is OK but you need to register two months in advance.

Yoga India (Abhyasa Yoga Shala; www.aananda.in; 7th Main, 3rd Stage, Gokulam) Offers Hatha and Ashtanga yoga with a young guru, Bharath Shetty, who learnt under the legendary BKS Iyengar from Pune.

Atma Vikasa (☎2341978; www.atmavikasayoga.com; 18, 80ft Rd, Ramakrishnanagar) 'Backbending expert' Yogacharya Venkatesh offers courses in yoga, Sanskrit and meditation. It has a new location in a peaceful suburb 5km southwest of the palace.

Sri Patanjala Yogashala (Yoga Research Institute; ☎2430721, 9986390093; www.bnsiyengar.org; 490 Devamba Agrahara, KR Mohalla; ⏲6-8am & 5-7pm) The baby of well-respected Ashtanga practitioner BNS Iyengar (not to be confused with BKS Iyengar, famed exponent of Iyengar yoga). Conveniently located in the city centre.

Sleeping & Eating

No yoga centres offer acccommodation, so you'll need to make own arrangements. Many foreign yoga students congregate stay in the residential suburb of Gokulam, where the following are located.

Anokhi Garden Guest House (☎4288923; www.anokhigarden.com; 408 Contour Rd, 3rd stage, Gokulam; s/d from ₹1700/2400; ⏲cafe 8am-12.30pm Thu-Sun; Wi-Fi) Boutique guesthouse with four rooms in leafy propery, and a lovely cafe that does yummy vegetarian meals, vegan breakfasts and brunches.

Urban Oasis (☎2410713; www.urbanoasis.co.in; 7 Contour Rd, 3rd Stage, Gokulam; r from ₹1500, monthly from ₹26,000; A/C Wi-Fi) More of a business hotel, but popular with students for its comfortable rooms.

Anu's Bamboo Hut (☎9900909428; anugan@gmail.com; 365, 2nd Main, 3rd Stage, Gokulam; lunch buffet ₹250, cooking class ₹450; ⏲1-3pm & 5-7pm Fri-Wed) Rooftop shack cafe catering to yoga students with healthy vegetarian lunch buffets, and evening smoothies. A great source of info and offers cooking classes.

Bollywood decor. Best of all, the profits are distributed to charity and environmental projects across India. It's 3km west of town.

Parklane Hotel HOTEL $$
(☎4003500; www.parklanemysore.com; 2720 Harsha Rd; r from ₹2000; A/C @ Wi-Fi pool) Travellers' central on Mysore's tourist circuit, the Parklane is over-the-top kitsch but it's hard to dislike with its massive rooms which are immaculate, ultracomfortable and thoughtfully outfitted with mobile-phone chargers and very useful toiletry kits. The restaurant on the 1st is always busy and has a lively atmosphere.

Hotel Maurya Residency HOTEL $$
(☎2523375; www.hotelmauryaresidency.com; Harsha Rd; d from ₹1400; A/C Wi-Fi) Along with Hotel Maurya Palace, its twin establishment next door, the Maurya Residency remains

a trusted name among the Harsha Rd midrange gang. It's a friendly place with budget-midrange decent rooms. **Veg Kourt**, the restaurant downstairs, serves a sumptuous all-you-can-eat breakfast for ₹85.

★ Lalitha Mahal Palace HERITAGE HOTEL $$$
(☎8212526100; turret room incl breakfast ₹4834, heritage classic room incl breakfast ₹12,080; ❄@📶) A former maharaja's guesthouse built in 1921, this grand majestic heritage building has been operating as a hotel since 1974. Old-world charm comes in bucketloads from the 1920s birdcage elevator to mosaic tiled floors. The 'standard' turret room offers good value with wooden floors and bright bathrooms, but the heritage classic rooms are where you'll feel the history. Spacious four-poster beds sit next to antique furniture, claw-foot baths sit on marble bathroom floors and shuttered windows look out to stately landscaped gardens. There's also a gym and tennis courts. Watch out for the cheeky monkeys here.

Royal Orchid Metropole HERITAGE HOTEL $$$
(☎4255566; www.royalorchidhotels.com; 5 Jhansi Lakshmi Bai Rd; s/d incl breakfast from ₹6568/7160; ❄📶🏊) Originally built by the Wodeyars to serve as the residence of the Maharaja's British guests, this is undoubtedly one of Mysore's leading heritage hotels. The charming colonial-era structure has 30 rooms oozing historical character, and there are performances of magic shows, music, dance and snake charming when tour groups pass through.

Eating & Drinking

Malgudi Café CAFE $
(Green Hotel; mains ₹60-80; ⏲10am-7pm; 📶) 🍃 Set around an inner courtyard within the Green Hotel, this ambient cafe brews excellent coffees and Himalayan teas to be enjoyed with tasty snacks, cakes or fresh bread baked on the premises daily. Staff here come from underprivileged backgrounds and are mostly women, and profits assist with downtrodden communities, so you can do your bit by ordering a second cuppa. Service can be slow.

Hotel RRR SOUTH INDIAN $
(Gandhi Sq; mains ₹75-102) Classic Andhra-style food is ladled out at this ever-busy eatery, and you may have to queue for a table during lunch. One item to try is the piping-hot veg thali (₹85) served on banana leaves. There's a second branch on Harsha Rd.

Vinayaka Mylari SOUTH INDIAN $
(769 Nazarbad Main Rd; mains ₹30-50; ⏲7.30-11.30am & 4-8pm) Local foodies say this is one of the best eateries in town to try South Indian classics of *masala dosa* (lentil-flour pancake filled with vegetables) and *idlis* (spongy, round, fermented rice cakes). There's a similar branch up the road run by the owner's brother.

Pelican Pub PUB $
(Hunsur Rd; mains ₹75-150; ⏲11am-11pm) A popular watering hole located en route to Green Hotel, this laid-back joint serves beer for ₹65 a mug in the indoor classic pub or al fresco style garden setting out back. Tasty food pairs nicely with a cold beer, try some sinful pork chilli for ₹135 a platter, or spinach balls in a sticky sauce. There's live music Wednesdays.

Hotel Sree Annapoorna SOUTH INDIAN $
(Sayyaji Rao Rd; mains ₹30-80; ⏲7.30am-10pm) 🍃 This typically busy South Indian eatery rolls out steaming breakfast platters for Mysore's office-goers, and welcomes them back in the evenings with aromatic filter coffee and a convoy of delicious snacks, including speciality dosa each day of the week.

★ Sapphire INDIAN $$
(mains ₹180-450; ⏲lunch 12.30-2.45pm, snacks 2.45-7.45pm, dinner 8-11pm) Dine in absolute royal Indian–style in the grand ballroom of the Lalitha Mahal Palace hotel. And grand it is, with high stained-glass ceilings, lace tablecloths and polished teak floors. Order the royal Mysore silver thali which gets you an assortment of vegetables, breads and sweets served on lavish brassware (₹390) while enjoying live Indian sitar performances over lunch and dinner.

Parklane Hotel MULTICUISINE $$
(2720 Harsha Rd, Parklane Hotel; mains ₹100-140) Mysore's most social restaurant with buzzing picnic-style garden tables, lit up moodily by countless lanterns. The food here is stock standard, with the usual Indian dishes, but live traditional music, and a fully stocked bar, make for a great night out.

Tiger Trail INDIAN $$
(5 Jhansi Lakshmi Bai Rd, Royal Orchid Metropole; mains ₹150-300; ⏲12.30-3.30pm & 7-11pm) This sophisticated restaurant works up delectable Indian dishes in a courtyard that twinkles with torches and fairy lights at night

and a menu comprising jungle recipes collected from different tiger reserves across India. Also has a lunch buffet from ₹450.

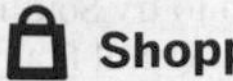

Shopping

Mysore is a great place to shop for its famed sandalwood products, silk saris and wooden toys. It is also one of India's major incense-manufacturing centres. Look for the butterfly-esque 'Silk Mark' on your purchase; it's an endorsement for quality silk.

Government Silk Factory CLOTHING
(Mananthody Rd, Ashokapuram; 10am-6.30pm Mon-Sat, outlet 10.30am-7.30pm Mon-Sat) Given that Mysore's prized silk is made under its very sheds, this is the best and cheapest place to shop for the exclusive textile. Behind the showroom is the factory, where you can drop by to see how the fabric is made.

Sandalwood Oil Factory SOUVENIRS
(Mananthody Rd, Ashokapuram; 9.30-1pm & 2-5pm Mon-Sat) A quality-assured place for sandalwood products such as incense, soap, cosmetics and the prohibitively expensive pure sandalwood oil. Guided tours are available to show you around the factory and explain how the products are made.

Cauvery Arts & Crafts Emporium CLOTHING
(Sayyaji Rao Rd; 10am-7.30pm) Not the cheapest place, but the selection is extensive, and there's no pressure to buy.

Fabindia CLOTHING
(2334451; www.fabindia.com; Jaya Lakshmi Vilas Rd, Chamrajpuram; 10.30am-8.30pm) A branch of the ever reliable clothing and homewares shop with North Indian items and fixed prices.

Shruthi Musical Works MUSIC STORE
(Irwin Rd, 1189 3rd Cross; 10am-9pm Mon-Sat) Sells a variety of traditional musical instruments including tabla sets and assorted percussion instruments.

Sapna Book House BOOKS
(1433 Narayana Shastri Rd; 10.30am-8.30pm) Paperbacks and magazines, as well guidebooks and yoga books; excellent for maps.

Information

INTERNET ACCESS

Pal Net (per hour ₹40; 9am-9pm Mon-Sat, to 2pm Sun)

KSE Internet (BN Rd, Hotel Ramanashree Complex; per hr ₹60; 8am-10pm)

LEFT LUGGAGE

The City bus stand's cloakroom, open from 6am to 11pm, costs ₹10 per bag for 12 hours.

MEDICAL SERVICES

Government Hospital (4269806; Dhanvanthri Rd) Has a 24-hour pharmacy.

MONEY

HDFC Bank (Devaraj Urs Rd) ATM.

ICICI Bank ATM (BN Rd) ATM at Hotel Pai Vista.

State Bank of Mysore (cnr Irwin & Ashoka Rds; 10.30am-2.30pm & 3-4pm Mon-Fri, 10.30am-12.30pm Sat) Changes cash and ATM.

Thomas Cook (2420090; 9/2 Ashoka Rd, Silver Tower; 9.30am-6pm Mon-Sat) Foreign currency.

POST

Main Post Office (cnr Irwin & Ashoka Rds; 10am-6pm Mon-Sat)

TOURIST INFORMATION

Karnataka Tourism (2422096; adtourism-mysore@gmail.com; Irwin Rd, Old Exhibition Bldg; 10am-5.30pm Mon-Sat) Extremely helpful, and plenty of brochures.

KSTDC Transport Office (2423652; 2 Jhansi Lakshmi Bai Rd; 8.30am-8.30pm) Offers general tourist information and provides a useful map. Has counters at the train station and Central bus stand, as well as this transport office next to Hotel Mayura Hoysala.

Getting There & Away

AIR

Mysore's airport was not operating any flights at the time of research but discussions were in place about the possibility of resuming commercial flights in future. Check with the tourism office for updates.

BUS

The **Central bus stand** (BN Rd) handles all KSRTC long-distance buses. The **City bus stand** (Sayyaji Rao Rd) is for city, Srirangapatnam and Chamundi Hill buses.

The **Private bus stand** (Sayyaji Rao Rd) also has services to Hubli, Bijapur, Mangalore, Ooty and Ernakulam. You'll find several ticketing agents around the stand.

TRAIN

From Mysore's **railway booking office** (131; 8am-8pm Mon-Sat, 8am-2pm Sun), buy a ticket on the 6.45am Chamundi Express (₹57/202) or the 11am Tippu Express to Bengaluru (2nd class/AC chair ₹66/233, three hours at 11am). The 2.15 Shatabdi Express also connects Bengaluru (AC chair/AC executive chair ₹285/620, two hours) and Chennai (AC chair/

AC executive chair ₹741/1535, seven hours) daily except Wednesday. Several passenger trains to Bengaluru (₹25, 3½ hours) stop at Srirangapatnam (₹15, 20 minutes). The 10.30pm Mysore Dharwad Express goes to Hubli (sleeper/2AC ₹212/880, 9½ hours).

Getting Around

Agencies at hotels and around town rent cabs for about ₹7 per kilometre, with a minimum of 250km per day, plus a daily allowance of ₹200 for the driver.

The flagfall on autorickshaws is ₹20, and ₹10 per kilometre is charged thereafter. Count on around ₹800 for a day's sightseeing.

Around Mysore

Srirangapatnam

08236

Steeped in bloody history, the fort town of Srirangapatnam, 16km from Mysore, is built on an island straddling the Cauvery River. The seat of Hyder Ali and Tipu Sultan's power, this town was the de facto capital of much of southern India during the 18th century. Srirangapatnam's glory days ended when the British waged an epic war again Tipu Sultan in 1799, when he was defeated and killed. However, the ramparts, battlements and some of the gates of the fort still stand, as do a clutch of monuments. The island is now linked to the mainland by bridge.

There's no real reason to stay overnight, but **Mayura River View** (252114; d from ₹2300, restaurant mains ₹100-120;) has a nice location on the riverbank and is a good place to lunch.

Sights

Daria Daulat Bagh PALACE

(Indian/foreigner ₹5/100; 9am-5pm) Set within lovely manicured grounds, Srirangapatnam's star attraction is Tipu's summer palace, 1km east of the fort. Built largely out of teak, the palace may not look like much from the outside, but the lavish decoration that covers every inch of its interiors is impressive. The ceilings are embellished with floral designs, while the walls bear murals depicting courtly life and Tipu's campaigns against the British. There's a small museum within displaying artefacts and interesting paintings.

Gumbaz MAUSEOLEUM

(admission free; 8am-6.30pm) FREE Located within a serene garden, the historically significant Gumbaz is the resting place of the legendary Tipu Sultan, his equally famed father, Hyder Ali, and his wife. The interior of the onion-dome mausoleum is painted in tiger-like motif as a tribute to the sultan. Aross from the tomb is the **Masjid-E-Aska** (mosque).

Sri Ranganathaswamy Temple HINDU TEMPLE

(7.30am-1pm & 4-8pm) Constructed in 894 AD, this attractive Vaishnavite temple has a mix of Hoysala and Vijayanagar design. Within are cavernous walkways, pillars and the centerpiece 4.5m-long reclining statue of Ranganatha, a manifestation of Vishnu.

Jamia Masjid MOSQUE

This cream-coloured mosque with two minarets was built by the sultan in 1787 and features an interesting blend of Islamic and

KSRTC BUSES FROM MYSORE

DESTINATION	FARE (₹)	DURATION (HR)	FREQUENCY
Bandipur	75 (O)/200 (V)	2	every 30min 6.30am-3.30pm
Bengaluru	110 (O)/162 (R)/270 (V)	3	every 20min
Channarayapatna	70 (O)	2	hourly
Chennai	930 (V)/ 531 (R)	12	4 daily
Ernakulam	593 (V)	11	4 daily
Gokarna	412 (O)	12	1 daily
Hassan	110 (O)	3	hourly
Hospet	372 (O)/491 (R)	10	4 daily
Mangalore	210 (O)/310 (R)/500 (V)	7	hourly
Ooty	127 (O) 191 (R)/300 (V)	5	8 daily

O – Ordinary, R – Rajahamsa Semideluxe, V – Airavath AC Volvo

Hindu architecture. Climb the stairs at the back for panoramic views of the site.

Colonel Bailey's Dungeon HISTORICAL SITE

FREE North of the island on the banks of the Cauvery is this well-preserved 18th-century white-walled dungeon used to hold British prisoners of war, including Colonel Bailey who died here in 1780. Jutting out from the walls are stone fixtures used to chain prisoners. East from here along the river is **Thomas Inman's Dungeon**, hidden away beneath undulating terrain, with a more undiscovered feel that's fun to explore.

Getting There & Away

Take buses 313 or 313a (₹15, 50 minutes) that depart every hour from Mysore's City bus stand. Passenger trains travelling from Mysore to Bengaluru (₹2, 20 minutes) also stop here. Bus 307 (₹18, 30 minutes) heading to Brindavan Gardens is just across from Srirangapatnam's main bus stand.

Getting Around

The sights are spread out, so hiring an autorickshaw is the best option (₹250 for three hours) of getting around.

Melkote

Life in the devout Hindu town of Melkote, about 50km north of Mysore, revolves around the atmospheric 12th-century **Cheluvanarayana Temple** (Raja St; ⏲8am-1pm & 5-8pm), with its rose-coloured *gopuram* (gateway tower) and ornately carved pillars. Get a workout on the hike up to the hilltop **Yoganarasimha Temple**, which offers fine views of the surrounding hills. The town really comes alive for the **Vairamudi Festival** (Melkote; ⏲Mar/Apr) in March or April, attracting 400,000 pilgrims for the crowning of the statue of Vishnu.

Three KSRTC buses shuttle daily between Mysore and Melkote (₹60, 1½ hours).

Somnathpur

The astonishingly beautiful **Keshava Temple** (Indian/foreigner ₹5/100; ⏲8.30am-5.30pm) is one of the finest examples of Hoysala architecture, on par with the masterpieces of Belur and Halebid. Built in 1268, this star-shaped temple, 33km from Mysore, is adorned with superb stone sculptures depicting various scenes from the Ramayana, Mahabharata and Bhagavad Gita, and the life and times of the Hoysala kings.

Somnathpur is 12km south of Bannur and 10km north of Tirumakudal Narsipur. Take one of the half-hourly buses from Mysore to either village (₹35, 30 minutes) and change there. There are also government-run day tours that visit from Mysore

Bandipur National Park

A part of the Nilgiri Biosphere Reserve, **Bandipur National Park** (Indian/foreigner ₹75/1000, video ₹100; ⏲6am-6pm) is one of South India's most famous wildernesses areas. Covering 880 sq km, it was once the Mysore maharajas' private wildlife reserve, and is now a protected zone for over 100 species of mammals, including tiger, elephant, leopard, gaur (Indian bison), chital (spotted deer), sambar, sloth bear and langur. It's also home to an impressive 350 species of bird. Only 80km south of Mysore on the Ooty road, it's very accessible from both Bengaluru and Mysore.

Only government vehicles are permitted to run safaris within the park, and the best option is to go on Bandipur Safari Lodge's (p201) two-hour drives for ₹2000, inclusive of park entry fees. The forest department also arrange **safaris** (2hr jeep safari ₹3000; ⏲6am & 4pm), but its rumbling minibus is simply best avoided.

Sleeping & Eating

It's also possible to stay at the **forest department bungalows** (☎236021; dc_bandipur@yahoo.com; 20-bed dm ₹1000, bungalow foreigner from ₹3000), but you're likely to pay a ₹1000 entry fee, making it terrible value given it's a 20-bed dorm.

Hotel Bandipur Plaza HOTEL $$

(☎8547680406; Ooty-Mysore Hwy; r ₹1500) Its highway location may not be what you hope for when visiting a national park, but its rooms are functional and affordable in an otherwise pricey destination. It's close to Bandipur Safari Lodge, so it's easy to book safaris in the park.

Tiger Ranch LODGE $$

(☎8095408505; www.tigerranch.net; Mangala Village; r incl full board ₹1105) The only place in Bandipur with a genuine outdoorsy feel to it, the *very* basic rooms here blend wonderfully into nature. It has an atmospheric thatched-roof dining hall, and evenings can be enjoyed around the bonfire. Be warned that monkeys are a nuisance here, so don't leave valuables (or food!) lying around your room. There's no alcohol here, but it's fine to bring your own. It's inconveniently located away from the park, so you'll need to call ahead to arrange a pickup (₹300).

★ **Dhole's Den** LODGE $$$
(☎8229-236062; www.dholesden.com; Kaniyanapura Village; s/d incl full board & safari from ₹9000/10,000;) With a boutique design that's lifted straight from the pages of an architectural magazine, Dhole's effectively mixes comfort and its lovely pastoral surrounds. Stylish rooms are decked out with art and colourful fabrics, plus couches and deck chairs that look out to the dam. It's environmentally conscious with solar power, tank water and organic veggies. A 20-minute drive from the park headquarters, rates include transfers and safaris, but not park entry (₹1000).

Bandipur Safari Lodge CAMPGROUND $$$
(www.junglelodges.com/index.php/resorts/bandipur.html; Mysore-Ooty Rd; r incl full board & safari Indian/foreigner ₹3750/7000;) This sprawling government-owned camp has well-maintained, comfortable cottages, but it lacks character and 'safari' atmosphere. However, it's conveniently located on the fringes of the park, and rates include two safaris per day.

Getting There & Away

Buses between Mysore and Ooty can drop you at Bandipur (₹65, three hours), an 88km journey. Skyway (p186) can arrange an overnight taxi from Mysore for about ₹2000.

Nagarhole National Park & Around

Blessed with rich wildlife, attractive jungle and a scenic lake, **Nagarhole National Park** (Rajiv Gandhi National Park; Indian/foreigner ₹200/1000, video ₹100; 6am-6pm), pronounced nag-ar-hole-eh, is one of Karnataka's best wildlife getaways. Adjoining **Kabini Lake**, it forms an important animal corridor that runs through neighbouring Bandipur National Park – making up a part of the Nilgiri Biosphere Reserve. Despite sharing the same wildlife, it sees much fewer visitors than Bandipur, making it all the more appealing. Set over 643 sq km, Nagarhole features a good blend of dense jungle and open sightlines along the river bank, which makes for fantastic wildlife-watching. Its lush forests are home to tigers, leopards, elephants, gaurs, barking deer, wild dogs, bonnet macaques and common langurs, plus 270 species of birds. The park can remain closed for long stretches between July and October, when the rains transform the forests into a giant slush-pit.

The traditional inhabitants of the land, the hunter-gatherer Jenu Kuruba people, still live in the park, despite government efforts to relocate them.

The best time to view wildlife is during summer (April to May), though winter (November to February) is more comfortable.

Government-run **jeep safaris** (2½hr jeep safari ₹1750) and **boat trips** (₹1750) are conducted from Kabini River Lodge between 6.30am and 9.30am and 4pm and 7pm, which are both good ways to see animals.

Sleeping & Eating

Since the government banning of private vehicles in the park, most people stay in lodges arond Kabini Lake. Unfortunately there's no genuine budget lodging; however, it's worth touching base with Waterwoods Lodge to see if it offers camping on its property.

★ **Bison Wilderness** LODGE $$$
(☎80-41278708; www.thebisonresort.com; Gundathur Village; s/d incl full board US$250/260;) Inspired by the luxury safari lodges in Africa, Bison succeeds in replicating the classic wilderness experience. It has a stunning location on the waterfront, with luxurious tents and stilted cottages linked by a rickety wooden platform. Each is done out in decadent touches of polished timber floors, throw rugs and clawfoot baths. It has a swimming pool built into a wooden decking, nightly bonfires and expert naturalists for safaris.

Waterwoods Lodge GUESTHOUSE $$$
(☎082-28264421; www.waterwoods.in; s/d incl full board ₹5500/7800;) A boutique guesthouse on the grassy embarkment of the scenic lake, Waterwoods has a homely atmosphere that makes for a relaxing stay. It's run by two likeable young, environmentally aware owners who are very knowledgeable about the area. It's kid-friendly with trampoline, infinity pool and woodfired pizzas. Each evening there's a bonfire to accompany a screening of wildlife docos.

OFF THE BEATEN TRACK

BILIGIRI RANGANNA (BR) HILLS

Much less known than Bandipur or Nagarhole, the **Biligiri Ranganna Temple Wildlife Sanctuary** in the BR Hills makes a great alternative to live out your *Jungle Book* fantasies. Set over 570 sq km, it was declared a tiger reserve in 2010 with a population of 36 tigers inhabiting the area – but like most parks, you'll need to be *extremely* lucky to spot one. Elephants, leopards, sloth bears and dholes (wild dogs) also roam the hills here.

The government-owned **K Gudi Wilderness Camp** (www.junglelodges.com; per person tented camp incl full board & activities ₹7000, huts ₹7500) has a fantastic site among the peaceful forest, with grazing warthog and spotted deer. Accommodation is in tented cottages or delightful stilted log cabins, and rates include meals, two safaris and wildlife screenings in the evening.

The wildlife sanctuary is a 4½-hour drive from Bengaluru. It's best to hire a vehicle although it is theoretically possible to get there by public transport. You can either catch a direct 7.45am bus from Mysore to K Gudi, or otherwise a bus to Chamarajanagar and connect to a 1.30pm bus to K Gudi. From Chamarajanagar you can arrange a jeep for ₹700.

Kabini River Lodge LODGE **$$$**
(☎080-40554055; www.junglelodges.co; per person India/foreigner incl full board & activities from ₹5000/9000; ❄) These attractive government-run bungalows have a prime location beside the lake in the serene, tree-lined grounds of the former Mysore maharaja's hunting lodge. It has large tented cottages and bungalows and an atmospheric colonial-style bar. Rates include safaris, boat rides and entry fees.

ℹ Getting There & Away

The park's main entrance is 93km southwest of Mysore. A few buses depart daily from Mysore to Kabini village, but you'll need transport for the last leg to the resorts.

Kodagu (Coorg) Region

Nestled amid ageless hills that line the southernmost edge of Karnataka is the luscious Kodagu (Coorg) region, gifted with emerald landscapes and acres of plantations. A major centre for coffee and spice production, this rural expanse is also home to the unique Kodava race, believed to have descended from migrating Persians and Kurds or perhaps Greeks left behind from Alexander the Great's armies. The uneven terrain and cool climate make it a fantastic area for trekking, birdwatching or lazily ambling down little-trodden paths winding around carpeted hills. All in all, Kodagu is rejuvenation guaranteed.

Kodagu was a state in its own right until 1956, when it merged with Karnataka. The region's chief town and transport hub is Madikeri, but for an authentic Kodagu experience, you have to venture into the plantations. Avoid weekends, when places can quickly get filled up by weekenders from Bengaluru.

Madikeri (Mercara)

☎08272 / POP 32,500 / ELEV 1525M

Also known as Mercara, this congested market town is spread out along a series of ridges. The only reason for coming here is to organise treks or sort out the practicalities of travel. A colourful time to visit is around November and December when the Kodava community celebrates **Huthri**, a week-long festival that commemorates the start of the rice harvesting season.

👁 Sights

Madikeri Fort HISTORICAL SITE
FREE Originally Tipu Sultan's fort in the 16th century, before Raja Lingarajendra II took over in 1812, today it's the less glamorous site of the municipal headquarters. Within the fort's walls are the hexagonal palace (now the dusty district commissioner's office) and colonial church, which houses a quirky **museum** (⏲10am-5.30pm Sun-Fri) FREE displaying eclectic exhibits.

Raja's Seat VIEWPOINT
(MG Rd; ₹5; ⏲6am-7.30pm) The place to come to watch sunset, as the raja himself did, with fantastic outlooks to rolling hills and endless valleys.

Raja's Tombs HISTORIC BUILDING

FREE Stop off en route to Abbi Falls at the quietly beautiful Raja's Tombs, better known as Gaddige. Built in Indo-Sarcenic style, the domed tombs are the resting place for Kodava royalty and dignitaries. Located 7km from town, an autorickshaw costs ₹200 return.

Abbi Falls WATERFALLS

A spectacular sight after the rainy season, these 21.3m-high falls can pack a punch. It's ₹250 for a return autorickshaw, including stop off at Raja's Tombs.

Activities

Coorg is all about enjoying the outdoors, and a novel approach is to head up into the skies via a microlight flight with **Coorg Sky Adventures** (☎9448954384; www.coorgskyadventures.com; 10/30 min ₹2250/4850).

Ayurveda

★Jiva Spa AYURVEDA

(☎0827-2665800; www.tajhotels.com/JivaSpas/index.html; Vivanta, Galibeedu) Surrounded by rainforest, the stunning Vivanta (p204) is *the* place to treat yourself with a range of rejuvenating treatments amid lavish atmosphere. Appointments essential.

Ayurjeevan AYURVEDA

(☎224466; www.ayurjeevancoorg.com; Kohinoor Rd; ⏲7.30am-7pm) Ayurjeevan, a short walk from ICICI Bank, is an ayurvedic 'hospital' that offers a whole range of intriguing and rejuvenating techniques; refer to its website for details. Hour-long treatments cost ₹900.

Swaasthaya Ayurveda Retreat Village AYURVEDA

(www.swaasthya.com; Bekkesodlur Village; s/d incl full board & yoga class ₹2500/3500) For an exceptionally peaceful and refreshing ayurvedic vacation, head to south Coorg to soothe your soul among the lush greenery on 4 acres of coffee and spice plantations. To get here from Madikeri, catch a bus to Gonikoppa (1½ hours) from where you'll need to transer to a bus heading to Kutta and disembark at Bekkesodlur Village.

Trekking

Exploring the region by foot is a highlight for many visitors to the area that offers part cultural experience, part nature encounter. The best season for trekking is October to March; there are no treks during monsoon. The most popular routes are to the peaks of Tadiyendamol (1745m) and Pushpagiri (1712m), and to smaller Kotebetta (1620m). As well as good walking shoes you'll need insect repellant. A trekking guide is essential for navigating the labyrinth of forest tracks.

V-Track TREKKING

(☎229102, 229974; v_track@reddiffmail.com; College Rd, opp Corporation Bank; ⏲10am-2pm & 4.30-8pm Mon-Sat) Veteran guides Raja Shekhar and Ganesh can arrange one- to 10-day treks, which include guide, accommodation and food. Lodging is a mix of village homestays and basic huts. Rates are ₹950 to ₹1250 per person per day, depending upon group size.

Coorg Trails TREKKING

(☎9886665459; www.coorgtrails.com; Main Rd; ⏲9am-8.30pm) Another recommended outfit, Coorg Trails can arrange day treks around Madikeri for ₹450 per person, and a 16km trek to Kotebetta, including an overnight stay in a village (₹850 per person).

Sleeping & Eating

With fantastic guesthouses in the surrounding area, there's no real reason to stay in Madikeri; though you may have to a spend a night if you arrive late.

Hotel Chitra HOTEL $

(☎225372; www.hotelchitra.net; School Rd; dm ₹200, d from ₹728, d with AC ₹1620; ❄) A short walk off Madikeri's main traffic intersection is this austere hotel, providing low-cost, no-frills rooms. The sheets are clean and service is efficient, which – coupled with its midtown location – makes it a good budget option.

Hotel Mayura Valley View HOTEL $$

(☎228387; d incl breakfast from ₹1600; ❄) On a secluded hilltop past Raja's Seat, this government hotel is one of Madikeri's best, with large bright rooms and fantastic valley views. Its restaurant-bar with terrace overlooking the valley is a great spot for a beer.

★Coorg Cuisine INDIAN $

(Main Rd; mains ₹70-90; ⏲noon-4pm & 7-10pm) Finally a place that makes an effort to serve regional dishes, cooking up unique Kodava specialities such as *pandhi barthadh* (pork dry fry) and *kadambuttu* (rice dumplings). It's above a shop on the 1st floor on the main road.

SPICE OF LIFE

If you have space in your bag, remember to pick up some local spices and natural produce from Madikeri's main market. There's a whole range of spices on offer at the shops lining the streets, including vanilla, nutmeg, lemongrass, pepper and cardamom, as well as the unbranded aromatic coffee that comes in from plantations. Sickly sweet homemade wines are also widely available.

Hotel Popular Guruprasad SOUTH INDIAN $
(Main Rd; mains ₹30-50; 6.30am-9.30pm) A hearty range of vegie options, including a value-for-money veg thali (₹50) make this a favourite with the locals.

Information

Travel Coorg (321009; www.travelcoorg.in; outside KSRTC bus stand; 24hr) provides excellent travel information, and can arrange homestays and guides.

State Bank of India (229959; College Rd) and **HDFC** (Racecourse Rd) have ATMs. **Cyber Inn** (Kohinoor Rd; per hour ₹20; 9am-9pm) has internet access, opposite from Ayurjeebah.

Getting There & Away

Seven deluxe buses a day depart from the KSRTC bus stand for Bengaluru (fan/AC ₹315/450 six hours), stopping in Mysore (₹195, 3½ hours) en route. Deluxe buses go to Mangalore (₹169/250, four hours, three daily), while frequent ordinary buses head to Hassan (₹95, four hours) and Shimoga (₹210, eight hours).

The Plantations

Spread around Madikeri are Kodagu's quaint and leafy spice and coffee plantations. Numerous estates here offer 'homestays', which are actually more B&Bs (and normally closed during monsoon). Some high-end resorts have begun to spring up too.

Sleeping

★Golden Mist HOMESTAY $$
(08272-265629; www.golden-mist.net; Galibeedu; s/d incl full board ₹2500/4000; @) One of Coorg's finest plantation stays, the friendly Indian-German-managed Golden Mist has character-filled loft-style cottages on its lovely 26-acre property of rice paddies and tea-, coffee- and spice-plantations. Meals are tasty rustic veg and nonveg dishes made from the farm's organic produce, including homemade cheese and bread. Rates include nature walks and plantation tours. You'll need to bring your own alcohol. A rickshaw costs ₹150 from Madikeri.

Rainforest Retreat GUESTHOUSE $$
(08272-265639; www.rainforestours.com; Galibeedu; dm ₹1000, s/d tent ₹1500/2000, r from ₹2000/4000) A nature-soaked refuge located on an organic plantation, the Rainforest Retreat is an NGO that devotes itself to exploring organic and ecofriendly ways of life. Organic farming, sustainable agriculture and waste management are catchphrases here; check the website for details. Accommodation is in tents and eco-chic cottages with solar power, and activities include plantation tours, birdwatching and treks. An autorickshaw from Madkeri is ₹200.

Honeypot Homes B&B $$
(9448720382; www.honeypothomes.com; off Bangalore Rd; d incl breakfast ₹4000;) Set over 225 acres of dense coffee and spice plantations, this quaint 'homestay' has three red-brick cottages that look out to lush surrounds. Walking tours and explanations of coffee production process is inclusive of rates. It's located 7km from Madikeri.

★Vivanta HOTEL $$$
(0827-665800; www.vivantabytaj.com; Galibeedu; r incl breakfast from ₹17,900; @) Another stunner by the Taj group, built across 180 acres of misty rainforest. Its stylish design incorporates principles of space and minimalism, and effectively blends itself into its environment. Old cattle tracks lead to rooms, with pricier ones featuring private indoor pools, fireplaces and butlers. Meanwhile the 9000 sq ft presidential suite, costing a cool lakh (₹100,000), is the size of a small village. Other highlights are its stunning views from the lobby and infinity pool, the outdoor amphitheatre surrounded by water, ayurvedic spa and Xbox room.

Kakkabe

08272

About 40km from Madikeri, the village of Kakkabe is an ideal base to plan an assault on Kodagu's highest peak, Tadiyendamol. At the bottom of the summit, 3km from Kakkabe, is the picturesque **Nalakunad Palace** (9am-5pm) FREE, the restored hunting lodge of a Kodagu king dating from 1794. The caretaker will happily show you around; bring a torch.

The **Honey Valley Estate** (☎08272-238 339; www.honeyvalleyindia.in; d from ₹800) has a wonderful location 1250m above sea level where you can wake to a chirpy dawn and cool, fresh air. The owners' friendliness, eco-mindedness and scrumptious organic food make things even better. Run by the same family, **Chingaara** (☎08272-204488; www.chingaara.com; r incl full board from ₹1800) is a delightful farmhouse on the same road, with spacious rooms and roaming donkeys. Both are great bases for treks, and guides are available for ₹400. It's a rough, steep road up here, so you'll need to call ahead to arrange transport from Kabbinakad (inclusive in room rates).

Regular buses run to Kabbinakad from Madikeri (₹35, 1½ hours) and from Virajpet (₹20, one hour).

Belur & Halebid

☎08177 / ELEV 968M

The Hoysala temples at Halebid (also known as Halebeedu) and Belur (also called Beluru) are the apex of one of the most artistically exuberant periods of ancient Hindu cultural development. Architecturally, they are South India's answer to Khajuraho in Madhya Pradesh and Konark near Puri in Odisha (Orissa).

Only 16km lie between Belur and Halebid; they are connected by frequent buses from 6.30am to 7pm (₹20, 40 minutes).

To get here you'll need to pass through the busy transport hub of **Hassan** – easily accesible from Mysore and Bengaluru, with buses departing every half-hour to Mysore (₹96, three hours), Bengaluru (semideluxe/deluxe ₹155/340, four hours) and Mangalore (₹150, 340). From Hassan's well-organised train station, three passenger trains head to Mysore daily (2nd class ₹120, three hours). For Bengaluru, take the 1.30am Yeshvantpur Express (sleeper ₹140, 5½ hours). It's also possible to visit on day trip from Bengaluru with KSTDC (p181) offering tours.

Belur

The **Channakeshava Temple** (Temple Rd; admission free; ⏲7.30am-7.30pm) was commissioned in 1116 to commemorate the Hoysalas' victory over the neighbouring Cholas. It took more than a century to build, and is currently the only one among the three major Hoysala sites still in daily use – try to be there for the ritual *puja* ceremonies at around 8.45am and 6.45pm. Some parts of the temple, such as the exterior lower friezes, were not sculpted to completion and are thus less elaborate than those of the other Hoysala temples. However, the work higher up is unsurpassed in detail and artistry, and is a glowing tribute to human skill. Particularly intriguing are the angled bracket figures depicting women in ritual dancing poses. While the front of the temple is reserved for images depicting erotic sections from the Kama Sutra, the back is strictly for gods. The roof of the inner sanctum is held up by rows of exquisitely sculpted pillars, no two of which are identical in design.

Scattered around the temple complex are other smaller temples, a marriage hall which is still used, and the seven-storey *gopuram,* which has sensual sculptures explicitly portraying the activities of dancing girls.

Guides can be hired for ₹250; they help to bring some of the sculptural detail to life.

Hotel Mayura Velapuri (☎222209; Kempegowda Rd; d ₹950, with AC ₹1200; ❄), a state-run hotel gleaming with postrenovation glory, is located on the way to the temple, and is the best place to camp in Belur. The restaurant-bar serves a variety of Indian dishes and snacks (₹70 to ₹90) to go with beer. The cheaper **Sumukha Residency** (Temple Rd; d with fan/AC ₹500/700) is another option.

There's an Axis ATM on the road leading to the temple.

There are buses to/from Hassan (₹24, one hour), 38km away, every half-hour.

Halebid

Construction of the stunning **Hoysaleswara Temple** (admission free; ⏲dawn-dusk), Halebid's claim to fame, began around 1121 and went on for more than 190 years. It was never completed, but nonetheless stands today as a masterpiece of Hoysala architecture. The interior of its inner sanctum, chiselled out of black stone, is marvellous. On the outside, the temple's richly sculpted walls are covered with a flurry of Hindu deities, sages, stylised animals and friezes depicting the life of the Hoysala rulers. Two statues of Nandi (Shiva's bull) sit to the left of the main temple, facing the inner sanctum. Guides are available to show you around for ₹250.

OFF THE BEATEN TRACK

BYLAKUPPE

Tiny Bylakuppe, 5km southeast of Kushalnagar, was among the first refugee camps set up in South India to house thousands of Tibetans who fled from Tibet following the 1959 Chinese invasion. Over 10,000 Tibetans live here (including some 3300 monks), making it South India's largest Tibetan settlement. The atmosphere is heart-warmingly welcoming, and home to much festivity during the **Tibetan New Year** (Bylakuppe; ⏲Feb) celebrations.

The area's highlight is the atmospheric **Namdroling Monastery** (www.palyul.org), home to the jaw-droppingly spectacular **Golden Temple** (Padmasambhava Buddhist Vihara; ⏲7am-8pm), presided over by three 18m-high gold-plated Buddha statues. The temple is at its dramatic best when prayer is in session and it rings out with gongs, drums and the drone of hundreds of young monks chanting. You're welcome to sit and meditate; look for the small blue guest cushions lying around. The **Zangdogpalri Temple** (⏲7am-8pm), a similarly ornate affair, is next door.

Foreigners are not allowed to stay overnight in Bylakuppe without a Protected Area Permit (PAP) from the Ministry of Home Affairs in Delhi, which can take up to five months to process. Contact the **Tibet Bureau Office** (☎11-26474798; www.tibetbureau.in; New Delhi) for details. Daytrippers are welcome to visit, however, and many base themselves in nearby Kushalnagar. If you have a permit, the simple **Paljor Dhargey Ling Guest House** (☎258686; pdguesthouse@yahoo.com; d from ₹350) is opposite the Golden Temple. There are many hotels in Kushalnagar, including **Iceberg** (☎9880260544; Main Rd; s/d from ₹550/750), with clean functional rooms, and located next door to a good veg restaurant.

For delicious momos or *thukpa* (noodle soup), pop into the Tibetan-run **Malaya Restaurant** (momos ₹60-90; ⏲7am-9pm).

Autorickshaws (shared/solo ₹10/40) run to Bylakuppe from Kushalnagar, 5km away. Buses frequently do the 34km run to Kushalnagar from Madikeri (₹40, 1½ hour) and Hassan (₹98, four hours). Most buses on the Mysore–Madikeri route stop at Kushalnagar.

The temple is set in large, well-tended gardens, adjacent to which is a small **museum** (admission ₹5; ⏲9am-5pm Sat-Thu) with a collection of beautiful sculptures from around Halebid.

Take some time out to visit the nearby, smaller **Kedareswara Temple**, or a little-visited enclosure containing three **Jain** temples about 500m away, which also have fine carvings.

Hotel Mayura Shanthala (☎273224; d ₹850), set around a leafy garden opposite the temple complex, is the best sleeping option.

Regular buses depart for Hassan (₹34, one hour), 33km away.

Sravanabelagola

☎08176

Atop the bald rock of Vindhyagiri Hill, the 17.5m-high statue of the Jain deity Gomateshvara (Bahubali), said to be the world's tallest monolithic statue, is visible long before you reach the pilgrimage town of Sravanabelagola. Viewing the statue close up is the main reason for heading to this sedate town, whose name means 'Monk of the White Pond'.

Sights

Gomateshvara Statue MONUMENT

(Bahubali; ⏲6.30am-6.30pm) FREE A steep climb up 614 steps takes you to the top of Vindhyagiri Hill, the summit of which is lorded over by the towering naked statue of the Jain deity Gomateshvara. Commissioned by a military commander in the service of the Ganga king Rachamalla and carved out of a single piece of granite by the sculptor Aristenemi in AD 981, its serenity and simplicity is in stark contrast to the Hoysala sites at Belur and Halebid.

Bahubali was the son of emperor Vrishabhadeva, who later became the first Jain *tirthankar* (revered teacher) Adinath. Embroiled in fierce competition with his brother Bharatha to succeed his father, Bahubali realised the futility of material gains and renounced his kingdom. As a recluse, he meditated in complete stillness in the forest until he attained enlightenment. His lengthy meditative spell is denoted by vines curling around his legs and an ant hill at his feet.

Leave shoes at the foot of the hill, but it's fine to wear socks.

Every 12 years, millions flock here to attend the **Mastakabhisheka** (Feb) ceremony, when the statue is dowsed in holy waters, pastes, powders, precious metals and stones. The next ceremony is slated for 2018.

Jain Temples JAIN TEMPLES

Apart from the Bahubali statue, there are several interesting Jain temples in town. The **Chandragupta Basti** (Chandragupta Community; 6am-6pm), on Chandragiri Hill opposite Vindhyagiri, is believed to have been built by Emperor Ashoka. The **Bhandari Basti** (Bhandari Community; 6am-6pm), in the southeast corner of town, is Sravanabelagola's largest temple. Nearby, **Chandranatha Basti** (Chandranatha Community; 6am-6pm) has well-preserved paintings depicting Jain tales.

Sleeping & Eating

The local Jain organisation **SDJMI** (257258) handles bookings for its 15 guesthouses (d/tr ₹210/260). The office is behind the Vidyananda Nilaya Dharamsala, past the post office.

Hotel Raghu HOTEL $

(257238; d from ₹500; restaurant 6am-9pm;) The only privately owned hotel around, offering basic but clean rooms. There's a vegetarian restaurant downstairs, which works up an awesome veg thali (₹50).

Getting There & Away

There are no direct buses from Sravanabelagola to Hassan or Belur – you must go to Channarayapatna (₹41, 20 minutes) and catch an onward connection there. Three daily buses run direct to Bengaluru (₹120, 3½ hours) and Mysore (₹80 2½ hours). Long-distance buses clear out before 3pm. If you miss these, catch a local bus to Channarayapatna and change there.

A 3pm train heads to Hassan (₹7), 48km from Sravanabelagola, for onward travel to Mysore or Mangalore.

KARNATAKA COAST

Mangalore

0824 / POP 484,785

Alternating from relaxed coastal town to hectic nightmare, Mangalore has a Jekyll and Hyde thing going, but it's a pleasant enough place to break up your trip. While there's not a lot to do here, it has an appealing off-the-beaten-path feel, and the spicy seafood dishes are sensational.

It sits at the estuaries of the picturesque Netravathi and Gurupur Rivers on the Arabian Sea coast and has been a major pit stop on international trade routes since the 6th century AD.

Sights

Ullal Beach BEACH

While it's no Om Beach, this stretch of golden sand is a good place to escape the city heat. It's best enjoyed from Summer Sands Beach Resort, which also has a pool for swimming (₹300). It's about an hour's drive south of town. An autorickshaw is ₹200 one way, or the frequent bus 44 (₹9) from the City bus stand will drop you right outside the gate.

St Aloysius College Chapel CHURCH

(Lighthouse Hill; 9am-6pm) Catholicism's roots in Mangalore date back to the arrival of the Portuguese in the early 1500s, and one of the most impressive legacies is the 1880 Sistine Chapel–like St Aloysius chapel, with its walls and ceilings painted with brilliant frescoes.

Sultan's Battery FORT

(Sultan Battery Rd; 6am-6pm) The only remnant of Tipu Sultan's fort is this small lookout with views over scenic backwaters. It's 4km from the city centre on the headland of the old port; bus 16 will get you there.

Kadri Manjunatha Temple HINDU TEMPLE

(Kadri; 6am-1pm & 4-8pm) This Kerala-style temple houses a 1000-year-old bronze statue of Lokeshwara.

Sleeping

Hotel Manorama HOTEL $

(2440306; KS Rao Rd; s/d from ₹530/650, with AC ₹884;) A decent, centrally located budget option, with clean, good-value rooms and a lobby decked out with replicas of artifacts.

Mangalore

Mangalore

Sights

1 Kadri Manjunatha Temple D1
2 St Aloysius College Chapel C2

Sleeping

3 Adarsh Hotel C3
4 Gateway Hotel B4
5 Hotel Manorama C3
6 Hotel Ocean Pearl C2
7 Nalapad Residency C3

Eating

8 Gajalee D1
9 Janatha Deluxe C3
Kadal .... (see 7)
10 Lalith Bar & Restaurant C3

Drinking & Nightlife

11 Liquid Lounge C3

Information

12 HDFC C3
13 ICICI Bank ATM C3
14 State Bank of Mysore ATM C3

Transport

15 Air India B1
16 City Bus Stand B4
17 Jet Airways C2
18 KSRTC Bus Stand C1

Adarsh Hotel HOTEL $

(2440878; Market Rd; s/d ₹230/330) Long-established cheapie with very basic rooms, but it gets the job done and is well maintained.

Nalapad Residency HOTEL $$

(2424757; www.nalapad.com; Lighthouse Hill Rd; s/d incl breakfast from ₹800/1000;) The best midrange option in Mangalore comes with spruce rooms featuring floor-to-ceiling win-

RANI ABBAKKA THE WARRIOR QUEEN

The legendary exploits of Rana Abbakka, one of India's first freedom fighters – who just so happens to be a female – is one that gets surprisingly little attention outside the Mangalore region. An Indian Joan of Arc, her inspiring story is just waiting to be picked up by a Bollywood/Hollywood screenwriter.

As the Portuguese consolidated its power along India's western coastline in the 16th century, seizing towns across Goa and down to Mangalore, their attempts to take Ullal proved more of a challenge. This was thanks to its 'fearless queen' who proved to be a major thorn in its grand plans to control the lucrative spice trade. Her efforts to continually repell their advances is the stuff of local legend.

Well trained in the art of war, both in strategy and combat, she knew how to brandish a sword, and while she was eventually defeated, this was a result of her treacherous ex-husband, who conspired against her in leaking intelligence to the enemy.

Her efforts to rally her people to defeat the powerful Portuguese is not forgotten by locals: she's immortalised in a bronze statue on horseback at the roundabout on the road to Ullal beach, and has an annual festival dedicated to her.

The shore temple that looks over the beautiful Someshwara beach a few kilometres south from Ullal was the former site of her fort, and only sections of its wall remains intact.

dows and heavy red curtains. The rooftop restaurant, **Kadal**, will spice up your stay with fantastic views.

Hotel Ocean Pearl HOTEL $$$
(☎2413800; www.theoceanpearl.in; Navabharath Circle; s/d from ₹4300/5280; ❄@📶) Designer hotel with mint-fresh rooms and all the creature comforts that are paraded by business hotels. Its **Jazz** bar is a good place for a drink.

Gateway Hotel HOTEL $$$
(☎6660420; www.tajhotels.com/gateway; Old Port Rd; s/d incl breakfast from ₹6570/7460; ❄@📶🏊) From plasma TVs and beds laden with pillows to swimming pool surrounded by lawn and deck chairs, it's high standards across the board at this reliable four-star chain. No need to go beyond the standard rooms.

Summer Sands Beach Resort HOTEL $$$
(☎2467690; www.summersands.in; d from ₹5971; ❄@🏊) Set amid palm groves on a remote patch along Ullal Beach, Summer Sands offers a series of comfortable bungalows arranged in a tropical-resort-style setup. Its restaurant has a great seafood selection, but nonguests have to pay a ridiculous ₹100 to eat here.

Eating & Drinking

Don't leave town without sampling Mangalorean delights such as masala fish fry smothered in saucy red coconut curry, or scrumptious deep-fried prawn *rawa* fry.

Janatha Deluxe SOUTH INDIAN $
(Hotel Shaan Plaza; mains ₹50-70; ⏲7am-11pm) A local favourite that serves tasty veg thali (₹70), and North and South Indian veg dishes in the comfort of air-con and cushioned seating.

Lalith Bar & Restaurant SEAFOOD $$
(Balmatta Rd; mains ₹150-400; ⏲11.30am-3.30pm & 6.30-11.30pm) First impressions can be deceiving, so ignore the divey basement decor and order the masala fish fry with a chilled beer and you'll instantly be transported to heaven. The day's special seafood is also a good choice.

Kadal SOUTH INDIAN $$
(Lighthouse Hill Rd, Nalapad Residency; mains ₹150-220; ⏲11.30am-3.30pm & 6.30-11pm) This high-rise restaurant has elegant and warmly lit interiors, with sweeping views all around. Try the spicy chicken *uruval* (a coconut coastal curry) or the yummy prawn ghee roast.

Gajalee SEAFOOD $$$
(www.gajalee.com/rest_mangalore.html; Circuit House, Kadri Hills; mains ₹150-1200; ⏲11am-3.30pm & 6.30-11pm) In a town famous for seafood, locals often cite this as the best. Its interior is fairly posh, while outdoor tables more low key.

Liquid Lounge PUB
(☎4255175; Balmatta Rd; ⏲7-11.30pm) A stiff Jack and Coke or a cold Corona will sort you

out at this trendy pub with funky posters and neon-lit interiors. Also does decent food.

Information

State Bank of Mysore, **HDFC** and **ICICI Bank** have ATMs on Balmatta Rd and Lighthouse Hill Rd.

There's cheap internet cafes along **Balmatta Rd** (per hour ₹15) and near KSTRC bus station

Getting There & Away

AIR

The airport is precariously perched atop a plateau in Bajpe, about 20km northeast of town. **Air India** (☎2451046; Hathill Rd), **Jet Airways** (☎2441181; KS Rao Rd, Ram Bhavan Complex) and **SpiceJet** (☎18001803333) all operate daily flights to Mumbai, Bengaluru, Hyderabad and Chennai.

BUS

The **KSRTC bus stand** (☎2211243; Bejai Main Rd) is on Bejai Main Rd, 3km from the city centre. Several deluxe buses depart every half-hour to Bengaluru (ordinary/semideluxe/deluxe ₹290/451/650, nine hours), via Madikeri (ordinary/semideluxe/deluxe ₹103/190, five hours) and Mysore every half-hour (ordinary/semideluxe/deluxe ₹220/320/396, seven hours). Semideluxe buses go to Hassan (₹175, five hours). A 10.30pm deluxe bus heads to Panaji (semideluxe/deluxe ₹440/586, seven hours).

From opposite the **City bus stand**, private buses connect Udupi (₹75, 1½ hours), Dharmasthala (₹55, 2½ hours) and Jog Falls. Buses to Gokarna (₹130, seven hours) depart at 11am and 1.30pm.

TRAIN

The main train station Mangalore Central is south of the city centre. The 6.25pm Malabar Express heads to Thiruvananthapuram (Trivandrum; sleeper/2AC ₹257/1085, 15 hours). The 9.30pm West Coast Express heads to Chennai (sleeper/2AC ₹317/1370, 18 hours).

Several Konkan Railway trains (to Mumbai, Margao, Ernakulam or Trivandrum) use Mangalore Junction (aka Kankanadi), 5km east of Mangalore. This includes the 12.20am Netravati Express, stopping at Margao in Goa (sleeper/2AC ₹214/800, 5½ hours) and continuing to Mumbai (sleeper/2AC ₹367/1620, 15 hours).

Getting Around

To get to the airport, take buses 47B or 47C from the City bus stand, or catch a taxi (₹500).

Flag fall for autorickshaws is ₹20, and ₹13 per kilometre thereafter. For late-night travel, add 50%. An autorickshaw to Kankanadi station costs around ₹60, or take bus 9 or 11B.

Dharmasthala

Inland from Mangalore are a string of Jain temple towns, such as Venur, Mudabidri and Karkal. The most interesting among them is Dharmasthala, 75km east of Mangalore by the Netravathi River. Some 10,000 pilgrims pass through this town every day. During holidays and major festivals such as the five-day pilgrim festival of **Lakshadeepotsava** (Dharmasthala; Nov), the footfall can go up tenfold.

The **Manjunatha Temple** (6.30am-2pm & 5-9pm) is Dharmasthala's main shrine, devoted to the Hindu lord Shiva. Men have to enter with legs covered. Simple free meals are available in the temple's **kitchen** (11.30am-2.15pm & 7.30-10pm), attached to a hall that can seat up to 3000.

Associated sights in town include the 12m-high statue of Bahubali at Ratnagiri Hill, and the **Manjusha Museum** (admission ₹5; 9am-1pm & 4.30-9pm), which houses an electic collection of everything from artefacts to quirky collections of vintage cameras, telephones and typewriters (better than it sounds!). Don't forget to visit the fantastic **Car Museum** (admission ₹3; 8.30am-1pm & 2-7pm), home to 48 vintage autos, including a 1903 Renault, a 1920s Studebaker President used by Mahatma Gandhi and a 1951 Jaguar.

Should you wish to stay, contact the helpful **temple office** (☎08256-277121; www.shridharmasthala.org) for accommodation (per person ₹50) in pilgrim lodges.

There are frequent buses to Dharmasthala from Mangalore (₹55, 2½ hours).

Udupi (Udipi)

☎0820

Udupi is a buzzing yet relaxed pilgrim town that's home to the atmospheric 13th-century **Krishna Temple** (Car St; 3.30am-10pm), which draws thousands of Hindu pilgrims through the year. Surrounded by eight *maths* (monasteries), it's a hive of ritual activity, with musicians playing at the entrance, elephants on hand for *puja*, and pilgrims constantly passing through. Non-Hindus are welcome inside the temple; men must enter bare-chested. Elaborate rituals are also performed in the temple during the **Udupi Paryaya festival** (Udupi; Jan) (held every even year) in which outgoing swamiji

WORTH A TRIP

SURFING SWAMIS

While there's always been a spiritual bond between surfer and Mother ocean, the **Surfing Swamis** (9880659130; www.surfingindia.net; 6-64 Kolachikambla, Mulki; s/d incl full board from ₹2500/3000;) at Mulki, 30km north of Mangalore, take things to a whole new plane. At this working ashram, which was established by its American guru who's been surfing since 1963 (and living in India for four decades), devotees follow a daily ritual of puja, chanting, mediation and a pure vegetarian diet in between catching barrels.

The best waves are May to June and September to October. The Swamis can also assist with information on surfing across India. Board hire is ₹500 per day (it also has bodyboards and stand-up paddleboards) and lessons are ₹1500 per day.

Accommodation is pricey , but it has a homely beach-house feel, and rates include meals.

All are welcome to visit, but it's important to be aware it's strictly a place of worship and there are guidelines to abide by, including no alcohol and refraining from sex during their stay. See the website for more details.

of each of the eight *math* transfer duties to new swamiji.

There are several pilgrim hotels near the temple including **Shri Vidyasamuda Choultry** (2520820; Car St; r ₹150), but they're often booked out. The smartest choice is **Hotel Sriram Residency** (2530761; www.hotelsriramresidency.com; r with fan/AC ₹780/1445) with a fantastic upstairs restaurant-bar.

Udupi is famed for its vegetarian food, and recognised across India for its sumptuous thali; it's also the birthplace of the humble dosa. A good place to sample the local fare is the subterranean **Woodlands** (Dr UR Rao Complex; mains ₹60-90; 8am-9.30pm), a short walk south of the temple.

ICICI (Car St) has an ATM near the temple.

Udupi is 58km north of Mangalore along the coast; regular buses ply the route (₹75, 1½ hours). Buses also head to Gokarna (₹170, six hours) and Bengaluru (₹350/500/720, 10 hours). Regular buses head to Malpe (₹7).

Malpe

0820

A laid-back fishing harbour on the west coast 4km from Udupi, Malpe has nice beaches ideal for flopping about in the surf. A good place to stay is the **Paradise Isle Beach Resort** (2538777; www.theparadiseisle.com; s/d from ₹1300/1500, with AC ₹3000/3500;); ask for a room with a sea view. It can also organise **houseboat cruises** (per couple ₹4000; Oct-Mar) on backwaters that are similarly scenic to Kerala's, yet untouched by tourism.

From Malpe pier you can take a boat (₹100 return, 45 minutes) every 30 minutes from 9.30am to 5.30pm out to tiny **St Mary's Island**, where Vasco da Gama supposedly landed in 1498. Over weekends the island is busy with locals inspecting the curious hexagonal basalt formations that jut out of the sand; during the week you might have it to yourself. No boats run between June and mid-October.

Buses to Udupi are ₹7, and an autorickshaw ₹70.

Jog Falls

08186

Nominally the highest waterfalls in India, the Jog Falls only come to life during the monsoon. At other times, the Linganamakki Dam further up the Sharavati River limits the water flow and spoils the show. The tallest of the four falls is the Raja, which drops 293m.

To get a good view of the falls, bypass the scrappy area close to the bus stand and hike to the foot of the falls down a 1200-plus step path. Watch out for leeches during the wet season.

Jog Falls has buses roughly every hour to Shimoga (₹65, three hours), and three daily to Karwar via Kumta (₹25, three hours), where you can change for Gokarna (₹21, one hour). For Mangalore, change at Shimoga. A return taxi from Gokarna will cost around ₹1800.

FORMULA BUFFALO

Call it an indigenous take on the Grand Prix. Kambla, or traditional buffalo racing, is a hugely popular pastime among villagers along the southern Karnataka coast. Popularised in the early 20th century and born out of local farmers habitually racing their buffaloes home after a day in the fields, the races have now hit the big time. Thousands of spectators attend each edition, and racing buffaloes are pampered and prepared like thoroughbreds.

Kambla events are held between November and March, usually on weekends. Parallel tracks are laid out in a paddy field, along which buffaloes hurtle towards the finish line. In most cases the man rides on a board fixed to a ploughshare, literally surfing his way down the track behind the beasts.

Keep your cameras ready, but don't even think of getting in the buffaloes' way to take that prize-winning photo. The faster creatures can cover the 120m-odd distance through water and mud in around 14 seconds!

Gokarna

☎08386

A regular nominee among travellers' favorite beaches in India, Gokarna is a more laid-back and less-commercialised version of Goa. It attracts a crowd for a low-key, chilled-out beach holiday and not full-scale parties. Most accommodation is in thatched bamboo huts set along several stretches of blissful coast.

In actual fact there are two Gokarnas. Foremostly it's a sacred Hindu pilgrim town, full of ancient temples and important festivals such as **Shivaratri** (⏲Feb/Mar) and **Ganesh Chaturthi** (Gokarna; ⏲Sep). While its lively bazaar is an interesting place to visit, 99% of foreign tourists don't hang around here, instead making a bee-line straight to the adjoining beaches.

Sights & Activities

Temples

Foreigners and non-Hindus are not allowed inside Gokarna's temples. However, there are plenty of colourful rituals to be witnessed around town. At the western end of Car St is the **Mahabaleshwara Temple**, home to a revered lingam (phallic representation of Shiva). Nearby is the **Ganapati Temple**, while at the other end of the street is the **Venkataraman Temple**. About 100m further south is **Koorti Teertha**, the large temple tank (reservoir) where locals, pilgrims and immaculately dressed Brahmins perform their ablutions next to washermen on the ghats (steps or landings).

Beaches

Popular with local tourists, Gokarna's 'town beach' is dirty, and not meant for casual bathing. A short walk north along here will bring you to a nicer stretch of sand with some basic bungalow accommodation. **Cocopelli Surf School** (☎8105764969; www.cocopelli.org) can arrange board rental (₹750) and surf lessons (1½ hour ₹1000).

The best beaches are due south of Gokarana town, with Om Beach and Kudle Beach being the most popular.

Don't walk around the paths after dark, and not alone at any time – it's easy to slip or get lost, and muggings have occurred.

OM BEACH

Gokarna's most famous beach twists and turns over several kilometres in a way that's said to resemble the outline of an Om symbol. It's a great mix of lovely long beach and smaller shady patches of sand, perfect for sunbathing and swimming. There's plenty of guesthouses and beach shack restaurants. It's a 20-minute walk to Kudle Beach, while an autorickhaw to Gokarana town is about ₹150.

KUDLE BEACH

Also lined with rows of restaurants and guesthouses, Kudle Beach has emerged as a popular alternative to Om Beach. It's Gokarna's longest and widest beach, with plenty of room to stretch out on its attractive sands. Unfortunately the odd jet-ski marrs what's an otherwise perfect beach.

It's a 20-minute hike from both Gokarna town or Om Beach along a path that heads atop along the barren headland with expansive sea views. Otherwise it's a ₹60 rickshaw ride to town.

HALF MOON & PARADISE BEACH

Well hidden away south of Om Beach lie the small sandy coves of Half Moon Beach and Paradise Beach. Half Moon is the more attractive of the two, with a lovely sweep of powdery sand, and basic hut accommodation. Paradise Beach is a mix of sand and rocks, and a haven with the long-term 'turn-on-tune-in-drop-out' crowd. However, unfortunate developments at time of research had seen the government destroying all the huts out this way, leaving it in a ramshackle state.

From Om Beach, these beaches are a 30-minute and one-hour walk, respectively. Watch out for snakes along the path and don't walk it after dark. A fishing boat (which can fit 10 people) from Om Beach will cost around ₹700.

Sleeping & Eating

With a few exceptions, the choice here is basic, but perfectly comfortable, beach shacks. Most close May to August.

There are also rudimentary huts (₹150) at Half Moon and north along Gorkana Beach. In town, there's slightly more comfortable concrete rooms, but they're lacking in atmosphere.

Om Beach

Om Shree Ganesh BUNGALOWS $

(☎838625/310; www.omshreeganesh.com; hut ₹500, without bathroom ₹300) A winning combination of cheap bungalows, friendly management and beachside location makes this place justifiably popular. It's atmospheric double-storey restaurant rocks at night and does tasty dishes such as tandoori prawns, mushroom tikka and *momos*.

Sangham BUNGALOWS $

(☎9448101099; r with/without bathroom ₹400/200) A blissful spot overlooking the water, with sandy path leading to the bungalows out the back among banana trees, life's definitely a beach at Sangham.

Dolphin Shanti GUESTHOUSE $

(☎973962790; r from ₹150) Occupying the last plot of land on Om Beach, this mellow guesthouse sits perched upon the rocks with fantastic ocean views, and lives up to its name with dolphins often spotted. It's run by a friendly family and rooms are basic yet appealing.

Nirvana Café GUESTHOUSE $

(☎329851; d ₹250, cottage ₹400-600; @) Located on the southern end of Om, Nirvana has el cheapo huts and spacious cottages set among a shady garden. Has internet for ₹40 per hour.

Namaste Café GUESTHOUSE $

(☎257141; Om Beach; s/d ₹300/936, r with AC ₹2000; ❄@) This well-established guesthouse at the beginning of Om has slightly overpriced rooms, but a good choice for those wanting air-con. Its popular open-air restaurant has cold beer and dreamy sea views.

★ **SwaSwara** HOTEL $$$

(☎257132, 0484-3011711; www.swaswara.com; Om Beach; s/d 5 nights €1725/18755; ❄@🛜≋) One of South India's finest retreats, this health resort offers a holiday based around yoga and ayurveda. No short stays are possible, but once you've set eyes upon its elegant private villas – some with forest views, others with river – you'll be happy to stay put. All have small garden courtyards full of basil and lemongrass, open-air showers and lovely sitting areas. There's an interactive kitchen here, and the artists in residence can help you hone your creative skills. Rates also include transport from Goa, leisure activities and daily yoga sessions.

Dolphin Bay Cafe MULTICUISINE $

(mains ₹60-180; ⏰8am-10pm) Literally plonked on the beach. Dolphin Bay is your classic chilled-out shack restaurant that's what makes Gokarna so great.

Kudle Beach

Sea Rock Cafe GUESTHOUSE $

(☎7829486382; r from ₹300) Yet more chilled-out bungalows, but this one with an option of more-comfortable rooms, and a beachside restaurant where the good times roll.

Ganga Guesthouse GUESTHOUSE $

(☎08386257195; r from ₹250 ; @🛜) Occupying the last spot on Kudle, relaxed Ganga is a perennial favourite. Has internet and wi-fi (per hour ₹50).

Goutami Prasad GUESTHOUSE $

(☎9379481358; huts from ₹150, r ₹500) Relaxed, family-run guesthouse with a prime spot in the centre of Kudle Beach. Choose between basic huts with sandy floors or more comfortable concrete rooms.

Gokarna

Kamat Lodge GUESTHOUSE $
(☎256035; Main St; s/d/tr ₹275/500/675, s/d with AC ₹1175/1325; ❄) On Gokarna's main drag, Kamat has clean rooms with fresh sheets and large windows. But don't expect room service and other such fluffs.

Shastri Guest House GUESTHOUSE $
(☎256220; narasimha.shastri@gmail.com; Main St; s/d/tr ₹150/250/350) A hostel-like place with good, airy doubles in the new block out back. The singles are cramped, though.

Shopping

Shree Radhakrishna Bookstore BOOKS
(⏲10am-6pm) A good selection of second-hand novels, postcards and maps

Information

Axis Bank (Main St)

SBI (Main St, Gorkana Town) Has an ATM.

Shama Internet Centre (Car St; per hr ₹40; ⏲10am-11pm) Fast internet connections.

Sub Post Office (1st fl, cnr Car & Main Sts; ⏲10am-4pm Mon-Sat)

Getting There & Away

Be aware that trains arriving from Mumbai or Goa, and private buses from Hampi/Hospet, may get you into Gokarna at the ungodly hour of 3am, so it might be worth notifying your guesthouse to see if there's someone who can check you in.

BUS

From the KSRTC bus stand, buses roll to Madgaon in Goa (₹100, four hours) at 8.15am or otherwise to Karwar (₹33, 1½ hours), which has connections to Goa. There are buses to Hospet (₹240, nine hours) for Hampi, Bengaluru (from ₹415, 12 hours) and Mangalore (₹200, 6½ hours), to Kunda (₹25) for Jog Falls (₹100) and frequent direct buses run to Hubli (₹134, four hours).

TRAIN

Many express trains stop at Gokarna Rd station, 9km from town; however, double check your ticket as some stop at Ankola, 26km away. Many of the hotels and small travel agencies in Gokarna can book tickets.

The 3am Matsyagandha Express goes to Mangalore (sleeper ₹200, 3½ hours); the return train leaves Kumta around 6pm for Margao (sleeper ₹200, 2½ hours) and Mumbai.

Autorickshaws charge ₹250 to go to Gokarna Rd station (or ₹500 from Ankola); a bus charges ₹35 and leaves every 30 minutes.

CENTRAL KARNATAKA

Hampi

☎08394

Unreal and bewitching, the forlorn ruins of Hampi dot an unearthly landscape that will leave you spellbound the moment you cast your eyes on it. Heaps of giant boulders perch precariously over miles of undulating terrain, their rusty hues offset by jade-green palm groves, banana plantations and paddy fields. A World Heritage Site, Hampi is a place where you can lose yourself among wistful ruins, or simply be mesmerised by the vagaries of nature.

Hampi is a major pit stop on the traveller circuit; November to March is the high season. While it's possible to see the main sites in a day or two, this goes against Hampi's relaxed grain. Plan on lingering for a while.

The main travellers' ghetto is Hampi Bazaar, a village crammed with budget lodges, shops and restaurants, and towered over by the majestic Virupaksha Temple. Across the river is also popular, a more tranquil setting that's love at first sight for many a traveller.

The Vijaya Utsav (p174) festival in January is a good time to visit, with three day spectacle of dance, music, puppetry and a grand finale procession. The **Virupaksha Car Festival** (⏲Mar/Apr) in March/April is another big event, a colurful procession characterised by a giant wooden chariot (the temple car from Virupaksha Temple) being pulled along the main strip of Hampi bazaar.

History

Hampi and its neighbouring areas find mention in the Hindu epic Ramayana as Kishkinda, the realm of the monkey gods. In 1336 Telugu prince Harihararaya chose Hampi as the site for his new capital Vijayanagar, which – over the next couple of centuries – grew into one of the largest Hindu empires in Indian history. By the 16th century it was a thriving metropolis of about 500,000 people, its busy bazaars dabbling in international commerce, brimming with precious stones and merchants from faraway lands. All this, however, ended in a stroke in 1565, when a confederacy of Deccan sultanates razed Vijayanagar to the ground, striking it a death blow from which it never recovered.

Sights

Set over 36 sq km, there are some 3700 monuments to explore here, and it would take months if you were to do it justice. The ruins are divided into two main areas: the Sacred Centre, around Hampi Bazaar; and the Royal Centre, towards Kamalapuram.

Be aware that the ₹250 ticket for Vittala Temple entitles you to same-day admission into most of the paid sites across the ruins, so don't lose your ticket.

Virupaksha Temple HINDU TEMPLE
(Map p218; admission ₹2, camera ₹50; ⌚dawn-dusk) The focal point of Hampi Bazaar is the Virupaksha Temple, one of the city's oldest structures, and Hampi's only remaining working temple. The main *gopuram,* almost 50m high, was built in 1442, with a smaller one added in 1510. The main shrine is dedicated to Virupaksha, an incarnation of Shiva.

If Lakshmi (the **temple elephant**) and her attendant are around, she'll smooch (bless) you for a coin. The adorable Lakshmi gets her morning bath at 8am, just down the way by the river ghats.

To the south, overlooking Virupaksha Temple, **Hemakuta Hill** has a few early ruins, including monolithic sculptures of Narasimha (Vishnu in his man-lion incarnation) and Ganesha. At the east end of Hampi Bazaar is a monolithic **Nandi statue** (Map p218), around which stand colonnaded blocks of the ancient marketplace. Overlooking the site is Matanga Hill, whose summit affords dramatic views of the terrain at sunrise. The Vijaya Utsav (p174) festival is held at the base of the hill in January.

Vittala Temple HINDU TEMPLE
(Map p216; Indian/foreigner ₹10/250; ⌚8.30am-5.30pm) The undisputed highlight of the Hampi ruins, the 16th-century Vittala Temple stands amid the boulders 2km from Hampi Bazaar. Though a few cement scaffolds have been erected to keep the main structure from collapsing, the site is in relatively good condition.

Work possibly started on the temple during the reign of Krishnadevaraya (r 1509–29). It was never finished or consecrated, yet the temple's incredible sculptural work remains the pinnacle of Vijayanagar art.

The ornate **stone chariot** that stands in the courtyard is the temple's showpiece and represents Vishnu's vehicle with an image of Garuda within. Its wheels were once capable of turning.

The outer 'musical' pillars reverberate when tapped, which supposedly were designed to replicate 81 different Indian instruments, but authorities have placed them out of tourists' bounds for fear of further damage, so no more do-re-mi. As well as the main temple, whose sanctum was illuminated using a design of reflective waters, here you'll find the marriage hall and prayer hall the structures to the left and right upon entry, respectively.

Sule Bazaar HISTORIC SITE
(Map p216) Halfway along the path from Hampi Bazaar to the Vittala Temple, a track to the right leads over the rocks to deserted Sule Bazaar, one of ancient Hampi's principal centres of commerce and reputedly the red-light district. At the southern end of this area is the atmospheric, deserted Achyutaraya Temple.

Royal Centre HISTORIC SITE
While it can be accessed by a 2km foot trail from the Achyutaraya Temple, the Royal Centre is best reached via the Hampi–Kamalapuram road. A number of Hampi's major sites stand here.

The **Mahanavami-diiba** (Map p216) is a 12m-high three-tired platform with intricate carvings and panoramic vistas of the walled complex of ruined temples, stepped tanks and the King's audience hall. The platform was used as Royal viewing area for the Dasara festivities, religious ceremonies and processions.

Further along is the **Hazarama Temple** (Map p216), with exquistive carvings that depict scenes from the Ramayana, and polished black granite pillars.

Northeast from here within the walled ladies' quarters is the **Zenana Enclosure** (Map p216; Indian/foreigner ₹10/250; ⌚8.30am-5.30pm). Its peaceful grounds and lush lawns feel like an oasis amid the arid surrounds. Here is the **Lotus Mahal** (Map p216), a delicately designed pavilion which was supposedly the queen's recreational mansion. It overlooks the 11 grand **Elephant Stables** (Map p216; ⌚8:30am-5:30pm) with arched entrances and domed chambers. There's also a small museum and army barracks within the high-walled enclosure.

Further south, you'll find various temples and elaborate waterworks, including the **Queen's Bath** (Map p216; ⌚8.30am-5.30pm),

Hampi & Anegundi

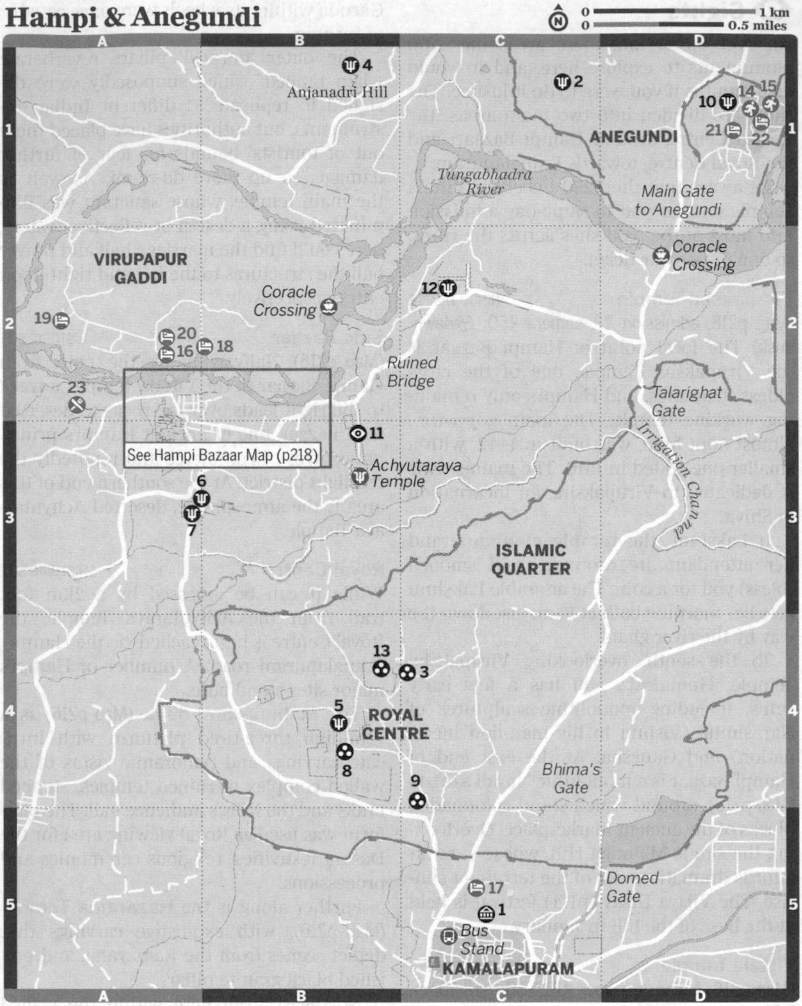

ANEGUNDI
Tungabhadra River
Main Gate to Anegundi
Coracle Crossing
VIRUPAPUR GADDI
Coracle Crossing
Anjanadri Hill
Ruined Bridge
Talarighat Gate
Irrigation Channel
See Hampi Bazaar Map (p218)
Achyutaraya Temple
ISLAMIC QUARTER
ROYAL CENTRE
Bhima's Gate
Domed Gate
Bus Stand
KAMALAPURAM

deceptively plain on the outside but amazing within, with its Indo-Islamic architecture.

Other interesting stop offs along the road to the Virupaksha Temple is the 6.7m monolithic statue of the bulging-eyed **Lakshimi Narasmiha** (Map p216) in a cross-legged yoga position and topped by a hood of seven snakes. Nearby is the **Krishna Temple** (Map p216) built in 1513, which is fronted by a D-cupped apsara and 10 incarnations of Vishnu

Archaeological Museum MUSEUM
(Map p216; Kamalapuram; ⏲10am-5pm Sat-Thu) Worth popping in for its quality collection of sculptures from local ruins, plus neolithic tools, fascinating coins, 16th-century weaponry and a large floor model of the Vijayanagar ruins.

Hampi Heritage Gallery GALLERY
(Map p218; ⏲10am-1pm & 3-6pm Tue-Sun) Books and photo albums on Hampi's history and architecture, and can arrange walking tours.

Activities

Get in touch with Kishkinda Trust (p220) for info on activities in the region.

Hampi & Anegundi

Sights

1 Archaeological Museum ... C5
2 Durga Temple ... C1
3 Elephant Stables ... C4
4 Hanuman Temple ... B1
5 Hazarama Temple ... B4
6 Krishna Temple ... A3
7 Lakshimi Narasmiha ... A3
Lotus Mahal ... (see 13)
8 Mahanavami-diiba ... B4
9 Queen's Bath ... C4
10 Ranganatha Temple ... D1
11 Sule Bazaar ... B3
12 Vittala Temple ... C2
13 Zenana Enclosure ... B4

Activities, Courses & Tours

14 Banana Fibre Craft Workshop ... D1
15 Kishkinda Trust ... D1

Sleeping

Champa Guest House ... (see 14)
16 Durga Huts ... A2
17 Hotel Mayura Bhuvaneshwari ... C5
18 Manju's Place ... B2
Peshagar Guest House ... (see 14)
19 Shanthi ... A2
20 Sunny Guesthouse ... A2
TEMA Guest House ... (see 14)
21 Uramma Cottage ... D1
22 Uramma House ... D1

Eating

Hoova Craft Shop & Café ... (see 14)
23 Mango Tree ... A2

Rock-Climbing ROCK CLIMBING

(Around Hampi) Hampi is the undisputed bouldering capital of India. The entire landscape is a climber's adventure playground made of granite crags and boulders, some bearing the marks of ancient stonemasons. **Tom & Jerry** (9481093862, 9482746697; luckykoushik1@gmail.com; Virupapur Gaddi; 3hr class ₹350) are two local lads who are doing great work in catering to climbers' needs, providing quality mats, shoes and local knowledge. They can also organise all-inclusive bouldering trips to Badami for ₹1600. Challenging rock faces can also be found in Ramnagar, 40km south of Bengaluru, Savandurga, 50km west of the capital, and Turahalli, on Bengaluru's southern outskirts.

Sleeping

Most guesthouses are cosy family-run digs, perfect for the budget traveller. A handful of places also have larger, more-comfortable rooms with air-con and TV. If you're needing something more comfortable, Hospet has more upmarket options.

Hampi Bazaar

★ **Padma Guest House** GUESTHOUSE $

(Map p218; 241331; padmaguesthouse@gmail.com; d from ₹500-800, with AC from ₹1600; wi-fi) In a quiet corner of Hampi Bazaar, the astute and amiable Padma has basic but squeaky-clean rooms and is a pleasant deviation from Hampi's usual offerings. Those on the 1st floor have good views of the Virupaksha Temple, while new rooms have creature comforts of TV and air-con. There's free wi-fi downstairs.

Archana Guest House GUESTHOUSE $

(Map p218; 241547; addihampi@yahoo.com; d from ₹500, with AC ₹1200; AC @ wi-fi) At the end of a lane on the riverfront, quiet and cheerful Archana is another friendly family-run affair, that makes for a fantastic budget choice. Decent rooms are painted in vivid purple and green, and there's a lovely rooftop hangout.

Pushpa Guest House GUESTHOUSE $

(Map p218; 9948795120; pushpaguesthouse99@yahoo.in; d from ₹750, with AC from ₹1100; AC) A top all-round option, Pushpa is a bit pricier than others, but it gets you a comfortable room and an extremely cordial family playing host. It has a lovely sit-out on the 1st floor, and a reliable travel agency.

Gopi Guest House GUESTHOUSE $

(Map p218; 241695; www.gopiguesthouse.com; r ₹500-700; @ wi-fi) Centrally located amid the bustle of the bazaar, this pleasant dive continues to provide commendable service to travellers. The new block is quite upscale for Hampi's standards, with ensuite rooms fronted by a sun-kissed terrace. The rooftop cafe – with a lovely view of the Virupaksha Temple – is a nice place to hang out.

Ranjana Guest House GUESTHOUSE $

(Map p218; 241696; r from ₹800, with AC ₹1200) Run by a friendly, tight-knit family, Ranjana is slightly overpriced, but it prides itself on well-appointed rooms and killer temple-views from its terrace.

Vicky's GUESTHOUSE $

(Map p218; 241694; vikkyhampi@yahoo.co.in; r ₹520; wi-fi) An old faithful with decent rooms, rooftop cafe and free wi-fi.

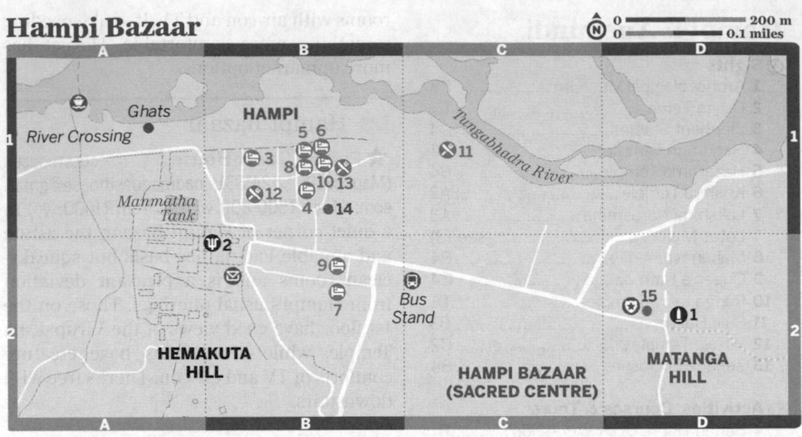

Hampi Bazaar

Sights

1 Nandi Statue D2
2 Virupaksha Temple B2

Sleeping

3 Archana Guest House B1
4 Gopi Guest House B1
5 Kiran Guest House B1
6 Netra Guesthouse B1
7 Padma Guest House B2
8 Pushpa Guest House B1
9 Ranjana Guest House B2
10 Vicky's B1

Eating

11 Garden Paradise C1
12 Prince Restaurant B1
13 Ravi's Rose B1

Information

14 Akash Art Gallery & Bookstore B1
15 Hampi Heritage Gallery D2
Internet .... (see 10)
Tourist Office .... (see 2)

Kiran Guest House GUESTHOUSE $
(Map p218; ☎9448143906; kiranhampi2012@gmail.com; r ₹400-600) Chilled-out guesthouse on the riverfront and banana groves.

Netra Guesthouse GUESTHOUSE $
(Map p218; ☎9483419731; r from ₹300, without bathroom from ₹200) Basic but relaxed option for shoestringers.

Virupapur Gaddi

Many travellers prefer the tranquil atmosphere of Virupapur Gaddi, across the river from Hampi Bazaar.

Sunny Guesthouse GUESTHOUSE $
(Map p216; ☎9448566368; www.sunnyguesthouse.com; r ₹200-750; @📶) Sunny both in name and disposition, this popular guesthouse is a hit among backpackers for its cheap rooms, tropical garden, hammocks and chilled-out restaurant. It has a good choice of rooms, all with attached bathroom.

Shanthi GUESTHOUSE $
(Map p216; ☎9449260162; www.shanthihampi.com; r without bathroom ₹200, cottage ₹500-1650; @📶) Shanthi's earth-themed, thatched cottages have sublime rice-field, river and sunset views, with couch swings dangling on their front porches. The restaurant does good thalis and pizzas.

Manju's Place GUESTHOUSE $
(Map p216; ☎9449247712; r ₹300, without bathroom from ₹100) The place for those who like things quiet, with a bucolic setting among rice fields and nearby boulders. Its attractive mud-brick huts are wonderful, and overall a top spot to chill out.

Durga Huts GUESTHOUSE $
(Map p216; ☎9482051515; durgahuts@yahoo.com; huts without bathroom ₹100, r ₹700) Relocating across the river following Hampi Bazaar being bulldozed, Durga's new offering is basic thatched huts with hammocks, that are perfect for those watching their rupees. Its restaurant gets good reviews.

Kamalapuram

Hotel Mayura Bhuvaneshwari HOTEL $$
(Map p216; ☎241474; s/d from ₹1200/1500; ❄) This tidy government operation, about 3km south of the Royal Centre, has well-appointed rooms, a lovely big garden, a much-appreciated beer bar, and good multicuisine restaurant.

Eating

Due to Hampi's religious significance, meat is strictly off the menu in all restaurants, and alcohol is banned (though some restaurants can order it for you).

★**Garden Paradise** INDIAN, MULTICUISINE $
(Map p218; mains from ₹120) Not only does it have a sublime riverside location, but easily the best food. Dine on outdoor tables under shady mango trees or indoors on cushions and psychedelic murals. It does the best pizzas outside Bangalore, while the signature *paneer lavadar* in creamy spinach sauce and cashews is unbelievable. Breakfasts are good too, with vegemite or marmite on toast, strong coffee and excellent juices. Also has accommodation here.

Ravi's Rose MULTICUISINE $
(Map p218; mains from ₹70) This slightly sketchy rooftop-restaurant is the bazaar's most social hangout, with a good selection of dosas, but most are here for the, erm, tasty lassis (cough, cough). It's built into a rockface, where you can scramble through under boulders to get incredible sunset views.

Laughing Buddha MULTICUISINE $
(mains from ₹100; ⏲8am-10pm) The other side of the river's equivalent to the Mango Tree, with serene river views that span beyond to the temples and ruins. Its menu is curries, burgers, pizzas, you know the drill...

Mango Tree MULTICUISINE $$
(Map p216; mains ₹80-150; ⏲7.30am-9.30pm) Creativity blends with culinary excellence at this legendary rural-themed chill-out joint, spread out under the eponymous mango tree by the river. Once a haven for hippies, now it's equally popular with Indian families. The terraced seating is perfect for whiling away a lazy afternoon, book in hand. Walk through a banana plantation to get here, and try the special vegetable curry or the spaghetti with cashew nuts and cheese (₹100).

OUT OF HARM'S WAY

Hampi Bazaar is an extremely safe area, but do not wander around the ruins after dark or alone. It's a dangerous terrain to get lost in; long-time guides have even sighted sloth bears prowling around Vittala Temple at night!

Local laws require all foreign travellers to report to the police station (Map p218) with their passports upon arrival, and notify the authorities about their proposed duration of stay.

Prince Restaurant MULTICUISINE $$
(Map p218; mains ₹70-180; ⏲7.30am-10pm) Food here takes ages to arrive, so thankfully this atmospheric shady hut is a good place to chill out with cushioned seating on the floor. Does *momos*, pizzas etc.

Shopping

Akash Art Gallery & Bookstore BOOKS
(Map p218; ⏲6am-9pm) Stocks an excellent selection of books on Hampi and India, plus secondhand fiction. It has a free Hampi map.

Information

There's no ATM in Hampi; the closest is 3km away in Kamalapuram – a ₹100 autorickshaw return trip.

Internet (per hour Rs40) is ubiquitous in Hampi Bazaar; some guesthouses have paid wi-fi. A good tourist resource for Hampi is www.hampi.in.

Tourist Office (Map p218; ☎241339; ⏲10am-5.30pm Sat-Thu) Dingy office inside Virupaskha Temple has brochures and can arrange guides for ₹600/1000 for a half-/full day.

Getting There & Away

A semideluxe bus connects Hampi Bazaar to Bengaluru (₹434, eight hours) leaving at 8pm. Overnight private sleeper buses ply to/from Goa and Gokarna occasionally departing from Hampi, but more likely Hospet. Numerous travel agents in Hampi Bazaar book onward tickets or arrange taxis.

The first bus from Hospet (₹15, 30 minutes, half-hourly) is at 6.30am; the last one back leaves Hampi Bazaar at 8.30pm. An autorickshaw costs ₹150 to ₹200.

Hospet is Hampi's nearest train station.

HAMPI BAZAAR

While in 1865 it was the Deccan sultanates who leveled Vijayanagar, today a different battle rages in Hampi between conservationists bent on protecting Hampi's architectural heritage and the locals who have settled there. In mid-2012 the master plan that had been in the works since mid-2000s, and which aims to classify all of Hampi's ruins as protected monuments, was finally put into action. Overnight many shops, hotels and homes in the bazaar were bulldozed, reducing the main strip to rubble overnight, as villagers who'd made the site a living monument were evicted.

While villagers were compensated with a small plot of land in Kaddirampur, 4km from the bazaar (where there is talk of new guesthouses eventually opening up), many locals remained displaced months later as they awaited their pay out.

So what does this mean for tourism, and are any guesthouses remaining in Hampi Bazaar? For now, thankfully little has changed in terms of tourist infrastructure. While at the time of research rubble from demolished buildings remained, and the main temple road resembled a bombed-out town, all hotels just back from the bazaar remained intact and the owners were confident of continuing to do so. There was talk, however, that height restrictions may be enforced, which would see three-storey buildings having to be cut back to two floors. This would mean a lot Hampi's appealing rooftop restaurants would disappear.

Getting Around

Bicycles cost about ₹30 per day in Hampi Bazaar, while mopeds can be hired for around ₹100 to ₹150. Petrol is ₹90 a litre.

A small **boat** (Map p218; person/bicycle/motorbike ₹15/10/20; 7am-6pm) shuttles frequently across the river to Virupapur Gaddi from 7am to 6pm. A large backpack will cost ₹5 extra, while a special trip after 6pm is ₹50 to ₹100 per person depending on how late you cross.

Walking the ruins is recommended too, but expect to cover at least 7km just to see the major sites. Autorickshaws and taxis are available for sightseeing, and will drop you as close to each of the major ruins as they can. Hiring an autorickshaw for the day costs ₹750.

Organised tours depart from Hospet.

Around Hampi

Anegundi

Across the Tungabhadra, about 5km northeast of Hampi Bazaar, sits Anegundi, an ancient fortified village that's part of the Hampi World Heritage Site but predates Hampi by way of human habitation. Gifted with a landscape similar to Hampi, quainter Anegundi has been spared the blight of commercialisation, and thus continues to preserve the local atmosphere minus the touristy vibe.

Sights & Activities

Hindu Temples HINDU TEMPLES

Mythically referred to as Kishkinda, the kingdom of the monkey gods, Anegundi retains many of its historic monuments, such as sections of its defensive wall and gates, and the **Ranganatha Temple** (Map p216; dawn-dusk) devoted to Rama. The whitewashed **Hanuman Temple** (Map p216; dawn-dusk), accessible by a 570-step climb up the Anjanadri Hill, has fine views of the rugged terrain around. Many believe this is the birthplace of the Hindu monkey god Hanuman. On the pleasant hike up, you'll be courted by impish monkeys, and within the temple you'll find a horde of chillum-puffing resident sadhus. Also worth visiting is the **Durga Temple** (Map p216; dawn-dusk), an ancient shrine closer to the village.

★Kishkinda Trust CULTURAL PROGRAMS, OUTDOOR ADVENTURE

(TKT; Map p216; 08533-267777; www.thekishkindatrust.org) The Kishkinda Trust, an NGO that promotes sustainable tourism in Anegundi, organises activities such as rock-climbing, treks, visits to prehistoric cave paintings, canal tours, birdwatching and other community initiatives such as performing arts sessions. Mountain bikes are available for ₹250 per day. Volunteers are also accepted.

Banana Fibre Craft Workshop HANDICRAFTS WORKSHOP
(Map p216; admission ₹10, camera ₹100 ; ⏲10am-1pm & 2-5pm Mon-Sat) Watch on at this small workshop as workers ply their trade making a range of handicrafts and accesories using the bark of a banana tree, and recycled materials. Of course they sell it all too.

Sleeping & Eating

A great place to escape the hippies in Hampi, Anegundi has fantastic homestays in restored heritage buildings that provide a lovely experience. The following are managed by Kishkinda Trust.

Peshagar Guest House GUESTHOUSE $
(Map p216; ☎09449972230; www.urammaheritagehomes.com; s/d ₹450/850) Six simple rooms done up in rural motifs open around a pleasant common area in this heritage house-now-budget guesthouse, with lovely courtyard garden.

TEMA Guest House GUESTHOUSE $
(Map p216; per person ₹350) The two rooms in this village heritage house are decked out in traditional style with plenty of colour and cow dung floors. Has a full kitchen.

Champa Guest House GUESTHOUSE $
(Map p216; s/d incl breakfast ₹350/650) Champa offers basic but pleasant accommodation in two rooms, and is looked after by an affable village family.

Uramma House GUESTHOUSE $$
(Map p216; www.urammaheritagehomes.com; house incl full board for 4-persons ₹8000; 📶) This 4th-century heritage house is a gem, with traditonal-style rooms featuring boutique touches throughout. It's a great deal for groups, and has an attractive dining room, rooftop area and even a butler!

★**Uramma Cottage** COTTAGE $$$
(Map p216; ☎08533-267792; www.urammaheritagehomes.com; s/d incl full board ₹3700/5500; ❄📶) Delightful thatched-roof cottages with rustic farmhouse charm that are both comfortable and attractive. Each has outdoor seating and hammocks, and there's a library with good reading material for the relaxed landscaped garden setting.

Hoova Craft Shop & Café CAFE $
(Map p216; mains ₹40-60; ⏲8.30am-9.30pm) A lovely place for an unhurried flavoursome local meal.

Getting There & Away

Anegundi can be reached by crossing the river on a coracle (₹10) from the pier east of the Vittala Temple. By far the most convenient way is to hire a moped or bicycle (if you're feeling energetic) from Virupapur Gaddi, or get an autorickshaw here for around ₹200.

Hospet

☎08394 / POP 206,159

The busy regional town of Hospet is the main transport hub for Hampi. Unless you're wanting to stay in an upmarket hotel, few choose to linger in Hospet as it's a dusty, unattractive town with not much going on.

Sleeping & Eating

Hotel Malligi HOTEL $$
(☎228101; www.malligihotels.com; Jabunatha Rd; r ₹450-2680; ❄@🏊) Hospet's premier luxury option builds its reputation around clean and well-serviced rooms, an aquamarine swimming pool and a good multicuisine restaurant. Also has some budget rooms.

Royal Orchid HOTEL $$$
(☎300100; www.royalorchidhotels.com; r incl breakfast ₹6890; ❄@📶🏊) If you're in

DAROJI SLOTH BEAR SANCTUARY

About 30km south of Hampi, amid a scrubby undulating terrain, lies the **Daroji Sloth Bear Sanctuary** (admission Indian/foreigner ₹50/300; ⏲1.30pm-6pm), which over 83 sq km nurses a population of around 150 free-ranging sloth bears. You have a very good chance of spotting them, as honey is slathered on the rocks to coincide with visitors' arrival. However, you can only see them from afar at the viewing platform. Bring binoculars, or basically there's no point turning up. Generally 4pm to 6pm is the best time to visit.

The sanctuary is also home to leopards, wild boars, hyenas, jackals and others animals, but you're unlikely to see anything other than peacocks. You'll need to arrange transport to get here, which should cost around ₹500 for an autorickshaw and ₹1000 for a car.

Hospet seeking comfort, look no further than Royal Orchid with its plush business-hotel standards of wi-fi, flat-screen TVs, gym, four restaurants and bar. It's popular with package tourists, and staff here are professional.

Udupi Sri Krishna Bhavan SOUTH INDIAN $
(Bus stand; mains ₹40-80; ⏲6am-11pm) Opposite the bus stand, this clean spot dishes out Indian vegie fare, including thalis for ₹45.

Information

There are ATMs along the main drag and Shanbagh Circle. Internet joints are common, costing ₹40 per hour.

Getting There & Away

BUS

The bus stand has services to Hampi every half-hour (₹15, 30 minutes). Several express buses run to Bengaluru (ordinary/deluxe ₹290/412, nine hours). Buses for Gokarna (₹315, eight hours) depart at 9.15am, or take a bus to Hubli (₹108, 4½ hours) and change. Two buses head to Badami (₹180, four hours) at 1pm and 1.30pm. There are frequent buses to Bijapur (₹210, six hours) and overnight services to Hyderabad (semideluxe/deluxe ₹435/654, 10 hours) at 8.30pm. For Mangalore or Hassan, take a morning bus to Shimoga (₹240, five hours) and change there.

For Goa, **Paulo Travels** (☎0832-6637777) has a 7pm bus (₹355, 11 hours) via Gokarna (₹700 to ₹800), but arrives at Gokarana at the inconvenient time of 3am, so it's best to go with the KSTRC bus.

TRAIN

Hospet's train station is a ₹30 autorickshaw journey from town. The 5.30am Rayalaseema Express heads to Hubli (2nd class ₹120, 3½ hours). For Bengaluru, take the 8.40pm Hampi Express (sleeper/2AC ₹191/785, nine hours). Every Monday, Wednesday, Thursday and Saturday, a 6.30am express train heads to Vasco da Gama (sleeper/2AC ₹194/715, 8½ hours).

For Badami, catch a Hubli train to Gadag and change there.

Hubli

☎0836 / POP 943,857

Prosperous Hubli is a hub for rail routes for Mumbai, Bengaluru, Goa and northern Karnataka. The train station is a 15-minute walk from the old bus stand. Most hotels sit along this stretch.

Sleeping & Eating

Ananth Residency HOTEL $$
(☎2262251; ananthresidencyhubli@yahoo.co.uk; Jayachamaraj Nagar; d from ₹1500; ❄) A comfortable option that sports a sleek business-hotel look and feel. Has good-value rooms and efficient service, and a cheerful restaurant with chilled beer.

Hotel Ajanta HOTEL $
(☎2362216; Jayachamaraj Nagar; s/d from ₹300/400) This well-run place near the train station has basic, functional rooms. Its popular ground-floor restaurant serves delicious regional-style thalis for ₹35.

Information

SBI has an ATM opposite the bus stand. On the same stretch are several internet cafes, charging around ₹30 per hour.

Getting There & Away

AIR

From Hubli's basic airport, SpiceJet has daily flights to Bengaluru.

BUS

Buses stop briefly at the old bus stand before moving to the new bus stand 2km away. There are numerous semideluxe services to Bengaluru (semideluxe/AC Volvo/sleeper ₹352/401/600, 10 hours), Bijapur (₹180, six hours) and Hospet (₹164, 4½ hours). There are regular connections to Mangalore (₹300, 10 hours, several daily), Borivali in Mumbai (semideluxe/sleeper ₹515/780, 14 hours, four daily), Mysore (₹320, 10 hours, three daily), Gokarna (₹175, five hours, two daily) and Panaji (₹161, six hours, six daily).

Private deluxe buses to Bengaluru run from opposite the old bus stand.

TRAIN

From the train station, expresses head to Hospet (2nd class ₹120, 3½ hours, six daily), Bengaluru (sleeper/2AC ₹203/910, 11 hours, four daily) and Mumbai (sleeper/2AC ₹285/1215, 14 hours). The 11pm Hubli-Vasco Link Express goes to Goa (sleeper ₹153, six hours).

NORTHERN KARNATAKA

Badami

☎08357 / POP 26,000

Once the capital of the mighty Chalukya empire, today Badami is famous for its mag-

WORTH A TRIP

WALK ON THE WILD SIDE

Located in the jungles of the Western Ghats about 100km from Goa, emerging **Dandeli** is a wildlife getaway that promises close encounters with diverse exotic wildlife such as elephants, leopards, sloth bears, gaur, wild dogs and flying squirrels. It's a chosen birding destination too, with resident hornbills, golden-backed woodpeckers, serpent eagles and white-breasted kingfishers. Also on offer are a slew of adventure activities ranging from kayaking to bowel-churning white-water rafting on the swirling waters of the Kali River.

Kali Adventure Camp (☎08-25597944; www.junglelodges.com/index.php/resorts/kali.html; per person incl full board & activities Indian/foreigner from ₹2500/4000; ❄) offers accommodation in tented cottages and rooms, done up lavishly while adhering to ecofriendly principles.

Frequent buses connect Dandeli to both Hubli (₹50, two hours) and Dharwad (₹42, 1½ hours), with onward connections to Goa, Gokarna, Hospet and Bengaluru.

nificent rock-cut cave temples, and red sandstone cliffs that resemble the Wild West. While the dusty main road is an eyesore that will have you wanting to get the hell out of there, its backstreets are a lovely area to explore with old houses, carved wooden doorways, an occasional Chalukyan ruin and flocks of curious kids.

History

From about AD 540 to 757, Badami was the capital of an enormous kingdom stretching from Kanchipuram in Tamil Nadu to the Narmada River in Gujarat. It eventually fell to the Rashtrakutas, and changed hands several times thereafter, with each dynasty sculpturally embellishing Badami in their own way.

The sculptural legacy left by the Chalukya artisans in Badami includes some of the earliest and finest examples of Dravidian temples and rock-cut caves. During Badami's heydays, Aihole and Pattadakal served as trial grounds for new temple architecture; the latter is now a World Heritage Site.

Sights

Cave Temples CAVES

(Indian/foreigner ₹5/100, video camera ₹25; ⏲6am-6pm) Badami's highlight is its beautiful cave temples. Nonpushy and informed guides ask ₹300 for a tour of the caves. Late afternoon is the best time to visit. Watch out for pesky monkeys and don't carry food on you.

Cave one, just above the entrance to the complex, is dedicated to Shiva. It's the oldest of the four caves, probably carved in the latter half of the 6th century. On the wall to the right of the porch is a captivating image of Nataraja striking 81 dance moves in the one pose. On the right of the porch area is a huge figure of Ardhanarishvara. The right half of the figure shows features of Shiva, while the left half has aspects of his wife Parvati. On the opposite wall is a large image of Harihara; half Shiva and half Vishnu.

Dedicated to Vishnu, **cave two** is simpler in design. As with caves one and three, the front edge of the platform is decorated with images of pot-bellied dwarfs in various poses. Four pillars support the verandah, their tops carved with a bracket in the shape of a *yali* (mythical lion creature). On the left wall of the porch is the bull-headed figure of Varaha, an incarnation of Vishnu and the emblem of the Chalukya empire. To his left is Naga, a snake with a human face. On the right wall is a large sculpture of Trivikrama, another incarnation of Vishnu.

Between the second and third caves are two sets of steps to the right. The first leads to a **natural cave**, where resident monkeys laze around. The eastern wall of this cave contains a small image of Padmapani (an incarnation of the Buddha). The second set of steps – sadly, barred by a gate – leads to the hilltop **South Fort**.

Cave three, carved in AD 578, is the largest and most impressive. On the left wall is a carving of Vishnu, to whom the cave is dedicated, sitting on a snake. Nearby is an image of Varaha with four hands. The pillars have carved brackets in the shape of *yalis*. The ceiling panels contain images, including Indra riding an elephant, Shiva on a bull and Brahma on a swan. Keep an eye out for the image of drunken revellers, in particular one lady being propped up by her husband. There's also original colour on the ceiling;

the divots on the floor at the cave's entrance were used as paint palettes.

Dedicated to Jainism, **cave four** is the smallest of the set and dates between the 7th and 8th centuries. The pillars, with their roaring *yalis,* are similar to the other caves. The right wall has an image of Suparshvanatha (the seventh Jain *tirthankar*) surrounded by 24 Jain *tirthankars*. The inner sanctum contains an image of Adinath, the first Jain *tirthankar*.

Other Sights HISTORIC SITES

Badami's caves overlook the 5th-century **Agastyatirtha Tank** and the waterside **Bhutanatha temples**. On the other side of the tank is an **archaeological museum** (admission ₹5; ⏲9am-5pm Sat-Thu), which houses superb examples of local sculpture, including a remarkably explicit Lajja-Gauri image of a fertility cult that once flourished in the area. The stairway behind the museum climbs through a sandstone chasm and fortified gateways to reach the ruins of the **North Fort**.

Activities

The bluffs and the horseshoe-shaped red sandstone cliff of Badami offer some great low-altitude climbing. For more information, visit www.indiaclimb.com.

Sleeping & Eating

Station Rd, Badami's main street, has several hotels and restaurants.

Mookambika Deluxe HOTEL $

(☎220067; Station Rd; d from ₹750, with AC ₹1650; ❄) Faux antique lampshades hang in the corridors of this friendly hotel, leading to comfy rooms done up in matte orange and green. Staff are a good source of travel info.

Hotel New Satkar HOTEL $

(☎220417; Station Rd; d with/without AC ₹1000/600; ❄) This once dive hotel now has decent budget rooms, but prices have tripled.

Hotel Mayura Chalukya HOTEL $$

(☎220046; Ramdurg Rd; d from ₹990, with AC ₹1600; ❄) A government issue buried behind civic offices away from the bustle, this renovated hotel has large and clean (though featureless) rooms. There's a decent restaurant serving Indian staples.

Hotel Badami Court HOTEL $$$

(☎220231; badamicourt@bsnl.in; Station Rd; d incl breakfast from ₹4403; ❄≋) This luxury hotel sits amid a pastoral countryside 2km from town. Rooms are more functional than plush. Nonguests can use the pool for ₹150.

Banashree INDIAN $

(Station Rd; mains ₹60-90; ⏲6.30am-10.30pm) The awesome North Indian thalis (₹80) at this busy and popular eatery in front of Hotel Rajsangam are tasty to the last morsel.

Golden Caves Cuisine MULTICUISINE $

(Station Rd; mains ₹55-100; ⏲8.30am-5pm & 7.30-11.30pm) A shabby place that produces good North and South Indian fare, and has a pleasant outdoor area that's perfect for a beer on a balmy evening.

Information

The **KSTDC tourist office** (☎220414; Ramdurg Rd; ⏲10am-5.30pm Mon-Sat), adjoining Hotel Mayura Chalukya, has a brochures on Badami, but otherwise is not useful.

SBI and Axis have ATMs on the main road.

Internet is available at **Hotel Rajsangam** (Station Rd; per hr ₹20) in the town centre.

Getting There & Away

Buses regularly shuffle off from Badami's bus stand on Station Rd to Kerur (₹20, 45 minutes), which has connections to Bijapur and Hubli. Three buses go direct to Hospet (₹180, six hours).

By train, the 7.30am Bijapur Express runs to Bijapur (sleeper/2nd class ₹120/39, 3½ hours), while the 11am Hubli Express goes to Hubli (2nd class ₹120, 3½ hours). For Bengaluru, take the 8pm Gol Gumbaz Express (2nd class ₹244, 13 hours).

Getting Around

Frequent, on-time local buses make sightseeing in the area quite affordable. You can visit Aihole and Pattadakal in a day from Badami if you get moving early. Start with Aihole (₹37, one hour) departing at 7.45am, then move to Pattadakal (₹15, 30 minutes), and finally return to Badami (₹18, one hour). The last bus from Pattadakal to Badami is at 5pm. Take food with you.

Taxis/autorickshaws cost around ₹1000/600 for a day trip to Pattadakal, Aihole and nearby Mahakuta. Badami's hotels can arrange taxis.

Around Badami

There's no accommodation or restaurants at either Pattadakal or Aihole.

Pattadakal

A secondary capital of the Badami Chalukyas, Pattadakal is known for its group of **temples** (Indian/foreigner ₹10/250, video camera ₹25; ⏲6am-6pm), which are collectively a World Heritage Site. Barring a few temples that date back to the 3rd century AD, most others in the group were built during the 7th and 8th centuries AD. Historians believe Pattadakal served as an important trial ground for the development of South Indian temple architecture. A guide here costs about ₹250.

Two main types of temple towers were tried out here. Curvilinear towers top the Kadasiddeshwra, Jambulinga and Galaganatha temples, while square roofs and receding tiers are used in the Mallikarjuna, Sangameshwara and Virupaksha temples.

The main **Virupaksha Temple** is a massive structure, its columns covered with intricate carvings depicting episodes from the Ramayana and Mahabharata. A giant stone sculpture of Nandi sits to the temple's east. The **Mallikarjuna Temple**, next to the Virupaksha Temple, is almost identical in design. About 500m south of the main enclosure is the Jain **Papanatha Temple**, its entrance flanked by elephant sculptures. The temple complex also serves as the backdrop to the annual **Classical Dance Festival** (Pattadakal; ⏲Jan/Feb), held between January and February.

Pattadakal is 20km from Badami, with buses (₹18) departing every 30 minutes until about 5pm. There are two buses to Aihole (₹15), 13 km away, at 8am and 2.30pm.

Aihole

Some 100 temples, built between the 4th and 6th centuries AD, speck the ancient Chalukyan regional capital of Aihole (*ay-ho-leh*). Most, however, are either in ruins or engulfed by the modern village. Aihole documents the embryonic stage of South Indian Hindu architecture, from the earliest simple shrines, such as the most ancient Ladkhan Temple, to the later and more complex buildings, such as the Meguti Temple.

The most impressive of them all is the 7th-century **Durga Temple** (Indian/foreigner ₹5/100, camera ₹25; ⏲8am-6pm), notable for its semicircular apse (inspired by Buddhist architecture) and the remains of the curvilinear *sikhara* (temple spire). The interiors house intricate stone carvings. The small **museum** (admission ₹5; ⏲9am-5pm Sat-Thu) behind the temple contains further examples of Chalukyan sculpture.

To the south of the Durga Temple are several other temple clusters, including early examples such as the Gandar, Ladkhan, Kontigudi and Hucchapaya groups – all pavilion type with slightly sloping roofs. About 600m to the southeast, on a low hillock, is the Jain **Meguti Temple**. Watch out for snakes if you're venturing up.

Aihole is about 40km from Badami and 13km from Pattadakal.

Bijapur

☎08352 / POP 326,360 / ELEV 593M

A fascinating open-air museum dating back to the Deccan's Islamic era, dusty Bijapur tells a glorious tale dating back some 600 years. Blessed with a heap of mosques, mausoleums, palaces and fortifications, it was the capital of the Adil Shahi kings from 1489 to 1686, and one of the five splinter states formed after the Islamic Bahmani kingdom broke up in 1482. Despite its strong Islamic character, Bijapur is also a centre for the Lingayat brand of Shaivism, which emphasises a single personalised god. The **Lingayat Siddeshwara Festival** runs for eight days in January/February.

Sights

There's a lot to see here, so you'll need to start early if you're going to cover it in a day.

★**Golgumbaz** MONUMENT

(Indian/foreigner ₹5/100, camera ₹25; ⏲6am-6pm) Set in tranquil gardens, the magnificent Golgumbaz is big enough to pull an optical illusion on you; despite the perfect engineering, you might just think it's ill-proportioned! Golgumbaz is actually a mausoleum, dating back to 1659, and houses the tombs of emperor Mohammed Adil Shah (r 1627–56), his two wives, his mistress (Rambha), one of his daughters and a grandson.

Octagonal seven-storey towers stand at each corner of the monument, which is capped by an enormous dome. An astounding 38m in diameter, it's said to be the largest dome in the world after St Peter's Basil-

Bijapur

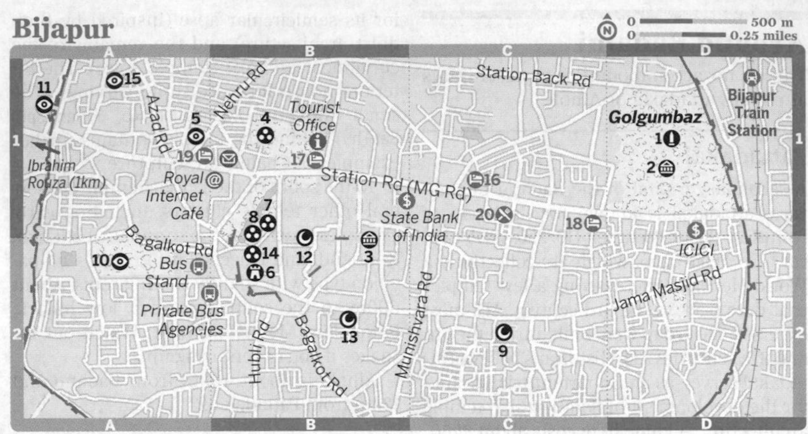

Bijapur

Top Sights
1 Golgumbaz ... D1

Sights
2 Archaeological Museum ... D1
3 Asar Mahal ... B2
4 Bara Kaman ... B1
5 Central Market ... A1
6 Citadel ... B2
7 Gagan Mahal ... B1
8 Jala Manzil ... B1
9 Jama Masjid ... C2
10 Jod Gumbad ... A2
11 Malik-e-Maidan ... A1
12 Mecca Masjid ... B2
13 Mihtar Mahal ... B2
14 Sat Manzil ... B2
15 Upli Buruj ... A1

Sleeping
Hotel Basava Residency ... (see 16)
16 Hotel Madhuvan International ... C1
17 Hotel Mayura Adil Shahi Annexe ... B1
18 Hotel Pearl ... C1
19 Hotel Tourist ... A1

Eating
Hotel Madhuvan International .. (see 16)
20 Kamat Restaurant ... C1
Swapna Lodge Restaurant ... (see 19)

ica in Rome. Climb the steep, narrow stairs up one of the towers to reach the 'whispering gallery' within the dome. An engineering marvel, its acoustics are such that if you whisper into the wall, a person on the opposite side of the gallery can hear you clearly. Unfortunately people like to test this out by hollering (its unnerving acoustics have the effect of a bad acid trip), so come early while most tourists are still snoozing. Be sure to take the stairs down from the back exit.

Set in the lawns fronting the monument is a fantastic **archaeological museum** (admission ₹5; ⏲10am-5pm Sat-Thu), with an excellent collection of artefacts, such as Persian carpets, china crockery, weapons, armours, scrolls and objects of daily use, dating back to Bijapur's heyday.

★ Ibrahim Rouza MONUMENT

(Indian/foreigner ₹5/100, video ₹25; ⏲6am-6pm) The beautiful Ibrahim Rouza is among the most elegant and finely proportioned Islamic monuments in India. Its tale is rather poignant: the monument was built by emperor Ibrahim Adil Shah II (r 1580–1627) as a future mausoleum for his queen, Taj Sultana. Ironically, he died before her, and was thus the first person to be rested there. Interred here with Ibrahim Adil Shah and his queen are his daughter, his two sons, and his mother, Haji Badi Sahiba.

Unlike the Golgumbaz, noted for its immense size, the emphasis here is on grace and architectural finery. Its 24m-high minarets are said to have inspired those of the Taj Mahal. For a tip (₹150 is fine), caretakers can show you around the monument, including the dark labyrinth around the catacomb where the actual graves are located.

Citadel FORT

FREE Surrounded by fortified walls and a wide moat, the citadel once contained the palaces, pleasure gardens and durbar (royal court) of the Adil Shahi kings. Now mainly in ruins, the most impressive of the remaining fragments is the colossal archway of **Gagan Mahal**, built by Ali Adil Shah I around 1561 as a dual-purpose royal residency and durbar hall. The gates here are locked, but someone will be on hand to let you in.

The ruins of Mohammed Adil Shah's seven-storey palace, the **Sat Manzil**, are nearby. Across the road stands the delicate **Jala Manzil**, once a water pavilion surrounded by secluded courts and gardens. On the other side of Station Rd (MG Rd) are the graceful arches of **Bara Kaman**, the ruined mausoleum of Ali Roza.

Central Market MARKET
(9am-9pm) A refreshing change in pace from historical ruins, this lively market is an explosion of colour and scents with flowers, spices and fresh produce on sale. It's a great mix of welcoming Muslim and Hindu people.

Jama Masjid MOSQUE
(Jama Masjid Rd; admission free; 9am-5.30pm) Constructed by Ali Adil Shah I (r 1557–80), the finely proportioned Jama Masjid has graceful arches, a fine dome and a vast inner courtyard with room for more than 2200 worshippers. You can take a silent walk through its assembly hall, which still retains some of the elaborate murals. Women should make sure to cover their heads and not wear revealing clothing.

Asar Mahal HISTORIC BUILDING
(admission free) Built by Mohammed Adil Shah in about 1646 to serve as a Hall of Justice, the Asar Mahal once housed two hairs from Prophet Mohammed's beard. The rooms on the upper storey are decorated with frescoes and a square tank graces the front. It's out of bounds for women.

Mecca Masjid MOSQUE
(admission free) On the eastern side of the citadel is the tiny, walled Mecca Masjid, thought to have been built in the early 17th century. Some speculate that this mosque, with high surrounding walls, may have been for women.

Upli Buruj HISTORIC SITE
(admission free) Upli Buruj is a 16th-century, 24m-high watchtower near the western walls of the city. An external flight of stairs leads to the top, where you'll find two hefty cannons and good views of other monuments around town.

Malik-e-Maidan HISTORIC SITE
(Monarch of the Plains) FREE Perched upon a platform is this beast of a cannon – over 4m long, almost 1.5m in diameter and estimated to weigh 55 tonnes. Cast in 1549, it was supposedly brought to Bijapur as a war trophy thanks to the efforts of 10 elephants, 400 oxen and hundreds of men!

Jod Gumbad HISTORIC SITE
FREE In the southwest of the city, off Bagalkot Rd, stand the twin Jod Gumbad tombs with handsome bulbous domes. An Adil Shahi general and his spiritual adviser, Abdul Razzaq Qadiri, are buried here.

Sleeping

Hotel Tourist HOTEL $
(250655; Station Rd; s/d ₹150/230) Bang in the middle of the bazaar, with scrawny (but clean) rooms. Service is apathetic, so bring that DIY manual along.

Hotel Mayura Adil Shahi Annexe HOTEL $
(250401; Station Rd; s/d from ₹519/577, with AC ₹831/923;) One of the better government hotels with massive rooms, balconies and a garden setting that lends an oasis feel. It has an appealing open-air restaurant that's a good place for a beer. Staff here are friendly.

Hotel Pearl HOTEL $$
(256002; www.hotelpearlbijapur.com; Station Rd; d with fan/AC from ₹936/1296;) Very good midrange hotel with clean and bright rooms around a central atrium, and conveniently located to Golgumbaz.

Hotel Madhuvan International HOTEL $$
(255571; Station Rd; d with fan/AC ₹988/1326;) Hidden down a lane off Station Rd, this pleasant hotel boasts lime-green walls, tinted windows, an amiable management and a lovely outdoor garden restaurant.

Hotel Basava Residency HOTEL $$
(243777; www.hotelbasavaresidency.com; Station Rd, Makund Nagar; s/d incl breakfast from ₹2160/2800;) The Basava Residency is a new boutique hotel found down a quiet street. It has spacious rooms with plasma TVs and patterned walls. It also has wi-fi in the lobby and a smart vegetarian restaurant.

Eating & Drinking

Kamat Restaurant SOUTH INDIAN $
(Station Rd; mains ₹60-80; 7am-10pm) Below Hotel Kanishka International, this popular joint serves diverse South Indian snacks and meals, including an awesome thali bursting with regional flavours.

Swapna Lodge Restaurant INDIAN $
(Station Rd; mains ₹90-160; noon-11pm) It's two floors up a dingy staircase next to Hotel Tourist, and has good grub, cold beer and a 1970s lounge feel. Its open-air terrace is a pleasant lounging spot, albeit a little noisy with maddening traffic below.

Hotel Madhuvan International INDIAN $
(Station Rd; mains ₹60-80; 9am-11am, noon-4pm & 7-11pm) Forget its motel-facade surrounds, this attractive outdoor garden restaurant does fantastic vegetarian dishes including eight different kinds of *dosa* and 14 paneer dishes. The downside is that there is no alcohol on offer.

Information

You'll find ATMs about town, including **SBI** (Station Rd) and **ICICI**. Cheap internet is at **Royal Internet Cafe** (Station Rd, below Hotel Pearl; per hr ₹30; 9.30am-9.30pm) near Golumbaz.

The **tourist office** (250359; Station Rd; 10am-5.30pm Mon-Sat) at Hotel Mayura Adil Shahi Annexe has a good brochure on Bijapur with useful map.

Getting There & Away

BUS

From the **bus stand** (251344), two evening buses at 10pm and 11pm head to Bidar (₹250, seven hours). Ordinary buses head frequently to Gulbarga (₹125, four hours) and Hubli (₹160, six hours). There are buses to Bengaluru (ordinary/sleeper ₹438/650, 12 hours, seven daily) via Hospet (₹180, five hours), Hyderabad (₹500, 11 hours, four daily) and Mumbai (₹500, 12 hours, eight daily) via Pune (₹380, 10 hours).

TRAIN

From Bijapur train station, express trains go to Sholapur (2nd class ₹80, 2½ hours, three daily), Bengaluru (sleeper/2AC ₹277/1190, 17 hours, three daily), 3pm service to Mumbai (2nd class ₹150; 12 hours, four weekly) and Hyderabad (sleeper ₹150, 14 hours, one daily) at 6pm. There are three trains to Badami (₹120).

Getting Around

Given the amount to see and distance to cover, ₹450 is a fair price to hire an autorickshaw for a day of sightseeing. Expect to pay ₹40 to get from the train station to the town centre, and ₹50 between Golgumbaz and Ibrahim Rouza.

Bidar

08482 / POP 211,944 / ELEV 664M

Tucked away in Karnataka's far northeastern corner, Bidar is a little gem that most travellers choose to ignore, and no one quite knows why. At most an afterthought on some itineraries, this old walled town – first the capital of the Bahmani kingdom (1428–87) and later the capital of the Barid Shahi dynasty – is drenched in history. That aside, it's home to some amazing ruins and monuments, including the colossal Bidar Fort, the largest in South India. Wallowing in neglect, Bidar sure commands more than the cursory attention it gets today. The old town has a conservative Islamic feel to it.

Sights

Bidar Fort FORT
(9am-5pm) FREE Keep aside a few hours for peacefully wandering around the remnants of this magnificent 15th-century fort. Sprawled across rolling hills 2km east of Udgir Rd, it was once the administrative capital of much of southern India. Surrounded by a triple moat hewn out of solid red rock and 5.5km of defensive walls (the second longest in India), the fort has a fairytale entrance that twists in an elaborate chicane through three gateways.

While entry to the fort is free, the catch is you'll need a guide (₹150 to ₹200) to unlock the gates to the most interesting ruins within the fort. These include the **Rangin Mahal** (Painted Palace), which sports elaborate tilework, teak pillars and panels with mother-of-pearl inlay, the **Solah Khamba Mosque** (Sixteen-Pillared Mosque) and **Tarkash Mahal** with exquistive Islamic inscriptions and wonderul roof-top views.

There's also a small **museum** in the former royal bath with local artefacts and crude wooden rifles. Clerks at the **archaeological office** beside the museum often double as guides.

Bahmani Tombs HISTORIC SITE

(⏲dawn-dusk) The huge domed tombs of the Bahmani kings in Ashtur, 3km east of Bidar, have a desolate, moody beauty that strikes a strange harmony with the rolling hills around them. These impressive mausoleums were built to house the remains of the sultans – their graves are still regularly draped with fresh satin and flowers – and are arranged in a long line along the edge of the road. The painted interior of Ahmad Shah Bahman's tomb is the most impressive, and is regularly prayed in.

About 500m prior to reaching the tombs, to the left of the road, is **Choukhandi** (admission free; ⏲dawn-dusk), the serene mausoleum of Sufi saint Syed Kirmani Baba, who travelled here from Persia during the golden age of the Bahmani empire. An uncanny air of calm hangs within the monument, and its polygonal courtyard houses rows of medieval graves, amid which women in hijab sit quietly and murmur inaudible prayers.

Khwaja Mahmud Gawan Madrasa RUINS, HISTORIC SITE

(admission free; ⏲dawn-dusk) Dominating the heart of the old town are the ruins of Khwaja Mahmud Gawan Madrasa, a college for advanced learning built in 1472 by Mahmud Gawan, then chief minister of the empire. It was later used as an armoury by Mughal emperor Aurangzeb, when a gunpowder explosion ripped the building in half. To get an idea of its former grandeur, check out the remnants of coloured tiles on the front gate and one of the minarets which still stands intact.

Sleeping & Eating

Hotel Mayura HOTEL $

(☎228142; Udgir Rd; d with fan/AC from ₹500/800; ❄) Smart and friendly, with cheerful and well-appointed rooms (though hard beds), this is the best hotel to camp at in Bidar. It's bang opposite the bus stand. Look out for its NBC-peacock symbol.

Hotel Mayura Barid Shahi HOTEL $

(☎221740; Udgir Rd; s/d ₹350/450, r with AC ₹785; ❄) Otherwise featureless with simple, minimalist rooms (service is OK, though), this place scores due to its central location. The lovely garden bar-restaurant to the rear brims over with joy and merriment every evening.

Jyothi Fort INDIAN $

(Bidar Fort; mains ₹45-90) Delightful outdoor restaurant with peaceful setting at the fort's entry. Tables are set up on the grass under sprawling banyan trees, while the kitchen is in an attractive stone-brick homestead-style building, and cooks up some delicious vegetarian meals. There's also seating in private stone chambers.

Information

You can find **ATMs** (Udgir Rd) and **internet** (per hr ₹ 20; ⏲9am-9pm) on the main road and opposite from Hotel Mayura Barid Shahi.

Getting There & Away

From the bus stand, frequent buses run to Gulbarga (₹110, three hours), which is connected to Mumbai and Bengaluru. Buses also go to Hyderabad (₹112, four hours), Bijapur (₹260, seven hours) and a 6am bus to Bengaluru (semideluxe/AC ₹700/900, 12 hours).

The train station, around 1km southwest of the bus stand, has services to Hyderabad (sleeper ₹120, five hours, three daily) and Bengaluru (sleeper ₹280, 17 hours, one daily).

Getting Around

Rent a very basic bicycle at **Sami Cycle Taxi** (Basveshwar Circle; per day ₹ 20; ⏲10am-10pm) against your proof of identity, or arrange a day tour in an autorickshaw for around ₹400.

Andhra Pradesh

Includes ➡

Best Places to Eat

- Hotel Shadab (p243)
- Shah Ghouse Cafe (p243)
- So. (p244)
- Southern Spice (p244)
- Dharani (p252)

Best Off the Beaten Track

- Maredumilli (p254)
- Guntupalli (p257)
- Sankaram (p253)
- Moula Ali Dargah (p236)
- Bhongir (p251)

Why Go?

Andhra Pradesh won't hit you over the head with its attractions. It doesn't have the flashiness of Rajasthan or the pride of Tamil Nadu; it doesn't brag. So when you come here – to see the ornate palaces, tombs and mosques of Hyderabad's bygone royal families, or to wander the deserted ruins of hilltop monasteries that once housed monks from across Asia – you might be the only traveller around. You might even be the only person around. And if the place is out of the way, as so many of Andhra's sights are, you might just feel like you've discovered it yourself.

So come, but be prepared to dig for the jewels; get ready to wend your way through paddy fields and 500-year-old urban markets, to climb towering smooth-granite hills, and to feel the liberating uncertainty of being off the tourist trail and in a wonderland of forgotten history.

When to Go

Hyderabad

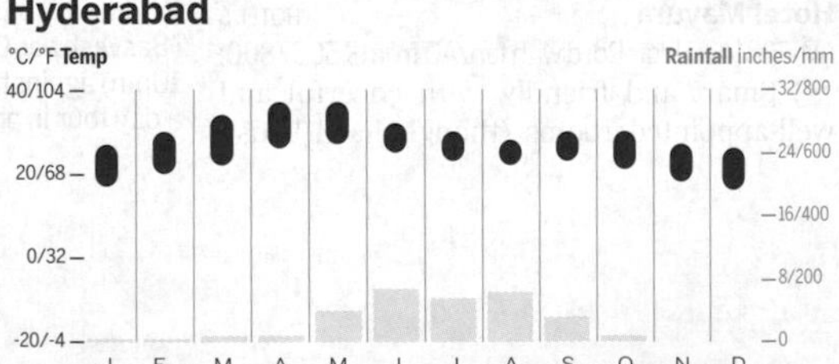

Dec–Jan Explore Hyderabad's sights in perfect 20–25°C weather.

Jun–July Join locals digging into *haleem*, a Ramzan (Ramadan) favourite.

Jun–Sep Rains make travel tough, but they also make for good surfing at Vizag beaches.

Food

Andhra Pradesh is known for its residents' love of good food, and Hyderabadis especially take great pride in their city's offerings. The state's cuisine has two major influences: The Mughals brought tasty biryanis, *haleem* (pounded, spiced wheat with goat or mutton) and kebabs. The Andhra style is vegetarian and famous across India for its delicious spiciness. If you're in Hyderabad during Ramadan (known locally as Ramzan), look out for the clay ovens called *bhattis*. You'll probably hear them before you see them. Men gather around, taking turns to vigorously pound *haleem* inside purpose-built structures. Come nightfall, the serious business of eating begins. The taste is worth the wait. In 2010, this love of the dish was taken a step further when 'Hyderabadi haleem' was given 'Geographical Indication' protection: it cannot be served by that name unless it meets strict quality guidelines.

DON'T MISS

The splendid architecture of **Hyderabad's** royal kingdoms – which ran from the 16th century to Indian independence – is what brings most visitors to the region. The Qutb Shahis produced some masterful architecture, including the stunning **Charminar**, **Golconda Fort** and their final resting place, the opulent **Qutb Shahi tombs**. The lavish nizam lifestyle is on display all over Hyderabad, especially at **Chowmahalla Palace**, **HEH the Nizam's Museum** and **Falaknuma Palace**, now an extravagant hotel. Before any of these wealthy princes came along, another prince held sway: the Buddha. Scenic monastic ruins at **Nagarjunakonda**, **Guntupalli** and **Sankaram** will bring you to a peaceful place.

Top State Festivals

- **Sankranti** (Jan, statewide) This important Telugu festival marks the end of harvest season. Kite-flying abounds, doorsteps are decorated with colourful *kolams* (rice-flour designs) and men adorn cattle with bells and fresh horn paint.
- **Brahmotsavam** (Sep/Oct, Tirumala, p256) This nine-day festival sees the Venkateshwara temple adorned in decorations. Special *pujas* and chariot processions are held, and it's an auspicious time for *darshan* (deity-viewing).
- **Muharram** (Oct/Nov; Hyderabad, p240) Muharram commemorates the martyrdom of Mohammed's grandson. Shiites wear black in mourning, and throngs gather at Badshahi Ashurkhana.
- **Visakha Utsav** (Dec/Jan, Visakhapatnam, p251) A celebration of all things Visakhapatnam, with classical and folk dance and music performances, some on the beach.

MAIN POINTS OF ENTRY

Hyderabad's Rajiv Gandhi International Airport, Nampally and Secunderabad train stations, and Mahatma Gandhi Bus Station (Imlibun) are the main arrival points.

Visakhapatnam has monthly ferries to Port Blair in the Andaman Islands.

Fast Facts

- **Population:** 84.7 million
- **Area:** 276,754 sq km
- **Capital:** Hyderabad
- **Main languages:** Telugu, Urdu, Hindi
- **Sleeping prices: $** below ₹1000, **$$** ₹1000 to ₹3000, **$$$** above ₹3000

Top Tip

Tea's gaining a foothold, but Andhra is traditionally coffee country. Skip the chai here and order the filter coffee when you see it.

Resources

- **APTDC** (www.aptdc.in)
- **Deccan Chronicle** (www.deccanchronicle.com)
- **Full Hyderabad** (www.fullhyderabad.com)
- **Zomato** (www.zomato.com)

Andhra Pradesh Highlights

1. Imagine a life of riches, pleasure gardens and poetry in **Hyderabad's** many palaces and royal structures (p233)

2. Soak up centuries-old ambience at Hyderabad's colourful **Laad Bazaar** (p235)

3. Absorb the meditative vibrations of monks past at **Sankaram** (p253), **Bavikonda** (p253) and **Thotlakonda** (p253), and **Guntupalli** (p257), destinations on a 2300-year-old monastic trail

4. Find devotion you didn't know you had alongside thousands of Hindu pilgrims at **Tirumala** (p256)

5. Enjoy the views as your train chugs through the spectacular Eastern Ghats to **Araku** (p254)

6. Get hypnotised by the lush intricacy and colours of *kalamkari* paintings in **Sri Kalahasti** (p258)

7. Learn about Andhra's rich ethnic diversity at tribal museums in **Hyderabad** (p237) and **Araku** (p254)

History

From the 3rd century BC the Satavahana empire, also known as the Andhras, reigned throughout the Deccan plateau. It evolved from the Andhra people, whose presence in southern India may date back to 1000 BC. Buddha's teaching took root here early on, and the Andhras fully embraced it, building huge edifices in its honour. In the coming centuries, the Andhras would develop a flourishing civilisation that extended from the west to the east coast of South India.

From the 7th to the 10th century, the Chalukyas ruled the area, establishing their Dravidian style of architecture, especially along the coast. The Chalukya and Chola dynasties merged in the 11th century to be overthrown by the Kakatiyas, who introduced pillared temples into South Indian religious architecture. The Vijayanagars then rose to become one of the most powerful empires in India.

By the 16th century the Islamic Qutb Shahi dynasty held the city of Hyderabad, but in 1687 was supplanted by Aurangzeb's Mughal empire. In the 18th century the post-Mughal rulers in Hyderabad, known as nizams, retained relative control as the British and French vied for trade, though their power gradually weakened. The region reluctantly became part of independent India in 1947, and in 1956 the state of Andhra Pradesh, an amalgamation of Telugu-speaking areas plus the predominantly Urdu-speaking capital, was created.

Telangana, one of the three main regions that combined to become Andhra Pradesh, is still being fought over: a movement to create a separate state got traction in 2009 when the split was approved by the federal government. But the new state's formation was shelved following protests from Andhra's coastal and northeastern regions. The issue is still being viciously debated.

Hyderabad

040 / POP 6.81 MILLION

Hyderabad, City of Pearls, is like an elderly, impeccably dressed princess with really faded, really expensive jewellery. Once the seat of the powerful and wealthy Qutb Shahi and Asaf Jahi dynasties, the city has seen centuries of great prosperity and innovation. Today, the 'Old City' is full of centuries-old Islamic monuments and even older charms. In fact, the whole city is laced with architectural gems: ornate tombs, mosques, palaces and homes from the past – some weathered and enchanting, others recently restored and gleaming – are peppered across town.

The 1990s saw the rise of Hyderabad's west side (the aged princess's fun, stylish granddaughter) and the emergence of a new decadence. 'Cyberabad', with Bengaluru (Bangalore) and Pune, is the seat of India's mighty software dynasty and has created a culture of good food and posh lounges for the city's new royalty.

Secunderabad, north of the Hussain Sagar, is the former British cantonment, now useful to travelers mainly for its huge train station.

Traffic is a problem here: keep in mind that even short distances can take a long time to cover.

History

Hyderabad owes its existence to a water shortage at Golconda in the late 16th century, when the reigning Qutb Shahis were forced to abandon Golconda Fort. They relocated to the banks of the Musi River. The new city of Hyderabad was established, with the brand-new Charminar as its centrepiece.

In 1687 the city was overrun by the Mughal emperor Aurangzeb, and subsequent rulers of Hyderabad were viceroys installed by the Mughal administration in Delhi.

In 1724 the Hyderabad viceroy, Asaf Jah, took advantage of waning Mughal power and declared Hyderabad an independent state with himself as leader. The dynasty of the nizams of Hyderabad began, and the traditions of Islam flourished. Hyderabad became a focus for the arts, culture and learning, and the centre of Islamic India. Its abundance of rare gems and minerals – the world-famous Kohinoor diamond is from here – furnished the nizams with enormous wealth. (William Dalrymple's *White Mughals* is a fascinating portrait of the city at this time.)

When Independence came in 1947, the then-nizam of Hyderabad, Osman Ali Khan, considered amalgamation with Pakistan, then opted for sovereignty. Tensions between Muslims and Hindus increased, however, and military intervention saw Hyderabad join the Indian union in 1948.

The city continues to fall victim to tensions and violence: several bombings in 2007, including at Mecca Masjid, killed 55 people, and two bombs in market areas

Hyderabad

ANDHRA PRADESH HYDERABAD

killed at least 16 commuters and shoppers in 2013. Anger over plans to expand a Hindu temple on the side of Charminar, the city's iconic Islamic monument, resulted in injuries, cars set on fire, and a police blockade of the old city for several days in late 2012.

Sights

★Charminar MONUMENT, MARKET

(Map p243; Indian/foreigner ₹5/100; 9am-5pm) Hyderabad's principal landmark was built by Mohammed Quli Qutb Shah in 1591 to commemorate the founding of Hyderabad and the end of epidemics caused by Golconda's water shortage. The dramatic four-column, 56m-high structure has four arches facing the cardinal points. Minarets sit atop each column. The 2nd floor, home to Hyderabad's oldest mosque, and upper columns are not open to the public. The structure is illuminated from 7pm to 9pm.

The crowded lanes around the Charminar – the neighbourhood is also known as Charminar – are the perfect place to get lost, with sidewalks full of everything from perfumes to kitchen implements to coconuts. Skilled wanderers may find the bird market, or the workshops where *varakh* (silver foil) is pounded out for use in sweets. **Laad Bazaar** (Map p243), west of the monument, is known across southern India as the last word in wedding saris, jewels and bangles, and the area is also the centre of India's pearl trade: some great deals can be had – if you know your stuff.

★Golconda Fort FORT

(Indian/foreigner ₹5/100, sound-and-light show adult/child ₹50/30; ⌚9am-5pm, English-language sound-and-light show 6.30pm Nov-Feb, 7pm Mar-Oct) Although most of this 16th-century fortress dates from the time of the Qutb Shah kings, its origins as a mud fort have been traced to the earlier reigns of the Yadavas and Kakatiyas.

Golconda was the capital of the eponymous independent state for nearly 80 years; in 1590, Sultan Mohammed Quli Qutb Shah abandoned the fort and moved to the new city of Hyderabad.

The citadel is built on a 120m-high granite hill and surrounded by crenellated ramparts constructed from large masonry blocks. Outside the citadel stands another crenellated rampart, with a perimeter of 11km, and yet another wall beyond this. The massive gates were studded with iron spikes to obstruct war elephants.

Survival within the fort was also attributable to water and sound. A series of concealed glazed earthen pipes ensured a reliable water supply, while the ingenious acoustics guaranteed that even the smallest sound from the entrance would echo across the fort complex.

Naya Qila (new fort) is home to a magnificent 400-year-old **baobab tree** (*hatiyan ka jhad*: elephant tree), with a circumference of 27m, said to have been brought from Abyssinia by Arab traders. The crumbling rampart here has great views of the fort and tombs.

Guides charge a whopping ₹600 per 90-minute tour. Small guidebooks to the fort are also available. A **sound-and-light show** is held nightly.

Mornings are best for peace and quiet. The fort is about 12km from Abids; take bus 119 from Nampally station, or 66G or Setwin bus 66 from Charminar (one hour). Autorickshaw drivers charge ₹400 return, including waiting.

Chowmahalla Palace MUSEUM

(Map p243; www.chowmahalla.com; Indian/foreigner ₹40/150, camera ₹50; ⌚10am-5pm Sat-Thu) In their latest act of architectural showmanship, the nizam family has restored this dazzling palace – or, technically, four *(char)* palaces *(mahalla)*. Begun in 1750, it was expanded over the next 100 years, absorbing Persian, Indo-Saracenic, Rajasthani and European styles. The southern courtyard has one *mahal* with period rooms containing the nizams' over-the-top furniture; another *mahal* with an exhibit on life in the *zenana* (women's quarters) that includes bejewelled clothes, carpets and a bride palanquin; antique cars (one nizam allegedly used a Rolls Royce as a garbage can); and curiosities like elephant seats.

In the northern courtyard is the **Khilwat Mubarak**, a magnificent durbar hall where nizams held ceremonies under 19 enormous chandeliers of Belgian crystal. Today the hall houses exhibitions of photos, arms and clothing. Hung with curtains, the balcony over the main hall once served as seating for the women of the family, who attended all durbars in purdah.

Stop by the **Royal Photo Studio** on your way out to dress up like royalty and have your sepia-tone photo taken (₹100).

Qutb Shahi Tombs HISTORIC SITE

(adult/child ₹10/5, camera/video ₹20/100; ⌚9.30am-5.30pm) These graceful domed tombs sit serenely in landscaped gardens about 1.5km northwest of the Golconda Fort entrance. Seven of the nine Qutb Shahi rulers were buried here, as well as members of the royal family and respected citizens, from entertainers to doctors. You could easily spend half a day here taking photos and wandering in and out of the mausoleums. The upper level of Mohammed Quli's tomb, reached via a narrow staircase, has good views of the area. The Qutb Shahi Tombs **booklet** (₹20) is available at the ticket counter.

The tombs are an easy walk from the fort; alternatively, take bus 80S or 142K, or an autorickshaw (about ₹30). From town, take bus 142M from Nampally or Setwin bus 66 from Charminar.

Paigah Tombs HISTORIC SITE

(Santoshnagar; ⌚10am-5pm) FREE The aristocratic Paigah family, purportedly descendents of the second Caliph of Islam, were fierce loyalists of the nizams, serving as statespeople, philanthropists and generals under and alongside them. The Paigahs' necropolis, in a quiet neighbourhood 4km

STATE OF GOOD KARMA

In its typically understated way, Andhra Pradesh doesn't make much of its vast archaeological – and karmic – wealth. But the state is packed with impressive ruins of its rich Buddhist history. Only a few of Andhra's 150 stupas, monasteries, caves and other sites have been excavated, turning up rare relics of Buddha with offerings such as golden flowers.

They speak of a time when Andhra Pradesh – or Andhradesa – was a hotbed of Buddhist activity, when monks came from around the world to learn from some of the tradition's most renowned teachers, and when Indian monks set off for Sri Lanka and Southeast Asia via the Krishna and Godavari Rivers to spread Buddha's teachings.

Andhradesa's Buddhist culture, in which *sangha* (the community of monks and nuns), laity and statespeople all took part, lasted around 1500 years from the 6th century BC. There's no historical evidence for it, but some even say Buddha himself visited the area.

Andhradesa's first practitioners were likely disciples of Bavari, an ascetic who lived on the banks of the Godavari River and sent his followers north to bring back Buddha's teachings. But the dharma really took off in the 3rd century BC under Ashoka, who dispatched monks across his empire to teach and construct stupas enshrined with relics of the Buddha. (Being near these was thought to help progress on the path to enlightenment.)

Succeeding Ashoka, the Satavahanas and then Ikshvakus were also supportive. At their capital at Amaravathi, the Satavahanas adorned Ashoka's modest stupa with elegant decoration. They built monasteries across the Krishna Valley and exported the dharma through their sophisticated maritime network.

It was also during the Satavahana reign that Nagarjuna lived. Considered the progenitor of Mahayana Buddhism, the monk was equal parts logician, philosopher and meditator, and he wrote several ground-breaking works that shaped contemporary Buddhist thought. Other important monk-philosophers would emerge from the area in the following centuries, making Andhradesa a sort of Buddhist motherland of the South.

Today, the state's many sites are ripe for exploring; even in ruins, you can get a sense of how large some of the stupas were, how expansive the monastic complexes, and how the monks lived, sleeping in caves and fetching rainwater from stone-cut cisterns. Most of the sites have stunning views across seascapes and countryside.

The once-flourishing Buddhist complexes of Nagarjunakonda (p249) and Amaravathi (p256) have good infrastructure and helpful museums on-site. For more ambience and adventure, head to the area around Vijayawada for Guntupalli (p257) or Bhattiprolu, and near Visakhapatnam for Thotlakonda (p253) and Bavikonda (p253), Sankaram (p253), and Ramatheertham.

southeast of Charminar, is a small compound of exquisite mausoleums made of marble and lime stucco. The main complex contains 27 tombs with intricate inlay work, surrounded by delicately carved walls and canopies, stunning filigree screens with geometric patterning and, overhead, tall, graceful turrets. The tombs are down a small lane across from Owasi Hospital. Look for the Preston Junior College sign. *The Paigah Tombs* (₹20) booklet is sold at the AP State Museum, but not here.

Moula Ali Dargah SACRED SITE

The top of Moula Ali hill has spectacular views of the cityscape, cool breezes and a dargah with an ornate interior covered in thousands of tiny mirrors. The dargah is also filled, it is said, with healing blessings. It all started one night in 1578, when an ill member of the Qutb Shahi court dreamt that Ali, the son-in-law of the Prophet Mohammed, visited the hill. The next day, not only was he cured, but Ali's handprints were found there, and the sultan immediately built a dargah over the prints and a mosque. Today, the hill is a pilgrimage site for the sick as well as one of the city's most dramatic sights, a smooth solid-rock mound towering 600m over the city (via 484 steps – avoid the midday heat).

The hill has an eastern approach, too, adjacent to the recently restored **mausoleum** of Mah Laqa Bai (1768–1824), a poet, courtesan and powerful member of the courts of the second and third nizams.

Moula Ali hill is about 10km northeast of Secunderabad. Frequent buses run from Secunderabad bus stand to the ECIL stop, as does bus 136H from Nampally. ECIL is 2km from the hill.

Salar Jung Museum MUSEUM

(Map p243; www.salarjungmuseum.in; Salar Jung Marg; Indian/foreigner ₹10/150; ⊙10am-5pm Sat-Thu) The huge and varied collection, dating back to the 1st century, was put together by Mir Yusaf Ali Khan (Salar Jung III), the grand vizier of the seventh nizam, Osman Ali Khan (r 1910–49). The 14,000 exhibits from every corner of the world include sculptures, wood carvings, devotional objects, Mughal miniature paintings, illuminated manuscripts, weaponry, toys and textiles. Cameras are not allowed. Avoid Sunday, when it's bedlam. From Abids, take bus 8 or 8A, which stop in front of the museum, or bus 7 to **Afzal Gunj bus stop** on the north side of the nearby Musi River bridge.

Just west of the bridge (on the north side) is the spectacular **Osmania General Hospital**, and, on the south, the **High Court** and **Government City College**, all built under the seventh nizam in the Indo-Saracenic style.

HEH The Nizam's Museum MUSEUM

(Purani Haveli; Map p243; adult/student ₹70/15, camera ₹150; ⊙10am-4.30pm Sat-Thu) The 16th-century Purani Haveli was home of the sixth nizam, Fath Jang Mahbub Ali Khan (r 1869–1911). He was rumoured to have never worn the same thing twice: hence the 72m-long, two-storey Burmese teak wardrobe. In the palace's former servants' quarters are personal effects of the seventh nizam, Osman Ali Khan, and gifts from his Silver Jubilee, lavish pieces that include an art deco silver letterbox collection. The museum's guides do an excellent job putting it all in context.

The rest of Purani Haveli is now a school, but you can wander around the grounds and peek in the administrative building, the nizam's former residence.

Badshahi Ashurkhana HISTORIC BUILDING

(Map p243) The 1594 Badshahi Ashurkhana (literally 'royal house of mourning') was one of the first structures built by the Qutb Shahs in the new city of Hyderabad. It's easy to miss, set back from the road in a corner of Charminar, but inside its walls are practically glowing with intricate, brightly-coloured tile mosaic. Look closely to see the faux-tile painting at the bottom: a 1908 flood destroyed the first two metres of tile. The Ashurkhana is packed during Muharram, as well as on Thursdays, when local Shiites gather to commemorate the martyrdom of Hussain Ibn Ali. You should remove your shoes and dress modestly (including a headscarf for women).

Nehru Centenary Tribal Museum MUSEUM

(Map p244; Masab Tank; Indian/foreigner ₹10/100; ⊙10.30am-5pm) Andhra Pradesh's 33 tribal groups, based mostly in the northeastern part of the state, comprise several million people. This museum, run by the government's Tribal Welfare Department, exhibits photographs, dioramas of village life, musical instruments and some exquisite Naikpod masks. It's basic, but you'll get a glimpse into the cultures of these fringe peoples. There's also an excellent **library** (library 1-2pm & 4-5pm).

AP State Museum MUSEUM

(Map p238; Public Gardens Rd, Nampally; admission ₹10, camera/video ₹100/500; ⊙10.30am-4.30pm Sat-Thu) This sprawling museum hosts a collection of important archaeological finds from the area, as well as an exhibit on Andhra's Buddhist history, with relics of Buddha himself. There are also Jain and bronze sculpture galleries, a decorative-arts gallery and a 4500-year-old Egyptian mummy.

The museum is in a fanciful building constructed in 1920 by the seventh nizam as a playhouse for one of his daughters. It, along with the gorgeous **Legislative Assembly** (Map p238) building nearby (also commissioned by the nizam), is floodlit at night.

Buddha Statue & Hussain Sagar MONUMENT, LAKE

(Map p238; boats adult/child ₹50/25) Set picturesquely on a plinth in the Hussain Sagar, a lake built by the Qutb Shahs, is one of the world's largest free-standing stone Buddha statues. It's an especially magnificent sight when illuminated at night.

Frequent **boats** make the 30-minute return trip to the statue from both **Eat Street** (Map p244; ⊙launches 2.30-8.15pm) and **Lumbini Park** (Map p238; admission ₹10; ⊙9am-9pm). It's a pleasant place to enjoy sunsets and the popular musical fountain and laser show. The Tankbund Rd promenade, on the eastern shore of Hussain Sagar, has great views of the statue.

Abids Area

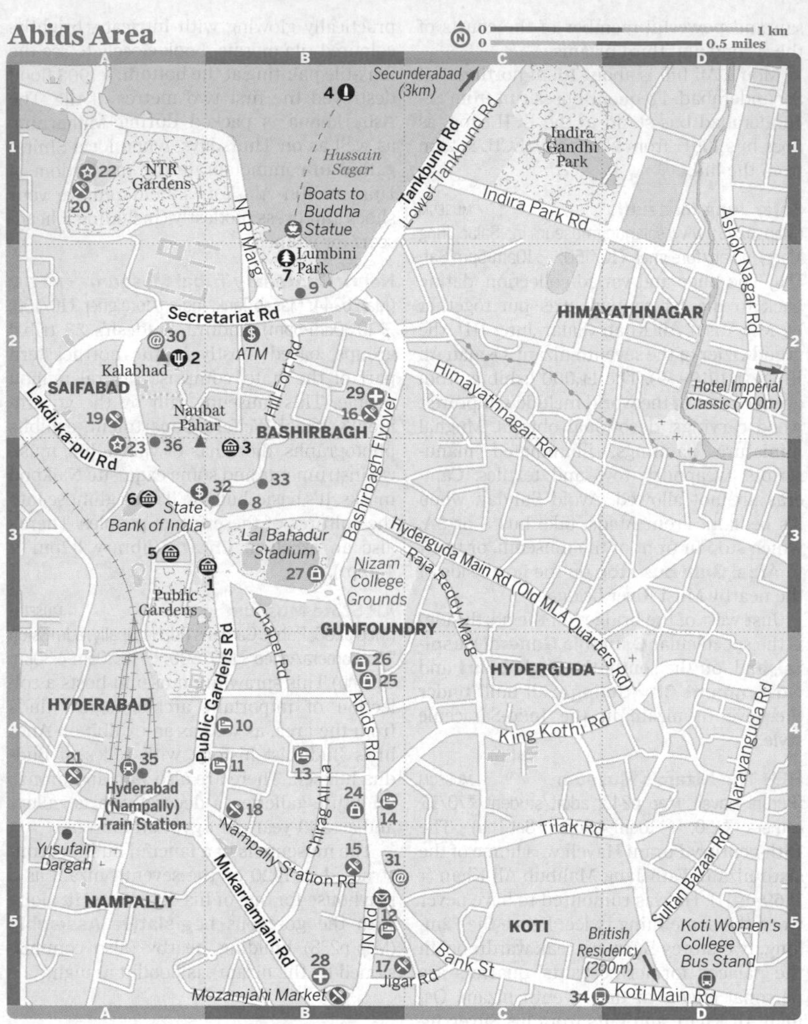

British Residency HISTORIC BUILDING
(☎24657813) This ornate home, built in 1803 by British Resident James Achilles Kirkpatrick, was featured in William Dalrymple's historical love story *White Mughals*. Kirkpatrick became enchanted by Mughal culture and eventually married Khair-un-Nissa, the teenage granddaughter of Hyderabad's prime minister. The Residency, now part of Koti Women's College, was in disrepair at research time but was about to undergo restoration. With its grand staircases and halls, it's fascinating to see, either way. Contact Principal Seetha for permission to visit.

Taramati Baradari HISTORIC BUILDING
(Ibrahimbagh; ⏲11.30am-8.30pm) According to legend, this elegant pavilion atop a hill 4km from Golconda Fort was built by Sultan Abdullah Qutb Shah for his courtesan, Taramati, whose singing and dancing performances the sultan watched from a perch at the fort. Autorickshaws charge ₹300 return from Golconda.

Birla Mandir HINDU TEMPLE
(Map p238; ⏲7am-noon & 2-9pm) The ethereal Birla Mandir, constructed of white Rajasthani marble in 1976, graces Kalabahad

Abids Area

(Black Mountain), one of two rocky hills overlooking the Hussain Sagar. Dedicated to Venkateshwara, the temple is a popular Hindu pilgrimage centre and affords magnificent views over the city, especially at sunset.

Birla Modern Art Gallery MUSEUM
(Map p238; www.birlasciencecentre.org; admission ₹40; ⏲10.30am-6pm) Formerly a so-so collection of local art, this museum was recently overhauled and now hosts a skilfully curated collection of modern and contemporary works – the best you'll see in South India. Look for paintings by superstars Jogen Chowdhury, Tyeb Mehta, Arpita Singh and Thota Vaikuntam.

Mecca Masjid MOSQUE
(Map p243; Shah Ali Banda Rd, Charminar; ⏲9am-5pm) This mosque is one of the world's largest, with space for 10,000 worshippers. Women are not allowed inside.

Several bricks embedded above the gate are made with soil from Mecca – hence the name. To the left of the mosque an enclosure contains the tombs of Nizam Ali Khan and his successors. Since the 2007 bomb blasts here, security is tight; no bags are allowed inside.

BM Birla Science Centre MUSEUM
(Map p238; www.birlasciencecentre.org; science museum/planetarium ₹35/40; ⏲museum 10.30am-8pm, planetarium shows 11.30am, 4pm & 6pm) The fun, retro Birla Science Centre comprises a museum of science, a planetarium, archaeology and fine-art exhibits and a 'dinosaurum'.

Volunteering

Blue Cross of Hyderabad VOLUNTEERING
(☎23544355; www.bluecrosshyd.in; Rd No 35, Jubilee Hills) This 2-acre shelter with 1000 animals rescues sick animals, and vaccinates and sterilises stray dogs. Volunteers can help in the shelter (grooming and feeding animals), in the adoption centre (walking and socialising dogs) or in the office.

Courses

Vipassana International Meditation Centre MEDITATION
(Dhamma Khetta; ☎24240290; www.khetta.dhamma.org; Nagarjuna Sagar Rd, Km12.6) Intensive 10-day meditation courses in peaceful grounds 20km outside the city. The centre is convenient but not as comfortable as the centre at Nagarjuna Sagar (p250). Apply

online. Bus 277 (from MGBS or Koti Women's College) runs to the centre; it's a 1km walk from the bus stop.

Tours

Andhra Pradesh Tourism Development Corporation TOURS
(APTDC; ☎24hr info 23450444; www.aptdc.in; ⊙7am-8pm) APTDC tours the city (₹300), Ramoji Film City (₹900), Nagarjuna Sagar (weekends, ₹500) and destinations across Andhra Pradesh. The Sound & Light tour (₹230) takes in Golconda Fort's sound-and-light show, but you get stuck in traffic. Reserve at the **Bashirbagh** (Map p238; ☎66746370; NSF Shakar Bhavan, opposite Police Control Room), **Secunderabad** (Map p241; ☎27893100; www.aptdc.in; Yatri Nivas Hotel, SP Rd) or **Tankbund Rd** (Map p238; ☎65581555) offices.

Heritage Walks WALKING TOUR
(☎9849728841; www.aptdc.in/heritage_walks; tours per person ₹50) These Sunday-morning tours were designed and are sometimes led by architect Madhu Vottery, whose *A Guide to Heritage of Hyderabad: The Natural and the Built* are part of a movement to preserve and illuminate Hyderabad's rich architectural heritage.

Society To Save Rocks WALKING TOUR
(☎23552923; www.saverocks.org; 1236 Rd No 60, Jubilee Hills) This NGO organises monthly walks through the Andhran landscape and its surreal-looking 2.5-billion-year-old boulders.

Abbas Tyabji HISTORIC TOUR
(☎9391010015; abbastyabji@gmail.com; 8hr tour incl transport ₹3500) Passionate local photojournalist Abbas Tyabji can take you to less touristy sights: historic caravan routes or natural areas in the city's outskirts to see toddy tappers.

Festivals & Events

Muharram MUSLIM
(⊙Oct/Nov) Muharram is the first month of the Islamic year and commemorates the martyrdom of Mohammed's grandson with mass mourning and all-night sermons. Hyderabad is known for its massive procession on the 10th day. which draws people from around the region.

Sankranti HINDU
(statewide; ⊙Jan) Hyderabad's skies fill with kites during this important Telugu harvest festival.

Sleeping

Gents can book a dorm bed (with/without air-con ₹100/60) at Mahatma Gandhi bus station (p248).

Hotel Suhail HOTEL $
(Map p238; ☎24610299; www.hotelsuhail.in; Troop Bazaar; s/d/tr from ₹475/650/945; ❄@) If all budget hotels were like the Suhail, we'd be much better off. Staff are friendly and there's cheap internet, while rooms are large, quiet and have balconies and hot water. It's tucked away on an alley behind the main post office and the Grand Hotel.

Hotel Rajmata HOTEL $
(Map p238; ☎66665555; royalrajmata@gmail.com; Public Gardens Rd; s/d ₹900/1012; ❄) Rajmata's

KITSCHABAD

Mixed in with Hyderabad's world-class sights are some attractions that err on the quirkier side.

Ramoji Film City (www.ramojifilmcity.com; adult/child from ₹600/500; ⊙9am-10pm) Andhra Pradesh's film industry, Tollywood, is massive, and its primary studio is fittingly huge. The 670-hectare Film City produces films and TV shows in Telugu, Tamil and Hindi, among others. The four-hour bus tour will take you through flimsy film sets and gaudy fountains, stopping for dance routines and stunt shows. Take bus 204A, 205/205A/205B, 206, 207 or 299 from Koti Women's College (one hour, 20km).

Health Museum (Map p238; Public Gardens Rd, Nampally; admission free; ⊙10.30am-5pm Sat-Thu) A throwback to a 1950s classroom, this place has a bizarre collection of medical and public-health paraphernalia, including a rather terrifying giant model of a crab louse.

Sudha Cars Museum (www.sudhacars.com; Bahadurpura; Indian/foreigner ₹40/150; ⊙9.30am-6.30pm) The genius work of Sudhakar includes cars in the shape of a computer, cricket bat, hamburger and condom, among other wacky designs. Poke your head into the workshop to see his latest project. The museum is east of Nehru Zoological Park.

Secunderabad

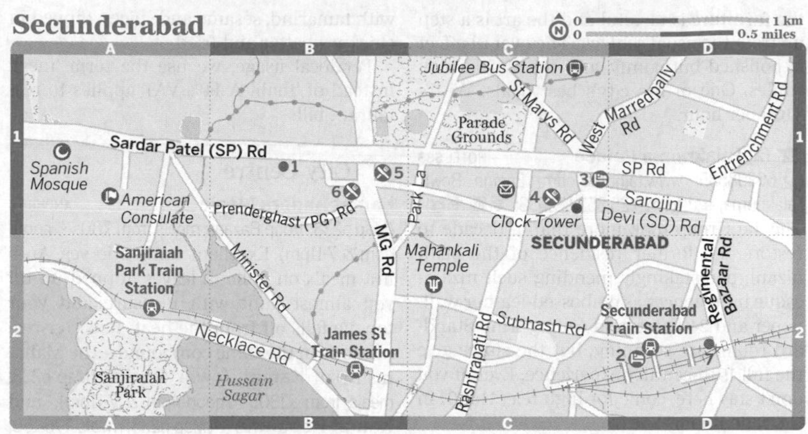

location is prime: across from Nampally station, but set back from the road, keeping things quiet. Standard rooms are aged but good-value; deluxe rooms (singles/doubles ₹2023/2248) are overpriced but fresh and roomy; some have views of the station. Popular with families.

YMCA HOSTEL $
(Map p241; ☎27806049; secunderabadymca@yahoo.co.in; SP Rd, Secunderabad; dm/s/d ₹125/500/650, s/d with shared bath ₹350/450; ❄) This cheery hostel in a quiet spot in Secunderabad has no-frills rooms that are clean-ish, some with balcony. It's near the clock tower.

Secunderabad Retiring Rooms RAILWAY RETIRING ROOM $
(Map p241; dm/s/d from ₹75/500/600; ❄) An excellent deal for late arrivals at Secunderabad, even with the 5am check-out.

★Taj Mahal Hotel HOTEL $$
(Map p238; ☎66120606; www.hoteltajmahalindia.com; Abids Rd; s/d with air-con from ₹1349/1855; ❄📶) This 1924 heritage building has a magnificent exterior, plants peppered about and some rooms with character (ie boudoirs, crystal-knobbed armoires and wood-beam ceilings). The hotel recently annexed a modern building next door and renovated, reducing the old timey feel. It's still the city's best value, with daily room cleaning, super-helpful reception, good wi-fi/broadband (₹100 per day) and a fabulous veg restaurant.

Hotel Imperial Classic HOTEL $$
(☎66137698/99; www.imperialclassic.in; RTC Cross Rd, Chikkadpally; s/d from ₹1012/1124; ❄)

Secunderabad

Activities, Courses & Tours
1 APTDC Secunderabad office B1

Sleeping
2 Secunderabad Retiring Rooms D2
3 YMCA C1

Eating
4 Kamat Hotel C1
5 Kamat Hotel B1
6 Paradise Persis Restaurant B1

Transport
7 Secunderabad Reservation Complex D2

In a commercial area removed from the usual tourist hoods, this simple place is keeping it real: friendly staff, reasonable prices, soundproofed windows and plain rooms that go more clean than character.

Golden Glory Guesthouse GUESTHOUSE $$
(Map p244; ☎23554765; www.goldengloryguesthouse.com; off Rd No 3, Banjara Hills; s/d incl breakfast from ₹900/1236, s without bathroom ₹393; ❄📶) This little hotel on a quiet residential street in ritzy Banjara Hills scores big on location. Rooms are modest, but clean and homey, and some have balconies. The downside: the welcome's not the warmest.

Hotel Harsha HOTEL $$
(Map p238; ☎23201188; www.hotelharsha.net; Public Gardens Rd; s/d incl breakfast from ₹1798/2023; ❄📶) Rooms don't have tons of character and can be noisy (ask for a rear-facing room) but they're bright, have fridges,

the furniture is tasteful and the art is a step up from the usual schlock. The overall effect is polished but comfy, and the staff are all smiles. One of the city's best deals. Wi-fi's ₹100 per hour.

★ **Taj Falaknuma Palace** HOTEL $$$
(☎66298585; www.tajhotels.com; Engine Bowli, Falaknuma; s/d from ₹25,852/27,538; ❄@📶🏊) The Taj Group took more than a decade to restore the former residence of the sixth nizam, painstakingly mending such nizamesque indulgences as embossed-leather wallpaper and 24-karat-gold ceiling trim. Standard rooms are stunning, but the suites give the full 19th-century experience. Even if you don't stay here, come for high tea (₹1500) in the Jade Room.

★ **Marigold** HOTEL $$$
(Map p244; ☎67363636; www.marigoldhotels.com; Greenlands Rd, Begumpet; s/d incl breakfast from ₹8430/9554; ❄@📶🏊) The new Marigold is as practical as it is stylish. Rooms are smart but not try-hard, with golds, neutrals and fresh flowers, while the lobby has vanishing-edge fountains, artful chandeliers and pod-like reservation counters. The rooftop pool was also a good idea. Rates listed are rack; they're often significantly lower.

GreenPark HOTEL $$$
(Map p244; ☎66515151; www.hotelgreenpark.com; Greenlands Rd, Begumpet; s/d incl breakfast from ₹6744/7868; ❄@📶) Don't bother going beyond the standard rooms here, which are comfy and classy, with sleek desks, bamboo flooring and flower petals in the bathroom. Good taste reigns (as does sensibleness, eg free wi-fi). The lobby, meanwhile, is a paragon of peace and gentle lighting, while smiley staff look on.

Mercure HOTEL $$$
(Map p238; ☎67122000; www.mercure.com; Chirag Ali Lane, Abids; s/d incl breakfast from ₹4496/5058; ❄@📶) The gargantuan black chandelier, mirrored elevators and jazz soundtrack in the Mercure's lobby give off a slight Manhattan vibe, while overlooking a busy (but very convenient) part of Abids. Rooms have stylish textiles and big glass showers. The hotel is veg and alcohol-free.

Eating

In the early evenings, look out for *mirchi bhajji* (chilli fritters), served at street stalls with tea. The Hyderabadi style is famous: chillis are stripped of their seeds, stuffed with tamarind, sesame and spices, dipped in chickpea batter and fried.

Per local usage, we use the term 'meal' instead of 'thali'. A 14% VAT applies to restaurant bills.

City Centre

Kamat Andhra Meals ANDHRA $
(Map p238; Troop Bazaar; meals from ₹80; ⏲noon-4pm & 7-11pm) Excellent authentic veg Andhra meals on banana leaves, topped up till you almost faint with pleasure and your tongue falls off from the heat. Its sister restaurants in the same compound – the Maharashtrian **Kamat Jowar Bhakri** (Map p238; meals from ₹130; ⏲noon-4pm & 7-11pm), and **Kamat Restaurant** (Map p238; meals ₹75-150; ⏲7am-10.30pm) – are also good. No relation to Kamat Hotel.

Kamat Hotel SOUTH INDIAN $
(Map p238; Nampally Station Rd; mains ₹60-120, meals ₹50-135; ⏲7am-11pm) Each Kamat is slightly different, but they're all cheap and good. There's also a **Kamat Hotel** (Map p241; SD Rd; mains ₹80-120; ⏲8am-10pm) near Secunderabad's Paradise Circle, another **Kamat** (Map p241; SD Rd, Secunderabad; mains ₹80-120; ⏲8am-10pm) near the clock tower, and **Kamat Hotel** (Map p238; meals ₹80-150, mains ₹125-175; ⏲8am-10pm) in Saifabad. Meals are reliably delish.

Subhan Bakery BAKERY $
(Map p238; www.subhanbakery.com; Yousufain Dargah Cross Rd, Nampally; baked goods ₹10-150; ⏲7am-11pm) The Osmania biscuit, so named because it was nizam Osman Ali Khan's favourite, is a Hyderabadi classic – a cardamom-inflected shortbread best eaten with tea – and Subhan's is famous. So is its *dil khush* – literally 'happy heart' – a pie filled with dried fruit that really will make your heart happy.

Eat Street FAST FOOD $
(Map p244; Necklace Rd; light meals from ₹40; ⏲7.30am-11pm) This kitschy food court has a Minerva Coffee Shop with excellent tiffins, a Café Coffee Day and fun fast food, as well as kids' rides, boat launches to the Buddha Statue and tables on a waterfront boardwalk.

G Pulla Reddy SWEETS $
(Map p238; www.gpullareddysweets.org; Nampally Station Rd, Abids; sweets from ₹10; ⏲8.30am-10pm) Sweets so good you'll die. Try the

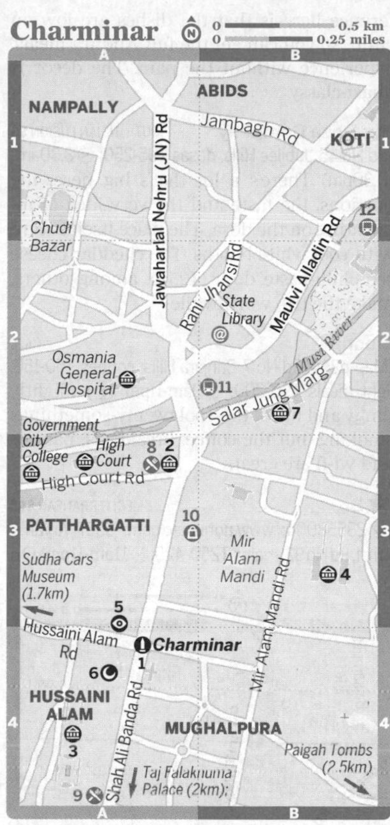

ariselu, a Telugu specialty made with rice flour, ghee and jaggery.

★Hotel Shadab HYDERABADI **$$**
(Map p243; High Court Rd, Charminar; mains ₹120-280; ⏲noon-midnight) One meal at Shadab and you'll be forever under its spell. This hopping restaurant is the capital of biryani, kebabs and mutton in all configurations and, during Ramzan (Ramadan), *haleem*. Packed with Old City families and good vibes.

★Shah Ghouse Cafe HYDERABADI **$$**
(Map p243; Shah Ali Banda Rd; mains ₹90-220; ⏲5am-midnight) During Ramzan, Hyderabadis line up for Shah Ghouse's famous *haleem*, but unusually, it also serves it outside of Ramzan. The biryani and other dishes are equally revered (and a bargain: 'half' portions feed two). Don't expect ambience: just good, hard-working, traditional food.

Charminar

Top Sights
1 Charminar A4

Sights
2 Badshahi Ashurkhana A3
3 Chowmahalla Palace A4
4 HEH The Nizam's Museum B3
5 Laad Bazaar A3
6 Mecca Masjid A4
7 Salar Jung Museum B2

Eating
8 Hotel Shadab A3
9 Shah Ghouse Cafe A4

Shopping
10 Hyderabad Perfumers A3

Transport
11 Afzal Gunj Bus Stop B2
12 Mahatma Gandhi Bus Station B1

Taj Mahal Hotel ANDHRA **$$**
(Map p238; Abids Rd; mains ₹120-180, meals from ₹130; ⏲7am-10.30pm) The Taj's restaurant is a beloved family spot for Andhra meals. You'll have a hard time finding a table at lunch, when an army of servers will bring you heap after heap of rice and refills of exquisite, burn-your-tongue-off veg dishes.

Paradise HYDERABADI **$$**
(Map p238; ☎66661138; www.paradisefoodcourt.com; NTR Gardens; mains ₹170-350; ⏲11.30am-11pm) Paradise is synonymous with biryani in these parts. **Paradise Secunderabad** (Map p241; cnr SD & MG Rds; mains ₹170-300; ⏲11.30am-11pm) is the mother ship, but this new location, part of the NTR Gardens complex with Prasads cinema (p246), is more fun.

Gufaa NORTH INDIAN **$$$**
(Map p238; Ohri's, Bashirbagh Rd; mains ₹250-350; ⏲12-3.30pm & 7-11pm) Gufaa has faux-rock walls, stars on the ceiling and Bollywood oldies playing in the background. And it serves Peshawari food. But somehow it works, and even the dhal here is special.

Waterfront MULTICUISINE **$$$**
(Map p244; ☎65278899; Necklace Rd; mains ₹175-575; ⏲noon-3.30pm & 6-11pm) The peaceful waterfront deck here has views of the Buddha Statue, Hussain Sagar and the city's twinkling lights. The tandoori, Chinese and Western food is adequate, but desserts include *qubani ka meetha*, a Hyderabadi speciality of stewed apricots and cream.

Banjara Hills & Jubilee Hills

24-Letter Mantra GROCERY $
(Map p244; www.24mantra.com; Rd No 12; ⏰9am-9pm) This tiny grocery shop has organic produce, snacks and juices, and is an organic-farming pioneer. Pick up spices, traditional soaps, beauty products and news about green happenings.

★Southern Spice SOUTH INDIAN $$
(Map p244; Rd No 3; mains ₹225-375; ⏰noon-3.30pm & 7-10.30pm) Southern Spice does a fine Andhra meal as well as specialities from all over the south. It's a good place to sample typical Andhra dishes, like *natu kodi iguru* ('country chicken') or *chapa pulusu*, a tasty, coconutty preparation of river fish.

Chutneys SOUTH INDIAN $$
(Map p244; Rd No 3; mains ₹170-215, meals ₹170; ⏰7am-11pm) Chutneys is famous for its South Indian thalis and tiffins. The difference here is that the dishes are low on chilli, so you can get the full 'Andhra meals' experience without the pain. The decor is quasi-classy.

Big Dosa Company SOUTH INDIAN FUSION $$
(Rd No 45, Jubilee Hills; dosas ₹95-250; ⏰8.30am-10.30pm) There's a lot that's big here: the portions, the taste and the very idea of innovating on the dosa. The place itself is tiny, with cool white booths. The cheddar cheese red-chilli-paste dosa (₹250), among others, make the trip worthwhile.

Mocha CAFE
(Map p244; Rd No 7, Banjara Hills; coffees ₹50-150, light meals ₹90-200; ⏰9am-11pm; 📶) Slightly dingy and full of too-cool twenty-somethings smoking, but the coffee, breakfasts, paninis and wi-fi are great.

★So. MEDITERRANEAN $$$
(☎23558004; www.notjustso.com; 550F Aryan's, 4th fl, Rd No 92; mains ₹250-425; ⏰11am-11pm) On

Banjara Hills

a quiet Jubilee Hills rooftop, with candles, loungy playlists and wooden tables surrounded by sugarcane and banana plants, So's the most atmospheric eating and drinking spot in town. *And* the Indian-inflected Mediterranean dishes are exquisite. Downstairs is the very popular **Little Italy** (☎23558001; www.littleitaly-india.com; Rd No 92, Jubilee Hills; mains ₹245-450; ⊙noon-3pm & 7-11pm), for pasta and wine.

Fusion 9 CONTINENTAL **$$$**

(Map p244; ☎65577722; www.fusion9.in; Rd No 1; mains ₹445-555; ⊙12.30-3.30pm & 7-11.30pm) Soft lighting and cosy decor set off Persian lamb kebabs on saffron rice (₹475) or Moroccan paneer steak with harissa-lemon couscous (₹445). One of the best international menus in town. Downstairs, **Deli 9** (Map p244; Rd No 1; snacks ₹35-100; ⊙9am-10.30pm; wi-fi) has quiches, cakes and wi-fi.

Barbeque Nation INDIAN **$$$**

(Map p244; ☎64566692; www.barbeque-nation.com; Rd No 1; veg/nonveg lunches ₹425/475, dinners ₹550/650; ⊙noon-3pm & 7-10.30pm) All-you-can-eat BBQ skewers in unpretentious surrounds. The menu changes often, but kebab options might include veg coconut or Goan prawn. Reserve on weekends; dinner discounts for early birds.

Drinking & Nightlife

Hyderabad's nightlife is limited by an 11.30pm curfew law. Some of the following charge covers (₹500 to ₹2000) on certain nights – for couples, that is: guys usually need a gal to enter.

★**Lamakaan** CAFE, THEATRE

(Map p244; www.lamakaan.com; off Rd No 1, Banjara Hills; teas & snacks ₹10-50; ⊙10am-10.30pm Tue-Sun; wi-fi) This 'noncommercial collective' is an open centre where artists stage plays, screen films, organize music-appreciation sessions and whatever else inspires. It's also a great cafe, with cheap tea and snacks, free wi-fi, artsy types collaborating on the leafy patio and a bulletin board with all of Hyderabad's most interesting possibilities. It's on a small lane off Rd No 1, north of GVK1 mall.

Beyond Coffee CAFE

(www.beyondcoffee.in; Rd No 36, Jubilee Hills, near Jubilee Checkpost; coffees ₹55-100, light meals ₹170-300; ⊙7am-10.30pm; wi-fi) Hyderabad has a zillion Baristas and Café Coffee Days, but the coffee here is in another league entirely, making it worth the trip. It also has rotating contemporary-art exhibitions, live music on Thursdays and free wi-fi.

Coco's BAR

(☎23540600; 217 Rd No 2, opp KBR Park, Banjara Hills; mains ₹145-295) The rooftop setting,

Banjara Hills

Sights
1 Nehru Centenary Tribal Museum C4

Activities, Courses & Tours
2 Eat Street Boating D2

Sleeping
3 Golden Glory Guesthouse B2
4 GreenPark C1
5 Marigold C1

Eating
6 24-Letter Mantra B3
7 Barbeque Nation C3
8 Chutneys C2
9 Deli 9 .... C3
10 Eat Street D2
Fusion 9 .... (see 9)
11 Southern Spice B2
12 Waterfront D2

Drinking & Nightlife
13 Aqua D2
14 Lamakaan C2
15 Mocha B3
16 Syn C3

Entertainment
Kismet .... (see 13)
17 Liquids Et Cetera C3

Shopping
18 Anokhi B3
19 Fabindia B3
Gandhi Handmade Papers .... (see 20)
20 Malkha C4
21 Suvasa B3

Information
22 Care Hospital Outpatient C3
23 Indiatourism C1

Transport
Boats to Buddha Statue .... (see 2)
24 Emirates C3
25 Etihad Airways C2
26 Qatar Airways C3
Thai Airways .... (see 9)

along with the cosy white-cushion bamboo couches, makes Coco's perfect for a cold drink on a balmy evening. There's live music daily, plus decent Indian and Continental dishes. (Reserve for dinner on weekends.)

Syn LOUNGE

(Map p244; Taj Deccan, Rd No 1, Banjara Hills; ⌚ Tue-Sun) Syn has sparkly black floors, blue lighting and futuristic white-vinyl seating, but it's still classy, in a space-age way. The outdoor seating is equally atmospheric. But it's the sushi, cocktails and weekend parties that have made it Hyderabad's new favourite scene.

Aqua BAR

(Map p244; www.theparkhotels.com/hyderabad; The Park, Raj Bhavan Rd, Somajiguda) The live music here goes well with the infinity pool, chaises longues, city views and late-night hookahs. Come in the early evening for a swim, a Thai starter and a sundowner, or on Saturdays, for the DJ pool party.

Kismet NIGHTCLUB

(Map p244; www.theparkhotels.com/hyderabad; The Park, Raj Bhavan Rd, Somajiguda; ⌚ Wed-Sun) Kismet is expensive and glamorous, but it also has macrame hanging chairs, chimneys leading to the illuminated glass-bottom pool overhead, passageways covered in mirrors and a secret smoking room (favoured by gals maintaining reputations). Friday's Bollywood night.

Liquids Et Cetera NIGHTCLUB

(Map p244; ☎ 66259907; www.liquidsetc.com; 5th fl, Bhaskar Plaza, Rd No 1, Banjara Hills) Regularly featured in the papers' society pages, Liquids doesn't bother with a sign; enter through the cellar.

☆ Entertainment

Ravindra Bharathi Theatre THEATRE

(Map p238; ☎ 23210295; www.ravindrabharathi.org; Public Gardens Rd) Regular music, dance and drama performances; check local papers.

Prasads Multiplex CINEMA

(Map p238; ☎ 23448888, booking 39895050; www.prasadz.com; NTR Gardens; tickets ₹150-250) Six theatres, one a monstrous Imax, plus shopping and food courts.

Shopping

Charminar's the most exciting place to shop: you'll find exquisite pearls, slippers, gold and fabrics alongside billions of bangles.

Hyderabad Perfumers PERFUMERY

(Map p243; Patthargatti; ⌚ 10am-8.30pm Mon-Sat) The family-run Hyderabad Perfumers, in business for four generations, can whip something up for you on the spot.

AA Husain & Co BOOKS

(Map p238; Abids Rd; ⌚ 10.30am-8.30pm Mon-Sat) A superbly curated collection of Indian and foreign authors, magically condensed into a tiny shop.

Malkha CLOTHING

(Map p244; www.malkha.in; Khadi Bhavan, Humayan Nagar, Masab Tank Rd, opposite NMDC; ⌚ 10.30am-7pm Mon-Sat) Unlike industrial cotton, Malkha cloth is made near the cotton fields, by hand and with natural dyes, which reduces strain to the cotton, the environment and on the rural job market. The result is gorgeous; pick up shawls or fabric at reasonable prices. Upstairs is **Gandhi Handmade Papers** (Map p244; Khadi Bhavan, Humayun Nagar; ⌚ 10.30am-7.30pm Mon-Sat), with papers, books and gifts.

Suvasa CLOTHING

(Map p244; www.suvasa.in; Rd No 12, Banjara Hills) Suvasa's block-printed kurtas (long shirt with a short/no collar), *patialas* (baggy, pleated pants) and *dupattas* are a step up – in styling, cut and prints – from the other mainstream boutiques. A Suvasa kurta plus some leggings equals your new favourite travel outfit.

Sheela's Arts & Crafts HANDICRAFTS

(Map p238; www.sheelashandicraftindia.com; No 17, Lal Bahadur Stadium; ⌚ 10am-8pm Mon-Sat) Tiny Sheela's is packed with handicrafts and souvenirs: some of it's great, some of it's schlock, but there's enough of it that you'll find stuff you like.

Lepakshi HANDICRAFTS

(Map p238; www.lepakshihandicrafts.gov.in; Gunfoundry; ⌚ 10am-8pm Mon-Sat) A great selection of Andhra crafts.

Bidri Crafts HANDICRAFTS

(Map p238; Abids Rd, Gunfoundry; ⌚ 11am-9pm Mon-Sat) Tiny shop selling bidriware at good prices.

Anokhi CLOTHING

(Map p244; www.anokhi.com; Rd No 10, Banjara Hills; ⌚ 10.30am-7.30pm Mon-Sat) Sophisticated clothes in hand-block prints.

Fabindia CLOTHING
(Map p244; www.fabindia.com; Rd No 9, Banjara Hills; ⌚11am-8.30pm) 🍃 Clothes and accessories in traditional artisanal fabrics.

Information

INTERNET ACCESS

Net World (Map p238; Taramandal Complex, Saifabad; per hr ₹15; ⌚10am-9pm)

Reliance Web World (Map p238; MPM Mall, Abids Circle; per 4hr ₹100; ⌚11am-9pm Mon-Sat, 12-7pm Sun)

State Library (Map p243; Digital Library section, 2nd fl, Maulvi Allaudin Rd; per hr ₹10; ⌚10.30am-5pm Mon-Sat) Check your email where Hyderabad's rare books and manuscripts (from as far back as 1650) are being digitised.

MEDIA

Good 'what's on' guides include **Channel 6** (₹25), *GO Hyderabad* and *City Info*. The juiciest is **Wow! Hyderabad** (www.wowhyderabad.com; ₹35). The *Hindu* is by far the best of the city's papers. The *Hyderabad Chronicle* insert in the *Deccan Chronicle* has info on happenings.

MEDICAL SERVICES

Care Hospital (www.carehospitals.com) Banjara Hills (Map p244; ☎30418888; Rd No 1); Banjara Hills Outpatient (Map p244; ☎39310444, 1800 1086666; 4th Lane); Nampally (Map p238; ☎30417777; Mukarramjahi Rd); Reputable hospital with a 24-hour pharmacy.

Mor Chemists (Map p238; ☎65547111; Bashirbagh Rd; ⌚9.30am-9.30pm Mon-Sat, 10am-2pm Sun) Helpful and well-stocked.

MONEY

The banks offer the best currency-exchange rates here. ATMs are everywhere.

State Bank of India (Map p238; HACA Bhavan, Saifabad; ⌚10.30am-4pm Mon-Fri)

POST

General Post Office (Map p238; Abids Circle; ⌚8am-8pm Mon-Sat, 10am-2pm Sun)

Secunderabad Post Office (Map p241; Rashtrapati Rd; ⌚8am-7pm Mon-Sat)

TOURIST INFORMATION

Indiatourism (Government of India; Map p244; ☎23409199; www.incredibleindia.org; Paryatak Bhavan, Tourism Plaza, Greenlands, Begumpet; ⌚9.30am-6pm Mon-Fri, to 1pm Sat) Very helpful, with information on Hyderabad, Andhra Pradesh and beyond.

Getting There & Away

AIR

Hyderabad's massive, modern **Rajiv Gandhi International Airport** (☎1800 4192008, 66546370; www.hyderabad.aero) is 22km southwest of the city in Shamshabad.

You'll get the best fares online or with a travel agent. Try **Neo Globe Tours & Travels** (Map p238; ☎66751786; Saifabad; ⌚10am-8pm Mon-Sat).

Most airline offices are open 9.30am to 5.30pm Monday to Friday, with a one-hour lunch break, and to 1.30pm Saturday.

Air India (Map p238; ☎23389744, airport 66605163; HACA Bhavan, Hill Fort Rd)

Emirates (Map p244; ☎33773377; Reliance Classic Building, Rd No 1, Banjara Hills)

Etihad Airways (Map p244; ☎1800 2090808; Rd No 1, Banjara Hills)

IndiGo (☎airport 24255052)

Jet Airways (Map p238; ☎39893333; Hill Fort Rd; ⌚9am-7pm Mon-Sat) Also handles bookings for JetKonnect.

Qatar Airways (Map p244; ☎7930616000, airport 66605121; Rd No 1, Banjara Hills)

Thai Airways (Map p244; ☎23333030, airport 66605022; Rd No 1, Banjara Hills)

MAJOR BUS ROUTES FROM HYDERABAD & SECUNDERABAD

BUS NO	ROUTE
65G, 66G	Charminar–Golconda, via Abids
87	Charminar–Nampally
2/2V, 8A/8U	Charminar–Secunderabad station
20D	Jubilee station–Nampally
142K	Koti–Golconda
142M	Nampally–Golconda
1P, 25	Secunderabad station–Jubilee station
1K, 1B, 3SS, 40	Secunderabad station–Koti
20P, 20V, 49, 49P	Secunderabad station–Nampally

BUSES FROM HYDERABAD

DESTINATION	FARE (₹)	DURATION (HR)	FREQUENCY (DAILY)
Bengaluru	640-905	10-12	20
Bidar	140	4½	half-hourly
Chennai	645-1010	12-14	4
Hospet	305-650	10	5
Mumbai	1065	15	1
Mysore	1215	14	3
Nagarjuna Sagar (Hill Station)	144	4	hourly
Tirupathi	550-1320	12	23
Vijayawada	265-390	6	half-hourly
Visakhapatnam	630-1500	14	18
Warangal	135	3½	frequent

BUS

Hyderabad's long-distance bus stations are mind-bogglingly efficient, and some of the **AP-SRTC** (Andhra Pradesh State Road Transport Corporation; ☎1800 2004599) air-con services are quite good. Visit www.apsrtc.co.in for timetables and fares; most long-distance services depart in the evening. When booking ahead, women should request seats up front as these are reserved for women.

Near Abids, **Mahatma Gandhi bus station** (Map p243; ☎23434268) (MGBS), more commonly known as Imlibun, has **advance booking offices** (MGBS; ☎23434269; ⏲8am-10pm). For trips to Karnataka, go with **KSRTC** (☎24656430; ⏲8am-9pm) near platform 30. See p248 for useful routes.

Secunderabad's **Jubilee bus station** (Map p241; ☎27802203) is smaller. Useful routes include the following:

Bengaluru (Volvo AC ₹895, 10 hours, three daily)
Mumbai ('express' ₹655, 14 hours, 2pm)
Tirupathi (express/Volvo AC ₹650/885, 14 hours, 7.30pm/7pm)
Visakhapatnam (Volvo AC ₹960, 12 hours, 5pm)

Private bus companies are on Nampally High Rd, near the train station.

TRAIN

Secunderabad, Hyderabad (also known as Nampally), and Kacheguda are Hyderabad's three major train stations. Most through trains stop at Kacheguda, which is convenient for Abids and Secunderabad. See p249 for key routes.

The **Nampally** (Map p238; ☎27829999) and **Secunderabad** (Rathifile; Map p241; Regimental Bazaar Rd, Secunderabad) reservation complexes have foreign-tourist-quota counters (bring passport and visa photocopies, along with originals). The Secunderabad reservation complex is around the corner from the station, next to the bus stand. For enquiries and PNR status, phone ☎139.

Getting Around

TO/FROM THE AIRPORT

The airport is about a 45-minute drive from town.

Bus

Frequent APSRTC buses (₹15 to ₹20) run from the airport to Jubilee and Imlibun stations.

APSRTC's new **Pushpak** air-conditioned services run to various points in the city, including Rd No 1 in Banjara Hills (₹150, half-hourly), Secretariat (₹200, hourly; convenient for Abids) and Secunderabad (₹200, twice hourly).

All buses stop running between 11pm and 3am.

Taxi

The **prepaid taxi booth** is inside the terminal; cabs to Abids and Banjara Hills cost ₹500.

Meru (☎44224422) and **Sky Cabs** (☎49494949) 'radio taxis' queue up outside arrivals and charge ₹18 per kilometre, ₹22.50 at night. The fare for Abids or Banjara Hills shouldn't exceed ₹700.

AUTORICKSHAW

Flag fall is ₹16 for the first kilometre, ₹9 for each additional kilometre. Between 10pm and 5am a 50% surcharge applies. Meters are often broken or uncalibrated and lots of drivers will not use them: so be prepared to negotiate.

BUS

Many local buses originate at **Koti bus stand** (Map p238; Turrebaz Khan Rd), so if you come here you might get a seat. The 'travel as you like' ticket (₹60), available from conductors, permits unlimited travel anywhere within the city on the day of purchase. *City Bus Route Guide* (₹20) is available at bookshops around Koti.

CAR

Arrange car hire through your hotel or with **Links Travels** (☎9348770007). At research time, the going rate for a non-aircon car and driver for sightseeing (eight hours/80km maximum) was ₹950.

TRAIN

MMTS trains (www.mmtstraintimings.in; ₹2-10) are convenient, particularly for the three main stations, but infrequent (every half-hour). There are two main lines: Hyderabad (Nampally) to Lingampalli (northwest of Banjara Hills) stops at Necklace Rd, Begumpet and Hitec City; the Falaknuma (south of Old City) to Begumpet line passes by Kacheguda and Secunderabad stations and joins the Hyderabad–Lingampalli line at Begumpet. Trains are labelled with start and end points, eg HF for Hyderabad–Falaknuma.

Nagarjunakonda

The Hill of Nagarjuna, 150km southeast of Hyderabad, is a peaceful island peppered with ancient Buddhist structures. From the 3rd century BC until the 4th century AD, the Krishna River valley was home to powerful empires that supported the sangha, including the Ikshvakus, whose capital was Nagarjunakonda. This area alone had some 30 monasteries.

The remains here were actually discovered in 1926 in the adjacent valley. In 1953, in anticipation of the new dam, which would flood the area with the **Nagarjuna Sagar** reservoir, an excavation was launched to unearth the area's many ruins: stupas, *viharas* (monasteries), *chaitya-grihas* (assembly halls with stupas) and *mandapas* (pillared pavilions), as well as some outstanding white-marble depictions of the Buddha's life. The finds were reassembled on Nagarjunakonda.

The thoughtfully laid-out **Nagarjunakonda Museum** (Indian/foreigner ₹5/100; ⌚8am-5pm, closed Fri) has Buddha statues and beautifully carved limestone slabs that once adorned stupas. The reassembled **monuments** are arranged around the hilltop outside.

Boats (₹90, one hour) depart for the island from Vijayapuri at 9.30am, 11.30am and 1.30pm, and stay for one hour. You'll want to take the morning launch out and the afternoon one back.

MAJOR TRAINS FROM HYDERABAD & SECUNDERABAD

DESTINATION	TRAIN NO & NAME	FARE (₹)	DURATION (HR)	DEPARTURE TIME & STATION
Bengaluru	12430 Rajdhani	1475/1037 (B)	12	6.50pm Secunderabad (Tue, Wed, Sat & Sun)
	12785 Bangalore Exp	274/742/1105 (A)	11½	7.05pm Kacheguda
Chennai	12604 Hyderabad–Chennai Exp	295/801/1200 (A)	12½	5.20pm Hyderabad
	12760 Charminar Exp	312/854/1285 (A)	14	6.30pm Hyderabad
Delhi	12723 Andhra Pradesh Exp	465/1298/2045 (A)	27	6.25am Hyderabad
	12429 Rajdhani	1789/2595 (B)	22	7.50am Secunderabad (Mon, Tue, Thu, Fri)
Kolkata	12704 Falaknuma Exp	442/1231/1925 (A)	26	4pm Secunderabad
Mumbai	12702 Hussainsagar Exp	313/883/1355 (A)	14½	2.45pm Hyderabad
	12220 Duranto Exp	892/1390 (B)	12	11.05pm Secunderabad (Tue, Fri)
Tirupathi	12734 Narayanadri Exp	284/772/1155 (A)	12	6.05pm Secunderabad
	12797 Venkatadri Exp	277/750/1115 (A)	11½	8.05pm Kacheguda
Visakhapatnam	12728 Godavari Exp	297/808/1210 (A)	13	5.15pm Hyderabad

Fares: (A) sleeper/3AC/2AC, (B) 3AC/2AC

Keeping Buddha's teachings alive in the region, **Dhamma Nagajjuna** (☎9440139329, 9348456780; www.nagajjuna.dhamma.org; Hill Colony) meditation centre offers free 10-day courses in charming flower-filled grounds overlooking Nagarjuna Sagar. Apply in advance. If you take a bus from Hyderabad, get down at Buddha Park.

At the convenient **Nagarjuna Resort** (☎08642242471; r without/with AC ₹674/1349; ❄), across the road from the boat launch, slightly shabby rooms have geysers and balconies with good views. Two kilometres up the hill from the bus stand is the government **Vijaya Vihar Haritha** (☎08680277362/3; r with AC on weekday/weekend from ₹1574/2810; ❄ ≋), with rooms overlooking the lake and APTDC on-site. Both hotels have restaurants.

The easiest way to visit Nagarjunakonda, other than with a private vehicle, is to go with APTDC (p240) (₹500) from Hyderabad; however, tours only run on weekends, when the site can be crowded.

To make your own way there from Hyderabad, take a bus to Hill Station/Nagarjuna Sagar (₹144, four hours, hourly); get down at Pylon and catch a ₹20 shared autorickshaw to Vijayapuri.

Warangal

☎0870 / POP 620,000

Warangal was the capital of the Kakatiya kingdom, which covered most of present-day Andhra Pradesh from the late 12th to early 14th centuries. The Hindu Kakatiyas were great builders and patrons of Telugu literature and arts, and during their reign the Chalukyan style of temple architecture reached its pinnacle.

Sights

Fort FORT

(Indian/foreigner ₹5/100; ⌚9am-6pm) Warangal's fort was a massive construction with three circular strongholds surrounded by a moat. Four paths with decorative gateways led to the Swayambhava, a huge Shiva temple. The gateways are still obvious, but most of the fort is in ruins. A **pillared hall** can be seen at the children's park across the street. From Warangal, take a bus (four daily) or autorickshaw (₹300 return). Admission includes entry to nearby **Kush Mahal**, a 16th-century royal hall.

1000-Pillared Temple HINDU TEMPLE

(⌚6am-6pm) Built in 1163, the 1000-Pillared Temple, on the slopes of Hanamkonda Hill, is a fine example of Chalukyan architecture in a leafy setting. Dedicated to Shiva, Vishnu and Surya, it has been carefully restored, with intricately carved pillars and an impressive black-granite Nandi (bull; Shiva's mount).

Down the hill and 3km to the right is the small **Siddheshwara Temple**. The lakeside **Bhadrakali Temple**, whose striking deity sits with a weapon in each of her eight hands, is on a hill between Hanamkonda and Warangal.

Sleeping & Eating

Vijaya Lodge HOTEL $

(☎2501222; Station Rd; s/d from ₹200/350) Close to the train station, the Vijaya is well organised with helpful staff and pin-striped hallways. Rooms are borderline dreary but workable.

Hotel Ashoka HOTEL $$

(☎2578491-94; hotelashoka_wgl@yahoo.co.in; Main Rd, Hanamkonda; r from ₹1349; ❄ @) Good-value rooms near the Hanamkonda bus stand and the 1000-Pillared Temple. Also in the compound are a restaurant, a bar-restaurant, a pub and the veg **Kanishka** (meals ₹90).

Sri Geetha Bhavan ANDHRA $

(Market Rd, Hanamkonda; mains ₹60-100; ⌚7am-11pm) Really good South Indian meals (₹75).

Information

ATMs and internet cafes are plentiful. **APTDC** (☎2571339; 1st fl, Hanamkonda-Kazhipet Rd, Hanamkonda; ⌚10.30am-5pm Mon-Sat), opposite Indian Oil, is helpful.

Getting There & Around

Frequent buses from **Hanamkonda bus stand** (☎9959226056) and hourly buses from **Warangal bus stand** (☎9959226057) go to Hyderabad (express/deluxe/luxury ₹120/130/140, four hours).

Warangal is a major rail junction, with several trains daily to the following (fares are sleeper/3AC/2AC) destinations:

Chennai (₹277/750/1115, 11 hours)
Delhi (₹442/1231/1925, 25 hours)
Hyderabad (₹140/292/640, three hours)
Vijayawada (₹144/328/610, four hours)

Shared autorickshaws (₹15) ply fixed routes around Warangal and Hanamkonda.

Around Warangal

Bhongir

Most Hyderabad–Warangal buses and trains stop at Bhongir, 50km from Hyderabad. It's worth jumping down for a couple of hours to climb the fantastical-looking 12th-century Chalukyan **hill fort** (admission ₹3; ⏲10am-5pm). Looking like a gargantuan stone egg, the smooth hill is mostly ringed by stairs. Legend has it that an (as-yet-undiscovered) underground tunnel leads from the fort to Golconda.

Palampet

About 65km northeast of Warangal, the stunning **Ramappa Temple** (⏲6am-6.30pm), built in 1234, is an attractive example of Kakatiya architecture. Its pillars are ornately carved and its eaves shelter fine statues of female forms. The Kakatiyas constructed a lake, **Ramappa Cheruvu**, 1km south, to serve as temple tank. It's popular with migrating birds. APTDC has a **guesthouse** (☎08715200200; r ₹950) here.

The easiest way to get here is by private car (₹1200), but frequent buses also run from Hanamkonda to Mulugu (₹40), then a further 13km to Palampet (₹15). The temple is about 500m from here.

Visakhapatnam

☎0891 / POP 1.73 MILLION

Visit Visakhapatnam – also called Vizag (*vie*-zag) – during the holiday season and you'll see domestic tourism in rare form: balloons, fairy floss (cotton candy) and, of course, weddings! But the crowds only enhance the area's kitschy coasts. The rundown boardwalk along Ramakrishna Beach has spunk, and nearby Rushikonda beach is Andhra's best.

The old beach-resort vibe exists despite the fact that Vizag is Andhra Pradesh's second-largest city, famous for shipbuilding and steel. It's big and dusty, but surrounded by little gems: sweet beaches, a gorgeous temple and, further out, the Araku Valley and several ancient Buddhist sites.

If you're here in December or January, seek out **Visakha Utsav**, the city's annual festival with events on the beach.

Yo! Vizag (₹25), available at bookshops, lists events.

Sights & Activities

Beaches BEACH

The long beaches of **Waltair** overlook the Bay of Bengal, with its mammoth ships and brightly-painted fishing boats. Its coastal **Beach Rd**, lined with parks, is great for long walks.

Kailasagiri Hill (Beach Rd; admission ₹5, cable car adult/child ₹60/30; ⏲11am-8.30pm) has a cable car with incredible views, playgrounds, a toy train and a gargantuan Shiva and Parvati. A Telugu-heritage museum is in the works.

Rushikonda, one of the nicest stretches of India's east coast, 10km north of town, is the best beach for swimming. Weekends are busy and festive. **Surfers** can rent decent boards from local surf pioneer, Melville, at **SAAP** (Sports Authority of Andhra Pradesh; ☎9848561052; Rushikonda; lessons/board rental ₹300/300). To avoid unwanted attention, gals should go for modest swim attire (T-shirts and shorts).

Submarine Museum MUSEUM

(Beach Rd; adult/child ₹40/20, camera ₹50; ⏲2-8.30pm Tue-Sat, 10am-12.30pm & 2-8.30pm Sun) The 91m-long Indian navy submarine *Kursura* saw battle in 1971 during the Liberation War (when India sided with East Pakistan in its struggle for independence). The museum is a fascinating look inside the vessel and its jumble of knobs, switches, gauges and dials.

Simhachalam Temple HINDU TEMPLE

(⏲6-10am & 4-6pm) Dedicated to Narasimha, an incarnation of Vishnu, this important 11th-century temple is atop Simhachalam (literally 'lion hill') 10km northwest of town. Bus 6A/H goes here.

Tours

The **APTDC** (www.aptdc.in) operates city tours (from ₹350) and several to Araku Valley from the RTC Complex (p253) and **train station** (☎2788821; ⏲6am-8.30pm).

Sleeping

Beach Rd is the place to stay, but it's low on inexpensive hotels.

Hotel Morya HOTEL $

(☎2731112; www.hotelmorya.com; Bowdara Rd; s/d from ₹438/618; ❄) Nothing special, but a good cheapie in town, close to the train station.

Railway Retiring Rooms RAILWAY RETIRING ROOM $
(dm/r ₹150/450, with air-con ₹225/750 ; ❄) Near the train station.

Haritha Hotel HOTEL $$
(☎2788824; Beach Rd, Appughar; r incl breakfast from ₹1236; ❄) This slightly tired APTDC hotel is near Kailasagiri Hill and across from the beach. The lowest-priced rooms (with no views) are only so-so; bump yourself up if you can.

Haritha Beach Resort HOTEL $$
(☎2788826; www.aptdc.in; Rushikonda; r with AC incl breakfast from ₹2136) The service is iffy, but the Haritha's location – high on a hill in Rushikonda – is sublime. Down the hill, **Vihar** (Rushikonda; mains ₹100-240; ⏲11am-10.30pm) is great for a beer or a meal: views from the terrace are insane.

Sai Priya Resort HOTEL $$
(☎2790333444; www.saipriyabeachresorts.com; cottages/r from ₹955/2136; ❄@≋) With a prime Rushikonda beach location, Sai Priya rests on its laurels. Some rooms have sea views and bamboo cottages are quaint, but everything here falls short of its potential – and checkout's 8am. Nonguests can use the **pool** (₹100).

Hotel Supreme HOTEL $$
(☎278247234; hotelsupreme@hotmail.co.in; Beach Rd, near Coastal Battery; s/d from ₹1461/1686; ❄) The rooms are more budget than the price would suggest, but the Supreme's spot across the street from the beach is worth a few bucks. Pricier rooms have sea views.

Park HOTEL $$$
(☎3045678; www.theparkhotels.com; Beach Rd; s/d from ₹7714/9918; ❄@≋) Vizag's best hotel is very elegant, very high-design, but also warm and inviting, with 6 acres of beachfront gardens. Rooms are cosy and sophisticated and have internet connectivity through the flatscreen TV.

Eating

At night snack stalls on Ramakrishna Beach are hopping.

Pastry, Coffee n' Conversation BAKERY $
(PCC; Dutt Island, Siripuram Junction; pastries ₹20-60, light meals ₹60-200; ⏲11am-10.30pm) This hangout spot for Vizag's hip young crowd is the place for coffee, pizza and a ridiculously good 'lava cake'.

New Andhra Hotel ANDHRA $
(Sree Kanya Lodge, Bowdara Rd; mains ₹50-125; ⏲11am-4pm & 7-10.30pm) An unassuming place with decent, spicy Andhra dishes; go for the meals (from ₹55) or biryani.

★ **Dharani** ANDHRA $$
(Daspalla Hotel, Suryabagh; mains ₹110-135; ⏲7am-3.30pm & 6.30-11.30pm) Words don't do justice to the super-deliciousness of the meals (₹98) at this family veg restaurant. The fabulous Daspalla Hotel has several other restaurants in the building too. Be sure to try the South Indian–style coffee: it's heavenly.

Masala INDIAN $$
(Signature Towers, 1st fl, Asilmetta; mains ₹100-190; ⏲11.30am-3.30pm & 7-10.30pm) Near Sampath Vinayaka Temple, Masala does out-of-this-world Andhra, tandoori and Chinese in a friendly family setting.

Sea Inn SEAFOOD $$
(Beach Rd, Rushikonda; mains ₹100-150; ⏲noon-3.30pm Tue-Sun) The chef here cooks Andhra-style seafood dishes the way her mom did, and serves it up in a simple dining room with bench seating. The restaurant is below street level and has no sign: look for the thatch roof and white gate 500m south of Sai Priya Resort.

Bamboo Bay ANDHRA $$$
(The Park, Beach Rd; mains ₹300-650; ⏲7-11pm) Excellent coastal Andhra, Chettinad and Mughlai food in gardens on the beach, framed by palms and magnolias. The less formal **Beach Shack** has drinks and grilled catches of the day.

Shopping

Tribes India HANDICRAFTS
(www.tribesindia.com; GCC, East Point Colony, Beach Rd; ⏲10.30am-8pm Mon-Sat) Unique textiles, artwork and crafts from tribal villages in Andhra and beyond.

Fabindia CLOTHING
(www.fabindia.com; 1st fl, Dutt Island, Siripuram Junction; ⏲11.30am-8.30pm) Traditional prints and modern cotton cuts for men and women.

Information

ATMs are everywhere. RTC Complex has several internet cafes (per hour ₹20).

Apollo Pharmacy (☎2788652; Siripuram Junction; ⏲24hr)

Thomas Cook (☎2588112; Eswar Plaza, Dwarakanagar; ⏰9am-6pm Mon-Sat) Near ICICI Bank.

ℹ Getting There & Around

You'll have to negotiate fares with autorickshaw drivers here. Most in-town rides are around ₹40. **Guide Tours & Travels** (☎9866265559, 2754477), reliable for car hire, is opposite the RTC Complex 'out gate'.

AIR

Take an autorickshaw (₹200), taxi (₹270) or bus 38 (₹10, 30 minutes) to Vizag's airport, 12km west of town. The arrivals hall has a prepaid taxi booth.

Nonstop flights run daily to Hyderabad, Chennai, Delhi, Bhubaneswar, Kolkota and Mumbai.

Air India (☎2746501, airport 2572521; LIC Bldg) The only airline with a town office.

BOAT

Boats depart monthly-ish for Port Blair in the Andaman Islands. Book for the 56-hour journey (₹2000 to ₹8000) at the **Shipping Office** (☎2565597, 9866073407; Av Bhanoji Row; ⏰9am-5pm Mon-Sat) in the port complex. Bring your passport.

BUS

Vizag's well-organised **RTC Complex** (☎9177101947) has frequent services to the following:

Hyderabad ('superluxury'/Volvo ₹629/987, 14/12 hours)

Rajahmundry (₹209, four hours)

Vijayawada ('superluxury'/Volvo ₹373/469, eight/seven hours)

TRAIN

The **train station** is on the western edge of town, near the port. The prepaid autorickshaw stand and cloak room are open 24 hours.

Vizag is on the main Kolkata–Chennai line; the 12841 Coromandel Express is the fastest in both directions.

Chennai (sleeper/3AC/2AC ₹312/854/1285, 12½-16 hours)

Kolkata (via Bhubaneswar; sleeper/3AC/2AC ₹333/914/1385, 14-16 hours)

Vijayawada (via Rajahmundry; sleeper/3AC/2AC ₹190/495/720, seven hours)

On Mondays and Fridays, the 18512 Visakhapatnam–Koraput Intercity Express heads near Chalikona, Onkadelli and Chandoori Sai in Odisha.

Around Visakhapatnam

Bheemunipatnam

This former Dutch settlement, 25km north of Vizag, is the oldest municipality in mainland India, with bizarre sculptures on the beach, an 1861 lighthouse, an interesting Dutch cemetery and Bheemli Beach, where local grommets surf on crude homemade boards. Catch bus 999 or 900 (₹22, 40 minutes) or a shared autorickshaw.

Bavikonda & Thotlakonda

The Vizag area's natural harbours have long been conducive to dropping anchor, which helped monks from Sri Lanka, China and Tibet come here to learn meditation. **Bavikonda** (⏰9am-5pm) and **Thotlakonda** (⏰8am-6pm) were popular hilltop monasteries on the coast that hosted up to 150 monks at a time – with the help of massive rainwater tanks and, at Thotlakonda, a natural spring.

The monasteries flourished from around the 3rd century BC to the 3rd century AD, and had votive stupas, congregation halls, *chaitya-grihas*, *viharas* and refectories. Today only the ruins of these monastic compounds remain, but they're impressive nonetheless, with a placid, almost magical, air and sea views to meditate on. Bavikonda and Thotlakonda are 14km and 16km, respectively, from Vizag on Bheemli Beach Rd. Vizag's autorickshaw drivers charge around ₹500 return from RTC Complex to see both.

Sankaram

Forty kilometres southwest of Vizag is this stunning **Buddhist complex** (⏰dawn-dusk), better known by the name of its two hills, Bojjannakonda and Lingalakonda. Used by monks from the 2nd to 9th centuries AD, the hills are covered with rock-cut caves, stupas, ruins of monastery structures and reliefs of Buddha that span the Theravada, Mahayana and Vajrayana periods. Bojjannakonda has a two-storey group of rock-cut caves flanked by *dwarapalakas* (doorkeepers) and containing a stupa and gorgeous carvings of Buddha. Atop the hill sit the ruins of a huge stupa and a monastery; you can still make out the individual cells where monks meditated. Lingalakonda is piled high with stupas, some of them enormous.

A private car from Vizag costs around ₹900. Or, take a frequent bus (₹32, 1½ hours) or train (₹30, one hour) to Anakapalle, 3km away, and then an autorickshaw (₹100 return including waiting).

Araku Valley

☎08936 / ELEV 975M

Andhra's best train ride is through the magnificent Eastern Ghats to the Araku Valley, 115km north of Vizag. The area is home to isolated tribal communities and a small **Museum of Habitat** (admission ₹10; ⏲8am-8pm) with exhibits on indigenous life.

The coffee from this area is excellent – mostly organic, with hints of berry and chocolate; pick up some at the roadside stands by the **Ananthagiri coffee plantations**, 28km from Araku. You can sample local coffee and chocolate-covered coffee beans at **Araku Valley Coffee House** (⏲8am-8pm), next to the tribal museum, which has a tiny coffee museum.

APTDC runs **tours** (from ₹550) from Vizag, which take in a performance of Dhimsa, a tribal dance, and the million-year-old limestone **Borra Caves** (adult/child ₹40/30, camera ₹25; ⏲10am-1pm & 2-5pm), 30km from Araku.

The most atmospheric place to stay is **Jungle Bells** (www.aptdc.in; Tyda; cottages incl breakfast from ₹1200; ❄), 45km from Araku, with cottages tucked away in woods. Book with APTDC (p251).

There are several hotels near the train station, including the unfriendly but well-maintained **Hotel Rajadhani** (☎249580; www.hotelrajadhani.com; d/tr from ₹700/900; ❄). APTDC's **Valley Resort** (☎249202; r incl breakfast from ₹1200; ❄) is closer to the town centre, such as it is. The train station has **retiring rooms** (₹225). The restaurant at **Hill Resort Mayuri** (☎249204; meals ₹100, cottages from ₹850; ❄) serves good Andhra meals.

The Kirandol passenger train (₹22, five hours) leaves Vizag at 6.50am and Araku at 3pm. It's a slow, spectacular ride; sit on the right-hand side coming out of Vizag for best views. For Jungle Bells, get off at Tyda station, 500m from the resort. Frequent buses (₹90, 4½ hours) leave Araku for Vizag every half-hour until 7pm.

Vijayawada

☎0866 / POP 1.05 MILLION

Vijayawada is a busy city and an important port, but it's also intersected by canals, lined with ghats and ringed by fields of rice and palm. The surrounding area is intensely lush and green.

Vijayawada is low on sights, but it has an important Durga temple and is considered by many to be the heart of Andhra culture and language. It's a good base for visiting the area's important Buddhist sites.

OFF THE BEATEN TRACK

MAREDUMILLI

A little **nature circuit** (☎088642449968; www.vanavihari.com; admission to all sites ₹25, guides per day ₹250, r & cottages ₹562-1124) has been set up in the village of Maredumilli by the local tribal community and AP's Forest Department. A guesthouse, with cottages in a woodsy setting and excellent meals (₹50), is at one end of a 16km road lined by eight lush natural sites, including: a 70-hectare coffee plantation with pepper vines, wild mango and orange trees, and great trekking; a medicinal-plant garden; two waterfalls tucked away in the forest; and a 260-hectare medicinal-plant conservation area, with walking trails, 203 plant species and 170 species of birds.

The sites have been developed mindfully, with natural materials, and it's easy to immerse yourself in the forest. Some trails require a guide, which the guesthouse can arrange; it also hires bicycles and can set up autorickshaw day hire (₹450).

The Maredumilli area is known for its 'bamboo chicken' – chicken roasted in a bamboo trunk. October to February is toddy season.

Maredumilli is about 80km from Rajahumundry, which is about halfway between Vijayawada and Visakhapatnam. From Rajahmundry, take any Bhadrachalam bus to Maredumilli (₹63, three hours, every two hours until 4pm). If you need to stay the night in Rajahmundry, **Akanksha Inn** (☎0883-2477775/6; akanksha.inn@gmail.com; Alcot Gardens, opp railway station, Rajahmundry; s/d with AC from ₹400/1000; ❄), across from the train station, will do fine.

Sights

Undavalli Cave Temples HISTORIC SITE, HINDU
(Indian/foreigner ₹5/100; ⏲9am-5pm) Seven kilometres southwest of Vijayawada, these stunning cave temples cut a fine silhouette against the palm trees and rice paddies. Shrines are dedicated to Brahma, Vishnu and Shiva, and one cave on the third level houses a huge reclining Vishnu. The caves, in their Hindu form, date to the 7th century, but they're thought to have been constructed for Buddhist monks 500 years earlier. Bus 301 (₹11, 20 minutes) goes here; autorickshaws ask ₹250 return.

Victoria Jubilee Museum MUSEUM
(MG Rd; Indian/foreigner ₹30/100, camera ₹3; ⏲10.30am-5pm Sat-Thu) The best part of this museum is the building itself, built in 1887 to honour Queen Victoria's coronation jubilee. The museum also has a small collection of art and arms, and a garden with temple sculptures from around the state.

Sleeping

Hotel Sripada HOTEL $
(☎6644222; hotelsripada@rediffmail.com; Gandhi Nagar; s/d from ₹913/1028; ❄) One of the only budget hotels in Vijayawada authorised to accept foreign guests, the Sripada has small but bright rooms, a decent restaurant and helpful staff. Near the train station.

Railway Retiring Rooms RAILWAY RETIRING ROOM $
(dm/s/d from ₹75/180/375; ❄) The train station's clean and spacious rooms are a great option.

Alankar Inn HOTEL $$
(www.alankarinn.com; Alankar Circle, Gandhi Nagar; s/d with AC from ₹1686/2248; ❄📶) The Alankar, new at the time of research, was still working out the kinks. Hopefully, they're sorted now, and the compact, semi-chic rooms and free wi-fi are all fulfilling their potential.

Hotel Golden Way HOTEL $$
(☎2576693; Purnanandapet; s/d incl breakfast from ₹1574/2019; ❄) A good midranger right near the train station.

Eating

★**Minerva Coffee Shop** INDIAN $
(Museum Rd; mains ₹75-170, meals ₹65-145; ⏲6.30am-11pm) Near Big Bazaar, this outpost of the fabulous Minerva chain has great North and South Indian cuisine, including top-notch dosas. A newer **Minerva** (MG Rd; mains ₹125-185; ⏲7am-11pm) serves similarly excellent food in airy, sophisticated surrounds.

Lotus Food City INDIAN $$
(www.lotusthefoodcity.com; Seethanagaram; mains ₹110-190; ⏲12.30pm-11pm) This APTDC food complex has a lovely spot on the Krishna River (over the Prakasam Barrage) where you can dine in or outdoors looking over the water.

Information

APTDC (☎2571393; MG Rd, opposite PWD Grounds; ⏲8am-8pm) Good for brochures.

Department of Tourism (☎2578880; train station; ⏲10.30am-5pm)

MagicNet (Swarnalok Complex, Eluru Rd; per hr ₹20; ⏲10am-10pm) Internet access.

Getting There & Around

BUS

Frequent bus services, most in the evening, run to the following destinations:

Amaravathi (ordinary/express ₹26/36, two hours)

Chennai (superluxury/Venella ₹453/1074, nine hours)

Hyderabad (express/Venella ₹197/630, seven/five hours)

Rajahmundry (express/superluxury ₹114/149, three hours)

Tirupathi (express/Indra ₹312/508, nine hours)

Visakhapatnam (express/Venella ₹281/895, nine hours)

TRAIN

Vijayawada is on the main Chennai–Kolkata and Chennai–Delhi railway lines. The Chennai–Kolkata 12842 Coromandal Express is quick. The **advance-booking office** (☎enquiry 2577775; ⏲8am-8pm Mon-Sat, till 2pm Sun) is in the basement. Fares below are for sleeper/3AC/2AC.

Chennai (₹214/564/830, seven hours)

Hyderabad (₹190/495/720, 6½ hours, 17 daily)

Kolkata (₹395/1093/1690, 20 hours)

Tirupathi (₹178/490/730, seven hours, 11 daily)

Warangal (₹144/359/640, three hours, 20 daily)

The train station has a prepaid autorickshaw stand.

Around Vijayawada

Eluru

Dhamma Vijaya MEDITATION
(Vipassana Meditation Centre; ☎9441449044, 08812225522; www.dhamma.org; Eluru-Chintalapudi Rd, Vijayarai) Intensive 10-day *vipassana* meditation courses are offered free of charge (donations are accepted) in lush palm- and cocoa-forested grounds; apply in advance. Buses depart Vijayawada for Eluru (₹50, 1½ hours, half-hourly, 64km), and Eluru for Vijayarai (₹15, 20 minutes, half-hourly). Call for details.

Amaravathi

Amaravathi was once the Andhran capital and a significant Buddhist centre. India's biggest **stupa** (Indian/foreigner ₹5/100; ⏲8am-6pm), measuring 30m high and 51m across, was constructed here in the 3rd century BC, when Emperor Ashoka sent monks south to spread Buddha's teaching. All that remains are a mound and some of the stones, but the nearby **museum** (admission ₹5; ⏲10am-5pm, closed Fri) has a small replica of the stupa, with its intricately carved pillars, marble-surfaced dome and carvings of scenes from Buddha's life. In the courtyard is a reconstruction of part of the surrounding gateway, which gives you an idea of the stupa's massive scale. It's worth the trip, but many of Amaravathi's best sculptures are in London's British Museum and Chennai's Government Museum.

About 1km down the road is the **Dhyana Buddha**, a 20m-high Buddha on the site where the Dalai Lama spoke in 2006.

Buses run from Vijayawada to Amaravathi half-hourly (ordinary/express ₹26/36, two hours), passing some lovely scenery.

Tirumala & Tirupathi

☎0877 / POP 287,000

The holy hill of **Tirumala** is, on any given day, filled with tens of thousands of blissed-out devotees, many of whom have endured long journeys to see the powerful **Lord Venkateshwara** here, at his home. It's one of India's most visited pilgrimage centres: 50,000 pilgrims come each day, and *darshan* runs 24/7. Temple staff alone number 14,000, and the efficient **Tirumala Tirupathi Devasthanams** (TTD; ☎2233333, 2277777; www.tirumala.org) brilliantly administers the crowds. As a result, although the throngs can be overwhelming, a sense of order, serenity and ease mostly prevails, and a trip to the Holy Hill can be fulfilling, even if you're not a pilgrim.

'It is believed that Lord Sri Venkateshwara enjoys festivals', according to the TTD. And so do his devotees: *darshan* queues during September/October's **Brahmotsavam** can run up to several kilometres, with up to 500,000 people visiting a day.

Tirupathi is the service town at the bottom of the hill, with hotels, restaurants and transport; a fleet of buses constantly ferries pilgrims the 18km up and down. You'll find most of your worldly needs around the Tirupathi bus station (TP Area) and, about 500m away, the train station.

Sights

Venkateshwara Temple HINDU TEMPLE
Devotees flock to Tirumala to see Venkateshwara, an avatar of Vishnu. Among the many powers attributed to him is the granting of any wish made before the idol at Tirumala. Many pilgrims also donate their hair to the deity – in gratitude for a wish fulfilled, or to renounce ego – so hundreds of barbers attend to devotees. Tirumala and Tirupathi are filled with tonsured men, women and children.

Legends about the hill itself and the surrounding area appear in the Puranas, and the temple's history may date back 2000 years. The main temple is an atmospheric place, though you'll be pressed between hundreds of devotees when you see it. The inner sanctum itself is dark and magical; it smells of incense, resonates with chanting and may make you religious. There, Venkateshwara inspires bliss and love among his visitors from the back of the sanctum. You'll have a moment to say a prayer and then you'll be shoved out again. Don't forget to collect your delicious *ladoo* from the counter: Tirumala *ladoos* (sweet ball made with chickpea flour, cardamom and dried fruits) are famous across India.

'Ordinary *darshan*' requires a wait of anywhere from two to eight hours in the claustrophobic metal cages ringing the temple. Several kinds of special-*darshan* tickets (₹300) will get you through the queue faster, though you'll still have to brave the gauntlet of the cage, which is part of the fun, kind of... Head to the Supatham complex or the Seeghra Darshan counters

OFF THE BEATEN TRACK

GUNTUPALLI

Getting here is a very scenic adventure. The former **monastic compound** (Indian/foreigner ₹5/100; 10am-5pm), high on a hilltop overlooking a vast expanse of forest and paddy fields, is noteworthy for its circular rock-cut *chaitya-griha*. The cave's domed ceiling is carved with 'wooden beams' designed to look like those in a hut. The *chaitya-griha* also has a well-preserved stupa and, like the monk dwellings that line the same cliff, a gorgeous arched facade also designed to look like wood (note the 'rafters'). Also check out the stone 'beds' in the monks' cells, and the compound's 60-plus votive stupas. The monastery was active from the 2nd century BC to the 3rd century AD.

Guntupalli is best reached from Eluru, on the main Vijayawada–Visakhapatnam train line. From Vijayawada, buses run half-hourly to Eluru (₹50, 1½ hours); from here, take another bus to Kamavarapukota (₹30, one hour, half-hourly, 35km). Guntupalli is 10km west of Kamavarapukota; catch a local bus or autorickshaw. A private car from Eluru costs around ₹900 return.

at Vaikuntam Queue Complex 1 for these tickets. There are special hours for special entry; call ahead.

Upon entry, you'll have to sign a form declaring your faith in Lord Vishnu.

Tours

If you're pressed for time, APTDC (p240) runs three-day tours (₹2300) to Tirumala from Hyderabad. KSTDC and TTDC offer the same from Bengaluru and Chennai, respectively. **APTDC** (2289126; Sridevi Complex, 2nd fl, Tilak Rd; 8.30am-8pm) also has a full-day tour (₹310) of temples in the Tirupathi area.

Sleeping & Eating

The TTD runs vast **dormitories** (beds free) and **guesthouses** (r ₹50-6000) around the temple in Tirumala, but these are intended for pilgrims. To stay, check in at the Central Reception Office. Huge **dining halls** (meals free) on the hill feed thousands of pilgrims daily; veg restaurants also serve meals for ₹25.

Small, inexpensive restaurants cluster around Tirupathi's train and bus stations. The following are all in Tirupathi.

Hotel Mamata Lodge HOTEL $
(2225873; 1st fl, 170 TP Area; s/d/tr/q ₹250/300/400/500) A friendly, spick-and-span cheapie. Some of the sheets are stained, but they're tucked in tight and lovingly patched with white squares. Avoid the downstairs lodge of the same name.

Railway Retiring Rooms RAILWAY RETIRING ROOM $
(dm/r from ₹75/225, with AC ₹225/450) The station retiring rooms are super value.

Hotel Annapurna HOTEL $$
(2250666; Nethaji Rd; r without/with AC ₹1236/1911;) Rooms at the convenient and well-organised Annapurna are clean and pink. Since it's on a corner across from the train station, nonair-con front rooms can be noisy, but air-con rooms are not as good-value. Its veg **restaurant** (mains ₹100 to ₹175) has fresh juices and excellent food.

★ **Minerva Grand** ANDHRA $$
(6688888; www.minervagrand.com; Renigunta Rd; mains & meals ₹130-185, s/d with AC from ₹3147/3822; 7am-11.30pm;) The dining room here is contemporary and somewhat cold – the Minerva is part of a new generation of sleek properties in town – but it's warmed up by the exquisite meals: dish after dish of Andhra food done good and right. Follow it with the dynamite filter coffee. The rooms here are the best in town.

Maya INDIAN $$
(Bhimas Deluxe Hotel; 2225521; bhimasdeluxe@rediffmail.com; G Car St; meals & mains ₹135-190, r with AC ₹1855-2023; 6am-10pm) Great veg meals in the basement of the Bhimas Deluxe, which also has good-value rooms (some without windows: beware) near the train station. Not to be confused with Bhimas Hotel.

Information

Anu Internet Centre (per hr ₹20; 9am-7.30pm) Next to the bus stand, along with several other internet cafes.

Apollo Pharmacy (G Car St; 24hr)

Getting There & Away

It's possible to visit Tirupathi on a (very) long day trip from Chennai. If travelling by bus or train, buy a 'link ticket', which includes transport from Tirupathi to Tirumala.

AIR

Renigunta Airport, 14km outside Tirupathi, was at research time being upgraded to an international airport. **Air India** (2283992, airport 2283992; Tirumala Bypass Rd; 9.30am-5.30pm), with an office 2km from Tirupathi, **SpiceJet** (airport 2275595) and **JetKonnect** (airport 2274155) all fly to Hyderabad daily. You can book with the mobile **Mitta Travels** (2225981; DR Mahal Rd; 11am-11pm).

BUS

Tirupathi's **bus station** (2289900) is a wonder of logistics. Useful routes include the following destinations:

Bengaluru (express/Volvo/night Volvo ₹201/400/450, four to six hours)

Chennai (express/Volvo ₹110/208, four hours)

Hyderabad (superluxury/Volvo ₹548/896, 10-12 hours)

Vijayawada (express/superluxury/Volvo ₹300/412/600, nine hours)

Private buses depart from TP Area, opposite the bus stand.

TRAIN

Tirupathi station is well served by express trains; the **reservation office** (8am-8pm Mon-Sat, 8am-2pm Sun) is across the street. Fares are for sleeper/3AC/2AC.

Bengaluru (₹168/470/665, seven hours)

Chennai (₹140/298/640, three hours)

Hyderabad (₹284/764/1075, 12 hours)

Vijayawada (₹198/502/730, seven hours)

Getting Around

There's a prepaid taxi booth outside the train station.

BUS

Tirumala Link buses have a stand next to the main bus stand and another outside the train station. The scenic 18km trip to Tirumala takes one hour (₹72 return); if you don't mind heights, sit on the left side for views.

WALKING

TTD has constructed probably the best footpath in India for pilgrims to walk up to Tirumala. It's about 15km from Tirupathi and takes four to six hours. Leave your luggage at the toll gate at Alipiri near the Hanuman statue. It will be transported free to the reception centre. There are shady rest points along the way, and a few canteens.

Around Tirumala & Tirupathi

Chandragiri Fort

Only a couple of buildings remain from this 15th-century **fort** (Indian/foreigner ₹10/100; 9am-5pm, Sat-Thu), 14km west of Tirupathi. Both the Rani Mahal and the Raja Mahal, which houses a small **museum** (9am-5pm Sat-Thu), were constructed under Vijayanagar rule and resemble structures in Hampi's Royal Centre. There's a nightly **sound-and-light show** (admission ₹35; 7pm Mar-Sep, 6.30pm Oct-Feb), narrated by Bollywood great Amitabh Bachchan. Buses for Chandragiri (₹14) leave Tirupathi every 15 minutes. Prepaid taxis are ₹450 return.

Sri Kalahasti

Around 36km east of Tirupathi, Sri Kalahasti is known for its important **Sri Kalahasteeswara Temple** and for being, along with Machilipatnam near Vijayawada, a centre for the ancient art of *kalamkari*. These paintings are made with natural ingredients: the cotton is primed with *myrabalam* (resin) and cow's milk; figures are drawn with a pointed bamboo stick dipped in fermented jaggery and water; and the dyes are made from cow dung, ground seeds, plants and flowers. See the artists at work in the Agraharam neighbourhood, 2.5km from the bus stand. **Sri Vijayalakshmi Fine Kalamkari Arts** (9441138380; door No 15-890) is an old family business with 40 artists.

Buses leave Tirupathi for Sri Kalahasti every 10 minutes (₹30, 45 minutes); a prepaid taxi is ₹700 return.

RICHARD I'ANSON / GETTY IMAGES ©

Kerala

Serene Kerala is a state shaped by its wonderful natural landscape: a long, luxurious coastline; wandering backwaters; lush palms and spice plantations; and cool mountain escapes. Add the kaleidoscope of culture best seen in the unique performing arts and you'll understand why Kerala is an experience not to be missed.

Contents

Above Backwater canals near Kumarakom (p294)

1

Beaches

Goa might pull in the package-holiday crowds, but Kerala's coastline – almost 600km of it – boasts a stunning string of golden-sand beaches, fringed by palms and washed by the Arabian Sea. The southern beaches are the busiest, while less-discovered, wilder choices await in the north.

Southern Beaches

Most established of the resorts along the coast is Kovalam, only a short hop from the capital, Thiruvananthapuram (Trivandrum). Once a quiet fishing village, Kovalam has two sheltered crescents of beach perfect for paddling that are now overlooked by a town that's almost entirely made up of hotels. If you're looking for something less built up: south of here are some lovely beaches and resorts, clustered in the area around Pulinkudi and Chowara, where ayurvedic treatments are popular.

Further north is Varkala, which straggles along its dramatic, streaked russet-and-gold cliffs. Although a holy town popular with Hindu pilgrims, Varkala has also developed into Kerala's backpacker bolthole and the cliffs are lined with guesthouses, open-front restaurants and bars all moving to a reggae, rock and trance soundtrack. For a quieter scene, travellers are drifting north to Odayam and Kappil beaches.

Even further north, Alappuzha (Alleppey) is best known for its backwaters, but also has a decent beach, while Kochi (Cochin) has Cherai Beach on Vypeen Island, a lovely stretch of white sand, with miles of lazy lagoons and backwaters only a few hundred metres from the seafront.

ANDERS BLOMQVIST / GETTY IMAGES ©

ANDERS BLOMQVIST / GETTY IMAGES ©

TIM MAKINS / GETTY IMAGES ©

1. Papanasham beach, Varkala (p280)
2. Idyllic Keralan coastline **3.** Beach at sunset, Kovalam (p276)

Far North & Islands

Fewer travellers make it to Kerala's far north, which means there are some beautifully deserted pockets of beach, where resorts are replaced by more traditional village life. Among the best are the peaceful white-sand beaches south of Kannur, or further north around the Valiyaparamba backwaters between Kannur and Bekal.

Even more far flung are the Lakshadweep Islands, a palm-fringed island archipelago 300km west of Kerala. As well as pristine beaches, the islands boast some of India's best scuba diving and snorkelling.

BEST BEACH TOWNS

Varkala (p280) The beautiful cliff-edged coastline of Varkala is a Hindu holy place as well as a lively backpacker-focused resort. Good base for yoga, surfing or just chilling out.

Kovalam (p276) Kerala's most commercial beach resort, but still fun and scenic despite the crowds and hawkers. Resorts here and further south have a strong focus on ayurvedic treatments.

Kannur (p324) While Kannur itself is not a particularly appealing beach town, head 8km south to Thottada for gorgeous beaches and seafront homestays in local villages. Kannur town's 4km-long Payyambalam Beach is popular with locals.

Backwaters

Kerala's 900km of waterways spread watery tendrils through the region's lusciously green landscape. Palm-shaded, winding canals are lined by back-in-time villages, many of which are accessible only by boat. It's an environment unique to Kerala and an unforgettable South India experience.

Houseboats

To glide along the canals in a punted canoe or sleep under a firmament of stars in a traditional houseboat is pure enchantment. The distinctive houseboats that cluster around the main hubs of Alleppey and Kollam (Quilon) are designed like traditional rice barges or *kettuvallam* ('boat with knots', so-called because the curvaceous structure is held together by knotted coir).

There are several ways to explore the backwaters. The most popular method is to rent a houseboat for a night or two; these sleep anything from two up to 14 or more people. They vary wildly in luxury and amenities. The hire includes staff (at least a driver and cook but usually additional kitchen staff and crew), catering is included, and you'll eat traditional Keralan meals of fish and vegetables cooked in coconut milk. However, the popularity of these tours can mean that the main waterways get very busy – even gridlocked – in peak season. An overnight houseboat trip won't get you far through the backwaters.

Ferries & Canoes

Another means of seeing the waterways is to take a public ferry. This is the cheapest way to travel, and you can take

SARAVANAN ALAGARSAM / GETTY IMAGES ©

PETER ADAMS / GETTY IMAGES ©

1. Houseboats cruising on Kerala's backwaters
2. Backwaters around Alleppey (p287)
3. Fishermen in Kollam (p285)

MITCHELL KANASHKEVICH / GETTY IMAGES ©

trips from town to town, though again you won't see much of the smaller canals where it is really tranquil. Two of the most popular trips are the all-day tourist cruise between Kollam and Alleppey, a scenic but slow trip, and the 2½-hour ferry from Alleppey to Kottayam.

The best way to explore deep into the network and escape the bigger boats is to take a canoe tour, as this will allow you to travel along the narrower canals and see village life in a way that's impossible on a houseboat or ferry. Village tours with a knowledgable guide are another tranquil way to explore the region and understand some of the local culture.

WHICH HOUSEBOAT?

The choice of houseboats – especially at Alleppey – is mind-boggling and the boat and operator you decide on can make or break the experience.

➡ Avoid booking a houseboat until you arrive at the backwaters; inspect a few boats before committing.

➡ Ask to see operators' certification: those houseboat owners who have a 'Green Palm' or 'Gold Star' certificate have met requirements such as solar panels, sanitary tanks and low-emission engines. Punt-powered boats are even better.

➡ Visit the houseboat dock in Alleppey, talk to returning travellers or guesthouse owners and search online to gauge costs and quality.

➡ Avoid peak season (mid-December to mid-January) when prices peak and the waterways are clogged.

Performing Arts

Kerala has an intensely rich culture of performing arts – living art forms that are passed on to new generations in specialised schools and arts centres.

Kathakali

Kathakali, with its elaborate ritualised gestures, heavy mask-like makeup, and dramatic stories of love, lust and power struggles based on the Ramayana, the Mahabharata and the Puranas, stems in part from 2nd-century temple rituals, though its current form developed in around the 16th century. The actors tell the stories through precise mudras (hand gestures) and facial expressions. Traditionally performances start in temple grounds at around 8pm and go on all night, though versions for those with shorter attention spans are performed in many tourist centres, to give a taste of the art.

Theyyam

Theyyam is an even earlier art, believed to be older than Hinduism, having developed from harvest folk dances. It's performed in *kavus* (sacred groves) in northern Kerala. The word refers to the ritual itself, and to the shape of the deity or hero portrayed, of which there are around 450. The costumes are magnificent, with face paint, armour, garlands and huge headdresses. The performance consists of frenzied dancing to a wild drumbeat, creating a trance-like atmosphere.

Kalarippayat

Taking its moves from both these ancient arts is the martial art of *kalarippayat*, a ritualistic discipline taught throughout

MITCHELL KANASHKEVICH / GETTY IMAGES ©

CHRISTOPHER PILLITZ / GETTY IMAGES ©

NEIL McCALLISTER / GETTY IMAGES ©

1. Artists applying makeup before a Kathakali performance
2. *Kalarippayat* martial artists
3. *Theyyam* ritual

Kerala. It's taught and displayed in an arena called a *kalari*, which combines gymnasium, school and temple.

Places to See Performing Arts

In the spring there are numerous festivals with the chance to see Kathakali, including Thirunakkara in Kottayam in March and the Pooram festival in Kollam in April. The easiest places for travellers to see performances are at cultural centres across Kerala, such as Kerala Kathakali Centre (p313), See India Foundation (p313) and Greenix Village (p313) in Kochi, Mudra Kathakali Centre (p298) in Kumily and Thirumeny Cultural Centre (p301) in Munnar. In Kovalam and Varkala there are short versions of the art in season.

If you're interested in learning more about the art of Kathakali, Kerala Kalamandalam (p319) near Thrissur and Margi Kathakali School (p271) in Trivandrum offer courses for serious students, or you can attend these schools to see performances and practice sessions. Both the Kochi and Kumily centres also have shows of *kalarippayat*, or you can visit the martial art training centres of CVN Kalari Sangham (p271) in Trivandrum and Ens Kalari (p313) in Nettoor, close to Ernakulam.

The best areas to see *theyyam* performances are around Kannur, Payyannur and Valiyaparamba, in the northern backwater area, where there are more than 500 *kavus*. The season is from October to May. For advice on finding performances, contact the Tourist Desk (p315) in Kochi or homestays at Thottada Beach.

Tea plantation near Top Station (p303)

Hill Stations & Sanctuaries

Kerala's hill towns are set in sumptuous natural landscapes and cooling altitudes and are incredibly soothing places to escape the cares of the world. Narrow roads wind up through jungle-thick vegetation providing dizzying views over deep peacock-green tea plantations. Spindly betel nut trees sway in the breeze and flame of the forest provides splashes of red.

Munnar

Best known is Munnar, with contoured green fields carpeting the hills as far as the eye can see. This is South India's tea-growing heartland, but also a great place to trek and discover viewpoints across epic mountain scenery. There are some wonderfully remote places to stay hidden in the hills, tucked deep into spice and flower gardens, or cardamom and coffee plantations.

Wayanad & Periyar

The northern area around Wayanad Wildlife Sanctuary has shimmering green rice paddies and plantations of coffee, cardamom, ginger and pepper everywhere you look. The rolling hills are fragrant with wild herbs and punctuated by mammoth clumps of bamboo. It's one of the best places to spot wild elephants and there are plenty of opportunities for trekking, such as up the area's highest mountain, Chembra Peak (2100m).

At Periyar Wildlife Sanctuary, a Project Tiger reserve since 1978 and Kerala's most-visited wildlife sanctuary, you can take a cruise on Periyar Lake, stay in an island palace, or embark on a jungle trek with a trained tribal guide.

Kerala

Includes ➡

Best Wildlife-Watching

- Wayanad Wildlife Sanctuary (p322)
- Thattekkad Bird Sanctuary (p316)
- Periyar Wildlife Sanctuary (p295)
- Neyyar Wildlife Sanctuary (p275)
- Parambikulam Wildlife Sanctuary (p302)

Best Homestays

- Green Woods Bethlehem (p308)
- Cherukara Nest (p290)
- Tranquil (p324)
- Graceful Homestay (p273)
- Rodo Residency (p309)

Why Go?

A sliver of a state in India's deep south, Kerala is shaped by its landscape – almost 600km of glorious Arabian Sea coast and beaches, a languid network of backwaters and the spice and tea-covered hills of the Western Ghats. As relaxing as an ayurvedic massage, just setting foot on this swath of soul-quenching green will slow your stride to a blissed-out amble. Kerala is a world away from the frenzy of elsewhere, as if India had passed through the Looking Glass and become an altogether more laid-back place.

Besides its famous backwaters, rice paddies, coconut groves, elegant houseboats and delicately spiced, taste-bud-tingling cuisine, Kerala is home to wild elephants, exotic birds and the odd tiger; and crazily vibrant traditions such as Kathakali plays and snake-boat races. Few visitors neglect to put Kerala on a South India itinerary – the biggest problem is choosing where to linger the longest.

When to Go

Thiruvananthapuram

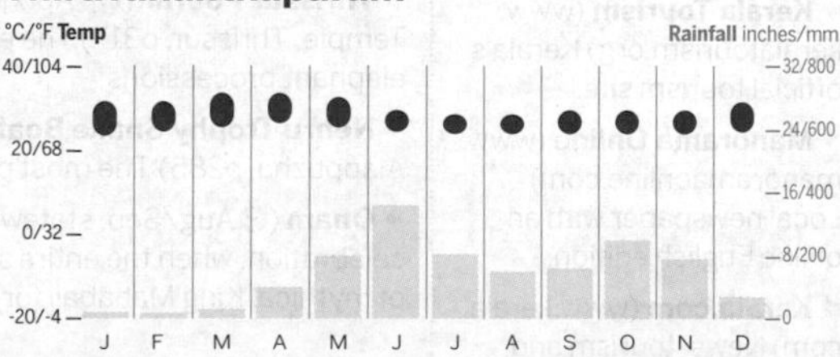

Jan–Feb Perfect beach and backwater weather. Ernakulathappan Utsavam festival in Kochi (Cochin).

Apr Kathakali at Kottayam and Kollam festivals, and the elephant procession in Thrissur.

Aug-Sep End of the monsoon period: Onam festival, snake-boat races.

MAIN POINTS OF ENTRY

Thiruvananthapuram (Trivandrum), Kozhikode (Calicut) and Kochi (Cochin) are Kerala's air and rail transport hubs.

Fast Facts

- **Population:** 33.34 million
- **Area:** 38,864 sq km
- **Capital:** Thiruvanan thapuram (Trivandrum)
- **Main Language:** Malayalam
- **Sleeping Prices: $** below ₹1000, **$$** ₹1000 to ₹3500, **$$$** above ₹3500

Planning Your Trip

High season in the backwaters and beach resorts is around November to March; between mid-December and mid-January prices creep up further. There are great deals during the monsoon (June to September).

Resources

- **Kerala Tourism** (www.keralatourism.org) Kerala's official tourism site.
- **Manorama Online** (www.manoramaonline.com) Local newspaper with an online English edition.
- **Kerala.com** (www.kerala.com) News, tourism and loads of links.
- **Lonely Planet** (www.lonelyplanet.com/india/kerala) Planning advice, reviews, recommendations and insider tips.

Food

Delicious South Indian breakfast dishes include *puttu* (steamed rice powder and coconut), *idlis* (spongy, round, fermented rice cakes), *sambar* (fragrant vegetable dhal), and dosas with coconut chutney.

Kerala's spice plantations, coconut-palm groves and long coastline shape the local cuisine, with deliciously delicate dishes such as fish *molee* or the spicy Malabar chicken curry. Fresh seafood, such as pomfret, kingfish and prawns, can be bought from fishing boats along the coast.

For dessert, *payasam* is made of brown molasses, coconut milk and spices, garnished with cashew nuts and raisins.

DON'T MISS

Fort Cochin is an extraordinary town, resonant with 500 years of colonial history. There are few more magical experiences than floating along **Kerala's backwaters** on a houseboat, canoe or even a kayak. For a true Keralan family welcome, try spending the night in a **homestay**, where you can eat (and cook) with the family.

Top State Festivals

- **Ernakulathappan Utsavam** (Jan/Feb, Shiva Temple, Ernakulam, Kochi, p307) Eight days of festivities culminating in a parade of elephants, music and fireworks.
- **Thirunakkara Utsavam** (Mar, Thirunakkara Shiva Temple, Kottayam, p292) All-night Kathakali dancing on the third and fourth nights of this 10-day festival.
- **Kollam Pooram** (Apr, Asraman Shri Krishna Swami Temple, Kollam, p285) A 10-day festival with all-night Kathakali performances and a procession of 40 ornamented elephants.
- **Thrissur Pooram** (Apr/May, Vadakkunathan Kshetram Temple, Thrissur, p317) The elephant procession to end all elephant processions.
- **Nehru Trophy Snake Boat Race** (2nd Sat in Aug, Alappuzha, p285) The most popular of Kerala's boat races.
- **Onam** (Aug/Sep, statewide) Kerala's biggest cultural celebration, when the entire state celebrates the golden age of mythical King Mahabali for 10 days.

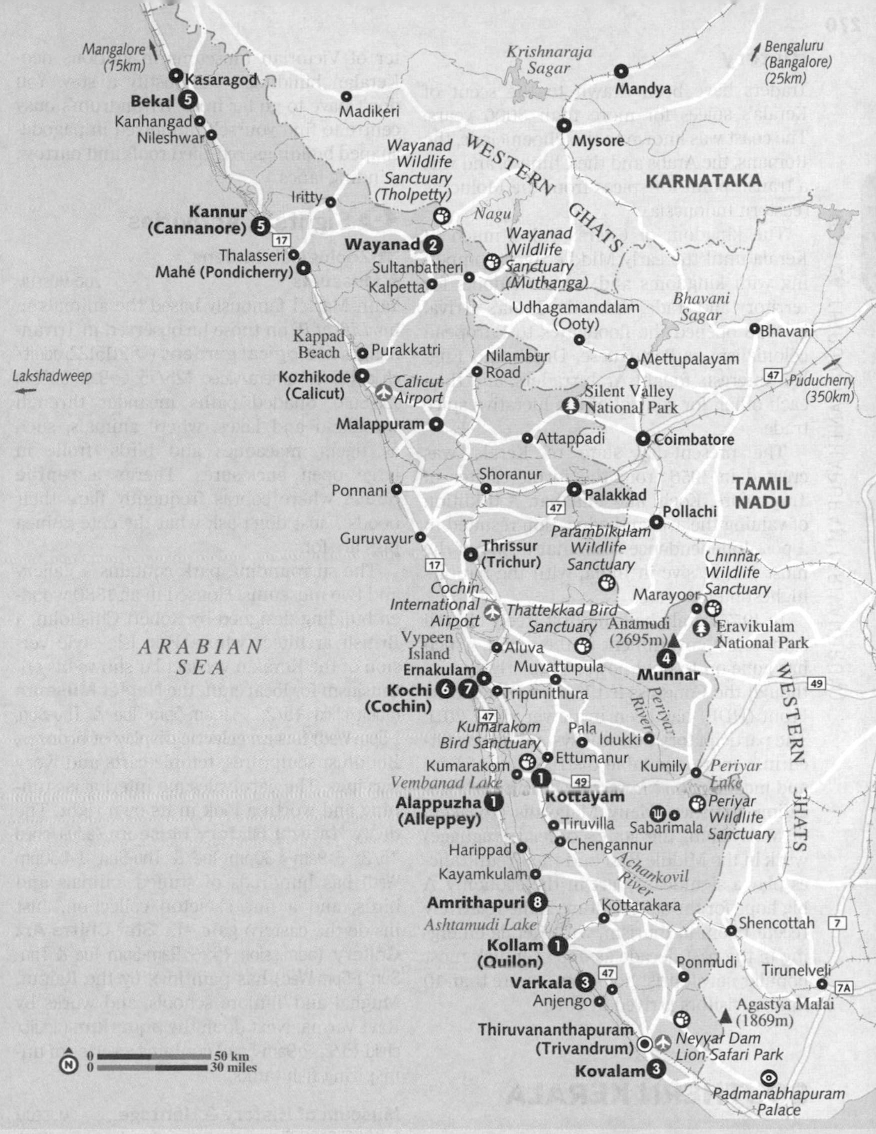

Kerala Highlights

1 Take a houseboat or canoe through Kerala's fabled **backwaters** (p292) from Alleppey, Kollam or Kottayam

2 Spot wild elephants at **Wayanad** (p322) amid spectacular scenery

3 Amble around the breathtaking beach resort of **Varkala** (p280) and have some laid-back fun in **Kovalam** (p276)

4 Bed down in a remote resort and trek through emerald tea plantations around **Munnar** (p299)

5 Explore the golden-sand beaches and backwaters around **Kannur** (p324) and **Bekal** (p327)

6 Relax in a homestay in **Fort Cochin** (p308) in Kochin

7 Experience the ritual of a **Kathakali** performance or martial arts **kalarippayat** in Kochi (p313)

8 Take the **cruise** between Kollam and Alleppey, stopping off at Amrithapuri to visit the 'Hugging Mother' (p287)

History

Traders have been drawn to the scent of Kerala's spices for more than 3000 years. The coast was known to the Phoenicians, the Romans, the Arabs and the Chinese, and was a transit point for spices from the Moluccas (eastern Indonesia).

The kingdom of Cheras ruled much of Kerala until the early Middle Ages, competing with kingdoms and small fiefdoms for territory and trade. Vasco da Gama's arrival in 1498 opened the floodgates to European colonialism as Portuguese, Dutch and English interests fought Arab traders, and then each other, for control of the lucrative spice trade.

The present-day state of Kerala was created in 1956 from the former states of Travancore, Kochi and Malabar. A tradition of valuing the arts and education resulted in a post-Independence state that is one of the most progressive in India, with the nation's highest literacy rate.

In 1957 Kerala had the first freely elected communist government in the world, which has gone on to hold power regularly since – though the Congress-led United Democratic Front (UDF) has been in power since 2011. The participatory political system has resulted in a more equitable distribution of land and income, and impressive health and education statistics. Many Malayalis (speakers of Malayalam, the state's official language) work in the Middle East and their remittances play a significant part in the economy. A big hope for the state's future is the relatively recent boom in tourism, with Kerala emerging in the past decade as one of India's most popular new tourist hot spots – more than 10 million visitors arrived in 2011.

SOUTHERN KERALA

Thiruvananthapuram (Trivandrum)

☎0471 / POP 752,500

Kerala's capital – for obvious reasons still often referred to by its colonial name, Trivandrum – is an energetic place and an easygoing introduction to city life down south. Most travellers merely springboard from here to the nearby beachside resorts of Kovalam and Varkala, but Trivandrum has enough sights – including its zoo and cluster of Victorian museums in glorious neo-Keralan buildings – to justify a stay. You don't have to go far from Trivandrum's busy centre to find yourself immersed in pagoda-shaped buildings, red-tiled roofs and narrow, winding lanes.

Sights & Activities

★Zoological Gardens & Museums ZOO, MUSEUM

Yann Martel famously based the animals in his *Life of Pi* on those he observed in Trivandrum's **zoological gardens** (☎2115122; adult/child ₹10/5, camera/video ₹25/75; ⏲9am-5.15pm Tue-Sun). Shaded paths meander through woodland and lakes, where animals, such as tigers, macaques and birds, frolic in large open enclosures. There's a **reptile house** where cobras frequently flare their hoods – just don't ask what the cute guinea pigs are for.

The surrounding park contains a gallery and two museums. Housed in an 1880 wooden building designed by Robert Chisholm, a British architect whose Fair Isle–style version of the Keralan vernacular shows his enthusiasm for local craft, the **Napier Museum** (adult/child ₹5/2; ⏲10am-5pm Tue & Thu-Sun, 1-5pm Wed) has an eclectic display of bronzes, Buddhist sculptures, temple carts and ivory carvings. The carnivalesque interior is stunning and worth a look in its own right. The dusty **Natural History Museum** (adult/child ₹5/2; ⏲9am-4.30pm Tue & Thu-Sun, 1-4.30pm Wed) has hundreds of stuffed animals and birds, and a fine skeleton collection. Just inside the eastern gate, the **Shri Chitra Art Gallery** (admission ₹5; ⏲9am-5pm Tue & Thu-Sun, 1-5pm Wed) has paintings by the Rajput, Mughal and Tanjore schools, and works by Ravi Varma. Next door, the **aquarium** (adult/child ₹5/2; ⏲9am-5pm) contains a series of uninspiring fish tanks.

Museum of History & Heritage MUSEUM

(☎9567019037; www.museumkeralam.org; Park View; Indian adult/child ₹20/10, foreigner adult/child ₹200/50, camera ₹25; ⏲10am-5.30pm Tue-Sun) In a lovely heritage building within the Kerala Tourism complex, this spacious new museum traces Keralan history and culture through superb static displays and interactive audiovisual presentations. Exhibits range from Iron Age implements to bronze and terracotta sculptures, murals, *dhulichitra* (floor paintings) and recreations of traditional Keralan homes. Admission is steep but it's all beautifully presented.

Shri Padmanabhaswamy Temple HINDU TEMPLE
(Hindus only 4am-7.30pm) This 260-year-old temple is Trivandrum's spiritual heart. Its main entrance is the 30m-tall, seven-tier eastern *gopuram* (gateway tower). In the inner sanctum, the deity Padmanabha reclines on the sacred serpent and is made from over 10,000 *salagramam* (sacred stones) that were purportedly transported from Nepal by elephant.

The path around to the right of the gate offers good views of the *gopuram.*

Puthe Maliga Palace Museum MUSEUM
(Fort; Indian/foreigner ₹15/50, camera/video ₹30/250; 8.30am-1pm & 3-5pm Tue-Sun) The 200-year-old palace of the Travancore maharajas has carved wooden ceilings, marble sculptures and even imported Belgian glass. Inside you'll find Kathakali images, an armoury, portraits of maharajas, ornate thrones and other artefacts. Admission includes a 45-minute guided tour, though you can skip that and just visit the outside of the palace grounds (free), where you'll also find the **Chitrali Museum** (₹50), a newly opened section of the palace containing loads of historical memorabilia, photographs and portraits from the Travancore dynasty.

An annual **classical music festival** is held here in January.

Courses

Ayushmanbhava Ayurvedic Centre AYURVEDA, YOGA
(4712556060; www.ayushmanbhava.com; Pothujanam; massage from ₹600; yoga classes 6.30am) This centre, 3km west of MG Rd, offers massage, daily therapeutic-yoga classes, as well as longer ayurvedic treatments.

Margi Kathakali School CULTURAL PROGRAM
(2478806; www.margitheatre.org; Fort) Conducts courses in Kathakali and *Kootiattam* (traditional Sanskrit drama) for beginner and advanced students. Fees average ₹300 per two-hour class. Visitors can peek at uncostumed practice sessions held from 10am to noon Monday to Friday. It's in an unmarked building behind the Fort School, 200m west of the fort.

CVN Kalari Sangham MARTIAL ARTS
(2474182; www.cvnkalari.in; South Rd; 15-day/1-mth course ₹1000/2000) Offers long-term courses in *kalarippayat* for serious students (aged under 30) with some experience in martial arts. Training sessions are held Monday to Saturday from 7am to 8.30am.

TRADITIONAL KERALAN ARTS

Kathakali

The art form of Kathakali crystallised at around the same time as Shakespeare was scribbling his plays. The Kathakali performance is the dramatised presentation of a play, usually based on the Hindu epics the Ramayana, the Mahabharata and the Puranas. All the great themes are covered – righteousness and evil, frailty and courage, poverty and prosperity, war and peace.

Drummers and singers accompany the actors, who tell the story through their precise movements, particularly *mudras* (hand gestures) and facial expressions.

Preparation for the performance is lengthy and disciplined. Paint, fantastic costumes, ornamental headpieces and meditation transform the actors both physically and mentally into the gods, heroes and demons they are about to play.

Traditional performances can last for many hours, but you can see cut-down performances in tourist hot spots all over the state, and there are Kathakali schools in Trivandrum (p271) and near Thrissur (p319) that encourage visitors.

Kalarippayat

Kalarippayat is an ancient tradition of martial arts training and discipline, still taught throughout Kerala. Some believe it is the forerunner of all martial arts, with roots tracing back to the 12th-century skirmishes among Kerala's feudal principalities.

Masters of *kalarippayat*, called Gurukkal, teach their craft inside a special arena called a *kalari*. You can see often *kalarippayat* performances at the same venues as Kathakali.

Thiruvananthapuram (Trivandrum)

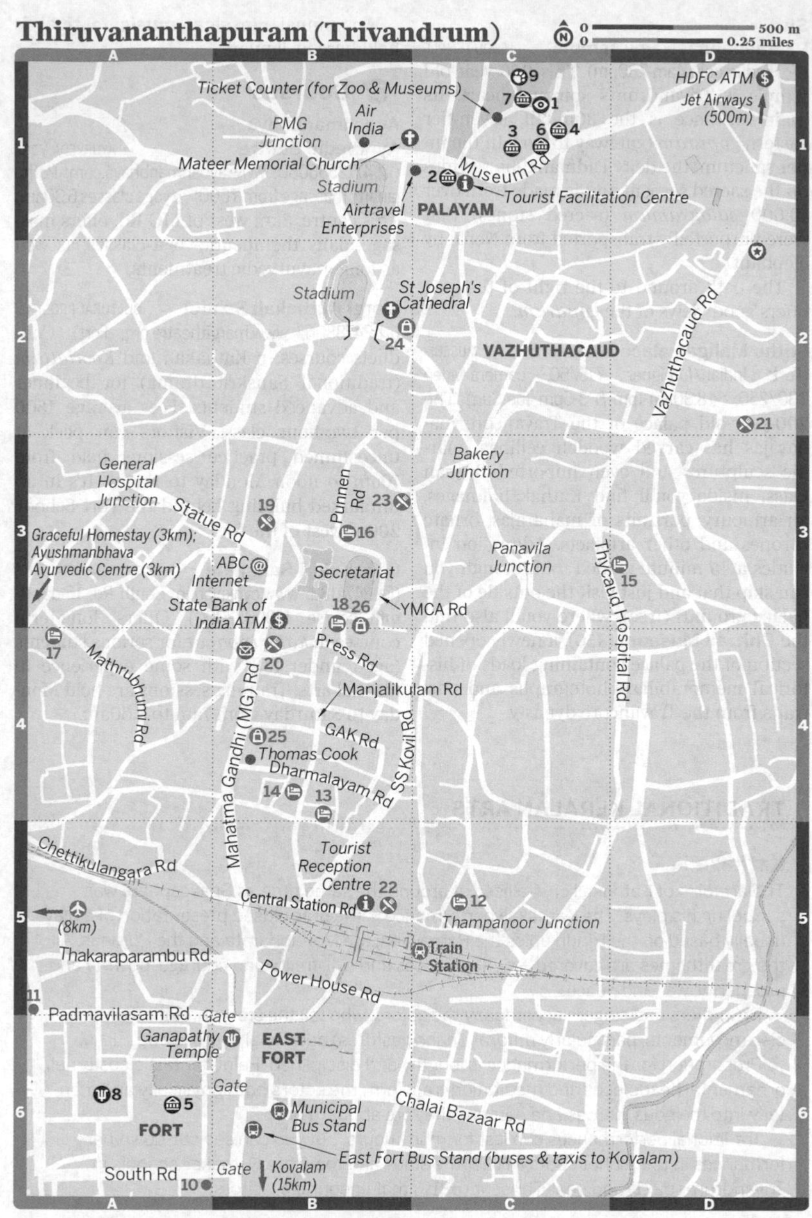

Tours

KTDC (Kerala Tourist Development Corporation) runs several tours, all leaving from the Tourist Reception Centre at the KTDC Hotel Chaithram on Central Station Rd. The City Tour (₹300) includes the zoo and other local sights; the Kanyakumari Day Tour (₹700) visits Padmanabhapuram Palace, Kanyakumari in Tamil Nadu and the nearby Suchindram Temple. Other trips include Neyyar Dam (₹400) and Kovalam (₹200).

Thiruvananthapuram (Trivandrum)

Sights
1 Aquarium........C1
2 Museum of History & Heritage........C1
3 Napier Museum........C1
4 Natural History Museum........C1
5 Puthe Maliga Palace Museum........A6
6 Reptile House........C1
7 Shri Chitra Art Gallery........C1
8 Shri Padmanabhaswamy Temple........A6
9 Zoological Gardens........C1

Activities, Courses & Tours
10 CVN Kalari Sangham........A6
11 Margi Kathakali School........A5

Sleeping
12 Greenland Lodge........C5
13 Hotel Regency........B4
14 Princess Inn........B4
15 Taj Vivanta........D3
16 Varikatt Heritage........B3
17 Wild Palms Home Stay........A4
18 YMCA International Guesthouse........B3

Eating
19 Ananda Bhavan........B3
Ariya Nivaas........(see 12)
20 Azad Restaurant........B4
21 Cherries & Berries........D2
22 Indian Coffee House........B5
23 Vibhav........B3

Shopping
24 Connemara Market........B2
25 Sankers Coffee & Tea........B4
26 SMSM Institute........B3

Sleeping

YMCA International Guesthouse HOSTEL $
(2330059; www.ymcatvm.org; YMCA Rd; s/d ₹376/732, with AC ₹788/1125;) Centrally located but down a relatively quiet street, this is one of the best budget deals in town; rooms are spacious, spotless and come with tiled bathrooms and TV. Both men and women accepted.

Princess Inn HOTEL $
(2339150; Manjalikulam Rd; s/d ₹350/600, with AC from ₹750/850;) In a glass-fronted building, the Princess Inn promises a relatively quiet sleep in a central sidestreet location. It's clean and comfortable, with satellite TV and immaculate bathrooms; the 'deluxe' rooms are spacious.

Hotel Regency HOTEL $
(2330377; www.hotelregency.com; Manjalikulam Cross Rd; s/d ₹600/900, with AC ₹1125/1350;) This tidy, welcoming place offers small but spotless rooms with satellite TV; the deluxe rooms are larger and there's wi-fi available downstairs.

Greenland Lodge HOTEL $
(2328114; Thampanoor Junction; s/d ₹435/680, with AC ₹900/1070;) Close to the muted mayhem of the train station and bus stand, Greenland is acceptable for the location with lots of serenity-inducing pastel colours. Rooms are cleanish but variable so ask to see a few. Officious staff demand a hefty two-night advance deposit.

★**Graceful Homestay** HOMESTAY $$
(2444358; www.gracefulhomestay.com; Pothujanam Rd, Philip's Hill; downstairs s/d ₹1300/1500, upstairs & ste s/d incl breakfast ₹2000/2500;) In Trivandrum's leafy western suburbs, this lovely, serene house set in a couple of hectares of garden is owned by Sylvia and run by her brother Giles. The four rooms are all neatly furnished with access to kitchen, living areas and balconies. The pick of the rooms has an amazing covered terrace with views overlooking a sea of palms.

Wild Palms Home Stay HOMESTAY $$
(2471175; www.wildpalmsonsea.com; Mathrubhumi Rd; s ₹1095-1495, d ₹1395-1795, ste s/d ₹1795/2195;) A leafy courtyard garden greets you in front of this ornate but cosy family home with plenty of character. The seven rooms are all spacious with enormous bathrooms – the best is the upstairs suite with balcony, reached by a spiral staircase. Breakfast included.

★**Varikatt Heritage** HOMESTAY $$$
(2336057; www.varikattheritage.com; Punnen Rd; r incl breakfast ₹3950-5050;) Trivandrum's most charismatic place to stay is the 250-year-old home of Colonel Roy Kuncheria. It's a wonderful Indo-Saracenic bungalow with four rooms flanked by verandahs facing a pretty garden. Every antique – and the home itself – has a family story attached. Lunch and dinner available (₹300).

Taj Vivanta HOTEL $$$
(6612345; www.vivantabytaj.com; Thycaud Hospital Rd; s/d incl breakfast from ₹9500/10,700, ste

THE INDIAN COFFEE HOUSE STORY

The Indian Coffee House is a place stuck in time. Its India-wide branches feature old India prices and waiters dressed in starched white with peacock-style headdresses. It was started by the Coffee Board in the early 1940s, during British rule. In the 1950s the Board began to close down cafes across India, making employees redundant. At this point, the communist leader Ayillyath Kuttiari Gopalan Nambiar began to support the workers and founded with them the India Coffee Board Worker's Co-operative Society. The intention was to provide them with better opportunities and promote the sale of coffee. The Coffee House has remained ever since, always atmospheric, and always offering bargain snacks and drinks such as Indian filter coffee, rose milk and *idlis*. It's still run by its employees, all of whom share ownership.

₹25,500; ❄@📶🏊) The lobby here is bigger than most hotels in town, so the Taj doesn't disappoint with the wow factor. Rooms are sufficiently plush, the lawn and pool area is well maintained, there's a gym and a couple of good restaurants.

Eating

For some unusual refreshments with your meal, look out for *karikku* (coconut water) and *sambharam* (buttermilk with ginger and chilli).

★Indian Coffee House INDIAN $
(Maveli Cafe; Central Station Rd; snacks ₹10-45; ⏰7am-11pm) The Central Station Rd branch of Indian Coffee House serves its strong coffee and snacks in a crazy red-brick tower that looks like a cross between a lighthouse and a pigeon coop, and has a spiralling interior lined with concrete benches and tables. You have to admire the hard-working waiters. There's another, more run-of-the-mill branch near the zoo.

Ariya Nivaas INDIAN $
(Manorama Rd; thalis ₹70; ⏰6.45am-10pm) Always busy thanks to its superb all-you-can-eat South Indian veg thalis, Ariya Nivaas is away from the main drag but convenient for the train station.

Ananda Bhavan INDIAN $
(☎2477646; MG Rd; dishes ₹28-40; ⏰lunch & dinner) A classic sit-down-and-dig-in-with-your-hands-type situation with dosas and veg snacks.

Cherries & Berries CAFE $$
(www.cherriesandberries.in; Carmel Towers, Cotton Hill; ₹45-130; ⏰9.45am-10pm; 📶) For serious comfort food, icy air-con and free wi-fi, take a trip east of the centre to Cherries & Berries. Waffles, mini-pizzas, toasties, good coffee and indulgent chocolate-bar milkshakes.

Azad Restaurant INDIAN $$
(Press Rd; dishes ₹75-145; ⏰noon-11.30pm) A busy family favourite serving up authentic Keralan fish dishes, like fish *molee*, and excellent biryanis and tandoori.

Vibhav MULTICUISINE $$
(☎4076000; Vanross Junction; mains ₹80-250; ⏰8am-10.30pm) This smart restaurant at Magic Days Hotel offers a terrific buffet for lunch and dinner, as well as à la carte Indian, Chinese and Continental.

Shopping

Wander around **Connemara Market** (MG Rd) to see vendors selling vegetables, fish, live goats, fabric, clothes, spices and more bananas than you can poke a hungry monkey at.

SMSM Institute HANDICRAFTS
(www.keralahandicrafts.in; YMCA Rd; ⏰9am-8pm Mon-Sat) Kerala Government–run handicraft emporium with an Aladdin's cave of well-priced goodies.

Sankers Coffee & Tea FOOD & DRINK
(☎2330469; MG Rd; ⏰9am-9pm Mon-Sat) You'll smell the fresh coffee well before you reach this dainty shop. It sells Nilgiri Export OP Leaf Tea (₹520 per kilo) and a variety of coffees and nuts.

Information

ABC Internet (MG Rd, Capital Centre; per hr ₹20; ⏰8.30am-9pm) One of several good internet places in this small mall.

KIMS (Kerala Institute of Medical Sciences; ☎3041000, emergency 3041144; www.kims-kerala.com; Kumarapuram; ⏰24hr) Best choice for medical problems; about 3km northwest of Trivandrum.

Main Post Office (☎2473071; MG Rd)

Thomas Cook (☎2338140, 2338141; MG Rd; ⏰10.30am-6pm Mon-Sat) Changes cash and travellers cheques.

Tourist Facilitation Centre (☎2321132; Museum Rd; ⏰24hr) Near the zoo; supplies maps and brochures.

Tourist Reception Centre (KTDC Hotel Chaithram; ☎2330031; Central Station Rd; ⏰7am-9pm) Arranges KTDC-run tours.

Getting There & Away

AIR

Between them, **Air India** (☎2317341; Mascot Sq), **Jet Airways** (☎2728864; Sasthamangalam Junction) and **SpiceJet** (☎09871803333; www.spicejet.com; Trivandrum airport) fly from Trivandrum airport to Mumbai (Bombay), Kochi, Bengaluru (Bangalore), Chennai (Madras) and Delhi.

There are also direct flights from Trivandrum to Colombo in Sri Lanka, Male in the Maldives and major Gulf regions such as Dubai, Kuwait and Bahrain.

All airline bookings can be made at the efficient **Airtravel Enterprises** (☎3011300; www.ate.travel; MG Rd, New Corporation Bldg).

BUS

For buses operating from the KSRTC bus stand, opposite the train station, see the table.

For Tamil Nadu destinations, State Express Transport Corporation (SETC) buses leave from the eastern end of the KSRTC bus stand.

Buses leave for Kovalam beach (₹15, 30 minutes, every 20 minutes) between 6am and 9pm from the southern end of the East Fort bus stand on MG Rd.

TRAIN

Trains are often heavily booked, so it's worth visiting the **reservation office** (☎139; ⏰8am-8pm Mon-Sat, to 2pm Sun) at the main train station. While most major trains arrive and depart at Trivandrum Central Station close to the city centre, some express services terminate at Vikram Sarabhai Station (Kochuveli), about 7km north of the city – check in advance.

Within Kerala there are frequent express trains to Varkala (sleeper/3AC ₹57/175, one hour), Kollam (₹64/175, 1¼ hours) and Ernakulam (₹128/342, 4½ hours), with trains passing through either Alleppey (₹120/267, three hours) or Kottayam (₹120/313, 3½ hours). There are also numerous daily services to Kanyakumari (sleeper/3AC ₹120/218, three hours).

Getting Around

The **airport** (☎2501424) is 8km from the city and 15km from Kovalam; take local bus 14 from the East Fort and City Bus stand (₹7). Prepaid taxi vouchers from the airport cost ₹350 to the city and ₹500 to Kovalam.

Autorickshaws are the easiest way to get around, with short hops costing ₹20 to ₹30.

Around Trivandrum

Neyyar Wildlife Sanctuary

Surrounding an idyllic lake created by the 1964 Neyyar Dam 35km north of Trivandrum, the main attraction at this sanctuary is the **Lion Safari Park** (☎2272182, 9744347582; Indian/foreigner ₹200/300; ⏰9am-4pm Tue-Sun). Admission includes a boat ride across the lake, lion safari by bus, a visit to a **deer park** and **Crocodile Production Centre** (named for Australian legend Steve Irwin). The fertile forest lining the shore is home to gaurs,

BUSES LEAVING FROM TRIVANDRUM (KSRTC BUS STAND)

DESTINATION	FARE (₹)	DURATION (HR)	FREQUENCY
Alleppey	100, AC 191	3½	every 15min
Chennai	560	17	10 daily
Ernakulam (Kochi)	135, AC 250	5	every 20min
Kanyakumari	50	2	6 daily
Kollam	43	1½	every 15min
Kumily (for Periyar)	200	8	2 daily
Munnar	250	7	2 daily
Neyyar Dam	30	1½	every 40min
Thrissur	200	7½	every 30min
Ooty (Udhagamandalam)	485	14	1 daily
Varkala	40	1¼	hourly

MAJOR TRAINS FROM TRIVANDRUM

DESTINATION	TRAIN NO & NAME	FARE (₹, SLEEPER/3AC/2AC)	DURATION (HR)	DEPARTURES (DAILY)
Bengaluru	16525 Bangalore Express	307/864/1320	18	1pm
Chennai	12696 Chennai Express	341/936/1425	16½	5.10pm
Coimbatore	17229 Sabari Express	191/524/785	9¼	7.15am
Delhi	12625 Kerala Express	595/1676/2780	50½	11.15am
Mangalore	16347 Mangalore Express	257/719/1085	14½	8.40pm

sambar deer, sloth, elephants, lion-tailed macaques and the occasional tiger.

Get here from Trivandrum's Kerala State Road Transport Corporation (KSRTC) bus stand by frequent bus (₹30, 1½ hours). A taxi is ₹900 return (with two hours' waiting time) from Trivandrum, ₹1300 from Kovalam. The KTDC office in Trivandrum also run tours to Neyyar Dam (₹400).

Sivananda Yoga Vedanta Dhanwantari Ashram

Just before Neyyar Dam, the superbly located **Sivananda Yoga Vedanta Dhanwantari Ashram** (☎0471-2273093; www.sivananda.org/ndam), established in 1978, is renowned for its hatha yoga courses. Courses start on the 1st and 16th of each month, run for a minimum of two weeks and cost ₹800 per day for accommodation in a double room (₹1500 with air-con) and ₹500 in a dormitory (meals are included). Low season (May to September) rates are ₹100 less. There's an exacting schedule (5.30am to 10pm) of yoga practice, meditation and chanting. Bookings are required. Month-long yoga-teacher training and ayurvedic massage courses are also available.

Kovalam

☎0471

Once a calm fishing village clustered around its crescent beaches, these days Kovalam is Kerala's most developed resort. The main stretch, **Lighthouse Beach**, is touristy with hotels and restaurants built up along the shore, while **Hawa Beach** to the north is usually crowded with day-trippers heading straight from the taxi stand to the sand. Neither beach is particularly clean, but at less than 15km from the capital it's a convenient place to have some fun by the sea, there's some promising surf and it makes a good base for ayurvedic treatments and yoga courses.

About 2km further north by road, **Samudra Beach** has several upmarket resorts and a peaceful but steep beach.

Dangers & Annoyances

Bikini-clad women are likely to attract male attention, though this is definitely more of an annoyance than a danger. Cover up with a sarong when you're out of the water.

There are strong rips at both ends of Lighthouse Beach that carry away several swimmers every year. Swim only between the flags in the area patrolled by lifeguards and avoid swimming during the monsoon.

Kovalam has frequent blackouts and the paths behind Lighthouse Beach are unlit, so carry a torch (flashlight) after dark.

Sights & Activities

Vizhinjam Lighthouse LIGHTHOUSE

(Indian/foreigner ₹10/25, camera/video ₹20/25; 10am-5pm) Kovalam's most distinguishing feature is the candy-striped lighthouse at the southern end of the beach. Climb the spiral staircase for endless views along the coast.

Santhigiri AYURVEDA

(☎2482800; www.santhigiriashram.org; Lighthouse Beach Rd; 9am-8pm) Excellent massages and ayurvedic treatments from ₹1000.

Sleeping

Kovalam is chock-a-block with hotels, though budget places here cost more than usual and are becoming a dying breed in high season. Beachfront properties are the most expensive, but look out for smaller places tucked away in the labyrinth of paths behind the beach among the palm groves and rice paddies; they're often much better value. All places offer big discounts outside the December–January high season, but call ahead in peak times.

Green Valley Cottages GUESTHOUSE $
(☎2480636; indira_ravi@hotmail.com; r ₹500-800) Back amongst the palm trees, this serene complex feels a little faded but it's quiet and good value at this price. Rooms are simple, but the upper rooms have good views from the front terraces.

Hotel Greenland GUESTHOUSE $
(☎2486442; hotelgreenlandin@yahoo.com; r ₹600-1200) This friendly family-run place has refurbished rooms in a multilevel complex just back from the beach. It's not flash but rooms have lots of natural light and the larger upstairs rooms have a balcony.

Hotel Sky Palace GUESTHOUSE $
(☎9745841222; hotelskypalace@yahoo.com; r ₹500-700) This little two-storey place lies down a small lane; rooms are well kept, brightly painted in greens and blues, some with TV; the ground-floor rooms are cheaper (but the same).

Dwaraka Lodge GUESTHOUSE $
(☎2480411; d ₹500) With regular licks of paint helping to cover up the war wounds of this tired old-timer attached to Rock Cafe, friendly Dwaraka is the cheapest and most basic oceanside property.

Kovalam

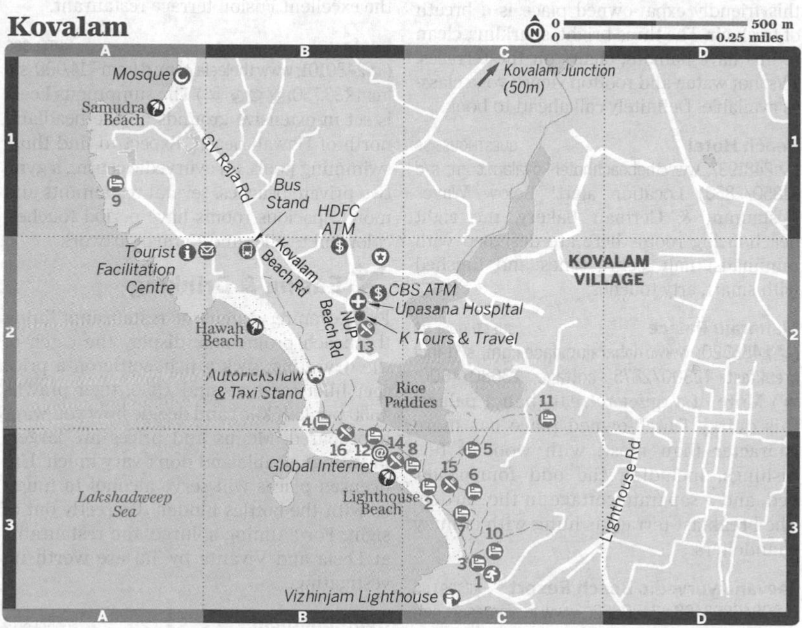

Kovalam

Activities, Courses & Tours
1 Santhigiri C3

Sleeping
2 Beach Hotel C3
3 Beach Hotel II C3
4 Dwaraka Lodge B2
5 Green Valley Cottages C3
6 Hotel Greenland C3
7 Hotel Sky Palace C3
8 Jeevan Ayurvedic Beach Resort C3
9 Leela A1
10 Maharaju Palace C3
11 Paradesh Inn C2
Sea Flower .... (see 3)
12 Sea Star Hotel B3
Treetops .... (see 11)

Eating
13 Devi Garden Restaurant B2
Fusion .... (see 3)
14 Malabar Cafe B3
15 Suprabhatham C3
16 Swiss Cafe B3
Waves Restaurant & German Bakery .... (see 2)

★Paradesh Inn GUESTHOUSE $$
(☎9995362952; inn.paradesh@yahoo.com; Avadu-thura; d incl breakfast ₹1600, ste ₹2500; @) Well back from the beach above the palms, tranquil Italian-run Paradesh Inn resembles a Greek island hideaway – a whitewashed house highlighted in blue. Each of the six fan-cooled rooms has a hanging chair outside, there are sweeping views from the rooftop, fab breakfasts and *satya* cooking ('yoga food') for guests.

Treetops GUESTHOUSE $$
(☎9847912398, 2481363; treetopsofkovalam@yahoo.in; r ₹1000; @) Indeed in the treetops high above the beach next to Paradesh Inn, this friendly expat-owned place is a breath of fresh air. The three bright, sparkling-clean rooms have hanging chairs on the terraces, TVs, hot water, and rooftop views; yoga classes available. Definitely call ahead to book.

Beach Hotel GUESTHOUSE $$
(☎2481937; www.thebeachhotel-kovalam.com; s/d ₹1850/2850) Location alert! Below Waves Restaurant & German Bakery, the eight beach-facing rooms here are designed with minimalist flair, ochre tones and finished with smart, arty touches.

Maharaju Palace GUESTHOUSE $$
(☎2485320; www.maharajupalace.com; s/d incl breakfast ₹2300/2875, cottage ₹3680/4600; ❄) More of a quiet retreat than a palace, this quirky Dutch-owned place has more character than most, with wooden furnishings, including the odd four-poster bed, and a separate cottage in the garden. The breakfast terrace is hung with chintzy chandeliers.

Jeevan Ayurvedic Beach Resort RESORT $$
(☎9846898498, 2480662; www.jeevanresort.net; d ₹2025-3150, with AC ₹3950-4150; ❄ 🏊) Expect inoffensively decorated, decent-sized rooms with bathtubs and an alluring pool – one of the few on the seafront. All but the cheapest ground-floor rooms have sea views and balconies.

Sea Flower HOTEL $$
(☎2480554; www.seaflowerkovalam.com; d ₹1150-2300, with AC ₹2600; ❄) At the southern end of Lighthouse Beach, this slightly dowdy place is reasonably priced for the beachfront location. Rooms are simple but fresh, with a premium for the upper-floor rooms.

Sea Star Hotel HOTEL $$
(☎2488088; www.patanjaliresort.com; Lighthouse Beach; r ₹1800-2500, with AC from ₹3000; ❄ @) In a handy location tucked down a laneway at the north end of Lighthouse Beach, Sea Star has spacious and immaculate rooms and a professional attitude. Yoga sessions with a view from the rooftop.

★Beach Hotel II HOTEL $$$
(☎9400031243, 2481937; www.thebeachhotel-kovalam.com; d ₹4500, with AC ₹5600; ❄) Tucked into the southern end of Lighthouse Beach, this stylish pad has 10 sea-facing rooms all with balcony and large sliding French windows. Decor is simple chic. It's also home to the excellent Fusion terrace restaurant.

Leela HOTEL $$$
(☎2480101; www.theleela.com; d from ₹14,000, ste from ₹33,750; ❄ @ 📶 🏊) The sumptuous Leela is set in extensive grounds on the headland north of Hawah beach. Expect to find three swimming pools, an ayurvedic centre, a gym, two private beaches, several restaurants and more. Spacious rooms have period touches, colourful textiles and Keralan artwork.

✖ Eating & Drinking

Each evening dozens of restaurants lining the beach promenade display the catch of the day – just pick a fish, settle on a price (per fillet serve around ₹350, tiger prawns ₹550 per half kilo) and decide how you want it prepared. Menus and prices are largely indistinguishable and don't vary much. Unlicensed places will serve alcohol in mugs, or with the bottles hidden discreetly out of sight. For a dining splurge, the restaurants at Leela and Vivanta by Taj are worth investigating.

Suprabhatham KERALAN $
(meals ₹60-125; ⏲9am-10pm) This little veg place hidden back from the beach doesn't look like much, but it dishes up excellent, dirt-cheap Keralan cooking in a rustic setting of dirt floor and plastic chairs.

Devi Garden Restaurant INDIAN $
(NUP Beach Rd; mains ₹30-170; ⏲7.30am-11pm) Garden is overstating it, but this tiny, family-run eatery just up the road from the taxi stand whips up great veg and nonveg Indian and Chinese food at refreshingly reasonable prices – most veg dishes are under ₹80.

Waves Restaurant & German Bakery MULTICUISINE $$
(Beach Hotel; breakfast ₹70-300, mains ₹150-550; ⏲7am-11pm) With its broad, burnt-orange balcony, ambient soundtrack and wide-roaming menu, Waves is always busy with foreigners. It morphs with the German Bakery, a great spot for breakfast with fresh bread, croissants, pastries and decent coffee, while dinner turns up Thai curries, German sausages and seafood. There's a small bookshop attached.

Swiss Cafe CAFE $$
(mains ₹70-390; ⏲7.30am-11pm) Swiss Cafe stands out for tasty Euro dishes like rosti, schnitzel, pasta and pizza, as well as the usual fresh seafood and Indian staples. The balcony with its wicker chairs is a good place to take in the action.

Malabar Cafe INDIAN $$
(mains ₹100-450; ⏲8am-11pm) The busy tables tell their own story: with candlelight at night and views through pot plants to the crashing waves, Malabar offers tasty food and good service.

Fusion MULTICUISINE $$
(mains ₹120-340; ⏲8.30am-10.30pm) The terrace restaurant at Beach Hotel II is one of the best dining experiences on Lighthouse Beach, with an inventive East-meets-West menu, a range of Continental dishes, Asian fusion and interesting seafood numbers like lobster steamed in vodka. Also serves French press coffee and herbal teas.

☆ Entertainment

During high season, an abridged version of Kathakali is performed most nights – enquire about locations and times at the Tourist Facilitation Centre.

ℹ Information

Almost every shop and hotel will change money. Near the hospital is a CBS ATM taking Visa cards. About 500m uphill from the beach are HDFC and Axis ATMs, and there are Federal Bank and ICICI ATMs at Kovalam Junction. There are several small internet cafes charging around ₹30 per hour.

Global Internet (Leo Restaurant; per hr ₹30; ⏲8.30am-11pm; wi-fi) Check your email with wi-fi over a cold beer.

Post Office (Kovalam Beach Rd; ⏲9am-1pm Mon-Sat)

Tourist Facilitation Centre (☎2480085; Kovalam Beach Rd; ⏲9.30am-5pm) Helpful; in the entrance to Government Guesthouse near the bus stand and Leela Hotel.

Upasana Hospital (☎2480632) Has English-speaking doctors who can take care of minor injuries.

ℹ Getting There & Around

BUS

Buses start and finish at an unofficial stand on the main road outside the entrance to Leela Hotel and all buses pass through Kovalam Junction, about 1.5km north of Lighthouse Beach. Buses connect Kovalam and Trivandrum every 20 minutes between 5.30am and 10.10pm (₹9, 30 minutes). There are two buses daily to Ernakulam (₹200, 5½ hours), stopping at Kallambalam (for Varkala, ₹70, 1½ hours), Kollam (₹80, 2½ hours) and Alleppey (₹120, four hours). There's another 6.30am bus to Ernakulam via Kottayam that bypasses Varkala.

MOTORBIKE HIRE

K Tours & Travel (☎2127003), next door to Devi Garden Restaurant, rents out scooters/Enfields for around ₹400/550 per day.

TAXI

A taxi between Trivandrum and Kovalam beach is around ₹400; an autorickshaw should cost ₹250. From the bus stand to Lighthouse Beach costs around ₹50.

Around Kovalam

Pulinkudi & Chowara

Around 8km south of Kovalam, amid seemingly endless swaying palms, colourful village life, and some empty golden-sand beaches, are some ayurvedic resorts that make tantalising high-end alternatives to Kovalam's crowded centre.

Dr Franklin's Panchakarma Institute (☎2480870; www.dr-franklin.com; Chowara; s/d hut €15/20, r from €25/32, with AC €38/55; internet, wi-fi) is a reputable and less expensive alternative to the flashier resorts. Daily treatment with full board costs €56. Accommodation is tidy and comfortable but not resort style.

Surya Samudra Private Retreats (☎2480413; www.suryasamudra.com; Pulinkudi; r incl breakfast ₹14,100-22,600; AC, pool) offers A-list-style seclusion, with 22 transplanted traditional Keralan homes, with four-poster beds and open-air bathrooms, set in a palm grove above sparkling seas. There's an infinity pool carved out of a single block of granite, ayurvedic treatments, gym and spectacular outdoor yoga platforms.

Bethsaida Hermitage (☎2267554; www.bethsaidahermitage.com; Pulinkudi; s €80-140, d €140-155; ❄) 🍃 is a resort with a difference: this is a charitable organisation that helps support two nearby orphanages and an old people's home. It's also an inviting, somehow old-fashioned beachside escape with sculpted gardens, a friendly welcome and putting-green perfect lawns.

Thapovan Heritage Home (☎2480453; www.thapovan.com; hillside s/d from ₹2700/3480, cottages ₹4500/5700, beachfront s/d cottage ₹4800/6000) has two properties about 100m apart – one has beachfront cottages in Keralan style and the other is on a gorgeous hilltop location, with teak cottages filled with handcrafted furniture and set amidst perfectly manicured grounds with wonderful views to the ocean and swaying palm groves.

Varkala

☎0470 / POP 42,270

Perched almost perilously along the edge of dizzying cliffs, the resort of Varkala has a naturally beautiful setting and the cliff-top stretch has steadily grown into Kerala's most popular backpacker hang-out. A strand of golden beach nuzzles Varkala's cliff edge, where restaurants play innocuous trance music and stalls sell T-shirts, baggy trousers and silver jewellery. While this kind of tie-dye commercialism can grate on the nerves – the daily wander along the cliff path is made a little less relaxing by the constant chants of 'come see my shop' – Varkala is still a great place to watch the days slowly turn into weeks, and it's not hard to escape the crowds further north or south.

Despite its backpacker vibe, Varkala is essentially a temple town, and the main Papanasham beach is a holy place where Hindus come to make offerings for passed loved ones, assisted by priests who set up shop beneath the Hindustan Hotel. You can while away days watching the mix of fishermen, Hindu rituals, volleyball-playing visitors, locals gazing at the sea and strolling backpackers that make up the traffic on the beach.

Dangers & Annoyances

The beaches at Varkala have strong currents; even experienced swimmers have been swept away here. This is one of the most dangerous beaches in Kerala; swim between the flags or ask locally. During the monsoon the beach all but disappears and the cliffs themselves are slowly being eroded. Take care walking on the cliff path, especially at night – much of it is unfenced and can be slippery in parts.

If women wear bikinis or even swimsuits on the beach at Varkala, they are likely to feel uncomfortably exposed to stares. Wearing a sarong when out of the water will help avoid offending local sensibilities. It pays to dress sensitively, especially if you're going into Varkala town.

Sights

Janardhana Temple HINDU TEMPLE

Varkala is a temple town and Janardhana Temple is the main event – its technicolour Hindu spectacle sits hovering above Beach Rd. The temple is closed to non-Hindus, but you may be invited into the temple grounds where there is a huge banyan tree and shrines to Ayyappan, Hanuman and other Hindu deities.

Sivagiri Mutt SACRED SITE

(☎2602807; www.sivagirimutt.org) Sivagiri Mutt is the headquarters of the Shri Narayana Dharma Sanghom Trust, the ashram devoted to Shri Narayana Guru (1855–1928), Kerala's most prominent guru. This is a popular pilgrimage site and the resident swami is happy to talk to visitors.

Activities

Yoga is offered at several guesthouses for ₹200 to ₹300 per session. **Boogie boards** can be hired from places along the beach for ₹100; plese be wary of strong currents. Many of the resorts and hotels along the north cliff offer ayurvedic treatments and massage.

Laksmi's MASSAGE

(☎9895948080; Clafouti Beach Resort; manicure/pedicure from ₹400/600, henna ₹300, massage ₹800; ⏲9am-7pm) This tiny place offers treatments such as threading and waxing as well as massages (women only).

Haridas Yoga YOGA

(www.pranayogavidya.com; Hotel Green Palace; classes ₹250; ⏲8am & 4.30pm Aug-May) Recommended 1½-hour hatha yoga classes with experienced teachers.

Eden Garden MASSAGE

(☎2603910; www.eden-garden.net; massage from ₹1000) Offers a more upmarket ayurvedic

Varkala

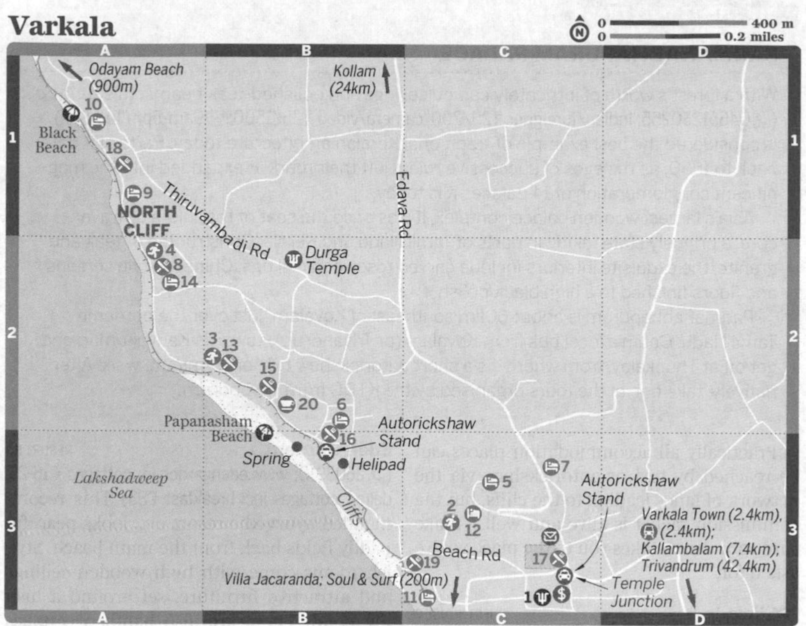

Varkala

Sights

1 Janardhana Temple C3

Activities, Courses & Tours

2 Eden Garden C3
3 Haridas Yoga B2
4 Laksmi's A2

Sleeping

Eden Garden .... (see 2)
5 Guest House Varkala C3
6 Jicky's B2
7 Kaiya House C3
8 Kerala Bamboo House A2
9 Puthooram A1
10 Sea Breeze A1
11 Sea Pearl Chalets C3
12 Taj Gateway Hotel C3

Eating

13 Café del Mar B2
14 Hungry Eye Kitchen A2
15 Juice Shack B2
16 Oottupura Vegetarian Restaurant B3
17 Sreepadman C3
18 Trattorias A1
19 Wait n Watch C3

Drinking & Nightlife

20 Coffee Temple B2

Entertainment

Rock n Roll Cafe .... (see 14)

experience, including single treatments and packages.

Soul & Surf SURFING, YOGA
(☎9746512584; www.soulandsurf.com; South Cliff; surf guide ₹800, with board rental ₹1200) This UK outfit organises surfing trips and yoga retreats in season, usually through packages with accommodation included, but if there's space, nonguests can join the regular surfing tours.

Sleeping

Most places to stay are crammed in along the north cliff where backpackers tend to congregate, but there are some nice places down by the southern cliffs; some are only open for the tourist onslaught in November. Less-developed Odayam beach, about 1km further north of Varkala's black beach, is a tranquil alternative.

OFF THE BEATEN TRACK

PADMANABHAPURAM PALACE

With a forest's worth of intricately carved ceilings and polished-teak beams, this **palace** (04651250255; Indian/foreigner ₹25/200, camera/video ₹25/1500; 9am-5pm Tue-Sun) is considered the best example of traditional Keralan architecture today. Parts of it date back to 1550; as the egos of successive rulers left their mark, it expanded into the magnificent conglomeration of 14 palaces it is today.

Asia's largest wooden palace complex, it was once the seat of the rulers of Travancore, a princely state taking in parts of Tamil Nadu and Kerala. Constructed of teak and granite, the exquisite interiors include carved rosewood ceilings, Chinese-style screens and floors finished to a high black polish.

Padmanabhapuram is about 60km southeast of Kovalam, just over the border in Tamil Nadu. Catch a local bus from Kovalam (or Trivandrum) towards Kanyakumari and get off at Thuckalay, from where it's a short autorickshaw ride or 15-minute walk. Alternatively, take one of the tours organised by the KTDC from Trivandrum.

Practically all accommodation places can be reached by taxi or autorickshaw via the network of lanes leading to the cliffs, but the commission racket is alive and well – make sure your driver takes you to the place you've asked for.

★Jicky's GUESTHOUSE $
(2606994; www.jickys.com; s ₹400, d ₹600-1000, cottage ₹1250-1750, r with AC ₹2500) In the palm groves just back from the cliffs and taxi stand, family-run Jicky's remains as friendly as they come and has spread into several buildings offering plenty of choice for travellers. The rooms in the main whitewashed building are lovely and fresh, and nearby are two charming octagonal double cottages, and some larger air-con rooms.

Guest House Varkala GUESTHOUSE $
(2602227; d ₹220, with AC ₹440) It would take a true budgeteer to trek to this government-run guesthouse (ironically close to the five-star Taj), but the spartan rooms here are bargain-basement in season if you don't mind the location and basic rooms.

★Kaiya House GUESTHOUSE $$
(9746126909, 9995187913; www.kaiyahouse.com; s/d incl breakfast ₹1500/2000, d with AC ₹2500;) Well back from the cliffs, what Kaiya House lacks in sea views it makes up for with charm, welcoming owners and sheer relaxation. Each of the five rooms is thoughtfully furnished and themed (African, Indian, Chinese, Japanese and English) with four-poster beds and artworks on the walls. There's a lovely rooftop terrace and rear courtyard with calming vibe. The cliff-top is 10 minutes' walk away.

Eden Garden RESORT $$
(2603910; www.edengarden.in; cottages €16-25, deluxe cottages incl breakfast €83) This recommended ayurvedic resort overlooks peaceful paddy fields back from the main beach. Stylish rooms come with high wooden ceilings and attractive furniture, set around a lush lily pond. There are also bamboo cottages and deluxe organically-shaped cottages like white space-mushrooms with intricate paintwork, round beds, and mosaic circular baths. Ayurvedic packages range from three- to 30-day packages.

Kerala Bamboo House RESORT $$
(9895270993; www.keralabamboohouse.com; huts d ₹1500-3000) For that bamboo-hut experience, this popular place squishes together dozens of pretty Balinese-style huts and a neatly maintained garden in a cliff-top compound. Some of the huts are nicer than others, so look at a few. Ayurvedic treatments, yoga and cooking class are on offer.

Puthooram RESORT $$
(3202007; www.puthooram.com; r ₹1150-2875, with AC ₹3450-4500; @) Puthooram's wood-lined bungalows are set around a charming little garden of pot plants. Rooms with sea view are pricier.

Sea Pearl Chalets RESORT $$
(2660105; www.seapearlchalets.com; d ₹1500) Perched on Varkala's quieter southern cliff, these basic, pod-like huts have unbeatable views and are surrounded by prim lawns. Worth checking out before they tumble into the ocean.

Sea Breeze GUESTHOUSE $$
(☎9746079790; www.seabreezevarkala.in; r ₹1725, with AC ₹2500-3450; ❄📶) The spacious, orderly, if dull rooms at this friendly guesthouse offer sea views and share a large verandah – perfect for nightly sunset adulation.

Villa Jacaranda GUESTHOUSE $$$
(☎2610296; www.villa-jacaranda.biz; d incl breakfast ₹5600-7000; 📶) The ultimate in understated luxury, this romantic retreat has just a handful of huge, bright rooms in a large two-storey house, each with a balcony and decorated with a chic blend of minimalist modern and period touches. The top-floor room has its own rooftop garden with sea views.

Blue Water Beach Resort COTTAGES $$$
(☎94468 48534; www.bluewaterstay.com; Odayam Beach; cottages ₹3000-5000) At quiet Odayam Beach, north of Varkala, Blue Water is the pick of the beachfront places with sturdy individual timber cottages with tiled roofs arranged in a pleasant lawn area sloping down to the beach.

Taj Gateway Hotel HOTEL $$$
(☎6673300; www.thegatewayhotels.com; d incl breakfast from ₹7700; ❄@📶🏊) Varkala's flashiest hotel is looking hot – refurbished rooms with gleaming linen and mocha cushions overlook the garden, while the more expensive rooms have sea views and private balconies. There's a fantastic pool with bar (nonguests ₹500), tennis court and well-regarded GAD restaurant.

Eating & Drinking

Most restaurants in Varkala offer the same mishmash of Indian, Asian and Western fare to a soundtrack of easy-listening trance and Bob Marley, but the quality of the cliffside 'shacks' has improved out of sight over the years and most offer free wi-fi. Join in the nightly Varkala saunter till you find a place that suits. Unlicensed places will usually serve alcohol discreetly.

Sreepadman SOUTH INDIAN $
(thali ₹40) To grab dirt-cheap and authentic Keralan fare – think dosas and thalis – where you can rub shoulders with rickshaw drivers rather than tourists, check out hole-in-the-wall Sreepadman opposite the Janardhana temple.

Oottupura Vegetarian Restaurant INDIAN $
(mains ₹35-80) Near the taxi stand, this budget eatery has a respectable range of cheap

AYURVEDA

With its roots in Sanskrit, the word ayurveda is from *ayu* (life) and *veda* (knowledge); the knowledge or science of life. Principles of ayurvedic medicine were first documented in the Vedas some 2000 years ago, but may have been practised centuries earlier.

Ayurveda sees the world as having an intrinsic order and balance. It argues that we possess three *doshas* (humours): *vata* (wind or air); *pitta* (fire); and *kapha* (water/earth), known together as the *tridoshas*. Deficiency or excess in any of them can result in disease: an excess of *vata* may result in dizziness and debility; an increase in *pitta* may lead to fever, inflammation and infection. *Kapha* is essential for hydration.

Ayurvedic treatment aims to restore the balance, and hence good health, principally through two methods: panchakarma (internal purification), and herbal massage. Panchakarma is used to treat serious ailments, and is an intense detox regime, a combination of five types of different therapies to rid the body of built-up endotoxins. These include: *vaman* – therapeutic vomiting; *virechan* – purgation; *vasti* – enemas; *nasya* – elimination of toxins through the nose; and *raktamoksha* – detoxification of the blood. Before panchakarma begins, the body is first prepared over several days with a special diet, oil massages (*snehana*) and herbal steam-baths (*swedana*). Although it may sound pretty grim, panchakarma purification might only use a few of these treatments at a time, with therapies like bloodletting and leeches only used in rare cases. Still, this is no spa holiday. The herbs used in ayurveda grow in abundance in Kerala's humid climate – the monsoon is thought to be the best time of year for treatment, when there is less dust in the air, the pores are open and the body is most receptive to treatment – and every village has its own ayurvedic pharmacy.

veg dishes, including breakfast *puttu* (flour with milk, bananas and honey).

Juice Shack CAFE $
(juices ₹50, snacks ₹30-150; ⏲7am-7pm; 📶) It's looking a little 'shack-like' next to the fancy new places, but this funky little health-juice bar still turns out great juices, smoothies and snacks such as Mexican wraps.

Café del Mar MULTICUISINE $
(dishes ₹80-350; 📶) It doesn't have the big balcony like some of its neighbours, but Café del Mar is always busy thanks to efficient service, good coffee and consistently good food, albeit from a 10-page menu.

Hungry Eye Kitchen MULTICUISINE $
(meals ₹70-250; ⏲8am-11pm) Hungry Eye is a reliable multilevel cliff-top choice where Tibetan momos meet Thai curries and steaks, along with the usual Indian and Chinese.

Trattorias MULTICUISINE $$
(meals ₹100-400; ⏲8.30am-11pm) Trattorias aims to specialise in Italian with a decent range of pasta and pizza but also offers Japanese – including sushi – and Thai dishes. This was one of the original places with an Italian coffee machine, and the wicker chairs and sea-facing terrace are cosy.

Wait n Watch INDIAN $$
(Hindustan Hotel; mains ₹120-280; ⏲11am-10pm) The top-floor restaurant and cocktail bar at this beachfront hotel block offer tasty-enough Indian fare and seafood, but the real reason to come here is the view from the balcony (with just a couple of tables) over the beach action. There's another alfresco restaurant by the pool.

Coffee Temple CAFE
(⏲from 6am; 📶) For your early morning coffee fix it's hard to beat this English-run place, where the beans are freshly ground. Also good cakes and fresh bread.

☆ Entertainment

Kathakali performances are organised during high season – look out for notices locally.

Rock n Roll Cafe LIVE MUSIC
(⏲24hr) Music is the thing at this otherwise unremarkable restaurant-bar. There's live music, DJs or movies on most nights in season, as well as tabla lessons. Cold beer and a good cocktail list.

ℹ Information

A 24-hour ATM at Temple Junction takes Visa cards, and there are more ATMs in Varkala town. Many of the travel agents lining the cliff do cash advances on credit cards and change travellers cheques. **Internet cafes** (per hr around ₹40) dot the cliff top but most of the restaurants and cafes offer free wi-fi – save emails often, as power cuts are not uncommon.

Post Office (⏲10am-2pm Mon-Sat) North of Temple Junction.

ℹ Getting There & Away

There are frequent local and express trains to Trivandrum (sleeper/3AC ₹140/249, one hour) and Kollam (₹140/249, 40 minutes), as well as four daily services to Alleppey (2nd-class/chair class ₹50/185, two hours). It's feasible to get to Kollam in time for the morning backwater boat to Alleppey. From Temple Junction, three daily buses pass by on their way to Trivandrum (₹40, 1½ to two hours), with one heading to Kollam (₹30, one hour).

A taxi to Trivandrum costs ₹1100 and to Kollam ₹800.

ℹ Getting Around

It's about 2.5km from the train station to Varkala beach, with rickshaws going to Temple Junction for ₹60 and north cliff for ₹80. Local buses also travel regularly between the train station and Temple Junction (₹4).

Many places along the cliff hire out scooters/Enfields for ₹250/350 per day.

Around Varkala

Kappil Beach

About 9km north of Varkala, Kappil Beach is a beautiful and, as yet, undeveloped stretch of sand. It's also the start of a mini network of backwaters. The **Kappil Lake Boat Club**, near the bridge, hires out boats for short trips on the lake.

Kappil Paradise Resort COTTAGES $$
(📱938775509; mohdrafi20@rediffmail.com; r ₹1200) Located just steps from the golden sand of Kappil and with very little around to disturb the peace, this is a pretty basic place with a handful of solid cottage-style rooms among the palms. Meals are available and the owner can help with transport to/from Varkala (around ₹150) and motorbike rental.

Kollam (Quilon)

0474 / POP 349,000

Untouristy Kollam (Quilon) is the southern approach to Kerala's backwaters and one end of a popular backwater ferry trip to Alleppey. One of the oldest ports in the Arabian Sea, it was once a major commercial hub that saw Roman, Arab, Chinese and later Portuguese, Dutch and British traders jostle into port – eager to get their hands on spices and the region's cashew crops. The centre of town is reasonably hectic, but surrounding it are the calm waterways of Ashtamudi Lake, fringed with coconut palms, cashew plantations and traditional villages – a great place to get a feel for the backwaters without the crowds.

Sights

The best thing to do from Kollam is explore the backwaters around **Munroe Island**. There's a rowdy **fish market** at Kollam Beach where customers and fisherfolk alike pontificate on the value of the day's catch; there's also an evening fish market from 5pm to 9pm. The average **beach** is 2km south of town, a ₹35 rickshaw ride away.

Activities

Santhigiri Ayurveda Centre AYURVEDA
(2763014; http://santhigiriashram.com; Asramam Rd, Kadappakada) An ayurvedic centre with more of an institutional than a spa vibe, popular for its seven- to 21-day treatment packages – accommodation is available for ₹500 a night. You can also just visit for a rejuvenation massage (₹1000).

Tours

★**Canal Cruise** BOATING
(www.dtpckollam.com; per person ₹400; 9am-1.30pm & 2-6.30pm) Excellent tours through the canals of Munroe Island and across Ashtamudi Lake are organised by the DTPC (District Tourism Promotion Council) and a few private operators. After a 25km drive to the starting point, you take a three-hour trip via punted canoe. On these guided excursions you can observe daily village life, see *kettuvallam* (rice barge) construction, toddy (palm beer) tapping, coir-making (coconut fibre), prawn and fish farming, and do some birdwatching on spice-garden visits.

Houseboat Cruises BOATING
(www.dtpckollam.com; 2/4/6 people overnight from ₹3000/4000/5500, Kollam to Alappuzha cruise ₹10,000/12,000/14,000) Kollam has far fewer houseboats than Alleppey, which can mean a less-touristy experience. The DTPC organises various houseboat cruise packages, both locally and to Alleppey and Kochi.

Festivals & Events

Kollam Pooram is a colourful annual temple festival held in April, featuring elephants and mock sword fights. Snake-boat races are common in villages around Kollam. The **President's Trophy Boat Race**, held on Ashtamudi Lake on 1 November, is the largest and most prestigious in the region.

Sleeping

The DTPC office keeps a list of **homestays** in and around Kollam.

Karuna Residency GUESTHOUSE $
(3263240; Main Rd; s/d ₹350/450, r with AC ₹700;) This little budgeteer is starting to show its age and is very basic, but it's still in reasonable condition and the owner is accustomed to travellers.

★**Ashtamudi Villas** GUESTHOUSE $$
(98471 32449, 2706090 www.ashtamudivillas.com; near Kadavoor Church, Mathilil; d ₹1000-1500;) These charming brick cottages on the water's edge are easily the best choice for a relaxing, affordable stay in Kollam. Ebullient host Prabhath Joseph offers a warm welcome and pulls out all the stops with thoughtful architectural design, colourful decor, gleaming bathrooms, hammocks swinging between palm trees by the lake and a library of books on Kerala. Access is by road or boat – call ahead for directions.

Nani Hotel HOTEL $$
(2751141; www.hotelnani.com; Chinnakada Rd; d incl breakfast ₹1300, with AC ₹2080-3650; @) This boutique business hotel is a surprise in Kollam's busy centre, and very good value. Built by a cashew magnate, it's beautifully designed and mixes traditional Keralan elements and modern lines for a sleek look. Even the cheaper rooms have flat-screen TVs, feathery pillows and sumptuous bathrooms.

Kollam (Quilon)

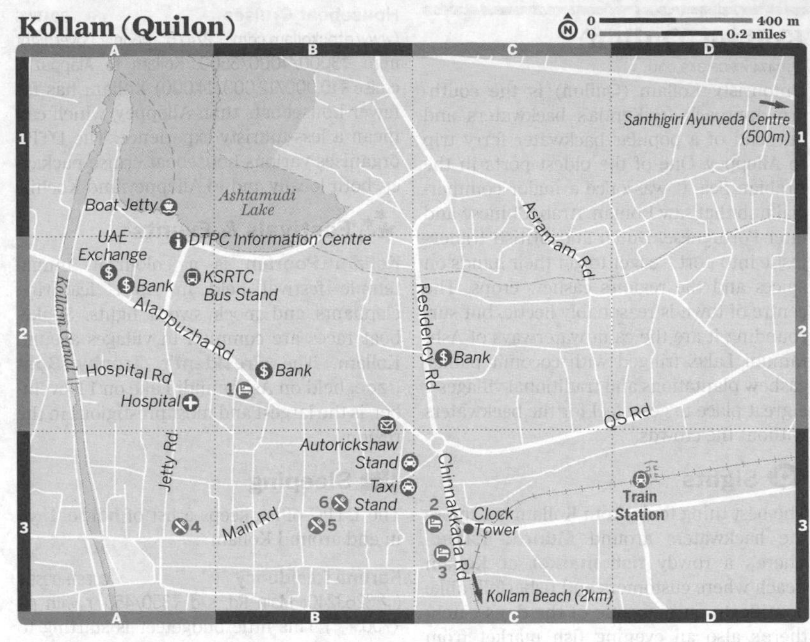

Kollam (Quilon)

Sleeping
1 Hotel Sudarsan B2
2 Karuna Residency C3
3 Nani Hotel C3

Eating
4 Fayalwan Hotel A3
5 Hotel Guru Prasad B3
6 Indian Coffee House B3
Kedar Restaurant .... (see 1)
Prasadam .... (see 3)

Hotel Sudarsan HOTEL $$
(☎2744322; www.hotelsudarsan.com; Alappuzha Rd; d ₹1100, s/d with AC from ₹1350/1460, ste ₹2250/2500; ❄@) Close to the boat jetty, Sudarsan is a decent-value midranger with rooms set around an inner carpark-courtyard. The spacious suites are a bargain at this price. There's a restaurant, bar and coffee shop on site and 24-hour checkout.

Eating

Indian Coffee House INDIAN $
(Main Rd; dishes ₹10-40; ⊙7am-10pm) Reliable for a decent breakfast and strong coffee.

Hotel Guru Prasad INDIAN $
(Main Rd; meals ₹10-25) In a neat colonial building, this busy lunchtime place draws (mostly male) punters with dirt-cheap set meals.

Fayalwan Hotel INDIAN $
(Main Rd; meals ₹15-50) This is a real Indian working-man's diner, packed to the rafters come lunchtime. There are concrete booths and long benches for sitting and tucking in – try the mutton biryani.

Prasadam MULTICUISINE $$
(☎2751141; Chinnakada Rd, Nani Hotel; mains ₹60-240; ⊙8am-10pm) The restaurant at the Nani Hotel has a slightly formal feel with high-backed chairs amid intricate copper-relief artwork depicting Kollam history. Meals, including Keralan dishes such as Travancore egg masala, as well as tandoori and Chinese, are well prepared and tasty thalis are available at lunchtime.

Kedar Restaurant INDIAN $$
(Hotel Sudarsan; meals ₹90-150; ⊙7am-11pm) This darkened air-con restaurant is recommended for its tasty veg and nonveg cuisine, thalis and Sunday lunch buffet. There's a less-formal coffee shop for snacks and the Golden Tavern bar in the same hotel complex.

Information

DTPC Information Centre (☎2745625; www.dtpckollam.com; ⏲8am-7pm) Helpful and can organise backwater trips; near the KSRTC bus stand and boat jetty.

Post Office (☎2746607; Alappuzha Rd)

UAE Exchange (☎2751240; Alappuzha Rd; ⏲9.30am-6pm Mon-Fri, to 4pm Sat, to 1.30pm Sun) For changing cash and travellers cheques.

Getting There & Away

BOAT

There are cruises to Alleppey (p292). From the main boat jetty there are frequent public ferry services across Ashtamudi Lake to Guhanandapuram (one hour). Fares are around ₹10 return, or ₹3 for a short hop.

BUS

Kollam is on the Trivandrum–Kollam–Alleppey–Ernakulam bus route, with buses departing every 10 or 20 minutes to Trivandrum (₹50, two hours), Alleppey (₹55, 2½ hours) and Ernakulam (Kochi, ₹95, 3½ hours). Buses depart from the **KSRTC bus stand** (☎2752008), conveniently near the boat jetty.

TAXI

A taxi to Alleppey costs ₹1200 and to Varkala ₹700.

TRAIN

There are frequent trains to Ernakulam (sleeper/3AC ₹140/308, 3½ hours, six daily) and Trivandrum (₹140/249, one hour) via Varkala (₹36/165, 30 minutes). A couple of trains daily go to Alappuzha (Alleppey; 2nd-class/AC chair ₹45/165, 1½ hours).

Around Kollam

Krishnapuram Palace Museum

Two kilometres south of Kayamkulam (between Kollam and Alleppey), this restored **palace** (☎04792441133; admission ₹10, camera/video ₹25/250; ⏲9am-1pm & 2-4.30pm Tue-Sun) is a fine example of grand Keralan architecture. Now a museum, inside are paintings, antique furniture, sculptures and a renowned 3m-high mural depicting the Gajendra Moksha (the liberation of Gajendra, chief of the elephants) as told in the Mahabharata.

Buses (₹26, one hour) leave Kollam every few minutes for Kayamkulam. Get off at the bus stand near the temple gate, 2km before the palace.

Alappuzha (Alleppey)

☎0477 / POP 174,200

Alappuzha – still more romantically known as Alleppey – is the hub of Kerala's backwaters, home to a vast network of waterways and more than 1000 houseboats. Wandering around the small but chaotic city centre, with its modest grid of canals, you'd be hard-pressed to agree with the 'Venice of the East'

MATHA AMRITHANANDAMAYI MISSION

Well worth a visit if you are doing the **backwater cruise** (p292) between Kollam and Alleppey is the incongruously pink **Matha Amrithanandamayi Mission** (☎04762897578; www.amritapuri.org; Amrithapuri). One of India's few female gurus, Amrithanandamayi is also known as Amma (Mother), or the 'Hugging Mother,' because of the *darshan* (audience) she offers, often hugging thousands of people in marathon all-night sessions. The ashram runs official tours daily – call ahead for times. It's a huge complex, with about 3000 people living here permanently – monks, nuns, students and families, both Indian and foreign. It offers food, ayurvedic treatments, yoga and meditation. Amma travels around for much of the year, so you might be out of luck if in need of a cuddle.

Visitors should dress conservatively and there is a strict code of behaviour. With prior arrangement – register online – you can stay at the ashram for ₹200 per day (including simple vegetarian meals) and pick up an onward or return cruise a day or two later. Alternatively, cross to the other side of the canal and grab a rickshaw 10km south to Karunagappally or 12km north to Kayankulam (around ₹200), from where you can catch onward buses or trains.

If you're not taking the cruise, catch a train to either Karunagappally or Kayankulam and take an autorickshaw (around ₹100) to Vallickavu and cross the pedestrian bridge or take the punt across the canal from there. Alternatively, if you intend to stay a while, you can book online for an ashram taxi – they pick up from as far away as Kochi or Trivandrum.

Alappuzha (Alleppey)

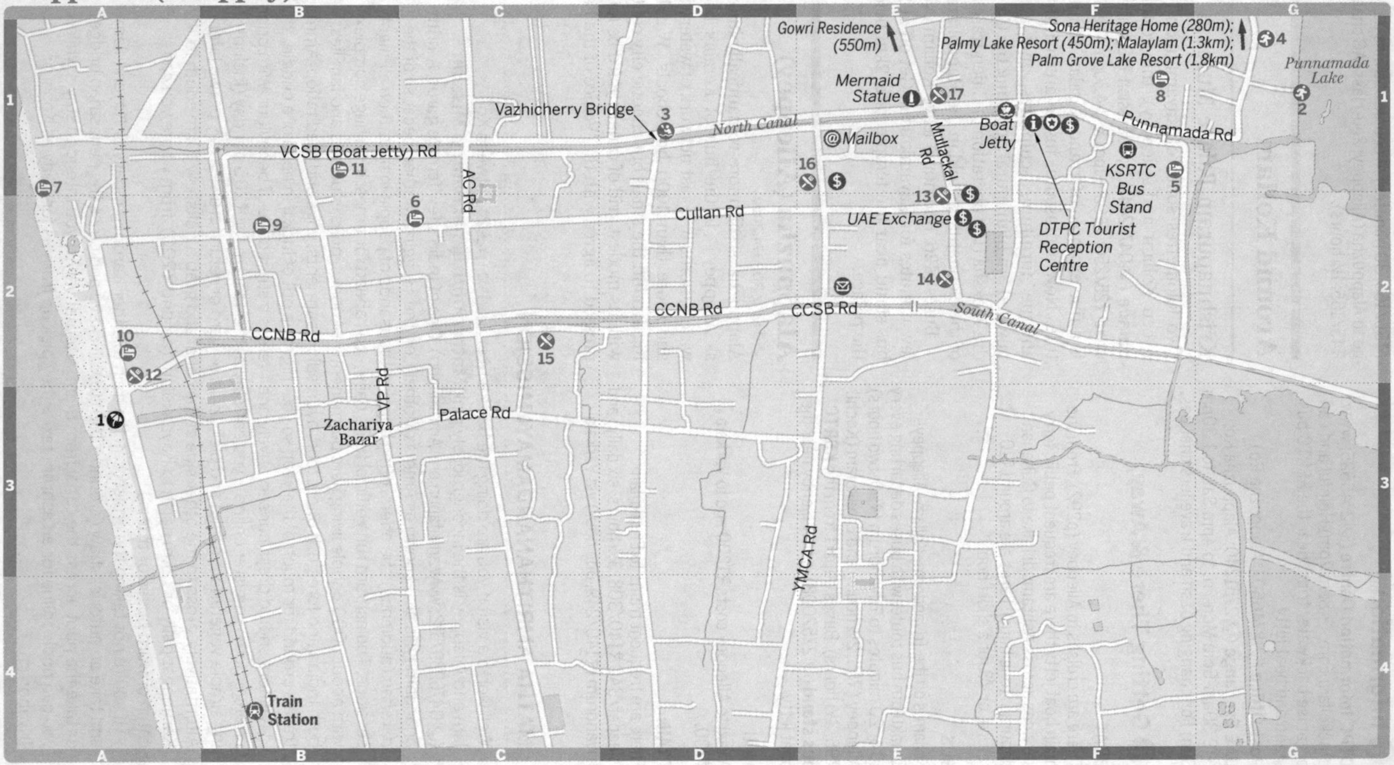
0 500 m
0 0.25 miles
Gowri Residence (550m)
Sona Heritage Home (280m); Palmy Lake Resort (450m); Malaylam (1.3km); Palm Grove Lake Resort (1.8km)
Punnamada Lake
Mermaid Statue
Vazhicherry Bridge
North Canal
@Mailbox
Mullackal Rd
Boat Jetty
Punnamada Rd
VCSB (Boat Jetty) Rd
KSRTC Bus Stand
AC Rd
Cullan Rd
UAE Exchange
DTPC Tourist Reception Centre
CCNB Rd
CCSB Rd
South Canal
CCNB Rd
VP Rd
Palace Rd
Zachariya Bazar
YMCA Rd
Train Station
1
2
3
4
5
6
7
8
9
10
11
12
13
14
15
16
17
A
B
C
D
E
F
G

Alappuzha (Alleppey)

Sights

1 Alleppey Beach A3

Activities, Courses & Tours

2 Houseboat Dock G1
3 Kerala Kayaking D1
4 Shri Krishna Ayurveda Panchkarma Centre G1

Sleeping

5 Cherukara Nest F1
6 Johnson's C2
7 Mandala Beach House A1
8 Mathews Palmy Residency F1
9 Nanni Beach Residence B2
10 Raheem Residency A2
11 Tharavad B1

Eating

Chakara Restaurant .... (see 10)
12 Harbour Restaurant A2
13 Indian Coffee House E2
14 Kream Korner Art Cafe E2
15 Mushroom C2
16 Royale Park Hotel E1
17 Thaff E1

tag. But step out of this mini-mayhem and head west to the beach – or in practically any other direction towards the backwaters – and Alleppey is graceful and greenery-fringed, disappearing into a watery world of villages, canoes, toddy shops and, of course, houseboats. Float along and gaze over rice fields of succulent green, curvaceous rice barges and village life along the banks. This is one of Kerala's most mesmerisingly beautiful and relaxing experiences.

Sights & Activities

Alleppey Beach BEACH

Alleppey's main beach is about 2km west of the city centre; there's no shelter at the beach itself and swimming is fraught, but the sunsets are good and there are a few places to stop for a drink or snack. The beach stretches up and down the coast.

Kerala Kayaking KAYAKING

(☎2245001, 9846585674; www.keralakayaking.com; per person 4-/7-/10-hour ₹1000/3000/4000) The first (and only) kayaking outfit in Alleppey, the young crew here offer excellent guided kayaking trips through narrow backwater canals. Paddles in single or double kayaks include a support boat and motorboat transport to your starting point.

Shri Krishna Ayurveda Panchkarma Centre AYURVEDA

(☎3290728; www.krishnayurveda.com) For ayurvedic treatments; one-hour rejuvenation massages are ₹800, but it specialises in three-, five- and seven-night packages with accommodation and yoga classes. It's near the Nehru race finishing point.

Tours

Any of the dozens of travel agencies in town, guesthouses, hotel, or the KTDC can arrange canoe or houseboat tours of the backwaters.

Festivals & Events

Nehru Trophy Boat Race BOAT RACE

(http://nehrutrophy.nic.in; tickets from ₹50) Held on the second Saturday in August on Punnamada Lake, this is the most popular and fiercely-contested of Kerala's snake-boat races.

Sleeping

Even if you're not planning on boarding a houseboat, Alleppey has some of the most charming and best-value accommodation in Kerala, from heritage homes and resorts to family-run homestays with backwater views.

The rickshaw-commission racketeers are at work here, particularly at the train and bus stations; ask to be dropped off at a landmark close to your destination, or if you're booked in, call ahead for a pick-up.

Mathews Palmy Residency GUESTHOUSE $

(☎2235938; www.palmyresidency.com; off Finishing Point Rd; r ₹400-700) One of the better budget deals in town, this place has six spotless rooms with Italian marble floors, three with garden-facing verandahs. The serene location is great too – north of the canal only five minutes' walk from the bus stand but set well back from the road amid lush greenery. Cross over the new Matha footbridge east of the bus station, turn right and take the first laneway to the left.

Mandala Beach House GUESTHOUSE $

(www.mandalabeachhouse.com; Alleppey Beach; d ₹600-900, cottage ₹750, ste ₹2000) Beachfront accommodation on a budget doesn't get much better than this in Alleppey. Super laid-back Mandala sits on the edge of the sand and has a range of simple rooms – the best being the glass-fronted 'penthouse' with unbeatable sunset views. Impromptu parties are known to crank up here in season.

Johnson's GUESTHOUSE $
(☎2245825; www.johnsonskerala.com; d ₹400-750; @📶) This backpacker favourite in a tumble-down mansion is as quirky as its owner, the gregarious Johnson Gilbert. It's a rambling residence with themed rooms filled with funky furniture, loads of plants outside and a canoe-shaped fish tank for a table. Johnson hires out his 'eco-houseboat' (₹6500 to ₹9000) and has a secluded riverside guest-house in the backwaters.

Palmy Lake Resort HOMESTAY $
(☎2235938; www.palmyresorts.com; Punnamada Rd East; cottages d ₹850) With six handsome individual cottages, some bamboo and some concrete, there's loads of charm and peace at this welcoming homestay, 3.5km north of Alleppey. Friendly owners (who also run Mathews Palmy Residency) offer free pick-up from town and home-cooked meals.

Nanni Beach Residence GUESTHOUSE $
(☎9895039767; nannitours@gmail.com; Cullan Rd; d ₹250-400) You can't beat the price at this basic guesthouse, a short walk from the beach and 1.5km north of the train station. The young owner Shibu is a good source of local information and works hard at sprucing the place up.

★ **Cherukara Nest** HOMESTAY $
(☎2251509; www.cherukaranest.com; d/tr incl breakfast ₹750/900, with AC ₹1200, AC cottage ₹1500; ❄@📶) Set in well-tended gardens, with a pigeon coop at the back, this lovely heritage home has the sort of welcoming family atmosphere that makes you want to stay. In the main house there are four large characterful rooms, with high ceilings, lots of polished wood touches and antediluvian doors with ornate locks – check out the spacious split-level air-con room. Owner Tony also has a good-value houseboat (₹5500 for two people) – one of the few that still uses punting power.

Gowri Residence GUESTHOUSE $
(☎2236371; www.gowriresidence.com; SH40; d ₹675-1350, AC cottages ₹1350-2250; ❄📶) This rambling complex about 800m north of North Canal has a startling array of rooms and cottages in a large garden: traditional wood-panelled rooms in the main house, several types of lovely bungalows made from either stone, wood, bamboo or thatch – the best with cathedral ceilings, air-con and flat-screen TV – and a very cool towering tree house. Good food is served, free bicycles and there's an aviary that even includes an emu.

Tharavad HOMESTAY $$
(☎242044; www.tharavadheritageresort.com; West of North Police Station; d ₹1200-1500, with AC ₹2000; ❄) In a quiet canalside location between the town centre and beach, this charming ancestral home has lots of glossy teak and antiques, shuttered windows, five characterful rooms and well-maintained gardens.

Sona Heritage Home GUESTHOUSE $
(☎2235211; www.sonahome.com; Lakeside, Finishing Point; r ₹800-900, with AC ₹1125; ❄📶) Run by the affable Joseph, this beautiful old heritage home has slightly shabby but high-ceilinged rooms with faded flowered curtains, Christian motifs and four-poster beds overlooking a well-kept garden.

Malayalam RESORT $$
(☎2234591; malayalamresorts@yahoo.com; Punnamada; r ₹1200-2500) This little family-run pad has four cute bamboo cottages, tree houses and a big new two-storey four-room house facing the lake near the Nehru Trophy Boat Race starting point. Views from the upstairs rooms with balcony are sweet. It's a bit hard to find: walk past the Keraleeyam resort reception and along the canal bank.

Palm Grove Lake Resort RESORT $$
(☎2235004; www.palmgrovelakeresort.com; Punnamada; cottages d ₹1970-2200, with AC ₹3320) Close to the starting point of the Nehru Trophy Boat Race on Punnamada Lake, the stylish individual double cottages here are set in a palm-filled garden with lake views.

★ **Raheem Residency** HOTEL $$$
(☎2239767; www.raheemresidency.com; Beach Rd; d €112-146; ❄📶🏊) This thoughtfully renovated 1860s heritage home is a joy to visit, let alone stay in. The 10 rooms have been restored to their former glory and have bathtubs, antique furniture and period fixtures. The common areas are airy and comfortable, there are pretty indoor courtyards, a well-stocked library, a great little pool and an excellent restaurant.

✕ Eating & Drinking

Mushroom ARABIAN, INDIAN $
(near South Police Station; mains ₹40-90; ⏲noon-midnight) Breezy open-air restaurant with wrought-iron chairs specialising in cheap, tasty and spicy halal meals like chicken kali

mirch, fish tandoori and chilli mushrooms. Lots of locals and travellers give it a good vibe.

Kream Korner Art Cafe MULTICUISINE $
(☎2252781; www.kreamkornerartcafe.com; Mullackal Rd; dishes ₹25-150; ⏰9am-10pm) The most colourful dining space in town, this food-meets-art restaurant greets you with brightly painted tables and contemporary local art on the walls. It's a relaxed, airy place popular with Indian and foreign families for its inexpensive and tasty menu of Indian and Chinese dishes. There's also a pint-sized **Cullan Rd** (veg thalis ₹45) branch of Kream Korner with just a few seats and popular.

Thaff INDIAN $
(YMCA Rd; meals ₹45-110) A popular hole-in-the-wall that has tasty Indian bites, with some Arabic flavours mixed in. It does succulent spit roast chicken, *shwarma* and brain-freezing ice-cream shakes. There's another location on Punnamada Rd.

Indian Coffee House CAFE $
(snacks ₹8-40; ⏰8am-9pm) Branches on Mullackal Rd, YMCA Rd and Beach Rd – the latter is a pavilion in a breezy beachside location.

Harbour Restaurant MULTICUISINE $$
(☎2230767; Beach Rd; meals ₹100-290; ⏰10am-10pm) This enjoyable beachside place is run by the nearby Raheem Residency. It's more casual and budget-conscious than the hotel's restaurant, but promises a range of well-prepared Indian, Chinese and Continental dishes, and some of the coldest beer in town.

Royale Park Hotel INDIAN $$
(YMCA Rd; meals ₹100-200; ⏰7am-10.30pm, bar 10.30am-10.30pm; 📶) There is an extensive menu at this air-con hotel restaurant, and the food is excellent, including scrumptious veg/fish thalis (₹120/150). You can order from the same menu in the surprisingly nice upstairs bar and wash down your meal with a cold Kingfisher.

Chakara Restaurant MULTICUISINE $$$
(☎2230767; Beach Rd; mini Kerala meal ₹420, mains from ₹450; ⏰12.30-3pm & 7-10pm) The restaurant at Raheem Residency is Alleppey's finest, with seating on a *bijou* open rooftop, reached via a spiral staircase, with views over to the beach. The menu creatively combines traditional Keralan and European cuisine, specialising in locally-caught fish.

ℹ Information

DTPC Tourist Reception Centre (☎2251796; www.dtpcalappuzha.com; Boat Jetty Rd; ⏰9am-5pm) Close to the bus stand and boat jetty. Staff are helpful and can advise on homestays and houseboats.

Mailbox (☎2339994; Boat Jetty Rd; per hr ₹20; ⏰9am-8pm) Internet access.

Tourist Police (☎2251161; ⏰24hr) Next door to the DTPC.

UAE Exchange (☎2264407; cnr Cullan & Mullackal Rds; ⏰9.30am-6pm, to 4pm Sat, to 1pm Sun) For changing cash and travellers cheques.

ℹ Getting There & Away

BOAT

Ferries run to Kottayam from the boat jetty on VCSB (Boat Jetty) Rd.

WORTH A TRIP

GREEN PALM HOMES

Kerala's backwaters snake in all directions from Alleppey and, while touring on a houseboat is a great experience, taking time to slow down and stay in a village can be just as rewarding.

Just 12km from Alleppey on a backwater island, **Green Palms Homes** (☎9495557675, 0477-2724497; www.greenpalmhomes.com; Chennamkary; r without bathroom incl full board ₹2250, r ₹3250-4000) is a series of homestays that seem a universe away, set in a picturesque village, where you sleep in simple rooms in villagers' homes among rice paddies (though 'premium' rooms with attached bathroom and air-con are available). It's splendidly quiet, there are no roads in sight and you can take a guided walk, hire bicycles (₹50 per hour) and canoes (₹100 per hour) or take cooking classes with your hosts (₹150).

To get here, call ahead and catch one of the hourly ferries from Alleppey to Chennamkary (₹5, 1¼ hours). It's also accessible by autorickshaw (around ₹150) then canoe across to the island. This is a traditional village; dress appropriately.

KERALA'S BACKWATERS

The undisputed highlight of a trip to Kerala is travelling through the 900km network of waterways that fringe the coast and trickle inland. Long before the advent of roads, these waters were the slippery highways of Kerala, and many villagers still use paddle-power as their main form of transport. Trips through the backwaters traverse palm-fringed lakes studded with cantilevered Chinese fishing nets, and wind their way along narrow, shady canals where coir (coconut fibre), copra (dried coconut kernels) and cashews are loaded onto boats. Along the way are isolated villages where farming life continues as it has for eons.

Tourist Cruises

The popular tourist cruise between Kollam and Alleppey (₹400) departs from either end at 10.30am, arriving at 6.30pm, daily from August to March and every second day at other times. Generally, there's a 1pm lunch stop (with a basic lunch provided) and a brief afternoon chai stop. The crew has an ice box full of fruit, soft drinks and beer to sell, but it pays to bring snacks, sunscreen and a hat.

It's a scenic and leisurely way – the journey takes eight hours – to get between the two towns, but the boat travels along only the major canals – you won't have many close-up views of the village life that makes the backwaters so magical. Another option is to take the trip halfway (₹250) and get off at the Matha Amrithanandamayi Mission (p287) and meet one of India's few female gurus.

Houseboats

If the stars align, renting a houseboat designed like a *kettuvallam* (rice barge) could well be one of the highlights of your trip to India. It can be an expensive experience (depending on your budget) but for a couple on a romantic overnight jaunt or split between a group of travellers, it's usually worth every rupee. Drifting through quiet canals lined with coconut palms, eating delicious Keralan food, meeting local villagers and sleeping on the water – it's a world away from the clamour of India.

Houseboats cater for couples (one or two double bedrooms) and groups (up to seven bedrooms!). Food (and an onboard chef to cook it) is generally included in the quoted cost, as is a driver/captain. Houseboats can be chartered through a multitude of private operators in Alleppey, Kollam and Kottayam. This is the biggest business in Kerala: some operators are unscrupulous. The quality of boats varies widely, from rust buckets to floating palaces – try to check out the boat before agreeing on a price. Travel-agency reps will be pushing you to book a boat as soon as you set foot in Kerala, but it's better to wait till you reach a backwater hub: choice is greater in Alleppey (an incredible 1000-plus boats

BUS

From the KSRTC bus stand, frequent buses head to Trivandrum (₹120, 3½ hours, every 20 minutes), Kollam (₹55, 2½ hours) and Ernakulam (Kochi, ₹50, 1½ hours). Buses to Kottayam (₹40, 1¼ hours, every 30 minutes) are much faster than the ferry. One bus daily leaves for Kumily at 6.40am (₹120, 5½ hours). The Varkala bus (₹100, 3½ hours) leaves at 9am and 10.40am daily.

TRAIN

There are several trains to Ernakulam (2nd-class/sleeper/3AC ₹39/120/218, 1½ hours) and Trivandrum (₹59/120/267, three hours) via Kollam (₹66/140/250, 1½ hours). Four trains a day stop at Varkala (2nd-class/AC chair ₹71/218, two hours). The train station is 4km west of town.

ℹ Getting Around

An autorickshaw from the train station to the boat jetty and KSRTC bus stand is around ₹60. Several guesthouses around town hire out scooters for ₹200 per day.

Kottayam

☎0481 / POP 172,878

Sandwiched between the Western Ghats and the backwaters, Kottayam is renowned for being the centre of Kerala's spice and rubber trade rather than for its aesthetic appeal. For most travellers it's a hub town, well connected to both the mountains and the backwaters, with many travellers taking the and counting), and you're much more likely to be able to bargain down a price if you turn up and see what's on offer. Most guesthouses and homestays can also book you on a houseboat.

In the high season you're likely to get caught in backwater-gridlock – some travellers are disappointed by the number of boats on the water. It's possible to travel by houseboat between Alleppey and Kollam and all the way to Kochi – the DTPC in Kollam can organise these trips. Expect a boat for two people for 24 hours to cost about ₹5000 to ₹8000 at the budget level; for four people, ₹8000 to to ₹12,000; for larger boats or for air-conditioning expect to pay from ₹12,000 to ₹30,000. Shop around to negotiate a bargain – though this will be harder in the peak season. Prices triple from around 20 December to 5 January.

Village Tours & Canoe Boats

More and more travellers are opting for village tours or canal-boat trips. Village tours usually involve small groups of five to six people, a knowledgable guide and an open canoe or covered *kettuvallam*. The tours (from Kochi, Kollam or Alleppey) last from 2½ to six hours and cost from around ₹400 to ₹800 per person. They include visits to villages to watch coir-making, boat building, toddy tapping and fish farming. The Munroe Island trip from Kollam is an excellent tour of this type; the tourist desk in Ernakulam also organises recommended tours.

In Alleppey, rented canoe boats offer a nonguided laze through the canals on a small, covered canoe for up to four people (two people for two/four hours ₹200/400).

Public Ferries

If you want the local backwater transport experience for just a few rupees, there are State Water Transport (www.swtd.gov.in) boats between Alleppey and Kottayam (₹10 to ₹12, 2½ hours) five times daily starting from Alleppey at 7.30am. The trip crosses Vembanad Lake and has a more varied landscape than the Kollam–Alleppey cruise.

Environmental Issues

Pollution from houseboat motors is becoming a major problem as boat numbers swell every season. The Keralan authorities have introduced an ecofriendly accreditation system for houseboat operators. Among the criteria an operator must meet before being issued with the 'Green Palm Certificate' are the installation of solar panels and sanitary tanks for the disposal of waste – ask operators whether they have the requisite certification. Consider choosing one of the few remaining punting, rather than motorised, boats if possible, though these can only operate in shallow water.

backwater cruise to or from Alleppey. The city itself has a crazy, traffic-clogged centre, but you don't have to go far to be in the villages and waterways.

Kottayam has a bookish history: the first Malayalam-language printing press was established here in 1820, and this was the first district in India to achieve 100% literacy. A place of churches and seminaries, it was a refuge for the Orthodox church when the Portuguese began forcing Keralan Christians to switch to Catholicism in the 16th century.

The **Thirunakkara Utsavam festival** is held in March at the Thirunakkara Shiva Temple.

Sleeping

The accommodation options are pretty average in Kottayam – you're better off heading to Kumarakom for some great lakeside accommodation.

Ambassador Hotel HOTEL $
(☎2563293; ambassadorhotelktm@yahoo.in; KK Rd; d from ₹560, with AC from ₹950) This old-school place gets our vote for best budget hotel in town. Rooms with TV are spartan but fairly clean, spacious and quiet for this price. It has a bar, an adequate restaurant, a pastry counter and a boat-shaped fish tank in the lobby.

Homestead Hotel HOTEL $
(2560467; KK Rd; s/d from ₹425/782, d with AC ₹1500;) This has reasonably well maintained rooms – though some are a little musty and come with eye-watering green decor – in a blissfully quiet building off the street.

Pearl Regency HOTEL $$
(2561123; www.pearlregency.in; MC Rd, TB Junction; s/d from ₹2430/2950;) This business-focused multistorey contender is efficient, decent value and a passable stay if you're stuck in Kottayam. Two restaurants and a 24-hour coffee shop mean you won't even need to leave the hotel.

Windsor Castle & Lake Village Resort HOTEL $$$
(2363637; www.thewindsorcastle.net; MC Rd; s/d from ₹3375/4500, cottages ₹6750;) This grandiose white box has some of Kottayam's best hotel rooms, but the more interesting accommodation is in the Lake Village behind the hotel. Deluxe cottages, strewn around the private backwaters and manicured gardens, are pricey but top notch. There's a pleasant restaurant overlooking landscaped waterways.

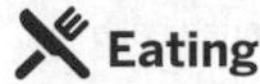

Eating

Thali SOUTH INDIAN $
(1st fl, KK Rd; meals ₹45-95; 8am-8.30pm) A lovely, spotlessly kept 1st-floor dining room with slatted blinds, Thali is a swankier version of the typical Keralan set-meal place. The food here is great, including Malabar fish curry and thalis.

Meenachil MULTICUISINE $
(2nd fl, KK Rd; dishes ₹50-125; noon-3pm & 6-9.30pm) A favourite place in Kottayam to fill up on Indian and Chinese fare. The family atmosphere is friendly, the dining room modern and tidy, and the menu expansive.

★ **Nalekattu** SOUTH INDIAN $$
(MC Rd, Windsor Castle; dishes ₹140-210; noon-3pm & 7-10pm) The traditional Keralan restaurant at the Windsor Castle overlooks some neat backwaters and serves tasty Keralan specialities like *chemeen* (mango curry). The hotel's more upmarket indoor restaurant, **Lake Paradise**, serves a spectacular multicuisine buffet at lunch and dinner for ₹300.

Information

The KSRTC bus stand is 1km south of the centre; the boat jetty is a further 2km (at Kodimatha). The train station is 1km north of Kottayam. There's a handful of ATMs around.

DTPC Office (2560479; www.dtpckottayam.com; 10am-5pm Mon-Sat) At the boat jetty. Offers daily backwater trips to Alleppey and Kumarakom for ₹250.

UAE Exchange (2303865; 1st fl, MC Rd; 9.30am-6pm Mon-Sat, 9.30am-1pm Sun) Changes cash and travellers cheques.

Getting There & Away

BOAT

Daily ferries (p292) run to Alleppey from the boat jetty.

BUS

The **KSRTC bus stand** has buses to Trivandrum (₹98, four hours, every 20 minutes), Alleppey (₹40, 1¼ hours, every 30 minutes) and Ernakulam (Kochi, ₹52, two hours, every 20 minutes). There are also frequent buses to nearby Kumarakom (₹15, 30 minutes, every 15 minutes), Thrissur (₹98, four hours), Calicut (₹190, seven hours, 13 daily), Kumily for Periyar Wildlife Sanctuary (₹71, four hours, every 30 minutes) and Munnar (₹100, five hours, five daily). There are also buses to Kollam (₹65, four daily), where you can change for Varkala.

TRAIN

Kottayam is well served by frequent trains running between Trivandrum (2nd-class/sleeper/3AC ₹82/140/307, 3½ hours) and Ernakulam (₹60/140/225, 1½ hours).

Getting Around

An autorickshaw from the jetty to the KSRTC bus stand is around ₹40, and from the bus stand to the train station about ₹30. Most trips around town cost ₹30.

Around Kottayam

Kumarakom

0481

Kumarakom, 16km west of Kottayam and on the shore of Vembanad Lake – Kerala's largest lake – is an unhurried backwater town with a smattering of dazzling top-end sleeping options and a renowned bird sanctuary. You can arrange houseboats through Kumarakom's less-crowded canals, but expect to pay considerably more than in Alleppey.

Arundhati Roy, author of the 1997 Booker Prize–winning *The God of Small Things*, was raised in the nearby Aymanam village.

Sights & Activities

Kumarakom Bird Sanctuary NATURE RESERVE
(Indian/foreigner ₹30/100, video ₹1000; 6am-5pm) This reserve on the five-hectare site of a former rubber plantation is the haunt of a variety of domestic and migratory birds. October to February is the time for travelling birds like the garganey teal, osprey, marsh harrier and steppe eagle; May to July is the breeding season for local species such as the Indian shag, pond herons, egrets and darters. Early morning is the best viewing time. A guide costs ₹200 for a two-hour tour (₹300 from 6am to 8am).

Buses between Kottayam's KSRTC stand and Kumarakom (₹15, 30 minutes, every 15 minutes) stop at the entrance to the bird sanctuary.

Sleeping

Cruise 'N Lake RESORT $$
(2525804; www.homestaykumarakom.com; Puthenpura Tourist Enclave, Cheepunkal; r ₹1500, with AC ₹2000;) Location, location. Surrounded by backwaters on one side and a lawn of rice paddies on the other, this is the ideal affordable Kumarakom getaway. The three double rooms are plain but have verandahs facing the water. Go a couple of kilometres past the sanctuary to Cheepunkal and take a left; it's then 2km down a rugged dirt road. Management can arrange pick-ups from Kottayam (₹450), and houseboats and all meals are available from here.

Tharavadu Heritage Home GUESTHOUSE $$
(2525230; www.tharavaduheritage.com; d ₹1070-2025, bamboo cottage ₹1575, d with AC ₹2475-2800;) Rooms are either in the superbly restored 1870s teak family mansion or in equally comfortable individual creek-side bamboo cottages. All are excellently crafted and come with arty touches. It's 4km before the bird sanctuary.

Santitheeram Heritage Home HOMESTAY $$
(04812525122; Pushpalayam, Kavanattinkara; r ₹1200) Just two rooms in this cosy and welcoming traditional family home on the water's edge just a few hundred metres from the KTDC boat jetty.

Ettumanur

The **Shiva Temple** at Ettumanur, 12km north of Kottayam, has inscriptions dating from 1542, but parts of the building may be even older. The temple is noted for its exceptional woodcarvings and murals similar to those at Kochi's Mattancherry Palace. The annual **festival** is held in February/March.

Sree Vallabha Temple

Devotees make offerings at this temple, 2km from Tiruvilla, in the form of traditional, regular all-night **Kathakali** performances that are open to all. Around 10km east of here, the **Aranmula Boat Race**, one of Kerala's biggest snake-boat races, is held during Onam in August/September.

THE WESTERN GHATS

Periyar Wildlife Sanctuary

04869

South India's most popular wildlife sanctuary, **Periyar** (224571; www.periyartigerreserve.org; Indian/foreigner ₹25/300; 6am-6pm, last entry 5pm) encompasses 777 sq km and a 26-sq-km artificial lake created by the British in 1895. The vast region is home to bison, sambar, wild boar, langur, 900 to 1000 elephants and 35 to 40 hard-to-spot tigers. Firmly established on both the Indian and foreigner tourist trails, the place can sometimes feel a bit like Disneyland-in-the-Ghats, but its mountain scenery and jungle walks make for an enjoyable visit. Bring warm and waterproof clothing.

Kumily, 4km from the sanctuary, is the closest town and home to a growing strip of hotels, spice shops, chocolate shops and Kashmiri emporiums. Thekkady is the sanctuary centre with the KTDC hotels and boat jetty. Confusingly, when people refer to the sanctuary they tend to use Kumily, Thekkady and Periyar interchangeably.

Sights & Activities

Various tours and trips access Periyar Wildlife Sanctuary. Most hotels and agencies around town can arrange all-day 4WD **jungle safaris** (per person ₹1600-2000; 5am-6.30pm), which cover over 40km of trails in jungle bordering the park, though many travellers complain that at least 30km of the trip is on sealed roads.

You can arrange **elephant rides** (per 30min/1-hr/2- ₹350/750/1000) at most hotels and agents in town. If you want the extended elephant experience, you can pay ₹2500 for a 2½-hour ride that includes elephant feeding and washing. **Cooking classes** (around ₹200-400) are offered by many local homestays.

Periyar Lake Cruise BOATING
(adult/child ₹150/50; departures 7.30am, 9.30am, 11.15am, 1.45pm & 3.30pm) These 1½-hour boat trips around the lake are the main way to tour the sanctuary without taking a guided walk. You might see deer, boar and birdlife but it's generally more of a cruise – often a rowdy one – than a wildlife-spotting experience. Boats are operated by the Forest Department and by KTDC – the **ticket counters** are together in the main building above the boat jetty, and you must buy a ticket before boarding the boat. In high season get to the ticket office 1½ hours before each trip to buy tickets. The first and last departures offer the best prospects for wildlife spotting, and October to March is generally the best time to see animals.

Ecotourism Centre OUTDOOR ADVENTURE
(224571; www.periyartigerreserve.org; Thekkady Rd; 9am-1pm & 2-5pm) A number of more adventurous explorations of the park can be arranged by the Ecotourism Centre, run by the Forest Department. These include border hikes (₹1000; from 8am to 5pm), 2½-hour nature walks (₹200), full-day bamboo rafting (₹1500) and 'jungle patrols' (₹750), which cover 4km to 5km and are the best way to experience the park close up, accompanied by a trained tribal guide. Trips usually require a minimum of four or five people. There are also overnight 'tiger trail' treks (per person ₹4000, solo ₹6000), which are run by former poachers retrained as guides, and cover 20km to 30km.

Gavi Ecotourism OUTDOOR ADVENTURE
(223270, 994792399; http://gavi.kfdcecotourism.com; treks ₹1000, jeep safaris ₹1500; 9am-8pm) This Forest Department venture offers jeep safaris, treks and boating to Gavi, a cardamom plantation and jungle area bordering the sanctuary about 45km from Kumily. Hotels can help organise the same trips.

Spice Gardens & Tea Plantation GARDENS, TEA ESTATE
This part of the ghats is an important spice-growing region – check out the many spice shops in Kumily's bazaar to see what's harvested. Several spice plantations are open to visitors and most hotels can arrange tours (₹450/750 by autorickshaw/taxi for two to three hours). If you want to see a tea factory in operation, do it from here – working tea-factory visits are not permitted in Munnar.

If you'd rather do a spice tour independently, you can visit a few excellent gardens outside Kumily. The one-hectare **Abraham's Spice Garden** (222919; www.abrahamspice.com; Spring Valley; tours ₹100; 7am-6.30pm) has been going for 56 years. **Highrange Spices** (222117; tours ₹100; 7am-6pm), 3km from Kumily, has 4 hectares where you can see ayurvedic herbs and vegetables growing. A rickshaw/taxi to either spice garden and back will be around ₹200/300. About 13km away from Kumily the working **Connemara Tea Plantation** (Vandiperiyar; tours ₹100; 8am-5pm) offers guided tours of the fields and tea-making process. Any bus heading towards Kottayam will stop at the tea factory in Vandiperiyar on request (₹11, every 15 minutes).

Santhigiri Ayurveda AYURVEDA
(223979; www.santhigiri.co.in; Munnar Rd, Vandanmedu Junction; 8am-8pm) An excellent and authentic place for the ayurvedic experience, offering top-notch massage (₹650 to ₹1500) and long-term treatments lasting seven to 14 days.

Sleeping

Inside the Sanctuary

The KTDC runs three steeply priced hotels in the park, including Periyar House, Aranya Nivas and the grand Lake Palace. Make reservations (at any KTDC office), particularly for weekends. Note that there's effectively a curfew at these places – guests are not permitted to roam the sanctuary after 6pm.

The Ecotourism Centre can arrange tented accommodation inside the park at the **Jungle Camp** (d tent ₹5000). Rates include trekking and meals but not the park entry fee. Also ask about **Bamboo Grove** (d ₹1500), a group of basic cottages and tree houses not far from Kumily town.

Lake Palace HOTEL $$$
(223887; www.lakepalacethekkady.com; r incl all meals ₹20,000-25,000) There's a faint whiff of royalty at this restored old summer palace, located on an island in the middle of the Periyar Lake. The six charismatic rooms are decorated with flair using antique furnishings and a selection of modern conveniences (like flat-screen TVs). Staying in the midst of the

sanctuary gives you a good chance of seeing wildlife from your private terrace, and rates include meals, boat trip and trekking.

Kumily

Mickey Homestay GUESTHOUSE $
(223196; www.mickeyhomestay.com; Bypass Rd; r ₹500-850) Mickey is a genuine homestay with just a handful of intimate rooms in a family house and a rear cottage, all with homely touches that make them some of the most comfortable in town. Balconies have rattan furniture and hanging bamboo seats and the whole place is surrounded by greenery.

Coffee Inn GUESTHOUSE $
(222763; coffeeinn@sancharnet.in; Thekkady Rd; r without bath ₹400, d ₹800-2000, tree house ₹600) This whimsical timber hotel and cafe has a range of neatly furnished and quirky wood-lined rooms, as well as rustic tree houses and cottages in a back garden overlooking a rather urban section of the sanctuary. Decent restaurant.

★ **Green View Homestay** HOMESTAY $
(224617; www.sureshgreenview.com; Bypass Rd; r incl breakfast ₹500-1750;) It has grown from its humble homestay origins but Greenview is a lovely place that manages to retain its personal and friendly family welcome from owners Suresh and Sulekha. The two buildings house several classes of beautifully maintained rooms with private balconies, some overlooking a lovely rear spice garden. Excellent vegetarian meals and cooking lessons (veg/nonveg ₹200/350) are available.

El-Paradiso HOMESTAY $
(222350; www.goelparadiso.com; Bypass Rd; d ₹750-1250, q ₹1850; @) This immaculate family homestay has fresh rooms with balconies and hanging chairs, or rooms opening onto a terrace overlooking greenery at the back. Cooking classes (₹400 including meal) are a speciality here.

Tranquilou HOMESTAY $$
(223269; www.tranquilouhomestay.com; off Bypass Rd; r incl breakfast ₹800-1200; @) Another friendly family homestay in a peaceful

Kumily & Periyar Wildlife Sanctuary

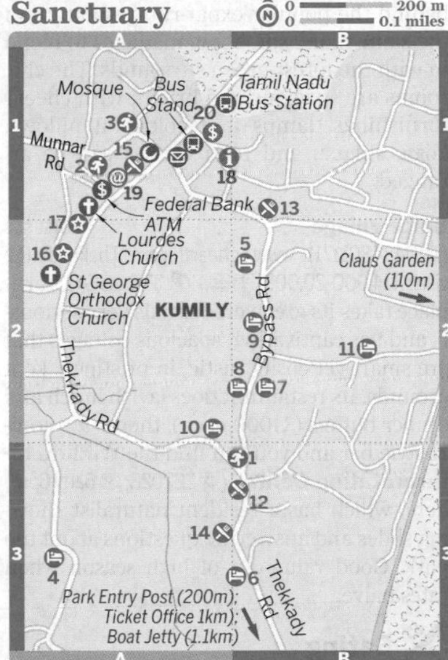

Kumily & Periyar Wildlife Sanctuary

Activities, Courses & Tours
1 Ecotourism Centre ... B3
2 Gavi Ecotourism ... A1
3 Santhigiri Ayurveda ... A1

Sleeping
4 Bamboo Grove ... A3
5 Chrissie's Hotel ... B2
6 Coffee Inn ... B3
7 El-Paradiso ... B2
8 Green View Homestay ... B2
9 Mickey Homestay ... B2
10 Spice Village ... A2
11 Tranquilou ... B2

Eating
12 Ambadi Restaurant ... B3
Chrissie's Cafe ... (see 5)
13 Ebony's Cafe ... B1
14 French Restaurant & Bakery ... A3
15 Shri Krishna ... A1

Entertainment
16 Kadathanadan Kalari Centre ... A2
17 Mudra Kathakali Centre ... A2

Information
18 DTPC Office ... A1
Ecotourism Centre ... (see 1)
19 Mt Sinai Cyber Cafe ... A1
20 State Bank of Travancore ... A1

location. Neatly furnished rooms surround a pleasant garden; the two doubles that adjoin a shared sitting room are a good family option.

Claus Garden HOMESTAY $$
(☎222320; www.homestay.in; s/d without bathroom ₹800/950, d/tr ₹1500/1600;) Set well away from the hustle and bustle and up a very steep hill, this lovely big building has gently curving balconies, splashes of colour and six rooms around a lush green garden.

Chrissie's Hotel GUESTHOUSE $$
(☎9447601304, 224155; www.chrissies.in; Bypass Rd; r ₹1920-2400) This four-storey building behind the popular expat-run restaurant of the same name somehow manages to blend in with the forest-green surrounds. The chic rooms are spacious and bright, with cheery furnishings, lamps and colourful pillows. Yoga, shiatsu and reiki classes can be arranged.

Spice Village HOTEL $$$
(☎04843011711; www.cghearth.com; Thekkady Rd; villas ₹14,000-20,000;) This CGH Earth place takes its green credentials very seriously and has captivating, spacious cottages that are smart yet cosily rustic, in pristinely kept grounds. Its restaurant does lavish lunch and dinner buffets (₹1000 each), there's a colonial-style bar and you can find the **Wildlife Interpretation Centre** (☎222028; ⏰6am-6pm) here, which has a resident naturalist showing slides and answering questions about the park. Good value out of high season when rates halve.

Eating

There are plenty of good cheap veg restaurants in the bazaar area, and some decent traveller-oriented restaurants on the road to the wildlife sanctuary.

Shri Krishna INDIAN $
(KK Rd; meals ₹60-120) A local favourite in the bazaar, serving up spicy pure veg meals including several takes on thali.

Ebony's Cafe MULTICUISINE $
(Bypass Rd; meals ₹40-240; ⏰8.30am-9.30pm) This friendly rooftop joint with lots of pot plants, check tablecloths and traveller-friendly tunes serves up a tasty assortment of Indian and Western food from mashed potato to pasta and cold beer (₹150).

French Restaurant & Bakery CAFE, BAKERY $
(meals ₹40-175; ⏰7.30am-10pm) This family-run shack set back from the main road is a good spot for breakfast or lunch, serving up croissants, pancakes and baguettes, along with decent pasta and noodle dishes.

Chrissie's Cafe MULTICUISINE $
(Bypass Rd; meals ₹80-200; ⏰8am-9.30pm) A perennially popular haunt, this airy 1st-floor cafe satisfies travellers with cakes and snacks, excellent coffee and well-prepared Western faves like pizza and pasta.

Ambadi Restaurant INDIAN $
(dishes ₹80-250; ⏰7.30am-9.30pm) At the hotel of the same name, Ambadi has a more formal feel than most with an almost church-like decor, but the broad menu of North and South Indian dishes are reasonably priced.

Entertainment

Mudra Kathakali Centre CULTURAL PROGRAM
(☎9446072901; www.mudraculturalcentre.com; Lake Rd; admission ₹200, camera/video free/₹200; ⏰shows 4.30pm & 7pm) Twice daily one-hour Kathakali shows at this cultural centre are highly entertaining. Make-up and costume starts 30 minutes before each show; very photogenic. Arrive early for a good seat.

Kadathanadan Kalari Centre CULTURAL PROGRAM
(www.kalaripayattu.co.in; Thekkady Rd; ₹200; ⏰shows 6pm) Hour-long demonstrations of the exciting Keralan martial art of *kalarippayat* are staged here every evening. Tickets are available from the box office throughout the day.

Information

There's a Federal Bank ATM at the junction with the road to Kottayam accepting international cards, and several internet cafes in the bazaar area.

DTPC Office (☎222620; ⏰10am-5pm Mon-Sat) Behind the bus stand, not as useful as the Ecotourism Centre.

Ecotourism Centre (☎224571; www.periyartigerreserve.org; ⏰9am-1pm & 2-5pm) For park tours, information and walks.

Mt Sinai Cyber Cafe (☎222170; Thekkady Junction; per hr ₹20; ⏰9am-10pm)

State Bank of Travancore (⏰10am-3.30pm Mon-Fri, to 12.30pm Sat) Changes travellers cheques and currency; has an ATM accepting foreign cards.

Getting There & Away

Kumily's KSRTC bus stand is at the eastern edge of town.

Eleven buses daily operate between Ernakulam (Kochi) and Kumily (₹120, five hours). Buses leave every 30 minutes for Kottayam (₹71, four hours), with two direct buses to Trivandrum at 8.45am and 11am (₹210, eight hours) and one daily bus to Alleppey at 1.10pm (₹120, 5½ hours). Private buses to Munnar (₹75, 4 to 5 hours) also leave from the bus stand at 6am, 6.30am and 9.45am.

Tamil Nadu buses leave every 30 minutes to Madurai (₹80, four hours) from the Tamil Nadu bus stand just over the border.

Getting Around

It's only about 1.5km from Kumily bus stand to the main park entrance, but another 3km from there to Periyar Lake; you might catch a bus (almost as rare as the tigers), but will more likely take an autorickshaw from the entry post (₹50) or set off on foot – but bear in mind there's no walking path so you'll have to dodge traffic on the road. Autorickshaws will take you on short hops around town for ₹30. **Bicycle hire** is available from many guesthouses.

Munnar

04865 / POP 68,200 / ELEV 1524M

South India's largest tea-growing region, the rolling hills around Munnar are carpeted in emerald-green tea plantations, contoured, clipped and sculpted like ornamental hedges. The low mountain scenery is magnificent – you're often up above the clouds watching veils of mist clinging to the mountaintops. Munnar itself is a scruffy administration centre, not unlike a North Indian hill station, but wander just a few kilometres out of town and you'll be engulfed in a sea of a thousand shades of green.

Once known as the High Range of Travancore, today Munnar is the commercial centre of some of the world's highest tea-growing estates. The majority of the plantations are now operated by the Kannan Devan Hills Plantation Company (KDHP), a local cooperative which succeeded corporate giant Tata Tea in 2005.

Sights & Activities

The main reason to visit Munnar is to explore the lush, tea-filled hillocks that surround it. Hotels, homestays, travel agencies, autorickshaw drivers and practically every passerby will want to organise a day of sightseeing for you: shop around. The best way to experience the hills is on a **guided trek**, which can range from a few hours' 'soft trekking' around tea plantations to more arduous full-day mountain treks, which open up some stupendous views. Trekking guides can easily be organised through hotels and guesthouses or the DTPC for around ₹100 per person per hour (usually a minimum of four hours).

Tea Museum MUSEUM
(230561; adult/child ₹75/35, camera ₹20; 10am-4pm Tue-Sun) About 1.5km northwest of town, this museum is about as close as you'll get to a working tea factory around Munnar. It's a demo model of the real thing, but it still shows the basic process. A collection of old bits and pieces from the colonial era, including photographs and a 1905 tea-roller, are also kept here. A 30-minute video explaining the history of Munnar, its tea estates and the programs put in place for its workers screens hourly. The short walk to or from town follows the road but passes some of the most accessible tea plantations from Munnar town. An autorickshaw charges ₹20 from the bazaar.

Tours

The DTPC (p302) runs three fairly rushed full-day tours to points around Munnar. The **Sandal Valley Tour** (per person ₹350; 9am-6pm) visits Chinnar Wildlife Sanctuary, several viewpoints, waterfalls, plantations, a sandalwood forest and villages. The **Tea Valley tour** (per person ₹300; 10am-6pm) visits Echo Point, Top Station and Rajamalai (for Eravikulam National Park), among other places. The **Village Sightseeing Tour**

> OFF THE BEATEN TRACK
>
> **SABARIMALA**
>
> Deep in the Western Ghats about 20km west of Gavi and some 50km from the town of Erumeli is a place called Sabarimala, home to the Ayyappan temple. It's said to be one of the world's most visited pilgrimage centres, with anywhere between 40 and 60 million Hindu devotees trekking here each year. Followers believe the god Ayyappan meditated at this spot. Strict rules govern the pilgrimage. For information see www.sabarimala.org.

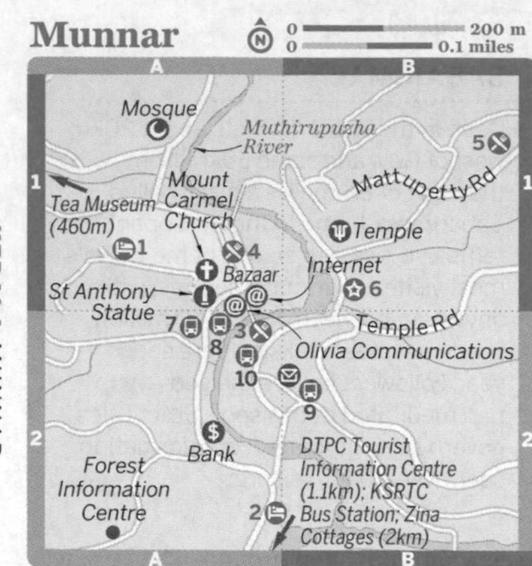

Munnar

Sleeping

1 Kaippallil Inn A1
2 Tea Sanctuary A2

Eating

3 Eastend A2
4 Rapsy Restaurant A1
5 Sree Mahaveer B1

Entertainment

6 Thirumeny Cultural Centre B1

Transport

Autorickshaw Stand .... (see 10)
7 Buses to Coimbatore A2
8 Buses to Ernakulam, Kottayam & Trtivandrum A2
9 Buses to Kumily & Madurai B2
10 Buses to Top Station A2

(₹400; ⌚9.30am-6pm) covers Devikulam, Anayirankal Dam, Ponmudy and a farm tour among others. You can hire a taxi to visit the main local sights for around ₹1200 per day.

Sleeping

Munnar has plenty of accommodation but the best budget options are just south of the town centre. If you really want to feel the serenity and are willing to pay a bit more, head for the hills.

Around Town

★JJ Cottage HOMESTAY $
(☎230104; jjcottagemunnar@sancharnet.in; d ₹350-800; @) The sweet family at this superb purple place a couple of kilometres south of town (but easy walking distance from the main bus stand) will go out of its way to make sure your stay is comfortable. The varied and uncomplicated rooms are ruthlessly clean, bright, great value and have TV and hot water. The one deluxe room on the top floor has a separate sitting room and sweeping views. Free internet but no wi-fi.

Green View GUESTHOUSE $
(☎230940; www.greenviewmunnar.com; d ₹450-700; @ wi-fi) This tidy guesthouse has 10 fresh budget rooms, a friendly welcome and reliable tour advice. The best rooms are on the upper floor and there's a super rooftop garden where you can sample 15 kinds of tea. The young owner organises trekking trips and also runs **Green Woods Anachal** (d incl breakfast ₹750) outside Munnar – a four-room budget option out in the tea and spice plantations.

Zina Cottages HOMESTAY $
(☎230349; r ₹700-900) On the outskirts of town but immersed in lush tea plantations and with fine views, this hospitable homestay is a good deal. Rooms are pretty basic with bucket hot water but the views are sensational. They offer free pick-up from town (an autorickshaw costs about ₹40).

Kaippallil Inn GUESTHOUSE $
(☎9495029259; www.kaippallil.com; r ₹300-800) A stiff walk or rickshaw ride uphill from the bazaar, Kaippallil is a good budget bet in the town centre, thanks mainly to the serene Benoy, who offers free yoga and meditation sessions and plenty of tea. It looks a little tatty from the outside but the rooms are clean and the top ones have little corner balconies with sweeping views.

Royal Retreat HOTEL $$
(☎230240; www.royalretreat.co.in; d ₹2200-2800, ste ₹3900; @) Away from the bustle just south of the main bus stand, Royal Retreat is a reliable midranger with pleasant ground-level rooms facing a pretty garden and others with tea plantation views.

Munnar Hills

Dew Drops GUESTHOUSE $$
(☎04842216455; wilsonhomes2003@yahoo.co.in; Kallar; r incl breakfast ₹1500) Set in thick forest around 20km south of Munnar, this fantastic, remote place lies on 97 hectares of spice

plantation and farmland. The resplendent building has eight bright, simple rooms each with a verandah on which you can sit and enjoy the chirping of birdlife and expansive views. The peace here is zen; call for a pick-up (₹50 per person).

Tea Sanctuary BUNGALOWS $$$
(☎230141; www.theteasanctuary.com; KDHP House; s/d incl breakfast ₹4500/5000) The KDHP operates four charming old heritage bungalows scattered around the Munnar hills under the banner of Tea Sanctuary. The secluded locations are amazing, surrounded by tea plantations. You can book through KDHP House in Munnar town.

★ **Rose Gardens** HOMESTAY $$$
(☎04864278243; www.munnarhomestays.com; NH49 Rd, Karadipara; r incl breakfast ₹4000; @ wifi) Despite its handy location on the main road to Kochi, around 10km south of Munnar and with good bus connections, this is a peaceful spot overlooking the owner Tomy's idyllic plant nursery, with over 240 types of plants, and his mini spice and fruit plantation. The five rooms are large and comfortable with balconies overlooking the valley, and the family is charming. Cooking lessons are free, including fresh coconut pancakes for breakfast and delicately spiced Keralan dishes for dinner.

Bracknell Forest GUESTHOUSE $$$
(☎9446951963; www.bracknellforestmunnar.com; Bison Valley Rd, Ottamaram; r incl breakfast ₹5000-6000; @ wifi) A remote-feeling 9.5km southeast of Munnar, this place houses 11 neat, handsome rooms with balconies and lovely views overlooking a lush valley and cardamom plantation. It's surrounded by deep forest on all sides. The small restaurant has wraparound views. A transfer from Munnar costs ₹350.

Windermere Estate RESORT $$$
(☎reservations 04842425237; www.windermeremunnar.com; Pothamedu; d incl breakfast ₹8300-14,000, villa ₹18,500; ❄ @ wifi) Windermere is a charming boutique-meets-country-retreat 4km southeast of Munnar. There are supremely spacious garden and valley view rooms, but the best are the suite-like 'Plantation Villas' with spectacular views, surrounded by 26 hectares of cardamom and coffee plantations. There's a cosy library above the country-style restaurant. Book ahead at its Kochi office.

Eating

Early-morning food stalls in the bazaar serve breakfast snacks and cheap meals.

Rapsy Restaurant INDIAN $
(Bazaar; dishes ₹30-140; ⏰8am-9pm) This spotless glass-fronted sanctuary from the bazaar is packed at lunchtime, with locals lining up for Rapsy's famous *paratha* or biryani (from ₹50). It also makes a decent stab at fancy international dishes like Spanish omelette, Israeli *shakshuka* (eggs with tomatoes and spices) and Mexican salsa.

SN Restaurant INDIAN $
(AM Rd; meals ₹35-90; ⏰7.30am-10pm) Just south of the DTPC office, SN is a cheery place with an attractive red interior, which seems to be perpetually full of people digging into masala dosas and other Indian veg and non-veg dishes.

Aromas INDIAN $
(www.royalretreat.co.in; Kannan Devan Hills; dishes ₹35-120; ⏰7.30-10am, noon-3pm, 7-9pm) In the Royal Retreat hotel, just south of town, this longstanding favourite has reliably tasty and fresh Indian cooking served in nicely twee rooms with checked tablecloths.

Sree Mahaveer INDIAN $
(Mattupetty Rd; meals ₹85-185; ⏰8.30am-10.30pm) This pure veg restaurant attached to SN Annex Hotel has a nice deep-orange look with slatted blinds on the windows. It's madly popular with families for its great range of thalis: take your pick from Rajasthani, Gujarati, Punjabi and more, plus a dazzling array of veg dishes.

Eastend INDIAN $$
(Temple Rd; dishes ₹110-250; ⏰7.30-10.30am, noon-3.30pm & 6.30-10.30pm) In the slightly fancy hotel of the same name, this brightly lit, smartish place is one of the best in town for nonveg Indian dishes, with Chinese, North and South Indian and Kerala specialities on the menu.

Entertainment

Thirumeny Cultural Centre CULTURAL PROGRAM
(☎9447827696; Temple Rd; shows ₹200; ⏰Kathakali shows 5-6pm & 7-8pm; kalarippayat 6-7pm & 8-9pm) On the road behind the Eastend Hotel, this theatre stages one-hour Kathakali shows and *kalarippayat* martial arts demonstrations twice nightly.

OFF THE BEATEN TRACK

PARAMBIKULAM WILDLIFE SANCTUARY

Possibly the most protected environment in South India – nestled behind three dams in a valley surrounded by Keralan and Tamil Nadu sanctuaries – **Parambikulam Wildlife Sanctuary** (www.parambikulam.org; Indian/foreigner ₹10/100, camera/video ₹25/150; ⏲7am-6pm last entry 4pm) constitutes 285 sq km of Kipling-storybook scenery and wildlife-spotting goodness. Far less touristed than Periyar, it's home to elephants, bison, gaur, sloths, sambar, crocodiles, tigers, panthers and some of the largest teak trees in Asia. The sanctuary is best avoided during monsoon (June to August) and it sometimes closes in March and April.

Contact the **Ecocare Centre** (☎04253245025) in Anappady to arrange tours of the park, **hikes** (1-/2-day trek from ₹3000/6000, shorter treks from ₹600) and stays on the reservoir's freshwater island (r ₹5000). There are 150 beds in **tree-top huts** (₹2500-3500) throughout the park; book through the Ecocare Centre. Boating or rafting costs ₹600 for one hour.

You have to enter the park from Pollachi (40km from Coimbatore and 49km from Palakkad) in Tamil Nadu. There are two buses in either direction between Pollachi and Parambikulam via Annamalai daily (₹17, 1½ hours).

Information

There are ATMs near the bridge, south of the bazaar.

DTPC Tourist Information Office (☎231516; keralatourismmunnardtpc@gmail.com; Alway-Munnar Rd; ⏲8.30am-7pm) Marginally helpful; operates a number of tours and can arrange trekking guides.

Forest Information Centre (☎231587; enpmunnar@gmail.com; ⏲10am-5pm) Wildlife Warden's Office, for accommodation bookings in Chinnar Wildlife Sanctuary.

Olivia Communications (per hr ₹35; ⏲9am-9pm) Cramped but surprisingly fast internet in the bazaar.

Getting There & Away

Roads around Munnar are in poor condition and can be affected by monsoon rains. The main **KSRTC bus station** (AM Rd) is south of town, but it's best to catch buses from stands in Munnar town (where more frequent private buses also depart). The main stand is in the bazaar.

There are around 13 daily buses to Ernakulam (Kochi, ₹81, 5½ hours), two direct buses to Alleppey (₹110, five hours) at 6.20am and 1.10pm, and five to Trivandrum (₹226, nine hours). Private buses go to Kumily (₹75, four hours) at 11.25am, 12.20pm and 2.25pm.

A taxi to Ernakulam costs around ₹2000, and to Kumily ₹1800.

Getting Around

Gokulam Bike Hire (☎9447237165; per day ₹250-300; ⏲7.30am-7.30pm), in the former bus stand south of town, has motorbikes and scooters for hire. Call ahead.

Autorickshaws ply the hills around Munnar with bone-shuddering efficiency; they charge up to ₹700 for a full day's sightseeing.

Around Munnar

Eravikulam National Park

Sixteen kilometres from Munnar, **Eravikulam National Park** (☎04865231587; www.eravikulam.org; Indian/foreigner ₹15/200, camera/video ₹25/2000; ⏲8am-5pm Mar-Dec) is home to the endangered, but almost tame, Nilgiri tahr (a type of mountain goat). From Munnar, an autorickshaw/taxi costs around ₹300/500 return; a government bus takes you the final 4km from the checkpoint (₹40).

Chinnar Wildlife Sanctuary

About 10km past Marayoor and 60km northeast of Munnar, this **wildlife sanctuary** (www.chinnar.org; Indian/foreigner ₹100/150, camera/video ₹25/150; ⏲7am-6pm) hosts deer, leopards, elephants and the endangered grizzled giant squirrel. Trekking and **tree house** (s/d ₹1000/1250) or hut accommodation within the sanctuary are available, as well as ecotour programs like river-trekking, cultural visits and waterfall treks (around ₹150). For details contact the Forest Information Centre in Munnar. Buses from Munnar can drop you off at Chinnar (₹35, 1½ hours), or taxi hire for the day will cost ₹1300.

Top Station

High above Kerala's border with Tamil Nadu, Top Station is popular for its spectacular views over the Western Ghats. From Munnar, four daily buses (₹35, from 7.30am, 1½ hours) make the steep 32km climb in around an hour, or you could book a return taxi (₹1000).

CENTRAL KERALA

Kochi (Cochin)

☎0484 / POP 601,600

Serene Kochi has been drawing traders and explorers to its shores for over 600 years. Nowhere else in India could you find such an intriguing mix: giant fishing nets from China, a 400-year-old synagogue, ancient mosques, Portuguese houses and crumbling remains of the British Raj. The result is an unlikely blend of medieval Portugal, Holland and an English village grafted onto the tropical Malabar Coast. It's a delightful place to spend some time and nap in some of India's finest homestays and heritage accommodation.

Mainland Ernakulam is the hectic transport and cosmopolitan hub of Kochi, while the historical towns of Fort Cochin and Mattancherry, though well-touristed, remain wonderfully serene – thick with the smell of the past. Other islands, including Willingdon and Vypeen, are linked by a network of ferries and bridges.

While you're here, the perfect read is Salman Rushdie's *The Moor's Last Sigh*, which bases much action around Mattancherry and the synagogue.

Sights

Fort Cochin

Fort Cochin has a couple of small, sandy beaches which are only really good for people-watching in the evening and gazing out at the incoming tankers. A popular promenade winds around to the unofficial emblems of Kerala's backwaters: cantilevered **Chinese fishing nets** (Map p304). A legacy of traders from the AD 1400 court of Kublai Khan, these enormous, spiderlike contraptions require at least four people to operate their counterweights at high tide. Unfortunately, modern fishing techniques are making these labour-intensive methods less and less profitable.

Kochi (Cochin)

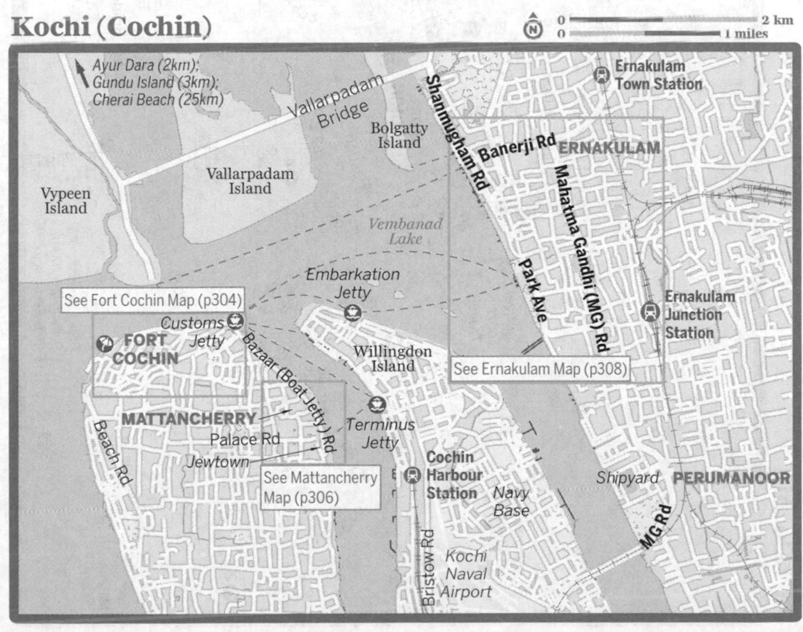

Fort Cochin

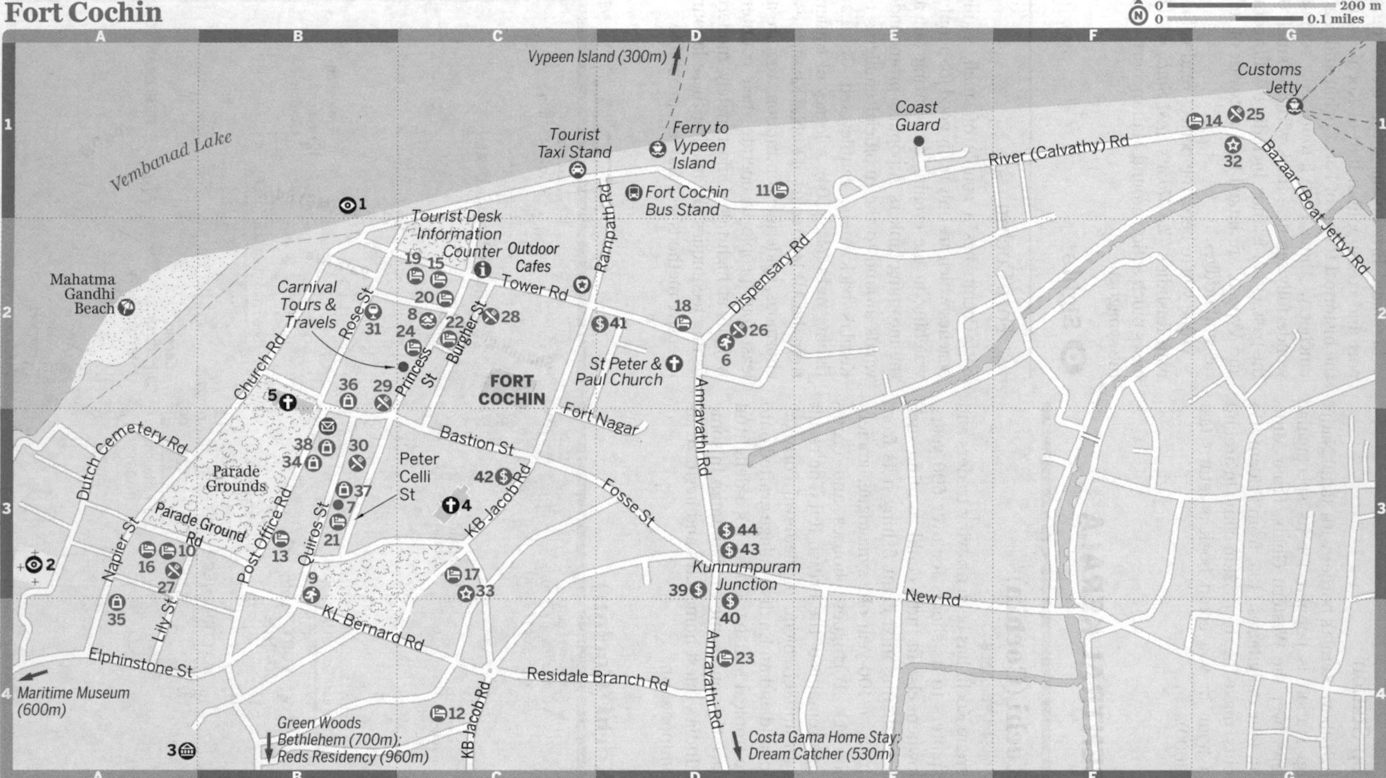
Vypeen Island (300m)
Customs Jetty
Coast Guard
Ferry to Vypeen Island
Tourist Taxi Stand
Vembanad Lake
Fort Cochin Bus Stand
River (Calvathy) Rd
Bazaar (Boat Jetty) Rd
Tourist Desk Information Counter
Outdoor Cafes
Tower Rd
Rampath Rd
Dispensary Rd
Mahatma Gandhi Beach
Carnival Tours & Travels
Rose St
Burgher St
Princess St
St Peter & Paul Church
FORT COCHIN
Fort Nagar
Church Rd
Bastion St
Dutch Cemetery Rd
Parade Grounds
Peter Celli St
KB Jacob Rd
Fosse St
Amravathi Rd
Parade Ground Rd
Post Office Rd
Quiros St
Napier St
Lily St
Kunnumpuram Junction
New Rd
KL Bernard Rd
Elphinstone St
Residale Branch Rd
Maritime Museum (600m)
Green Woods Bethlehem (700m); Reds Residency (960m)
Costa Gama Home Stay; Dream Catcher (530m)
200 m
0.1 miles

Fort Cochin

Sights

1 Chinese Fishing Nets ... B1
2 Dutch Cemetery ... A3
3 Indo-Portuguese Museum ... A4
4 Santa Cruz Basilica ... C3
5 St Francis Church ... B2

Activities, Courses & Tours

6 Ayush ... D2
7 Cook & Eat ... B3
8 Grande Residencia Hotel ... C2
9 SVM Ayurveda Centre ... B3

Sleeping

10 Bernard Bungalow ... A3
11 Brunton Boatyard ... D1
12 Daffodil ... C4
13 Delight Home Stay ... B3
14 Fort House Hotel ... G1
15 Koder House ... C2
16 Malabar House ... A3
17 Mother Tree ... C3
18 Noah's Ark ... D2
19 Old Harbour Hotel ... C2
20 Princess Inn ... C2
21 Raintree Lodge ... B3
Royal Grace Tourist Home ... (see 6)
22 Sonnetta Residency ... C2
23 Tea Bungalow ... D4
24 Walton's Homestay ... C2

Eating

25 Arca Nova ... G1
26 Casa Linda ... D2
27 Dal Roti ... A3
28 Kashi Art Cafe ... C2
29 Loafers Corner ... B2
Malabar Junction ... (see 16)
30 Teapot ... B3

Drinking & Nightlife

31 XL Fishnet Bar ... B2

Entertainment

32 Greenix Village ... G1
33 Kerala Kathakali Centre ... C3

Shopping

34 Cinnamon ... B3
35 Fabindia ... A4
36 Idiom Bookshop ... B2
37 Niraamaya ... B3
38 Tribes India ... B3

Information

39 Federal Bank ATM ... D3
40 ICICI ATM ... D4
41 SBI ATM ... D2
42 South India Bank ATM ... C3
43 UAE Exchange ... D3
44 UAE Exchange ... D3

Indo-Portuguese Museum MUSEUM
(Map p304; 2215400; Indian/foreigner ₹10/25; 9am-1pm & 2-6pm Tue-Sun) This museum in the garden of the Bishop's House preserves the heritage of one of India's earliest Catholic communities, including vestments, silver processional crosses and altarpieces from the Cochin diocese. The basement contains remnants of the Portuguese Fort Immanuel.

Maritime Museum MUSEUM
(Beach Rd; admission ₹75, camera/video ₹100/150; 9.30am-12.30pm & 2.30-5.30pm) In a pair of former bomb shelters, this museum traces the history of the Indian navy, as well as maritime trade dating back to the Portuguese and Dutch, through a series of relief murals and information panels. There's plenty of naval memorabilia, including a couple of model battleships outside in the garden.

St Francis Church CHURCH
(Map p304; Church Rd; 8.30am-5pm) Believed to be India's oldest European-built church, it was originally constructed in 1503 by Portuguese Franciscan friars. The edifice that stands here today was built in the mid-16th century to replace the original wooden structure. Explorer Vasco da Gama, who died in Cochin in 1524, was buried in this spot for 14 years before his remains were taken to Lisbon – you can still visit his tombstone in the church.

Santa Cruz Basilica CHURCH
(Map p304; cnr Bastion St & KB Jacob Rd; 7am-8.30pm) The imposing Catholic basilica was originally built on this site in 1506, though the current building dates to 1902. Inside you'll find artefacts from the different eras in Kochi and a striking pastel-coloured interior.

Dutch Cemetery HISTORIC SITE
(Map p304; Beach Rd) Consecrated in 1724, this cemetery near Kochi beach contains the worn and dilapidated graves of Dutch traders and soldiers. Its gates are normally locked but a caretaker might let you in, or ask at St Francis Church.

Mattancherry & Jew Town

About 3km southeast of Fort Cochin, Mattancherry is the old bazaar district and centre of the spice trade. These days it's packed with spice shops and overpriced Kashmiri-run emporiums that autorickshaw drivers will fall over backwards to take you to for a healthy commission. In the midst of this, Jew Town is a bustling port area with a fine synagogue. Scores of small firms huddle together in old, dilapidated buildings and the air is filled with the biting aromas of ginger, cardamom, cumin, turmeric and cloves, though the lanes around the Dutch Palace and synagogue are packed with antique and tourist-curio shops rather than spices. Look out for the Jewish names on some of the buildings.

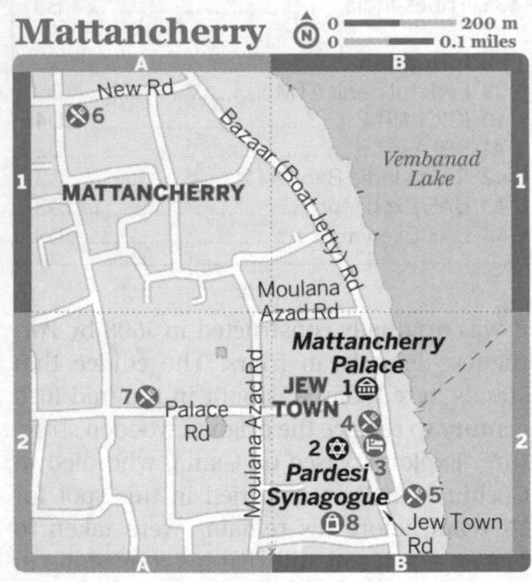

Mattancherry

Top Sights
1 Mattancherry Palace....B2
2 Pardesi Synagogue....B2

Sleeping
3 Caza Maria....B2

Eating
4 Café Jew Town....B2
Caza Maria....(see 3)
5 Ginger House....B2
6 Ramathula Hotel....A1
7 Shri Krishna....A2

Shopping
8 Niraamaya....B2

★Mattancherry Palace MUSEUM
(Dutch Palace; Map p306; ☎2226085; Palace Rd; adult/child ₹5/free; ⊙9am-5pm Sat-Thu) Mattancherry Palace was a generous gift presented to the Raja of Kochi, Veera Kerala Varma (1537–61), as a gesture of goodwill by the Portuguese in 1555. More probably, it was used as a sweetener to securing trading privileges. The Dutch renovated the palace in 1663, hence its alternative name, the Dutch Palace.

The star attractions here are the astonishingly preserved Hindu **murals**, depicting scenes from the Ramayana, Mahabharata and Puranic legends in intricate detail. The central hall on the 1st floor is now a portrait gallery of maharajas from 1864. There's an impressive collection of palanquins (hand-carried carriages), bejewelled outfits and splendidly carved ceilings in every room. Information panels detail the history of the Kochi royal dynasty. Photography is prohibited.

★Pardesi Synagogue SYNAGOGUE
(Map p306; admission ₹5; ⊙10am-1pm & 3-5pm Sun-Thu, closed Jewish hols) Originally built in 1568, this synagogue was partially destroyed by the Portuguese in 1662, and rebuilt two years later when the Dutch took Kochi. It features an ornate gold pulpit and elaborate hand-painted, willow-pattern floor tiles from Canton, China, which were added in 1762. It's magnificently illuminated by chandeliers (from Belgium) and coloured-glass lamps. The graceful clock tower was built in 1760. There is an upstairs balcony for women who worshipped separately according to Orthodox rites. Note that shorts, sleeveless tops, bags and cameras are not allowed inside.

Ernakulam

Kerala Folklore Museum MUSEUM
(☎04842665452; www.folkloremuseum.org; Folklore Junction, Thevara; Indian/foreigner ₹100/200, performances Indian/foreigner ₹100/400; ⊙9.30am-7pm, performances 6-7.30pm Oct-Mar) It's a shame that this interesting place is a bit off the tourist trail on the southeast outskirts of Ernakulam, but it's worthy of the journey. The private museum is created in Keralan style from ancient temples and beautiful old houses collected by its owner, an antique dealer. It includes over 4000 artefacts and covers three architectural

styles: Malabar on the ground floor, Kochi on the 1st, Travancore on the 2nd. Upstairs is a beautiful wood-lined theatre, with a 17th-century wooden ceiling, where nightly performances take place. A rickshaw from Ernakulam should cost ₹80, or you can take any bus to Thevara from where it's a ₹20 rickshaw ride. An autorickshaw from Fort Cochin should cost ₹180.

Activities

Grande Residencia Hotel SWIMMING
(Map p304; Princess St, Fort Cochin; 7am-6.30pm) Nonguests can swim at the hotel's small pool for ₹350 per person.

Cherai Beach (Vypeen Island) SWIMMING
For a dip in the ocean, you can make a day trip out to Cherai Beach (p316), 25km away on Vypeen Island.

Ayur Dara AYURVEDA
(2502362, 9447721041; www.ayurdara.com; Murikkumpadam, Vypeen Island; 9am-5.30pm) Run by third-generation ayurvedic practitioner Dr Subhash, this delightful waterside treatment centre specialises in treatments of one to three weeks (₹9100 per week). By appointment only. It's 3km from the Vypeen Island ferry (autorickshaw ₹35).

Ayush AYURVEDA
(Map p304; 6456566; Amaravathi Rd, Fort Cochin; massage from ₹900; 8am 8pm) Part of an India-wide chain of ayurvedic centres, this place also does long-term treatments.

SVM Ayurveda Centre AYURVEDA
(Kerala Ayurveda Pharmacy Ltd; Map p304; 9847371667; www.svmayurveda.com; Quieros St; massage from ₹600, Hatha yoga ₹400,1½hr; 9.30am-7pm) A small Fort Cochin centre, this offers relaxing massages and Hatha yoga daily at 8am. Longer rejuvenation packages are also available.

Courses

The Kerala Kathakali Centre (p313) has lessons in classical Kathakali dance, music and make-up (short and long-term courses from ₹350 per hour).

For a crash course in the martial art of *kalarippayat*, head out to Ens Kalari (p313), a famed training centre, which offers short intensive courses from one week to one month.

Cook & Eat COOKING
(Map p304; 2215377; www.leelahomestay.com; Quiros St; classes veg/nonveg ₹550; 11am & 6pm) Mrs Leelu Roy runs popular two-hour cooking classes in her big family kitchen, teaching five dishes to classes of five to 10 people. Several of the homestays in towns are also happy to organise cooking classes for their guests.

Tours

Most hotels and tourist offices can arrange the popular day trip out to the **Elephant training camp** (7am-6pm) at Kudanadu, 50km from Kochi. Here you can go for a ride (₹200) and even help out with washing the gentle beasts if you arrive at 8am. Entry is free, though the elephant trainers will expect a small tip. A return trip out here in a taxi should cost around ₹1000 to ₹1200.

Tourist Desk Information Counter BOAT TOUR, WILDLIFE-WATCHING
(2371761; www.touristdesk.in) This private tour agency runs the popular full-day **Water Valley Tour** (₹650) through local backwater canals and lagoons. A canoe trip through smaller canals and villages is included, as is lunch and hotel pick-ups. It also offers a two night **Wayanad Wildlife tour** (₹6000), and an overnight **Munnar Hillstation tour** (₹3000). Prices include accommodation, transport and meals.

KTDC BOAT TOUR
(2353234; backwater tours half-day ₹450, motor boat tours 2½hr ₹250, houseboat backwater trips day tour ₹650) The KTDC has **backwater tours** at 8.30am and 2pm, and **motor-boat tours** around Fort Cochin at 9am and 2pm. Its full-day **houseboat backwater trips** (8am-6.30pm) visit local weaving factories, spice gardens and toddy tappers.

Kerala Bike Tours BIKE TOUR
(04842356652, 9388476817; www.keralabiketours.com; Kirushupaly Rd, Ravipuram) Organises motorcycle tours in Kerala and the Western Ghats and hires out touring-quality Enfield Bullets (from US$155 per week) with unlimited mileage, full insurance and free recovery/maintenance options.

Festivals & Events

The eight-day **Ernakulathappan Utsavam festival** (January/February) culminates in a procession of 15 decorated elephants, ecstatic music and fireworks. The **Cochin Carnival** (www.cochincarnival.org; 21-31 Dec) is Fort Cochin's biggest bash, a 10-day festival culminating on New Year's Eve. Street parades,

Ernakulam

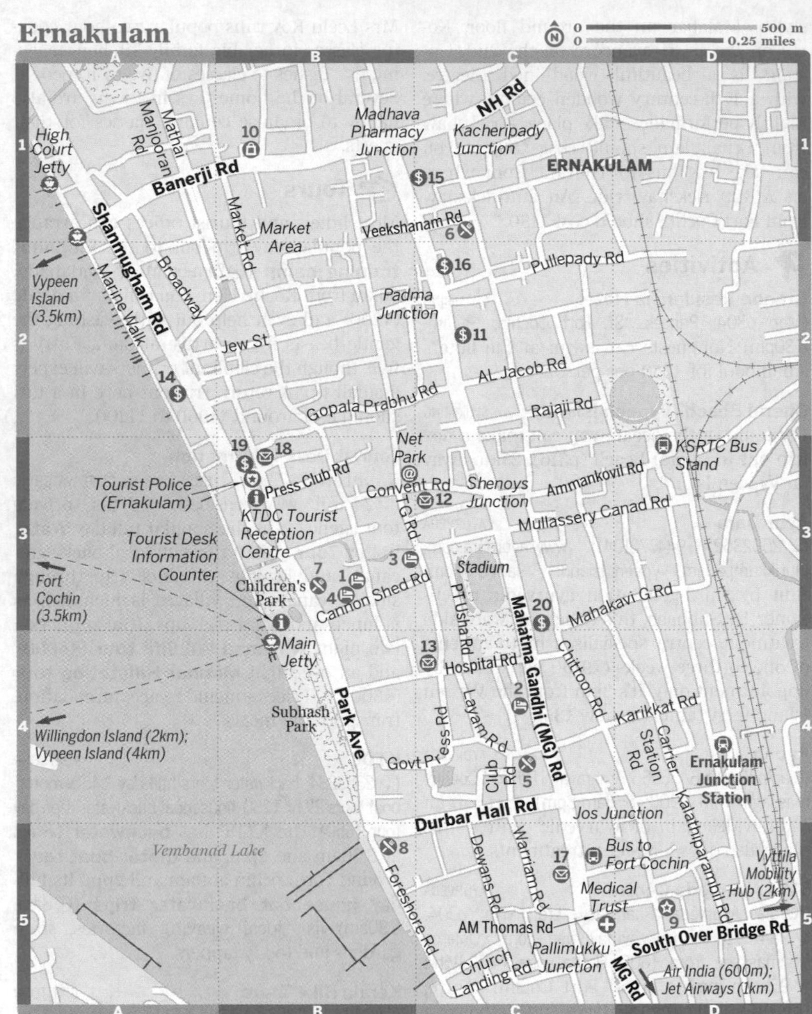

colourful costumes, embellished elephants, music, folk dancing and lots of fun.

Sleeping

Fort Cochin can feel a bit touristy and crowded in season but it's an ideal place to escape the noise and chaos of the mainland – tranquil and romantic, with some of Kerala's finest accommodation. This could be India's homestay capital, with dozens of family houses offering large and clean budget rooms and a hearty welcome.

Ernakulam is cheaper and more convenient for onward travel, but the ambience and accommodation choices are less inspiring. Regardless of where you stay, book ahead during December and January. At other times you can bargain for a discount.

Fort Cochin

★Green Woods Bethlehem HOMESTAY **$**
(☎3247791; greenwoodsbethlehem1@vsnl.net; opposite ESI Hospital; s/d incl breakfast ₹800/900) With a smile that brightens weary travellers, welcoming owner Sheeba looks ready to sign your adoption papers the minute you walk through her front door. Down a quiet lane-

Ernakulam

Sleeping
1 Bijus Tourist Home B3
2 Grand Hotel C4
3 John's Residency B3
4 Saas Tower B3

Eating
5 Chillies C4
6 Frys Village Restaurant C1
Grand Pavilion .... (see 2)
7 Kochin Food Mall B3
8 Subhiksha B5

Entertainment
9 See India Foundation D5

Shopping
10 DC Books B1

Information
11 Citibank C2
12 College Post Office C3
13 Ernakulam Post Office Branches C4
14 Federal Bank ATM A2
15 HDFC Bank ATM C1
16 Idbi Bank ATM C2
17 Post Office C5
18 Post Office B3
19 SBI ATM B3
20 UAE Exchange C3

way and with a walled garden thick with plants and palms, this is one of Kochi's most serene homestays. The rooms are humble but cosy; breakfast is served in the fantastic, leafy rooftop cafe, where cooking classes/demonstrations are often held.

Princess Inn GUESTHOUSE $
(Map p304; ☎2217073; princessinnfortkochi@gmail.com; Princess St; r ₹400-800) Sticking to its budget guns, the friendly Princess Inn spruces up its dull, tiny rooms with cheery bright colours. The comfy communal spaces are a treat, and the three large, front-facing rooms are great value for this location.

Mother Tree HOMESTAY $
(Map p304; ☎9447464906; www.hotelmothertree.com; off KL Bernard Master Rd; d incl breakfast ₹700, with AC ₹1000; ❄@📶) There are just a few minuscule rooms in this compact homestay, but the cleanliness and neat rooftop chill-out space make it worth seeking out.

Dream Catcher HOMESTAY $
(☎2217550; www.dreamcatcherhomestays.com; Vasavan Lane; r ₹800-1000, with AC from ₹2000; ❄) Tucked away on a narrow laneway, this rambling old colonial house has spotless midpriced rooms, an almost gothic sitting room and balconies lined with pot plants: it offers a warm backpacker-friendly welcome from the Portuguese-descended family.

Costa Gama Home Stay HOMESTAY $
(☎2216122; www.stayIncochin.com; Thamaraparambu Rd; r without/with AC ₹800/1200; ❄📶) With just three rooms, this cosy little place gets good reviews. Across the road are another three rooms in a heritage-style building with a nice terrace.

Royal Grace Tourist Home GUESTHOUSE $
(Map p304; ☎2216584; Amaravathi Rd; r ₹350-500, with AC ₹1200; ❄) This old-timer is one of the rare budget stalwarts still left in Fort Cochin. There are loads of staid rooms on offer in the off-white four-storey building, each with little more than a bed, four walls and a pint-sized bathroom. The best open onto a balcony.

★ **Reds Residency** HOMESTAY $$
(☎3204060; www.redsresidency.in; 11/372 A, KJ Herschel Rd; d incl breakfast ₹800-1000, with AC ₹1000-1200, AC cottage ₹1500; ❄@📶) Reds is a relatively new homestay with hotel-quality rooms but a true family welcome from knowledgable hosts Philip and Maryann. The five double rooms are modern and immaculate, and there's a self-contained 'penthouse' cottage with kitchen on the rooftop. It's in a peaceful location near the Maritime Museum.

Noah's Ark HOMESTAY $$
(Map p304; ☎2215481; www.noahsarkcochin.com; 1/508 Fort Kochi Hospital Rd; r incl breakfast ₹2800-3000; ❄@📶) This large modern family home comes with a friendly welcome but plenty of privacy. There's a sweeping spiral staircase from the reception room and four immaculate, upmarket rooms – two with a balcony.

Walton's Homestay GUESTHOUSE $$
(Map p304; ☎2215309; www.waltonshomestay.com; Princess St; r incl breakfast ₹1200-2600; ❄📶) The fastidious Mr Walton offers big wood-furnished rooms in his lovely old house that's painted a nautical white with blue trim and buried behind a bookshop. Downstairs

rooms open onto a lush garden while upstairs rooms have a balcony, and there's a nice communal breakfast room.

Raintree Lodge GUESTHOUSE $$
(Map p304; ☎3251489; www.fortcochin.com; Peter Celli St; r ₹2800; ❄) The intimate and elegant rooms at this historic place flirt with boutique-hotel status. Each room has a great blend of contemporary style and heritage carved-wood furniture and the front upstairs rooms have gorgeous vine-covered *Romeo and Juliet* balconies. Good value.

Bernard Bungalow HOMESTAY $$
(Map p304; ☎2216162; www.bernardbungalow.com; Parade Ground Rd; d incl breakfast ₹2000-3000, with AC ₹2500-3500; ❄@✆) This gracious place has the look of a 1940s summer cottage, housed in a fine 350-year-old family home with a collection of interesting rooms. The house has polished floorboards, wooden window shutters, balconies and verandahs, and is filled with lovely period furniture. Top-floor rooms are the best.

Sonnetta Residency GUESTHOUSE $$
(Map p304; ☎2215744; www.sonnettaresidency.com; 1/387 Princess St; s/d/f ₹900/1000/1500, with AC ₹1500-2000; ❄✆) Right in the thick of the Fort Cochin action, the six rooms at this friendly Portuguese-era place are immaculately kept and well-presented, with nice, chintzy touches like curtains, colourful bedspreads and indoor plants. Every room has air-con but you can choose not to use it at the cheaper rate.

Delight Home Stay GUESTHOUSE $$
(Map p304; ☎2217658; www.delightfulhomestay.com; Post Office Rd; r ₹1400-1800, with AC ₹2500; ❄✆) And delightful it is. This grand house's exterior is adorned with frilly white woodwork, and the rooms are spacious and polished. There's a charming little garden, elegant breakfast room and an imposing sitting room covered in wall-to-wall teak. Good food is served and cooking classes are offered in the open kitchen.

Daffodil GUESTHOUSE $$
(Map p304; ☎2218686; Njaliparambu Junction; d incl breakfast without/with AC ₹2000/2500; ❄@✆) Run by a local couple, Daffodil has eight big and brightly painted modern rooms, but the best feature is the carved-wood Keralan balcony upstairs.

★**Malabar House** HOTEL $$$
(Map p304; ☎2216666; www.malabarhouse.com; Parade Ground Rd; r €230, ste incl breakfast €330-380; ❄@≋) What may just be one of the fanciest boutique hotels in Kerala, Malabar flaunts its über-hip blend of modern colours and period fittings like it's not even trying. While the suites are huge and lavishly appointed, the standard rooms are more snug. The award-winning restaurant and wine bar are top notch.

★**Brunton Boatyard** HOTEL $$$
(Map p304; ☎2215461; bruntonboatyard@cghearth.com; River Rd; r ₹21,000, ste ₹28,000; ❄@✆≋) This imposing hotel faithfully reproduces 16th- and 17th-century Dutch and Portuguese architecture in its grand complex. All of the rooms look out over the harbour, and have bathtub and balconies with a refreshing sea breeze that beats air-con any day. It has the excellent History Restaurant and Armoury Bar, along with a couple of open-air cafes.

Tea Bungalow HOTEL $$$
(Map p304; ☎3019200; www.teabungalow.in; 1/1901 Kunumpuram; r US$340; ❄@✆≋) This mustard-coloured colonial building was built in 1912 as headquarters of a UK spice trading company before being taken over by Brooke Bond tea. The 10 graceful boutique rooms – all named after sea ports – are decorated with flashes of strong colour and carved colonial wooden furniture, and have Bassetta-tiled bathrooms. Off-season rates drop by 60%.

Old Harbour Hotel HOTEL $$$
(Map p304; ☎2218006; www.oldharbourhotel.com; Tower Rd; r ₹9250-13,050; ❄@≋) Set around an idyllic garden with lily ponds and a small pool, the dignified Old Harbour is housed in a 300-year-old Dutch/Portuguese heritage building. The elegant mix of period and modern styles lends it a more intimate feel than some of the more grandiose competition. There are 13 rooms, some facing directly onto the garden and some with plant-filled, open-air bathrooms.

Koder House HOTEL $$$
(Map p304; ☎2217988; www.koderhouse.com; Tower Rd; r from ₹8000-9000; ❄≋) A historic 200-year-old mansion overlooking the Chinese fishing nets, this fine heritage property has six characterful suites and an atmospheric, high-ceiling restaurant. Overpriced in season, but worth a splurge at other times.

Fort House Hotel HOTEL $$$
(Map p304; ☎2217103; www.hotelforthouse.com; 2/6A Calvathy Rd; r incl breakfast ₹5520; ❄@) Close to the ferry point, this is one of the few truly waterfront hotels, though the 16 smart air-con rooms are set back in a lush garden, with the restaurant taking prime waterside position.

Mattancherry & Jew Town

Caza Maria HOMESTAY $$$
(Map p306; ☎9846050901; cazamaria@rediffmail.com; Jew Town Rd, Mattancherry; r incl breakfast ₹4500; ❄) Right in the heart of Jew Town, this unique place has just two enormous, gorgeous heritage rooms overlooking the bazaar. Fit for a maharaja, the rooms feature an idiosyncratic style – with each high-ceilinged room painted in bright colours, filled to the brim with antiques.

Ernakulam

John's Residency HOTEL $
(Map p308; ☎2355395; TD Rd; s/d from ₹450/550, with AC ₹1350; ❄) With a cool yellow foyer featuring interesting clutter such as vintage fans, this is a refreshing backpacker place. Rooms are small (deluxe rooms are bigger) but decorated with flashes of colour that give them a funky feel that's a welcome surprise in this price bracket.

Bijus Tourist Home HOTEL $
(Map p308; ☎2361661; www.bijustouristhome.com; Market Rd; s/d from ₹700/850, with AC ₹1575/1750; ❄@) This friendly, popular choice is handy for the main jetty and has reasonable, drab but clean rooms and a friendly welcome.

Saas Tower HOTEL $$
(Map p308; ☎2365319; www.saastower.com; Cannon Shed Rd; s/d ₹880/1460, with AC from ₹1755/2100; ❄@) The flashy lobby is more promising than the rooms in this low-end business hotel but if you're after a step up from the budget hotels near the jetty, this isn't a bad option. Clean rooms filled with wooden furniture. There's a restaurant, business centre and day spa with ayurvedic treatments.

Grand Hotel HOTEL $$$
(Map p308; ☎2382061; www.grandhotelkerala.com; MG Rd; s/d from ₹3000/3600, ste ₹5400; ❄@📶) This 1960s hotel, with its polished original art deco fittings, oozes the sort of retro cool that modern hotels would kill to recreate. The spacious rooms have gleaming parquet floors and large modern bathrooms, and there's a good restaurant and Ernakulam's most sophisticated bar.

Around Kochi

★**Olavipe** HOMESTAY $$
(☎04782522255; www.olavipe.com; Olavipe; s/d incl meals ₹5100/8500) This gorgeous 1890s traditional Syrian-Christian home is on a 16-hectare farm surrounded by backwaters, 28km south of Kochi. A restored mansion of rosewood and glistening teak, it has several large and breezy rooms beautifully decorated in original period decor. There are lots of shady awnings and sitting areas, a fascinating archive with six generations of family history, and the gracious owners will make you feel like a welcome friend rather than a guest.

Eating & Drinking

Some of Fort Cochin's best dining can be found in the homestays, but there are lots of good restaurants and cafes. Covert beer consumption in teapots is de rigueur in many of Fort Cochin's cheaper restaurants, and more expensive in the licensed ones.

Fort Cochin

Behind the Chinese fishing nets are several **fishmongers**, from whom you can buy fish (or prawns, scampi, lobster), then take your selection to one of the row of simple but popular restaurants on nearby Tower Rd where the folks there will cook it and serve it to you for an additional charge. Market price varies.

Kashi Art Cafe CAFE $
(Map p304; Burgher St; breakfast & snacks ₹80-110; ⊙8.30am-7.30pm) An institution in Fort Cochin, this natural light-filled place has a zen-but-casual vibe and solid wood tables that spread out into a semi-courtyard space. The coffee is as strong as it should be and the daily Western breakfast and lunch specials are excellent. A small gallery shows off local artists.

Teapot CAFE $
(Map p304; Peter Celli St; mains ₹60-250) This atmospheric cafe is the perfect venue for 'high tea', with 16 types of tea, sandwiches, cake and full meals served in chic, airy rooms. Witty tea-themed accents include loads of

antique teapots, tea chests for tables and a gnarled, tea-tree-based glass table.

Loafers Corner CAFE $

(Map p304; cnr Bastion & Princess Sts; ₹40-90; ⏲11am-10pm) If you can grab one of the three window seats there are few better people-watching spots than this corner cafe with a beautiful timber ceiling and earthy tones. The menu is mostly snacks like dosas and kati rolls, as well as shakes, juice and lassis.

★Dal Roti INDIAN $$

(Map p304; ☎9746459244; 1/293 Lily St; meals ₹100-230; ⏲noon-3.30pm & 6.30-10.30pm Wed-Mon) There's a lot to like about busy Dal Roti. Friendly and knowledgable owner Ramesh will hold your hand through his expansive North Indian menu, which even sports its own glossary, and help you dive into his delicious range of vegetarian, eggetarian and nonvegetarian options. From kati rolls to seven types of thali, you won't go hungry. No alcohol.

Arca Nova SEAFOOD $$

(Map p304; 2/6A Calvathy Rd; mains ₹220-380; ⏲7.30am-10.30pm) The waterside restaurant at the Fort House Hotel is a prime choice for a leisurely lunch. It specialises in fish dishes and you can sit out at tables overlooking the water or in the serenely spacious covered garden area.

Casa Linda MULTICUISINE $

(Map p304; Dispensary Rd; mains ₹95-450; ⏲7-10.30pm) This modern dining room above the hotel of the same name might not be much to look at, but it's all about the Indo-European food here. Chef Dipu once trained with a Frenchman and whips up delicious local Keralan dishes alongside French fusion.

★Malabar Junction INTERNATIONAL $$$

(Map p304; ☎2216666; Parade Ground Rd; mains ₹350-650) Set in an open-sided pavilion, the restaurant at Malabar House is movie-star cool, with white-tableclothed tables in a courtyard close to the small pool. There's a seafood-based, European-style menu – the signature dish is the impressive seafood platter with grilled vegetables. Upstairs, the wine bar serves upmarket snacks such as tapioca-and-cumin fritters in funkily clashing surroundings.

XL Fishnet Bar BAR

(Map p304; Rose St; ⏲10am-10.30pm) This slightly dingy 1st-floor bar-restaurant is a popular place to settle down with a cold Kingfisher, palatable snacks and meals such as beef deep fry. The downstairs restaurant also serves alcohol at slightly higher prices.

Mattancherry & Jew Town

Ramathula Hotel INDIAN $

(Map p306; Kayees Junction, Mattancherry; biryani ₹40-60; ⏲lunch & dinner) This place is legendary among locals for its chicken and mutton biryanis – get here early or miss out. It's better known by the chef's name, Kayikka's.

Shri Krishna INDIAN $

(Map p306; dishes ₹10-55; ⏲7.30am-9.30pm) Simple, busy, basic, but tasty thalis.

Caza Maria MULTICUISINE $$

(Map p306; Bazaar Rd; mains around ₹150-290; ⏲10am-8pm) This enchanting 1st-floor place across from the hotel of the same name is a bright-blue, antique-filled space with funky music and a changing daily menu of North Indian, South Indian and French dishes.

Café Jew Town CAFE $$

(Map p306; Bazaar Rd; snacks around ₹120-150; ⏲9.30am-6pm) Walk through chic antique shops and galleries to reach this sweet Swiss-owned cafe; the few tables proffer good cakes, snacks and Italian coffee.

Ginger House INDIAN $$$

(Map p306; Bazaar Rd; mains ₹300-700; ⏲8.30am-6pm) Hidden behind a massive antique-filled godown (warehouse) is this fantastic waterfront restaurant, where you can feast on Indian dishes and snacks – ginger prawns, ginger ice cream... you get the picture. Less about the pricey food and more about the sculptures – check out the giant snake-boat canoe.

Ernakulam

Frys Village Restaurant KERALAN $

(Map p308; Veekshanam Rd; dishes ₹75-120; ⏲noon-3.30pm & 7-10.30pm) This brightly decorated and breezy place with an arched ceiling is a great family restaurant with authentic Keralan food, especially seafood like *pollichathu* or crab roast. Fish/veg thalis are available for lunch.

Subhiksha INDIAN $

(Map p308; DH Road, Gandhi Sq; dishes ₹40-120; ⏲7.30am-3.30pm & 7-11pm) At Bharat Hotel, this popular pure-veg restaurant is a smart place to dig into tasty thalis.

Kochin Food Mall MALL $
(Map p308; www.cochinfoodmall.com; Park Avenue Rd, Ernakulam; ₹70-170; ⏲10.30am-11pm) Opposite the boat jetty, this super-modern new food mall gives you the choice of 10 food outlets, including North and South Indian, Chinese, pizza and, most interesting of all, Ooru, specialising in tribal foods from Wayanad district.

Chillies INDIAN $$
(Map p308; meals ₹100-210; ⏲11.30am-3.30pm & 7.30-10pm) A dark, buzzing 1st-floor place, serving spicy Andhra cuisine on banana leaves. Try a thali, for all-you-can-eat joy.

★ **Grand Pavilion** INDIAN $$$
(Map p308; MG Rd; meals ₹180-500) The restaurant at the Grand Hotel is as elegant and retro-stylish as the hotel itself, with cream-coloured furniture and stiff tablecloths. It serves a tome of a menu that covers dishes from the West, North India, South India and most of the rest of the Asian continent.

Entertainment

There are several places in Kochi where you can view Kathakali. The performances are certainly made for tourists, but they're a good introduction to this intriguing art form. The standard program starts with the intricate make-up application and costume-fitting, followed by a demonstration and commentary on the dance and then the performance – usually two hours in all. The fast-paced traditional martial art of *kalarippayat* can also be easily seen in Fort Cochin.

Fort Cochin

Kerala Kathakali Centre CULTURAL PROGRAM
(Map p304; ☎2217552; www.kathakalicentre.com; KB Jacob Rd, Fort Cochin; admission ₹250; ⏲make-up from 5pm, show 6-7.30pm) In an intimate, wood-lined theatre, this place provides a useful introduction to Kathakali, complete with amazing demonstrations of eye movements, plus handy translations of the night's story. The centre also hosts performances of the martial art of *kalarippayat* from 4pm to 5pm daily, traditional music from 8pm to 9pm Sunday to Friday and classical dance at 8pm from 9pm on Saturday.

Greenix Village CULTURAL PROGRAM
(Map p304; ☎2217000; www.greenix.in; Kalvathy Rd, Fort Cochin; ⏲10am-6pm, shows from 5pm) This touristy 'cultural village' seeks to put the full gamut of Keralan music and arts under one roof with a small cultural museum, performances of Kathakali and *kalarippayat* and other cultural shows in an impressive complex.

Ernakulam

See India Foundation CULTURAL PROGRAM
(Map p308; ☎2376471; devankathakali@yahoo.com; Kalathiparambil Lane, Ernakulam; admission ₹200; ⏲make-up 6pm, show 7-8pm) One of the oldest Kathakali theatres in Kerala, it has small-scale shows with an emphasis on the religious and philosophical roots of Kathakali.

Ens Kalari CULTURAL PROGRAM
(☎2700810; www.enskalari.org.in; Nettoor, Ernakulam; admission by donation; ⏲demonstrations 7.15-8.15pm) If you want to see real professionals have a go at *kalarippayat,* it's best to travel out to this renowned *kalarippayat* learning centre, 8km southeast of Ernakulam. There are one-hour demonstrations daily (one day's notice required).

Shopping

Broadway in Ernakulam is good for local shopping, spice shops and clothing, and around Convent and Market Rds is a huddle of tailors. On Jew Town Rd in Mattancherry there's a plethora of Gujarati-run shops selling genuine antiques mingled with knock-offs and copies. Most of the shops in Fort Cochin are identikit Kashmiri-run shops selling a mixed bag of North Indian crafts. Many shops around Fort Cochin and Mattancherry operate lucrative commission rackets, with autorickshaw drivers getting huge kickbacks (added to your price) for dropping tourists at their door. Any driver who offers to take you on a factory tour or to a special viewpoint will be heading straight to a shop.

Niraamaya CLOTHING
Fort Cochin (Map p304; ☎3263465; Quiros St, Fort Cochin; ⏲10am-5.30pm Mon-Sat); **Mattancherry** (Map p306; VI/217 AB Salam Rd, Jew Town, Mattancherry) Popular throughout Kerala, Niraamaya sells 'ayurvedic' clothing and fabrics – all made of organic cotton, coloured with natural herb dyes, or infused with ayurvedic oils.

DC Books BOOKS
(Map p308; ☎2391295; Banerji Rd, Ernakulam; ⏲9am-7.30pm Mon-Sat, 11am-6pm Sun) Excellent English-language selection of fiction and nonfiction. Also branches in Fort Cochin and Mattancherry.

MAJOR BUSES FROM ERNAKULAM

The following bus services operate from the KSRTC bus stand and Vyttila Mobility Hub.

DESTINATION	FARE (₹)	DURATION (HR)	FREQUENCY/TIME
Alleppey	41	1½	every 10min
Bengaluru	405-495	14	4 daily
Calicut	133	5	hourly
Chennai	555	16	2pm
Coimbatore	139	4½	hourly
Kannur	210	8	2 daily
Kanyakumari	210	8	2 daily
Kollam	94	3½	every 30min
Kothamangalam	35	2	every 10min
Kottayam	51	2	every 30min
Kumily (for Periyar)	120	5	8 daily
Mangalore	305	12	6.30pm
Munnar	90	4½	every 30min
Thrissur	51	2	every 10min
Trivandrum	138	5	every 30min

Idiom Bookshop BOOKS
(Map p304; ⊙10.30am-9pm Mon-Sat) Huge range of quality new and used books.

Fabindia CLOTHING, HOMEWARES
(Map p304; ☎2217077; www.fabindia.com; Napier St, Fort Cochin; ⊙10.30am-8.30pm) Fine Indian textiles, fabrics, clothes and household linen from this renowned brand.

Cinnamon CLOTHING
(Map p304; Post Office Rd, Fort Cochin; ⊙10am-7pm Mon-Sat) Opposite the parade ground, Cinnamon sells gorgeous Indian-designed clothing, jewellery and homewares in an ultrachic white retail space.

Tribes India HANDICRAFTS
(Map p304; ☎2215077; Head Post Office, Fort Cochin; ⊙10am-6.30pm Mon-Sat) Tucked behind the post office, this TRIFED (Ministry of Tribal Affairs) enterprise sells tribal artefacts, paintings, shawls, figurines etc, at reasonable fixed prices and the profits go towards supporting the artisans.

ℹ Information

INTERNET ACCESS

There are several internet cafes around Princess St in Fort Cochin charging ₹40 per hour, and a number of homestays offer free wi-fi.

Net Park (Map p308; Convent Rd, Ernakulam; per hr ₹15; ⊙9am-8pm)

MEDICAL SERVICES

Lakeshore Hospital (☎2701032; www.lakeshorehospital.com; NH Bypass, Marudu) Modern hospital 8km southeast of central Ernakulam.

Medical Trust Hospital (Map p308; ☎2358001; www.medicaltrusthospital.com; MG Rd)

MONEY

UAE Exchange (⊙9.30am-6pm Mon-Fri, to 4pm Sat) Ernakulam (☎2383317; MG Rd, Perumpillil Bldg, Ernakulam); Ernakulam (☎3067008; Chettupuzha Towers, PT Usha Rd Junction, Ernakulam); Fort Cochin (Map p304; ☎2216231; Amravathi Rd, Fort Cochin) Foreign exchange and travellers cheques.

POST

College Post Office (Map p308; ☎2369302; Convent Rd, Ernakulam; ⊙9am-5pm Mon-Sat)

Ernakulam Post Office Branches (Map p308; ☎2355467; Hospital Rd; ⊙9am-8pm Mon-Sat, 10am-5pm Sun) Also branches on MG Rd and Broadway.

Main Post Office (Map p304; Post Office Rd, Fort Cochin; ⊙9am-5pm Mon-Fri, to 3pm Sat) Main post office.

TOURIST INFORMATION

There's a tourist information counter at the airport. Many places distribute a free brochure that includes a map and walking tour entitled *Historical Places in Fort Cochin*.

KTDC Tourist Reception Centre (Map p308; ☎2353234; Shanmugham Rd, Ernakulam;

⌚8am-7pm) Also organises tours. There's another office at the jetty at Fort Cochin.

Tourist Desk Information Counter Ernakulam (Map p308; ☎2371761; www.touristdesk.in; Boat Jetty, Ernakulam; ⌚8am-6pm); Fort Cochin (Map p304; ☎2216129; Fort Cochin; ⌚8am-7pm) A private tour agency that's very knowledgable and helpful about Kochi and beyond. Runs several popular and recommended tours, and its Ernakulam office displays recommended cultural events on in town that day, and has a secondhand book exchange.

Tourist Police Ernakulam (Map p308; ☎2353234; Shanmugham Rd, Ernakulam; ⌚8am-6pm); Fort Cochin (Map p304; ☎2215055; Fort Cochin; ⌚24hr)

Getting There & Away

AIR

Kochi International Airport is a popular hub, with international flights to the Gulf states, Sri Lanka and Singapore. Between them Jet Airways, Air India and Spicejet fly direct daily to Chennai, Mumbai and Bengalaru. Jet Airways and Spicejet also fly to Hyderabad, while IndiGo flies to Trivandrum. Air India flies to Delhi daily and to Agatti in the Lakshadweep islands six times a week. The following airlines have offices in Ernakulam:

Air India (☎2351295; MG Rd)

Jet Airways (☎2359334; MG Rd)

BUS

At the time of writing there were plans afoot for buses to operate directly between Fort Cochin and places like Munnar, Alleppey and Periyar. Until then, all long-distance services operate from Ernakulam. The **KSRTC bus stand** (Map p308; ☎2372033; ⌚reservations 6am-10pm) is next to the railway, halfway between the two train stations. There's a separate window for reservations to Tamil Nadu. Government and private buses pull into the massive new **Vyttila Mobility Hub** (☎2306611; www.vyttilamobilityhub.com; ⌚24hr), a state-of-the-art transport terminal about 2km east of Ernakulam Junction train station. Numerous private bus companies have super-deluxe, air-con, video and Volvo buses to long distance destinations such as Bengaluru, Chennai, Mangalore, Trivandrum and Coimbatore; prices vary depending on the standard but the best buses are about 50% higher than government buses. Agents in Ernakulam and Fort Cochin sell tickets. Private buses also use the **Kaloor bus stand**, 1km north of the city.

A prepaid autorickshaw from Vyttila costs ₹67 to the boat jetty, ₹62 to the train station and ₹171 to Fort Cochin.

TRAIN

Ernakulam has two train stations, **Ernakulam Town** and **Ernakulam Junction**. Reservations for both are made at the Ernakulam Junction **reservations office** (☎132; ⌚8am-8pm Mon-Sat, 8am-2pm Sun).

There are local and express trains to Trivandrum (2nd-class/AC chair ₹73/264, 4½ hours), via either Alleppey (₹39/171, 1½ hours) or Kottayam (₹39/171, 1½ hours). Trains also run to Thrissur (₹64/205, 1½ hours), Calicut (₹67/237, 4½ hours) and Kannur (₹105/341, 6½ hours).

Getting Around

TO/FROM THE AIRPORT

Kochi International Airport (☎2610125; http://cochinairport.com) is at Nedumbassery, 30km northeast of Ernakulam. A new bus services runs between the airport and Fort Cochin (₹70, one hour, eight daily), some going via Ernakulam. Taxis to/from Ernakulam cost around ₹650, and to/from Fort Cochin around ₹900.

BOAT

Ferries are the fastest, most enjoyable form of transport between Fort Cochin and the mainland. The jetty on Willingdon Island's eastern side is called **Embarkation** (Map p303); the west one, opposite Mattancherry, is **Terminus** (Map p303); and Fort Cochin's main stop is **Customs** (Map p304), with another stop at the **Mattancherry Jetty** near the synagogue. One-way fares are

MAJOR TRAINS FROM ERNAKULAM

The following are major long-distance trains departing from Ernakulam Town.

DESTINATION	TRAIN NO & NAME	FARE (₹, SLEEPER/ 3AC/2AC)	DURATION (HR)	DEPARTURES (DAILY)
Bengaluru	16525 Bangalore Express	257/719/1085	13	5.55pm
Chennai	12624 Chennai Mail	292/793/1185	12	6.40pm
Delhi	12625 Kerala Express (A)	579/1630/2685	46	3.50pm
Goa	16346 Netravathi Express (A)	305/858/1315	15	2.05pm
Mumbai	16382 Mumbai Express	469/1337/2130	40	1.30pm

(A) Departs from Ernakulam Junction

₹2.50 (₹3.50 between Ernakulam and Mattancherry).

Ernakulam

There are services to both Fort Cochin jetties (Customs and Mattancherry) every 25 to 50 minutes (⏲5.55am to 9.30pm) from Ernakulam's main jetty.

Ferries also run every 20 minutes or so to Willingdon and Vypeen Islands (Map p308; ⏲6am to 10pm).

Fort Cochin

Ferries run from Customs Jetty to Ernakulam (⏲6.20am to 9.50pm). Ferries also hop between Customs Jetty and Willingdon Island 18 times a day (⏲6.40am to 9.30pm, Monday to Saturday).

Car and passenger ferries cross to Vypeen Island from Fort Cochin virtually nonstop (Map p304; ⏲6am to 10pm).

LOCAL TRANSPORT

There are no real bus services between Fort Cochin and Mattancherry Palace, but it's an enjoyable 30-minute walk through the busy warehouse area along Bazaar Rd. Autorickshaws should cost around ₹40, much less if you promise to look in a shop. Most autorickshaw trips around Ernakulam shouldn't cost more than ₹35.

To get to Fort Cochin after ferries stop running you'll need to catch a taxi or autorickshaw – Ernakulam Town train station to Fort Cochin should cost around ₹300; prepaid autorickshaws during the day cost ₹150.

Scooters/Enfields can be hired for ₹250/350-600 per day from a number of agents in Fort Cochin.

Around Kochi

Cherai Beach

On Vypeen Island, 25km from Fort Cochin, Cherai Beach makes a fantastic day trip or getaway from Kochi. It's a lovely stretch of as-yet undeveloped white sand, with miles of lazy backwaters just a few hundred metres from the seafront. Cherai is easily visited on a day trip from Kochi – it's an excellent ride if you hire a scooter or motorbike in Fort Cochin – but a growing number of low-key resorts along the single road running paral-

WORTH A TRIP

THATTEKKAD BIRD SANCTUARY

A serene 25-sq-km park in the foothills of the Western Ghats, cut through by two rivers and two streams, **Thattekkad Bird Sanctuary** (☎04852588302; Indian/foreigner ₹10/100, camera/video ₹25/150; ⏲6.30am-6pm) is home to over 320 fluttering species – unusual in that they are mostly forest, rather than water birds – including Malabar grey hornbills, Ripley owls, jungle nightjars, grey drongos, darters and rarer species like the Sri Lankan frogmouth. There are kingfishers, flycatchers, warblers, sunbirds and flower peckers (which weigh only 4g). To stay in the **Treetop Machan** (Indian/foreigner dm ₹80/150, d incl meals ₹1500-2500) in the sanctuary, contact the **assistant wildlife warden** (☎04852588302) at Kothamangalam. Another option is the **Jungle Bird Homestay** (☎08452588143, 9947506188; per person incl meals ₹900), located inside the park and run by the enthusiastic Ms Sudah and son Gireesh, who will meet guests at the gate. Ms Sudah also offers guided birdwatching trips for ₹600.

For more luxury, visit the lovely **Soma Birds Lagoon** (☎04712268101; www.somabirdslagoon.com; Palamatton, Thattekkad; s/d incl breakfast €70/85, with AC from €75/90; ❄🏊). Set deep in the villages near Thattekkad, this low-key resort lies on a seasonal lake among spacious and manicured grounds. The basic rooms here are roomy and the whole place feels refreshingly remote but is just 16km from Kothamangalam. There's also the tented **Hornbill Camp** (☎04842092280; www.thehornbillcamp.com; d full board US$110), with accommodation in large permanent tents in a sublimely peaceful location facing the Periyar River. Kayaking, cycling and a spice-garden tour are included in the price. Birdwatching guides cost ₹1500. It's around 8km from Thattekkad by road.

Thattekkad is on the Ernakulam–Munnar road. Take a direct bus from either Ernakulam (₹30, two hours) or Munnar (₹55, three hours) to Kothamangalam, from where a Thattekkad bus travels the final 12km (₹8, 25 minutes), or catch an autorickshaw for around ₹150.

lel to the beach make it worth hanging out a few days.

Brighton Beach House (☎9946565555; www.brightonbeachhouse.org; d ₹1100) has five basic rooms in a small building by the shore. The beach is rocky here, but the place is wonderfully secluded, filled with hammocks to loll in, and has a neat, elevated stilt-restaurant overlooking the seawall.

A collection of distinctive cottages lying around a meandering lagoon, **Cherai Beach Resort** (☎04842416949; www.cheraibeachresorts.com; Cherai Beach, Vypeen Island; villas from ₹3750, with AC from ₹4500; ❄@) has the beach on one side and backwaters on the other. Bungalows are individually designed using natural materials, and there's a bar and restaurant.

Hidden back from the beach but with the backwaters on your doorstep, **Les 3 Elephants** (☎04842480005, 9349174341; www.3elephants.in; Convent St; cottages ₹4000-8000; ❄📶) is a superb French-run ecoresort. The 11 beautifully designed boutique cottages are all different but have private sit outs, thoughtful personal touches and lovely backwater views. The restaurant serves home-cooked French-Indian fare. Worth the trip!

For European-style comfort food by the beach – think burgers, pizzas and barbecue – **Chilliout Cafe** (mains ₹180-250; 🕘9am-late Oct-May) is a cool hangout with sea breezes and a relaxed vibe.

To get here from Fort Cochin, catch the vehicle-ferry to Vypeen Island (per person ₹2) and either hire an autorickshaw from the jetty (around ₹350) or catch one of the frequent buses (₹15, one hour) and get off at Cherai village, 1km from the beach. Buses also go here direct from Ernakulam via the Vallarpadam bridge.

Tripunithura

At Tripunithura, 16km southeast of Ernakulam, **Hill Palace Museum** (☎04842781113; admission ₹20; 🕘9am-12.30pm & 2-4.30pm Tue-Sun) was formerly the residence of the Kochi royal family and is an impressive 49-building palace complex. It now houses the collections of the royal families, as well as 19th-century oil paintings, old coins, sculptures and paintings, and temple models. From Ernakulam catch the bus to Tripunithura from MG Rd or Shanmugham Rd, behind the Tourist Reception Centre (₹5 to ₹10, 45 minutes); an autorickshaw should cost around ₹300 return with one-hour waiting time.

Parur & Chennamangalam

Nowhere is the tightly woven religious cloth that is India more apparent than in **Parur**, 35km north of Kochi. One of the oldest **synagogues** (admission ₹5; 🕘9am-5pm Tue-Sun) in Kerala, at **Chennamangalam**, 8km from Parur, has been fastidiously renovated. Inside you can see door and ceiling wood-reliefs in dazzling colours, while just outside lies one of the oldest tombstones in India – inscribed with the Hebrew date corresponding to 1269. The Jesuits first arrived in Chennamangalam in 1577 and there's a **Jesuit church** and the ruins of a Jesuit college nearby. Nearby are a **Hindu temple** on a hill overlooking the Periyar River, a 16th-century **mosque**, and Muslim and Jewish **burial grounds**.

In Parur town, you'll find the **agraharam** (place of Brahmins) – a small street of closely packed and brightly coloured houses originally settled by Tamil Brahmins.

Parur is compact, but Chennamangalam is best visited with a guide. Travel agencies in Fort Cochin can organise tours. **Carnival Tours & Travels** (Map p304; ☎9895224922; www.carnivaltourskochi.com; Princess St) runs a full-day Jewish Heritage Tour to Parur, Chennamangalam and other sites for ₹3000 per person, starting with the ferry to Vypeen Island. A taxi tour for the day can be done for around ₹1000.

Thrissur (Trichur)

☎0487 / POP 315,600

While the rest of Kerala has its fair share of celebrations, untouristy, slightly chaotic Thrissur is the cultural cherry on the festival cake. With a list of energetic festivals as long as a temple-elephant's trunk, the region supports several institutions nursing the dying classical Keralan performing arts back to health. Centred around a large park (known as the 'Round') and temple complex, Thrissur is home to a Nestorian Christian community whose denomination dates to the 3rd century AD. There's not much to see when there's no festivities so plan to arrive during the rambunctious festival season (November to mid-May).

Sights & Activities

Thrissur is renowned for its central temple, as well as for its numerous impressive

Thrissur (Trichur)

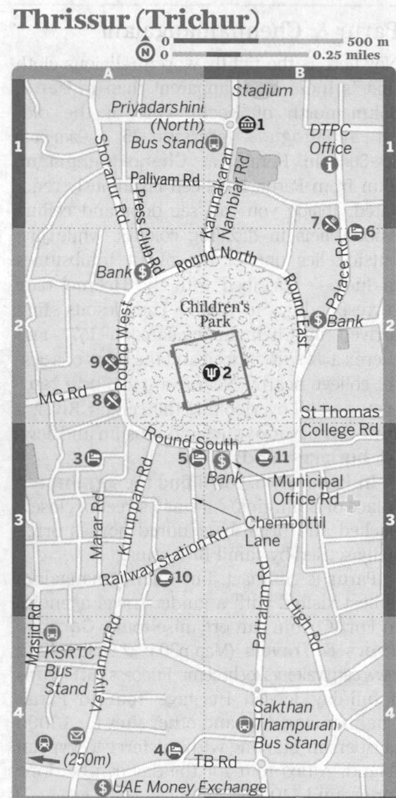

churches, including the massive **Our Lady of Lourdes Cathedral**, towering, whitewashed **Puttanpalli (New) Church** and the **Chaldian (Nestorian) Church**.

Vadakkunathan Kshetram Temple HINDU TEMPLE

One of the oldest in the state, Vadakkunathan Kshetram Temple crowns the hill at the epicentre of Thrissur. Finished in classic Keralan architecture, only Hindus are allowed inside, though the mound surrounding the temple has sweeping views and is a popular spot to linger.

Archaeology Museum MUSEUM

(admission ₹10, camera/video ₹25/50; 9am-1pm & 2-4.30pm Tue-Sun) The Archaeology Museum is housed in the wonderful 200-year-old Sakthan Thampuran Palace. Its mix of artefacts include fragile palm-leaf manuscripts, 12th-century Keralan bronze sculptures and giant earthenware pots. It was closed for renovation at the time of research but should be open by the time you read this.

Thrissur (Trichur)

Sights

1 Archaeology Museum B1
2 Vadakkunathan Kshetram Temple B2

Sleeping

3 Hotel Luciya Palace A3
4 Joys Palace A4
5 Pathans Hotel A3
6 YMCA International Guesthouse B2

Eating

7 India Gate B1
8 Navaratna Restaurant A2
9 New Ambady Restaurant A2
Pathans Restaurant .... (see 5)

Drinking & Nightlife

10 Indian Coffee House A3
11 Indian Coffee House B3

Festivals & Events

In a state where festivals are a way of life, Thrissur still manages to stand out for temple revelry. Highlights include **Thrissur Pooram** (April/May) – the most colourful and biggest of Kerala's temple festivals with wonderful processions of elephants; **Uthralikavu Pooram** (March/April), whose climactic day sees 20 elephants circling the shrine; and **Thypooya Maholsavam** (January/February), with a *kavadiyattam* (a form of ritualistic dance) procession in which dancers carry tall, ornate structures called *kavadis*.

Sleeping

Pathans Hotel HOTEL $

(2425620; www.pathansresidentialhotel.com; Round South; s/d from ₹480/644, with AC ₹840/1200;) No-frills rooms at no-frills prices and the location is unbeatable across from the central park. The basic and cleanish rooms are on the 5th and 6th floors (served by a painfully slow lift) and have TV and occasional hot water.

YMCA International Guesthouse GUESTHOUSE $

(2331190; www.ymcathrissur.org; Palace Rd; d ₹650, with AC ₹1000) Clean, comfortable and secure. A good budget choice.

Hotel Luciya Palace HOTEL $$
(☎2424731; www.hotelluciyapalace.com; Marar Rd; s/d with AC ₹1400/1600, ste ₹2600; ❄) In a cream, colonial-themed building, this is one of the few places in town that has some genuine character, and it's great value. Sitting in a quiet cul-de-sac but close to the temple action, it has comfortable and spacious air-con rooms, a neat lawn garden, a decent restaurant and two of Thrissur's best bars.

Joys Palace HOTEL $$
(☎2429999; www.joyshotels.com; TB Rd; s/d incl breakfast from ₹2800/3400, ste ₹6500/7000; ❄@📶) This ornate 10-storey whitewashed meringue caters to Thrissur's jet set. Rooms have big windows to enjoy the upper floor's sweeping views. There's a 2nd-floor restaurant with an outdoor balcony, a bar and a cool glass-fronted elevator.

Eating & Drinking

Pathans Restaurant INDIAN $
(1st fl, Round South; dishes ₹30-70; ⏲6.30am-9.30pm) On the first floor of the Pathans Hotel building, this easygoing place opens early for a cheap breakfast and is popular with families for lunch (thali ₹40).

New Ambady Restaurant SOUTH INDIAN $
(Round West; dishes ₹25-70; ⏲8am-9pm) Set back from the main street, this dark-brown place is a huge hit with families tucking into several different varieties of cheap set veg meals.

India Gate INDIAN $
(Palace Rd; dishes ₹55-125; ⏲8am-10pm) In the Kalliyath Royal Square building, this bright, pure-veg place has a vintage feel and an extraordinary range of dosas, including jam, cheese and cashew versions. In the same complex is a Chinese restaurant (China Gate) and a fast food joint (Celebrations).

Navaratna Restaurant MULTICUISINE $
(Round West; dishes ₹80-140; ⏲noon-9.30pm) Cool, dark and intimate, this is one of the classiest dining experiences in town, with seating on raised platforms. Downstairs is veg and upstairs is nonveg, with lots of North Indian specialities, Chinese and a few Keralan dishes.

Indian Coffee House CAFE
(₹25-90; ⏲7.30am-9.30pm) Has branches at Round South and Railway Station Rd.

Information

There are several ATMs and internet cafes around town.

DTPC Office (☎2320800; Palace Rd; ⏲10am-5pm Mon-Sat)

UAE Money Exchange (TB Rd; ⏲9am-6.30pm Mon-Fri, to 1pm Sat, to 4pm Sun)

Getting There & Away

BUS

KSRTC buses leave around every 30 minutes from the **KSRTC bus stand** bound for Trivandrum (₹182, 7½ hours), Ernakulam (Kochi, ₹50, two hours), Calicut (₹86, 3½ hours), Palakkad (₹45, 1½ hours) and Kottayam (₹86, four hours). Hourly buses go to Coimbatore (₹79, three hours).

Regular services also chug along to Guruvayur (₹20, one hour), Irinjalakuda (₹22, one hour) and Cheruthuruthy (₹20, 1½ hours). Two private bus stands (**Sakthan Thampuran** and **Priyadarshini**) have more frequent buses to these destinations, though the chaos involved in navigating each station hardly makes using them worthwhile.

TRAIN

Services run regularly to Ernakulam (2nd-class/AC chair ₹64/205, 1½ hours) and Calicut (₹74/220, three hours).

Around Thrissur

The Hindu-only **Shri Krishna Temple** at Guruvayur, 33km northwest of Thrissur, is among the most famous in Kerala. Said to have been created by Guru, preceptor of the gods, and Vayu, god of wind, the temple is believed to date from the 16th century and is renowned for its healing powers. A spectacular annual **Elephant Race** is held here in February or March.

Kerala Kalamandalam (☎04884262418; www.kalamandalam.org; ⏲June-Mar), 32km northeast of Thrissur at Cheruthuruthy, is a champion of Kerala's traditional-art renaissance. Using an ancient Gurukula system of learning, students undergo intensive study in Kathakali, *mohiniyattam* (dance of the enchantress), *Kootiattam*, percussion, voice and violin. **A Day with the Masters** (per person including lunch ₹1000; ⏲9.30am-1pm) is a morning program allowing visitors to tour the theatre and classes and see various art and cultural presentations. Individually tailored **introductory courses** (per month around ₹2500) are offered one subject at a time and last from six to 12 months. The school can help you find local homestay accommodation. For visits, email to book in advance.

Natana Kairali Research & Performing Centre for Traditional Arts (☎04802825559; natanakairali@gmail.com), 20km south of Thrissur near Irinjalakuda, offers training in traditional arts, including rare forms of puppetry and dance. Short **appreciation courses** (per class about ₹400) lasting up to a month are sometimes available to keen foreigners. In December each year, the centre holds five days of *mohiniyattam* **performances**.

River Retreat (☎04884262244; www.riverretreat.in; Palace Rd, Cheruthuruthy; s/d from ₹2600/3300) is only 1km from Kerala Kalamandalam. It's a hotel and ayurvedic resort in the former summer palace of the Maharajas of Cochin.

Regular bus services connect each of these destinations with Thrissur.

NORTHERN KERALA

Kozhikode (Calicut)

☎0495 / POP 432,100

Northern Kerala's largest city, Calicut (as it's most commonly known), was always a prosperous trading town and was once the capital of the formidable Zamorin dynasty. Vasco da Gama first landed near here in 1498, on his way to snatch a share of the subcontinent for king and country (Portugal that is). These days, trade depends mostly on exporting Indian labour to the Middle East, while agriculture and the timber industry are economic mainstays. For travellers it's a jumping off point for Wayanad or for the long trip over the ghats to Mysore or Bengaluru.

Sights

Mananchira Square, a large central park, was the former courtyard of the Zamorins and preserves the original spring-fed tank. South of the centre, the 650-year-old **Kuttichira Mosque** is in an attractive wooden four-storey building that is supported by impressive wooden pillars and painted brilliant aqua, blue and white. The central **Church of South India** was established by Swiss missionaries in 1842 and has unique Euro-Keralan architecture.

About 1km west of Mananchira Square is **Kozhikode Beach** – not much for swimming but good for an evening promenade along the foreshore.

Sleeping

Alakapuri HOTEL **$**
(☎2723451; www.alakapurihotels.com; MM Ali Rd; s/d from ₹300/900, with AC ₹750/1000; ❄) Built motel-style around a green lawn (complete with fountain!), this place is set back from a busy road and quieter than most. Various rooms are a little scuffed and dingy, but reasonable value.

Beach Hotel HOTEL **$$**
(☎2762055; www.beachheritage.com; Beach Rd; r with seaview or AC ₹3000; ❄@) Built in 1890 to house the Malabar British Club, this is a slightly worn but charming 10-room hotel. Some have bathtubs and secluded sea-facing verandahs; others have original polished wooden floors and private balconies. All are tastefully furnished and drip with character.

Hyson Heritage HOTEL **$$**
(☎4081000; www.hysonheritage.com; Bank Rd; s/d from ₹1300/1700, deluxe ₹2500/3250; ❄ wi-fi) You get a fair bit of swank for your rupee at this central business hotel. All rooms are spick and span, while the massive deluxe rooms have views over town. There's a good restaurant and a gym.

★ **Harivihar** HOMESTAY **$$$**
(☎2765865; www.harivihar.com; Bilathikulam; s/d incl full board €100/125) In northern Calicut, the ancestral home of the Kadathanadu royal family is as serene as it gets, a traditional Keralan family compound with pristine lawns. The seven rooms are large and beautifully furnished with dark-wood antiques. There's an ayurvedic and yoga centre, with packages available. The pure veg food is delicious and cooking classes are available.

Eating & Drinking

Paragon Restaurant INDIAN **$**
(Kannur Rd; dishes ₹50-220; ⏲11.45am-midnight) You might struggle to find a seat at this always-packed restaurant, founded in 1939. The overwhelming menu is famous for fish dishes such as fish in tamarind sauce, and its legendary chicken biryani.

Kozhikode (Calicut)

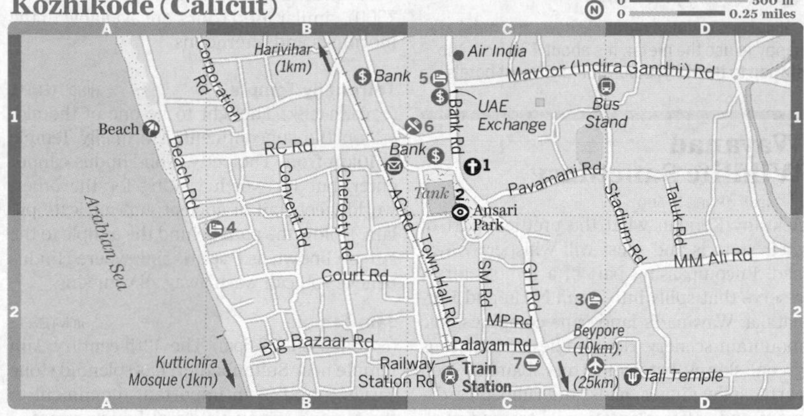

Kozhikode (Calicut)

Sights
1 Church of South India C1
2 Mananchira Square C1

Sleeping
3 Alakapuri C2
4 Beach Hotel B2
5 Hyson Heritage C1

Eating
Beach Hotel .... (see 4)
6 Paragon Restaurant C1

Drinking & Nightlife
7 Indian Coffee House C2

Beach Hotel INDIAN $$
(Beach Rd; ₹85-250; ⏲7am-10.30pm) At the back of the Beach Hotel is a cool open-sided bamboo 'hut' restaurant-bar serving a big range of fish and chicken dishes and Malabari cuisine. It's a breezy place for an informal lunch or cold beer.

Indian Coffee House CAFE
(GH Rd; ₹10-60; ⏲8am-9pm) For tasty snacks and great coffee.

Information

There are HDFC and State Bank of India ATMs in town, and several internet cafes.

UAE Exchange (☎2762772; Bank Rd; ⏲9.30am-6pm Mon-Fri, to 4pm Sat, to 1pm Sun) Close to the Hyson Heritage hotel.

Getting There & Away

AIR

Calicut airport is about 25km south of the city in Karipur. It serves major domestic routes as well as international flights to the Gulf. **Air India** (☎2771974; 5/2521 Bank Rd, Eroth Centre) flies daily to Mumbai and Chennai, and twice-weekly to Kochi. **Jet Airways** (☎2712375; Calicut Airport) has one daily flight to Mumbai, while **Spicejet** (www.spicejet.com; Calicut airport) also flies to Chennai and Mumbai.

BUS

The **bus stand** (Mavoor Rd) has government buses to Bengaluru (via Mysore, ordinary/AC ₹256/355, eight hours, 10 daily), Mangalore (₹250, seven hours, three daily) and to Ooty (₹100, 5½ hours, three daily). There are frequent buses to Thrissur (₹70, 3½ hours) and Trivandrum (via Alleppey and Ernakulam; ordinary/express/deluxe ₹270/300/350, 10 hours, eight daily). For Wayanad district, buses leave every 15 minutes heading to Sultanbatheri (₹55, three hours) via Kalpetta (₹35, two hours). Private buses for various long-distance locations also use this stand.

TRAIN

The train station is 1km south of Mananchira Sq. There are frequent trains to Kannur (2nd-class/sleeper/3AC ₹67/140/250, two hours), Mangalore (sleeper/3AC/2AC ₹147/365/625, five hours), Ernakulam (₹140/343/640, 4½ hours) via Thrissur (₹140/275/625, three hours), and all the way to Trivandrum (₹181/498/745, 11 hours).

Heading southeast, trains go to Coimbatore (sleeper/3AC/2AC ₹120/303/610, 4½ hours), via Palakkad (₹140/278/625, 3½ hours).

Getting Around

Calicut has a glut of autorickshaws and most are happy to use the meter. It's about ₹30 from the station to the KSRTC bus stand or most hotels.

Wayanad Wildlife Sanctuary

04936 / POP 816,500

Ask any Keralan what the prettiest part of their state is and most will whisper: Wayanad. Encompassing part of a remote forest reserve that spills into Tamil Nadu and Karnataka, Wayanad's landscape combines epic mountain scenery, rice paddies of ludicrous green, skinny betel nut trees, bamboo, red earth, spiky ginger fields, and rubber, cardamom and coffee plantations. Foreign travellers are making it here in increasing numbers, partly because it provides easy access between Mysore or Bengaluru and Kerala, but it's still fantastically unspoilt and satisfyingly remote. Importantly, it's also one of the few places you're almost guaranteed to spot wild elephants.

The 345-sq-km sanctuary has two separate pockets – **Muthanga** in the east bordering Tamil Nadu, and **Tholpetty** in the north bordering Karnataka. Three main towns in Wayanad district make good bases and transport hubs for exploring the sanctuary – **Kalpetta** in the south, **Sultanbatheri** (Sultan Battery) in the east and **Mananthavadi** in the northwest – though the best of the accommodation is scattered throughout the region.

Most hotels and homestays can arrange guided jeep tours (7am and 3pm) to various parts of Wayanad.

Sights & Activities

★Wayanad Wildlife Sanctuary NATURE RESERVE

(www.wayanadsanctuary.org; admission to each part Indian/foreigner ₹150/200, camera/video ₹25/150; 7-10am & 3-5pm) Entry to both parts of the sanctuary is only permitted as part of a guided trek or jeep safari, both of which can be arranged at the sanctuary entrances. Both Tholpetty and Muthanga close during the June to August monsoon period.

At **Tholpetty** (04935250853; jeep ₹450, guide ₹300), the two-hour **jeep tours** can be rough going but are a great way to spot wildlife. Rangers organise **guided treks** (up to 5 people ₹1500, extra people ₹400) from here.

At **Muthanga** (271010; jeep ₹450, guide ₹300), similar **jeep tours** are available in the mornings and afternoons.

Thirunelly Temple HINDU TEMPLE

(dawn-dusk) Thought to be one of the oldest on the subcontinent, Thirunelly Temple is 10km from Tholpetty. Non-Hindus cannot enter, but it's worth visiting for the otherworldly cocktail of ancient and intricate pillars. Follow the path behind the temple to the stream known as **Papanasini**, where Hindus believe you can wash away all your sins.

Jain Temple JAIN TEMPLE

(8am-noon & 2-6pm) The 13th-century Jain temple near Sultanbatheri has splendid stone carvings and is an important monument to the region's strong historical Jain presence.

Edakal Caves CAVE

(admission ₹40; 9am-5pm) Close to the Jain temple, near Ambalavayal, these caves have petroglyphs thought to date back over 3000 years and views of Wayanad district.

Wayanad Heritage Museum MUSEUM

(Ambalavayal; admission ₹15; 9am-5pm) In the same area as the caves, this museum exhibits headgear, weapons, pottery, carved stone and other artefacts dating back to the 15th century that shed light on Wayanad's significant Adivasi population.

Uravu HANDICRAFTS CENTRE

(04936231400; www.uravu.net; Thrikkaippetta; 8.30am-5pm Mon-Sat) Around 6km southeast of Kalpetta a collective of workers creates all sorts of artefacts from bamboo. You can visit the artists' workshops, where they work on looms, painting and carving, and support their work by buying vases, lampshades, bangles and baskets.

Trekking & Rafting OUTDOOR ACTIVITY

There are some top opportunities for independent **trekking** around the district, including a climb to the top of **Chembra Peak** (2100m), the area's tallest summit; **Vellarimala**, with great views and lots of wildlife-spotting opportunities; and **Pakshipathalam**, a seven-hour return mountain trek that takes you to a formation of large boulders high in the forest. Permits are necessary and can be arranged at forest offices in South or North Wayanad. The standard cost for permit and guide is ₹1500 for up to five people – try to arrange a group in advance. The **DTPC office** in Kalpetta also

Wayanad District

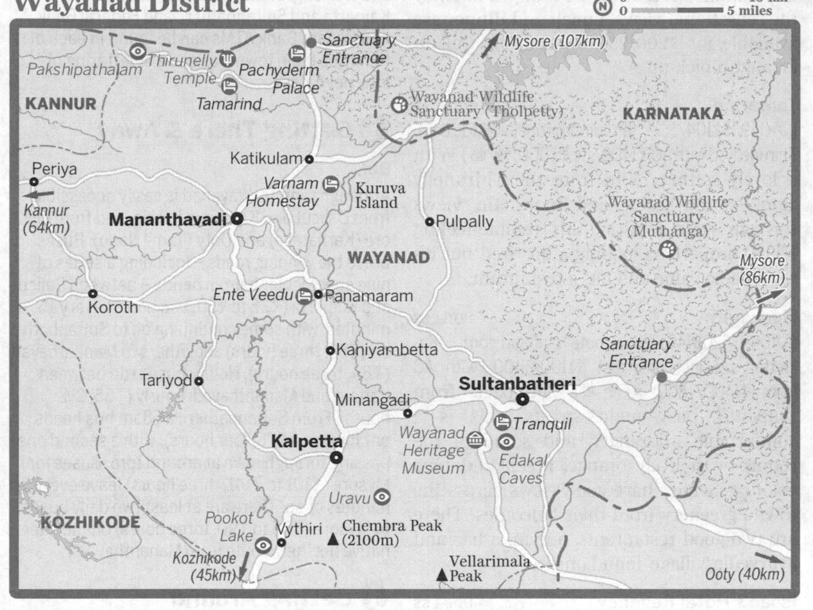

organises trekking guides and transport, as well as tame rafting excursions on inflatable rafts (half-/full-daytrip ₹2500/5000 for six people).

Kannur Ayurvedic Centre AYURVEDA
(☎0436203001; www.ayurvedawayanad.com; Kalpetta; massage from ₹500-800, yoga & meditation ₹750; ⏰yoga classes 6-7am) For rejuvenation and curative ayurvedic treatments, visit this excellent, small, government-certified and family-run clinic in the leafy backstreets of Kalpetta. Accommodation and yoga classes available.

Sleeping & Eating

PPS Tourist Home HOTEL $
(☎04936203431; www.ppstouristhome.com; Kalpetta; s/d ₹250/400, d with AC ₹900; ❄) This friendly budget place in the middle of Kalpetta has a variety of reasonably clean rooms in a motel-like compound as well as a popular multicuisine restaurant and a bar. Helpful management can arrange trips around Wayanad.

★ **Varnam Homestay** HOMESTAY $$
(☎04935215666; www.varnamhomestay.com; Kadungamalayil House, Payyampally; per person incl meals ₹1000,) This oasis of peace and calm is a lovely place to stay only a few kilometres from Katikulam in northern Wayanad. Varghese and Beena will look after you with Wayanad stories, local information and delicious home-cooking. The four rooms in a traditional family home are simple but cosy, and the property is surrounded by jungle and spice plantations. Forest drives and trekking to tribal villages can be arranged.

Pachyderm Palace GUESTHOUSE $$
(☎reservations 04842371761; touristdesk@satyam.net.in; Tholpetty; s/d incl meals ₹1250-2500, tree house ₹2500) This fine old Keralan house lies just outside the gate of Tholpetty Wildlife Sanctuary – handy for early-morning treks, tours and wildlife viewing. The varied rooms include two secluded stilt-bungalow 'tree houses' surrounded by forest and another private cottage. Venu is a stupendous cook, and his son Dilip is a great guide who can organise village and mountain treks.

Ente Veedu HOMESTAY $$
(☎04935220008; www.enteveedu.co.in; Panamaram; r incl breakfast ₹2500-3500; @) Isolated and set in a stunning location overlooking sprawling banana plantations and rice paddies, this homestay halfway between Kalpetta and Mananthavadi is definitely worth seeking out. Several large rooms and two bamboo-lined rooms with private balconies,

and hammocks and wicker lounges to enjoy the sensational views. Lunch and dinner are available for ₹200/250 veg/nonveg. Call to arrange a pick-up.

Tamarind HOTEL **$$**
(☎04935210475; tamarindthirunelly@ktdc.com; Thirunelly; d with AC ₹1400, ste ₹2000; ❄@) With a lovely setting 750m from the Thirunelly Temple, and forest and mountain views through your window, this remote-feeling KTDC property is looking a bit tired but it's reasonable value and has a restaurant.

Haritagiri HOTEL **$$**
(☎04936203145; www.hotelharitagiri.com; Kalpetta; s/d incl breakfast ₹1100/1400, with AC from ₹1400/1800; ❄📶🏊) Set back from Kalpetta's busy main streets, this is a comfortable midranger, and some of the rooms, with lively orange, green and blue colour schemes, have good views across the town's greenery from their balconies. There are two good restaurants, a gym, a bar and ayurvedic 'village' found on-site.

Isaac's Hotel Regency HOTEL **$$**
(☎04936220512; www.issacsregency.com; Sultanbatheri; s/d/tr from ₹1000/1400/1600, with AC from ₹1400/1800/2000; ❄@🏊) The pick of Sultanbatheri's motley bunch of hotels, this quiet and no-nonsense place has routine, large and relatively tidy rooms in a U-shaped building. The deluxe rooms differ from the standard ones in price only.

★ **Tranquil** HOMESTAY **$$$**
(☎04936220244; www.tranquilresort.com; Kuppamudi Estate, Kolagapara; full board s/d from ₹10,101/13,750, tree house ₹13,000/17,900, tree villa ₹14,850/19,500; 🏊) This wonderfully serene and exclusive homestay is in the middle of an incredible lush 160 hectares of pepper, coffee, vanilla and cardamom plantations. The elegant house has sweeping verandahs filled with plants and handsome furniture, and there are two tree houses that have to be the finest in the state – the most romantic has sublime views through panoramic windows and a branch growing through the bathroom. A network of marked walking trails meander around the plantation.

ℹ Information

The **DTPC office** (☎04936202134; www.dtpcwayanad.com; Kalpetta; ⏰10am-5pm Mon-Sat) at Kalpetta can help organise tours, permits and trekking. There are UAE Exchange offices in Kalpetta and Sultanbatheri, and Federal Bank and Canara Bank ATMs can be found in each of the three main towns, as can a smattering of internet cafes.

ℹ Getting There & Away

BUS

Although remote, Wayanad is easily accessible from Calicut and Kannur in Kerala, and from Mysore (Karnataka) and Ooty (Tamil Nadu). Buses brave the winding roads – including a series of nine spectacular hairpin bends – between Calicut and Kalpetta (₹35 to ₹50, two hours) every 15 minutes, with some continuing on to Sultanbatheri (₹55, three hours) and others to Mananthavadi (₹64, three hours). Hourly buses run between Kannur and Mananthavadi hourly (₹55, 2½ hours). From Sultanbatheri, an 8am bus heads out for Ooty (₹76, four hours), with a second one passing through town at around 1pm. Buses for Mysore (₹101 to ₹141, three hours) leave every 30 minutes or so. There are at least two daily buses to Mysore (₹85 to ₹90, three hours) on the alternative northern route from Mananthavadi.

ℹ Getting Around

The Wayanad district is quite spread out but plenty of private buses connect Mananthavadi, Kalpetta and Sultanbatheri every 10 to 20 minutes during daylight hours (₹15 to ₹25, 45 minutes to one hour). From Mananthavadi, regular buses also head to Tholpetty (₹15, one hour). You can hire jeeps or taxis to get between towns for ₹500 to ₹700 each way, or hire a vehicle to tour the region for around ₹2000 per day.

There are plenty of autorickshaws and taxis for short hops within the towns.

Kannur & Around

☎0497 / POP 1.6 MILLION

The main draw in this part of coastal Kerala are the undeveloped beaches and the enthralling *theyyam* possession rituals. Under the Kolathiri rajas, Kannur (Cannanore) was a major port bristling with international trade – explorer Marco Polo christened it a 'great emporium of spice trade'. Since then, the usual colonial suspects, including the Portuguese, Dutch and British, have had a go at exerting their influence on the region. Today it is an unexciting, though agreeable, town known mostly for its weaving industry and cashew trade.

Beaches to the south and north of Kannur – some of the nicest in Kerala – and the growing number of family homestays are

THEYYAM

Kerala's most popular ritualistic art form, *theyyam* is believed to pre-date Hinduism, originating from folk dances performed during harvest celebrations. An intensely local ritual, it's often performed in *kavus* (sacred groves) throughout northern Kerala.

Theyyam refers both to the shape of the deity/hero portrayed, and to the actual ritual. There are around 450 different *theyyams*, each with a distinct costume; face paint, bracelets, breastplates, skirts, garlands and especially headdresses are exuberant, intricately crafted and sometimes huge (up to 6m or 7m tall). During performances, each protagonist loses their physical identity and speaks, moves and blesses the devotees as if they were that deity. Frenzied dancing and wild drumming create an atmosphere in which a deity indeed might, if it so desired, manifest itself in human form.

During October to May there are annual rituals at each of the hundreds of *kavus*. *Theyyams* are often held to bring good fortune to important events such as marriages and housewarmings.

The best place for visitors to see *theyyam* is in village temples in the Kannur region of northern Kerala (most frequently between late November and mid-April).

Although tourists are welcome to attend, this is not a dance performance but a religious ritual, and the usual rules of temple behaviour apply: dress appropriately, avoid disturbing participants and villagers; refrain from displays of public affection. Photography is allowed but avoid using a flash.

the big attractions. Bear in mind you can't swim during the monsoon season because of rough seas. This is a predominantly Muslim area, so local sensibilities should be kept in mind: wear a sarong over your bikini on the beach.

Sights & Activities

Kannur's main town beach is the 4km-long **Payyambalam Beach**, which starts about 1.5km east of the train station, just past the military cantonment.

St Angelo Fort FORT

(9am-6pm) FREE The Portuguese built the St Angelo Fort in 1505 from brilliantly red laterite stone on a promontory a few kilometres south of town.

Loknath Weavers' Co-operative HANDICRAFTS WORKSHOP

(2726330; 8.30am-5.30pm Mon-Sat) Established in 1955, this is one of the oldest co-operatives in Kannur and occupies a large building busily clicking with the sound of looms. You can stop by for a quick (free) tour and visit the small shop here that displays the fruits of their labours. It's 4km south of Kannur town.

Kerala Dinesh Beedi Co-Operative HANDICRAFTS WORKSHOP

(2835280; www.keraladinesh.com; 8am-6pm Tue-Sat) This region is also known for the manufacture of *beedis*, those tiny Indian cigarettes deftly rolled inside green leaves. This is one of the largest and purportedly best manufacturers, with a factory at Thottada, 7km south of Kannur and about 4km from Thottada beach. A skilled individual can roll up to 1000 a day! An autorickshaw should cost around ₹100 return from Kannur town.

Theyyam Rituals RELIGIOUS

The Kannur region is the best place to see the spirit-possession ritual called *theyyam*; on most nights of the year there should be a *theyyam* ritual on at a village temple somewhere in the vicinity. The easiest way to find out is to contact Kurien at Costa Malabari guesthouse or by asking at your accommodation.

Kerala Folklore Academy ARTS SCHOOL

(04972778090; http://keralafolkloreakademy.com; Chirakkal) At this training academy near Chirakkal Pond Valapattanam, about 6km north of Kannur, you can see vibrantly coloured folklore costumes up close and sometimes catch a performance.

Sleeping & Eating

Although there a plenty of hotels in Kannur, the best places to stay are homestays near the beach at Thottada (8km south) and towards Thalassery.

Kannur Town

Hotel Meridian Palace HOTEL $
(☎2761676; www.hotelmeridianpalace.com; Bellard Rd; s from ₹300/400, with AC from ₹900-1000) In the market area opposite the main train station, this is hardly palatial but friendly enough and offers a cornucopia of clean budget rooms and a Punjabi restaurant.

Mascot Beach Resort HOTEL $$
(☎2708445; www.mascotresort.com; d ₹1350, with AC from ₹1800, ste ₹4500;) All rooms are sea-facing at this compact, midrange hotel looking over the small, rocky Baby Beach. Facilities are good, including a pool and restaurant.

Thottada Beach & Around

★**Blue Mermaid Homestay** HOMESTAY $$
(☎9497300234; www.bluemermaid.in; Thottadda Beach; full board s/d ₹1850/2700, d with AC ₹3200;) With a prime location in the palms facing Thottada Beach, Blue Mermaid is a charming and immaculate guesthouse with rooms in a traditional home, bright air-con rooms in a lovely new building and a whimsical stilted 'honeymoon cottage'. Friendly young owners cook up Keralan meals.

Costa Malabari GUESTHOUSE $$
(☎09447775691, reservations 04842371761; touristdesk@satyam.net.in; Thottada Beach; s/d incl meals ₹1500/2750, d with AC ₹3000 ;) Surrounded by lush greenery above the beach, Costa Malabari pioneered tourism in this area. Spacious rooms in an old hand-loom factory, a huge communal space and comfy lounging areas outside. Extra rooms are offered in two other buildings. The home-cooked Keralan food is plentiful, varied and delicious. Manager Kurien is an expert on the *theyyam* ritual and can help arrange a visit.

Waves Beach Resort HOMESTAY $$
(☎9447173889; s/d incl meals ₹1250/2500;) If the crashing waves don't lull you to sleep they might just keep you awake at this very cute pair of hexagonal laterite brick huts overlooking a semi-private little crescent beach. There are four rooms here (two up, two down). The welcoming owners also have rooms in two other nearby properties, including cheaper rooms in an old Keralan house.

Kannur Beach House HOMESTAY $$
(☎04972708360, 9847184535; www.kannurbeachhouse.com; Thottada Beach; s/d ₹2200/3000) The original beachfront homestay, rooms in this traditional Keralan building have handsome wooden shutters, but are looking a little

OFF THE BEATEN TRACK

VALIYAPARAMBA BACKWATERS

For those seeking to escape the burgeoning commercialism around Alleppey, what are often referred to as the northern backwaters offer an intriguing alternative. This large body of water is fed by five rivers and fringed by ludicrously green lands punctuated by rows of nodding palms. One of the nearest towns is **Payyanur**, 50km north of Kannur. It's possible to catch the ferry from Kotti, from where KSWTD operates local ferries to the surrounding islands. It's five minutes' walk from Payyanur railway station. The 2½-hour trip (₹10) from Kotti takes you to the Ayitti Jetty, 8km from Payyanur; then catch the return ferry.

You can stay at the tiny **Valiyaparamba Retreat** (☎2371761; www.touristdesk.in/valiyaparambaretreat.htm; d full board ₹3000), a secluded place 15km north of Payyanur and 3km from Ayitti Jetty. It has two simple rooms and two stilted bungalows, fronted by an empty golden-sand beach. Kochi's Tourist Desk (p315) also runs **day trips** (per person incl lunch ₹600) for groups of four to 15 people, on a traditional houseboat around the Valiyaparamba Backwaters.

Around 22km south of Bekal, **Bekal Boat Stay** (☎04672282633, 9447469747; www.bekalboatstay.com; Kottappuram, Nileshwar) is one of the few operators in the region to offer overnight **houseboat trips** (2/4 people per 24hr ₹8500/10,500) around the Valiyaparamba backwaters. Sunset/day cruises (₹3000/6000 for up to six people) are also available. It's about 2km from Nileshwar – get off any bus between Kannur and Bekal and take an autorickshaw from there (₹20).

worn. Still, you can enjoy sensational ocean sunset views from your porch or balcony. Breakfast and dinner included.

Ezhara Beach House HOMESTAY $$
(☎04972835022; www.ezharabeachhouse.com; 7/347 Ezhara Kadappuram; s/d incl meals ₹1250/2500;) Beside the unspoilt Kizhunna Ezhara beach, midway between Kannur and Thalassery railway stations (11km from each) the blue Ezhara Beach House is run by no-nonsense Hyacinth. The five rooms are simple and small, but the house has character and there's a terrace where you can sit and gaze out to sea and enjoy home cooking.

Information

The **DTPC Office** (☎2706336; www.dtpckannur.com; ⏲10am-5pm Mon-Sat), opposite the KSRTC bus stand, supplies basic maps of Kannur. There are Federal Bank and State Bank of India ATMs adjacent to the bus stand. A **UAE Exchange** (☎2709022; Fort Rd, City Centre; ⏲9.30am-6pm Mon-Sat, 11am-1pm Sun) office changes travellers cheques and cash; it's located in City Centre mall, five minutes from the train station.

Getting There & Away

BUS

Kannur has several bus stands but the enormous **central bus stand** – the largest in Kerala – is the place to catch long-distance buses, both private and government. It's about 500m southeast of the train station. Some government buses also use the **KSRTC bus stand** near the Caltex junction, 1km northeast of the train station.

There are daily buses to Mysore (₹190, eight hours, five daily), Mangalore (₹92, four hours, two daily), Madikeri (₹63, 2½ hours, 11am) and Mananthavadi (₹55, 2½ hours, hourly) for Wayanad. There's one daily bus to Ooty (via Wayanad, ₹171, nine hours) at 10pm.

For Thottada Beach, take bus No 29 (₹7) from Plaza Junction opposite the train station and get off at Adikatalayi village.

TRAIN

There are several daily trains to Calicut (2nd-class/AC chair ₹67/205, 1½ hours), Mangalore (sleeper/3AC/2AC ₹140/283/625, three hours) and Ernakulam (₹166/420/625, 6½ hours).

Bekal & Around

☎0467

Bekal and nearby Palakunnu and Udma, in Kerala's far north, have some long white-sand beaches begging for DIY exploration. The area is gradually being colonised by glitzy five-star resorts catering to fresh-from-the-Gulf millionaires, but it's still worth the trip for off-the-beaten-track adventurers intent on discovering the beaches before they get swallowed up by developers.

The laterite-brick **Bekal Fort** (Indian/foreigner ₹5/100; ⏲8am-5pm), built between 1645 and 1660, sits on Bekal's rocky headland and houses a small Hindu temple and plenty of goats. Next door, **Bekal Beach** (admission ₹5) encompasses a grassy park and a long, beautiful stretch of sand that turns into a circus on weekends and holidays when local families descend here for rambunctious leisure time. Isolated **Kappil Beach**, 6km north of Bekal, is a beautiful, lonely stretch of fine sand and calm water, but beware of shifting sandbars.

There are lots of cheap, poor quality hotels scattered between Kanhangad (12km south) and Kasaragod (10km north), with a few notable exceptions.

Gitanjali Heritage HOMESTAY $$
(☎9447469747, 04672234159; www.gitanjaliheritage.com; s/d full-board ₹3500/5000; @) This lovely place lies surrounded by rice paddies, deep among Kasaragod's inland villages. It is just 5km from Bekal and is an intimate heritage home with three comfortable rooms filled with ancestral furniture and polished wood.

★ **Neeleshwar Hermitage** RESORT $$$
(☎04672287510; www.neeleshwarhermitage.com; Ozhinhavalappu, Neeleshwar; s/d cottages from ₹10,600/12,600, seaview ₹16,000/17,300;) This spectacular beachfront ecoresort consists of 16 beautifully designed thatch-roof cottages modelled on Keralan fisherman's huts but with modern comforts like iPod docks and a five-star price tag. Built according to the principles of Kerala Vastu, the resort has an infinity pool that gazes out to sea, nearly 5 hectares of lush gardens fragrant with frangipani, superb organic food and Ayurvedic massage, meditation and yoga programs.

Getting There & Around

A couple of local trains stop at Fort Bekal station, right on Bekal beach. Kanhangad, 12km south, is a major train stop, while Kasaragod, 10km to the north, is the largest town in the area. Frequent buses run from Bekal to both Kanhangad and Kasaragod (around ₹10, 20 minutes), from where you can pick up major trains to Mangalore or south to Kochi. An auto-

DIVING

Lakshadweep is a diver's dream, with excellent visibility and an embarrassment of marine life living on undisturbed coral reefs. The best time to dive is between November and mid-May when the seas are calm and visibility is 20m to 40m.

Dive Lakshadweep (☎94460 55972; http://divelakshadweep.com; Agatti Island; single dive ₹3000, PADI open water course ₹24,000) is based on Agatti Island and offers a variety of PADI courses and dive packages, including Discover Scuba (₹1700) dives for beginners. Unfortunately, at the time of writing foreigners were not permitted on Agatti Island and not able to use this outfit under a dispute with Lakshadweep administration, but this situation is likely to change.

rickshaw from Bekal Junction to Kappil beach is around ₹50.

LAKSHADWEEP

POP 64,500

Comprising a string of 36 palm-covered, white-sand-skirted coral islands 300km off the coast of Kerala, Lakshadweep is as stunning as it is isolated. Only 10 of these islands are inhabited, mostly with Sunni Muslim fishermen, and foreigners are only allowed to stay on a few of these. With fishing and coir production the main sources of income, local life on the islands remains highly traditional, and a caste system divides the islanders between Koya (land owners), Malmi (sailors) and Melachery (farmers).

The real attraction of the islands lies under the water: the 4200 sq km of pristine archipelago lagoons, unspoiled coral reefs and warm waters are a magnet for flipper-toting travellers and divers alike.

Lakshadweep can only be visited on a prearranged package trip. At the time of research, only the resorts on Kadmat and Minicoy islands were open to tourists – most visits to the islands are boat-based packages which include a cruise from Kochi, island visits, watersports, diving and nights spent on board the boat. Packages include permits and meals, and can be arranged through SPORTS.

ℹ Information

SPORTS (Society for the Promotion of Recreational Tourism & Sports; ☎9495984001, 04842668387; www.lakshadweeptourism.com; IG Rd, Willingdon Island; ⏲10am-5pm Mon-Sat) is the main organisation for tourist information and package tours.

PERMITS

At the time of writing, foreigners were only allowed to stay at the government resorts on Kadmat and Minicoy islands, though Agatti (which has a private resort and the only airport), Kavaratti and Bangaram should reopen in the future; enquire at SPORTS. Any visits require a special permit (one month's notice) which can be organised by tour operators or SPORTS in Kochi.

ℹ Getting There & Away

Air India flies between Kochi and Agatti Island (from ₹7000 return) daily except Sunday. Boat transport between Agatti and Kadmat is included in the package tours available, and the same goes for transport from Kochi to Kadmat and the Minicoy Islands. See the package section of www.lakshwdeeptourism.com for more details.

Kadmat Island

Kadmat Beach Resort (☎04844011134; www.kadmat.com; 4 nights from €512 per person; ❄) has 28 modern cottages, administered by Mint Valley (www.mintvalley.com) and can be reached by overnight boat from Kochi, or by boat transfer from Agatti airport on Tuesday and Saturday.

Minicoy Island

You can stay on the remote island of Minicoy, the second-largest island and the closest to the Maldives, in modern cottages or a 20-room guesthouse at **Minicoy Island Resort** (☎04842668387; www.lakshadweeptourism.com; s/d ₹3000/4000, with AC ₹5000/6000; ❄) via SPORTS Swaying Palms and Coral Reef Packages.

Tamil Nadu & Chennai

Includes ➡

Best Temples

- Meenakshi Amman Temple (p384)
- Brihadishwara Temple (p374)
- Sri Ranganathaswamy Temple (p379)
- Arunachaleshwar Temple (p360)
- Nataraja Temple (p371)

Best Places to Stay

- Visalam (p383)
- Les Hibiscus (p366)
- Bungalow on the Beach (p372)
- 180° McIver (p401)

Why Go?

Tamil Nadu is the homeland of one of humanity's living classical civilisations, stretching back uninterrupted for two millennia and very much living on today in the Tamils' language, dance, poetry and Hindu religion.

But this state with its age-old trading vocation is as dynamic as it is immersed in tradition. Fire-worshipping devotees who smear tikka on their brows in the famously spectacular Tamil temples may then head off to IT offices to develop new software applications – and afterwards unwind in a stylish nocturnal haunt in rapidly modernising Chennai (Madras).

When the heat and noise of Tamil Nadu's temple towns overwhelm, escape to the very end of India where three seas mingle, or up to the cool, forest-clad, wildlife-prowled Western Ghats. It's all packed into a state that remains proudly distinct from the rest of India, while at the same time being among the most welcoming.

When to Go

Chennai

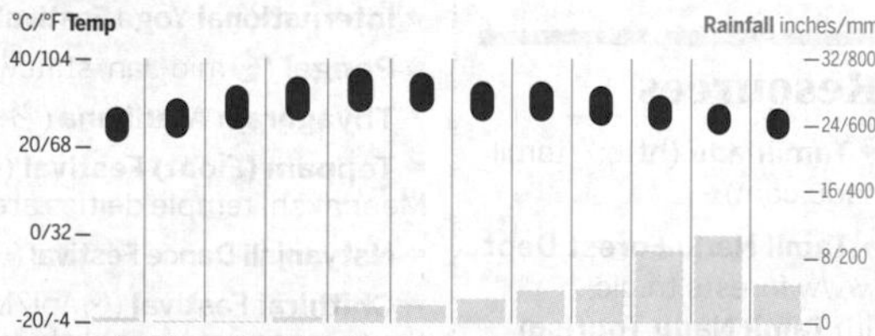

Jan The weather is at its (relative) coolest and Pongal (harvest) celebrations spill into the streets.

Jul–Sep Head to the hill stations after the crowded, expensive 'season', weather is still good.

Nov–Dec The full-moon festival of lights.

MAIN POINTS OF ENTRY

Chennai Airport will be your probable entry point if you're flying into Tamil Nadu from overseas, although Trichy, Madurai and Coimbatore also have (limited) international services. The same four cities are also the state's major train junctions.

Fast Facts

- **Population:** 72.1 million
- **Area:** 130,058 sq km
- **Capital:** Chennai (Madras)
- **Main language:** Tamil
- **Sleeping prices:** **$** below ₹1000, **$$** ₹1000 to ₹5000**, $$$** above ₹5000

Top Tip

If you need train tickets in a hurry, the Foreign Tourist Cell at Chennai Central is the most helpful and efficient we've ever come across; tickets for booked-up trains anywhere in India seem to become magically available here.

Resources

- **Tamilnadu** (http://tamilnadu.com)
- **Tamil Nadu Forest Dept** (www.forests.tn.nic.in) **Tamil Nadu Tourism** (http://tamilnadutourism.org)
- **Lonely Planet** (www.lonelyplanet.com.au/india)

Food

Tamil Nadu's favourite foods are overwhelmingly vegetarian, with lots of coconut and chilli. You'll find dosas, *idlis* (spongy, round fermented rice cakes) and *vadas* (deep-fried lentil-flour doughnuts), all served with coconut chutney and *sambar* (lentil broth). Almost as ubiquitous is the *uttapam*, a thick, savoury rice pancake that typically comes with chopped onions, green chillies and coriander. South Indian 'meals' – thalis based around rice, lentil dishes, *rasam* (hot and sour tamarind soup) and chutneys, often served on a banana leaf – are also good. The main local exception to the all-veg diet is Chettinad food, originating from the Chettinadu region south of Trichy but available at restaurants in bigger towns. The dishes are spicy but not fiery. For a state growing a lot of tea, Tamil Nadu really loves its coffee; filtered coffee (mixed with milk and sugar, of course, and a dash of chicory) is often more readily available than tea. Restaurant prices include the taxes added to menu rates at some places.

DON'T MISS

Few parts of India are as fervent in their worship of the Hindu gods as Tamil Nadu. Great temples stun with their spectacular architecture, the colour of their crowds of worshippers, and their noisy, chaotic festivals. For artistry don't miss the World Heritage–listed trio at **Thanjavur**, **Darasuram** village (near Kumbakonam) and **Gangaikondacholapuram**. For spectacle and contemporary fervour, head to **Madurai**, **Chidambaram**, **Srirangam** (Trichy) and **Tiruvannamalai**. Escape from the heat of the plains to the hill stations in the cool, misty **Western Ghats**. The Nilgiri Mountain Railway, alias the 'toy train', snaking its way up nearly 2000m of forest-clothed mountain, makes a trip to **Ooty** (Udhagamandalam) unforgettable; **Kodaikanal** is a smaller, prettier, quirkier alternative to Ooty.

Top State Festivals

- **International Yoga Festival** (4–7 Jan, Puducherry, p362)
- **Pongal** (mid-Jan, statewide) Harvest festival.
- **Thyagaraja Aradhana** (Jan, Thiruvaiyaru, p375)
- **Teppam (Float) Festival** (Jan/Feb, Madurai, p386) Meenakshi temple deities are taken on a tour of the town.
- **Natyanjali Dance Festival** (Feb/Mar, Chidambaram, p371)
- **Chithirai Festival** (Apr/May, Madurai, p386) Celebrates the marriage of Meenakshi to Sundareswarar (Shiva).
- **Karthikai Deepam Festival** (Nov/Dec, statewide) Festival of lights.
- **Chennai Festival of Music & Dance** (mid-Dec–mid-Jan, Chennai, p340) Celebrates southern music and dance.
- **Mamallapuram Dance Festival** (Dec–Jan, Mamallapuram, p354) Four-weeks of dance, drama and music.

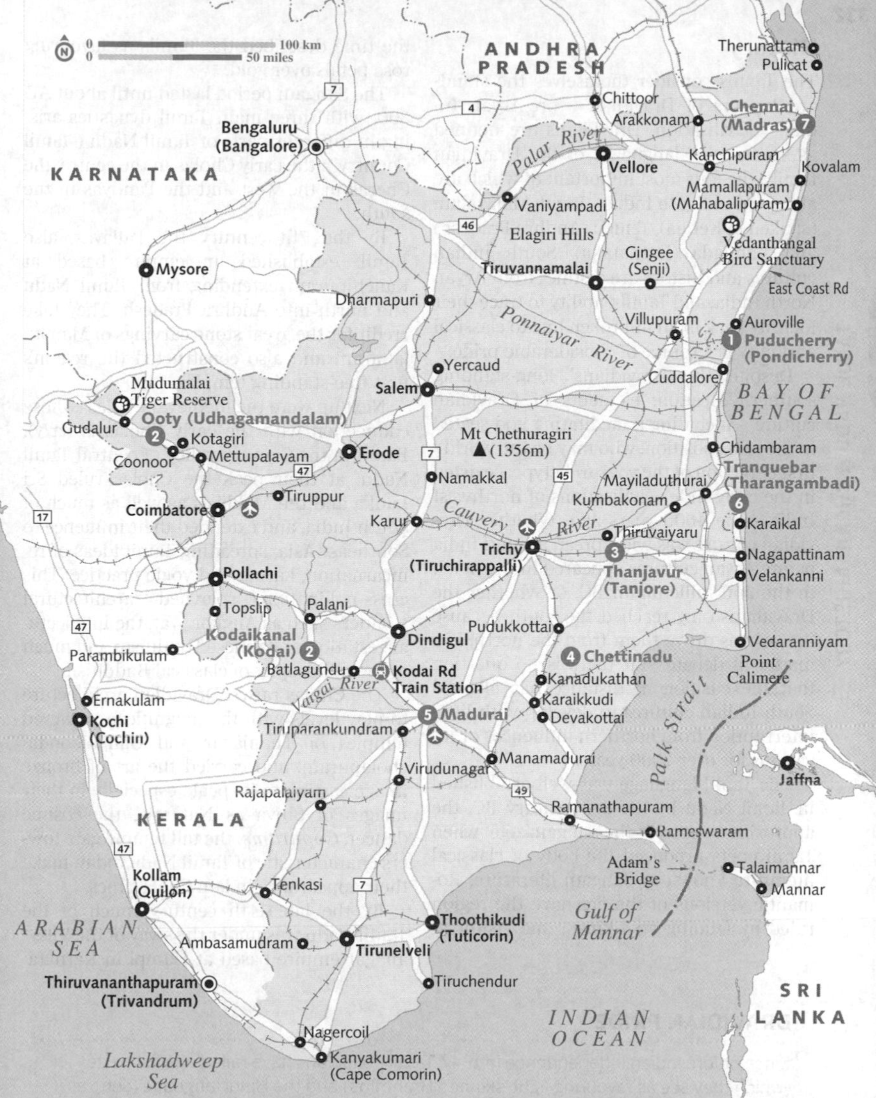

Tamil Nadu Highlights

1. Soak up the unique Franco-Indian style of **Puducherry** (Pondicherry, p362)
2. Climb into the cool forests of the Western Ghats at **Kodaikanal** (p393) or **Ooty** (Udhagamadalam, p403)
3. Admire the magnificence of Chola architecture at Thanjavur's **Brihadishwara Temple** (p374)
4. Spend the night in an opulent mansion in **Chettinadu** (p382)
5. Immerse yourself in the colour of Tamil temple life at Madurai's **Meenakshi Amman Temple** (p384)
6. Relax at tranquil **Tranquebar** (p372), a quirky old Danish colony
7. Get acquainted with the many faces of traditional but increasingly cosmoplitan and contemporary **Chennai** (p333)

History

The Tamils consider themselves the standard bearers of Dravidian – pre-Aryan Indian – civilisation. Dravidians are defined as speakers of languages of the Dravidian family, the four most important of which are all rooted in South India – Tamil, Malayalam (spoken in Kerala), Telugu (Andhra Pradesh) and Kannada (Karnataka). South Indian cultures and history are distinct from Aryan North India, and Tamils' ability to trace their identity back in an unbroken line to classical antiquity is a source of considerable pride.

Despite the Dravidians' long-standing southern location, elements of Dravidian culture – including a meditating god seated in the lotus position, who may be the world's first depiction of the yogi archetype – existed in the early Indus civilisations of northwest India some 4000 years ago. Whether Dravidian culture was widespread around India before Aryan cultures appeared in the north in the 2nd millennium BC, or whether the Dravidians only reached the south because the Aryans drove them from the north, is a matter of debate. But there is no question that the cushion of distance has allowed South Indian cultures to develop with little interruption from northern influences or invasions for over 2000 years.

The Tamil language was well established in Tamil Nadu by the 3rd century BC, the approximate start of the Sangam Age, when Tamil poets produced the body of classical literature known as Sangam literature. Romantic versions of the era have the region ruled by feuding poet-kings; one visitor at the time described the Tamils as favouring rose petals over gold.

The Sangam period lasted until about AD 300, with three main Tamil dynasties arising in different parts of Tamil Nadu ('Tamil Country'): the early Cholas in the centre, the Cheras in the west and the Pandyas in the south.

By the 7th century the Pallavas, also Tamil, established an empire based at Kanchipuram extending from Tamil Nadu and north into Andhra Pradesh. They take credit for the great stone carvings of Mamallapuram and also constructed the region's first free-standing temples.

Next up were the medieval Cholas (whose connection with the early Cholas is hazy). Based in the Cauvery valley of central Tamil Nadu, at their peak the Cholas ruled Sri Lanka and the Maldives as well as much of South India, and extended their influence to Southeast Asia, spreading Tamil ideas of reincarnation, karma and yogic practice. This cross-pollination spawned architectural wonders such as Angkor Wat, the intellectual gestation of Balinese Hinduism and much of the philosophy of classical Buddhism.

The Cholas raised Dravidian architecture to new levels with the magnificent towered temples of Thanjavur and Gangaikondacholapuram, and carried the art of bronze image casting to its peak, especially in their images of Shiva as Nataraja, the cosmic dancer. *Gopurams,* the tall temple gate towers characteristic of Tamil Nadu today, make their appearance in late Chola times.

By the late 14th century much of the Tamil Nadu was under the sway of the Vijayanagar empire based at Hampi in Karnata-

DRAVIDIAN PRIDE

Since before Indian independence in 1947, Tamil politicians have railed against caste (which they see as favouring light-skinned Brahmins) and the Hindi language (seen as North Indian cultural imperialism). The pre-Independence 'Self Respect' movement and Justice Party, influenced by Marxism, mixed South Indian communal values with class-war rhetoric, and spawned Tamil political parties that remain the major powers in Tamil Nadu today. In the early post-Independence decades there was even a movement for an independent Dravida Nadu nation comprising the four main South Indian peoples, but today Dravidian politics is largely restricted to Tamil Nadu, where parties are often led by former film stars.

During the conflict in nearby Sri Lanka, many Indian Tamil politicians loudly defended the Tamil Tigers, the organisation that assassinated Rajiv Gandhi in a village near Chennai in 1991. There is still considerable prejudice among the generally tolerant Tamils towards anything Sinhalese.

Throughout the state, male politicians don a white shirt and white *mundu* (sarong), the official uniform of Tamil pride.

ka. As the Vijayanagar state weakened in the 16th century, some of their local governors, the Nayaks, set up strong independent kingdoms, notably at Madurai and Thanjavur. Vijayanagar and Nayak sculptors carved wonderfully detailed statues and reliefs at many Tamil temples.

Europeans first came sniffing around Tamil shores in the 16th century, when the Portuguese settled at San Thome. The Dutch, British, French and Danes followed in the 17th century, striking deals with local rulers to set up coastal trading colonies. Eventually it came down to a contest between the British, based at Madras (now Chennai), and the French, based at Pondicherry (Puducherry), for supremacy among the colonial rivals. The British won out in the three Carnatic Wars, fought between the two European powers in alliances with various Indian princes, between 1744 and 1763. By the end of the 18th century British dominance over the majority of Tamil lands was assured.

The area governed by the British from Madras, the Madras Presidency, included parts of Andhra Pradesh, Kerala and Karnataka, an arrangement that continued after Indian independence in 1947, until the four existing southern states were created on linguistic lines in the 1950s.

CHENNAI (MADRAS)

☎ 044 / POP 7.7 MILLION

The 'capital of the south' has always been the rather dowdy sibling among India's four biggest cities, with its withering southern heat, roaring traffic, and scarcity of outstanding sights. For many travellers, it is as much a gateway as a destination in itself. If you're just caught here between connections, it's certainly worth poking around one of the museums or taking a sunset stroll along Marina Beach. If you have more time to explore Chennai's varied neighbourhoods and appreciate its role as keeper of South Indian artistic and religious traditions, the odds are this 70-sq-km conglomerate of urban villages will grow on you. Recent years have added a new layer of cosmopolitan glamour in the shape of luxury hotels, shiny boutiques, classy contemporary restaurants and even a smattering of clubs and bars open into the wee hours.

One of Chennai's biggest assets is its people, infectiously enthusiastic about their hometown. They won't hit you with a lot of hustle and hassle, and they will mostly treat you as a guest rather than a commodity.

The old British Fort St George and the jumble of narrow streets and bazaars that is George Town constitute the historic hub of the city. The two main train stations, Egmore and Central, sit inland from the fort. Much of the best eating, shopping and accommodation lies in the leafier southern and southwestern suburbs such as Nungambakkam, T Nagar (Thyagaraya Nagar) and Alwarpet. The major thoroughfare linking northern with southern Chennai is Anna Salai (Mount Rd).

History

The southern neighbourhood of Mylapore existed long before most of the rest of Chennai and there is evidence that it traded with Roman and even Chinese and Greek merchants. The Portuguese established their San Thome settlement on the coast nearby in 1523. Another century passed before the British East India Company, searching for a good southeast Indian trading base, struck a deal with the local Vijayanagar ruler to build a fort-cum–trading post at the fishing village of Madraspatnam. This was Fort St George, erected between 1640 and 1653.

The three Carnatic Wars between 1744 and 1763 saw Britain and its colonialist rival France allying with competing South Indian princes in their efforts to get the upper hand over the locals and each other. The French occupied Fort St George from 1746 to 1749 but the British eventually won out, with the French withdrawing to Pondicherry (now Puducherry).

As capital of the Madras Presidency, one of the four major divisions of British India, Madras grew into an important naval and commercial centre. After Independence, it became capital of Madras state and its successor Tamil Nadu. The city itself was renamed Chennai in 1996. IT and motor-vehicle manufacture are its industrial mainstays today.

ℹ Dangers & Annoyances

Unless the city's authorities and its autorickshaw drivers manage to strike a deal over fares, convincing a driver to use the meter will remain a Vatican-certified miracle, with fares bordering on the astronomical. Avoid paying upfront, and never get into an autorickshaw before agreeing the fare.

Chennai (Madras)

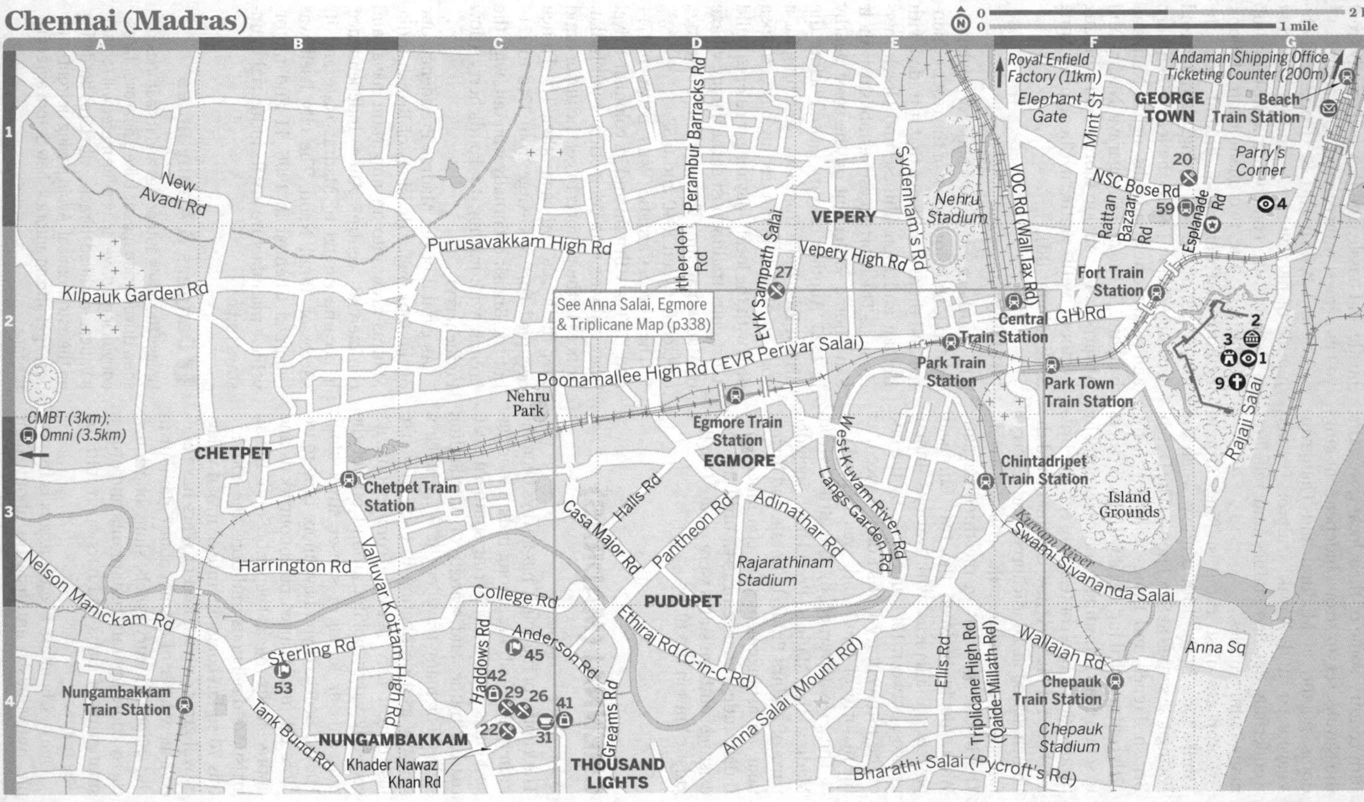

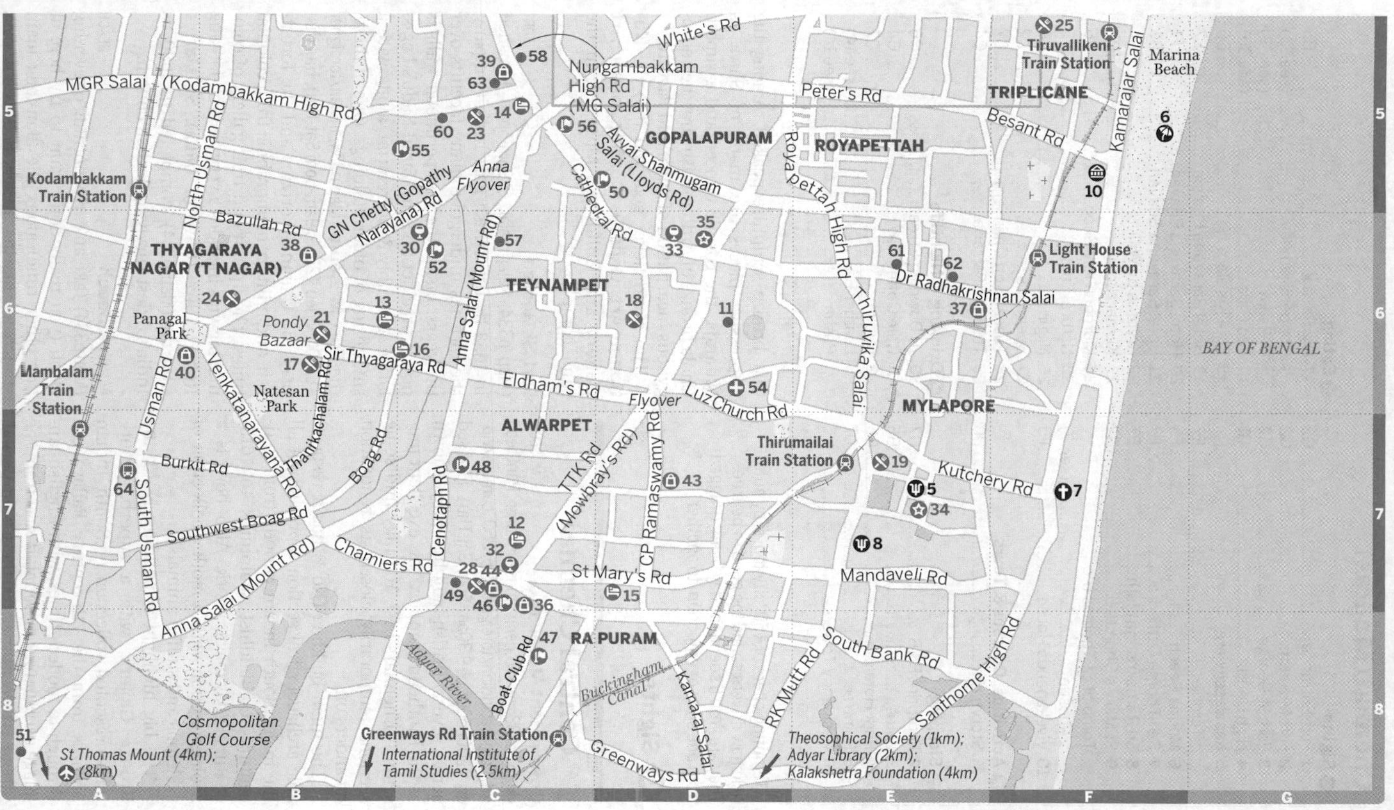
White's Rd
Nungambakkam High Rd (MG Salai)
MGR Salai (Kodambakkam High Rd)
Peter's Rd
TRIPLICANE
Tiruvallikeni Train Station
Kamarajar Salai
Marina Beach
Besant Rd
GOPALAPURAM
ROYAPETTAH
Avvai Shanmugam Salai (Lloyds Rd)
Royapettah High Rd
Kodambakkam Train Station
North Usman Rd
Anna Flyover
GN Chetty (Gopathy Narayana) Rd
Cathedral Rd
Bazullah Rd
THYAGARAYA NAGAR (T NAGAR)
Anna Salai (Mount Rd)
Light House Train Station
Dr Radhakrishnan Salai
TEYNAMPET
Panagal Park
Pondy Bazaar
Sir Thyagaraya Rd
BAY OF BENGAL
Mambalam Train Station
Usman Rd
Venkatanarayana Rd
Natesan Park
Thanikachalam Rd
Eldham's Rd
Flyover
Luz Church Rd
Thiruvika Salai
MYLAPORE
ALWARPET
Boag Rd
Burkit Rd
TTK Rd (Mowbray's Rd)
CP Ramaswamy Rd
Thirumailai Train Station
Kutchery Rd
Cenotaph Rd
South Usman Rd
Southwest Boag Rd
Chamiers Rd
St Mary's Rd
Mandaveli Rd
Anna Salai (Mount Rd)
RA PURAM
South Bank Rd
Santhome High Rd
Boat Club Rd
Adyar River
Buckingham Canal
Kamaraj Salai
RK Mutt Rd
Cosmopolitan Golf Course
Greenways Rd Train Station
Greenways Rd
St Thomas Mount (4km); (8km)
International Institute of Tamil Studies (2.5km)
Theosophical Society (1km); Adyar Library (2km); Kalakshetra Foundation (4km)
A
B
C
D
E
F
G
5
6
7
8

Chennai (Madras)

Sights

1 Fort Entrance G2
2 Fort Museum G2
3 Fort St George G2
4 High Court G1
5 Kapaleeshwarar Temple E7
6 Marina Beach F5
7 San Thome Cathedral F7
8 Sri Ramakrishna Math E7
9 St Mary's Church G2
Tomb of St Thomas the Apostle .... (see 7)
10 Vivekananda House F5

Activities, Courses & Tours

11 Storytrails D6

Sleeping

12 Footprint B&B C7
13 Lotus B6
14 Park Hotel C5
15 Raintree D7
16 Residency Towers C6

Eating

17 Big Bazaar B6
Copper Chimney .... (see 33)
Dakshin .... (see 32)
Eco Cafe .... (see 36)
18 Enté Keralam D6
19 Hotel Saravana Bhavan E7
20 Hotel Saravana Bhavan F1
21 Hotel Saravana Bhavan B6
22 Kryptos by Willi C4
23 Kumarakom C5
24 Murugan Idly Shop B6
25 Natural Fresh F5
26 Nilgiri's C4
27 Spencer's D2
28 Tuscana on Chamiers C7
29 Tuscana Pizzeria C4

Drinking & Nightlife

30 10 Downing Street C6
31 Café Coffee Day C4
32 Dublin C7
Leather Bar .... (see 14)
Pasha .... (see 14)

Tempting offers of ₹50 'city tours' by auto-rickshaw drivers sound too good to be true. They are. You'll spend the day being dragged from one shop or emporium to another.

Sights

Central Chennai

Government Museum MUSEUM
(Map p338; www.chennaimuseum.org; Pantheon Rd, Egmore; Indian/foreigner ₹15/250, camera/video ₹200/500; 9.30am-5pm Sat-Thu) Housed across several British-built buildings known as the Pantheon Complex, this excellent museum is Chennai's best. You may find some sections temporarily closed as renovation meanders on.

The main building (No 1) has a respectable archaeological section representing all the major South Indian periods from 2nd-century-BC Buddhist sculptures to 16th-century Vijayanagar work. Also here is a zoology section with a motley collection of skeletons and stuffed animals.

The big highlight is building No 3, the **Bronze Gallery**, with a superb, beautifully presented collection of South Indian bronzes from the 7th-century Pallava era through to modern times, with English-language explanatory material. It was from the 9th to 11th centuries, in the Chola period, that bronze sculpture peaked. Among the impressive pieces are many of Shiva as Nataraja, the cosmic dancer, and a superb Chola bronze of Ardhanarishvara, the androgynous incarnation of Shiva and Parvati.

The same ticket gets you into the **National Art Gallery**, **Contemporary Art Gallery** and **Children's Museum**, in the same complex.

Fort St George FORT
(Map p334; Rajaji Salai; 9am-5pm) Finished in 1653 by the British East India Company, the fort has undergone many facelifts over the years. Inside the vast perimeter walls is now a precinct housing Tamil Nadu's Legislative Assembly & Secretariat, along with a smattering of older buildings. One of these, the **Fort Museum** (Map p334; Indian/foreigner ₹5/100, video ₹25; 9am-5pm Sat-Thu), has displays on Chennai's origins and the fort itself, and military memorabilia from colonial times. The upstairs portrait gallery of colonial bigwigs includes a very assured-looking Robert Clive (Clive of India). **St Mary's Church** (Map p334), completed in 1680, is India's oldest surviving British church.

Marina Beach BEACH
(Map p334) Take an early-morning or evening stroll (you really don't want to fry here at any other time) along the 3km-long main stretch of Marina Beach and you'll pass

cricket matches, flying kites, fortune-tellers, fish markets and families enjoying the sea breeze. Try a cob of roast corn with lime and chilli powder from one of the vendors – delicious. Don't swim: strong rips make it dangerous.

Vivekananda House MUSEUM

(Vivekanandar Illam, Ice House; Map p334; www.vivekanandahouse.org; Kamarajar Salai; adult/child ₹10/5; ⏲10am-12.15pm & 3-7.15pm Thu-Tue) The Vivekananda House is interesting not only for its displays on the famous 'wandering monk', Swami Vivekananda, but also for its semicircular form, built in 1842 to store ice imported from the USA. Vivekananda stayed here briefly in 1897 and preached his ascetic Hindu philosophy to adoring crowds. The exhibits include a pictorial overview of Hindu philosophy and sacred literature, a photo exhibition on the swami's life, and the room where Vivekananda stayed, now used for meditation. Free one-hour meditation classes are held on Wednesdays at 7pm.

High Court NOTABLE BUILDING

(Map p334; Parry's Corner) Completed in 1892, this imposing red Indo-Saracenic structure is said to be the largest judicial building in the world after the Courts of London. Depending on current regulations, you may or may not be allowed to enter the buildings or even the grounds. If you fancy trying, take your passport.

Southern Chennai

Kalakshetra Foundation ARTS SCHOOL

(☎24524057; www.kalakshetra.net; Muthulakshmi St, Thiruvanmiyur; admission ₹50; ⏲campus 8.45am-11.15am Mon-Sat late Jun–mid-Mar, craft centre 9am-1pm & 2-5pm Mon-Sat, all closed 2nd & 4th Sat of month) Founded in 1936, Kalakshetra is a leading serious school of Tamil classical dance and music (courses last four to six years), set in beautiful, shady grounds in the far south of the city. During morning class times visitors can walk around the grounds (without interrupting classes), and visit the **Rukmini Devi Museum**. Across the road is the Kalakshetra Craft Centre where you can witness Kanchipuram-style hand-loom weaving, textile block-printing and the fascinating, rare art of Kalamkari (hand-painting on textiles with vegetable dyes). The Thiruvanmiyur bus stand, terminus of many city bus routes, is 500m west of the Kalakshetra entrance.

While here it's also worth visiting the **Book Building** (☎42601033; www.tarabooks.com; Plot 9, CGE Colony, Kuppam Beach Rd, Thiruvanmiyur; ⏲10am-7.30pm Mon-Sat), 700m south

Anna Salai, Egmore & Triplicane

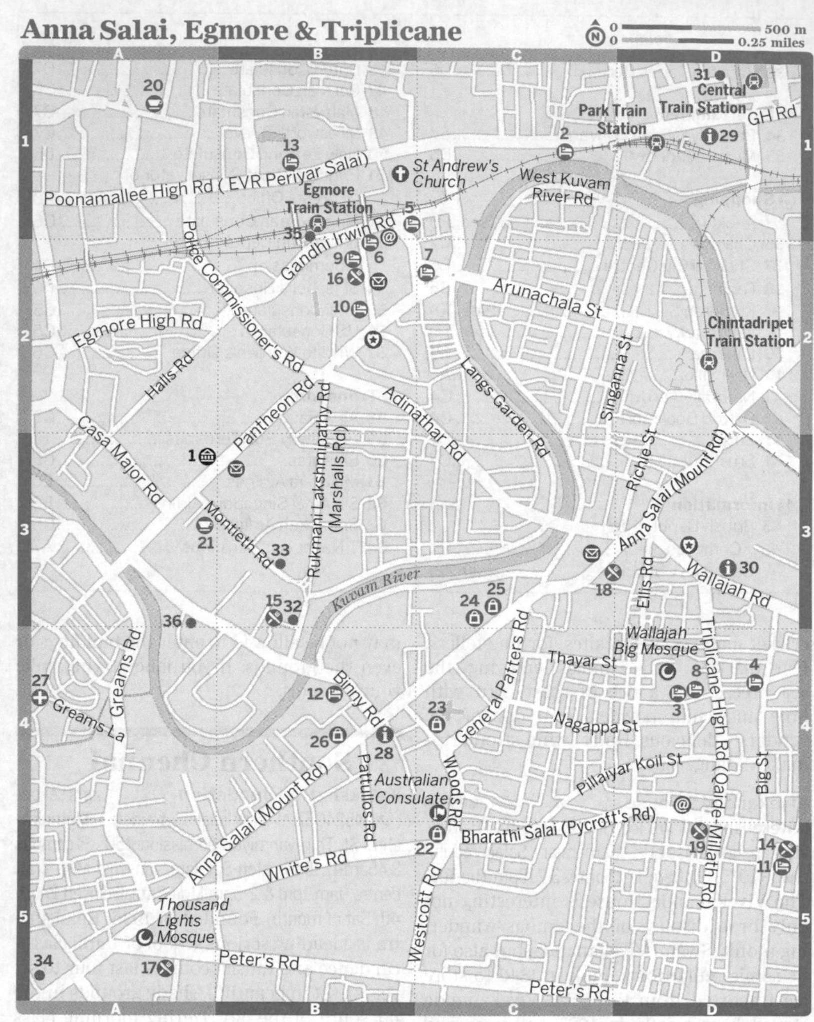

of Kalakshetra, where Tara Books stages exhibitions and events as well as displaying its own highly original, attractive handmade books. With prior notice, you can visit the workshop where the books are created (10 minutes' drive away).

Kapaleeshwarar Temple HINDU TEMPLE
(Map p334; Ponnambala Vathiar St, Mylapore; ⏲5am-noon & 4-9.30pm) The Mylapore neighbourhood is one of Chennai's most characterful and traditional; it predated colonial Madras by several centuries. Kapaleeshwarar Temple is Chennai's most active and impressive temple. It displays the main architectural elements of many a Tamil Nadu temple – a rainbow-coloured *gopuram* (gateway tower), pillared *mandapas* (pavilions) inside and out, and a huge tank – and it's dedicated to the state's most popular deity, Shiva. Legend tells that in a fit of pique Shiva once turned his consort Parvati into a peacock, and instructed her to worship him here in order to regain her normal form. Parvati supposedly did as instructed at a spot just outside the northeast corner of the temple's central block, where a shrine commemorates the event.

Anna Salai, Egmore & Triplicane

San Thome Cathedral CHURCH

(Map p334; www.santhomechurch.com; Santhome High Rd) This soaring Roman Catholic cathedral, a stone's throw from the beach, was founded by the Portuguese in the 16th century, then rebuilt in neo-Gothic style in the 1890s. Behind the cathedral is the entrance to the **tomb of St Thomas the Apostle** (Map p334; admission free; tomb & museum 6am-8.30pm). It's believed 'Doubting Thomas' brought Christianity to the subcontinent and was killed at St Thomas Mount, Chennai, in AD 72. Although most of his mortal remains are apparently now in Italy, a small cross on the chapel wall containing a tiny bone fragment is marked 'Relic of St Thomas'. A museum above contains various Thomas-related artefacts including the lancehead believed to have killed him.

Sri Ramakrishna Math HINDU TEMPLE

(Map p334; www.chennaimath.org; 31 RK Mutt Rd; Universal Temple 5-11.45am & 3.30-9pm, evening prayers 6.30-7.30pm) The tranquil, leafy grounds of the Ramakrishna Math are a world away from the chaos and crazy rickshaw drivers outside. Monks glide around and there's a reverential feel here. The Math is a monastic order following the teachings of the 19th-century sage Sri Ramakrishna who preached the essential unity of all religions. The Universal Temple here is a handsome modern building incorporating architectural elements from several different religions. It's open to all, to participate in worship or pray or meditate in silence.

Theosophical Society GARDEN

(www.ts-adyar.org; south of Thiru Vi Ka Bridge, Adyar; admission free; grounds 8.30-10am & 2-4pm Mon-Sat) Between the Adyar River and the coast, the 100-hectare grounds of the Theosophical Society provide a green and peaceful retreat from the city. A lovely spot just to wander, they contain a church, mosque, Buddhist shrine and Hindu temple as well as a huge variety of native and introduced trees. The **Adyar Library** (1yr reader's card ₹50 (deposit ₹250); ⌚9am-5pm Tue-Sun) here has an immense collection of books on religion and philosophy, some of which are on display, from 1000-year-old Buddhist scrolls to intricate, handmade 19th-century Bibles.

St Thomas Mount SACRED SITE
(Parangi Malai; off Lawrence Rd) The reputed site of St Thomas' martyrdom rises in the southwest of the city, 2.5km north of St Thomas Mount train station. The St Thomas Shrine, built by the Portuguese in 1523, contains what are supposed to be a fragment of Thomas' bone and a cross he carved; the views across the city are wonderful.

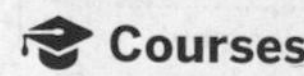

Courses

International Institute of Tamil Studies LANGUAGE
(☎22542781; www.ulakaththamizh.org; CIT Campus, 2nd Main Rd, Tharamani) Runs intensive three-month and six-month courses in Tamil.

Kalakshetra Foundation TEXTILE PAINTING
(☎24524057;www.kalakshetra.net;MuthulakshmiSt, Thiruvanmiyur) The crafts centre here offers one- or two-month courses in the old art of Kalamkari – hand-painting of textiles using vegetable inks – which survives in only a handful of places. Courses usually occupy three hours per day for around ₹10,000 a month.

Tours

The Tamil Nadu Tourism Development Corporation (p346) conducts half-day city tours (non-AC/AC ₹215/235) and day trips to Mamallapuram (₹275/350). Book ahead for weekends and holidays; be ready for cancellations on quiet weekdays. Every full moon there's an overnight pilgrimage trip to Tiruvannamalai (₹650/780).

TRADITIONAL TRADERS

Even as Chennai expands relentlessly to the south, west and north, George Town, the local settlement that grew up near the British Fort St George, remains the city's wholesale centre. Many streets are entirely given over to selling one particular type of merchandise as they have for hundreds of years – paper goods in Anderson St, fireworks in Badrian St, jewellery on NSC Bose Rd and so on. Even if you're not in the market for anything, wander the maze-like streets to see Indian life flowing seamlessly from the past into the present.

Storytrails WALKING TOURS
(Map p334; ☎42124214, 9940040215; http://storytrails.in; 1, 2nd Cross St, CIT Colony, Mylapore; 3hr tour ₹695-795.) Runs entertaining and informative neighbourhood walking tours based around themes such as dance, temples, jewellery and bazaars, as well as tours specially aimed at children.

Royal Enfield Factory FACTORY TOUR
(☎42230400; www.royalenfield.com; Tiruvottiyur High Rd, Tiruvottiyur) The classic Enfield Bullet motorcycle has been manufactured since 1955 at the Royal Enfield Factory, in far northern Chennai. Tours (per person ₹600) run on the second and fourth Saturdays of each month for about two hours from 10.30am. It's essential to book.

Festivals & Events

Chennai Festival of Music & Dance MUSIC, DANCE
(Madras Music & Dance Season; ⌚mid-Dec–mid-Jan) One of the largest of its type in the world, this festival is a celebration of South Indian music and dance.

Sleeping

Hotels in Chennai are pricier than in the rest of Tamil Nadu and don't, as a rule, offer much bang for your buck. The Triplicane High Rd area is best for budget accommodation. There are some cheapies in Egmore, where you'll also find a good number of midrange options. Most top-end hotels are in the more middle-class areas to the south.

It's always a good idea to call ahead; many hotels in Chennai fill up by noon. For the most expensive hotels, check their websites for good discounts.

Egmore & Around

Raj Residency HOTEL **$**
(Map p338; ☎28192219; www.rajresidencyhotel.com; 2/22 Kennet Lane; s ₹675-1315, d ₹785-1555; ❄) The non-AC rooms here are reasonable value, a bit dingy and worn but kept clean enough, in shades of brown.

Regal Lodge HOTEL **$**
(Map p338; ☎28191122; 15 Kennet Lane; s/d ₹380/490) If you're in need of a cheap room near Egmore station, the Regal can give you a small, dingy one with grubby walls. At least they change the sheets and clean the rooms between occupants.

YWCA International Guest House GUESTHOUSE $$
(Map p338; ☎25324234; ywcaigh@indiainfo.com; 1086 Poonamallee High Rd; s/d incl breakfast ₹785/1045, with AC ₹1300/1500; ❄@📶) The YWCA guesthouse, set in green and shady grounds, offers a calm atmosphere and exceptionally good value. Very efficiently run by an amiable staff, it provides good-sized, impeccably clean rooms, spacious common areas and good-value meals (₹150/225 for veg/nonveg lunch or dinner). Wi-fi (in the lobby) costs ₹100 per day.

Hotel Park Plaza HOTEL $$
(Map p338; ☎30777777; www.hotelparkplaza.in; 29 Whannels Rd; s/d incl half-board ₹3238/3837; ❄📶) With dinner and wi-fi included in rates as well as breakfast, and good, spacious rooms, the Park Plaza is a decent deal.

Hotel Chandra Park HOTEL $$
(Map p338; ☎28191177; www.hotelchandrapark.com; 9 Gandhi Irwin Rd; s ₹1319-2279, d ₹1499-2578, all incl breakfast; ❄) Chandra Park's prices remain mysteriously lower than most comparable establishments. Standard rooms are small but have air-con, clean towels and tight, white sheets. Throw in a decent bar and a hearty buffet breakfast and this is good value by Chennai standards.

Bell Central HOTEL $$
(Map p338; ☎40412200; www.bellhotels.in; 47 Poonamallee High Rd; s ₹2399-2999, d ₹2999-3598, all incl breakfast; ❄📶) The Bell is a welcome relief from the typical dreary midrange decor. Rooms are smallish, but they're cheerfully contemporary, bright and colourful and have tea/coffee makers. The hotel is convenient for Chennai Central station and has a multicuisine restaurant. Wi-fi costs ₹50 per hour.

Vivanta by Taj – Connemara HERITAGE HOTEL $$$
(Map p338; ☎66000000; www.vivantabytaj.com; Binny Rd; s/d from ₹11,992/13,191; ❄@📶🏊) The top-end Taj group has four hotels in and around Chennai but this is the only one with historical ambience, built in the 1850s as the British governor's residence. There's a beautiful pool in tropical gardens, and even the smallest rooms are large and very comfy, with all mod cons.

Fortel HOTEL $$$
(Map p338; ☎30242424; www.fortelhotels.com; 3 Gandhi Irwin Rd; s ₹4197-6596, d ₹4797-7195, all incl breakfast; ❄📶) Conveniently close to Egmore train station, the Fortel is cool and stylish in a wood, mirrors and white walls way, with comfy cushion-laden beds and two good restaurants. Wi-fi costs ₹200/500 per one/24 hours.

Triplicane

Paradise Guest House HOTEL $
(Map p338; ☎28594252; paradisegh@hotmail.com; 17 Vallabha Agraharam St; s ₹400-500, d ₹500-600; ❄) Paradise offers some of Triplicane's best-value digs – simple rooms with clean tiles, a breezy rooftop, friendly staff and hot water by the steaming bucket.

Broad Lands Lodge HOTEL $
(Map p338; ☎28545573; broadlandshotel@yahoo.com; 18 Vallabha Agraharam St; s ₹350-400, d ₹400-525; 📶) In business since 1951, Broad Lands was a hippie-era stalwart and may not have had a fresh coat of pale-blue paint or a good spring clean since. But this colonial-era mansion with three leafy courtyards, and rooms located up several rambling staircases, still has its devotees, who love its laid-back atmosphere and don't seem to mind the bare-bone, idiosyncratic rooms, dank bathrooms, colony of cats or the high-volume muezzins of Wallajah Big Mosque. Wi-fi (a concession to the 21st century) is ₹20 per hour.

Royal City HOTEL $
(Map p338; ☎28443819; 10 Venkatachalam St; s ₹368-968, d ₹605-1089; ❄) A friendly place on a fairly quiet street with smallish but very clean, marble-floored rooms.

Cristal Guest House HOTEL $
(Map p338; ☎28513011; 34 CNK Rd; r ₹300, with AC ₹650; ❄) The clean, pink abodes in this modern building are not quite the cheapest rooms in Chennai, but they're only about ₹10 more expensive than many others close by - and that difference means the hotel is more likely to have vacancies.

Southern Chennai

★ **Footprint B&B** B&B $$
(Map p334; ☎9840037483; http://chennaibedandbreakfast.com; Gayatri Apartments, 16 South St, Alwarpet (behind Sheraton Park Hotel); r incl breakfast ₹4045; ❄@📶) This is a wonderfully comfortable and relaxed base for your Chennai explorations, in a quiet street in a leafy

neighbourhood. Bowls of pretty flowers and old-Madras drawings set the scene. The nine cosy, spotless rooms have king-size or wide twin beds. Breakfasts (Western or Indian) are generous, wi-fi is free and the hospitable owners can tell you all you need to make the most of your time. Phone or email in advance; walk-ins are discouraged.

★Lotus HOTEL **$$**
(Map p334; 28157272; www.thelotus.in; 15 Venkatraman St, T Nagar; s ₹2980-4170, d ₹3930-4470, all incl breakfast;) An absolute gem, the Lotus offers a quiet setting away from the main roads, a good veg restaurant, and fresh, stylish rooms with wood floors and cheerful decor. Wi-fi is free (but doesn't reach all rooms).

★Residency Towers HOTEL **$$$**
(Map p334; 28156363; www.theresidency.com; Sir Thyagaraya Rd, T Nagar; s ₹7135-8994, d ₹7675-8994, all incl breakfast;) Residency Towers combines five-star elegance with personality at very good prices for this level of accommodation. Rooms have sliding doors in front of windows to block out noise, walnut-veneer furniture, weighing scales and other thoughtful touches. Also here are three restaurants, a nice outdoor pool and a 'pub' that becomes a heaving weekend night spot. Wi-fi is free.

★Park Hotel BOUTIQUE HOTEL **$$$**
(Map p334; 42676000; www.theparkhotels.com; 601 Anna Salai; s ₹12,592-17,988, d ₹13,791-17,988, ste from ₹19,187;) We love this super-stylish large boutique hotel, which flaunts design everywhere you look, from the bamboo, steel and gold cushions of the towering lobby to the posters from classic South Indian movies shot in Gemini Studios, the previous incarnation of the hotel site. Rooms have lovely lush bedding, all mod cons and stylish touches including glass-walled bathrooms. It's all pretty swish, and that goes for the three restaurants, large open-air pool, luxurious spa and two night spots too!

Raintree HOTEL **$$$**
(Map p334; 24304050; www.raintreehotels.com; 120 St Mary's Rd, Alwarpet; s ₹10,000-12,500, d ₹11,250-13,750, all incl breakfast;) At this 'ecosensitive' hotel, floors are made of bamboo or rubber, water and electricity conservation hold pride of place, and the heat generated by the AC warms the bathroom water. The sleek, minimalist rooms are stylish and comfortable, and the rooftop sports a sea-view infinity pool (which doubles as insulation) as well as a restaurant.

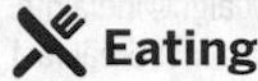

Eating

Chennai is packed with inexpensive 'meals' joints, serving thalis for lunch and dinner, and tiffin (snacks) such as *idlis* and dosas for the rest of the day. It's feasible to eat every meal at Chennai's 20 Hotel Saravana Bhavan restaurants, where you can count on quality vegetarian food. In the Muslim area around Triplicane High Rd you'll find great biryani joints every few steps.

Classier and more stylish Indian restaurants are growing in number, and international cuisines have finally taken off in Chennai, so there's a reasonable choice of more upmarket eating. Big top-end hotels always have a variety of reliably good eating options.

Useful supermarkets for picking up your own supplies include **Spencer's** (Map p334; 15 EVK Sampath Salai, Vepery; 9am-10pm), not too far from Egmore and Central stations, **Big Bazaar** (Map p334; 34 Sir Thyagaraya Rd; 10.30am-9.30pm) in T Nagar and **Nilgiri's** (Map p334; 14 Wallace Garden 3rd St, Nungambakkam; 10am-8pm) off Nungambakkam High Rd.

Egmore

★Hotel Saravana Bhavan INDIAN **$**
(Map p338; www.saravanabhavan.com; 21 Kennet Lane; mains ₹60-150; 6am-10pm) Dependably delish, lunchtime and evening South Indian thali 'meals' at the Saravana Bhavans usually run ₹80 to ₹100. This famous Chennai vegetarian chain is also excellent for South Indian breakfasts (*idlis* and *vadas* for ₹49), ice cream, filter coffee and other Indian vegetarian fare including biryanis and pilaus. Branches include **George Town** (Map p334; 209 NSC Bose Rd; 6am-10.30pm), **Triplicane** (Map p338; Shanthi Theatre Complex, 44 Anna Salai; 7am-11pm), **Thousand Lights** (Map p338; 293 Peter's Rd; 11.30am-11pm), **Mylapore** (Map p334; 70 North Mada St; 6am-11pm) and **T Nagar** (Map p334; 102 Sir Thyagaraya Rd; 6am-11pm), not to mention London, Paris and New York! The Thousand Lights branch is more upscale than most, with silver cutlery.

Annalakshmi INDIAN **$$**
(Map p338; 28525109; www.annalakshmichennai.co.in; 1st fl, Sigapi Achi Bldg, 18/3 Rukmani Lakshmipathy Rd; mains ₹180-240, set/buffet lunch ₹575/400; noon-3pm & 7-9pm) Very fine

South and North Indian vegetarian fare in a beautiful dining room adorned with carvings and paintings, inside a high-rise behind the Air India building. The buffet option is served in another part of the same premises. Annalakshmi is run by devotees of Swami Shanthanand Saraswathi; proceeds support medical programs for the poor.

Basil MULTICUISINE **$$**
(Map p338; Fortel, 3 Gandhi Irwin Rd; mains ₹150-250; ⏲7am-11pm) This restaurant at the Fortel hotel has an impressive Western breakfast range, if you're really after hash browns, as well as tasty North Indian and Continental dishes in a pleasant setting.

Triplicane & Around

Ratna Café SOUTH INDIAN **$**
(Map p338; 255 Triplicane High Rd; dishes ₹25-70; ⏲6am-10.30pm) Though often crowded and cramped, Ratna is renowned for its scrumptious *idlis* and the hearty doses of *sambar* that go with it – people sit down to this ₹26.50 dish at all times of day.

A2B SOUTH INDIAN **$**
(Map p338; 47/23 Bharathi Salai; mains ₹75-110; ⏲6am-11.30pm) Sit down to South Indian classics or veg biryani in the clean AC hall upstairs, or get a big choice of sweets downstairs. If you've got any room left, head to nearby **Natural Fresh** (Map p334; 35 Bharathi Salai; scoop ₹50-60; ⏲11am-11pm) for excellent ice cream.

Express Avenue Garden MULTICUISINE **$$**
(Map p338; Express Avenue Shopping Centre, White's Rd, Royapettah; dishes ₹100-300; ⏲10am-11pm) This food court on the top floor of Chennai's newest shopping mall has about 30 Indian and international outlets. With picture windows and trees in pots it's quite a pleasant place for a bite.

Nungambakkam & Around

Kumarakom KERALAN **$$**
(Map p334; www.kumarakomrestaurant.com; 9 Kodambakkam High Rd; mains ₹75-300; ⏲noon-4pm & 6.30-11pm) You may have to queue for a table at this popular Keralan restaurant with dark-wood furniture, cool AC and busy waiters. The seafood is the standout – try the prawns masala or *karimeen pollichathu* (pearl-spot fish marinated and steamed in a banana leaf) – but everything's fresh and tasty.

★**Tuscana Pizzeria** ITALIAN **$$$**
(Map p334; ☎45038008; www.tuscana.in; 19, 3rd St, Wallace Garden; pizzas & pasta ₹315-690; ⏲noon-11.30pm) This, my pizza-loving friends, is the real deal, and Chennai has embraced it enthusiastically. Tuscana serves authentic thin-crust pizzas with toppings such as prosciutto, as well as interesting takes such as hoison chicken pizza. Pasta and desserts are also top-notch. There's another branch, **Tuscana on Chamiers** (Map p334; ☎45000008; www.tuscanaonchamiers.in; 89 Chamiers Rd, Alwarpet; ⏲12.30-3.15pm & 6.30-11.15pm), in Alwarpet. Reservations are a good idea at both.

Kryptos by Willi GREEK **$$$**
(Map p334; ☎45038001; www.kryptosbywilli.com; Basement, Yafa Tower, Khader Nawaz Khan Rd; mains ₹380-690; ⏲12.30-3.30pm & 6.30-11.30pm) From the same stable as the nearby Tuscana Pizzeria comes another successfully authentic Mediterranean restaurant. There's good seafood as well as Greek favourites such as *spanakopita* (spinach and cheese pastries), souvlaki and baklava.

Raintree CHETTINAD **$$$**
(Map p338; www.vivantabytaj.com; Vivanta by Taj – Connemara, Binny Rd; mains ₹475-700; ⏲12.30-2.45pm & 7.30-11.40pm) This hotel restaurant is probably the best place in Chennai to savour the delicious flavours of Tamil Nadu's Chettinadu region. Chettiar cuisine is superbly spicy without being chilli-laden, and includes a good number of meat dishes. In good weather you can sit out in the leafy courtyard.

South Chennai

Murugan Idly Shop SOUTH INDIAN **$**
(Map p334; 77 GN Chetty Rd, T Nagar; dishes ₹25-75; ⏲7am-11.30pm) Those in the know generally agree this particular branch of the small chain serves some of the best *idlis* and South Indian meals in town. We heartily concur.

★**Eco Cafe** MULTICUISINE **$$**
(Map p334; Chamiers, 106 Chamiers Rd, RA Puram; mains ₹250-375, breakfasts ₹175-305; ⏲8.30am-9.30pm) This 1st-floor cafe feels a continent

away from Chennai, except that Chennaites love it too. Leafy wallpaper, leaves through the windows, discreetly spaced tables, wonderful banana nut bread and cappuccino, English breakfasts, American pancakes, pasta, quesadillas, waffles, salads…

Enté Keralam KERALAN $$
(Map p334; ☎ 32216591; www.orientalcuisines.in; 1 Kasturi Estate 1st St, Poes Garden; mains ₹175-475; ⊙ noon-3pm & 7.30-11.30pm) A calm ambience prevails in the four orange-toned rooms of this Keralan restaurant, holding just three or four tables each. Try the lightly spiced *pachakkari* vegetable stew or *kozhi porichatu* (deep-fried marinated chicken) and wind up with *paal ada payasam*, a kind of sweet rice pudding.

★**Copper Chimney** NORTH INDIAN $$$
(Map p334; ☎ 28115770; 74 Cathedral Rd, Gopalapuram; mains ₹200-575; ⊙ noon-3pm & 7-11.30pm) The vegetarian dishes aren't the priority here, but meat eaters will drool over the yummy North Indian tandoori dishes served in stylishly minimalist surroundings. The *machchi* tikka – skewers of tandoori-baked fish – is superb.

Dakshin SOUTH INDIAN $$$
(Map p334; Sheraton Park Hotel, 132 TTK Rd, Alwarpet; mains ₹550-900; ⊙ 12.30-2.45pm & 7-11.15pm) Dakshin specialises in the cuisine of the four states of South India. Traditional sculptures set the scene, and flute and tabla musicians play nightly except Monday. Food suggestion: the Andhra Pradesh fish curry.

Drinking & Nightlife

Cafes

Café Coffee Day (www.cafecoffeeday.com; ⊙ 9am-11pm) provides a range of reliably good hot and cold coffees and teas for ₹60 to ₹120, and usually some tempting cakes, in pleasant ambience at several locations, including **Egmore** (Map p338; Alsa Mall, Montieth Rd), **Vepery** (Map p338; 92 Dr Alagappa Rd), **Nungambakkam** (Map p334; Khader Nawaz Khan Rd) and **Express Avenue Mall** (Map p338; 1st, 2nd & 3rd fl, Express Avenue Mall, White's Rd).

Bars & Nightclubs

Chennai has possibly the most liberal licensing laws in India – for five-star hotels. Bars and clubs at these hotels can serve alcohol 24 hours a day, seven days a week, and so that's where most of the jumping joints are found. Other hotel bars mostly close at midnight. There are very few salubrious places to get a drink without loud music after about 6pm. For listings see www.timescity.com/chennai.

Zara the Tapas Bar BAR
(Map p334; ☎ 28111462; zaratapasbar.in; 71 Cathedral Rd; cocktails ₹400-500, tapas ₹225-375; ⊙ 12.30-3pm & 6.30pm-midnight) Where else in the world would you find DJs playing club music beneath bullfight posters next to TVs showing cricket? Zara is packed with a happy 20s and 30s crowd most nights. There's a small space to dance but most of the acreage is occupied by tables, and it's a good idea to reserve one. And the tapas? The *jamón serrano* is sacrilegiously minced into a paste, but the *tortilla española* is authentically good.

Leather Bar BAR
(Map p334; Park Hotel, 601 Anna Salai; ⊙ 11am-4am) 'Leather' refers to floor and wall coverings rather than anything kinky. This tiny, modish pad has mixologists serving up fancy drinks and DJs spinning dance tunes from around 9pm. How half of Chennai fits into it on Friday and Saturday nights is a mystery.

Dublin PUB, NIGHTCLUB
(Map p334; Sheraton Park Hotel, 132 TTK RD, Alwarpet; nightclub per person ₹1500; ⊙ from 6pm Wed-Sat) A long-running favourite with 30- and 40-somethings, including a fair sprinkling of expats, this Irish pub and nightclub has three levels of dancing and music from hip hop to Bollywood. Until 10pm it's a pub, then it becomes a club, alive to 2am or 3am on Saturday nights. No unaccompanied men, or 'stags' as they call them.

10 Downing Street PUB
(10D; Map p334; North Boag Rd, T Nagar; drinks ₹250-500, food ₹200-650; ⊙ noon-midnight) An English-themed pub (pictures of Big Ben on the wall, fish fingers on the menu) with a small dance floor, 10D is often packed with a mixed bag of 20s-to-40s professionals and some expats. Wednesday is Ladies' Night (free drinks for women), Friday Retro Night ('70s/'80s) and Saturday Club Night.

Pasha NIGHTCLUB
(Map p334; Park Hotel, 601 Anna Salai; men ₹2000 incl ₹500 drink voucher, women free; ⊙ 9pm-4am Wed-Mon) A fashionable, mostly 20s, even late-teens bunch crowds into this two-level, Moroccan-themed club and tries to get onto the small dance floor.

★ Entertainment

There's *bharatanatyam* (Tamil classical dance) and/or a Carnatic music concert going on somewhere in Chennai almost every evening. Check listings in the *Hindu* or *Times of India*, or the website www.timescity.com/chennai. The **Music Academy** (Map p334; ☎28112231; www.musicacademymadras.in; 168 (old 306) TTK Rd, Royapettah) is the most popular venue; the Kalakshetra Foundation (p337) and **Bharatiya Vidya Bhavan** (Map p334; ☎24643420; www.bhavanchennai.org; East Mada St, Mylapore) also stage many events, often free.

Shopping

Thyagaraya Nagar (aka T Nagar) has great shopping, especially at Pondy Bazaar and around Panagal Park. Nungambakkam's shady Khader Nawaz Khan Rd is a pleasant lane of designer shops, cafes and galleries.

The best shopping malls include **Express Avenue** (Map p338; White's Rd), **Chennai Citi Centre** (Map p334; 10 Dr Radhakrishnan Salai, Mylapore) and **Spencer Plaza** (Map p338; Anna Salai), all full of major international and Indian apparel chains. They normally open from 10am to 9pm. Spencer Plaza is a bit downmarket from the others, and includes many smaller craft and souvenir shops.

Handicrafts

Srushti (Map p334; www.srushtihandicrafts.com; 86 Chamiers Rd, Alwarpet; ⏲10.30am-8.30pm) is an artisan outlet with some very good (and some less good) bronze and wooden sculptures, and **Shilpi** (Map p334; 29 CP Ramaswamy Rd, Alwarpet; ⏲10am-8pm) has beautiful saris, salwars and kurtas in silk and cotton.

Fabindia CLOTHING, HANDICRAFTS
(Map p338; www.fabindia.com; Woods Rd; ⏲10.30am-8.30pm) This nationwide chain sells attractively contemporary, village-made crafts. This branch has ceramics, table and bed linen and personal care products, as well as fabulous clothes. Fabindia is also at **Spencer Plaza** (Map p338; 2nd fl, Phase 3, Spencer Plaza, Anna Salai; ⏲11am-8.30pm), **Express Avenue** (Map p338; 1st fl, Express Avenue Mall, White's Rd; ⏲11am-9pm) and **T Nagar** (Map p334; 84 GN Chetty Rd, T Nagar; ⏲10.30am-8.30pm).

Naturally Auroville HANDICRAFTS
(Map p334; 8 Khader Nawaz Khan Rd, Nungambakkam; ⏲10am-8pm Mon-Sat, 11.30am-7.30pm Sun) *Objets* (pottery, bedspreads, scented candles) and a few teas, cheeses and pastries, all from Auroville, near Puducherry.

Chamiers CLOTHING, HANDICRAFTS
(Map p334; 106 Chamiers Rd, RA Puram; ⏲10am-8pm) Upstairs, next to the Eco Cafe, is a shop with some original gifts including witty Chennaigaga T-shirts. Downstairs is **Anokhi** (Map p334; ☎24311495; 85/47 Chamiers Rd; ⏲10am-8pm), with wonderful and well-priced hand-block-printed and other clothes in light fabrics.

Poompuhar HANDICRAFTS
(Map p338; 108 Anna Salai; ⏲10am-8pm Mon-Sat, 11am-7pm Sun) This large branch of the fixed-price state-government handicrafts chain is good for everything from cheap technicolor plaster deities to a ₹200,000, 1m-high bronze Nataraja.

Silk

Many of the finest Kanchipuram silks turn up in Chennai, and the streets around Panagal Park are filled with silk shops; if you're lucky enough to be attending an Indian wedding this is where you buy your sari.

Nalli Silks TEXTILES
(Map p334; www.nalli.com; 9 Nageswaran Rd, T Nagar; ⏲9.30am-9.30pm) The huge, super-colourful granddaddy of silk shops, with a jewellery branch next door.

Kumaran Silks TEXTILES
(Map p334; 12 Nageswaran Rd, T Nagar; ⏲9.30am-9.30pm) Saris, saris (including 'budget saris') and plenty of Kanchipuram silk.

Bookshops

Higginbothams BOOKS
(Map p338; higginbothams@vsnl.com; 116 Anna Salai; ⏲9am-8pm Mon-Sat, 10.30am-7.30pm Sun) Open since 1844, this is reckoned to be India's oldest bookshop. It has a decent English-language selection, including Lonely Planet guides, and a good range of maps.

Oxford Bookstore BOOKS
(Map p334; www.oxfordbookstore.com; 39/12 Haddows Rd, Nungambakkam; ⏲9.30am-9.30pm) A big English-language selection and a nice cafe.

Landmark BOOKS
(Map p338; www.landmarkonthenet.com; 1st fl, Phase II, Spencer Plaza, Anna Salai; ⏲10.30am-9pm) Landmark has several large shops selling DVDs and CDs as well as lots of English-language books. Also at **Thousand**

Lights (Map p334; Apex Plaza, Nungambakkam High Rd; ⏲10.30am-9.30pm) and **Mylapore** (Map p334; Chennai Citi Centre, Dr Radhakrishnan Rd; ⏲10.30am-9pm).

Information

INTERNET ACCESS

'Browsing centres' are dotted all over town.

Cyber Palace (Map p338; 114 Bharathi Salai; per hr ₹25; ⏲8am-10.30pm)

Internet (Map p338; 6 Gandhi Irwin Rd, Egmore; per hr ₹30; ⏲7.30am-10pm) In the Hotel Imperial yard.

LEFT LUGGAGE

Egmore and Central train stations have left-luggage offices (signed 'Cloakroom') for those with journey tickets. The airport also has left-luggage facilities.

MEDICAL SERVICES

Apollo Hospital (Map p338; ☎28293333, emergency 1066; www.apollohospitals.com; 21 Greams Lane) State-of-the-art, expensive hospital popular with 'medical tourists'.

St Isabel's Hospital (Map p334; ☎24991081; www.stisabelshospital.in; 49 Oliver Rd, Mylapore) Affordable quality care.

MONEY

ATMs are everywhere, including at Central train station, the airport and the main bus station.

Thomas Cook (Map p338; Phase I, Spencer Plaza, Anna Salai; ⏲10am-6pm Mon-Sat, 10am-4pm Sun) Charges only ₹50 commission on all foreign cash exchanges. Also changes American Express travellers cheques.

POST

DHL (Map p338; ☎42148886; www.dhl.co.in; 85 VVV Sq, Pantheon Rd, Egmore; ⏲8am-11pm Mon-Sat, 9am-6pm Sun) For secure international parcel delivery. There are several branches around town.

Main Post Office (Map p334; Rajaji Salai, George Town; ⏲8am-8.30pm Mon-Sat, 10am-6pm Sun)

TOURIST INFORMATION

Indiatourism (Map p338; ☎28460285; www.incredibleindia.org; 154 Anna Salai; ⏲9am-6pm Mon-Fri) Maps and information on all of India; helpful on Chennai too.

ATMS

Axis Bank, Canara Bank, HDFC Bank, ICICI Bank and State Bank of India ATMs are the best for withdrawing cash with foreign cards in Tamil Nadu.

HOLIDAY TRANSPORT

All kinds of transport in, to and from Tamil Nadu can get booked up weeks in advance for the periods around major festivals including Pongal, Karthikai Deepam and Diwali. Plan ahead.

Tamil Nadu Tourism Development Corporation (TTDC; Map p338; ☎25383333; www.tamilnadutourism.org; Tamil Nadu Tourism Complex, 2 Wallajah Rd, Triplicane; ⏲24hr) The state tourism body's main office takes bookings for its own bus tours and mediocre hotels, and also answers questions and hands out a few leaflets. In the same building are state tourist offices from all over India, mostly open 9am to 6pm Monday to Friday. The TTDC has 24-hour office (Map p338; ☎25384356; 4 Poonamallee High Rd; ⏲24hr) near Central train station and counters at Central and Egmore stations.

TRAVEL AGENCIES

Milesworth Travel (Map p334; ☎24320522; http://milesworth.com; RM Towers, 108 Chamiers Rd, Alwarpet; ⏲9.30am-6pm Mon-Sat) A very professional and amiable agency that can help with just about any travel need you have.

Getting There & Away

AIR

Chennai Airport (☎22560551) is at Tirusulam in the far southwest of the city. A brand-new domestic terminal was due to open soon, with the international terminal expanding to occupy the whole of the old building.

There are direct flights to over 20 Indian cities, including Trichy, Madurai, Coimbatore and Thoothikudi (Tuticorin) within Tamil Nadu. Internationally, Chennai has plenty of direct flights to/from Colombo, Singapore, Kuala Lumpur and Bangkok, as well as the Gulf states. The best fares from Europe are often on Jet Airways (with connections at Mumbai or Delhi) or Emirates (via Dubai). Cathay Pacific flies to Hong Kong, and Maldivian to Male.

Airlines

Air Asia (Map p334; ☎33008000; www.airasia.com; Ispahani Centre, 123/12 Nungambakkam High Rd; ⏲9.30am-1pm & 2-6pm Mon-Fri, 9.30am-1.30pm Mon-Sat)

Air India (Map p338; ☎23453301; www.airindia.com; 19 Rukmani Lakshmipathy Rd, Egmore; ⏲9.30am-1pm & 2-5.15pm Mon-Sat)

Air India Express (Map p338; ☎23453375; www.airindiaexpress.in; 19 Rukmani Lakshmipathy Rd, Egmore; ⏲9.30am-1pm & 2-5.15pm Mon-Sat)

Emirates (Map p334; ☎33773377; www.emirates.com; 1st fl, Riaz Garden, 12 & 13 Kodambakkam High Rd; ⏰9am-5.30pm Mon-Sat)

Go Air (☎1800 222111, 22560293; www.goair.in)

IndiGo (☎09910383838; www.goindigo.in)

Jet Airways (Map p338; ☎39893333; www.jetairways.com; 43/44 Montieth Rd, Egmore; ⏰10am-6pm Mon-Sat)

JetKonnect (☎39893333; www.jetkonnect.com)

Malaysia Airlines (Map p334; ☎42191919; www.malaysiaairlines.com; 90 Dr Radhakrishnan Salai; ⏰9am-5.30pm Mon-Sat)

Maldivian (Map p338; ☎45028833; www.maldivian.aero; Spencer's Travel Services, Lakshmi Bhavan, Sundaram Ave, 609 Anna Salai)

SilkAir & Singapore Airlines (Map p334; ☎45921921; www.silkair.com; Westminster, 108 Dr Radhakrishnan Salai, Mylapore; ⏰9.15am-5.45pm Mon-Fri, 9.15am-1pm Sat)

SpiceJet (☎1800 1803333; spicejet.com)

SriLankan Airlines (Map p334; ☎43921241; www.srilankan.com; 4 Kodambakkam High Rd; ⏰9am-5.30pm Mon-Sat, 9am-1pm Sun)

Thai Airways International (Map p338; ☎42063311; www.thaiair.com; 4th fl, KGN Towers, Ethiraj Rd, Egmore; ⏰9.30am-5.30pm Mon-Fri)

BOAT

Passenger ships sail from the George Town harbour direct to Port Blair in the Andaman Islands twice a month. The Andaman Shipping Office Ticketing Counter (p413) sells tickets (₹2160 to ₹8420) for the 60-hour trip. Book several days ahead to ensure a place, and take three copies each of your passport data page and Indian visa. It can be a long process.

BUS

Most government buses operate from the large but surprisingly orderly **CMBT** (Chennai Mofussil Bus Terminus; Jawaharlal Nehru Rd, Koyambedu), 6km west of the centre. The most comfortable and expensive are the AC buses, followed by the UD ('Ultra Deluxe'), and these can generally be reserved in advance. The **T Nagar Bus Terminus** (Map p334; South Usman Rd) has a few daily departures to Bengaluru, Madurai, Mysore, Thanjavur and Trichy, plus bus 599 to Mamallapuram (₹27, two hours, about hourly).

Private buses offer generally greater comfort than non-AC government buses to many destinations, at up to double the price. Service information is available at www.redbus.in, and tickets can be booked at many travel agencies. Their main terminal is the **Omni Bus Stand** (off Kaliamman Koil St, Koyambedu), 500m west of the CMBT, but some companies also pick up and drop off elsewhere in the city. Parveen Travels, for example, has services to Ernakulam (Kochi), Kodaikanal, Madurai, Puducherry, Trichy and Trivandrum for which it picks up passengers at its **Egmore office** (Map p338; ☎28193538; www.parveentravels.com; 11/5 Kennet Lane, Egmore).

CAR

Renting a car with a driver is the easiest way of going almost anywhere and is easily arranged through most travel agents, midrange or top-end hotels, or the airport's prepaid taxi desks. Sample rates for non-AC/AC cars are ₹1300/1550 to Mamallapuram (Mahabalipuram) and ₹2700/3200 to Puducherry.

MOVING ON?

For further information, head to shop.lonelyplanet.com to purchase a downloadable PDF of the West Coast chapter from Lonely Planet's *Sri Lanka* guide.

NONSTOP DOMESTIC FLIGHTS FROM CHENNAI

DESTINATION	AIRLINES	FARE FROM (₹, ONE WAY)	DURATION (HR)	FREQUENCY (DAILY)
Bengaluru	AI, SG, S2, 6E	2668	1	8
Delhi	AI, SG, 6E, 9W	4840	2¾	16
Goa	AI, SG	2668	1¼-2	1-2
Hyderabad	AI, SG, S2, 6E	2668	1-1½	13
Kochi	SG, S2, 9W	2668	1½	6
Kolkata	AI, SG, S2, 6E	4137	2¼	8
Mumbai	AI, G8, SG, 6E, 9W	4136	2	16
Port Blair	AI, G8, SG, 9W	4137	2¼	4
Trivandrum	AI, SG, 6E, 9W	2668	1¼	5

Airline codes: AI – Air India, G8 – Go Air, SG – SpiceJet, S2 – JetKonnect, 6E – IndiGo, 9W – Jet Airways

GOVERNMENT BUSES FROM CMBT

DESTINATION	FARE (₹)	DURATION (HR)	FREQUENCY
Bengaluru	355-650	8	60 daily
Coimbatore	420	11	10 daily (6pm to 10pm)
Ernakulam (Kochi)	565	16	3pm
Kanchipuram	47	2	38 daily
Kodaikanal	495	13	5pm
Madurai	350-420	10	33 daily
Mamallapuram	80	2	every 30min
Mysore	530-900	11	7 daily (7pm to 11.30pm)
Ooty	430	13	4.30pm, 5.45pm, 7.15pm
Puducherry	100	4	every 30min
Thanjavur	260-340	8½	40 daily
Tirupathi	100-180	4	55 daily
Trichy	260-300	7	every 30min
Trivandrum	570	16	hourly, 10am to 9pm
Vellore	81	3½	58 daily

TRAIN

Interstate trains and those heading west generally depart from Central station, while trains heading south mostly leave from Egmore. The **advance reservations office** (Map p338; 1st fl, Chennai Central local station; ⌚8am-8pm Mon-Sat, 8am-2pm Sun), with its extremely helpful Foreign Tourist Cell, is in a separate 11-storey building just west of the main Central station building. The **Passenger Reservation Office** (Map p338; ☎28194579) at Egmore station keeps the same hours.

Getting Around

TO/FROM THE AIRPORT

The Chennai Metro Rail system, expected to open in 2014, will provide a cheap and easy link between the airport and city. Meanwhile, the cheapest option is a suburban train to or from Tirusulam station, connected by a pedestrian underpass to the parking areas outside the international terminal. Trains run several times hourly from 4am to midnight to/from Chennai Beach station (₹7, 42 minutes) with stops including Kodambakkam, Egmore, Chennai Park and Chennai Fort.

Prepaid taxi kiosks at the airport charge ₹380/515 for a non-AC/AC cab to Egmore, and slightly less to T Nagar.

AUTORICKSHAW

The city authorities have been trying to negotiate a deal with autorickshaw drivers for fixed fares of ₹10 per kilometre, with a minimum charge of ₹20. If no deal eventuates, drivers will doubtless continue refusing to use their meters and instead quote astronomical fares for locals and tourists alike: you can expect to pay at least ₹40 for a short trip down the road, around ₹80 for a 3km trip and ₹100 to ₹120 for 5km. Prices are at least 25% higher after 10pm. There are prepaid booths outside the CMBT (₹160 to Egmore) and Central station.

BUS

Chennai's city bus system is worth getting to know, although buses get packed to overflowing at busy times. Fares are between ₹3 and ₹14 (up to double for express and deluxe services, and multiplied by five for AC services). Route information is online at http://busroutes.in/chennai. See also p350.

METRO RAIL

Chennai Metro Rail, a new, part-underground rapid transit system, is expected to open in 2014 and should make moving around the city significantly easier. Line 1 goes from the airport to Teynampet, Thousand Lights, Central train station, the High Court and Washermanpet in the north of the city, running beneath Anna Salai for several kilometres. Line 2 goes from Central train station west to Egmore and the CMBT then south to St Thomas Mount.

TRAIN

Efficient, cheap suburban trains run from Beach station to Fort, Park (near Central station), Egmore, Chetpet, Nungambakkam, Kodambakkam, Mambalam, Saidapet, Guindy, St Thomas Mount, Tirusulam (for the airport), and on down to Tambaram. At Egmore station, the suburban platforms (10 and 11) and ticket office are on the north side of station. A second line branches south after Fort to Parktown, Chepauk, Tiruvallikeni (for Marina Beach), Light House and Thirumailai (near Kapaleeshwarar Temple). Trains run from 4am to midnight, several times hourly; rides cost between ₹4 and ₹7.

NORTHERN TAMIL NADU

Chennai to Mamallapuram

Chennai's sprawl peters out after an hour or so heading south on the East Coast Road (ECR), at which point Tamil Nadu becomes green fields, trees, red dirt, blue skies and not a few towns and villages (or, if you take the 'IT Expressway' inland, huge new buildings).

There's a tropical bohemian groove floating around Injambakkam village, site of the **Cholamandal Artists' Village** (☎044-24490092; Injambakkam; museum ₹20; ⊙museum & galleries 9am-6.30pm), 10km south of the Adyar River. This 3-hectare artists' cooperative – founded in 1966 by artists of the Madras Movement, pioneers of modern art in South India – is a serene muse away from the world, and the art in its museum and galleries is very much worth inspection. Look especially for work by KCS Paniker, SG Vasudev, M Senathipathi and S Nandagopal. You can have a very good Iranian meal in a lovely garden at **Shiraz** (mains ₹150-300, Sunday lunch buffet ₹600; ⊙11am-11pm Wed-Mon), just along the lane past the museum.

As Cholamandal is to contemporary artistic expression, **DakshinaChitra** (☎044-27472603; www.dakshinachitra.net; East Coast Rd, Muttukadu; Indian adult/student ₹75/30, foreign ₹200/70; ⊙10am-6pm Wed-Mon), 12km further south, is to South India's traditional arts and crafts. This jumble of open-air museum, traditional architecture, artisan workshops (including pottery, silk weaving, puppet building and basket making) and live theatre and dance performances is another stop that's well worth it (including for kids).

Kovalam, a fishing village 4km south of DakshinaChitra, has probably the best surfing waves on the Tamil Nadu coast. Waves get up to 2m and rides of 200m aren't uncommon. For classes or surf companionship,

MAJOR TRAINS FROM CHENNAI

DESTINATION	TRAIN NO & NAME	FARE (₹)	DURATION (HR)	DEPARTURE
Bengaluru	12007 Shatabdi Express*	529/1155	5	6am CC
	12609 Chennai-Bangalore Intercity Express	110/386	6½	1.35pm CC
Coimbatore	12675 KovaiExpress	132/488	7½	6.15am CC
	12671 Nilgiri Express	232/616/910	7½	9.15pm CC
Delhi	12621 Tamil Nadu Express	528/1482/2375	33	10pm CC
Goa	17311 Vasco Express (Friday only)	343/971/1500	22	2.10pm CC
Hyderabad	12759 Charminar Express	312/854/1285	14	6.10pm CC
Kochi	16041 Alleppey Express	275/770/955	12¼	8.45pm CC
Kolkata	12842 Coromandel Express	461/1242/1955	27	8.45am CC
Madurai	12635 Vaigai Express	132/488	8	1.20pm CE
	12637 Pandyan Express	232/594/880	9	9.20pm CE
Mumbai	11042 Mumbai Express	383/1085/1700	26	11.55am CC
Mysore	12007 Shatabdi Express*	679/1470	7	6am CC
	16222 Kaveri Express	212/564/850	10¼	9.30pm CC
Tirupathi	16053 Tirupathi Express	60/206	3¼	1.50pm CC
Trichy	12635 Vaigai Express	104/381	5	1.20pm CE
Trivandrum	12623 Trivandrum Mail	337/925/1405	15¾	7.45pm CC

Departure codes: CC – Chennai Central, CE – Chennai Egmore
*Daily except Wednesday
Shatabdi fares: chair/executive; Express and Mail fares are 2nd/chair car for day trains, sleeper/3AC/2AC for overnight trains

look up villager Murthy, Kovalam's original local surf pioneer, who runs the 'social surfing school' **Kovelong Point** (☎9840975916; www.covelongpoint.com).

Madras Crocodile Bank (☎044-27472447; www.madrascrocodilebank.org; Vadanemmeli; adult/child ₹35/10, camera/video ₹20/100; ⏰8.30am-5.30pm Tue-Sun) , 6km on down the ECR from Kovalam, is a fascinating peep into a world of reptiles, and an incredible conservation and research trust to boot. With 18 of the world's 23 species of crocodilian (crocodiles and similar creatures) now here, the Bank does crucial work in maintaining genetic reserves of these animals, several of which are endangered. There are thousands of reptiles here, including gharials (a rare North Indian river crocodilian with a long, thin snout), Indian muggers (a marsh croc) and saltwater crocs of the Andaman and Nicobar Islands – plus turtles, tortoises and snakes. The Croc Bank has openings for volunteers with an interest in wildlife (minimum two weeks): email volunteer.mcbt@gmail.com for more information if you're interested.

Nine kilometres past the Croc Bank (just 5km short of Mamallapuram), the **Tiger Cave** (Saluvankuppam; admission free; ⏰6am-6pm) is an unfinished but impressive rock-cut shrine, probably dating from the 7th century. What's special is the 'necklace' of 11 monstrous heads framing its central shrine-cavity. At the north end of the park-like grounds is a rock-cut **Shiva shrine** from the same era. Just beyond this, outside the fence, lies the recently excavated **Subrahmanya Temple**, comprising an 8th-century granite shrine built over a Sangam-era brick temple dedicated to Murugan, which is one of the two oldest known temples in Tamil Nadu.

To reach these places, take any bus heading south from Chennai to Mamallapuram and ask to be let off at the appropriate point(s). Another option is the TTDC's Chennai–Mamallapuram round-trip bus tour (₹275, 10 hours), which visits several of the sites as well as Mamallapuram itself. A full-day taxi tour from Chennai costs around ₹3000. It's unwise to swim along the coast because of strong currents and tides.

Mamallapuram (Mahabalipuram)

☎044 / POP 17,666

Mamallapuram was the major seaport of the ancient Pallava kingdom based at Kanchipuram, and a wander round the town's great, World Heritage–listed temples and carvings inflames the imagination, especially at sunset.

CHENNAI BUS ROUTES

BUS NO	ROUTE
A1	Central–Anna Salai–Rd (Mylapore) –Theosophical Society–Thiruvanmiyur
1B	Parry's–Central–Anna Salai–Airport
10A	Parry's–Central–Egmore(S)–Pantheon Rd–T Nagar
11	Broadway–Central–Anna Salai–T Nagar
12	TNagar–Pondy Bazaar–Eldham's Rd–Vivekananda House
15B &15F	Broadway–Central–Egmore (N)–CMBT
21H	Broadway–FortSt George–Kamarajar Salai–San Thome Cathedral–Theosophical Society
27B	CMBT–Egmore(N)–Central–Bharathi Salai (Triplicane)
27C	TNagar–CMBT
27D	Egmore(S)–Anna Salai–Cathedral Rd–Dr Radhakrishnan Salai–San Thome Cathedral
32& 32A	Central–Triplicane High Rd–Vivekananda House

Routes operate in both directions.
Broadway – Broadway Bus Terminus, George Town
Central – Central Station
Egmore (N) – Egmore station (north side)
Egmore (S) – Egmore station (south side)
Parry's – Parry's Corner
T Nagar – T Nagar Bus Terminus

And then, in addition to ancient archaeological wonders, there's the traveller ghetto of Othavadai and Othavadai Cross Sts. Restaurants serve pasta, pizza and pancakes, shops sell hand sanitiser and things from Tibet, and you know you have landed, once again, in the Kingdom of Backpackistan.

'Mahabs', as some call it, is only two hours by bus from Chennai, and many travellers make a beeline straight here. The town is small and laid-back, and its sights can be explored on foot or by bicycle.

Sights

You can easily spend a full day exploring Mamallapuram's marvellous temples and rock carvings. Most of them were carved from the rock in the 7th century during the reign of Pallava king Narasimhavarman I, whose nickname Mamalla (Great Wrestler) gave the town its name. Apart from the Shore Temple and Five Rathas, admission is free. Official Archaeological Survey of India guides can be hired at the sites for around ₹50; they're worth the money.

★Shore Temple HINDU TEMPLE
(combined 1-day ticket with Five Rathas Indian/foreigner ₹10/250, video ₹25; ⏲6am-6pm) Standing like a magnificent fist of rock-cut elegance overlooking the sea, the two-towered Shore Temple symbolises the heights of Pallava architecture and the maritime ambitions of the Pallava kings. Its small size belies its excellent proportion and the supreme quality of the carvings, many of which have been eroded into vaguely Impressionist embellishments. Built under Narasimhavarman II in the 8th century, it's the earliest significant free-standing stone temple in Tamil Nadu. The two towers rise above shrines to Shiva and their original linga (phallic symbols of Shiva) captured the sunrise and sunset. Between the Shiva shrines is one to Vishnu, shown sleeping.

★Five Rathas HINDU TEMPLE
(Pancha Ratha; Five Rathas Rd; combined 1-day ticket with Shore Temple Indian/foreigner ₹10/250, video ₹25; ⏲6am-6pm) Huddled together at the south end of Mamallapuram, the Five Rathas look like buildings, but they were, astonishingly, all carved from single large rocks. Each of these 7th-century temples was dedicated to a Hindu god and is now named after one or more of the Pandavas, the five hero-brothers of the epic Mahabharata, or their common wife, Draupadi. Outside each one is a carving of its god's animal mount.

Ratha is Sanskrit for chariot, and may refer to the temples' form or to their function as vehicles for the gods. The *rathas* were hidden in the sand until excavated by the British 200 years ago. It's thought they didn't originally serve as actual places of worship, but were created as models for structures to be built elsewhere.

The first *ratha* on the left after you enter the gate is the **Draupadi Ratha**, in the form of a stylised South Indian hut. It's dedicated to the demon-fighting goddess Durga, who looks out from inside, standing on a lotus. A huge sculpted lion, Durga's mount, stands guard outside.

Next in line is the 'chariot' of the most important Pandava, the **Arjuna Ratha**, dedicated to Shiva. Its pilasters, miniature roof shrines, and small, octagonal dome make it a precursor of many later temples in South India. A huge Nandi bull, vehicle of Shiva, stands behind. Shiva (with Nandi) and other gods are depicted on the temple's outer walls.

The barrel-roofed **Bhima Ratha** was never completed, as is evidenced by the missing colonnade on its north side. Inside is a shrine to Vishnu. The **Dharmaraja Ratha**, tallest of the temples, is similar in form to the Arjuna Ratha but one storey higher. Large carvings on its outer walls mostly represent gods, including the androgynous Ardhanarishvara (half Shiva, half Parvati) on the east side. King Narasimhavarman I appears at the west end of the south side.

The **Nakula-Sahadeva Ratha** (named after two twin Pandavas) stands aside from the other four and is dedicated to Indra. The life-size stone elephant beside it is one of the most perfectly sculpted elephants in India. Approaching from the gate to the north you see its back end first, hence its nickname Gajaprishthakara (elephant's backside).

★Arjuna's Penance HINDU, MONUMENT
(West Raja St) The crowning masterpiece of Mamallapuram's stonework, this giant relief carving is one of the greatest works of ancient art in India. Inscribed on a huge boulder, the Penance bursts with scenes of Hindu myth and everyday vignettes of South Indian life. In the centre *nagas,* or snake-beings, descend a cleft once filled with water, meant to represent the Ganges. To the left Arjuna performs self-mortification (fasting and standing on one leg), so that the

Mamallapuram (Mahabalipuram)

four-armed Shiva will grant him his most powerful weapon, the god-slaying Pasupata. (Some scholars believe the carving shows not Arjuna but the sage Bagiratha, who did severe penance to obtain Shiva's help in bringing the Ganges to earth.) Shiva is attended by dwarves, and celestial beings fly across the upper parts of the carving, including the moon god (above Shiva) and sun god (right of the cleft) with orbs behind their heads. Below Arjuna/Bagiratha appears a temple to Vishnu, mythical ancestor of the Pallava kings. The many wonderfully carved animals include a small herd of elephants and – humour amid the holy – a cat performing penance to a crowd of appreciative mice.

South along the road from Arjuna's Penance are the **Panch Pandava Mandapa** (6.30am-6pm), an unfinished cave temple; the **Krishna Mandapa** (6.30am-6pm), with a famous carving depicting Krishna lifting Govardhana Hill above villagers and cows to protect them from a storm sent by the god Indra; an **unfinished relief carving** similar in size to Arjuna's Penance; and the **Dharmaraja Cave Temple** (6.30am-6pm).

Mamallapuram Hill

Many interesting monuments are scattered over the rock-strewn hill on the west side of the town. It takes an hour or so to walk round the main ones. The hill area is open from 6am to 6pm and has two entrances: a northern one on West Raja St, and a southern one just off Five Rathas Rd.

Straight ahead inside the northern entrance you can't miss the huge boulder that bears the inspired name of **Krishna's Butterball**. Immovable, but apparently balancing precariously, it's a favourite photo opportunity. Pass between some rocks north of here to the **Trimurti Cave Temple**, honouring the Hindu 'trinity', with a shrine for

Mamallapuram (Mahabalipuram)

Top Sights
1 Arjuna's Penance ... B3
2 Shore Temple ... D3

Sights
3 Dharmaraja Cave Temple ... A4
4 Ganesh Ratha ... B2
5 Krishna Mandapa ... B3
6 Krishna's Butterball ... B2
7 Lighthouse ... A4
8 Mahishamardini Mandapa ... A4
9 Panch Pandava Mandapa ... B3
10 Ramanuja Mandapa ... A3
11 Raya Gopura ... A3
12 Trimurti Cave Temple ... B2
13 Unfinished Relief Carving ... A4
14 Varaha Mandapa ... A3

Activities, Courses & Tours
15 Hi! Tours ... B2
16 Sri Durga ... C1

Sleeping
17 Butterball Bed 'n Breakfast ... B2
18 Hotel Daphne ... C2
19 Hotel Mahabs ... B3
20 Hotel Mamalla Heritage ... B2
21 La Vie en Rose ... B3
22 Lakshmi Cottage ... D2
23 Sri Harul Guest House ... D2
24 Tina Blue View Lodge & Restaurant ... D1

Eating
Blue Elephant ... (see 31)
25 Freshly 'n Hot ... D1
26 Gecko Café ... C3
27 Gecko Café ... C3
28 Le Yogi ... D1
29 Moonrakers ... C1

Shopping
30 Apollo Bookshop ... D1
31 Ponn Tailoring ... C1
32 Shriji Art Gallery ... C2
33 Southern Arts & Crafts ... B3

Transport
34 Bicycle Hire ... B1
35 Southern Railway Reservation Centre ... B3

each deity: Brahma (left), Shiva (centre) and Vishnu (right). Around the back of the same rock is a beautiful group of carved elephants, with a monkey and peacock.

Back south of Krishna's Butterball you reach the **Ganesh Ratha**, carved from a single rock. Once a Shiva temple, it became a shrine to Ganesh (Shiva's elephant-headed son) after the original lingam was removed. Southwest of here, the **Varaha Mandapa** houses some of Mamallapuram's finest carvings. The left panel shows Vishnu's boar avatar, Varaha, lifting the earth out of the oceans. The outward-facing panels show Vishnu's consort Lakshmi (washed by elephants) and Durga, while the right-hand panel has Vishnu in his eight-armed giant form, Trivikrama, overcoming the demon king Bali.

A little further south, then up to the left, is the 16th-century **Raya Gopura** (Olakkanatha Temple), which is probably an unfinished *gopuram* (tall temple entrance tower). The main path continues south to the **Ramanuja Mandapa** and up to Mamallapuram's **lighthouse**, which offers fine panoramas. Just southwest of the lighthouse is the **Mahishamardini Mandapa**, carved from the rock with excellent scenes from the Puranas (Sanskrit stories from the 5th century AD). The left-side panel shows Vishnu sleeping on the coils of a snake; on the right, Durga bestrides her lion vehicle while killing the demon-buffalo Mahisha. Inside the central shrine, Murugan is depicted sitting between his parents Shiva and Parvati.

Activities

Beach

The beach fronting the village isn't exactly pristine and gets downright grubby in some spots, but south of the Shore Temple it clears into very fine sand. You'll also be further away from the leers of men who spend their days gawking at tourists. Like most of Tamil Nadu's coast, these beaches are not great for swimming, as there are dangerous rips.

Therapies

Numerous places offer massage, reiki, yoga and ayurvedic practices.

Sri Durga (☎9840288280; sridurgamassageyoga1999@yahoo.com; 35 Othavadai St; 45min massage ₹700-900, 1hr yoga ₹200) offers massages and ayurvedic treatments (with male therapists for men and female for women), as well as yoga sessions at 7am and 7pm. Several other operators in town have similar rates and timings. As always, and especially for such an intimate service, ask fellow travellers, question the therapist carefully and if you have any misgivings, don't proceed.

The Radisson resort has a branch of the popular ayurvedic treatment centre Ayush as well as a spa with a wide range of massages, mud rubs and more – both open to nonguests.

Tours

Hi! Tours CYCLING, BIRDWATCHING
(☎27443360; www.hi-tours.com; 123 East Raja St; bicycle tours ₹350-400; ⌚9.30am-6pm Mon-Fri, 9.30am-2pm Sat) Runs half-day bicycle tours to nearby villages, observing activities like rice- and masala-grinding and kolam drawing (the 'welcome' patterns outside doorways, also called rangoli). It also organises day trips to places including Kanchipuram and Vedantangal Bird Sanctuary and can put together longer packages with reasonable prices on accommodation and transport.

Festivals & Events

Mamallapuram Dance Festival DANCE
(⌚late Dec-late Jan) A four-week dance festival showcasing classical and folk dances from all over India, with many performances on an open-air stage against the imposing backdrop of Arjuna's Penance. Dances include the Bharata Natyam (Tamil Nadu), Kuchipudi (Andhra Pradesh) tribal dance, Kathakali (Kerala drama); there are also puppet shows and classical music performances. Performances are held only from Friday to Sunday.

Sleeping

Hotel Daphne HOTEL $
(☎27442811; www.moonrakersrestaurants.com; 17 Othavadai Cross St; r ₹300-1500; ❄) Most of the Daphne's rooms are quite acceptable if nothing special, but the new, top-floor AC rooms 12 and 13 are great value, with four-poster beds, balconies and cane swing chairs. The leafy courtyard is another drawcard.

Tina Blue View Lodge & Restaurant GUESTHOUSE $
(☎27442319; 34 Othavadai St; s/d/tr ₹400/500/600) Tina is one of Mamallapuram's originals and kind of looks it, with some frayed and faded edges, but remains deservedly popular for its whitewashed walls, blue accents and tropically pleasant garden, as well as tireless original owner Xavier ('I am same age as Tony Wheeler!').

Sri Harul Guest House GUESTHOUSE $
(Sea View Guest House; ☎9384620173; 181 Bajanai Koil St, Fishermen's Colony; r ₹500-1000) Surf crashes on to the rocks right below your balcony if you get one of the half-dozen sea-view rooms at Sri Harul, one of the best of several seafront cheapies. Rooms are basic, medium-sized and quite clean.

La Vie en Rose HOTEL $
(☎9444877544; Old College Rd; d without/with AC ₹700/1200; ❄) Simple, decent-sized, clean rooms (though a bit worn), a nice leafy entrance and friendly staff.

Lakshmi Cottage HOTEL $
(☎27442463; lakshmilodge2002@yahoo.co.in; 5 Othavadai Cross St; r ₹400-800, with AC ₹1200; ❄) One of the better of several backpacker-oriented places along Othavadai Cross St, the Lakshmi has lots of rooms in primary colours, and assorted travel services on the ground floor. Beds range from concrete to carved wood.

Butterball Bed 'n Breakfast B&B $$
(☎9094792525; suhale2009@gmail.com; 9/26 West Raja St; s/d incl breakfast ₹1600/1800; ❄📶) There's a great view of the eponymous giant rock from the roof terrace, and a nice lawn. The smallish but clean, pleasant rooms have old English prints, writing desks and blue-tiled bathrooms. Breakfast is a good Western-style affair; also welcome is the civilised 24-hour checkout, rare in Mamallapuram. Free wi-fi throughout.

Hotel Mahabs HOTEL $$
(☎27442645; www.hotelmahabs.com; 68 East Raja St; r ₹1319, with AC ₹2159-2518; ❄@📶🏊) Friendly Mahabs is centred on an attractive pool (₹300 for nonguests) surrounded by trees, plants and murals. Rooms are in shades of brown but very clean and comfy. There's a decent in-house restaurant; internet use is ₹50/200 per hour/24 hours.

Hotel Mamalla Heritage HOTEL $$
(☎27442060; www.hotelmamallaheritage.com; 104 East Raja St; s ₹2136-2611, d ₹2374-3086, all incl breakfast; ❄📶🏊) Popular with tour groups, the Mamalla has large, comfortable rooms with spotless bathrooms. The pool's a decent size, and there's a quality rooftop restaurant. Wi-fi costs ₹50/200 per hour/24 hours.

★Radisson Blu Resort Temple Bay RESORT $$$
(☎27443636; http://radissonblu.com/hotel-mamallapuram; 57 Kovalam Rd; s/d incl breakfast

TAMIL NADU TEMPLES

Tamil Nadu is a gold mine for anyone wanting to explore Indian temple culture. Not only does this state have some of the country's most spectacular temple architecture and sculpture, its people are among the most devout and fervent in their Hindu beliefs. Tamil Nadu's 5000-odd temples are constantly busy with worshippers flocking in for *puja* (offering or prayer), and colourful temple festivals abound. Among the plethora of Hindu deities, Shiva probably has most Tamil temples dedicated to him, in a multitude of aspects including Nataraja, the cosmic dancer, who dances in a ring of fire with two of his four hands holding the flame of destruction and the drum of creation, while the third makes the *abhaya mudra* (fear not) gesture and the fourth points to the dwarf of ignorance being trampled beneath Shiva's foot. Tamils also have a soft spot for Shiva's peacock-riding son Murugan (also called Kartikeya or Skanda).

The special significance of many Tamil temples makes them goals of countless Hindu pilgrims from all over India. The Pancha Sabhai Sthalangal are the five temples where Shiva is believed to have performed his cosmic dance (chief among them Chidambaram). Then there's the Pancha Bootha Sthalangal, the five temples where Shiva is worshipped as a manifestation of one of the five elements – land, water, air, sky/space, fire. Each of the nine Navagraha temples in the Kumbakonam area is the abode of one of the nine celestial bodies of Hindu astronomy – key sites given the importance of astrology in Hindu faith.

Typical Tamil temple design features tall stepped entrance towers called *gopurams*, encrusted with often colourfully painted sculptures of gods and demons; halls of richly carved columns called *mandapas*; a sacred water tank; and a ground plan comprising a series of compounds *(prakarams)* of diminishing size, one within the next, with the innermost containing the central sanctum where the temple's main deity resides. The earliest Tamil temples were small shrines sculpted direct from the living rock; the first free-standing temples were built in the 8th century AD; *gopurams* began to appear around the 12th century.

Admission to almost all temples is free, but non-Hindus are often not allowed inside inner sanctums, which can be disappointing for many travellers. At other temples priests may invite you in and in no time you are doing *puja*, having a *tilak* daubed on your forehead and being asked for a donation.

Temple touts are fairly common and can be a nuisance, but there are also many excellent guides who deserve both your time and rupees; use your judgement, talk to other travellers and be on the lookout for badge-wearing official guides, who tend to be excellent resources.

A South Indian Journey by Michael Wood is a great read if you're interested in learning more about Tamil culture. TempleNet (www.templenet.com) is one of the best online resources.

from ₹8934/9893; ❄@📶🏊) The Radisson's 144 luxurious chalets, villas and bungalows are spread around manicured gardens stretching 500m to the beach. Somewhere in the midst is India's longest swimming pool, all 220m of it. Rooms range from large to enormous and the most expensive have private pools. The Radisson also offers Mamallapuram's finest (and most expensive) dining and two top-notch spas (one exclusively ayurvedic). It's a popular getaway for well-heeled Chennai-ites. Free wi-fi throughout.

Ideal Beach Resort RESORT **$$$**
(☎27442240; www.idealresort.com; East Coast Rd; s/d from ₹5934/6527; ❄@🏊) With a landscaped garden setting and its own stretch of (pretty nice) beachfront, this laid-back resort, 3km north of town, is popular with families and couples. There's a lovely poolside restaurant where live classical music is sometimes performed. Internet costs ₹100 per 24 hours.

Eating

Eateries on Othavadai and Othavadai Cross Sts provide semi-open-air settings, decent

Western mains and bland Indian curries. Most of them can serve you a beer. For real Indian food, there are a few decent cheap veg and biryani places near the bus stand.

Le Yogi MULTICUISINE **$$**
(19 Othavadai St; mains ₹120-350; ⏰7.30am-11pm) This is some of the best Western food in town; the steaks, pasta, pizzas and crepes are genuine and tasty (if small), service is good, and the airy setting, with bamboo posts and pretty hanging lamps, has a touch of the romantic.

Gecko Café MULTICUISINE **$$**
(www.gecko-web.com; 14 Othavadai Cross St; mains ₹150-290; ⏰8am-10.30pm) Two friendly brothers run this cute little spot on a thatch-covered rooftop overlooking a large pond. The offerings and prices aren't that different from other tourist-oriented spots, but there's more love put into the cooking here and it comes out tastier. At research time they were building a **second location** around the corner.

Freshly 'n Hot CAFE **$$**
(Othavadai Cross St; mains ₹60-225; ⏰7.30am-9pm) Yes, the name makes no sense, but the ambience is relaxed and the decor clean and fresh. A comparatively small menu of perfectly OK pizza, pasta, sandwiches, egg items and crepes accompanies a long list of coffees. The iced coffees are excellent.

Moonrakers MULTICUISINE **$$**
(34 Othavadai St; mains ₹100-300; ⏰10am-11.30pm) You're likely to end up here at some stage; it's the sort of place that dominates the backpacker-ghetto streetscape. The food won't win any prizes but it's OK, and the three floors of tables keep pretty busy. For a change of scene try the same owners' **Blue Elephant** (Othavadai St), opposite, with almost identical food and nicer decor.

Water's Edge Cafe MULTICUISINE **$$$**
(Radisson Blu Resort Temple Bay, 57 Kovalam Rd; mains ₹250-700; ⏰24hr) Offers everything from American breakfast to lamb goulash and Indian veg dishes. Also in the Radisson is the **Wharf** (mains ₹550-2000; ⏰noon-3pm & 7-11pm), a gourmet multicuisine seaside restaurant.

Shopping

The roar of electric stone-grinders has replaced the tink-tink of chisels in Mamallapuram's stone-carving workshops, enabling them to turn out ever more granite sculptures of varying quality, from ₹100 pendants to a ₹400,000 Ganesh that needs to be lifted with a crane. There are also some good art galleries, tailors and antique shops here. For clothes, we recommend **Ponn Tailoring** (Othavadai St; ⏰9.30am-10pm). Nice prints, cards and original art can be found at **Shriji Art Gallery** (14/21 Othavadai St; ⏰9am-10pm), and expensive but beautiful curios culled from local homes, along with quality new sculptures, at **Southern Arts & Crafts** (☎27443675; www.southernarts.in; 72 East Raja St; ⏰9am-7.30pm).

Apollo Bookshop (89 Fishermen's Colony; ⏰9am-9pm) has a decent range of books in several languages to sell and swap.

Information

Head to East Raja St for ATMs.

Hi Tech Net-Centre (Othavadai St; internet per hr ₹30; ⏰8am-9.30pm) Welcome spacious conditions.

Ruby Forex (East Raja St; ⏰9.30am-7pm Mon-Sat) Currency exchange.

Suradeep Hospital (☎27442448; 15 Thirukula St; ⏰24hr) Recommended by travellers.

Tourist Office (☎27442232; Kovalam Rd; ⏰10am-5.45pm Mon-Fri) Quite helpful and friendly.

Getting There & Away

From the **bus stand** (East Raja St), bus 599 heads to Chennai's T Nagar Bus Terminus (₹27, two hours) 24 times daily, and AC bus 568C (588C on Saturday and Sunday) runs to Chennai's CMBT (₹85, two hours) about hourly, 8am to 9pm. For Chennai Airport take bus 515 to Tambaram (every 30 minutes, 6.20am to 9.30pm), then a taxi, autorickshaw or suburban train from there. There are also nine daily buses to Kanchipuram (₹31, two hours) from the bus stand. Buses to Puducherry (₹50, two hours) stop about every half-hour at the junction of Kovalam Rd and the Mamallapuram bypass, 1km north of the town centre.

Taxis are available from the bus stand, travel agents and hotels. It's about ₹1000 to ₹1200 to Chennai, or ₹1500 to Puducherry.

You can make train reservations at the **Southern Railway Reservation Centre** (32 East Raja St, 1st fl; ⏰10am-1pm & 2.30-5pm Mon-Sat, 8am-2pm Sun)

Getting Around

The easiest way to get around is on foot, though on a hot day it's quite a hike to see all the monuments. Bicycles can be hired at some guesthouses and hotels, and at a few rental stalls, usually for ₹50 per day.

Vedanthangal Bird Sanctuary

About 55km southwest of Mamallapuram, this 30-hectare **sanctuary** (admission ₹5, camera/video ₹25/150; ⏲6am-6pm) is a spectacular breeding ground for many kinds of water birds, which migrate here from October to March. Some years as many as 100,000 birds mass at Vedanthangal Lake and its marshy surrounds. The best viewing times are early morning and late afternoon; head for the watchtower and look down on the noisy nests across the water.

Three basic AC rooms are available at the **Forest Department Resthouse** (r ₹750) 500m before the sanctuary. For these you're supposed to book in advance with the **Wildlife Warden's Office** (Map p334; ☎044-24321471; DMS Compound, 259 Anna Salai, Teynampet) in Chennai. It's worth phoning the office beforehand, as it may be changing location – or just book through a travel agency such as Hi! Tours (p354) in Mamallapuram, or Chennai's Milesworth Travel (p346). If you just turn up the caretaker may just find a room if one's available. You should bring all food and drinks with you.

Visitors often make a day trip by taxi from Mamallapuram; this should cost around ₹1500. To get here by public transport, first get to Chengalpattu, an hour's bus ride from Mamallapuram en route to Kanchipuram. From here you can take a bus to Vedanthangal via Padalam, where you may have to change buses again. Most Vedanthangal buses go to the sanctuary entrance, but some stop at the village bus station, 1km away.

Kanchipuram

☎ 044 / POP 164,225

Kanchipuram, 80km southwest of Chennai, was capital of the Pallava dynasty during the 6th to 8th centuries, when the Pallavas were creating the great stone monuments of Mamallapuram. Today a typically hectic modern Indian town, it's famed for its numerous important and busy temples, some dating from Pallava, Chola or Vijayanagar times, and also for its high-quality silk saris, woven on hand looms by thousands of families in the city and nearby villages. Silk and sari shops are strung along Gandhi Rd, southeast of the centre, though their wares are generally no cheaper than at silk shops in Chennai. Kanchi can easily be visited in a day trip from Mamallapuram or Chennai.

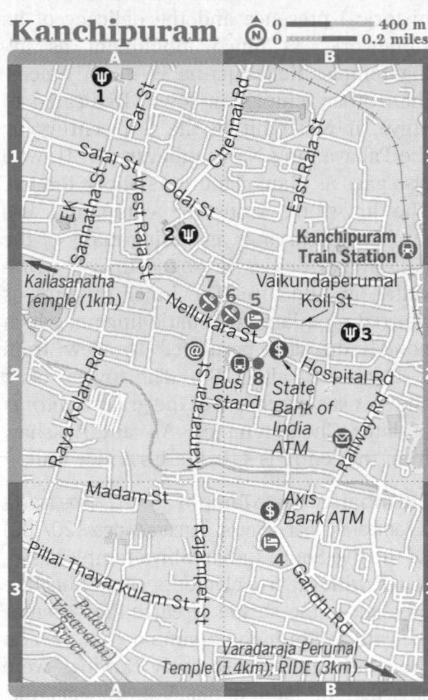

Kanchipuram

Sights

1 Ekambareshwara Temple A1
2 Kamakshi Amman Temple A1
3 Vaikunta Perumal Temple B2

Sleeping

4 GRT Regency B3
5 Sree Sakthi Residency B2

Eating

Dakshin .... (see 4)
6 Sangeetha Restaurant B2
7 Saravana Bhavan A2

Transport

8 Bicycle Hire B2

Sights

All temples are open from 6am to noon and 4pm to 8pm. All have free admission, though you may have to pay small amounts for shoe-keeping and/or cameras.

Kailasanatha Temple HINDU TEMPLE

Kanchi's oldest temple is its most impressive, not for its size but for its weight of historical presence and the delicacy of its stonework. As much monument as living temple, Kailasanatha is much quieter than other temples in town. Dedicated to Shiva, it was built in the 8th century by the Pallava king Narasimhavarman II, who also gave us Mamallapuram's Shore Temple. The low-slung sandstone compound has fascinating carvings, including many of the half-animal deities in vogue in early Dravidian architecture. The inner sanctum is centred on a large prismatic lingam, which non-Hindus are permitted to view from a distance of about 8m. The tower rising above it is a precursor of the great *vimanas* of later Chola temples. An autorickshaw from the centre is ₹40, but it's a nice walk.

Ekambareshwara Temple HINDU TEMPLE
(Ekambaranathar Temple; camera/video ₹20/100) Of the five South Indian Shiva temples associated with the five elements, this 12-hectare precinct is the shrine of earth. You'll enter beneath a 59m-high unpainted *gopuram* on the south side, whose lively carvings were chiselled in 1509 under Vijayanagar rule. Inside, a columned hall leads left into the central compound: non-Hindus cannot go into the inner sanctum, which includes a mirror chamber whose central Shiva image is reflected in endless repetition, alluding to his infinite presence.

According to legend, the goddess Kamakshi (She Whose Eyes Awaken Desire; a form of Parvati, Shiva's consort) worshipped Shiva under a mango tree here. The temple's name means 'Lord of the Mango Tree' and in one courtyard behind the inner sanctum you can see a mango tree said to be 3500 years old, with four branches representing the four Vedas (sacred Hindu texts).

Kamakshi Amman Temple HINDU TEMPLE
This imposing temple, dedicated to Kamakshi/Parvati, is one of India's most important places of *shakti* (female energy/deities) worship. It's thought to have been founded by the Pallavas. The entire main building inside is off-limits to non-Hindus, but the small, square marriage hall, to the right inside the temple's southeast entrance, is worth a good look for its wonderful ornate pillars. Each February/March carriages bearing the temple deities are hauled through the streets; don't miss this procession if you're in the vicinity.

Varadaraja Perumal Temple HINDU TEMPLE
(Devarajaswami Temple; 100-pillared hall ₹1, camera/video ₹5/100) The enormous Varadaraja Perumal Temple in the southeast of the city is dedicated to Vishnu and was built by the Cholas in the 11th century. The main central compound is off-limits to non-Hindus, but the artistic highlight is the '100-pillared' marriage hall, added in the 16th century just inside the western entrance. Its pillars (actually 96) are superbly carved with countless animals and monsters; at its corners hang four stone chains each carved from a single rock.

Every 40 years the waters of the temple tank are drained, revealing a huge wooden statue of Vishnu that is worshipped for 48 days. Next viewing: 2019. Meantime, very popular processions carrying temple idols through the streets happen several times a year.

Vaikunta Perumal Temple HINDU TEMPLE
Roughly 1200 years old, this Vishnu temple is a Pallava creation. A passage around the central shrine has lion pillars and a wealth of weathered wall panels, some showing historical scenes. The main shrine, uniquely spread over three levels, contains images of Vishnu standing, sitting, reclining and riding his preferred mount, the garuda (half-eagle, half-man).

Volunteering

RIDE VOLUNTEERING
(Rural Institute for Development Education; ☎27268223; www.rideindia.org; 48 Periyar Nagar, Little Kanchipuram) Kanchipuram's celebrated silk-weaving industry has traditionally depended heavily on child labour. The NGO RIDE has been a leader in reducing child labour numbers in the industry from over 40,000 in 1997 to less than 1000 by 2010, by its own estimates. RIDE also works to empower the rural poor through education and women's self-help groups. It welcomes volunteers from one week to two years to work in a wide variety of projects. Volunteers pay between ₹1500 and ₹7000 per week (depending how long they are staying) for accommodation, food and other costs.

Tours

RIDE offers original and fascinating **tours** (per person incl lunch half/full day ₹600/900) covering diverse themes from silk weaving and temples to released child labour or an Indian cookery class with market visit.

Sleeping & Eating

RIDE GUESTHOUSE $
(Rural Institute for Development Education; ☎27268223; www.rideindia.org; 48 Periyar Nagar, Little Kanchipuram; s/d incl breakfast ₹350/700; ❄) This NGO has several simple but clean and sizeable rooms for travellers, at its base in a residential area about 5km southeast of the city centre (signposted from the main road about 1km past Varadaraja Perumal Temple). Contact them a day ahead if possible. Home-cooked lunch and dinner are available (₹250 each).

GRT Regency HOTEL $$
(☎27225250; www.grthotels.com; 487 Gandhi Rd; s/d incl breakfast ₹3000/3500; ❄📶) The GRT has the cleanest and most comfortable rooms you'll find in Kanchi, boasting marble floors and bathroom fittings and tea/coffee makers. The hotel's **Dakshin** (mains ₹185-390; ⏰7am-11pm) restaurant is a tad overpriced but offers a big multicuisine menu including Western-style breakfast, good seafood and tasty tandoori.

Sree Sakthi Residency HOTEL $$
(☎27233799; www.sreesakthiresidency.com; 71 Nellukara St; s ₹1319-1439, d ₹1559; ❄) Simple blonde-wood furniture and coloured walls make the rooms fairly modern, and they're good and clean. The **Sangeetha Restaurant** (mains ₹50-140; ⏰6am-10.30pm) here, with AC and non-AC sections, does very good veg food.

Saravana Bhavan SOUTH INDIAN $$
(66 Nellukara St; meals ₹80-230; ⏰6am-10pm) A reliable veg restaurant with a welcome AC dining room.

Getting There & Away

Suburban trains to Kanchipuram (₹15, 2½ hours) leave Chennai's Egmore station (platform 10) six times daily.

The busy **bus stand** is in the centre of town. Departures:

Chennai ₹47, two hours, every 15 to 30 minutes
Mamallapuram ₹42, two hours, 10 daily
Puducherry ₹75, three hours, 11 daily
Tiruvannamalai ₹70, three hours, 11 daily
Vellore ₹41, two hours, every 15 minutes

Getting Around

Bike hire (per hour ₹5) is available at stall around the bus stand. An autorickshaw for a half-day tour of the five main temples (around ₹400) will inevitably involve a stop at a silk shop.

Vellore

☎0416 / POP 185,895

For a dusty bazaar town, Vellore feels kinda cosmopolitan, thanks to a couple of tertiary institutions and the Christian Medical College (CMC), one of India's finest hospitals, attracting medical students as well as patients from all over the country. On the main Chennai–Bengaluru road, Vellore is worth a stop mainly for its massive Vijayanagar fort.

Central Vellore is bounded on the north by Ida Scudder Rd (Arcot Rd), home to the hospital and cheap sleeping and eating options; and on the west by Officer's Line (Anna Salai), with Vellore Fort on its west side. Buses arrive at the New Bus Stand, 1.5km north.

Sights

Vellore Fort FORT
A circuit of the moat-surrounded ramparts (nearly 2km) of the splendid fort is the most peaceful experience available in Vellore. The fort was built in the 16th century and passed through Maratha and Mughal hands before the British occupied it in 1760. These days it houses, among other things, government offices, two parade grounds (capable of hosting a dozen simultaneous games of cricket), a church and a police recruiting school. Also inside is the **Jalakantesvara Temple** (⏰6am-1pm & 3-8.30pm), a gem of late Vijayanagar architecture, built about 1566. Check out the small, detailed sculptures on the walls of the marriage hall in the southwest corner. The fort contains two museums: the dusty exhibits in the **Government Museum** (Indian/foreigner ₹5/100; ⏰9.30am-5pm Sat-Thu) have seen better days, but the **Archaeological Survey Museum** (admission free; ⏰9am-5pm Sat-Thu) has a good collection of Pallava, Chola and Nayak stone sculptures, plus exhibits on the 1806 Vellore Mutiny, the earliest anti-British uprising by Indian troops. Next door, pretty **St John's Church** (1846) is only open for Sunday services.

Sleeping & Eating

Vellore's cheap hotels are concentrated along Ida Scudder Rd and in the busy, narrow streets south of there. The cheapest are pretty grim, and the better ones fill up quickly.

Hotel Solai HOTEL $
(☎2222996; hotelsolai@gmail.com; 26 Babu Rao St; s/d ₹315/473, with AC ₹520/825; ❄) If you can get a room, this almost-new hotel is probably the best value, near the hospital. It has clean rooms, reasonably airy walkways, and a back-up generator for those power cuts.

Darling Residency HOTEL $$
(☎2213001; www.darlingresidency.com; 11/8 Officer's Line; s ₹1882-2118, d ₹2235-2471, all incl breakfast; ❄@🛜) It's not five-star, but rooms are clean and comfortable (if forgettable), staff are friendly and the hotel has four restaurants, including the cool and breezy **Aaranya Roof Garden Restaurant** (mains ₹100-150; ⏰6.30-10.45pm). It's 1.5km south of Vellore Fort entrance.

Hotel Palm Tree HOTEL $$
(☎2222960; www.hotelpalmtree.co.in; 10 Thennamaram St; s/d ₹524/770, with AC s ₹1079-1319, d ₹1187-1499; ❄) On a narrow street off Officer's Line, 750m south of Vellore Fort entrance, the Palm Tree offers clean, spruce rooms with IKEA-style furniture, and its staff are very helpful.

Hotel Arthy INDIAN $
(Ida Scudder Rd; dishes ₹20-60, meals ₹45-75; ⏰6.30am-10.30pm) A bunch of cheap veg restaurants line Ida Scudder Rd, but this is one of the cleanest, with tasty North and South Indian favourites including good thalis and cheap, yummy biryani.

Information

Sri Apollo (Ida Scudder Rd; internet per hr ₹30.; ⏰8.30am-9pm)

State Bank of India ATM (Officer's Line) About 700m south of Vellore Fort entrance.

Getting There & Away

BUS

Departures from the New Bus Stand:

Bengaluru ₹138, five hours, every 30 minutes

Chennai AC Volvo buses ₹161, 2½ hours, about hourly; other buses ₹81, three hours, every 10 to 20 minutes

Kanchipuram ₹41, two hours, every 15 minutes

Tiruvannamalai ₹47, two hours, every 15 minutes

TRAIN

Vellore's main station is 5km north at Katpadi. There are at least 20 daily superfast or express trains to/from Chennai Central (2nd class/AC chair ₹64/226, 2¼ to 3¾ hours), most with a big choice of classes, and 10 trains to/from Bangalore City station. Bus 192 shuttles between the station and town.

Tiruvannamalai

☎04175 / POP 144,683

There are temple towns, there are mountain towns, and there are temple-mountain towns where God appears as a phallus of fire. Welcome to Tiruvannamalai. Set below boulder-strewn Mt Arunachala, this is one of South India's five 'elemental' cities of Shiva; here the god is worshipped in his fire incarnation as Arunachaleshwar. At every full moon 'Tiru' swells with thousands of pilgrims who come to circumnavigate the base of Arunachala in a purifying ritual known as Girivalam, but at any time you'll see Shaivite priests, sadhus (holy people) and devotees gathered around the big Arunachaleshwar Temple. The area's reputation for strong spiritual energies has engendered numerous ashrams, and Tiruvannamalai is attracting growing numbers of spiritual-minded travellers. Around the main cluster of ashrams, on and near Chengam Rd about 2km southwest of the centre, you'll find a few congenial cafes and sleeping options.

Sights & Activities

★**Arunachaleshwar Temple** HINDU TEMPLE
(Annamalaiyar Temple; http://arunachaleswarar.org; ⏰5am-12.30pm & 3.30-9.30pm) During festivals the Arunachaleshwar is awash in golden flames and the roasting scent of burning ghee, as befits the fire incarnation of the Destroyer of the Universe. This 10-hectare temple is one of the largest in India. Its oldest parts date back to the 9th century and the site was a place of worship long before that. Four large unpainted *gopurams* mark the entrances, with the main, eastern one rising 13 storeys and an astonishing 66m. Inside the complex are five more *gopurams*, two tanks and a profusion of sub-temples and shrines (the interactive map at www.arunachaleswarar.com/earunastructure.html is a help). To reach the innermost sanctum, with its huge lingam, worshippers must pass through five surrounding *prakarams* (compounds). The temple elephant gives blessings inside the second *gopuram* coming from the east.

Mt Arunachala MOUNTAIN
This 800m-high extinct volcano dominates Tiruvannamalai and local conceptions of the

element of fire, which supposedly finds its sacred abode in Arunachala's heart. Devout barefoot pilgrims, especially on full-moon and festival days, make the 14km circumambulation of the mountain, stopping at eight famous linga along the route. If you're not quite that devoted, buy a Giripradakshina map (₹15) from the bookshop at Sri Ramana Ashram (p361), hire a bicycle on the roadside nearby, and ride your way around. Or make an autorickshaw circuit for about ₹250 (up to double at busy times).

For a superb view of the Arunachaleshwar Temple and Tiruvannamalai, climb part or all the way up the hill. The hot ascent to the top and back takes five or six hours: start early and take water. A 'Skandasramam & Virupakshi Cave' sign, across the road from the northwest corner of Arunachaleshwar Temple, points the way up past homes and two caves, **Virupaksha** (about 20 minutes up) and **Skandasramam** (30 minutes). Sri Ramana Maharshi lived and meditated in these caves from 1899 to 1922.

Sri Ramana Ashram ASHRAM

(Sri Ramanasramam; ☎237200; www.sriramanamaharshi.org; Chengam Rd; ⊙office 7.30am-12.30pm & 2-8pm) This tranquil ashram, in green surrounds 2km southwest of the city centre, draws devotees of Sri Ramana Maharshi, one of the first Hindu gurus to gain an international following, who died here in 1950 after half a century in contemplation. Visitors can meditate or attend daily *pujas* and chantings, mostly in the samadhi hall where the guru's body is enshrined. A limited amount of free accommodation (donations accepted; maximum three days) is available: write at least a month ahead (email is acceptable).

Sri Seshadri Swamigal Ashram ASHRAM

(☎236999; www.tiruvarunaimahan.org; Chengam Rd) Dedicated to a contemporary and helper of Sri Ramana. It has meditation platforms and some accommodation. It is located in the southwest of town near the famous Sri Ramana Ashram.

Other Ashrams ASHRAMS

Side by side 7km west of town, just off the Krishnagiri road, are two ashrams that are places for retreat rather than permanent communities, both with good Arunachala views and personable young staff accustomed to foreigners. **Sri Anantha Niketan** (☎9444862276; gopi.chitra@yahoo.com; Periya Paliyapattu Village; by donations) has tree-shaded grounds, homey rooms and daily chanting in an attractive meditation hall. **Singing Heart Ashram** (☎9443969220; www.cosmicairport.com; Periya Paliyapattu Village; per person per day incl meals from ₹450; ⊙Oct-Mar) sits on a spacious, open site with simple rooms. You can join organised meditation retreats, or just participate in morning meditation, help with running the place and 'relax in the energy field'.

Sleeping & Eating

Many visitors prefer to stay in the less hectic Chengam Rd area, but there are also some typical temple-town options near the Arunachaleshwar Temple. During Karthikai Deepam (November/December) prices at some places multiply several times.

Hill View Residency HOTEL $

(☎9442712441; www.hillviewresidency.com; 120 Seshatri Mada St; r from ₹400, with AC from ₹750) Extremely good value, Hill View has large, clean, cool, marble-floored rooms round two small garden patios, up a lane off Chengam Rd. Upstairs under a big palm roof, **Tasty Café** (dishes ₹50-130; ⊙7am-10pm; wi-fi) does well-prepared Indian and Western food.

Arunachala Ramana Home HOTEL $

(☎236120; www.arunachalaramanahome.co.in; 70 Ramana Nagar; s/d ₹400/600, with AC r ₹1000; air-con) Basic, clean and friendly, this popular place is down a lane off Chengam Rd. It has a rooftop restaurant.

Hotel Ganesh HOTEL $

(☎226701; lingam100@indiatimes.com; 111A Big St; s/d ₹250/500, with AC d/tr ₹825/1210; air-con) Set 400m northeast of the Arunachaleshwar Temple's east gate. Some rooms are small and most have squat toilets, but they're clean enough, management is friendly and the inner courtyard balcony is pleasant. The sign atop the building says 'Hotel Kanna'.

Arunachala Inn HOTEL $$

(Hotel Arunachala; ☎228300; www.hotelarunachala.com; 5 Vada Sannathi St; s/d ₹525/770, with AC ₹880/1100, deluxe d ₹1687; air-con) This place right next to the Arunachaleshwar Temple's east entrance is clean and fine with pretentions to luxury in the marblesque floors and ugly furniture. Many of the slightly faded standard rooms are being upgraded to deluxe. **Hotel Sri Arul Jothi** (dishes ₹35-60; ⊙6.30am-10.30pm), the veg restaurant downstairs, has simple, very good, South Indian dishes.

Shanti Café CAFE $
(www.shanticafe.com; 115A Chengam Rd; food items ₹50-100, drinks ₹30-70; ⊙8.30am-8.30pm;) This relaxed cafe with floor-cushion seating, up a lane off Chengam Rd, is highly popular among short- and long-term visitors and serves wonderful croissants, cakes, pies, baguettes, omelettes, pancakes, juices, coffees, teas and breakfasts. Wi-fi is ₹25 per hour; there's also an **internet cafe** (⊙8.30am-2pm & 3.30-8pm) downstairs.

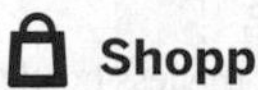

Shopping

Shantimalai Handicrafts Development Society HANDICRAFTS
(www.smhds.org; 83/1 Chengam Rd; ⊙8.30am-7pm Mon-Sat, 9am-2pm Sun) Attractive bedspreads, incense, oils, bangles, scarves and more, made by local village women.

Getting There & Around

A taxi to Puducherry with a two- to three-hour stop at Gingee costs around ₹2000.

The bus stand is in the north of town, 800m north of Arunachaleshwar Temple, and a ₹50 to ₹60 autorickshaw ride from the main ashram area.

Chennai ₹100 to ₹110, 3½ hours, every 15 minutes
Puducherry ₹63, three hours, about hourly
Trichy ₹120, five to six hours, 12 daily
Vellore ₹47, two hours, every 15 minutes

Gingee (Senji)

With three separate hilltop citadels and a 6km perimeter of cliffs and thick walls, the ruins of enormous **Gingee Fort** (Indian/foreigner ₹5/100; ⊙9am-5.30pm) poke out of the Tamil plain, 37km east of Tiruvannamalai, like castles misplaced by the *Lord of the Rings*. It was constructed mainly in the 16th century by the Vijayanagars and was later occupied by the Marathas, Mughals, French and finally the British before being abandoned in the 19th century.

Today the main road from Tiruvannamalai towards Puducherry slices through the fort, just before Gingee town. Of the three citadels, the easiest to reach, Krishnagiri, rises north of the road. To the south are the highest of the three, Rajagiri, and the most distant and least interesting, Chakklidurg.

Remains of numerous buildings stand in the lower parts of the site, especially at the foot of Rajagiri, where the main landmark of the old palace area is the white, restored, seven-storey Kalyana Mahal (Marriage Hall). Just east of the palace area is an 18th-century mosque, and southeast of that is the large, abandoned, 16th-century Venkataramana Temple.

It's a good hike to the top of Krishnagiri and even more so to the top of Rajagiri (more than 150m above the plain) and you need half a day to cover both hills. Start early and bring water.

Gingee is on the Tiruvannamalai–Puducherry bus route, with buses from Tiruvannamalai (₹20, 1½ hours) running about every half-hour. Get off at the fort to save a trip back out from Gingee town.

Puducherry (Pondicherry)

☎0413 / POP 241,773

Let's get something clear: if you came to Puducherry (formerly called Pondicherry and almost always referred to as 'Pondy') expecting a Provençal village on the Bay of Bengal, you're in for a disappointment, *mon ami*. Pondy is South India: honk-roar-haggle-honk South India. That said, the older part of this former French colony (where you'll probably spend most of your time) does

THE LINGAM OF FIRE

Legend has it Shiva appeared as the original lingam of fire on Mt Arunachala to restore light to the world after his consort Parvati had playfully plunged everything into darkness by closing Shiva's eyes. Each November/December full moon, the **Karthikai Deepam Festival** (statewide; ⊙Nov/Dec) celebrates this legend throughout India but becomes particularly significant at Tiruvannamalai. The lighting of a huge fire atop Mt Arunachala on the full moon night, from a 30m wick immersed in 3 tonnes of ghee, culminates a 10-day festival with nightly processions for which many hundreds of thousands of people converge on Tiruvannamalai. Huge crowds scale the mountain or circumnavigate its base. On the upward path, steps quickly give way to jagged, unstable rocks. The sun is relentless and the journey must be undertaken barefoot – none of which deters the thousands of pilgrims who joyfully make their way to the top and the abode of their deity.

have a lot of quiet, clean, shady, cobbled streets, lined with mustard-yellow colonial townhouses numbered in an almost logical manner. In fact, if you've come from Chennai or some of the inland cities, old Pondy may well seem a sea of tranquillity.

Puducherry was under French rule until 1954 and some people here still speak French (and English with French accents). Hotels, restaurants and 'lifestyle' shops sell a seductive vision of the French-subcontinental aesthetic, enhanced by Gallic creative types whose presence has in turn attracted Indian artists and designers. Thus Pondy's vibe: less faded colonial-era *ville,* more a bohemian-chic, New Age–cum–Old World node on the international travel trail. Part of the vibe stems from the presence of the internationally famous Sri Aurobindo Ashram and its offshoot just out of town, Auroville. These draw large numbers of spiritually minded visitors and are responsible for a lot of the creative artisanry. Enjoy the shopping, the French food (hello steak!), the beer (goodbye Tamil Nadu alcohol taxes – Pondy is a Union Territory), the sea air and, if you like, some yoga and meditation.

Puducherry is split from north to south by a partially covered canal. The more 'French' part of town is on the east side (towards the sea). Nehru (JN) St and Lal Bahadur Shastri St (better known as Rue Bussy) are the main east–west streets; Mahatma Gandhi (MG) Rd and Mission St (Cathedral St) are the chief north–south thoroughfares. Many streets change names as they go along and may also have English, French and Tamil names all at the same time.

Sights

French Quarter NEIGHBOURHOOD

Pocketed away just behind the seafront is a series of cobbled streets, white and mustard buildings in various states of romantic dishevelment, and a slight sense of Gallic glory gone by, otherwise known as the French Quarter. A do-it-yourself **heritage walk** through this area could start at the French Consulate near the north end of Goubert Ave, the seafront promenade. Head south then turn inland to shady **Bharathi Park**, with the neoclassical governor's residence, **Raj Nivas**, facing its north side. Return to the seafront at the **Gandhi Memorial**, pass the **Hôtel de Ville** (City Hall) and then it's a matter of pottering south through what's known as the 'white town' – Dumas, Romain Rolland, Suffren and Labourdonnais Sts. Quite a lot of restoration has been going on down here: if you're interested in Pondy's history and architectural heritage check out **INTACH Pondicherry** (www.intachpondicherry.org). The Tourist Info Bureau (p369) also details heritage walks on its website.

Seafront PROMENADE

(Goubert Ave) Pondy is a seaside town, but that doesn't make it a beach destination; the city's sand is a thin strip of dirty brown that slurps into a seawall of jagged rocks. But Goubert Ave (Beach Rd) is a killer stroll, especially at dawn and dusk when half the town takes a constitutional or romantic amble there. In a stroke of genius the city council has banned traffic here from 6pm to 7.30am.

There are a few sandy beaches north and south of town, but they're not places for sunbathing due to crowds of men and boys, nor for swimming due to possible undertow or rip tides.

Sri Aurobindo Ashram ASHRAM

(www.sriaurobindoashram.org; Marine St; ⏲ general visits 8am-noon & 2-6pm) Founded in 1926 by Sri Aurobindo and a French-born woman known as 'the Mother', this spiritual community now has about 1200 members who work in the ashram's many departments including its commercial sections and large education centre. Aurobindo's teachings focus on an 'integral yoga' as the path towards a 'supramental consciousness which will divinise human nature'. Devotees work in the world, rather than retreating from it.

General visits to the main ashram building on Marine St are cursory – you just see the flower-festooned samadhi of Aurobindo and the Mother, then the bookshop, then you leave. People staying in ashram guesthouses have access to other areas and activities. Collective meditation around the samadhi from 7.25pm to 7.50pm Monday, Tuesday, Wednesday and Friday is open to all.

The ashram's **Bureau Central** (☎2233604; bureaucentral@sriaurobindoashram.org; Ambour Salai; ⏲6am-8pm) has interesting exhibitions on the lives and teachings of Sri Aurobindo and the Mother.

Puducherry Museum MUSEUM

(St Louis St; Indian/foreigner ₹10/50; ⏲10am-1pm & 2-5pm Tue-Sun) Goodness knows how this cute little museum keeps its artefacts from rotting, considering there's a whole floor of

Puducherry (Pondicherry)

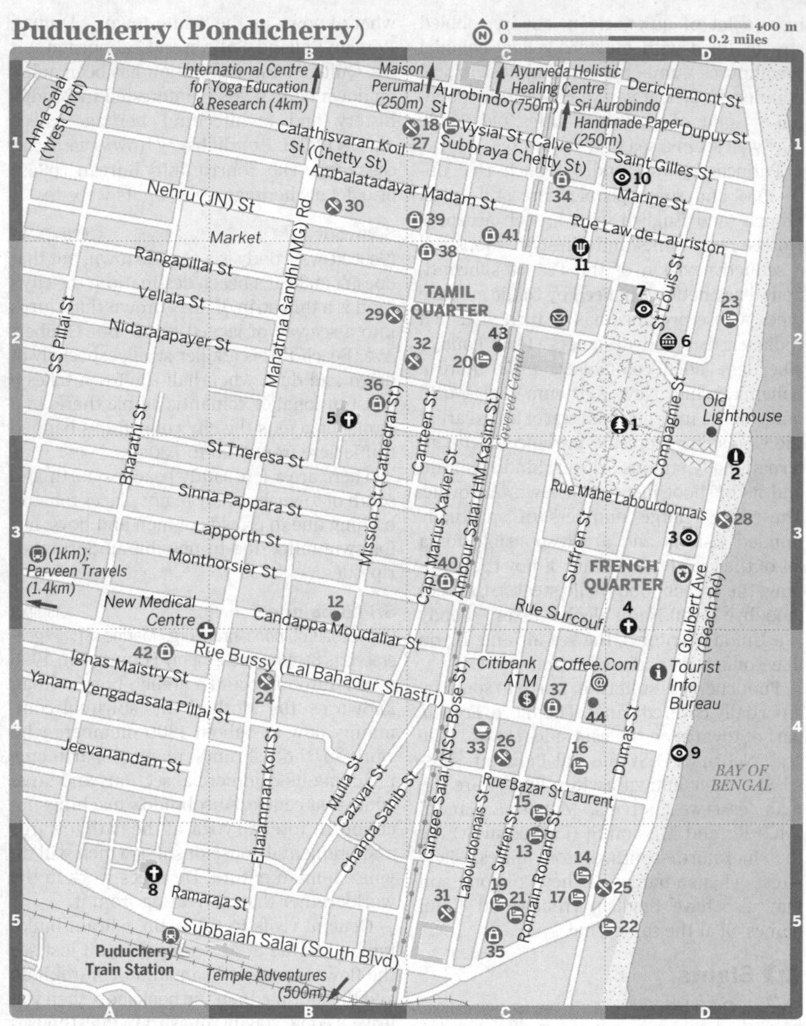

French-era furniture and decorations sitting in the South Indian humidity. On the ground floor look especially for the Chola, Vijayanagar and Nayak bronzes, and the pieces of ancient Greek and Spanish pottery and amphorae (storage vessels) excavated from Arikamedu, a once-major trading port a few kilometres south of Puducherry.

Sri Manakula Vinayagar Temple HINDU TEMPLE
(Manakula Vinayagar Koil St; ⌚5.45am-12.30pm & 4-9.30pm) Pondy may have more churches than most towns, but this is still India, and the Hindu faith still reigns supreme. Don't miss the chance to watch tourists, pilgrims and the curious get a head pat from the temple elephant at this temple dedicated to Ganesh. The temple also contains over 40 skilfully painted friezes.

Churches CHURCHES
Puducherry has one of the best collections of over-the-top cathedrals in India. *Merci,* French missionaries. **Our Lady of the Immaculate Conception Cathedral** (Mission St), completed in 1791, is a robin's-egg-blue-and-cloud-white typically Jesuit edifice in a

Puducherry (Pondicherry)

Sights

1	Bharathi Park	D2
2	Gandhi Memorial	D3
3	Hôtel de Ville	D3
4	Notre Dame des Anges	D3
5	Our Lady of the Immaculate Conception Cathedral	B2
6	Puducherry Museum	D2
7	Raj Nivas	D2
8	Sacred Heart Basilica	A5
9	Seafront	D4
10	Sri Aurobindo Ashram	D1
11	Sri Manakula Vinayagar Temple	C2

Activities, Courses & Tours

12	Sita	B3

Sleeping

13	Coloniale Heritage Guest House	C5
14	Dumas Guest House	C5
15	Gratitude	C4
16	Hotel De L'Orient	C4
17	Hotel de Pondichéry	C5
18	Kailash Guest House	C1
19	Les Hibiscus	C5
20	Meeranjali	C2
21	New Guest House	C5
22	Park Guest House	D5
23	Sea Side Guest House	D2

Eating

24	Baker Street	B4
25	Café de Flore	C5
26	Café des Arts	C4
	Carte Blanche Restaurant	(see 16)
	Kasha Ki Aasha	(see 40)
27	La Pasta	C1
28	Le Café	D3
	Le Club	(see 17)
	Le Hidesign	(see 38)
29	Nilgiri's	B2
30	Saravana Bhavan	B1
31	Satsanga	C5
32	Surguru	C2

Drinking & Nightlife

33	L'e-Space	C4

Shopping

34	Auroshikha Agarbathies	C1
35	Fabindia	C5
36	Focus the Book Shop	B2
37	Geethanjali	C4
38	Hidesign	C2
39	Kalki	C1
40	Kasha Ki Aasha	C3
41	La Boutique d'Auroville	C1
42	Libraire Kailash	A4

Information

43	Bureau Central	C2
44	Shanti Travel	C4

Goa-like Portuguese style, while the brown-and-white grandiosity of the **Sacred Heart Basilica** (Subbayah Salai) is set off by stained glass and a Gothic sense of proportion. The twin towers and dome of the mellow pink-and-cream **Notre Dame des Anges** (Dumas St), built in the 1850s, look sublime in the late-afternoon light. The smooth limestone interior was made using eggshells in the plaster.

Activities

Sita ARTS, COOKING

(☎9944016128; www.pondicherry-arts.com; 22 Candappa Moudaliar St; single class ₹250-1000) This energetic young Franco-Indian cultural centre runs a host of activities and classes for adults and kids, which visitors are welcome to join. You can try Indian or French cooking, *bharatanatyam* or Bollywood dance, *kolam* making, *mehndi* (henna 'tattoos'), yoga, ayurveda and more. For most activities,it's possible to do a single session.

Temple Adventures DIVING

(☎9940219449; www.templeadventures.com; 5 Veeramamunivar St, Colas Nagar; 1-day Discover Scuba Diving ₹7500, 2-dive day for qualified divers ₹5000; ⊙9am-6.30pm) The waters off Puducherry contain coral reefs and plenty of tropical fish. Experienced, multilingual Temple Adventures offers fun dives for qualified divers and a full range of PADI and NAUI diving courses, from beginners up. Best months: February to April and September to November.

Yoga & Ayurveda

You can practise (and study) yoga at Sri Aurobindo Ashram (p363) and Auroville. The **Ayurveda Holistic Healing Centre** (☎6537651; www.ayurojas.org; 6 Sengeniamman Koil St, Vazhakulam; ⊙9am-7.30pm) performs ayurvedic and varma-point treatments for all manner of ailments, and offers courses in yoga, ayurveda and varma. The **International Centre for Yoga Education & Research** (Ananda Ashram; ☎2241561; www.icyer.com; 16A Mettu St, Chinnamudaliarchavady,

Kottukuppam), 5km north of town, conducts annual six-month yoga-teacher-training courses and three-week introductory courses (₹550 including food and lodging).

Tours

Shanti Travel (p369) offers recommended two-hour **walking tours** (per person ₹400) of Puducherry with English- or French-speaking guides.

Festivals & Events

International Yoga Festival YOGA
(4-7 Jan) Puducherry's ashrams and yoga culture are put on show with workshops, demonstrations and music and dance events. The event attracts experts from all over India and beyond.

Bastille Day PARADE
(14 Jul) Street parades and a bit of French pomp and ceremony are part of the fun at this celebration.

Sleeping

If you've been saving for a special occasion, this is the place for it, because Puducherry's lodgings are as good as South India gets. Local heritage houses manage to combine colonial-era romanticism with comfort and, dare we say, French playfulness; many of these rooms would cost four or five times as much back in Europe. It's smart to book ahead if you're arriving at a weekend.

Sri Aurobindo Ashram (p363) runs several simple but clean guesthouses. They're primarily intended for ashram visitors, but many accept other guests who are willing to abide by their rules: 10.30pm curfew and no smoking, alcohol or drugs. Only some accept advance bookings. The ashram's Bureau Central (p363) has a list.

Kailash Guest House HOTEL $
(2224485; http://kailashguesthouse.in; 43 Vysial St; s/d ₹600/800, with AC d ₹1000;) The best value for money in this price range; Kailash has simple, super-clean rooms with well mosquito-proofed windows, and friendly management. It's geared to traveller needs, with communal areas, clothes-drying facilities and laundry service.

Park Guest House ASHRAM GUESTHOUSE $
(2233644; 1 Goubert Ave; r ₹600, with AC ₹800-900;) The most sought-after ashram guesthouse in town thanks to its wonderful seafront position. All front rooms face the sea and have a porch or balcony, and there's a large garden suitable for yoga or meditation. These are the best-value AC rooms in town. No advance bookings, though.

New Guest House ASHRAM GUESTHOUSE $
(2233634; newguesthouse@gmail.com; 64 Romain Rolland St; d/tr ₹300/450, r for 6 ₹850) Sparse, huge and packed with ashram faithful; this is a great spot for those who love the monastery cubicle school of lodging. You can book up to two months ahead.

★ **Les Hibiscus** HERITAGE GUESTHOUSE $$
(2227480; www.leshibiscus.in; 49 Suffren St; s/d incl breakfast ₹2200/2500;) Hibiscus has just four pristine, high-ceilinged rooms with gorgeous antique beds, coffee-makers and a mix of quaint Indian art and old-Pondy photos. The whole place is immaculately tasteful, the breakfast is fabulous, internet is free and management is genuinely friendly and helpful. Well worth booking ahead for.

Gratitude HERITAGE GUESTHOUSE $$
(9442065029; www.gratitudeheritage.in; 52 Romain Rolland St; s ₹3335-5448, d ₹3891-6671, all incl breakfast;) A wonderfully tranquil 19th-century house (no TVs, no children) with welcoming staff, Gratitude has been painstakingly restored to a state probably even more charming than the original. The eight good-sized, spotless rooms are set on two floors around a shady courtyard, and there's a lovely roof terrace. Free wi-fi.

Coloniale Heritage Guest House HERITAGE GUESTHOUSE $$
(2224720; http://colonialeheritage.com; 54 Romain Rolland St; r incl breakfast ₹2000-4000;) This colonial home with six comfy rooms is chock-full of character thanks to the owner's amazing collection of gem-studded Tanjore paintings, Ravi Varma lithographs and other 19th- and 20th-century South Indian art. Breakfast is served in a sunken patio next to the leafy garden. Free wi-fi.

Hotel de Pondichéry HERITAGE HOTEL $$
(2227409; www.hoteldepondicherry.com; 38 Dumas St; s ₹2000, d ₹2800-3800, all incl breakfast;) A heritage spot with comfy, quiet, high-ceilinged, colonial-style rooms and a dash of original modern art. The large front courtyard area houses the good restaurant, Le Club (p368). Staff are lovely and there's free wi-fi in the lobby.

Meeranjali HOMESTAY $$
(☎2334009; www.meeranjali.com; 9 Capitaine Marius Xavier St; r incl breakfast ₹2500-3000; ❄📶) This lovely modern town house was designed and built by its welcoming owners, who are full of good ideas on how to spend your time here. Rooms have comfy beds, good blue-tiled bathrooms and fine Burmese teak furniture. Free wi-fi.

Dumas Guest House HERITAGE GUESTHOUSE $$
(☎2225726; www.dumasguesthouse.com; 36 Dumas St; r ₹2400; ❄) All whitewash and dark wood, the antique-filled Dumas has real personality to which the odd patch of flaking paint kind of contributes. Enjoy the carved doors, quiet gardens, slightly quirky decor and friendly multilingual staff. All rooms have three beds.

Sea Side Guest House ASHRAM GUESTHOUSE $$
(☎2231700; seaside@aurosociety.org; 14 Goubert Ave; s ₹1208-1746, d ₹1396-1934, all incl breakfast; ❄📶) A cut above your typical ashram guesthouse, Sea Side has pristine, neat, freshly decorated rooms, and looks straight across the road to the sea. Sea-facing rooms have balconies. Advance bookings are accepted; wi-fi is ₹300 per 24 hours.

Hotel De L'Orient HERITAGE HOTEL $$$
(☎2343067; www.neemranahotels.com; 17 Romain Rolland St; r incl breakfast ₹3760-8056; ❄📶) A grand restored colonial mansion with breezy verandahs, charming rooms kitted out with antique furniture and *objets*, and a large, pretty courtyard at its heart. A place to get that old Pondy feel while enjoying polished service and French, Italian or creole (French-Indian) food in the courtyard **Carte Blanche Restaurant** (mains ₹250-400; ⏲7.15-10.30am, noon-6pm, 7-9.30pm).

Maison Perumal HERITAGE HOTEL $$$
(☎2227519; www.cghearth.com; 44 Perumal Koil St; r incl breakfast ₹9500; ❄📶) The old Tamil Quarter has almost as many mansions as the French Quarter but is off most tourists' radars. This recently renovated 200-year-old building has cool, pleasant rooms above two lovely pillared patios. The excellent Tamil/French **restaurant** (dinner ₹990, lunch mains ₹300-400) cooks everything to order from fresh ingredients. Staff are charming and wi-fi is free. From March to Christmas rates dip by 30% or more.

Eating

Puducherry is a culinary highlight of Tamil Nadu; you get good South Indian cooking plus several restaurants specialising in well-prepped French and Italian cuisine. If you've been missing cheese or have a hankering for pâté, you're in luck, and *everyone* in the French quarter offers crepes and good brewed coffee.

Baker Street CAFE $
(123 Rue Bussy; items ₹40-130; ⏲7am-10pm) A very popular upmarket, French-style bakery with delectable cakes, croissants and eclairs. Baguettes, brownies and quiches aren't bad either. Eat in or take away.

Surguru SOUTH INDIAN $
(235 (old 99) Mission St; mains ₹65-110; ⏲7.30am-10.30pm) Simple South Indian served in a relatively posh setting. Surguru is the fix for thali and dosa addicts who like their veg accompanied by good strong AC. Thali is available at lunchtime.

Saravana Bhavan SOUTH INDIAN $
(Hotel Pondicherry; Nehru St; dishes ₹30-120; ⏲11am-10.30pm) A clean, AC setting with good, cheap South Indian food – all the thalis, dosas and *vadas* you could want.

★ **Satsanga** MULTICUISINE $$
(☎2225867; www.satsanga.co.in; 54 Labourdonnais St; mains ₹150-340; ⏲8am-11pm) Deservedly popular for its excellent Continental cuisine, Satsanga, like most places in this genre, offers a full Indian menu as well. It's especially strong on steaks, fish, prawns and pâtés. There are good vegetarian options too, and the homemade bread and butter goes down a treat. Some have complained of slow service, but we found it fine. For a table on the breezy terrace, it's a good idea to book.

Café des Arts CAFE $$
(Labourdonnais St; light dishes ₹100-190; ⏲8.30am-7pm Mon & Wed-Fri, 9am-5pm Sat & Sun; 📶) Good brekky and coffee, free wi-fi and a nice outdoor/verandah setting outside a small gallery.

Café de Flore CAFE $$
(Maison de Colombani, 37 Dumas St; dishes ₹90-290; ⏲8.30am-7.30pm) In the gallery and building of Pondy's Alliance Française, on an airy verandah overlooking a grassy garden, you'll find mocktails, great coffee, salads, *croques monsieur*, pasta and vegie burgers.

Kasha Ki Aasha CAFE $$

(23 Rue Surcouf; mains ₹165-295; ⏲8am-7pm) You'll get a great pancake breakfast, good lunches and delicious cakes on the pretty rooftop of this colonial-house-cum-craft-shop-cum-cafe. Fusion food includes chips with chutney, 'European-style thali' and 'Indian enchilada'. The heat in some dishes has been dialled back for Western tastes, but it's all tasty.

Le Café CAFE $$

(Goubert Ave; dishes ₹30-210; ⏲24hr) This seafront spot is good for baguettes, croissants, salads, cake and organic South Indian coffee (hot or iced), plus welcome fresh breezes from the Bay of Bengal. It's popular, so sometimes you have to wait for, or share, a table.

La Pasta ITALIAN $$

(http://lapastapondy.blogspot.com; 55 Vysial St; mains ₹125-350; ⏲noon-2pm & 6-9.30pm Tue-Sun) Pasta aficionados, make a little pilgrimage to this spot with just three check-cloth tables, where a real Italian whips up her own yummy sauces and concocts her own perfect pasta in an open kitchen as big as the dining area. No alcohol: it's all about the food, and she even has wholemeal options.

Le Club CONTINENTAL, INDIAN $$$

(38 Dumas St; mains ₹330-440; ⏲8.30am-10.30pm) The steaks (with sauces such as Béarnaise or blue cheese), pizzas and crepes are all top-class at this romantically lit garden restaurant. Tempting local options include creole prawn curry and Malabar-style fish, and there are plenty of cocktails and even wine to go with your meal.

Self-Catering

Nilgiri's SUPERMARKET

(23 Rangapillai St; ⏲9.30am-9pm) A well-stocked place to shop for groceries (and toiletries) in AC comfort.

Drinking & Nightlife

Although this is one of the better spots in Tamil Nadu to sink a beer, closing time is a decidedly un-Gallic 11pm. Despite low taxes on alcohol, you'll really only find cheap beer in 'liquor shops' or the darkened bars attached to them.

L'e-Space CAFE, BAR

(2 Labourdonnais St; cocktails ₹200, pancakes ₹100; ⏲5-11pm) A quirky little semi-open-air upstairs cafe that serves decent cocktails and where some people may be away on something other than alcohol. Locals and tourists congregate here, and during the season it can be a social traveller spot.

Shopping

With all the yoga yuppies congregating here, Pondy specialises in the boutique-chic-meets-Indian-bazaar school of fashion and souvenirs, and there is some appealing and original stuff, quite a lot of it produced by Sri Aurobindo Ashram or Auroville.

★ **Kalki** CLOTHING, ACCESSORIES

(134 Mission St; ⏲9.30am-8.30pm) Beautiful, jewel-coloured silk and cotton clothes, as well as incense, essential oils, handmade-paper products and more, nearly all made at Auroville.

Fabindia TEXTILES

(www.fabindia.com; 59 Suffren St; ⏲10am-8pm) This shop has a good variety of silk, cotton and wool clothes in Indian and Western styles, plus quality tablecloths and bags, predominantly made by villagers using traditional craft techniques but with a contemporary feel. The Fabindia chain has been in operation since 1960, and one of its selling points is its emphasis on handmade products and promoting rural employment.

La Boutique d'Auroville HANDICRAFTS

(38 Nehru St; ⏲9.30am-1pm & 3.30-8pm Mon-Sat) It's fun browsing through the crafts here, including jewellery, clothes, slippers and pretty wooden trays.

Hidesign BAGS

(www.hidesign.com; 69 Nehru St; ⏲9am-10pm) Established in Pondy in the 1970s, Hidesign sells beautifully made designer leather bags, briefcases, purses and belts in a range of colours, at very reasonable prices for what you get. It now has outlets in many countries. The top-floor cafe, **Le Hidesign** (69 Nehru St; mains ₹135-170; ⏲9.30am-9.30pm; wi-fi), serves delicious tapas and excellent coffee.

Auroshikha Agarbathies INCENSE

(17 Gingee Salai; ⏲8.30am-12.30pm & 3-7pm Tue-Sun) A wonderful array of incense, perfumed candles and essential oils, produced by Sri Aurobindo Ashram.

Geethanjali ANTIQUES

(20 Rue Bussy; ⏲9am-8.30pm) The sort of place where Indiana Jones gets the sweats, this antique and curio shop sells sculptures, carved doors, wooden chests, paintings and

furniture culled from Puducherry's colonial and even pre-colonial history. It ships to Europe for ₹12,000 per cubic metre and can obtain export permits for free.

Kasha Ki Aasha CLOTHING, HANDICRAFTS
(23 Rue Surcouf; 8am-7pm) Fabulous fabrics, gorgeous garments and comfy leather sandals are sourced directly from their makers and sold by an all-female staff in a lovely colonial-era house.

Focus the Book Shop BOOKS
(204 Mission St; 9.30am-1.30pm & 3.30-9pm Mon-Sat) A great collection of India-related and other books in English (including Lonely Planet guides).

Libraire Kailash BOOKS
(169 Rue Bussy; 9am-1pm & 3-7.30pm Mon-Sat) Good selection of India and Asia titles in French.

Information

ATMs are plentiful and there are numerous currency-exchange offices on Mission St near the corner of Nehru St.

Rue Bussy between Bharathi St and MG Rd is packed with clinics and pharmacies.

Citibank ATM (22 Rue Bussy) This ATM can dispense ₹30,000 in one go, saving on bank charges.

Coffee.Com (11A Romain Rolland St; per hr ₹80; 9am-10pm) A genuine internet cafe, with good coffee and light food (₹60 to ₹100) to help your browsing.

New Medical Centre (2225289; www.nmcpondy.com; 470 MG Rd; 24hr) Recommended private clinic and hospital.

Shanti Travel (4210401; www.shantitravel.com; 13 Romain Rolland St; 10am-7pm) Professional agency offering transport ticketing, walking tours, cultural activities, day trips and Chennai airport pick-ups.

Tourist Info Bureau (2339497; http://tourism.puducherry.gov.in; 40 Goubert Ave; 9am-6pm) Has enthusiastic staff and the website has some worthwhile maps.

Getting There & Away

BUS

The **bus stand** (Maraimalai Adigal Salai) is in the west of town, 2km from the French Quarter. Private bus companies, running mostly overnight to various destinations, have offices along Maraimalai Adigal Salai west of the bus stand. The only service to Kodaikanal (₹600, eight hours) is an 11pm semisleeper with **Parveen Travels** (www.parveentravels.com; 288 Maraimalai Adigal Salai).

TRAIN

Puducherry station has only a few services. Two daily trains run to Chennai Egmore, with unreserved seating only (₹28 to ₹53, four to five hours). You can connect at Villupuram, 38km west of Puducherry, for many more services north and south. Puducherry station has a computerised booking office for trains throughout India.

Getting Around

One of the best ways to get around Pondy's flat streets is by walking. Autorickshaws are plentiful. Official metered fares are ₹20 for up to 2km and ₹1 for each further 100m, which should mean ₹25 maximum from bus stand to French Quarter. If drivers refuse to use their meters, you'll probably have to pay ₹50 or ₹60 for that trip.

Auroville

0413 / POP 2249

Auroville is one of those ideas that anyone with idealistic leanings will love: an international community dedicated to peace, harmony, sustainable living and 'divine consciousness', where people from around the globe, ignoring creed, colour and nationality, work together to build a universal, cash-free, non-religious township and realise good old human unity.

BUSES FROM PUDUCHERRY (PONDICHERRY) BUS STAND

DESTINATION	FARE (₹)	DURATION (HR)	FREQUENCY (DAILY)
Bengaluru	188-200 (Volvo AC 500-600)	8	6 (Volvo AC 8.30am, 10.30pm)
Chennai	97 (Volvo AC 190)	4	124 (25 Volvo AC)
Chidambaram	42	2½	40
Kumbakonam	80	4	6
Mamallapuram	50	2	70
Tiruvannamalai	63	3	11
Trichy	138	5	5

Making reality out of such a dream would never be easy. Imagine over 100 small settlements scattered across an area of Tamil countryside, with 2100 residents of more than 40 nationalities. Nearly 60% of Aurovillians are foreign, and most new members require more funds than most Indians are ever likely to have. Outside opinions of Auroville's inhabitants range from admiration to accusations of self-indulgent escapism. But the vibe you will receive on a visit is likely to be positive, and the energy driving the place is palpable.

Some 12km northwest of downtown Puducherry, Auroville was founded in 1968 on the inspiration of 'the Mother', co-founder of Puducherry's Sri Aurobindo Ashram, and her philosophy still guides it. Aurovillians run a huge variety of projects ranging from schools and IT to organic farming, renewable energy and handicrafts production, and they employ at least 4000 people from nearby villages.

The **Auroville website** (www.auroville.org) is an encyclopedic resource.

Sights & Activities

Auroville in general is not geared for tourism – most inhabitants are just busy getting on with their lives – but it does have a good **Visitors Centre** (2622239; 9am-6pm) with information services, exhibitions and a few shops selling Auroville products. You can buy a handbook and map here, and after watching a 10-minute video you can get a pass for external viewing of the **Matrimandir** (passes issued 9.30am-12.30pm daily & 2-4pm Mon-Sat), Auroville's 'soul', a 1km walk away through the woodlands.

The large, golden, almost spherical Matrimindir has been likened to a golf ball or a UFO. You might equally feel that its grand simplicity of form, surrounded by pristine green parkland, does indeed evoke the divine consciousness it's intended to represent. The orb's main inner chamber, lined with white marble, houses a large glass crystal that suffuses a beam of sunlight around the chamber. It's conceived as a place for individual silent concentration and if, after viewing the Matrimandir from the gardens, you want to spend time inside, you must make a reservation at least one day ahead at the **Matrimandir access office** (2622268; Visitors Centre; 10-11am & 2-3pm Wed-Mon).

Visitors are quite free to wander round Auroville's network of roads and tracks and look at some of the unusual and original buildings. It's a large area, about 20 sq km, but with two million trees planted since Auroville's foundation it has an attractive forested ambience.

If you're interested in getting to know more about Auroville, they recommend you stay at least 10 days and join one of their introduction programs or retreats. To get seriously involved, you normally need to come as a volunteer, in any of a wide variety of programs, usually for two to 12 months.The **Auroville Guest Service** (2622675; www.aurovilleguestservice.org; Solar Kitchen Bldg, 2km east of Visitors Centre; 9.30am-12.45am Mon-Sat) provides information and help on active participation.

Sleeping & Eating

Auroville has over 40 **guesthouses** (per person ₹300-1000) of varying comfort levels, offering from two to 46 beds. You can book them through the **Guest Accommodation Service** (2622704; www.aurovilleguesthouses.org; Visitors Centre; 9.30am-12.30pm & 2-5pm) or directly with individual guesthouses. For the peak seasons, December to March and August and September, reservations three or four months ahead are advised.

TYPICALLY TAMIL FESTIVALS

As well as local festivals (often temple-centred) and national ones that are celebrated here, Tamil Nadu has a couple of important state-wide festivals of its own.

Pongal (statewide; mid-Jan), the harvest festival, is held over four days in mid-January and is one of the year's most important occasions for families to get together. It's named after a Tamil rice-and-lentil dish cooked at this time in new clay pots. For many, the celebrations begin with temple rituals, followed by family gatherings. Later it's the animals, especially cows, that are honoured for their contribution to the harvest.

Held during full moon in November/December, Karthikai Deepam (p362) is Tamil Nadu's 'festival of lights'. It is celebrated throughout the state with earthenware lamps and firecrackers, but the best place to see it is Tiruvannamalai, where the legend began.

The **Right Path Cafe** (Visitors Centre; mains ₹60-340; ⏰12.15-3pm & 6.30-9pm) serves decent Indian and Western food.

Getting There & Away

The main turning to Auroville from the East Coast Rd is at Periyar Mudaliarchavadi village, 6km north of Puducherry. From there it's about 6km west to the Visitors Centre. An autorickshaw one way from Puducherry is about ₹250, or you could take a Kottukuppam bus northbound on Ambour Salai to the Auroville turnoff (₹6), then an autorickshaw for ₹150. A good way to explore Auroville used to be by rented two-wheeler from outlets on and around northern MG Rd and Mission St in Puducherry, but the Puducherry authorities banned such rentals in 2012. If they relent, expect to pay around ₹50/150/250 per day for a bicycle/scooter/motorbike.

CENTRAL TAMIL NADU

Chidambaram

☎ 04144 / POP 82,458

There's basically one reason to visit here: the great temple complex of Nataraja, Shiva as the Dancer of the Universe. One of the holiest of all Shiva sites, this also happens to be a Dravidian architectural highlight.

Of the town's many festivals, the two largest are the 10-day **chariot festivals** in June/July and December/January. In February/March the five-day **Natyanjali Dance Festival** attracts classical dancers from all over India to the Nataraja Temple.

Most accommodation is close to the temple or the bus stand (500m southeast of the temple). The train station is about 1km further southeast.

Sights

★Nataraja Temple HINDU TEMPLE

(⏰inner compound 6am-noon & 4.30-10pm) The legend goes: one day Shiva and Kali got into a dance-off that was judged by Vishnu. Shiva dropped an earring and picked it up with his foot, a move that Kali could not duplicate, so Shiva won the title Nataraja (Lord of the Dance). It is in this form that he is worshipped at this great temple, which draws an endless stream of pilgrims and worshippers. The temple was erected during Chola times (Chidambaram was a Chola capital), but the shrines at its heart date back to at least the 6th century.

The high-walled 22-hectare complex has four towering *gopurams* decked out in schizophrenic Dravidian stone and stucco work. The main entrance is through the east *gopuram,* off East Car St. In its passageway are carved the 108 sacred positions of classical Tamil dance. To your right through the *gopuram* are the 1000-pillared **Raja Sabha** (King's Hall; ⏰festival days), and the large temple tank, the **Sivaganga**.

The central compound (no cameras allowed) is entered from the east. In its southern part (left from the entrance) is the **Nritta Sabha** (Dance Hall), in the form of a chariot with 56 very fine carved pillars. Some say this is the very spot where Shiva outdanced Kali.

Through a door north of the Nritta Sabha you enter the inner courtyard. In front of you is the **Kanaka Sabha**, a pavilion where many temple rituals are performed. At *puja* times devotees crowd into and around the pavilion to witness the rites performed by the temple's hereditary Brahmin priests, the Dikshithars, who shave off some of their hair but grow the rest of it long and tie it into topknots.

Behind (north of) the Kanaka Sabha is the innermost sanctum, the golden-roofed **Chit Sabha**, which holds the temple's central bronze image of Nataraja – Shiva the cosmic dancer, ending one cycle of creation, beginning another and uniting all opposites.

Priests may offer to guide you around the temple complex. Since they work as a kind of cooperative to fund the temple, you may wish to support this magnificent building by hiring one (for anything between ₹30 and ₹300, depending on their language skills and knowledge).

Sleeping & Eating

Many cheap pilgrims' lodges are clustered around the temple, but some of these are pretty dire. If there's anywhere really nice to stay in Chidambaram, we haven't found it yet. There are lots of cheap veg eats in the area surrounding the temple, but the best places to eat are in hotels.

Hotel Saradharam HOTEL $$

(☎221336; www.hotelsaradharam.co.in; 19 VGP St; r incl breakfast ₹990, with AC ₹2100; ❄📶) The busy, friendly Saradharam is as good as it gets, and is conveniently located across from the bus stand. It's a bit worn but comfortable enough, and a welcome respite from the frenzy of the town centre. Breakfast is

OFF THE BEATEN TRACK

TRANQUIL TRANQUEBAR

South of Chidambaram the many-armed delta of the Cauvery River stretches 180km along the coast and deep into the hinterland. The Cauvery is the beating heart of Tamil agriculture and its valley was the heartland of the Chola empire. Today the delta is one of the prettiest, poorest and most traditional parts of Tamil Nadu.

Easily the most appealing base is the little coastal town of Tharangambadi, still mostly known by its old name Tranquebar. A great place to recharge from the sweaty, crowded towns inland, this former Danish colony is quiet, orderly, pretty and set right on a long sandy beach with a few fishing boats and delicious sea breezes. The old part of town inside the 1791 Landporten gate makes an enjoyable stroll, and has seen a lot of restoration since the 2004 tsunami, which killed about 800 people here. INTACH Pondicherry (p363) has an excellent downloadable map. The old Danish fort, **Dansborg** (Indian/foreigner ₹5/50, camera/video ₹30/100; ⌚10am-1pm & 2-5.30pm Sat-Thu), dates from 1624 and contains an interesting little museum. Other notable buildings include **New Jerusalem Church** (Tamil Evangelical Lutheran Church; King's St), an interesting mix of Indian and European styles built in 1718, and the 14th-century beachside **Masilamani Nathar Temple**, recently repainted in kaleidoscopic colours.

All accommodation is run by the **Bungalow on the Beach** (☎04364-288065; http://neemranahotels.com; 24 King's St; r incl breakfast ₹3600-7195, budget r ₹990; ❄🏊), in the former residence of the British administrator (Denmark sold Tranquebar to the British East India Company in 1845). This amounts to 17 lovely heritage-style rooms in the main building and two other locations in town, plus five clean, sizeable, budget rooms in the Hotel Tamil Nadu, opposite the main building. All rooms are AC. The main building has a lovely swimming pool and a good multicuisine **restaurant** (mains ₹150-250; ⌚7.30-9.30am, 12.30-2.30pm, 7.30-9.30pm). For weekends and holidays you should book ahead.

Tranquebar is a good base for exploring the delta area. At Velankanni, 47km south, the **Basilica of Our Lady of Health** stands where a young buttermilk boy glimpsed the Virgin Mary in the 16th century. The Virgin's image supposedly has curative powers and this is a big pilgrimage spot, with some distinctly Hindu styles of worship. A 10-day festival culminates on 8 September. Tamil Nadu's largest temple chariot is hauled around Thiruvarur during the Thyagararaja Temple's 10-day car festival in April/May.

Buses in this region are often extremely crowded, but Tranquebar has regular connections with Chidambaram (₹23, two hours, hourly) and Karaikal (₹11, 30 minutes, half-hourly). From Karaikal there are buses to Kumbakonam (₹26, 2¼ hours, 36 daily), Thanjavur (₹68, 3½ hours, three daily) and Puducherry (₹65, four hours, five daily).

a good buffet, there's free wi-fi in the lobby, and the hotel has three restaurants – two vegetarian places plus the good multicuisine, AC **Anupallavi** (mains ₹145-280; ⌚7-10am, noon-3pm, 6-10.30pm).

Hotel Akshaya HOTEL **$$**
(☎220192; www.hotel-akshaya.com; 17-18 East Car St; r incl breakfast ₹1090, with AC ₹2050-2400; ❄) Close to the temple, this hotel has a wide range of rooms in various states of preservation. Some non-AC rooms are in better condition than some AC ones. The **Annapoorani Restaurant** (mains ₹65-90; ⌚7-10am, 11am-3pm, 6-9.30pm) here does an excellent ₹75 South Indian lunch and other good vegetarian fare. Next door, **Dravidian Handicrafts** (www.dravidiansculpturescom; 9 East Sannathi) sells quality reproduction bronzes.

ℹ Information

ICICI Bank ATM (Hotel Saradharam, VGP St)

ℹ Getting There & Away

Buses head to Chennai (₹140, six hours) every half-hour, most going via Puducherry (₹42, 2½ hours). Other destinations include Kumbakonam (₹48, 2½ hours, every 20 minutes), Thanjavur (₹90, four hours, every 30 minutes) and Tranquebar (Tharangambadi; ₹23, two hours, hourly). Universal Travels, opposite the bus stand, has three daily comfortable Volvo AC departures to Chennai (₹450).

Three or more daily trains head to Trichy (2nd-class/3AC/2AC ₹61/277/610, 3½ hours) via Kumbakonam and Thanjavur, and five to Chennai (₹78/362/610, 5½ hours).

Kumbakonam

☎ 0435 / POP 140,113

At first glance Kumbakonam is another Indian junction town, but then you notice the dozens of colourful *gopurams* pointing skyward from Kumbakonam's 18 temples, a reminder that this was once a seat of medieval South Indian power. With two World Heritage–listed Chola temples nearby, it's worth staying at least one night.

Sights

Most of the temples are dedicated to Shiva or Vishnu. All are open from 6.30am to 12.30pm and 4.30pm to 8.30pm, with free admission.

The largest Vishnu temple, with a 45m-high eastern *gopuram* as its main entrance, is **Sarangapani Temple** (no photography allowed inside). Past the temple cowshed, another *gopuram* and a pillared hall you reach the inner sanctuary, a 12th-century Chola creation, which is given a chariot appearance by large carved elephants, horses and wheels.

Kumbeshwara Temple, entered via a nine-storey *gopuram*, is the largest Shiva temple. It dates from the 17th and 18th centuries and contains a lingam said to have been made by Shiva himself when he mixed the nectar of immortality with sand.

The **Nageshwara Temple**, founded by the Cholas in 886, is Kumbakonam's oldest temple, and is dedicated to Shiva in the guise of Nagaraja, the serpent king. On three days of the year (in April or May) the sun's rays fall on the lingam..

The huge **Mahamaham Tank**, surrounded by 17 pavilions, is one of Kumbakonam's most sacred sites. It's believed that every 12 years the waters of the Ganges flow into the tank, and at this time a festival is held; the next is due in 2016.

Sleeping & Eating

Pandian Hotel HOTEL $
(☎2430397; 52 Sarangapani East Sannathi St; s/d ₹294/473, d with AC ₹990; ❄) It feels a bit institutional, but in general you're getting fair value at this clean-enough budget standby.

Hotel Raya's HOTEL $$
(☎2423170; www.hotelrayas.com; 18 Head Post Office Rd; r ₹990, with AC ₹1320-2280; ❄) Friendly service and reliably spacious, clean rooms make this your best lodging option in town. They have a convenient car service for out-of-town trips. **Sathars Restaurant** (mains ₹85-175; ⏰11.30am-11.30pm) here does good veg and nonveg fare in clean surroundings.

Hotel Kanishka HOTEL $$
(☎2425231; 18/450 Ayekulam Rd; r ₹770-880, AC ₹1100-1238; ❄📶) A cheerful place with smallish, simple but stylish rooms with yellow or pink feature walls. It's owned by a young couple who keep the hotel family-friendly. Free wi-fi in the reception area.

Paradise Resort RESORT $$$
(☎3291354; www.paradiseresortindia.com; Tanjore Main Rd, Darasuram; s ₹5396-10,193, d ₹5996-10,193; ❄📶🏊) Five kilometres west of downtown, this charming resort occupies large, lush grounds that even include a small village. The luxurious rooms have antique doors, carved wood furnishings and lovely big bathrooms. You can enjoy cooking demos, bullock-cart rides, ayurveda and yoga, and the high-class multicuisine restaurant has some great South Indian specialities.

Hotel Sri Venkkatramana INDIAN $
(TSR Big St; thalis ₹50-65; ⏰5.30am-10pm Mon-Sat) Serves good fresh veg food and is very popular with locals.

Taj Samudra INDIAN $$
(80 Nageswaran South St; mains ₹100-170; ⏰11am-3pm & 7-11pm) Here you can get tasty veg and nonveg dishes from all over India, in neat, even stylish surroundings – and the pictures on the menu and screen will help if you're not familiar with their names!

Information

Speed Systems (Sarangapani East St; internet per hr ₹20; ⏰9.30am-9.30pm) Take your passport.

Getting There & Away

Eleven daily trains head to Thanjavur (2nd-class/3AC/2AC ₹35/218/610, 30 minutes to one hour) and Trichy (₹46/218/610, two to 2½ hours). Four daily trains to/from Chennai Egmore include the overnight Rock Fort Express (sleeper/3AC/2AC/1AC ₹191/524/785/1340, 9½ hours), via Thanjavur and Trichy, and the daytime Chennai Express/Trichy Express (₹158/428/635/1075, six to seven hours).

Government buses from the **bus stand**:

Chennai ₹156 to ₹230, seven to eight hours, every 15 minutes

Chidambaram ₹48, 2½ hours, every 20 minutes

Karaikal ₹26, 2¼ hours, every 30 minutes

Thanjavur ₹29, 1½ hours, every 10 minutes

Kumbakonam

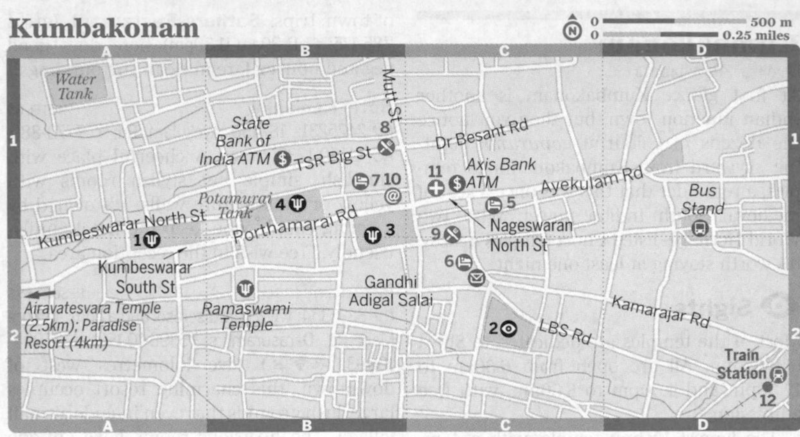

Kumbakonam

Sights

1 Kumbeshwara Temple A2
2 Mahamaham Tank C2
3 Nageshwara Temple B1
4 Sarangapani Temple B1

Sleeping

5 Hotel Kanishka C1
6 Hotel Raya's C2
7 Pandian Hotel B1

Eating

8 Hotel Sri Venkkatramana B1
Sathars Restaurant .... (see 6)
9 Taj Samudra C1

Information

10 Speed Systems B1
11 STH Hospital C1

Transport

12 Train Station D2

Thanjavur (Tanjore)

04362 / POP 222,619

Here are the ochre foundation blocks of perhaps the most remarkable civilisation of Dravidian history, one of the few kingdoms to expand Hinduism beyond India, a bedrock for aesthetic styles that spread from Madurai to the Mekong. A dizzying historical legacy was forged from Thanjavur, capital of the great Chola Empire during its heyday, which is today...a hectic, crowded, noisy, modern Indian town. But the past is still very much present: every day thousands of people still worship at the Cholas' grand Brihadishwara Temple, and Thanjavur's labyrinthine royal palace preserves memories of other powerful dynasties from later centuries.

Sights

★Brihadishwara Temple HINDU TEMPLE

(admission free; 6am-8.30pm) Come here twice: in the morning, when the tawny granite begins to assert its dominance over the white dawn sunshine, and in the evening, when the rocks capture a hot palette of reds, oranges, yellows and pinks on the crowning glory of Chola temple architecture. The World Heritage–listed Brihadishwara Temple was built between 1003 and 1010 by Rajaraja I (whose name means 'king of kings'), a monarch so organised he had the names and addresses of all his dancers, musicians, barbers and poets inscribed into the temple wall. The outer fortifications were put up by Thanjavur's later Nayak and British regimes.

You enter through a Nayak gate, followed by two original *gopurams* with elaborate stucco sculptures. You'll often find the temple elephant below one of the *gopurams*, dispensing good luck with a dab of his trunk to anyone who puts a rupee in it. Several shrines are dotted around the extensive grassy areas of the walled temple compound, including one with one of India's largest statues of Nandi (Shiva's sacred bull) facing the main temple building. Cut from a single rock, this 16th-century Nayak creation is 6m long.

A long, columned assembly hall leads to the central shrine with its 4m-high Shiva lingam, beneath the superb 61m-high *vimana* (tower). The assembly hall's southern steps are flanked by two huge *dvarapalas* (temple guardians). Many lovely, graceful deity images stand in niches around the *vimana's* lower levels, including Shiva emerging from the lingam (beside the southern steps); Shiva as the beggar Bhikshatana (first image, south side); Harihara (half Shiva, half Vishnu) on the west wall; and Ardhanarishvara (Shiva as half-man, half-woman), leaning on Nandi, on the north side. Set between the deity images are panels showing positions of classical dance.

The compound also contains a worthwhile interpretation centre along the south wall and, in the colonnade along the west and north walls, hundreds more linga as well as some good Nayak-era murals. North of the temple compound, but still within the outer fortifications, is a park containing the **Sivaganga tank** and 18th-century **Schwartz's Church**.

★Royal Palace PALACE

(Indian/foreigner/camera ₹10/50/30; 9am-5pm) Thanjavur's royal palace is a mixed bag of decrepitude and renovation, superb art and random royal paraphernalia, with a frequent whiff of dung and decay. The labyrinthine complex was constructed partly by the Nayaks who took over Thanjavur in 1535, and partly by a local Maratha dynasty that ruled from 1676 to 1855.

Seven different sections of the palace can be visited, and you need four separate tickets to see them all! The two don't-miss sections are the Art Gallery and Saraswati Mahal Library Museum. The main entrance is from the north, via a lane off East Main St. On the way in you'll find the ticket office for the Maratha Palace Museum, which comprises three of the seven sections: the Mahratta Dharbar Hall, the bell tower and the Saarjah Madi (this last under reconstruction at research time).

Past this ticket office, a passage to the left leads to, first, the **Royal Palace Museum** (admission ₹1; 9am-6pm), a small miscellany of sculptures, weaponry, elephant bells and rajas' headgear; second, the **Maharaja Serfoji Memorial Hall** (admission ₹4; 9am-6pm), commemorating the enlightened Maratha scholar-king Serfoji II (1798–1832), with a better miscellany overlooking a once-splendid, now overgrown courtyard; and third, the **Mahratta Dharbar Hall**, where Maratha rulers gave audience in a pavilion adorned with colourful murals, including their own portraits behind the dais and hunting scenes on the north wall.

As you exit the passage from the above, the **Saraswati Mahal Library Museum** (admission free; 10am-1pm & 1.30-5.30pm) (no photos allowed) is on your left. Perhaps Serfoji II's greatest contribution to posterity, this is testimony both to the 19th-century obsession with knowledge accumulation and to an eclectic mind that collected prints of Chinese torture methods, Audubon-style paintings of Indian flora and fauna, and sketches of the London skyline. Serfoji amassed more than 65,000 books and 50,000 palm-leaf and paper manuscripts in Indian and European languages, though these aren't included in the exhibit.

Exiting the library, turn left again for the **Art Gallery** (Indian/foreigner ₹7/60, camera ₹30/100; 9am-1pm & 3-6pm). Set around the courtyard of the Nayak palace, this contains a large collection of superb, mainly Chola, bronzes and stone carvings. One of the rooms is the Nayak Durbar Hall, built in 1600, which also contains a statue of Serfoji II. From the courtyard, steps lead about halfway up a large *gopuram*-like tower affording good views over Thanjavur. The Maratha bell tower, outside the Art Gallery entrance, can be climbed with your Palace Museum ticket.

Festivals & Events

Thyagaraja Aradhana MUSIC FESTIVAL

(Jan) At Thiruvaiyaru, 13km north of Thanjavur, this important eight-day Carnatic music festival honours the saint and composer Thyagaraja.

Sleeping

Hotel Ramnath HOTEL $

(272567; hotel_ramnath@yahoo.com; 1335 South Rampart; r ₹900, with AC ₹1200;) The best of a bunch of places facing the local bus stand downtown (the attendant noise is not as bad as you might expect), the Ramnath is a decent 'upmarket budget' option with clean, not very big, pine-furnished rooms.

Hotel Valli HOTEL $

(231580; www.hotelvalli.com; 2948 MKM Rd; s ₹504, d ₹605-715, r with AC ₹1463;) Near the train station, green-painted Valli has good-value, spick-and-span rooms. Staff are personable, and the hotel has a decent restaurant. It's in a reasonably peaceful location beyond a bunch of greasy backstreet workshops.

Thanjavur (Tanjore)

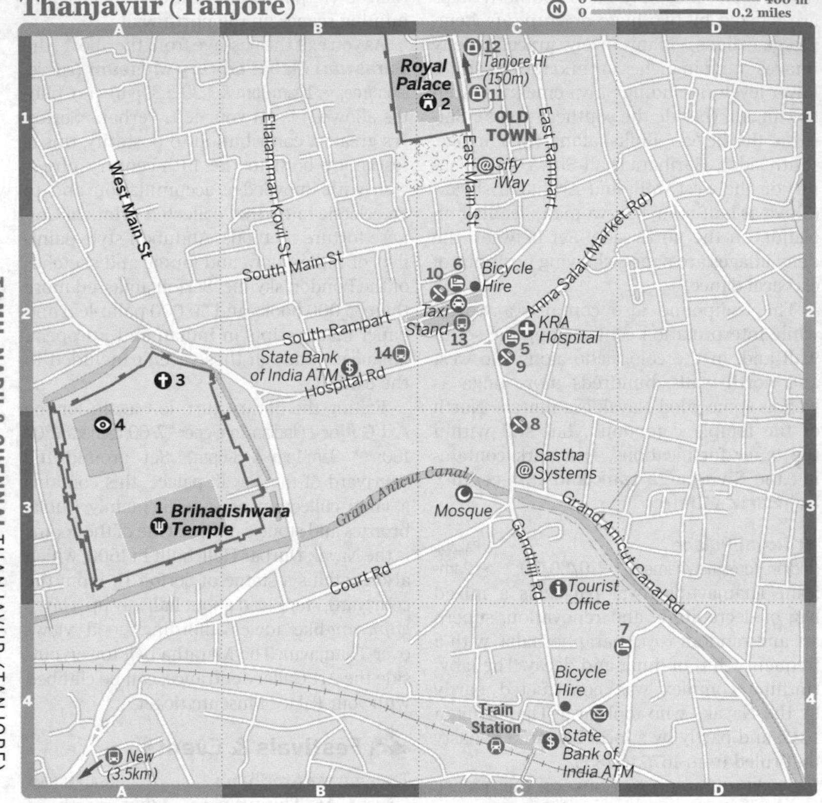

Hotel Gnanam — HOTEL $$

(☎278501; www.hotelgnanam.com; Anna Salai; s/d incl breakfast from ₹2159/2518; ❄📶) With the best overall value in town, the Gnanam has stylish, comfy rooms (the more expensive ones with lovely clean bath-tubs) and is perfect for anyone needing wi-fi (in the lobby; free), good meals and other modern amenities while they're plopped in Thanjavur's geographic centre.

Tanjore Hi — BOUTIQUE HOTEL $$$

(☎252111; http://tanjorehihotel.com; 464 East Main St; r incl breakfast from ₹9341; ❄📶) A 1926 house revamped by a German architect, Tanjore Hi has lovely, stylish, all-different rooms in blue and white, with solid wood floors, large contemporary art prints and free wi-fi. The bright top-floor **restaurant** (mains ₹200-320; ⏰7.30-10am, 12.30-2.30pm, 7.30-10-30pm) serves appetising international and Indian dishes.

Eating

Sri Venkata Lodge — SOUTH INDIAN $

(Gandhiji Rd; thalis ₹50; ⏰5.15am-10pm) A friendly, popular, veg-only place near the centre of everything, that does a nice thali.

Vasanta Bhavan — INDIAN $

(1338 South Rampart; mains ₹50-70; ⏰6am-11pm) The most appealing of several veg places facing the local bus stand downtown, Vasanta Bhavan has welcome AC and offers biryani and North Indian curries as well as your usual southern favourites.

Sahana — INDIAN $$

(Anna Salai, Hotel Gnanam; mains ₹95-115; ⏰7am-11pm) This classy hotel restaurant does a very nice line in fresh, tasty, mainly Indian veg dishes. The hotel's pricier nonveg **Diana** (mains ₹140-250; ⏰11am-3pm & 6.30-10pm) is also very good, with a wide range of north-

Thanjavur (Tanjore)

Top Sights

1	Brihadishwara Temple	A3
2	Royal Palace	C1

Sights

3	Schwartz's Church	A2
4	Sivaganga Tank	A3

Sleeping

5	Hotel Gnanam	C2
6	Hotel Ramnath	C2
7	Hotel Valli	D4

Eating

	Diana	(see 5)
	Sahana	(see 5)
8	Sathars	C3
9	Sri Venkata Lodge	C2
10	Vasanta Bhavan	C2

Shopping

11	Chola Art Galerie	C1
12	Kandiya Heritage	C1

Transport

13	Local Bus Stand	C2
14	SETC Bus Stand	B2

ern dishes and local Chettinad fare – and beer too.

Sathars INDIAN $$

(167 Gandhiji Rd; mains ₹80-160; noon-4pm & 6.30-11.30pm) Good service and quality food make this place popular, and the upper floor has a bit of fresh air. You can get biryanis, five types of chicken tikka kebab, good *parathas* (flaky bread stuffed with veg), and mutton, seafood and plenty of veg dishes.

Shopping

Thanjavur is a good place to shop for handicrafts, especially near the palace, where shops such as **Kandiya Heritage** (634 East Main St; 9am-7.30pm Mon-Sat) and **Chola Art Galerie** (78/799 East Main St; 10am-7pm) sell antiques, reproduction bronzes, brightly painted wooden horses, old European pottery and more.

Information

Sify iWay (927 East Main St; internet per hr ₹20; 9am-9pm)

Tourist Office (230984; Gandhiji Rd; 10am-5pm Mon-Fri) One of Tamil Nadu's more helpful offices.

Getting There & Away

BUS

The downtown **SETC bus stand** (reservation office 7.30am-9.30pm) has AC express buses to Chennai (₹260, eight hours) every 45 minutes from 5.30am to 1pm, and five times between 8pm and 10.45pm. Buses for other cities leave from the New Bus Station, 5km southwest of the centre. Many arriving buses can let you off in the city centre before heading out there. Services from the New Bus Station:

Chidambaram ₹90, four hours, every 30 minutes

Karaikal ₹45, 3½ hours, 11 daily

Kumbakonam ₹29, 1½ hours, every 15 minutes

Madurai ₹90, four hours, every 15 minutes

Trichy ₹31, 1½ hours, every 10 minutes

TRAIN

The station is reasonably central at the end of Gandhiji Rd. Five daily trains head to Chennai Egmore (seven to nine hours) including the 8.30pm Rock Fort Express (sleeper/3AC/2AC/1AC ₹190/490/730/1225). Eighteen trains head to Trichy (2nd-class/3AC/2AC ₹37/218/610, 1½ hours), and 12 to Kumbakonam (2nd-class/3AC/2AC ₹35/218/610, 40 minutes to 1½ hours).

Getting Around

Bus 74 (₹6) shuttles between the New Bus Station and the local bus stand downtown. An autorickshaw can cost ₹100.

Trichy (Tiruchirappalli)

0431 / POP 846,915

Welcome to (more or less) the geographic centre of Tamil Nadu. Tiruchirappalli, universally known as Trichy or Tiruchi, isn't just a travel junction; it also mixes up a throbbing bazaar with some major must-see temples. It's a big, crowded, busy city, and the fact that most hotels are grouped around the large bus station isn't exactly a plus point. But Trichy has a strong character and long history and a way of overturning first impressions.

Trichy may have been a capital of the early Cholas in the 3rd century BC. It passed through the hands of the Pallavas, medieval Cholas, Pandyas, Delhi Sultanate and Vijayanagars before the Madurai Nayaks really brought it to prominence, making it a capital in the 17th century and building its famous Rock Fort Temple.

Trichy stretches a long way from north to south, and most of what matters to travellers

DON'T MISS

CHOLA TEMPLES NEAR KUMBAKONAM

Two of the three great monuments of Chola civilisation stand in villages near Kumbakonam. Unlike the also World Heritage–listed Brihadishwara Temple at Thanjavur, these temples receive relatively few worshippers today. They are wonderful both for their overall form (with pyramidal towers rising at the heart of rectangular walled compounds) and for the exquisite detail of their carved stone.

Only 3km west of Kumbakonam in Darasuram village, the **Airavatesvara Temple** (admission free; ⌚6.30am-8.30pm), dedicated to Shiva, was constructed by Rajaraja II (1146–63). Guides can explain everything inside for around ₹100. The steps of the Rajagambhira Hall are carved with vivid elephants and horses pulling chariots. This pavilion's 108 all-different pillars have a plethora of detailed carving including dancers, acrobats and the five-in-one beast Yali who has an elephant's head, lion's body, goat's horns, pig's ears and the backside of a cow. On the outside of the main shrine are several fine carved images of Shiva. Inside the **shrine** (⌚6am-noon & 4-7pm) you can pay your respects to the central lingam and receive a *tilak* mark for ₹10. The **Nataraja Mandapa** contains a museum of sculptures from the site plus boards of historical information.

The **temple** (admission free; ⌚6.30am-8.30pm) at Gangaikondacholapuram ('City of the Chola who Conquered the Ganges'), 35km north of Kumbakonam, is also dedicated to Shiva. It was built by Rajendra I in the 11th century when he moved the Chola capital here from Thanjavur after successful campaigns in northern India. The temple has many similarities to the earlier Brihadishwara at Thanjavur. Its beautiful 49m-tall main tower, however, has a slightly concave curve, in contrast to the mildly convex one at Thanjavur. Gangaikondacholapuram is thus considered the 'feminine' counterpart to the Thanjavur edifice.

A large Nandi bull (Shiva's vehicle) faces the temple from the surrounding grassy lawns. The main shrine, beneath the tower, contains a huge lingam and is approached through a long, gloomy, 17th-century hall. The complex's artistic highlights are the wonderfully graceful sculptures around the tower's exterior. These include Shiva as the beggar Bhikshatana, immediately left of the southern steps; Ardhanarishvara (Shiva as half-man, half-woman), and Shiva as Nataraja, on the south side; and Shiva with Ganga, Shiva emerging from the lingam, and Vishnu with Lakshmi and Bhudevi (the first three images on the west side). Most famous of all is the beatiful panel of Shiva garlanding the head of his follower, Chandesvara, beside the northern steps.

From Kumbakonam bus stand, frequent buses heading to nearby villages will drop you at Darasuram; buses to Gangaikondacholapuram (₹19, 1½ hours) go every half-hour. An autorickshaw to Darasuram costs about ₹120 round trip. A half-day car trip to both temples, through Hotel Raya's (p373), is ₹950 (₹1100 with AC).

is split into three distinct areas. The Trichy Junction, or Cantonment, area in the south has most of the hotels and restaurants and the main bus and train stations. The Rock Fort Temple and main bazaar area is 4km north of here; the other important temples are in Srirangam, a further 4km north again, across the Cauvery River. Fortunately, the whole lot is connected by a good bus service.

Sights

★Rock Fort Temple HINDU TEMPLE

(Map p380; admission ₹3, camera/video ₹20/100; ⌚6am-8pm) The Rock Fort Temple, perched 83m high on a massive outcrop, lords over Trichy with stony arrogance. The ancient rock was first hewn by the Pallavas and Pandyas, who cut small cave temples on its south side, but it was the war-savvy Nayaks who later made strategic use of the naturally fortified position. There are over 400 stone-cut steps to climb to the top. From NSB Rd on the south side, you pass between small shops and cross a street before entering the temple precinct proper. Then it's 180 steps up to the Thayumanaswamy Temple (Swami Amman Sannathi) on the left (closed to non-Hindus). This is the rock's biggest temple and prominently visible from below and above. A gold-topped tower rises over its sanctum, which houses a 2m-high Shiva lingam. Heading on up, you pass the 6th-century Pallava cave temple on the left – it's often railed off but should you get inside, check out the famous Gangadhara panel on the left, showing Shiva restraining the waters of the Ganges with a single strand of his hair. From here it's just another 183 steps to the small Uchipillaiyar Temple at the summit, dedicated to Ganesh. The view is wonderful, with eagles wheeling beneath and Trichy sprawling all around.

★ Sri Ranganathaswamy Temple HINDU TEMPLE
(Map p380; camera/video ₹50/100; ⏲6am-9pm) All right temple-philes, here's the one you've been waiting for: quite possibly the biggest temple in India – so large, it feels like a self-enclosed city. It has 49 separate shrines, all dedicated to Vishnu, and reaching the inner sanctum from the south, as most worshippers do, requires passing through seven *gopurams*. The first, the **Rajagopuram** (Map p380), was added to the 20 older ones in 1987, and is claimed to be Asia's tallest temple tower at 73m high. You pass through streets with shops, restaurants and cars until you reach the temple proper at the fourth *gopuram*. Inside here is the ticket desk for the nearby **roof viewpoint** (ticket ₹10; ⏲8am-6pm), which gives a semi-panoramic view of the complex. Non-Hindus cannot pass the sixth *gopuram* so won't see the innermost sanctum whose image shows Vishnu as Lord Ranganatha, lying on a five-headed snake.

Turn right just before the fifth *gopuram* to the small but intriguing **Art Museum** (admission ₹5; ⏲9am-1pm & 2-6pm), with good bronzes, tusks of bygone temple elephants, and a collection of superb 17th-century Nayak ivory figurines depicting gods, demons, kings and queens (some of them erotically engaged) and even a portly Portugese soldier. Continue round to the left past the museum to the **Sesha Mandapa**, a 16th-century pillared hall with magnificent, large but detailed Vijayanagar carvings of rearing horses in battle.

The temple's most important festival is the 21-day Vaikunta Ekadasi (Paradise Festival) in December/January, when the celebrated Vaishnavaite text, Tiruvaimozhi, is recited before an image of Vishnu.

Bus 1 from or to the Central Bus Station or the Rock Fort stops right outside the Rajagopuram.

Sri Jambukeshwara Temple HINDU TEMPLE
(Tiruvanakoil; camera/video ₹30/200; ⏲6am-8pm) If you're visiting Tamil Nadu's five elemental temples of Shiva, you need to visit Sri Jambukeshwara, dedicated to Shiva, Parvati and the medium of water. The liquid theme is realised in the central shrine (closed to non-Hindus), whose Shiva lingam reputedly issues a nonstop trickle of water. If you're taking bus 1, ask for 'Tiruvanakoil'; the temple is 350m east of the main road.

Lourdes Church CHURCH
(Map p380; College Rd) The hush of this 19th-century church makes an interesting contrast to the frenetic activity of Trichy's Hindu temples. In the green, cool campus of Jesuit St Joseph's College next door, an eccentric and dusty **museum** (Map p380; admission free; ⏲9am-noon & 2-4pm Mon-Sat) contains the natural history collections of the Jesuit priests' excursions to the Western Ghats in the 1870s. Bang on the door and the caretaker will let you in (if he's there).

Sleeping & Eating

Most hotels are near the Central Bus Station, a short walk north from Trichy Junction train station.

The most enjoyable eateries are in the better hotels, but there are some decent cheaper places too.

Hotel Abbirami HOTEL $
(Map p382; ☎2415001; 10 McDonald's Rd; r ₹770-990, with AC ₹1439-2159; ❄) Most appealing are the 1st-floor renovated rooms with light wood and colourful glass panels adding a touch of fun. Older rooms have darker wood and are a bit worn, but all are kept clean. It's a busy place with friendly staff.

Hotel Mathura HOTEL $
(Map p382; ☎2414737; www.hotelmathura.com; 1 Rockins Rd; r ₹680, with AC ₹1100; ❄) Rooms are very ordinary but tolerably clean. Those on the 2nd floor, at least, have had a fairly recent coat of paint. Next door, **Hotel Meega** (Map p382; ☎2414092; 3 Rockins Rd; s ₹446, d ₹605-660, s/d with AC ₹715/880; ❄) is on similar lines.

Hotel Ramyas HOTEL $$
(Map p382; ☎2414646; www.ramyas.com; 13-D/2 Williams Rd; r ₹1089, with AC s ₹2039-2518, d ₹2878-3118, all incl breakfast; ❄@📶) Excellent rooms, service and facilities make this business-oriented hotel a fine choice. 'Business class' singles are small but it's only another ₹200-odd for an excellent executive room. The **Thendral** (Map p382; mains ₹90-195; ⏲noon-3.30pm & 7-11pm) roof-garden restaurant is lovely, breakfast is an excellent buffet,

Trichy (Tiruchirappalli)

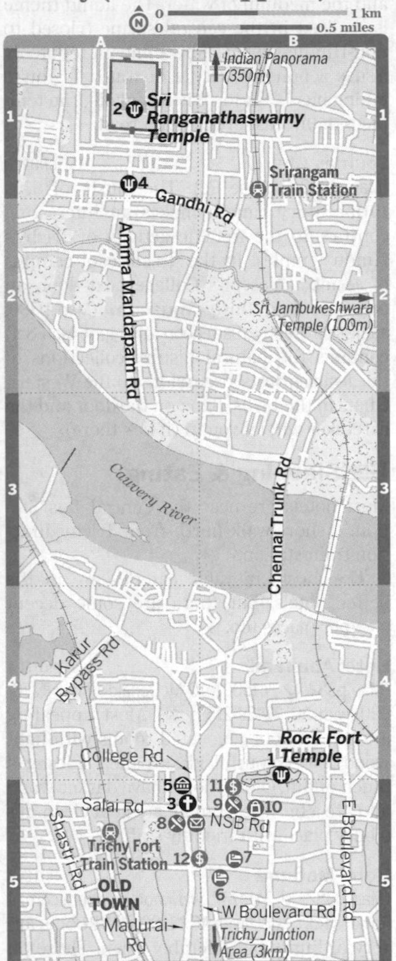

Trichy (Tiruchirappalli)

Top Sights
1 Rock Fort Temple B4
2 Sri Ranganathaswamy Temple A1

Sights
3 Lourdes Church A5
4 Rajagopuram A1
5 St Joseph's College Museum A5

Sleeping
6 Hotel Royal Sathyam B5
7 Hotel Susee Park B5

Eating
8 Banana Leaf A5
9 Vasanta Bhavan B5

Shopping
10 Saratha's B5

Information
11 Canara Bank ATM B5
12 ICICI Bank ATM A5

and the **Chola Bar** (Map p382; ⏲11am-3.30pm & 6.30-11pm) is livelier and less dingy than most hotel bars (though still male-dominated). In-room wi-fi is ₹50 per three hours,

Hotel High Point BOUTIQUE HOTEL $$
(☎2416766; www.hotelhighpoint.in; Manghalam Towers, 9 Reynolds Rd; s ₹2159-3238, d ₹2998-3957, all incl breakfast; ❄📶) In a relatively upmarket, leafy neighbourhood, High Point provides very comfy, stylish rooms incorporating pop-art prints, red-and-yellow-striped walls, free wi-fi and glassed-in showers. There's a good multicuisine restaurant and a spacious bar. It's a cut above other midrange hotels, and singles are as big as doubles. Autorickshaws charge ₹40 from the bus station; it's on the top floor of the Reliance supermarket building.

Femina Hotel HOTEL $$
(Map p382; ☎2414501; www.feminahotels.in; 109 Williams Rd; s ₹1559-2998, d ₹2039-4797, all incl breakfast; ❄@🏊) The Femina looks 1950s outside but renovations have given the inside quite a contemporary look. Facilities are good and staff helpful. Economy rooms are closest to the busy street, and a bit jaded. Standard rooms are cosier and have a much lower honk factor. There's a nice outdoor **pool** (nonguests per hr ₹100; ⏲7am-7pm Tue-Sun) and eateries include the stylish coffee-shop-cum-veg-restaurant **Round the Clock** (Map p382; mains ₹90-110; ⏲24hr).

PLA Krishna Inn HOTEL $$
(Map p382; ☎2406666; www.plakrishnainn.com; 8A Rockins Rd; s ₹2099-2758, d ₹2392-2758, all incl breakfast; ❄📶) New in 2012, PLA Krishna has bright, spacious rooms sporting trendy rectangular white washbasins and plus-size shower heads. With two restaurants, a bar, polished service and free in-room wi-fi, you won't go wrong here.

Breeze Residency HOTEL $$
(Map p382; ☎2414414; www.breezeresidency.com; 3/14 McDonald's Rd; s/d ₹2998/3478, ste ₹4197-

5996, all incl breakfast; ❄@📶🏊) The Breeze is enormous, semiluxurious and in a relatively quiet location. The best rooms are on the top floor,s but all are well appointed. Facilities include a gym, the good **Madras Restaurant** (Map p382; mains ₹100-300; ⏰12.30-3.30pm & 7-11pm) and a bizarre Wild West theme bar.

Hotel Royal Sathyam HOTEL **$$**
(Map p380; ☎4011414; www.sathyamgrouphotels.com; 42A Singarathope; s ₹1439-1919, d ₹1679-2998, all incl breakfast; ❄📶) The classiest option if you want to be close to the temple and market action. Rooms are small but stylish, with extra-comfy mattresses and a fresh wood-and-whitewash theme. There's free wi-fi in the lobby. Nearby **Hotel Susee Park** (Map p380; ☎2812345; www.hotelsuseepark.com; 45 Singarathope; r ₹1079, with AC ₹1498-2278) is also fine.

Vasanta Bhavan INDIAN **$**
(Map p380; 3 NSB Rd; mains ₹50-80, thalis ₹80-110; ⏰6am-11pm) A good spot for a meal with a view and, with luck, a breeze near the Rock Fort. Tables on the outer gallery overlook the Teppakulam Tank. It's good for North Indian veg food – that of the *paneer* and naan genre – as well as South Indian. It gets very busy at lunchtime when people crowd in for the good thalis. There's another **branch** (Map p382; Rockins Rd; mains ₹40-55, thalis ₹60-90; ⏰6am-11pm) in the Cantonment.

Banana Leaf INDIAN **$$**
(Map p382; McDonald's Rd; mains ₹80-175; ⏰11am-midnight) A big menu of veg and nonveg regional favourites is served in two small AC rooms. The speciality is the fiery, vaguely vinegary cuisine of Andhra Pradesh. Another **branch** (Map p380; Madurai Rd) is near the Rock Fort.

Shopping

The main bazaar, immediately south of the Rock Fort, is as chaotic and crowded as you could want; it constantly feels as if all of Trichy is strolling the strip. While you'here, do have a look round **Saratha's** (Map p380; 45 NSB Rd; ⏰9am-9.30pm), which claims to be (and may indeed be) the 'largest textile showroom in India' and sells men's and women's clothes of every conceivable kind.

Information

Indian Panorama (☎4226122; www.indianpanorama.in; 5 Annai Avenue, Srirangam) Trichy-based and covering all of India, this professional, reliable travel agency/tour operator is run by an Indian–New Zealander couple.

Kauvery Hospital (Map p382; KMC Speciality Hospital; ☎4077777; www.kmcspecialityhospital.in; 6 Royal Rd) A large, well-equipped, private hospital.

Tourist Office (Map p382; ☎2460136; McDonald's Rd; ⏰10am-5.45pm Mon-Fri)

Getting There & Away

AIR

Trichy's airport has a few international flights, as well as daily flights to Chennai on **JetKonnect** (www.jetkonnect.com), **Air India Express** (☎2341744; www.airindiaexpress.in) and **SpiceJet** (www.spicejet.com), and Bengaluru SpiceJet. To Colombo, **SriLankan Airlines** (Map p382; ☎2460844; 14C Williams Rd; ⏰9am-5.30pm Mon-Fri) flies twice daily, and **Mihin Lanka** (☎4200606; www.mihinlanka.com; Reynolds Rd, Translanka Air Travels; ⏰9.30am-6pm Mon-Fri, 9.30am-2pm Sat) four times weekly. **Air Asia** (Map p382; ☎4540393; www.airasia.com; 18/3-5 Ivory Plaza, Royal Rd) flies to Kuala Lumpur, **Tiger Airways** (www.tigerairways.com) to Singapore, and Air India Express to Singapore and Dubai, all daily.

GOVERNMENT BUSES FROM TRICHY

DESTINATION	FARE (₹)	DURATION (HR)	FREQUENCY
Bengaluru	350 Ultra Deluxe (UD)	8	6 UD daily
Chennai	180 regular, 235 UD, 350 AC	6-7	15 UD, 4 AC daily
Coimbatore	140	5-6	every 30min
Kodaikanal	110	5	6.40am, 8.30am, 11.50am
Madurai	80	3	every 15min
Ooty	260 UD	8	10.15pm UD
Rameswaram	180	6½	hourly
Thanjavur	31	1½	every 10min

Trichy Junction Area

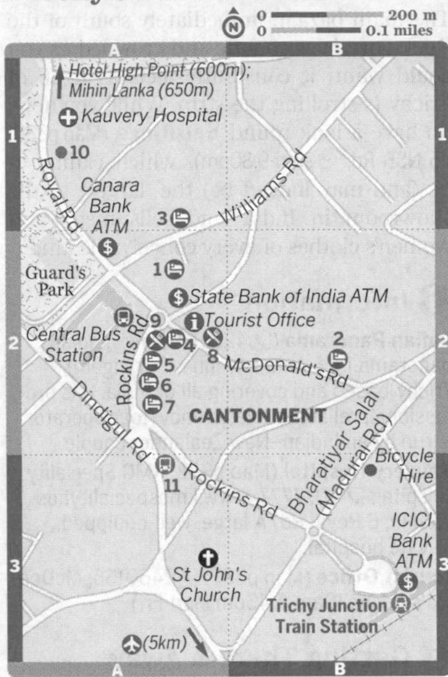

Trichy Junction Area

Sleeping
1 Hotel Ramyas A2
2 Breeze Residency B2
3 Femina Hotel A1
4 Hotel Abbirami A2
5 Hotel Mathura A2
6 Hotel Meega A2
7 PLA Krishna Inn A2

Eating
8 Banana Leaf A2
Madras Restaurant .... (see 2)
Round the Clock .... (see 3)
Thendral .... (see 1)
9 Vasanta Bhavan A2

Drinking & Nightlife
Chola Bar .... (see 1)

Transport
10 Air Asia A1
Femina Travels .... (see 3)
11 Parveen Travels A3
SriLankan Airlines .... (see 3)

BUS

Government buses use the busy **Central Bus Station** (Map p382; Rockins Rd). The best services for most longer trips are the UD ('ultra deluxe'), which have softer seats than regular buses. There's a booking office for these in the southwest corner of the station. For Kodaikanal, a good option is to take one of the frequent buses to Dindigul (₹30, two hours) and change there. Several private bus companies have offices near the Central Bus Station, including **Parveen Travels** (Map p382; www.parveentravels.com; 12 Ashby Complex) which offers AC services to Chennai (₹560 to ₹720, four daily), Coimbatore (₹260, 11.30pm), Bengaluru (₹650, 11pm) and Trivandrum (₹1300 to ₹1400, 12.30am and 1am).

TAXI

Plenty of travel agencies can provide a car and driver. **Femina Travels** (Map p382; ☎2418532; 109 Williams Rd) has an efficient, reasonably priced service. AC cars for up to 10 hours start at ₹1000 plus ₹6 per kilometre.

TRAIN

Trichy Junction station is on the main Chennai–Madurai line. Of 15 daily express or SuperFast services to Chennai, the best daytime option is the Vaigai Express (2nd/chair class ₹104/381, 5¾ hours) departing at 9am. The overnight Rock Fort Express (sleeper/3AC/2AC/1AC ₹164/430/640/1085, seven hours) leaves at 10.20pm. Twelve daily trains to Madurai include the 7.15am Bharathi Express (2nd/chair class ₹71/244, 2¼ hours) and the 1.15pm Guruvaya Express (2nd-class/sleeper/3AC/2AC ₹62/120/282/610, 3¼ hours). Eighteen trains head to Thanjavur (2nd-class/3AC ₹37/218, 40 minutes to 1½ hours).

Getting Around

The 5km ride between the airport and Central Bus Station area is about ₹300 by taxi and ₹150 by autorickshaw; there's a prepaid taxi stand at the airport. Or take bus K1.

Bus 1 from Rockins Rd outside the Central Bus Station goes every few minutes to Sri Ranganathaswamy Temple (₹6) and back, stopping close to the Rock Fort Temple and Sri Jambukeshwara Temple en route.

SOUTHERN TAMIL NADU

Chettinadu

The Chettiars, a community of traders based in and around Karaikkudi, 95km south of Trichy, really hit the big time back in the 19th century as financiers and entrepreneurs in colonial Sri Lanka and Southeast Asia. They lavished their fortunes on building at least 10,000, maybe 20,000 opulent mansions in the 90-odd towns and villages of their rural homeland, Chettinadu. No expense was spared on bringing the finest materials to adorn these palatial homes – Burmese teak, Italian marble, Indian rosewood, Belgian chandeliers, English steel, and art and sculpture from everywhere. In the aftermath of WW II, the Chettiars' business networks collapsed and many families had to leave Chettinadu to seek new opportunities. Disused mansions fell into decay and were demolished or sold off piecemeal. Awareness of their value started to revive around the turn of the 21st century, and several have now been turned into gorgeous heritage hotels where, among other things, you can enjoy authentic Chetttinad cuisine, known throughout India for its brilliant use of spices.

Sights & Activities

Hotels can give cooking demos or classes, and provide bicycles or bullock carts for rural rambles. They can also arrange visits to sari-weavers, temples, the Athangudi tileworks (producing the colourful handmade tiles you see in many Chettiar mansions), and shrines of the popular pre-Hindu deity Ayyanar (identifiable by their large terracotta horses, Ayyanar's vehicle). The antique shops in Karaikkudi's Muneeswaran Koil St will give you a feel for how much of the Chettiar heritage is still being sold off.

The nondescript town of Pudukkottai, 51km south of Trichy and 44km north of Karaikkudi, has historical significance in inverse proportion to its current obscurity; it was the capital of the only princely state in Tamil Nadu to remain officially independent throughout British rule.

Vijayalaya Cholisvaram HINDU TEMPLE

(Narthamalai) **FREE** This small but stunning 8th-century temple stands on a rock slope 1km southwest of Narthamalai village, about 16km north of Pudukkottai. Reminiscent of the Shore Temple at Mamallapuram, without the crowds, it was probably built in late Pallava times. The caretaker, if present, will open two rock-cut Shiva shrines in the adjacent rock face, one with 12 impressively large reliefs of Vishnu. The walk from the village is lovely, with panoramas of fields, water tanks and dramatic rock outcrops unfolding as you go. The Narthamalai turn-off is 7km south of Keeranur on the Trichy–Pudukkottai road; it's 2km west to the village.

Pudukkottai Museum MUSEUM

(Indian/foreigner ₹5/100; 9.30am-5pm Sat-Thu) The relics of bygone days are on display in this wonderful museum, in a renovated palace building in Pudukkottai town. Its eclectic collection includes musical instruments, megalithic burial artefacts, and some remarkable paintings and miniatures.

Thirumayam Fort FORT

(Indian/foreigner ₹5/100; 9am-5.30pm) Simple and imposing, the renovated Thirumayam Fort, about 20km south of Pudukkottai, is worth a climb for the 360-degree views from the battlements over the surrounding countryside. There's a rock-cut Shiva shrine up some metal steps on the west side of the small hill.

Sleeping & Eating

To get a feel for the palatial life, book a night or two in one of Chettinadu's top-end hotels; they're pricey but they provide a fantastic experience.

★**Visalam** HERITAGE HOTEL **$$$**

(04565-273301; www.cghearth.com; Local Fund Rd, Kanadukathan; r incl breakfast ₹9000-15,000;) Stunningly restored and professionally run by a Malayali hotel chain, Visalam is a relatively young Chettiar mansion, done in the fashionable art-deco style of the 1930s. It's still decorated with the original owners' photos, furniture and paintings, and staff can tell you the sad story of the young woman the house was built for. The garden is lovely, the rooms large and stylish, and the pool setting is magical, with a low-key cafe alongside it. There's free in-room wi-fi. Kanadukathan is 9km south of Thirumayam.

★**Bangala** BOUTIQUE HOTEL **$$$**

(04565-220221; www.thebangala.com; Devakottai Rd, Karaikkudi; r ₹6400;) This lovingly restored whitewashed 'bungalow' isn't a typical mansion but has all the requisite charm, with quirky decorations, antique furniture and fascinating old family photos. It's famous for its food: the ₹700 set lunch or dinner is actually a Chettiar wedding feast and worth every single paisa (it's available to nonguests from noon to 3pm for ₹1000; call at least two hours ahead). The Bangala has a lovely pool and there's free in-room wi-fi.

Saratha Vilas BOUTIQUE HOTEL **$$$**

(9884203175, 9884936158; www.sarathavilas.com; 832 Main Rd, Kothamangalam; r incl breakfast ₹6050-7060; ❄@📶) A different style of Chettiar charm inhabits this French-run mansion 6km east of Kanadukathan. Rooms combine traditional and contemporary with distinct French panache and the food is an enticing mix of Chettiar and French. The owners are very active in the conservation and promotion of Chettinad heritage through the NGO **ArcHeS** (www.arche-s.com), which they founded (and which has volunteer openings for the likes of historians, geographers and architects, especially Tamil-speaking ones!).

Chidambara Vilas HERITAGE HOTEL **$$$**
(☎0433-3267070; www.chidambaravilas.com; TSK House, Kadiapatti; s/d incl breakfast ₹11,000/12,000; ❄@🏊) This mansion in a village 5km east of Thirumayam has been restored into a luxurious hotel with plenty of original Burmese teak, rosewood, stained glass and colourful paintwork. Most rooms are in a new block but still full of Chettiar atmosphere, including punka fans that you can operate yourself from your four-poster bed. A bar, pool and recreation room help you to relax in style. Check for discount offers.

Chettinadu Mansion HERITAGE HOTEL **$$$**
(☎04565-273080; www.chettinadumansion.com; 11 AR St, SARM House, Kanadukathan; s/d incl breakfast ₹5200/7050, half-board ₹5800/8250; ❄📶) Slightly shabbier than some other Chettiar joints, but very colourfully decorated, this century-old house is still owned by the original family. Service is top-notch, and all 12 sizeable rooms have private balconies looking over other village mansions. Wi-fi is ₹100 per day. The owners also run **Chettinadu Court** (☎04565-283776; www.deshadan.com; Raja's St, Kanadukathan; s/d incl breakfast ₹3350/3850, half-board ₹3800/4750; ❄📶) a few blocks away, with eight pleasant new rooms sporting a few heritage touches, and free wi-fi.

ℹ Getting There & Away

Car is the best way to get to and around this area. Renting one with a driver from Trichy, Thanjavur or Madurai for two days should cost around ₹3500. Otherwise there are buses about every 10 minutes from Trichy to Pudukkottai (₹31, 1½ hours) and Karaikkudi (₹56, 2½ hours) and you can get off and on along the way. There are also buses from Thanjavur, Madurai and Rameswaram.

Madurai

☎ 0452 / POP 1.02 MILLION

Chennai may be the capital of Tamil Nadu, but Madurai claims its soul. Madurai is Tamil-born and Tamil-rooted, one of the oldest cities in India, a metropolis that traded with ancient Rome and was a great capital long before Chennai was even dreamt of.

Tourists, Indian and foreign, usually come here to see the Meenakshi Amman Temple, a labyrinthine structure ranking among the greatest temples of India. Otherwise, Madurai, perhaps appropriately given her age, captures many of India's glaring dichotomies with a centre dominated by a medieval temple and an economy increasingly driven by IT, all overlaid with the energy and excitement of a large Indian city and slotted into a much more manageable package than Chennai's sprawl.

History

Ancient documents record the existence of Madurai from the 3rd century BC. It was a trading town, especially in spices, and according to legend was the home of the third *sangam* (gathering of Tamil scholars and poets). Over the centuries Madurai came under the sway of the Cholas, Pandyas, local Muslim sultans, Hindu Vijayanagar kings, and the Nayaks, who ruled until 1736. Under Tirumalai Nayak (1623–59) the bulk of the Sri Meenakshi Temple was built, and Madurai became the hub of Tamil culture, playing an important role in the development of the Tamil language.

In 1840 the British East India Company razed Madurai's fort and filled in its moat. The four broad Veli streets were constructed on top of this fill and to this day define the limits of the old city.

👁 Sights

★**Meenakshi Amman Temple** HINDU TEMPLE
(camera/video ₹50/250; ⏰4am-12.30pm & 4-9.30pm) The abode of the triple-breasted goddess Meenakshi ('fish-eyed' – an epithet for perfect eyes in classical Tamil poetry) is considered by many to be the height of South Indian temple architecture, as vital to the aesthetic heritage of this region as the Taj Mahal is to North India. It's not so much a temple as a 6-hectare complex with 12 tall *gopurams,* all encrusted with a staggering array of gods, goddesses, demons and heroes (1511 of them on the south *gopuram* alone).

Madurai

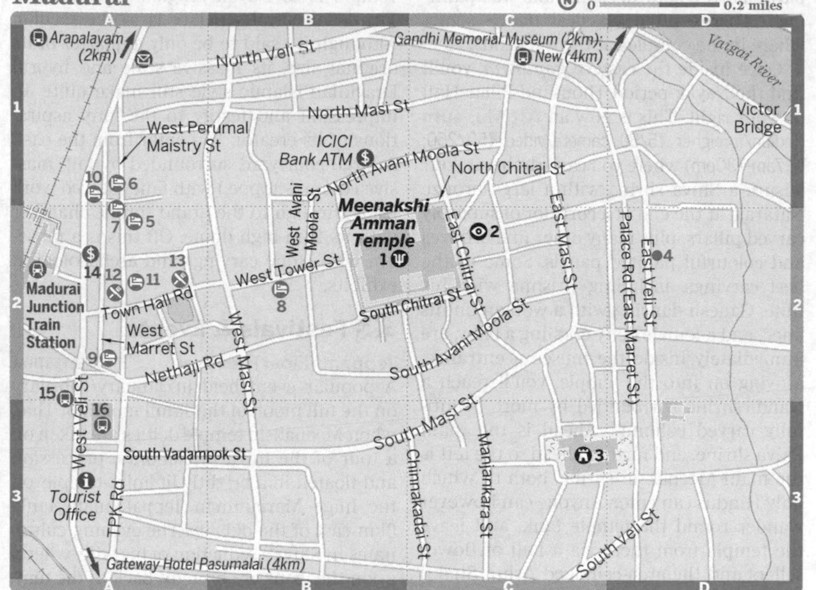

According to legend, the beautiful Meenakshi (a version of Parvati) was born with three breasts and this prophecy: her superfluous breast would melt away when she met her husband. The event came to pass when she met Shiva and took her place as his consort. The existing temple was built during the 17th-century reign of Tirumalai Nayak, but its origins go back 2000 years to when Madurai was a Pandyan capital.

The four streets surrounding the temple are pedestrian-only. The main entrance is by the eastern *gopuram*. First, have a look round the **Pudhu Mandapa** (East Chitrai St), the 100m-long, 16th-century pillared hall facing the *gopuram*. It's filled with colourful textile and craft stalls and tailors at sewing machines, partly hiding some of the lovely pillar sculptures, but it's easy to find the triple-breasted Meenakshi near the southeast corner, and her marriage to Shiva, accompanied by Vishnu, just inside the western entrance. A particularly handsome light-blue Nandi bull (Shiva's vehicle) sits outside the *mandapa's* eastern entrance.

Dress codes are fairly strict for the temple itself: no women's shoulders, or legs of either gender, may be exposed. Despite this the temple has a happier, more joyful atmosphere than some of Tamil Nadu's more solemn shrines, and is adorned with

Madurai

Top Sights
- 1 Meenakshi Amman Temple ... B2

Sights
- Art Museum ... (see 1)
- 2 Pudhu Mandapa ... C2
- 3 Tirumalai Nayak Palace ... C3

Activities, Courses & Tours
- 4 Foodies Day Out ... D2

Sleeping
- 5 Hotel Keerthi ... A2
- 6 Hotel Park Plaza ... A1
- 7 Hotel Supreme ... A2
- 8 Hotel West Tower ... B2
- 9 Madurai Residency ... A2
- 10 Royal Court ... A1
- 11 TM Lodge ... A2

Eating
- 12 Anna Meenakshi Restaurant ... A2
- 13 Dhivya Mahal Restaurant ... A2
- Surya Restaurant ... (see 7)

Information
- 14 State Bank of India ... A2
- Supreme Web ... (see 7)

Transport
- Air India ... (see 14)
- 15 Periyar Bus Stand ... A2
- 16 Shopping Complex Bus Stand ... A3

particularly colourful ceiling and wall paintings. There's often classical dance somewhere in the complex at the weekends.

Once inside the eastern *gopuram*, you'll find the Nayak-period Thousand Pillar Hall on your right. This is now an **Art Museum** (Indian/foreigner ₹5/50, camera/video ₹50/250; ⏲7am-7.30pm) where you can admire at your leisure a Shiva shrine with a large bronze Nataraja at the end of a corridor of superbly carved pillars, plus many other fine bronzes and colourful painted panels. Some of the best carvings, including Krishna with his flute, Ganesh dancing with a woman on his knee, and a female deity cradling a baby, are immediately inside the museum entrance. Moving on into the temple, you'll reach a Nandi shrine surrounded by more beautifully carved columns. Ahead is the main Shiva shrine, and further ahead to the left is the main Meenakshi shrine, both of which only Hindus can enter. Anyone can however wander round the temple tank, and leave the temple from there via a hall of flower sellers and the arch-ceilinged Ashta Shakti Mandapam, which is actually used as the temple entrance by most worshippers and is lined with relief carvings of the goddess's eight attributes and has perhaps the loveliest of all the temple's brightly painted ceilings.

Gandhi Memorial Museum MUSEUM
(Gandhi Museum Rd; camera ₹50; ⏲10am-1pm & 2-5.45pm Tue-Sun) FREE Housed in a 17th-century Nayak queen's palace, this excellent museum contains an impressively moving and detailed account of India's struggle for independence from 1757 to 1947, and the English-language text pulls no punches about British rule. Included in the exhibition is the blood-stained dhoti (long loincloth) that Gandhi was wearing when he was assassinated in Delhi in 1948; it's here because it was in Madurai, in 1921, that he first took up wearing the dhoti as a sign of native pride. The small **Madurai Government Museum** (Indian/foreigner ₹5/100, camera ₹20; ⏲9.30am-5pm Sat-Thu) is next door, and the **Gandhian Literary Society Bookshop** (⏲10am-1pm & 2.30-6.30pm Mon-Sat) behind. Bus 75 from Periyar Bus Stand goes to the Tamukkam bus stop on Alagarkoil Rd, 600m from the museum.

Tirumalai Nayak Palace PALACE
(Palace Rd; Indian/foreigner ₹10/50, camera/video ₹30/100; ⏲9am-5pm) What the Meenakshi Temple is to Nayak religious architecture, Tirumalai Nayak's palace is to the secular. Although it's said to be only a quarter of its original size, its massive scale and hybrid Dravidian-Islamic style still make quite an impression and testify to the lofty aspirations of its creator. You enter from the east. A large courtyard surrounded by tall, massive columns topped with fancy stucco work leads through to the grand throne chamber with its 25m-high dome. Off this is a museum with stone carvings and archaeological exhibits.

Festivals & Events

Teppam (Float) Festival TEMPLE FESTIVAL
A popular event held in January/February on the full moon of the Tamil month of Thai, when Meenakshi temple deities are taken on a tour of the town in elaborate procession and floated in a brightly lit 'mini-temple' on the huge Mariamman Teppakkulam tank, 3km east of the old city. The evening culminates in Shiva's seduction of his wife, whereupon the icons are brought back to the temple to make love and, in so doing, regenerate the universe (Meenakshi's diamond nose stud is even removed so it doesn't irritate her lover).

Chithirai Festival TEMPLE FESTIVAL
The main event on Madurai's busy festival calendar is this two-week event in April/May celebrating the marriage of Meenakshi to Sundareswarar (Shiva). The deities are wheeled around the Meenakshi Amman Temple in massive chariots that form part of long, colourful processions.

Sleeping

Budget hotels in the central area are mostly dreary and unloved, but there is a big choice of good and near-identical midrange places along West Perumal Maistry St, not far from the train station. Most of them have rooftop restaurants with temple and sunset views.

Hotel West Tower HOTEL $
(☎2346908; 42/60 West Tower St; s/d ₹473/825, r with AC ₹1238; ❄) The West Tower's best asset is that it's very near the temple, but it's also acceptably clean and friendly.

TM Lodge HOTEL $
(☎2341651; http://hellomadurai.in/tmlodge; 50 West Perumal Maistry St; s/d ₹399/605, r with AC ₹1294; ❄) The walls are a bit grubby, but the

sheets are clean. TM is efficiently run, even with a lift operator!

Madurai Residency HOTEL $$
(☎438000; www.madurairesidency.com; 15 West Marret St; s ₹2039-2518, d ₹2398-2878, all incl breakfast; ❄📶) The service is stellar and the rooms are comfy and fresh at this winner, which has one of the the highest rooftop restaurants in town. It's very popular, so book at least two days ahead. There's wi-fi in the lobby.

Hotel Park Plaza HOTEL $$
(☎3011111; www.hotelparkplaza.net; 114 West Perumal Maistry St; s/d incl half-board ₹2878/3358; ❄📶) The Plaza's rooms are comfortable and simply but attractively furnished, with free wi-fi. Four have temple views. It also boasts a good multicuisine rooftop restaurant and the (inappropriately named) Sky High Bar – on the 1st floor.

Hotel Supreme HOTEL $$
(☎2343151; www.hotelsupreme.in; 110 West Perumal Maistry St; s ₹2278-3118, d ₹2578-3298, all incl breakfast; ❄📶) The Supreme is a well-presented hotel with friendly service that is very popular with domestic tourists. Don't miss the chance to walk into Apollo 96, a bar built to look like a spaceship, and wonder if someone laced your lassi last night. There's good food at the inhouse Surya Restaurant, and free in-room wi-fi.

Hotel Keerthi HOTEL $$
(☎4377788; http://hellomadurai.in/hotelkeerthi; 40 West Perumal Maistry St; r incl breakfast ₹1379-1918; ❄) This shiny, modern hotel has decent prices, small 'classic' rooms and large 'deluxe'. They're almost stylish thanks to their minimalist lines, funky wall mirrors and feature walls. No wi-fi though.

Royal Court HOTEL $$$
(☎4356666; www.royalcourtindia.com; 4 West Veli St; s ₹3957-4917, d ₹4797-5636, all incl breakfast; ❄@📶) The Royal Court manages to blend a bit of white-sheeted, hardwood-floored colonial elegance with comfort, good eating options, professional service and free in-room wi-fi. It's an excellent, central choice for someone who needs a bit of spoiling.

Gateway Hotel Pasumalai HOTEL $$$
(☎6633000; www.thegatewayhotels.com; 40 TPK Rd, Pasumalai; s ₹5996-8394, d ₹7195-9594) A lovely escape from city scramble, the Gateway is spread over hilltop gardens 4km southwest of the centre. The views, outdoor pool and resident peacocks are just great, the rooms are well equipped, very comfy and mostly large, and the panoramic **Garden All Day** (⏱6.30am-11pm) restaurant does a terrific multicuisine dinner buffet for ₹717.

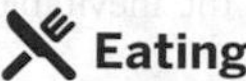

Eating

The hotel-rooftop restaurants along West Perumal Maistry St offer breezy night-time dining and temple views (don't forget the mosquito repellent); most of the hotels also have AC restaurants open for breakfast and lunch. For a great evening tasting Madurai specialities with a local food enthusiast, call or email **Foodies Day Out** (☎9840992340; www.foodiesdayout.com; 2nd fl, 56 East Veli St; tour per person ₹1500). They'll pick you up around 5.30pm and take you to seven or eight restaurants and stalls to sample the signature dish at each. Vegetarian tours are available; at least two people are needed.

Dhivya Mahal Restaurant MULTICUISINE $
(☎2342700; 21 Town Hall Rd; mains ₹50-150; ⏱noon-11pm) One of the better multicuisine restaurants not attached to a hotel, Dhivyar Mahal is clean, bright, air-conditioned and friendly. The curries go down a treat, and where else are you going to find roast leg of lamb in Madurai?

Anna Meenakshi Restaurant INDIAN $
(West Perumal Maistry St; mains ₹60-100; ⏱6am-11pm) With marginally more attention to decor and ambience than other cheapies along the street, Anna Meenakshi is a busy spot where you can get a decent South Indian thali for ₹60.

Surya Restaurant MULTICUISINE $$
(110 West Perumal Maistry St; mains ₹70-160; ⏱4pm-midnight) The rooftop restaurant of Hotel Supreme offers a superb view over the city, stand-out service and good pure-veg food, but the winner here has got to be the iced coffee, which might have been brewed by God when you sip it on a dusty, hot day.

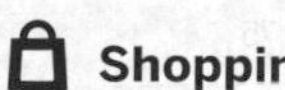

Shopping

Madurai teems with cloth stalls and tailors' shops, as you may notice upon being approached by tailor touts. A great place for getting clothes made up is the Pudhu Mandapa. Here you'll find rows of tailors busily treadling away and capable of whipping up a good replica of whatever you're wearing in an hour or two. A cotton top or shirt can cost as little as ₹350. Drivers, guides and touts will also be keen to lead you to the Kashmiri craft shops in North Chitrai St, offering to show you the temple view from the rooftop – the views are good, and so is the inevitable sales pitch.

Information

State Bank of India (West Veli St) Has foreign-exchange desks and an ATM.

Supreme Web (110 West Perumal Maistry St; per hr ₹30; ⏲7am-11pm) An efficient place with browsing, printing, scanning and photocopying. Take your passport.

Tourist Office (☎2334757; 1 West Veli St; ⏲10am-5.45pm Mon-Fri) Reasonably helpful.

Getting There & Away

AIR

SpiceJet (www.spicejet.com) flies at least once daily to Bengaluru, Chennai, Colombo, Delhi, Hyderabad and Mumbai. Further Chennai flights are operated by **JetKonnect** (☎2690771; www.jetkonnect.com; Airport) three or four time daily, and **Air India** (☎2341795; www.airindia.com; 7A West Veli St) once daily.

BUS

Most government buses arrive and depart from the **New Bus Stand** (Melur Rd), 4km northeast of the old city. Services to Coimbatore, Kodaikanal and Ooty go from the **Arapalayam bus stand** (Puttuthoppu Main Rd), 2km northwest of the old city. Tickets for more expensive (and mostly more comfortable) private buses are sold by agencies on the south side of the **Shopping Complex Bus Stand** (btwn West Veli St & TPK Rd). Most travel overnight.

TRAIN

From Madurai Junction station, 13 daily trains head north to Trichy (two to five hours) and nine to Chennai, the fastest being the 6.45am Vaigai Express (Trichy 2nd/chair class ₹71/253, two hours; Chennai ₹132/488, eight hours). A good overnight train for Chennai is the 8.35pm Pandyan Express (sleeper/3AC/2AC/1AC ₹232/730/880/1500, nine hours). To Kanyakumari the only daily train departs at 1.55am (sleeper/3AC/2AC ₹157/398/640, five hours), though there's a later train some days (at varying times). Trivandrum (three trains daily), Coimbatore (two daily) and Bengaluru (onedaily) are other destinations.

Getting Around

The airport is 12km south of town and taxis cost ₹300 to the centre. Alternatively, buses 15 and 16 run to/from the **Periyar Bus Stand** (West Veli St). From the New Bus Stand (p388), bus 5 (₹4) shuttles into the city; an autorickshaw is ₹100.

Rameswaram

☎ 04573 / POP 46,461

Rameswaram was once the southernmost point of sacred India; to leave its boundaries was to abandon caste and fall below the status of the lowliest skinner of sacred cows. Then Rama, incarnation of Vishnu and hero of the Ramayana, led an army of monkeys and bears across a monkey-built bridge to the island of (Sri) Lanka, where he defeated the demon Ravana and rescued his wife, Sita. Afterwards, prince and princess came to this spot to offer thanks to Shiva.

If all this seems like so much folklore, it's absolute truth for millions of Hindus, who flock to the Ramanathaswamy Temple to worship where a god worshipped a god.

GOVERNMENT BUSES FROM MADURAI

DESTINATION	FARE (₹)	DURATION (HR)	FREQUENCY
Chennai	325	9-10	40 daily
Coimbatore	125	6	every 15min
Ernakulam (Kochi)	340	8	9am & 9pm
Kanyakumari	140-150	4	31 daily
Kodaikanal	75	4	14 buses 5am-2pm, & 5.50pm
Mysore	280-360	16	7 buses 4.30-9.45pm
Ooty	170	9	/7.30am & 9.30pm
Puducherry	265	8	8.45pm & 9.30pm
Rameswaram	110	5	every 30min
Trichy	90	3	40 daily

WORTH A TRIP

DHANUSHKODI

The promontory stretching 22km southeast from Rameswaram narrows to a thin strip of sand dunes about halfway along, and near the end stands the ghost town of Dhanushkodi. Once a thriving port, Dhanushkodi was washed away by the tidal waves of a monster cyclone in 1964. The shells of its train station, church, post office and other ruins still stand among a scattering of fishers' shacks, and Adam's Bridge (or Rama's Bridge), the chain of reefs, sandbanks and islets that almost connects India with Sri Lanka, stretches away to the east.

Autorickshaws charge about ₹400 round trip (including waiting time) to Moonram Chattram, a collection of fishers' huts about 14km from town. From there to Dhanushkodi it's a hot 4km walk along the beautiful sands, or a ₹100 two-hour round trip in a truck or minibus which will go when it fills up with 12 to 20 customers. It's tempting to swim, but beware of strong rips.

Apart from these pilgrims, Rameswaram is a small fishing town on an island, Pamban, which is connected to the mainland by a 2km-long road and rail bridges. The town smells of drying fish and has a lot of flies, and if you're not a pilgrim, the temple alone would barely merit the journey here. But the eastern point of the island, Dhanushkodi, only 30km from Sri Lanka, has a natural magic that adds considerably to Rameswaram's attractions.

Most hotels and eateries are clustered around the Ramanathaswamy Temple, which is surrounded by North, East, South and West Car Streets. Middle St heads west towards the bus stand (2km). The train station is 1.5km southwest of the temple.

Sights

Ramanathaswamy Temple HINDU TEMPLE
(camera ₹25; ⏲5am-9.30pm) When Rama decided to worship Shiva, he figured he'd need a lingam to do the thing properly. Being a god, he sent Hanuman to find the biggest lingam around – a Himalayan mountain. But the monkey took too long, so Rama's wife Sita made a simple lingam of sand, which is enshrined today in this temple's inner sanctum (open to Hindus only). Besides housing the world's holiest sand mound, the temple, dating mainly from the 16th to 18th centuries, is notable for its long, long, 1000-pillar halls and 22 *theerthams* (tanks and wells). Pilgrims are expected to bathe in all 22 as well as the sea before visiting the deity. The temple bathing takes the form of attendants tipping pails of water over the (often fully dressed) faithful, who then hurry on to the next *theertham*. All this water sloshing around makes the temple floors pretty wet, and you'll have a less slippery amble round the corridors if you go when the inner sanctum is closed (12.30pm to 4.30pm).

Sleeping & Eating

Many hotels are geared towards pilgrims, and some cheapies (which are mostly pretty dire) refuse to take in single travellers, but there's a string of reasonable midrange hotels. Book ahead before festivals. Budget travellers can try heading to the **rooms booking office** (East Car St; ⏲24hr), which can score doubles for as low as ₹500 a night.

A number of inexpensive vegetarian restaurants such as **Vasantha Bhavan** (East Car St; dishes ₹28-50; ⏲6am-10.30pm) and **Ananda Bhavan** (West Car St) serve vegetarian thali lunches for around ₹40, and evening dosai and *uttapams* for around ₹30. You might find fish in some restaurants, but other flesh is hard to come by.

Hotel Venkatesh HOTEL $
(☎221296; SV Koil St; r ₹420-550, with AC ₹770; ❄) The lemon-walled rooms here are reasonably clean and not bad value for the price, and it accepts single travellers. It's on the westward continuation of South Car St.

Hotel Royal Park HOTEL $$
(☎221680; www.hotelroyalpark.in; Ramnad Hwy; s ₹1919-2638, d ₹2398-3358; ❄@) Away from the temple action, this place on the main road 400m west of the bus stand is one of the most peaceful in town. Rooms are good and clean with some nice artwork, and the AC veg restaurant is good value (mainly South Indian, but the cheese and tomato toastie is perfect too).

Hotel Sri Saravana HOTEL $$
(223367; http://srisaravanahotel.com; 1/9A South Car St; r ₹1395-2815; ❄) The best of the town-centre hotels, Sri Saravana is friendly and clean with good service and spacious, colourful rooms. Those towards the top have sea views (and higher rates).

Hotel Sunrise View HOTEL $$
(223434; www.hotelsunriseview.com; 1/3G East Car St; r ₹1463; ❄) This has sparkling wall tiles and wooden furniture that's a tad better quality than at some other spots. It's acceptably clean and some rooms do indeed have sunrise (and sea) views; just try to look at the ocean rather than the rubbish on the ground.

Information

Siva Net (Middle St; per hr ₹40; 8am-9pm Mon-Sat)

State Bank of India ATM (South Car St) Accepts international cards.

Getting There & Around

Buses run to Madurai (₹110, five hours) every 30 minutes, and to Trichy (₹180, 6½ hours) every hour. 'Ultra Deluxe' (UD) services are scheduled twice daily to Chennai (₹450, 12 hours) and Kanyakumari (₹250, eight hours), but don't always run.

The three daily trains to/from Madurai (₹24, four hours) have unreserved seating only. The Sethu Express departs daily at 8pm for Chennai (sleeper/3AC/2AC ₹246/665/1000, 12½ hours) via Trichy and Thanjavur. The Rameswaram–Kanyakumari Express leaves at 8.45pm Monday, Thursday and Saturday, reaching Kanyakumari (sleeper/3AC ₹204/519) at 4.05am.

Bus 1 (₹4) shuttles between the bus stand and East Car St. Autorickshaws to the centre from the bus stand or train station should be ₹40.

Kanyakumari (Cape Comorin)

04652 / POP 23,844

There's a sense of accomplishment on making it to the point of the subcontinent's 'V', past the final dramatic flourish of the Western Ghats and the green fields, glinting rice paddies and slow-looping wind turbines of India's deep south. Like all edges, there is a sense of the surreal here. At certain times of year you can see the sun set and the moon rise over three seas simultaneously. The Temple of the Virgin Sea Goddess and the 'Land's End' symbolism draw crowds of pilgrims and tourists to Kanyakumari, but it remains a small-scale, refreshing respite from the hectic Indian road.

Sights & Activities

Kumari Amman Temple HINDU TEMPLE
(4.30am-12.30pm & 4-8.15pm) The legends say the *kanya* (virgin) goddess Kumari, a manifestation of the Great Goddess Devi, single-handedly conquered demons and secured freedom for the world. At this temple at the tip of the subcontinent, pilgrims give her thanks in an intimately spaced, beautifully decorated temple, where the crash of waves from three seas can be heard behind the twilight glow of oil fires clutched in vulva-shaped votive candles (a reference to the sacred femininity of the goddess). You're likely to be asked for a donation to enter the inner precinct, where men must remove their shirts, and cameras are forbidden.

The shoreline around the temple has a couple of tiny, sandy beaches, and bathing ghats where some worshippers immerse themselves before visiting the temple. A *mandapa* south of the temple is a highly popular spot for sunset-watching and grabbing a bit of daytime shade. A small bazaar of souvenir shops leads back from here to the main road.

Vivekananda Memorial MONUMENT
(admission ₹10; 8am-5pm) Four hundred metres offshore is the rock where the famous Hindu apostle Swami Vivekananda meditated from 25 to 27 December 1892, and decided to take his moral message beyond India's shores. A two-*mandapa* memorial was built in Vivekananda's memory in 1970, and reflects architectural styles from all over India. With all the tourist crowds this brings, Vivekananda would undoubtedly choose somewhere else to meditate today.

The huge **statue** on the smaller island next door, looking like an Indian Colossus of Rhodes, is of the ancient Tamil poet Thiruvalluvar. The work of more than 5000 sculptors, it was erected in 2000 and honours the poet's 133-chapter work *Thirukural* – hence its height of exactly 133ft (40.5m).

Ferries shuttle out to the Vivekananda island (₹30 return) between 7.45am and 4pm, but there's no regular service to Thiruvalluvar.

Gandhi Memorial MONUMENT
(admission free; 7am-7pm) Appropriately placed at the end of the nation that Gan-

Kanyakumari (Cape Comorin)

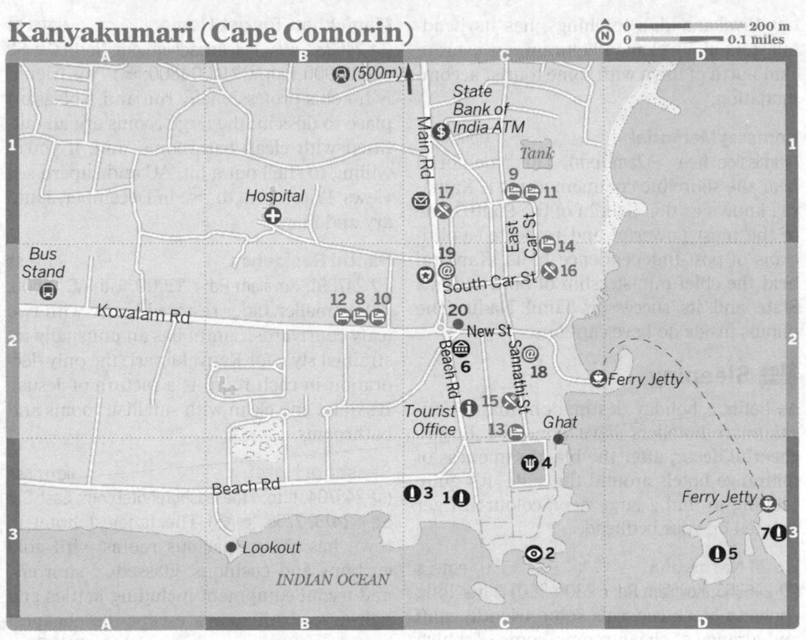

Kanyakumari (Cape Comorin)

Sights
1 Gandhi Memorial C3
2 Ghat C3
3 Kamaraj Memorial C3
4 Kumari Amman Temple C3
5 Statue of Thiruvalluvar D3
6 Swami Vivekananda Wandering Monk Exhibition C2
7 Vivekananda Memorial D3

Sleeping
8 Hotel Narmadha B2
9 Hotel Sivamurugan C1
10 Hotel Tri Sea B2
11 Manickhan Tourist Home C1
12 Santhi Residency B2
13 Saravana Lodge C2
14 Seashore Hotel C2

Eating
15 Hotel Saravana C2
16 Hotel Sea View C2
17 Sangam Restaurant C1
Seashore Hotel .... (see 14)

Information
18 Tony Travels Internet Cafe C2
19 Xerox, Internet, Fax C2

Transport
20 SETC Booking Office C2

dhi fathered, this lemon-and-pink memorial is designed in the form of an Odishan temple embellished by Hindu, Christian and Muslim architects. The central plinth was used to store some of the Mahatma's ashes, and each year, on Gandhi's birthday (2 October), the sun's rays fall on the stone. Exhibits are limited to a few uncaptioned photos; the tower is a popular sunset-viewing position.

Swami Vivekananda Wandering Monk Exhibition MUSEUM
(Main Rd; admission ₹10; 8am-noon & 4-8.15pm)
This newly refurbished exhibition details Swami Vivekananda's wisdom, sayings and encounters with the mighty and the lowly during his five years as a wandering monk around India from 1888 to 1893. The spiritual organisation **Vivekananda Kendra** (www.vivekanandakendra.org), devoted to carrying

out Vivekananda's teachings, has its headquarters at Vivekanandapuram, an ashram 1km north of town with some tourist accommodation.

Kamaraj Memorial MONUMENT
(admission free; ⌚7am-7pm) This memorial near the shoreline commemorates K Kamaraj, known as the 'Gandhi of the South'. One of the most powerful and respected politicians of post-Independence India, Kamaraj held the chief ministership of both Madras State and its successor, Tamil Nadu. The photos inside do have captions.

Sleeping

As befits a holiday destination, many Kanyakumari hoteliers have gone for bright, cheerful decor; after the bland sameness of midrange hotels around the state, it's quite exciting to find a large neon-coloured tiger painted on your bedhead.

Hotel Narmadha HOTEL $
(☎246365; Kovalam Rd; r ₹300-500) This long concrete block conceals some friendly staff and a range of cheap rooms, some of which are cleaner and have less dank bathrooms than others; the ₹500 sea-view doubles with spearmint-stripe sheets are decent value.

Saravana Lodge HOTEL $
(☎246007; Sannathi St; r ₹300-500, with AC ₹1000; ❄) It's basic, but you can get a reasonable deal here, just outside the temple entrance. All rooms have private bathrooms, though there's no hot water. The better rooms are on the upper floors of the new block at the far end from the entrance.

Hotel Tri Sea HOTEL $$
(☎246586; www.triseahotel.com; Kovalam Rd; d ₹800-1800; ❄🏊) You can't miss the high-rise Tri Sea, whose sea-view rooms are huge, spotless and airy, with particularly hectic colour schemes. The top-floor triples are even grander. The rooftop pool is a welcome bonus, though the restaurant is a sad afterthought.

Hotel Sivamurugan HOTEL $$
(☎246862; www.hotelsivamurugan.com; 2/93 North Car St; r ₹1000-1200, with AC ₹1600-2000; ❄) A welcoming, well-appointed new hotel, with spacious, spotless, marble-floored rooms. The 'super-deluxes' have sea views past a couple of buildings. There's 24-hour hot water, which not all competitors can claim.

Manickhan Tourist Home HOTEL $$
(☎246387; www.hotelmaadhini.com; North Car St; r ₹800-900, with AC ₹1400-1800; ❄) This friendly hotel is professionally run and a pleasant place to doss in; the large rooms are all outfitted with clean bathrooms, and, if you're willing to shell out a bit, AC and superb sea views. Prices tend to rise in December, January and May.

Santhi Residency HOTEL $$
(☎247091; Kovalam Rd; r ₹1000, with AC ₹1500; ❄) A smaller, older restored house with two leafy courtyards, Santhi has an unusually restrained style for Kanyakunari (the only decoration in each room is a picture of Jesus). It's quiet and clean with smallish rooms and bathrooms.

Seashore Hotel HOTEL $$$
(☎246704; http://theseashorehotel.com; East Car St; r ₹4137-7795; ❄📶) The fanciest hotel in town has shiny, spacious rooms with gold curtains and cushions, glassed-in showers, and useful equipment including kettles and hair-dryers. All rooms except the cheapest have panoramic sea views and the 7th-floor restaurant is one of Kanyakumari's best. Free wi-fi in the lobby.

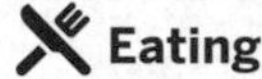

Eating

Hotel Saravana INDIAN $
(Sannathi St; mains ₹54-91; ⌚6am-10pm) A clean, very popular spot with plenty of North and South Indian vegetarian dishes, and lunchtime thalis.

Hotel Sea View MULTICUISINE $$
(East Car St; mains ₹90-250; ⌚6am-11pm) This AC hotel restaurant doesn't have a sea view, but it does do excellent fresh seafood and versions of North and South Indian faves. The vibe is upmarket and the service professional. It's also probably the best breakfast spot in town, with buffet, Continental and American options.

Seashore Hotel MULTICUISINE $$
(East Car St; mains ₹160-600; ⌚7am-10.45pm) Amazingly, the 7th-floor restaurant here is the only one in Kanyakumari with a sea view. And a fabulous view it is. What's more, the food and service are worthy of it. There's very good grilled fish and plenty of Indian veg and nonveg choices, plus a few Continental options.

Sangam Restaurant INDIAN $$
(Main Rd; mains ₹75-200; ⌚7.30am-11pm) It's as if the Sangam started in Kashmir, trekked the length of India, and stopped here to offer top veg and nonveg picks from every province along the way. The food is good, the seats are soft and the joint is bustling.

Information

State Bank of India ATM (Main Rd) Accepts international cards.

Tony Travels Internet Cafe (Sannathi St; per hr ₹60; ⌚7.30am-10pm) Friendly – possibly over-friendly (but not unsafe) for lone women.

Tourist Office (☎246276; Beach Rd; ⌚10am-5.15pm Mon-Fri) Helpful.

Xerox, Internet, Fax (Main Rd; per hr ₹30; ⌚7.30am-11pm Mon-Sat) Staffed by women, and does what its name says.

Getting There & Away

BUS

The sedate **bus stand** (Kovalam Rd) is a 10-minute walk west of the centre and there's a handy **SETC booking office** (cnr Main Rd & New St; ⌚7am-9pm) in town. Ordinary buses go about hourly to both Madurai (₹110 to ₹150) and Trivandrum (₹65, 2½ hours). The most comfortable buses are the so-called Ultra Deluxe (UD), which includes the following:

Chennai ₹520, 12 to 15 hours, seven daily

Kodaikanal ₹300, 10 hours, 8.15pm

Madurai ₹210, four hours, seven daily

TAXI

Drivers ask ₹1500 for a ride to Kovalam.

TRAIN

The train station is a walkable distance north of the centre. The one daily northbound train, the Kanyakumari Express, departs at 5.20pm for Chennai (sleeper/3AC/2AC/1AC ₹305/831/1245/2125, 13½ hours) via Madurai (₹157/398/640/1080, 4½ hours) and Trichy (₹204/538/790/1345, 7¼ hours). Two daily express trains depart in the morning for Trivandrum (2nd-class/sleeper/3AC/2AC ₹31/120/218/610, 2¼ hours), both continuing to Kollam and Ernakulam. Several more trains go from Nagercoil Junction, 15km northwest of Kanyakumari.

For real long-haulers or train buffs, the Vivek Express runs all the way to Dibrugarh in Assam, 4241km and 85 hours away – the longest single train ride in India. It departs from Kanyakumari at 2.45pm Saturday (sleeper/3AC/2AC ₹673/1948/3340).

THE WESTERN GHATS

Welcome to the lush Western Ghats, some of the most welcome heat relief in India. Rising like an impassable bulwark of evergreen and deciduous tangle from north of Mumbai to the tip of Tamil Nadu, the Ghats (with an average elevation of 915m) contain 27% of India's flowering plants and an incredible array of endemic wildlife. In Tamil Nadu they rise to 2000m and more in the Palni Hills around Kodaikanal and the Nilgiris around Ooty. British influence lingers a little stronger up in these hills, where the colonists covered the slopes in neatly trimmed tea bushes and created their 'hill stations' to escape the heat of the plains. It's not just the air and (relative) lack of pollution that's refreshing – there's a certain acceptance of quirkiness and eccentricity in the hills that is rarer in the lowlands. Think organic farms, handlebar-moustached trekking guides and tiger-stripe earmuffs for sale in the bazaars.

Kodaikanal (Kodai)

☎04542 / POP 41,882 / ELEV 2100M

There are few more refreshing Tamil Nadu moments than boarding a bus in the heat-soaked plains and disembarking in the sharp pinch of a Kodaikanal night or morning. It's not all cold though; during the day the weather is positively pleasant, more reminiscent of deep spring than early winter. This misty hill station, 120km northwest of Madurai in the Palni hills, is more relaxed and more intimate than its big sister Ooty (brochures call Kodai the 'Princess of Hill Stations', while Ooty is the Queen). The renowned Kodaikanal International School provides a bit of cosmopolitan influence, with students from around the globe.

Centred on a very pretty lake, Kodai rambles up and down hillsides with patches of *shola* forest, unique to the Western Ghats in South India, and evergreen broadleaf trees such as magnolia, mahogany, myrtle and rhododendron. Another plant speciality around here (in the grasslands) is the *kurinji* shrub, whose lilac-blue blossoms only appear every 12 years: next due date 2018.

Kodai is popular with honeymooners, who flock to the spectacular lookout points and waterfalls in and around town.

Kodaikanal (Kodai)

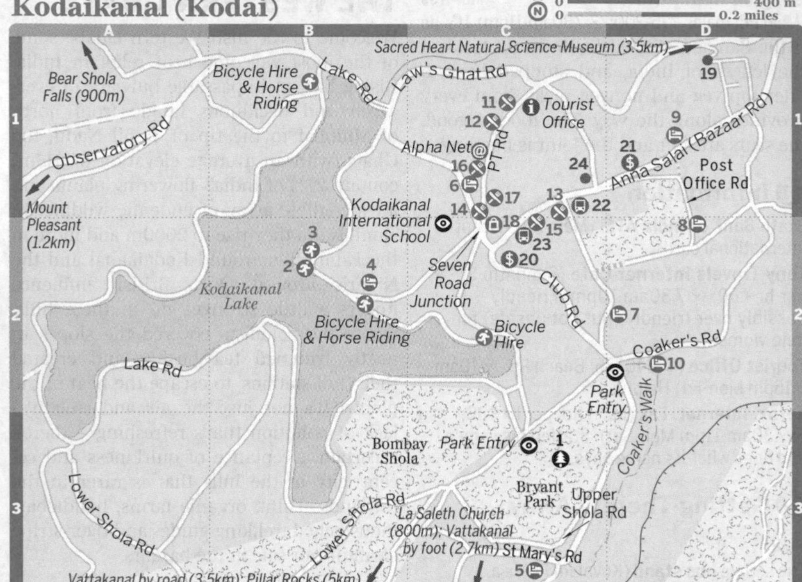

Sights & Activities

Sacred Heart Natural Science Museum MUSEUM

(Sacred Heart College, Law's Ghat Rd; admission ₹10; ⌚9am-5pm) In the grounds of a former Jesuit seminary about 4km downhill east of town, this museum has a ghoulishly intriguing miscellany of flora and fauna put together over more than 100 years by priests and trainees. Displays range over bottled snakes, human embryos (!), giant moths, stuffed animal carcasses and black-and-white photos of solemn priests with huge snakes draped over them. You can also see some pressed *kurinji* flowers *(Strobilanthes kunthiana)* in case you're not around for their flowering.

Parks & Waterfalls

Bryant Park (adult/child ₹20/10, camera/video ₹30/75; ⌚9am-6.30pm), landscaped and stocked by the British officer after whom it's named, is pretty, and often busy with canoodling couples as well as tourists.

Several beauty spots around Kodai are very popular with Indian tourists and crowded with souvenir and snack stalls too. They're best visited by taxi unless you like walking along busy roads. Taxi drivers offer a tour of eight 'sightseeing places' for ₹500 (₹600 April to June). **Green Valley View** (6km from downtown), **Pillar Rocks** (7km) and less visited **Moir's Point** (13km), all along the same road west of town, have spectacular views to the plains far below. To go beyond Moir's Point to pretty, forest-surrounded **Berijam Lake** requires a Forest Department permit. Taxi drivers can organise this, if asked the day before, and do four-hour 'forest tours' to Berijam, via a couple more lookouts, for ₹1600. Access to the lake is closed on Tuesdays.

The river that empties Kodaikanal Lake tumbles dramatically down **Silver Cascade**, on the Madurai road 7km from town. Compact **Bear Shola Falls** are in a pocket of forest on the northwest edge of town.

Walking

Assuming it's not cloaked in opaque mist, the views from paved **Coaker's Walk** (admission ₹5, camera ₹10; ⌚7am-6.30pm) are magnificent, all the way down to the plains 2000m below. The stroll takes all of five minutes.

Kodai's lake is very pretty and the 5km lake circuit is pleasant in the early morning when you can count the kingfishers before the tourist traffic starts. A walk along Lower Shola Rd will take you through the Bombay

Kodaikanal (Kodai)

Sights

1 Bryant Park C3

Activities, Courses & Tours

2 Kodaikanal Boat & Rowing Club B2
3 Tamil Nadu Tourist Development Corporation B2

Sleeping

4 Carlton Hotel B2
5 Greenlands Youth Hostel C3
6 Hilltop Towers C1
7 Hotel Cokkers Tower D2
8 Hotel Sunrise D2
9 Snooze Inn D1
10 Villa Retreat D2

Eating

Carlton Hotel .... (see 4)
11 Cloud Street C1
12 Eco Nut C1
13 Hotel Astoria C1
14 Hotel New Punjab C1
15 Pastry Corner C2
16 Pot Luck C1
17 Tava C1

Shopping

Cottage Craft Shop .... (see 16)
18 Re Shop C2

Information

19 District Forest Office D1
20 HDFC Bank ATM C2
21 State Bank of India ATM D1

Transport

22 Bus Stand C1
23 Raja's Tours & Travels C2
Taxi Stand .... (see 22)
24 Train Booking Office C1

Shola, the nearest surviving patch of *shola* to downtown Kodai.

Most serious trekking routes in the Kodai area require Forest Department permits which can only be obtained with considerable time, patience and luck. Contact the **Principal Chief Conservator of Forests** (Map p334; ☎044-24321174; Panagal Maaligai, Anna Salai, Saidapet) office in Chennai, then Kodai's **District Forest Office** (☎240287; Muthaliarpuram; ⏲10am-5.45pm Mon-Fri). Kodai's tourist office (p397) and accommodation places such as Greenlands Youth Hostel (p395) can put you in touch with local guides who may be able to offer interesting off-road local routes for ₹1000 to ₹1500 per full day.

Boating, Cycling & Horse Riding

If you're sappy in love like a bad Bollywood song, the thing to do in Kodai is rent a pedal boat (₹50 per half-hour for two people), rowboat (₹90 including boatman) or Kashmiri *shikara*, aka 'honeymoon boat' (₹260 including boatman) from the **Kodaikanal Boat & Rowing Club** (⏲9am-5.30pm) or **Tamil Nadu Tourist Development Corporation** (⏲9am-5.30pm); screechy crooning is strictly optional.

Around the lake are a few **bicycle-rental** (₹20/200 per hour/day) and **horse-riding stands** (₹60 per 500m, or ₹300 per hour).

Sleeping

Some hotel prices rise by up to 100% during the high season (April to June). There are some lovely heritage places, and some good-value midrange options if you can live without colonial-era ambience. Most hotels have a 9am or 10am checkout time in high season, but the rest of the year it's usually 24 hours.

Hotel Cokkers Tower HOTEL $
(☎240374; cokkers.tower@yahoo.com; Woodville Rd; dm/d ₹110/825) A straightforward hotel with simple, very clean, light-coloured rooms (no colonial wood here). The dorm has narrow beds reminiscent of train bunks, and is best avoided during the monsoon when its roof may leak, but its bathroom is sparkling and you can't beat the price.

Snooze Inn HOTEL $
(☎240873; www.jayarajgroup.com; Anna Salai; r ₹770-935; wi-fi) The outside has a bit more character than the rooms, but this is a decent-value budget choice with clean bathrooms, plenty of blankets and free wi-fi.

Greenlands Youth Hostel HOSTEL $
(☎240899; www.greenlandskodaikanal.com; St Mary's Rd; dm ₹250, d ₹600-1800) This long-running spot has a nice garden and excellent views, but the accommodation is very bare and basic, hot water is only available from 8am to 10am, and washing in the dorms is by buckets of cold water.

★ **Villa Retreat** HOTEL $$
(☎243556, 240940; www.villaretreat.com; Club Rd; r incl breakfast ₹2878-4677; wi-fi) You can enjoy the awesome Coaker's Walk views from your garden breakfast table at this lovely old stone-built family hotel, right next to the walk's northern end. It's a friendly place

WORTH A TRIP

VATTAKANAL WALK

This is a lovely walk of about 4.5km (each way) from the centre of town, on which you might, if lucky, spot gaur (bison) or giant squirrels in the forested bits. Follow St Mary's Rd west then southwest from the south end of Coaker's Walk, passing La Saleth Church after 1.2km. At a fork 400m after the church, go left downhill on what quickly becomes an unpaved track passing through part of the Pambar Shola forest. After 450m you emerge on a road by a bridge above some falls. Across the bridge you'll find snack stalls selling fruit, tea, coffee, bread omelettes, and roasted corn with lime and masala – all yummy! Follow the road 1km downhill, with panoramas opening up as you go, to Vattakanal village. Take the path down past Altaf's Cafe and in about 15 minutes you'll reach the Dolphin's Nose, a rock lookout overhanging a precipitous drop.

with comfy, good-sized rooms and free wi-fi in the dining room. Checkout time is 9am.

Hilltop Towers HOTEL **$$**
(☎240413; www.hilltopgroup.in; Club Rd; r incl breakfast ₹2160-2700) Although it's bland on the outside, rustic accents like polished teak floors and wooden embellishments, plus friendly staff, in-room coffee-makers and 90-channel TV make the Hilltop a good midrange choice.

Mount Pleasant BOUTIQUE HOTEL **$$**
(☎242023, 9655126023; www.kodaikanalheritage.com; 19/12-20 Observatory Rd; r incl breakfast ₹2278-3718; wi-fi) A lot of perfectly decent hotels are scattered around the outer reaches of Kodai's spaghetti-like street map. In most cases the inconvenient distance outweighs their appeal, but Mount Pleasant is worth finding for its quiet setting, comfy rooms and the amiable Keralan owner's slightly quirky taste – colourful wall weavings, coconut-wood beds, coir matting. Tasty buffet dinners are available. It's advisable to book.

Hotel Sunrise HOTEL **$$**
(☎241358; www.kodaihotelsunrise.com; 8/62 Post Office Rd; r ₹1438-2877) Cosy red-and-brown rooms, amiable staff, 24-hour hot water and sunrise views from about half the rooms make this a worthy option.

★ **Carlton Hotel** HOTEL **$$$**
(☎240056; www.krahejahospitality.com; Lake Rd; d/cottages incl half-board ₹9550/14,500; wi-fi) The cream of Kodai's hotels is a magnificent five-star colonial-era mansion that overlooks the lake. Rooms are bright and spacious and some have private balconies. The common areas and grounds very much succeed at recreating hill-station ambience, with stone walls, housie (bingo) by the fireplace at 6.30pm, billiards, badminton, putting green and a bar that might make you want to demand a scotch now, dammit, from the eager staff.

Vattakanal

Little Vattakanal village, about 4.5km southwest of the town centre, is a great rural retreat for budget travellers. It's very popular with, among others, Israeli travellers, and a party atmosphere develops here at busy times. Several village houses have rooms to rent for about ₹400 to ₹600. Altaf's Cafe (p396) has a few sizeable three-bed rooms accommodating up to five or six people (sometimes more!) with private bathroom for ₹1000.

Eating

PT Rd is best for cheap restaurants and it's here that most travellers and students from the international school congregate.

Hotel New Punjab NORTH INDIAN **$**
(PT Rd; mains ₹55-200; ⏲12.30-10pm) For North Indian cuisine, including tandoori (and any nonveg curries in general), this little place is Kodai's favourite. It serves the best tandoori chicken in South India, according to locals.

Tava INDIAN **$**
(PT Rd; mains ₹40-90; ⏲11am-9pm) A clean, fast and cheap veg option, Tava has a wide menu; try the spicy, cauliflower-stuffed *gobi paratha* or *sev puri* (crisp, puffy fried bread with potato and chutney).

Altaf's Cafe MULTICUISINE **$**
(☎9488569632; Vattakanal; dishes ₹50-150; ⏲7.30am-8pm; wi-fi) This open-air cafe does Indian and Middle Eastern dishes including *sabich* (Israeli aubergine-and-egg pita sandwiches) and assorted breakfasts, for the hungry travellers at Vattakanal.

Pot Luck CAFE $
(PT Rd; snacks & light meals ₹30-130; ⏰11am-7pm Wed-Mon) Sandwiches, pancakes, coffee, omelettes and quesadillas (!) served up on a pretty, tiny terrace attached to a pottery shop.

Cloud Street MULTICUISINE $$
(PT Rd; mains ₹175-300; ⏰8.30am-10.30pm) Why yes, that is a real Italian-style wood-fire pizza oven. And yes, that's hummus, felafel and nachos on the menu, alongside pasta, Spanish omelette and pepper steak – it's all great food in a simple, relaxed setting.

Hotel Astoria INDIAN $$
(Anna Salai; mains ₹85-135; ⏰7am-10pm) This veg restaurant is always packed with locals and tourists, especially at lunchtime when it serves excellent all-you-can-eat thalis.

★ **Carlton Hotel** MULTICUISINE $$$
(buffet lunch/dinner ₹720/810; ⏰7-10am, 1-3pm, 7.30-10.30pm) The buffet meals here provide a big variety of excellent Indian and Continental dishes in limitless quantity. Definitely the place to come for a splash-out fill-up.

Self-Catering

Pastry Corner BAKERY $
(Anna Salai; ⏰10am-2pm & 3-7pm) Pick up great picnic sandwiches and yummy muffins and croissants at this highly popular bakery, or squeeze onto the benches with a cuppa to watch the world go by.

Eco Nut ORGANIC $
(PT Rd; ⏰9.30am-5.30pm Mon-Sat) This interesting shop sells a wide range of local organic food – wholewheat bread, muffins, marmalade, spices – and oils, herbs and herb remedies.

Shopping

Shops and stalls all over town sell spices, homemade chocolate and natural oils. Some also reflect a low-key but long-term commitment to social justice.

Re Shop HANDICRAFTS
(www.bluemangoindia.com; Seven Roads Junction; ⏰10am-7pm Mon-Sat) Stylish jewellery, T-shirts, cards and more, at reasonable prices, made by and benefiting marginalised village women around Tamil Nadu.

Cottage Craft Shop HANDICRAFTS
(PT Rd; ⏰10am-7.30pm Mon-Sat, 11am-7.30pm Sun) This shop sells hats, incense, embroidery and other goods crafted by disadvantaged groups, with about 80% of the purchase price returned to the makers.

Information

Alpha Net (PT Rd; per hr ₹60; ⏰9am-8.30pm)

Tourist Office (☎241675; PT Rd; ⏰10am-5.45pm Mon-Fri) Doesn't look too promising but they're surprisingly helpful.

Getting There & Away

The nearest train station is Kodai Road, down in the plains about 80km east of Kodaikanal. There are nine daily trains to/from Chennai Egmore including the overnight Pandiyan Express (sleeper/3AC/2AC/1AC ₹220/561/825/1419, eight hours), departing Chennai at 9.20pm and departing Kodai Road northbound at 9.10pm. For most closer destinations, it's quicker and easier to get a bus. Taxis to/from the station cost ₹1100. There are plenty of buses between the station and Batlagundu, which is on the Kodai–Madurai bus route. There's a **train booking office** (off Anna Salai; ⏰8am-noon & 2.30-5pm Mon-Sat, 8am-noon Sun) in town.

Government buses from Kodai's **bus stand** (Anna Salai):

Bengaluru ₹425-450, 11 hours, 5.30pm and 6pm
Chennai ₹380, 11 hours, 6.30pm
Coimbatore ₹120, five hours, 8.30am and 4.30pm
Madurai ₹68, four hours, 15 daily
Trichy ₹111, 5½ hours, four daily

Raja's Tours & Travels (☎242422; Anna Salai) runs 20-seat minibuses with push-back seats to Ooty (₹350, eight hours) at 7.30pm, to Madurai (₹250) at 4pm and to Kochi (₹600, 10 hours) at 6pm. It also sells tickets for overnight AC sleeper buses to Chennai (₹820) and Bengaluru (₹830).

Getting Around

The central part of Kodaikanal is compact and easy to get around on foot. There are no autorickshaws (believe it or not), but plenty of taxis. Trips within town generally cost ₹100.

Around Kodaikanal

One of the better escapes in the area, about three hours' drive below Kodaikanal off the Dindigul–Batlagundu road, is fabulous **Cardamom House** (☎9360691793, 0451-2556765; www.cardamomhouse.com; near Athoor Village; r ₹3300-4000 Apr-Nov, ₹4500-5500 Dec-Mar) 🍃. Created with love and care by a retired Brit, this comfortable guesthouse – at the end of a scenic road beside bird rich

Lake Kamarajar – runs on solar power, uses water wisely, farms organically, and trains and employs only locals (who produce terrific meals). Book well ahead, hire a driver to take you there, and prepare for some serious relaxation.

Coimbatore

☎ 0422 / POP 1.06 MILLION

This large business and junction city – the second largest in Tamil Nadu, sometimes known as the Manchester of India for its textile industry – is friendly enough, but the dearth of interesting sights means that for most travellers it's just a stepping stone towards Ooty or Kerala. It has plenty of accommodation and eating options if you need to spend the night.

Sleeping

Legend's Inn HOTEL $$
(☎4350000; legends_inn@yahoo.com; Geetha Hall Rd; r ₹1089-1439, s/d with AC ₹1799/2040; ❄) One of the best-value midrange options, with spacious, clean, comfortable rooms at good prices for what you get. It gets busy, so it's worth booking ahead.

Hotel ESS Grande HOTEL $$
(☎2230271; www.hotelessgrande.co.in; 358-360 Nehru St; s/d incl breakfast from ₹2159/2518; ❄@) Near a few of the bus stands, the ESS has small but very clean, fresh rooms, and possibly the sparkliest bathrooms in Coimbatore. Free cable internet in rooms. There are several other midrange and budget hotels on this street.

Hotel AP HOTEL $$
(☎2301773; hotelap@yahoo.com; Geetha Hall Rd; s/d ₹990/1440; ❄) One of at least 10 places on this lane opposite the train station, the AP has renovated all its rooms, which are now all AC, with white paint and light wood, and reasonable value. If you don't need AC and price is the priority, try **Sree Subbu Hotel** (☎2300006; Geetha Hall Rd; s/d ₹420/605) a few doors away.

Residency HOTEL $$$
(☎2241414; www.theresidency.com; 1076 Avinashi Rd; s/d incl breakfast from ₹6596/7075; ❄@📶🏊) The Residency is top choice for, among other things, its friendly staff, attractive and well-equipped rooms, swimming pool, free wi-fi and excellent eating and drinking options: the buffet meals in the **Pavilion** (buffet breakfast/lunch/dinner ₹450/670/670; ⏲24hr) restaurant are very good value. Check the website for discounts.

Eating

Naalukattu SOUTH INDIAN $
(Nehru St; mains ₹65-140; ⏲11am-11pm) Like a dark-wood-accented Keralan verandah, with Malayalam-inspired food that's all good – especially the seafood.

That's Y On The Go MULTICUISINE $$
(167 Racecourse Rd; mains ₹100-250; ⏲12.30-3pm & 7-11pm) With a clean, contemporary, cheerful ambience, this is a good place to enjoy tasty North Indian dishes and global fare from Italian to Southeast Asian to Middle Eastern. Tempting chocolatey desserts, too.

Hot Chocolate WESTERN $$
(734 Avinashi Rd; mains ₹90-300; ⏲10am-10.30pm) This place is not bad at all if you're hankering after Tex-Mex, pasta, sandwiches or indulgent cakes.

Information

ATMs (State Bank Rd) State Bank of India and Canara Bank, among others, have ATMs outside the train station.

Travel Gate (Geetha Hall Rd; per hr ₹25; ⏲9am-10pm) Cramped and sweaty internet cafe.

MAJOR TRAINS FROM COIMBATORE

DESTINATION	TRAIN NO & NAME	FARE (₹)	DURATION (HR)	DEPARTURE
Bengaluru	16525 Island Express	194/533/800	8	10.55pm
Chennai Central	12676 Kovai Express	132/471*	7½	2.20pm
	12674 Cheran Express	232/594/880	8½	10.20pm
Ernakulam	17230 Sabari Express	122/323/610	5	8.30am
Madurai	16610 Nagercoil Express	155/419/-	5½	8.30pm

*2nd-class/AC chair
All other fares are sleeper/3AC/2AC

Getting There & Away

AIR

The airport is 10km east of town, with daily direct flights to domestic destinations including Bengaluru, Chennai, Delhi, Hyderabad and Mumbai on **Air India** (☎2303569; www.airindia.com), **IndiGo** (www.goindigo.in), **JetKonnect** (☎2243465; www.jetkonnect.com) or **SpiceJet** (www.spicejet.com). **SilkAir** (☎4370271; www.silkair.com) flies three times weekly to/from Singapore.

BUS

From the **SETC Bus Stand** (Thiruvalluvar Bus Stand; Bharathiyar Rd), government express buses head to Bengaluru (₹367 to ₹700, nine hours, five daily), Chennai (₹360, 11 hours, nine buses 5.30pm to 10pm), Ernakulam (₹139, 5½ hours, three daily), Mysore (₹147 to ₹300, six hours, 13 daily) and Trivandrum (₹300, 10½ hours, eight daily). The **Ooty Bus Stand** (New Bus Stand; Mettupalayam (MTP) Rd), northwest of the centre, has services to Ooty (₹52, four hours) via Mettupalayam (₹21, one hour) and Coonoor (₹40, three hours) every 20 to 30 minutes from 1.30am to 9pm, plus hourly buses to Kotagiri (₹32, three hours, 5.15am to 7.15pm), 18 daily to Mysore and eight to Bengaluru. Buses to Trichy (₹140, six hours) and Madurai (₹125, six hours), both every 15 minutes from 5.30am to 6.30pm, go from the **Singanallur Bus Stand** (Kamaraj Rd), 6km east of the centre: take city bus 80 from the **Town Bus Stand** (cnr Dr Nanjappa & Bharathiyar Rds).

Ukkadam Bus Station (NH Rd), southwest of the centre, has buses to southern destinations including Pollachi (₹25, 1¼ hours, every 10 minutes), Kodaikanal (₹120, six hours, 10am) and Munnar (₹140, 6½ hours, two daily), plus some services to Madurai and Ernakulam.

Private buses to Bengaluru, Ernakulam, Chennai and Trivandrum start from the **Omni Bus Stand** (Sathy Rd), 500m north of the Town Bus Stand. Many agencies on Sathy Rd sell tickets.

TAXI

A taxi up the hill to Ooty (three hours) costs about ₹1800; Ooty buses are often so crowded that it's an option worth considering.

TRAIN

Coimbatore Junction is on the main line between Chennai and Ernakulam (Kochi, Kerala), with at least 12 daily trains in each direction. The 5.15am Nilgiri Express to Mettupalayam connects with the miniature railway departure from Mettupalayam to Ooty at 7.10am. The whole trip to Ooty takes about seven hours.

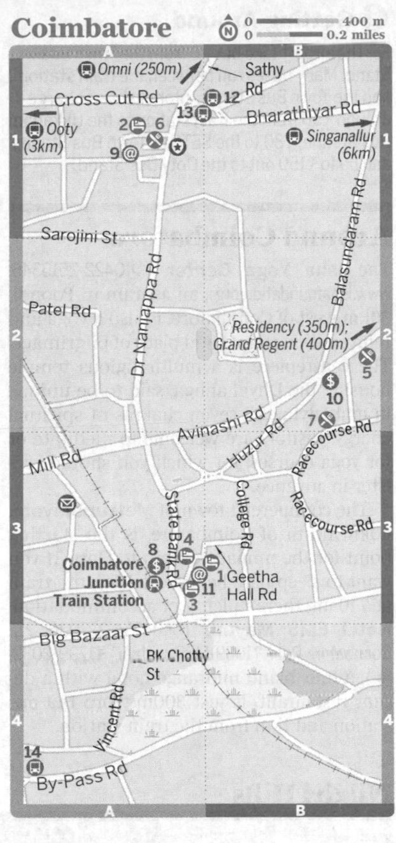

Coimbatore

Sleeping
1 Hotel AP B3
2 Hotel ESS Grande A1
3 Legend's Inn A3
4 Sree Subbu Hotel A3

Eating
5 Hot Chocolate B2
6 Naalukattu A1
7 That's Y On The Go B2

Information
8 ATMs A3
9 Oscar Browsing Centre A1
10 State Bank of India ATM B2
11 Travel Gate A3

Transport
12 SETC Bus Stand B1
13 Town Bus Stand A1
14 Ukkadam Bus Station A4

Getting Around

For the airport take bus 20 from the Town Bus Stand. Many buses run between the train station and the Town Bus Stand. Autorickshaws charge around ₹50 from the train station to the Ukkadam Bus Station, ₹80 to the SETC or Town Bus Stands, and up to ₹150 out to the Ooty Bus Stand.

Around Coimbatore

The **Isha Yoga Center** (☎0422-2515345; www.ishafoundation.org), an ashram in Poondi, 30km west of Coimbatore, is also a yoga and rejuvenation retreat and place of pilgrimage. The centrepiece is a multireligious temple housing the Dhyanalinga, said to be unique in embodying all seven chakras of spiritual energy. Visitors are welcome to meditate or for yoga courses, for which you should register in advance.

The commercial town of **Mettupalayam**, 40km north of Coimbatore, is the starting point for the miniature train to Ooty. If you want to sleep here before catching the train at 7.10am, there's plenty of accommodation. **Hotel EMS Mayura** (☎04254-227936; 212 Coimbatore Rd; r ₹1089-1439, with AC ₹1799-2039; ❄), a fine, bland midrange hotel with a decent restaurant, is just 300m from the bus station and 1km from the train station.

Coonoor

☎ 0423 / POP 54,355 / ELEV 1720M

Coonoor is one of the three Nilgiri hill stations – Ooty, Kotagiri and Coonoor – that sit high above the southern plains. Smaller and quieter than Ooty, it has some terrific small hotels and guesthouses, from which you can do just the same kind of things as you would do from bigger, busier Ooty. From upper Coonoor, 1km to 2km above the town centre, you can look down over the sea of red-tile rooftops to the slopes beyond and soak up the peace, cool climate and beautiful scenery. Just note you get none of the above in central Coonoor, which is a bustling, honking mess.

Sights & Activities

The **Dolphin's Nose viewpoint**, about 10km from town, exposes a vast panorama encompassing Catherine Falls (p401) across the valley. On the same road, **Lamb's Rock**, a favourite picnic spot in a pretty patch of forest, has amazing views past the hills to the hazy plains. The easiest way to see these sights is a rickshaw tour for around ₹600. If you like, walk the 6km or so back into town from Lamb's Rock (it's mostly downhill).

Nilgiri Hills

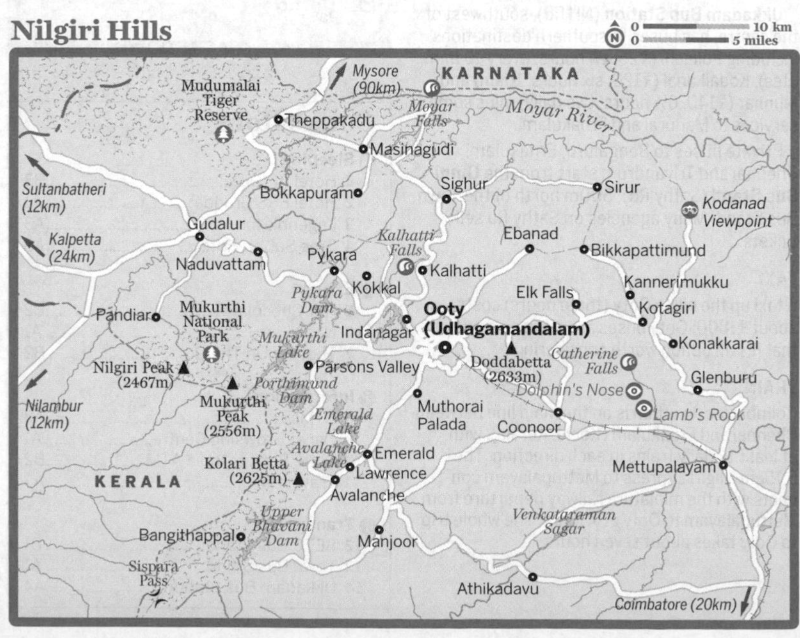

Sim's Park PARK
(adult/child ₹20/10, camera/video ₹30/75; ⌚8am-6.30pm) Upper Coonoor's 12-hectare Sim's Park, established in 1874, is a peaceful oasis of manicured lawns sloping down to a small lake, with more than 1000 plant species from several continents, including magnolia, tree ferns and camellia. Kotagiri-bound buses can drop you here.

Sleeping & Eating

You'll need a rickshaw, car or good legs to reach any of these places. If you're self-catering, visit the **Green Shop** (www.lastforest.in; Jograj Bldg, Bedford Circle; ⌚9.30am-7pm Mon-Sat) for fair-trade local tribal products like wild honey, nuts, spices and organic tea (plus attractive tribal crafts). The well-stocked supermarket in **Tulsi Mall** (31 Mount Pleasant Rd) has a range of packaged Western goods.

YWCA Wyoming Guesthouse HOSTEL $
(☎2234426; ywcacoonoor@gmail.com; Bedford; dm/s/d ₹150/345/810; @) A ramshackle, 150-year-old gem, the Wyoming is ageing and draughty but oozes character with wooden terraces and serene views through trees over the town. Staff are welcoming and the rooms are good and clean, with geysers for hot water. Meals available with two or three hours' notice.

★**180° McIver** BOUTIQUE HOTEL $$
(☎2233323; http://serendipityo.com; Orange Grove Rd; r incl breakfast ₹3857-5875;) A classic 1880s British bungalow at the top of town has been turned into something special with a *soupçon* of French taste. The six lovely, large rooms sport antique furniture, working fireplaces and big fresh bathrooms, and the panoramas from the wraparound front lawn are fabulous. The in-house restaurant, **La Belle Vie** (mains ₹150-450; ⌚noon-2.45pm & 7-10pm), uses organic produce and has guests driving a long way to sample its European-Indian-Southeast Asian menu. There's free wi-fi throughout.

Acres Wild FARMSTAY $$
(☎9443232621; www.acres-wild.com; Upper Meanjee Estate, Kannimariamman Kovil St; r incl breakfast ₹2398-4797;) This gorgeously situated farm on the southeast edge of town is run on sustainable lines with solar heating, rain harvesting and cheese like you've never tasted in India from the milk of its own cows. Guests can take a two-day cheese-making course. The five rooms, in three cottages, are ample and stylish, with kitchens and fireplaces, and your friendly hosts have lots of ideas for things to do away from tourist crowds. Advance booking advisable.

Tryst GUESTHOUSE $$$
(☎2207057; http://trystindia.com; Carolina Tea Estate; s/d incl breakfast & dinner ₹5500/6600; ⌚Oct-Apr; @) If you're looking for a gregarious accommodation experience that's quirky and classy, check out the website of this highly original and welcoming guesthouse and book ahead. It's beautifully located in a former tea-plantation manager's bungalow, in a valley about 4km west of town, with lovely local walks.

Getting There & Away

Coonoor is on the miniature train line between Mettupalayam (27km) and Ooty (19km), with three daily trains just to/from Ooty as well as the daily Mettupalayam–Ooty–Mettupalayam service. Buses to and from Ooty (₹10, one hour) run about every 10 minutes; buses to Kotagiri (₹11, one hour) and Coimbatore (₹40, three hours) go roughly every 20 minutes.

Kotagiri

☎04266 / POP 29,777 / ELEV 1800M

The oldest and smallest of the three Nilgiri hill stations, Kotagiri is a quiet, unassuming place with a forgettable town centre – the appeal is the escape to red dirt tracks in the pines, blue skies and the high green walls of the Nilgiris.

You can visit **Catherine Falls**, 8km south, off the Mettupalayam road (the last 3km is on foot, and the falls only flow after rain), **Elk Falls** (6km) and **Kodanad Viewpoint** (22km), where there's a view over both the Coimbatore Plains and the Mysore Plateau. A half-day taxi tour to all three costs around ₹1000. The scenery on the road to Mettupalayam is gorgeous, too.

If you've any interest in the history of the Nilgiris, do visit the **Sullivan Memorial** (☎9942545085; www.sullivanmemorial.org; Kannerimukku; admission ₹10; ⌚10am-5pm Mon-Sat), 2km north of Kotagiri centre. The house built in 1819 by John Sullivan, founder of Ooty, has been refurbished and filled with fascinating photos and artefacts about local tribal groups, European settlement and icons such as the toy train.

Also here are the offices of the **Keystone Foundation** (☎272277; www.keystone-foundation.org; Groves Hill Rd), an NGO working

THE NILGIRIS & THEIR TRIBES

The forest-clothed, waterfall-threaded walls of the Nilgiris (Blue Mountains) rise abruptly from the surrounding plains, ascended only by winding ghat roads and the famous Nilgiri Mountain Railway which snakes up the relatively less steep eastern slope. The Nilgiris stand between the lowland towns of Mettupalayam to the southeast and Gudalur to the northwest, with the Sispara Pass and Kodanad Viewpoint marking their approximate southwest and northeast extremities. The upland territory, a jumble of valleys and hills with more than 20 peaks above 2000m, is a botanist's dream with 2300 flowering plant species, although a lot of the native *shola* forest and grasslands have been displaced by tea, eucalyptus and cattle.

The Unesco-designated Nilgiri Biosphere Reserve is a larger, 5520-sq-km area that also includes lowland areas and parts of Kerala and Karnataka states. It contains several important tiger reserves, national parks and wildlife sanctuaries, and is rated one of the world's biodiversity hot spots.

The Nilgiris' tribal inhabitants were left pretty much to themselves in their isolated homeland until the British arrived two centuries ago. Today, the effects of colonialism and migration from the lowlands have reduced many tribal cultures to the point of collapse, and some have assimilated to the point of invisibility. Some, however, continue at least a semi-traditional lifestyle, practising small-scale agriculture or herding, or gathering wild forest produce. Organisations such as the Keystone Foundation (p401) are helping to promote traditional activities and crafts.

Best known of the tribes, thanks to anthropologists' interest and their proximity to Ooty, are the Toda, who now number around 1000. Some still inhabit tiny villages of their traditional barrel-shaped huts made of bamboo, cane and grass. Toda women wear their hair in long, shoulder-length ringlets, and both sexes wear characteristic black-and-red-embroidered shawls of homespun cotton. The water buffalo is at the centre of Toda life. Buffalo milk and ghee are integral to their diet and are also bartered for grain, tools and medical services. The dairy produce also provides offerings to the gods. Traditionally, it is only at funerals that the strictly vegetarian Toda kill a buffalo, not for food but to provide company for the deceased.

The 350,000-strong Badaga are believed to have migrated into the Nilgiris from the north around 1600 AD, and are thus not usually considered truly indigenous. Their traditional dress is of white cloth with a border of narrow coloured stripes. They worship the mother goddess Hetti Amman, to whom their six-day Hettai habba festival in December or January is dedicated.

The Kota live in seven settlements in the Kotagiri area. Cultivators, they still undertake ceremonies in which the gods are beseeched for rains and bountiful harvests. They have adapted relatively well to modernity, with a significant number holding government jobs.

The Kurumba inhabit the thick forests of the south and are traditional gatherers of forest products such as bamboo and wild honey, which they collect from cliffs, rocky crevices and trees.

to improve environmental conditions in the Nilgiris while working with, and creating better living standards for, indigenous communities. It has some openings for volunteers with communications, design and other skills. The foundation's **Green Shop** (Johnstone Sq; 9.30am-7pm Mon-Sat) in Coonoor has goodies for picnics (local organic cheese, wild honey and more) plus appealing tribal crafts.

Hope Park (271229; www.hopeparkhotel.com; Hope Park; r ₹1679-2398) has big, clean rooms, a decent restaurant and friendly staff. French-owned **La Maison** (273347; Hadatharai; s/d ₹7425/8910;) is a beautifully renovated 1890s Scottish bungalow, in the countryside about 5km southwest of town: the Franco-Indian fusion food is one of the attractions here.

Buses to and from Ooty run half-hourly (₹13, 1½ hours), crossing one of Tamil Nadu's highest passes. Buses to Mettupalayam leave hourly.

Ooty (Ootacamund, Udhagamandalam)

☎ 0423 / POP 111,918 / ELEV 2240M

Ooty may be a bit bustling for some tastes, and the town centre is, frankly, an ugly mess, but it doesn't take long to get up into the greener, quieter areas where tall pines rise above what might almost be mistaken for English country lanes. Ooty combines Indian bustle and Hindu temples with lovely parks and gardens and charming Raj-era bungalows, the latter providing its most memorable (and generally most expensive) places to stay.

The town was established by the British in the early 19th century as the summer headquarters of the Madras government, and memorably nicknamed 'Snooty Ooty'. Development ploughed in a few decades ago, but somehow old Ooty survives. You just have to walk a bit further out from the centre to find it.

The journey up here on the celebrated miniature train is romantic and the scenery stunning. Even the road up from the plains is pretty impressive. From April to June (the *very* busy season) Ooty is a welcome relief from the hot plains, and in the colder months (October to March) you'll need warm clothing, which you can buy cheap here, as overnight temperatures occasionally drop to 0°C.

The train and bus stations are at the west end of Ooty's racecourse, in almost the lowest part of town. To their west is the lake, while the streets of the town snake upwards all around. From the bus station it's a 20-minute walk to Ooty's commercial centre, Charing Cross. Like Kodaikanal, Ooty has an international school whose students can often be seen around town.

Sights

Botanical Gardens GARDEN

(adult/child ₹20/10, camera/video ₹30/75; ⏲7am-6.30pm) Established in 1848, these lovely gardens are a living gallery of the natural flora of the Nilgiris. Look out for a fossilised tree trunk believed to be around 20 million years old, and on busy days, roughly 20 million Indian tourists.

Doddabetta Lookout VIEWPOINT

(admission ₹5; ⏲7am-6pm) This is it: the highest point (2633m) of the Nilgiris and one of the best viewpoints around, assuming the day is clear (go early for better chances of a mist-free view). It's about 7km from the town centre: Kotagiri buses will drop you at the Dodabetta junction, then you have a fairly energetic 3km walk or a quick jeep ride. Taxis will do the round trip from Charing Cross for ₹400.

Rose Garden GARDEN

(Selbourne Rd; admission ₹20, camera/video ₹30/75; ⏲8.30am-6pm) With its terraced lawns and over 20,000 rose bushes of 2200 varieties – best between May and July – the large Rose Garden is a pleasant place for a stroll. There are good views over Ooty from the hilltop location.

Tribal Research Centre Museum MUSEUM

(Muthorai Palada; ⏲10am-1pm & 2-5pm Sat-Thu) FREE It's hard to say why you should love this museum more: for its decently executed exhibits on Nilgiri and Andaman tribal groups, or the decomposing corpses of badly stuffed local wildlife. Seriously, the artefacts are fantastic – you may never get the chance to hold a Stone Age bow in your life again – and descriptions of the tribes are good, albeit academically anthropological. It's just beyond the village of Muthorai Palada (M Palada), 11km south of Ooty on the way to Emerald and served by frequent buses. A rickshaw costs around ₹350 return. Note that opening times can be a bit fluid.

St Stephen's Church CHURCH

(⏲10.30am-5pm, services 8am & 11am Sun) Perched above the town centre, the immaculate St Stephen's, built in 1829, is the oldest church in the Nilgiris. It has lovely stained glass, huge wooden beams hauled by elephant from the palace of Tipu Sultan some 120km away, and the sometimes kitschy, sometimes touching, slabs and plaques donated by colonial-era churchgoers. In the quiet, overgrown cemetery you'll find headstones commemorating many an Ooty Brit.

Nilgiri Library LIBRARY

(Hospital Rd; ⏲reading room 9.30am-1pm & 2.30-6pm Sat-Thu) This quaint little haven in a crumbling 1867 building has more than 60,000 books, including rare titles on the Nilgiris and hill tribes. Visitors can consult books in the reading room in return for a donation (whatever you want to give).

Ooty (Udhagamandalam)

Activities

Hiking & Trekking

To make the most of Ooty, you should get out into the beautiful Nilgiris. Ooty's tourist office and many accommodation places can put you in touch with local guides who do day trips for ₹400 to ₹450 per person including lunch. You'll normally drive out of town and walk around hills, tribal villages and tea plantations. The tourist office can give basic information about some self-guided hikes but doesn't have any leaflets or decent maps of them.

More serious trekking in the best forest areas with plenty of wildlife – such as beyond Avalanche to the south or Parsons Valley to the west, or in Mukurthi National Park – requires Tamil Nadu Forest Department permits and you will probably need to take a guide from the department. Take a written application and your passport to the **District Forest Office Nilgiris South Division** (2444083; dfosouth@sancharnet.in; Mount Stuart Hill) or **District Forest Office Nilgiris North Division** (2443968; dfonlg@tn.nic.in; Mount Stuart Hill): permits, if granted, are normally issued the same day. The department has basic accommodation available in some locations. A great trek of three to five days, if you can organise it, is the 'Silent Valley' route southwest from Bangithappal in Mukurthi National Park, to the Sispara Pass and down to Walakkad and Sairandhri in Kerala's Silent Valley National Park.

The **Nilgiri Wildlife & Environment Association** (2447167; http://nwea.in; Mount Stuart Hill; 10am-1pm & 3-5pm Mon-Fri, 10am-1pm Sat) can be helpful with trekking advice. Its members can act as guides for ₹2000 to ₹3000 per day (including food).

Boating

Rowboats can be rented from the **Boathouse** (admission ₹5, camera/video ₹10/100; 9am-6pm) by Ooty's lake. Prices start from

₹100 (with a ₹100 deposit) for a two-seater pedal boat (30 minutes).

Horse Racing

Ooty's racecourse dominates the valley between Charing Cross and the lake. Racing season runs from mid-April to mid-June, and on the two or three race days each week the town is a hive of activity; it's an event you can't miss if you're in town. Racing happens between about 10.30am and 2.30pm.

Tours

Fixed taxi tour rates are ₹800 for four hours tootling around Ooty, ₹950 for Coonoor (four hours), or ₹1600 for Mudumalai Tiger Reserve.

Sleeping

Ooty has some gorgeous colonial-era residences at the high end and some decent backpacker dosses. There's not much on offer in the lower midrange though. Be warned: it's a sellers' market in the high season (1 April to 15 June), when many hotels hike their rates and checkout time is often 9am.

Ooty (Udhagamandalam)

Sights
1 Nilgiri Library D2
2 Rose Garden E3
3 St Stephen's Church D1
4 St Thomas Church B4

Activities, Courses & Tours
5 Boathouse A3

Sleeping
6 Hotel Sweekar C4
7 Hotel Welbeck Residency C1
8 Lymond House B1
9 Mount View Hotel B4
10 Reflections Guest House B4
11 Savoy Hotel B1
12 YWCA Anandagiri D4

Eating
13 Garden Restaurant E2
14 Kabab Corner E2
15 Modern Stores E1
16 Shinkow's Chinese Restaurant D2
17 Virtue Bakes E1
18 Willy's Coffee Pub E2

Drinking & Nightlife
Café Coffee Day .... (see 15)
19 Café Coffee Day D2

Shopping
20 Green Shop C2
21 Higginbothams E2
22 Higginbothams D2
23 K Mahaveer Chand C4
24 Mohan's D1

Information
25 Axis Bank ATM E2
26 Canara Bank ATM C3
27 District Forest Office Nilgiris North Division E2
District Forest Office Nilgiris South Division .... (see 27)
28 Nilgiri Wildlife & Environment Association E2
Office of the Field Director .... (see 28)
29 State Bank of India ATM D2

Transport
30 Jeep Taxi Stand D3
31 Jeep Taxi Stand C4
32 Royal Tours C3
33 Taxi Stand D3

YWCA Anandagiri HOSTEL $
(☎2442218; www.ywcaagooty.com; Ettines Rd; dm ₹99-110, s ₹230-960, d ₹345-960) This former brewery and sprawling complex of cottages is dotted with flower gardens; throw in spacious common areas including a restaurant with good-value meals (book ahead for these), and you've got some excellent budget accommodation going on. Rooms are clean and mostly quite spacious, though high ceilings can mean cold nights; ask for extra blankets if you might need them.

Reflections Guest House GUESTHOUSE $
(☎2443834; reflectionsin@yahoo.co.in; 1B North Lake Rd; s ₹500-600, d ₹550-800) A long-running budget haunt, Reflections sits across the road from Ooty's lake, and most of its 12 clean and decent rooms have lake views. It also serves Indian and Continental food at fair prices (₹60 to ₹180). Hot showers are available for two hours per day; there's a ₹20 charge for toilet paper and towels.

Hotel Sweekar HOTEL $
(☎2442348; hotelsweekar@gmail.com; 236 Race View Rd; r ₹350-550) The Sweekar hosts guests in small but clean rooms in a traditional Ooty cottage at the end of a flower-lined path. Hot water is limited to 7.30am to 9.30am, but the Sweekar is good value for its prices, and is run by a very helpful Bahai manager.

★ **Lymond House** HERITAGE HOTEL $$
(☎2223377; http://serendipityo.com; 77 Sylks Rd; r incl breakfast ₹4137-4797; 📶) What is it about this 1850s British bungalow that gives it the edge over its peers? The cosy cottage ambience with flowers, four-poster beds, fireplaces, white linen and warm lighting? The contemporary fittings and free wi-fi accompanying the old-world style in the spacious rooms and bathrooms? The bright dining room and pretty country garden? All of those, no doubt – plus an informal yet efficient management style that helps you feel right at home.

Hotel Welbeck Residency HOTEL $$
(☎2223300; www.welbeck.in; Welbeck Circle, Club Rd; r incl breakfast ₹2878-4257; @📶) An attractive older building that's been thoroughly tarted up with comfortable and cosy rooms, a touch of colonial-era class (a 1920 Austin saloon at the front door!), a decent restaurant and helpful staff.

Mount View Hotel HOTEL $$
(☎2442077; www.hotelmountviewooty.com; Ettines Rd; r ₹1971-3943; 📶) Perched on a quiet driveway convenient to the bus and train stations, the nine enormous, wood-lined, high-ceilinged rooms in this elegant old bungalow have recently been renovated to a good standard of comfort. It's a pity they still aren't using the fireplaces, though.

Willow Hill HOTEL $$
(☎2223123; www.willowhill.in; 58/1 Havelock Rd; s ₹1319-3598, d ₹1559-3957, all incl breakfast) Sitting high above town, Willow Hill's large windows provide great views of Ooty if you're on one of the upper floors. The 10 rooms have a distinct alpine-chalet chic, with the most expensive offering a private garden.

★ **Savoy Hotel** HERITAGE HOTEL $$$
(☎2225500; www.tajhotels.com; 77 Sylks Rd; s ₹5341-10,088, d ₹5934-12,275, all incl breakfast; @📶) The Savoy is one of Ooty's oldest hotels, with parts dating back to 1829. Big cottages are arranged around a beautiful garden of flowerbeds, lawns and clipped hedges. The quaint rooms have large bathrooms, log fires and bay windows. Service is very good, and modern facilities include a bar, wi-fi (chargeable), plenty of games for kids and adults, and an excellent multicuisine dining room. During high season, full-board arrangements may be obligatory.

Ferrnhills Palace HERITAGE HOTEL $$$
(☎2443910; www.welcomheritagehotels.com; Fern Hill; r incl breakfast ₹11,192-33,576; @📶) The Maharaja of Mysore's splendiferous Anglo-Indian summer palace has been lovingly restored in gorgeous, over-the-top princely colonial style; if you can afford to stay here, you really should. All rooms are large suites, with antique furnishings, fireplaces and Jacuzzis. Play billiards, walk in the huge, forest-surrounded grounds and dine on regal multicuisine fare beneath vivid murals.

King's Cliff HERITAGE HOTEL $$$
(☎2452888; www.littlearth.in; Havelock Rd; r incl breakfast ₹2129-5966; 📶) High above Ooty on Strawberry Hill is this classic colonial-era house with wood panelling, antique furnishings and cosy lounge. The cheaper ones don't have quite the same old-world charm as the more expensive ones, however.

Eating & Drinking

Top-end hotels such as the Savoy and Fernhills Palace have atmospheric, multicuisine restaurants that are the best places to go for a classy meal.

Garden Restaurant SOUTH INDIAN $
(Commercial Rd; mains ₹50-130; ⏲7.30am-9.30pm) Very good South Indian food in a clean setting behind the Nahar Nilgiris Hotel, along with juices, ice creams, snacks and moderate pizza.

Kabab Corner NORTH INDIAN $$
(Commercial Rd; mains ₹70-300; ⏲1-11pm) This is the place for meat eaters who are tiring of South Indian vegetarian food. It doesn't look much from the outside, but here you can tear apart perfectly grilled and spiced chunks of lamb, chicken and, if you like, paneer, sopping up the juices with pillowy triangles of naan. The ₹640 tandoori platter is exceptionally good for a group; if there are fewer than four of you, it may defeat you.

Shinkow's Chinese Restaurant CHINESE $$
(38/83 Commissioner's Rd; mains ₹100-250; ⏲noon-3.45pm & 6.30-9.45pm) Shinkow's is an Ooty institution and the simple menu of chicken, pork, beef, fish, noodles and rice dishes is reliably good and quick to arrive at your table.

Willy's Coffee Pub CAFE $
(KCR Arcade, Walsham Rd; dishes ₹20-80; ⏲10am-9.30pm) Climb the stairs and join international students and local cool kids for board games, a small lending library and very reasonably priced pizzas, fries, toasted sandwiches, cakes and cookies.

Café Coffee Day CAFE $
(Garden Rd; coffee ₹60-110; ⏲9am-11pm; 📶) Reliably fine coffee, tea and cakes. There's another **branch** (Church Hill Rd; ⏲9am-11pm; 📶) on Church Hill Rd.

Self-Catering

Modern Stores (144 Garden Rd; ⏲9.30am-8.30pm) is a mini-supermarket with all kinds of Western foods from muesli to Seville orange marmalade, as well as Nilgiri-produced bread and cheese. The fair-trade and organic-oriented **Green Shop** (Sargan Villa, off Club Rd; ⏲9.30am-7pm Mon-Sat) has excellent wild honey, plus attractive crafts and also a bee museum. **Virtue Bakes** (Garden Rd; ⏲10.30am-8.30pm) sells excellent cakes, pastries and bread to take away.

Shopping

The main shopping street is Commercial Rd, where you'll find Kashmiri shops as well as outlets for Keralan crafts and *khadi* (handspun cloth). Elsewhere, **K Mahaveer Chand** (291 Main Bazaar Rd; ⏲9.30am-8pm) has been selling particularly attractive Toda tribal and silver jewellery for over 40 years, and **Mohan's** (Commissioner's Rd; ⏲10am-8pm) has a curious assortment of antique telephones, radios and beer tankards as well as warm clothes. Near the botanical gardens entrance, Tibetan refugees sell sweaters and shawls, which you may appreciate on a chilly Ooty evening. **Higginbothams** (☎2443736; Commercial Rd; ⏲9am-1pm & 3.30-7.30pm Mon-Sat) has a good English-language book selection (including Lonely Planet guides), and another **branch** (☎2442546; Commissioner's Rd; ⏲9am-1pm & 2-6pm Mon-Sat) up the hill.

Information

Cyber Planet (Garden Rd; per hr ₹30; ⏲9.30am-6.30pm)

Global Net (Commercial Rd; per hr ₹30; ⏲9am-9.30pm)

Tourist Office (☎2443977; Wenlock Rd; ⏲10am-5.45pm Mon-Fri; 📶) Good for maps and information.

Getting There & Away

The fun way to arrive in Ooty is aboard the miniature train from Mettupalayam. Buses also run regularly up and down the mountain from other parts of Tamil Nadu, from Kerala and from Mysore and Bengaluru in Karnataka. Taxis cluster at several stands in town and there are fixed one-way fares to many destinations, including Coonoor (₹600), Kotagiri (₹700), Coimbatore (₹1500) and Mudumalai Tiger Reserve (₹1000).

BUS

For Kochi (Cochin, Kerala) take the 7am or 8am bus to Palakkad (₹80, six hours) and change there. **Royal Tours** (☎2446150), opposite the train station, runs a 9am minibus to Kodaikanal (₹500, eight hours).

The Tamil Nadu, Kerala and Karnataka state bus companies all have reservation offices at the busy **bus station**. Departures include:

Bengaluru ₹350-600, eight hours, 12 daily

Chennai ₹450, 14 hours, three daily

Coimbatore ₹52, four hours, every 30 minutes, 5.30am to 8.30pm

Mysore ₹135, five hours, about every 45 minutes, 6.15am to 5.45pm

TRAIN

The miniature (or 'toy') train from Mettupalayam to Ooty – one of the Mountain Railways of India given World Heritage status by Unesco – is the best way to get here. Called the Nilgiri Mountain Railway, it requires special cog wheels on the locomotive, meshing with a third, 'toothed' rail on the ground, to manage the exceptionally steep gradients There are marvellous views of forest, waterfalls, mountainsides and tea plantations along the way. The section between Mettupalayam and Coonoor uses steam engines, which push, rather than pull, the train up the hill.

For the high season, try to book the train several weeks ahead; at other times a few days ahead is advisable, though not always essential. The train departs Mettupalayam for Ooty at 7.10am daily (1st/2nd class ₹155/23, five hours). From Ooty to Mettupalayam the train leaves at 2pm and takes 3½ hours. Departures and arrivals at Mettupalayam connect with those of the Nilgiri Express to/from Chennai Central. There are also three daily passenger trains each way just between Ooty and Coonoor (₹18, 1¼ hours).

Note that Ooty is usually listed as Udagamandalam in train timetables.

Getting Around

There are plenty of autorickshaws and taxis: autorickshaw fare charts are posted outside the bus station and botanical gardens and elsewhere. An autorickshaw from the train or bus station to Charing Cross costs about ₹60.

There are jeep taxi stands near the bus station and municipal market: expect to pay about 1.5 times local taxi fares.

Mudumalai Tiger Reserve

☎ 0423

In the foothills of the Nilgiris, this 321-sq-km reserve is like a classical Indian landscape painting given life: thin, spindly trees and light-slotted leaves concealing spotted chital deer and grunting wild boar. Also here are around 50 tigers, giving Mudumalai the highest tiger population density in India – though you'll still be very lucky to see one. Overall the reserve is the best place for spotting wildlife in Tamil Nadu. The creatures you're most likely to see include deer, peacocks, wild boar, langurs and Malabar giant squirrels. There's also a significant chance of sighting wild elephants (the park has several hundred) and gaur (Indian bison).

Along with Karnataka's Bandipur and Nagarhole and Kerala's Wayanad, Mudumalai forms part of an unbroken chain of protected areas comprising an important wildlife refuge.

Mudumalai sometimes closes for fire risk in April, May or June. Rainy July and August are the least favourable months for visiting.

The reserve's **reception centre** (☎ 2526235; ⏰ 6.30am-6pm), and some government-run accommodation, is at Theppakadu, on the main road between Ooty and Mysore. The closest village to Theppakadu is Masinagudi, 7km east.

Sights & Activities

Hking in the reserve is not allowed and private vehicles are only allowed on the main Ooty–Gudalur–Theppakadu–Mysore road and the Theppakadu–Masinagudi and Masinagudi–Moyar River roads. Some wildlife can be seen from these roads, but the best way to see the reserve is on the enjoyable official 45-minute **minibus tours** (per person ₹35; ⏰ 7am, 8am, 3pm, 4pm & 5pm), which make a 15km loop in camouflage-striped 26-seat buses. Get to the reception centre 30 minutes beforehand to ensure a seat. Half-hour **elephant rides** (for 4 people ₹460; ⏰ 7-8am & 4-5pm) are also available from the reception centre. At 6pm you can watch the reserve's working elephants being fed at the nearby **elephant camp** (minibus-tour customers free, others ₹15).

Some operators may offer treks in the buffer zone around the reserve, but these are potentially dangerous and the reserve authorities advise very strongly against them. Jeep safaris organised through the better resorts, with expert guides, are a safer option.

Sleeping & Eating

The reserve runs some simple accommodation along a track just above the Moyar River at Theppakadu. For these it's advisable to book in advance at the **Office of the Field Director** (Map p404; ☎ 0423-2444098; fdmtr@tn.nic.in; Mount Stuart Hill, Ooty; ⏰ 10am-6pm Mon-Fri, 10am-1pm Sat) in Ooty, though the reception centre will accept walk-in bookings if there are vacancies. Best is the well maintained **Theppakadu Log House** (d/q ₹1100/1600), whose comfortable rooms have private bathrooms. **Sylvan Lodge** (d ₹600) is on similar lines though less comfortable. The caretaker can arrange meals at both places (dinner costs ₹40 to ₹50). Also here is the extremely basic, government-run **Hotel Tamil Nadu** (☎ 2526580; htn-mdm@ttdconline.com; dm/d/q ₹125/550/950), with a restaurant.

Better accommodation is provided by numerous lodges and forest resorts outside the park's fringes, many of them family-run businesses with a warm atmosphere, high standards and breathtaking views. Many of the best cluster in Bokkapuram village, 5km from Masinagudi at the foot of the mountains. Don't wander outside your resort at night; leopards, among other wild animals, are present. Meals at the resorts, where not included in room rates, cost between ₹250 and ₹450 each.

★The Wilds at Northernhay LODGE $$
(☎9843149490; http://serendipityo.com; Singara; r incl breakfast ₹4035-4747) A wonderful lodge 8km southwest of Masinagudi, in a converted coffee warehouse on a coffee plantation with many tall trees that give it a deep-in-the-forest feel. Cosy rooms (two of them up in the trees) and excellent meals complement the two-hour morning and evening jeep safaris (₹2750), on which you can expect to see a very good variety of wildlife.

Jungle Retreat RESORT $$
(☎2526469; www.jungleretreat.com; Bokkapuram; dm ₹524, r ₹2941-4706;) One of the most stylish resorts in the area, with accommodation in sturdy bamboo huts or lovingly built stone cottages or even a high treehouse, all spread out to give a feeling of seclusion. The bar, restaurant and common area are great places to meet fellow travellers, and the owners are knowledgeable and friendly. The beautiful pool has a stunning setting, and elephants and leopards have been known to visit it for a drink.

Forest Hills Guest House RESORT $$
(☎2526216; www.foresthillsindia.com; Bokkapuram; d ₹2177-4430) Forest Hills is a family-run, family-sized guesthouse (14 rooms on 5 hectares) with a few cute bamboo huts and treehouses, some clean spacious rooms, and a watchtower room that's great for wildlife-watching and birdwatching. There's a slight colonial-era air here with a gazebo-style bar, games rooms and evening bonfires.

Jungle Hut RESORT $$$
(☎2526463; www.junglehut.in; Bokkapuram; full board s ₹3400-5300, d ₹5000-6900;) Along with spacious rooms in cottages scattered around a large property, and a sociable common area, this welcoming resort has probably the best food in Bokkapuram (if you're visiting the restaurant from another resort after dark, don't walk home on your own!). A herd of chital deer grazes the grounds morning and evening, and jeep safaris, treks and birdwatching walks can be organised.

ℹ Getting There & Around

You can do a taxi day-trip to Mudumalai from Ooty for around ₹1600. Do go at least one way by the alternative Sighur Ghat road with its spectacular 36-hairpin hill. A one-way taxi from Ooty to Theppakadu should be ₹1000.

Buses between Ooty and Mysore go via Gudalur and stop at Theppakadu (₹45, three hours from Ooty). Smaller buses that can manage the Sighur Ghat road run from Ooty to Masinagudi (₹10, 1½ hours, eight daily). Local buses run every two hours between Masinagudi and Theppakadu (₹5); shared jeeps also ply this route for ₹10 per person if there are enough passengers, or you can have one to yourself for about ₹100. Costs are similar for jeeps between Masinagudi and Bokkapuram.

Andaman Islands

Includes ➡

Best Beaches

- Radhanagar (p419)
- Merk Bay (p426)
- Ross & Smith Islands (p427)
- Butler Bay (p428)
- Beach 5 (p421)

Best Places to Stay

- Emerald Gecko (p422)
- Aashiaanaa Rest Home (p417)
- Pristine Beach Resort (p427)
- Blue View (p428)
- Blue Planet (p426)

Why Go?

Long fabled among travellers for its legendary beaches, world-class diving and far-flung location in the middle of nowhere, the Andaman Islands are still the ideal place to get away from it all.

Its lovely opaque emerald waters are surrounded by primeval jungle and mangrove forest, and snow-white beaches that melt under flame-and-purple sunsets. The population is a friendly masala of South and Southeast Asian settlers, as well as Negrito ethnic groups whose arrival here still has anthropologists baffled. Adding to the intrigue is its remote location, some 1370km from the mainland, meaning the islands are geographically more Southeast Asia – 150km from Indonesia and 190km from Myanmar.

While the archipelago comprises some 300 islands, only a dozen or so are open to tourists, Havelock by far being the most popular for its beaches and diving. The Nicobars are strictly off limits to tourists, as are the tribal areas.

When to Go

Port Blair

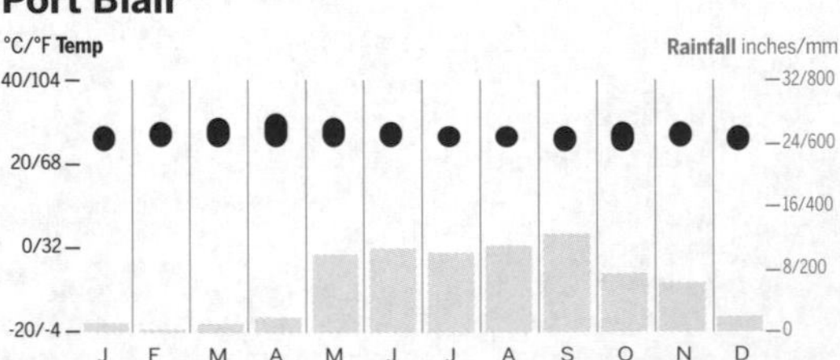

Dec–Mar Perfect sunny days, optimal diving conditions, and turtle nesting.

Oct–Dec & Mar–mid-May Weather's a mixed bag, but fewer tourists and lower costs.

May–Aug Pumping waves on Little Andaman for experienced surfers.

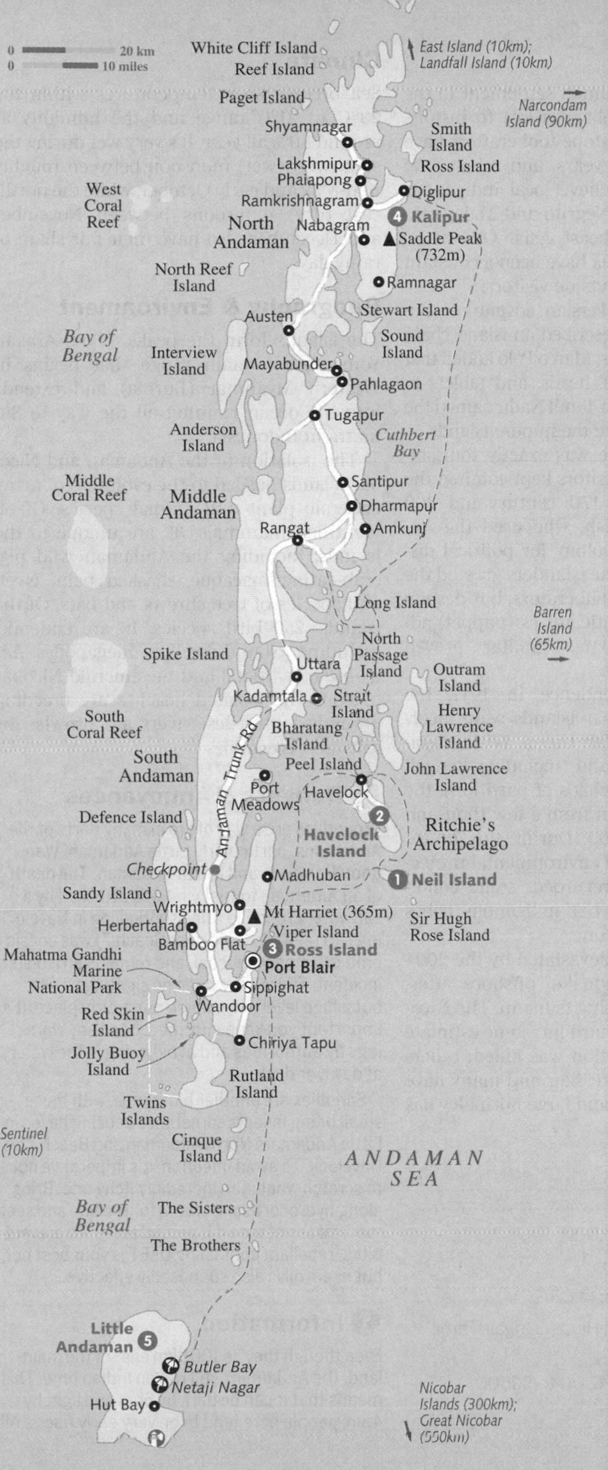

Andaman Islands Highlights

1. Regress to infantile laziness and happiness on **Neil Island** (p424)
2. Dive, snorkel and socialise on **Havelock Island** (p419)
3. Glimpse Port Blair's colonial history at **Ross Island** (p416)
4. Experience the true wilds of Northern Andaman in **Kalipur** (p427) while island-hopping to pristine beaches and coral reefs
5. Find Butler Bay and paradise on **Little Andaman** (p427)

History

The date of initial human settlement in the Andamans and Nicobars is lost to history. Anthropologists say stone-tool crafters have lived here for 2000 years, and scholars of human migration believe local indigenous tribes have roots in Negrito and Malay ethnic groups in Southeast Asia. Otherwise, these specks in the sea have been a constant source of legend to outside visitors.

The 10th-century Persian adventurer Buzurg Ibn Shahriyar described an island chain inhabited by cannibals, Marco Polo added that the natives had dogs' heads, and tablets in Thanjavur (Tanjore) in Tamil Nadu named the archipelago Timaittivu: the Impure Islands.

None of the above was exactly tourism-brochure stuff, but visitors kept coming: the Marathas in the late 17th century and, 200 years later, the British, who used the Andamans as a penal colony for political dissidents. In WWII some islanders greeted the invading Japanese as liberators, but despite installing Indian politicians as (puppet) administrators, the Japanese military proved to be harsh occupiers.

Following Independence in 1947, the Andaman and Nicobar Islands were incorporated into the Indian Union. With migration from the mainland (including Bengali refugees fleeing the chaos of partition), the population has grown from a few thousand to more than 350,000. During this influx, tribal land rights and environmental protection were often disregarded; some conditions are improving but indigenous tribes remain largely in decline.

The islands were devastated by the 2004 Indian Ocean earthquake, offshore aftershocks and the resulting tsunami. The Nicobars were especially hard hit; some estimate a fifth of the population was killed; others were relocated to Port Blair and many have yet to return. But by and large normalcy has returned.

FAST FACTS

- **Population:** 380,000
- **Area:** 8248 sq km
- **Telephone code:** 03192
- **Main languages:** Hindi, Bengali, Tamil
- **Sleeping prices:** **$** below ₹800, **$$** ₹800 to ₹2500, **$$$** above ₹2500

Climate

Sea breezes keep temperatures within the 23°C to 31°C range and the humidity at around 80% all year. It's very wet during the southwest (wet) monsoon between roughly mid-May and early October, while the northeast (dry) monsoons between November and December also have their fair share of rainy days.

Geography & Environment

The islands form the peaks of the Arakan Yoma, a mountain range that begins in Western Myanmar (Burma) and extends into the ocean running all the way to Sumatra in Indonesia.

The isolation of the Andaman and Nicobar Islands has led to the evolution of many endemic plant and animal species. Of 62 identified mammals, 32 are unique to the islands, including the Andaman wild pig, crab-eating macaque, masked palm civet, and species of tree shrews and bats. Of the islands' 250 bird species, 18 are endemic, including ground-dwelling megapodes, *hawabills* (swiftlets) and the emerald Nicobar pigeon. The isolated beaches are breeding grounds for turtles; rivers are prowled by saltwater crocodiles.

Dangers & Annoyances

Crocodiles are a way of life in many parts of the Andamans, particularly Little Andaman, Wandoor, Baratang and North Andaman. The death of an American tourist who was attacked by a saltwater crocodile while snorkelling in Havelock in 2010 (at Neils Cove near Beach 7) was considered extremely unusual, and remains an isolated incident. There have been no sightings since, but a high level of vigilance remains in place. It's important you keep informed, heed any warnings by authorities and avoid being in the water at dawn or dusk.

Sandflies are another hindrance, with these small biting insects sometimes causing havoc in Little Andaman, North Andaman and Beach 7 on Havelock. To avoid infection, it's imperative not to scratch what is an incredibly itchy bite. Bring along hydrocortisone cream for the bite and seek medical assistance if it gets infected. To prevent bites, repellant containing DEET is your best bet, but neem oil is also supposedly effective.

Information

Even though they're 1000km east of the mainland, the Andamans still run on Indian time. This means that it can be dark by 5pm and light by 4am; people here tend to be very early risers. All telephone numbers must include the ☎ 03192 area code, even when dialling locally.

ACCOMMODATION

Prices here are listed for high season (December to March), though be aware tariffs can rise during peak season of mid-December to January. In peak season accommodation on the islands can be stretched, so reservations are a good idea. May to November is low to mid-season, which brings healthy discounts. Camping is not permitted on the islands.

PERMITS

All foreigners need a permit to visit the Andaman Islands; it's issued free on arrival. The 30-day permit allows foreigners to stay in Port Blair, South and Middle Andaman (excluding tribal areas), North Andaman (Diglipur), Long Island, North Passage, Little Andaman (excluding tribal areas), and Havelock and Neil Islands. It's possible to get a 15-day extension from the **Immigration Office** (☎ 03192-239247; ⏰ 8.30am-1pm & 2-5.30pm Mon-Fri, to 1pm Sat) in Port Blair, or at police stations elsewhere.

The permit also allows day trips to Jolly Buoy, South Cinque, Red Skin, Ross, Narcondam, Interview and Rutland Islands, as well as the Brothers and the Sisters.

Boat passengers will probably be met by an immigration official on arrival; if not, seek out the immigration office at Haddo Jetty immediately. Keep your permit on you at all times – you won't be able to travel without it. Police frequently ask to see it, especially when you're disembarking on other islands, and hotels will need permit details. Check current regulations regarding permits with the following agencies:

Andaman & Nicobar Tourism (☎ 03192-232694; www.and.nic.in/newtourism; Kamaraj Rd; ⏰ 8.30am-12.30pm & 1.30-4.30pm Mon-Fri, 8.30am-noon Sat)

Foreigner's Registration Office (☎ Chennai 044-23454970, Kolkata 033-22470549; www.immihelp.com/nri/protected-restricted-area-permit-india.html)

Additional permits are required to visit some national parks and sanctuaries. The tourism office in Port Blair can tell you whether a permit is needed and how to go about getting it. If you plan to do something complicated, you'll be sent to the **Chief Wildlife Warden** (CWW; ☎ 03192-233321; Haddo Rd, Port Blair; ⏰ 8.30am-noon & 1-4pm Mon-Fri).

For most day permits it's not the hassle but the cost. For areas such as Mahatma Gandhi Marine National Park, and Ross and Smith Islands near Diglipur, the permits cost ₹50/500 for Indians/foreigners. For Saddle Peak National Park, also near Diglipur, the cost is ₹25/250. Students with valid ID pay minimal entry fees, so don't forget to bring your card.

PERMIT COPIES

At the time of research it was a requirement to produce a photocopy of your permit when booking ferry tickets. While you're not always asked to provide it, to avoid the trauma of having to re-queue, it's worth taking five or so copies before arriving at Port Blair's ferry office: you'll likely need them later in your trip.

The Nicobar Islands are off-limits to all except Indian nationals engaged in research, government business or trade.

Getting There & Away

AIR

There are daily flights to Port Blair from Delhi, Kolkata and Chennai, although flights from Delhi and Kolkata are often routed through Chennai. Round-trip fares are between US$250 and US$600 depending on how early you book; some airlines offer one-way flights for as low as US$80, but these need to be booked months in advance. Airlines that head to Port Blair include **SpiceJet** (☎ 1800 1803333; www.spicejet.com), **GoAir** (☎ 1800 222111; www.goair.in), **Air India** (☎ Port Blair 03192-233108; www.airindia.com), **Jet Airways** (☎ 22-39893333; www.jetairways.com) and **JetLite** (☎ 03192-242707; www.jetlite.com). Kingfisher flights were suspended at time of research.

There are no international flights from Port Blair to Southeast Asia

BOAT

Depending on who you ask, the infamous boat to Port Blair is either 'the only *real* way to get to the Andamans' or a hassle and a half. The truth lies somewhere in between. There are usually three to four sailings a month between Port Blair and Chennai (60 hours) and Kolkata (64 hours), plus a monthly ferry to Vizag (56 hours). All ferries from the mainland arrive at Haddo Jetty.

➡ For Chennai you can book tickets through the **Andaman Shipping Office** (☎ 25226873; www.and.nic.in; 2nd fl, Shipping Corporation of India, Jawahar Bldg, 17 Rajaji Salai, George Town; ⏰ 9am-1pm & 2-3pm Mon-Fri, 9am-noon Sat)

➡ Kolkata and Vizag are booked through **Shipping Corporation of India** (☎ in Kolkata 033-22484921, in Vizag 0891-2565597; www.shipindia.com; 13 Strand Rd, Kolkata)

Take sailing times with a large grain of salt – travellers have reported sitting on the boat at Kolkata harbour for up to 12 hours, or waiting to dock near Port Blair for several hours. With hold-ups and variable weather and sea conditions, the trip can take 2½ to five days.

You can organise your return ticket at the ferry booking office (p418) at Phoenix Bay. Bring two passport photos and a photocopy of your permit. Updated schedules and fares can be found at www.and.nic.in/newtourism or www.shipindia.com.

Classes vary slightly between boats, but the cheapest is bunk (₹2160), followed by 2nd class B (₹4280), 2nd class A (₹5540), 1st class (₹6320) and deluxe cabins (₹7640). The MV *Akbar* also has AC dorm berths (₹3620). Higher-end tickets cost as much as, if not more than, a plane ticket. If you go bunk, prepare for waking up to a chorus of men 'hwwaaaaching' and spitting, little privacy and toilets that tend to get… unpleasant after three days at sea. That said, it's a good way to meet locals, and is one for proponents of slow, adventure travel.

Food (tiffin for breakfast, thalis for lunch and dinner) costs around ₹150/200 per day for bunk/cabin class, though bring something (fruit in particular) to supplement your diet. Some bedding is supplied, but if you're travelling bunk class bring a sleeping sheet. Many travellers take a hammock to string up on deck.

There is no ferry between Port Blair and Thailand, but private yachts can get clearance. You can't legally get from the Andamans to Myanmar (Burma) by sea, although we hear it's been done by those with their own boat. Be aware you risk imprisonment or worse from the Indian and Burmese navies if you give this a go.

Getting Around

AIR

Two modes of air transport link Port Blair with the rest of the islands. If your budget allows it, it's worth it for the views.

The new amphibious **Sea Plane** (☎03192-244312; andamanseaplane@gmail.com; ⊙Mon-Sat) links Port Blair with Havelock (₹4100), Little Andaman (₹7170) and Diglipur (₹10,500), landing and taking off on the water, and the runway in Port Blair

There's also the interisland helicopter service that runs from Port Blair to Little Andaman (₹2625, 35 minutes), Havelock (₹1500, 20 minutes), Diglipur (₹4125, one hour) and Mayabunder (₹3375). Priority is given to government workers and the 5kg baggage limit precludes most tourists from using this service. You can chance your luck by applying at the **Secretariat** (☎03192-230093) in Port Blair.

BOAT

Most islands can only be reached by water. While this sounds romantic, ferry ticket offices can be hell: expect hot waits, slow service, queue-jumping and a rugby scrum to the ticket window. To hold your spot and advance you need to be a little aggressive (but don't be a jerk) – or be a woman; ladies' queues are a godsend, but they really only apply in Port Blair. You can buy tickets the day you travel by arriving at the appropriate jetty an hour beforehand, but it's risky, and normally one or two days in advance is recommended. You can't prebook ferry tickets until you've been issued your island permit upon arrival in the Andamans; see p413.

There are regular boat services to Havelock and Neil Islands, as well as Rangat, Mayabunder, Diglipur and Little Andaman. A schedule of inter-island sailing times can be found at the website www.and.nic.in/spsch/iisailing.htm.

The private ferry **Makruzz** (www.makruzz.com; from ₹775) runs a daily boat to Havelock, which is quicker but triple the cost. At the time of research, **Coastal Cruise** (☎03192-241333; www.coastalcruise.in) was another private operator that was set to begin a fast boat service linking Havelock with Neil Island and Port Blair.

CAR & MOTORCYCLE

Hiring a car and driver costs ₹ 550 per 35km, or around ₹10,000 for a return trip to Diglipur from Port Blair (including stopovers along the way). Mopeds can hired from ₹300 per day.

BUS

All roads – and ferries – lead to Port Blair, and you'll inevitably spend a night or two here booking onward travel. The main island group – South, Middle and North Andaman – is connected by road, with ferry crossings and bridges. Cheap state and more expensive private buses run south from Port Blair to Wandoor, and north to Bharatang, Rangat, Mayabunder and finally to Diglipur, 325km north of the capital. The Jarawa reserve closes to most traffic at around 3pm; thus, buses that pass through the reserve leave from around 4am up till 11am.

FERRY CANCELLATIONS

Bad weather can seriously muck up your itinerary, with ferry services often cancelled if the sea is too rough. Build in a few days' buffer to avoid being marooned and missing your flight.

PORT BLAIR

POP 100,608

Though surrounded by attractive lush forest and rugged coastline, Port Blair itself is a somewhat gritty town that serves as the

Port Blair

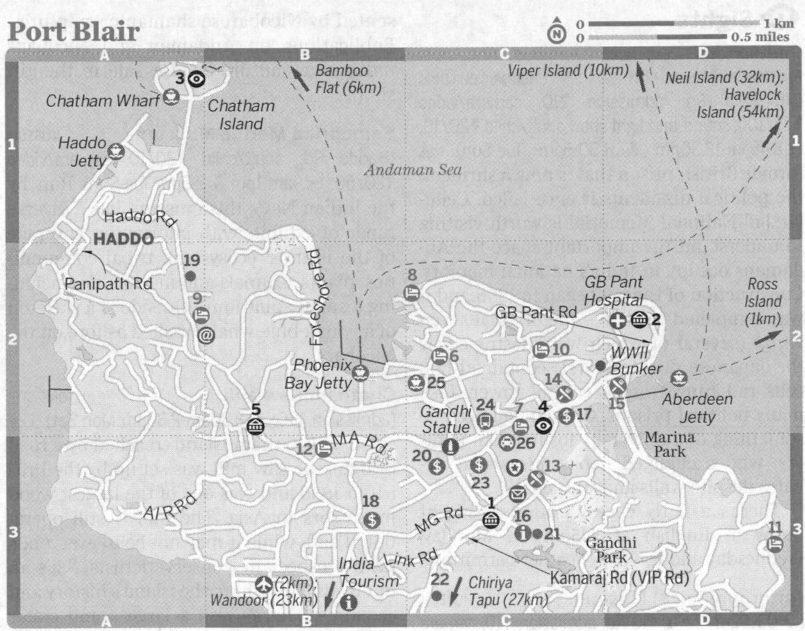

Port Blair

Sights

- 1 Anthropological Museum C3
- 2 Cellular Jail National Memorial D2
- 3 Chatham Saw Mill A1
- 4 Clock Tower C2
- 5 Samudrika Marine Museum B2

Sleeping

- 6 Aashiaanaa Rest Home C2
- Amina Lodge .... (see 7)
- 7 Azad Lodge C2
- 8 Fortune Resort – Bay Island C2
- 9 Hotel Driftwood A2
- 10 Hotel Lalaji Bay View C2
- 11 Hotel Sinclairs Bayview D3
- 12 TSG Emerald B3

Eating

- 13 Annapurna C3
- Bayview .... (see 11)
- Excel Restaurant .... (see 10)
- Gagan Restaurant .... (see 4)
- 14 Lighthouse Residency C2
- Mandalay Restaurant .... (see 8)
- 15 New Lighthouse Restaurant D2

Information

- 16 Andaman & Nicobar Tourism C3
- 17 Axis Bank ATM C2
- 18 Axis Bank ATM B3
- 19 Chief Wildlife Warden A2
- E-Cafe .... (see 4)
- Green Island Tours .... (see 4)
- 20 ICICI ATM C3
- 21 Immigration Office C3
- 22 Secretariat C3
- 23 State Bank of India C3

Transport

- 24 Bus Stand C2
- 25 Ferry Booking Office C2
- 26 Taxi & Autorickshaw Stand C3

provincial capital of the Andamans. It's a vibrant mix of Indian Ocean inhabitants – Bengalis, Tamils, Telugus, Nicobarese and Burmese. Most travellers don't hang around any longer than necessary (usually one or two days while waiting to book onward travel in the islands, or returning for departure), instead hell-bent on heading straight to the islands. And while 'PB' can't compete with the beaches of Havelock, its fascinating history makes for some outstanding sightseeing that warrants a day or two spent here.

Sights

Cellular Jail National Memorial HISTORIC BUILDING

(GB Pant Rd; admission ₹10, camera/video ₹25/100, sound-and-light show adult/child ₹20/10; 8.45am-12.30pm & 1.30-5pm Tue-Sun) A former British prison that is now a shrine to the political dissidents it once jailed, Cellular Jail National Memorial is worth visiting to understand the important space the Andamans occupy in India's national memory. Construction of the jail began in 1896 and it was completed in 1906 – the original seven wings (several of which were destroyed by the Japanese during WWII) contained 698 cells radiating from a central tower. Like many political prisons, Cellular Jail became something of a university for freedom fighters, who exchanged books, ideas and debates despite walls and wardens.

There's a fairly cheesy **sound-and-light show** in English at 7.15pm on Monday, Wednesday and Friday – weather permitting.

Anthropological Museum MUSEUM

(03192-232291; MG Rd; admission ₹10, camera ₹20; 9am-1pm & 1.30-4.30pm Tue-Sun) The best museum in Port Blair provides a thorough and sympathetic portrait of the islands' indigenous tribal communities. The glass display cases may be old school, but they don't feel anywhere near as ancient as the simple geometric patterns etched into a Jarawa chest guard, a skull left in a Sentinelese lean-to or the totemic spirits represented by Nicobarese shamanic sculptures. Publications on Andaman and Nicobar's indigenous culture are for sale in the gift shop.

Samudrika Marine Museum MUSEUM

(Haddo Rd; adult/child ₹20/10, camera/video ₹20/50; 9am-1pm & 2-5pm Tue-Sun) Run by the Indian Navy, this museum has a diverse range of exhibits with informative coverage of the islands' ecosystem, tribal communities, plants, animals and marine life (including a small aquarium). Outside is a skeleton of a young blue whale washed ashore on the Nicobars.

Chatham Saw Mill HISTORIC SITE

(admission ₹10; 8.30am-2.30pm Mon-Sat) Located on Chatham Island (reached by a road bridge), the saw mill was set up by the British in 1836 and was one of the largest wood processors in Asia. The mill is still operational and, while it may not be to everyone's taste – especially conservationists – it's an interesting insight to the island's history and economy. There's also a large bomb crater from WWII, accessed via the path alongside the forest museum.

Corbyn's Cove BEACH

No one comes to Port Blair for the beach, but if you need a break from town, Corbyn's Cove has a small curve of sand backed by palms. It's not really a beach you'll want to laze on, but the coastal road here makes for

DON'T MISS

ROSS ISLAND

Just a 20-minute boat ride from Port Blair, visiting Ross Island (not to be confused with its namesake island in North Andaman) feels like discovering a jungle-clad Lost City, à la Angkor Wat. Here the ruins happen to be Victorian English rather than ancient Khmer. The former administrative headquarters for the British in the Andamans, Ross Island in its day was fondly called the 'Paris of the East' (along with Pondicherry, Saigon etc etc...). But the cute title, vibrant social scene and tropical gardens were all wiped out by the double whammy of a 1941 earthquake and the invasion of the Japanese (who left behind some machine-gun nests that are great fun to poke around in).

Today the old English architecture is still standing, even as it is swallowed by a green wave of fast-growing jungle. Landscaped paths cross the island and most of the buildings are labelled. There's a small **museum** with historical displays and photos of Ross Island in its heyday, and a small park where resident deer nibble on bushes.

Ferries to Ross Island (₹90, 20 minutes) depart from Aberdeen Jetty behind the aquarium in Port Blair at 8.30am, 10.30am, 12.30pm and 2pm every day other than Wednesday.

You can tack on a visit to **Viper Island** (₹75), where you'll find the ruins of gallows built by the British in 1867, but it's a fairly forgettable excursion.

a scenic journey, and passes several **Japanese WWII bunkers** along the way. Located 7km from town, an autorickshaw here costs ₹200, or you can rent a scooter.

Tours

Andaman & Nicobar Tourism TOURS
(IP&T; ☎03192-232694; www.and.nic.in/newtourism; Kamaraj Rd) Popular with Indian mainland tourists, these tours include day trips to Mt Harriet (₹250), Wandoor via spice and rubber plantations (₹200), Chiriya Tapu (₹200), Baratang limestone caves (₹525) and snorkelling trips to Jolly Buoy or Redskin Islands (₹500).

Sleeping

★ **Aashiaanaa Rest Home** GUESTHOUSE $
(☎09474217008; shads_maria@hotmail.com; Marine Hill; r without bathroom ₹300, with AC from ₹600; ❄📶) Port Blair's most comfortable budget choice has homely rooms decked out in marine, and a convenient location uphill from Phoenix Bay jetty. Most have cable TV and reliable hot water, while pricier rooms get you a balcony and air-con. Staff can help out with booking ferry tickets and takeaway food delivery, though a restaurant was planned at the time of research.

Hotel Lalaji Bay View GUESTHOUSE $
(☎9476005820, 03192-236333; www.lalajibayview.com; RP Rd; s/d ₹300/400, r with AC ₹800; ❄📶) Set among ramshackle colonial buildings, just up from the mosque, this popular budget hotel is run by the friendly Nirman, a young entrepreneur who's an excellent source of travel information. The rooms are small and basic, but good value, and it has a sociable rooftop restaurant with paid wi-fi access.

Amina Lodge GUESTHOUSE $
(☎9933258703; aminalodge@ymail.com; Aberdeen Bazaar; s/d ₹350/450) Run by an entertaining couple, Amina has good-value, clean rooms with TV and a handy, though sometimes noisy, location in the heart of the bazaar. Prices are fixed.

Azad Lodge GUESTHOUSE $
(☎03192-242646; MA Rd, Aberdeen Bazaar; s/d without bathroom ₹200/300, d with bathroom ₹500, r with AC ₹850) An old budget favourite that's popular for its simple and clean rooms; though singles without bathroom are like prison cells.

Hotel Driftwood HOTEL $$
(☎03192-244044; hoteldriftwood@rediffmail.com; JN Rd, Haddo; r from ₹2150; ❄📶) The midrange Driftwood makes a fine choice with sunny, decent-sized rooms; the pricier ones have lovely views of lush jungle. It has smiley staff, a good restaurant with an attached outdoor bar (beware Saturday night karaoke), and wi-fi access in the lobby.

TSG Emerald HOTEL $$
(☎03192-246488; www.andamantsghotels.com; MA Rd, Haddo; r from ₹2470; ❄📶) While a business-chic hotel may not necessarily suit the Andamans, this place is pretty plush with sleek, sparkling, modern rooms. Also has a nautical-themed bar upstairs.

Hotel Sinclairs Bayview HOTEL $$$
(☎03192-227824; www.sinclairshotels.com; South Point; s/d incl breakfast from ₹6900/7520; ❄📶🏊) Located on the road to Corbyn's Cove, 2km outside town, Sinclairs' big comfy rooms have the best views in town, opening right out to the water. It has a nice seaside garden with hammocks to lounge in, and several Japanese WWII bunkers on-site. Airport transfer is free.

Fortune Resort – Bay Island HOTEL $$$
(☎03192-234101; www.fortunehotels.in; Marine Hill; s/d incl breakfast from ₹6445/7300; ❄📶🏊) One of PB's finest, with lovely bay views, tropical garden and modern rooms with polished floors; ask for a sea-facing room.

Eating & Drinking

Gagan Restaurant INDIAN $
(Clock tower, Aberdeen Bazaar; mains from ₹30; ⏰7am-10pm) Popular with locals, this hole-in-the-wall place serves up great food at good prices, including seafood curries, coconut chicken, and dosas for breakfast. There's also air-con seating upstairs.

Excel Restaurant INTERNATIONAL, INDIAN $
(RP Rd; meals from ₹60; ⏰7am-11pm) Not to be confused with the seedy downstairs bar, the popular Excel rooftop restaurant above Hotel Lalaji Bay brings a 'Havelock' menu to the city. Burgers, grilled seafood, and Israeli dishes are all good, and its fully stocked bar makes it a great place to meet fellow travellers.

Annapurna INDIAN $
(MG Rd; mains from ₹40) An excellent veg option that looks like a high-school cafeteria

and serves consistently good dosas and rich North Indian–style curries.

★Lighthouse Residency INDIAN $$
(MA Rd; mains ₹80-800; ⏲11am-11pm) The best place for seafood in Port Blair, if not the Andamans, where you select from the display of red snapper, crab or tiger prawns to barbecue, grill or cook in the tandoor and served with rice, chips and a cold Kingfisher. There's a cheaper **second branch** (Marina Park; mains ₹80-400) in an outdoor shack near the water.

Bayview MULTICUISINE $$$
(Hotel Sinclairs Bayview; mains ₹110-500; ⏲11am-11pm) Right on the water with a lovely cool sea breeze, the Bayview is a great spot for lunch. While the grilled fish is delicious and the beer cold, this place is much more about the location than the food. Ask the friendly staff to show you the Japanese WWII bunkers on the premises. An autorickshaw here costs ₹40.

Mandalay Restaurant INDIAN, MULTICUISINE $$$
(Marine Hill; mains ₹160-480; ⏲7am-11pm) A good place to while away an afternoon, with sensational sea views from the outdoor deck (the ₹20 note is actually based on this spot). Food is pricey, but it does a tasty Goan prawn curry, plus sandwiches and burgers.

ℹ Information

There are several ATMs around town including SBI and Axis that accept foreign cards. You can find internet cafes in Aberdeen Bazaar, including the air-conditioned **Green Island Tours** (per hour ₹30; ⏲9am-9pm Mon-Sat; 📶) and **E-Cafe** (internet & wi-fi per hr ₹40; ⏲8am-10pm) near the clock tower; both have wi-fi. Green Island can also book flights.

Aberdeen Police Station (☎03192-232400; MG Rd)

Andaman & Nicobar Tourism (☎03192-232694; www.and.nic.in/newtourism; Kamaraj Rd; ⏲8.30am-12.30pm & 1.30-4.30pm Mon-Fri, 8.30am-noon Sat) The main island tourist office is the place to book permits for areas around Port Blair. It also sells the useful tourist booklet *Emerald Islands* (₹120), which you can also pickup from the airport.

Axis Bank ATM (Netaji Rd, Aberdeen Bazar)

Axis Bank ATM (MG Rd)

GB Pant Hospital (☎emergency 03192-232102, 03192-233473; GB Pant Rd)

Main Post Office (MG Rd; ⏲9am-7pm Mon-Sat)

State Bank of India (MA Rd; ⏲9am-noon & 1-3pm Mon-Fri, 10am-noon Sat) Foreign currency can be changed here.

ℹ Getting There & Away

The airport is about 4km south of town.

BOAT

Most interisland ferries depart from **Phoenix Bay Jetty**. Tickets can be purchased from the **ferry booking office** (⏲9am-1pm & 2-4pm Mon-Sat); inexplicably closed Sundays. Ferries can be prebooked one to three days in advance; if sold out you can chance your luck with a same-day ticket issued an hour before departure from outside the ticket office at the end door.

Most people head straight to Havelock (₹195, 2½ hours), with ferries departing daily at 6.20am, 11.30am and 2pm.

Otherwise there's the privately owned **Makruzz** (www.makruzz.com; from ₹775), departing daily at 8.45am (1½ hours). Tickets are available from the airport or travel agents in Aberdeen Bazaar.

There are also daily services to Neil Island and Little Andaman, which regularly sell out, and several boats a week to Diglipur and Long Island.

Those not wanting to hang around Port Blair should make the jetty their first port of call to book tickets.

BUS

There are buses all day from the **bus stand** at Aberdeen Bazaar to Wandoor (₹18, one hour) and Chiriya Tapu (₹18, one hour). Two buses run at 4am and 4.15am to Diglipur (₹230, 12 hours) and 4.30am for Mayabunder (₹180, 10 hours) via Rangat (₹130, six hours) and Baratang (₹80, three hours). More-comfortable, and pricier, private buses are also available; their 'offices' (a guy with a ticket book) are located across from the main bus stand.

ℹ Getting Around

TO & FROM THE AIRPORT

A taxi or autorickshaw from the airport to Aberdeen Bazaar costs around ₹70. There are also hourly buses (₹10) to/from airport, located 100m outside the complex, to the main bus stand.

AUTORICKSHAW

Aberdeen Bazaar to Phoenix Bay Jetty is about ₹20, and to Haddo Jetty it's around ₹40.

MOTORBIKE

You can hire a scooter from Green Island Tours for ₹400 per day.

AROUND PORT BLAIR & SOUTH ANDAMAN

Wandoor

Wandoor, a tiny speck of a village 29km southwest of Port Blair, has a nice beach (though at the time of research, swimming was prohibited due to crocodiles), and some chilled-out guesthouses. It's better known as a jumping-off point for **Mahatma Gandhi Marine National Park** (Indian/foreigner ₹50/500). Covering 280 sq km it comprises 15 islands of mangrove creeks, tropical rainforest and reefs supporting 50 types of coral. Depending upon the time of year, the marine park's snorkelling sites alternate between Jolly Buoy and Red Skin, allowing the other to regenerate. Both are popular day trips from Wandoor Jetty (₹450; Tuesday to Sunday), That said, if Havelock or Neil Islands are on your Andamans itinerary, it's probably easier and cheaper to wait until you reach them for your underwater experience; particularly due to Red Skin and Jolly Bouy's popularity with package tourists and damage suffered from coral bleaching.

However, for serious divers, **Lacadives** (☎9679532104; www.lacadives.com) is well worth checking out to visit more-remote areas of Mahatma Gandhi National Park.

Genuine nature lovers – the kind who like snakes and insects – will want to stay at **ANET** (Andaman & Nicobar Environmental Team; ☎03192-280081; www.anetindia.org; North Wandoor; per person incl full board ₹1100; @ 📶). Led by an inspiring team of dynamic young Indian ecologists, this is the place to gain a true sense of the Andamans' wilderness as you'll learn about the mangroves and intertidal zones, snakes, birds and crocs, and go on night walks. All activities are inclusive, but volunteers are given priority to the bamboo-hut accomodation. Reservations are essential.

Buses run from Port Blair to Wandoor (₹18, one hour).

Chiriya Tapu

Chiriya Tapu, 30km south of Port Blair, is a tiny village fringed by beaches and mangroves, and is famous for celestial sunsets. It also has some of the best **diving** outside Havelock. Lacadives and **Infinity Scuba** (☎03192-281183; www.infinityscubandamans.com) are two reputable dive companies that visit spectacular **Cinque Island, Rutland Island** and a wrecked ship. Snorkelling is also reportedly very good off the beach at sunset point, though like many places coral bleaching has occurred; enquire at the dive shops for more info.

There's also the **biological park** (Indian/foreigner ₹20/50; ⏲9am-4pm Tue-Sun), essentially a zoo, but with a pleasant forested setting and natural enclosures for crocodiles, Andaman wild pig, water monitors and spotted deer.

Most visit as a day trip from Port Blair, but **Wild Grass** (☎9474204508; r incl breakfast ₹4500; ❄) has double-storey cottages looking out to green surrounds.

There are seven buses a day to Port Blair (₹18, one hour); last bus is 6pm.

HAVELOCK ISLAND

POP 5500

With snow-white beaches, teal shallows, a coast crammed with beach huts and some of the best diving in Asia, Havelock has a well-deserved reputation as a backpacker paradise. For many, Havelock is *the* Andamans, and is what lures most tourists across the Bay of Bengal, many of whom are content to stay here for the entirety of their trip.

Sights & Activities

Most come to Havelock for some serious R and R, whether lazing on the beach, or diving or snorkelling.

Some resorts can organise guided **jungle treks** for keen walkers or birdwatchers, but be warned the forest floor turns to glug after rain. The inside rainforest is a spectacular, emerald cavern, and the **birdwatching** – especially on the forest fringes – is rewarding; look out for the blue-black racket-tailed drongo or golden oriole.

Sport fishing is another option, with **Captain Hook's** (☎9434280543; www.andamansportsfishing.com; Beach 3; half-day for 2 people ₹5500) offering the most reasonable rates for its boat trips.

Beaches

The prettiest and most popular stretch of sand is the critically acclaimed **Radhanagar Beach (Beach 7)**. It's a beautiful curve of sugar fronted by perfectly spiraled waves, all backed by native forest. Late afternoon is the best time to visit to avoid the heat and

ISLAND INDIGENES

The Andaman and Nicobar Islands' indigenous peoples constitute 12% of the population and, in most cases, their numbers are decreasing. The Onge, Sentinelese, Andamanese and Jawara are all of Negrito ethnicity, who share a strong resemblance to people from Africa. Tragically, numerous groups have become extinct over the past century. In February 2010 the last survivor of the Bo tribe passed away, bringing an end to both the language and 65,000 years of ancestry.

Onge

Two-thirds of Little Andaman's Onge Island was taken over by the Forest Department and 'settled' in 1977. The 100 or so remaining members of the Onge tribe live in a 25-sq-km reserve covering Dugong Creek and South Bay. Anthropologists say the Onge population has declined due to demoralisation through loss of territory.

Sentinelese

The Sentinelese, unlike the other tribes in these islands, have consistently repelled outside contact. For years, contact parties arrived on the beaches of North Sentinel Island, the last redoubt of the Sentinelese, with gifts of coconuts, bananas, pigs and red plastic buckets, only to be showered with arrows, although some encounters have been a little less hostile. About 150 Sentinelese remain.

Andamanese

As they now number only about 50, it seems impossible the Andamanese can escape extinction. There were around 7000 Andamanese in the mid-19th century, but friendliness to colonisers was their undoing, and by 1971 all but 19 of the population had been swept away by measles, syphilis and influenza epidemics. They've been resettled on tiny Strait Island.

Jarawa

The 350 remaining Jarawa occupy the 639-sq-km reserve on South and Middle Andaman Islands. In 1953 the chief commissioner requested that an armed sea plane bomb Jarawa settlements and their territory has been consistently disrupted by the Andaman Trunk Rd, forest clearance and settler and tourist encroachment. In 2012, a video went viral showing an exchange between Jarawa and tourists, whereby a policeman orders them to dance in exchange for food. This resulted in a government inquest that saw to the end of the so-called 'human safari' tours. Most Jarawa remain hostile to contact.

Shompen

Only about 250 Shompen remain in the forests on Great Nicobar. Semi-nomadic hunter-gatherers who live along the riverbanks, they have resisted integration and avoid areas occupied by Indian immigrants.

Nicobarese

The 30,000 Nicobarese are the only indigenous people whose numbers are not decreasing. The majority have converted to Christianity and been partly assimilated into contemporary Indian society. Living in village units led by a head man, they farm pigs and cultivate coconuts, yams and bananas. The Nicobarese, who probably descended from people of Malaysia and Myanmar, inhabit a number of islands in the Nicobar group, centred on Car Nicobar, the region worst affected by the 2004 tsunami – with an estimated one fifth of the population killed or missing.

crowds, as well as for its sunset. The further you walk from the main entry the more privacy you'll get. **Elephant rides** are possible in high season with work elephants, or, if you have a spare ₹30,000, you can swim with Rajan, Barefoot Resort's elephant. Radhanagar is on the northwestern side of the island about 12km.

Northwest of Radhanagar is the gorgeous 'lagoon' at **Neils Cove**, another gem of sheltered sand and crystalline water. Swimming is prohibited dusk and dawn; and take heed of any warnings regarding crocodiles (p412).

On the other side of the island from Radhanagar, the palm-ringed **Beach 5** has your more classic tropical vibe, with the bonus of shady patches and less sandflies. However, swimming is very difficult in low tide when water becomes shallow for miles. Most of the island's accommodation is out this way.

About 5km beyond No 5 Village, you'll find the low-key **Kalapathar**, another pristine beach. There's an elephant training camp out this way, but not much action to see at the time of research.

Diving & Snorkelling

Havelock is the premier spot for scuba diving in the Andamans. It's world renowned as much for its relative isolation as for its crystal-clear waters, deep-sea corals, schools of fish, turtles and kaleidoscope of colourful marine life. Diving here is suitable for all levels.

The main dive season is roughly November to April, but trips still occur year-round.

Prices are standardised, so it's a matter of finding a dive operator you feel comfortable with. Recommended operators include **Andaman Bubbles** (☎03192-282140; www.andamanbubbles.com; No 5 Village), a quality outfit with professional, personable staff; long-established **Barefoot Scuba** (☎9566088560; www.diveandamans.com; No 3 Village), with budget dive-accommodation packages in A-frame huts; **Dive India** (☎9932082205; www.diveindia.com; btwn No 3 & 5 Village), the original PADI company in Havelock, and still one of the best; and new operator **Ocean Tribe** (☎9531836695; www.ocean-tribe.com; No 3 Village), run by legendary local Karen divers.

All offer fully equipped boat dives, and prices vary depending on the location, number of participants and duration of the course. Diving starts from around ₹4725 for a two-tank dive, with options of discover scuba (one hour ₹4500), PADI open-water (four dives ₹20,000) and a range of advanced courses (three dives ₹12,000).

Popular sites are **Pilot Reef** with its abundance of coral, **South Button** for macro dives and rock formations, **Jackson Bar** for sharks, rays and turtles and **Minerva's Delight** for a bit of everything. Keep an eye out for trips further afield such as **Barren Island**, home to India's only active volcano whose ash produces an eerie underwater spectacle and regarded as one of the best.

While coral bleaching has been a major issue since 2010, diving remains world-class. The shallows may not have bright corals, but all the colourful fish are still here, and for depths beyond 20m, corals remain as vivid as ever. The Andamans fully recovered from a similar bleaching in 1998, and today things are likewise slowly repairing themselves.

Dive companies can arrange **snorkelling** trips, but it's cheaper to organise a *dunghi* (motorised wooden boat) through your guesthouse. Trips cost ₹1500 to ₹2000, depending on the number of people going, distance involved etc – if you go with a good-sized group you may pay as low as ₹300 per head. Snorkelling gear is widely available on Havelock from resorts and small restaurants, but is generally very low quality.

Most boats head to Elephant Beach for snorkelling, which can also be reached by a 40-minute walk through a muddy elephant logging trail; it's well marked (off the cross-island road), but turns to bog if it's been raining. At high tide it's also impossible to reach – ask locally. Lots of snorkelling charters, and even jet skis, come out this way, so be prepared, it can be bit of a circus.

Sleeping

Most lodges in Havelock are of the cluster-of-beach-huts genre. They all claim to be 'eco' huts ('eco' apparently meaning 'cheap building material'), but they're great value for money, especially in low season. Hammocks are available from the bazaar at Beach 3 for ₹150.

Orient Legend Resort GUESTHOUSE **$**
(☎03192-282389; Beach 5; huts ₹300, r ₹800-2000, with AC ₹3000) This popular sprawling place on Beach 5 covers most budgets, from doghouse A-frame huts, to concrete rooms and double-storey cottages that give a glimpse of the ocean.

Coconut Grove GUESTHOUSE **$**
(☎9474269977; huts ₹400, without bathroom ₹300;) Popular with Israeli travellers, Coconut Grove has an appealing communal vibe with psychedelic-painted huts

Havelock Island

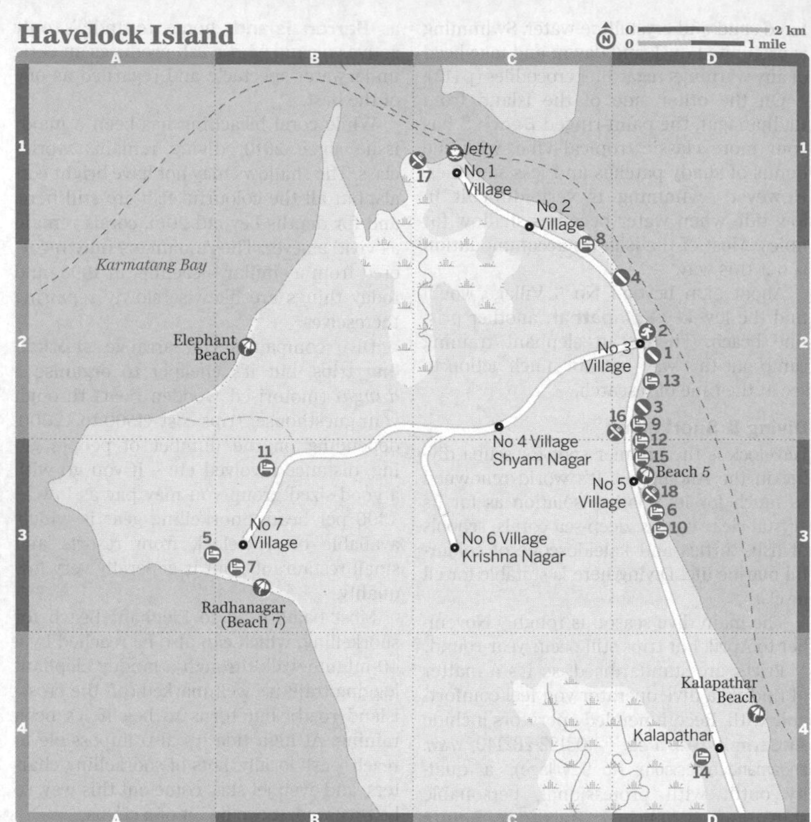

arranged in a circular outlay that directs everyone to the raised, concrete restaurant.

Dreamland Resort GUESTHOUSE $
(☎9474224164; Beach 7; huts without bathroom ₹400) In a prime location, only 50m from Beach 7, Dreamland is an old backpacker favourite with simple blue thatched bungalows and friendly owners.

Pellicon Beach Resort BUNGALOWS $
(☎9932081673; www.pelliconbeachresort.com; Beach 5; huts from ₹500) Attractive beach-side bungalows, and Nicobari huts with private porches on a peaceful plot of land close to the beach.

El Dorado BUNGALOWS $
(☎03192-282451; Beach 5; r from ₹350, with AC ₹3000) Chilled-out budget bamboo huts set in a tropical garden leading to Beach 5. Also has a restaurant-bar and fancier concrete air-con rooms.

Green Land Resort GUESTHOUSE $
(☎9933220625; huts ₹200-250, without bathroom ₹150-200) A taste of village life, with simple huts 2km from Radhanagar.

★ **Emerald Gecko** BUNGALOWS $$
(☎03192-282170; www.emerald-gecko.com; huts from ₹1200) On an island where very little thought goes into design, Emerald Gecko stands miles ahead. Comfortable double-storey bungalows have couches on its upper balcony looking to the water, while pricier rooms have sumptuous lighting and outdoor bathrooms that feel like Gilligan's Island. All are lovingly constructed from bamboo rafts drifted ashore from Myanmar. The concrete-floored rooms at the back are much less attractive. Staff are friendly, its restaurant quality and there's free filtered water.

Eco Villa BUNGALOWS $$
(☎03192-282212; www.havelock.co.in/ecovilla; Beach 2; r from ₹3000) Backpacker turned

Havelock Island

Activities, Courses & Tours

Sleeping

Eating

Information

overpriced resort with plush beachfront duplexes.

Wild Orchid HOTEL $$$
(☎03192-282472; www.wildorchidandaman.com; r incl breakfast from ₹5000; ❄@🛜) One of the Andamans' premier resorts, with thoughtfully furnished Andamanese-style cottages, or modern rooms with TV and air-con, all set around a fabulous tropical garden a stone's throw from the beach. It has the Red Snapper restaurant.

Barefoot at Havelock RESORT $$$
(☎044-24341001; www.barefootindia.com; Beach 7; tented cottage incl breakfast ₹5050, Nicobari cottages ₹8920, with AC ₹11,820; ❄) Havelock's most luxurious resort, boasting beautifully designed timber and bamboo-thatched cottages just back from the famed Radhanagar Beach. Its romantic restaurant is a good place to splurge. Barefoot also has attractive beachside duplexes at its dive resort on Beach 3.

People Tree BUNGALOWS, RETREAT $$$
(Kalapathar; r ₹2500-3500) Hidden away on Kalapathar beach, in a pastoral setting of rice paddies and betel palms, this yoga and meditation retreat was just opening its doors at time of research. Its elegant bamboo duplexes are constructed from driftwood and feature outdoor stone-garden bathrooms. A menu of healthy organic food was on the cards. It's a few minutes' walk from the beach.

Eating

There are *dhabas* (snack bars) near the jetty or try the main bazaar (No 3 Village) for local meals.

Anju-coco Resto INDIAN, CONTINENTAL $
(mains ₹120-250; ⏲8am-10.30pm) Having expanded to a much bigger restaurant, Anju-coco is still popular and is run by a friendly owner. There's a varied menu, with standouts being BBQ fish and its big breakfasts (₹60). Its original shack restaurant up the road does tasty Indian dishes.

Welcome Restaurant INDIAN, SEAFOOD $
(No 3 Village; mains from ₹50; ⏲7.30am-9.30pm) Just across from the market, this small eatery does delicious seafood curries and prawn rolls with rolled-up *parathas*.

Rony's INDIAN $
(Beach 5; mains from ₹40) Popular family-run cheapie serving up inexpensive seafood curries.

Fat Martin's SOUTH INDIAN $
(Beach 5; mains from ₹60; ⏲7.30am-8pm) Squeaky-clean open-air shack serving up a good selection of dosas, including paneer tikka and nutella dosas.

Why Like This? INDIAN, ISRAELI $
(Beach 5; mains from ₹100) Named as a tribute to the Israeli traveller, with a menu of schnitzels (including a fish version), and BBQ seafood dishes.

★**Red Snapper** SEAFOOD, MULTICUISINE $$
(Wild Orchid; mains ₹200-800; ⏲breakfast, lunch & dinner) Easily Havelock's best restaurant, with its atmospheric polished-bamboo decor and thatched-roof exuding a romantic island ambience. Pick from lavish seafood platters, BBQ fish and handmade pastas, accompanied by delicious cheese-and-olive naan. The outdoor deck seating is a

good spot to catch a breeze, and watch the glassed-in tandoori kitchen.

B3 – Barefoot Bar & Restaurant PIZZA **$$**
(No 1 Village; ⏲11am-4pm & 6-9.30pm) Modern decor with classic movie posters on the walls; there's a Western-heavy menu, with the best pizzas in Havelock, and it's a good place to wait for your ferry.

Information

There are two ATMs side by side in No 3 Village. Internet is insanely pricey (per hour ₹350!), so try to send all your emails in Port Blair.

Havelock Tourist Service (Beach 3) in the bazaar can arrange air tickets and has the schedule for government ferries.

Getting There & Away

Government ferries run from Havelock to Port Blair two to three times a day (₹195, 2½ hours), and you're best to book tickets from the **port** (⏲9.15am-noon & 2-4pm Mon-Sat, to 2pm Sun) at least a day in advance. Otherwise Makruzz (p418) has a daily service at 4pm.

One to two ferries a day link Havelock with Neil Island (₹195, one hour 10 minutes), while four boats a week head to Long Island (₹195, two hours) en route to Rangat.

Getting Around

A local bus (₹10, 40 minutes) connects the jetty, villages and Radar Nagar on a roughly hourly circuit until 6pm. Otherwise you can rent a scooter (per day from ₹300) or bicycle (per day ₹60).

An autorickshaw from the jetty to No 3 Village is ₹40, to No 5 ₹60 and to No 7 ₹200.

NEIL ISLAND

Happy to laze in the shadows of its more famous island neighbour, tranquil Neil is still the place for that added bit of relaxation. Its beaches may not be as luxurious as Havelock's, but they have ample character and are a perfect distance apart to explore by bicycle. There's a lovely unhurried pace of life here; cycling through picturesque villages you'll get many friendly hellos. In Neil Island you're about 40km from Port Blair, a short ferry ride from Havelock and several universes away from life at home

There's no ATM or moneychanging facilities on Neil, so bring plenty of cash. There's pricey satellite **internet** (per 30min ₹150; ⏲8.30am-9pm) and a post office in the bazaar. The main bazaar has a mellow vibe, and is a popular gathering spot in the early evening.

Sights & Activities

Neil Island's five beaches (numbered one to five) all have their unique charms, though they're not necessarily great for swimming.

Beach 1 (Lamanpur) is a long sweep of sandy beach and mangrove, a 40-minute walk west of the jetty and village. The island's best **snorkelling** is around the coral reef at the far (western) end of this beach at high tide. If you're extremely lucky you may spot a dugong feeding in the shallows at high tide. There's a good sunset viewpoint out this way accessed via Pearl Park Resort, which becomes a communal spot in the sand for tourists and locals come early evening.

Beach 2, on the north side of the island, has the **Natural Bridge** rock formation, accessible only at low tide by walking around the rocky cove. To get here by bicycle take the side road that runs through the bazaar, then take a left where the road forks.

Beach 3 (Ram Nagar) is a secluded powdery sand cove, which is best accessed via Blue Sea Restaurant. There's also good snorkelling here.

The best swimming beach is at **Beach 4 (Bharatpur)**, though its proximity to the jetty is a slight turn-off.

Further ahead the more wild and rugged **Beach 5 (Sitapur)**, 5km from the village, and reached via the village road to the eastern side of the island, is a nice place to walk along the beach, with small limestone caves accessible at low tide.

You can dive with **India Scuba Explorers** (☎9474238646; www.indiascubaexplorers.com) or **Dive India** (☎9932082205; www.diveindia.com/neil.html), which both have snorkelling gear for ₹150. Those interested in free diving can contact Sanjay at Gayan Garden. Hiring a fishing boat to go to offshore snorkelling or fishing will costs around ₹1500.

Cooking classes (from ₹200) can be arranged at Gayan Garden Restaurant, where you can learn to cook your favourite Indian dishes; reservations essential.

Sleeping

Pearl Park Beach Resort BUNGALOWS **$**
(☎9434260132; www.andamanpearlpark.com; Beach 1; huts with/without bathroom ₹500/250,

Nicobari cottages ₹1500) One of Neil's original bamboo-bungalow 'resorts', with pleasant huts arranged around a flower-filled garden and the best sunset point on the island.

Breakwater Beach Resort BUNGALOWS $
(Beach 3; r ₹400) Family-run bungalows on Beach 3 wins rave reviews for its chilled-out ambience and delicious food.

A-N-D Beach Resort BUNGALOWS $
(☎214722; Beach 4; huts with/without bathroom ₹600/200) Just to the left of the pier, on an attractive stretch of beach, these laid-back thatched bungalows have friendly staff and a good restaurant.

Gayan Garden BUNGALOWS $
(Beach One; r ₹300) Attractive bamboo cottages are situated between the bazaar and Beach 1, with a relaxed garden, seafood restaurant and filtered coffee. Also has excellent recycling initiatives and free filtered water.

Tango Beach Resort HOTEL $
(☎9474212842; www.tangobeachandaman.com; Beach 1; huts ₹500, cottages from ₹1000) Famous for its sea breeze, this Beach 1 classic is a bit pricier than most, but its sea-facing rooms are still a fine choice. Has a good map on its website.

Kalapani BUNGALOWS $
(☎9474274991; Beach 3; huts ₹350) Another reason why travellers are heading to Beach 3, with relaxed bungalows run by a friendly couple, a sandy garden, free snorkelling gear and a book exchange.

Seashell RESORT $$$
(☎9933239625; www.seashellneil.com; Beach 1; r incl breakfast ₹5370) It was only a matter of time before a fancy resort arrived at Neil, but thankfully it's nice and unobtrusive, with tented cottages leading down to the mangrove-lined beach.

Eating

Moonshine SEAFOOD, INDIAN $
(mains ₹40-150) On the road to Beach 1, this backpacker favourite has excellent home-made pastas, fish thalis and cold beer.

Blue Sea SEAFOOD, INDIAN $
(Beach 3; mains from ₹90; 8.30am-10.30pm) Old-school beach shack with sandy floor and dangling beach curios, and all the usual dishes. The path here leads to arguably Neil's best beach.

Chand Restaurant INDIAN, CONTINENTAL $
(Bazaar; mains ₹50-200; 6am-10.30pm) Best place in the market with good mix of international and Indian dishes, strong filtered coffee and delicious seafood.

Getting There & Around

A ferry heads to Port Blair two or three times a day (₹195, two hours). There's also one or two daily ferries to Havelock (₹195, one hour), and three ferries a week to Long Island (₹260, five hours). There's talk the Makruzz ferry might commence a service to/from Port Blair.

Hiring a bicycle (per day from ₹50) is the best way to get about; roads are flat and distances short. You'll be able to find one in the bazaar, or guesthouses. An autorickshaw will take you to Beach 1 or 3 from the jetty for ₹50 to ₹60.

MIDDLE & NORTH ANDAMAN

The Andamans aren't just sun and sand. They're also jungle that feels as primeval as the Jurassic, a green tangle of ancient forest that could have been birthed in Mother Nature's subconscious. This shaggy, wild side of the islands can be seen on a long, loping bus ride up the Andaman Trunk Rd (ATR), framed by antediluvian trees and roll-on, roll-off ferries that cross red-tannin rivers prowled by saltwater crocodiles.

But there's a negative side to riding the ATR: the road cuts through the homeland of the Jarawa and has brought the tribe into incessant contact with the outside world. Modern India and tribal life do not seem able to coexist – every time Jarawa and settlers interact, misunderstandings have led to friction, confusion and, at worst, violent attacks and death. Indian anthropologists and indigenous rights groups such as Survival International have called for the ATR to be closed; its status continues to be under review at time of writing. At present, vehicles are permitted to travel only in convoys at set times from 6am to 3pm. Photography is strictly prohibited, as is stopping or any other interaction with the Jarawa people – who are becoming increasingly reliant on handouts from passing traffic.

The first place of interest north of Port Blair is the impressive **limestone caves** (closed Mon) at Baratang. It's a 45-minute boat trip (₹300) from the jetty, a scenic trip through mangrove forest. A permit is required, organised at the jetty.

Rangat is the next main town, a transport hub with not much else going for it. If you do get stuck here, **UK Nest** (☎9434276356; Rangat; r from ₹400) has clean rooms. There's an ATM nearby. Ferries depart Long Island (₹7) from Yeratta Jetty, 8km from Rangat. Otherwise Rangat Bay, 10km outside town, has ferries to/from Port Blair (₹55, six hours) and Havelock (₹195, two hours). A daily bus goes to Port Blair (₹95, seven hours) and Diglipur (₹90, four hours).

Long Island

With its friendly island community and lovely slow pace of life, Long Island is perfect for those wanting to take the pace down even a few more notches. Other than the odd motorcycle, there's no motorised vehicles on the island, and at times you may be the only tourist here.

A 1½-hour trek in the jungle (not advisable after heavy rain) will lead you to the secluded **Lalaji Bay**, a beautiful white-sand beach with good swimming; follow the red arrows to get here. Hiring a *dunghi* (₹2000 return) makes it much easier – especially if you don't like leeches. There's a closer, OK beach reached via the yellow arrows.

You can also get a *dunghi* to North Passage island for snorkelling at the stunning **Merk Bay** (₹2500) with blinding white sand and translucent waters.

Blue Planet now offers **diving**, charging ₹4000 for two dives, and visits Campbell Shoal for its schools of trevally and barracuda.

There are four ferries a week to Havelock, Neil and Port Blair (₹195). From Yerata, there are two daily boats to Long Island (₹9, one hour) at 9am and 4pm, returning at 7am and 2pm.

Sleeping

Construction of a luxury hotel at Lalaji Bay was about to commence at the time of research.

★ **Blue Planet** GUESTHOUSE $
(☎9474212180; www.blueplanetandamans.com; r with/without bathroom from ₹1000/350; @) The only place to stay on the island, so fortunately it's a gem, with thatched-bamboo rooms and hammocks set around a lovely Padauk tree. It sets an excellent example by incorporating bottles washed ashore into its architecture, and provides free filtered water. Follow the blue arrows from the jetty to get here. It also has wonderful double-storey bamboo cottages (from ₹2000) at a nearby location.

Diglipur & Around

Those who make it this far north are well rewarded with some impressive attractions in the area. It's a giant outdoor adventure playground designed for nature lovers: home to Andaman's highest peak, a network of caves, a famous turtle nesting site and crocodile

OFF THE BEATEN TRACK

MAYABUNDER & AROUND

In 'upper' Middle Andaman, Mayabunder is most famous for its villages inhabited by Karen, members of a Burmese hill tribe who were relocated here during the British colonial period. **Sea'n'Sand** (☎03192-273454, fax 03192-273455; thanzin_the_great@yahoo.co.in; r from ₹200; ❄) is easily the best place to stay with comfortable rooms, and attractive bamboo restaurant and bar. It's run by Titus and Elizabeth (and their extended Karen family), who are a good source for everything Mayabunder. It's a low-key destination and will appeal to travellers looking for an experience away from the crowds.

You can go on a range of day tours, with the highlight being jungle trekking at creepy **Interview Island** (boat ₹4000 fits eight people), inhabited by a population of 42 wild elephants, released after a logging company closed for business in the 1950s. You'll feel very off the beaten track here. Armed guards accompany you in case of elephant encounters. A permit (₹500) is required, which is best organised by faxing your details to Titus at Sea'n'Sand. Other trips include **Forty One Caves**, where hawabills make their highly prized edible nests, and snorkelling off **Avis Island**.

Mayabunder, 71km north of Rangat, is linked by daily buses from Port Blair (₹180, 10 hours) and by thrice-weekly ferries. There's an unreliable ATM here.

sanctuaries, to go with white-sandy beaches and the best snorkelling in the Andamans.

However, don't expect anything of Diglipur, the northernmost major town in the Andamans, which is a sprawling, gritty bazaar town with an ATM and slow internet connection (per hour ₹40). You should instead head straight for the tranquil coastal village of **Kalipur**.

Ferries arrive at Aerial Bay Jetty, from where it's 11km to Diglipur, and 8km to Kalipur in the other direction.

Sights & Activities

Diglipur has huge tourist potential, and those who hang around will have plenty to discover. Get in touch with Pristine Beach Resort, who are involved with the Darted grassroots tourist initiative to promote Alfred Caves, mud volcanoes and crocodile habitats. It's also possible to visit elephant work camps.

Ross & Smith Islands BEACH, SNORKELLING
(Indian/foreigner ₹50/500; Forest Office 6am-2pm Mon-Sat) Like lovely tropical counterweights, the twin islands of Smith and Ross are connected by a narrow sandbar of dazzling white sand, and are up there with the best in the Andamans.

Since this is designated as a marine sanctuary, you need a ₹500 permit from the Forest Office opposite Aerial Bay Jetty. However, at time of research, you could apply in writing to the Forest Office to visit Smith Island for free (which is duly linked to Ross...); Pristine Beach Resort can assist with this process.

You can organise a boat from Aerial Bay for ₹2000, but if you're staying at Pristine Resort it's easier and cheaper to take its *dunghi* for ₹1800, meaning you don't have to travel to Aerial Bay.

Craggy Island, a small island off Kalipur, also has good snorkelling. Strong swimmers can make it across (flippers recommended), otherwise a *dunghi* is available (₹200 return).

Saddle Peak TREKKING
(Indian/foreigner ₹25/250) At 732m, Saddle Peak is the highest point in the Andamans. You can trek through subtropical forest to the top and back from Kalipur in about six hours; the views from the peaks onto the archipelago are incredible. Again, a permit is required from the Forest Office and a local guide will make sure you don't get lost. Otherwise follow the red arrows marked on the trees.

DON'T MISS

TURTLE NESTING

Reputedly the only beach in the world where leatherback, hawksbill, olive ridley and green turtles all nest along the same coastline, Kalipur is a fantastic place to observe this evening show between mid-December and April. Turtles can be witnessed most nights, and you can assist with collecting eggs, or with the release of hatchlings. Contact Pristine Beach Resort for more information.

There's also turtle breeding grounds at Cuthbert Bay, a 45-minute drive from Rangat.

Sleeping & Eating

A new budget guesthouse in Kalipur was about to open a few doors down from Pristine at time of research.

★**Pristine Beach Resort** GUESTHOUSE $
(9474286787; www.andamanpristineresorts.com; huts ₹300-1000, r ₹2500-3500; ❄@) Huddled among the palms between paddy fields and the beach, this relaxing resort has simple bamboo huts, more romantic bamboo 'tree houses' and upmarket rooms. Its attractive restaurant-bar serves up delicious Nicobari fish and cold beer. Alex, the super-friendly owner, is a top source of information. It also rents bicycles/motorcycles (per day ₹60/250).

Getting There & Around

Diglipur, located about 80km north of Mayabunder, is served by daily buses to/from Port Blair (₹230, 12 hours), as well as buses to Mayabunder (₹50, 2½ hours) and Rangat (₹100, 4½ hours). There are also ferries to Port Blair (seat/bunk ₹110/310, nine hours) three times a week.

Buses run the 18km journey from Diglipur to Kalipur (₹13, 30 mintues) every 45 minutes; an autorickshaw costs ₹200.

LITTLE ANDAMAN

As far south as you can go in the islands, Little Andaman has an appealing end-of-the-world feel. It's a gorgeous fist of mangroves, jungle and teal, ringed by beaches as fresh as bread out of the oven.

Badly hit by the 2004 Boxing Day tsunami, Little Andaman has slowly rebuilt itself. Located about 120km south of Port Blair, the main settlement here is **Hut Bay**, a pleasant small town that primarily produces smiling Bengalis and Tamils.

Sights & Activities

Little Andaman has a coastline of uninterrupted white sandy beach. **Netaji Nagar Beach**, 11km north of Hut Bay, and **Butler Bay** (₹20), a further 3km north, are gorgeous, deserted (apart from the odd cow) and great for surfing.

Inland, the **White Surf** and **Whisper Wave waterfalls** offer a forest experience (the latter involves a 4km jungle trek and a guide is highly recommended); they're pleasant falls and you may be tempted to swim in the rock pools, but beware of local crocodiles.

Little Andaman lighthouse, 14km from Hut Bay, is another worthwhile excursion. Standing 41m high, exactly 200 steps spiral up to magnificent views over the coastline and forest. The easiest way to get here is by motorcycle, or otherwise a sweaty bicycle journey. You could also take an autorickshaw until the road becomes unpassable, and walk for an hour along the blissful stretch of deserted beach.

Kalapathar lagoon is a popular enclosed swimming area with shady patches of sand. Look for the cave in the cliff face that you can scamble through for stunning ocean views. It's just located before Butler Bay, and accessed via a side road that runs past modern housing constructed post-tsunami.

Harbinder Bay and **Dugong Creek** are designated tribal areas for the Nicobarese and Onge, respectively, and are off-limits.

Intrepid surfing travellers have been whispering about Little Andaman since it first opened up to foreigners several years ago. The reef breaks are legendary, but best suited for more experienced surfers. **Surfing Little Andaman** (9609688970; www.surfinglittleandaman.com; 2hr lessons ₹1000, board rental half-/full day ₹500/900), based in Hut Bay, hire out boards, conduct lessons and have all the info on waves for Little Andaman and around.

Sleeping & Eating

There are plenty of cheap and tasty thali and tiffin places in town. None of the following serve alcohol, but you can stock up from a 'wine shop' in Hut Bay.

★ **Blue View** BUNGALOWS $
(9734480840; Km11.5; r without bathroom ₹350-500) Prime real estate across the road from Netaji Nagar Beach, Blue View's simple thatched bungalows are run by the lovely Azad and his wife. It has surfboards (per hour/day ₹100/500) and rents out bicycles/motorbikes (per day ₹50/300). The food here is very good.

Jina Resort BUNGALOWS $
(9476038057; Netaji Nagar 11km; r from ₹150) This newcomer also has chilled-out bungalows sprawled out over a lovely garden, just across from a lovely beach. Also rents out bikes.

Hotel Sea Land HOTEL $
(03192-284525; Hut Bay; s/d ₹250/400, with AC ₹700) In town, Sea Land offers more-comfortable concrete rooms, but lacks atmosphere, though it has a nice gazebo with a sea breeze and hammocks.

Palm Groove INDIAN $
(Hut Bay; 6am-9pm) Attractive heritage-style bungalow with outdoor garden gazebo serving up a good selection of biriyanis and thalis.

Getting There & Around

Ferries land at Hut Bay Jetty on the east coast; from there the beaches lay to the north. Buses (₹10) to Netaji Nagar usually coincide with ferry arrivals, or otherwise pass by every hour or so. Shared jeeps (₹50) are the other option. Failing that, an autorickshaw from the jetty to Netaji Nagar is ₹250, or ₹50 to town. Motorbikes and bicycles are available from most lodges.

Boats sail to Port Blair daily, alternating between afternoon and evening departures on vessels ranging from big ferries with four-/two-bed rooms (₹220/260, 8½ hours) to faster 5½-hour government boats (₹30); all have air-con. The ferry office is closed Sundays.

There's an ATM in Hut Bay, but no internet.

Understand South India

South India Today

With a tremendously diverse regional mix of people, customs, religions and perspectives, South India always has a lot going on. While each state has its own unique set of economic, political, cultural and environmental characteristics, government decisions made in the nation's capital, Delhi, still percolate right through the southern states. In this chapter we cover some of the major issues you're most likely to hear being discussed, no matter where your travels take you.

Best in Film

Fire (1996), **Earth** (1998) and **Water** (2005) The Deepa Mehta–directed trilogy was popular abroad, but controversial in India.

Pyaasa (Thirst; 1957) and **Kaagaz Ke Phool** (Paper Flowers; 1959) Two bittersweet films directed by and starring film legend Guru Dutt.

Gandhi (1982) The classic.

Best in Print: Fiction

Midnight's Children Salman Rushdie's allegory about Independence and Partition.

The Guide and **The Painter of Signs** Classic RK Narayan novels set in the fictional town of Malgudi.

A Fine Balance Rohinton Mistry's tragic Mumbai-based story.

White Tiger Aravind Adiga's Booker-winning novel about class struggle in globalised India.

Best in Print: Nonfiction

India after Gandhi: The History of the World's Largest Democracy An elegant post-Gandhi history by Ramachandra Guha.

The Nehrus and the Gandhis Tariq Ali's astute portrait-history of these powerful families.

Behind the Beautiful Forevers Katherine Boo's fascinating account of life in one of Mumbai's slums.

The Kashmir Impasse

In January 2013 Indian officials published a notice in newspapers in Kashmir about preparing for nuclear war, with tips on constructing shelters, stockpiling supplies and what to do if caught outside during an explosion. Delhi officials claimed that the notice was a normal public-education announcement – and not a response to recent border skirmishes, the worst in a decade, that killed three Pakistanis and two Indian soldiers, one of whom was beheaded.

This was only the latest in a long series of tragic events here: the predominantly Muslim Kashmir Valley is claimed by India and Pakistan (as well as the much less powerful Kashmiris themselves), and the impasse has plagued relations between the two countries since Partition in 1947.

Three India–Pakistan wars – in 1947, 1965 and 1971 – resolved little, and by 1989 Kashmir had its own Pakistan-backed armed insurgency. Tens of thousands were killed in the conflicts, and India has maintained hundreds of thousands of troops in Indian-administered Kashmir ever since. India–Pakistan relations sunk even lower in 1998 when both governments tested nuclear devices in a muscle-flexing show: nukes were now in the picture.

Talks that might have created an autonomous region were derailed in 2008, when terrorists killed at least 163 people around Mumbai (Bombay) during three days of coordinated bombings and shootings. The one sniper caught alive, a Pakistani, had ties to Lashkar-e-Taiba, a militant group that formed to assist the Pakistani army in Kashmir in the 1990s. Pakistan denied any involvement. The dust was beginning to settle in 2012, and talks were making headway. But in late 2012, India secretly executed the Pakistani sniper, and then, in early 2013, a Kashmiri man convicted for involvement in a 2001 attack on Parliament was also hanged, heightening – once again – tensions between the countries.

Communal Tension

While Kashmir is the site of India's most persistent conflict, religion-based confrontation further south may be its most insidious. One of the most violent episodes occurred in 1992, when Hindu extremists destroyed a mosque, the Babri Masjid, in Ayodhya, Uttar Pradesh, revered by Hindus as the birthplace of Rama. The Hindu-revivalist BJP, then the main opposition, did little to discourage the acts, and rioting in the north killed thousands.

The BJP grew in popularity and won elections in 1998 and 1999. Prime Minister Atal Bihari Vajpayee appeared moderate, but many BJP members and supporters took a more belligerent posture. In 2002, when 58 Hindus died in a suspicious train fire, more than 2000 people, mostly Muslims, were killed in subsequent riots; according to the nonprofit Human Rights Watch, some BJP government officials were directly involved.

The year 2008 was one of India's darkest: bomb blasts in Jaipur, Ahmedabad and Delhi each killed dozens of people. Investigations pointed at hard-line Islamist groups. Tensions seemed to be cooling in 2010, when a court stated that the Ayodhya site would be split between Hindus and Muslims and the response was peaceful. The ruling was suspended by the Supreme Court in 2011 after appeals by both Hindus and Muslims. But blasts in Mumbai and Delhi in 2011 were reminders that extremism isn't dead.

Congress Today & the Economy

When the Congress Party regained power in 2004, it was under the leadership of Sonia Gandhi – the Italian-born wife of the late Rajiv Gandhi, who served as prime minister from 1984 to 1989. The BJP's planned national agitation campaign against Sonia Gandhi's foreign origins was subverted when she stepped aside to allow Manmohan Singh to be sworn in as prime minister. With a reputation for transparency and intelligence, Singh is reasonably popular among Indians, though many believe that Gandhi still wields considerable influence over the actual decisions. Under Singh's leadership, India has carried out a program of economic liberalisation along with a number of education, health and other social-reform initiatives.

In 1991, Singh, then finance minister, floated the rupee against a basket of 'hard' currencies. State subsidies were phased out and the economy was opened up to foreign investment, with multinationals drawn by India's multitudes of educated professionals and low wages. India became the world's second-fastest growing economy (after China). But in recent years that growth has dropped off, the rupee has slumped and inflation has soared. Some economists see

POPULATION: **1.21 BILLION**

GDP: **US$1.85 TRILLION (2011)**

UNEMPLOYMENT RATE: **9.8%**

EMPLOYED IN AGRICULTURE: **52%**

LITERACY RATE: **65/82% (FEMALE/MALE)**

GENDER RATIO: **940/1000 (FEMALE/MALE)**

if India were 100 people

55 would speak one of 21 other official languages
41 would speak Hindi
4 would speak one of 400 other official languages

belief systems

(% of population)

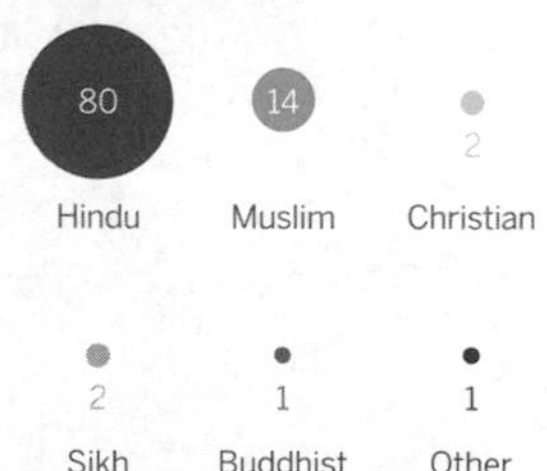

population per sq km

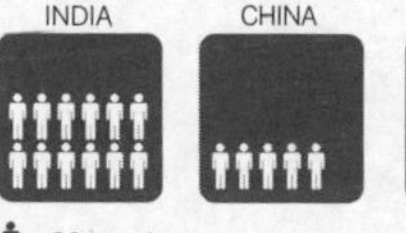

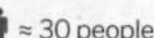 ≈ 30 people

Dos & Don'ts

Dress modestly Avoid tight clothes and keep shoulders and knees covered, especially at holy places.
PDA Public displays of affection – kissing, cuddling or holding hands – are not condoned.
Pure feet Remove shoes before entering people's homes and sacred sites.
Photos Always ask before photographing people or holy places.
That head wobble It can mean 'yes', 'maybe' or 'I have no idea'. Go with the flow!

Niceties

Namaste Saying *namaste* with hands together in a prayer gesture is a traditional, respectful Hindu greeting and a universally accepted way to say hello.
Hugs Hugs between strangers are not the norm.
Pure hands Use your right hand for eating and shaking hands; the left hand is the 'toilet' hand.
Bad vibes Avoid pointing the soles of your feet towards people or deities, or touching anyone with your feet.
Good Manners If you're invited to someone's home for a meal, it's nice to take flowers and/or sweets.

benefits to slower growth: it could slow down inflation and reduce economic disparity. Huge sections of the country's billion-plus population benefited little from the boom, and the gap between the haves and the have-nots continues to be vast.

In January 2013 Rahul Gandhi, Sonia's son, assumed the post of Vice President of the Congress Party. The move didn't surprise anyone: the Nehru-Gandhi name has become synonymous with the party. But he's not considered a charismatic or strategic figure, and it's expected to be a struggle to get a Gandhi back in the PM seat in 2014.

Violence Against Women

In December 2012 a 23-year-old paramedic and her male friend boarded a bus on their way home from the movies in Delhi only to find that it was a fake city bus, where six men awaited them. The men beat the two friends, and raped the woman so brutally that she died 12 days later. The woman became known in India as Nirbhaya, or 'fearless one', and the event set off massive protests and soul-searching nationwide.

Within weeks, India passed a package of new but controversial laws to deter violence against women: rape now carries a seven-year minimum sentence, with the death penalty in cases where the victim dies. But in the months following the murder, more crimes took place, including violent rapes of girls as young as four. And while some Indian politicians condemned the rapists, others made comments that downplayed rape or blamed the victim.

Many in India are also now reflecting on other abuses of women (tens of thousands die over dowry disputes alone each year), widespread police and justice-system mishandling of cases (of the more than 600 reported rapes in Delhi in 2012, just one resulted in a conviction), and the larger problems of gender inequality. The situation for women's violence isn't good, but many are hopeful that, now that the issues are out in the open, change will follow.

History

South India has always laid claim to its own unique history, largely resulting from its insulation, by distance, from the political developments up north. The cradle of Dravidian culture, it has a long and colourful historical tapestry of wrangling dynasties and empires, interwoven with the influx of traders and conquerors arriving by sea, all of which have richly contributed to shaping a remarkable mix of southern traditions that exist to the present day.

Indus Valley Civilisation

India's first major civilisation flourished around 2500 BC in the Indus River valley, much of which lies within present-day Pakistan. This civilisation, which continued for a thousand years and is known as the Harappan culture, appears to have been the culmination of thousands of years of settlement. The Harappan civilisation fell into decline from the beginning of the 2nd millennium BC. Some historians attribute the end of the empire to floods or decreased rainfall, which threatened the Harappans' agricultural base. The more enduring, if contentious, theory is that an Aryan invasion put paid to the Harappans, despite little archaeological proof or written reports in the ancient Indian texts to that effect. As a result, some nationalist historians argue that the Aryans (from a Sanskrit word meaning 'noble') were in fact the original inhabitants of India and that the invasion theory was invented by self-serving foreign conquerors. Others say that the arrival of the Aryans was more of a gentle migration that gradually subsumed Harappan culture, rather than an invasion. Those who defend the invasion theory believe that from around 1500 BC Aryan tribes from Afghanistan and Central Asia began to filter into northwest India. Despite their military superiority, their progress was gradual, with successive tribes battling over territory and new arrivals pushing further east into the Ganges plain. Eventually these tribes controlled northern India as far as the Vindhya Range. As a consequence, many of the original inhabitants, the Dravidians, were forced south.

To learn more about the ancient Indus Valley civilisation, ramble around Harappa, (www.harappa.com), which presents an illustrated yet scholarly overview

TIMELINE

2600–1700 BC

The heyday of the Indus Valley civilisation, which spans parts of Rajasthan, Gujarat and the Sindh province in present-day Pakistan, and includes cities such as Harappa and Moenjodaro.

1500 BC

The Indo-Aryan civilisation takes root in the fertile plains of the Indo-Gangetic basin. Settlers speak an early form of Sanskrit, from which several Indian vernaculars, including Hindi, later evolve.

1500–1200 BC

The *Rig-Veda,* the first and longest of Hinduism's canonical texts, the Vedas, is written; three more books follow. Earliest forms of priestly Brahmanic Hinduism emerge.

Influences from the North

While the Indus Valley civilisation may not have affected South India, the same cannot be said for the Aryan invasion. The Aryanisation of the south was a slow process, but it had a profound effect on the social order of the region and the ethos of its inhabitants. The northerners brought their literature (the four Vedas – a collection of sacred Hindu hymns), their gods (Agni, Varuna, Shiva and Vishnu), their language (Sanskrit) and a social structure that organised people into castes, with Brahmins at the top.

India: A History by John Keay is an astute and readable account of subcontinental history spanning from the Harappan civilisation to Indian Independence.

Over the centuries other influences flowed from the north, including Buddhism and Jainism. Sravanabelagola in Karnataka, an auspicious place of pilgrimage to this day, is where over 2000 years ago the northern ruler Chandragupta Maurya, who had embraced Jainism and renounced his kingdom, arrived with his guru. Jainism was then adopted by the trading community (its tenet of ahimsa, or nonviolence, precluded occupations tainted by the taking of life), who spread it through South India.

Emperor Ashoka, a successor of Chandragupta who ruled for 40 years from about 272 BC, was a major force behind Buddhism's inroads into the south. Once a campaigning king, his epiphany came in 260 BC when, overcome by the horrific carnage and suffering caused by his campaign against the Kalingas (a powerful kingdom), he renounced violence and

ASHOKA: AN ENLIGHTENED EMPEROR

Apart from the Mughals and then the British many centuries later, no other power controlled more Indian territory than the Mauryan empire. It's therefore fitting that it provided India with one of its most significant historical figures.

Emperor Ashoka's rule was characterised by flourishing art and sculpture, while his reputation as a philosopher-king was enhanced by the rock-hewn edicts he used both to instruct his people and to delineate the enormous span of his territory.

Ashoka's reign also represented an undoubted historical high point for Buddhism: he embraced the religion in 269 BC, declaring it the state religion and cutting a radical swath through the spiritual and social body of Hinduism. The emperor also built thousands of stupas and monasteries across the region. Ashoka sent missions abroad, and he is revered in Sri Lanka because he sent his son and daughter to carry Buddha's teaching to the island.

The long shadow this emperor of the 3rd century BC still casts over India is evident from the fact that the central design of the Indian national flag is the Ashoka Chakra, a wheel with 24 spokes. Ashoka's standard, which topped many pillars, is also the seal of modern-day India (four lions sitting back-to-back atop an abacus decorated with a frieze and the inscription 'truth alone triumphs') and its national emblem, chosen to reaffirm the ancient commitment to peace and goodwill.

1000 BC

Indraprastha, Delhi's first incarnation, comes into being. Archaeological excavations at the site, where the Purana Qila now stands, continue even today, as more facts about this ancient capital keep emerging.

599–528 BC

The life of Mahavir, the 24th and last *tirthankar* (enlightened teacher) who established Jainism. Like Buddha, he preaches compassion and a path to enlightenment for all castes.

563–483 BC

The life of Siddhartha Gautama. The prince is born in modern-day Nepal and attains enlightenment beneath the Bodhi Tree in Bodhgaya (Bihar), thereby transforming into Buddha (Awakened One).

326 BC

Alexander the Great invades India. He defeats King Porus in Punjab to enter the subcontinent, but a rebellion within his army keeps him from advancing beyond Himachal Pradesh's Beas River.

embraced Buddhism. He sent Buddhist missionaries far and wide, and his edicts (carved into rock and incised into specially erected pillars) have been found in Andhra Pradesh and Karnataka. Stupas were also built in South India under Ashoka's patronage, mostly along the coast of Andhra Pradesh, although at least one was constructed as far south as Kanchipuram in Tamil Nadu.

The appeal of Jainism and Buddhism was that they rejected the Vedas and condemned the caste system. Buddhism, however, gradually lost favour with its devotees, and was replaced with a new brand of Hinduism, which emphasised devotion to a personal god. This bhakti (surrendering to the gods) order developed in South India around AD 500. Bhakti adherents opposed Jainism and Buddhism, and the movement hastened the decline of both in South India.

Mauryan Empire & Southern Kingdoms

Chandragupta Maurya was the first in a line of Mauryan kings to rule what was effectively the first Indian empire. The empire's capital was in present-day Patna in Bihar. Chandragupta's son, Bindusara, who came to the throne around 300 BC, extended the empire as far as Karnataka. However, he seems to have stopped there, possibly because the Mauryan empire was on cordial terms with the southern chieftains of the day.

The identity and customs of these chiefdoms have been gleaned from various sources, including archaeological remains and ancient Tamil literature. These literary records describe a land known as the 'abode of the Tamils', within which resided three major ruling families: the Pandyas (Madurai), the Cheras (Malabar Coast) and the Cholas (Thanjavur and the Cauvery Valley). The region described in classical Sangam literature (written between 300 BC and AD 200) was still relatively insulated from Sanskrit culture, but from 200 BC this was starting to change.

A degree of rivalry characterised relations between the main chiefdoms and the numerous minor chiefdoms, and there were occasional clashes with Sri Lankan rulers. Sangam literature indicates that Sanskrit traditions from the old Aryan kingdoms of the north were taking root in South India around 200 BC. Ultimately, the southern powers all suffered at the hands of the Kalabhras, about whom little is known except that they appeared to have originated from somewhere north of the Tamil region.

By around 180 BC the Mauryan empire, which had started to disintegrate soon after the death of Emperor Ashoka in 232 BC, had been overtaken by a series of rival kingdoms that were subjected to repeated invasions from northerners such as the Bactrian Greeks. Despite this apparent instability, the post-Ashokan era produced at least one line of royalty whose patronage of the arts and ability to maintain a relatively

The concepts of zero and infinity are widely believed to have been devised by eminent Indian mathematicians during the reign of the Guptas.

321–185 BC

Rule of the Maurya kings. Founded by Chandragupta Maurya, this pan-Indian empire is ruled from Pataliputra (present-day Patna) and briefly adopts Buddhism during the reign of Emperor Ashoka.

c 235 BC

Start of Chola reign. The Tamil dynasty, known for the power and territory it accreted in the 9th to 13th centuries, ruled in India's south for more than 1500 years.

3rd century BC

The Satavahana empire, of Andhran origin, rules over a huge central Indian area. Their interest in art and maritime trade combines to influence artistic development regionally and in Southeast Asia.

1st century AD

International trade booms: the region's elaborate overland trade networks connect with ports linked to maritime routes. Trade to Africa, the Gulf, Socotra, Southeast Asia, China and even Rome thrives.

high degree of social cohesion have left an enduring legacy. This was the Satavahanas, who eventually controlled all of Maharashtra, Madhya Pradesh, Chhattisgarh, Karnataka and Andhra Pradesh. Under their rule, between 200 BC and AD 200, the arts blossomed, especially literature, sculpture and philosophy. Buddhism reached a peak in Maharashtra under the Satavahanas, although the greatest of the Buddhist cave temples at Ajanta and Ellora were built later by the Chalukya and Rashtrakuta dynasties.

Most of all, the subcontinent enjoyed a period of considerable prosperity. South India may have lacked vast and fertile agricultural plains on the scale of North India, but it compensated by building strategic trade links via the Indian Ocean.

The Fall & Rise of the Chola Empire

After the Kalabhras suppressed the Tamil chiefdoms, South India split into numerous warring kingdoms. The Cholas virtually disappeared and the Cheras on the west coast appear to have prospered through trading, although little is known about them. It wasn't until the late 6th century AD, when the Kalabhras were overthrown, that the political uncertainty in the region ceased. For the next 300 years the history of South India was dominated by the fortunes of the Chalukyas of Badami, the Pallavas of Kanchi (Kanchipuram) and the Pandyas of Madurai.

Pallava Architecture in Tamil Nadu

- *Shore Temple, Mamallapuram (Mahabalipuram)*
- *Arjuna's Penance, Mamallapuram*
- *Five Rathas, Mamallapuram*
- *Temples, Kanchipuram*
- *Rock Fort Temple, Trichy (Tiruchirappalli)*

The Chalukyas were a far-flung family. In addition to their base in Badami, they established themselves in Bijapur, Andhra Pradesh and near the Godavari Delta. The Godavari branch of the family is commonly referred to as the Eastern Chalukyas of Vengi. It's unclear from where the Pallavas originated, but it's thought they may have emigrated to Kanchi from Andhra Pradesh. After their successful rout of the Kalabhras, the Pallavas extended their territory as far south as the Cauvery River, and by the 7th century were at the height of their power, building monuments such as the Shore Temple and Arjuna's Penance at Mamallapuram (Mahabalipuram). They engaged in long-running clashes with the Pandyas, who, in the 8th century, allied themselves with the Gangas of Mysore. This, combined with pressure from the Rashtrakutas (who were challenging the Eastern Chalukyas), had by the 9th century snuffed out any significant Pallava power in the south.

At the same time as the Pallava dynasty came to an end, a new Chola dynasty was establishing itself and laying the foundations for what was to become one of the most significant empires on the subcontinent. From their base at Thanjavur, the Cholas spread north absorbing what was left of the Pallavas' territory, and made inroads into the south. But it wasn't until Rajaraja Chola I (r 985–1014) ascended the throne that the Chola kingdom really started to emerge as a great empire. Rajaraja Chola I

AD 52

Possible arrival of St Thomas the Apostle on the coast of Kerala. Christianity thought to have been introduced to India with his preaching in Kerala and Tamil Nadu.

319–510

The golden era of the Gupta dynasty, the second of India's great empires after the Mauryas. This era is marked by a creative surge in literature and the arts.

SHRAVYAN CLICKS / GETTY IMAGES ©

➡ Shore Temple (p351), Mamallapuram

successfully waged war against the Pandyas in the south, the Gangas of Mysore and the Eastern Chalukyas. He also launched a series of naval campaigns that resulted in the capture of the Maldives, the Malabar Coast and northern Sri Lanka, which became a province of the Chola empire. These conquests gave the Cholas control over critical ports and trading links between India, Southeast Asia, Arabia and East Africa. They were therefore in a position to grab a share of the huge profits involved in selling spices to Europe.

Rajaraja Chola's son, Rajendra Chola I (r 1014–44), continued to expand the Cholas' territory, conquering the remainder of Sri Lanka and campaigning up the east coast as far as Bengal and the Ganges River. Rajendra also launched a campaign in Southeast Asia against the Srivijaya kingdom (Sumatra), reinstating trade links that had been interrupted and sending trade missions as far as China. In addition to both its political and economic superiority, the Chola empire produced a brilliant legacy in the arts. Sculpture, most notably bronze sculpture, reached astonishing new heights of aesthetic and technical refinement.

Music, dance and literature flourished and developed a distinctly Tamil flavour, enduring in South India long after the Cholas had faded from the picture. Trade wasn't the only thing the Cholas brought to the shores of Southeast Asia; they also introduced their culture. That legacy lives on in Myanmar (Burma), Thailand, Bali (Indonesia) and Cambodia in dance, religion and mythology.

But the Cholas, eventually weakened by constant campaigning, succumbed to expansionist pressure from the Hoysalas of Halebid and the Pandyas of Madurai, and by the 13th century were finally supplanted by the Pandyas. The Hoysalas were themselves eclipsed by the Vijayanagar empire, which arose in the 14th century. The Pandyas prospered and their achievements were much admired by Marco Polo when he visited in 1288 and 1293. But their glory was short-lived, as they were unable to fend off the Muslim invasion from the north.

History and Society in South India by Noboru Karashima is an academic compilation focusing on the development of South Indian society during the Chola dynasty and the rule of the Vijayanagars.

Muslim Invasion & the Vijayanagar Empire

The Muslim rulers in Delhi campaigned in South India from 1296, rebuking a series of local rulers, including the Hoysalas and Pandyas, and by 1323 had reached Madurai.

Mohammed Tughlaq, the sultan of Delhi, dreamed of conquering the whole of India, something not even Emperor Ashoka had managed. He rebuilt the fort of Daulatabad in Maharashtra to keep control of South India, but eventually his ambition led him to overreach his forces. In 1334 he had to recall his army in order to quash rebellions elsewhere and, as a result, local Muslim rulers in Madurai and Daulatabad declared their independence.

4th–9th centuries

The Pallavas enter the shifting landscape of southern power centres, eventually establishing dominance in Andhra Pradesh and northern Tamil Nadu from their base in Kanchipuram.

610

Prophet Mohammed establishes Islam. He soon invites the people of Mecca to adopt the new religion under the command of God, and his call is met with eager response.

850

The Chola empire emerges anew in South India, establishing itself as a formidable economic and military presence in Asia under Rajaraja Chola I and his son Rajendra Chola I.

12th–19th centuries

Africans are brought to the Konkan coast as part of trade with the Persian Gulf; the slaves become servants, dock workers and soldiers, and are known as Siddis or Habshis.

At the same time, the foundations of what was to become one of South India's greatest empires, Vijayanagar, were being laid by Hindu chiefs at Hampi.

The Vijayanagar empire is generally said to have been founded by two chieftain brothers who, having been captured and taken to Delhi, converted to Islam and were sent back south to serve as governors for the sultanate. The brothers, however, had other ideas; they reconverted to Hinduism and in around 1336 set about establishing a kingdom that was eventually to encompass southern Karnataka, Tamil Nadu and part of Kerala. Seven centuries later, the centre of this kingdom – the ruins and temples of Hampi – is now one of South India's biggest tourist drawcards.

The Bahmanis, who were initially from Daulatabad, established their capital at Gulbarga in Karnataka, relocating to Bidar in the 15th century. Their kingdom eventually included Maharashtra and parts of northern Karnataka and Andhra Pradesh – and they took pains to protect it.

Not unnaturally, ongoing rivalry characterised the relationship between the Vijayanagar and Bahmani empires until the 16th century when both went into decline. The Bahmani empire was torn apart by factional fighting and Vijayanagar's vibrant capital of Hampi was laid to waste in a six-month sacking by the combined forces of the Islamic sultanates of Bidar, Bijapur, Berar, Ahmednagar and Golconda. Much of the conflict centred on control of fertile agricultural land and trading ports; at one stage the Bahmanis wrested control of the important port of Goa from their rivals (although in 1378 the Vijayanagars seized it back).

The Vijayanagar empire is notable for its prosperity, which was the result of a deliberate policy of giving every encouragement to traders from afar, combined with the development of an efficient administrative system and access to important trading links, including west-coast ports. Hampi became quite cosmopolitan, with people from various parts of India as well as from abroad mingling in the bazaars.

Portuguese chronicler Domingo Paez arrived in Vijayanagar during the reign of one of its greatest kings, Krishnadevaraya (r 1509–29). During his rule Vijayanagar enjoyed a period of unparalleled prosperity and power.

Paez recorded the achievements of the Vijayanagars and described how they had constructed large water tanks and irrigated their fields. He also described how human and animal sacrifices were carried out to propitiate the gods after one of the water tanks had burst repeatedly. He included detail about the fine houses that belonged to wealthy merchants and the bazaars full of precious stones (rubies, diamonds, emeralds, pearls), textiles (including silk) and 'every other sort of thing there is on earth and that you may wish to buy'.

Architecture of the Deccan Sultanates

Bijapur *Citadel, Golgumbaz, Ibrahim Rouza, Jama Masjid*

Bidar *Fort, Bahmani Tombs*

Hyderabad *Golconda Fort, Qutb Shahi Tombs, Charminar*

A History of South India from Prehistoric Times to the Fall of Vijayanagar by KA Nilakanta Sastri is arguably the most thorough history of this region; especially recommended if you're heading for Hampi.

13th century

The Pandyas, a Tamil dynasty dating to the 6th century BC, assumes control of Chola territory, expanding into Andhra Pradesh, Kalinga (Odisha) and Sri Lanka from their capital in Madurai.

1336

Foundation of the mighty Vijayanagar empire, named after its capital city, the ruins of which can be seen today in the vicinity of Hampi (in modern-day Karnataka).

1345

Bahmani sultanate is established in the Deccan following a revolt against the Tughlaqs of Delhi. The capital is set up at Gulbarga, in today's northern Karnataka, later shifting to Bidar.

1469

Guru Nanak, founder of the Sikh faith, which has millions of followers within and beyond India to the present day, is born in a village near Lahore (in modern-day Pakistan).

Like the Bahmanis, the Vijayanagar kings invested heavily in protecting their territory and trading links. Krishnadevaraya employed Portuguese and Muslim mercenaries to guard the forts and protect his domains. He also fostered good relations with the Portuguese, upon whom he depended for access to trade goods, especially the Arab horses he needed for his cavalry.

Arrival of the Europeans & Christianity

And so began a new era of European contact with the East. After Vasco da Gama's arrival in 1498 came Francisco de Ameida and Alfonso de Albuquerque, who established an eastern Portuguese empire that included Goa (first taken in 1510). Albuquerque waged a constant battle against the local Muslims in Goa, finally defeating them. But perhaps his greatest achievement was in playing off two deadly threats against each other – the Vijayanagars (for whom access to Goa's ports was extremely important) and the Bijapuris (who had split from the Bahmanis in the early 16th century and who controlled part of Goa).

The Career and Legend of Vasco da Gama by Sanjay Subrahmanyam is one of the better recent investigations of the person credited with 'discovering' the sea route to India.

The Bijapuris and Vijayanagars were sworn enemies, and Albuquerque skilfully exploited this antipathy by supplying Arab horses, which had to be constantly imported because they died in alarming numbers once on Indian soil. Both kingdoms bought horses from the Portuguese to top

ENTER THE PORTUGUESE

By the time Krishnadevaraya ascended to the throne, the Portuguese were well on the way to establishing a firm foothold in Goa. It was only a few years since they had become the first Europeans to sail across the Indian Ocean from the east coast of Africa to India's shores.

On 20 May 1498 Vasco da Gama dropped anchor off the South Indian coast near the town of Calicut (Kozhikode). It had taken him 23 days to sail from the east coast of Africa, guided by a pilot named Ibn Masjid, sent by the ruler of Malindi in Gujarat.

The Portuguese sought a sea route between Europe and the East so they could trade directly in spices. They also hoped they might find Christians cut off from Europe by the Muslim dominance of the Middle East, while at the same time searching for the legendary kingdom of Prester John, a powerful Christian ruler with whom they could unite against the Muslim rulers of the Middle East. However, in India they found spices and the Syrian Orthodox community, but not Prester John.

Vasco da Gama sought an audience with the ruler of Calicut, to explain himself, and seems to have been well received. The Portuguese engaged in a limited amount of trading, but became increasingly suspicious that Muslim traders were turning the ruler of Calicut against them. They resolved to leave Calicut, which they did in August 1498.

1484
Bahmani sultanate begins to break up following independence movements; Berar is the first to revolt. By 1518 there are five Deccan sultanates: Berar, Ahmadnagar, Bidar, Bijapur and Golconda.

1498
Vasco da Gama, a Portuguese voyager, discovers the sea route from Europe to India. He arrives in (present-day) Kerala and engages in trade with the local nobility.

1510
Portuguese forces capture Goa under the command of Alfonso de Albuquerque, whose initial attempt was thwarted by then-ruler Sultan Adil Shah of Bijapur. He succeeds following Shah's death.

1526
Babur becomes the first Mughal emperor after conquering Delhi. He stuns Rajasthan by routing its confederate force, gaining an edge with the introduction of matchlock muskets in his army.

up their warring cavalry, thus keeping Portugal's Goan ports busy and profitable.

The Portuguese also introduced Catholicism, and the arrival of the Inquisition in 1560 marked the beginning of 200 years of religious suppression in the Portuguese-controlled areas on the west coast of India. Not long after the beginning of the Inquisition, events that occurred in Europe had major repercussions for European relations with India. In 1580 Spain annexed Portugal and, until it regained its independence in 1640, Portugal's interests were subservient to Spain's. After the defeat of the Spanish Armada in 1588, the sea route to the East lay open to the English and the Dutch.

GOA INQUISITION

Thousands were burned at the stake during the Goa Inquisition, which lasted more than 200 years. The judgment ceremony took place outside the Se Cathedral in Old Goa.

Today the Portuguese influence is most obvious in Goa, with its chalk-white Catholic churches dotting the countryside, Christian festivals and unique cuisine, although the Portuguese also had some influence in Kerala in towns such as Kochi (Cochin). By the mid-16th century Old Goa had grown into a thriving city said to rival Lisbon in magnificence: although only a ruined shadow of that time, its churches and buildings are still a stunning reminder of Portuguese rule. It wasn't until 1961 – 14 years after national Independence – that the Portuguese were finally forced out by the Indian military.

The Dutch got to India first but, unlike the Portuguese, were more interested in trade than in religion and empire. Indonesia was used as the main source of spices, and trade with South India was primarily for pepper and cardamom. So the Dutch East India Company set up a string of trading posts (called factories), which allowed them to maintain a complicated trading structure all the way from the Persian Gulf to Japan. They set up trading posts at Surat (Gujarat) and on the Coromandel Coast in South India, and entered into a treaty with the ruler of Calicut. In 1660 they captured the Portuguese forts at Cochin (now Kochi) and Kodungallor.

The English also set up a trading venture, the British East India Company, which in 1600 was granted a monopoly. Like the Dutch, the English were at that stage interested in trade, mainly in spices, and Indonesia was their main goal. But the Dutch proved too strong there and the English turned instead to India, setting up a trading post at Madras (now Chennai). The Danes traded off and on at Tranquebar (on the Coromandel Coast) from 1616, and the French acquired Pondicherry (now Puducherry) in 1673.

Mughals Versus Marathas

Around the late 17th century the Delhi-based Mughals were making inroads into South India, gaining the sultanates of Ahmednagar, Bijapur and Golconda (including Hyderabad) before moving into Tamil Nadu.

1542–45

St Francis Xavier's first mission to India. He preaches Catholicism in Goa, Tamil Nadu and Sri Lanka, returning in 1548–49 and 1552 in between travels in the Far East.

1560–1812

Portuguese Inquisition in Goa. Trials focus on converted Hindus and Muslims thought to have 'relapsed'. Thousands were tried and several dozen were executed before it was abolished in 1812.

MAX PADDLER / GETTY IMAGES ©

➡ Basilica of Bom Jesus (p136), Old Goa

But it was here that Emperor Aurangzeb (r 1658–1707) came up against the Marathas who, in a series of guerrilla-like raids, captured Thanjavur and set up a capital at Gingee near Madras.

Although the Mughal empire gradually disintegrated following Aurangzeb's death, the Marathas went from strength to strength, and they set their sights on territory to the north. But their aspirations brought them into conflict with the rulers of Hyderabad, the Asaf Jahis, who had entrenched themselves here when Hyderabad broke away from the declining Mughal rulers of Delhi in 1724. The Marathas discovered that the French were providing military support to the Hyderabadi rulers in return for trading concessions on the Coromandel Coast. However, by the 1750s Hyderabad had lost a lot of its power and became landlocked when much of its coast was controlled by the British.

Down in the south, Travancore (Kerala) and Mysore were making a bid to consolidate their power by gaining control of strategic maritime regions and access to trade links. Martanda Varma (r 1729–58) of Travancore created his own army and tried to keep the local Syrian Orthodox trading community onside by limiting the activities of European traders. Trade in many goods, with the exception of pepper, became a royal monopoly, especially under Martanda's son Rama Varma (r 1758–98).

Amar Chitra Katha, a popular publisher of comic books about Indian folklore, mythology and history, has several books about Shivaji, including *Shivaji: The Great Maratha*, *Tales of Shivaji* and *Tanaji, the Maratha Lion*, about Shivaji's close friend and fellow warrior.

MIGHTY SHIVAJI

The name Chhatrapati Shivaji is revered in Maharashtra, with statues of the great warrior astride his horse gracing many towns, and street names and monuments being named (or renamed in the case of Mumbai's Victoria Terminus, among others) after him.

Shivaji was responsible for leading the powerful Maratha dynasty, a sovereign Hindu state that controlled the Deccan region for almost two centuries, at a time when much of India was under Islamic control. A courageous warrior and charismatic leader, Shivaji was born in 1627 to a prominent Maratha family at Shivneri. As a child he was sent to Pune with his mother, where he was given land and forts and groomed as a future leader. With a very small army, Shivaji seized his first fort at the age of 20 and over the next three decades he continued to expand Maratha power around his base in Pune, holding out against the Muslim invaders from the north (the Mughal empire) and the south (the forces of Bijapur) and eventually controlling the Deccan. He was shrewd enough to play his enemies (among them Mughal emperor Aurangzeb) off against each other, and in a famous incident in 1659 he killed Bijapuri general Afzal Khan in a face-to-face encounter at Pratapgad Fort.

In 1674 Shivaji was crowned Chhatrapati (Lord of the Universe) of the Marathas at Raigad Fort. He died six years later and was succeeded by his son Sambhaji, but almost immediately the power Shivaji had built up began to wane.

1600

Britain's Queen Elizabeth I grants the first trading charter to the East India Company, with the maiden voyage taking place in 1601 under the command of Sir James Lancaster.

1673

The Compagnie française des Indes orientales (French East India Company) establishes an outpost at Pondicherry (now Puducherry), which the French, Dutch and British fight over.

1674

Shivaji establishes the Maratha kingdom, spanning western India and parts of the Deccan and North India. He assumes the imperial title of Chhatrapati, which means 'Great Protector'.

1707

Death of Aurangzeb, the last of the Mughal greats. His demise triggers the gradual collapse of the Mughal empire, as anarchy and rebellion erupts across the country.

Mysore started off as a landlocked kingdom, but in 1761 a cavalry officer, Hyder Ali, assumed power and set about acquiring coastal territory. Hyder Ali and his son Tipu Sultan eventually ruled over a kingdom that included southern Karnataka and northern Kerala. Tipu conducted trade directly with the Middle East through the west-coast ports he controlled. But Tipu was prevented from gaining access to ports on the eastern seaboard and the fertile hinterland by the British East India Company.

The British Take Hold

The British East India Company at this stage was supposedly interested only in trade, not conquest. But Mysore's rulers proved something of a vexation. In 1780 the Nizam of Hyderabad, Hyder Ali, and the Marathas joined forces to defeat the Company's armies and take control of Karnataka. The Treaty of Mangalore, signed by Tipu Sultan in 1784, restored the parties to an uneasy truce. But meanwhile, within the Company there was a growing body of opinion that only total control of India would really satisfy British trading interests. This was reinforced by fears of a renewed French bid for land in India following Napoleon's Egyptian expedition of 1798–99. It was the governor general of Bengal, Lord Richard Wellesley, who launched a strike against Mysore, with the Nizam of Hyderabad as an ally (who was required to disband his French-trained troops and in return gained British protection). Tipu, who may have counted on support from the French, was killed when the British stormed the river-island fortress of Seringapatam (present-day Srirangapatnam, near Mysore) in 1799.

Wellesley restored the old ruling family, the Wodeyars, to half of Tipu's kingdom – the rest went to the Nizam of Hyderabad and the British East India Company – and laid the foundations for the formation of the Madras Presidency. Thanjavur and Karnataka were also absorbed by the British, who, when the rulers of the day died, pensioned off their successors. By 1818 the Marathas, racked by internal strife, had collapsed.

In 1839 the British government offered to buy Goa from the Portuguese for half a million pounds.

By now most of India was under British influence. In the south the British controlled the Madras Presidency, which stretched from present-day Andhra Pradesh to the southern tip of the subcontinent, and from the east coast across to the western Malabar Coast. Meanwhile, a fair chunk of the interior was ruled by a bundle of small princely states. Much of Maharashtra was part of the Bombay Presidency, but there were a dozen or so small princely states scattered around, including Kolhapur, Sawantwadi, Aundh and Janjira. The major princely states were Travancore, Hyderabad and Mysore, though all were closely watched by the Resident (the British de facto governor, who officially looked after areas under British control).

1757

The East India Company registers its first military victory on Indian soil. Siraj-ud-Daulah, nawab of Bengal, is defeated by Robert Clive in the Battle of Plassey.

1857

The First War of Independence against the British. In the absence of a national leader, freedom fighters coerce the Mughal king, Bahadur Shah Zafar, to proclaim himself emperor of India.

1858

British government assumes control over India – with power officially transferred from the East India Company to the Crown – beginning the period known as the British Raj.

1869

The birth of Mohandas Karamchand Gandhi in Porbandar (Gujarat) – the man who would later become popularly known as Mahatma Gandhi and affectionately dubbed 'Father of the Nation'.

The First War of Independence: The Indian Uprising

In 1857, half a century after having established firm control of India, the British suffered a serious setback. To this day, the causes of the Uprising (known at the time as the Indian Mutiny and subsequently labelled by nationalist historians as a War of Independence) are the subject of debate. The key factors included the influx of cheap goods, such as textiles, from Britain that destroyed many livelihoods; the dispossession of territories from many rulers; and taxes imposed on landowners.

The incident that's popularly held to have sparked the Uprising, however, took place at an army barracks in Meerut in Uttar Pradesh on 10 May 1857. A rumour leaked out that a new type of bullet was greased with what Hindus claimed was cow fat, while Muslims maintained that it came from pigs; pigs are considered unclean to Muslims, and cows are sacred to Hindus. Since loading a rifle involved biting the end off the waxed cartridge, these rumours provoked considerable unrest.

In Meerut, the situation was handled with a singular lack of judgment. The commanding officer lined up his soldiers and ordered them to bite off the ends of their issued bullets. Those who refused were immediately marched off to prison. The following morning, the soldiers of the garrison rebelled, shot their officers and marched to Delhi. Of the 74 Indian battalions of the Bengal army, seven (one of them Gurkhas) remained loyal, 20 were disarmed and the other 47 mutinied. The soldiers and peasants rallied around the ageing Mughal emperor in Delhi. They held Delhi for some months and besieged the British Residency in Lucknow for five months before they were finally suppressed. The incident left festering sores on both sides.

Almost immediately the East India Company was wound up, and direct control of the country was assumed by the British government, which announced its support for the existing rulers of the princely states, claiming they would not interfere in local matters as long as the states remained loyal to the British.

The Road to Independence

The desire among many Indians to be free from foreign rule remained. Opposition to the British began to increase at the turn of the 20th century, spearheaded by the Indian National Congress (Congress Party), the nation's oldest political party. The fight for independence gained momentum when, in April 1919, following riots in Amritsar (Punjab), a British Army contingent was sent to quell the unrest. Under direct orders of the officer in charge the army ruthlessly fired into a crowd of unarmed protesters attending a meeting, killing an estimated 1500 people. News

1869

Opening of the Suez Canal accelerates trade from Europe and makes Bombay India's first port of call; journey from England goes from three months to three weeks. Bombay's economic importance skyrockets.

1885

The Indian National Congress, India's first home-grown political organisation, is set up. It brings educated Indians together and plays a key role in India's enduring freedom struggle.

1891

BR Ambedkar, activist, economist, lawyer and writer, is born to a poor outcaste family. He earns several advanced degrees, becomes a Buddhist and advocates forcefully for Dalit rights.

1919

The massacre, on 13 April, of unarmed Indian protesters at Jallianwala Bagh in Amritsar (Punjab). Gandhi responds with his program of civil (nonviolent) disobedience against the British government.

of the massacre spread rapidly throughout India, turning huge numbers of otherwise apolitical Indians into Congress supporters. At this time, the Congress movement found a new leader in Mohandas Gandhi.

After some three decades of intense campaigning for an independent India, Mahatma Gandhi's dream finally materialised. However, despite Gandhi's plea for a united India – the Muslim League's leader, Mohammed Ali Jinnah, was demanding a separate Islamic state for India's sizeable Muslim population – the decision was made to split the country.

The Partition of India in 1947 contained all the ingredients for an epic disaster, but the resulting bloodshed was far worse than anticipated. Massive population exchanges took place. Trains full of Muslims, fleeing westward, were held up and slaughtered by Hindu and Sikh mobs. Hindus and Sikhs fleeing to the east suffered the same fate. By the time the chaos had run its course, more than 10 million people had changed sides and at least 500,000 had been killed.

THE KASHMIR CONFLICT

Kashmir is the most enduring symbol of the turbulent Partition of India. In the lead-up to Independence, the delicate task of drawing the India–Pakistan border was complicated by the fact that India's 'princely states' were nominally independent. As part of the settlement process, local rulers were asked which country they wished to belong to. Kashmir was a predominantly Muslim state with a Hindu maharaja, Hari Singh, who tried to delay his decision. A ragtag Pashtun (Pakistani) army crossed the border, intent on racing to Srinagar and annexing Kashmir for Pakistan. In the face of this advance, the maharaja panicked and requested armed assistance from India. The Indian army arrived only just in time to prevent the fall of Srinagar, and the maharaja signed the Instrument of Accession, tying Kashmir to India, in October 1947. The legality of the document was immediately disputed by Pakistan, and the two nations went to war, just two months after Independence.

In 1948 the fledgling UN Security Council called for a referendum (which remains a central plank of Pakistani policy) to decide the status of Kashmir. A UN-brokered ceasefire in 1949 kept the countries on either side of a demarcation line, called the Cease-Fire Line (later to become the Line of Control, or LOC), with little else resolved. Two-thirds of Kashmir fell on the Indian side of the LOC, which remains the frontier, but neither side accepts this as the official border. The Indian state of Jammu & Kashmir, as it has stood since that time, incorporates Ladakh (divided between Muslims and Buddhists), Jammu (with a Hindu majority) and the 130km-long, 55km-wide Kashmir Valley (with a Muslim majority and most of the state's inhabitants). On the Pakistani side live over three million Kashmiris. Since the frontier was drawn, incursions across the LOC have occurred with dangerous regularity.

1940

The Muslim League adopts its Lahore Resolution, which champions greater Muslim autonomy in India. Subsequent campaigns for the creation of a separate Islamic nation follow.

1942

Mahatma Gandhi launches the Quit India campaign, demanding that the British leave India without delay and allow the country to get on with the business of self-governance.

1947

India gains independence on 15 August. Pakistan is formed a day earlier. Partition is followed by mass cross-border exodus, as Hindus and Muslims migrate to their respective nations.

1947–48

First war between India and Pakistan takes place after the (procrastinating) Maharaja of Kashmir signs the Instrument of Accession that cedes his state to India. Pakistan challenges the document's legality.

India and Pakistan became sovereign nations under the British Commonwealth in August 1947 as planned, but the violence, migrations and the integration of a few states, especially Kashmir, continued. The Constitution of India was at last adopted in November 1949 and went into effect on 26 January 1950 and, after untold struggle, independent India officially became a republic.

Mahatma Gandhi

One of the great figures of the 20th century, Mohandas Karamchand Gandhi was born on 2 October 1869 in Porbandar, Gujarat. After studying in London (1888–91), he worked as a barrister in South Africa. Here, the young Gandhi became politicised, railing against the discrimination he encountered. He soon became the spokesman for the Indian community and championed equality for all.

Gandhi returned to India in 1915 with the doctrine of ahimsa (nonviolence) central to his political plans, and committed to a simple and disciplined lifestyle. He set up the Sabarmati Ashram in Ahmedabad, which was innovative for its admission of Untouchables (the lowest caste Dalits).

Within a year, Gandhi had won his first victory, defending farmers in Bihar from exploitation. It's said that this was when he first received the title 'Mahatma' (Great Soul) from an admirer. The passage of the discriminatory Rowlatt Acts (which allowed certain political cases to be tried without juries) in 1919 spurred him to further action and he organised a national protest. In the days that followed this hartal (strike), feelings ran high throughout the country. After the massacre of unarmed protesters in Amritsar (Punjab), a deeply shocked Gandhi immediately called off the movement.

By 1920 Gandhi was a key figure in the Indian National Congress, and he coordinated a national campaign of noncooperation or satyagraha (passive resistance) to British rule, with the effect of raising nationalist feeling while earning the lasting enmity of the British. In early 1930 Gandhi captured the imagination of the country, and the world, when he led a march of several thousand followers from Ahmedabad to Dandi on the coast of Gujarat. On arrival, Gandhi ceremoniously made salt by evaporating sea water, thus publicly defying the much-hated salt tax; not for the first time, he was imprisoned. Released in 1931 to represent the Indian National Congress at the second Round Table Conference in London, he won the hearts of many British people but failed to gain any real concessions from the government.

Disillusioned with politics, he resigned his parliamentary seat in 1934. He returned spectacularly to the fray in 1942 with the Quit India campaign, in which he urged the British to leave India immediately. His

GANDHI

A golden oldie, *Gandhi*, directed by Richard Attenborough, is one of the few films to engagingly capture the grand canvas that is India in tracing the country's rocky road to Independence.

1948
Mahatma Gandhi is assassinated in New Delhi by Nathuram Godse on 30 January. Godse and his co-conspirator Narayan Apte are later tried, convicted and executed (by hanging).

17 September 1948
Asaf Jah VII, the last Nizam of Hyderabad, surrenders to the Indian government. The Muslim dynasty was receiving support from Pakistan but had refused to join either new nation.

November 1949
The Constitution of India, drafted over two years by a 308-member Constituent Assembly, is adopted. The Assembly included dozens of members from Scheduled Castes.

26 January 1950
India becomes a republic. Date commemorates the Purna Swaraj Declaration, or Declaration of Independence, put forth by the Indian National Congress in 1930.

actions were deemed subversive and he and most of the Congress leadership were imprisoned.

In the frantic Independence bargaining that followed the end of WWII, Gandhi was largely excluded and watched helplessly as plans were made to partition the country – a dire tragedy in his eyes. Gandhi stood almost alone in urging tolerance and the preservation of a single India, and his work on behalf of members of all communities drew resentment from some Hindu hardliners. On his way to a prayer meeting in Delhi on 30 January 1948, he was assassinated by a Hindu zealot.

In 21st-century India, Mahatma Gandhi continues to be an iconic figure and is still widely revered as the 'Father of the Nation'.

Carving up the South

While the chaos of Partition was mostly felt in the north – mainly in Punjab and Bengal – the south faced problems of its own. Following Independence, the princely states and British provinces were dismantled and South India was reorganised into states along linguistic lines. Though most of the princely states acceded to India peacefully, an exception was that of the Nizam of Hyderabad. He wanted Hyderabad to join Islamic Pakistan, although only he and 10% of his subjects were Muslims. Following a time of violence between Hindu and Islamic hardliners, the Indian army moved in and forcibly took control of Hyderabad state in 1949.

The Nehrus and the Gandhis is Tariq Ali's astute portrait-history of these families and the India over which they cast their long shadow.

The Wodeyars in Mysore, who also ruled right up to Independence, were pensioned off. But they were so popular with their subjects that the maharaja became the first governor of the post-Independence state of Mysore. The boundaries of Mysore state were redrawn on linguistic grounds in 1956, and the extended Kannada-speaking state of Greater Mysore was established, becoming Karnataka in 1972.

Kerala, as it is today, was created in 1956 from Travancore, Cochin (now Kochi) and Malabar (formerly part of the Madras Presidency). The maharajas in both Travancore and Cochin were especially attentive to the provision of basic services and education, and their legacy today is India's most literate state. Kerala also blazed a trail in post-Independence India by becoming the first state in the world to freely elect a communist government in 1957.

Andhra Pradesh was declared a state in 1956, having been created by combining Andhra state (formerly part of the Madras Presidency) with parts of the Telugu-speaking areas of the old Nizam of Hyderabad's territory.

Tamil Nadu emerged from the old Madras Presidency, although until 1969 Tamil Nadu was known as Madras State. In 1956, in a nationwide reorganisation of states, it lost Malabar district and South Canara to the fledgling state of Kerala on the west coast. However, it also gained new

1961

In a military action code-named 'Operation Vijay' the Indian government sends armed troops into Goa and – with surprisingly little resistance – ends over four centuries of Portuguese colonial rule in the region.

1965

Skirmishes in Kashmir and the disputed Rann of Kutch in Gujarat flare into the Second India-Pakistan War, said to have involved the biggest tank battles since WWII. The war ends with a UN-mandated ceasefire.

1966

Indira Gandhi, daughter of independent India's first prime minister, Jawaharlal Nehru, becomes prime minister of India. She has so far been India's only female prime minister.

1971

East Pakistan seeks independence from West Pakistan. India gets involved, sparking the Third India-Pakistan War. West Pakistan surrenders, losing sovereignty of East Pakistan, which becomes Bangladesh.

areas in Trivandrum (now Thiruvananthapuram) district including Kanyakumari. In 1960, 1049 sq km of land in Andhra Pradesh was exchanged for a similar amount of land in Salem and Chengalpattu districts.

The creation of Maharashtra was one of the most contested issues of the language-based demarcation of states in the 1950s. After Independence, western Maharashtra and Gujarat were joined to form Bombay state, but in 1960, after agitation by pro-Marathi supporters, the modern state of Maharashtra was created, separating from Gujarat while gaining parts of Hyderabad and Madhya Pradesh.

The French relinquished Pondicherry in 1954 – 140 years after claiming it from the British. It's a Union Territory (controlled by the government in Delhi), though a largely self-governing one. Lakshadweep was granted Union Territory status in 1956, as were the Andaman and Nicobar Islands.

Throughout most of this carve-up, the tiny enclave of Goa was still under the rule of the Portuguese. Although a rumbling Independence movement had existed in Goa since the early 20th century, the Indian government was reluctant to intervene and take Goa by force, hoping the Portuguese would leave of their own volition. The Portuguese refused, so in December 1961 Indian troops crossed the border and liberated the state with surprisingly little resistance. It became a Union Territory of India, but after splitting from Daman and Diu (Gujarat) in 1987, it was officially recognised as the 25th state of the Indian Union.

In 1997 KR Narayanan became India's president, the first member of the lowest Hindu caste (the Dalits; formerly known as Untouchables) to hold the position.

1984

Prime Minister Indira Gandhi is assassinated by two of her Sikh bodyguards after her highly controversial decision to have Indian troops storm Amritsar's Golden Temple, the Sikhs' holiest shrine.

May 2004

Belonging to the Sikh faith, Manmohan Singh of the Congress Party becomes the first member of any religious minority community to hold India's highest elected office.

December 2004

On 26 December a catastrophic tsunami batters coastal parts of eastern and South India as well as the Andaman and Nicobar Islands, killing over 10,000 people and leaving hundreds of thousands homeless.

2008

On 26 November a series of coordinated bombing and shooting attacks on landmark Mumbai sites begins; the terrorist attacks last three days and kill at least 163 people.

The Way of Life

Spirituality is the common thread in the richly diverse tapestry that is India. It, along with family, lies at the heart of society – for most Indians, the idea of being unmarried by one's mid-30s is somewhat unpalatable. Despite the rising number of nuclear families – primarily in the more cosmopolitan cities such as Mumbai (Bombay) and Bengaluru (Bangalore) – the extended family remains a cornerstone in both urban and rural India, with males – usually the breadwinners – generally considered the head of the household.

The Wonder That Was India by AL Basham gives descriptions of Indian civilisations, major religions and social customs – a good thematic approach to weave the disparate strands together.

Marriage, Birth & Death

Marriage is an auspicious event for Indians and although 'love marriages' have spiralled upwards in recent times (mainly in urban hubs), most Hindu marriages are still arranged. Discreet enquiries are made within the community. If a suitable match is not found, the help of professional matchmakers may be sought and/or advertisements may be placed in the media. The horoscopes of both potential partners are checked and, if propitious, there's a meeting between the two families.

Dowry, although illegal, is still a key issue in more than a few arranged marriages, with some families plunging into debt to raise the required cash and merchandise. Health workers claim that India's high rate of abortion of female foetuses (despite sex identification medical tests being banned in India, they still clandestinely occur in some clinics) is predominantly due to the financial burden of providing a daughter's dowry.

The Hindu wedding ceremony is officiated over by a priest and the marriage is formalised when the couple walk around a sacred fire seven times. Despite the existence of nuclear families, it's still the norm for a wife to live with her husband's family once married and assume the household duties outlined by her mother-in-law.

Matchmaking has embraced the cyber age, with popular sites including www.shaadi.com, www.bharatmatrimony.com and, more recently, www.secondshaadi.com – for those seeking a partner again.

Divorce and remarriage is becoming more common (primarily in bigger cities), but divorce is still not granted by courts as a matter of routine and is generally not looked upon very favourably by society. Among the higher castes, widows are traditionally expected not to remarry and are admonished to wear white and live pious, celibate lives.

The birth of a child, in Hindu-majority India, is another momentous occasion, with its own set of special ceremonies, which take place at various auspicious times during the early years of childhood. These include the casting of the child's first horoscope, name-giving, feeding the first solid food, and the first hair cutting.

Hindus cremate their dead, and funeral ceremonies are designed to purify and console both the living and the deceased. An important aspect of the proceedings is the *sharadda,* paying respect to ancestors by offering water and rice cakes. It's an observance that's repeated at each anniversary of the death. After the cremation the ashes are collected and, 13 days after the death (when blood relatives are deemed ritually pure), a member of the family usually scatters them in a holy river such as the Ganges or in the ocean.

The Caste System

Although the Indian constitution does not recognise the caste system, caste still wields considerable influence, especially in rural India, where the caste you are born into largely determines your social standing in the community. It can also influence your vocational and marriage prospects. Castes are further divided into thousands of *jati*, groups of 'families' or social communities, which are sometimes but not always linked to occupation. Conservative Hindus will only marry someone of the same *jati*.

According to tradition, caste is the basic social structure of Hindu society. Living a righteous life and fulfilling your dharma (moral duty) raises your chances of being reborn into a higher caste and thus into better circumstances. Hindus are born into one of four varnas (castes): Brahmin (priests and scholars), Kshatriya (soldiers and administrators), Vaishya (merchants) and Shudra (labourers). The Brahmins were said to have emerged from the mouth of Lord Brahma at the moment of creation, Kshatriyas were said to have come from his arms, Vaishyas from his thighs and Shudras from his feet.

Beneath the four main castes are the Dalits (formerly known as Untouchables), who hold menial jobs such as sweepers and latrine cleaners. The word 'pariah' is derived from the name of a Tamil Dalit group, the Paraiyars. Some Dalit leaders, such as the renowned Dr BR Ambedkar (1891–1956), sought to change their status by adopting another faith; in his case it was Buddhism. At the bottom of the social heap are the Denotified Tribes. They were known as the Criminal Tribes until 1952, when a reforming law officially recognised 198 tribes and castes. Many are nomadic or seminomadic tribes, forced by the wider community to eke out a living on society's fringes.

To improve the Dalits' position, the government reserves a number of public-sector jobs, parliamentary seats and university places for them. Today these quotas account for almost 25% of government jobs and university (student) positions. The situation varies regionally, as different political leaders chase caste vote-banks by promising to include them in reservations. The reservation system, while generally regarded in a favourable light, has also been criticised for unfairly blocking tertiary and employment opportunities for those who would have otherwise got positions on merit.

CASTES

If you want to learn more about India's caste system these two books are a good start: *Interrogating Caste* by Dipankar Gupta and *Translating Caste* edited by Tapan Basu.

Pilgrimage

Devout Hindus are expected to go on a *yatra* (pilgrimage) at least once a year. Pilgrimages are undertaken to implore the gods or goddesses to grant a wish, to take the ashes of a cremated relative to a holy river, or to gain spiritual merit. India has thousands of holy sites to which pilgrims travel; the elderly often make Varanasi their final one, as it's believed that dying in this sacred city releases a person from the cycle of rebirth.

RANGOLIS

Rangolis, the striking and breathtakingly intricate chalk, rice-paste or coloured powder designs (also called *kolams)* that adorn thresholds, especially in South India, are both auspicious and symbolic. *Rangolis* are traditionally drawn at sunrise and are sometimes made of rice-flour paste, which may be eaten by little creatures – symbolising a reverence for even the smallest living things. Deities are deemed to be attracted to a beautiful *rangoli,* which may also signal to sadhus (ascetics) that they will be offered food at a particular house. Some people believe that *rangolis* protect against the evil eye.

ADIVASIS

India's Adivasis (tribal communities; Adivasi translates to 'original inhabitant' in Sanskrit) have origins that precede the Vedic Aryans and the Dravidians of the south. Today they constitute less than 10% of the population and are comprised of more than 400 different tribal groups. The literacy rate for Adivasis falls significantly below the national average.

Historically, contact between Adivasis and Hindu villagers on the plains rarely led to friction as there was little or no competition for resources and land. However, in recent decades an increasing number of Adivasis have been dispossessed of their ancestral land and turned into impoverished labourers. Although they still have political representation thanks to a parliamentary quota system, the dispossession and exploitation of Adivasis has reportedly sometimes been with the connivance of officialdom – an accusation the government denies. Whatever the arguments, unless more is done, the Adivasis' future is an uncertain one.

Read more about Adivasis in *Archaeology and History: Early Settlements in the Andaman Islands* by Zarine Cooper, *The Tribals of India* by Sunil Janah and *Tribes of India: The Struggle for Survival* by Christoph von Fürer-Haimendorf.

Most festivals in India are rooted in religion and are thus a magnet for throngs of pilgrims. This is something that travellers should keep in mind, even at those festivals that may have a carnivalesque sheen.

Women in India

Unique in many ways, Kerala is the most literate state in India and is also known for its tradition of matrilineal kinship. Exactly why the matrilineal family became established in this region is subject to conjecture, although one explanation is that it was in response to ongoing warfare in the 10th and 11th centuries. With the military men absent, women invariably took charge of the household. It has also been argued that the men would very likely form alliances wherever they found themselves and that the children of these unions would become the responsibility of the mother's family. Whatever the reason, by the 14th century a matrilineal society was firmly established in many communities across Kerala, and it lasted pretty much unchallenged until the 20th century.

In other parts of South India, such as Tamil Nadu, women also had more freedom than was the norm elsewhere in India. Matriarchy was a long-standing tradition within Tamil communities and the practice of marriage between cousins meant that young women did not have to move away and live among strangers

Dowry deaths and female infanticide were virtually unknown in India until relatively recent times, but the imposition of consumerism on old customs and conventions, making dowries more expensive, has resulted in increased instances.

Sati: A Study of Widow Burning in India by Sakuntala Narasimhan explores the history of *sati* (a widow's suicide on her husband's funeral pyre; now banned) on the subcontinent.

According to the most recent census, India's population is comprised of 586 million women, with an estimated 68% of those working (mostly as labourers) in the agricultural sector. Women in India are entitled to vote and own property. While the percentage of women in politics has risen over the past decade, they're still notably underrepresented in the national parliament, accounting for around 10% of parliamentary members.

Although the professions are male dominated, women are steadily making inroads, especially in urban centres, which includes a collection of South Indian hubs. Kerala was India's first state to break societal norms by recruiting female police officers in 1938. It was also the first state to establish an all-female police station (1973). For village women, right across India, it's much more difficult to get ahead. In low-income families, especially, girls can be regarded as a serious financial liability because at marriage a dowry must often be supplied.

For the urban middle-class woman, life is materially much more comfortable, but pressures still exist. Broadly speaking, she is far more likely to receive a tertiary education, but once married is still usually expected to 'fit in' with her in-laws and be a homemaker above all else. Like her village counterpart, if she fails to live up to expectations – even if it's just not being able to produce a grandson – the consequences can sometimes be dire, as demonstrated by the extreme practice of 'bride burning', wherein a wife is doused with flammable liquid and set alight. Reliable statistics are unavailable, but some women's groups claim that for every reported case, roughly 300 go unreported, and that less than 10% of the reported cases are pursued through the legal system.

Although the constitution allows for divorcees (and widows) to remarry, relatively few reportedly do so, simply because divorcees are traditionally considered outcasts from society, most evidently so beyond big cities. Divorce rates in India are among the world's lowest, despite having risen from around seven in 1000 in 1991, to roughly 12 in 1000 in 2012. Most divorces take place in urban centres and are generally deemed less socially unacceptable among those occupying the upper echelons of society.

In October 2006, following women's civil rights campaigns, the Indian parliament passed a landmark bill (on top of existing legislation) which gives women who are suffering domestic violence increased protection and rights. Prior to this legislation, although women could lodge police complaints against abusive spouses, they weren't automatically entitled to a share of the marital property or to ongoing financial support. The new law purports that any form of physical, sexual (including marital rape), emotional and economic abuse entails not only domestic violence, but also human rights violations. Perpetrators face imprisonment and fines. Under this law, abused women are legally permitted to remain in the marital house. In addition, the law prohibits emotional and physical bullying in relation to dowry demands. Critics claim that many women, especially those outside India's larger cities, are still reluctant to seek legal protection because of the social stigma involved. And despite the good intentions of the law reforms, the conviction rate for crimes against women remains relatively low; around 25% in 2011 as compared to 45% in the 1970s.

According to India's National Crime Records Bureau (NCRB), crimes against women have jumped by 7.1% from 2010 to 2011, with an increase in the number of rapes reported too. Human rights analysts say that many sexual assaults go unreported, largely due to family pressure and/or shame, especially if the perpetrator is known to the family. The NCRB reported that 228,650 of the total 256,329 violent crimes recorded in 2011 were against women. Of these, 8,618 were dowry-related deaths, 24,206

TRIBAL COMMUNITIES

Read more about India's tribal communities at www.tribal.nic.in, a site maintained by the Indian government's Ministry of Tribal Affairs.

HIJRAS

India's most visible nonheterosexual group is the *hijras*, a caste of transvestites and eunuchs who dress in women's clothing. Some are gay, some are hermaphrodites and some were unfortunate enough to be kidnapped and castrated. Since it has long been frowned upon to live openly as a gay man in India, *hijras* get around this by becoming, in effect, a third sex of sorts. They work mainly as uninvited entertainers at weddings and celebrations of the birth of male children, and possibly as prostitutes.

Read more about *hijras* in *The Invisibles* by Zia Jaffrey and *Ardhanarishvara the Androgyne* by Dr Alka Pande.

Women in saris, Mumbai

were rape (an increase of 9% from the previous year) and 42,968 were molestation.

Following the highly publicised brutal gangrape (and subsequent death) of a 23-year-old Indian student in Delhi in December 2012, tens of thousands of people protested in the capital and beyond, demanding swift government action to address the country's escalating gender-based violence. The government was criticised for its slow response to the public outrage and later vowed to deliver harsher punishments (including the death penalty) for sex offenders.

Sport

In India, it's all about cricket! Cutting across all echelons of society, cricket is more than just a national sporting obsession – it's a matter of enormous patriotism, especially evident whenever India plays against Pakistan. Matches between these South Asian neighbours – which have had rocky relations since Independence – attract especially passionate support, and the players of both sides are under immense pressure to do their respective countries proud. The most celebrated contemporary Indian cricketer is Sachin Tendulkar – fondly dubbed the 'Little Master' – who, in 2012, became the world's only player to have scored one hundred international centuries. Tendulkar announced his retirement from one-day internationals in December 2012.

In South India, football (soccer) has a reasonably strong following, especially in Kerala and Goa. In 2013 India occupied the 166th spot in the FIFA world rankings.

India's first recorded cricket match was in 1721. It won its first test series in 1952 in Chennai against England. Today cricket – especially the recently rolled out Twenty20 format (www.cricket20.com) – is big business in India, attracting lucrative sponsorship deals and celebrity status for its players. The sport has not been without its murky side though, with Indian cricketers among those embroiled in match-fixing scandals

INDIAN ATTIRE

Widely worn by Indian women, the elegant sari comes in a single piece (between 5m and 9m long and 1m wide) and is ingeniously tucked and pleated into place without the need for pins or buttons. Worn with the sari is the choli (tight-fitting blouse) and a drawstring petticoat. The *palloo* is the part of the sari draped over the shoulder. Also commonly worn is the *salwar kameez*, a traditional dresslike tunic and trouser combination accompanied by a *dupatta* (long scarf).

Traditional attire for men includes the dhoti, and in the south the lungi and the *mundu* are also quite often worn. The dhoti is a loose, long loincloth pulled up between the legs. The lungi is more like a sarong, with its end usually sewn up like a tube. The *mundu* is like a lungi but is always white.

There are regional and religious variations in costume – for example, you may see Muslim women wearing the all-enveloping burka.

over past years. International games are played at various centres – see Indian newspapers or check online for details about matches that coincide with your visit. Keep your finger on the cricketing pulse at www.espncricinfo.com (rated most highly by many cricket aficionados) and www.cricbuzz.com.

While cricket is the overwhelmingly favourite sport of contemporary India, the country is also known for its historical links to horse polo, which intermittently thrived in the subcontinent (especially among nobility) until Independence, after which patronage steeply declined due to dwindling funds. Today there's a renewed interest in polo thanks to beefed-up sponsorship and, although it still remains an elite sport, it's attracting more attention from the country's burgeoning upper middle class. The origins of polo are not completely clear. Believed to have its roots in Persia and China around 2000 years ago, in the subcontinent it's thought to have first been played in Baltistan (in present-day Pakistan). Some say that Emperor Akbar (who reigned in India from 1556 to 1605) first introduced rules to the game, but that polo, as it's played today, was largely influenced by a British cavalry regiment stationed in India during the 1870s. A set of international rules was implemented after WWI. The world's oldest surviving polo club, established in 1862, is in Kolkata (Calcutta) – see the Calcutta Polo Club website (www.calcuttapolo.com).

Despite being India's national sport, field hockey no longer enjoys the same fervent following it once did, largely due to the unassailable popularity of cricket, which snatches most of India's sponsorship funding. During its golden era, between 1928 and 1956, India won six consecutive Olympic gold medals in hockey; it later bagged two further Olympic gold medals, one in 1964 and the other in 1980. Recent initiatives to ignite renewed interest in the game have had mixed results. At the time of writing, India's national men's/women's hockey world rankings were 11/12 respectively. Tap into India's hockey scene at Indian Hockey (www.indianhockey.com) and Indian Field Hockey (www.bharatiyahockey.org).

Other sports which are growing in popularity in India include tennis (the country's star performers are Sania Mirza, Leander Paes and Mahesh Bhupathi) – to delve deeper, click www.aitatennis.com; football (soccer), which is particularly strong in the country's east and south; and horse racing, which is reasonably popular in the larger cities such as Mumbai and Bengaluru.

If you're interested in catching a sporting event during your time in India, consult local newspapers (or ask at a tourist office) for current details about dates and venues.

INDIAN DIASPORA

India has one of the world's largest diasporas – over 25 million people – with Indian banks holding upwards of US$50 billion in Non-Resident Indian (NRI) accounts.

Spiritual India

From elaborate city shrines to simple village temples, spirituality suffuses almost every facet of life in India. The nation's major faith, Hinduism, is practised by around 80% of the population and it, along with Buddhism, Jainism and Zoroastrianism, is one of the world's oldest extant religions, with roots extending beyond 1000 BC. The mind-stirring sight of sacred architecture and the soul-warming sound of bhajans and *qawwali* are bound to burn bright in your memory long after you've left India.

The Hindu pantheon is said to have a staggering 330 million deities; those worshipped are a matter of personal choice or tradition.

Hinduism

Hinduism has no founder or central authority and it isn't a proselytising religion. Essentially, Hindus believe in Brahman, who is eternal, uncreated and infinite. Everything that exists emanates from Brahman and will ultimately return to it. The multitude of gods and goddesses are merely manifestations – knowable aspects of this formless phenomenon.

Hindus believe that earthly life is cyclical: you are born again and again (a process known as 'samsara'), the quality of these rebirths being dependent upon your karma (conduct or action) in previous lives. Living a righteous life and fulfilling your dharma (moral code of behaviour; social duty) will enhance your chances of being born into a higher caste and better circumstances. Alternatively, if enough bad karma has accumulated, rebirth may take animal form. But it's only as a human that you can gain sufficient self-knowledge to escape the cycle of reincarnation and achieve moksha (liberation).

Gods & Goddesses

All Hindu deities are regarded as a manifestation of Brahman, who is often described as having three main representations, the Trimurti: Brahma, Vishnu and Shiva.

Brahman

The One; the ultimate reality. Brahman is formless, eternal and the source of all existence. Brahman is *nirguna* (without attributes), as opposed to all the other gods and goddesses, which are manifestations of Brahman and therefore *saguna* (with attributes).

Brahma

Only during the creation of the universe does Brahma play an active role. At other times he is in meditation. His consort is Saraswati, the goddess of learning, and his vehicle is a swan. He is sometimes shown sitting on a lotus that rises from Vishnu's navel, symbolising the interdependence of the gods. Brahma is generally depicted with four (crowned and bearded) heads, each turned towards a point of the compass.

Vishnu

The preserver or sustainer, Vishnu is associated with 'right action'. He protects and sustains all that is good in the world. He is usually depicted with four arms, holding a lotus, a conch shell (it can be blown like a trumpet so symbolises the cosmic vibration from which existence emanates), a discus and a mace. His consort is Lakshmi, the goddess of wealth, and his vehicle is Garuda, the man-bird creature. The Ganges is said to flow from his feet.

Shiva

Shiva is the destroyer – to deliver salvation – without whom creation couldn't occur. Shiva's creative role is phallically symbolised by his representation as the frequently worshipped lingam. With 1008 names, Shiva takes many forms, including Nataraja, lord of the *tandava* (cosmic victory dance), who paces out the creation and destruction of the cosmos.

Sometimes Shiva has snakes draped around his neck and is shown holding a trident (representative of the Trimurti) as a weapon while riding Nandi, his bull. Nandi symbolises power and potency, justice and moral order. Shiva's consort, Parvati, is capable of taking many forms.

Shiva is sometimes characterised as the lord of yoga, a Himalaya-dwelling ascetic with matted hair, an ash-smeared body and a third eye symbolising wisdom.

Other Prominent Deities

Elephant-headed Ganesh is the god of good fortune, remover of obstacles, and patron of scribes (the broken tusk he holds was used to write sections of the Mahabharata). His animal vehicle is Mooshak (a ratlike creature). How Ganesh came to have an elephant's head is a story with several variations. One legend says that Ganesh was born to Parvati in the absence of his father Shiva, and so grew up not knowing him. One day, as Ganesh stood guard while his mother bathed, Shiva returned and asked to be let into Parvati's presence. Ganesh, who didn't recognise Shiva, refused. Enraged, Shiva lopped off Ganesh's head, only to later discover, much to his horror, that he had slaughtered his own son. He vowed to replace Ganesh's head with that of the first creature he came across, which happened to be an elephant.

Another prominent deity, Krishna is an incarnation of Vishnu sent to earth to fight for good and combat evil. His alliances with the *gopis* (milkmaids) and his love for Radha have inspired countless paintings and songs. Depicted with blue-hued skin, Krishna is often seen playing the flute.

Hanuman is the hero of the Ramayana and loyal ally of Rama. He embodies the concept of bhakti (devotion). He's the king of the monkeys, but is capable of taking on other forms.

Among the Shaivite (followers of the Shiva movement), Shakti, the goddess as mother and creator, is worshipped as a force in her own right. The concept of *shakti* is embodied in the ancient goddess Devi (divine mother), who is also manifested as Durga and, in a fiercer evil-destroying incarnation, Kali. Other widely worshipped goddesses include Lakshmi, the goddess of wealth, and Saraswati, the goddess of learning.

One of Shiva's sons, Murugan is a popular deity in South India, especially in Tamil Nadu. He is sometimes identified with another of Shiva's

Did you know that blood-drinking Kali is another form of milk-giving Gauri? *Myth = Mithya: A Handbook of Hindu Mythology* by Devdutt Pattanaik sheds light on this and other fascinating Hindu folklore.

THE SACRED SEVEN

The number seven has special significance in Hinduism. There are seven sacred Indian cities, which are all major pilgrimage centres: Varanasi, associated with Shiva; Haridwar, where the Ganges enters the plains from the Himalaya; Ayodhya, birthplace of Rama; Dwarka with the legendary capital of Krishna thought to be off the Gujarat coast; Mathura, birthplace of Krishna; Kanchipuram, site of the historic Shiva temples; and Ujjain, venue of the Kumbh Mela every 12 years.

There are also seven sacred rivers: the Ganges (Ganga), Saraswati (thought to be underground), Yamuna, Indus, Narmada, Godavari and Cauvery.

sons, Skanda, who enjoys a strong following in North India. Murugan's main role is that of protector, and he is depicted as young and victorious.

Ayyappan is another of Shiva's sons who is identified with the role of protector. It's said that he was born from the union of Shiva and Vishnu, both male. Vishnu is said to have assumed female form (as Mohini) to give birth. Ayyappan is often depicted riding on a tiger and accompanied by leopards, symbols of his victory over dark forces. Today the Ayyappan following has become something of a men's movement, with devotees required to avoid alcohol, drugs, cigarettes and general misbehaviour before making the pilgrimage.

Unravelling the basic tenets of Hinduism are two books both called *Hinduism: An Introduction* – one is by Shakunthala Jagannathan, the other by Dharam Vir Singh.

Sacred Texts

Hindu sacred texts fall into two categories: those believed to be the word of god (*shruti,* meaning 'heard') and those produced by people (smriti, meaning 'remembered'). The Vedas are regarded as *shruti* knowledge and are considered the authoritative basis for Hinduism. The oldest of the Vedic texts, the Rig-Veda, was compiled over 3000 years ago. Within its 1028 verses are prayers for prosperity and longevity as well as an explanation of the universe's origins. The Upanishads, the last parts of the Vedas, reflect on the mystery of death and emphasise the oneness of the universe. The oldest of the Vedic texts were written in Vedic Sanskrit (related to Old Persian). Later texts were composed in classical Sanskrit, but many have been translated into the vernacular.

The smriti texts comprise a collection of literature spanning centuries and include expositions on the proper performance of domestic ceremonies as well as the proper pursuit of government, economics and religious law. Among its well-known works are the Ramayana and Mahabharata, as well as the Puranas, which expand on the epics and promote the notion of the Trimurti. Unlike the Vedas, reading the Puranas is not restricted to initiated higher-caste males.

Tribal religions have so merged with Hinduism and other mainstream religions that very few are now clearly identifiable. Some basic tenets of Hinduism are believed to have originated in tribal culture.

The Mahabharata

Thought to have been composed around 1000 BC, the Mahabharata focuses on the exploits of Krishna. By about 500 BC the Mahabharata had evolved into a far more complex creation with substantial additions, including the Bhagavad Gita (where Krishna proffers advice to Arjuna before a battle).

The story centres on conflict between the heroic gods (Pandavas) and the demons (Kauravas). Overseeing events is Krishna, who has taken on human form. Krishna acts as charioteer for the Pandava hero Arjuna, who eventually triumphs in a great battle against the Kauravas.

The Ramayana

Composed around the 3rd or 2nd century BC, the Ramayana is believed to be largely the work of one person, the poet Valmiki. Like the Mahabharata, it centres on conflict between the gods and the demons.

OM

One of Hinduism's most venerated symbols is 'Om'. Pronounced 'aum', it's a highly propitious mantra (sacred word or syllable). The 'three' shape symbolises the creation, maintenance and destruction of the universe (and thus the holy Trimurti). The inverted *chandra* (crescent or half moon) represents the discursive mind and the *bindu* (dot) within it, Brahman.

Buddhists believe that, if intoned often enough with complete concentration, it will lead to a state of blissful emptiness.

Meenakshi Amman Temple (p384), Madurai

The story goes that Dasharatha, the childless king of Ayodhya, called upon the gods to provide him with a son. His wife duly gave birth to a boy. But this child, named Rama, was in fact an incarnation of Vishnu, who had assumed human form to overthrow the demon king of Lanka (now Sri Lanka), Ravana.

As an adult, Rama, who won the hand of the princess Sita in a competition, was chosen by his father to inherit his kingdom. At the last minute Rama's stepmother intervened and demanded her son, Barathan, take Rama's place. Rama, Sita and Rama's brother, Lakshmana, were exiled and went off to the forests, where Rama and Lakshmana battled demons and dark forces. Ravana's sister attempted to seduce Rama but she was rejected and, in revenge, Ravana captured Sita and spirited her away to his palace in Lanka.

Rama, assisted by an army of monkeys led by the loyal monkey god Hanuman, eventually found the palace, killed Ravana and rescued Sita. All returned victorious to Ayodhya, where Rama was welcomed by Barathan and crowned king.

Two recommended publications containing English translations of holy Hindu texts are *The Bhagavad Gita* by S Radhakrishnan and *The Valmiki Ramayana* by Romesh Dutt.

Naturally Sacred

Animals, particularly snakes and cows, have long been worshipped on the subcontinent. For Hindus, the cow represents fertility and nurturing, while snakes (especially cobras) are associated with fertility and welfare. Naga stones (snake stones) serve the dual purpose of protecting humans from snakes and appeasing snake gods.

Plants can also have sacred associations, such as the banyan tree, which symbolises the Trimurti, while mango trees are symbolic of love – Shiva is believed to have married Parvati under one. Meanwhile, the lotus flower is said to have emerged from the primeval waters and is connected to the mythical centre of the earth through its stem. Often found in the most polluted of waters, the lotus has the remarkable ability to blossom above murky depths. The centre of the lotus corresponds to the centre of the universe, the navel of the earth: all is held together by the stem and the eternal waters. The fragile yet resolute lotus is an embodiment of beauty and strength and a reminder to Hindus of how their own lives should be. So revered has the lotus become that today it's India's national flower.

Worship

Worship and ritual play a paramount role in Hinduism. In Hindu homes you'll often find a dedicated worship area, where members of the family pray to the deities of their choice. Beyond the home, Hindus worship at temples. *Puja* is a focal point of worship and ranges from silent prayer to elaborate ceremonies. Devotees leave the temple with a handful of *prasad* (temple-blessed food) which is shared among others. Other forms of worship include *aarti* (the auspicious lighting of lamps or candles) and the playing of bhajans (devotional songs).

SADHUS

A sadhu is someone who has surrendered all material possessions in pursuit of spirituality through meditation, the study of sacred texts, self-mortification and pilgrimage. Explore further in *Sadhus: India's Mystic Holy Men* by Dolf Hartsuiker.

Islam

Islam is India's largest minority religion, followed by approximately 13.4% of the population. It's believed that Islam was introduced to northern India by Muslim rulers (in the 16th and 17th centuries the Mughal empire controlled much of North India) and to the south by Arab traders.

Islam was founded in Arabia by the Prophet Mohammed in the 7th century AD. The Arabic term *islam* means to surrender, and believers (Muslims) undertake to surrender to the will of Allah (God), which is revealed in the scriptures, the Quran. In this monotheistic religion, God's word is conveyed through prophets (messengers), of whom Mohammed was the most recent.

Following Mohammed's death, a succession dispute split the movement, and the legacy today is the Sunnis and the Shiites. Most Muslims in India are Sunnis. The Sunnis emphasise the 'well-trodden' path or the orthodox way. Shiites believe that only imams (exemplary leaders) can reveal the true meaning of the Quran.

All Muslims, however, share a belief in the Five Pillars of Islam: the shahada (declaration of faith: 'There is no God but Allah; Mohammed is his prophet'); prayer (ideally five times a day); the zakat (tax), in the form of a charitable donation; fasting (during Ramadan) for all except the sick, young children, pregnant women, the elderly and those undertaking arduous journeys; and the haj (pilgrimage) to Mecca, which every Muslim aspires to do at least once.

Sikhism

Sikhism, founded in Punjab by Guru Nanak in the 15th century, began as a reaction against the caste system and Brahmin domination of ritual. Sikhs believe in one god and although they reject the worship of idols, some keep pictures of the 10 gurus as a point of focus. The Sikhs' holy book, the Guru Granth Sahib, contains the teachings of the 10 Sikh gurus, among others. Like Hindus and Buddhists, Sikhs believe in rebirth and karma. In Sikhism, there's no ascetic or monastic tradition ending the cycles of rebirth. Almost 2% of India's citizens are Sikhs, with most living in Punjab.

Born in present-day Pakistan, Guru Nanak (1469–1539), the founder of Sikhism, was largely dissatisfied with both Muslim and Hindu religious practices. He believed in family life and the value of hard work – he married, had two sons and worked as a farmer when not travelling around, preaching and singing self-composed *kirtan* (Sikh devotional songs) with his Muslim musician, Mardana. He is said to have performed miracles and he encouraged meditation on God's name as a prime path to enlightenment.

Nanak believed in equality centuries before it became socially fashionable and campaigned against the caste system. He was a practical guru – 'a person who makes an honest living and shares earnings with others recognises the way to God'. He appointed his most talented disciple to be his successor, not one of his sons.

His *kirtan* are still sung in gurdwaras (Sikh temples) today and his picture is kept in millions of homes in and beyond the subcontinent.

To grasp the intricacies of Sikhism read Volume One (1469–1839) or Volume Two (1839–2004) of *A History of the Sikhs* by Khushwant Singh.

Buddhism

The 2011 census in India revealed that 0.8% of the country's population is Buddhist. Bodhgaya, in the state of Bihar, is one of Buddhism's most sacred sites, drawing pilgrims from right across the world.

Buddhism arose in the 6th century BC as a reaction against the strictures of Brahminical Hinduism. Buddha (Awakened One) is believed to have lived from about 563 to 483 BC. Formerly a prince (Siddhartha Gautama), the Buddha, at the age of 29, embarked on a quest for emancipation from the world of suffering. He achieved nirvana (the state of full awareness) at Bodhgaya, aged 35. Critical of the caste system and the unthinking worship of gods, the Buddha urged his disciples to seek truth within their own experiences.

The Buddha taught that existence is based on Four Noble Truths: that life is rooted in suffering, that suffering is caused by craving, that one can find release from suffering by eliminating craving, and that the way to eliminate craving is by following the Noble Eightfold Path. This path consists of right understanding, right intention, right speech, right action, right livelihood, right effort, right awareness and right concentration. By successfully complying with these one can attain nirvana.

Buddhism had somewhat waned in parts of India by the turn of the 20th century. However, it saw a revival in the 1950s among intellectuals and Dalits who were disillusioned with the caste system. The number of

RELIGIOUS ETIQUETTE

Whenever visiting a sacred site, dress and behave respectfully – don't wear shorts or sleeveless tops (this applies to men and women) – and refrain from smoking. Loud and intrusive behaviour isn't appreciated, and neither are public displays of affection or kidding around.

Before entering a holy place, remove your shoes (tip the shoe-minder a few rupees when retrieving them) and check if photography is allowed. You're permitted to wear socks in most places of worship – often necessary during warmer months, when floors can be uncomfortably hot.

Religious etiquette advises against touching locals on the head, or directing the soles of your feet at a person, religious shrine or image of a deity. Protocol also advises against touching someone with your feet or touching a carving of a deity.

Head cover (for women and sometimes men) is required at some places of worship – especially gurdwaras (Sikh temples) and mosques – so carry a scarf just to be on the safe side. There are some sites that don't admit women and some that deny entry to non-adherents of their faith – enquire in advance. Women may be required to sit apart from men. Jain temples request the removal of leather items you may be wearing or carrying and may also request that menstruating women not enter.

Taking photos inside a shrine, at a funeral, at a religious ceremony or of people taking a holy dip can be offensive – ask first. Flash photography may be prohibited in certain areas of a shrine, or may not be permitted at all.

Parsi temple, Mumbai

followers has been further increased with the influx of Tibetan refugees. Both the current Dalai Lama and the 17th Karmapa reside in India.

Jainism

Jainism arose in the 6th century BC as a reaction against the caste restraints and rituals of Hinduism. It was founded by Mahavira, a contemporary of the Buddha.

Jains believe that liberation can be attained by achieving complete purity of the soul. Purity means shedding all *karman,* matter generated by one's actions that binds itself to the soul. By following various austerities (eg fasting and meditation) one can shed *karman* and purify the soul. Right conduct is essential, and fundamental to this is ahimsa (nonviolence) in thought and deed towards any living thing.

The religious disciplines of followers are less severe than for monks (some Jain monks go naked). The slightly less ascetic maintain a bare minimum of possessions which include a broom to sweep the path before them to avoid stepping on any living creature, and a piece of cloth tied over their mouth to prevent the accidental inhalation of insects.

Today, around 0.4% of India's population is Jain, with the majority living in Gujarat and Mumbai (Bombay). Some notable Jain holy sites include Sravanabelagola, Palitana, Ranakpur and the temples of Mt Abu.

Christianity

There are various theories circulating about Christ's link to the subcontinent. Some, for instance, believe that Jesus spent his 'lost years' in India, while others say that Christianity came to South India with St Thomas the Apostle in AD 52. However, many scholars say it's more likely Christianity is traced to around the 4th century with a Syrian merchant, Thomas Cana, who set out for Kerala with around 400 families to establish what later became a branch of the Nestorian church. Today the Christian community is fractured into a multitude of established churches and new evangelical sects.

The Nestorian church sect survives today; services are in Armenian, and the Patriarch of Baghdad is the sect's head. Thrissur is the church's centre. Other Eastern Orthodox sects include the Jacobites and the Syrian Orthodox churches.

Catholicism established a strong presence in South India in the wake of Vasco da Gama's visit in 1498. Catholic orders that have been active in the region include the Dominicans, Franciscans and Jesuits. The faith is most noticeable in Goa, not only in the basilicas and convents of Old Goa, but in the dozens of active whitewashed churches scattered through towns and villages.

Protestant missionaries are believed to have arrived in South India from around the 18th century and today most of this minority group belong to the 'Church of South India', which is comprised of various denominations including Anglican, Methodist and Presbyterian.

Evangelical Christian groups have made inroads both into the other Christian communities, and lower caste and tribal groups across South India. According to various news reports over the years, some congregations have been regarded as being aggressive in seeking converts, and in 'retaliation' a number of Christian communities have been targeted by Hindu nationalist groups.

Zoroastrianism

Zoroastrianism, founded by Zoroaster (Zarathustra), had its inception in Persia in the 6th century BC and is based on the concept of dualism, whereby good and evil are locked in a continuous battle. Zoroastrianism isn't quite monotheistic: good and evil entities coexist, although believers are urged to honour only the good. Both body and soul are united in this struggle of good versus evil. Although humanity is mortal it has components that are timeless, such as the soul. On the day of judgment the errant soul is not called to account for every misdemeanour – but a pleasant afterlife does depend on one's deeds, words and thoughts during earthly existence.

Zoroastrianism was eclipsed in Persia by the rise of Islam in the 7th century and its followers, many of whom openly resisted this, suffered persecution. Over the following centuries, some immigrated to India, where they became known as Parsis. Historically, Parsis settled in Gujarat and became farmers; however, during British rule they moved into commerce, forming a prosperous community in Mumbai.

In recent decades the Parsi population has been spiralling downward; there are now believed to be only between 40,000 and 45,000 Parsis left in India, with most residing in Mumbai.

TOWERS OF SILENCE

The Zoroastrian funerary ritual involves the 'Towers of Silence' where the corpse is laid out and exposed to vultures that pick the bones clean.

Delicious South India

South India's culinary terrain – with its especially impressive patchwork of vegetarian cuisine – is not only intensely delectable, it's also richly steeped in history. From the inventively prepared deep-sea delights of coastal regions to the classically cooked southern vegetarian fare, it's the sheer diversity of what's on offer that makes eating your way through South India so deliciously rewarding.

Containing handy tips, including how to best store spices, Monisha Bharadwaj's *The Indian Spice Kitchen* is a slick cookbook with more than 200 traditional recipes.

A Culinary Carnival

South India's culinary story is an ancient one. The cuisine that exists today reflects an amalgam of regional and global influences. From the traditional Indian food prepared in simple village kitchens, to the piled-high Italian-style pizzas served in cosmopolitan city restaurants, the carnival of flavours available on the subcontinent is nothing short of spectacular.

Although South Indian meals may at times appear quite simple – mounds of rice, spiced vegetables, curd and a splodge of fresh pickles, sometimes served on a banana-leaf plate – within this deceptive simplicity hides a sensual and complex repertoire of taste sensations. Add to this the distinct regional variations, from the colonial-influenced fare of Goa to the traditional seafood specialities of Kerala – along with a bounty of exotic fruits and vegetables – and there's more than enough to get the tastebuds tingling.

Land of Spices

Christopher Columbus was actually searching for the black pepper of Kerala's Malabar Coast when he stumbled upon America. The region still grows the finest quality of the world's favourite spice, and it's integral to most savoury Indian dishes.

Turmeric is the essence of the majority of Indian curries, but coriander seeds are the most widely used spice and lend flavour and body to just about every savoury dish. Indian 'wet' dishes – commonly known as curries in the West – usually begin with the crackle of cumin seeds in hot oil. Tamarind is sometimes known as the 'Indian date' and is a popular souring agent in the south. The green cardamom of Kerala's Western Ghats is regarded as the world's best, and you'll find it in savouries, desserts and warming chai (tea). Saffron, the dried stigmas of crocus flowers grown in Kashmir, is so light it takes more than 1500 hand-plucked flowers to yield just one gram.

Spotlighting rice, *Finest Rice Recipes* by Sabina Sehgal Saikia shows just how versatile this humble grain is, with classy creations such as rice-crusted crab cakes.

Rice Paradise

Rice is a common staple, especially in South India. Long-grain white rice varieties are the most popular, served hot with just about any 'wet' cooked dish. From Assam's sticky rice in the far northeast to Kerala's red grains in the extreme south, you'll find countless regional varieties that locals will claim to be the best in India, though this honour is usually conceded to basmati, a fragrant long-grain variety which is widely exported around the world.

Flippin' Fantastic Bread

Although rice is the mainstay of the south, traditional breads are also widely eaten. Roti, the generic term for Indian-style bread, is a name used interchangeably with chapati to describe the most common variety, the irresistible unleavened round bread made with whole-wheat flour and cooked on a *tawa* (hotplate). It may be smothered with ghee (clarified butter) or oil. In some places, rotis are bigger and thicker than chapatis and possibly cooked in a tandoor.

Dhal-icious!

The whole of India is united in its love for dhal (curried lentils or pulses). You may encounter up to 60 different pulses: the most common are *channa,* a slightly sweeter version of the yellow split pea; tiny yellow or green ovals called *moong* (mung beans); salmon-coloured *masoor* (red lentils); the ochre-coloured southern favourite, *tuvar* (yellow lentils; also known as *arhar*); *rajma* (kidney beans); *urad* (black gram or lentils); and *lobhia* (black-eyed peas).

Meaty Matters

Although India probably has more vegetarians than the rest of the world combined, it still has an extensive repertoire of carnivorous fare. Chicken, lamb and mutton (sometimes actually goat) are the mainstays; religious taboos make beef forbidden to devout Hindus and pork to Muslims.

In some southern restaurants you'll probably come across meat-dominated northern Mughlai cuisine, which includes rich curries, kebabs, koftas and biryanis. This spicy food traces its history back to the (Islamic) Mughal empire that once reigned supreme in India.

Tandoori meat dishes are another North Indian favourite which have also made their way south. The name is derived from the clay oven, or tandoor, in which the marinated meat is cooked.

Deep-Sea Delights

India has around 7500km of coastline, so it's no surprise that seafood is an important staple, especially on the west coast, from Mumbai (Bombay) down to Kerala. Kerala is the biggest fishing state, while Goa boasts particularly succulent prawns and fiery fish curries, and the fishing communities of the Konkan Coast – sandwiched between these two states – are renowned for their seafood recipes.

The Fruits (& Vegetables) of Mother Nature

A visit to any South Indian market will reveal a vast and vibrant assortment of fresh fruit and vegetables, overflowing from large baskets or stacked in neat pyramids. The south is especially well known for its abundance of tropical fruits such as pineapples and papaya. Mangos abound during the summer months (especially April and May), with

PONGAL

Pongal, the major harvest festival of the south, is most closely associated with the dish of the same name, made with the season's first rice, along with jaggery, nuts, raisins and spices.

Fish is a staple of non-vegetarian Marathi food; Maharashtra's signature fish dish is *bombil* (Bombay duck; a misnomer for this slimy, pikelike fish), which is eaten fresh or sun-dried.

PAAN

Meals are often rounded off with *paan,* a fragrant mixture of betel nut (also called areca nut), lime paste, spices and condiments wrapped in an edible, silky *paan* leaf. Peddled by *paan*-wallahs, who are usually strategically positioned outside busy restaurants, *paan* is eaten as a digestive and mouth-freshener. The betel nut is mildly narcotic and some aficionados eat *paan* the same way heavy smokers consume cigarettes – over the years these people's teeth can become rotted red and black.

There are two basic types of *paan: mitha* (sweet) and *saadha* (with tobacco). A parcel of *mitha paan* is a splendid way to finish a meal. Pop the whole parcel in your mouth and chew slowly, allowing the juices to oooooooze.

India boasting more than 500 varieties, the pick of the luscious bunch being the sweet Alphonso.

Naturally in a region with so many vegetarians, *sabzi* (vegetables) make up a predominant part of the diet. Vegetables can be fried, roasted, curried, baked, mashed and stuffed into dosas or wrapped in batter to make deep-fried *pakoras* (fritters). Potatoes are ubiquitous and popularly cooked with various masalas, mixed with other vegetables, or mashed and fried for the street snack *aloo tikki* (mashed-potato patties). Onions are fried with other vegetables, ground into a paste for cooking with meats, and served raw as relishes. Heads of cauliflower are usually cooked dry on their own, with potatoes to make *aloo gobi* (potato-and-cauliflower curry), or with other vegetables such as carrots and beans. Also popular is *saag* (a generic term for leafy greens), which can include mustard, spinach and fenugreek. Something a little more unusual is the bumpy-skinned *karela* (bitter gourd) which, like the delicious *bhindi* (okra), is commonly prepared dry with spices.

Technically speaking, there's no such thing as an Indian 'curry' – the word, an anglicised derivative of the Tamil word *kari* (sauce), was used by the British as a term for any dish including spices.

Vegetarians & Vegans

South India is king when it comes to vegetarian fare. There's little understanding of veganism (the term 'pure vegetarian' means without eggs), and animal products such as milk, butter, ghee and curd are included in most Indian dishes. If you are vegan your first problem is likely to be getting the cook to completely understand your requirements.

For further information, surf the web – good places to begin include Indian Vegan (www.indianvegan.com) and Vegans World Network (www.vegansworldnetwork.org).

Pickles, Chutneys & Relishes

Pickles, chutneys and relishes are accompaniments that add zing to meals. A relish can be anything from a tiny pickled onion to a delicately crafted fusion of fruit, nuts and spices. One of the most popular side dishes is yoghurt-based raita, which makes a tongue-cooling counter to spicy food. *Chatnis* (chutneys) can come in any number of varieties (sweet or savoury) and can be made from many different vegetables, fruits, herbs and spices. But you should proceed with caution before polishing off that pickled speck sitting on your thali; it may quite possibly be the hottest thing that you've ever tasted.

Sweet at Heart

India has a fabulously colourful kaleidoscope of, often sticky and squishy, *mithai* (Indian sweets), most of them sinfully sugary. The main catego-

SOUTHERN BELLES

Dosas (also spelt dosai), a family of large papery rice-flour crêpes, usually served with a bowl of hot *sambar* (soupy lentil dish with cubed vegetables) and another bowl of cooling coconut *chatni* (chutney), are a South Indian speciality that can be eaten at any time of day. The most popular is the *masala dosa* (stuffed with spiced potatoes), but there are also other fantastic dosa varieties – the *rava dosa* (batter made with semolina), the Mysore dosa (like *masala dosa* but with more vegetables and chilli in the filling), and the *pessarettu dosa* (batter made with mung-bean dhal) from Andhra Pradesh.

The humble *idli*, a traditional South Indian snack, is low-cal and nutritious, providing a welcome alternative to oil, spice and chilli. *Idlis* are spongy, round, white fermented rice cakes that you dip in *sambar* and coconut *chatni*. *Dahi idli* is an *idli* dunked in lightly spiced yoghurt – brilliant for tender tummies. Other super southern snacks include *vadas* (doughnut-shaped deep-fried lentil savouries) and *appams* or *uttappams* (thick, savoury South Indian rice pancake with finely chopped onions, green chillies, coriander and coconut).

FEASTING INDIAN-STYLE

Most people in India eat with their right hand. In the south, they use as much of the hand as is necessary, while elsewhere they use the tips of the fingers. The left hand is reserved for unsanitary actions such as removing shoes. You can use your left hand for holding drinks and serving yourself from a communal bowl, but it shouldn't be used for bringing food to your mouth. Before and after a meal, it's good manners to wash your hands.

Once your meal is served, mix the food with your fingers. If you are having dhal and *sabzi* (vegetables), only mix the dhal into your rice and have the *sabzi* in small scoops with each mouthful. If you are having fish or meat curry, mix the gravy into your rice and take the flesh off the bones from the side of your plate. Scoop up lumps of the mix and, with your knuckles facing the dish, use your thumb to shovel the food into your mouth.

ries are *barfi* (a fudgelike milk-based sweet), soft *halwa* (made with vegetables, cereals, lentils, nuts or fruit), *ladoos* (sweet balls made with gram flour and semolina), and those made from *chhana* (unpressed paneer), such as *rasgullas*. There are also simpler – but equally scrumptious – offerings such as crunchy *jalebis* that you'll see all over the country.

Payasam (called *kheer* in the north) is one of the most popular after-meal desserts. It's a creamy rice pudding with a light, delicate flavour, enhanced with cardamom, saffron, pistachios, flaked almonds, chopped cashews or slivered dried fruit. Other favourites include hot *gulab jamuns* and refreshing *kulfi*.

Each year, an estimated 14 tonnes of pure silver is converted into the edible foil that decorates many Indian sweets, especially during the Diwali festival.

KERALA DELICACIES

101 Kerala Delicacies, by G Padma Vijay, is a detailed recipe book of vegetarian and non-vegetarian dishes from this tropical coast-hugging state.

Where to Fill Up?

South India has oodles of restaurants, from ramshackle street eateries to swish five-star hotel offerings. Most midrange restaurants serve one of two basic genres: South Indian (which usually means the vegetarian food of Tamil Nadu and Karnataka) and North Indian (which largely comprises Punjabi/Mughlai fare). You'll also find the cuisines of neighbouring regions and states. Indians frequently migrate in search of work and these restaurants cater to the large communities seeking the familiar tastes of home.

Not to be confused with burger joints and pizzerias, restaurants in the south advertising 'fast food' are some of India's best. They serve the whole gamut of tiffin (snack) items and often have separate sweet counters. Many upmarket hotels have outstanding restaurants, usually with pan-Indian menus so you can explore various regional cuisines. Meanwhile, the independent restaurant dining scene keeps mushrooming in India's larger cities, with menus sporting everything from Mexican and Mediterranean to Japanese and Italian.

Dhabas (basic snack bars) are oases to millions of truck drivers, bus passengers and sundry travellers going anywhere by road. The original *dhabas* dot the North Indian landscape, but you'll find versions of them throughout the country. The rough-and-ready but satisfying food served in these happy-go-lucky shacks has become a genre of its own known as '*dhaba* food'.

Street Food

Whatever the time of day, food vendors are frying, boiling, roasting, peeling, simmering, mixing, juicing or baking some type of food and drink to lure peckish passers-by. Small operations usually have one special that

STREET FOOD: TIPS

Tucking into street eats is a glowing highlight of travelling in South India – here are some tips to help avoid tummy troubles.

- Give yourself a few days to adjust to the local cuisine, especially if you're not used to spicy food.
- You know the rule about following a crowd – if the locals are avoiding a particular vendor, you should too. Also take notice of the profile of the customers – any place popular with families will probably be your safest bet.
- Check how and where the vendor is cleaning the utensils, and how and where the food is covered. If the vendor is cooking in oil, try to have a peek to check it's clean. If the pots or surfaces are dirty, there are food scraps about or too many buzzing flies, don't be shy to make a hasty retreat.
- Don't be put off when you order some deep-fried snack and the cook throws it back into the wok. It's common practice to partly cook the snacks first and then finish them off once they've been ordered. In fact, frying them hot again kills germs.
- Unless a place is reputable (and busy), it's best to avoid eating meat from the street.
- The hygiene standard at juice stalls varies, so exercise caution. Have the vendor press the juice in front of you and steer clear of anything stored in a jug or served in a glass (unless you're confident in the washing standards).
- Don't be tempted by glistening pre-sliced melon and other fruit, which keeps its luscious veneer with regular dousing of (often dubious) water.

they serve all day, while other vendors have different dishes for breakfast, lunch and dinner. The fare varies as you venture between neighbourhoods, towns and regions; it can be as simple as puffed rice or peanuts roasted in hot sand, as unexpected as a fried-egg sandwich, or as complex as the riot of different flavours known as *chaat* (savoury snack).

Railway Snack Attack

One of the thrills of travelling by rail right across India is the culinary circus that greets you at almost every station. Roving vendors accost arriving trains, yelling and scampering up and down the carriages; fruit, *namkin* (savoury nibbles), omelettes, nuts and sweets are offered through the grills on the windows; and platform cooks try to lure you from the train with the sizzle of spicy goodies such as samosas. Frequent rail travellers know which station is famous for which food item: Lonavla station in Maharashtra, for example, is known for *chikki* (rock-hard toffeelike confectionery).

Dakshin Bhog by Santhi Balaraman offers a yummy jumble of southern stars, from iconic dosas and *idlis* to *kootan choru* (vegetable rice).

Daily Dining Habits

Three main meals a day is the norm in South India. Breakfast is usually fairly light, maybe *idlis* and *sambar* or simply fruit, cereal and/or eggs. Lunch can be substantial (perhaps the local version of the thali) or light, especially for time-strapped office workers. Dinner is usually the main meal of the day. It's generally comprised of a few different preparations – several curried vegetable (maybe also meat or seafood) dishes and dhal, accompanied by rice and/or chapatis. Dishes are served all at once rather than as courses. Desserts are optional and most prevalent during festivals or other special occasions. Fruit may wrap up a meal. In many Indian homes dinner can be a rather late affair (post 9pm) depending on personal preference and possibly the season (eg late dinners during the warmer months). Restaurants usually spring to life after 9pm.

Above Making chapatis, Andaman Islands
Right Vegetarian thali, Mumbai

GRAHAM CROUCH / GETTY IMAGES ©

Spiritual Sustenance

For many in India, food is considered just as critical for fine-tuning the spirit as it is for sustaining the body. Broadly speaking, Hindus traditionally avoid foods that are thought to inhibit physical and spiritual development, although there are few hard-and-fast rules. The taboo on eating beef (the cow is holy to Hindus) is the most rigid restriction. Jains avoid foods such as garlic and onions, which, apart from harming insects in their extraction from the ground, are thought to heat the blood and arouse sexual desire. You may come across vegetarian restaurants that make it a point to advertise the absence of onion and garlic in their dishes for this reason. Devout Hindus may also avoid garlic and onions. These items are also banned from many ashrams.

Some foods, such as dairy products, are considered innately pure and are eaten to cleanse the body, mind and spirit. Ayurveda, the ancient science of life, health and longevity, also influences food customs.

The fiery cuisine of the Karnatakan coastal city of Mangalore is famed for its flavour-packed seafood dishes. Mangalorean cuisine is diverse, distinct and characterised by its liberal use of chilli and fresh coconut.

Pork is taboo for Muslims and stimulants such as alcohol are avoided by the most devout. Halal is the term for all permitted foods, and haram for those prohibited. Fasting is considered an opportunity to earn the approval of Allah, to wipe the sin-slate clean and to understand the suffering of the poor.

Buddhists and Jains subscribe to the philosophy of ahimsa (nonviolence) and are mostly vegetarian. Jainism's central tenet is ultravegetarianism, and rigid restrictions are in place to avoid even potential injury to any living creature – Jains abstain from eating vegetables that grow underground because of the potential to harm insects during cultivation and harvesting.

India's Sikh, Christian and Parsi communities have little or no restrictions on what they can eat.

Drinks, Anyone?

Gujarat is India's only dry state but there are drinking laws in place all over the country, and each state may have regular dry days when the sale of alcohol from liquor shops is banned. To avoid paying high taxes, head for Goa, where booze isn't subject to the exorbitant levies of other states.

You'll find impressive watering holes in most big cities, especially Mumbai and Bengaluru (Bangalore), which are usually at their liveli-

THE GREAT SOUTH INDIAN THALI

In South India the thali is a favourite lunchtime meal. Inexpensive, satiating, wholesome and incredibly tasty, this is Indian food at its simple best. Whereas in North India the thali is usually served on a steel plate with indentations for the various side dishes (thali gets its name from the plate), in the south a thali is traditionally served on a flat steel plate that may be covered with a fresh banana leaf. Or on a banana leaf itself.

In a restaurant, when the steel plate is placed in front of you, you may like to follow local custom and pour some water on the leaf then spread it around with your right hand. Soon enough a waiter with a large pot of rice will come along and heap mounds of it onto your plate, followed by servings of dhal, *sambar* (soupy lentils), *rasam* (dhal-based broth flavoured with tamarind), vegetable dishes, chutneys, pickles and *dahi* (curd/yoghurt). Using the fingers of your right hand, start by mixing the various side dishes with the rice, kneading and scraping it into mouth-sized balls, then scoop it into your mouth using your thumb to push the food in. It is considered poor form to stick your hand right into your mouth or to lick your fingers. Observing fellow diners will help get your thali technique just right. If it's all getting a bit messy, there should be a finger bowl of water on the table. Waiters will continue to fill your plate until you wave your hand over one or all of the offerings to indicate you have had enough.

est on weekends. The more upmarket bars serve a great selection of domestic and imported drinks as well as draught beer. Many bars turn into music-thumping nightclubs anytime after 8pm although there are quiet lounge-bars to be found in most large cities. In smaller towns the bar scene can be a seedy, male-dominated affair – not the kind of place thirsty female travellers should venture into alone.

Wine-drinking is steadily on the rise, despite the domestic wine-producing industry still being relatively new. The favourable climate and soil conditions in certain areas – such as parts of Maharashtra and Karnataka – have spawned some commendable Indian wineries including those of the Grover and Sula Vineyards.

Stringent licensing laws discourage drinking in some restaurants but places that depend on the tourist rupee may covertly serve you beer in teapots and disguised glasses – but don't assume anything, at the risk of causing offence.

Very few vegetarian restaurants serve alcohol.

Dakshin: Vegetarian Cuisine from South India, by Chandra Padmanabhan, is an easy-to-read and beautifully illustrated book of southern recipes.

Nonalcoholic Beverages

Chai (tea), the much-loved drink of the masses, is made with copious amounts of milk and sugar. A glass of steaming, frothy chai is the perfect antidote to the vicissitudes of life on the Indian road; the disembodied voice droning '*garam* chai, *garam* chai' (hot tea, hot tea) is likely to become one of the most familiar and welcome sounds of your trip.

South India grows both tea and coffee, but unlike in North India, where it has only fairly recently become all the rage to guzzle cappuccinos and lattes, coffee has long been popular down south. In the larger cities you'll find ever-multiplying branches of hip coffee chains, such as Barista and Café Coffee Day, widely found in what were once chai strongholds.

Masala soda is the quintessentially Indian soft drink. It's a freshly opened bottle of fizzy soda, pepped up with lime, spices, salt and sugar. Also refreshing is *jal jeera,* made of lime juice, cumin, mint and rock salt. Sweet and savoury lassi, a yoghurt-based drink, is especially popular nationwide and is another wonderfully rejuvenating beverage.

Falooda is an interesting rose-flavoured drink made with milk, cream, nuts and strands of vermicelli, while *badam* milk (served hot or cold) is flavoured with almonds and saffron.

India has zillions of fresh-fruit juice vendors, but be wary of hygiene standards. Some restaurants think nothing of adding salt or sugar to juice to intensify the flavours; ask the waiter to omit these if you don't want them.

WINE

The subcontinent's wine industry is an ever-evolving one – take a cyber-sip of Indian wine at www.indianwine.com.

Homegrown Brews

An estimated three-quarters of India's drinking population quaffs 'country liquor' such as the notorious arak (liquor distilled from coconut-palm sap, potatoes or rice) of the south. This is widely known as the poorman's drink and millions are addicted to the stuff. Each year, many people are blinded or even killed by the methyl alcohol in illegal arak.

An interesting local drink is a clear spirit with a heady pungent flavour called *mahua,* distilled from the flower of the *mahua* tree. It's brewed in makeshift village stalls all over central India during March and April, when the trees bloom. *Mahua* is safe to drink as long as it comes from a trustworthy source. There have been cases of people being blinded after drinking *mahua* adulterated with methyl alcohol.

Toddy, the sap from the palm tree, is drunk in coastal areas, especially Kerala, while feni is the primo Indian spirit, and the preserve of laid-back Goa. Coconut feni is light and rather unexceptional but the more popular cashew feni – made from the fruit of the cashew tree – is worth a try.

Menu Decoder

achar	pickle
aloo	potato; also *alu*
aloo tikki	mashed-potato patty
appam	South Indian rice pancake
arak	liquor distilled from coconut milk, potatoes or rice
baigan	eggplant/aubergine; also known as *brinjal*
barfi	fudgelike sweet made from milk
bebinca	Goan 16-layer cake
besan	chickpea flour
betel	nut of the betel tree; also called areca nut
bhajia	vegetable fritters
bhang lassi	blend of lassi and bhang (a derivative of marijuana)
bhelpuri	thin fried rounds of dough with rice, lentils, lemon juice, onion, herbs and chutney
bhindi	okra
biryani	fragrant spiced steamed rice with meat or vegetables
bonda	mashed-potato patty
chaat	savoury snack, may be seasoned with *chaat masala*
chach	buttermilk beverage
chai	tea
channa	spiced chickpeas
chapati	round unleavened Indian-style bread; also known as roti
chawal	rice
cheiku	small, sweet brown fruit
dahi	curd/yoghurt
dhal	spiced lentil dish
dhal makhani	black lentils and red kidney beans with cream and butter
dhansak	Parsi dish; meat, usually chicken or lamb, with curried lentils, pumpkin or gourd, and rice
dosa	large South Indian savoury crêpe
falooda	rose-flavoured drink made with milk, cream, nuts and vermicelli
faluda	long chickpea-flour noodles
feni	Goan liquor distilled from coconut milk or cashews
ghee	clarified butter
gobi	cauliflower
gulab jamun	deep-fried balls of dough soaked in rose-flavoured syrup
halwa	soft sweet made with vegetables, lentils, nuts or fruit
idli	South Indian spongy, round, fermented rice cake
imli	tamarind
jaggery	hard, brown, sugarlike sweetener made from palm sap
jalebi	orange-coloured coils of deep-fried batter dunked in sugar syrup; served hot
karela	bitter gourd
keema	spiced minced meat
kheer	creamy rice pudding
khichdi	blend of lightly spiced rice and lentils; also *khichri*
kofta	minced vegetables or meat; often ball-shaped
korma	currylike braised dish

kulcha	soft leavened Indian-style bread
kulfi	flavoured (often with pistachio) firm-textured ice cream
ladoo	sweet ball made with gram flour and semolina; also *ladu*
lassi	yoghurt-and-iced-water drink
masala dosa	large South Indian savoury crêpe (dosa) stuffed with spiced potatoes
mattar paneer	unfermented cheese and pea curry
methi	fenugreek
mishti doi	Bengali sweet; curd sweetened with jaggery
mithai	Indian sweets
momo	savoury Tibetan dumpling
naan	tandoor-cooked flat bread
namak	salt
namkin	savoury nibbles
pakora	bite-sized vegetable pieces in batter
palak paneer	unfermented cheese chunks in a puréed spinach gravy
paneer	soft, unfermented cheese made from milk curd
pani	water
pappadam	thin, crispy lentil or chickpea-flour circle-shaped wafer; also *pappad*
paratha	flaky flatbread (thicker than chapati); often stuffed
phulka	a chapati that puffs up on an open flame
pilau	rice cooked in spiced stock; also *pulau*, *pilao* or *pilaf*
pudina	mint
puri	flat savoury dough that puffs up when deep-fried; also *poori*
raita	mildly spiced yoghurt, often containing shredded cucumber or diced pineapple
rasam	dhal-based broth flavoured with tamarind
rasgulla	cream-cheese balls flavoured with rose-water
rogan josh	rich, spicy lamb curry
saag	leafy greens
sabzi	vegetables
sambar	South Indian soupy lentil dish with cubed vegetables
samosa	deep-fried pastry triangles filled with spiced vegetables
sonf	aniseed; used as a digestive and mouth-freshener; also *saunf*
tandoor	clay oven
tawa	flat hotplate/iron griddle
thali	all-you-can-eat meal; stainless steel (sometimes silver) compartmentalised plate
thukpa	Tibetan noodle soup
tiffin	snack; also refers to meal container often made of stainless steel
tikka	spiced, often marinated, chunks of chicken, paneer etc
toddy	alcoholic drink, tapped from palm trees
tsampa	Tibetan staple of roast-barley flour
upma	*rava* (semolina) cooked with onions, spices, chilli peppers and coconut
uttapam	thick savoury South Indian rice pancake with finely chopped onions, green chillies, coriander and coconut
vada	South Indian doughnut-shaped deep-fried lentil savoury
vindaloo	Goan dish; fiery curry in a marinade of vinegar and garlic
wazwan	traditional Kashmiri banquet

The Great Indian Bazaar

India's bazaars and emporiums sell a staggering range of goodies: from woodwork to silks, chunky tribal jewellery to finely embroidered shawls, sparkling gemstones to rustic village handicrafts. The array of arts and handicrafts is vast, with every region – sometimes every village – having its own traditions, some of them ancient. Get ready to encounter – and bring home – some spectacular items. India's shopping opportunities are as inspiring and multifarious as the country itself.

Be cautious when buying items that include international delivery, and avoid being led to shops by smooth-talking touts, but don't worry about too much else – except your luggage space!

Bronze Figures, Pottery, Stone Carving & Terracotta

In southern India and parts of the Himalaya, small images of deities are created by the age-old lost-wax process. A wax figure is made, a mould is formed around it, and the wax is melted, poured out and replaced with molten metal; the mould is then broken open to reveal the figure inside. Figures of Shiva as dancing Nataraja are the most popular, but you can also find images of Buddha and numerous deities from the Hindu pantheon.

The West Bengalese also employ the lost-wax process to make Dokra tribal bell sculptures, while in Chhattisgarh's Bastar region, the Ghadwa Tribe has an interesting twist on the lost-wax process: a fine wax thread covers the metal mould, leaving a lattice-like design on the final product.

In Buddhist areas, you'll find striking bronze statues of Buddha and the Tantric deities, finished off with finely polished and painted faces.

In Mamallapuram (Mahabalipuram) in Tamil Nadu, craftsmen using local granite and soapstone have revived the ancient artistry of the Pallava sculptors; souvenirs range from tiny stone elephants to enormous deity statues weighing half a tonne. Tamil Nadu is also known for bronzeware from Thanjavur and Trichy (Tiruchirappalli).

A number of places produce attractive terracotta items, ranging from vases and decorative flowerpots to images of deities, and children's toys. At temples across India you can buy small clay or plaster effigies of Hindu deities.

Carpets, Carpets, Carpets!

Carpet-making is a living craft in India, with workshops throughout the country producing fine wool and silkwork. The finest carpets are produced in Kashmir, Ladakh, Himachal Pradesh, Sikkim and West Bengal. Carpet-making is also a major revenue earner for Tibetan refugees; most refugee settlements have cooperative carpet workshops. You can also find reproductions of tribal Turkmen and Afghan designs in some states. Antique carpets usually aren't antique – unless you buy from an internationally reputable dealer; stick to 'new' carpets.

The price of a carpet is determined by the number and the size of the hand-tied knots, the range of dyes and colours, the intricacy of the design and the material. Silk carpets cost more and look more luxurious, but wool carpets usually last longer. Expect to pay upwards of US$250 for a good quality 90cm by 1.5m (or 90cm by 1.8m, depending on the region) wool carpet, and around US$2000 for a similar-sized carpet in silk. Tibetan carpets are cheaper, reflecting the relative simplicity of the designs; many refugee cooperatives sell the same size for around US$100.

Some people buy carpets thinking that they can be sold for a profit back home, but unless you really know your carpets, you're better off just buying a carpet because you love it. Many places can ship carpets home for a fee – although it may be safest to send things independently to avoid scams (follow your instincts) – or you can carry them in the plane's hold (allow 5kg to 10kg of your baggage allowance for a 90cm by 1.5m carpet).

You may come across coarsely woven woollen *numdas* (or *namdas*), which are much cheaper than knotted carpets. Various regions manufacture flat-weave *dhurries* (kilim-like cotton rugs) and striking *gabbas* (rugs with appliqué), made from chain-stitched wool or silk.

Children have been employed as carpet weavers in the subcontinent for centuries. The carpets produced by Tibetan refugee cooperatives are almost always made by adults; government emporiums and charitable cooperatives are usually the best places to buy.

BIDRI

Bidri, a method of damascening where silver wire is inlaid in gunmetal (a zinc alloy) and rubbed with soil from Bidar, Karnataka, is used to make jewellery, boxes and ornaments.

Jewellery

Virtually every town in India has at least one bangle shop selling an extraordinary variety, ranging from colourful plastic and glass to brass and silver.

Heavy folk-art silver jewellery can be bought in various parts of the country, with tourist centres often selling silver jewellery pitched at foreign tastes. Chunky Tibetan jewellery made from silver (or white metal) and semiprecious stones is sold all over India. Many pieces feature Buddhist motifs and text in Tibetan script, including the famous mantra *Om Mani Padme Hum* (Hail to the Jewel in the Lotus). Some of the pieces are genuine antiques, but there's a huge industry in India, Nepal and China making artificially aged souvenirs. For creative types, loose beads of agate,

THE ART OF HAGGLING

Government emporiums, fair-trade cooperatives, department stores and modern shopping centres almost always charge fixed prices. Anywhere else you need to bargain. Shopkeepers in tourist hubs are accustomed to travellers who have lots of money and little time to spend it, so you can often expect to be charged double or triple the going rate. Souvenir shops are generally the most notorious.

The first 'rule' to haggling is to never show too much interest in the item you've got your heart set upon. Secondly, resist purchasing the first thing that takes your fancy. Wander around several shops and price items, but don't make it too obvious: if you return to the first shop, the vendor will know it's because they are the cheapest (resulting in less haggling leeway).

Decide how much you would be happy paying, and then express a casual interest in buying. If you have absolutely no idea of the going rate, a common approach is to start by slashing the price by half. The vendor will, most likely, look utterly aghast, but you can now work up and down respectively in small increments until you reach a mutually agreeable price. You'll find that many shopkeepers lower their so-called 'final price' if you head out of the store saying you'll 'think about it'.

Haggling is a way of life in India and is usually taken in good spirit. It should never turn ugly. Always keep in mind how much a rupee is worth in your home currency, and how much you'd pay for the item back home, to put things in perspective. If a vendor seems to be charging an unreasonably high price, simply look elsewhere.

turquoise, carnelian and silver are widely available. Buddhist meditation beaded strings made of gems or wood also make good souvenirs.

Pearls are produced by most Indian seaside states, but they're a particular speciality of Hyderabad. You'll find them at most state emporiums across the country. Prices vary depending on the colour and shape: you pay more for pure white pearls or rare colours like black, and perfectly round pearls are generally more expensive than misshapen or elongated pearls. A single strand of seeded pearls can cost as little as ₹500, but better-quality pearls start at around ₹1000.

Throughout India you can find finely crafted gold and silver rings, anklets, earrings, toe rings, necklaces and bangles, and pieces can often be crafted to order.

Leatherwork

As cows are sacred in India, leatherwork is made from buffalo, camel, goat or some other animal skin. Kanpur in Uttar Pradesh is the country's major leatherwork centre.

Most large cities offer a smart range of modern leather footwear at very reasonable prices, some stitched with zillions of sparkly sequins – marvellous partywear!

The states of Punjab and Rajasthan (especially Jaipur) are famed for *jootis* (traditional, often pointy-toed slip-on shoes), which can also be found in some South Indian markets. *Chappals*, wonderful (often curly-toed) leather sandals, are sold throughout India but are particularly good in the cities of Kolhapur, Pune and Matheran.

In Bikaner in Rajasthan, artisans decorate camel hide with gold to produce beautiful mirror frames, boxes and bottles, while in Indore in Madhya Pradesh, craftspeople stretch leather over wire-and-cloth frameworks to make cute toy animals.

Metal & Marble Masterpieces

You'll find copper and brassware throughout India. Candleholders, trays, bowls, tankards and ashtrays are particularly popular buys.

Many Tibetan religious objects are created by inlaying silver in copper; prayer wheels, ceremonial horns and traditional document cases are all inexpensive buys. Resist the urge to buy *kangling* (Tibetan horns) and *kapali* (ceremonial bowls) made from inlaid human leg bones and skulls – they are illegal!

In all Indian towns you can find *kadhai* (Indian woks, also known as *balti*) and other cookware for incredibly low prices. Beaten-brass pots are particularly attractive, while steel storage vessels, copper-bottomed cooking pans and steel thali trays are also popular souvenirs. Be sure to have your name engraved on them (free of charge)!

The people of Bastar in Chhattisgarh use an iron-smelting technique, similar to the one discovered 35,000 years ago, to create abstract sculptures of spindly animal and human figures. These are often also made into functional items such as lamp stands and coat racks.

Crafts aren't necessarily confined to their region of origin; artists migrate and are sometimes influenced by regional aesthetics, resulting in some interesting stylistic combinations.

Musical Instruments

Quality Indian musical instruments are mostly available in the larger cities; prices vary according to the quality and sound of the instrument.

Decent tabla sets (pair of drums) with a wooden tabla (tuned treble drum) and metal *doogri* (bass tone drum) cost upwards of ₹5000. Cheaper sets are generally heavier and often sound inferior.

Sitars range anywhere from ₹5000 to ₹20,000 (possibly even more). The sound of each sitar will vary with the wood used and the shape of the gourd, so try a few. Note that some cheaper sitars can warp in colder or hotter climates. On any sitar, make sure the strings ring clearly and check the gourd carefully for damage. Spare string sets, sitar plectrums and a screw-in 'amplifier' gourd are sensible additions.

Saturday Night Market (p145), Arpora, Goa

Other popular instruments include the *shehnai* (Indian flute), the sarod (like an Indian lute), the harmonium and the *esraj* (similar to an upright violin). Conventional violins are great value – prices start at ₹3500, while Kolkata (Calcutta) is known for its quality acoustic guitars (from ₹2500).

Exquisite Paintings

India is known for its rich painting history. Reproductions of Indian miniature paintings are widely available, but the quality varies: the cheaper ones have less detail and are made with inferior materials.

In regions such as Kerala and Tamil Nadu, you'll come across miniature paintings on leaf skeletons that portray domestic life, rural scenes and deities. In Andhra Pradesh, *cheriyal* paintings, in bright, primary colours, were originally made as scrolls for travelling storytellers.

The artists' community of Raghurajpur near Puri (Odisha) preserves the age-old art of *patachitra* painting. Cotton or *tassar* (silk cloth) is covered with a mixture of gum and chalk; it's then polished, and images of deities and scenes from Hindu legends are painted on with exceedingly fine brushes. Odisha also produces *chitra pothi*, where images are etched onto dried palm-leaf sections with a fine stylus. Some South Indian bazaars sell these.

Bihar's unique folk art is Mithila (or Madhubani) painting, an ancient art form preserved by the women of Madhubani. These captivating paintings are most easily found in Patna but are also sold in big city emporiums around the country.

Exquisite *thangkas* (rectangular Tibetan paintings on cloth) of Tantric Buddhist deities and ceremonial mandalas are sold in Tibetan Buddhist areas. Some perfectly reproduce the glory of the murals in India's medieval gompas (Tibetan Buddhist monasteries); others are simpler. Prices vary, but bank on at least ₹4000 for a decent quality *thangka* of A3 size,

KALAMKARI

In Andhra Pradesh, intricately drawn, graphic cloth paintings called *kalamkari* depict deities and historic events.

PUTTING YOUR MONEY WHERE IT COUNTS

Overall, a comparatively small proportion of the money brought to India by tourism reaches people in rural areas. Travellers can make a greater contribution by shopping at community cooperatives, set up to protect and promote traditional cottage industries and provide education, training and a sustainable livelihood at the grassroots level. Many of these projects focus on refugees, low-caste women, tribal people and others living on society's fringes.

The quality of products sold at cooperatives is high and the prices are usually fixed, which means you won't have to haggle. A share of the sales money is channelled directly into social projects such as schools, healthcare, training and other advocacy programs for socially disadvantaged groups. Shopping at the national network of Khadi and Village Industries Commission emporiums will also contribute to rural communities.

Wherever you travel, keep your eyes peeled for fair-trade cooperatives.

and a lot more for large, intricate *thangkas*. The selling of antique *thangkas* is illegal, and you would be unlikely to find the real thing anyway.

In big cities like Mumbai (Bombay) and Bengaluru (Bangalore), look out for shops and galleries selling contemporary paintings by local artists.

Sumptuous Shawls, Silk & Saris

Indian shawls are famously warm and lightweight – they're often better than the best down jackets. It's worth buying one to use as a blanket on cold night journeys. Shawls are made from all sorts of wool, and many are embroidered with intricate designs.

The undisputed capital of the Indian shawl is the Kullu Valley in Himachal Pradesh, with dozens of women's cooperatives producing very fine woollen pieces that are sold across the country.

Be aware that it's illegal to buy shahtoosh shawls, as rare Tibetan antelopes are slaughtered to provide the wool. If you come across anyone selling these shawls, inform local authorities.

Ladakh and Kashmir are major centres for *pashmina* (wool shawl) production (sold throughout India) – you'll pay at least ₹6000 for the authentic article – however, be aware that many so-called *pashminas* are actually made from a mixture of yarns. Gujarat's Kutch region produces some particularly distinctive woollen shawls, patterned with subtle embroidery and mirrorwork.

Saris are a very popular souvenir, especially given that they can be easily adapted to other purposes (from cushion covers to skirts). Real silk saris are the most expensive, and the silk usually needs to be washed before it becomes soft. The 'silk capital' of India is Kanchipuram in Tamil Nadu, but you can also find fine silk saris (and cheaper scarves) in other centres including Mysore. You'll pay upwards of ₹3000 for a quality embroidered silk sari.

Patan in Gujarat is the centre for the ancient and laborious craft of *patola*-making. Every thread in these fine silk saris is individually hand-dyed before weaving, and patterned borders are woven with real gold. Slightly less involved versions are produced in Rajkot.

Aurangabad, in Maharashtra, is the traditional centre for the production of *himroo* shawls, sheets and saris, made from a blend of cotton, silk and silver thread. Silk and gold-thread saris produced at Paithan (near Aurangabad) are some of India's finest – prices range from around ₹7000 to a mind-blowing ₹300,000. Other regions famous for sari production include Madhya Pradesh for its cotton Maheshwari (from Maheshwar) and silk Chanderi saris (from Chanderi), and West Bengal for its *baluchari* saris from Bishnupur, which employ a traditional form of weaving with untwisted silk thread.

Terrific Textiles

Textile production is India's major industry and around 40% takes place at the village level, where it's known as *khadi* (homespun cloth) – hence the government-backed *khadi* emporiums around the country. These inexpensive superstores sell all sorts of items made from *khadi*, including the popular Nehru jackets and kurta pyjamas (long shirt and loose-fitting trousers), with sales benefiting rural communities.

You'll find a truly amazing variety of weaving and embroidery techniques around India. In tourist centres such as Goa, textiles are stitched into popular items such as shoulder bags, wall hangings, cushion covers, bedspreads, clothes and much more.

Appliqué is an ancient art in India, with most states producing their own version, often featuring abstract or anthropomorphic patterns. The traditional lampshades and *pandals* (tents) used in weddings and festivals are usually produced using the same technique.

In Adivasi (tribal) areas of Gujarat and Rajasthan, small pieces of mirrored glass are embroidered onto fabric, creating eye-catching bags, cushion covers and wall hangings. Gujarat has a diversity of textile traditions: Jamnagar is famous for its vibrant *bandhani* (tie-dye work) used for saris and scarves, among other things, and Vadodara is renowned for block-printed fabrics, used for bedspreads and clothing. These glorious creations are sold in shops right around the country, so keep your eyes peeled.

Block-printed and woven textiles are sold by fabric shops all over India: each region has its own speciality. The India-wide retail chain-store Fabindia (www.fabindia.com) is striving to preserve traditional patterns and fabrics, transforming them into home-decor items and Indian- and Western-style fashions.

Traditional Indian Textiles, by John Gillow and Nicholas Barnard, explores India's beautiful regional textiles and includes sections on tie-dye, weaving, beadwork, brocades and even camel girths.

Odisha has a reputation for bright appliqué and *ikat* (a Southeast Asian technique where thread is tie-dyed before weaving). The town of Pipli, between Bhubaneswar and Puri, produces striking appliqué work. The techniques used to create *kalamkari* cloth paintings in Andhra Pradesh (a centre for this ancient art is Sri Kalahasti) and Gujarat are also used to make lovely wall hangings and lampshades.

Lucknow, in Uttar Pradesh, is noted for hand-woven embroidered *chikan* cloth, which has intricate floral motifs. Punjab is famous for the attractively folksy *phulkari* embroidery (flowerwork with stitches in diagonal, vertical and horizontal directions), while women in West Bengal use chain stitches to make complex figurative designs called *kantha*. A similar technique is used to make *gabbas*, women's kurtas (long shirts) and men's wedding jackets in Kashmir.

Batik can be found throughout India. It's often used for saris and *salwar kameez* (traditional dresslike tunic and trouser combination for

GANDHI'S CLOTH

More than 80 years ago Mahatma Gandhi urged Indians to support the freedom movement by ditching their foreign-made clothing and turning to *khadi* – homespun cloth. *Khadi* became a symbol of Indian independence, and the fabric is still closely associated with politics. The government-run, nonprofit group Khadi and Village Industries Commission (www.kvic.org.in) serves to promote *khadi*, which is usually cotton, but can also be silk or wool.

Khadi outlets are simple, no nonsense places where you can pick up genuine Indian clothing such as kurta pyjamas, headscarves, saris and, at some branches, assorted handicrafts – you'll find them all over India. Prices are reasonable and are often discounted in the period around Gandhi's birthday (2 October). A number of outlets also have a tailoring service.

Flea market in Anjuna (p149), Goa

women). City boutiques flaunt trendy *salwar kameez* in a staggering array of fabrics and styles. Pick up haute couture by Indian designers, as well as moderately priced Western fashions, in Mumbai, Bengaluru and Hyderabad.

Beautiful Woodcarving

Woodcarving is an ancient art form throughout India. In Kashmir, walnut wood is used to make finely carved wooden screens, tables, jewellery boxes and trays, inspired by the decorative trim of houseboats. Kashmiri handicrafts are sold throughout India.

Sandalwood carvings of Hindu deities are one of Karnataka's specialities, but you'll pay a king's ransom for the real thing – a 10cm-high Ganesh costs around ₹3000 in sandalwood, compared to roughly ₹300 in kadamb wood. However, the sandalwood will release fragrance for years.

Buddhist woodcarvings are a speciality of Tibetan refugee areas. You'll find wall plaques of the eight lucky signs, dragons and *chaam* masks, used for ritual dances. Most of the masks are cheap reproductions, but you can sometimes find genuine *chaam* masks made from lightweight whitewood or papier mâché from ₹3000.

Other Great Finds

It's little surprise that Indian spices are snapped up by tourists. Virtually all towns have shops and bazaars selling locally made spices at great prices. Karnataka, Kerala and Tamil Nadu produce most of the spices that go into *garam masala* (the 'hot mix' used to flavour Indian dishes), while the Northeast States and Sikkim are known for black cardamom and cinnamon bark. Note that some countries, such as Australia, have stringent rules regarding the import of animal and plant products. Check with your country's embassy for details.

Shops selling attar (essential oil, mostly made from flowers) can be found around the country. Mysore in Karnataka is famous for its sandalwood oil, while Mumbai is a major centre for the trade of traditional fragrances, including valuable *oud,* made from a rare mould that grows on the bark of the agarwood tree. In Tamil Nadu, Ooty (Udhagamandalam) and Kodaikanal produce aromatic and medicinal oils from herbs, flowers and eucalyptus.

Indian incense is exported worldwide, with Bengaluru and Mysore, both in Karnataka, being major producers. Incense from Auroville in Tamil Nadu is also well regarded.

Meanwhile, a speciality of Goa is feni (liquor distilled from coconut milk or cashews) – it's a head-spinning spirit that often comes in decorative bottles.

Quality Indian tea can be found in centres such as Munnar in Kerala. There are also commendable tea retailers in major South Indian cities.

Artisans in Jammu and Kashmir have been producing lacquered papier mâché for centuries, and papier-mâché bowls, boxes, letter holders, coasters, trays and Christmas decorations are now sold right across India.

Fine-quality handmade paper – often fashioned into cards, boxes and notebooks – is worth seeking out. Puducherry (Pondicherry) in Tamil Nadu and Mumbai are good places to start.

India has a phenomenal range of books at very competitive prices, including leather-bound titles. Asian Educational Services publishes old (from the 17th century) and out-of-stock titles in original typeface.

The Arts

Over the millennia India's many ethnic groups have spawned a rich artistic heritage, and today you'll experience art both lofty and humble around every corner: from intricately painted trucks on dusty roads to harmonic chanting from an ancient temple to wedding-season hands adorned with *mehndi* (henna). The wealth of creative expression is a highlight of travelling here, and today's artists fuse ancient and modern influences to create art, dance, literature and music that are as evocative as they are beautiful.

Dance

Indian Classical Dance by Leela Venkataraman and Avinash Pasricha is a lavishly illustrated book covering various Indian dance forms, including BharataNatyam, Odissi and Kathakali.

The ancient Indian art of dance is traditionally linked to mythology and classical literature. Dance can be divided into two main forms: classical and folk.

Classical dance is essentially based on well-defined traditional disciplines. Some classical dance styles:

- *Bharatanatyam*, which originated in Tamil Nadu, has been embraced throughout India.
- *Kathak* has Hindu and Islamic influences and was particularly popular with the Mughals. *Kathak* suffered a period of notoriety when it moved from the courts into houses where nautch (dancing) girls tantalised audiences with renditions of the Krishna-and-Radha love story. It was restored as a serious art form in the early 20th century.
- Kathakali, which has its roots in Kerala, is sometimes just referred to as 'dance' but is essentially a type of classical dance-drama.
- Kuchipudi is a 17th-century dance-drama that originated in the Andhra Pradesh village from which it takes its name. The story centres on the envious wife of Krishna.
- Odissi, from Odisha (Orissa), is thought to be India's oldest classical dance form. It was originally a temple art, and was later also performed at royal courts.

India's second major dance form, folk, is widespread and varied. It ranges from the high-spirited bhangra dance of Punjab to the theatrical dummy-horse dances of Karnataka and Tamil Nadu, and the graceful fishers' dance of Odisha.

Pioneers of modern dance forms in India include Uday Shankar (older brother of the late sitar master Ravi), who once partnered with Russian ballerina Anna Pavlova. The dance you'll most commonly see, though, is in films. Dance has featured in Indian movies since the dawn of 'talkies' and often combines traditional, folk, modern and contemporary choreography.

Music

Indian classical music traces its roots back to Vedic times, when religious poems chanted by priests were first collated in an anthology called the Rig-Veda. Over the millennia classical music has been shaped by many influences, and the legacy today is Carnatic (characteristic of South India) and Hindustani (the classical style of North India) music. With common origins, they share a number of features. Both use the raga (the melodic shape of the music) and *tala* (the rhythmic meter characterised by the number of beats); *tintal*, for example, has a *tala* of 16 beats. The audience follows the *tala* by clapping at the appropriate beat, which in *tintal* is at beats one, five and 13. There's no clap at the beat of nine; that's the *khali* (empty section), which is indicated by a wave of the hand. Both the raga and the *tala* are used as a basis for composition and improvisation.

Both Carnatic and Hindustani music are performed by small ensembles, generally comprising three to six musicians, and both have many instruments in common. There's no fixed pitch, but there are differences between the two styles. Hindustani has been more heavily influenced by Persian musical conventions (a result of Mughal rule); Carnatic music, as it developed in South India, cleaves more closely to theory. The most striking difference, at least for those unfamiliar with India's classical forms, is Carnatic's greater use of voice.

One of the best-known Indian instruments is the sitar (large stringed instrument), with which the soloist plays the raga. Other stringed instruments include the sarod (which is plucked) and the sarangi (which is played with a bow). Also popular is the tabla (twin drums), which provides the *tala*. The drone, which runs on two basic notes, is provided by the oboelike *shehnai* or the stringed *tampura* (also spelt tamboura). The hand-pumped keyboard harmonium is used as a secondary melody instrument for vocal music.

Indian regional folk music is widespread and varied. Wandering musicians, magicians, snake charmers and storytellers often use song to entertain their audiences; the storyteller usually sings the tales from the great epics.

You may possibly come across *qawwali* (Sufi devotional singing), performed in mosques or at musical concerts.

A completely different genre altogether, filmi (music from films) includes modern, slower-paced love serenades along with hyperactive dance songs.

Painting

Around 1500 years ago artists covered the walls and ceilings of the Ajanta caves, in Maharashtra, with scenes from the Buddha's past lives. The figures are endowed with an unusual freedom and grace, and contrast with the next major style that emerged from this part of India in the 11th century.

The Indo-Persian style – characterised by geometric design coupled with flowing form – developed from Islamic royal courts, although the depiction of the elongated eye is one convention that seems to have been

MEHNDI

Mehndi is the traditional art of painting a woman's hands (and sometimes feet) with intricate henna designs for auspicious ceremonies, such as marriage. If quality henna is used, the design, which is orange-brown, can last up to one month.

In touristy areas, *mehndi*-wallahs are adept at applying henna tattoo 'bands' on the arms, legs and lower back. If you get *mehndi* applied, allow at least a few hours for the design process and required drying time (during drying you can't use your hennaed hands).

It's always wise to request the artist do a 'test' spot on your arm before proceeding: nowadays some dyes contain chemicals that can cause allergies. (Avoid 'black henna', which is mixed with some chemicals that may be harmful.) If good-quality henna is used, you shouldn't feel any pain during or after the application.

Painting of Aurangzeb hunting lions (c 1670-80)

retained from indigenous sources. The Persian influence blossomed when artisans fled to India following the 1507 Uzbek attack on Herat (in present-day Afghanistan), and with trade and gift-swapping between the Persian city of Shiraz, an established centre for miniature production, and Indian provincial sultans.

The 1526 victory by Babur at the Battle of Panipat ushered in the era of the Mughals in India. Although Babur and his son Humayun were both patrons of the arts, it's Humayun's son Akbar who is generally credited with developing the characteristic Mughal style. This painting style, often in colourful miniature form, largely depicts court life, architecture, battle and hunting scenes, as well as detailed portraits. Akbar recruited artists from far and wide, and artistic endeavour first centred on the production of illustrated manuscripts (topics varied from history to mythology), but later broadened into portraiture and the glorification of everyday events. European painting styles influenced some artists, and this influence occasionally reveals itself in experiments with motifs and perspective.

Get arty with *Indian Art* by Roy C Craven, *Contemporary Indian Art: Other Realities* edited by Yashodhara Dalmia, and *Indian Miniature Painting* by Dr Daljeet and Professor PC Jain.

Akbar's son Jehangir also patronised painting, but he preferred portraiture, and his fascination with natural science resulted in a vibrant legacy of paintings of flowers and animals. Under Jehangir's son Shah Jahan, the Mughal style became less fluid and, although the bright colouring was eye-catching, the paintings lacked the vigour of before.

Various schools of miniature painting (small paintings crammed with detail) emerged in Rajasthan from around the 17th century. The subject matter ranged from royal processions to shikhar (hunting expeditions), with many artists influenced by Mughal styles.

Mural painting in particular flourished throughout the south from the 17th century, with temple art – drawing on multifarious historical and mythological themes – especially prolific. By the 19th century, painting in North India was notably influenced by Western styles (especially English watercolours), giving rise to what has been dubbed the Company School, which had its centre in Delhi.

In 21st-century India, paintings by modern and contemporary Indian artists have been selling at record numbers (and prices) around the world. One very successful online art auction house is the Mumbai-based Saffronart (www.saffronart.com).

Cinema

India's film industry was born in the late 19th century – the first major Indian-made motion picture, *Panorama of Calcutta,* was screened in 1899. India's first real feature film, *Raja Harishchandra,* was made during the silent era in 1913 and it's ultimately from this film that Indian cinema traces its vibrant lineage.

Today, India's film industry is the biggest in the world – twice as big as Hollywood. Mumbai (Bombay), the Hindi-language film capital, aka 'Bollywood', is the biggest producer, but India's other major film-producing cities – Chennai (Madras; Kollywood), Hyderabad (Tollywood) and Bengaluru (Bangalore; Sandalwood) – also have a huge output. A number of other centres produce films in their own regional vernaculars too. Big-budget films are often partly or entirely shot abroad, with some countries vigorously wooing Indian production companies because of the potential spin-off tourism revenue these films generate.

An average of 1000 feature films are produced annually in India. Apart from hundreds of millions of local Bolly-, Tolly- and Kollywood buffs, there are also millions of Non-Resident Indian (NRI) fans, who have played a significant role in catapulting Indian cinema onto the international stage.

Broadly speaking, there are two categories of Indian films. Most prominent is the mainstream 'masala' movie – named for its 'spice mix' of elements. Designed to have something for every member of the family, the films tend to have a mix of romance, action, slapstick humour and moral themes. Three hours and still running, these blockbusters are often tear-jerkers and are packed with dramatic twists interspersed with numerous song-and-dance performances. There's no explicit sex, or even kissing (although smooching is creeping into some Bollywood movies) in Indian films made for the local market; however, lack of nudity is often compensated for by heroines dressed in skimpy or body-hugging attire, and lack of overt eroticism is more than made up for with heaps of intense flirting and loaded innuendoes.

The second Indian film genre is art house, which adopts Indian 'reality' as its base. Generally speaking they are, or at least are supposed to be, socially and politically relevant. Usually made on infinitely smaller budgets than their commercial cousins, these films are the ones that win kudos at global film festivals and award ceremonies. The late Bengali director Satyajit Ray, most famous for his 1950s work, is the father of Indian art films.

FILM HISTORY

Encyclopedia of Indian Cinema by Ashish Rajadhyaksha and Paul Willemen chronicles India's dynamic cinematic history, spanning from 1897 to the 21st century.

Literature

India has a long tradition of Sanskrit literature, although works in the vernacular have contributed to a particularly rich legacy. In fact, it's claimed there are as many literary traditions as there are written languages.

Bengalis are traditionally credited with producing some of India's most celebrated literature, a movement often referred to as the Indian or Bengal Renaissance, which flourished from the 19th century with works by Bankim Chandra Chatterjee. But the man who to this day is mostly credited with first propelling India's cultural richness onto the world stage is the Bengali Rabindranath Tagore.

One of the earliest Indian authors writing in English to receive an international audience, in the 1930s, was RK Narayan, whose deceptively simple writing about small-town life is subtly hilarious. Keralan Kamala Das (aka Kamala Suraiyya) wrote poetry and memoir in English; her frank approach to love and sexuality, especially in the 1960s and '70s, broke ground for women writers.

The prolific writer and artist Rabindranath Tagore won the Nobel Prize in Literature in 1913 for *Gitanjali*. For a taste of Tagore's work, read *Selected Short Stories*.

India has an ever-growing list of internationally acclaimed contemporary authors. Particularly prominent writers include Vikram Seth, best known for his epic novel *A Suitable Boy,* and Amitav Ghosh, who has won a number of accolades; his *Sea of Poppies* was shortlisted for the 2008 Man Booker Prize. Indeed, recent years have seen a number of Indian-born authors win the prestigious Man Booker Prize, the most recent being Aravind Adiga, who won in 2008 for his debut novel, *The White Tiger*. The prize went to Kiran Desai in 2006 for *The Inheritance of Loss;* Kiran Desai is the daughter of the award-winning Indian novelist Anita Desai, who has thrice been a Booker Prize nominee. In 1997 Arundhati Roy won the Booker Prize for her novel, *The God of Small Things,* while Salman Rushdie took this coveted award in 1981 for *Midnight's Children*.

Architectural Splendour

From looming temple gateways adorned with a rainbow of delicately carved deities to whitewashed cube-like village houses, South India has a rich architectural heritage. Traditional buildings, such as temples, often have a superb sense of placement within the local environment, whether perched on a boulder-strewn hill or standing by a large artificial reservoir. British bungalows with corrugated iron roofs and wide verandahs are a feature of many hill stations, but more memorable are the attempts to meld European and Indian architecture, such as the breathtaking Maharaja's Palace in Mysore.

Sacred Creations

South India has a remarkable assortment of historic and contemporary sacred architecture that draws inspiration from a variety of religious denominations. Although few of the wooden and occasionally brick temples built in early times have weathered the vagaries of nature, by the advent of the Guptas (4th to 6th centuries AD), sacred structures of a new type – better engineered to withstand the elements – were being constructed, and these largely set the standard for temples for several hundred years.

Masterpieces of Traditional Indian Architecture by Satish Grover and *The History of Architecture in India* by Christopher Tadgell proffer interesting insights into temple architecture.

For Hindus, the square is a perfect shape, and complex rules govern the location, design and building of each temple, based on numerology, astrology, astronomy and religious principles. Essentially, a temple represents a map of the universe. At the centre is an unadorned space, the *garbhagriha* (inner sanctum), which is symbolic of the 'womb-cave' from which the universe is believed to have emerged. This provides a residence for the deity to which the temple is dedicated.

Above a Hindu temple's shrine rises a tower superstructure known as a *vimana* in South India, and a *sikhara* in North India. The *sikhara* is curvilinear and topped with a grooved disk, on which sits a pot-shaped finial, while the *vimana* is stepped, with the grooved disk being replaced by a solid dome. Some temples have a *mandapa* (forechamber) connected to the sanctum by vestibules. The *mandapa* may also contain *vimanas* or *sikharas*.

A *gopuram* is a soaring pyramidal gateway tower of a Dravidian temple. The towering *gopurams* of various South Indian temple complexes, such as the nine-storey *gopurams* of Madurai's Meenakshi Amman Temple, took ornamentation and monumentalism to new levels.

Commonly used for ritual bathing and religious ceremonies, as well as adding aesthetic appeal, temple tanks have long been a focal point of temple activity. These often-vast, angular, engineered reservoirs of water, sometimes fed by rain, sometimes fed – via a complicated drainage system – by rivers, serve both sacred and secular purposes. The waters of some temple tanks are believed to have healing properties, while others are said to have the power to wash away sins. Devotees (as well as travellers) may be required to wash their feet in a temple tank before entering a place of worship.

Gopuram sculptures, Meenakshi Amman Temple (p384), Madurai

From the outside, Jain temples can resemble Hindu ones, but inside they're often a riot of sculptural ornamentation, the very opposite of ascetic austerity.

Buddhist shrines have their own unique features. Stupas, composed of a solid hemisphere topped by a spire, characterise Buddhist places of worship and essentially evolved from burial mounds. They served as repositories for relics of the Buddha and, later, other venerated souls. A further innovation is the addition of a *chaitya* (assembly hall) leading up to the stupa itself. Bodhgaya, where Siddhartha Gautama attained enlightenment and became the Buddha, has a collection of particularly notable Buddhist monasteries and temples.

In 262 BC the Mauryan emperor Ashoka embraced Buddhism, and as a penance built the Great Stupa at Sanchi, in the central Indian state of Madhya Pradesh. It is among the oldest surviving Buddhist structures in the subcontinent. Buddhist architecture found in the south includes Amaravathi in Andhra Pradesh, the Buddhist caves of Ajanta and the Buddha Statue in Hyderabad.

Discover more about India's diverse temple architecture (in addition to other temple-related information) at Temple Net (www.templenet.com).

India also has a rich collection of Islamic sacred sites, as its Muslim rulers contributed their own architectural conventions, including arched cloisters and domes. The Mughals uniquely melded Persian, Indian and provincial styles. Emperor Shah Jahan was responsible for some of India's most spectacular architectural creations, most notably the milky white Taj Mahal.

Islamic art eschews any hint of idolatry or portrayal of God, and it has evolved a vibrant heritage of calligraphic and decorative designs. In terms of mosque architecture, the basic design elements are similar worldwide. A large hall is dedicated to communal prayer and within the hall is a mihrab (niche) indicating the direction of Mecca. The faithful are called to prayer from minarets, placed at cardinal points. Islamic structures in the south include the Charminar in Hyderabad; the Qutb Shahi and Paigah Tombs in Hyderabad; and the Haji Ali Mosque in Mumbai.

The Sikh faith was founded by Guru Nanak, the first of 10 gurus, in the 15th century. Sikh temples, called gurdwaras, can usually be identified by a *nishan sahib* (a flagpole flying a triangular flag with the Sikh insignia). Amritsar's stunning Golden Temple is Sikhism's holiest shrine.

Architecture and Art of Southern India, by George Michell, provides details on the Vijayanagar empire and its successors, encompassing a period of some 400 years.

Forts & Palaces

A typical South Indian fort is situated on a hill or rocky outcrop, ringed by moated battlements. It usually has a town nestled at its base, which would have developed after the fortifications were built. Gingee (Senji) in Tamil Nadu is a particularly good example. Vellore Fort, also in Tamil Nadu, is one of India's best-known moated forts, while Bidar and Bijapur in Karnataka are home to great metropolitan forts.

Daulatabad in Maharashtra is another magnificent structure, with 5km of walls surrounding a hilltop fortress. The fortress is reached by passageways filled with ingenious defences, including spike-studded doors and false tunnels, which in times of war led either to a pit of boiling oil or to a crocodile-filled moat!

Few old palaces remain in South India, as conquerors often targeted these for destruction. The remains of the royal complex at Vijayanagar, near Hampi, indicate that local engineers weren't averse to using the sound structural techniques and fashions (such as domes and arches) of their Muslim adversaries, the Bahmanis. Travancore's palace of the maharajas at Padmanabhapuram, which dates from the 16th century, has private apartments for the king, a zenana (women's quarters), rooms dedicated to public audiences, an armoury, a dance hall and temples. Meanwhile, the Indo-Saracenic Maharaja's Palace in Mysore is the best known and most opulent in the south, its interior a kaleidoscope of stained glass, mirrors and mosaic floors.

Indian Wildlife

The wildlife of South India comprises a fascinating melting pot of animals from Europe, Asia and ancient Gondwanaland all swirled together in a mix of habitats ranging from steamy mangrove forests and jungles to expansive plains and flower-filled meadows.

India's national animal is the tiger, its national bird is the peacock and its national flower is the lotus. The national emblem of India is a column topped by three Asiatic lions.

India is celebrated for its big, bold, eminent species – tigers, elephants, rhinos, leopards, bears and monkeys. But there is much, much more, including a mesmerising collection of colourful birds and some of the nation's most endangered and intriguing wildlife, such as the Gangetic dolphin and Asiatic lion.

Signature Species

If you had to pick India's most charismatic species, the list would inevitably include tigers, elephants and rhinos, all of which are scarce and in need of stringent protection.

It's fortunate that Asian elephants – a thoroughly different species to the larger African elephant – are revered in Hindu custom and were able to be domesticated and put to work, otherwise they may well have been hunted into extinction long ago, as they were in neighbouring China. It's true that many Indian elephants survive in the wild; however, because elephants migrate long distances in search of food, these 3000kg animals require huge parks and run into predictable conflict when herds of them attempt to follow ancestral paths that are now occupied by villages and farms. One of the best parks for elephant viewing in South India is Nagarhole National Park in Karnataka.

There are far fewer one-horned rhinos left and two-thirds (just shy of 2000) of the world's total population can be found in Kaziranga National Park (in Assam), where they serenely wander the park's lush alluvial grasslands at the base of the Himalayas. They may look sedate but rhinos are unpredictably dangerous; they're built like battering rams, covered in plates of armour-like skin and use their sharp teeth to tear off chunks of flesh when they attack – let's just say that it's safest to watch rhinos from the back of an elephant.

India harbours some of the richest biodiversity in the world. There are 397 species of mammals, 1250 birds, 460 reptiles, 240 amphibians and 2546 fish – among the highest species count for any country.

Cool for Cats

India is justifiably famous for its tigers, and just admit it – you secretly hope to see one. But India is also home to 14 other species of cats, so don't miss out on any opportunity to see one of the other gorgeous felines.

It could be said that the global effort to protect tigers all started in India, and many experts agree that India's sizeable population of tigers is the species' last great stronghold. Unfortunately, despite a massive and well-funded conservation effort, the black market in tigers remains an irresistible temptation for both wildlife-poaching gangs and impoverished villagers, so tiger numbers continue to fall at a precipitous rate, even in supposedly secure sanctuaries.

Protection efforts have been successfully made on behalf of the Asiatic lion, a close relative of the more familiar African lion.

Hoofed & Handed

By far, the most abundant forms of wildlife you'll see in India are deer (nine species), antelope (six species), goats and sheep (10 species), and primates (15 species). In the open grasslands of many parks look for the stocky nilgai (bluebull), India's largest antelope, or elegantly horned blackbucks.

India's primates range from the extremely rare hoolock gibbon and golden langur of the northeast, to species that are so common as to be a pest – most notably the stocky and aggressive rhesus macaque and the elegant grey (Hanuman) langur. In the south, the pesky monkeys that loiter around temples and tourist sites are bonnet macaques.

Books

Mammals of India by Vivek Menon

A Guide to the Birds of India and Pocket Guide to the Birds of the Indian Subcontinent by Richard Grimmett, Carol Inskipp and Tim Inskipp

Treasures of Indian Wildlife by AS Kothari and BF Chhapgar

Endangered Species

Despite having amazing biodiversity, India faces a growing challenge from its exploding human population. Wildlife is severely threatened by poaching and habitat loss. A recent count suggested India had over 500 threatened species, including 247 species of plants, 53 species of mammals, 78 species of birds, 22 species of reptiles, 68 species of amphibians, 35 species of fish and 22 species of invertebrates. In 2012 the International Union for Conservation of Nature released a list of the 100 most threatened species in the world. It included four Indian species: a spider, a turtle and two birds, the great Indian bustard and white-bellied heron.

Although much touted as a success story, even the massively resourced Project Tiger faces an uphill battle every day. And every good news story seems to be followed by yet another story involving poor villagers and corrupt officials. All of India's wild cats, from leopards to snow leopards, panthers and jungle cats, are facing extinction from habitat loss and poaching for the lucrative trade in skins and body parts for Chinese medicine (a whole tiger carcass can fetch upwards of UK£32,000). Government estimates suggest that India is losing 1% of its tigers every year to poachers.

Even highly protected rhinos are poached for the medicine trade – rhino horn is highly valued as an aphrodisiac in China and as a material for making handles for daggers in the Gulf. Elephants are regularly poached for ivory, and 320 elephants were poached from 2000 to 2008 – we implore you not to support this trade by buying ivory souvenirs. Various species of deer are threatened by hunting for food and trophies, and the chiru, or Tibetan antelope, is nearly extinct because its hair is woven into wool for expensive shahtoosh shawls.

India has 238 species of snake, of which about 50 are poisonous. Of the various species of cobra, the king cobra is the world's largest venomous snake, attaining a length of 5m!

PROJECT TIGER

When naturalist Jim Corbett first raised the alarm in the 1930s, no one believed that tigers would ever be threatened. At the time it was believed there were 40,000 tigers in India, although no one had ever conducted a census. Then came Independence, which put guns into the hands of villagers who pushed into formerly off-limits hunting reserves to hunt for highly profitable tiger skins. By the time an official census was conducted in 1972, there were only 1800 tigers left and international outcry prompted Indira Gandhi to make the tiger the national symbol of India and set up **Project Tiger** (http://projecttiger.nic.in). The project has since established 39 tiger reserves totalling over 32,000 sq km that not only protect this top predator but all animals that live in the same habitats. After an initial round of successes (perhaps owing to counting anomalies), tiger numbers have continuously plummeted from 3600 in 2002 to around 1700 due to relentless poaching. And although numbers were supposedly up in the 2011 census, and though countless rupees and high-tech equipment continue to be devoted to the effort, the slide towards extinction in the wild appears inevitable as available tiger habitat continues to shrink.

The Bengal tiger – the national animal of India

India's bear species remain under threat although sloth bears will experience a reprieve with the official demise of the dancing bear industry. In the rivers, India's famous freshwater dolphins are in dire straits from pollution, habitat alteration and direct human competition. The sea-turtle populations that nest on the Odisha (Orissa) coast also face environmental challenges.

Threatened primate species clinging on in rainforests in the south include lion-tailed macaques, glossy black Nilgiri langurs and slender loris, an adept insect-catcher with huge eyes for nocturnal hunting.

Internet Resources

Raising awareness about wildlife, conservation and environment at www.sanctuaryasia.com

The Wildlife Trust of India news at www.wti.org.in

Top birdwatching information and photo galleries at www.birding.in

Birds

With well over 1000 species of birds, India is a birdwatcher's dream. Many birds are thinly spread over this vast country, but wherever critical habitat has been preserved in the midst of dense human activity you might see phenomenal numbers of birds in one location. Winter can be a particularly good time, as wetlands throughout the country host northern migrants arriving to kick back in the lush subtropical warmth of the Indian peninsula.

Plants

India was once almost entirely covered in forest; now its total forest cover is estimated at around 20%. Despite widespread clearing of native habitats, the country still boasts 49,219 plant species, of which some 5200 are endemic. Species on the southern peninsula largely show Malaysian ancestry.

Outside of mountain forests found in the Himalaya, nearly all the lowland forests of India are subtypes of tropical forest, with native sal forests forming the mainstay of the timber industry. Some of these tropical for-

UNBEARABLY GOOD NEWS

In 2012 the Indian government announced that the dancing bear industry was extinct. After several centuries, a cultural tradition has finally died out with few lamenting its demise. In fact the practice was bought out when the few remaining bear-handling communities, known as Kalandars, were redirected into more profitable enterprises. Although the dancing bear entertainment was outlawed in 1972, it has taken decades for the tradition to end.

ests are true rainforest, staying green year-round, such as in the Western Ghats and in the Northeast States, but most forests are deciduous, for example, the teak forests of central India, and can look surprisingly dusty and forlorn in the dry season. Fortunately, the leaf fall and dry vegetation makes wildlife viewing easier in otherwise dense woodlands.

High-value trees such as Indian rosewood, Malabar kino and teak have been virtually cleared from the Western Ghats, and sandalwood is endangered across India due to illegal logging for the incense and wood-carving industries. A bigger threat on forested lands is firewood harvesting, often carried out by landless peasants who squat on gazetted government land.

Around 2000 plant species are described in Ayurveda (traditional Indian herbal medicine) texts.

Several trees have significant religious value in India, including the silk-cotton tree, a huge tree with spiny bark and large red flowers under which Pitamaha (Brahma), the creator of the world, sat after his labours. Two well-known figs, the banyan and peepal, grow to immense size by dangling roots from their branches and fusing into massive multi-trunked jungles of trunks and stems – one giant is nearly 200m across. It is said that Buddha achieved enlightenment while sitting under a peepal (also known as the Bodhi tree).

National Parks & Wildlife Sanctuaries

Prior to 1972 India had only five national parks, so the Wildlife Protection Act was introduced that year to set aside parks and stem the abuse of wildlife. The Act was followed by a string of similar pieces of legislation with bold ambitions but few teeth with which to enforce them.

India now has about 100 national parks and 500 wildlife sanctuaries, which constitute around 5% of India's territory. An additional 70 parks have been authorised on paper but not yet implemented on the ground or only implemented to varying degrees. There are also 14 biosphere reserves, overlapping many of the national parks and sanctuaries, providing safe migration channels for wildlife and allowing scientists to monitor biodiversity.

Wildlife reserves tend to be off the beaten track and infrastructure can be limited – book transport and accommodation in advance, and check opening times, permit requirements and entry fees before you visit. Many parks close to conduct a census of wildlife in the low season, and monsoon rains can make wildlife-viewing tracks inaccessible.

Almost all parks offer jeep/van tours, but you can also search for wildlife on guided treks, boat trips and elephant safaris. New rules introduced in 2012 put an end to 'tiger shows', whereby resting tigers became sitting ducks for tourists that were radioed in, taken off their jeep and put on elephants to get close to the, presumably peeved, resting tiger. Also, in many reserves, safari vehicle visits have been cut and for one day in the week, some tiger sanctuaries will be closed to safaris. These new rules are in flux, so do find out the latest situation before booking your safari.

Top Parks

- *Mahatma Gandhi Marine National Park*
- *Nagarhole National Park*
- *Periyar Wildlife Sanctuary*

The Landscape

India is an incredibly diverse country with everything from steamy jungles and tropical beaches to arid deserts and the soaring icy peaks of the Himalaya. At 3,287,263 sq km it is the second-largest Asian country (after China), and forms the vast bulk of the South Asian subcontinent – an ancient block of earth crust that carried a wealth of unique plants and animals like a lifeboat across a prehistoric ocean before slamming into Asia about 40 million years ago.

India is home to 18% of the world's population, crowded together on 2.5% of the world's landmass.

The Lie of The Land

The three major geographic features that define modern-day India are the Himalayan peaks and hills along the northern borders, the alluvial floodplains of the Indus and Ganges Rivers in the north, and the elevated Deccan Plateau that forms the core of India's triangular southern peninsula.

The Himalaya

As the world's highest mountains – with the highest peak in India (Khangchendzonga) reaching 8598m – the Himalaya create an almost impregnable boundary separating India from its neighbours to the north. These mountains formed when the Indian subcontinent broke away from Gondwanaland, a supercontinent in the southern hemisphere that included Africa, Antarctica, Australia and South America. All by itself, India drifted north and finally slammed slowly, but with immense force, into the Eurasian continent about 40 million years ago, buckling the ancient seafloor upward to form the Himalaya and many lesser ranges that stretch 2500km from Afghanistan to Myanmar (Burma).

When the Himalaya reached its great heights during the Pleistocene (less than 150,000 years ago), it blocked and altered weather systems, creating the monsoon climate that dominates India today, as well as forming a dry rainshadow to the north.

The Indo-Gangetic Plains

Covering most of northern India, the vast alluvial plains of the sacred Ganges River are so flat that they drop a mere 200m between Delhi and the waterlogged wetlands of West Bengal, where the river joins forces with the Brahmaputra River from India's northeast before dumping into the sea in Bangladesh. Vast quantities of eroded sediments from the neighbouring highlands accumulate on the plains to a depth of nearly 2km, creating fertile, well-watered agricultural land. This densely populated region was once extensively forested and rich in wildlife.

The Andoman and Nicobar Islands comprise 572 islands and are the peaks of a vast submerged mountain range extending almost 1000km between Myanmar (Burma) and Sumatra.

The Deccan Plateau

South of the Indo-Gangetic (northern) plain, the land rises to the Deccan Plateau, marking the divide between the Mughal heartlands of North India and the Dravidian civilisations of the south. The Deccan is bound on either side by the Western and Eastern Ghats, which come together in their southern reaches to form the Nilgiri Hills in Tamil Nadu.

On the Deccan's western border, the Western Ghats drop sharply down to a narrow coastal lowland, forming a luxuriant slope of rainforest.

The Islands

Offshore from India are a series of island groups, politically part of India but geographically linked to the landmasses of Southeast Asia and islands of the Indian Ocean. The Andaman and Nicobar Islands sit far out in the Bay of Bengal, while the coral atolls of Lakshadweep (300km west of Kerala) are a northerly extension of the Maldives islands, with a land area of just 32 sq km.

Get the inside track on Indian environmental issues at Down to Earth (www.downtoearth.org.au), an online magazine that delves into stories overlooked by mainstream media.

Environmental Issues

With well over a billion people, ever-expanding industrial and urban centres, and growth in chemical-intensive farming, India's environment is under tremendous pressure. An estimated 65% of the land is degraded in some way. Many current problems are a direct result of the Green Revolution of the 1960s, when chemical fertilisers and pesticides enabled huge growth in agricultural output, at enormous cost to the environment.

Despite numerous environmental laws, corruption continues to exacerbate environmental degradation – exemplified by the flagrant flouting of laws by companies involved in hydroelectricity and mining. Usually, the people most affected are low-caste rural farmers and Adivasis (tribal people).

Agricultural production has been reduced by soil degradation from overfarming, rising soil salinity, loss of tree cover and poor irrigation. The human cost is heart rending, and lurking behind all these problems is a basic Malthusian truth: there are far too many people for India to support.

Climate Change

Changing climate patterns – linked to global carbon emissions – have been creating dangerous extremes of weather in India. While India's per-capita carbon emissions still rank far behind that of the USA, Australia and Europe, its sheer size of population makes it a major polluter.

It has been estimated that by 2030 India will see a 30% increase in the severity of its floods and droughts. Islands in the Lakshadweep group as well as the low-lying plains of the Ganges delta are being inundated by rising sea levels.

Deforestation

Since Independence, over 50,000 sq km of India's forests have been cleared for logging and farming, or destroyed by urban expansion, mining, industrialisation and river dams. Even in the well-funded, highly protected Project Tiger parks, the amount of forest cover classified as 'degraded' has tripled due to illegal logging. The number of mangrove forests has halved since the early 1990s, reducing the nursery grounds for the fish that stock the Indian Ocean and Bay of Bengal.

India's first Five Year Plan in 1951 recognised the importance of forests for soil conservation, and various policies have been introduced to increase forest cover. Almost all have been flouted by officials or criminals and by ordinary people clearing forests for firewood and grazing in forest areas.

AIR POLLUTION

Air pollution in many Indian cities has been measured at more than double the maximum safe level recommended by the World Health Organization.

Water Resources

Arguably the biggest threat to public health in India is inadequate access to clean drinking water and proper sanitation. With the population set to double by 2050, agricultural, industrial and domestic water usage are all expected to spiral. The World Health Organization estimates that, out of more than 3000 cities in India, only eight have adequate wastewater treatment facilities. Many cities dump untreated sewage and partially cremated bodies directly into rivers, while open defecation is a simple fact of life in most rural (and many urban) areas.

Noise pollution in major cities has been measured at over 90 decibels – more than 1½ times the recognised 'safe' limit. Bring earplugs!

Rivers are also affected by run-off, industrial pollution and sewage contamination. In recent years, drought has devastated parts of the subcontinent and has been a driving force for rural-to-urban migration.

Water distribution is another volatile issue. Since 1947 an estimated 35 million people in India have been displaced by major dams, mostly built to provide hydroelectricity for this increasingly power-hungry nation. While hydroelectricity is one of the greener power sources, valleys across India are being sacrificed to create new power plants, and displaced people rarely receive adequate compensation.

Survival Guide

Women & Solo Travellers

Women and solo travellers may encounter a few extra hurdles when visiting India – from cost (for those travelling alone) to maintaining appropriate dress codes (women). As with anywhere else in the world, it pays to be prepared.

Women Travellers

Although Bollywood might suggest otherwise, India remains a largely conservative society. Female travellers should be aware that their behaviour and attire choice are likely to be under constant scrutiny, particularly away from tourist centres.

Attention

➡ Be prepared to be stared at; it's something you'll simply have to live with so don't allow it to get the better of you.

➡ Refrain from returning male stares; this can be considered a come-on.

➡ Dark glasses, phones, electronic devices and books are useful for averting unwanted conversations.

Clothing

Avoiding culturally inappropriate clothing will help avert undesirable attention.

➡ Steer clear of sleeveless tops, shorts, miniskirts (ankle-length skirts are recommended) and anything else that's skimpy, see-through or tight-fitting.

➡ Wearing Indian-style clothes is viewed favourably and can help deflect harassment.

➡ Draping a dupatta (long scarf) over T-shirts is another good way to avoid stares – it's also handy if you visit a shrine that requires your head to be covered.

➡ Wearing a *salwar kameez* (traditional dresslike tunic and trousers) will help you blend in.

➡ If you're not keen on wearing a *salwar kameez*, a smart alternative is a kurta (long shirt) worn over jeans or trousers.

➡ Avoid going out in public wearing a choli (sari blouse) or a sari petticoat (which some foreign women mistake for a skirt); it's like strutting around half-dressed.

➡ Aside from at pools, many Indian women wear long shorts and a T-shirt when swimming in public view; it's wise to wear a sarong from the beach to your hotel.

Health & Hygiene

Sanitary pads are widely available but tampons are usually restricted to pharmacies in big cities and tourist towns (even then, the choice may be limited). Carry additional stocks for travel off the beaten track.

Sexual Harassment

Many female travellers have reported some form of sexual harassment while in India.

➡ Most cases are reported in urban centres and prominent tourist towns, and have involved lewd comments, invasion of privacy and groping.

➡ Other cases have included provocative gestures, jeering, getting 'accidentally' bumped into on the street and being followed.

➡ Incidents are particularly common at exuberant (and crowded) public events such as the Holi festival.

➡ Women travelling with a male partner are less likely to be hassled.

Staying Safe

The following tips will hopefully help you avoid uncomfortable situations during your journey:

➡ Keep conversations with unknown men short – getting involved in an inane conversation with someone you barely know can be misinterpreted as a sign of sexual interest.

➡ Questions and comments such as 'Do you have a boyfriend?' or 'You're very beautiful' are indicators that the conversation may be taking a steamy tangent.

➡ Some women wear a pseudo wedding ring, or

announce early on in the conversation that they're married or engaged (regardless of the reality).

➡ If you feel that a guy is encroaching on your space, he probably is. A firm request to keep away usually does the trick, especially if your tone is loud and curt enough to draw the attention of passers-by.

➡ The silent treatment can also be very effective.

➡ Follow local women's cues and instead of shaking hands say *namaste* – the traditional, respectful Hindu greeting.

➡ Avoid wearing expensive-looking jewellery and carrying flashy accessories.

➡ Check the reputation of any teacher or therapist before going to a solo session (get recommendations from travellers). Some women have reported being molested by masseurs and other therapists. If you feel uneasy at any time, leave.

➡ At hotels keep your door locked, as staff (particularly at budget and midrange places) can knock and automatically walk in without waiting for your permission.

➡ Arrive in towns before dark. Don't walk alone at night and avoid wandering alone in isolated areas even during daylight.

➡ Act confidently in public; to avoid looking lost (and thus more vulnerable) consult maps at your hotel (or at a restaurant) rather than on the street.

Taxis & Public Transport

Being female has some advantages; women can usually queue-jump for buses and trains without consequence and on trains there are special ladies-only carriages.

➡ Solo women should prearrange an airport pick-up from their hotel, especially if their flight is scheduled to arrive after dark.

➡ India's larger cities may have prepaid radio cab services such as Easycabs – they're more expensive than the regular prepaid taxis, but promote themselves as being safe, with drivers who have been vetted as part of their recruitment.

➡ If you do catch a regular prepaid taxi, make a point of writing down the car registration and driver's name – in front of the driver – and giving it to one of the airport police.

➡ Avoid taking taxis alone late at night and never agree to have more than one man (the driver) in the car – ignore claims that this is 'just my brother' etc.

➡ Solo women have reported less hassle by opting for the more expensive classes on trains.

➡ If you're travelling overnight in a three-tier carriage, try to get the uppermost berth, which will give you more privacy (and distance from potential gropers).

➡ On public transport, don't hesitate to return any errant limbs, put an item of luggage between you and others, be vocal (attracting public attention, thus shaming the pest), or to simply find a new spot.

Solo Travellers

One of the joys of travelling solo in India is that you're more likely to be 'adopted' by families, especially if you're commuting together on a long rail journey. It's a great opportunity to make friends and get a deeper understanding of local culture. If you're keen to hook up with fellow travellers, tourist hubs such as Goa and Kerala are some popular places to do so. You may also be able to find travel companions on Lonely Planet's Thorn Tree Travel Forum (www.lonelyplanet.com/thorntree).

Cost

The most significant issue facing solo travellers is cost.

➡ Single-room accommodation rates are sometimes not much lower than double rates.

➡ Some midrange and top-end places don't even offer a single tariff.

➡ It's always worth trying to negotiate a lower rate for single occupancy.

Safety

Most solo travellers experience no major problems in India but, like anywhere else, it's wise to stay on your toes in unfamiliar surroundings.

➡ Some less honourable souls (locals and travellers alike) view lone tourists as an easy target for theft and sexual assault.

➡ Single men wandering around isolated areas have been mugged, even during the day.

Transport

➡ You'll save money if you find others to share taxis and autorickshaws, as well as when hiring a car for longer trips.

➡ Solo bus travellers may be able to get the 'co-pilot' seat (near the driver) on buses, which not only has a good view out front, but is also handy if you've got a big bag.

HANDY WEBSITES

Peruse personal experiences proffered by fellow female travellers at www.journeywoman.com and www.wanderlustandlipstick.com.

Scams

Scams, both classic and newfangled, are known to exist in India. Of course, most can be avoided with a little bit of common sense and caution. Chat with fellow travellers to keep abreast of the latest cons. Look at the India branch of Lonely Planet's Thorn Tree Travel Forum (www.lonelyplanet.com/thorntree), where travellers often post timely warnings about problems they've encountered on the road.

Contaminated Food & Drink

➡ While in transit, try to carry packed food if possible. If you must eat at bus or train stations, follow the crowd and buy food only from fast-moving places. Never eat food that either looks stale or is exposed to the elements.

➡ Most bottled water is legit, but ensure the seal is intact and the bottom of the bottle hasn't been tampered with. Crush plastic bottles after use to prevent them being misused. Better still, use your own water bottle and water-purification tablets to avoid adding to India's plastic waste mountain.

Credit Card Con

➡ Be careful when paying for souvenirs with a credit card. While government shops are usually legitimate, private souvenir shops have been known to surreptitiously run off copies of credit-card imprint slips and use them for phoney transactions later. Ask the trader to process the transaction in front of you. Memorising the CVV/CVC2 number and scratching it off the card is also a good idea, to avoid misuse.

Druggings

➡ Occasionally, tourists (especially solo ones) are drugged and robbed on train or bus trips. A spiked drink is the most commonly used method for sending them to sleep – chocolates, chai from a co-conspiring vendor and 'homemade' food are also used. Use your instincts, and if you're unsure, politely decline drinks or food offered by strangers.

Gem Scams

➡ This classic scam involves charming con artists who promise foolproof 'get rich quick' schemes. Travellers are asked to carry or mail gems home and then sell them to the trader's (nonexistent) overseas representatives at a profit. Without exception, the goods – if they arrive at all – are worth a fraction of what you paid, and the 'representatives' never materialise.

➡ Don't believe hard-luck stories about an inability to obtain an export licence, and

KEEPING SAFE

➡ A good travel-insurance policy is essential.

➡ Email copies of your passport identity page, visa and airline tickets to yourself, and keep copies on you.

➡ Keep your money and passport in a concealed money belt or secure place under your shirt.

➡ Store at least US$100 separately from your main stash.

➡ Don't publicly display large wads of cash when paying for services or checking into hotels.

➡ Consider using your own padlock at cheaper hotels.

➡ If you can't lock your hotel room securely from the inside, stay somewhere else.

OTHER TOP SCAMS

➡ Gunk (dirt, paint, poo) suddenly appears on your shoes, only for a shoe cleaner to magically appear and offer to clean it off – for a price.

➡ Shops and restaurants 'borrow' the name of their more successful and popular competitor.

➡ Touts claim to be 'government-approved' guides or agents, and sting you for large sums of cash. Enquire at the local tourist office about licensed guides and ask to see identification from guides themselves.

➡ This one's a gem: some souvenir sellers have reportedly offered commissions to tourists to pose as satisfied customers and lure other travellers to their stores!

don't believe the testimonials they show you from other travellers – they are all fake. Carpets, curios and *pashmina* woollens are other favourites for this con.

Overpricing

➡ Always agree on prices beforehand while availing services that don't have regulated tariffs. This particularly applies to friendly neighbourhood guides, snack bars at places of touristy interest, and autorickshaws and taxis without meters.

Photography

➡ Use your instincts (better still, ask permission) while photographing people. The common argument – voiced only after you've snapped your photos – is you're going to sell them to international magazines, so it's only fair that you pay a posing fee.

Theft

➡ Theft is a risk in India, as anywhere else. Keep luggage locked and chained on buses and trains. Remember that snatchings often occur when a train is pulling out of the station, as it's too late for you to give chase.

➡ Take extra care in dormitories and never leave valuables unattended. Use safe deposit boxes if you can.

➡ For lost or stolen credit cards, call the international lost/stolen number. For lost/stolen travellers cheques, contact the American Express or Thomas Cook offices in Delhi.

Touts & Commission Agents

➡ Touts come in many avatars and operate in mysterious ways. Cabbies and autorickshaw drivers often coerce you to put up at a budget hotel of their choice, only to collect a commission (included within your room tariff) from the receptionists afterward.

➡ Wherever possible, arrange hotel bookings (if only for the first night), and request a hotel pick-up. You'll often hear stories about hotels of your choice being 'full' or 'closed' – check things out yourself.

➡ Be very sceptical of phrases like 'my brother's shop' and 'special deal at my friend's place'. Many fraudsters operate in collusion with souvenir stalls, so be careful while making expensive purchases in private stores.

➡ Avoid friendly people in train and bus stations who offer unsolicited help. Look confident, and if anyone asks if this is your first trip to India, say you've been here several times, even if you haven't. Telling touts that you have already prepaid your transfer/tour/onward journey can dissuade them.

➡ Touts can be particularly bothersome in major tourist centres.

Transport Scams

➡ Upon arriving at train stations and airports, always book transport from government-approved booths. All major airports now have radio cab, prepaid taxi and airport shuttle bus counters within the arrival lounge. Never go with a loitering cabbie who offers you a cheap ride into town, especially at night.

➡ While booking multiday sightseeing tours, stick to itineraries offered by tourism offices, or those that come recommended in this book or by friends who've personally used them.

➡ When buying a bus, train or plane ticket anywhere other than the registered office of the transport company, make sure you're getting the ticket class you paid for. Use online booking facilities where possible.

➡ Some tricksters pose as Indian Railways officials and insist you pay to have your e-ticket validated on the platform; ignore them.

Directory A–Z

Accommodation

Accommodation in South India ranges from grungy backpacker hostels with concrete floors and cold 'bucket' showers to opulent heritage hotels. We've listed reviews by author preference within price categories; standout options are indicated by ★.

Categories

As a general rule, budget ($) covers everything from basic hostels, hotels and guesthouses in urban areas to traditional homestays in villages. Midrange hotels ($$) tend to be modern concrete-and-glass affairs that usually offer extras such as cable/satellite TV and air-conditioning (although some just have noisy 'air-coolers' that cool air by blowing it over cold water). Top-end places ($$$) stretch from luxury five-star chains to gorgeous heritage palaces and resorts.

Costs

Costs vary widely across South India; prices are highest in large cities (especially Mumbai), lowest in rural areas. Costs are also highly seasonal – hotel prices can drop by 20% to 50% outside of peak season. Most establishments raise tariffs annually, so the prices may have risen by the time you read this.

Reservations

➡ The majority of top-end and some midrange hotels require a deposit at the time of booking. The figure can range from a day's tariff to the full amount. This can usually be done with a credit card.

➡ Some midrange places may ask for a cheque or cash deposit into a bank account to secure a reservation. This is usually more hassle than it's worth. Some places honour phone reservations – call to re-confirm the day before you arrive, especially during high tourist seasons.

➡ Some budget options won't take reservations as they don't know when people are going to check-out; call ahead to check or just turn up around check-in time.

➡ Other places will want a deposit at check-in – ask for a receipt and be wary of any request to sign a blank impression of your credit card. If the hotel insists, consider going to the nearest ATM and paying cash.

➡ Verify the check-out time when you check-in – some hotels have a fixed check-out time (usually 10am or noon), while others offer 24-hour check-out. In some places, check-out can be as early as 9am.

Seasons

➡ Rates given are full price in high season. For places like Goa and Kerala high season is basically one month before and two months after Christmas; in the hill stations it's usually from around April to July.

➡ In areas popular with foreign tourists, there's an additional peak period over Christmas and New Year; make reservations well in advance.

➡ At other times you may find significant discounts; if the hotel seems quiet, ask for one.

➡ Some hotels in places like Goa largely shut during the

SLEEPING PRICE RANGES

The following price ranges refer to a double room with private bathroom in high season. Exceptions are noted in reviews.

CATEGORY	KERALA	KARNATAKA	GOA
$ budget	less than ₹1000	less than ₹1000	less than ₹1200
$$ midrange	₹1000-3500	₹1000-4000	₹1200-4000
$$$ top end	more than ₹3500	more than ₹4000	more than ₹4000

monsoon period. Certain hill stations close down during winter.

➡ Many temple towns have additional peak seasons around major festivals and pilgrimages.

Taxes & Service Charges

➡ State governments slap a variety of taxes on hotel accommodation (except at the cheaper hotels), and these are added to the cost of your room.

➡ Taxes vary from state to state. Even within a state, prices can vary across price ranges, with more expensive hotels levying higher taxes.

➡ Many upmarket hotels also add an additional 'service charge' (usually around 10%).

➡ Rates quoted in this book include taxes, unless noted.

➡ Some upscale restaurants may add a service charge (between 10% and 13%) on meals.

Budget & Midrange Hotels

➡ Apart from some traditional wood or stone guesthouses in remote mountain areas, most budget and midrange hotels are modern-style concrete blocks with requisite creature comforts. Some are charming, clean and good value; others less so.

➡ Room quality can vary considerably within a hotel so try to inspect a few rooms first; avoid carpeted rooms at cheaper hotels unless you like the smell of mouldy socks.

➡ Shared bathrooms (often with squat toilets) are usually only found at the cheapest lodgings.

➡ Most rooms have ceiling fans and better rooms have electric mosquito killers and/or window nets, though cheaper rooms may lack windows altogether.

➡ If you're mostly staying in budget places, bring your own sheet or sleeping-bag liner. Sheets and bedcovers at cheap hotels can be stained, well worn and in need of a wash.

➡ An insect repellent and a torch (flashlight) are recommended for budget hotels.

➡ Noise pollution can be irksome (especially in urban hubs); pack good-quality earplugs and request a room that doesn't face a busy road.

➡ It's wise to keep your door locked, as some staff (particularly in budget hotels) may knock and automatically walk in without awaiting your permission.

➡ Blackouts are common (especially during summer and the monsoon) so double-check that the hotel has a back-up generator if you're paying for electric 'extras' such as air-conditioners, TVs and wi-fi.

➡ Note that some hotels lock their doors at night. Members of staff might sleep in the lobby but waking them up can be a challenge. Let the hotel know in advance if you'll be arriving late at night, or leaving early in the morning.

➡ Away from tourist areas, cheaper hotels may not take foreigners because they don't have the necessary foreigner-registration forms.

Camping

➡ There are few official camping sites in South India. On the other hand, wild camping is often the only accommodation option on trekking routes. Seek safety advice in advance.

➡ In some mountain areas, you'll also find summer-only tented camps, with accommodation in semi-permanent 'Swiss tents' with attached bathrooms.

Dormitory Accommodation

➡ A number of hotels have cheap dormitories, although these may be mixed and, in less touristy places, full of drunken males – not ideal conditions for women.

➡ More traveller-friendly dorms are found at the handful of hostels run by the YMCA, YWCA and Salvation Army as well as at those associated with HI or YHAI (Youth Hostels Association of India).

Government Accommodation & Tourist Bungalows

➡ The Indian government maintains a network of guesthouses for travelling officials and public workers, known variously as rest houses, dak bungalows, circuit houses, PWD (Public Works Department) bungalows and forest rest houses.

➡ These places may accept travellers if no government employees need the rooms, but permission is sometimes required from local officials and you'll probably have to find the *chowkidar* (caretaker) to open the doors. Besides, there's always the risk of being thrown out if officials suddenly arrive during your stay!

➡ 'Tourist bungalows' are run by state governments – rooms are usually midpriced (some with cheap dorms) and have varying standards of cleanliness and service.

BOOK YOUR STAY ONLINE

For more accommodation reviews by Lonely Planet authors, check out http://lonelyplanet.com/hotels. You'll find independent reviews, as well as recommendations on the best places to stay. Best of all, you can book online.

PRACTICALITIES

- **Newspapers & Magazines** Major English-language dailies include the *Hindustan Times, Times of India, Indian Express, Hindu, Statesman, Telegraph, Daily News & Analysis (DNA)* and *Economic Times*. Regional English-language and local-vernacular publications are found nationwide. Incisive current-affairs magazines include *Frontline, India Today, Week, Open, Tehelka* and *Outlook*.
- **Radio** Government-controlled All India Radio (AIR), India's national broadcaster, has over 220 stations broadcasting local and international news. Private FM channels broadcast music, current affairs, talkback and more.
- **TV & Video** The national (government) TV broadcaster is Doordarshan. More people watch satellite and cable TV; English-language channels include BBC, CNN, Star World, HBO, National Geographic and Discovery.
- **Weights & Measures** Officially India is metric. Terms you're likely to hear are: lakhs (one lakh = 100,000) and crores (one crore = 10 million).

- Some state governments also run chains of more expensive hotels, including some lovely heritage properties. Details are normally available through the state tourism offices.

Homestays/B&Bs For Paying Guests

- These family-run guesthouses will appeal to those seeking a small-scale, uncommercial setting with home-cooked meals.
- Standards range from mud-and-stone village huts with hole-in-the-floor toilets to comfortable middle-class homes in cities.
- Be aware that some hotels market themselves as 'homestays' but are run like hotels with little (or no) interaction with the family.
- Contact local tourist offices for full lists of participating families.

Railway Retiring Rooms

- Most large train stations have basic rooms for travellers holding an ongoing train ticket or Indrail Pass. Some are grim, others are surprisingly pleasant, but suffer from the noise of passengers and trains.
- They're useful for early-morning train departures and there's usually a choice of dormitories or private rooms (24-hour checkout) depending on the class you're travelling in.
- Some smaller stations may have waiting rooms instead of retiring rooms. These are large halls with rows of chairs (similar to an airport lounge but with substantially lower degrees of comfort and cleanliness), and are usually located in the vicinity of toilets and cafeterias. Once again, there may be different waiting rooms for passengers travelling in different classes.

Temples & Pilgrims' Rest Houses

- Accommodation is available at some ashrams (spiritual retreats), gurdwaras (Sikh temples) and *dharamsalas* (pilgrims' guesthouses) for a donation or a nominal fee. Vegetarian meals are usually available at the refectories.
- These places have been established for genuine pilgrims so please exercise judgment about the appropriateness of staying.
- Always abide by any protocols. Smoking and drinking within the premises are a complete no-no.

Top-End & Heritage Hotels

- South India has plenty of top-end properties, from modern five-star chain hotels to glorious palaces and unique heritage abodes.
- Most top-end hotels have rupee rates for Indian guests and US dollar rates for foreigners, including Non-Resident Indians (NRIs).
- Officially, you're supposed to pay the dollar rates in foreign currency or by credit card, but many places will accept rupees adding up to the dollar rate (verify this when checking in).
- The Government of India tourism website, **Incredible India** (www.incredibleindia.org), has a useful list of palaces, forts and other erstwhile royal retreats that accept paying guests – go to the 'Travel' page and click on the 'Royal Retreats' link.
- In recent times, India has also seen a mushrooming of luxury eco- and forest resorts in and around several national parks.

Customs Regulations

- Technically you're supposed to declare any amount of cash/travellers cheques over US$5000/10,000 on arrival.
- Indian rupees shouldn't be taken out of India; however, this is rarely policed.

➡ Officials very occasionally ask tourists to enter expensive items such as video cameras and laptop computers on a 'Tourist Baggage Re-export' form to ensure they're taken out of India at the time of departure.

Electricity

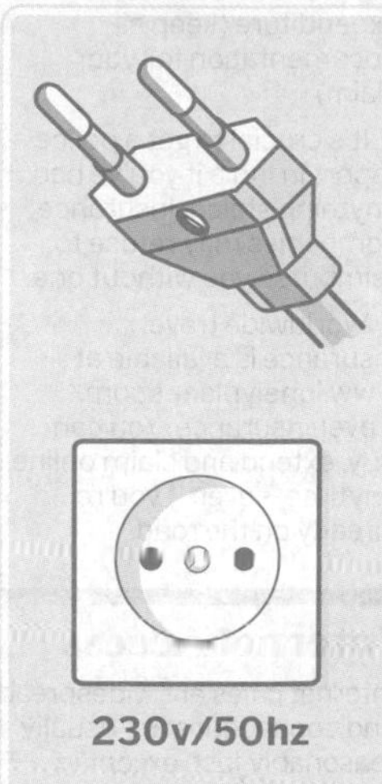

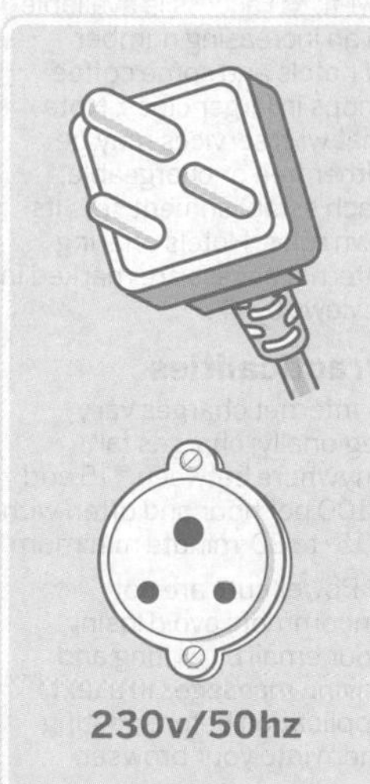

Embassies & Consulates

Most foreign diplomatic missions are based in Delhi, but several nations operate consulates in other Indian cities (see websites, where provided, for more details). Many missions have certain timings for visa applications, usually mornings: phone for details. The following are just some of the many foreign missions found in India.

Australian (www.india.highcommission.gov.au); Chennai (☎044-45921300, 9th fl, Express Chambers, Whites Rd, Royapettah); Delhi (☎011-41399900, 1/50G Shantipath, Chanakyapuri); Mumbai (☎022-67574900, 10th fl, A Wing, Crescenzo Bldg, G Block, Plot C 38-39, Bandra Kurla Complex)

Canadian (www.canadainternational.gc.ca/india-inde); Chennai (☎044-28330888; 18, 3rd fl YAFA Tower, Khader Nawaz Khan Rd); Delhi (☎011-41782000; 7/8 Shantipath, Chanakyapuri); Mumbai (☎022-67574900; 10th fl, A Wing, Crescenzo Bldg, G Block, Plot C 38-39, Bandra Kurla Complex)

French (http://ambafrance-in.org); Delhi (☎011-24196100; 2/50E Shantipath, Chanakyapuri); Mumbai (☎022-56694000; Wockhardt Towers, East Wing, 5th fl, Bandra Kurla Complex); Puducherry (☎0413-2231000; 2 Marine St)

German (www.new-delhi.diplo.de); Chennai (☎044-24301600; 9 Boat Club Rd, RA Puram); Delhi (☎011-44199199; 6/50G Shantipath, Chanakyapuri); Kolkata (☎033-24791141; 1 Hastings Park Rd, Alipore); Mumbai (☎022-22832422; 10th fl, Hoechst House, Nariman Point)

Israeli (http://delhi.mfa.gov.il); Delhi (☎011-30414500; 3 Aurangzeb Rd); Mumbai (☎022-22819994; Earnest House, 16th fl, NCPA Marg, 194 Nariman Point)

Nepali Delhi (☎011-23327361; Mandi House, Barakhamba Rd); Kolkata (☎033-24561224; 1 National Library Ave, Alipore)

Netherlands (www.holland-india.org); Chennai (☎044-42112770; 8B Adyar Club Gate Rd, RA Puram); Delhi (☎011-24197600; 6/50F Shantipath, Chanakyapuri); Mumbai (☎022-22194200; Forbes Bldg, Charanjit Rai Marg, Fort)

New Zealand (www.nzembassy.com/india); Chennai (☎044-28112472; Rane Engine Valves Ltd, Maithri, 132 Cathedral Rd); Delhi (☎011-46883170; Sir Edmund Hillary Marg, Chanakyapuri); Mumbai (☎022-61316666; Level 2, Maker Maxity, 3 North Ave, Bandra Kurla Complex)

Singaporean (www.mfa.gov.sg/newdelhi); Chennai (☎044-28158207; 17A North Boag Rd, T Nagar); Delhi (☎011-46000915; E6 Chandragupta Marg, Chanakyapuri); Mumbai (☎022-22043205; 152, Maker Chambers IV, 14th fl, 222 Jamnalal Bajaj Rd, Nariman Point)

UK (http://ukinindia.fco.gov.uk); Chennai (☎044-42192151; 20 Anderson Rd); Delhi (☎011-24192100; Shantipath, Chanakyapuri); Kolkata (☎033-22885172; 1A Ho Chi Minh Sarani); Mumbai (☎022-66502222; Naman Chambers, C/32 G Block, Bandra Kurla Complex)

US (http://newdelhi.usembassy.gov); Chennai (☎044-28574000; Gemini Circle, 220 Anna Salai); Delhi (☎011-24198000; Shantipath, Chanakyapuri); Kolkata (☎033-39842400; 5/1 Ho Chi Minh Sarani); Mumbai (☎022-2672 4000; C49, G Block, Bandra Kurla Complex)

Food

See Delicious South India (p462) for information about food in South India.

EATING PRICE RANGES

The following price ranges refer to a standard main course.

$ less than ₹100

$$ ₹100–₹300

$$$ more than ₹300

Gay & Lesbian Travellers

➡ Homosexuality is legal in India, although the country remains largely conservative. Public displays of affection are generally frowned upon for gay and lesbian couples (and even for heterosexual couples).

➡ There are gay scenes in a number of South Indian cities including Mumbai (Bombay), Chennai (Madras) and Bengaluru (Bangalore) – Gay Pride marches may be held annually at some of these centres. *Time Out Mumbai* (www.timeoutmumbai.net) has information about gay events in Mumbai.

Websites

Gay Bombay (www.gaybombay.org) Lists gay events as well as offering support and advice.

Gaysi (http://gaysifamily.com) Started as a forum for LGBT South Asians, it has excellent news, reviews and features.

Indian Dost (www.indiandost.com/gay.php) News and information including contact groups in India.

Indja Pink (www.indjapink.co.in) India's first 'gay travel boutique', founded by a well-known Indian fashion designer.

Queer Azaadi Mumbai (http://queerazaadi.wordpress.com) Mumbai's queer pride blog, with news.

Queer Ink (www.queer-ink.com) Online bookshop specialising in gay- and lesbian-interest books from the subcontinent, including the story collection *Out!*, which it published.

Support Groups

Chennai Dost (www.chennaidost.blogspot.com) Organises varied events, including parties, exhibitions, campaigns and the Chennai Rainbow Pride march every June.

Humsafar Trust (☎022-26673800; www.humsafar.org; Old BMC Bldg, 1st fl, Nehru Rd, Vakola, Santa Cruz East) Runs gay and transgender support groups and advocacy programs. The drop-in centre in Santa Cruz East hosts workshops and has a library – pick up a copy of the pioneering LGBT magazine *Bombay Dost*.

Nigah (http://nigahdelhi.blogspot.com) Autonomous collective that holds monthly queer events and organises the annual Nigah Queerfest.

Sangama (www.sangama.org) Deals with crisis intervention and provides a community outreach service for gay and bisexual men and women, transgenders and *hijras* (transvestites and eunuchs).

Sappho (www.sapphokolkata.org) Operates as a support group for lesbian, bisexual and transgender women.

Wajood Society (www.wajoodsociety.com) Hyderabad's budding queer-support organisation organises get-togethers.

Insurance

➡ Comprehensive travel insurance to cover theft, loss and medical problems (as well as air evacuation) is strongly recommended.

➡ Some policies specifically exclude potentially dangerous activities such as scuba diving, skiing, motorcycling, paragliding and even trekking: read the fine print.

➡ Some trekking agents may only accept customers who have cover for emergency helicopter evacuation.

➡ If you plan to hire a motorcycle in India, make sure the rental policy includes at least third-party insurance.

➡ Check in advance whether your insurance policy will pay doctors and hospitals directly or reimburse you later for overseas health expenditure (keep all documentation for your claim).

➡ It's crucial to get a police report in India if you've had anything stolen; insurance companies may refuse to reimburse you without one.

➡ Worldwide travel insurance is available at www.lonelyplanet.com/travel-insurance. You can buy, extend and claim online anytime – even if you're already on the road.

Internet Access

Internet cafes are widespread and connections are usually reasonably fast, except in more remote areas. Wireless (wi-fi; 📶) access is available in an increasing number of hotels and some coffee shops in larger cities. Note that wi-fi services may be either free or chargeable; each establishment sets its own rules. Hotels offering internet access are marked in reviews by @.

Practicalities

➡ Internet charges vary regionally; charges fall anywhere between ₹15 and ₹100 per hour and often with a 15- to 30-minute minimum.

➡ Power cuts are not uncommon; avoid losing your email by writing and saving messages in a text application before pasting them into your browser.

➡ Bandwidth load tends to be lowest in the early morning and early afternoon.

- Some internet cafes may ask to see your passport.

Security

- Be wary of sending sensitive financial information from internet cafes; some places are able to use keystroke-capturing technology to access passwords and emails.
- Avoid sending credit-card details or other personal data over a wireless connection; using online banking on any non-secure system is generally unwise.
- If you must use public peripherals to carry out financial transactions during your trip, be sure to change all passwords (email, netbanking, credit card 3-D Secure code etc) the moment you get back home.

Laptops

- Many internet cafes can supply laptop users with internet access over a LAN ethernet cable; alternatively, take out an account with a local internet service provider (ISP).
- Companies that offer prepaid wireless 2G and 3G modem sticks (called dongles) include Reliance, Airtel, Tata Docomo and Vodafone. Just plug one into the USB port of your laptop and you can access the internet.
- To subscribe for a connection, you have to submit your identity proof and address in India – usually a letter or receipt from your hotel will suffice. A nonrefundable activation fee (around ₹1200) has to be paid, which includes the price of the dongle.
- Tariffs for broadband internet start from ₹150 per month for 4GB up to ₹1000 per month for 11GB.
- Make sure the areas you will be travelling to are covered by your service provider.
- Consider purchasing a fuse-protected universal AC adaptor to protect your circuit board from power surges.
- Plug adaptors are widely available throughout India, but bring spare plug fuses from home.

Legal Matters

If you're in a sticky legal situation, contact your embassy as quickly as possible. However, be aware that all your embassy may be able to do is monitor your treatment in custody and arrange a lawyer. In the Indian justice system, the burden of proof can often be on the accused and stints in prison before trial are not unheard of.

Antisocial Behaviour

- Smoking in public places is illegal throughout India but this is very rarely enforced; if caught you'll be fined ₹200.
- People can smoke inside their homes and in most open spaces such as streets (heed any signs stating otherwise).
- A number of Indian cities have banned spitting and littering, but this is also variably enforced.

Drugs

- Indian law does not distinguish between 'hard' and 'soft' drugs; possession of any illegal drug is regarded as a criminal offence.
- If convicted, the *minimum* sentence is 10 years, with very little chance of remission or parole.
- Cases can take months, even several years, to appear before a court while the accused may have to wait in prison. There's also usually a hefty monetary fine on top of any custodial sentence.
- Be aware that travellers have been targeted in sting operations in Goa and other backpacker enclaves.
- Marijuana grows wild in various parts of India, but consuming it is still an offence, except in towns where bhang is legally sold for religious rituals.
- Police are getting particularly tough on foreigners who use drugs, so you should take this risk very seriously.

PROHIBITED EXPORTS

To protect India's cultural heritage, the export of certain antiques is prohibited, especially those which are verifiably more than 100 years old. Reputable antique dealers know the laws and can make arrangements for an export-clearance certificate for old items that are OK to export. Detailed information on prohibited items can be found on the government webpage www.asi.nic.in/pdf_data/8.pdf. The rules may seem stringent but the loss of ancient artworks and sculptures due to the international trade in antiques has been alarming. Look for quality reproductions instead.

The Indian Wildlife Protection Act bans any form of wildlife trade. Don't buy any product that endangers threatened species and habitats – doing so can result in heavy fines and even imprisonment. This includes ivory, shahtoosh shawls (made from the down of chirus or rare Tibetan antelopes), and anything made from the fur, skin, horns or shell of any endangered species. Products made from certain rare plants are also banned.

WARNING: BHANG LASSI

Although it's rarely printed in menus, some restaurants in popular tourist centres will clandestinely whip up bhang lassi, a yoghurt and iced-water beverage laced with cannabis (occasionally other narcotics). Commonly dubbed 'special lassi', this often-potent concoction can cause varying degrees of ecstasy, drawn-out delirium, hallucination, nausea and paranoia. Some travellers have been ill for several days, robbed, or hurt in accidents, after drinking this fickle brew. A few towns have legal (controlled) bhang outlets.

Police

- You should always carry your passport; police are entitled to ask you for identification at any time.
- It is illegal to pay a bribe in India. Many people deal with an on-the-spot fine by just paying it to avoid trumped-up charges. Corruption is rife so the less you have to do with local police the better; try to avoid all potentially risky situations.

Maps

Maps available inside India are of variable quality. Throughout India, most state-government tourist offices stock basic local maps. These are some of the better map series, which are available at good bookshops.

Eicher (http://maps.eicher-world.com/)

Nelles (www.nelles-verlag.de)

Nest & Wings (www.nestwings.in)

Survey of India (www.surveyofindia.gov.in)

TTK (www.ttkmaps.com)

Money

The Indian rupee (₹) is divided into 100 paise (p), but paise coins are becoming increasingly rare. Coins come in denominations of 1, 2, 5 and 10 (the 1s and 2s look almost identical); notes come in 5, 10, 20, 50, 100, 500 and 1000 (the last is handy for paying large bills but can pose problems when getting change for small services). The Indian rupee is linked to a basket of currencies and has been subject to fluctuations in recent years.

ATMs

- ATMs are found in most urban centres.
- Visa, MasterCard, Cirrus, Maestro and Plus are the most commonly accepted cards.
- ATMs at the following banks recognise foreign cards: Axis Bank, Citibank, HDFC, HSBC, ICICI and the State Bank of India. Other banks may accept major cards (Visa, MasterCard etc) but not necessarily all types of cards.
- Before your trip, check whether your card can reliably access banking networks in India and ask for details of charges.
- Notify your bank that you'll be using your card in India (provide dates) to avoid having your card blocked; take along your bank's phone number just in case.
- Always keep the emergency lost-and-stolen numbers for your credit cards in a safe place, separate from your cards, and report any loss or theft immediately.
- Away from major towns, always carry cash (including rupees) or travellers cheques as back-up.

Black Market

Black-market moneychangers exist but legal moneychangers are so common that there's no reason to use them, except perhaps to change small amounts of cash at land border crossings. If someone approaches you on the street and offers to change money, you're probably being set up for a scam.

Cash

- Major currencies such as US dollars, pounds sterling and euros are easy to change throughout India, although some bank branches insist on travellers cheques only.
- Some banks also accept other currencies such as Australian and Canadian dollars, and Swiss francs.
- Private moneychangers deal with a wider range of currencies, but Pakistani, Nepali and Bangladeshi currency can be harder to change away from the border.
- When travelling off the beaten track, always carry an adequate stock of rupees.
- Whenever changing money, check every note. Don't accept any filthy, ripped or disintegrating notes, as these may be difficult to use.
- It can be tough getting change in India so keep a stock of smaller currency; ₹10, ₹20 and ₹50 notes are helpful.
- Officially you cannot take rupees out of India, but this is laxly enforced. You can change any leftover rupees back into foreign currency, most easily at the airport (some banks have a ₹1000 minimum). You may have to present encashment certificates or credit-card/ATM receipts, and show your passport and airline ticket.

Credit Cards

- Credit cards are accepted at a growing number of shops, upmarket restaurants, and midrange and top-end hotels, and they can usually be used to pay for flights and train tickets.
- Cash advances on major credit cards are also possible at some banks.
- MasterCard and Visa are the most widely accepted cards.

Encashment Certificates

- Indian law states that all foreign currency must be changed at official moneychangers or banks.
- For every (official) foreign-exchange transaction, you'll receive an encashment certificate (receipt), which will allow you to change rupees back into foreign currency when departing India.
- Encashment certificates should cover the amount of rupees you intend to change back to foreign currency.
- Printed receipts from ATMs are also accepted as evidence of an international transaction at most banks.

International Transfers

- If you run out of money, someone back home can wire you cash via moneychangers affiliated with **Moneygram** (www.moneygram.com) or **Western Union** (www.westernunion.com). A fee is added to the transaction.
- To collect cash, bring your passport and the name and reference number of the person who sent the funds.

Moneychangers

- Private moneychangers are usually open for longer hours than banks, and are found almost everywhere (many also double as internet cafes and travel agents).
- Upmarket hotels may also change money, but their rates are usually not as competitive.

Tipping, Baksheesh & Bargaining

- In tourist restaurants or hotels, a service fee is usually already added to your bill and tipping is optional. Elsewhere, a tip is appreciated.
- Hotel bellboys and train/airport porters appreciate anything around ₹50; hotel staff should be given similar gratuities for services above and beyond the call of duty.
- It's not mandatory to tip taxi or rickshaw drivers, but it's good to tip drivers who are honest about the fare.
- If you hire a car with driver for more than a couple of days, a tip is recommended for good service.
- Baksheesh can loosely be defined as a 'tip'; it covers everything from alms for beggars to bribes.
- Many Indians implore tourists not to hand out sweets, pens or money to children, as it encourages them to beg. To make a lasting difference, donate to a reputable school or charitable organisation.
- Except in fixed-price shops (such as government emporiums and fair-trade cooperatives), bargaining is the norm.

Travellers Cheques

- All major brands are accepted, but some banks may only accept cheques from American Express (Amex) and Thomas Cook.
- Euro, pounds sterling and US dollars are the safest currencies, especially in smaller towns.
- Keep a record of the cheques' serial numbers separate from your cheques, along with the proof-of-purchase slips, encashment vouchers and photocopied passport details. If you lose your cheques, contact the Amex or Thomas Cook office in Delhi.
- To replace lost travellers cheques, you need the proof-of-purchase slip and the numbers of the missing cheques (some places require a photocopy of the police report and a passport photo). If you don't have the numbers of your missing cheques, the issuing company (eg Amex) will contact the place where you bought them.

Opening Hours

- Official business hours are from 10am to 5pm Monday to Friday but many offices open later and close earlier.

STANDARD OPENING HOURS

General opening hours are as follows:

BUSINESS	OPENING HOURS
Airline offices	9.30am-5.30pm Mon-Sat
Banks (nationalised)	10am-2pm or 4pm Mon-Fri, to noon or 1pm Sat
Government offices	9.30am-1pm & 2-5.30pm Mon-Fri, closed 2nd and 4th Sat in some places
Museums	10am-5pm Tue-Sun
Post offices	10am-4pm Mon-Fri, to noon Sat
Restaurants	lunch noon-3pm, dinner 7-10pm or 11pm
Shops	10am-7pm or 8pm, some closed Sun
Sights	10am-5pm or dawn-dusk

- Most offices have an official lunch hour from around 1pm.
- Bank opening hours vary from town to town so check locally; foreign-exchange offices may open longer and operate daily.
- Some larger post offices have a full day on Saturday and a half-day on Sunday.
- In some places with six-day weeks, establishments may be closed on the second and fourth Saturdays of the month.
- All timings vary regionally. In remote areas, shops may open and close depending on the weather, local political situation or the proprietor's mood.

Photography

For useful tips and techniques on travel photography, read Lonely Planet's guide to *Travel Photography*.

Digital

- Memory cards for digital cameras are available from photographic shops in most large cities and towns. However, the quality of memory cards is variable – some don't carry the advertised amount of data.
- Expect to pay upwards of ₹500 for a 4GB card.
- To be safe, regularly back up your memory card to CD; internet cafes may offer this service for ₹60 to ₹120 per disk.
- Some photographic shops make prints from digital photographs for roughly the standard print-and-processing charge.

Restrictions

- India is touchy about anyone taking photographs of military installations – this can include train stations, bridges, airports, military sites and sensitive border regions.
- Photography from the air is mostly OK, unless you're taking off from (or landing in) airports actively shared by defence forces.
- Many places of worship – such as monasteries, temples and mosques – also prohibit photography. Taking photos inside a shrine, at a funeral, at a religious ceremony or of people publicly bathing (including rivers) can also be offensive – ask first.
- Flash photography may be prohibited in certain areas of shrines or historical monuments, or may not be permitted at all.
- Exercise sensitivity when taking photos of people, especially women, who may find it offensive – obtain permission in advance.
- It is not uncommon these days for people in touristy areas to demand a posing fee in return for being photographed. Exercise your discretion in these situations: if you think the money would make a positive difference in the lives of your subjects and their families, then go ahead and donate by all means. Alternately, if it looks like a scam to earn a quick buck, refrain. In any case, ask first to avoid misunderstandings later.

Post

India has the biggest postal network on earth, with over 155,500 post offices. Mail and poste-restante services are generally good, although the speed of delivery will depend on the efficiency of any given office. Airmail is faster and more reliable than sea mail, although it's best to use courier services (such as DHL and TNT) to send and receive items of value – expect to pay around ₹3000 per kilogram to Europe, Australia or the USA. Smaller private couriers are often cheaper, but goods may be repacked into large packages to cut costs and things sometimes go missing.

Receiving Mail

- To claim mail you'll need to show your passport.
- Ask senders to address letters to you with your surname in capital letters and underlined, followed by poste restante, GPO (main post office), and the city or town in question.
- Many 'lost' letters are simply misfiled under given/first names, so check under both your names and ask senders to provide a return address.
- Letters sent via poste restante are generally held for around one to two months before being returned.
- It's best to have any parcels sent to you by registered post.

Sending Mail

LETTERS

- Posting letters/aerogrammes to anywhere overseas costs ₹20/15.
- International postcards cost around ₹7.
- For postcards, stick on the stamps *before* writing on them, as post offices can give you as many as four stamps per card.
- Sending a letter overseas by registered post costs an extra ₹15.

PARCELS

- Posting parcels can either be relatively straightforward or involve multiple counters and lots of queuing; get to the post office in the morning.
- Prices depend on weight (including packing material). Packing the article safely is your responsibility.
- A small package (unregistered) costs ₹40 (up to 100g) to any country and ₹30 per additional 100g (up to a maximum of 2000g; different charges apply for higher weights).

- Parcel post has a maximum of 20kg to 30kg depending on the destination.
- Airmail takes one to three weeks, sea mail two to four months and Surface Air-Lifted (SAL) – a curious hybrid where parcels travel by both air and sea – around one month.
- Express mail service (EMS; delivery within three days) costs around 30% more than the normal airmail price.
- All parcels sent through the government postal service must be packed up in white linen and the seams sealed with wax – agents outside the post office usually offer this service for a small fee.
- Customs declaration forms, available from the post office, must be stitched or pasted to the parcel. No duty is payable by the recipient for gifts under the value of ₹1000.
- Carry a permanent marker to write on the parcel any information requested by the desk.
- Books or printed matter can go by international book post for ₹350 (maximum 5kg), but the package must be wrapped with a hole that reveals the contents for inspection by customs – tailors can do this in such a way that nothing falls out. **India Post** (www.indiapost.gov.in) has an online calculator for domestic and international postal tariffs.

Public Holidays

There are officially three national public holidays. Every state celebrates its own official holidays, which cover bank holidays for government workers as well as major religious festivals. Most businesses (offices, shops etc) and tourist sites close on public holidays, but transport is usually unaffected. It's wise to make transport and hotel reservations well in advance if you intend visiting during major festivals.

Republic Day 26 January
Mahavir Jayanti (Jain) February
Holi (Hindu) March
Easter (Christian) March/April
Buddha Jayanti (Buddhist) April/May
Independence Day 15 August
Eid al-Fitr (Muslim) August/September
Dussehra (Hindu) September/October
Gandhi Jayanti 2 October
Diwali (Hindu) October/November
Guru Nanak Jayanti (Sikh) November
Christmas (Christian) 25 December

Safe Travel

Travellers to India's major cities may fall prey to petty and opportunistic crime but most problems can be avoided with a bit of common sense and an appropriate amount of caution. Women and solo travellers should read p496; for scams, see p498. Also have a look at the India branch of Lonely Planet's Thorn Tree Travel Forum (www.lonelyplanet.com/thorntree), where travellers often post timely warnings about problems they've encountered on the road. Always check your government's travel advisory warnings.

Rebel Violence

India has a number of (sometimes armed) dissident groups championing various causes, who have employed the same tried and tested techniques of rebel groups everywhere: assassinations and bomb attacks on government infrastructure, public transport, religious centres, tourist sites and markets.

Curfews and strikes can close the roads (as well as banks, shops etc) for days on end in sensitive regions.

International terrorism is as much of a risk in Europe or the USA, so this is no reason not to go to India, but it makes sense to check the local security situation carefully before travelling (especially in high-risk areas).

Telephone

- There are few payphones in South India (apart from in airports), but private

GOVERNMENT TRAVEL ADVICE

The following government websites offer travel advice and information on current hotspots.

- **Australian Department of Foreign Affairs** (www.smarttraveller.gov.au)
- **British Foreign Office** (www.gov.uk/fco)
- **Canadian Department of Foreign Affairs** (www.voyage.gc.ca)
- **German Foreign Office** (www.auswaertiges-amt.de)
- **Japan Ministry of Foreign Affairs** (www.mofa.go.jp)
- **Netherlands Ministry of Foreign Affairs** (www.government.nl)
- **Swiss Department of Foreign Affairs** (www.eda.admin.ch)
- **US State Department** (http://travel.state.gov)

STD/ISD/PCO call booths do the same job, offering inexpensive local, interstate and international calls at lower prices than calls made from hotel rooms.

➡ These booths are found around the country. A digital meter displays how much the call is costing and usually provides a printed receipt when the call is finished.

➡ Costs vary depending on the operator and destination but can be from ₹1 per minute for local calls and between ₹5 and ₹10 for international calls.

➡ Some booths also offer a 'call-back' service – you ring home, provide the phone number of the booth and wait for people at home to call you back, for a fee of around ₹20 on top of the cost of the preliminary call.

➡ Getting a line can be difficult in remote country and mountain areas – an engaged signal may just mean that the exchange is overloaded or broken, so keep trying.

➡ Useful online resources include the **Yellow Pages** (www.indiayellowpages.com) and **Justdial** (www.justdial.com).

Mobile Phones

➡ Indian mobile phone numbers usually have 10 digits, mostly beginning with 9 (but sometimes also with 7 or 8).

➡ There's roaming coverage for international GSM phones in most cities and large towns.

➡ To avoid expensive roaming costs (often highest for incoming calls), get hooked up to the local mobile-phone network by applying for a local prepaid SIM card.

➡ Mobiles bought in some countries may be locked to a particular network; you'll have to get the phone unlocked, or buy a local phone (available from ₹2000) to use an Indian SIM card.

GETTING CONNECTED

➡ Getting connected is inexpensive but complicated, owing to security concerns, and involves some amount of paperwork.

➡ Foreigners must supply between one and five passport photos, their passport, and photocopies of their passport identity and visa pages.

➡ You must also supply a residential address, which can be the address of your hotel (ask the management for a letter confirming this).

➡ Some phone companies send representatives to the listed address; others call to verify that you are actually staying there.

➡ Some travellers have reported their SIM cards being 'blocked' once the company realised they had moved from the hotel where they registered their phone. Others have been luckier for the entire duration of their travels.

➡ Another option is to get a friendly local to obtain a connection in their name.

➡ Prepaid mobile phone kits (SIM card and phone number, plus an allocation of calls) are available in most towns for about ₹200 from a phone shop, local STD/ISD/PCO booth or grocery store.

➡ You must then purchase more credit, sold as direct credit. You pay the vendor and the credit is deposited straight into your account, minus some taxes and service charge.

CHARGES

➡ Calls made within the state or city where you bought the SIM card are less than ₹1 a minute. You can call internationally for less than ₹10 a minute.

➡ SMS messaging is even cheaper. International outgoing messages cost ₹5. Incoming calls and messages are free.

➡ Most SIM cards are state-specific. If you use them in another state, you have to pay (nominal) roaming charges for both incoming and outgoing communications.

➡ The government may have done away with roaming charges altogether by 2013, making calls on the move cheaper.

➡ Unreliable signals and problems with international texting (messages or replies not coming through or being delayed) are not uncommon.

➡ The leading service providers are Airtel, Vodafone, Reliance, Idea and BSNL.

➡ As the mobile-phone industry continues to evolve, rates, coverage and suppliers are all likely to develop during the life of this book.

Phone Codes

➡ When calling India from abroad dial your country's international access code, then ☎91 (India's country code), then the area code (without the initial zero), then the local number. For mobile phones, the area code and initial zero are not required.

➡ If calling internationally from India dial ☎00 (the international access code), then the country code of the country you're calling, the area code (without the initial zero) and the local number.

➡ Land phone numbers have an area code followed by up to eight digits.

➡ Toll-free numbers begin with ☎1800.

➡ To make interstate calls to a mobile phone, add 0 before the 10-digit number.

➡ To call a land phone from a mobile phone, you always have to add the area code (with the initial zero).

➡ Some call centre numbers might require the initial zero (eg calling an airline ticketing service based in Delhi from Karnataka).

➡ A Home Country Direct service, which gives you access to the international operator in your home country, exists for the US (☎000 117) and the UK (☎000 4417).

➡ To access an international operator elsewhere, dial ☎000 127. The operator can place a call to anywhere in the world and allow you to make collect calls.

Time

India uses the 12-hour clock and the local standard time is known as Indian Standard Time (IST). IST is 5½ hours ahead of GMT/UTC. The floating half-hour was added to maximise daylight hours over such a vast country.

Toilets

➡ Public toilets are most easily found in major cities and tourist sites; the cleanest (usually with sit-down and squat choices) are usually at modern restaurants, shopping complexes and cinemas.

➡ Beyond urban centres, toilets are of the squat variety and locals may use the 'hand-and-water' technique, which involves carrying out ablutions with a small jug of water and the left hand. It's always a good idea to carry your own toilet paper and hand sanitiser, just in case.

GET TO KNOW YOUR BATHROOM

➡ Most South Indian midrange hotels and all top-end ones have sit-down toilets with toilet paper and soap supplied. In ultracheap hotels, and in places off the tourist trail, squat toilets (described as 'Indian style', as opposed to 'Western style') are the norm and toilet paper is rarely provided.

➡ Terminology for hotel bathrooms varies across India. 'Attached bath' or 'private bath' means the room has its own en suite bathroom. 'Common bath' or 'shared bath' means communal bathroom facilities.

➡ Not all rooms have hot water. 'Running', '24-hour' or 'constant' water means hot water is available round-the-clock (not always the case in reality). 'Bucket' hot water is only available in buckets (sometimes for a small charge).

➡ Many places use wall-mounted electric geysers (water heaters) that need to be switched on up to an hour before use. The geyser's switch can sometimes be located outside the bathroom.

➡ The hotel rooms we have listed have their own private bathroom unless otherwise indicated.

Tourist Information

In addition to Government of India tourist offices (also known as 'India Tourism'), each state maintains its own network of tourist offices. These vary in their efficiency and usefulness – some are run by enthusiastic souls who go out of their way to help, others are little more than a means of drumming up business for State Tourism Development Corporation tours.

The first stop for information should be the tourism website of the Government of India, **Incredible India** (www.incredibleindia.org); for details of its regional offices around India, click on the 'Help Desk' tab at the top of the homepage.

Travellers with Disabilities

India's crowded public transport, crush of humanity and variable infrastructure can test even the hardiest able-bodied traveller. If you have a physical disability or are vision impaired, these can pose even more of a challenge. If your mobility is considerably restricted, you may like to ease the stress by travelling with an able-bodied companion.

Accommodation Hotels that are wheelchair-friendly are almost exclusively top end. Make pre-trip enquiries and book ground-floor rooms at hotels that lack adequate facilities.

Accessibility Some restaurants and offices have ramps but most tend to have at least one step. Staircases are often steep; lifts frequently stop at mezzanines between floors.

Footpaths Where pavements exist, they can be riddled with holes, littered with debris and packed with pedestrians. If using crutches, bring along spare rubber caps.

Transport Hiring a car with a driver will make moving around a lot easier; if you use a wheelchair, make sure the car-hire company can provide an appropriate vehicle to carry it.

For further advice pertaining to your specific requirements, consult your doctor before heading to India.

The following organisations may be able to proffer further information or at least point you in the right direction.

Accessible Journeys (www.disabilitytravel.com)

Access-Able Travel Source (www.access-able.com)

Global Access News (www.globalaccessnews.com)

Mobility International USA (MIUSA; www.miusa.org)

Royal Association for Disability & Rehabilitation (RADAR; www.radar.org.uk)

Visas

Citizens of Finland, Japan, Luxembourg, New Zealand, Singapore, Cambodia, Vietnam, the Philippines, Laos, Myanmar (Burma) and Indonesia are currently granted a 30-day single-entry visa on arrival at Mumbai (Bombay), Chennai (Madras), Kolkata (Calcutta) and New Delhi airports. All other nationals – except Nepali and Bhutanese – must get a visa *before* arriving in India. These are available at Indian missions worldwide. Note that your passport needs to be valid for at least six months beyond your intended stay in India, with at least two blank pages.

Entry Requirements

➡ In 2009 a large number of foreigners were found to be working in India on tourist visas, so regulations surrounding who can get a visa and for how long have been tightened.

➡ Most people travel on the standard six-month tourist visa.

➡ Student and business visas have strict conditions (consult the Indian embassy for details).

➡ Tourist visas are valid from the date of issue, not the date you arrive in India. You can spend a total of 180 days in the country.

➡ Five- and 10-year tourist visas are available to US citizens *only* under a bilateral arrangement; however, you can still only stay in the country for up to 180 days continuously.

➡ Currently you are required to submit two passport photographs with your visa application; these must be in colour and must be 2in x 2in.

➡ An onward travel ticket is a requirement for most visas, but this isn't always enforced (check in advance).

➡ Additional restrictions apply to travellers from Bangladesh and Pakistan, as well as certain Eastern European, African and Central Asian countries. Check any special conditions for your nationality with the Indian embassy in your country.

➡ Visas are priced in the local currency and may have an added service fee (contact your country's Indian embassy for current prices).

➡ Extended visas are possible for people of Indian origin (excluding those in Pakistan and Bangladesh) who hold a non-Indian passport and live abroad.

➡ For visas lasting more than six months, you're supposed to register at the Foreigners' Regional Registration Office (FRRO) within 14 days of arriving in India; enquire about these special conditions when you apply for your visa.

Re-Entry Requirements

A law barring re-entry of foreigners into India within two months of the date of their previous exit was scrapped in late 2012, allowing tourists on subcontinental or South Asian itineraries to transit freely between India and its neighbouring countries. However, the 60-day-gap law still applies to citizens of China, Pakistan, Iraq, Iran, Afghanistan, Bangladesh and Sudan.

Visa Extensions

India has traditionally been very stringent with visa extensions. At the time of writing, the government was granting extensions only in circumstances such as medical emergencies or theft of passport just before the applicant planned to leave the country (at the end of his/her visa).

If you do need to extend your visa due to any such exigency, you should contact the **Foreigners' Regional Registration Office** (FRRO; ☎011-26711443; frrodli@nic.in; East Block VIII, Level II Sector 1, RK Puram) in Delhi. This is also the place to come for a replacement visa, and if you need your lost/stolen passport replaced (required before you can leave the country). Regional FRROs are even less likely to grant an extension.

Assuming you meet the stringent criteria, the FRRO is permitted to issue an extension of 14 days (free for nationals of most countries; enquire on application). You must bring your confirmed air ticket, one passport photo (take two, just in case), and a photocopy of your passport identity and visa pages. Note that this system is designed to get you out of the country promptly with the correct official stamps, not to give you two extra weeks of travel and leisure.

Transport

GETTING THERE & AWAY

South India is most easily accessed via its major international airports in Mumbai (Bombay) and Chennai (Madras). Some countries may offer charter flights to Goa. The South can also be reached overland from elsewhere in and near India. Flights, tours and other tickets can be booked online at www.lonelyplanet.com/bookings.

Entering India

Entering India by air or land is relatively straightforward, with standard immigration and customs procedures. A frustrating law barring re-entry into India within two months of the previous date of departure has now been done away with (except for citizens of some Asian countries), thus allowing travellers to freely combine their India tour with side trips to neighbouring countries.

Passport

- To enter India you need a valid passport, a visa and an onward/return ticket.
- Your passport should be valid for at least six months beyond your intended stay in India. If your passport is lost or stolen, immediately contact your country's representative.
- Keep photocopies of your airline ticket and the identity and visa pages of your passport in case of emergency. Better yet, scan and email copies to yourself.
- Check with the Indian embassy in your home country for any special conditions that may exist for your nationality.

Air

Airports & Airlines

As India is a big country, it makes sense to fly into the airport that's nearest to the area you'll be visiting. South India has four main gateways for international flights (see the following list); however, a number of other centres such as Goa, Kochi (Cochin) and Thiruvananthapuram (Trivandrum) also service international carriers. For detailed information log on to www.aai.aero.

India's national carrier is **Air India** (☎1800 1801407; www.airindia.com), of which the former state-owned domestic carrier, Indian Airlines, is now a part. Air travel in India has had a relatively decent safety record in recent years.

Bengaluru (Bangalore; BLR; ☎1800 4254425; www.bengaluruairport.com; Bengaluru International Airport)

Chennai (Madras; MAA; ☎044-22560551; www.chennaiairportguide.com; Anna International Airport)

Hyderabad (HYD; www.hyderabad.aero; Rajiv Gandhi International Airport)

Mumbai (Bombay; BOM; ☎022-26264000; www.csia.in; Chhatrapati Shivaji International Airport)

Land

Border Crossings

- Although most visitors fly into India, it is possible to travel overland between India and Bangladesh, Bhutan, Nepal and Pakistan. The overland route from Nepal is the most popular. For more on these routes, consult Lonely Planet's *Istanbul to Kathmandu*, or see the 'Europe to India overland' section on www.seat61.com/India.htm.
- If you enter India by bus or train, you'll be required to disembark at the border for standard immigration and customs checks.
- You *must* have a valid Indian visa in advance, as no visas are available at the border.
- Drivers of cars and motorbikes will need the vehicle's registration papers, liability insurance and an international drivers' permit in addition to their domestic licence. You'll also need a *Carnet de passage en douane*, which acts as a

CLIMATE CHANGE & TRAVEL

Every form of transport that relies on carbon-based fuel generates CO_2, the main cause of human-induced climate change. Modern travel is dependent on aeroplanes, which might use less fuel per kilometre per person than most cars but travel much greater distances. The altitude at which aircraft emit gases (including CO_2) and particles also contributes to their climate change impact. Many websites offer 'carbon calculators' that allow people to estimate the carbon emissions generated by their journey and, for those who wish to do so, to offset the impact of the greenhouse gases emitted with contributions to portfolios of climate-friendly initiatives throughout the world. Lonely Planet offsets the carbon footprint of all staff and author travel.

temporary waiver of import duty on the vehicle.

➡ To find out the latest requirements for the paperwork and other important driving information, contact your local automobile association.

Sea

There are several sea routes between India and surrounding islands but none leave Indian sovereign territory. After a 28-year hiatus, a ferry service between southern India and Sri Lanka began again in 2011, linking Thoothikudi (Tuticorin) in Tamil Nadu with Colombo. However, it was suspended after five months. A new service between the same ports, or on the old route between Rameswaram and Talaimannar, may start; check the internet to see if there has been any progress.

GETTING AROUND

Air

Airlines in South India

➡ India has a competitive domestic airline industry. Well-established players are Air India (which now includes Indian Airlines), GoAir, IndiGo, Jet Airways and Spicejet.

➡ Airline seats can be booked cheaply over the internet, through travel agencies or by telephone. In fact, private operators – in a bid to reduce operational costs – are slowly doing away with city offices in favour of online or phone bookings. Several authorised agents, however, still continue to book tickets on their behalf. Domestic airlines set rupee fares for Indian citizens, while foreigners may be charged US dollar fares (usually payable in rupees).

➡ Apart from airline sites, bookings can be made through reliable ticketing portals such as **Cleartrip** (www.cleartrip.com), **Make My Trip** (www.makemytrip.com) and **Yatra** (www.yatra.com).

➡ Security norms require you to produce your ticket and your passport at the time of entering an airport. Airline counters at airports can issue you a printed copy of your ticket (if you don't have one) for ₹50.

➡ At the time of writing, the following airlines were operating across various destinations in India. Keep in mind, however, that the competitive nature of the aviation industry means that fares fluctuate dramatically. Holidays, festivals and seasons also have a serious effect on ticket prices so check for the latest fares online.

➡ Security at airports is generally stringent. In smaller airports, all hold baggage must be x-rayed prior to check-in (major airports now have in-line baggage screening facilities). Every item of cabin baggage needs a label, which must be stamped as part of the security check (don't forget to collect tags at the check-in counter).

➡ Keeping peak hour congestion in mind, the recommended check-in time for domestic flights is two hours before departure – the deadline is 45 minutes. The usual baggage allowance is 20kg (10kg for smaller aircraft) in economy class.

Air India (☎1800 1801407; www.airindia.com) India's national carrier operates many domestic and international flights.

GoAir (☎1800 222111; www.goair.in) Reliable low-cost carrier servicing Goa and Kochi among other destinations.

IndiGo (☎099-10383838; www.goindigo.in) The best and trendiest of the lot, with plenty of flights across India and to select overseas destinations. Has an untarnished reputation for being on time.

Jet Airways (☎1800 225522; www.jetairways.com) Operates flights across India and to select overseas destinations.

JetKonnect (☎1800 223020; www.jetkonnect.com) Jet Airways' budget carrier flies to numerous destinations.

Spicejet (☎1800 1803333; www.spicejet.com) Destinations include Bengaluru

(India), Colombo (Sri Lanka) and Kathmandu (Nepal).

Bicycle

There are no restrictions on bringing a bicycle into the country. However, bicycles sent by sea can take a few weeks to clear customs in India, so it's better to fly them in. It may actually be cheaper – and less hassle – to hire or buy a bicycle in India itself. Read up on bicycle touring before you travel: Rob Van Der Plas' *Bicycle Touring Manual* and Stephen Lord's *Adventure Cycle-Touring Handbook* are good places to start. Consult local cycling magazines and clubs for useful information and advice. The **Cycling Federation of India** (www.cyclingfederationofindia.org) can provide local information.

Hire

- Tourist centres and traveller hang-outs are the easiest spots to find bicycles for hire – simply enquire locally.
- Prices vary: between ₹40 and ₹100 per day for a roadworthy, Indian-made bicycle; mountain bikes, where available, are usually upwards of ₹350 per day.
- Hire places may require a cash security deposit (avoid leaving your airline ticket or passport).

Practicalities

- Mountain bikes with off-road tyres give the best protection against India's puncture-prone roads.
- Roadside cycle mechanics abound but you should still bring spare tyres, brake cables, lubricating oil, a chain repair kit, and plenty of puncture-repair patches.
- Bikes can often be carried for free, or for a small luggage fee, on the roof of public buses – handy for uphill stretches.
- Contact your airline for information about transporting your bike and customs formalities in your home country.

Purchase

- Mountain bikes with reputable brands that include Hero and Atlas generally start at around ₹5000.
- Reselling is usually fairly easy – ask at local cycle or hire shops or put up an advert on travel noticeboards. If you purchased a new bike and it's still in reasonably good condition, you should be able to recoup around 50% of what you originally paid.

Road Rules

- Vehicles are driven on the left in India but otherwise road rules are virtually nonexistent.
- Cities and national highways can be hazardous places to cycle so, where possible, stick to back roads.
- Be conservative about the distance you expect to cover – an experienced cyclist can manage around 60km to 100km a day on the plains, 40km to 60km on all-weather mountain roads and 40km or less on dirt roads.

RIDING THE RAILS WITH YOUR BIKE

For long hauls, transporting your bike by train can be a convenient option. Buy a standard train ticket for the journey, then take your bike to the station parcel office with your passport, registration papers, driver's licence and insurance documents. Packing-wallahs will wrap your bike in protective sacking for around ₹200 to ₹500 and you must fill out various forms and pay the shipping fee – around ₹2500 to ₹3500 (charges are less on an ordinary train) – plus an insurance fee of 1% of the declared value of the bike. Bring the same paperwork to collect your bike from the goods office at the other end. If the bike is left waiting at the destination for more than 24 hours, you'll pay a storage fee of around ₹100 per day.

Boat

- Scheduled ferries connect mainland India to Port Blair in the Andaman Islands.
- There are sporadic ferries from Visakhapatnam (Andhra Pradesh) to the Andaman Islands.
- Between October and May there are boat services from Kochi (Kerala) to the Lakshadweep Islands.
- There are also numerous shorter ferry services across rivers, from chain pontoons to coracles, and various boat cruises.

Bus

- Buses go almost everywhere in India and are the only way to get around many mountainous areas. They tend to be the cheapest way to travel. Services are generally fast and frequent.
- Roads in curvaceous terrain can be especially perilous; buses are often driven with wilful abandon, and accidents are always a risk.
- Avoid night buses unless there's no alternative: driving conditions are more hazardous and drivers may be inebriated or suffering from lack of sleep.
- All buses make snack and toilet stops (some more

frequently than others), providing a break but possibly adding hours to journey times.

➡ Shared jeeps complement the bus service in many mountain areas.

Classes

➡ State-owned and private bus companies both offer several types of buses, graded loosely as 'ordinary', 'semi-deluxe', 'deluxe' or 'super deluxe'. These are usually open to interpretation, and the exact grade of luxury offered in a particular class can vary from place to place.

➡ In general, ordinary buses tend to be ageing rattletraps while the deluxe grades range from less decrepit versions of ordinary buses to flashy Volvo buses with AC and reclining (locally called 'push-back') two-by-two seating.

➡ Buses run by the state government are usually the more reliable option (if there's a breakdown, another bus will be sent to pick up passengers), and seats can usually be booked up to a month in advance. Many state governments now operate super-deluxe buses.

➡ Private buses are either more expensive (but more comfortable), or cheaper but with kamikaze drivers and conductors who cram on as many passengers as possible to maximise profits.

➡ Travel agencies in many tourist towns offer relatively expensive private two-by-two buses, which tend to leave and terminate at convenient central stops.

➡ Take earplugs on long-distance buses to muffle the often deafening music or movies played in some buses.

➡ On any bus, try to sit upfront to minimise the bumpy effect of potholes. Avoid sitting directly above the wheels.

Costs

➡ The cheapest buses are 'ordinary' government buses, but prices vary from state to state.

➡ Add around 50% to the ordinary fare for deluxe services, double the fare for AC, and triple or quadruple the fare for a two-by-two super-deluxe service.

Luggage

➡ Luggage is stored in compartments underneath the bus (sometimes for a small fee) or carried on the roof.

➡ Arrive at least an hour before departure time – some buses cover roof-stored bags with a canvas sheet, making last-minute additions inconvenient/impossible.

➡ If your bags go on the roof, make sure they're securely locked, and tied to the metal baggage rack – unsecured bags can fall off on rough roads.

➡ Theft is a (minor) risk: watch your bags at snack and toilet stops. Never leave day-packs or valuables unattended inside the bus.

Reservations

➡ Most deluxe buses can be booked in advance – government buses usually a month ahead – at the bus station or local travel agencies.

➡ Online bookings are now possible in select states such as Karnataka or at the excellent portal **Redbus** (☎1800 30010101; www.redbus.in).

➡ Reservations are rarely possible on 'ordinary' buses; travellers can be left behind in the mad rush for a seat.

➡ To secure a seat, send a travelling companion ahead to claim some space, or pass a book or article of clothing through an open window and place it on an empty seat. This 'reservation' method rarely fails.

➡ If you board a bus midway through its journey, you may have to stand until a seat becomes free.

➡ Many buses only depart when full – passengers might suddenly leave yours to join one that looks nearer to departing.

➡ Many bus stations have a separate women's queue (not always obvious when signs are in Hindi and men join the melee).

➡ Women have an unspoken right to elbow their way to the front of any bus queue in India, so don't be shy, ladies!

Car

Few people bother with self-drive car hire – not only because of the hair-raising driving conditions, but also because hiring a car with driver is wonderfully affordable in India, particularly if several people share the cost. Seatbelts are either nonexistent or of variable quality. **Hertz** (www.hertz.com) is one of the few international companies with representatives in India.

Hiring a Car & Driver

➡ Most towns have taxi stands or car-hire companies where you can arrange short or long tours.

➡ Not all hire cars are licensed to travel beyond their home state. Those that are will pay extra state taxes, which are added to the hire charge.

➡ Ask for a driver who speaks some English and knows the region you intend visiting, and try to see the car and meet the driver before paying anything.

➡ A wide range of cars now ply as taxis. From a proletarian Tata Indica hatchback to a comfy Toyota Innova SUV, there's a model to suit every pocket.

➡ Hire charges for multiday trips cover the driver's

meals and accommodation. Drivers should make their own sleeping and eating arrangements.

➡ To help avoid misunderstandings, it's important to set the ground rules from day one; politely but firmly let the driver know that you're boss.

Costs

➡ Car hire costs depend on the distance and the terrain (driving on mountain roads uses more petrol, hence the higher cost).

➡ One-way trips usually cost the same as return ones (to cover the petrol and driver charges for getting back).

➡ Hire charges vary from state to state. Some taxi unions set a minimum time limit or a minimum kilometre distance for day trips – if you go over, you'll have to pay extra. Prices also vary according to the make and model of the taxi; luxury cabs and SUVs cost more than ordinary hatchbacks.

➡ To avoid potential misunderstandings, get *in writing* what you've been promised (quotes should include petrol, sightseeing stops, all your chosen destinations, and meals and accommodation for the driver). If a driver asks you for money for petrol en route because he is short of cash, get receipts for reimbursement later. If you're travelling by the kilometre, always check the odometer reading before you set out so as to avoid confusions while paying up.

➡ For sightseeing day trips around a single city, expect to pay upwards of ₹1000/1200 for a non-AC/AC car with an eight-hour, 80km limit per day (extra charges apply). For multiday trips, operators usually peg a 250km minimum running distance per day and charge around ₹8/10 per kilometre for a non-AC/AC car. If you overshoot, you pay extra.

➡ A tip is customary at the end of your journey; ₹100 per day is fair (more if you're really pleased with the driver's service).

Hitching

For a negotiable fee, truck drivers supplement the bus service in some remote areas. However, as drivers rarely speak English, you may have difficulty explaining where you wish to go, and working out a fair price to pay. Be aware that truck drivers have a reputation for driving under the influence of alcohol. As anywhere, women are strongly advised against hitching alone or even in pairs. Always use your instincts.

Local Transport

➡ Buses, cycle-rickshaws, autorickshaws, taxis, boats and urban trains provide transport around South India's cities.

➡ Costs for public transport vary from town to town.

➡ For any transport without a fixed fare, agree on the price *before* you start your journey and make sure that it covers your luggage and every passenger.

➡ Even where meters exist, drivers may refuse to use them, demanding an elevated 'fixed' fare. Insist on the meter; if that fails, find another vehicle. Or just bargain hard.

➡ Fares usually increase at night (by up to 100%) and some drivers charge a few rupees extra for luggage.

➡ Carry plenty of small bills for taxi and rickshaw fares as drivers rarely have change.

➡ In some places, taxi/autorickshaw drivers are involved in the commission racket.

Autorickshaw, Tempo & Vikram

➡ Similar to the tuk-tuks of Southeast Asia, the Indian autorickshaw is a three-wheeled motorised contraption with tin or canvas roof and sides, with room for two passengers (although you'll often see many more squeezed in) and limited luggage.

➡ They are also referred to as autos, scooters and riks.

➡ They are mostly cheaper than taxis and usually have a meter, although getting it turned on can be a challenge.

➡ Travelling by auto is great fun but, thanks to the open windows, can be noisy and hot (or severely cold!).

➡ Tempos and *vikrams* (large tempos) are outsized autorickshaws with room for more passengers, shuttling on fixed routes for a fixed fare.

➡ In country areas you may also see the fearsome-looking 'three-wheeler' – a crude tractor-like tempo with a front wheel on an articulated arm – or the Magic, a cute minivan that can take up to a dozen passengers.

Boat

Various kinds of local boats offer transport across and down rivers in South India, from big car ferries to wooden canoes and wicker coracles. Most of the larger boats carry bicycles and motorcycles for a fee.

Bus

Urban buses range from fume-belching, human-stuffed mechanical monsters that travel at breakneck speed to sanitised AC vehicles with comfortable seating and smoother ride quality. In any case, it's usually far more convenient to opt for an autorickshaw or taxi, as they are quicker and more frequent.

Cycle-Rickshaw

- A cycle-rickshaw is a pedal cycle with two rear wheels, supporting a bench seat for passengers. Most have a canopy that can be raised in wet weather, or lowered to provide extra space for luggage.
- Fares must be agreed upon in advance – speak to locals to get an idea of what is a fair price for the distance you intend to travel.
- Kolkata (Calcutta) is the last bastion of the hand-pulled rickshaw, known as the *tana* rickshaw. This is a hand-cart on two wheels pulled directly by the rickshaw-wallah.

Taxi

Most towns have taxis, and these are usually metered; however, getting drivers to use the meter can be a hassle. To avoid fare-setting shenanigans, use prepaid taxis where possible.

Prepaid Taxis & Radio Cabs

- Most major Indian airports and train stations now incorporate prepaid-taxi and radio cab booths. Here, you can book a taxi for a fixed price (which will include baggage) and thus avoid commission scams. Hold onto your receipt until you reach your destination, as proof of payment.
- Radio cabs cost marginally more than prepaid taxis, but are air-conditioned and manned by the company's chauffeurs. Cabs have electronic, receipt-generating fare meters and are fitted with GPS units, so the company can monitor the vehicle's movement around town. These minimise chances of errant driving or unreasonable demands for extra cash by the driver afterward.
- Smaller airports and stations may have prepaid autorickshaw booths instead.

Other Local Transport

In some towns, tongas (horse-drawn two-wheelers) and victorias (horse-drawn carriages) still operate. Mumbai and Chennai, among other centres, have suburban trains that leave from ordinary train stations.

Motorcycle

Despite traffic challenges, India is an amazing country for long-distance motorcycle touring. However, it can be quite an undertaking; there are some popular motorcycle tours for those who don't want the rigmarole of going it alone.

Weather is an important factor and you should check for the best times to visit different areas. To cross from neighbouring countries, check the latest regulations and paperwork requirements from the relevant diplomatic mission.

Driving Licence

To hire a motorcycle in India, technically you're required to have a valid international drivers' permit in addition to your domestic licence. In tourist areas, some places may rent out a motorcycle without asking for a driving permit/licence, but you won't be covered by insurance in the event of an accident, and may also face a fine.

Hire

The classic way to motorcycle around India is on a Royal Enfield, built to both vintage and modern specs. As well as making a satisfying chugging sound, these bikes are fully manual, making them easy to repair (parts can be found almost everywhere in India). On the other hand, Enfields are often less reliable than many of the newer, Japanese-designed bikes.

- Plenty of places rent out motorcycles for local trips and longer tours. Japanese- and Indian-made bikes in the 100cc to 150cc range are cheaper than the big 350cc to 500cc Enfields.
- As security, you'll need to leave a large cash deposit (ensure you get a receipt that stipulates the refundable amount), your passport or air ticket. We strongly advise not leaving these documents, in particular your passport which you need for hotel check-ins and if asked by the police.
- For three weeks' hire, a 500cc Enfield costs from ₹22,000; a 350cc costs ₹15,000. The price includes excellent advice and an invaluable crash course in Enfield mechanics and repairs.
- Helmets are available for ₹500 to ₹2000; extras (panniers, luggage racks, protection bars, rear-view mirrors, lockable fuel caps, petrol filters, extra tools) are also easy to come by.
- A useful website for Enfield models is **www.royalenfield.com**. In Mumbai, **Allibhai Premji Tyrewalla** (☎022-23099313; www.premjis.com; 205 Dr D Bhadkamkar (Lamington) Rd) sells new and

MANNING THE METER

Getting a metered ride is only half the battle. Meters are almost always outdated, so fares are calculated using a combination of the meter reading and a complicated 'fare adjustment card'. Predictably, this system is open to abuse. To get a rough estimate of fares in advance, try the portal www.taxiautofare.com.

secondhand motorcycles with a buy-back option.

Purchase

For longer tours, purchasing a motorcycle may sound like a great idea. However, sales of motor vehicles to foreigners come with reams of complicated paperwork, and in many situations, procuring a motorcycle might not be possible or feasible at all.

➡ Secondhand bikes are widely available (and paperwork is simpler than for a new machine). To find a secondhand motorcycle, check travellers' noticeboards and ask motorcycle mechanics and other bikers.

➡ A well-looked-after secondhand 350cc Enfield costs ₹40,000 to ₹50,000. The 500cc model ranges between ₹50,000 and ₹65,000. You will also have to pay for insurance.

OWNERSHIP PAPERS

➡ There's plenty of paperwork associated with owning a motorcycle. The process is complicated and time-consuming, so it's wise to seek advice from the agent selling the bike.

➡ Registration papers are signed by the local registration authority when the bike is first sold; you need these when you buy a secondhand bike.

➡ Foreign nationals cannot change the name on the registration but you must fill out forms for change of ownership and transfer of insurance.

➡ Registration must be renewed every 15 years (for around ₹5000); make absolutely sure that it states the 'road-worthiness' of the vehicle, and that there are no outstanding debts or criminal proceedings associated with the bike.

Insurance

➡ Only hire a bike that has third-party insurance – if you hit someone without insurance, the consequences can be very costly. Reputable companies will include third-party cover in their policies; those that don't probably aren't trustworthy.

➡ You must also arrange insurance if you buy a motorcycle (usually you can organise this through the person selling the bike).

➡ The minimum level of cover is third-party insurance – available for around ₹600 per year. This will cover repair and medical costs for any other vehicles, people or property you might hit, but won't cover you for your own machine. Comprehensive insurance (recommended) costs upwards of ₹1200 per year.

Fuel, Spare Parts & Extras

➡ Petrol and engine oil are widely available in the plains, but petrol stations are fewer in the mountains. If travelling to remote regions, carry enough extra fuel (seek local advice about fuel availability before setting off). At the time of writing, petrol cost around ₹70 to ₹75 per litre in different states.

➡ If you're going to remote regions it's also important to carry basic spares (valves, fuel lines, piston rings etc). Parts for Indian and Japanese machines are widely available in cities and larger towns.

➡ Get your machine serviced regularly (particularly older ones). Indian roads and engine vibration work things loose quite quickly.

➡ Check the engine and gearbox oil level regularly (at least every 500km) and clean the oil filter every few thousand kilometres.

➡ Given the road conditions, the chances are you'll make at least a couple of visits to a puncture-wallah – start your trip with new tyres and carry spanners to remove your own wheels.

➡ It's a good idea to bring your own protective equipment (jackets, gloves etc).

Road Conditions

Given the varied road conditions, India can be challenging for novice riders.

➡ Hazards range from cows and chickens crossing the carriageway to broken-down trucks, unruly traffic, pedestrians on the road, and ubiquitous potholes and unmarked speed humps.

➡ Rural roads sometimes have grain crops strewn across them to be threshed by passing vehicles – a serious sliding hazard for bikers.

➡ Try not to cover too much territory in one day and never ride in the dark – many vehicles drive without lights, and dynamo-powered motorcycle headlamps are useless at low revs while negotiating around potholes.

➡ On busy national highways, expect to average 40km/h to 50km/h without stops; on winding back roads and dirt tracks this can drop to 10km/h.

Organised Motorcycle Tours

Dozens of companies offer organised motorcycle tours around India with a support vehicle, mechanic and guide. Here are some reputable outfits (see websites for contact details, itineraries and prices):

Blazing Trails (www.blazingtrailstours.com)

Classic Bike Adventure (www.classic-bike-india.com)

Ferris Wheels (www.ferriswheels.com.au)

H-C Travel (www.hctravel.com)

Himalayan Roadrunners (www.ridehigh.com)

Lalli Singh Tours (www.lallisingh.com)

Moto Discovery (www.motodiscovery.com)

Royal Expeditions (www.royalexpeditions.com)

Saffron Road Motorcycle Tours (www.saffronroad.com)

Wheel of India (www.wheelofindia.com)

Shared Jeeps

➡ In mountain areas, shared jeeps supplement the bus service, charging similar fixed fares.

➡ Although nominally designed for five to six passengers, most shared jeeps squeeze in more. The seats beside and immediately behind the driver are more expensive than the cramped bench seats at the rear.

➡ Jeeps only leave when full; people often bail out of a half-full jeep and pile into one with more passengers that is ready to depart. Drivers will leave immediately if you pay for all the empty seats and 'reserve' a vehicle for yourself.

➡ Jeeps run from jeep stands and 'passenger stations' at the junctions of major roads; ask locals to point you in the right direction.

➡ In some states, jeeps are known as 'sumos' after the Tata Sumo, a popular vehicle.

➡ Travel sickness, particularly on winding mountain roads, may mean you'll be asked to give up your window seat to queasy fellow passengers.

Tours

Tours are available all over South India, run by tourist offices, local transport companies and travel agencies. Organised tours can be an inexpensive way to see several places on one trip, although you rarely get much time at each place. If you arrange a tailor-made tour, you'll have more freedom about where you go and how long you stay.

Drivers may double as guides, or you can hire a qualified local guide for a fee. In tourist towns, be wary of touts claiming to be professional guides.

International Tour Agencies

Many international companies offer tours to India, from straightforward sightseeing trips to adventure tours and activity-based holidays. To find current tours that match your interests, quiz travel agents and surf the web. Some good places to start your tour hunt:

Dragoman (www.dragoman.com) One of several reputable overland tour companies offering trips in customised vehicles.

Exodus (www.exodus.co.uk) A wide array of specialist trips, including tours with a holistic, wildlife or adventure focus.

India Wildlife Tours (www.india-wildlife-tours.com) All sorts of wildlife tours, plus jeep, horse or camel safaris and birdwatching.

Indian Encounter (www.indianencounters.com) Special-interest tours that include wildlife-spotting, river-rafting and ayurvedic treatments.

Intrepid Travel (www.intrepidtravel.com) Endless possibilities, from wildlife tours to sacred rambles.

Peregrine Adventures (www.peregrineadventures.com) Popular cultural and trekking tours.

Sacred India Tours (www.sacredindiatours.com) Includes tours with a holistic focus such as yoga and ayurveda, as well as architectural and cultural tours.

Shanti Travel (www.shantitravel.com/en) A range of tours including family and adventure run by a Franco-Indian team.

World Expeditions (www.worldexpeditions.com) An array of options that includes trekking and cycling tours.

Train

Travelling by train is a quintessential Indian experience. Trains offer a smoother ride than buses and are especially recommended for long journeys that include overnight travel. India's rail network is one of the largest and busiest in the world and Indian Railways is the largest utility employer on earth, with roughly 1.5 million workers. There are around 6900 train stations scattered across the country.

We've listed useful trains but there are hundreds more. The best way of sourcing updated railway information is to use relevant internet sites such as **Indian Railways** (www.indianrail.gov.in) and the excellent **India Rail Info** (www.indiarailinfo.com), with added offline browsing support. There's also *Trains at a Glance* (₹45), available at many train station bookstands and better bookshops/newsstands, but it's published annually so it's not as up to date as websites. Nevertheless, it offers comprehensive timetables covering all the main lines.

Booking Tickets in India

➡ You can either book tickets through a travel agency or hotel (for a commission) or in person at the train station.

➡ You can also book online through **IRCTC** (www.irctc.co.in), the e-ticketing division of Indian Railways, or portals such as **Make My Trip** (www.makemytrip.com) and **Yatra** (www.yatra.com).

➡ Remember, however, that online booking of train tickets has its share of glitches: travellers have reported problems with registering themselves on some portals and using certain overseas credit cards.

➡ Big stations often have English-speaking staff who can help with reservations; at smaller stations, the stationmaster and their deputies usually speak English. It's also worth approaching tourist-office staff if you need advice.

AT THE STATION

Get a reservation slip from the information window, fill in the name of the departure station, destination station, the class you want to travel and the name and number of the train. Join the long queue for the ticket window where your ticket will be printed. Women should take advantage of the separate women's queue – if there isn't one, go to the front of the regular queue.

TOURIST RESERVATION BUREAU

Larger cities and major tourist centres have an International Tourist Bureau, which allows you to book tickets in relative peace – check www.indianrail.gov.in for a list of these stations.

Reservations

➡ Bookings open 120 days before departure and you must make a reservation for chair-car, sleeper, 1AC, 2AC and 3AC carriages. No reservations are required for general (2nd-class) compartments; you have to grab seats here the moment the train pulls in.

➡ Trains are always busy so it's wise to book as far in advance as possible, especially for overnight journeys. There may be additional services to certain destinations during major festivals but it's still worth booking well in advance.

➡ Reserved tickets show your seat/berth and carriage number. Carriage numbers are written on the side of the train (station staff and porters can point you in the right direction). A list of names and berths is posted on the side of each reserved carriage.

➡ Refunds are available on any ticket, even after departure, with a penalty – rules are complicated, check when you book.

➡ Trains can be delayed at any stage of the journey; to avoid stress, factor some leeway into your plans.

➡ Be mindful of potential drugging and theft.

➡ If the train you want to travel on is sold out, enquire about other options.

TOURIST QUOTA

A special (albeit small) tourist quota is set aside for foreign tourists travelling between popular stations. These seats can only be booked at dedicated reservation offices in major cities, and you need to show your passport and visa as ID. Tickets can be paid for in rupees (some offices may ask to see foreign exchange certificates – ATM receipts will suffice), British pounds, US dollars or euros in cash, or Thomas Cook and American Express travellers cheques.

TAKTAL TICKETS

Indian Railways holds back a small number of tickets on key trains and releases them at 10am one day before the train is due to depart. A charge of ₹10 to ₹300 is added to each ticket price. First AC tickets are excluded from the scheme.

RESERVATION AGAINST CANCELLATION (RAC)

Even when a train is fully booked, Indian Railways sells a handful of seats in each class as 'Reservation Against Cancellation' (RAC). This means that if you have an RAC ticket and someone cancels before the departure date, you will get his or her seat (or berth). You'll have to check the reservation list at the station on the day of travel to see if you've been allocated a confirmed seat/berth. Even if no one cancels, you can still board the train

FARE FINDER

Go to www.indiarailinfo.com and type in the name of the two destinations. You'll promptly get a list of every train (with the name, number, arrival/departure times and journey details) plying the route, as well as fares for each available class.

EXPRESS TRAIN FARES (₹)

DISTANCE (KM)	1AC	2AC	3AC	EXECUTIVE CHAIR	CHAIR CAR (CC)	SECOND (II)
100	848	500	155	353	120	90
200	848	500	251	559	196	90
300	848	500	342	755	266	122
400	1064	627	425	937	331	151
500	1279	754	509	1121	396	182
1000	2140	1255	829	1853	644	295
1500	2780	1624	1049	NA	816	374
2000	3420	1993	1270	NA	987	452

as an RAC ticket holder and travel without a seat.

WAITLIST (WL)

If the RAC quota is maxed out as well, you will be handed a waitlisted ticket. This means that if there are enough cancellations, you may eventually move up the order to land a confirmed berth, or at least an RAC seat. Check your booking status at www.indianrail.gov.in/pnr_stat.html by entering your ticket's PNR number. You can't board the train on a waitlisted ticket, but a refund is available – ask the ticket office about your chances.

Costs

- Fares are calculated by distance and class of travel; some are slightly more expensive, but the price includes meals.
- Most air-conditioned carriages have a catering service (meals are brought to your seat). In unreserved classes, it's a good idea to carry portable snacks.
- Seniors (those over 60) get 30% off all fares in all classes on all types of trains. Children below the age of five travel free, those aged between five and 12 are charged half price.

Health

There is huge geographical variation in India, so environmental issues like heat, cold and altitude can cause health problems. Hygiene is generally poor so food and water-borne illnesses are fairly common. Various insect-borne diseases are present, particularly in tropical regions. Medical care is basic in many areas (especially beyond the larger cities) so it's essential to be well prepared.

Pre-existing medical conditions and accidental injury (especially traffic accidents) account for most life-threatening problems. Becoming ill in some way, however, is common. Fortunately, most travellers' illnesses can be prevented with some common-sense behaviour or treated with a well-stocked travellers' medical kit – however, never hesitate to consult a doctor while on the road, as self-diagnosis can be hazardous.

Many parts of South India are hot and humid throughout the year. For most people it takes around two weeks to adapt to the hot climate. Swelling of the feet and ankles is common, as are muscle cramps caused by excessive sweating. Prevent these by avoiding dehydration and excessive activity in the heat. Don't eat salt tablets (they aggravate the gut); drinking rehydration solution or eating salty food helps. Treat cramps by resting, rehydrating with double-strength rehydration solution and gently stretching. Prickly heat is a common skin rash in the tropics, caused by sweat trapped under the skin. Treat it by moving out of the heat for a few hours and by having cool showers. Creams and ointments clog the skin so they should be avoided. Locally bought prickly-heat powder can be helpful.

The following advice is a general guide only and certainly does not replace the advice of a doctor trained in travel medicine.

BEFORE YOU GO

You can buy many medications over the counter in India without a doctor's prescription, but it can be difficult to find some of the newer drugs, particularly the latest antidepressant drugs, blood-pressure medications and contraceptive pills. Bring the following:

- medications in their original, labelled containers
- a signed, dated letter from your physician describing your medical conditions and medications, including generic names
- a physician's letter documenting the medical necessity of any syringes you bring
- if you have a heart condition, a copy of your ECG taken just prior to travelling
- any regular medication (double your ordinary needs)

Insurance

Don't travel without health insurance. Emergency evacuation is expensive. Consider the following when buying insurance:

- You may require extra cover for adventure activities such as rock climbing and scuba diving.
- In India, doctors usually require immediate payment in cash. Your insurance plan may make payments directly to providers or it will reimburse you later for overseas health expenditures. If you do have to claim later, make sure you keep all relevant documentation.
- Some policies ask that you telephone back (reverse charges) to a centre in your home country where an immediate assessment of your problem will be made.

Vaccinations

Specialised travel-medicine clinics are your best source of up-to-date information; they stock all available vaccines and can give specific recommendations for your trip. Most vaccines don't give immunity until *at least* two weeks after they're given, so visit a doctor well before departure. Ask your doctor for an International Certificate of Vaccination (also known as the 'yellow booklet'), which will list all the vaccinations you've received.

Medical Checklist

Recommended items for a personal medical kit:

- antifungal cream, eg Clotrimazole
- antibacterial cream, eg Mupirocin
- antibiotic for skin infections, eg Amoxicillin/Clavulanate or Cephalexin
- antihistamine – there are many options, eg Cetrizine for daytime and Promethazine for night
- antiseptic, eg Betadine
- antispasmodic for stomach cramps, eg Buscopam
- contraceptive
- decongestant, eg Pseudoephedrine
- DEET-based insect repellent
- diarrhoea medication – consider an oral rehydration solution (eg Gastrolyte), diarrhoea 'stopper' (eg Loperamide) and antinausea medication (eg Prochlorperazine). Antibiotics for diarrhoea

REQUIRED & RECOMMENDED VACCINATIONS

The only vaccine required by international regulations is **yellow fever**. Proof of vaccination will only be required if you have visited a country in the yellow-fever zone within the six days prior to entering India. If you are travelling to India from Africa or South America, you should check to see if you require proof of vaccination.

The World Health Organization (WHO) recommends the following vaccinations for travellers going to India (as well as being up to date with measles, mumps and rubella vaccinations):

Adult diphtheria & tetanus Single booster recommended if none in the previous 10 years. Side effects include sore arm and fever.

Hepatitis A Provides almost 100% protection for up to a year; a booster after 12 months provides at least another 20 years' protection. Mild side effects such as headache and sore arm occur in 5% to 10% of people.

Hepatitis B Now considered routine for most travellers. Given as three shots over six months. A rapid schedule is also available, as is a combined vaccination with Hepatitis A. Side effects are mild and uncommon, usually headache and sore arm. In 95% of people lifetime protection results.

Polio Only one booster is required as an adult for lifetime protection. Inactivated polio vaccine is safe during pregnancy.

Typhoid Recommended for all travellers to India, even those only visiting urban areas. The vaccine offers around 70% protection, lasts for two to three years and comes as a single shot. Tablets are also available, but the injection is usually recommended as it has fewer side effects. Sore arm and fever may occur.

Varicella If you haven't had chickenpox, discuss this vaccination with your doctor.

These immunisations are recommended for long-term travellers (more than one month) or those at special risk (seek further advice from your doctor):

Japanese B Encephalitis Three injections in all. Booster recommended after two years. Sore arm and headache are the most common side effects. In rare cases, an allergic reaction comprising hives and swelling can occur up to 10 days after any of the three doses.

Meningitis Single injection. There are two types of vaccination: the quadravalent vaccine gives two to three years' protection; meningitis group C vaccine gives around 10 years' protection. Recommended for long-term backpackers aged under 25.

Rabies Three injections in all. A booster after one year will then provide 10 years' protection. Side effects are rare – occasionally headache and sore arm.

Tuberculosis (TB) A complex issue. Adult long-term travellers are usually recommended to have a TB skin test before and after travel, rather than vaccination. Only one vaccine given in a lifetime.

HEALTH ADVISORIES

It's a good idea to consult your government's travel-health website before departure, if one is available:

- **Australia** (www.smartraveller.gov.au)
- **Canada** (www.travelhealth.gc.ca)
- **New Zealand** (www.mfat.govt.nz/travel)
- **UK** (www.fco.gov.uk/en/travelling-and-living-overseas)
- **US** (www.cdc.gov/travel)

include Ciprofloxacin; for bacterial diarrhoea, Azithromycin; for giardia or amoebic dysentery, Tinidazole

- first-aid items such as scissors, elastoplasts, bandages, gauze, thermometer (but not mercury), sterile needles and syringes, safety pins and tweezers
- Ibuprofen or another anti-inflammatory
- iodine tablets (unless you are pregnant or have a thyroid problem) to purify water
- migraine medication if you suffer from migraines
- Paracetamol
- pyrethrin to impregnate clothing and mosquito nets
- steroid cream for allergic or itchy rashes, eg 1% to 2% hydrocortisone
- high-factor sunscreen
- throat lozenges
- thrush (vaginal yeast infection) treatment, eg Clotrimazole pessaries or Diflucan tablet
- Ural or equivalent if prone to urine infections

Websites

There is a wealth of travel-health advice on the internet; www.lonelyplanet.com is a good place to start. Some other suggestions:

Centers for Disease Control and Prevention (CDC; www.cdc.gov) Good general information.

MD Travel Health (www.mdtravelhealth.com) Provides complete travel-health recommendations for every country, updated daily.

World Health Organization (WHO; www.who.int/ith) Its helpful book *International Travel & Health* is revised annually and is available online.

Further Reading

Lonely Planet's *Healthy Travel – Asia & India* is a handy pocket size and packed with useful information, including pre-trip planning, emergency first aid, immunisation and disease information, and what to do if you get sick on the road. Other recommended references include *Travellers' Health* by Dr Richard Dawood and *Travelling Well* by Dr Deborah Mills – check out the website of **Travelling Well** (www.travellingwell.com.au).

IN INDIA

Availability & Cost of Health Care

Medical care is hugely variable in India. Some cities now have clinics catering specifically to travellers and expatriates; these clinics are usually more expensive than local medical facilities, and offer a higher standard of care. Additionally, they know the local system, including reputable local hospitals and specialists. They may also liaise with insurance companies should you require evacuation. It is usually difficult to find reliable medical care in rural areas.

Before buying medication over the counter, check the use-by date, and ensure the packet is sealed and properly stored (eg not exposed to the sunshine).

Infectious Diseases

Malaria

This is a serious and potentially deadly disease. Before you travel, seek expert advice according to your itinerary (rural areas are especially risky) and on medication and side effects.

Malaria is caused by a parasite transmitted by the bite of an infected mosquito. The key symptom of malaria is fever, but general symptoms, such as headache, diarrhoea, cough or chills, may also occur. Diagnosis can only be properly made by taking a blood sample.

Two strategies should be combined to prevent malaria: mosquito avoidance and antimalarial medications. Most people who catch malaria are taking inadequate or no antimalarial medication.

Travellers are advised to prevent mosquito bites by taking these steps:

- Use a DEET-containing insect repellent on exposed skin. Wash this off at night, as long as you are sleeping under a mosquito net. Natural repellents such as citronella can be effective, but must be applied more frequently than products containing DEET.
- Sleep under a mosquito net impregnated with pyrethrin.
- Choose accommodation with proper screens and fans (if not air-conditioned).
- Impregnate clothing with pyrethrin in high-risk areas.

- Wear long sleeves and trousers in light colours.
- Use mosquito coils.
- Spray your room with insect repellent before going out for your evening meal.

There are a variety of medications available:

Chloroquine & Paludrine combination Limited effectiveness in many parts of South Asia. Common side effects include nausea (40% of people) and mouth ulcers.

Doxycycline (daily tablet) A broad-spectrum antibiotic that helps prevent a variety of tropical diseases, including leptospirosis, tick-borne disease and typhus. Potential side effects include photosensitivity (a tendency to sunburn), thrush (in women), indigestion, heartburn, nausea and interference with the contraceptive pill. More serious side effects include ulceration of the oesophagus – take your tablet with a meal and a large glass of water, and never lie down within half an hour of taking it. It must be taken for four weeks after leaving the risk area.

Lariam (mefloquine) This weekly tablet suits many people. Serious side effects are rare but include depression, anxiety, psychosis and seizures. Anyone with a history of depression, anxiety, other psychological disorders or epilepsy should not take Lariam. It is considered safe in the second and third trimesters of pregnancy. Tablets must be taken for four weeks after leaving the risk area.

Malarone A combination of atovaquone and proguanil. Side effects are uncommon and mild, most commonly nausea and headache. It is the best tablet for scuba divers and for those on short trips to high-risk areas. It must be taken for one week after leaving the risk area.

Other Diseases

Avian Flu 'Bird flu' or Influenza A (H5N1) is a subtype of the type A influenza virus. Contact with dead or sick birds is the principal source of infection and bird-to-human transmission does not easily occur. Symptoms include high fever and flu-like symptoms with rapid deterioration, leading to respiratory failure and death in many cases. Immediate medical care should be sought if bird flu is suspected. Check www.who.int/en/or www.avianinfluenza.com.au.

Dengue Fever This mosquito-borne disease is becomingly increasingly problematic, especially in the cities. As there is no vaccine available it can only be prevented by avoiding mosquito bites at all times. Symptoms include high fever, severe headache and body ache and sometimes a rash and diarrhoea. Treatment is rest and paracetamol – do not take aspirin or ibuprofen as it increases the likelihood of haemorrhaging. Make sure you see a doctor to be diagnosed and monitored.

Hepatitis A This food- and water-borne virus infects the liver, causing jaundice (yellow skin and eyes), nausea and lethargy. There is no specific treatment for hepatitis A, you just need to allow time for the liver to heal. All travellers to India should be vaccinated against hepatitis A.

Hepatitis B This sexually transmitted disease is spread by body fluids and can be prevented by vaccination. The long-term consequences can include liver cancer and cirrhosis.

Hepatitis E Transmitted through contaminated food and water, hepatitis E has similar symptoms to hepatitis A, but is far less common. It is a severe problem in pregnant women and can result in the death of both mother and baby. There is no commercially available vaccine, and prevention is by following safe eating and drinking guidelines.

HIV Spread via contaminated body fluids. Avoid unsafe sex, unsterile needles (including in medical facilities) and procedures such as tattoos. The growth rate of HIV in India is one of the highest in the world.

Japanese B Encephalitis This viral disease is transmitted by mosquitoes and is rare in travellers. Most cases occur in rural areas and vaccination is recommended for travellers spending more than one month outside of cities. There is no treatment, and it may result in permanent brain damage or death. Ask your doctor for further details.

Rabies This fatal disease is spread by the bite or possibly even the lick of an infected animal – most commonly a dog or monkey. You should seek medical advice immediately after any animal bite and commence postexposure treatment. Having pre-travel vaccination means the postbite treatment is greatly simplified. If an animal bites you, gently wash the wound with soap and water, and apply iodine-based antiseptic. If you are not pre-vaccinated you will need to receive rabies immunoglobulin as soon as possible, and this is very difficult to obtain in much of India.

Tuberculosis While TB is rare in travellers, those who have significant contact with the local population (such as medical and aid workers and long-term travellers) should take precautions. Vaccination is usually only given to children under the age of five, but adults at risk are recommended to have pre- and post-travel TB testing. The main symptoms are fever, cough, weight loss, night sweats and fatigue.

Typhoid This serious bacterial infection is also spread via food and water. It gives a high and slowly progressive fever and headache, and may be accompanied by a dry cough and stomach pain. It is diagnosed by blood tests and treated with antibiotics. Vaccination is recommended for all travellers who are spending more than a week in India. Be aware that vaccination is not 100% effective, so you must still be careful with what you eat and drink.

Travellers' Diarrhoea

This is by far the most common problem affecting travellers in India – between 30% and 70% of people will suffer from it within two weeks of starting their trip. It's usually caused by a bacteria, and thus responds promptly to treatment with antibiotics.

Travellers' diarrhoea is defined as the passage of more than three watery bowel actions within 24 hours, plus at least one other symptom, such as fever, cramps, nausea, vomiting or feeling generally unwell.

Treatment consists of staying well hydrated; rehydration solutions like Gastrolyte are the best for this. Antibiotics such as Ciprofloxacin or Azithromycin should kill the bacteria quickly. Seek medical attention quickly if you do not respond to an appropriate antibiotic.

Loperamide is just a 'stopper' and doesn't get to the cause of the problem. It can be helpful, though (eg if you have to go on a long bus ride). Don't take Loperamide if you have a fever or blood in your stools.

Amoebic Dysentery Amoebic dysentery is very rare in travellers but is often misdiagnosed by poor-quality labs. Symptoms are similar to bacterial diarrhoea: fever, bloody diarrhoea and generally feeling unwell. You should always seek reliable medical care if you have blood in your diarrhoea. Treatment involves two drugs: Tinidazole or Metronidazole to kill the parasite in your gut and then a second drug to kill the cysts. If left untreated complications such as liver or gut abscesses can occur.

Giardiasis Giardia is a parasite that is relatively common in travellers. Symptoms include nausea, bloating, excess gas, fatigue and intermittent diarrhoea. The parasite will eventually go away if left untreated but this can take months; the best advice is to seek medical treatment. The treatment of choice is Tinidazole, with Metronidazole being a second-line option.

Environmental Hazards

Air Pollution

Air pollution, particularly vehicle pollution, is an increasing problem in most of India's urban hubs. If you have severe respiratory problems, speak with your doctor before travelling to India.

Diving & Surfing

Divers and surfers should seek specialised advice before they travel to ensure their medical kit contains treatment for coral cuts and tropical ear infections. Divers should ensure their insurance covers them for decompression illness – get specialised dive insurance through an organisation such as **Divers Alert Network** (DAN; www.danasiapacific.org). Certain medical conditions are incompatible with diving; check with your doctor.

Food

Ways to help avoid food-related illness, including diarrhoea:

- eat only freshly cooked food
- avoid shellfish and buffets
- peel fruit
- cook vegetables
- soak salads in iodine water for at least 20 minutes
- eat in busy restaurants with a high turnover of customers

Insect Bites & Stings

Bedbugs They don't carry disease but their bites can be very itchy. They live in furniture and walls and then migrate to the bed at night. You can treat the itch with an antihistamine.

DRINKING WATER

- Never drink tap water.
- Bottled water is generally safe – but check the seal is intact at purchase.
- Avoid ice unless you know it has been safely made.
- Be careful of fresh juices served at street stalls in particular – they may have been watered down or may be served in unhygienic jugs/glasses.
- Boiling water is usually the most efficient method of purifying it.
- The best chemical purifier is iodine. It should not be used by pregnant women or those with thyroid problems.
- Water filters should also filter out most viruses. Ensure your filter has a chemical barrier such as iodine and a small pore size (less than four microns).

CARBON-MONOXIDE POISONING

Some mountain areas rely on charcoal burners for warmth, but these should be avoided due to the risk of fatal carbon-monoxide poisoning. The thick, mattress-like blankets used in many mountain areas are amazingly warm once you get beneath the covers. If you're still cold, improvise a hot-water bottle by filling your drinking-water bottle with boiled water and covering it with a sock.

Lice Most commonly appear on the head and pubic areas. You may need numerous applications of an antilice shampoo such as pyrethrin. Pubic lice are usually contracted from sexual contact.

Ticks Contracted walking in rural areas. Ticks are commonly found behind the ears, on the belly and in armpits. If you have had a tick bite and have a rash at the site of the bite or elsewhere, or fever or muscle aches, you should see a doctor. Doxycycline prevents tick-borne diseases.

Leeches Found in humid rainforest areas. They do not transmit any disease but their bites are often intensely itchy for weeks and can easily become infected. Apply an iodine-based antiseptic to any leech bite to help prevent infection.

Bee and wasp stings Anyone with a serious bee or wasp allergy should carry an injection of adrenalin (eg an Epipen). For others pain is the main problem – apply ice to the sting and take painkillers.

Skin Problems

Fungal rashes There are two common fungal rashes that affect travellers. The first occurs in moist areas, such as the groin, armpits and between the toes. It starts as a red patch that slowly spreads and is usually itchy. Treatment involves keeping the skin dry, avoiding chafing and using an antifungal cream such as Clotrimazole or Lamisil. The second, *Tinea versicolor,* causes light-coloured patches, most commonly on the back, chest and shoulders. Consult a doctor.

Cuts and scratches These become easily infected in humid climates. Immediately wash all wounds in clean water and apply antiseptic. If you develop signs of infection (increasing pain and redness), see a doctor.

Sunburn

Even on a cloudy day sunburn can occur rapidly. Always adhere to the following:

- use a strong sunscreen (factor 30) and reapply after a swim
- wear a wide-brimmed hat and sunglasses
- avoid lying in the sun during the hottest part of the day (10am to 2pm)
- be vigilant above 3000m – you can get burnt very easily at altitude

If you become sunburnt, stay out of the sun until you have recovered, apply cool compresses and, if necessary, take painkillers for the discomfort. Hydrocortisone cream (1%) applied twice daily is also helpful.

Women's Health

For gynaecological health issues, seek out a female doctor.

Birth control Bring adequate supplies of your own form of contraception.

Sanitary products Pads, rarely tampons, are readily available.

Thrush Heat, humidity and antibiotics can all contribute to thrush. Treatment is with antifungal creams and pessaries such as Clotrimazole. A practical alternative is a single tablet of Fluconazole (Diflucan).

Urinary-tract infections These can be precipitated by dehydration or long bus journeys without toilet stops; bring suitable antibiotics.

Language

The number of languages spoken in India helps explain why English is still widely spoken here, and why it's still in official use. Another 22 languages are recognised in the constitution, and more than 1600 other languages are spoken throughout the country.

While Hindi is the predominant language in the north, it bears little relation to the Dravidian languages of India's south and few people in the south speak Hindi. The native languages of the southern regions covered in this book (and in this chapter) are Tamil, Kannada, Konkani, Malayalam, Marathi and Telugu. Most of them belong to the Dravidian language family, although they have been influenced to varying degrees by Hindi and Sanskrit. As the predominant languages in specific geographic areas, they have in effect been used to determine the regional boundaries for the southern states.

Many educated Indians speak English as virtually their first language and for a large number of Indians it's often their second tongue, so you'll also find it very easy to get by in South India with English.

Pronunciation

The pronunciation systems of all languages covered in this chapter include a number of 'retroflex' consonants (pronounced with the tongue bent backwards), and all languages except for Tamil also have 'aspirated' consonants (pronounced with a puff of air). Our simplified pronunciation guides don't distinguish the retroflex consonants from their nonretroflex counterparts. The aspirated sounds are indicated with an apostrophe (') after the consonant. If you read our coloured pronunciation guides as if they were English, you'll be understood. The stressed syllables are indicated with italics for languages that have noticeable word stress; for others, all syllables should be equally stressed.

WANT MORE?

For in-depth language information and handy phrases, check out Lonely Planet's *India Phrasebook*. You'll find it at **shop.lonelyplanet.com**, or you can buy Lonely Planet's iPhone phrasebooks at the Apple App Store.

TAMIL

Tamil is the official language in the South Indian state of Tamil Nadu (as well as a national language in Sri Lanka, Malaysia and Singapore). It is one of the major Dravidian languages of South India, with records of its existence going back more than 2000 years. Tamil has about 62 million speakers in India.

A pronunciation tip: aw is pronounced as in 'law' and ow as in 'how'.

Basics

Hello.	வணக்கம்.	va·*nak*·kam
Goodbye.	போய் வருகிறேன்.	*po*·i va·*ru*·ki·reyn
Yes./No.	ஆமாம்./இல்லை.	*aa*·maam/*il*·lai
Excuse me.	தயவு செய்து.	ta·ya·*vu* sei·*du*
Sorry.	மன்னிக்கவும.	*man*·nik·ka·vum
Please.	தயவு செய்து.	ta·ya·*vu* chey·*tu*
Thank you.	நன்றி.	*nan*·dri

How are you?
நிங்கள் நலமா? *neeng*·kal na·*la*·maa

Fine, thanks. And you?
நலம், நன்றி. na·*lam nan*·dri
நீங்கள்? *neeng*·kal

What's your name?
உங்கள் பெயர் என்ன? *ung*·kal pe·*yar en*·na

My name is ...
என் பெயர் ... en pe·*yar* ...

Do you speak English?
நீங்கள் ஆங்கிலம் பேசுவீர்களா? — *neeng*·kal *aang*·ki·lam *pey*·chu·*veer*·ka·la

I don't understand.
எனக்கு விளங்கவில்லை. — e·*nak*·ku vi·*lang*·ka·vil·*lai*

Accommodation

Where's a ... nearby?	அருகே ஒரு ... எங்கே உள்ளது?	a·ru·*ke* o·*ru* ... *eng*·ke *ul*·la·tu
guesthouse	விருந்தினர் இல்லம	vi·*run*·ti·nar *il*·lam
hotel	ஹோட்டல	*hot*·tal

Do you have a ... room?	உங்களிடம் ஓர் ... அறை உள்ளதா?	*ung*·ka·li·tam awr ... a·*rai* *ul*·la·taa
single	தன	ta·*ni*
double	இரட்டை	i·rat·*tai*

How much is it per ...?	ஓர் ... என்னவிலை?	awr ... *en*·na·vi·lai
night	இரவுக்கு	i·ra·*vuk*·ku
person	ஒருவருக்கு	o·ru·va·*ruk*·ku

bathroom	குளியலறை	ku·li·*ya*·la·rai
bed	படுக்கை	pa·*tuk*·kai
window	சன்னல	*chan*·nal

Directions

Where's the ...?
... எங்கே இருக்கிறது? — ... *eng*·key i·*ruk*·ki·ra·tu

What's the address?
விலாசம் என்ன? — vi·*laa*·cham *en*·na

Can you show me (on the map)?
எனக்கு (வரைபடத்தில்) காட்ட முடியுமா? — e·*nak*·ku (va·*rai*·pa·*tat*·til) *kaat*·ta mu·ti·yu·*maa*

How far is it?
எவ்வளவு தூரத்தில் இருக்கிறது? — *ev*·va·la·vu too·*rat*·til i·*ruk*·ki·ra·tu

It's ...	அது இருப்பது ...	a·*tu* i·*rup*·pa·tu ...
behind ...	... க்குப் பின்னால	... kup *pin*·naal
in front of ...	... க்கு முன்னால	... ku *mun*·naal
near (to ...)	(... க்கு) அருகே	(... ku) a·ru·*key*
on the corner	ஓரத்தில	aw·*rat*·til
straight ahead	நேரடியாக முன்புறம்	*ney*·ra·di·*yaa*·ha *mun*·pu·ram

Turn ...	... புறத்தில் திரும்புக.	pu·*rat*·til *ti*·rum·pu·ka
left	இடது	i·ta·*tu*
right	வலது	va·la·*tu*

Eating & Drinking

Can you recommend a ...?	நீங்கள் ஒரு ... பரிந்துரைக்க முடியுமா?	*neeng*·kal o·*ru* ... pa·rin·tu·*raik*·ka mu·ti·*yu*·maa
bar	பார்	paar
dish	உணவு வகை	u·na·*vu* va·*kai*
place to eat	உணவகம்	u·na·va·*ham*

I'd like (a/the) ..., please.	எனக்கு தயவு செய்து ... கொடுங்கள்.	e·*nak*·ku ta·ya·*vu* chey·*tu* ... ko·*tung*·kal
bill	விலைச்சீட்டு	vi·*laich*·cheet·tu
menu	உணவுப்–பட்டியல்	u·na·*vup*·pat·ti·yal
that dish	அந்த உணவு வகை	*an*·ta u·na·*vu* va·*hai*

(cup of) coffee/tea ...	(கப்) காப்பி/ தேனீர் ...	(kap) *kaap*·pi/ *tey*·neer ...
with milk	பாலுடன்	paa·lu·*tan*
without sugar	சர்க்கரை–இல்லாமல	*chark*·ka·rai·*il*·laa·mal

a bottle/glass of ... wine	ஒரு பாட்டில்/ கிளாஸ ... வைன்	o·*ru* *paat*·til/ ki·*laas* ... vain
red	சிவப்பு	chi·*vap*·pu
white	வெள்ளை	*vel*·lai

Do you have vegetarian food?
உங்களிடம சைவ உணவு உள்ளதா? — *ung*·ka·li·tam *chai*·va u·na·*vu* *ul*·la·taa

I'm allergic to (nuts).
எனக்கு (பருப்பு வகை) உணவு சேராது. — e·*nak*·ku (pa·*rup*·pu va·*kai*) u·na·*vu* *chey*·raa·tu

beer	பீர்	peer
breakfast	காலை உணவு	kaa·*lai* u·na·*vu*
dinner	இரவு உணவு	i·ra·*vu* u·na·*vu*
drink	பானம்	paa·*nam*
fish	மீன்	meen
food	உணவு	u·na·*vu*
fruit	பழம்	pa·*zam*
juice	சாறு	chaa·*ru*
lunch	மதிய உணவு	ma·*ti*·ya u·na·*vu*
meat	இறைச்சி	i·*raich*·chi

milk	பால்	paal
soft drink	குளிர் பானம்	ku·*lir* paa·*nam*
vegetable	காய்கறி	*kai*·ka·ri
water	தண்ணீர்	*tan*·neyr

Emergencies

Help!	உதவ!	u·ta·*vi*
Go away!	போய் விடு!	*pow*·i *vi*·tu

Call a doctor!
ஐ அழைக்கவும் ஒரு மருத்துவர்! — i a·*zai*·ka·vum o·*ru* ma·*rut*·tu·var

Call the police!
ஐ அழைக்கவும் போலிஸ! — i a·*zai*·ka·vum pow·*lees*

I'm lost.
நான் வழி தவறி போய்விட்டேன். — naan va·*zi* ta·va·*ri* pow·i·*vit*·teyn

I have to use the phone.
நான் தொலைபேசியை பயன்படுத்த வேண்டும். — naan *to*·lai·pey·*chi*·yai pa·*yan*·pa·*tut*·ta veyn·*tum*

Where are the toilets?
கழிவறைகள் எங்கே? — ka·*zi*·va·rai·kal *eng*·key

Shopping & Services

Where's the market?
எங்கே சந்தை இருக்கிறது? — *eng*·key *chan*·tai i·*ruk*·ki·ra·tu

Can I look at it?
நான் இதைப் பார்க்கலாமா? — naan i·*taip* *paark*·ka·laa·maa

How much is it?
இது என்ன விலை? — i·*tu* en·na vi·*lai*

That's too expensive.
அது அதிக விலையாக இருக்கிறது. — a·*tu* a·*ti*·ka vi·*lai*·yaa·ka i·*ruk*·ki·ra·tu

There's a mistake in the bill.
இந்த விலைச்சீட்டில் ஒரு தவறு இருக்கிறது. — *in*·ta vi·*laich*·cheet·til o·*ru* *ta*·va·ru i·*ruk*·ki·ra·tu

bank	வங்கி	*vang*·ki
internet	இணையம்	i·nai·*yam*
post office	தபால் நிலையம்	ta·*paal* ni·*lai*·yam
tourist office	சுற்றுப்பயண அலுவலகம்	chut·*rup*·pa·ya·na a·lu·va·la·*kam*

Numbers

1	ஒன்று	on·*dru*
2	இரண்டு	*i*·*ran*·tu
3	மூன்று	*moon*·dru
4	நான்கு	naan·*ku*
5	ஐந்து	ain·*tu*
6	ஆறு	*aa*·ru
7	ஏழு	ey·*zu*
8	எட்டு	et·*tu*
9	ஒன்பது	on·pa·*tu*
10	பத்து	pat·*tu*
20	இருபது	i·ru·pa·*tu*
30	முப்பது	mup·pa·*tu*
40	நாற்பது	naar·pa·*tu*
50	ஐம்பது	aim·pa·*tu*
60	அறுபது	a·ru·pa·*tu*
70	எழுபது	e·zu·pa·*tu*
80	எண்பது	en·pa·*tu*
90	தொன்னூறு	ton·noo·*ru*
100	நூறு	noo·*ru*
1000	ஓராயிரம்	*aw*·raa·yi·ram

Time & Dates

What time is it?
மணி என்ன? — ma·*ni* *en*·na

It's (two) o'clock.
மணி (இரண்டு). — ma·*ni* (i·*ran*·tu)

Half past (two).
(இரண்டு) முப்பது. — (i·*ran*·tu) mup·pa·*tu*

morning	காலை	kaa·*lai*
evening	மாலை	maa·*lai*
yesterday	நேற்று	*neyt*·tru
today	இன்று	in·*dru*
tomorrow	நாளை	*naa*·lai

Monday	திங்கள்	*ting*·kal
Tuesday	செவ்வாய்	chev·*vai*
Wednesday	புதன்	pu·*tan*
Thursday	வியாழன்	vi·*yaa*·zan
Friday	வெள்ளி	vel·*li*
Saturday	சனி	cha·*ni*
Sunday	ஞாயிறு	*nyaa*·yi·ru

Transport

Is this the ... to (New Delhi)?
இது தானா (புது– டில்லிக்குப்) புறப்படும் ...? — i·*tu* taa·*naa* (pu·*tu* til·lik·*kup*) pu·*rap*·pa·tum ...

bus	பஸ்	pas
plane	விமானம்	vi·*maa*·nam
train	இரயில்	i·ra·*yil*

One ... ticket (to Madurai), please.	(மதுரைக்கு) தயவு செய்து ... டிக்கட் கொடுங்கள்.	(ma·tu·raik·*ku*) ta·ya·*vu* chey·*tu* ... tik·*kat* ko·tung·*kal*
one-way	ஒரு வழிப்பயண	o·*ru* va·*zip*·pa·ya·na
return	இரு வழிப்பயண	i·*ru* va·*zip*·pa·ya·na

What time's the first/last bus?
எத்தனை மணிக்கு முதல்/இறுதி பஸ் வரும்?
et·ta·nai ma·*nik*·ku mu·*tal*/i·ru·*ti* pas va·*rum*

How long does the trip take?
பயணம் எவ்வளவு நேரம் எடுக்கும்?
pa·ya·*nam* ev·*va*·la·vu ney·*ram* e·*tuk*·kum

How long will it be delayed?
எவ்வளவு நேரம் அது தாமதப்படும்?
ev·*va*·la·vu *ney*·ram a·*tu* taa·ma·*tap*·pa·tum

Please tell me when we get to (Ooty).
(ஊட்டிக்குப்) போனவுடன் தயவு செய்து எனக்குக கூறுங்கள்.
(oot·tik·*kup*) paw·na·vu·*tan* ta·ya·*vu* chey·*tu* e·*nak*·kuk *koo*·rung·kal

Please take me to (this address).
தயவு செய்து என்னை இந்த (விலாசத்துக்குக்) கொண்டு செல்லுங்கள்.
ta·ya·*vu* chey·*tu en*·nai *in*·ta (vi·*laa*·chat·tuk·kuk) *kon*·tu *chel*·lung·kal

Please stop/wait here.
தயவு செய்து இங்கே நிறுத்துங்கள்/ காத்திருங்கள்.
ta·ya·*vu* chey·*tu ing*·key ni·*rut*·tung·kal/ *kaat*·ti·rung·kal

I'd like to hire a car (with a driver).
நான் ஒரு மோட்டார் வண்டி (ஓர் ஓட்டுநருடன்) வாடகைக்கு எடுக்க விரும்புகிறேன்.
naan o·*ru mowt*·taar *van*·ti (awr aw·*tu*·na·ru·tan) vaa·ta·*haik*·ku e·*tuk*·ka vi·*rum*·pu·ki·reyn

Is this the road to (Mamallapuram)?
இது தான் (மாமல்லபுரத்துக்கு) செல்லும் சாலையா?
i·*tu* taan (maa·mal·*la*·pu·rat·*tuk*·ku) *chel*·lum chaa·lai·*yaa*

airport	விமான நிலையம்	*vi*·maa·na *ni*·lai·yam
bicycle	சைக்கிள்	*chaik*·kil
boat	படகு	pa·ta·*ku*
bus stop	பஸ் நிறுத்தும்	pas ni·*rut*·tum
economy class	சிக்கன வகுப்பு	*chik*·ka·na va·*kup*·pu
first class	முதல் வகுப்பு	mu·*tal* va·*kup*·pu
motorcycle	மோட்டார் சைக்கிள்	*mowt*·taar *chaik*·kil
train station	நிலையம்	ni·*lai*·yam

KANNADA

Kannada is the official language of the state of Karnataka. It has 38 million speakers.

The symbol oh is pronounced as the 'o' in 'note' and ow as in 'how'.

Basics

Hello.	ನಮಸ್ಕಾರ.	na·mas·kaa·ra
Goodbye.	ಸಿಗೋಣ.	si·goh·na
Yes./No.	ಹೌದು./ಇಲ್ಲ.	how·du/il·la
Please.	ದಯವಿಟ್ಟು.	da·ya·vit·tu
Thank you.	ಥ್ಯಾಂಕ್ಯೂ.	t'ank·yoo
Excuse me.	ಸ್ವಲ್ಪ ದಾರಿ ಬಿಡಿ.	sval·pa daa·ri bi·di
Sorry.	ಕ್ಷಮಿಸಿ.	ksha·mi·si

What's your name?
ನಿಮ್ಮ ಹೆಸರೇನು? nim·ma he·sa·rey·nu

My name is ...
ನನ್ನ ಹೆಸರು ... nan·na he·sa·ru ...

Do you speak English?
ನೀವು ಇಂಗ್ಲೀಷ್ ಮಾತಾಡುತ್ತೀರ? nee·vu ing·lee·shu maa·taa·dut·tee·ra

I don't understand.
ನನಗೆ ಅರ್ಥವಾಗುವುದಿಲ್ಲ. na·na·ge ar·t'a·aa·gu·vu·dil·la

How much is it?
ಎಷ್ಟು ಇದು? esh·tu i·du

Where are the toilets?
ಟಾಯ್ಲೆಟ್ಟುಗಳು ಎಲ್ಲಿ? taay·let·tu·ga·lu el·li

Emergencies

Help!	ಸಹಾಯ ಮಾಡಿ!	sa·haa·ya maa·di
Go away!	ದೂರ ಹೋಗಿ!	doo·ra hoh·gi
Call ...!	... ಕಾಲ್ ಮಾಡಿ!	... kaal maa·di
a doctor	ಡಾಕ್ಟರಿಗೆ	daak·ta·ri·ge
the police	ಪೋಲೀಸಿಗೆ	poh·lee·si·ge

I have to use the phone.
ನಾನು ಫೋನ್ ಬಳಸಬೇಕು. naa·nu foh·nu ba·la·sa·bey·ku

I'm lost.
ನಾನು ಕಳೆದುಹೋಗಿರುವೆ. naa·nu ka·le·du·hoh·gi·ru·ve

Numbers

1	ಒಂದು	on·du
2	ಎರಡು	e·ra·du
3	ಮೂರು	moo·ru
4	ನಾಲ್ಕು	naa·ku
5	ಐದು	ai·du
6	ಆರು	aa·ru

7	ಏಳು	ey·lu
8	ಎಂಟು	en·tu
9	ಒಂಬತ್ತು	om·bat·tu
10	ಹತ್ತು	hat·tu
20	ಇಪ್ಪತ್ತು	ip·pat·tu
30	ಮೂವತ್ತು	moo·vat·tu
40	ನಲವತ್ತು	na·la·vat·tu
50	ಐವತ್ತು	ai·vat·tu
60	ಅರವತ್ತು	a·ra·vat·tu
70	ಎಪ್ಪತ್ತು	ep·pat·tu
80	ಎಂಬತ್ತು	em·bat·tu
90	ತೊಂಬತ್ತು	tom·bat·tu
100	ನೂರು	noo·ru
1000	ಸಾವಿರ	saa·vi·ra

KONKANI

Konkani is the official language of the state of Goa. It has 2.5 million speakers. The Devanagari script (also used to write Hindi and Marathi) is the official writing system for Konkani in Goa. However, many Konkani speakers in Karnataka use the Kannada script, as given in this section.

Pronounce eu as the 'u' in 'nurse', oh as the 'o' in 'note' and ts as in 'hats'.

Basics

Hello.	ಹಲ್ಲೋ.	*hal*·lo
Goodbye.	ಮೆಳ್ಯಾಂ.	*mel*·yaang
Yes./No.	ವ್ಹಯ್./ನಾಂ.	*weu*·i/naang
Please.	ಉಪ್ಕಾರ್ ಕರ್ನ್.	*up*·kaar keurn
Thank you.	ದೇವ್ ಬರೆಂ ಕರುಂ.	*day*·u *bo*·reng *ko*·roong
Excuse me.	ಉಪ್ಕಾರ್ ಕರ್ನ್.	*up*·kaar keurn
Sorry.	ಚೂಕ್ ಜ಼ಾಲಿ, ಮಾಫ಼್ ಕರ್.	ts'ook *zaa*·li maaf keur

What's your name?
ತುಜೆಂ ನಾಂವ್ಂ ಕಿತೆಂ? — *tu*·jeng *naang*·ung *ki*·teng

My name is ...
ಮ್ಹುಜೆಂ ನಾಂವ್ಂ ... — *m'eu*·jeng *naang*·ung ...

Do you speak English?
ಇಂಗ್ಲಿಶ್ ಉಲೈತಾಯ್ಗೀ? — *ing*·leesh *u*·leuy·taay·gee

Do you understand?
ಸಮ್ಜಾಲೆಂಗೀ? — *som*·zaa·leng·gee

I understand.
ಸಮ್ಜಾಲೆಂ. — *som*·zaa·leng

I don't understand.
ನಾಂ, ಸಮ್ಜೊಂಕ್–ನಾಂ. — naang *som*·zonk·naang

How much is it?
ತಾಕಾ ಕಿತ್ಲೆ ಪೈಶೆ? — *taa*·kaa *kit*·le *peuy*·she

Where are the toilets?
ಟೊಯ್ಲೆಟ್ ಖ್ಯೆಂಚರ್ ಆಸಾತ್? — *toy*·let *k'eu*·ing·ts'eur *aa*·saat

Emergencies

Help!	ಮ್ಹಾಕಾ ಕುಮಕ್ ಕರ್!	*m'aa*·kaa *ku*·meuk keur
Go away!	ವಸ್!	weuts'
Call ...!	... ಆಪೈ!	... *aa*·pai
a doctor	ದಾಕ್ತೆರಾಕ್	*daak*·te·raak
the police	ಪೊಲಿಸಾಂಕ್	*po*·li·saank

I have to use the phone.
ಮ್ಹಾಕಾ ಫೊನಾಚಿ ಘರ್ಜ್ ಆಸಾ. — *m'aa*·kaa *fo*·na·chi g'eurz *aa*·saa

I'm lost.
ಮ್ಹುಜೀ ವಾಟ್ ಚುಕ್ಲ್ಯಾ. — *m'eu*·ji waat *ts'uk*·lyaa

Could you help me, please?
ಮ್ಹಾಕಾ ಇಲ್ಲೊಚೊ ಉಪ್ಕಾರ್ ಕರ್ಶಿಗೀ? — *m'aa*·kaa *il*·lo·ts'o *up*·kaar *keur*·shi·gee

Numbers

1	ಏಕ್	ayk
2	ದೋನ್	dohn
3	ತೀನ್	teen
4	ಚಾರ್	chaar
5	ಪಾಂಚ್	paants'
6	ಸೊ	so
7	ಸಾತ್	saat
8	ಆಟ್	aat'
9	ನೋವ್	nohw
10	ಧಾ	d'aa
20	ವೀಸ್	wees
30	ತೀಸ್	tees
40	ಚಾಳೀಸ್	*ts'aa*·lees
50	ಪನ್ನಾಸ್	*pon*·naas
60	ಸಾಟ್	saat'
70	ಸತ್ತರ್	*seut*·teur
80	ಐಂಶಿಂ	*euyng*·shing
90	ನೊವ್ವೋದ್	*no*·wod
100	ಶೆಂಭರ್	*shem*·bor
1000	ಹಜ಼ಾರ್	*ha*·zaar

MALAYALAM

Malayalam is the official language of the state of Kerala. It has around 33 million speakers.

Note that zh is pronounced as the 's' in 'measure'.

Basics

Hello.	ഹലോ.	ha·*lo*
Goodbye.	ഗുഡ് ബൈ.	good bai
Yes.	അതെ.	a·*t'e*
No.	അല്ല.	al·*la*
Please.	ദയവായി.	da·ya·va·*yi*
Thank you.	നന്ദി.	nan·*n'i*
Excuse me.	ക്ഷമിക്കണം.	ksha·mi·ka·*nam*
Sorry.	ക്ഷമിക്കുക.	ksha·mi·ku·*ka*

Do you speak English?
നിങ്ങൾ ഇംഗ്ലീഷ് സംസാരിക്കുമോ? — ning·*al* in·*glish* sam·*saa*·ri·ku·*mo*

I don't understand.
എനിക്ക് മനസ്സിലാകില്ല. — e·ni·*ku* ma·na·*si*·la·ki·la

What's your name?
താങ്കളുടെ പേര് എന്താണ്? — t'ang·a·lu·*te* pey·*ru* en·t'aa·*nu*

My name is ...
എന്റെ പേര് ... — en·*te* pey·*ru* ...

How much is it?
എത്രയാണ് ഇതിന്? — et'·ra·yaa·*nu* i·t'i·*nu*

Where are the toilets?
എവിടെയാണ് കക്കൂസ്? — e·vi·de·yaa·*nu* ka·koo·*su*

Emergencies

Help!	സഹായിക്കൂ!	sa·ha·yi·*koo*
Go away!	ഇവിടുന്ന് പോകൂ!	i·vi·du·*nu* po·*koo*

Call ...!	... വിളിക്കൂ!	... vi·li·*koo*
a doctor	ഒരു ഡോക്ടറെ	o·*ru* dok·ta·*re*
the police	പൊലീസിനെ	po·li·si·*ne*

I have to use the phone.
എനിക്ക് ഈ ഫോൺ ഒന്നു വേണമായിരുന്നു. — e·ni·*ku* ee fon o·*nu vey*·na·maa·yi·ru·*nu*

I'm lost.
എനിക്ക് വഴി അറിഞ്ഞുകൂട. — e·ni·*ku* va·*zhi* a·ri·*nyu*·koo·*da*

Numbers

1	ഒന്ന്	*on*·na
2	രണ്ട്	*ran*·d'a
3	മൂന്ന്	*moo*·na
4	നാല്	*naa*·la
5	അഞ്ച്	*an*·ja
6	ആറ്	*aa*·ra
7	ഏഴ്	e·zha
8	എട്ട്	e·t'a
9	ഒമ്പത്	*on*·pa·t'a
10	പത്ത്	*pa*·t'a
20	ഇരുപത്	i·*ru*·pa·t'a
30	മുപ്പത്	*mu*·p'a·t'a
40	നാൽപത്	*naal*·pa·t'a
50	അമ്പത്	*an*·ba·t'a
60	അറുപത്	a·*ru*·pa·t'a
70	എഴുപത്	e·*zhu*·pa·t'a
80	എൺപത്	*en*·pa·t'a
90	തൊണ്ണൂറ്	t'on·*noo*·ra
100	നൂറ്	*n'oo*·ra
1000	ആയിരം	*aa*·ye·ram

MARATHI

Marathi is the official language of the state of Maharashtra. It is spoken by an estimated 71 million people. Marathi is written in the Devanagari script (also used for Hindi).

Keep in mind that oh is pronounced as the 'o' in 'note'.

Basics

Hello.	नमस्कार.	na·mas·*kaar*
Goodbye.	बाय.	bai
Yes.	होय.	hoy
No.	नाही.	naa·*hee*
Please.	कृपया.	kri·pa·*yaa*
Thank you.	धन्यवाद.	d'an·ya·*vaad*
Excuse me.	क्षमस्व.	ksha·mas·*va*
Sorry.	खेद आहे.	k'ed aa·*he*

What's your name?
आपले नांव ? — aa·pa·*le* naa·*nav*

My name is ...
माझे नांव ... — maa·*j'e* naa·*nav* ...

Do you speak English?
आपण इंग्रजी बोलता का ? — aa·*pan* ing·re·*jee* bol·*taa* kaa

I don't understand.
मला समजत नाही. — ma·*laa* sam·*jat* naa·*hee*

How much is it?
याची काय किंमत आहे ? — yaa·*chee* kaay ki·*mat* aa·*he*

Where are the toilets?
शौचालय कुठे आहे ? — shoh·chaa·*lai* ku·*t'e* aa·*he*

Emergencies

Help!	मदत !	ma·*dat*
Go away!	दूर जा !	door jaa

Call ...!	कॉल करा ...!	kaal ka·*raa* ...
a doctor	डॉक्टरांना	dok·ta·raan·*naa*
the police	पोलिसांना	po·li·saa·*naa*

I have to use the phone.
मला फोन वापरायचा आहे. — ma·*laa* fon vaa·pa·raa·ya·*chaa* aa·*he*

I'm lost.
मी हरवले आहे. — mee ha·ra·va·*le* aa·*he*

Numbers

1	एक	ek
2	दोन	don
3	तीन	teen
4	चार	chaar
5	पाच	paach
6	सहा	sa·*haa*
7	सात	saat
8	आठ	aat'
9	नऊ	na·*oo*
10	दहा	da·*haa*
20	वीस	vees
30	तीस	tees
40	चाळीस	chaa·*lees*
50	पन्नास	pan·*naas*
60	साठ	saat'
70	सत्तर	sat·*tar*
80	ऐंशी	ain·*shee*
90	नव्वद	nav·*vad*
100	शंभर	sham·*b'ar*
1000	एक हजार	ek ha·*jaar*

TELUGU

Telugu is the official language of the state of Andhra Pradesh. It has 70 million speakers.

Remember to pronounce oh as the 'o' in 'note'.

Basics

Hello.	నమస్కారం.	na·mas·kaa·ram
Goodbye.	వెళ్ళొస్తాను.	vel·loh·staa·nu
Yes./No.	అవును./కాదు.	a·vu·nu/kaa·du
Please.	దయచేసి.	da·ya·chay·si
Thank you.	ధన్యవాదాలు.	d'an·ya·vaa·daa·lu
Excuse me.	ఏమండి.	ay·an·di
Sorry.	క్షమించండి.	ksha·min·chan·di

What's your name?
మీ పేరేంటి? — mee pay·rayn·ti

My name is ...
నా పేరు ... — naa pay·ru ...

Do you speak English?
మీరు ఇంగ్లీషు మాట్లాడుతారా? — mee·ru ing·lee·shu maat·laa·du·taa·raa

I don't understand.
అర్థం కాదు. — ar·t'am kaa·du

How much is it?
అది ఎంత? — a·di en·ta

Where are the toilets?
బాత్రూములు ఎక్కడ ఉన్నాయి? — baat·room·lu ek·ka·da un·naa·yi

Emergencies

Help!	సహాయం కావాలి!	sa·haa·yam kaa·vaa·li
Go away!	వెళ్ళిపో!	vel·li·poh
Call ...!	... పిలవండి!	... pi·la·van·di
a doctor	డాక్టర్ని	daak·tar·ni
the police	పోలీసుల్ని	poh·lee·sul·ni

I have to use the phone.
నేను ఫోను వాడుకోవాలి. — nay·nu p'oh·nu vaa·du·koh·vaa·li

I'm lost.
నేను దారి తప్పి పోయాను. — nay·nu daa·ri tap·pi poh·yaa·nu

Numbers

1	ఒకటి	oh·ka·ti
2	రెండు	ren·du
3	మూడు	moo·du
4	నాలుగు	naa·lu·gu
5	ఐదు	ai·du
6	ఆరు	aa·ru
7	ఏడు	ay·du
8	ఎనిమిది	e·ni·mi·di
9	తొమ్మిది	tohm·mi·di
10	పది	pa·di
20	ఇరవై	i·ra·vai
30	ముప్పై	mup·p'ai
40	నలభై	na·la·b'ai
50	యాభై	yaa·b'ai
60	అరవై	a·ra·vai
70	డెబ్బై	deb·b'ai
80	ఎనభై	e·na·b'ai
90	తొంభై	tohm·b'ai
100	వంద	van·da
1000	వెయ్యి	vey·yi

GLOSSARY

Adivasi – tribal person
Agni – major deity in the *Vedas*; mediator between men and the gods; also fire
ahimsa – discipline of non-violence
air-cooler – noisy water-filled cooling fan
Ananta – serpent on whose coils *Vishnu* reclined
apsara – heavenly nymph
Arjuna – *Mahabharata* hero and military commander who married Subhadra (*Krishna*'s incestuous sister), took up arms and overcame many demons; he had the *Bhagavad Gita* related to him by *Krishna*, led *Krishna*'s funeral ceremony and finally retired to the Himalaya
Aryan – Sanskrit for 'noble'; those who migrated from Persia and settled in northern India
Ashoka – ruler in the 3rd century BC; responsible for spreading Buddhism throughout South India
ashram – spiritual community or retreat
autorickshaw – noisy, three-wheeled, motorised contraption for transporting passengers, livestock etc for short distances; found throughout the country, they are cheaper than taxis
avatar – incarnation, usually of a deity
ayurveda – the ancient and complex science of Indian herbal medicine and healing
azad – free (Urdu), as in Azad Jammu & Kashmir

baba – religious master or father; term of respect
bagh – garden
baksheesh – tip, donation (alms) or bribe
banyan – Indian fig tree; spiritual to many Indians
Bhagavad Gita – Hindu Song of the Divine One; *Krishna*'s lessons to *Arjuna*, the main thrust of which was to emphasise the philosophy of *bhakti*; it's part of the *Mahabharata*
bhajan – devotional song
bhakti – surrendering to the gods; faith
bhang – dried leaves and flowering shoots of the marijuana plant
bhavan – house, building; also spelt *bhawan*
BJP – Bharatiya Janata Party; political party
bodhisattva – literally 'one whose essence is perfected wisdom'; in Early Buddhism, bodhisattva refers only to the Buddha during the period between his conceiving the intention to strive for Buddhahood and the moment he attained it; in *Mahayana* Buddhism, it is one who renounces nirvana in order to help others attain it
Bollywood – India's answer to Hollywood; the film industry of Mumbai (Bombay)
Brahma – Hindu god; worshipped as the creator in the *Trimurti*
Brahmin – member of the priest/scholar caste, the highest Hindu caste
Buddha – Awakened One; the originator of Buddhism; also regarded by Hindus as the ninth incarnation of *Vishnu*

cantonment – administrative and military area of a Raj-era town
Carnatic music – classical music of South India
caste – a Hindu's hereditary station (social standing) in life; there are four castes: the *Brahmins*, the *Kshatriyas*, the *Vaishyas* and the *Shudras;* the Brahmins occupy the top spot
chaitya – Sanskrit form of 'cetiya', meaning shrine or object of worship; has come to mean temple, and more specifically, a hall divided into a central nave and two side aisles by a line of columns, with a votive *stupa* at the end
chappals – sandals or leather thonglike footwear; flip-flops
charas – resin of the marijuana plant; also referred to as 'hashish'
chital – spotted deer
choli – sari blouse
chowk – town square, intersection or marketplace

dagoba – see *stupa*
Dalit – preferred term for India's *Untouchable* caste
dargah – shrine or place of burial of a Muslim saint
darshan – offering or audience with someone; auspicious viewing of a deity
Deccan – meaning 'South', this refers to the central South Indian plateau
Devi – *Shiva*'s wife; goddess
dhaba – basic restaurant or snack bar; especially popular with truck drivers
dharamsala – pilgrims' rest house
dharma – for Hindus, the moral code of behaviour or social duty; for Buddhists, following the law of nature, or path, as taught by the Buddha
dhobi – person who washes clothes; commonly referred to as *dhobi-wallah*
dhobi ghat – place where clothes are washed by the *dhobi*
dhoti – like a *lungi*, but the ankle-length cloth is then pulled up between the legs; worn by men
dhurrie – rug
dowry – money and/or goods given by a bride's parents to their son-in-law's family; it's illegal but still exists in many arranged marriages
Dravidian – general term for the cultures and languages of the deep south of India, including Tamil, Malayalam, Telugu and Kannada
dupatta – long scarf for women often worn with the *salwar kameez*
durbar – royal court; also a government
Durga – the Inaccessible; a form of *Shiva*'s wife, *Devi*, a beautiful, fierce goddess riding a tiger/lion

filmi – slang term describing anything to do with Indian movies

Ganesh – Hindu god of good fortune and remover of obstacles; popular elephant-headed son of *Shiva* and *Parvati*, he is also known as Ganpati; his vehicle is a ratlike creature

Ganga – Hindu goddess representing the sacred Ganges River; said to flow from *Vishnu*'s toe

Garuda – man-bird vehicle of *Vishnu*

gaur – Indian bison

ghat – steps or landing on a river, range of hills, or road up hills

giri – hill

gopuram – soaring pyramidal gateway tower of *Dravidian* temples

gurdwara – Sikh temple

guru – holy teacher; in Sanskrit literally *goe* (darkness) and *roe* (to dispel)

Hanuman – Hindu monkey god, prominent in the *Ramayana*, and a follower of *Rama*

Indo-Saracenic – style of colonial architecture that integrated Western designs with Islamic, Hindu and Jain influences

Indra – significant and prestigious Vedic god; god of rain, thunder, lightning and war

Jagannath – Lord of the Universe; a form of *Krishna*

ji – honorific that can be added to the end of almost anything as a form of respect; thus 'Babaji', 'Gandhiji'

Kailasa – sacred Himalayan mountain; home of *Shiva*

kalamkari – designs painted on cloth using vegetable dyes

Kali – the ominous-looking evil-destroying form of *Devi*; commonly depicted with dark skin, dripping with blood, and wearing a necklace of skulls

kameez – woman's shirtlike tunic

Kannada – state language of Karnataka

karma – Hindu, Buddhist and Sikh principle of retributive justice for past deeds

khadi – homespun cloth; Mahatma Gandhi encouraged people to spin this rather than buy English cloth

Khan – Muslim honorific title

kolam – elaborate chalk, rice-paste or coloured powder design; also known as *rangoli*

Konkani – state language of Goa

Krishna – *Vishnu's* eighth incarnation, often coloured blue; he revealed the *Bhagavad Gita* to *Arjuna*

Kshatriya – Hindu caste of soldiers or administrators; second in the caste hierarchy

kurta – long shirt with either short collar or no collar

lakh – 100,000

Lakshmana – half-brother and aide of *Rama* in the *Ramayana*

Lakshmi – *Vishnu's* consort, Hindu goddess of wealth; she sprang forth from the ocean holding a lotus

lama – Tibetan Buddhist priest or monk

lingam – phallic symbol; auspicious symbol of *Shiva*; plural 'linga'

lungi – worn by men, this loose, coloured garment (similar to a sarong) is pleated at the waist to fit the wearer

maha – prefix meaning 'great'

Mahabharata – Great Hindu Vedic epic poem of the Bharata dynasty; containing approximately 10,000 verses describing the battle between the Pandavas and the Kauravas

mahal – house or palace

maharaja – literally 'great king'; princely ruler

mahatma – literally 'great soul'

Mahavir – last *tirthankar*

Mahayana – the 'greater vehicle' of Buddhism; a later adaptation of the teaching which lays emphasis on the *bodhisattva* ideal, teaching the renunciation of nirvana (ultimate peace and cessation of rebirth) in order to help other beings along the way to enlightenment

mahout – elephant rider or master

maidan – open (often grassed) area; parade ground

Malayalam – state language of Kerala

mandapa – pillared pavilion; a temple forechamber

mandir – temple

Maratha – central Indian people who controlled much of India at various times and fought the *Mughals* and *Rajputs*

marg – road

masjid – mosque

mehndi – henna; ornate henna designs on women's hands (and often feet), traditionally for certain festivals or ceremonies (eg marriage)

mela – fair or festival

moksha – liberation from samsara

mudra – ritual hand movements used in Hindu religious dancing; gesture of Buddha figure

Mughal – Muslim dynasty of subcontinental emperors from Babur to Aurangzeb

Naga – mythical serpentlike beings capable of changing into human form

namaste – traditional Hindu greeting (hello or goodbye), often accompanied by a respectful small bow with the hands together at the chest or head level

Nandi – bull, vehicle of *Shiva*

Narasimha – man-lion incarnation of *Vishnu*

Narayan – incarnation of *Vishnu* the creator

Nataraja – *Shiva* as the cosmic dancer

nizam – hereditary title of the rulers of Hyderabad

NRI – Non-Resident Indian

Om – sacred invocation representing the essence of the divine principle; for Buddhists, if repeated often enough with complete concentration, it leads to a state of emptiness

Pali – the language; related to Sanskrit, in which the Buddhist scriptures were recorded; scholars still refer to the original Pali texts

Parsi – adherent of the Zoroastrian faith

Partition – formal division of British India in 1947 into two separate countries, India and Pakistan

Parvati – a form of *Devi*

PCO – Public Call Office from where to make local, interstate and international phone calls

Pongal – Tamil harvest festival

pradesh – state

prasad – temple-blessed food offering

puja – literally 'respect'; offering or prayers

Puranas – set of 18 encyclopaedic Sanskrit stories, written in verse, relating to the three gods, dating from the 5th century AD

Radha – favourite mistress of *Krishna* when he lived as a cowherd

raga – any of several conventional patterns of melody and rhythm that form the basis for freely interpreted compositions

raj – rule or sovereignty; British Raj (sometimes just Raj) refers to British rule

raja – king; sometimes *rana*

Rajput – Hindu warrior caste, former rulers of northwestern India

Rama – seventh incarnation of *Vishnu*

Ramadan – the Islamic holy month of sunrise-to-sunset fasting (no eating, drinking or smoking); also referred to as Ramazan

Ramayana – the story of *Rama* and *Sita* and their conflict with *Ravana* is one of India's best-known epics

rana – king; sometimes *raja*

rangoli – see *kolam*

rani – female ruler or wife of a king

rathas – rock-cut *Dravidian* temples

Ravana – demon king of Lanka who abducted *Sita*; the titanic battle between him and *Rama* is told in the *Ramayana*

rickshaw – small, two- or three-wheeled passenger vehicle

sadhu – ascetic, holy person; one who is trying to achieve enlightenment; often addressed as *swamiji* or *babaji*

sagar – lake, reservoir

sahib – respectful title applied to a gentleman

salwar – trousers usually worn with a *kameez*

salwar kameez – traditional dresslike tunic and trouser combination for women

samadhi – in Hinduism, ecstatic state, sometimes defined as 'ecstasy, trance, communion with God'; in Buddhism, concentration; also a place where a holy man has been cremated/buried, usually venerated as a shrine

sambar – deer

Sangam – ancient academy of Tamil literature; means literally 'the meeting of two hearts'

sangha – community of monks and nuns

Saraswati – wife of *Brahma*; goddess of learning; sits on a white swan

Sati – wife of *Shiva*; became a *sati* ('honourable woman') by immolating herself; although banned more than a century ago, the act of *sati* is still (very) occasionally performed

satyagraha – nonviolent protest involving a hunger strike, popularised by Mahatma Gandhi; from Sanskrit, literally meaning 'insistence on truth'

Scheduled Castes – official term used for the *Untouchables* or *Dalits*

shahadah – Muslim declaration of faith ('There is no God but Allah; Mohammed is his prophet')

Shaivite – follower of *Shiva*

Shakti – creative energies perceived as female deities; devotees follow Shaktism

Shiv Sena – Hindu nationalist political party

Shiva – the Destroyer; also the Creator, in which form he is worshipped as a lingam

Shivaji – great Maratha leader of the 17th century

shola – virgin forest

Shudra – caste of labourers

sikhara – Hindu temple-spire or temple

Sita – the Hindu goddess of agriculture; more commonly associated with the *Ramayana*

sitar – Indian stringed instrument

Sivaganga – water tank in temple dedicated to *Shiva*

Skanda – Hindu god of war, *Shiva's* son

stupa – Buddhist religious monument composed of a solid hemisphere topped by a spire, containing relics of the Buddha; also known as a *dagoba* or pagoda

Sufi – Muslim mystic

Surya – the sun; a major deity in the *Vedas*

swami – title of respect meaning 'lord of the self'; given to initiated Hindu monks

tabla – twin drums

Tamil – language of Tamil Nadu; people of *Dravidian* origin

tandava – *Shiva's* cosmic victory dance

tank – reservoir; pool or large receptacle of holy water found at some temples

tempo – noisy three-wheeler public-transport vehicle; bigger than an *autorickshaw*

Theravada – orthodox form of Buddhism practiced in Sri Lanka and Southeast Asia that is characterised by its adherence to the *Pali* canon; literally, 'dwelling'

tilak – auspicious forehead mark of devout Hindu men

tirthankars – the 24 great Jain teachers

tonga – two-wheeled horse or pony carriage

toy train – narrow-gauge train; mini-train

Trimurti – triple form; the Hindu triad of *Brahma*, *Shiva* and *Vishnu*

Untouchable – lowest caste or 'casteless', for whom the most menial tasks are reserved; the name derives from the belief that higher castes risk defilement if they touch one; now known as *Dalit*

Vaishya – member of the Hindu caste of merchants

Vedas – Hindu sacred books; collection of hymns composed in preclassical Sanskrit during the second millennium BC and divided into four books: Rig-Veda, Yajur-Veda, Sama-Veda and Atharva-Veda

vihara – Buddhist monastery, generally with central court or hall off which open residential cells, usually with a Buddha shrine at one end

Vijayanagar empire – one of South India's greatest empires; lasted from the 14th to 17th centuries

vikram – *tempo* or a larger version of the standard *tempo*

vimana – principal part of Hindu temple; a tower over the sanctum

vipassana – the insight meditation technique of *Theravada* Buddhism in which mind and body are closely examined as changing phenomena

Vishnu – part of the *Trimurti*; Vishnu is the Preserver and Restorer who so far has nine *avatars*: the fish Matsya, the tortoise Kurma, the wild boar Naraha, *Narasimha*, Vamana, Parasurama, *Rama*, *Krishna* and *Buddha*

wallah – man; added onto almost anything, eg *dhobi*-wallah, chai-wallah, taxi-wallah

yali – mythical lion creature

yatra – pilgrimage

zenana – area of a home where women are secluded; women's quarters

Behind the Scenes

SEND US YOUR FEEDBACK

We love to hear from travellers – your comments keep us on our toes and help make our books better. Our well-travelled team reads every word on what you loved or loathed about this book. Although we cannot reply individually to postal submissions, we always guarantee that your feedback goes straight to the appropriate authors, in time for the next edition. Each person who sends us information is thanked in the next edition – the most useful submissions are rewarded with a selection of digital PDF chapters.

Visit **lonelyplanet.com/contact** to submit your updates and suggestions or to ask for help. Our award-winning website also features inspirational travel stories, news and discussions.

Note: We may edit, reproduce and incorporate your comments in Lonely Planet products such as guidebooks, websites and digital products, so let us know if you don't want your comments reproduced or your name acknowledged. For a copy of our privacy policy visit lonelyplanet.com/privacy.

OUR READERS

Many thanks to the travellers who used the last edition and wrote to us with helpful hints, useful advice and interesting anecdotes:
Phil Almond, Paul Anderson, Jonna Bang, Andrew Barnes, Emilia Bober, Juliette Bogers, John Brankin, Mark Brawler, Lizzie Cawley, Jane Clarke, Tony Clarke, Jan de Jong, Gemma Eisner, Jo Garvey, Gabrielle George, Christine Gibson, Stephanie Gillespie, Lars Haarr, Tage Hansen, Scott Harper, Luke Haskett, Rüdiger Hess, Mat Hines, Daniel Isherwood, Victoria Kjos, Tim Laslavic, Rod Lee, Luca Misasi, Pieter Mols, Maureen Moon, Nia Murphy, Malcolm Noden, Karin Nyfort-Hansen, Mahendra Prabhu K, Vendula Prokopcova, Bharath Punyamurthy, Lynda Purvis, Lieve Roeland, Christina Ronnberg, Chris Rust, Patricia F Sheafor, Sarah-Jane Smiles, Vanessa Stilwell, Joe Thomas, Gert Van Reck, Jens Wieland, Suzie Williams, Leena Zarowiecki

AUTHOR THANKS

Sarina Singh

A big thank you to everyone at Lonely Planet – with special mention to Suzannah and Brigitte – who worked so hard on this book. Gratitude, also, goes to the many readers across the world who took the time to write to us. Finally, warm thanks to the fantastic team of authors – you made this edition a delight for me to coordinate.

Lindsay Brown

I am very grateful for the assistance of various hotel managers, travel desks and tourism centres for putting up with all my questions. I would particularly like to thank Homi in Mumbai, coordinating author Sarina Singh, fellow traveller and Kingfisher fancier Stephen Nicholson, and Jenny, Pat and Sinead at home.

Paul Harding

Thanks to the many lovely people in Kerala and Goa who helped with tips, advice and a drink or two. In particular Debra, Johnson, Shibu, Niaz, Philip and Maryann, Suresh, Varghese and Beena, Walter, Ajit, Jack and family. But mostly thanks to Hannah and my beautiful daughter, Layla, who made Goa so much more enjoyable.

Trent Holden & Kate Morgan

First up thanks to Suzannah and Glenn for commissioning us to work on our dream book again. Cheers also to Sarina for her great work in piecing this together. In the Andamans, a massive thanks to all who helped out with tips and assistance in organising ferry schedules etc. Big sing out to Steve, too, for his trailblazing efforts. While in Karnataka we're also indebted to those who helped us get around and for all the leads and feedback.

Amy Karafin

I'm deeply grateful to the people of Andhra Pradesh and Bombay for all their help and for making such interesting places. Special thanks to Sandhya Kanneganti, Ram Babu, Jayasri Anand and Gayatri, Taps and Devi Vasireddy, Dr Kishore and Sandeep Kishore, Asif Husain Arastu, Saaz Aggarwal, Malini and Hari Hariharan, Akash Bhartiya, Surekha and Manik Bhartiya, Naresh Fernandes, Mujju, Satish Asi, Sarina Singh, Suzannah Shwer, Brigitte Ellemor, and everyone at Dhamma Khetta, Dhamma Vijaya and the Global Pagoda. *Bhavatu sabba mangalam!*

John Noble

Extra special thanks to super-efficient research assistant and perfect travelling companion Isabella Noble; Ashish Gupta and colleagues; V Rangaraj Pillai; the Chennai autorickshaw driver who insisted on a fare lower than I offered; and, during write-up, to Coley, Hilary, Josh and Nala for the witty conversation, and to Jack for meals in the home stretch.

ACKNOWLEDGMENTS

Climate map data adapted from Peel MC, Finlayson BL & McMahon TA (2007) 'Updated World Map of the Köppen-Geiger Climate Classification', *Hydrology and Earth System Sciences*, 11, 163344.

Illustration p192 by Michael Weldon.

Cover photograph: Backwaters near Kochi (Cochin), Kerala, PitGreenwood/Getty Images.

THIS BOOK

This 7th edition of Lonely Planet's *South India & Kerala* guidebook was coordinated by Sarina Singh, who wrote the planning and background chapters for this and the last three editions, and co-written by Lindsay Brown, Paul Harding, Trent Holden, Amy Karafin, Kate Morgan and John Noble.

This guidebook was commissioned in Lonely Planet's Melbourne office, and produced by the following:

Commissioning Editors Suzannah Shwer, Glenn van der Knijff

Coordinating Editors Nigel Chin, Andrea Dobbin

Senior Cartographer David Kemp

Coordinating Layout Designer Carol Jackson

Managing Editors Brigitte Ellemor, Martine Power

Senior Editor Catherine Naghten

Managing Cartographer Adrian Persoglia

Managing Layout Designer Chris Girdler

Assisting Layout Designer Mazzy Prinsep

Cover Research Naomi Parker

Internal Image Research Kylie McLaughlin

Language Content Branislava Vladisavljevic

Thanks to Ryan Evans, Larissa Frost, Genesys India, Jouve India, Elizabeth Jones, Trent Paton, Ian Posthumus, Kerrianne Southway, Gina Tsarouhas, Gerard Walker, Amanda Williamson

Index

Map Pages **000**
Photo Pages **000**

Map Legend

Sights

- Beach
- Buddhist
- Castle
- Christian
- Hindu
- Islamic
- Jewish
- Monument
- Museum/Gallery
- Ruin
- Winery/Vineyard
- Zoo
- Other Sight

Activities, Courses & Tours

- Diving/Snorkelling
- Canoeing/Kayaking
- Skiing
- Surfing
- Swimming/Pool
- Walking
- Windsurfing
- Other Activity/ Course/Tour

Sleeping

- Sleeping
- Camping

Eating

- Eating

Drinking

- Drinking
- Cafe

Entertainment

- Entertainment

Shopping

- Shopping

Information

- Bank
- Embassy/ Consulate
- Hospital/Medical
- Internet
- Police
- Post Office
- Telephone
- Toilet
- Tourist Information
- Other Information

Transport

- Airport
- Border Crossing
- Bus
- Cable Car/ Funicular
- Cycling
- Ferry
- Monorail
- Parking
- Petrol Station
- Taxi
- Train/Railway
- Tram
- Underground Train Station
- Other Transport

Routes

- Tollway
- Freeway
- Primary
- Secondary
- Tertiary
- Lane
- Unsealed Road
- Plaza/Mall
- Steps
- Tunnel
- Pedestrian Overpass
- Walking Tour
- Walking Tour Detour
- Path

Geographic

- Hut/Shelter
- Lighthouse
- Lookout
- Mountain/Volcano
- Oasis
- Park
- Pass
- Picnic Area
- Waterfall

Population

- Capital (National)
- Capital (State/Province)
- City/Large Town
- Town/Village

Boundaries

- International
- State/Province
- Disputed
- Regional/Suburb
- Marine Park
- Cliff
- Wall

Hydrography

- River, Creek
- Intermittent River
- Swamp/Mangrove
- Reef
- Canal
- Water
- Dry/Salt/ Intermittent Lake
- Glacier

Areas

- Beach/Desert
- Cemetery (Christian)
- Cemetery (Other)
- Park/Forest
- Sportsground
- Sight (Building)
- Top Sight (Building)

Amy Karafin

Mumbai (Bombay), Andhra Pradesh Indian in several former lives, Amy first fell for the country in 1996, when she discovered *idlis* (spongy, round, fermented rice cakes), meditation and endless train rides. In many visits since, she has written about everything from Bollywood to *mithai* (Indian sweets), contemporary art to ancient religions, and yoga ghettoes to nizams' palaces; read more at www.amykarafin.com. When not on the road, she can be found watching Guru Dutt movies or singing filmi in Brooklyn, where she mostly lives.

Read more about Amy at:
lonelyplanet.com/members/amykarafin

John Noble

Tamil Nadu & Chennai John, from England, lives in Spain and has written about 20-odd countries for Lonely Planet. He first experienced Tamil Nadu in the 1980s when Chennai's Triplicane High Rd was clogged with bullock carts and families milked their buffaloes beside it. Autorickshaws have replaced bullock carts now, but the bustle of Tamil cities remains as exhilarating and exhausting as ever, and the thrill of reaching cool, green Kodaikanal will never pall. Best discovery of the trip: the tranquillity of Tranquebar.

OUR STORY

A beat-up old car, a few dollars in the pocket and a sense of adventure. In 1972 that's all Tony and Maureen Wheeler needed for the trip of a lifetime – across Europe and Asia overland to Australia. It took several months, and at the end – broke but inspired – they sat at their kitchen table writing and stapling together their first travel guide, *Across Asia on the Cheap*. Within a week they'd sold 1500 copies. Lonely Planet was born.

Today, Lonely Planet has offices in Melbourne, London and Oakland, with more than 600 staff and writers. We share Tony's belief that 'a great guidebook should do three things: inform, educate and amuse'.

OUR WRITERS

Sarina Singh

Coordinating Author After finishing a business degree in Melbourne, Sarina travelled to India where she pursued a hotel corporate traineeship before working as a journalist. After five years she returned to Australia and completed postgraduate journalism qualifications before coauthoring Lonely Planet's first edition of *Rajasthan*. Apart from numerous Lonely Planet books, she has written for a raft of newspapers and magazines, and has been a high-profile travel columnist. Sarina is also the author of two prestigious books – *Polo in India* and *India: Essential Encounters*. Her award-nominated documentary film premiered at the Melbourne International Film Festival before being screened internationally.

Read more about Sarina at:
lonelyplanet.com/members/sarinasingh

Lindsay Brown

Maharashtra Lindsay, a former conservation biologist and Publishing Manager at Lonely Planet, has been a frequent visitor to India for more than 25 years. Lindsay has trekked, jeeped, ridden and stumbled across many a mountain pass and contributed to Lonely Planet's *Bhutan*, *Nepal*, *South India*, *Rajasthan*, *Delhi & Agra* and *Pakistan & the Karakoram Highway* guides, among others.

Paul Harding

Goa, Kerala Paul has explored India and all its mayhem many times over the past 15 years, frequently writing about it. He still has a soft spot for the south, where the pace of life is that little bit slower. For this trip he investigated Kerala's backwaters at close range, was charged by wild elephants in Wayanad, and carefully inspected all of Goa's beautiful beaches while taste-testing fresh seafood. Tough life! Paul also wrote the Itineraries chapter and Kerala colour section.

Trent Holden & Kate Morgan

Karnataka & Bengaluru, Andaman Islands Having worked together on books from Zimbabwe to Japan, Trent and Kate were thrilled to be assigned to India again for Lonely Planet, this time working as coauthors. In Karnataka they had the not-so-shabby task of testing Bengaluru's countless bars and classy restaurants, spotting leopards on safari and taking in Hampi's famous ruins. Trent also returned to the Andamans for more sun, surf and sand. Based in Melbourne, in between travels they write about food and music.

OVER PAGE MORE WRITERS

Published by Lonely Planet Publications Pty Ltd
ABN 36 005 607 983
7th edition – Oct 2013
ISBN 978 1 74220 413 0

10 9 8 7 6 5 4 3 2
Printed in Singapore